EMPLOYMENT DISCRIMINATION LAW AND PRACTICE

By

Harold S. Lewis, Jr.

Walter F. George Professor of Law
Mercer University

and

Elizabeth J. Norman

Member of the Georgia Bar

HORNBOOK SERIES®

WEST
GROUP

ST. PAUL, MINN., 2001

Hornbook Series, *WESTLAW*, and the West Group symbol
are registered trademarks used herein under license.

COPYRIGHT © 2001 By WEST GROUP
                      610 Opperman Drive
                      P.O. Box 64526
                      St. Paul, MN 55164–0526
                      1–800–328–9352

ISBN 0–314–25403–X

TEXT IS PRINTED ON 10% POST
CONSUMER RECYCLED PAPER

Dedication

To Leslie, for unflagging cheer and support. The authors also dedicate this work to the spirit animating the Supreme Court's opinion in *Reeves v. Sanderson Plumbing Products, Inc.*, __ U.S. __, 120 S.Ct. 2097, 147 L.Ed.2d 105 (2000). Fairly applied, *Reeves* has the potential to reinvigorate employment discrimination litigation by significantly increasing the number of cases in which the merits may be determined at trial.

*

Preface

This work surveys the claims, defenses, procedures and remedies fundamental to an understanding of the contemporary federal law of employment discrimination. It is intended, first, to offer guidance, structure, judicial authority and critical commentary for law students coming fresh to this intricate and fascinating field. For seasoned students, including practitioners, the text selectively ventures analysis of more challenging points of doctrine, procedural essentials, remedial choices, and synthesis of the overlapping statutory tools. Because of the rapid pace of change in this field, an unusually high proportion of the cited cases we've included were decided within the past several years. Students will recognize among these the Supreme Court's critically important year 2000 decision, <u>Reeves v. Sanderson Plumbing Products, Inc.</u>; its 1999 trilogy of Americans With Disabilities Act cases, <u>Sutton</u>, <u>Murphy</u>, and <u>Albertsons</u>; and the 1998 sexual harassment duo of <u>Faragher</u> and <u>Burlington</u>.

To serve the needs of law students, the book tracks the coverage of the most important issues canvassed in the principal employment discrimination casebooks. These include Zimmer, Sullivan, Richards and Calloway's *Cases and Materials on Employment Discrimination* (5th ed. Little, Brown 2000); Smith, Craver and Clark's *Employment Discrimination Law: Cases and Materials* (5th ed. Michie 2000); Friedman and Strickler's *The Law of Employment Discrimination: Cases and Materials* (4th ed. Foundation Press 1997); and Player, Shoben and Lieberwitz's *Employment Discrimination Law: Cases and Materials* (2d ed. West 1995). Recent additions of great merit are Belton and Avery's *Employment Discrimination Law: Cases and Materials on Equality in the Workplace* (West 1999) and Estreicher's *Cases and Materials on Employment Discrimination and Employment Law* (West 2000). With law school course emphasis uppermost in mind, one lengthy chapter is devoted entirely to the distinct and overlapping modes of proof that have been held sufficient to establish individual and systemic disparate treatment discrimination, and to mount and resist challenges to neutral practices having disproportionate adverse impact.

It is of course customary for employment discrimination casebooks to cover Title VII of the Civil Rights Act of 1964, as amended, the Equal Pay Act of 1963, and the Age Discrimination in Employment Act of 1968. We also consider the comparative advantages and pitfalls of proceeding under the Reconstruction Civil Rights Acts most conducive to employment discrimination claims—42 U.S.C. Sections 1981(a), as amended by the Civil Rights Act of 1991, and 1983. The book also presents compact coverage of Title IX, insofar as it reaches sex-based employment discrimination in federally funded education programs, and more comprehensive treatment of the Americans With Disabilities Act. Special attention is given to the interconnections between and among the statutes. For example, we consider the combined or alternative use, as against private, state and local government, and federal employers, of Title VII and Section 1981, Title VII and Section 1983, and Section 1981 and 1983.

This book proceeds from an assumption that guides most contemporary law school courses: the procedural, remedial and technical features of employment discrimination actions shape the resulting judicial decisions at least as much as substantive decisional doctrine. Thus the text considers the basic elements of a civil lawsuit—prerequisites to suit; jurisdictional and quasi-jurisdictional limitations; class actions and other party joinder problems; the elements of statutory claims and defenses; summary judgment; jury trial and available forms of relief; appeal; and the effect of administrative rulings and judicial judgments on subsequent state or federal proceedings. Three separate chapters address Title VII administrative procedures and available remedies, the Civil Rights Attorneys' Fees Act of 1976, and a complex of related procedural issues commonly encountered in formal litigation. Topic choices within this coverage were dictated by the likely frequency that the law student would confront an issue and its general significance to law practice.

H.L. and E.N.

Acknowledgements

The authors gratefully acknowledge the support of the Walter F. George Foundation and Mercer Law School.

*

WESTLAW® Overview

Employment Discrimination Law and Practice offers a detailed and comprehensive treatment of basic rules, principles and issues relating to employment discrimination law and practice. To supplement the information contained in this book, you can access Westlaw, a computer-assisted legal research service of West Group. Westlaw contains a broad array of legal resources, including case law, statutes, expert commentary, current developments and various other types of information.

Learning how to use these materials effectively will enhance your legal research abilities. To help you coordinate the information in the book with your Westlaw research, this volume contains an appendix listing Westlaw databases, search techniques and sample problems.

THE PUBLISHER

*

Research References

Key Number System: Civil Rights ⊂141–180, 205(2) (78I(B), 78k205(2))

Am Jur 2d, Americans with Disabilities Act §§ 1 et seq.; Civil Rights §§ 1 et seq.; Constitutional Law § 831; Job Discrimination §§ 1 et seq.; Labor and Labor Relations §§ 57, 921, 3478, 4055, 4071, 4118, 4159, 4164, 4707; Military and Civil Defense § 239; Pensions and Retirement Funds §§ 122, 420; Sheriffs, Police and Constables § 156; Wrongful Discharge §§ 154–156

Corpus Juris Secundum, Civil Rights §§ 1 et seq.; Constitutional Law §§ 412, 928, 1224; Judgments §§ 911, 927, 1012; Juries §§ 88-93; Labor Relations § 7; Schools and School Districts §§ 716–721; United States § 192

ALR Index: Age Discrimination; Civil Rights and Discrimination; Civil Rights Attorney's Fees Awards Act; Employment Discrimination; Equal Pay Act; Sex Discrimination

ALR Digest: Civil Rights §§ 1 et seq.; Criminal Law § 216.6; Limitation of Actions § 198.5

Am Jur Legal Forms 2d, Compromise and Settlement § 63:185; Job Discrimination §§ 1 et seq.

Am Jur Pleading and Practice (Rev), Associations and Clubs § 35; Civil Rights §§ 1 et seq.; Civil Service § 12; Constitutional Law § 12; Injunctions §§ 33, 34, 56, 57; Labor and Labor Relations, Forms 241–277; Master and Servant §§ 233.1, 235.1; Schools §§ 212–215; Sheriffs, Police, and Constables §§ 140–142

65 Am Jur Trials 65, Taking the Deposition of the Sexual Harassment Plaintiff; 64 Am Jur Trials 425, Asserting Claims of Unconstitutional Prision Conditions Under 42 USCA § 1983; 63 Am Jur Trials 127, Efficiently and Effectively Defending Employment Discrimination Cases; 63 Am Jur Trials 257, Defendant Class Actions in Title VII Cases; 62 Am Jur Trials 235, Workplace Sexual Harassment: Quid Pro Quo; 61 Am Jur Trials 489, Individual Liability for Sexual Harassment; 57 Am Jur Trials 255, Alternative Dispute Resolution: Employment Law; 53 Am Jur Trials 299, Sex Discrimination Based Upon Sexual Stereotyping; 49 Am Jur Trials 171, Defense of Claim Brought Under the Americans With Disabilities Act; 33 Am Jur Trials 257, Sexual Harassment On The Job; 29 Am Jur Trials 1, Age Discrimination in Employment Action Under ADEA; 29 Am Jur Trials 267, Negligent Hiring and Retention of an Employee; 28 Am Jur Trials 1, Housing Discrimination Litigation; 21 Am Jur Trials 1, Employment Discrimination Action Under Federal Civil Rights Acts

57 POF3d 1, Hate Crimes and Liability for Bias-Motivated Acts; 56 POF3d 1, Proof of Employer Negligence in Hiring and Supervision of

Employee with Propensity Toward Workplace Sexual Harassment; 52 POF3d 1, Proof of Employer Liability for Sexual Harassment Claims Under Title VII of the Civil Rights Act of 1964; 49 POF3d 1, Discrimination in Provision of Medical Services on Basis of Disability; 48 POF3d 1, Employment Discrimination on the Basis of Mental Disability Under the Americans with Disabilities Act; 48 POF3d 75, Proof of Racial Discrimination in Employment Promotion Decisions Under Title VII of the Civil Rights Act of 1964; 46 POF3d 99, Sex Discrimination in Employment Promotion Practices; 44 POF3d 79, Proof of Discrimination Under Age Discrimination in Employment Act; 39 POF3d 55, Proof of Sex Discrimination in Job Assignment or Transfer Under Title VII of the Civil Rights Act of 1964; 26 POF3d 269, Proof of Violation of Equal Pay Act; 25 POF3d 415, Employment Handicap Discrimination Based on Gender Dysphoria (Transsecualism); 24 POF3d 393, Proof of Damages For Sexual Harassment under the Civil Rights Act of 1991; 23 POF3d 499, Discrimination on the Basis of Handicap Under the Fair Housing Act; 20 POF3d 361, Disability Discrimination Under the Americans With Disabilities Act

50 POF2d 127, Sex Discrimination: Sexual Harassment Creating a Hostile Work Environment; 35 POF2d 209, Harassment or Termination of Employee Due to Religious Beliefs or Practices; 12 POF2d 49, "Business Necessity" Justifying Prima Facie Discriminatory Employment Practice; 12 POF2d 645, Sex Discrimination in Employment-Promotion Practices; 10 POF2d 1, Discrimination under Age Discrimination in Employment Act; 1 POF2d 549, Discharge from Employment Because of Garnishment of Earnings

Summary of Contents

*

Table of Contents

EMPLOYMENT DISCRIMINATION LAW AND PRACTICE

*

Chapter One

AN INTRODUCTION TO TITLE VII OF THE 1964 CIVIL RIGHTS ACT AND THE CIVIL RIGHTS ACT OF 1991

Analysis

* * *

§ 1.1 An Overview

Federal judges afforded a generous early reception to claims under Title VII of the Civil Rights Act of 1964,[1] the nation's first full-scale legislation prohibiting private sector employment discrimination. Since 1977, however, Title VII decisionmaking has frequently reverted to the cramped mode of construction traditional in the American law of "master" and "servant."[2] The predominant theme in the Supreme Court's jurisprudence has been the impulse to free employers from the dread hand of government regulation.[3] Thus more than half the judicial life of this landmark legislation has been devoted primarily to restriction, retrenchment, and restoration of traditional management prerogatives.

Indeed the lone apparent exception in the last decade, the Supreme Court's curious flirtation with affirmative action, is in fact not an exception at all. Rather, affirmative action has been embraced by larger employers as an inexpensive, relatively efficient means of securing or

---

§ 1.1

1. 42 U.S.C.A. §§ 2000e to 2000e–15 (1988) [hereafter, Title VII].

2. Although the number of federal court employment discrimination filings tripled between 1990 and 1998, the likelihood of a case reaching trial declined to approximately 5%. *Civil Rights Complaints in U.S. District Courts, 1990–1998*, Bureau of Justice Statistics Special Report, January 2000, available at http://www.ojp.usdoj.gov/bjs/pub/pdf/crcusdc.pdf on the Department of Justice website.

3. *See, e.g., Watson v. Fort Worth Bank & Trust*, 487 U.S. 977, 108 S.Ct. 2777, 101 L.Ed.2d 827 (1988) (plurality opinion); *Texas Dept. of Community Affairs v. Burdine*, 450 U.S. 248, 259, 101 S.Ct. 1089, 1096, 67 L.Ed.2d 207 (1981); *Furnco Constr. Corp. v. Waters*, 438 U.S. 567, 98 S.Ct. 2943, 57 L.Ed.2d 957 (1978); *cf. United Steelworkers of Am. v. Weber*, 443 U.S. 193, 99 S.Ct. 2721, 61 L.Ed.2d 480 (1979) (employer voluntary affirmative action program justified as exercise of traditional management prerogatives).

maintaining government contracts, or reducing the risk and magnitude of more direct governmental interference in the form of Title VII litigation by blacks or women.[4]

From the impassioned rhetoric surrounding the vetoed Civil Rights Act of 1990 and its somewhat strengthened successor, the Civil Rights Act of 1991,[5] [hereafter, the Act], one might think that Congress has reentered the fray. The Act does, after all, respond to the Supreme Court's 1989 decisions that frontally assaulted both Title VII and the Reconstruction era statute, 42 U.S.C.A. § 1981, that for well over a decade stood as a bulwark against race and ancestry discrimination in private employment. Further, the 1991 legislation for the first time authorizes jury trials and compensatory and punitive damages as a remedy for intentional violations. And to some uncertain degree it attempts to restore the formal, more lenient standards of proof that had prevailed in disparate impact cases before the Court's 1988 Term decisions.

Yet most of the latest liberalizing changes are offset by restrictive counterprovisions added as part of a compromise orchestrated by Senator Danforth. In addition, key Court-approved restrictions on attorney's fees, slated for abolition in earlier versions of the legislation, escaped unscathed. Also fallen by the wayside is a proposed legislative directive to the courts to give Title VII an expansive interpretation. The bill does offer substantial evidentiary and remedial support for the individual plaintiff's action based on intentional discrimination. But it provides only an equivocal endorsement of the group protection concept that is implemented through the disproportionate adverse impact mode of proof, although it does reaffirm "voluntary" employer affirmative action as well as group-based relief to settle partially or fully litigated claims. On balance, then, the changes fail fully to restore the pre–1989 status quo for claims that challenge neutral practices having disproportionate adverse effect on protected groups. Instead, it ploughs new ground only at the margins by enhancing the remedies available for traditional, noncontroversial forms of intentional discrimination.[6] In sum, the legislation appears dramatic only in relation to the congressional passivity and resurgent judicial reaction of the preceding decade.

The depth of Congress' commitment to eradicate employment discrimination is drawn into question by its failure to expand domestic

---

4. Executive Order 11246, 30 F.R. 12319 (1965), as amended, together with the Secretary of Labor's implementing rules and regulations, 41 C.F.R. § 60–1.1 et seq. (1980), impose detailed affirmative action obligations, *see* 41 C.F.R. § 60–2.10 et seq., on government contractors and subcontractors with 50 or more employees and contracts equal to or exceeding $50,000. *See* 41 C.F.R. § 60–1.40(a). Title VII itself applies only to employers with 15 or more employees each working day in each of 20 or more weeks in the current or preceding calendar year. Section 701(b) of Title VII, 42 U.S.C.A. § 2000e(b).

5. Pub.L. 102–166, 105 Stat. 1071.

6. Indeed even the more far-reaching proposals embodied in H.R. 1, the version introduced in January 1991 by Representative Brooks, would have worked only modest, reactive changes that were unlikely to usher in a new era of meaningful antidiscrimination enforcement. Textual references to the Brooks Bill are to H.R. 1, 102d Cong., 1st Sess. (1991) [hereinafter H.R. 1].

coverage to smaller employers.[7] This failure comes despite Congress' evident awareness that small employers are still free to practice religious, gender and national origin discrimination with impunity from federal law.[8] New legislation is far more likely to enlarge the reach of federal employment discrimination laws than judicial interpretation of existing statutes.[9] Yet even after a quarter century's experience with Title VII, Congress is content to deny federal protection from gender, national origin, or religious discrimination to the millions of Americans who work or seek to work for employers with fewer than fifteen employees or, in the case of age discrimination, twenty employees.[10] Second, as mentioned in passing above, the legislation does not fully revive the plaintiff's ability to challenge neutral practices. Third, even in the realm of intentional discrimination, it does not afford gender, religion, or national origin plaintiffs full parity with those complaining of discrimination based on race. More fundamentally, the Act fails to come to grips with three enduring tensions in the goals, nature, and means of antidiscrimination law, tensions that were revealed sharply in the elaboration of Title VII during its first quarter century.

The first of these issues is whether antidiscrimination legislation should be confined to eradicating particular unlawful employer practices or should also set minimum standards to meet such employee needs as child care and remedial training and thereby enable minority group members and others to take advantage of nondiscriminatory employment opportunities. The current legislation ignores this alternative, continuing to focus on nondiscrimination alone.

The second key dilemma is endemic to the antidiscrimination concept: does it protect individuals or groups? The tension between the two theories is shot through Title VII's history, and the residue is rampant jurisprudential schizophrenia. The current legislation compounds the confusion. On balance the 1991 Act stands foresquare behind disparate treatment—the classic proof mode designed to show one-on-one intentional discrimination. It reaffirms the individual protection model, principally by reinvigorating the single-plaintiff case of "disparate treatment" where an employer's motives are mixed, although it fails to overturn earlier Supreme Court decisions that impeded proof of intentional discrimination in the efficient class action form and denied full, certain "make-whole" seniority relief to proven victims.

No similar consensus emerged in support of the Title VII "disproportionate adverse impact" case that evolved in the wake of the Supreme Court's decision in *Griggs v. Duke Power Co.*[11] This approach strives for

7. With certain exemptions, the Act does for the first time expand coverage to U.S. citizens working overseas for American employers or enterprises they control. Section 109 of the Act.

8. Even small employers may not intentionally discriminate based on race or ancestry, because of 42 U.S.C.A. § 1981, discussed in Chapter 5.

9. Donohue and Siegelman, *The Changing Nature of Employment Discrimination Litigation,* 43 Stan.L.Rev. 983, 1000 (1991).

10. *See infra* Chapters 2 (Title VII) and 7 (ADEA).

11. 401 U.S. 424, 91 S.Ct. 849, 28 L.Ed.2d 158 (1971).

relative equality of achievement, not merely opportunity. It seeks to redress historic group disadvantage by banning practices that perpetuate the effects of past discrimination. Thus, "impact" theory condemns neutral employer practices that produce disproportionately adverse results and cannot be adequately justified by job or business need, even when those practices treat different groups alike and are adopted with benign motivation.[12]

By insisting that historically disfavored groups enjoy rough equality of achievement, the disproportionate adverse impact proof mode departs from and even impinges on the classic model of the "equal opportunity" principle that animated Title VII's initial passage.[13] In this vein, the business community and the Bush Administration continually objected that the provisions strengthening the disparate impact case would encourage employers to resort to quota hiring or promotion. The argument is that quotas would yield "bottom lines" favorable to minorities and women, which in turn would reduce the likelihood of employer liability for particular practices shown to have disproportionate adverse impact on these groups.[14]

At the same time, the Act does advance the group protection model in several other ways. It revives, though only partially, challenges to facially neutral employer practices that disproportionately adversely impact protected groups and perpetuate their historic handicaps. Further, it endorses employer discrimination against whites or men through "voluntary"[15] affirmative action plans designed to enhance the representation of blacks or women in job categories from which they were previously excluded or under-represented. In other words, even as it leaves some obstacles in the path of groups of black or women plaintiffs in their attempts to prove the discriminatory impact of employer practices on their groups, Congress continues to countenance race-and gender-based preferences that confer benefits on blacks and women (regardless of whether they were victims of unlawful discrimination) as members of a group, at the expense of individual whites and males. Finally, the legislation advances the group protection model by providing partial procedural insulation to most court decrees that afford race-or gender-based relief. Whites or males disadvantaged by those decrees will no longer be able to attack them "collaterally"—that is, in subsequent reverse discrimination litigation—if they failed to join as parties to the earlier litigation after notice and opportunity to do so.

---

12. *See* Blumoff & Lewis, *The Reagan Court and Title VII: A Common–Law Outlook on a Statutory Task*, 69 N.C.L.Rev. 1, 12–15 (1990).

13. *Id.* at 15.

14. One flaw in this argument is that an individual minority plaintiff who can demonstrate that she was screened out of a selection process as the result of a neutral practice that has disproportionate adverse impact on her group states a Title VII claim even if her group as a whole is well repre-

sented on the employer's staff. *Connecticut v. Teal*, 457 U.S. 440, 102 S.Ct. 2525, 73 L.Ed.2d 130 (1982).

15. Terming the plans "voluntary" overlooks the fact that employers are often motivated to adopt them in order to satisfy requirements or avoid penalties imposed by law—for example, to comply with government contracting requirements or to avoid liability in actions brought by minorities and women under Title VII.

There is a third fundamental issue raised by the experience under Title VII: Whether the goals of antidiscrimination legislation should be met primarily through public and compulsive mechanisms, or through incentives for employers to revise their practices. Here, too, the legislation cuts in opposite directions. On one hand, its acceptance of affirmative action and encouragement of alternative dispute resolution may facilitate consensual compliance. Similarly, the provisions that bar or burden collateral attacks on consent decrees by white or male victims of reverse discrimination should stimulate settlements by instilling greater confidence in the durability of the parties' bargains.

By contrast, the Act's failure unequivocally to restore the "neutral practices" case to its complete pre–1989 vigor, or to revive the class action and provide certain, make-whole seniority remedies for proven discriminatees, removes some of the litigation exposure that motivates "voluntary" employer affirmative action in the first place. Yet the legislation does create new incentives to litigate, and hence to settle by: (1) authorizing jury trials and compensatory and punitive damages in cases of intentional discrimination; and (2) providing for the recovery of uncapped expert witness fees by prevailing plaintiffs.

The legislation is therefore a peculiar pastiche of individual and group protection concepts left for further elucidation in assorted public and private arenas. At the formal level, Congress continues to prefer the model that offers relief to individual victims of intentional discrimination. Waning in importance is the model that redresses group disadvantage by subjecting today's employers to liability for neutral practices that carry forward historical discrimination in the society at large. Nevertheless, the group protection concept persists in the somewhat resuscitated "neutral practice" case, in the benign congressional neglect of reverse discrimination by private employers, and in provisions that may encourage some employers to enter into consent decrees that require affirmative action. In these three ways, the Act places the force of law behind arrangements that conflict with the concept of equal opportunity in order to achieve equality of result. This somewhat incoherent approach at once facilitates litigation designed to punish classic disparate treatment discrimination against individual minority group members and women, while at the same time allowing employers to engage in the same kind of discrimination against individual whites or men when they find it advantageous to enhance the employment opportunities of historically disfavored groups at the expense of individual whites or men.

Some states have minimum standards laws that require employers to provide specified leave, reinstatement or benefits to employees during and after pregnancy. The 1978 amendments to Title VII, known as the Pregnancy Discrimination Act ("PDA"), adopt an equal treatment principle that requires employers to distribute burdens and benefits associated with pregnancy-related disabilities in the same fashion as with any other disability.[16] Most (but not all) federal courts reject the view that

---

16. *See generally, International Union, United Auto. Workers v. Johnson Controls,* *Inc.*, 499 U.S. 187, 111 S.Ct. 1196, 113 L.Ed.2d 158 (1991); *Newport News Ship*

the PDA requires employers to provide preferential treatment; pregnancy-related disabilities are subject to the same restrictions, penalties, and benefits limitations, including outright denial, as any other.[17] But PDA's nondiscrimination floor does not preclude state-mandated preferential treatment,[18] provided that the preference is limited to periods of actual physical disability related to the pregnancy.[19]

Neither does the legislation address underlying societal impediments that prevent racial minorities from translating the legal command of equal treatment into realized employment gains. If fair employment law is to bear fruit for lesser-educated and lower-skilled minorities residing predominantly in inner-city areas, for example, when virtually all the recent growth in low-skilled jobs has been suburban,[20] the amendments would have had to include significant changes in national housing policy.[21] Similarly, government recognition that a high proportion of minority employees are educated and trained only for entry-level service jobs might have suggested the desirability of minimum standards legislation aimed at raising the general wage level of service employment.[22] Alfred Blumrosen contends that Congress' failure to address these issues in the past explains why Title VII has not improved the relative wages or unemployment levels of black workers, even as it has improved their occupational distribution.[23]

The current legislation skirts these underlying structural issues, as well as Professor Blumrosen's more tangential suggestions for adjustments to tax and bankruptcy laws that would soften their adverse effects on poorer minority employees.[24] Apart from vaguely instructing the Equal Employment Opportunity Commission to "carry out educational and outreach activities,"[25] Congress has simply shored up the existing framework of nondiscrimination. The Act makes no attempt to chart a broader approach by mandating minimum standards keyed to the histor-

building & Dry Dock Co. v. E.E.O.C., 462 U.S. 669, 103 S.Ct. 2622, 77 L.Ed.2d 89 (1983).

17. *See California Fed. S & L Ass'n v. Guerra*, 479 U.S. 272, 107 S.Ct. 683, 93 L.Ed.2d 613 (1987).

18. *Id.*

19. *Schafer v. Board. of Pub. Educ.*, 903 F.2d 243 (3d Cir.1990).

20. *See* Kasarda, *Jobs, Migration and Emerging Urban Mismatches*, Urban Change & Poverty 148, 193 (McGeary & Lynn eds., 1988), cited by Blumrosen, *Society In Transition I: A Broader Congressional Agenda for Equal Employment–The Peace Dividend, Leapfrogging, and Other Matters*, 8 Yale L. & Pol'y Rev. 257, 266 (1990).

21. Blumrosen, 8 Yale L. & Pol'y Rev. at 266. He suggests that a realistic employment initiative should encompass such re-

lated concerns as subsidized housing, relocation assistance, enforcement of housing discrimination laws, and pooled transportation to suburban jobs.

22. *Id.* at 269.

23. *Id.* at 262–264.

24. *Id.* at 270. Indeed the legislation even fails to revive a proposal abandoned by EEOC that would have recognized a prima facie case when a company's transfer of operations from a high-density to a low-density minority area adversely affects the incumbent minority work force or, more controversially, simply results in a lesser minority applicant pool for future employment. *Id.* at 268 (citing Weiss, *Risky Business: Age and Race Discrimination in Redeployment Decisions*, 48 Md.L.Rev. 901, 921–22 (1989)).

25. Section 111 of the Act (amending § 705(h) of Title VII, 42 U.S.C.A. § 2000e–4(h)).

ic disadvantages or contemporary needs of minority or women employees.

As the succeeding chapters illustrate, the courts are constrained to construe Title VII without any Congressional moral compass on the question of race. Two principal competing moral visions have been advanced. The first, reflected in employment discrimination law in the still dominant nondiscrimination, or "equal opportunity" model, holds that racial preference of any kind in divvying up scarce jobs or job benefits is wrong. The second, reflected in the "equality of result" model, proceeds from a moral imperative that government should coercively redistribute society's benefits in favor of today's members of previously enslaved or oppressed races or groups at the expense of today's descendants of an assumed historic oppressor group, whites males. Unfortunately, in the course of the three-decade dialectic about these principles, Congress and the courts have compromised both of them regularly.

The equal opportunity principle, the rhetorical bedrock of the system, is often half-heartedly enforced. On one hand, the Congressional/court complex seems insufficiently serious about the equal opportunity principle to approve (1) the use of proof methods calculated to root out less readily detectable forms of traditional, anti-minority discrimination; (2) party joinder devices designed to afford proven victims remedies as a group; or (3) full, assured make-whole remedies for all proven victims of discrimination. One example on the proof issue is the Supreme Court's requirement that "systemic treatment" plaintiffs raise an inference of discrimination only when the statistical evidence of their underrepresentation rises to the magnitude of "two or three" standard deviations from their expected representation based on interest and qualifications. Another example is furnished by Congress' fudging in the 1991 Act about the extent to which it overturned *Wards Cove*, leaving it to the courts to sort out the nature of the employer defense from a hotchpot of contradictory Supreme Court decisions.[26] The signal procedural example of the Court's faint allegiance to the antidiscrimination principle is its decision in *Falcon v. General Telephone* that erected major roadblocks to Title VII class actions. And the most noteworthy remedial example is the Court's flinching, in *United States v. Teamsters*, from immediately ordering retroactive seniority or back pay in favor of the minority members who were proven victims of the equal-opportunity brand of discrimination.

On the other hand, a circuit court rule that requires additional evidence of "background circumstances" to prove discrimination against

---

26. This example must be qualified. It has been widely argued that the neutral practice/disproportionate adverse impact proof mode addressed by *Wards Cove* and the referenced provisions of the 1991 Act does not really embody an equal opportunity principle at all, but the more controversial standard of equality of result. *See* Blumoff and Lewis, 69 N.C.L.Rev. 1. Nevertheless, as first articulated by the Supreme Court in *Griggs v. Duke Power* and subsequent decisions, the impact proof mode is simply another way, separate from a demonstration of discriminatory intent, to demonstrate that an employer practice unlawfully discriminates on one of the grounds prohibited by Title VII.

whites reflects judicial skepticism that members of the traditionally oppressed minority, when they attain positions of influence, are as likely to act in the same discriminatory fashion as their historic oppressors. In other words, the equal-opportunity principle is not applied evenhandedly when the plaintiff is white. This rule contrasts starkly with the Supreme Court's formal admonition, expressed by Justice Marshall in *McDonald v. Santa Fe Trail Corp.*, that the equal opportunity model should be applied in any direction on the same terms. There is a far more significant example of the Supreme Court's own faltering fidelity to the equal opportunity principle when the gored ox is a member of the traditional oppressor group: its strained construction of Title VII, in the *Weber* and *Johnson* decisions, that permits employers "voluntarily" to give explicit racial or gender preference in distributing job benefits.

Still less have Congress and the courts shaped the employment discrimination laws to mandate equality of result. That norm would require a defendant employer to offer racial or gender preferences despite the absence of proof that it had discriminatorily denied minorities or women equal opportunity. Yet as we shall see, Title VII, EPA, and the ADEA as conceived by the Supreme Court, with Congress' acquiescence, all rest on premises largely inimical to equality of result. Instead, they have been interpreted so as to maximize managerial prerogatives and free employers from undue governmental interference, except to the limited extent that the defendant employer, rather than the society at large, has discriminated on a basis prohibited by statute.[27]

True, the Supreme Court's *Weber* and *Johnson* decisions hold that Title VII *permits* employers, including covered public employers, to implement race-and gender-based preferences within judge-made sanitizing limits. But more recently, in its *Wygant* decision, fortified by *Croson*, the Court has expressly repudiated that approach by holding that under the Equal Protection Clause a government employer can implement race-based preferences usually only if there is firm evidence of its own prior discrimination. General societal discrimination will not justify a voluntary race-based government preference under the Equal Protection Clause, although it will under Title VII.[28]

The combined residue of *Weber/Johnson* and *Wygant/Croson*, then, appears to be that Title VII deviates from the Court's general view of the 14th Amendment by permitting private employers to make decisions dictated by equality of result, but only when those decisions favor minorities whose ancestors suffered historic discrimination by the general society. Yet there are indications that the Court's cramped understanding of the requirements of equal protection has of late also influ-

---

27. *See* Chapters 2 and 3 (Title VII); 7 (ADEA); and 8 (EPA). In *Mardell v. Harleysville Life Ins. Co.*, 31 F.3d 1221, 1233 n. 20 (3d Cir.1994), *vacated in part,* 65 F.3d 1072 (3d Cir.1995), the court wrote: "The federal anti-employment discrimination laws were designed not to impinge directly upon employer free choice; that is, not to interfere unnecessarily with legitimate business operations and decisions." (citations omitted).

28. *See* discussion of *Wygant* and *Croson* in Chapter 4.

enced the lower courts' appraisal under Title VII of judicially ordered race-based relief.[29] If the Supreme Court follows suit, leading to the overruling of *Weber/Johnson*, Title VII will no more countenance equality of result than does the Equal Protection clause as currently understood by the Supreme Court.

29. *See* Chapter 4 on Title VII remedies.

Chapter Two

TITLE VII OF THE 1964 CIVIL RIGHTS ACT: COVERAGE, PROHIBITED GROUNDS OF DISCRIMINATION, SPECIALLY TREATED PRACTICES, AND DEFENSES

Analysis

Sec.

---

§ 2.1   In General

Title VII of the Civil Rights Act of 1964 is the most broadly based and influential federal statute prohibiting discrimination in employment. Its prohibitions on discrimination based on race, color, sex, religion or national origin extend to all "terms, conditions or privileges" of employment,[1] a phrase the federal courts have construed quite broadly to embrace any benefit actually conferred or burden actually imposed in the workplace, whether or not provided for by contract.[2] The statute there-

§ 2.1

1. Section 703(a)(1), 42 U.S.C.A. § 2000e–2(a)(1).

2. *See, e.g., Hishon v. King & Spalding,* 467 U.S. 69, 104 S.Ct. 2229, 81 L.Ed.2d 59 (1984) and opinion of Powell, J., concurring (after a specified number of years employed a law firm associate had the right to be considered for partnership without regard to gender because that was the firm's practice, even if such consideration was not specifically promised). From the tenor of the *Hishon* decision, it is extremely doubtful that the relationship among partners is regulable by the employment discrimination statutes. Nevertheless, appellate decisions since *Hishon* appear to assume that a court may order partnership as a remedy for discrimination against an associate or employee respecting the decision to admit to membership as a partner. *See Hopkins v. Price Waterhouse,* 920 F.2d 967 (D.C.Cir.1990); *Ezold v. Wolf, Block, Schorr & Solis–Cohen,* 751 F.Supp. 1175 (E.D.Pa.1990), *supplemented,* 758 F.Supp. 303 (1991), *reversed on other grounds,* 983 F.2d 509 (3d Cir.1992), *cert. denied,* 510 U.S. 826, 114 S.Ct. 88, 126 L.Ed.2d 56 (1993). The circuits are divided as to whether the corporate form decisively determines that employees of a corporation, including professional corporations, are per se protected by the employment discrimination statutes. *Compare EEOC v. Johnson & Higgins, Inc.,* 91 F.3d 1529 (2d Cir.1996), cert. denied, 522 U.S. 808, 118 S.Ct. 47, 139 L.Ed.2d 13 (1997) (case under ADEA) (stock-owning directors whose compensation is tied to profits but who also work as officers and continue to perform work typical of employees are not sufficiently like "partners" to forfeit protection); *Serapion v. Martinez,* 119 F.3d 982 (1st Cir.1997), cert. denied, 522 U.S. 1047, 118 S.Ct. 690, 139 L.Ed.2d 636 (1998) (plaintiff denominated "partner" cannot claim Title VII protection where she had equity interest, her compensation turned substantially on firm profits, she was exposed to liability for firm losses, and participated "meaningfully" in firm governance); *Devine v. Stone, Leyton & Gershman P.C.,* 100 F.3d 78 (8th Cir.1996), cert. denied, 520 U.S. 1211, 117 S.Ct. 1694, 137 L.Ed.2d 821 (1997) (form of the organization does not dictate conclusion that plaintiff is a covered "employee" and court should instead apply economic realities tests); *Simpson v. Ernst & Young,* 100 F.3d 436 (6th Cir.1996), cert. denied, 520 U.S. 1248, 117 S.Ct. 1862, 137 L.Ed.2d 1062 (1997) (applying common-law principles, including right and duty to participate in management, or to act as an agent for or expose to liability other partners, and whether compensation geared to profits, and finding that a particular "partner" functioned in fact as a protected "employee"); *Wheeler v. Hurdman,* 825 F.2d 257, 263 (10th Cir.), *cert. denied,* 484 U.S. 986,

fore protects against discrimination across the full range of employment practices or decisions, embracing such intangible aspects of employment as workplace assignments, environment, and even mentoring opportunities[3] as well as more tangible problems like refusals to hire or promote, unequal pay or discriminatory discharge. Still, the plaintiff must present persuasive evidence that any unlawful conduct on the part of the employer caused a real detriment to her employment.[4] The requirement

108 S.Ct. 503, 98 L.Ed.2d 501 (1987) ("partners" not protected where plaintiff participated in profits, possessed voting rights, and was exposed to liability); *Fountain v. Metcalf, Zima & Co. P.A.*, 925 F.2d 1398 (11th Cir.1991) (individuals who function as partners will not be classified as employees, even if they also possess important indicia of common-law "employee" status, because partners own and manage firm). *See generally* EEOC Enforcement Guidance, *Whether Individuals Who Are Partners, Officers, Directors or Major Shareholders in Organizations May Be Considered Employees Under Title VII, ADEA, and the EPA*, No. 915.007 (July 14, 1987).

3. *Jensvold v. Shalala*, 829 F.Supp. 131 (D.Md.1993) (gender discrimination in affording plaintiff less adequate mentoring than male employees actionable). Despite the generally broad interpretation courts have accorded the phrase "terms and conditions" of employment under both Title VII and ADEA, recent decisions have recognized a de minimis exception that has extended to a lateral transfer, *Brown v. Brody*, 199 F.3d 446 (D.C.Cir.1999); *Galabya v. New York City Bd. of Educ.*, 202 F.3d 636, 640–41 (2d Cir.2000) (ADEA); *Williams v. Bristol–Myers Squibb Co.*, 85 F.3d 270 (7th Cir.1996) and even lower performance ratings. *See Primes v. Reno*, 190 F.3d 765, 767 (6th Cir.1999); *Rabinovitz v. Pena*, 89 F.3d 482 (7th Cir.1996); *Smart v. Ball State Univ.*, 89 F.3d 437 (7th Cir.1996). *See also Ledergerber v. Stangler*, 122 F.3d 1142 (8th Cir.1997) (where employer replaced a supervisor's subordinate staff and placed a statement in supervisor's file that discrimination would not be tolerated, supervisor did not suffer an adverse employment action); *Dobbs–Weinstein v. Vanderbilt Univ.*, 185 F.3d 542 (6th Cir.1999), *cert. denied*, ___ U.S. ___, 120 S.Ct. 1421, 146 L.Ed.2d 313 (2000) (intermediate adverse promotion recommendation ultimately reversed through internal grievance procedure not actionable). The trend is particularly pronounced in retaliation cases under § 704, as discussed in § 2.40, *infra. See especially Mattern v. Eastman Kodak Co.*, 104 F.3d 702 (5th Cir.), *cert. denied*, 522 U.S. 932, 118 S.Ct. 336, 139 L.Ed.2d 260 (1997) (§ 704 retaliation protection extends only

to employer "discrimination" affecting "ultimate employment decisions" of the kind prohibited by Section 703(a)(1), not to the broader proscription of Section 703(a)(2) against tangential interference with employment "opportunities").

4. *See, e.g., Boone v. Goldin*, 178 F.3d 253 (4th Cir.1999) (transfer did not constitute an actionable adverse employment action under Title VII despite the increased stress on plaintiff, because she suffered no demotion, compensation decrease, reduction in job title or supervisory responsibility); *Bragg v. Navistar Int'l Transp. Corp.*, 164 F.3d 373 (7th Cir.1998); cases cited *supra. But see Jones v. School Dist. of Phila.*, 198 F.3d 403, 411–12 (3d Cir.1999) (a transfer resulting in a lost opportunity to teach infield, coupled with a second transfer to a school with a reputation of being difficult suffices to show an adverse employment action).

Title VII's "a person claiming to be aggrieved" language, 42 U.S.C. § 2000e–5(b), has been broadly interpreted by the courts to allow claims by those who suffer a pecuniary loss as a result of discrimination aimed at others. For example, in *Anjelino v. New York Times Co.*, 200 F.3d 73 (3d Cir. 1999), male workers who were hired as daily extras from a list of union workers claimed that they were denied opportunities to work because they were sandwiched between women on the list. The defendant allegedly stopped hiring extras from the list when it reached women's names. The Third Circuit rejected defendant's contention that the men lacked standing because they were merely indirect victims of the discrimination. The court analogized Title VII with Title VIII, the Fair Housing Act, which the Supreme Court had interpreted to permit standing to such indirect victims of housing discrimination. *See Trafficante v. Metropolitan Life Ins. Co.*, 409 U.S. 205, 209–10, 93 S.Ct. 364, 34 L.Ed.2d 415 (1972) (holding that two tenants who alleged a loss of the social and professional benefits of living in an integrated community, due to landlords' alleged discrimination against racial minorities, had standing to sue under Title VIII). *See also EEOC v. Mississippi College*, 626

of proving adverse employment action has proven far more problematic, however, in cases alleging retaliation under § 704 than in proving primary or underlying discrimination under § 703.[5]

This broad sweep distinguishes Title VII from statutes, like EPA, that prohibit employment discrimination solely with respect to one term or condition of employment, such as compensation. Further, the Title VII prohibitions on race, color, sex, religious and national origin discrimination set it apart from single-focus statutes that ban only sex discrimination (EPA and Title IX); age discrimination (the Age Discrimination in Employment Act of 1967, or "ADEA"); race, ancestry and possibly national origin discrimination (42 U.S.C.A. §§ 1981 and 1985(3) and Title VI);[6] or handicap discrimination (the Rehabilitation Act of 1973 as expanded and partially supplanted by the Americans with Disabilities Act of 1990, or "ADA").

Title VII was amended by the Civil Rights Act of 1991. The principal stated purposes of the Act were to "provide appropriate remedies for intentional discrimination and unlawful harassment in the workplace:" to "confirm statutory authority and provide statutory guidelines for the adjudication of disparate impact suits under Title VII.... ;" and to "respond to recent decisions of the Supreme Court by expanding the scope of relevant civil rights statutes."[7]

This chapter gives a broad overview of Title VII as amended by the Civil Rights Act of 1991. Specifically, this chapter addresses which employees and employers are within the scope of Title VII and what actions fall within the boundaries of Title VII. The following chapter, Chapter 3, discusses the modes of proving a Title VII claim. Chapter 4

F.2d 477, 482 (5th Cir.1980), *cert. denied*, 453 U.S. 912, 101 S.Ct. 3143, 69 L.Ed.2d 994 (1981) ("We agree with other circuits that have held that the strong similarities between the language, design, and purposes of Title VII and [Title VIII] require that the phrase 'a person claiming to be aggrieved' in [Title VII] must be construed in the same manner *Trafficante* construed the term 'aggrieved person' in [Title VIII]."); *accord Clayton v. White Hall Sch. Dist.*, 875 F.2d 676, 679–80 (8th Cir.1989) (holding that white woman who was not object of discrimination, but who alleged injury because of race discrimination against another, was a "person aggrieved" within the meaning of Title VII); *Stewart v. Hannon*, 675 F.2d 846, 850 (7th Cir.1982) (finding white woman who had been deprived of interracial associations in workplace a "person aggrieved" within meaning of Title VII); *EEOC v. Bailey Co.*, 563 F.2d 439, 451–54 (6th Cir.1977), *cert. denied*, 435 U.S. 915, 98 S.Ct. 1468, 55 L.Ed.2d 506 (1978) (holding that white female had standing under Title VII to challenge her employee's alleged racial discrimination against blacks); *Waters v. Heublein, Inc.*, 547 F.2d 466, 469 (9th Cir.1976), *cert. denied*, 433 U.S. 915, 97 S.Ct. 2988, 53 L.Ed.2d 1100 (1977) (holding that white woman who sued under Title VII to enjoin racially discriminatory employment practices was "aggrieved person" within meaning of the statute); *Gray v. Greyhound Lines, East*, 545 F.2d 169, 175 (D.C.Cir.1976) (holding that blacks who were not subjected to racial discrimination had standing under Title VII to sue over discrimination against other blacks).

5. See § 2.40, *infra*.

6. As explained in more detail in Chapter 5 discussing the two cited Reconstruction Act statutes, their protection extends somewhat beyond our current conception of race as such. Generally speaking, the § 1981 prohibition extends as well to ancestry, although perhaps not to national origin; the § 1985(3) prohibition includes protection for those discriminated against on the basis of racial advocacy even if they do not suffer race discrimination per se.

7. Civil Rights Act of 1991, Pub.L. 102–166, §§ 3(1), (3), and (4), 105 Stat. 1071.

then looks at administrative prerequisites and procedures as well as Title VII remedies.

A. COVERAGE

§ 2.2 Protection for Individuals

Title VII's principal provisions defining unlawful employment practices, contained in § 703, extend protection to any "individual," whether or not an employee. This is somewhat curious because the statute contains a separate, if singularly unilluminating definition of employee: "any individual employed by an employer." Relying on § 703's broad protection of "any individual," courts have had no difficulty according plaintiff status and standing on former employees as well as applicants. Further, they have sometimes even recognized claims on behalf of persons who fall outside any common-law understanding of the employee-employer relationship, provided the circumstances satisfy an "economic realities" test that protects those in a position to suffer the kind of discrimination Title VII was designed to prevent. The key factor in the inquiry is the employer's right to control the means and manner of the plaintiff's performance of his work.[1] Occasionally, however, a court will rely on the "employee" definition to deny protection to persons, mainly independent contractors, who do not satisfy the common law's test for employee status, the "totality of the working relationship."[2] For exam-

§ 2.2

1. *See Atchley v. Nordam Group, Inc.*, 180 F.3d 1143, 1152 (10th Cir.1999). And work need not be compensated to constitute a covered employment relationship, provided the putative employee receives job-related benefits like health coverage, pension, and life and disability insurance. *See Pietras v. Board of Fire Comm'rs of Farmingville Fire Dist.* 180 F.3d 468 (2d Cir.1999).

2. *See, e.g., Schwieger v. Farm Bureau Ins. Co. of Nebraska*, 207 F.3d 480 (8th Cir.2000) (insurance agent who hired own support staff, was paid solely on commission and whose contract stated she was independent contractor could not hold corporation liable); *Adcock v. Chrysler Corp.*, 166 F.3d 1290 (9th Cir.), *cert. denied*, 528 U.S. 816, 120 S.Ct. 55, 145 L.Ed.2d 48 (1999) (automobile dealership applicant not covered by Title VII where as dealer he would have owned and controlled daily operations of the dealership); *EEOC v. North Knox Sch. Corp.*, 154 F.3d 744 (7th Cir. 1998) (bus drivers deemed independent contractors, and school district therefore not their employer, where drivers furnished their own buses, absorbed all costs and had no expectation of being engaged for a long term and where district exercised no significant control over daily work); *Cilecek v. Inova Health Sys. Servs.*, 115 F.3d 256 (4th Cir.1997), *cert. denied*, 522 U.S. 1049, 118 S.Ct. 694, 139 L.Ed.2d 639 (1998) (hospital staff physician's independence in setting his own maximum hours and his right to work for other employer's makes him independent contractor rather than covered "employee" despite hospital's right to determine his particular hours of work and insistence that he comply with hospital regulations and use its instruments and supplies); *Alexander v. Rush N. Shore Med. Ctr.*, 101 F.3d 487 (7th Cir.1996), *cert. denied*, 522 U.S. 811, 118 S.Ct. 54, 139 L.Ed.2d 19 (1997) (same conclusion concerning staff physician who billed and collected fees directly from his own patients, received no hospital benefits, and could associate with other hospitals); *Swallows v. Barnes & Noble Book Stores, Inc.*, 128 F.3d 990, 992 (6th Cir.1997) (state university and independent contractor operating college bookstore were not single employer where university had no authority to hire or fire book store employees and there was no common ownership or control); *Dykes v. DePuy Inc.*, 140 F.3d 31 (1st Cir.1998) (sales representative who set own hours and compensation, hired own staff, and maintained own office was independent contractor, not an employee); *Barnhart v. New York Life Ins. Co.*, 141 F.3d 1310 (9th Cir.1998) (even though company provided

ple, employees working for independent contractors are not generally considered employees of the other contracting party.[3]

Relying on the statutory language "any individual," courts have permitted plaintiffs to sue for harm respecting employment with third parties.[4] These courts reason that while the Title VII defendant must be a defined "employer," the plaintiff need not be an "employee" but

benefits usually associated with employment, insurance agent was independent contractor; he was under contract which specifically classified him as independent contractor, he was paid exclusively on a commission basis, and company did not control daily operations).

A circuit court has held that the "employee"/"independent contractor" issue is a question of fact for a jury, provided there is a genuine issue about any of the facts potentially determinative of the plaintiff's status. *Garcia v. Copenhaver, Bell & Assocs.*, 104 F.3d 1256 (11th Cir.1997). *See generally* EEOC Enforcement Guidance, *Title VII Coverage of Independent Contractors and Independent Businesses*, No. 915 (September 4, 1987). *But see Scarfo v. Ginsberg*, 175 F.3d 957 (11th Cir.1999), *cert. denied*, ___ U.S. ___, 120 S.Ct. 1267, 146 L.Ed.2d 217 (2000) (holding that whether a defendant is an "employer" covered by Title VII is a question for the court).

For idiosyncratic reasons, courts have also sometimes excluded particular persons from protected "employee" status even when they do otherwise satisfy the common law indicia of employee status. *See, e.g., Daniels v. Browner*, 63 F.3d 906 (9th Cir. 1995) (ADEA did not explicitly waive federal agency's sovereign immunity with respect to plaintiff whose work for agency was under cooperative agreement with private non-profit organization authorized by separate legislation designed to promote community service activities; hence plaintiff not "employee"); *Wilde v. County of Kandiyohi*, 15 F.3d 103 (8th Cir.1994). *See also O'Connor v. Davis*, 126 F.3d 112 (2d. Cir.1997), *cert. denied*, 522 U.S. 1114, 118 S.Ct. 1048, 140 L.Ed.2d 112 (1998) (denying employee status to college student who was required to participate in unpaid work/study internship at hospital but whose financial aid package took into account the work/study program because no financial benefit was obtained by the purported employee from the employer; "compensation by the putative employer ... is an essential condition to the existence of an employer-employee relationship.")

The EEOC, for example, takes the position that "employee" status should be denied to prison inmates who perform mandatory, on-site labor. A recent appellate decision suggests, however, that voluntary prison labor not conforming to the characteristics outlined by EEOC may confer "employee" status on an inmate. *See Moyo v. Gomez*, 32 F.3d 1382 (9th Cir.1994), *amended*, 32 F.3d 1382 (9th Cir.), *cert. denied*, 513 U.S. 1081, 115 S.Ct. 732, 130 L.Ed.2d 635 (1995).

Circuit courts have rejected defendant's position that an in-house counsel is excluded from the Title VII definition of employee by virtue of the attorney's knowledge of confidential information. *See Kachmar v. SunGard Data Sys., Inc.*, 109 F.3d 173 (3d Cir.1997); *Jones v. Flagship Int'l*, 793 F.2d 714 (5th Cir.1986), *cert. denied*, 479 U.S. 1065, 107 S.Ct. 952, 93 L.Ed.2d 1001 (1987) (in-house counsel may sue under Title VII, even if, in course of action, proof of claim may require her to reveal client confidence).

3. *See, e.g., Zinn v. McKune*, 143 F.3d 1353 (10th Cir.1998) (using a multiple factor totality of the working relationship test to find that prison nurse was employed by the contractor and not the prison despite prison's control over nurse's work rules and conditions); and cases cited *supra*.

4. *See, e.g., Christopher v. Stouder Mem. Hosp.*, 936 F.2d 870, 874–75 (6th Cir.), *cert. denied*, 502 U.S. 1013, 112 S.Ct. 658, 116 L.Ed.2d 749 (1991); *Zaklama v. Mt. Sinai Med. Ctr.*, 842 F.2d 291, 294–95 (11th Cir. 1988); *Gomez v. Alexian Bros. Hosp. of San Jose*, 698 F.2d 1019, 1021–22 (9th Cir. 1983); *Spirt v. Teachers Ins. & Annuity Ass'n*, 691 F.2d 1054, 1062–63 (2d Cir. 1982), *vacated on other grounds*, 463 U.S. 1223, 103 S.Ct. 3565, 77 L.Ed.2d 1406 (1983); *Sibley Memorial Hospital v. Wilson*, 488 F.2d 1338 (D.C.Cir.1973). *See also Graves v. Lowery*, 117 F.3d 723, 728 (3d Cir.1997) (discussing standing per *Sibley*). *But cf. Fields v. Hallsville Ind. Sch. Dist.*, 906 F.2d 1017, 1018–1019 (5th Cir.1990), *cert. denied*, 498 U.S. 1026, 111 S.Ct. 676, 112 L.Ed.2d 668 (1991) and *Diggs v. Harris Hospital–Methodist, Inc.*, 847 F.2d 270, 271–272 (5th Cir.), *cert. denied*, 488 U.S. 956, 109 S.Ct. 394, 102 L.Ed.2d 383 (1988) (finding no direct employment relationship, but not directly passing on standing per *Sibley*).

instead is referred to in the statute as a "person aggrieved."[5] (For the same reason, the statute applies to defendant labor unions and employment agencies, which also have no direct employment relationship with a plaintiff.) For example, in *Sibley Memorial Hosp. v. Wilson*,[6] a hospital was found liable for interfering with a private nurse in his relationship with his privately-paying patients despite the court's recognition that there was no employment relationship between the hospital and the nurse. "While neither hiring nor reinstatement may be relevant outside the context of direct employment, both injunctive and [compensatory damages] may be available, in an appropriate case, against respondents who are neither actual nor potential direct employers of particular complainants, but who control access to such employment and who deny such access by reference to invidious criteria."[7] The plaintiff attempting to invoke such *"Sibley* standing" must show that a defined Title VII "employer" used a position of power and control over a third party to wrongfully interfere with that party's employment relationship with the plaintiff.[8]

By contrast, the § 704 protection against retaliation for opposing unlawful employment practices or participating in proceedings to protest them extends to "employees or applicants for employment."[9] The Su-

---

5. The Seventh Circuit has accorded Title VII standing to testers in *Kyles v. J.K. Guardian Security Servs., Inc.*, 222 F.3d 289, 299–300 (7th Cir.2000). Analogizing the testers' Title VII claim to similar claims brought under Title VIII or the Fair Housing Act, the court reasoned that functionally, the two statutes are equivalent in that they both create a broad substantive right that can be enforced through private attorneys general. *See also Molovinsky v. Fair Employment Council of Greater Washington, Inc.*, 683 A.2d 142, 146 (D.C.1996) (per curiam) (testers have standing to sue for sexual harassment under local ordinance, akin to Title VII, prohibiting sex discrimination in employment). *But see Sledge v. J.P. Stevens & Co.*, 585 F.2d 625, 641 (4th Cir.1978), *cert. denied*, 440 U.S. 981, 99 S.Ct. 1789, 60 L.Ed.2d 241 (1979) (" 'tester' plaintiffs are not, of course, harmed by a refusal to hire since they are not seriously interested in the job for which they apply"); *Parr v. Woodmen of the World Life Ins. Soc'y*, 657 F.Supp. 1022, 1032–33 (M.D.Ga. 1987) (plaintiff who had no genuine interest in employment with defendant could not make prima facie case of employment discrimination); *Allen v. Prince George's County, Maryland*, 538 F.Supp. 833, 841–43 (D.Md.1982), *judgment aff'd. on other grounds*, 737 F.2d 1299 (4th Cir.1984) (same).

6. 488 F.2d 1338 (D.C.Cir.1973).

7. *Id.* at 1342. *See also Bender v. Suburban Hosp. Inc.*, 159 F.3d 186 (4th Cir.1998) (rejecting staff physician's claim that a hospital's denial of privileges which interfered with her *prospective* ability to get other work was prohibited by Title VII; court acknowledged that such an "indirect" sex discrimination claim is cognizable, but only if plaintiff can show an *existing* employment relationship with some third party).

8. See *Sibley*, 488 F.2d at 1342. While courts that recognize *Sibley* standing are clear that the plaintiff need not have a direct employment relationship with the defendant, they do tend to require that the plaintiff have such a direct relationship with the third party. That relationship may be shown, however, through a test that considers the economic realities of employment but also relies on the degree of the third party's control over the plaintiff's conduct. *See, e.g., Alexander v. Rush N. Shore Med. Ctr.*, 101 F.3d 487, 492–493 (7th Cir. 1996), *cert. denied*, 522 U.S. 811, 118 S.Ct. 54, 139 L.Ed.2d 19 (1997); *Cobb v. Sun Papers, Inc.*, 673 F.2d 337, 341 (11th Cir.), *cert. denied*, 459 U.S. 874, 103 S.Ct. 163, 74 L.Ed.2d 135 (1982); *Spirides v. Reinhardt*, 613 F.2d 826, 831–832 (D.C.Cir.1979).

9. *See, e.g., Moyo v. Gomez*, 32 F.3d 1382 (9th Cir.1994), *amended*, 40 F.3d 982 (9th Cir.), *cert. denied*, 513 U.S. 1081, 115 S.Ct. 732, 130 L.Ed.2d 635 (1995) (prison guard stated retaliation claim for protesting prison's practice of denying black inmates showers after job shifts on same terms as white inmates).

preme Court has agreed with the overwhelming view of the circuit courts that, despite the possible implication that "employees" refers only to those currently working, former employees also enjoy protection from retaliation.[10]

The Court wrote that in context, some Title VII sections use "employee" to mean something more inclusive than current employees, while others use the term more restrictively. Accordingly, the Court concluded, the term as used in § 704 is ambiguous. It then resolved that ambiguity in favor of covering former employees, reasoning that the broader structure of Title VII presupposes their eligibility to file charges. In particular, the Court observed, discriminatory discharge is expressly made the basis of a "charge" under § 703, and § 704 prohibits retaliation for, among other things, filing a § 703 "charge." Excluding former employees from § 704's protection would also undermine Title VII's effectiveness by "allowing the threat of post-employment retaliation to deter victims of discrimination from complaining to EEOC" about the single most serious adverse employment discipline, namely, discharge, thereby providing employers the "perverse incentive to fire employees who might bring Title VII claims."[11] Although the decision itself involved a former employee who alleged retaliation (in the form of adverse references) for filing an EEOC charge, the "employees" language should now embrace former employees' claims of retaliation for informal "opposing" activity as well. This follows not only from the text of § 704— the protection against opposition, although more limited in scope than the protection against formal participation,[12] is made available to the same "employees"—but from the Court's rationale that antiretaliation provisions are designed to maintain unfettered access to statutory remedial mechanisms.[13] The standing of spouses and others to pursue claims under Title VII or ADEA is discussed in Chapter 12.

---

10. *Robinson v. Shell Oil Co.,* 519 U.S. 337, 117 S.Ct. 843, 136 L.Ed.2d 808 (1997).

11. *Id.,* at 346, 117 S.Ct. at 848. But a questionable circuit decision issued before *Robinson* held that former employees are not protected from post-employment discrimination respecting employer-provided fringe benefits under the Americans with Disabilities Act, despite that statute's relevant similarities with Title VII. *See Gonzales v. Garner Food Servs., Inc.,* 89 F.3d 1523 (11th Cir.1996), *cert. denied,* 520 U.S. 1229, 117 S.Ct. 1822, 137 L.Ed.2d 1030 (1997). *But see Ford v. Schering–Plough Corp.,* 145 F.3d 601 (3d Cir.1998), *cert. denied,* 525 U.S. 1093, 119 S.Ct. 850, 142 L.Ed.2d 704 (1999) (holding that the ADA allows former employees to sue former employers regarding disability benefits).

12. *See* § 2.40 *infra.*

13. This last concern has led EEOC categorically to prohibit employee agreements not to file a charge or participate in an EEOC proceeding. The agency treats such agreements as "null and void" regardless of whether they are contained in employee handbooks, individual contracts, or waiver agreements entered into as part of a settlement agreement. EEOC Guidance, *Waivers Under Civil Rights Laws,* No. 915.002 (April 10, 1997). The federal courts, too, consistently treat the right to file EEOC charges as nonwaivable. *See EEOC v. Astra USA, Inc.,* 94 F.3d 738, 744 (1st Cir.1996) (affirming injunction prohibiting employer from enforcing settlement agreement provisions that purported to bar employees from assisting EEOC in investigating charges); *EEOC v. Cosmair, Inc.,* 821 F.2d 1085, 1090 (5th Cir.1987) (invalidating employee promise not to file EEOC charge). The Supreme Court has recognized the invalidity of such an agreement even where the employee has also agreed to arbitrate a statutory discrimination claim and is accordingly required to arbitrate on the employer's demand before pursuing (or perhaps in lieu of pursuing) a judicial action. *See Gilmer v. Inter-*

§ 2.3 Employers Governed by Title VII/ADEA

Title VII applies to employers, employment agencies, apprenticeship programs and labor organizations whose activities affect interstate commerce. There are very few categorical exclusions from the definition of "employer" in either Title VII or ADEA. Title VII expressly exempts private membership clubs[1] exempt from taxation under the Internal Revenue Code and Indian tribes.[2] ADEA contains neither such exemption in express terms, but Indian tribes have been exempted by judicial construction.[3] By far the most significant exclusion is numerical: an employer is covered by Title VII only if it has 15 or more employees, and by ADEA only if it has 20 or more employees, for each working day in 20 or more calendar weeks in the current or prior calendar year.[4] Persons holding an employment relationship with the employer during a calendar week (usually manifested by presence on the payroll) are counted regardless of how many of them actually worked or received compensation on any particular working day in that week.[5]

Courts have wrestled with whether to aggregate for coverage purposes the number of employees employed by affiliated enterprises, for example by subjecting a parent corporation to potential liability for the conduct of a subsidiary;[6] whether to consider all of an employer's

---

state/Johnson Lane Corp., 500 U.S. 20, 28, 111 S.Ct. 1647, 1653, 114 L.Ed.2d 26 (1991), discussed in § 4.6, *infra*; *Adams v. Philip Morris, Inc.*, 67 F.3d 580 (6th Cir. 1995). On the other hand, the Commission and the courts recognize that an employer who has secured an otherwise valid settlement waiver agreement can effectively shield itself from further recovery sought by an employee filing an employment discrimination charge. EEOC Guidance, *supra*; *EEOC v. Astra USA*, 94 F.3d at 744.

§ 2.3

1. *See generally* 42 U.S.C.A. § 2000e(b)(2) (Title VII exemption for private membership clubs). As long as a club is "private" in the sense of being owned and run by a restricted membership, not advertising publicly to solicit members, and limiting use of facilities to members and their guests, the exemption applies even if the club is of large size and even though no exemption is needed to protect the members' constitutional associational rights. *See EEOC v. The Chicago Club*, 86 F.3d 1423 (7th Cir.1996).

2. *See generally* 42 U.S.C.A. § 2000e(b)(1) (explicit Title VII tribal exemption). In addition to the exemption of tribes from coverage as employers, private employers may prefer Indians over non-Indians pursuant to 42 U.S.C.A. § 2000e–2(i). A circuit court has agreed with the policy of EEOC, however, that this latter provision does not permit a non-Indian em-

ployer to prefer members of one tribe over another. *Dawavendewa v. Salt River Project Agric. Improvement and Power Dist.*, 154 F.3d 1117 (9th Cir.1998), *cert. denied*, 528 U.S. 1098, 120 S.Ct. 843, 145 L.Ed.2d 708 (2000).

3. *See EEOC v. Fond du Lac Heavy Equip. and Const. Co., Inc.*, 986 F.2d 246 (8th Cir.1993) (implied ADEA tribal exemption despite lack of express one and presence of express exemption in Title VII). By contrast, it appears that private clubs are amenable to suit under the ADEA. *See Lindsey v. Prive Corp.*, 987 F.2d 324 (5th Cir.1993).

4. The phrase "current calendar year" refers to the year in which the alleged discrimination takes place and not, even for a new business, the calendar year after the year the discrimination occurred. *See Komorowski v. Townline Mini–Mart and Rest.*, 162 F.3d 962 (7th Cir.1998).

5. *See Walters v. Metropolitan Educ. Enters., Inc.*, 519 U.S. 202, 117 S.Ct. 660, 136 L.Ed.2d 644 (1997).

6. *See Schweitzer v. Advanced Telemarketing Corp.*, 104 F.3d 761 (5th Cir. 1997) (assess interrelation of operations, common management, centralized control of labor relations, and common ownership and financial control to decide whether parent corporation should be considered "employer" of employee of subsidiary); *Cook v.*

employees when the alleged unlawful employment practice is confined to a discrete operating location;[7] whether to impose liability on a successor employer after a sale of the business or bankruptcy;[8] whether a government-appointed receiver is a Title VII "employer" of employees of a failed financial institution;[9] whether a contractor is liable for a subcontractor's unlawful employment practice;[10] whether a nonprofit organization qualifies as an "employer";[11] and whether an employment agency or

---

Arrowsmith Shelburne, Inc., 69 F.3d 1235 (2d Cir.1995) (sustaining claim against parent that controlled labor relations of wholly owned subsidiary); *Childs v. Local 18, Int'l Bhd. of Elec. Workers,* 719 F.2d 1379 (9th Cir.1983); *Armbruster v. Quinn,* 711 F.2d 1332 (6th Cir.1983) (where evidence of interrelationship between subsidiary and corporate parent is sufficient, the two entities are jointly responsible for acts of subsidiary); *Lusk v. Foxmeyer Health Corp.,* 129 F.3d 773 (5th Cir.1997) (evidence of common ownership and management insufficient to find parent and subsidiary a single employer where parent company was simply a holding company with no involvement in daily operations). The Seventh Circuit has rejected this "integrated enterprises" four-factor test as "vague" and "useless." It now holds that otherwise too-small employers are subject to liability based on affiliating with a larger parent only when (1) a court could pierce the corporate veil because of neglect of corporate formalities or the parent's holding itself out as responsible for the affiliate's debts; (2) if the enterprise division was devised in order to avoid employment discrimination liability; or (3) the parent directed the alleged unlawful employment practice. *Papa v. Katy Indus., Inc.,* 166 F.3d 937 (7th Cir.), *cert. denied,* 528 U.S. 1019, 120 S.Ct. 526, 145 L.Ed.2d 408 (1999) (case under ADEA and ADA). *But see Herman v. Blockbuster Entertainment Group,* 182 F.3d 899, 1999 WL 385765, at *1–2 (2d Cir.), *cert. denied,* 528 U.S. 1020, 120 S.Ct. 529, 145 L.Ed.2d 409 (1999) (applying four factor test). At least two circuits have rejected the four factor test when considering governmental entities. *See Lyes v. City of Riviera Beach, Florida,* 166 F.3d 1332, 1343 (11th Cir.1999); *Trevino v. Celanese Corp.,* 701 F.2d 397, 404 n. 10 (5th Cir.1983). In *Lyes,* the Eleventh Circuit held that two or more government entities will be aggregated where one entity exerts or shares control over the fundamental aspects of the employment relationships of another entity, to such a substantial extent that it clearly outweighs the presumption that the entities are distinct. Interrelation of operations; centralized control of labor operations; the authority to

hire, transfer, promote, discipline or discharge; the authority to establish work schedules or direct work assignments; and the obligation to pay or the duty to train the charging party are factors to be considered. 166 F.3d at 1345.

7. *See Owens v. Rush,* 636 F.2d 283 (10th Cir.1980) (sheriff's department named as defendant in Title VII action which employed less than 15 people was considered an "employer" for Title VII purposes because the county employed more than 15 people).

8. *See, e.g., Rojas v. TK Communications, Inc.,* 87 F.3d 745 (5th Cir.1996) (declining to impose liability on corporation that met the standard indicia of successor because predecessor continued as viable entity and plaintiff sought only monetary relief, not reinstatement); *EEOC v. G–K–G, Inc.,* 39 F.3d 740 (7th Cir.1994) (affirming general rule that a mere purchaser of corporate assets does not acquire the seller's liability for unlawful employment practices unless, as was the case there, the successor receives notice of the claim before the sale and maintains "substantial continuity" of operations).

9. *See Nowlin v. Resolution Trust Corp.,* 33 F.3d 498 (5th Cir.1994) (holding that the appropriate standard is the "hybrid test," which considers all relevant factors including the right to control terms of the plaintiffs' employment, rather than the "borrowed servant" doctrine from common law tort).

10. *See Fitzgerald v. Mountain States Tel. & Tel. Co.,* 68 F.3d 1257 (10th Cir. 1995) (absent ratification or approval of subcontractor's alleged discriminatory misconduct, contracting company not liable under § 1981); *Zinn v. McKune,* 143 F.3d 1353 (10th Cir.1998) (using a multiple factor totality of the working relationship test to find that prison nurse was employed by the contractor and not the prison despite prison's control over nurse's work rules and conditions).

11. *See EEOC v. Association of Community Orgs. for Reform Now,* 1995 WL 107075 (E.D.La.1995), *aff'd sub nom.*

union meets the statutory "employer" definition even when it has fewer than 15 employees.[12] These and other coverage questions are capably discussed in detail in several standard works.[13]

Unions may be liable as labor organizations representing employees in collective bargaining without regard to the number of employees represented, but are liable in their capacity as "employer" only if they satisfy the employer definition, including the requirement of at least 15 employees under Title VII.[14]

Answering an increasingly important question in an economy depending heavily on temporary employees referred through employment agencies, federal courts have permitted such employees to recover under Title VII from the firms to which they are assigned, provided that firm exercises sufficient control over the means and manner of their performance or interferes with any employment relation they have established with the referring agency.[15] An EEOC Guidance explains that both temporary staffing firms and their clients may be jointly liable for unlawful discrimination if both have the right to control the worker and each meets the statutory minimum number of employees. And according to the EEOC, employees who are assigned jobs in welfare-to-work programs are also protected by federal discrimination statutes in the same way as other workers.[16]

States, their political subdivisions, and agencies of each are also employers under Title VII.[17] The constitutionality of applying Title VII

NLRB v. Pilgrim Indus., 83 F.3d 418 (5th Cir.1996) (organization is covered "employer" because of its involvement in and relationship to commerce despite nonprofit status).

12. *See Greenlees v. Eidenmuller Enters., Inc.*, 32 F.3d 197 (5th Cir.1994) and *Kern v. City of Rochester,* 93 F.3d 38 (2d Cir.1996), *cert. denied*, 520 U.S. 1155, 117 S.Ct. 1335, 137 L.Ed.2d 494 (1997) (rejecting this interpretation in the case of employment agencies and unions, respectively, contrary to the view of the EEOC).

13. *See generally,* Player, *Employment Discrimination Law* (West 1990).

14. *See Yerdon v. Henry*, 91 F.3d 370 (2d Cir.1996).

15. *See Reynolds v. CSX Transp., Inc.,* 115 F.3d 860, 868 n. 12 (11th Cir.1997), *judgment vacated in light of Faragher*, 524 U.S. 947, 118 S.Ct. 2364, 141 L.Ed.2d 732 (1998); *Amarnare v. Merrill Lynch, Pierce, Fenner & Smith, Inc.*, 611 F.Supp. 344, 349 (S.D.N.Y.1984), *aff'd*, 770 F.2d 157 (2d Cir. 1985).

16. EEOC Enforcement Guidance, *Application of EEO Laws to Contingent Workers Placed by Temporary Employment Agencies and Other Staffing Firms*, date issued 12/8/97, available at http://www.eeoc.gov/docs/conting.txt.

17. Title VII § 701(b) and (a), 42 U.S.C.A. § 2000e(b), (a). Whether one or another government entity is the sole or a coemployer of the plaintiff is determined functionally, in sharp contrast to the practice under Section 1983, where the form of state law controls. *Compare Graves v. Lowery*, 117 F.3d 723 (3d Cir.1997) (county a de facto Title VII coemployer of court clerks where it maintained and communicated personnel policies to plaintiffs that led them to believe that county had hiring, termination, and reinstatement authority) *with McMillian v. Monroe Co., Ala.,* 520 U.S. 781, 117 S.Ct. 1734, 138 L.Ed.2d 1 (1997) (the form of state law allocating authority between state and local government determines which entity a final policymaker acts on behalf of). But where the local entity would functionally be viewed as the plaintiff's primary employer, the state is not liable for indirect support of those functions. Thus it is not liable for aiding and abetting a local school district's mandatory retirement of a plaintiff teacher, either because it failed to repeal legislation preempted by ADEA or on a theory that the state was the plaintiff's de facto employer as ultimate regulator of the local school district.

to state defendants, and their amenability to suit in federal court is settled. Even before *Garcia v. San Antonio Metropolitan Transit Authority*[18] determined that the Tenth Amendment does not supersede Congress' Commerce Clause authority to regulate the wages and hours of state employees, the Supreme Court had held in *Fitzpatrick v. Bitzer*,[19] that Title VII's grounding in § 5 of the Fourteenth Amendment empowered Congress to override the Eleventh Amendment barrier to state liability in federal court.[20]

The federal government and its agencies are not defined "employers,"[21] but special provisions in each statute[22] mandate that personnel actions affecting most federal employees be made free from discrimination based on any of the grounds those statutes address. Title VII generally does not apply to uniformed members of the armed services.[23]

Both Title VII and ADEA define a covered "employer" to include

EEOC v. Illinois, 69 F.3d 167 (7th Cir. 1995).

18. 469 U.S. 528, 105 S.Ct. 1005, 83 L.Ed.2d 1016 (1985). *But cf. Alden v. Maine*, 527 U.S. 706, 119 S.Ct. 2240, 144 L.Ed.2d 636 (1999) (holding that a nonconsenting state is immune from a damages claim under the FLSA in its own state courts). The *Alden* holding makes the principle espoused in *Garcia* a practical nullity with regards to retrospective damages actions because the FLSA cannot be enforced against a state in federal court under the Eleventh Amendment nor in a state court under *Alden*. Only an *Ex parte Young* suit can be utilized to enforce a state's compliance with FLSA. *See* the discussion of the Eleventh Amendment in Chapter 12.

19. 427 U.S. 445, 96 S.Ct. 2666, 49 L.Ed.2d 614 (1976).

20. The Eleventh Circuit recently held that Title VII validly abrogated states' immunity for disparate impact claims as well. *See In re Employment Discrimination Litigation Against the State of Ala.*, 198 F.3d 1305 (11th Cir.1999). The case was decided, however, before the Supreme Court's decision in *Kimel v. Florida Bd. Of Regents*, 528 U.S. 62, 120 S.Ct. 631, 145 L.Ed.2d 522 (2000), wherein the Court held that the ADEA did not validly abrogate states' immunity for age discrimination suits in federal court. The Eleventh Amendment issues are fully discussed in Chapter 12.

21. Title VII § 701(b), 42 U.S.C.A. § 2000e(b), and ADEA § 11(b)(2), 29 U.S.C.A. § 630(b)(2).

22. Title VII § 717, 42 U.S.C.A. § 2000e–16 and ADEA § 15, 29 U.S.C.A. § 633a. But while § 717(a) bans discrimination respecting "all personnel activities" against civilian employees in military departments, the federal security clearance process has been held beyond Title VII scrutiny. *See Ryan v. Reno*, 168 F.3d 520 (D.C.Cir.1999) (denial of security clearance is a nonreviewable Department of Justice decision); *Brazil v. United States Dep't of the Navy*, 66 F.3d 193 (9th Cir.1995), *cert. denied*, 517 U.S. 1103, 116 S.Ct. 1317, 134 L.Ed.2d 470 (1996). Similarly, a civilian employee of the National Guard who was denied a military promotion was held to have failed to state a Title VII claim. *Mier v. Owens*, 57 F.3d 747 (9th Cir.1995), *cert. denied sub nom. Mier v. Van Dyke*, 517 U.S. 1103, 116 S.Ct. 1317, 134 L.Ed.2d 470 (1996). *See also Hupp v. United States Dep't of the Army*, 144 F.3d 1144 (8th Cir.1998) (National Guard could not be held liable for sex discrimination for denying a female National Guard member a position as a civilian technician where the hiring process included consideration of both military and civilian qualifications). *Accord Randall v. United States*, 95 F.3d 339 (4th Cir.1996), *cert. denied*, 519 U.S. 1150, 117 S.Ct. 1085, 137 L.Ed.2d 219 (1997) (held, in case alleging racially motivated failure to promote, that statute applies only to civilian, not uniformed, members of military departments). But a civilian employee's right to be free of sexual harassment extends to harassment by a uniformed co-worker. *See Yamaguchi v. United States Dep't of the Air Force*, 109 F.3d 1475 (9th Cir.1997). The court explained that an adverse judgment would not indirectly impose discipline on military personnel but would merely require the military to compensate the plaintiff.

23. *See, e.g., Taylor v. Jones*, 653 F.2d 1193, 1200 (8th Cir.1981); *Johnson v. Alexander*, 572 F.2d 1219, 1224 (8th Cir.), *cert.*

any "agent" of an employer.[24] At a minimum, this definition makes the employer as an entity liable for the acts of subordinates by means of respondeat superior. The circuits that have confronted the issue have uniformly concluded, however, that a supervisor is not such an "agent" who can be subjected to personal liability.[25] The argument favoring individual liability is arguably slightly stronger now that the 1991 Civil Rights Act affords, in cases of intentional discrimination, elements of relief (namely compensatory and punitive damages) that individual defendants may provide.[26] Nevertheless, the provisions of that Act that add damages liability do not refer to individual liability. Further, the retention of a fifteen-employee threshold for employer liability suggests the continuing Congressional reluctance to impose liability on small entities, and therefore presumably also individual employees.[27] Where supervisory employees are held subject to Title VII their liability has been limited to conduct deemed to have been undertaken in their official capacities[28] and where they exercised independent authority or were unmistakably acting as "agent" of the employer.[29] Two recent Fourth Circuit cases neatly illustrate how a court may read the term "agent" broadly for purposes of imposing liability on the employer[30] yet exclude from its reach the personal liability of an employer officer.[31]

denied, 439 U.S. 986, 99 S.Ct. 579, 58 L.Ed.2d 658 (1978).

24. 42 U.S.C.A. § 2000e(b) (Title VII); 29 U.S.C.A. § 630(b) (ADEA).

25. *See Lissau v. Southern Food Serv., Inc.*, 159 F.3d 177 (4th Cir.1998) (no individual Title VII liability); *Wathen v. General Elec.*, 115 F.3d 400 (6th Cir.1997) (same); *Dici v. Pennsylvania*, 91 F.3d 542, 552 (3d Cir.1996) (same); *Williams v. Banning*, 72 F.3d 552 (7th Cir.1995) (same); *Tomka v. Seiler Corp.*, 66 F.3d 1295 (2d Cir.1995) (same); *Gary v. Long*, 59 F.3d 1391 (D.C.Cir.), *cert. denied*, 516 U.S. 1011, 116 S.Ct. 569, 133 L.Ed.2d 493 (1995); *Greenlaw v. Garrett*, 59 F.3d 994 (9th Cir.1995), *cert. denied sub nom Greenlaw v. Dalton*, 519 U.S. 836, 117 S.Ct. 110, 136 L.Ed.2d 63 (1996); *Grant v. Lone Star Co.*, 21 F.3d 649 (5th Cir.), *cert. denied*, 513 U.S. 1015, 115 S.Ct. 574, 130 L.Ed.2d 491 (1994) (same); *Smith v. St. Bernards Regional Med. Ctr.*, 19 F.3d 1254 (8th Cir.1994); *Sauers v. Salt Lake County*, 1 F.3d 1122, 1125 (10th Cir. 1993) (same); *Busby v. City of Orlando*, 931 F.2d 764, 772 (11th Cir.1991). *But see Wyss v. General Dynamics Corp.*, 24 F.Supp.2d 202, 205 (D.R.I.1998); *Iacampo v. Hasbro, Inc.*, 929 F.Supp. 562, 572 (D.R.I.1996). *See also Alberte v. Anew Health Care Servs., Inc.*, 232 Wis.2d 587, 605 N.W.2d 515 (Wis. 2000) (no individual liability under ADA); *Carrisales v. Department of Corrections*, 21 Cal.4th 1132, 90 Cal.Rptr.2d 804, 988 P.2d

1083 (Cal.1999) (no individual liability for employment discrimination under California Fair Employment and Housing Act).

26. In *U.S. EEOC v. AIC Security Investigations, Ltd.*, 823 F.Supp. 571 (N.D.Ill. 1993), the District Court accepted the argument that the 1991 Act allowed individual liability. The Seventh Circuit reversed. *U.S. EEOC v. AIC Security Investigations, Ltd.*, 55 F.3d 1276 (7th Cir.1995).

27. *See Miller v. Maxwell's Int'l, Inc.*, 991 F.2d 583 (9th Cir.1993), *cert. denied sub nom Miller v. La Rosa*, 510 U.S. 1109, 114 S.Ct. 1049, 127 L.Ed.2d 372 (1994); *Stefanski v. R.A. Zehetner & Assocs., Inc.*, 855 F.Supp. 1030 (E.D.Wis.1994).

28. *See Harvey v. Blake*, 913 F.2d 226, 227–28 (5th Cir.1990), *limiting Hamilton v. Rodgers*, 791 F.2d 439, 442–43 (5th Cir. 1986); *Stefanski v. R.A. Zehetner*, 855 F.Supp. 1030.

29. *See Dirschel v. Speck*, 1994 WL 330262 (S.D.N.Y.1994).

30. *See EEOC v. Watergate at Landmark Condominium*, 24 F.3d 635 (4th Cir.), *cert. denied*, 513 U.S. 866, 115 S.Ct. 185, 130 L.Ed.2d 119 (1994) (resident owners of condominium treated as employer "agents" for purposes of imposing ADEA liability on condominium).

31. *See Birkbeck v. Marvel Lighting Corp.*, 30 F.3d 507 (4th Cir.), *cert. denied*,

a. American Corporations' Employees Working Abroad and "Foreign" Employers' Personnel Stationed in U.S. and Overseas: Of National Origin, Alienage and Ancestry Discrimination Under Title VII/ADEA, IRCA, and 42 U.S.C.A. § 1981

Discrimination on any ground against an *alien* (for this purpose, someone who has not yet attained full American citizenship) working *outside* the United States for either an American or non-U.S. company is not prohibited by either Title VII or ADEA. This results from an exemption to Title VII[32] and a restriction in the ADEA's definition of "employee."[33] Somewhat more difficult questions concern the statutory protection available to citizen employees of American companies stationed overseas and to the American-and overseas-based employees of foreign enterprises.

Unlike the ADEA, which was amended in 1984 to apply to the overseas work of American corporations and American-controlled foreign corporations,[34] Title VII until recently had no language specifically extending its application to work performed for the more than 2000 U.S. firms operating more than 21,000 foreign subsidiaries abroad.[35] These include U.S. citizens who work overseas for an American employer on a long-term basis, those who maintain their American residency during temporary assignments overseas, and American-based employees who routinely travel outside U.S. territorial limits in the course of their employment. If given a choice, the plaintiff would usually find it more advantageous to litigate in the United States under U.S. employment discrimination law than to litigate overseas under foreign law, as the foreign tribunals customarily place far greater limits on discovery (particularly depositions) and relief (especially injunctions directing reinstatement and punitive damages). The Supreme Court, reviving a nineteenth-century presumption against extraterritorial application of American statutes absent express statutory direction, limited Title VII's scope to unlawful employment practices arising in connection with work performed in the United States.[36] The Civil Rights Act of 1991 overturns that decision by defining most covered employees[37] to include U.S.

---

513 U.S. 1058, 115 S.Ct. 666, 130 L.Ed.2d 600 (1994) (vice president of employer not a proper ADEA defendant).

32. Section 702, 42 U.S.C.A. § 2000e–1.

33. ADEA § 11(f), 29 U.S.C.A. § 630(f).

34. ADEA § 4(h), 29 U.S.C.A. § 623(h). *See also Morelli v. Cedel*, 141 F.3d 39 (2d Cir.1998) (ADEA protects employees of U.S. branches of foreign employers with more than 20 workers worldwide); *Denty v. SmithKline Beecham Corp.*, 109 F.3d 147 (3d Cir.), *cert. denied*, 522 U.S. 820, 118 S.Ct. 74, 139 L.Ed.2d 34 (1997) (ADEA does not apply when a foreign parent corporation controls an American subsidiary corporation and employee seeks promotion to work for the foreign corporation abroad).

35. See 1 World Trade Academy Press, Directory of American Firms Operating in Foreign Countries (10th ed. 1984).

36. *EEOC v. Arabian American Oil Co.*, 499 U.S. 244, 111 S.Ct. 1227, 113 L.Ed.2d 274 (1991).

37. The 1991 amendment does not appear to extend to federal employees covered under § 717 of Title VII. Thus if the presumption against extraterritorial application of federal statutes announced in *EEOC v. Arabian American Oil Co.*, 499 U.S. 244, 111 S.Ct. 1227, 113 L.Ed.2d 274 (1991) survives the 1991 Act, federal employees may be unprotected with respect to their work overseas. *See* Street, *U.S. Corporations on Foreign Soil*, NBA Magazine, May 1991, at 8.

citizens "with respect to employment in a foreign country."[38]

This protection for U.S. citizens is now coextensive with that earlier provided by the ADEA. The 1991 Act subjects to Title VII jurisdiction not only U.S. corporations but also those foreign corporations "controlled" by American employers,[39] and it appears to provide dual defendants in this situation by presuming that unlawful employment practices of the controlled foreign affiliate are engaged in by the controlling (American) employer as well.[40] But it exempts conduct that would cause any employer to violate the national law of the foreign workplace.[41] This exemption is not triggered simply because the type of discrimination in question (e.g., gender or religious) is permitted by foreign law; rather, that law must affirmatively prohibit the particular employer conduct (e.g., hiring a woman as a driver in Saudi Arabia) that compliance with Title VII would otherwise require the employer to permit. But the foreign "law" that would be violated if ADEA were respected may include a collective bargaining agreement with a foreign labor union.[42]

Truly foreign corporations—those not "controlled" by a U.S. business—are not subject to Title VII with respect to work *outside* the United States. U.S. citizens working abroad meet the amended § 701 definition of "employee," and firms chartered in other nations are not excluded from the definition of "employer." To relieve foreign corporations of liability with respect to foreign work, therefore, Congress in 1991 had to specifically provide that the basic prohibitions of the Title do not apply "with respect to the foreign operations of an employer that is a foreign person."[43]

If the employer is not shielded by a treaty authorizing discrimination in the selection of executives on the basis of citizenship,[44] the more than half a million American-based employees of foreign corporations[45] may rely on Title VII and ADEA. But those statutes may not afford them

---

38. Section 701(f), 42 U.S.C.A. § 2000e(f).

39. This follows indirectly from § 702(c)(2), 42 U.S.C.A. § 2000e–1(c)(2), which provides that the "title shall *not* apply with respect to the foreign operations of an employer that is a foreign person *not* controlled by an American employer." Section 702(c)(3) identifies four factors critical to the determination of "control" of the foreign enterprise by the American company: interrelationship of operations, common management, centralized control of labor relations, and common ownership or financial control. This unweighted, multi-factor approach obviously leaves undecided the status of firms that were "American" in origin, as measured by locus of operations and number of employees, but then became predominantly transnational. It also sheds little light on the relative importance of such factors as principal place of business and residency or citizenship of directors or shareholders.

40. Section 702(c)(1), 42 U.S.C.A. § 2000e–1(c)(1).

41. Section 702(b), 42 U.S.C.A. § 2000e–1(b).

42. *See Mahoney v. RFE/RL, Inc.,* 47 F.3d 447 (D.C.Cir.), *cert. denied,* 516 U.S. 866, 116 S.Ct. 181, 133 L.Ed.2d 120 (1995).

43. Sections 702(c)(2), 42 U.S.C.A. § 2000e–1(c)(2). The foreign corporation's *United States* operations are not exempted. *See EEOC v. Kloster Cruise Ltd.,* 888 F.Supp. 147 (S.D.Fla.1995) (ADEA).

44. Such treaties are discussed below.

45. *See* Street, *Extraterritoriality, Conflict of Laws and Anti–Discrimination Laws,* Presentation by Lairold M. Street, EEOC Office of Legal Counsel, at Association of American Law Schools Annual Meeting, January 6, 1995.

protection against some of the more common forms of discrimination they may encounter. In the first place, although Title VII prohibits national origin discrimination, it does not reach discrimination based on alienage status (i.e. noncitizenship), which is dealt with by § 1981 and the Immigration Reform and Control Act of 1986 ("IRCA") or ancestry (i.e., ethnic or physiognomic characteristic transcending national borders, e.g., against Arabs or Jews), covered by § 1981. Title VII therefore will not avail a plaintiff whose employer, whether U.S. or foreign, excludes applicants solely because they lack U.S. citizenship or belong to a distinct cultural subgroup. Further, although Title VII and IRCA prohibit discrimination on the basis of national origin,[46] evidence that the plaintiff's compatriots are as well as or better represented in such an employer's workforce than others can defeat a claim that a U.S. citizenship requirement is in fact a smokescreen for intentional discrimination based on national origin.[47] It may be, however, that a neutral practice has the effect of discriminating on the basis of national origin; and if that is the case, a plaintiff excluded as a result of that practice may be able to state a prima facie national origin claim notwithstanding the fair or favorable treatment of her group.[48]

Since 1988, limited protection against discrimination in hiring because of alienage, i.e. citizenship status, is separately provided to lawfully admitted aliens, and a few others, by IRCA.[49] But unlike the IRCA protection against national origin, which extends to "any individual," the protection against alienage discrimination applies only to a rather narrowly defined "protected individual" who is well on the way to achieving full U.S. citizenship or has been granted refugee or asylum status.[50] Correlatively, IRCA imposes fines and imprisonment on employers who knowingly hire or employ undocumented persons or fail to check their authorization to work—in other words, it requires employers to discriminate against those aliens.[51]

A charge of discrimination under IRCA may be filed within 180 days after the occurrence of a violation before a U.S. Justice Department

---

46. *See, e.g., Hasham v. California State Bd. of Equalization,* 200 F.3d 1035 (7th Cir.2000).Title VII protection on this basis applies only with respect to an "employer" defined by that statute, that is, one with 15 or more employees in 20 or more calendar weeks in the current or preceding year. By contrast, IRCA § 102's prohibition of national origin discrimination against any individual, 8 U.S.C.A. § 274b(a)(3), applies to employers with as few as four employees. 8 U.S.C.A. § 1324b(a)(2)(A).

47. *See Espinoza v. Farah Mfg. Co.,* 414 U.S. 86, 94 S.Ct. 334, 38 L.Ed.2d 287 (1973). Compare the discussion of § 1981 in Chapter 5 (Section 1981 reaches ancestry but not national origin and perhaps not alienage discrimination).

48. *See Connecticut v. Teal,* 457 U.S. 440, 102 S.Ct. 2525, 73 L.Ed.2d 130 (1982),

discussed in Chapter 3. *But see Muzquiz v. W.A. Foote Memorial Hosp., Inc.,* 70 F.3d 422 (6th Cir.1995) (practice with assumed disproportionate impact on physicians trained in Mexico not tantamount to national origin discrimination against Mexicans or Mexican Americans).

49. Section 102, 8 U.S.C.A. § 1324a.

50. Sections 102(a)(1)(B) and 103, 8 U.S.C.A. § 1324b(a)(3).

51. Section 101, 8 U.S.C.A. § 1324a. It does not provide penalties against the undocumented workers themselves for accepting U.S. employment. Only the fraudulent presentation of employment verification documents is criminalized. 8 U.S.C.A. § 1324c.

Office of Special Counsel for Immigration–Related Unfair Employment Practices.[52] The Special Counsel has 120 days within which to investigate and determine whether there is reasonable cause to believe the charge is true and whether to file a complaint with a specially trained administrative law judge designated by the Attorney General. If the Special Counsel does not file such a complaint, the charging party may do so directly within 90 days after receiving notice to that effect from the Special Counsel. If the administrative law judge finds a violation after hearing, the employer may be ordered to hire the charging party with or without back pay, to pay attorney's fees, and to pay civil penalties of amounts that vary with the number of persons discriminated against and the number of prior offenses.[53] An anti-duplication provision is designed to ensure that national origin discrimination claims may be brought only before EEOC, if the complainant proceeds under Title VII, or to the Justice Department, if the complainant proceeds under IRCA, but not both.[54] Protection against retaliation is also provided,[55] as is judicial review in the United States court of appeals for the circuit in which the violation allegedly occurred or where the employer resides or transacts business.[56] A March, 2000 report by the Special Counsel's office reported that in the thirteen years of its existence, it had processed over 6,000 complaints, but had collected a mere $2.1 million in back pay and had levied less than $1.8 million in civil penalties.[57]

It has been contended that the fact that an alien is neither lawfully admitted for permanent U.S. residence within the meaning of IRCA nor authorized by law to work does not deprive him of capacity to sue and receive remedies under Title VII for the kinds of discrimination that are prohibited by that statute.[58] This follows not only from the fact that Title VII defines "employees" broadly as "individuals" employed by an

52. The EEOC has jurisdiction under Title VII to process national origin charges. The Office of Special Counsel has the authority to act on discrimination charges on the bases of national origin, citizenship status, unfair document practices and intimidation or retaliation under the Immigration and Nationality Act (INA). The EEOC and the Office of Special Counsel serve as the agent for the other agency for the purpose of receiving discrimination charges under Title VII and the INA. *See* 63 Fed. Reg. 5518 (1998).

53. *See* § 1324b(c) through (h).

54. 8 U.S.C.A. § 1324b(b)(2).

55. § 1324b(a)(5).

56. § 1324b(i)(1).

57. *See Special Report, BNA Daily Labor Report,* No.79, 4/24/00, at B–1.

58. *See EEOC v. Hacienda Hotel,* 881 F.2d 1504 (9th Cir.1989) (decided under pre-IRCA law); *Rios v. Enterprise Ass'n Steamfitters Local Union 638 of U.A.,* 860 F.2d 1168, 1173 (2d Cir.1988); *EEOC v. Tortilleria "La Mejor",* 758 F.Supp. 585 (E.D.Cal.1991) (decided after IRCA, and relying on legislative history to the effect that IRCA was not intended to limit the powers of state or federal labor standards agencies, including specifically the EEOC). *But see Egbuna v. Time–Life Libraries, Inc.,* 153 F.3d 184 (4th Cir.1998), *cert. denied,* 525 U.S. 1142, 119 S.Ct. 1034, 143 L.Ed.2d 43 (1999) (holding that an applicant who is unauthorized to work has no cause of cation under Title VII for discriminatory failure to hire). An October, 1999 EEOC Enforcement Guidance states that federal discrimination laws, including Title VII, ADEA, ADA, EPA, and the Rehabilitation Act, protect all employees in the United States regardless of their citizenship or work eligibility, and specifically disagrees with *Egbuna. See EEOC Enforcement Guidance on Remedies Available to Undocumented Workers Under Federal Employment Discrimination Laws,* No. 915.002 (10/26/99), at n.11.

employer but also from a negative implication of its alien exemption clause, which precludes application of the statute to the employment of aliens *outside* the United States.[59] The problem is that alien victims of the kinds of discrimination Title VII bans will often as a practical matter be ineligible for important Title VII remedies. If reinstatement would require the employer to violate IRCA, Title VII's mixed-motive or after-acquired evidence doctrines[60] would probably preclude a reinstatement order. A worker's undocumented status may also effect her eligibility for or the appropriate amount of back or front pay, since she may be "unavailable" for work after termination—either literally (e.g., out of the country) or legally, because of IRCA.[61] Recent Fourth Circuit decisions go further, holding that undocumented aliens working in violation of IRCA have no failure to hire claim under Title VII.[62] But EEOC takes the position that the plaintiff's undocumented status has no effect on the availability of injunctive relief or other more appropriate damages, and precludes the ordinary presumption favoring reinstatement or instatement only if the worker is unable to satisfy IRCA's verification requirements within a reasonable period of time and limits back pay only where the worker is unavailable in the sense of "being out of the company." The Commission does recognize that the worker's unauthorized status may form the basis for limited remedies in a mixed motives or after-acquired evidence case.[63] A claim alleging private employer alienage discrimination under 42 U.S.C. § 1981 has been held not to offend IRCA even though the plaintiff was an unauthorized alien where the court deemed him not to be complaining of discrimination because of his unauthorized status.[64]

As observed above, discrimination against aliens in general is not, absent adverse impact, treated as discrimination on the basis of any particular national origin, and is therefore not condemned by Title VII. There is sauce for the gander, however, even though the goose gets none:

---

59. The Supreme Court relied on that implication in writing broadly that Title VII affords protection for aliens against discrimination based on national origin. *Espinoza v. Farah Manufacturing Co.,* 414 U.S. 86, 95, 94 S.Ct. 334, 340, 38 L.Ed.2d 287 (1973). On the other hand, that implication was not sufficient in the Court's opinion to overcome the ordinary presumption against extraterritorial application of U.S. statutes. *See EEOC v. Arabian American Oil Co.,* 499 U.S. 244, 111 S.Ct. 1227, 113 L.Ed.2d 274 (1991). The Civil Rights Act of 1991 overturns *Arabian American*'s result by the addition to § 701(f), defining "employee," of a sentence that includes citizens, but not aliens, "with respect to employment in a foreign country." 42 U.S.C.A. § 2000e(f).

60. *See* Chapter 3.

61. *See generally* Ontiveros, *To Help Those Most in Need: Undocumented Workers' Rights and Remedies Under Title VII,* 20 N.Y.U. Rev. of Law & Social Change 607, 631–638 (1993–94).

62. *See Chaudhry v. Mobil Oil Corp.,* 186 F.3d 502 (4th Cir.1999) (Title VII and ADEA); *Egbuna v. Time–Life Libraries, Inc.,* 153 F.3d 184 (4th Cir.1998), *cert. denied,* 525 U.S. 1142, 119 S.Ct. 1034, 143 L.Ed.2d 43 (1999). The Fourth Circuit's opinion in *Egbuna* did intimate, however, that post-hire discrimination against an unauthorized alien might state a Title VII claim.

63. *EEOC Enforcement Guidance on Remedies Available to Undocumented Workers Under Federal Employment Discrimination Laws,* No. 915.002 (10/26/99).

64. *Anderson v. Conboy,* 156 F.3d 167 (2d Cir.1998), *cert. dismissed sub. nom. United Bhd. of Carpenters v. Anderson,* 527 U.S. 1030, 119 S.Ct. 2418, 144 L.Ed.2d 789 (1999).

discrimination *against* U.S. citizens, in favor of citizens of a particular nation, does amount to prohibited national origin discrimination under Title VII[65] as well as IRCA.[66] The rationale may be that only in the latter situation can it be said with some confidence that the discrimination relates to a particular national origin—putting aside the dubious assumption that U.S. citizenship corresponds to any particular national origin. Title VII protection from this "anti-American" discrimination based on national origin is limited, however, by treaty exemptions designed to give foreign companies operating in the United States a free hand in selecting their own citizens for executive positions.

The U.S.-Japanese Treaty of Friendship, Commerce and Navigation, for example, authorizes "companies of either party," such as a Japanese-chartered employer, "to engage, within the territories of the other Party ... executive personnel ... of their choice."[67] A U.S.-chartered American subsidiary of a foreign corporation will ordinarily not be deemed a company of the signatory entitled to this exemption.[68] But in a case where the foreign parent admitted[69] that it dictated the American subsidiary's discriminatory discharges of executives, the subsidiary was allowed to assert the parent's treaty rights.[70] These treaties have in other respects been construed narrowly, though, so as to permit only discrimination based on citizenship and not, for example, based on race, sex or age.[71] Nevertheless, they have been read to permit citizenship discrimination even when it has a statistical adverse impact on the basis of national origin. This happens, for example, where the executives preferred by the treaty hail from a homogeneous ethnic population, so that all or virtually all those preferred by virtue of their citizenship also share the same national origin.[72] Thus while companies of signatory countries are, despite these treaties, subject to liability, in their executive hiring and firing, for *intentional* discrimination based on national origin (but not citizenship), they cannot be liable for a citizenship-

65. *MacNamara v. Korean Air Lines*, 863 F.2d 1135 (3d Cir.1988), *cert. denied*, 493 U.S. 944, 110 S.Ct. 349, 107 L.Ed.2d 337 (1989).

66. *See* Zimmer, Sullivan, Richards and Calloway, *Cases and Material on Employment Discrimination* 695 (Little Brown, 3d ed. 1994) (asserting that "plain language" of IRCA forbids such discrimination).

67. *See also Weeks v. Samsung Heavy Indus. Co., Ltd.*, 126 F.3d 926 (7th Cir. 1997) (U.S.-Korea Treaty of Friendship, Commerce and Navigation authorizes Korean companies to select executives of their choice).

68. *Sumitomo Shoji America, Inc. v. Avagliano*, 457 U.S. 176, 102 S.Ct. 2374, 72 L.Ed.2d 765 (1982).

69. Such an admission may be rare, because a parent company may justifiably fear that in other proceedings the admission that the subsidiary is not independent would forfeit the foreign parent corporation's usual limited liability protection under state corporation law. That is, it might then become liable for the debts of its dominated subsidiary.

70. *Fortino v. Quasar Company*, 950 F.2d 389 (7th Cir.1991). *Accord Papaila v. Uniden America Corp.*, 51 F.3d 54 (5th Cir.), *cert. denied*, 516 U.S. 868, 116 S.Ct. 187, 133 L.Ed.2d 124 (1995); *Bennett v. Total Minatome Corp.*, 138 F.3d 1053 (5th Cir.1998).

71. *MacNamara*, 863 F.2d 1135; *cf. Spiess v. C. Itoh & Co.*, 643 F.2d 353, 362–363 (5th Cir.1981), *vacated by* 457 U.S. 1128, 102 S.Ct. 2951, 73 L.Ed.2d 1344 (1982).

72. *See Fortino*, 950 F.2d 389 and *MacNamara*, 863 F.2d 1135 (Japanese and Korean executives, respectively).

preference practice that merely has a disproportionate adverse impact on a particular national origin.[73] Courts have reached this result in order to avoid indirect nullification of the guest company's treaty right to discriminate in favor of its own country's citizens.[74]

The schematic that follows summarizes the complex set of relationships among the Title VII, IRCA and § 1981 protections for alien and citizen plaintiffs, against foreign or domestic employers, respecting work in the United States or abroad, on grounds of national origin, citizenship, and ancestry:

73. *MacNamara*, 863 F.2d 1135.   **74.** *Fortino*, 950 F.2d 389.

Coverage Under Title VII/ADA, ADEA, IRCA and Section 1981 of U.S. and Foreign Employers in Suits By Alien and Citizen Plaintiffs Respecting Work in U.S. and Abroad

	Ground Protected	U.S. Def't or U.S.-Controlled Corp.	Foreign Def't Not Controlled by U.S. Corp.	In U.S.	Work Abroad
I. TITLE VII, ADA and ADEA **A. Citizen Plaintiff**	Title VII: Race, Sex, Religion, National Origin ADA: Disability ADEA: Age	Potentially Prohibited if 15+ Employees; (ADEA 20+ Employees)	↑	Prohibited by ADA, ADEA and Title VII, absent treaty exemption allowing de facto national origin discrimination in hiring executives	Prohibited unless foreign law bans conduct that Title VII, ADEA, or ADA requires. Title VII § 702(b); ADA § 102(c)(1); ADEA § 630(f)
	Title VII: Race, Sex, Religion, National Origin ADA: Disability ADEA: Age		Title VII/ADA: Potentially Prohibited if 15+ Employees (ADEA: If 20+ Employees)	Prohibited by ADA, ADEA and Title VII, absent treaty exemption allowing de facto national origin discrimination in hiring executives	No coverage: Title VII § 702(c)(2); ADA § 702(c)(2)(B); ADEA § 623(h)(2)
B. Legal or Illegal Alien Plaintiff	Title VII: Race, Sex, Religion, National Origin ADA: Disability ADEA: Age	Potentially Prohibited if 15+ Employees; (ADEA: 20+)		Prohibited by ADA, ADEA and Title VII, absent treaty exemption allowing de facto national origin discrimination in hiring executives	No coverage. See Title VII, § 701(f) and 702(a); ADA § 101(4); ADEA § 630(f)
	Title VII: Race, Sex, Religion, National Origin ADA: Disability ADEA: Age		Title VII/ADA: Potentially Prohibited if 15+ Employees ADEA: No coverage: § 623(h)(2)	Prohibited by ADA and Title VII, absent treaty exemption allowing de facto national origin discrimination in hiring executives	No coverage: Title VII, § 701(f). ADA: § 102(c)(2)(B), see § 101(4)
II. IRCA **A. Any Individual Plaintiff**	National Origin	Prohibited if 4+ Employees			Presumably not, based on presumption against extraterritorial application in EEOC v. Arabian American Oil Co., 499 U.S. 244 (1991).
B. "Protected Person" Plaintiff	Alienage	Prohibited if 4+ Employees			
III. SECTION 1981 Any Plaintiff	Intentional Race and Ancestry and Maybe Alienage but not Gender, Religion, or National Origin	Prohibited, no employee minimum			

b. *Religious Employers: Coverage, Exemptions, Defenses*

Religious organizations are also viewed as Title VII "employers," and as such may be subject to a specially defined duty not to discriminate on that ground.[75] But they are specifically permitted to make certain employment decisions on the basis of religion. A welter of related and somewhat overlapping statutory and constitutional provisions afford different kinds of covered employers exemptions from or exceptions to liability for religious discrimination. In addition, the special prohibition on religious discrimination—subsuming the ordinary imperative not to discriminate and a duty to make "reasonable accommodation" to an employee's religious beliefs and practices—is subject to the general affirmative defense that permits an employer to discriminate under circumstances where the exclusion is a "bona fide occupational qualification." The nature of the two-part prima facie prohibition on religious discrimination is discussed in § 2.23 below. The exemptions, exceptions and BFOQ defense for religious and other employers will be treated here. The following schematic depicts the relationships among the statutory and constitutional exemptions, the prima facie case, and the BFOQ defense.

OVERVIEW: DISCRIMINATION BECAUSE OF RELIGION

Statutory Exemptions and Constitutional Overrides

—The § 702 exemption, strictly limited to pervasively religious institutions like churches, missions and seminaries (*Kamehemaha*), declares Title VII inapplicable with respect to the employment "of individuals of a particular religion" in any of its activities, for any position. [It does not exempt from regulation for sex, race, national origin (or age) discrimination.] Section 702 upheld as against the objection that it unconstitutionally "establishes" the institutions it protects, at least with respect to their nonprofitmaking activities. *Corporation of Presiding Bishop v. Amos*, 483 U.S. 327, 107 S.Ct. 2862, 97 L.Ed.2d 273 (1987).

—§ 703(e)(2) excludes from the definition of "unlawful employment practice" the hiring of employees of a particular religion by educational institutions insufficiently religious to qualify for the § 702 exemption but that are (a) substantially owned, supported, controlled or managed by a particular religion or (b) direct their curriculum "toward the propagation of" a particular religion. [Again, race, sex, national origin (and age) discrimination are still prohibited.] *Kamehemaha*

—If the ground alleged is sex, race, national origin, or age—where, that is, the foregoing statutory exemptions will not avail the employer—it may invoke a Free Exercise or Establishment Clause (excessive government entanglement) override of Title VII or ADEA regulation. These may succeed where the position (e.g., minister) or duties (e.g., teacher of theology) in question lie close to the religious core of the institution, or perhaps where the reason for discharge relates to malperformance of subsidiary religious duties. See *McClure* (Free Exercise Clause) and

---

75. *See* § 2.23, below, discussing the way in which the definition of "religion" in § 701(j) modifies the duty not to discriminate on the basis of religion as set forth in § 703.

Southwestern Baptist Theological Seminary (Establishment Clause) line of cases.

Prima Facie Prohibitions

—If no statutory or constitutional exemption applies, turn to the prima facie case: Section 703(a)(1), amplified by the 701(j) definition of "religion":

A. Has employer drawn a distinction because of "religion" (see Posner, J. concurring in *Pime*) (discrimination based on non-membership in Jesuit order not because of "religion") or imposed a neutral practice with adverse impact on a particular religion or persons outside a favored faith?

B. Even if employer has made no hostile discrimination, has it breached the 701(j) duty to accommodate:

    1. "Reasonable accommodation" need not fully meet needs of employee's religious belief or practice without cost to employee, and employer need not accept the particular accommodation proposed by employee (*Philbrook*); and

    2. A reasonable accommodation works "undue hardship" and is thus not required if it requires employer to incur more than de minimis cost. (*Trans World Airlines, Inc. v. Hardison*)

So diluted, § 701(j) does not violate Establishment Clause—*Protos*.

BFOQ Defense

In a refusal to hire case, if statutory exemptions and constitutional overrides fail and plaintiff establishes prima facie religious discrimination, employer has BFOQ defense of § 703(e)(1). As restrictively construed by *Johnson Controls*, employer must show that its religious exclusion relates to the "essence" of its business and that all or substantially all persons of the excluded faiths could not fulfill the requirements of the job in question. *Kamehemaha*; *cf. Pime* (pre-*Johnson Controls*)

§ 2.4 "Purely" Religious Organizations

In general, the more thoroughly "religious" the employer, the more widely it is insulated from liability with respect to terms and conditions of employment and even wholly sectarian activities. This discussion will identify those employers in descending degree of religiosity, and hence insulation.

First, any pervasively "religious" employer—paradigmatically a church, mission, seminary or one of their branches or subunits—is exempt by virtue of § 702(a)[1] from liability for religious discrimination. This section exempts a "religious corporation, association, educational institution, or society" from Title VII "with respect to the employment of individuals of a particular religion to perform work connected with the carrying on" of any of the institution's "activities." But the exemption

§ 2.4
1. 42 U.S.C.A. § 2000e–1(a).

has been widely interpreted not to ban discrimination based on race, gender, or national origin,[2] with important exceptions.[3]

For the most part, only churches or institutions owned or partly owned by them have qualified for the § 702 exemption.[4] The determination whether an organization, including an educational institution, is eligible for its sweeping protection hinges on whether "the corporation's purpose and character are primarily religious." That question, in turn, is answered on a case-by-case basis, with the court weighing "[a]ll significant religious and secular characteristics."[5] A nondenominational school that was established under a will requiring all trustees and teachers to be Protestants and that began classes with daily prayer but whose purpose, curriculum, and activities had evolved over the years from primarily religious to predominantly secular and most of whose students were not Protestant was held to reflect "a primarily secular rather than a primarily religious orientation" and hence held ineligible for the exemption.[6]

The § 702 exemption extends to any of the religious employer's activities, secular or sectarian, and applies regardless of the particular term and condition of employment involved. A 1972 amendment to § 702 deleted the word "religious" that had appeared before "activities" in the original 1964 legislation, and so the exemption has since been understood to shield a covered institution from liability for religious discrimination even with respect to its secular activities, provided those are non-profitmaking.[7] It has nevertheless withstood challenge as an unconstitu-

---

2. *See Martin v. United Way of Erie County*, 829 F.2d 445, 449 (3d Cir.1987); *Rayburn v. General Conference of Seventh-Day Adventists*, 772 F.2d 1164, 1170–71 (4th Cir.1985), *cert. denied*, 478 U.S. 1020, 106 S.Ct. 3333, 92 L.Ed.2d 739 (1986); *EEOC v. Pacific Press Publ'g Ass'n*, 676 F.2d 1272 (9th Cir.1982); *McClure v. Salvation Army*, 460 F.2d 553 (5th Cir.), *cert. denied*, 409 U.S. 896, 93 S.Ct. 132, 34 L.Ed.2d 153 (1972). *Cf. DeMarco v. Holy Cross High Sch.*, 4 F.3d 166, 173 (2d Cir. 1993) (discussing § 702 of Title VII in ADEA case).

3. The religious employer may be exempt from liability even for discriminating on these others grounds if discrimination on any such ground is a tenet of its religion. In that event, what appears at first blush to be race or gender discrimination ultimately is viewed as discrimination because of religion; in that event, the employer may be entitled to the statutory exemption, or the practice may simply not be regulable at all because of the religion clauses of the First Amendment. See § 2.10, *infra; cf. Geary v. Visitation of Blessed Virgin Mary Parish Sch.*, 7 F.3d 324, 328 (3d Cir.1993) (ADEA claim against Catholic school not barred by First Amendment where no claim that Catholic doctrine mandated age discrimina-

tion). Alternatively, if the discrimination is alleged with respect to the terms and conditions of employment of clergy, any Title VII regulation, including investigation by EEOC, may conflict with the demands of the First Amendment. *See* text § 2.10 *infra*.

4. *EEOC v. Kamehameha Sch./Bishop Estate*, 990 F.2d 458, 461 n. 7 (9th Cir.), *cert. denied*, 510 U.S. 963, 114 S.Ct. 439, 126 L.Ed.2d 372 (1993), and cases cited therein; *Killinger v. Samford Univ.*, 113 F.3d 196 (11th Cir.1997) (educational institution found to qualify for both the owned by a religious association exemption and the religious educational exemption).

5. *Kamehameha*, 990 F.2d at 460.

6. *Id.* at 461.

7. *See generally EEOC v. Fremont Christian Sch.*, 781 F.2d 1362, 1366 (9th Cir.1986); *Rayburn v. General Conference of Seventh–Day Adventists*, 772 F.2d 1164, 1169 (4th Cir.1985), *cert. denied*, 478 U.S. 1020, 106 S.Ct. 3333, 92 L.Ed.2d 739 (1986); *EEOC v. Pacific Press Publ'g Ass'n*, 676 F.2d 1272 (9th Cir.1982); *EEOC v. Mississippi College*, 626 F.2d 477, 485 (5th Cir.1980), *cert. denied*, 453 U.S. 912, 101 S.Ct. 3143, 69 L.Ed.2d 994 (1981).

tional establishment of religion.[8] The Court in *Amos* reasoned that § 702, by lifting what would otherwise be government regulation of religion, merely permits the religious organization to advance its own religion and does not result in the government itself advancing a particular religion.

The distinctions among the grounds on which Title VII bans discrimination, the § 702 exemption, and a separate, nonstatutory overriding defense based on the First Amendment are pointed up by a recent case in which a parochial school's married librarian was terminated for being pregnant by someone other than her husband. Even though the employer decision to fire the plaintiff was driven by its religious beliefs, it appeared that the discrimination was on the ground of pregnancy and therefore, in Title VII terms, because of sex rather than religion. Accordingly, the court ruled that the § 702 defense was not available. But if it turned out that the real reason for termination was her adultery rather than her pregnancy, the ground of discrimination would be sex-neutral and therefore not prohibited by Title VII.[9] (Then there would be no Title VII violation even if the adultery ground were not tantamount to religious discrimination—that is, even if the defendant could not avail itself of the § 702 exemption from liability for discrimination because of religion.) Moreover, the court added that ultimately the First Amendment might halt the action in any event if the proceedings, or a judgment of liability, were determined to interfere unduly with the church school's free exercise of religion.

An overlapping defense based on the religion clauses of the First Amendment is available to truly "religious" institutions, educational or not, where litigation raises the spectre of excessive government monitoring of religious decisionmaking or matters of doctrine. Where a university's canon law department was governed by the Vatican, for instance, the claim of a faculty member in that department who alleged sexually discriminatory tenure denial was rejected, wholly apart from § 702(a), because the court decided it lacked competence to review competing opinions about materially religious subjects in published articles. Both the Free Exercise and Establishment Clauses would be violated by scrutiny under Title VII that would "impair a religious institution's choice of those who teach its doctrine and participate in church governance."[10]

§ 2.5 Religiously Affiliated Educational Institutions

Because relatively few organizations are sufficiently religious to qualify for the broad exemption from Title VII afforded by § 702, Congress added a limited exception from liability designed to benefit religiously affiliated schools.

8. *Corporation of Presiding Bishop v. Amos*, 483 U.S. 327, 107 S.Ct. 2862, 97 L.Ed.2d 273 (1987).

9. *Vigars v. Valley Christian Ctr.*, 805 F.Supp. 802 (N.D.Cal.1992).

10. *EEOC v. Catholic Univ. of America*, 856 F.Supp. 1 (D.D.C.1994), *aff'd*, 83 F.3d 455 (D.C.Cir.1996).

Under § 703(e)(2) of Title VII,[1] an *educational* institution not qualifying as sufficiently religious to be exempt under § 702(a) but which is substantially supported or directed by a particular religion, or has a religiously oriented curriculum, may "hire and employ" persons of the particular religion with which it is affiliated.[2] Section 702(a), it will be remembered, provides that Title VII "shall not apply" to the "purely" religious institutions it protects. By contrast, § 703(e)(2) more modestly states that it is not an "unlawful employment practice" for an "educational institution or institution of learning to hire and employ employees of a particular religion" if that employer is "in whole or in substantial part, owned, supported, controlled, or managed by a particular religion"[3] (hereinafter, the "structure clause") or maintains a curriculum "directed toward the propagation of a particular religion" (the "curriculum clause").[4]

It is only somewhat easier for a religiously affiliated educational institution to qualify for the more limited § 703(e)(2) hiring immunity than for a religious organization or school to qualify for the broader exemption under § 702. One court, for example, declined to decide whether the defendant university qualified for the § 703(e)(2) exemption even though it had a long history as a Jesuit institution, until 1970 had only Jesuit trustees, still required that more than one-third of the trustees and the President be Jesuit, and enrolled students of predominantly Catholic background.[5] It further appears that to qualify under the curriculum clause it is not enough that a school require religious education courses, schedule prayers and services, and employ Protestant teachers for principally secular subjects. "Courses *about* religion and a general effort to teach good values do not constitute a curriculum that propagates religion, especially in view of the Schools' express disclaimer of any effort to convert their non-Protestant students."[6]

The courts have consistently held that the § 703(e)(2) exception to the definition of an unlawful employment practice by a religiously affiliated school, like the § 702 exemption from Title VII for a religious organization, does not shield the defendant from Title VII liability when the institution discriminates against an employee or applicant (say one who seeks a secular job like science teacher or custodian of a seminary or university) on some basis *other* than religion—sex, race, national origin, or retaliation.[7]

§ 2.5

1. 42 U.S.C.A. § 2000e–2(e)(2).

2. *See, e.g., Killinger v. Samford Univ.,* 113 F.3d 196 (11th Cir.1997) (educational institution found to qualify for both the owned by a religious association exemption and the religious educational exemption).

3. *See Pime v. Loyola Univ. of Chicago,* 803 F.2d 351 (7th Cir.1986).

4. *See EEOC v. Kamehameha Sch./Bishop Estate,* 990 F.2d 458, 464–65 (9th Cir.),

cert. denied, 510 U.S. 963, 114 S.Ct. 439, 126 L.Ed.2d 372 (1993).

5. *Pime v. Loyola Univ. of Chicago,* 803 F.2d 351 (7th Cir.1986).

6. *EEOC v. Kamehameha Sch./Bishop Trust,* 990 F.2d at 465.

7. *EEOC v. Fremont Christian Sch.,* 781 F.2d 1362, 1366 (9th Cir.1986); *Martin v. United Way of Erie County,* 829 F.2d 445 (3d Cir.1987) (dictum); *EEOC v. Southwestern Baptist Theological Seminary,* 651 F.2d 277 (5th Cir.1981), *cert. denied,* 456 U.S.

ADEA has no express exemption for religious or religiously affiliated institutions. But because ADEA's substantive prohibitions are derived *in haec verba* from Title VII,[8] courts have crafted an immunity from age discrimination liability of the same scope, and with the same limitations, for religious organizations that meet the § 702 (or, apparently, § 703(e)(2)) requirements.[9]

§ 2.6 The "BFOQ" Affirmative Defense Based on Religion

Under § 703(e)(1),[1] *any* employer, even one wholly sectarian, may "hire and employ" (a labor organization may "admit or employ" in apprenticeship or retraining programs) on the basis of religion where religion is a "bona fide occupational qualification ['BFOQ'] reasonably necessary to the normal operation" of the enterprise. The principal discussion of the BFOQ defense, as it applies to express gender and national origin discrimination, is set forth in Chapter 3 immediately following. The discussion here will be confined to its role in defending against express discrimination based on religion.

Section 703(e)(1) has the same textual limitation to hiring as does Section 703(e)(2). Accordingly, the BFOQ affirmative defense protects employers from liability only for certain religiously discriminatory hiring decisions; it does not excuse discrimination concerning subsequent terms and conditions of employment like compensation, promotion, discipline, harassment or discharge.[2]

Moreover, the Supreme Court's decision in *International Union, United Auto. Workers v. Johnson Controls*[3] confirms the narrowness of the BFOQ exception—in any context, i.e., gender or national origin as well as religion. The bare language of § 703(e)(1) would appear satisfied if an employer can show that a refusal to hire based on religion, sex, or national origin is reasonably necessary to the normal operation of the defendant's overall "enterprise." As a textual matter, that is, the employer need not show that the exclusion on those grounds is conducive to the sound performance of the particular plaintiff's job, only that it will further general business goals. Nor does the text of the BFOQ defense suggest that the discriminatory job qualification must relate to the heart of employer's business, only to its "normal operation." Yet the Court has concluded that to prevent the exception from virtually eliminating an

905, 102 S.Ct. 1749, 72 L.Ed.2d 161 (1982); *EEOC v. Mississippi College*, 626 F.2d 477, 482 (5th Cir.1980), *cert. denied*, 453 U.S. 912, 101 S.Ct. 3143, 69 L.Ed.2d 994 (1981).

8. *See Lorillard v. Pons*, 434 U.S. 575, 584, 98 S.Ct. 866, 872, 55 L.Ed.2d 40 (1978).

9. *See DeMarco v. Holy Cross High Sch.*, 4 F.3d 166, 173 (2d Cir.1993); *Geary v. Visitation of the Blessed Virgin Mary Parish Sch.*, 7 F.3d 324, 331 (3d Cir.1993); *Martin*, 829 F.2d 445 (dictum).

§ 2.6

1. 42 U.S.C.A. § 2000e–2(e)(1) (which also applies to discrimination based on sex or national origin, but not race).

2. *See EEOC v. Fremont Christian Sch.*, 781 F.2d at 1367.

3. 499 U.S. 187, 111 S.Ct. 1196, 113 L.Ed.2d 158 (1991).

applicant's protection against these forms of express discrimination, the employer must show that its discriminatory rule bears a "high correlation" to the plaintiff's ability to perform the job in question *and* relates to the "essence" or "central mission" of the employer's business.[4] Relying on *Johnson Controls*, an appellate court has denied the BFOQ defense to schools that insisted on hiring Protestant teachers to maintain a Protestant "presence" assertedly important to their general educational operations. First, the court defined the real mission of the schools as providing native Hawaiians "a solid education in traditional secular subjects" and "moral guidance" useful for developing a "system of values," rather than educating the students "from the Protestant point of view." It could find no correlation in the record between the employer's insistence on "nominally Protestant" teachers and the provision of superior instruction or moral guidance. And it concluded that even assuming maintenance of a Protestant "presence" went to the essence of the schools' business, the 100% presence mandated by the employer's Protestant-only hiring rule exceeded the requirements of its mission and actual daily operations.[5]

§§ 2.7–5.9   [Reserved]

B.   CONSTITUTIONAL PROBLEMS SURROUNDING REGULATION OF RELIGIOUS DISCRIMINATION

§ 2.10   In General

Subjecting a religiously based institution to Title VII regulation (and hence to the administrative scrutiny of EEOC and indirect regulation by the courts) for discrimination on grounds other than religion has survived most challenges based on the Free Exercise Clause. The critical inquiry under that clause concerns the impact of statutory regulation on the institution's exercise of its sincerely held religious beliefs. Because of the statutory exemptions, the statutory regulation will not extend to employment practices motivated or compelled by the religious beliefs of the employer or its affiliated church. Accordingly, although defense of an

---

4. 499 U.S. at 201, 111 S.Ct. at 1205 (quoting *Dothard v. Rawlinson*, 433 U.S. 321, 333, 335, 97 S.Ct. 2720, 2728, 2729, 53 L.Ed.2d 786 (1977) and *Western Air Lines, Inc. v. Criswell*, 472 U.S. 400, 413, 105 S.Ct. 2743, 2751, 86 L.Ed.2d 321 (1985)).

5. *EEOC v. Kamehameha Sch./Bishop Estate*, 990 F.2d at 465–466. In reaching the last conclusion, the court distinguished *Pime v. Loyola Univ. of Chicago*, 803 F.2d 351 (7th Cir.1986). In *Pime* the Seventh Circuit upheld a university's BFOQ defense to a Jesuit hiring preference on the ground that the discriminatory qualification served to maintain a small minority Jesuit presence on the faculty. But the Ninth Circuit,

observing that *Pime* was decided before *Johnson Controls*, also suggested that apart from whether the schools in the case before it needed an exclusively Protestant faculty "presence" to meet their overall business needs, the defendants' religious requirement was infirm because it did not relate to the plaintiff's capacity to perform the duties of a substitute French teacher. Under *Johnson Controls*, in other words, the employer claiming a BFOQ must show a strong correlation between its discriminatory rule and the plaintiff's ability to do the job in question as well as a link to the business as a whole.

employment discrimination charge may have substantial adverse impact on a church or other religious institution, the administrative proceeding or action should have slight or no impact on the religious practices or beliefs of its adherents. Any such incidental impact has been held outweighed by the government's "compelling" interest in ending employment discrimination.[1]

Where, however, the challenged employment practice relates to a staff member who occupies the functional status of clergy within the employer's denominational structure or belief system, courts have construed Title VII, the ADA, and the ADEA not to reach the practice in order to avoid transgressing the free exercise rights of the religious organization or its members.[2] On occasion, a lower court has permitted a discrimination claim to move forward when the plaintiff occupies a sensitive position but one that lies somewhat less close to the core of the religious enterprise[3] or where the plaintiff sought only money damages for sexual harassment.[4] But all regulation has been barred as burdening a religious school's right to free exercise when pursuit of the claim would entail government intrusion into the sponsoring church's choice of a teacher of theology.[5] The opinion, terming the plaintiff a "ministerial" employee with "pervasive" religious duties, distinguished cases in which

§ 2.10

1. *See, e.g., EEOC v. Fremont Christian Sch.*, 781 F.2d 1362, 1366 (9th Cir.1986); *EEOC v. Pacific Press Publ'g Ass'n*, 676 F.2d 1272 (9th Cir.1982); *EEOC v. Mississippi College*, 626 F.2d 477, 482 (5th Cir. 1980), *cert. denied*, 453 U.S. 912, 101 S.Ct. 3143, 69 L.Ed.2d 994 (1981).

2. *See, e.g., Gellington v. Christian Methodist Episcopal Church, Inc.*, 203 F.3d 1299, 1302–03 (11th Cir.2000); *Starkman v. Evans*, 198 F.3d 173, 175 (5th Cir.1999), *cert. denied*, ___ U.S. ___, 121 S.Ct. 49, 148 L.Ed.2d 18 (2000) (free exercise clause bars choir minister's ADA claim of disability discrimination because she performed tasks that were ecclesiastical); *Combs v. Central Texas Annual Conference of United Methodist Church*, 173 F.3d 343 (5th Cir.1999) (free exercise clause deprived federal court of jurisdiction to hear Title VII case brought against church by member of its clergy); *EEOC v. Catholic Univ. of Am.*, 83 F.3d 455 (D.C.Cir.1996) (plaintiff faculty member was a nun who acted as functional equivalent of a minister); *Young v. Northern Ill. Conference of United Methodist Church*, 21 F.3d 184 (7th Cir.1994), *cert. denied*, 513 U.S. 929, 115 S.Ct. 320, 130 L.Ed.2d 281 (1994); *Rayburn v. General Conference of Seventh–Day Adventists*, 772 F.2d 1164, 1170–71 (4th Cir.1985), *cert. denied*, 478 U.S. 1020, 106 S.Ct. 3333, 92 L.Ed.2d 739 (1986); *EEOC v. Southwestern*

Baptist Theological Seminary, 651 F.2d 277 (5th Cir.1981), *cert. denied*, 456 U.S. 905, 102 S.Ct. 1749, 72 L.Ed.2d 161 (1982); *EEOC v. Mississippi College*, 626 F.2d 477, 482 (5th Cir.1980), *cert. denied*, 453 U.S. 912, 101 S.Ct. 3143, 69 L.Ed.2d 994 (1981); *McClure*, 460 F.2d 553 (Title VII cases); *Scharon v. St. Luke's Episcopal Presbyterian Hosps.*, 929 F.2d 360, 363 (8th Cir.1991); *Minker v. Baltimore Annual Conference of United Methodist Church*, 894 F.2d 1354, 1356–58 (D.C.Cir.1990) (ADEA cases); *Natal v. Christian and Missionary Alliance*, 878 F.2d 1575 (1st Cir.1989) (concluding that clergyman is barred by First Amendment from suing not-for-profit religious organization for wrongful termination).

3. *Elbaz v. Congregation Beth Judea, Inc.*, 812 F.Supp. 802, (N.D.Ill.1992).

4. *Bollard v. California Province of the Society of Jesus*, 196 F.3d 940 (9th Cir. 1999). The court found that Title VII was not overridden by constitutional concerns because the defendant church was neither exercising its constitutionally protected right to choose its ministers, nor embracing the behavior at issue as a constitutionally protected religious practice. Plaintiff was not complaining that the Jesuits refused to ordain him or took an other adverse employment action against him.

5. *Powell v. Stafford*, 859 F.Supp. 1343 (D.Colo.1994) (case under ADEA).

the federal employment discrimination regulation concerned lay teachers of secular subjects.

The distinct question remains whether judicial regulation under Title VII, ADA, or ADEA that is not challenged, or survives a challenge, under §§ 702 or 703(e)(2) violates the Establishment Clause by fostering "an excessive government entanglement with religion."[6] In *N.L.R.B. v. Catholic Bishop of Chicago*,[7] where lay faculty sought to unionize under the protection of federal law, the Supreme Court construed the National Labor Relations Act as not affording jurisdiction over religiously associated organizations absent an affirmative, clearly expressed contrary intention of Congress. Yet it later intimated in dictum that the First Amendment does leave room for some degree of state intrusion into religious schools' employment practices.[8] We know for sure, then, only that subjecting a religiously affiliated organization to the full regulatory umbrella of the national laws governing employee self-organization and collective bargaining falls on the prohibited side of the line.

Lower courts have muddled through this quagmire by generally extending protection against employment discrimination to those teaching staff and supporting personnel of schools and seminaries who have no religious duties or whose religious duties, if any, are "easily isolated and defined" rather than pervasive.[9] *Catholic Bishop* has been distinguished on the ground that regulation of the labor relations of parochial schools by the National Labor Relations Board under the National Labor Relations Act is far more comprehensive and ongoing than the "limited inquiry required in anti-discrimination disputes."[10] But where a terminated Catholic school teacher brought Title VII charges alleging *religious* discrimination, the religion clauses were held too implicated to permit

---

6. *See Lemon v. Kurtzman*, 403 U.S. 602, 612–613, 91 S.Ct. 2105, 2111–2112, 29 L.Ed.2d 745 (1971).

7. 440 U.S. 490, 99 S.Ct. 1313, 59 L.Ed.2d 533 (1979).

8. *Ohio Civil Rights Comm'n v. Dayton Christian Sch., Inc.*, 477 U.S. 619, 106 S.Ct. 2718, 91 L.Ed.2d 512 (1986).

9. *See Weissman v. Congregation Shaare Emeth*, 38 F.3d 1038 (8th Cir.1994) (rejecting excessive entanglement defense to ADEA action brought by administrator of synagogue whose duties were principally or entirely non-sectarian, absent specific allegation that he was terminated for reasons related to arguably religious duties or for other religious reasons); *Geary v. Visitation of the Blessed Virgin Mary Parish Sch.*, 7 F.3d 324 (3d Cir.1993) (allowing ADEA claim to proceed by terminated lay teacher in church-operated elementary school, distinguishing cases where religious discrimination was alleged, where plaintiff had religious duties, or clergy were involved); *DeMarco v. Holy Cross High Sch.*,

4 F.3d 166 (2d Cir.1993) (holding that the *Catholic Bishop* presumption against coverage does not bar the ADEA claim of a math teacher in a religious school even though the faculty were also expected to serve as spiritual exemplars); *EEOC v. Fremont Christian Sch.*, 781 F.2d 1362 (9th Cir.1986); *EEOC v. Mississippi College*, 626 F.2d 477 (5th Cir.1980), *cert. denied*, 453 U.S. 912, 101 S.Ct. 3143, 69 L.Ed.2d 994 (1981) (largely secular schools); *EEOC v. Southwestern Baptist Theological Seminary*, 651 F.2d 277 (5th Cir.1981), *cert. denied*, 456 U.S. 905, 102 S.Ct. 1749, 72 L.Ed.2d 161 (1982) (sectarian school).

10. *DeMarco*, 4 F.3d 166; *Soriano v. Xavier Univ. Corp.*, 687 F.Supp. 1188, 1189 (S.D.Ohio 1988). *See also Geary*, 7 F.3d 324 (permitting ADEA action by lay employee of church-operated elementary school but noting the school's light burden of showing that a religious reason actually motivated the challenged employment action).

determination by secular courts.[11] At least one appellate opinion permitting an age discrimination action to go forward notwithstanding the entanglement objection[12] has nevertheless expressed concern that government could become an arbiter of the truth or validity of religious beliefs when a court determines whether a religious employer's stated justification for an employment action is "implausible"[13] or "false."[14] The Second Circuit sought to alleviate this problem by declaring that the factfinder will be required "to presume that an asserted religious motive is plausible in the sense that it is reasonably or validly held."[15] Thus while the factfinder may determine whether an employer took adverse action against the plaintiff because of a failure to fulfill religious duties, a lawful reason, or because of age, an unlawful one, the court may not question the validity or necessity of the duties themselves.[16] These cases suggest that counsel for such religious or religiously affiliated institutions would be well advised, whenever consistent with the facts, to plead specifically that the duties at issue in an adverse disciplinary action are religious or that the action was taken for religious reasons.[17]

As we shall see,[18] the substance of the employer's Title VII duty not to discriminate because of religion—particularly the "reasonable accommodation" feature of that duty—has been distinctly diluted by judicial interpretation, perhaps to ensure that the statute, so construed, will survive these First Amendment challenges.

C. THE BASIC SUBSTANTIVE PROHIBITIONS

§ 2.11 In General

The deceptively simple substantive prohibitions of Title VII are contained in § 703(a). Section 703(a)(1) declares it an "unlawful employment practice" for a covered employer

> to fail or refuse to hire or to discharge any individual, or otherwise to discriminate against any individual with respect to his compensa-

11. *Little v. Wuerl*, 929 F.2d 944 (3d Cir.1991).

12. *DeMarco*, 4 F.3d 166.

13. *See Hazen Paper Co. v. Biggins*, 507 U.S. 604, 613, 113 S.Ct. 1701, 1708, 123 L.Ed.2d 338 (1993).

14. *See* discussion under "Individual Disparate Treatment," Chapter 3 below, concerning *St. Mary's Honor Ctr. v. Hicks*, 509 U.S. 502, 502, 113 S.Ct. 2742, 2744, 125 L.Ed.2d 407 (1993).

15. *Id.; cf. DeMarco*, 4 F.3d at 171.

16. *Id.; cf. Estate of Thornton v. Caldor, Inc.*, 472 U.S. 703, 105 S.Ct. 2914, 86 L.Ed.2d 557 (1985) (O'Connor, J., concurring) (observing in dictum that a court, in ruling on a plaintiff's claimed entitlement to accommodation under § 701(j) of Title VII, discussed in section B.3., below, need only ascertain whether the belief is religious and sincerely held, and may not inquire into its verity). But where the court

finds that the suit will require only a limited inquiry into employment matters and the factfinder will not be asked to evaluate religious doctrine or the reasonableness of religious practices, the establishment clause will not bar the claim. *See Bollard v. California Province of the Society of Jesus*, 196 F.3d 940 (9th Cir.1999).

17. *See, e.g., Bollard v. California Province of the Society of Jesus*, 196 F.3d 940 (9th Cir.1999) (excessive entanglement can arise from a protracted legal process and protracted government surveillance of church activities); *Weissman v. Congregation Shaare Emeth*, 38 F.3d 1038 (8th Cir. 1994) (allegation that employer dissatisfied with plaintiff's job performance insufficient to trigger entanglement concern absent specific allegation that plaintiff's performance was deficient respecting any religious duties or that he was terminated for other religious reasons).

18. *See* § 2.23, *infra* this chapter.

tion, terms, conditions or privileges of employment, because of such individual's race, color, religion, sex, or national origin.

Section 703(a)(2) forbids limiting the employment "opportunities" of an applicant or incumbent employee on any of the same grounds. The controversies addressed by the case law have centered on two intertwined issues. First, what employer conduct or classifications correspond to the forbidden kinds of discrimination—what, in other words, constitutes discrimination on the grounds of "race, color, religion, sex or national origin"? As we shall see, the answers to these questions are not always self-evident. Discrimination based on alienage status, for example, is not tantamount to the prohibited discrimination based on national origin, even though a non-U.S. citizen would not have that status unless she or an ancestor recently arrived here from another nation. Whites may sue for race discrimination, as may blacks, based on the racial animus directed against them by other blacks.

The second pervasive issue concerns the nature and degree of the nexus that must exist between prohibited employer conduct and harm to a plaintiff's employment status. When, in other words, is adverse action taken by the employer "because of" prohibited discrimination? For example, the Supreme Court has treated as prohibited gender discrimination certain forms of employer speech and action characterized by sex stereotyping; but it has simultaneously demanded evidence that the employer actually relied on the stereotype as a factor in the challenged employment decision before that decision could constitute an unlawful employment practice under Title VII.[1]

Punishing an employee for voicing views associated with women does not unlawfully discriminate against her because of her sex.[2] Similarly, the Seventh Circuit, for example, has held that an interviewer's questions about child-bearing and child-rearing plans, asked only of women, did not violate Title VII where the interviewer was apparently reassured by the plaintiff's answers and she could not otherwise show that her rejection was attributable to the employer's stereotypical beliefs.[3] In this respect Title VII contrasts with some state and local antidiscrimination laws, as well as the Americans With Disabilities Act, which treat such questions as per se violations. The same court has also ruled that the plaintiff must show a nexus between a supervisor's occasional or sporadic slurs related to an employee's protected characteristic and a subsequent adverse employment action. Thus a supervisor's repeated directive that a Korean–American "learn to speak English"

§ 2.11

1. *Price Waterhouse v. Hopkins*, 490 U.S. 228, 109 S.Ct. 1775, 104 L.Ed.2d 268 (1989); *Panis v. Mission Hills Bank N.A.*, 60 F.3d 1486 (10th Cir.1995), *cert. denied*, 516 U.S. 1160, 116 S.Ct. 1045, 134 L.Ed.2d 192 (1996) (plaintiff failed to offer facts warranting trial on whether bank relied on gender-based stereotype by terminating her on "customer confidence" grounds after her

husband was indicted for scheming to defraud another bank's customers).

2. *Carpenter v. Federal Nat. Mortg. Ass'n*, 165 F.3d 69 (D.C.Cir.), *cert. denied*, 528 U.S. 823, 120 S.Ct. 69, 145 L.Ed.2d 59 (1999).

3. *Bruno v. Crown Point, Ind.*, 950 F.2d 355 (7th Cir.1991), *cert. denied*, 505 U.S. 1207, 112 S.Ct. 2998, 120 L.Ed.2d 874 (1992).

constituted circumstantial evidence of prohibited national-origin based animus but did not suffice to establish unlawful discrimination absent evidence that the employer ultimately relied on the impermissible criterion in discharging the employee.[4]

In a similar vein the Seventh Circuit has declared a per se rule that will almost always insulate employers from liability for word-of-mouth hiring. The court appeared to agree that an employer's virtually complete reliance on word-of-mouth recruiting by a largely Korean workforce resulted in the overwhelming exclusion of persons of other national origins.[5] But as long as the employer had evidence that this method of recruiting was cost efficient, the disparate result was held not to be evidence of intentional discrimination "even if the employer would prefer to employ people drawn predominantly or even entirely from his own ethnic or, here, national-origin community." The court explained that discrimination "is not preference or aversion; it is acting on the preference or aversion."

The courts have answered the statute's definitional silence on this causation or nexus question by developing different evidentiary allocations and burdens that are deemed equivalent to proof that adverse action was imposed "because of" an employer's reliance on a prohibited characteristic. These proof modes are discussed in Chapter 3 below.

Because Title VII applies so comprehensively to employment decisions affecting millions of private employees and is therefore invoked and litigated so pervasively, decisions interpreting its conceptual framework of discrimination, and even some of its defenses, have frequently served as interpretive models for other statutes. These include not only the cognate ADEA—constructions of which have also cross-pollinated Title VII[6]—but also the Reconstruction Acts, notably 42 U.S.C.A. §§ 1981 and 1983. For example, courts have transplanted the evolving judicial elaboration of unlawful individual disparate treatment under Title VII to both of these nineteenth century statutes,[7] and even imported into § 1981 the explicit textual Title VII defense for bona fide seniority systems.

§§ 2.12–5.19 [Reserved]

D. THE MEANING OF DISCRIMINATION BECAUSE OF "RACE," "COLOR," "NATIONAL ORIGIN," "SEX," AND "RELIGION"

§ 2.20 The Meaning of "Race"

For the most part the Supreme Court has defined the concept of 'race" in connection with actions under 42 U.S.C.A. § 1981, the 1866

---

4. *Hong v. Children's Memorial Hosp.,* 993 F.2d 1257 (7th Cir.1993), *cert. denied,* 511 U.S. 1005, 114 S.Ct. 1372, 128 L.Ed.2d 48 (1994).

5. *EEOC v. Consolidated Serv. Sys.,* 989 F.2d 233 (7th Cir.1993). *See also Foster v. Dalton,* 71 F.3d 52 (1st Cir.1995) (discrimination based on cronyism not prohibited).

6. *See Western Air Lines, Inc. v. Criswell,* 472 U.S. 400, 105 S.Ct. 2743, 86 L.Ed.2d 321 (1985).

7. *See St. Mary's Honor Ctr. v. Hicks,* 509 U.S. 502 n. 1, 113 S.Ct. 2742 n. 1, 125 L.Ed.2d 407 (1993).

statute which secures to all persons the same right to make and enforce contracts, including contracts of employment, as is enjoyed by white citizens. See discussion in Chapter 5. In one of those decisions, however, *McDonald v. Santa Fe Trail Transportation Co.*,[1] the Court held that the Title VII prohibition on race discrimination is enforceable by whites as well as blacks.[2] And whites have been granted standing to assert discrimination based on their association with or marriage to blacks, where the court is persuaded that a black plaintiff with those associations would not have endured similar treatment.[3] But some circuits have required in cases alleging discrimination against whites evidence of "background circumstances" tending to prove that the defendant is the "unusual employer who discriminates against the majority."[4] In a failure to promote situation, the white or male plaintiff can meet this burden by proving that the plaintiff's qualifications were superior to those of the successful minority applicant[5]—a showing the Supreme Court has specifically ruled is not required in the ordinary Title VII case.[6] The same skepticism about anti-white animus under current social conditions has led one circuit court to doubt that the inferential mode of proving intentional discrimination authorized by the *McDonnell Douglas* formula discussed in detail in Chapter 3 is available at all in cases of reverse

§ 2.20

1. 427 U.S. 273, 96 S.Ct. 2574, 49 L.Ed.2d 493 (1976).

2. Examples of claims of "reverse discrimination" by white or male plaintiffs are discussed in Chapters 3 (concerning race- or gender-based employment decisions made pursuant to an agreement settling a prior charge of discrimination) and 4 (concerning the lawfulness of employment decisions made pursuant to "voluntary" and court-decreed affirmative action programs).

3. *See Tetro v. Elliott Popham Pontiac, Oldsmobile, Buick, and GMC Trucks, Inc.*, 173 F.3d 988 (6th Cir.1999) (discrimination against a white man with a biracial child); *Deffenbaugh-Williams v. Wal–Mart Stores, Inc.*, 156 F.3d 581, 588–89 (5th Cir.1998), *vacated on grant of reh'g en banc*, 169 F.3d 215 (5th Cir.1999), *reinstated in relevant part*, 182 F.3d 333 (5th Cir.1999); *Parr v. Woodmen of the World Life Ins. Co.*, 791 F.2d 888 (11th Cir.1986); *Rosenblatt v. Bivona & Cohen, P.C.*, 946 F.Supp. 298 (S.D.N.Y.1996). *But see Childress v. City of Richmond*, 134 F.3d 1205 (4th Cir.) (en banc), *cert. denied*, 524 U.S. 927, 118 S.Ct. 2322, 141 L.Ed.2d 696 (1998) (affirming district court's ruling that white male police officers cannot maintain Title VII claims of hostile work environment directed against black and women officers by an equally divided en banc vote).

4. *See, e.g., Mills v. Health Care Serv. Corp.*, 171 F.3d 450 (7th Cir.1999); *Duffy v. Wolle*, 123 F.3d 1026, 1037 (8th Cir.1997), *cert. denied*, 523 U.S. 1137, 118 S.Ct. 1839, 140 L.Ed.2d 1090 (1998); *Reynolds v. Sch. Dist. No. 1*, 69 F.3d 1523 (10th Cir.1995); *Murray v. Thistledown Racing Club, Inc.*, 770 F.2d 63 (6th Cir.1985); *Parker v. Baltimore & Ohio R.R.*, 652 F.2d 1012, 1017 (D.C.Cir.1981); *Notari v. Denver Water Dep't*, 971 F.2d 585 (10th Cir.1992). At one time, the Fifth Circuit required white plaintiffs to produce prima facie evidence that they were in the racial minority at the workplace. *See, e.g., Switzer v. Texas Commerce Bank*, 850 F.Supp. 544, 547 (N.D.Tex.1994), *aff'd without opinion*, 42 F.3d 642 (5th Cir.1994); *Flanagan v. Aaron E. Henry Cmty. Health Servs. Ctr.*, 876 F.2d 1231, 1233 (5th Cir.1989). This requirement has since been rejected by the circuit. *See Byers v. Dallas Morning News, Inc.*, 209 F.3d 419, 426 (5th Cir.2000); *Singh v. Shoney's, Inc.*, 64 F.3d 217, 219 (5th Cir.1995).

5. *Harding v. Gray*, 9 F.3d 150, 154 (D.C.Cir.1993).

6. *Patterson v. McLean Credit Union*, 491 U.S. 164, 109 S.Ct. 2363, 105 L.Ed.2d 132 (1989).

discrimination.[7] Direct evidence, of course, will support a reverse discrimination claim.[8]

A particular species of race discrimination—harassment affecting the plaintiff's work environment or tangible terms of employment—is condemned on the same terms as sexual harassment.[9] The EEOC and the courts apply the same "subjective" and "objective" standards developed in sexual harassment cases to assess claims of unlawful harassment based on race, religion or national origin.[10] The majority's recognition in *Faragher v. City of Boca Raton*[11] that the elements of actionable sexual harassment derive from earlier race and national origin decisions have also resulted in the use of the *Faragher/Burlington*[12] standards to determine employer liability for racial or national origin harassment.[13] See § 2.22, *infra*.

The race concept has been viewed broadly under § 1981 as well. In *St. Francis College v. Al–Khazraji*[14] and *Shaare Tefila Congregation v. Cobb*,[15] the Court held that the § 1981 ban on race discrimination could be enforced by Arabs and Jews, respectively, if they could prove adverse treatment on the basis of their ancestry. Observing that these holdings in effect mean that whites can maintain a viable § 1981 claim against other whites, one court has concluded that a black plaintiff may maintain a Title VII claim based on alleged race discrimination by a black supervisor.[16] And the distinct Title VII prohibition on discrimination

7. *See, e.g., Hill v. Burrell Communications Group, Inc.,* 67 F.3d 665, 668 n. 2 (7th Cir.1995). By contrast, the Third and Eleventh Circuits apply the ordinary *McDonnell Douglas/Burdine* formula to a white plaintiff's claim of race discrimination, with no mention of any required "background circumstances." *See Alexander v. Fulton County,* 207 F.3d 1303 (11th Cir.2000); *Iadimarco v. Runyon,* 190 F.3d 151 (3d Cir. 1999) and *Schoenfeld v. Babbitt,* 168 F.3d 1257, 1267–68 (11th Cir.1999). *See also Pierce v. Commonwealth Life Ins. Co.,* 40 F.3d 796 (6th Cir.1994) (doubting the soundness of requiring heightened showing by white plaintiffs).

8. *See McGarry v. Board of County Comm'rs of County of Pitkin,* 175 F.3d 1193 (10th Cir.1999).

9. *See, e.g.,Hafford v. Seidner,* 183 F.3d 506 (6th Cir.1999) (applying, in racial harassment case, the *Burlington/Faragher* affirmative defense to environmental sexual harassment).

10. *See Enforcement Guidance on Harris v. Forklift Sys., Inc.,* March 8, 1994; *Hafford v. Seidner,* 183 F.3d 506 (6th Cir. 1999).

11. 524 U.S. 775, 118 S.Ct. 2275, 141 L.Ed.2d 662 (1998).

12. *Burlington Indus. v. Ellerth,* 524 U.S. 742, 118 S.Ct. 2257, 141 L.Ed.2d 633 (1998).

13. *See Wright–Simmons v. Oklahoma City,* 155 F.3d 1264 (10th Cir.1998) (applying *Burlington/Faragher* to racial hostile environment claim); *Booker v. Budget Rent–A–Car Sys.,* 17 F.Supp.2d 735 (M.D.Tenn. 1998) (applying both sexual hostile environment and employer liability standards in case of racial harassment); *Ngeunjuntr v. Metropolitan Life Ins. Co.,* 146 F.3d 464 (7th Cir.1998) (pre-*Ellerth* and *Faragher,* but applying *Harris, Meritor,* and *Oncale* to a claim of harassment on the basis of national origin). *But see Hardin v. S.C. Johnson & Son, Inc.,* 167 F.3d 340 (7th Cir. 1999), *cert. denied,* 528 U.S. 874, 120 S.Ct. 178, 145 L.Ed.2d 150 (1999) (black female harassment plaintiff required to show disparate treatment against blacks or women, that is by reference to white women or black men, rather than against blacks who are also women).

14. 481 U.S. 604, 107 S.Ct. 2022, 95 L.Ed.2d 582 (1987).

15. 481 U.S. 615, 107 S.Ct. 2019, 95 L.Ed.2d 594 (1987).

16. *Hansborough v. City of Elkhart Parks and Recreation Dep't,* 802 F.Supp. 199 (N.D.Ind.1992).

because of "color" has supported claims by lighter-or darker-skinned blacks based on discrimination by a black employer agent with skin of a different hue.[17] There is authority permitting proof of discrimination on a compound basis—e.g., gender and race.[18]

§ 2.21   Accent or Language Rules as National Origin Discrimination

Discrimination because of national origin presents special difficulties because it is relatively seldom that defendants refer explicitly to the particular country of origin of the plaintiff or his ancestors.[1] One example we saw above, an employer rule requiring citizenship as a precondition to hire, is an example. Because citizenship as such is not a forbidden ground of discrimination, the rule might violate Title VII if but only if in operation it has disproportionate adverse impact on persons of an identifiable national origin.[2] Similarly, ethnic slurs more commonly stain an individual's ancestry (e.g., slurs pertaining to Arabs, Jews, or persons hailing from Asia, Africa, Central or South America, Mexico, or Puerto Rico), another basis of discrimination not forbidden by Title VII, than her particular national origin. In addition, employer practices or rules based on language characteristics will usually also be neutral on their face. They therefore could violate Title VII only if applied in ways that are designed to injure or that have disproportionate adverse impact on persons of a particular national origin.

Two language problems of this kind have surfaced in the cases—discrimination based on foreign accent, and "speak-English-only" rules. Several circuit courts have considered discrimination because of accent, where the adverse employer action is typically meted out ad hoc, rather than pursuant to an across-the-board rule. Consequently, the decisions evaluate the evidence in these cases under the theory of individual disparate treatment, rather than disproportionate adverse impact. The leading case, *Fragante v. City and County of Honolulu*,[3] relied on an EEOC Guideline[4] in assuming without deciding that proof of discrimination based on foreign accent establishes a prima facie case of discrimination based on national origin. But it upheld the employer's bona fide

---

17. *See Walker v. Secretary of the Treasury*, 713 F.Supp. 403 (N.D.Ga.1989).

18. *Lam v. University of Hawaii*, 40 F.3d 1551 (9th Cir.1994). *But see Hardin*, 167 F.3d 340.

§ 2.21

1. In one circuit decision, though, discrimination on the basis of plaintiff's national origin was inferred simply from the fact that his supervisor called him a "foreigner." *Afzal v. Atlantic Coast Airlines, Inc.*, 176 F.3d 475 (4th Cir.1999).

2. *See* Chapter 3 below on the several Title VII proof modes. Some courts require identifiability of plaintiff's particular country of origin with more specificity than do

others. *See Gomez v. Allegheny Health Servs.*, 71 F.3d 1079 (3d Cir.1995), *cert. denied*, 518 U.S. 1005, 116 S.Ct. 2524, 135 L.Ed.2d 1049 (1996). Discrimination against a particular Indian tribe has been held actionable national origin discrimination because tribes were and to some degree still are considered separate nations. *Dawavendewa v. Salt River Project*, 154 F.3d 1117, 1119 (9th Cir.1998), *cert. denied*, 528 U.S. 1098, 120 S.Ct. 843, 145 L.Ed.2d 708 (2000).

3. 888 F.2d 591 (9th Cir.1989), *cert. denied*, 494 U.S. 1081, 110 S.Ct. 1811, 108 L.Ed.2d 942 (1990).

4. *See* 29 C.F.R. § 1606.1 *et seq.*

occupational qualification defense, writing that an adverse employment decision taken because of accent is lawful only when the accent "interferes materially with job performance."[5] Nevertheless, because accent and national origin "are obviously inextricably intertwined in many cases," the Court cautioned that a "searching look" is demanded to ensure that employer assertions about a candidate's poor communications skills are not used as a cover or pretext for national origin discrimination.[6]

The few appellate opinions on the issue treat English-only rules as neutral employer practices that are subject to evaluation on the theory of disproportionate adverse impact because of their potential adverse effect on non-English speakers as well as bilinguals.[7] Even if the rule is limited to certain times, the guideline gives it the same prima facie effect and says it must be "justified by business necessity."[8] Moreover, failure to give employees advance notification of the required circumstances and consequences of violation will be considered "evidence of" national origin discrimination.[9]

The part of this guideline that specifies a business necessity defense would appear to be of no current import. Title VII itself, as amended by the Civil Rights Act of 1991, requires the employer, once a prima facie case of disproportionate adverse impact is made, to "demonstrate that the challenged practice is job related for the position in question *and* consistent with business necessity."[10] While there will continue to be great uncertainty about the content of "business necessity" under the new statute, it is clear that neutral practices will now also have to be justified as "job related for the position in question," a requirement absent from the EEOC Guideline. See Chapter 3 for a fuller discussion of the concepts of "business necessity" and "job relatedness."

The currently significant issue raised by the guideline is its presumption that an English-only rule has adverse impact in all circumstances, particularly as applied to bilingual employees. This presump-

---

5. *Fragante*, 888 F.2d at 596.

6. 888 F.2d at 596 (citing 29 C.F.R. § 1606.6(b)(1)). *Accord Odima v. Westin Tucson Hotel Co.*, 991 F.2d 595, 600 (9th Cir.1993); *Ang v. Procter & Gamble Co.*, 932 F.2d 540, 550 (6th Cir.1991). *See also Carino v. University of Oklahoma Bd. of Regents*, 750 F.2d 815, 819 (10th Cir.1984); *Berke v. Ohio Dep't of Pub. Welfare*, 628 F.2d 980, 981 (6th Cir.1980). *Cf. Stephen v. PGA Sheraton Resort, Ltd.*, 873 F.2d 276 (11th Cir.1989) (race discrimination claim rebutted by credible evidence that plaintiff did not speak or understand English sufficiently to perform assigned duties).

7. *See, e.g., Garcia v. Gloor*, 618 F.2d 264 (5th Cir.1980), *cert. denied*, 449 U.S. 1113, 101 S.Ct. 923, 66 L.Ed.2d 842 (1981); *Garcia v. Spun Steak Co.*, 998 F.2d 1480 (9th Cir.1993), *cert. denied*, 512 U.S. 1228, 114 S.Ct. 2726, 129 L.Ed.2d 849 (1994);

Long v. First Union Corp., 86 F.3d 1151 (4th Cir.1996); and *Gonzalez v. Salvation Army*, 985 F.2d 578 (11th Cir.), *cert. denied*, 508 U.S. 910, 113 S.Ct. 2342, 124 L.Ed.2d 252 (1993). Generally, appellate courts have held that English-only rules do not have a disparate impact on the basis of national origin, particularly as applied to multilingual employees who can choose whether to violate the employer's rule.

8. *See, e.g., Kania v. Archdiocese of Phila.*, 14 F.Supp.2d 730 (E.D.Pa.1998) (church's English-only rule was intended to improve interpersonal relations and prevent bilingual employees from alienating monolingual coworkers and church members).

9. 29 C.F.R. § 1606.7.

10. 42 U.S.C.A. § 2000e–2(k)(1)(A) (emphasis added).

tion, if accepted, establishes the plaintiff's prima facie case, thereby casting on the employer the burden of justification. The early opinions, *Garcia v. Gloor*,[11] *Garcia v. Rush–Presbyterian–St. Luke's Medical Center*[12] and *Jurado v. Eleven–Fifty Corporation*,[13] concluded that employees fluent in both English and Spanish were not adversely impacted by even sweeping English-only rules, because they could readily comply with the employer's directive and thus avoid tangible employment detriment. Later, the Ninth Circuit, relying on the EEOC's Guideline, struck down a rule that forbade Spanish-speaking translators from speaking Spanish except while on break, at lunch, or actually translating.[14] The court found the prima facie case met the EEOC presumption and rejected the proffered employer justifications that the rule was necessary to promote racial harmony and to prevent the workplace from becoming a "Tower of Babel." Specifically disagreeing with the Fifth Circuit in *Garcia v. Gloor*, the court held that the mere fact that the plaintiff was bilingual and could comply with the employer's rule did not shield the rule from liability, because bilinguality "does not eliminate the relationship between his primary language and the culture that is derived from his national origin."

Subsequently, however, the Ninth Circuit repudiated this approach and rejected the EEOC Guideline in *Garcia v. Spun Steak Co.*[15] The Supreme Court denied certiorari despite the urging of the Justice Department. The Ninth Circuit in *Spun Steak* expressly subscribed to the Fifth Circuit's approach in *Garcia v. Gloor*[16] and insisted that adverse impact must be proved and not merely presumed. The Ninth Circuit's approach is likely to stand as a leading opinion because it represents the view of a circuit with an enormous immigrant population that will feel the brunt of such workplace rules.[17] But the scope of *Spun Steak* as applied to varying employer rules is uncertain. For example, there the court found, with somewhat curious logic,[18] that the employer's English-only rule had no disproportionate adverse impact because the plaintiff, being bilingual, could readily comply without jeopardizing his employment. That rationale would of course not pertain to monolingual Spanish speakers. Further, the *Spun Steak* policy was justified as a business

---

11. 618 F.2d 264 (5th Cir.1980), *cert. denied*, 449 U.S. 1113, 101 S.Ct. 923, 66 L.Ed.2d 842 (1981).

12. 660 F.2d 1217, 1222 (7th Cir.1981) (upholding employer rule requiring the ability to speak English as not having a disproportionate adverse impact on Latinos and in any event as job related).

13. 813 F.2d 1406 (9th Cir.1987).

14. *Gutierrez v. Municipal Court*, 838 F.2d 1031 (9th Cir.1988), *vacated as moot*, 490 U.S. 1016, 109 S.Ct. 1736, 104 L.Ed.2d 174 (1989).

15. 998 F.2d 1480 (9th Cir.1993), *cert. denied*, 512 U.S. 1228, 114 S.Ct. 2726, 129 L.Ed.2d 849 (1994).

16. 618 F.2d 264 (5th Cir.1980), *cert. denied*, 449 U.S. 1113, 101 S.Ct. 923, 66 L.Ed.2d 842 (1981).

17. More recently the Ninth Circuit has declared unconstitutional a state constitutional provision purporting to enshrine English as the state's official language and requiring all government employees to "act" in English only. *Yniguez v. Arizonans for Official English*, 42 F.3d 1217 (9th Cir. 1994), *vacated as moot*, *Arizonans for Official English v. Arizona*, 520 U.S. 43, 117 S.Ct. 1055, 137 L.Ed.2d 170 (1997).

18. *Spun Steak Co.*, 13 F.3d at 298 (Reinhardt, J., dissenting from denial of rehearing en banc).

necessity because it facilitated worker safety on a production line. That defense might not be available where a similar rule is applied to office personnel or to off-duty inter-employee conversations.[19]

Another circuit has held that an English-only rule challenged by Spanish-speaking employees cannot constitute unlawful disparate treatment absent evidence that English speakers were permitted to speak in languages other than English.[20] A related contention is that a policy of *permitting* employees to speak their native foreign language on the job may violate the right of English speakers to be free from discrimination based on national origin. The argument is said to draw support from the EEOC's national origin guideline which identifies an individual's primary language as an "essential national origin characteristic." A claim to this effect survived an employer's motion for summary judgment.[21] But a claim that an employer practice requiring employees with fluency in Spanish to use that skill on the job unlawfully discriminates failed where non-Hispanics also used Spanish-speaking skills on the job, at least in the absence of a pattern of systematic disparate treatment.[22]

§ 2.22 Discrimination Based on Sex

Whereas the problem with national origin discrimination is that it is often not relied on expressly, the definitional problem with many permutations of sex discrimination frequently is that sex, while an explicit part of an employer's decision or rule, is not the sole factor. For example, the employer's rule in *Phillips v. Martin Marietta Corp.*,[1] disqualified from employment women, though not men, with pre-school-aged children. The rule, then, excluded only women, but not all women; the question was whether this was the kind of express discrimination on the basis of sex that would require the greatest level of employer justification. The Supreme Court, reversing the court of appeals, found express discrimination, holding that the rule impermissibly created "one hiring policy for women and another for men." It was no defense that the policy discriminated not because of sex alone but because of a compound "sex-plus"— with the plus factor here being the early stages of motherhood. In reaching this conclusion, the Court noted that Congress had rejected proposed amendments to the statute that would have forbidden only discrimination that is "solely" on one of the prohibited grounds.

Although Title VII does not expressly prohibit employers from using marital status to make employment distinctions, the logic of *Martin Marietta* and decisions of other federal courts and the EEOC demon-

---

19. Alternatively, a policy that applies only to on-duty conversations may be upheld as having minimal restrictive impact, as in *Jurado*, 813 F.2d 1406.

20. *Long v. First Union Corp. of Virginia*, 86 F.3d 1151 (4th Cir.1996) (unpublished).

21. *McNeil v. Aguilos*, 831 F.Supp. 1079 (S.D.N.Y.1993).

22. *Morales v. Human Rights Div.*, 878 F.Supp. 653 (S.D.N.Y.1995); *Cota v. Tucson Police Dep't*, 783 F.Supp. 458, 473–74 (D.Ariz.1992).

§ 2.22

1. 400 U.S. 542, 544, 91 S.Ct. 496, 27 L.Ed.2d 613 (1971).

strate that such distinctions may constitute unlawful discrimination if sex is one of the factors the employer took into account when making such distinctions.[2] For example, it is unlawful sex discrimination to reject applicants or fail to promote employees who are married women, but not married men.[3] In *Sprogis*,[4] the airline-employer enforced a no-marriage rule for female flight attendants but not for male flight attendants. The Seventh Circuit recognized that disparity of treatment under Title VII may exist whether such disparity is universal among women or confined to a particular subclass of women.

An important lesson for plaintiff's counsel in sex-plus disparate treatment cases can be gleaned from several marital status circuit court cases: plaintiff must produce evidence of a similarly situated comparator group. In *Fisher v. Vassar College*,[5] plaintiff alleged she was denied tenure in the biology department at Vassar College because Vassar had a policy of not promoting married women in the "hard" sciences. The Second Circuit in reversing the district court pointed out that at best Fisher may have shown lawful discrimination on the basis of marital status. The absence of any comparison between married males and married females rendered plaintiff's proffered statistics of unlawful gender-based discrimination meaningless. Citing *St. Mary's Honor Center v. Hicks*,[6] the court concluded that Fisher had failed to carry the burden of proving that Vassar's stated reason for the denial of tenure was a pretext for unlawful "sex-plus" discrimination. In *Bryant v. International Schools Services*,[7] plaintiffs again failed to show that married women were treated differently from similarly situated males. Rather, the court found, the employer's policy of offering fewer benefits to applicants hired at the job site in Iran, than to those hired through the home office in Princeton, New Jersey, was equally applied to all persons—male and female, married and single. Similarly, where an airline hired only females as flight attendants, the enforcement of a no-marriage rule for flight attendants did not constitute unlawful sex-plus-marital status discrimination because there was no gender-based dissimilarity in treatment—there were no males in the work force![8]

A sex-plus-marital status case demonstrates the difficulty this burden may present. In *Coleman v. B–G Maintenance Management of Colorado, Inc.*,[9] plaintiff supervised maintenance workers, including her

---

2. *Sprogis v. United Air Lines*, 444 F.2d 1194, 1197–98 (7th Cir.), *cert. denied*, 404 U.S. 991, 92 S.Ct. 536, 30 L.Ed.2d 543 (1971). *See* EEOC Decisions No. 71–2048 (1971) and CCH EEOC Decision ¶ 6244. *See also* 29 CFR § 1604.4(a). In *Sprogis*, the court specifically adopted this EEOC regulation as reasonable and consistent with the legislative purpose of Title VII. 444 F.2d at 1198.

3. *Sprogis*, 444 F.2d at 1198.

4. *Id.* at 1196.

5. 70 F.3d 1420, 1448 (2d Cir.1995), *aff'd en banc*, 114 F.3d 1332 (2d Cir.1997),

cert. denied, 522 U.S. 1075, 118 S.Ct. 851, 139 L.Ed.2d 752 (1998) ..

6. 509 U.S. 502, 113 S.Ct. 2742, 125 L.Ed.2d 407 (1993). See discussion, § 3.10, *infra*.

7. 675 F.2d 562, 575 (3d Cir.1982).

8. *Stroud v. Delta Air Lines, Inc.*, 544 F.2d 892, 893–94 (5th Cir.), *cert. denied*, 434 U.S. 844, 98 S.Ct. 146, 54 L.Ed.2d 110 (1977).

9. 108 F.3d 1199 (10th Cir.1997). *See also Foray v. Bell Atlantic*, 56 F.Supp.2d 327 (S.D.N.Y.1999) (providing benefits to

husband. She was fired, the employer claimed, because she allowed her husband to leave the work site during his shift. Claiming sex-plus-marital status discrimination, plaintiff put forth evidence showing that male supervisors whose subordinates had left the work site during their shifts had not been fired; indeed, no other supervisor, male or female, had been terminated. The difficulty was that there was no male supervisor similarly situated—no other supervisor had any kind of personal relationship with any subordinate employee. Having lost a jury verdict on sex discrimination, without a comparator group for the sex-plus claim, plaintiff could not demonstrate any dissimilarity in treatment between the sexes, resulting in the failure of her claim.

Since only women become pregnant, it might seem that a distinction on the basis of pregnancy would be tantamount to express or facial discrimination because of gender. That result might clearly have been expected after *Martin Marietta*, which seemingly would have considered it irrelevant that pregnancy discrimination also draws a distinction on the basis of the "plus" characteristic of pregnancy. The Supreme Court held otherwise, however, in *General Electric Co. v. Gilbert*,[10] when it concluded that a pregnancy exclusion from an otherwise comprehensive disability insurance plan did not discriminate against women because it distinguished on a "gender-neutral" basis between pregnant women and non-pregnant persons. Congress legislatively overruled this result in the Pregnancy Discrimination Act of 1978, discussed in § 2.31 below.

Relying on the *Gilbert* reasoning, employers also contended that pension plan provisions requiring greater contributions by female employees, or awarding them lesser retirement benefits despite their equal contributions, are geared to the neutral factor of greater average female longevity rather than to gender. The Supreme Court, however, found gender an inadequate proxy for greater female longevity, noting that a significant part of the differential might be explainable by other factors, such as the heavier incidence of smoking among men. In any event, again stressing Title VII's focus on the individual, the Court expressed concern that even an accurate generalization about greater female longevity obscures the fact that many women will live less long than many men, and each such woman is entitled to benefits calculated without regard to gender-based averages. Accordingly, the Court has invalidated plans that require women to make greater contributions or that award them lesser benefits.[11] These decisions have revolutionized the employer-sponsored pension industry, forcing many insurers to offer plans featuring gender-neutral annuity assumptions.

Lower courts have long held, with substantial unanimity, that discrimination because of one's sexual orientation or behaviors does not

---

employees' same-sex partners but not to unmarried male heterosexual discriminates on basis of plaintiff's ability to receive benefits by marrying, not because of his sex).

10. 429 U.S. 125, 97 S.Ct. 401, 50 L.Ed.2d 343 (1976).

11. *See, respectively, Los Angeles Dep't of Water & Power v. Manhart*, 435 U.S. 702, 98 S.Ct. 1370, 55 L.Ed.2d 657 (1978); *Arizona Governing Committee v. Norris*, 463 U.S. 1073, 103 S.Ct. 3492, 77 L.Ed.2d 1236 (1983).

amount to gender discrimination prohibited by Title VII.[12] These courts have relied heavily on the repeated failure in Congress of bills that would have prohibited sexual orientation discrimination.[13] For these courts, unless an antihomosexual policy is disparately enforced in favor of or against members of a particular gender, the employer rule is simply not on the basis of gender. Efforts to circumvent this barrier, either by proceeding on a disparate impact theory or by asserting that a campaign of anti-homosexual hostility amounted to unlawful environmental harassment based on gender, have also failed.[14] For example, an anti-homosexual practice, gender-neutral on its face and neutrally applied, may nevertheless result in disproportionately greater exclusion of male homosexuals (as will be the case, if, for example, they are more readily identifiable) and might therefore be said to discriminate because of gender. But since the impetus for the discrimination is anti-homosexual rather than anti-male animus, the circuit opinions accordingly conclude that recognizing the impact theory would amount to an end-run around the Congressional purpose not to forbid discrimination based on sexual orientation.[15] By contrast, disparate enforcement of an anti-homosexual policy in favor of or against members of a particular gender would presumably violate the statute.[16] Despite the absence of national protection, numerous state and local laws provide protection from this type of

---

12. *See Higgins v. New Balance Athletic Shoe, Inc.*, 194 F.3d 252 (1st Cir.1999); *Garcia v. Elf Atochem N. America*, 28 F.3d 446 (5th Cir.1994) (alternative holding); *Dillon v. Frank*, 952 F.2d 403 (6th Cir.1992); *Williamson v. A.G. Edwards and Sons, Inc.*, 876 F.2d 69 (8th Cir.1989), *cert. denied*, 493 U.S. 1089, 110 S.Ct. 1158, 107 L.Ed.2d 1061 (1990); *DeCintio v. Westchester County Med. Ctr.*, 807 F.2d 304 (2d Cir.1986), *cert. denied*, 484 U.S. 825, 108 S.Ct. 89, 98 L.Ed.2d 50 (1987); *Ulane v. Eastern Airlines, Inc.*, 742 F.2d 1081 (7th Cir.1984), *cert. denied*, 471 U.S. 1017, 105 S.Ct. 2023, 85 L.Ed.2d 304 (1985); *DeSantis v. Pacific Tel. & Tel. Co.*, 608 F.2d 327 (9th Cir.1979); *Smith v. Liberty Mut. Ins. Co.*, 569 F.2d 325 (5th Cir.1978). *See also Hopkins v. Baltimore Gas & Elec. Co.*, 871 F.Supp. 822 (D.Md. 1994), *aff'd*, 77 F.3d 745 (4th Cir.), *cert. denied*, 519 U.S. 818, 117 S.Ct. 70, 136 L.Ed.2d 30 (1996); *Vandeventer v. Wabash Nat'l Corp.*, 867 F.Supp. 790 (N.D.Ind. 1994), *on reconsideration*, 887 F.Supp. 1178 (N.D.Ind.1995); *Goluszek v. Smith*, 697 F.Supp. 1452 (N.D.Ill.1988). *But see Joyner v. AAA Cooper Transp.*, 597 F.Supp. 537 (M.D.Ala.1983), *affirmed without opinion*, 749 F.2d 732 (11th Cir.1984); *Wright v. Methodist Youth Servs., Inc.*, 511 F.Supp. 307 (N.D.Ill.1981).

13. Efforts to pass a federal anti-discrimination statute continue. In 1997, identical bills were introduced in both houses of Congress that will, if enacted into law, prohibit employment discrimination on the basis of sexual orientation. Introduced with broad bi-partisan support in both houses, the "Employment Non–Discrimination Act of 1997" would prohibit discrimination against an individual on the basis of that individual's sexual orientation or on the basis of the sexual orientation of a person that individual is associated with. The bill specifically prevents use of the disparate impact mode of proof, stating that an employment practice with a disparate impact on the basis of sexual orientation does not establish a prima facie violation of the law. H. 1858, 105th Cong. (1997); S. 869, 105th Cong. (1997). As of November 1999, both bills remain in Congressional committees.

14. *See, respectively, DeSantis*, 608 F.2d 327 and *Dillon*, 952 F.2d 403.

15. *See, e.g.*, the majority's response in *DeSantis v. Pacific Tel. & Tel. Co.*, 608 F.2d 327 (9th Cir.1979) to the partial dissenting opinion of Judge Sneed.

16. However, a voluntary employer practice that provides medical and related benefits to same-sex but not to heterosexual unmarried domestic partners has been upheld under Title VII as differentiating only on the basis of legal capacity to marry, and not on the basis of sex. *Foray v. Bell Atlantic*, 56 F.Supp.2d 327 (S.D.N.Y.1999).

employment discrimination.[17]

Rules prohibiting the employment of spouses in the same office, department or plant of one company have been viewed as neutral on their face, actionable only if they are disparately enforced against members of a particular gender or if they have the statistical effect of disproportionately adversely impacting wives or husbands.[18] A no-dating rule is likewise neutral on its face and could violate Title VII only if disparately enforced or disproportionately impacting.[19]

Grooming and dress code regulations that on their face pertain only to one gender—men must have short hair, for example—have nevertheless been judicially assessed as neutral rather than as a form of express disparate treatment. The leading case, *Willingham v. Macon Telegraph Publishing Co.,*[20] offered a variety of reasons in support of this conclusion, none of which withstands hard scrutiny. For example, the court wrote that men could readily comply with a short-hair rule because it related to a "mutable" characteristic, and the statute was concerned only with assuring that employment opportunities not be denied on the basis of "immutable" characteristics like race or sex. This view has been otherwise expressed as asserting that the "primary thrust"[21] of Title VII is to ban employer reliance on sex stereotypes that pose "distinct employment disadvantages for one sex."[22] Yet religion, also prohibited by Title VII, is clearly mutable. And although gender, too, is within limits mutable (through the agency of transsexual surgery), the court certainly did not suggest that any other gender-based rules were outside the scope of the statute.

17. Approximately one-third of Americans live in jurisdictions that have enacted laws providing protection against discrimination on the basis of sexual orientation. *See, e.g.*, Cal.Lab.Code § 1102.1 (West Supp.1996); Conn.Gen.Stat. § 46a–81c (1995); D.C.Code Ann. § 1–2512 (1992); Haw.Rev.Stat. § 378–2 (1993); Mass.Gen.L. ch. 151B § 4 (1994); Minn.Stat. § 363.03 (1994); N.H.Rev.Stat.Ann. § 354–A:7 (1998); N.J.Stat.Ann. § 10:5–12 (West 1993); R.I.Gen. Laws § 28–5–7 (1995); Vt. Stat.Ann. tit. 21, § 495 (1994); Wisc.Stat. §§ 111.321, 111.36(1)(d)1 (1997). Over 150 cities and counties have passed similar statutes. American Civil Liberties Union, *Lesbian and Gay Rights* (visited November 10, 1999) <http://www.aclu.org/issues/gay/gaylaws.html>.

18. *See Yuhas v. Libbey–Owens–Ford*, 562 F.2d 496 (7th Cir.1977), *cert. denied*, 435 U.S. 934, 98 S.Ct. 1510, 55 L.Ed.2d 531 (1978) (holding that such a disparate adverse impact was justifiable because the no-spouse rule plausibly improved the work environment). *Cf. Scott v. Dynasty Transp. Inc.*, 1994 WL 160545 (E.D.La.1994), where the court rejected a retaliation claim resulting from the plaintiff's protest of his wife's discharge on the ground that discrimination because of "familial relations" is not a Title VII unlawful employment practice. This ruling evidently overlooked the fact that retaliation claims under § 704 lie regardless of whether the underlying employer conduct against which the retaliation plaintiff protested is itself a violation of the statute. See discussion of Retaliation, *infra*.

19. *See Sarsha v. Sears, Roebuck & Co.*, 3 F.3d 1035 (7th Cir.1993).

20. 507 F.2d 1084 (5th Cir.1975) (en banc). The *Willingham* holding was followed in *Harper v. Blockbuster Entertainment Corp.*, 139 F.3d 1385, 1388 (11th Cir.), *cert. denied*, 525 U.S. 1000, 119 S.Ct. 509, 142 L.Ed.2d 422 (1998) (citing cases) and *Tavora v. New York Mercantile Exchange*, 101 F.3d 907 (2d Cir.1996), *cert. denied*, 520 U.S. 1229, 117 S.Ct. 1821, 137 L.Ed.2d 1029 (1997) (per curiam).

21. *Craft v. Metromedia, Inc.*, 766 F.2d 1205 (8th Cir.1985), *cert. denied*, 475 U.S. 1058, 106 S.Ct. 1285, 89 L.Ed.2d 592 (1986).

22. *Knott v. Missouri Pac. R.R.*, 527 F.2d 1249, 1251 (8th Cir.1975).

Perhaps recognizing the frailty of this distinction, the court fell back on the assertion that hair length did not relate to a "fundamental right." But Title VII is designed precisely to go beyond the minimal fundamental rights that enjoy constitutional protection; it does so by assuring that employment status is not disadvantaged by any distinction based on race, sex, religion or national origin.[23] Neither the text nor history of the statute supports the distinction that conduct or behavior protected by the statute must be deemed "fundamental" from any other legal perspective.

The same approach has disadvantaged women with respect to regulations governing attire and grooming. Even when the employer's rule specifically imposes more demanding clothing and coiffure requirements on one gender than the other, the tendency has been for the courts to assert that the employer has one omnibus grooming regime that naturally has distinctive variations to account for gender differences. In a variation on this theme, courts will observe that the employer has *some* grooming standard for each gender and will treat that standard as the common, neutral employer practice. The fact that the employer imposes different, or more stringent, or differentially applied dress or grooming requirements on its employees of different genders is usually just ignored or minimized.[24] Plaintiffs have also been compelled to litigate no-beard rules within the framework of disproportionate adverse impact rather than disparate treatment.[25] The consequence of these decisions is that employers are far more easily able to justify such rules as a matter of business necessity or job relatedness than they would be if the rules were classified as discriminating facially on the basis of gender.[26]

The general judicial rejection of women's gender discrimination complaints about harsher grooming or clothing requirements represents an exception to the Supreme Court's general recognition that employer practices driven by sex stereotyping unlawfully discriminate because of

23. Of course it must be acknowledged that in the realm of voluntary employer affirmative action, white and male employees seem to enjoy *less* protection from reverse discrimination under Title VII than they do under the Constitution. Compare the *Weber* and *Johnson* decisions with *Wygant* and *Croson* in the section on affirmative action in Chapter 4.

24. *Craft v. Metromedia, Inc.*, 766 F.2d 1205 (8th Cir.1985), *cert. denied*, 475 U.S. 1058, 106 S.Ct. 1285, 89 L.Ed.2d 592 (1986); *Carroll v. Talman Fed. Sav. & Loan Ass'n*, 604 F.2d 1028 (7th Cir.1979), *cert. denied*, 445 U.S. 929, 100 S.Ct. 1316, 63 L.Ed.2d 762 (1980); *Barker v. Taft Broadcasting Co.*, 549 F.2d 400 (6th Cir.1977); *Earwood v. Continental Southeastern Lines, Inc.*, 539 F.2d 1349 (4th Cir.1976); *Fagan v. National Cash Register Co.*, 481 F.2d 1115 (D.C.Cir.1973). Similarly, the Court in *Willingham* accepted as an alternative ground that the employer maintained "[some, al-

beit different] grooming standards for female employees; thus in this respect each sex is treated equally." 507 F.2d at 1091–1092. *But see Frank v. United Airlines, Inc.*, 216 F.3d 845, 854–55 (9th Cir.2000) (rejecting defendant airline's argument that facially discriminatory flight attendant weight standards were mere grooming requirements where the standards imposed unequal burdens on men and women); *Hollins v. Atlantic Co., Inc.*, 188 F.3d 652 (6th Cir.1999) (African–American female states claim where subjected to grooming standards not imposed on white women).

25. *See, e.g., Bradley v. Pizzaco of Nebraska, Inc.*, 7 F.3d 795 (8th Cir.1993); *Fitzpatrick v. City of Atlanta*, 2 F.3d 1112 (11th Cir.1993).

26. This difference is well illustrated in *Frank*, 216 F.3d 845, 854–55.

gender.[27] A Third Circuit decision illustrates the continuing vitality of the concept in other contexts.[28] A female employee was ostracized by co-workers and received an adverse evaluation because of rumors that she was having an affair with her male supervisor; those rumors were fueled by the fact that the supervisor repeatedly borrowed money from her in private. The court held that she could proceed to trial with a claim of discrimination. A reasonable jury, the court explained, could conclude that she suffered the adverse effects of the rumors because she was a woman, even though the supervisor's practice of borrowing money would have been gender neutral had he borrowed from a man. In the court's view, the harm or "sting" of the practice derived from traditional negative stereotypes that linked women's workplace advancement and their sexual behavior. In this way the employer risks liability for creating a sexually hostile work environment absent any showing of sexual misconduct: the supervisor's practice was confined to the clearly gender-neutral act of borrowing money, and the rumors that surrounded that practice were not attributable to the supervisor or the employer! Before the reader concludes, however, that the court went overboard on punishing sex stereotyping, one last point should be made: the defendant employer was the EEOC. Perhaps then this is simply a case of a sometimes overscrupulous enforcer being held to overscrupulous standards.

There are a number of other frequently litigated issues that wrestle with the question when grounds of discrimination that correlate differentially or exclusively with one gender amount to the prohibited discrimination "because of sex." Most of these are specially treated by Title VII or related statutes and will be considered now.

a. Sexual[29] Harassment

Early decisions doubted whether a supervisor's imposition of adverse terms and conditions of employment on a subordinate employee for resisting the superior's sexual advances constituted discrimination "be-

27. *Price Waterhouse v. Hopkins*, 490 U.S. 228, 109 S.Ct. 1775, 104 L.Ed.2d 268 (1989).

28. *Spain v. Gallegos, EEOC*, 26 F.3d 439 (3d Cir.1994).

29. Because the federal courts have for the most part applied the same standards in cases alleging sexual and racial harassment, *see Hafford v. Seidner*, 183 F.3d 506 (6th Cir.1999) (applying sexual harassment standards to a racial harassment claim); *Allen v. Michigan Dep't of Corrections*, 165 F.3d 405, 411 (6th Cir.1999) (applying *Burlington* and *Faragher* in racial harassment case); *Wright-Simmons v. The City of Oklahoma City*, 155 F.3d 1264, 1270 (10th Cir. 1998) (stating that "[a]lthough *Burlington* and *Faragher* involved sexual harassment, the principles established in those cases ap-

ply with equal force to this case of racial harassment"); *Wallin v. Minnesota Dep't of Corrections*, 153 F.3d 681, 687–88 (8th Cir. 1998), *cert. denied*, 526 U.S. 1004, 119 S.Ct. 1141, 143 L.Ed.2d 209 (1999) (applying *Faragher* to an harassment claim under the ADA), some of the decisions cited *infra*, this section, concern allegations of racial harassment. Further, EEOC applies the Supreme Court decisions fixing the terms of employer liability for sexual harassment to age, race, national origin, disability and nonsexual but gender-based discrimination cases, as well as to harassment claims based on opposition or participation in complaint procedures. *EEOC Guidance on Vicarious Employer Liability for Unlawful Harassment by Supervisors*, No. 915.002, Pt. II (6/18/99).

cause of sex" even where the superior and subordinate were of different genders. After all, these cases reasoned, the selection of a "target" would usually not be based on the factor of gender alone, except perhaps if the superior targeted *all* subordinate employees of the opposite gender. That is, there would usually be a "plus" factor in the superior employee's calculus, usually the target's relative attractiveness or vulnerability to the superior. Subsequently, however, the Supreme Court has appeared to assume that, as in *Martin Marietta*, the target's gender need not be the sole motivating factor in the superior's advance in order for the subsequent reprisal to be actionable. The court held in *Meritor Savings Bank, FSB v. Vinson*[30] that it is sufficient if gender is a "but-for" cause of the advance. This of course would be the case in the most commonly charged sexual harassment scenario, an advance by a heterosexual directed toward a person of the opposite gender.

Nevertheless, the requirement that the discrimination be based on and directed against a particular gender, and not merely against sexual behavior attributable to persons of either gender, has some continuing significance in the law governing harassment.[31] It undercuts claims based on anti-homosexual harassment unless the discrimination is limited to homosexuals of one gender, e.g., lesbians, or there is evidence that homosexuality by an employee of a different gender would be tolerated.[32] It apparently also exempts from Title VII scrutiny sexual advances or reprisals made by a bisexual supervisor, who by hypothesis would not usually be selecting a target because of the target's particular gender.[33] Yet claims have been upheld based on nonsexually oriented "equal opportunity harassment" of both men and women where the evidence supports the conclusion that the harasser would not have sought to

---

30. 477 U.S. 57, 106 S.Ct. 2399, 91 L.Ed.2d 49 (1986).

31. *See, e.g., Pasqua v. Metropolitan Life Ins. Co.,* 101 F.3d 514 (7th Cir.1996) (sexual harassment claim of males sales manager demoted because of rumors surrounding his sexual relationship with female subordinate fails for want of evidence that rumors were spread because of his gender).

32. *See, e.g., Higgins v. New Balance Athletic Shoe, Inc.,* 194 F.3d 252 (1st Cir. 1999); *Garcia v. Elf Atochem N. America,* 28 F.3d 446 (5th Cir.1994); *DeSantis v. Pacific Telephone & Telegraph Co.,* 608 F.2d 327 (9th Cir.1979); *Hopkins v. Baltimore Gas & Elec. Co.,* 871 F.Supp. 822 (D.Md.1994), *aff'd,* 77 F.3d 745 (4th Cir.), *cert. denied,* 519 U.S. 818, 117 S.Ct. 70, 136 L.Ed.2d 30 (1996); *but see Barnes v. Costle,* 561 F.2d 983 (D.C.Cir.1977). *Cf. James v. Ranch Mart Hardware, Inc.,* 1994 WL 731517 (D.Kan.1994) (a male-to-female transsexual could state a claim under state law analogous to Title VII by alleging that a

female-to-male transsexual would not have faced similar discrimination). *But cf. Schmedding v. Tnemec Co., Inc.,* 187 F.3d 862 (8th Cir.1999) (male employee allegedly taunted by male and female co-workers to debase his masculinity stated claim despite other allegations that they were motivated by his perceived gay sexual orientation).

33. *See Holman v. State of Indiana,* 211 F.3d 399 (7th Cir.2000), *cert. denied,* —— U.S. ——, 121 S.Ct. 191, 148 L.Ed.2d 132 (2000) (where supervisor solicited sex from both a male and female, no gender discrimination claim will lie; Title VII does not cover the "equal opportunity" or "bisexual" harasser); *Vinson v. Taylor,* 760 F.2d 1330, 1333 n. 7 (D.C.Cir.1985), *affirmed sub nom. Meritor Sav. Bank v. Vinson,* 477 U.S. 57, 106 S.Ct. 2399, 91 L.Ed.2d 49 (1986); *Rabidue v. Osceola Refining Co.,* 805 F.2d 611, 620 (6th Cir.1986), *cert. denied,* 481 U.S. 1041, 107 S.Ct. 1983, 95 L.Ed.2d 823 (1987) (dictum); *Henson v. City of Dundee,* 682 F.2d 897, 902 (11th Cir.1982) (dictum); *Bundy v. Jackson,* 641 F.2d 934, 942 n. 7 (D.C.Cir.1981).

demean either victim except for their respective genders.[34] By the same token, where a male supervisor's nonsexual but gender-based harassing conduct is in fact directed only against women, it is no defense to conjecture that men might find the supervisor's conduct equally offensive.[35]

"Same-sex harassment" is actionable when a male harasses another male (or a female harasses another female) not because of the harassee's sexual orientation but because of the harassee's gender. As the EEOC's Compliance Manual asserts, "the crucial inquiry is whether the harasser treats . . . members . . . of one sex differently from members of the other sex."[36] A unanimous Supreme Court recently endorsed this reasoning in *Oncale v. Sundowner Offshore Services, Inc.*[37] The victim's gender must be a "but-for" factor in the harassment.[38] Thus, workplace harassment does not automatically constitute sex discrimination "merely because the words used have sexual content or connotations."[39] This evidentiary minimum is exactly, and only, what the Supreme Court in *Meritor* required in the classic case of opposite gender heterosexual harassment. Thus, conduct motivated by the harasser's homosexual interest in the harassee (rather than by the plaintiff-harassee's own sexual orientation) falls on the actionable side of the line because such conduct would not occur unless the victim were of a particular gender. By contrast, same-sex harassment inspired by the particular victim's prudishness, shyness or apparent relative vulnerability to sexually tinged teasing or taunting would generally not be actionable if the particular harasser would for the same reasons harass members of the other gender, too.

34. *Steiner v. Showboat Operating Co.,* 25 F.3d 1459 (9th Cir.1994), *cert. denied,* 513 U.S. 1082, 115 S.Ct. 733, 130 L.Ed.2d 636 (1995); *Chiapuzio v. BLT Operating Corp.,* 826 F.Supp. 1334 (D.Wyo.1993).

35. *Hutchison v. Amateur Electronic Supply, Inc.,* 42 F.3d 1037 (7th Cir.1994). *See also Williams v. General Motors Corp.,* 187 F.3d 553 (6th Cir.1999) (female employee subjected to nonsexual but gender-based epithets and conduct can maintain hostile environment sex discrimination claim).

36. EEOC Compliance Manual, § 615.2(b)(3). *See also Llampallas v. Mini-Circuits, Inc.,* 163 F.3d 1236 (11th Cir. 1998), *cert. denied,* 528 U.S. 930, 120 S.Ct. 327, 145 L.Ed.2d 255 (1999) (claim prosecuted as a same-sex sexual harassment case fails where evidence showed that actual ground for termination was employer's desire to retain managerial rather than subordinate employee).

37. 523 U.S. 75, 118 S.Ct. 998, 140 L.Ed.2d 201 (1998). Prior to *Oncale,* several circuits held likewise. *See, e.g., Fredette v. BVP Mgmt. Assocs.,* 112 F.3d 1503 (11th Cir.1997), *cert. denied,* 523 U.S. 1003, 118 S.Ct. 1184, 140 L.Ed.2d 315 (1998); *Yeary v. Goodwill Indus.–Knoxville, Inc.,* 107 F.3d

443 (6th Cir.1997); *Wrightson v. Pizza Hut of America,* 99 F.3d 138 (4th Cir.1996) (same-sex claim lies where male perpetrator is homosexual and advance is therefore at least in part because of victim's male gender); *Baskerville v. Culligan Int'l Co.,* 50 F.3d 428 (7th Cir.1995); *Steiner v. Showboat Operating Co.,* 25 F.3d 1459 (9th Cir. 1994), *cert. denied,* 513 U.S. 1082, 115 S.Ct. 733, 130 L.Ed.2d 636 (1995).

38. *See Johnson v. Hondo, Inc.,* 125 F.3d 408 (7th Cir.1997) (coworkers' isolated taunts of and references to plaintiff as homosexual insufficient to create genuine issue of fact that harassment was gender based).

39. *Oncale,* 118 S.Ct. at 1002. *See also Butler v. Ysleta Ind. Sch. Dist.,* 161 F.3d 263, 270 (5th Cir.1998) (sexual context of challenged conduct not sufficient to make it actionable unless directed at plaintiff because of plaintiff's gender); *Holman v. State of Indiana,* 211 F.3d 399 (7th Cir.2000), *cert. denied,* ___ U.S. ___, 121 S.Ct. 191, 148 L.Ed.2d 132 (2000) (where supervisor solicited sex from both a male and female, no gender discrimination claim will lie; Title VII does not cover the "equal opportunity" or "bisexual" harasser).

The Court in *Oncale* identified several ways that a same-sex harassee can prove that he was targeted "because of" his gender. The most direct way of course is to prove that men and women were treated differently. In single gender workplaces, like the offshore drilling platform in *Oncale*, this type of evidence is impossible to produce. Alternatively, a plaintiff can proffer credible evidence that the harasser is gay or lesbian; courts can reasonably assume that such a harasser would not sexually harass members of the other sex. A third approach, useful in cases factually similar to *Oncale*, is to prove that the harassee was harassed "in such sex-specific and derogatory terms" as to make it clear that the harasser is motivated by a general animus toward persons of plaintiff's gender.[40] Sometimes a combination of two or more approaches is necessary to survive a summary judgment motion. For example, the Seventh Circuit overturned a grant of summary judgment to the defendant in a same-sex hostile work environment claim despite the absence of proof that the harasser treated men and women differently; the plaintiff proffered some reliable evidence that the harasser was gay in combination with some evidence of vulgar and sexually charged derogatory remarks directed at the plaintiff.[41] But reliance on the third approach requires the plaintiff to adduce evidence of the specific nature of the allegedly derogatory comments.[42]

The same "because of sex" requirement will also usually defeat the typical claim of sexual favoritism, in which a plaintiff denied a job or benefit alleges that another employee was hired or promoted because he or she participated in a consensual romantic relationship with a supervisory or managerial agent of the employer.[43] In that situation both women and men are disadvantaged for a reason other than, or in addition to, their gender, viz., they were not the object of the agent's

---

40. *Oncale*, 118 S.Ct. at 1002.

41. *See Shepherd v. Slater Steels Corp.*, 168 F.3d 998 (7th Cir.1999). *See also Bailey v. Runyon*, 167 F.3d 466 (8th Cir.1999) (same-sex co-worker harassment).

42. *See Shermer v. Illinois Dep't of Transp.*, 171 F.3d 475 (7th Cir.1999) (claim fails where no evidence regarding the substance of the alleged comments or the context in which they were made).

43. *See Womack v. Runyon*, 147 F.3d 1298 (11th Cir.1998); *Galdieri–Ambrosini v. National Realty & Dev. Corp.*, 136 F.3d 276 (2d Cir.1998); *Taken v. Oklahoma Corp. Comm'n*, 125 F.3d 1366 (10th Cir.1997); *Becerra v. Dalton*, 94 F.3d 145 (4th Cir. 1996), *cert. denied*, 519 U.S. 1151, 117 S.Ct. 1087, 137 L.Ed.2d 221 (1997); *Mundy v. Palmetto Ford Inc.*, 998 F.2d 1010 (4th Cir. 1993); *DeCintio v. Westchester County Med. Ctr.*, 807 F.2d 304 (2d Cir.), *cert. denied*, 484 U.S. 965, 108 S.Ct. 455, 98 L.Ed.2d 395 (1987); *Ayers v. AT & T*, 826 F.Supp. 443 (S.D.Fla.1993); *EEOC: Policy Guide on Employer Liability For Sexual Favoritism Under Title VII*, 405 FEP Man. (1/12/90). In *Taken*, female plaintiffs alleged sex discrimination when their male boss promoted his girlfriend, while in *DeCintio*, male plaintiffs complained that their male boss promoted his female paramour. Even the difference in gender in *DeCintio* failed to persuade the court that this sexual favoritism constituted gender discrimination. In *Herman v. Western Fin. Corp.*, 254 Kan. 870, 869 P.2d 696 (Kan.1994), the claim that failed was that the plaintiff was subjected to additional work burdens because her supervisor was preoccupied by an affair with one of the plaintiff's co-workers. Such a claim could amount to gender discrimination, the court wrote, only if those additional burdens were experienced by women and not men. *But see King v. Palmer*, 778 F.2d 878 (D.C.Cir. 1985) (inexplicably, though only implicitly, finding preferential treatment of paramour actionable under Title VII).

sexual interest.[44] Thus in these settings the "gender-plus" liability avoidance persists, despite the Supreme Court's repudiation of it in *Phillips* and *Meritor*. If, however, an employee is coerced into sexual participation as a condition of receiving a job benefit, other employees of the same gender could prevail with a variant on the standard sexual harassment theme if they could prove that sexual favors were demanded generally as the "quid pro quo" for advancement.[45]

Ultimately the judicial rationale for relieving employers of liability based on sexual orientation and sexual favoritism discrimination is extratextual. It rests instead on a judicial perception about the underlying or motivating purposes of Title VII: to free applicants and employees from the imposition of adverse (thus excluding sexual favoritism discrimination) working conditions on the basis of the very few characteristics protected by Title VII (thus excluding sexual orientation discrimination).[46]

Courts have also been cautious before deciding that sexual harassment constitutes unlawful gender discrimination because in some cases the alleged harasser's proposition or advance may have been invited or received as welcome. Any sexual harassment plaintiff must therefore show that she or he subjectively perceived a proposition or advance as "unwelcome." (This requirement does not of course apply to a claim of racial harassment.) This requires first a showing that there was in fact a sexual advance. On this question Congress has balanced the scales against the defendant by approving the admission of evidence of past similar conduct by the alleged harasser. An amendment to the Federal Rules of Evidence, applicable to trials commencing on or after December 1, 1994, eases the plaintiff's proof on this issue in those harassment cases that are "predicated on a party's alleged commission of conduct constituting an offense of sexual assault...." In such cases, F.R.E. 415 provides that "evidence of that party's commission of another offense or offenses of sexual assault ... is admissible and may be considered as provided in Rule 413 ... of these rules." In turn, Rule 413, which authorizes the use of such evidence in criminal cases, provides that evidence concerning a defendant's prior sexual assault "may be considered for its bearing on any matter to which it is relevant."[47] Further, Congress has directed that Rule 413 itself "shall not be construed to limit the admission or consideration of evidence under any other rule."[48] The last quoted provision seems strikingly at odds with explicit legisla-

44. Sometimes these claims fail on the separate ground that the plaintiff's terms and conditions of employment were not harmed by a supervisor's romantic relationship with a co-worker. *Candelore v. Clark County Sanitation Dist.*, 975 F.2d 588 (9th Cir.1992). For another case, a related claim that the plaintiff was fired because of her *knowledge* of an apparently voluntary supervisor-subordinate relationship, failed as also not asserting discriminating treatment based on gender. *Ellert v. University of Texas*, 52 F.3d 543 (5th Cir.1995).

45. *See, e.g., Dirksen v. City of Springfield*, 842 F.Supp. 1117 (C.D.Ill.1994); EEOC Policy Guide, 405 FEP Manual.

46. *See DeCintio*, 807 F.2d 304.

47. Rule 413(a).

48. Rule 413(c).

tive history[49] which reflects Congress' understanding that Rule 415 simply creates an exception, in cases involving sex offenses, to Rule 404(b)'s exclusion of evidence of other crimes or acts that are offered to prove character and current action conforming thereto. But textually Rules 415 and 413 taken together override all other rules of evidence that ordinarily might result in the exclusion of such evidence—for example, where the prejudicial effect of the evidence outweighs its probative value, or where the evidence is introduced in the form of hearsay (not eligible for one of the usual hearsay exceptions), or where it is admissible only in the form of reputation or opinion testimony.[50]

If there was an advance, its welcomeness vel non is determined by a subjective test. Until recently, sufficient evidence of the plaintiff's off-hours conduct and attitudes has sufficed to refute her assertion that workplace harassment was unwelcome. An employer may attempt to overcome a showing that an actionable level of interference was unwelcome with evidence about the plaintiff's past sexual conduct, "fantasies," or failure to object to sexual advances.[51] But recent decisions caution against equating participation in off-duty sex-related activities with acquiescence to sexual advances on the job. For example, evidence that the plaintiff had posed nude for a magazine did not negate her evidence that she did not welcome the employer's sexual advances in the workplace.[52] Indeed even a plaintiff's "vulgar and unladylike" language and behavior on the job did not negate her showing that she did not welcome the crude sexual epithets, sexually insulting messages, and offensive demonstrative conduct (including urination and self-exposure) directed at her by her male co-workers. On this issue it was important to

49. See, e.g., 140 Cong.Rec. § 12990 (Sept. 20, 1994) (Sen. Dole); 140 Cong.Rec. H8968–01, 8991 (August 21, 1994) (Rep. Molinari).

50. Duane, *The New Federal Rules of Evidence On Prior Acts Of Accused Sex Offenders: A Poorly Drafted Version Of A Very Bad Idea,* 157 F.R.D. 95, 115–118 (1994). That conclusion is reinforced by the contrasting textual approach of new Rule 412, discussed immediately following, which specifies that evidence of the alleged *victim's* sexual behavior *is* admissible, but only "if otherwise admissible under these rules." The absence of any comparable caveat to § 415—for example, "except if such evidence is otherwise inadmissible under these rules"—could be read to suggest that Congress intended Rule 415 as an absolute, overriding rule of admissibility that trumps otherwise applicable rules of exclusion. *Id.* at 118–119. On February 9, 1995, the Judicial Conference of the United States issued a report sharply critical of the new provisions and calling for Congress to reconsider them. *But see Frank v. County of Hudson,* 924 F.Supp. 620 (D.N.J.1996) (despite FRE 413 and 415, evidence of alleged harasser's abuse of stepdaughter several years before the events in question held inadmissible in employment discrimination action alleging his harassment of adult subordinates because probative value found outweighed by potential for prejudice).

51. *Meritor,* 477 U.S. 57, 106 S.Ct. 2399, 91 L.Ed.2d 49.

52. *Burns v. McGregor Electronic Indus.,* 989 F.2d 959 (8th Cir.1993); *Swentek v. USAIR, Inc.,* 830 F.2d 552 (4th Cir.1987) (use of foul language or sexual innuendo in consensual setting does not waive plaintiff's protections against unwelcome on-the-job harassment); *cf. Williams v. District Court,* 866 P.2d 908 (Colo.1993) (information about plaintiff's sexual history discoverable because it may lead to admissible evidence about his reputation relevant to his claim for damages, even if sexual history information not admissible on the issue whether employer failed promptly to investigate sexual harassment allegations against him).

the court that the plaintiff plainly resented their conduct and complained of it repeatedly to her supervisor.[53]

Federal Rule of Evidence 412(b)(2), applicable to trials commencing after December 1, 1994, may rule out all but the most probative evidence of the *plaintiff's* prior sexual behavior. Rule 412 provides that in a civil action, "evidence offered to prove the sexual behavior or sexual predisposition of any alleged victim is admissible if ... its probative value *substantially* outweighs the danger of harm to any victim and of unfair prejudice to any party."[54] The FRE 412 amendment tilts the scales against admissibility in three respects, as compared to standard probative value-prejudicial impact balancing under FRE 403. First, it reverses the presumptive weighting, by requiring the proponent to justify admissibility rather than requiring the opponent to justify exclusion. Second, the prerequisites for admissibility are more stringent, because the value of the proffered evidence must "substantially" outweigh the specified dangers. Third, harm to the victim must be explicitly placed on the exclusion side of the balance, in addition to party prejudice.

This alteration of the rules' usual neutrality in weighing probative value against prejudice strongly suggests that evidence of consensual sexual conduct in a plaintiff's prior or even contemporaneous private life will seldom if ever be admissible.[55] The amendment casts doubt on the likelihood that a court would admit evidence of plaintiff's response to or initiation of sexual jokes, sexually tinged language, or erotic pictorial displays in the workplace, which may be regarded as tangential to her receptivity to an unconsented touching or sexual proposition. Indeed it may lead to the exclusion of evidence of plaintiff's consensual sexual relationships with co-employees, including even the alleged harasser.[56]

Of course the potential inadmissibility of any such evidence would not necessarily prevent the employer from pursuing these topics in discovery.[57] But the amendment to the evidence rules should strengthen a plaintiff's motion for a protective order[58] designed to eliminate or limit

---

53. *Carr v. Allison Gas Turbine Div.*, 32 F.3d 1007 (7th Cir.1994).

54. F.R.E. 412 (b)(2) (emphasis added). The section also provides that evidence of the alleged victim's "reputation is admissible only if it has been placed in controversy by the alleged victim." That, however, would seem to be met whenever a plaintiff alleges sexual harassment, since unwelcomeness is an essential element of that claim.

55. For example, in *Wolak v. Spucci*, 217 F.3d 157, 160 (2d Cir.2000), the court stated that "[w]hether a sexual advance was welcome, or whether an alleged victim in fact perceived an environment to be sexually offensive, does not turn on the private sexual behavior of the alleged victim, because a woman's expectations about her work environment cannot be said to change

depending upon her sexual sophistication." Although the appellate court found error where the district court admitted such evidence, the court held it was harmless error, despite the jury's failure to award damages after finding a hostile environment.

56. *See Excel Corp. v. Bosley*, 165 F.3d 635 (8th Cir.1999) (evidence of plaintiff's non-workplace sexual relations with her ex-husband inadmissible in her action alleging he harassed her at work).

57. Federal Rule of Civil Procedure 26(b)(1) provides that information sought in discovery "need not be admissible at the trial if the information sought appears reasonably calculated to lead to the discovery of admissible evidence."

58. Federal courts may issue such orders "to protect a party or person from annoyance, embarrassment, oppression, or

inquiry into her past or contemporaneous sexual habits or history where the court is persuaded that the evidence is unlikely to be admitted at trial and is being sought principally to embarrass or intimidate.

1. Quid Pro Quo (Tangible Benefit) Harassment: Conduct Constituting

It is clearest that Title VII is violated when submission to an employer's sexual demands is expressly made the "quid pro quo" of gaining a job, promotion, continued employment, pay increase, work assignment or other economic job benefit, or of avoiding demotion, diminished compensation, a disadvantageous transfer, or formal discipline or discharge.[59] The Court in *Burlington Industries v. Ellerth* stated that a tangible employment action "constitutes a significant change in employment status, such as hiring, firing, failing to promote, reassignment with significantly different responsibilities, or a decision causing a significant change in benefits."[60] EEOC's Guidelines assert that quid pro quo harassment also occurs when submission to unwelcome sexual advances or conduct is "implicitly" made a term of condition of the target's employment and made the basis for an employment decision.[61] Relying on the Guidelines, a circuit opinion has held that "quid pro quo sexual harassment occurs whenever an individual explicitly or implicitly conditions a job, a job benefit, or the absence of a job detriment, upon an employee's acceptance of sexual conduct."[62]

The Ninth Circuit has adopted a per se rule that "a supervisor's intertwining of a request for the performance of sexual favors with a discussion of actual or potential job benefits or detriments in a single conversation constitutes quid pro quo harassment."[63] On this theory, quid pro quo discrimination may occur even though, by submitting to the superior's sexual demands, the employee suffers no tangible economic loss.[64] More recently, however, where a harassing superior officer of

undue burden or expense." Federal Rule of Civil Procedure 26(c).

59. *See Meritor; Burlington Indus. v. Ellerth,* 524 U.S. 742, 118 S.Ct. 2257, 141 L.Ed.2d 633 (1998); *Faragher v. City of Boca Raton,* 524 U.S. 775, 118 S.Ct. 2275, 141 L.Ed.2d 662 (1998).

60. *Burlington Indus.,* 118 S.Ct. at 2268.

61. 29 C.F.R. §§ 106.11(a)(1) to (2) (1993).

62. *Nichols v. Frank,* 42 F.3d 503 (9th Cir.1994). *See also Robinson v. City of Pittsburgh,* 120 F.3d 1286, 1296 (3d Cir.1997). *Compare Durham Life Ins. Co. v. Evans,* 166 F.3d 139 (3d Cir.1999) (displacing insurance agent from her office, dismissing her secretary, denying her access to her client files, and changing job assignments that resulted in a fifty percent pay decrease sufficient to constitute a tangible job loss) *and Crady v. Liberty Nat. Bank & Trust Co.*

of Ind., 993 F.2d 132, 136 (7th Cir.1993) ("A materially adverse change might be indicated by a termination of employment, a demotion evidenced by a decrease in wage or salary, a less distinguished title, a material loss of benefits, significantly diminished material responsibilities, or other indices that might be unique to a particular situation"), *with Flaherty v. Gas Research Institute,* 31 F.3d 451, 456 (7th Cir.1994) (a "bruised ego" is not enough); *Kocsis v. Multi-Care Mgmt., Inc.,* 97 F.3d 876, 887 (6th Cir.1996) (demotion without change in pay, benefits, duties, or prestige insufficient) and *Harlston v. McDonnell Douglas Corp.,* 37 F.3d 379, 382 (8th Cir.1994) (reassignment to more inconvenient job insufficient).

63. *Nichols v. Frank,* 42 F.3d 503, 513 (9th Cir.1994).

64. *Karibian v. Columbia Univ.,* 14 F.3d 773 (2d Cir.), *cert. denied,* 512 U.S. 1213, 114 S.Ct. 2693, 129 L.Ed.2d 824 (1994).

the employer did not carry out threats to adversely alter the plaintiff's tangible terms of employment despite her refusal to submit, the Supreme Court treated the discrimination as an instance of a hostile work environment, limiting the "quid pro quo" classification to situations in which the threat is consummated.[65] This suggests that the Court might analyze "submission" scenarios as non-quid pro quo, unless perhaps the employer agent does adversely alter the target's terms of employment despite her submission.

In sum, the "quid pro quo" or "tangible terms" sexual harassment plaintiff must prove that (1) he or she encountered verbal, visual or physical propositions or advances of a sexual nature; (2) the harassment was based on her or his gender, and not, for example, sexual orientation; (3) she or he experienced the propositions or advances as subjectively unwelcome; and (4) the harassment was perpetrated by a supervisor, manager or other high-ranking agent of the employer[66] who had the authority to and did in fact give the plaintiff a tangible employment benefit for submitting, or imposed a tangible detriment for resisting, the proposition or advance.

Since *Burlington*, an appellate decision has held that merely assigning extra work to the plaintiff was not sufficiently "tangible" to impute automatic, vicarious liability to an employer.[67] But another has held that forcing the plaintiff to give up her office and her secretary was a tangible adverse action.[68] Where harassment is recognized as tangible, the available remedies would include back pay representing the economic loss of a lost job or promotion; injunctive relief directing the award of any lost position; emotional distress and, for a willful or reckless violation, punitive damages, with the sum of both types of damages capped at

EEOC takes same position. *EEOC Guidance on Vicarious Employer Liability for Unlawful Harassment by Supervisors*, No. 915.002, Pt. IV (6/18/99) (citing *Nichols*, 42 F.3d 503). *But see Reinhold v. Commonwealth of Virginia*, 151 F.3d 172 (4th Cir. 1998) (assigning extra work to employee did not constitute tangible employment action sufficient to give rise to an automatic imputation of liability against an employer for a supervisor's sexual harassment because the extra work was not akin to a demotion or reassignment entailing significantly different job responsibilities).

65. *Burlington Indus. v. Ellerth*, 524 U.S. 742, 118 S.Ct. 2257, 141 L.Ed.2d 633 (1998).

66. To be a supervisor for purposes of imputing liability to an employer, a harasser must possess at least some of the standard indicia of supervisory authority, e.g., the power to hire, fire, demote, promote, transfer, or discipline, or effectively recommend those actions. *See Pacheco v. New Life Bakery, Inc.*, 187 F.3d 1063 (9th Cir.

1999); *Parkins v. Civil Constructors of Ill., Inc.*, 163 F.3d 1027 (7th Cir.1998). *But see Caridad v. Metro–North Commuter R.R.*, 191 F.3d 283 (2d Cir.1999), *cert. denied sub nom.* Metro–North Commuter Railroad Co. v. Norris, ___ U.S. ___, 120 S.Ct. 1959, 146 L.Ed.2d 791 (2000) (if constructive discharge is caused by co-workers, no tangible employment action, so employer retains *Burlington* affirmative defense).

67. *Reinhold v. Commonwealth of Virginia*, 151 F.3d 172 (4th Cir.1998). *See also Jones v. Clinton*, 869 F.Supp. 690 (E.D.Ark. 1994), *aff'd in part and rev'd in part on other grounds*, 72 F.3d 1354 (8th Cir.1996) (plaintiff failed to prove that defendant's statements "constitute a clear threat that clearly conditions concrete job benefits or detriments on compliance with sexual demands.")

68. *See Durham Life Ins. Co. v. Evans*, 166 F.3d 139 (3d Cir.1999) (finding automatic liability for supervisor's gender-based, but non-sexual, interference with plaintiff's earning potential).

$50,000 to $300,000 depending on the number of persons employed by the defendant; and attorney's fees and costs.

2.   *Quid Pro Quo (Tangible Benefit) Harassment: Employer Liability For*

Because only supervisors or managers can alter such tangible terms of employment, and they are clothed by the employer with at least apparent authority to do so, a finding of quid pro quo harassment results, as with most other violations of Title VII, in automatic or "strict" liability of the employer.[69] Dictum in companion cases decided by the Supreme Court in June 1998 confirms that the employer is not only vicariously but strictly or "automatically" liable without more for quid pro quo harassment by a supervisor or other employer agent who has the means to and does in fact alter the plaintiff's tangible terms and conditions of employment.[70] Strict liability means that if the plaintiff demonstrates that her obtaining a tangible job benefit or avoiding a tangible job detriment turned on her compliance or noncompliance with an unwelcome sexual advance, and the employer agent carried out such a promise or threat, the employer, even if it was unaware of the harassment, will have no affirmative defense.[71] In a "tangible terms" case, the Court reasons, "there is assurance the injury could not have been inflicted absent the agency relation" between the supervisor and a defendant employer.[72]

3.   *Hostile Work Environment Harassment: Conduct Constituting*

Suppose the victim is subjected to worsened working conditions or other "environmental" harassment that affects only intangible aspects of the job? Until Title VII was amended by the Civil Rights Act of 1991, a plaintiff who could prove only an abusive or hostile work environment, without tangible detriment to her employment status, could recover no monetary relief. There was thus little incentive to sue under Title VII for environmental sexual harassment, unaccompanied by termination, demotion, or other adverse action resulting in a reduction or loss of pay or benefits. But Section 102 of the Civil Rights Act of 1991 authorized compensatory and, if appropriate, punitive damages, for all intentional forms of unlawful discrimination, including harassment. (Punitives are not available against government employers). These damages are capped in amounts that vary with the number of employees employed by the defendant.

In *Meritor* and *Oncale* the Supreme Court reaffirmed its traditional broad interpretation of covered "terms and conditions of employment,"

---

69. *Nichols,* 42 F.3d 503 (citing cases); *Pierce v. Commonwealth Life Ins. Co.,* 40 F.3d 796, 803 (6th Cir.1994); 29 CFR § 1604.11(c); *EEOC Policy Guidance on Current Issues of Sexual Harassment,* 8 FEP (BNA) 405:6681, 6694 (1990).

70. *Burlington Indus. v. Ellerth,* 524 U.S. 742, 118 S.Ct. 2257, 141 L.Ed.2d 633

(1998); *Faragher v. City of Boca Raton,* 524 U.S. 775, 118 S.Ct. 2275, 141 L.Ed.2d 662 (1998).

71. *Id.*

72. *Id.*

holding that harassment is actionable, even if it does not affect a tangible term of employment, provided it is sufficiently severe or pervasive to create a hostile or abusive working environment. The "hostile environment" label defines all actionable sexual harassment claims other than "quid pro quo." Thus it includes situations in which the harasser is (a) a co-worker, customer or subordinate without authority to reward or punish with tangible job benefits or detriments; (b) a supervisor whose conduct consists of unwanted verbal or physical sexually oriented advances (or of speech or conduct demeaning to the abilities or status of women), unaccompanied by a tangible job detriment, as in *Faragher*; or (c) a supervisor who threatens but does not fulfill a threat respecting the target's tangible terms of employment, as in *Burlington*. The Court explains that labeling a harasser's conduct as "hostile environment" rather than "quid pro quo" means that the plaintiff will have to show more aggravated or persistent conduct to prove sex discrimination violating Title VII, but does not by itself control whether the employer is liable for that conduct.

The "hostile environment" sexual harassment plaintiff must prove that (1) she or he encountered verbal, visual or physical propositions, advances, insults or invasions of person; (2) those propositions or insults were based on her or his gender, as distinct from, for example, her or his sexual orientation; (3) he or she experienced the alleged harasser's conduct as *subjectively* unwelcome; (4) the harassment was of sufficient nature and magnitude (e.g., on one hand, a one-time flagrant physical assault or intimate touching, or, on the other, ongoing, relatively frequent or continual physical or verbal propositions, advances, or insults) to have created an *objectively* intimidating, hostile, offensive, or abusive work environment of a kind that would have unreasonably interfered with the work performance, working conditions, or general well being of a reasonable person in her position; and (5) the harassment was perpetrated either by a supervisor, manager or high-ranking agent of the employer, or by a co-worker, subordinate, customer or other business invitee in circumstances that fasten liability on the employer under general principles of agency law.[73]

The plaintiff's most formidable obstacle here is usually establishing the objectively hostile or abusive work environment, element (4).[74] Whether conduct reaches a level of unreasonable interference with the employee's ability to work, or creates a sufficiently intimidating work environment, "should be evaluated from the objective standpoint of a

---

73. *See Meritor,* 477 U.S. 57, 106 S.Ct. 2399, 91 L.Ed.2d 49, *Burlington,* 524 U.S. 742, 118 S.Ct. 2257, 141 L.Ed.2d 633; *Faragher,* 524 U.S. 775, 118 S.Ct. 2275, 141 L.Ed.2d 662.

74. This was a stumbling block for Paula Jones's claim against President Clinton. The district court held that while Clinton's conduct was "certainly boorish and offensive," it was not sufficiently pervasive or severe to create a sexually hostile work environment. *Jones v. Clinton,* 869 F.Supp. 690 (E.D.Ark.1994), *aff'd in part and rev'd in part on other grounds,* 72 F.3d 1354 (8th Cir.1996). *See also Shepherd v. Comptroller of Pub. Accounts of State of Texas,* 168 F.3d 871 (5th Cir.), *cert. denied,* 528 U.S. 963, 120 S.Ct. 395, 145 L.Ed.2d 308 (1999) ("boorish and offensive comments" by a co-worker did not rise to actionable sexual harassment).

'reasonable person.' "[75]Thus a "normal" level of workplace obscenity, isolated sexual suggestiveness or propositions, and even some single instances of unwelcome touching, may not amount to unreasonable interference.[76] The circuit courts are still sorting out whether the "person" from whose standpoint reasonableness should be assessed is the genderless prototype of torts litigation (the "reasonable man") or a reasonable victim–usually, in this context, a woman.[77] The EEOC blurs

75. *EEOC Policy Guidance on Current Issues of Sexual Harassment*, 8 FEP 405:6681. But the employer cannot insulate itself from sexual harassment liability simply because the work environment is rough or male-dominated. *See Conner v. Schrader–Bridgeport Int'l, Inc.*, 227 F.3d 179 (4th Cir.2000).

76. *Compare Hostetler v. Quality Dining, Inc.*, 218 F.3d 798 (7th Cir.2000) (in a one week period, one vulgar remark and two incidents of forcible, unwelcome touching sufficed to create actionable work environment); *Leopold v. Baccarat, Inc.*, 174 F.3d 261 (2d Cir.1999) (threats to replace staff with young and sexy new hires were sufficient to demonstrate sexually hostile environment); *Davis v. United States Postal Serv.*, 142 F.3d 1334 (10th Cir.1998) (being subjected to regular unwelcome hugging and kissing suffices to show a subjectively hostile work environment); *Smith v. Norwest Fin. Acceptance Inc.*, 129 F.3d 1408 (10th Cir.1997) (plaintiff's testimony that harasser's comments were intolerable, publicly made, and caused humiliation and a loss of self-respect were sufficient to establish objectively hostile environment); *Spain v. Gallegos*, 26 F.3d 439 (3d Cir.1994) (employee may demonstrate that there is sexually hostile work environment without proving blatant sexual misconduct) *with Mendoza v. Borden, Inc.*, 195 F.3d 1238 (11th Cir.1999) (en banc), *cert. denied,* ___ U.S. ___, 120 S.Ct. 1674, 146 L.Ed.2d 483 (2000) (at least five episodes of inappropriate behavior, including comments, touching and other offensive behavior over an eleven month period was insufficient to state a claim for sexual harassment); *Burnett v. Tyco Corp.*, 203 F.3d 980 (6th Cir.2000), *petition for cert. filed*, June 14, 2000 (three alleged incidents over a six month period, including two vulgar comments and one incident of unwelcome touching did not constitute actionable work environment); *Minor v. Ivy Tech State College*, 174 F.3d 855 (7th Cir.1999) (plaintiff's "nebulous impressions concerning tone of voice, body language, and other nonverbal, nontouching modes of signaling" are not actionable); *Shepherd v. Comptroller of Pub. Accounts*, 168 F.3d 871 (5th Cir.), *cert. denied*, 528 U.S. 963, 120 S.Ct. 395, 145 L.Ed.2d 308

(1999) (male co-worker's sexual harassment of female employee, which included incidents of unwanted touching on employee's arm, attempting to look down employee's clothing and making offensive remarks, did not render employee's work environment objectively hostile or abusive); *Penry v. Federal Home Loan Bank of Topeka*, 155 F.3d 1257 (10th Cir.1998), *cert. denied*, 526 U.S. 1039, 119 S.Ct. 1334, 143 L.Ed.2d 498 (1999) (one gender based comment and three instances of unwanted physical touching over a three year period was insufficient to show severe and pervasive sexual harassment, particularly when plaintiffs cannot show any adverse employment action); *Ngeunjuntr v. Metropolitan Life Ins. Co.*, 146 F.3d 464 (7th Cir.1998) (sporadic but offensive comments insufficient to establish hostile working environment claim); *McKenzie v. Illinois Dep't of Transp.*, 92 F.3d 473 (7th Cir.1996) (reasonable person could not perceive any unreasonable interference with work environment as a result of three sexually suggestive comments over three-month period); *Gross v. Burggraf Constr. Co.*, 53 F.3d 1531, 1542 (10th Cir. 1995) (isolated incident of gender-based conduct in which harasser stated "sometimes don't you just want to smash a woman in the face" did not establish hostile work environment); *DeAngelis v. El Paso Mun. Police Officers Ass'n*, 51 F.3d 591 (5th Cir.), *cert. denied*, 516 U.S. 974, 116 S.Ct. 479, 133 L.Ed.2d 403 (1995) (derogatory references to plaintiff in police association newsletter too sporadic and infrequent and insufficiently offensive to alter working condition objectively); *Baskerville v. Culligan Intern. Co.*, 50 F.3d 428 (7th Cir.1995) (nine derogatory comments over seven months did not constitute sexual harassment because supervisor never touched employee or invited employee to have sex with him or to go out on date with him).

77. *Contrast Richardson v. New York State Dep't of Correctional Serv.*, 180 F.3d 426, 436 n. 3 (2d Cir.1999) (reasonable person rather than "reasonable African-American" standard in racial harassment case) and *Rabidue v. Osceola Refining Co.*, 805 F.2d 611 (6th Cir.1986), *cert. denied*, 481

this division in its Policy Guidance, advocating a "reasonable person" standard but adding that in applying that standard the factfinder "should consider the victim's perspective and not stereotyped notions of acceptable behavior."

The Supreme Court has upheld a "hostile environment" claim when workplace intimidation, ridicule and insult are "sufficiently severe or pervasive to alter the conditions of the victim's environment *and* create an abusive working environment."[78] The plaintiff suffered a series of gender-related insults and unwanted sexual innuendos. Because in totality this conduct may have been sufficient to create an abusive work environment from the standpoint of a hypothetical reasonable person, the Court held that the plaintiff was not required to show that it seriously affected her psychological well-being. The Court located the required level of injury somewhere "between making actionable any conduct that is merely offensive and requiring the conduct to cause a tangible psychological injury." Psychological harm is just another, nonessential factor relevant to the issue of abusiveness. A plaintiff can meet the *Harris* threshold without showing that the harassment affected her psychologically, diminished her work performance, or caused her to quit or even want to quit her job.

Justice O'Connor's opinion for the *Harris* majority emphasizes that when the defendant's conduct consists entirely of epithets or sexual innuendo, those must be sufficiently severe or pervasive "to create an objectively hostile or abusive work environment," one that a "reasonable person would find hostile or abusive." (In addition, the victim must "subjectively perceive the environment to be abusive.") The opinion does little more than identify a number of unweighted, nonexhaustive factors relevant to the objective question of an "abusive" or "hostile" work environment: the nature of the discriminatory conduct, i.e., whether it is merely offensive or also physically threatening or humiliating; the conduct's frequency and severity; and whether it unreasonably interfered with the plaintiff's work performance. None of these is identified as indispensable or even preeminent, and this leads the EEOC to conclude that none is.[79]

Justice Ginsburg, concurring, opined that the inquiry should "center, dominantly, on whether the discriminatory conduct has interfered with the plaintiff's work performance." For her this would mean that the plaintiff need show only that the defendant's conduct made it more difficult for her to do her job, and not that the plaintiff's productivity actually declined. At least two court of appeals decisions appear to hold

---

U.S. 1041, 107 S.Ct. 1983, 95 L.Ed.2d 823 (1987) (reasonable person) *with Steiner v. Showboat Operating Co.,* 25 F.3d 1459, 1465 (9th Cir.1994), *cert. denied,* 513 U.S. 1082, 115 S.Ct. 733, 130 L.Ed.2d 636 (1995); *Burns v. McGregor Electronic Indus.,* 989 F.2d 959 (C.A.8 1993); *Ellison v. Brady,* 924 F.2d 872 (9th Cir.1991); *Andrews v. City of Philadelphia,* 895 F.2d 1469 (3d Cir.1990); and *Yates v. Avco Corp.,* 819 F.2d 630 (6th Cir.1987) (reasonable woman).

78. *Harris v. Forklift Sys., Inc.,* 510 U.S. 17, 114 S.Ct. 367, 126 L.Ed.2d 295 (1993).

79. *See* Enforcement Guidance on *Harris v. Forklift Sys., Inc.,* March 8, 1994.

just that: a supervisor's sexual innuendo and banter was actionable because it was unwelcome and made it more difficult for plaintiff to do her job, even though it was not of sufficient severity to prevent her from timely meeting her work obligations.[80] But the *Harris* majority did not hold that a showing that the plaintiff's job has been made more difficult suffices. On the other hand, interference with the plaintiff's work performance is not essential to the required demonstration of hostility or abusiveness. It is enough if the offensive conduct is shown, through the totality of the circumstances, to create, cumulatively or in the aggregate, an abusive work environment, or even just that it adversely affected plaintiff's daily working conditions.[81]

Because no bright line separates merely vulgar banter (usually lawful) from a consistently hostile or severely abusive environment (usually unlawful), some circuits confide the pervasiveness and severity questions to a jury, so long as the district judge is satisfied that the harasser's comments or conducts were "because of sex."[82] Others, however, consider actionable harassment a question of law and accordingly reserve decision on the sufficiency of severity and pervasiveness for the district courts or for themselves.[83]

---

80. *See Smith v. Norwest Fin. Acceptance, Inc.*, 129 F.3d 1408, 1418–19 (10th Cir.1997) (if derogatory remarks were humiliating, intolerable, publicly made and caused a loss of self respect, plaintiff does not also have to show that the comments caused her work productivity or performance to decrease); *King v. Hillen*, 21 F.3d 1572 (Fed.Cir.1994). *See also Hafford v. Seidner*, 183 F.3d 506 (6th Cir.1999) (considering whether racial harassment adversely affected plaintiff's ability to do job).

81. *See Conner v. Schrader–Bridgeport Int'l, Inc.*, 227 F.3d 179 (4th Cir.2000) (criticizing lower court's failure to consider discreet incidents through the totality of the circumstances and reversing lower court's grant of employer's summary judgment motion); Williams v. General Motors Corp., *187 F.3d 553 (6th Cir.1999);* O'Shea v. Yellow Technology Servs., Inc., *185 F.3d 1093 (10th Cir.1999);* Richardson v. New York State Dep't of Correctional Serv., *180 F.3d 426 (2d Cir.1999) (applying totality of circumstances test, and cautioning against carving the plaintiff's claim into discrete incidents);* Carr v. Allison Gas Turbine Div., *32 F.3d 1007 (7th Cir.1994).* But see Saxton v. AT & T Co., *10 F.3d 526 (7th Cir.1993) (arguably ignoring the totality and instead considering harassing incidents in isolation);* Hopkins v. Baltimore Gas & Elec. Co., *77 F.3d 745 (4th Cir.),* cert. denied, *519 U.S. 818, 117 S.Ct. 70, 136 L.Ed.2d 30 (1996);* Butler v. Ysleta Indep. Sch. Dist., *161 F.3d 263, 269 (5th Cir.1998) (frightening letters sent to homes of teachers by their principal does not amount to harassment;*

workplace is central to the wrong of sexual harassment).

One commentator has argued that courts, especially in the Seventh Circuit, have misapplied the Rule 56 summary judgment standard in hostile environment cases. She contends that these courts have invaded the province of the jury by deciding as a matter of law that the conduct at issue is not sufficiently pervasive or severe for a reasonable jury to find for the plaintiff. She especially faults these courts for dividing up plaintiff's evidence into discrete parts, failing to consider the totality of the circumstances. *See* Theresa M. Beiner, *The Misuse of Summary Judgment in Hostile Environment Cases,* 34 Wake Forest L.Rev. 71 (1999).

82. *See Gallagher v. Delaney,* 139 F.3d 338 (2d Cir.1998); *Hathaway v. Runyon,* 132 F.3d 1214 (8th Cir.1997) (question of hostile work environment is for the jury); *Schwapp v. Town of Avon,* 118 F.3d 106 (2d Cir.1997) (racial harassment); *Torres v. Pisano,* 116 F.3d 625 (2d Cir.), cert. denied, 522 U.S. 997, 118 S.Ct. 563, 139 L.Ed.2d 404 (1997); *Smith v. St. Louis Univ.,* 109 F.3d 1261 (8th Cir.1997); *Baskerville v. Culligan Int'l Co.,* 50 F.3d 428 (7th Cir. 1995).

83. *Konstantopoulos v. Westvaco Corp.,* 112 F.3d 710 (3d Cir.1997), cert. denied, 522 U.S. 1128, 118 S.Ct. 1079, 140 L.Ed.2d 137 (1998); *Black v. Zaring Homes, Inc.,* 104 F.3d 822 (6th Cir.), cert. denied, 522 U.S. 865, 118 S.Ct. 172, 139 L.Ed.2d 114 (1997);

Commentators and courts alike have begun to criticize courts for carving up incidents of harassing conduct and analyzing each incident in isolation, an analysis that can lead to improperly granted (and affirmed) judgments as a matter of law. A vigorous dissenter in an en banc Eleventh Circuit sexual harassment case recently stated that the majority erred in examining each incident of sexual harassment in isolation, rather than looking at the evidence cumulatively, claiming that the opinion marked "a major departure from established" law.[84] One commentator posits that lower courts have disregarded the totality of the circumstances test and instead have transformed the "underlying factors identified by the Supreme Court as relevant to the inquiry" into "an exhaustive list of 'elements' any of whose absence dooms the claim."[85] Yet another commentator suggests a "tendency of the judiciary to 'look down' on harassment cases, discounting plaintiffs, their testimony, and their theory of litigation."[86] Both commentators make the point that fact-intensive issues such as whether a reasonable person would find a particular environment to be harassing are inappropriate for summary judgment,[87] and cite numerous examples of what they view as improvidently granted judgments as a matter of law.[88]

The environmental brand of sexual harassment, then, "is often a cumulative process rather than a onetime event. In its early stages, it may not ... cross the threshold that separates the nonactionable from the actionable, ... or may not cause sufficient distress ..., or may not have gone on long enough to charge the employer with knowledge and a negligent failure to take effective remedial measures."[89] To avoid encouraging premature litigation, therefore, courts will give plaintiffs complaining of slowly unfolding environmental sexual harassment the benefit of the continuing violation theory. That approach permits suit on conduct that occurred before the beginning of the applicable limitations period where that conduct could only have reasonably been recognized subsequently, within that period, as actionable harassment.[90] The theory has

Weller v. Citation Oil & Gas Corp., 84 F.3d 191 (5th Cir.1996), *cert. denied*, 519 U.S. 1055, 117 S.Ct. 682, 136 L.Ed.2d 607 (1997).

84. *See Mendoza v. Borden, Inc.*, 195 F.3d 1238, 1269 (11th Cir.1999) (Tjoflat, J., dissenting in part), *cert. denied*, ___ U.S. ___, 120 S.Ct. 1674, 146 L.Ed.2d 483 (2000). *See also Conner v. Schrader–Bridgeport Int'l Inc.*, 227 F.3d 179 (4th Cir.2000).

85. *See* M. Isable Medina, *A Matter of Fact: Hostile Environments and Summary Judgments*, 8 S.Cal. R.L. & Women's Stud. 311, 314–15 (1999).

86. Theresa M. Beiner, *The Misuse of Summary Judgment in Hostile Environment Cases*, 34 Wake Forest L.Rev. 71, 119 (1999) (positing that courts often grant motions for summary judgment and for judgment as a matter of law improperly because, in part, "the courts have seen a

marked increase in Title VII claims generally, and in harassment claims in particular").

87. Beiner, 34 Wake Forest L.Rev. at 102; Medina, 8 S.Cal. R.L. & Women's Stud. at 316.

88. *See, e.g,.* Beiner, 34 Wake Forest L.Rev. at 103–17; Medina, 8 S.Cal. R.L. & Women's Stud. at 313 n.13.

89. *Galloway v. General Motors Serv. Parts Operations,* 78 F.3d 1164, 1166 (7th Cir.1996).

90. *Id.* Another recent circuit decision endorses treating sexual harassment as a continuing violation where it consists of continual, intermittent, and substance-related episodes rather than unrelated, isolated incidents or flagrant one-time violations. *Rush v. Scott Specialty Gases*, 113 F.3d 476 (3d Cir.1997). *See also Anderson v. Reno,*

been denied, however, to plaintiffs who suffer harassment recognizable as such without the light of subsequent events.[91] Where environmental harassment is severe and obvious, as with intensive physical sexual abuse, assault, or rape, the limitations period begins to run immediately. But where such conduct is so severe as to disable a plaintiff from taking the steps necessary to prosecute a claim, equitable tolling may extend the duration of the period.[92]

4. Hostile Work Environment Harassment: Employer Liability For

The plaintiff will ordinarily receive no remedy for sexually harassing conduct of the "hostile environment type" unless the employer as an entity is liable for that conduct. This is because most of the federal appellate circuits addressing the question have held that supervisors, managers and most high officials of a covered "employer" cannot be held individually liable, even though the statute defines a covered "employer" to include "any agent of" that employer.[93] So the requirements of employer liability for environmental harassment are critical.

While recognizing that a supervisor's sexually harassing conduct is probably a "frolic and detour" outside the scope of his authority, the Supreme Court has nevertheless held that an employer "is subject to vicarious liability to a victimized employee for an actionable hostile environment created by a supervisor with immediate (or successively higher) authority over the employee."[94] As observed above, where the supervisor's harassment culminates in a tangible employment detriment to the victim—where it is "quid pro quo"—employer liability is not only vicarious but strict. But where the supervisor does not impose a tangible employment detriment for nonsubmission to a sexual demand–in, that is, an "intangible" or "hostile environment" case–the employer may avoid liability if by a preponderance of the evidence it carries *both* elements of the following affirmative defense:[95] "(a) that the employer exercised reasonable care to prevent and correct promptly any sexually harassing behavior, and (b) that the plaintiff employee unreasonably failed to take

190 F.3d 930, 930–31 (9th Cir.1999) (finding a long-standing, unabated pattern of unwanted, sexually-oriented teasing, harassment, and ridicule that were neither isolated nor different in kind); *Draper v. Coeur Rochester, Inc.*, 147 F.3d 1104, 1107 (9th Cir.1998); *Van Steenburgh v. Rival Co.*, 171 F.3d 1155 (8th Cir.1999) (even where there are no incidents within the limitations period that are explicitly sexual, continuing violation doctrine available when harasser "stared at" the plaintiff and "kept her in constant fear of retaliation"). Continuing violations are more fully discussed in § 4.3.

91. *Garrison v. Burke*, 165 F.3d 565 (7th Cir.1999) (prior incident included forcible touching and kissing).

92. *Stoll v. Runyon*, 165 F.3d 1238 (9th Cir.1999).

93. See § 2.3.

94. *See Burlington Indus. v. Ellerth*, 524 U.S. 742, 118 S.Ct. 2257, 141 L.Ed.2d 633 (1998); *Faragher v. City of Boca Raton*, 524 U.S. 775, 118 S.Ct. 2275, 141 L.Ed.2d 662 (1998).

95. And it seems certain that the defendant must carry both prongs of the defense by a preponderance. *See Booker v. Budget Rent-A-Car Sys.*, 17 F.Supp.2d 735 (M.D.Tenn.1998).

advantage of any corrective opportunities provided by the employer or to avoid harm otherwise."[96]

This test will likely expand employer liability for unlawful hostile environment harassment by supervisors or other high officials. If the compound prongs of the affirmative defense are applied literally, an employer would avoid liability for otherwise actionable supervisory harassment only when it exercised reasonable care to "prevent" and "correct" unlawful environmental harassment *and* when the plaintiff unreasonably failed to use available employer-provided channels of complaint or other remedies. To show that it took "reasonable care to prevent" under prong (a), and to meet prong (b)—that the plaintiff "unreasonably" failed to utilize corrective opportunities—the employer will typically prove that it had in place a policy that specifically condemned sexual harassment, and maintained an internal complaints procedure that assured victims a means of bypassing the alleged harasser to register a complaint,[97] was widely disseminated among employees, and was adequately enforced (with appropriate training of managers) in a climate that did not discourage complaints.[98] But because alleged victims will usually take advantage of such policies and procedures, the defense would frequently founder on this second prong.[99] Unreasonable failure to invoke the employer's procedures has been widely found where plaintiffs failed to report ongoing harassment because they fear retaliation or were uncertain allegations would be held confidential, especially where employers' anti-harassment policies contain express anti-retaliation provisions.[100] Indeed, employers may be at risk in honoring com-

---

96. *See Burlington* and *Faragher, supra.*

97. *See, e.g., Sharp v. City of Houston,* 164 F.3d 923 (5th Cir.1999) (finding city's policy lacking because it failed to provide complainant with an adequate means of reporting harassment by supervisor because complaints were channeled through existing management).

98. *See, e.g., Brown v. Perry,* 184 F.3d 388 (4th Cir.1999) (anti-harassment policy and procedure adequate because not "dysfunctional" or adopted or administered in bad faith); *Shaw v. AutoZone, Inc.,* 180 F.3d 806 (7th Cir.1999), *cert. denied,* 528 U.S. 1076, 120 S.Ct. 790, 145 L.Ed.2d 666 (2000) (policy distributed and managers trained); *Greene v. Dalton,* 164 F.3d 671 (D.C.Cir. 1999) (because "the rigor with which the Navy enforces its strict anti-harassment policy is unquestioned," the Navy was able to satisfy this aspect of prong (b)). EEOC delineates recommended features of effective harassment policies and complaint procedures in Guidance No. 915.002 (6/18/99). The Supreme Court observed in *Faragher* that maintaining an adequate policy and procedure is not invariably required to meet prong (a)'s "reasonable care to prevent"

element, but then strongly suggests that only small employers with compact workplaces can satisfy that duty without such a policy and procedure. 524 U.S. at 807–08, 118 S.Ct. at 2293. *See also Sharp v. City of Houston,* 164 F.3d 923 (5th Cir.1999) (where female police officer failed to report harassment because procedure lacked an adequate bypass mechanism, court imputed constructive knowledge of harassment because defendant knew of past complaints and failed to adequately supervise the harasser).

99. And a one month delay in reporting sexual harassment does not constitute an unreasonable failure. *See Greene,* 164 F.3d 671. *But see Scrivner v. Socorro Indep. Sch. Dist.,* 169 F.3d 969 (5th Cir.1999) (employer carries second prong where employee failed to complain for several months and lied during an internal investigation); *Corcoran v. Shoney's Colonial, Inc.,* 24 F.Supp.2d 601 (W.D.Va.1998) (where sexual harassment becomes intolerable or impossible to ignore, employee must complain in order to defeat second prong of employer's defense).

100. *See Montero v. AGCO Corp.,* 19 F.Supp.2d 1143 (E.D.Cal.1998), *aff'd,* 192 F.3d 856 (9th Cir.1999); *Fierro v. Saks*

plainants' requests for strict confidentiality, since doing so impedes full investigation which in turn may prevent them from taking the prompt and appropriate corrective action required by *Burlington/Faragher* to satisfy the affirmative defense.[101] It has even been held that an employee cannot maintain a work environment claim if she coupled an internal complaint with a request for confidentiality, at least absent evidence of the kind of egregious harassment that would predictably lead to serious physical or psychological harm if the employer does not act.[102] And the employer will be able to show plaintiff's noncompliance under prong (b) if her complaint, although timely, does not provide notice that the agent's offensive conduct was of sexual or perhaps gender-based nature.[103]

But there may be considerably more flexibility as to when the employee must complain where harassment has been extreme. In the statute of limitations context, equitable tolling may extend the time in which plaintiff may comply with prerequisites to suit where the harassment is so severe as to be disabling.[104] This concept might easily be transplanted to enable a plaintiff to resist the employer's evidence that she unreasonably failed timely to invoke an available internal complaints procedure.

If a literal reading prevails, the new affirmative defense would seem to deprive employers of the complete defense that circuit courts and EEOC previously recognized when an employer takes prompt and appropriate corrective action after an alleged victim did complain of a supervisor's hostile environment harassment. When the victim complains,[105] or when her failure to complain is not unreasonable, an employer could now be liable for a supervisor's unlawful hostile environment discrimination even if it *has* taken prompt appropriate remedial action. It may be doubted, however, whether the Court's two-pronged defense will be applied so literally.[106] A literal application reduces an employer's incen-

---

Fifth Ave., 13 F.Supp.2d 481, 492 (S.D.N.Y. 1998); *Coates v. Sundor Brands, Inc.*, 164 F.3d 1361, 1366 (11th Cir.1999) (the "great psychological burden" that the duty to complain places on the alleged victim does not excuse a failure to complain).

101. *Gallagher v. Delaney*, 139 F.3d 338 (2d Cir.1998).

102. *Torres v. Pisano*, 116 F.3d 625 (2d Cir.), *cert. denied*, 522 U.S. 997, 118 S.Ct. 563, 139 L.Ed.2d 404 (1997).

103. *Cf. Kunin v. Sears, Roebuck & Co.*, 175 F.3d 289 (3d Cir.), *cert. denied*, 528 U.S. 964, 120 S.Ct. 398, 145 L.Ed.2d 310 (1999) (telling manager that co-worker cursed at her, without specifying the sexual substance of the curse, does not put employer on notice or therefore trigger a duty to respond).

104. *Stoll v. Runyon*, 165 F.3d 1238 (9th Cir.1999).

105. Even though an employee had reported her supervisor's sexual harassment to a co-worker, rather than the person identified in the policy, the employer may still be charged with adequate notice if the employer led the employee to reasonably belief that the co-worker had the authority to handle the complaint. *See Sims v. Health Midwest Physician Servs. Corp.*, 196 F.3d 915, 920–21 (8th Cir.1999).

106. Several circuits have followed the literal reading of the defense. *See Greene v. Dalton*, 164 F.3d 671 (D.C.Cir.1999) (reversing grant of summary judgment on the defense, finding that the plaintiff did not unreasonably fail to use policy where she delayed one month to report incident); *Lissau v. Southern Food Serv., Inc.*, 159 F.3d 177 (4th Cir.1998) (remanding for additional discovery on defense; instructing trial court that summary judgment is inappropriate if it finds there was no effective anti-

tives to adopt and maintain a fair internal complaints policy by empowering a complainant unilaterally to defeat the defense simply by using a complaint procedure.[107] It would also render employers almost as susceptible to automatic liability for supervisory hostile environment as for tangible discrimination. These consequences run counter to the Court's stated goal in *Faragher* and *Burlington* of encouraging internal resolution of environmental harassment grievances. They also blur the Court's distinction between liability for supervisory tangible harassment, which is strict as well as vicarious, and liability for supervisory environmental harassment, which is also vicarious but potentially defensible.

In the presumably rare situation where a potential plaintiff does unreasonably fail to utilize a fair internal grievance mechanism, how is the employer supposed to learn about alleged harassment in order to carry the distinct burden under prong (a) to "correct promptly any sexually harassing behavior"? Perhaps in such cases the Court will conclude that the plaintiff has deprived the employer of the knowledge it needs to "correct"; it might hold accordingly that the employer has met prong (a) simply by having exercised reasonable care to "prevent."[108]

The "correct promptly" part of the first prong of the affirmative defense (prong a) continues to require district courts to determine the content of prompt and appropriate corrective action. Because the Supreme Court furnished no additional guidance on this question, the decisions after *Burlington* and *Faragher* are understandably as inconsistent as the decisions prior to those cases. A typical *pre-Burlington/Faragher* formulation asked whether the employer's combined response constituted prompt remedial action " 'reasonably likely to prevent the misconduct from recurring.' "[109] But the inquiry proceeded case by case, with the appropriateness determination turning on such facts as "the

harassment policy *or* if the plaintiff did avail herself of the policy). *But see Indest v. Freeman Decorating, Inc.*, 164 F.3d 258 (5th Cir.1999) where the court ignored the second prong of the defense and allowed the employer to carry the defense based on its prompt and appropriate remedial action after the employee complained. The court distinguished *Burlington* and *Faragher*—those cases "both involve complaints of longstanding supervisor misbehavior, and the plaintiffs either never utilized or claimed not to be aware of the company policies. But for purposes of imposing vicarious liability, a case presenting only an incipient hostile environment corrected by prompt remedial action should be distinct from a case in which a company was never called upon to react to a supervisor's protracted or extremely severe acts that created a hostile environment." *Id.* at 265. *See also Brown v. Perry*, 184 F.3d 388 (4th Cir.1999) (plaintiff subjected herself to a repetition of sexual advances she had previously rebuffed, without a compulsion to do so, enabling employer to satisfy second prong by showing her failure to "avoid harm otherwise").

107. *But see Harris v. L & L Wings, Inc.*, 132 F.3d 978 (4th Cir.1997) (where employer had no policy, called such policies "a ridiculous thing", and disavowed any responsibility to respond to repeated, specific complaints of a torrent of vulgarities, crude remarks, regular fondling, groping and other physical assaults, punitive damages were warranted).

108. *See Farley v. American Cast Iron Pipe Co.*, 115 F.3d 1548 (11th Cir.1997) (no employer Title VII hostile environment liability absent top management's actual knowledge of unlawful harassment, when plaintiff failed to use comprehensive, well publicized, vigorously enforced and fair anti-discrimination policy).

109. *See Adler v. Wal–Mart Stores, Inc.*, 144 F.3d 664, 673 (10th Cir.1998) (employer met reasonably calculated standard where its measures stopped unlawful conduct by the initial harassers but failed to deter harassment by other co-workers).

severity and persistence of the harassment, and the effectiveness of any initial steps."[110] Another circuit relieved the employer of liability for sexual harassment by a supervisor where it found that the supervisor was not wielding "actual" authority, the plaintiff did not subjectively attribute his acts to the company, and she thought she had an available avenue of complaint to the company president.[111] The post *Burlington/Faragher* decisions are similarly fact sensitive and diverse in their views as to what constitutes sufficiently prompt and appropriate corrective action.[112]

While a literal reading of the two-pronged defense would commonly prevent even explicit, fair and fairly enforced internal grievance procedures from avoiding liability altogether,[113] employers still have an incentive to adopt them. Such procedures will encourage internal complaints, thereby enhancing the employer's ability to take prompt corrective action that will limit its exposure for emotional distress, punitive damages and attorney's fees. Of course a complete avoidance of liability for supervisory environmental harassment is still possible, even when the plaintiff invokes a complaints procedure and a court applies the literal

110. For indications of the uncertainty surrounding the case-by-case appraisal of "appropriate" corrective action, *compare Perry v. Ethan Allen, Inc.*, 115 F.3d 143 (2d Cir.1997); *Zirpel v. Toshiba America Information Sys., Inc.*, 111 F.3d 80 (8th Cir. 1997) (investigation and warning to harasser adequate to negate employer liability); *Hirras v. National R.R. Passenger Corp.*, 95 F.3d 396 (5th Cir.1996) (investigatory efforts by employer suffice to avoid liability); *Spicer v. Virginia Dep't of Corrections*, 66 F.3d 705 (4th Cir.1995) (en banc) (counseling and training of supervisors deemed adequate response to co-worker harassment) and *Jeffries v. Metro–Mark, Inc.*, 45 F.3d 258 (8th Cir.), *cert. denied*, 516 U.S. 830, 116 S.Ct. 102, 133 L.Ed.2d 56 (1995) (employer response to co-worker racial harassment adequate where plaintiff reported only two of alleged multiple incidents) *with Smith v. St. Louis Univ.*, 109 F.3d 1261 (8th Cir.1997) (mere warning of harasser not sufficient to avoid trial) and *Karibian v. Columbia Univ.*, 14 F.3d 773, 779 (2d Cir.), *cert. denied*, 512 U.S. 1213, 114 S.Ct. 2693, 129 L.Ed.2d 824 (1994) (employer liable for a supervisor's harassment of the "quid pro quo" variety despite prompt investigation and fair resolution of plaintiff's charge).

111. *Bouton v. BMW of N. America, Inc.*, 29 F.3d 103 (3d Cir.1994).

112. *See Hill v. American General Finance*, 218 F.3d 639 (7th Cir.2000) (defendant carries affirmative defense where it had policies that were accessible to all employees, and promptly responded to complaint by transferring supervisor and reducing his compensation); *Tutman v. WBBM-TV, Inc.*, 209 F.3d 1044 (7th Cir.2000) (where employer conducted prompt investigation and reprimanded harasser, employer was not held liable); *Caudillo v. Continental Bank/Bank of America Illinois*, 191 F.3d 455 (7th Cir.), *cert. denied*, 528 U.S. 1048, 120 S.Ct. 584, 145 L.Ed.2d 485 (1999) (prompt response included thorough investigation, restrictions on alleged harasser's contact with plaintiff, written warning, and offer to transfer plaintiff); *Skidmore v. Precision Printing and Packaging, Inc.*, 188 F.3d 606 (5th Cir.1999) (instructing alleged harasser to leave plaintiff alone, and moving alleged harasser to new shift adequate, even though investigation delayed for months and alleged harasser not reprimanded); *Mikels v. City of Durham*, 183 F.3d 323 (4th Cir.1999) (prompt and adequate remedial action where alleged harasser reprimanded and transferred, and sexual harassment ceased, even though further sanctions against alleged harasser were set aside on internal appeal); *Indest v. Freeman Decorating, Inc.*, 164 F.3d 258 (5th Cir. 1999) (employer met the standard when it removed the plaintiff from harasser's supervision, issued the harassing supervisor verbal and written reprimands, suspended him without pay for a week, and excluded him from his own sales meeting); *Wilson v. Tulsa Junior College*, 164 F.3d 534 (10th Cir. 1998) (employer response untimely).

113. But proof of the existence of a policy with an adequate complaint procedure may not always be necessary to carry prong (a). *Harrison v. Eddy Potash*, 158 F.3d 1371 (10th Cir.1998). See discussion *supra*.

reading of the compound affirmative defense, for the plaintiff must still carry her prima facie burden of showing a sufficiently severe or hostile environment. The Court hinted in *Faragher* itself that it intended to continue to insist on palpable harm to the plaintiff's work environment, observing that the *Harris* standards for judging actionable interference "are sufficiently demanding to ensure that Title VII does not become a 'general civility code.' "

5. Hostile Environmental Harassment by Co–Workers, Customers, and Other Third Parties: Employer Liability For

In dictum in *Faragher* the Court confirmed the "negligence" standard widely used by most circuit courts[114] and EEOC to determine employer liability for actionable environmental harassment by a plaintiff's co-worker (or subordinate or customer).[115] This negligence standard has been carried forward in post-*Burlington/Faragher* circuit decisions.[116] Because a co-worker, subordinate or customer cannot indepen-

114. *See Hendry v. Schneider*, 116 F.3d 446 (10th Cir.1997) (upholding compensatory damages award based on sexual harassment of a waiter by a restaurant patron); *Reed v. A.W. Lawrence & Co.*, 95 F.3d 1170 (2d Cir.1996) (employer knowledge of co-employee's unlawful behavior permits employer liability); "EEOC Guidelines on Discrimination Because of Sex," 29 C.F.R. § 1604.11(d) (1993); *Doe v. R.R. Donnelley & Sons Co.*, 42 F.3d 439 (7th Cir.1994) (co-employee harassment not actually witnessed by plaintiff's supervisor who otherwise brought to employer's attention); *Pierce v. Commonwealth Life Ins. Co.*, 40 F.3d 796, 803 (6th Cir.1994). *See also Sauers v. Salt Lake County*, 1 F.3d 1122, 1125 (10th Cir.1993); *Levendos v. Stern Entertainment, Inc.*, 909 F.2d 747, 752 (3d Cir.1990); *Vance v. Southern Bell Tel. & Tel. Co.*, 863 F.2d 1503, 1512 (11th Cir.1989) (applying the standards of "co-worker" cases where a low-level supervisor uses no actual or apparent authority to further the harassment); *Menchaca v. Rose Records*, 1995 WL 151847 (N.D.Ill.1995) (employer liable when manager stood by while regular customer allegedly harassed cashier). In one recent state court case an employer was even held liable for a *subordinate's* environmental harassment of a *supervisor* where the employer, despite knowledge, failed to take prompt remedial measures and indeed punished the supervisor! *Hanlon v. Chambers*, 195 W.Va. 99, 464 S.E.2d 741 (W.Va.1995). *But see Folkerson v. Circus Circus Enters., Inc.*, 107 F.3d 754 (9th Cir.1997) (employer not liable for casino patron's harassment of plaintiff unless employer either ratifies or acquiesces in the harassment by failing to take prompt corrective action upon actual

or constructive notice); *Zimmerman v. Cook County Sheriff's Dep't*, 96 F.3d 1017 (7th Cir.1996) (plaintiff must draw co-worker harassment to employer's attention through specific notice or complaint); *McKeown v. Dartmouth Bookstore, Inc.*, 975 F.Supp. 403 (D.N.H.1997) (wearing of skimpy, provocative clothing by other female employees does not rise to necessary level of hostility).

115. Even the behavior of prison inmates which contributes to a hostile work environment can be attributed to the employer. *See Slayton v. Ohio Dep't of Youth Servs.*, 206 F.3d 669, 678 (6th Cir.2000). In *Slayton*, prison personnel intentionally manipulated inmates in ways that created a discriminatory environment, and prison supervisors failed to take steps to remedy known discrimination. A prison guard had, with tacit approval of supervisors, continually played misogynistic rap music, displayed sexually explicit music videos, called plaintiff derogatory names, and instigated inmates to engage in similar conduct.

116. *See, e.g., Curry v. District of Columbia*, 195 F.3d 654, 659 (D.C.Cir.1999), *cert. denied*, ___ U.S. ___, 120 S.Ct. 2219, 147 L.Ed.2d 251 (2000) (noting agreement among the circuits after *Faraher*); *Dhyne v. Meiners Thriftway, Inc.*, 184 F.3d 983, 987 (8th Cir.1999) (noting distinction between types of harassment and stating "[o]ur court has long recognized that an employer may be directly liable ... if it knew or should have known of the conduct and failed to take proper remedial action"); *Hafford v. Seidner*, 183 F.3d 506, 513 (6th Cir.1999) (stating "[e]mployer liability for co-worker harassment is based directly on

dently adversely alter the plaintiff's tangible terms of employment, the underlying violation here is of the "hostile environment" rather than "quid pro quo" variety.[117] It is even clearer with co-worker as with supervisory environmental harassment that the harasser is not acting on behalf of the employer or carrying out its business. In those cases, therefore, the circuit courts, with the Supreme Court's apparent approval, are unanimous that the employer will be liable only if it actually knew or should have known of the co-worker's (or subordinate's or customer's or supplier's) unlawful harassment and failed to take prompt and effective corrective action.[118] In co-worker or subordinate cases, then, the employer can assure its nonliability by its own unilateral action.

A key question that arises then is whether the harasser is a supervisor or a co-worker. If the harasser is only a co-worker, then the burden is on the plaintiff to prove that the employer was negligent, i.e., that the employer knew or should have known of the harassment yet the employer failed to take prompt corrective action. But if the harasser is a supervisor, the burden is on the defendant to establish the two-pronged *Burlington/Faragher* affirmative defense.[119] A confused Eleventh Circuit panel decision illustrates the difference. In *Coates v. Sundor Brands,*

the employer's conduct" and employer is liable if it "knew or should have known of the charged sexual harassment and failed to implement prompt and appropriate corrective action"); *Mikels v. City of Durham,* 183 F.3d 323, 331–32 (4th Cir.1999) (no vicarious liability for co-worker harassment); *Richardson v. New York State Dep't of Correctional Serv.,* 180 F.3d 426, 441 (2d Cir. 1999) (discussing *Faragher* and then concluding if the harasser is the victim's co-worker, "the employer will be liable only if it is negligent, that is, if it either provided no reasonable avenue for complaint or knew of the harassment and did nothing about it"); *Wilson v. Chrysler Corp.,* 172 F.3d 500, 508 (7th Cir.1999) ("Liability for co-worker harassment requires a showing of negligence . . . [so] a plaintiff must show that her employer failed to take reasonable steps to discover and remedy the harassment."); *Burrell v. Star Nursery, Inc.,* 170 F.3d 951, 955 (9th Cir.1999) (employer liable only for what management knew or should have known in co-worker harassment scenario); *Bailey v. Runyon,* 167 F.3d 466 (8th Cir.1999) (co-worker); *Sharp v. City of Houston,* 164 F.3d 923 (5th Cir. 1999) (noting *Faragher* did not disturb "negligence standard govern[ing] employer liability for co-worker harassment"); *Wilson v. Tulsa Junior College,* 164 F.3d 534, 541 n. 4 (10th Cir.1998) (noting distinction between vicarious liability and negligence standard); *Adusumilli v. City of Chicago,* 164 F.3d 353 (7th Cir.1998), *cert. denied,* 528 U.S. 988, 120 S.Ct. 450, 145 L.Ed.2d

367 (1999); *Lockard v. Pizza Hut Inc.,* 162 F.3d 1062 (10th Cir.1998) (customer). *But see Quinn v. Green Tree Credit Corp.,* 159 F.3d 759, 768 (2d Cir.1998) (employer not liable for co-worker harassment unless employer either knew of harassment and did nothing or provided no reasonable avenue of complaint).

117. *See Burlington.*

118. *See Faragher; Bailey v. Runyon,* 167 F.3d 466 (8th Cir.1999) (employer must act promptly; delayed action will not relieve employer of liability); *Parkins v. Civil Constructors of Ill., Inc.,* 163 F.3d 1027, 1035 (7th Cir.1998) ("employer's legal duty in co-employee harassment cases will be discharged if it takes reasonable steps to discover and rectify acts of sexual harassment by its employees"). *But see Whitmore v. O'Connor Mgmt., Inc.,* 156 F.3d 796 (8th Cir.1998) (acknowledging negligence standard but seemingly requiring actual knowledge; "employees have some obligation to inform their employers, either directly or otherwise, of behavior that they find objectionable before employers can be held responsible for failing to correct that behavior").

119. *See Pfau v. Reed,* 167 F.3d 228 (5th Cir.) (per curiam), *cert. denied,* 528 U.S. 813, 120 S.Ct. 49, 145 L.Ed.2d 43 (1999) (remanding for determination if harasser was supervisor or co-worker, and, if former, whether employer carried the *Burlington/Faragher* defense).

Incorporated,[120] the per curiam opinion analyzes the case as involving co-worker harassment; it employs the standard negligence framework under which the employee has the burden of showing that the employer knew or should have known of the harassment yet failed to react timely and appropriately. However, in a special concurrence, one judge applies the *Burlington/Faragher* framework for supervisory harassment (but apparently mistakenly places the burden on the plaintiff to disprove the two-pronged affirmative defense). It is not clear in the opinion whether the court carefully considered the status of the harasser. But the characterization of the harasser is critical at summary judgment or post-trial: summary judgment or judgment as a matter of law is uncommon when the moving party has the burden at trial as would the defendant-employer in a supervisory environmental harassment case that turns on the *Burington/Faragher* affirmative defense.[121]

Although the circuits have articulated various formulations for identifying supervisory status, a central question is whether the harasser had the authority to affect the terms and conditions of the harassee's work environment.[122] The Tenth Circuit has limited the term "supervisor" to those persons having actual and immediate authority over the plaintiff. In *Harrison v. Eddy Potash, Incorporated,*[123] the court rejected both an "alter ego" and apparent authority jury instruction requested by the plaintiff. The court relied on *Burlington,* and stated that employer liability cannot be grounded on a theory that a supervisor was an alter ego of the employer. The court further stated that to be a supervisor, the person must have actual authority; the false impression of authority is not sufficient. Only the misuse of actual authority can create employer liability.[124] The Tenth Circuit recently found such a misuse of actual authority where a bank vice president who harassed plaintiffs was not only their supervisor but also had ultimate hiring and firing authority in his department, was a member of policymaking committees, and an-

120.   164 F.3d 1361 (11th Cir.1999).

121.   *See, e.g., Dadurian v. Underwriters At Lloyd's, London,* 787 F.2d 756 (1st Cir. 1986) ("this circuit, like most courts, is reluctant to direct a verdict for the party having the burden of proof"). *But cf. Simblest v. Maynard,* 427 F.2d 1 (2d Cir.1970) (granting judgment as a matter of law to defendant on contributory negligence).

122.   *See Parkins v. Civil Constructors of Ill., Inc.,* 163 F.3d 1027, 1034 (7th Cir.1998) (essence of supervisory status is authority to affect terms and conditions of victim's employment; authority primarily consists of power to hire, fire, demote, promote, transfer, or discipline an employee); *Phillips v. Taco Bell Corp.,* 156 F.3d 884, 888 (8th Cir.1998) (harasser, who was the store manager, was a supervisor based on the authority he had over the plaintiff); *Wright-Simmons v. City of Oklahoma City,* 155 F.3d 1264, 1271 (10th Cir.1998) (the operative question in determining supervisory status is whether the employee in question "had sufficient control over the plaintiff to be considered her supervisor ..."); *Swentek v. USAIR, Inc.,* 830 F.2d 552, 558 (4th Cir.1987) (although pilots exercised some authority, it did not include the authority to "hire, fire, promote, or demote flight attendants"); *Yates v. Avco Corp.,* 819 F.2d 630, 636 (6th Cir.1987) (the employer is liable for hostile environment sexual harassment carried out "by someone with the authority to hire, fire, promote and discipline the plaintiffs"); *Alverio v. Sam's Warehouse Club,* 9 F.Supp.2d 955, 961 (N.D.Ill.1998) (harasser classified as supervisor where evidence showed he had authority to reprimand employees).

123.   158 F.3d 1371 (10th Cir.1998).

124.   *Id.*

swered only to the president.[125]

6. Ancillary Sexual Harassment Issues

Employers have asserted rights to indemnity or contribution with respect to supervisory conduct that has resulted in employer liability. But the Supreme Court has held that no such right is provided by Title VII itself or at common law.[126] Claims by supervisors disciplined for violating their employer's anti-sexual harassment policy have generally not fared well,[127] most courts reasoning that the employer must enjoy reasonable latitude to conduct a vigorous internal examination without risking additional charges of sexual harassment. Thus even a hostile, unprofessional and abusive employer investigation of sexual harassment charges ultimately determined to be unfounded could not support a separate sexual harassment claim by the exonerated suspect.[128]

On the other hand, unsuccessful sexual harassment charges in litigation have spawned defamation suits by the alleged harasser against accusers and against employers who placed stock in the charges and took unilateral corrective action.[129] In one case, the Virginia Supreme Court

125. See Mallinson–Montague v. Pocrnick, 224 F.3d 1224 (10th Cir.2000) (upholding employer liability on this "alter ego" alternative method).

126. Northwest Airlines, Inc. v. Transport Workers Union, AFL–CIO, 451 U.S. 77, 101 S.Ct. 1571, 67 L.Ed.2d 750 (1981); Atchley v. Nordam Group, Inc., 180 F.3d 1143, 1152 (10th Cir.1999). But see Jacobus v. Krambo Corp., 78 Cal.App.4th 1096, 93 Cal.Rptr.2d 425 (Cal.Ct.App.2000) (California state indemnification law mandates that employer pay legal costs in accused harasser's successful defense against charges of sexual harassment).

127. See, e.g., Biolchini v. General Elec. Co., 167 F.3d 1151 (7th Cir.1999) (plaintiff's violation of policy, together with his inadequate technical skills, prevented him from establishing prima facie case because he failed to meet employer's legitimate job expectations); Pierce v. Commonwealth Life Ins. Co., 40 F.3d 796 (6th Cir.1994) (disciplined male supervisor's claim that his female subordinate engaged in even more egregious conduct but was not disciplined fails to state claim under Kentucky law because the female employee, who had no duty to enforce the employer's sexual harassment policy, was not "similarly situated"). See also Stroehmann Bakeries, Inc. v. Local 776, Int'l Bhd. of Teamsters, 969 F.2d 1436 (3d Cir.), cert. denied, 506 U.S. 1022, 113 S.Ct. 660, 121 L.Ed.2d 585 (1992); Newsday, Inc. v. Long Island Typographical Union, 915 F.2d 840 (2d Cir. 1990), cert. denied, 499 U.S. 922, 111 S.Ct. 1314, 113 L.Ed.2d 247 (1991) (explicit, well

defined statutory policy against harassment must be taken into account by labor arbitrators hearing grievances by disciplined harassers). But see Westvaco Corp. v. United Paperworkers Int'l Union, Local Union 676, 171 F.3d 971 (4th Cir.1999) (no public policy exception to arbitrator's authority to reinstate union-represented employee fired for sexual harassment; employer must use reasonable care in correcting unlawful harassing behavior); Chrysler Motors Corp. v. International Union, 959 F.2d 685 (7th Cir.), cert. denied, 506 U.S. 908, 113 S.Ct. 304, 121 L.Ed.2d 227 (1992); Communication Workers of Am. v. Southeastern Elec. Coop., 882 F.2d 467 (10th Cir.1989) (arbitrator may award relief to harasser provided the public policy against sexual harassment is considered).

128. McDonnell v. Cisneros, 84 F.3d 256 (7th Cir.1996). See also Ribando v. United Airlines, Inc., 200 F.3d 507, 511 (7th Cir. 1999) (accused harasser has no Title VII claim arising from the investigation, counseling and mediation hearing following the sexual harassment complaint).

The distinct potential that supervisor and employer defendants may have adverse interests and legal positions in sexual harassment litigation based on the hostile environment theory also strongly suggests that they should be represented by separate counsel.

129. See, e.g., Rausman v. Baugh, 248 A.D.2d 8, 682 N.Y.S.2d 42 (N.Y.App.Div. 1998) (harasser could not hold employer liable under respondeat superior theory for

upheld a verdict against the plaintiff's female subordinate, rejecting her contention that sexual harassment is an "inherently subjective concept" that as such represents a pure expression of opinion absolutely protected by the First Amendment.[130] But another plaintiff who was fired in the wake of allegations of sexual harassment by two female employees failed to survive summary judgment for want of sufficient evidence of the "actual malice" Texas law required to recover for defamation. At most, the court found, the employer may have been hasty or mistaken, but there was no evidence that it took that action for any ulterior motive reflecting animus against the plaintiff.[131] And a discharged executive failed to prove a violation of ERISA in connection with his loss of severance benefits even though his conduct, although violative of company policy, was too sporadic to violate Title VII.[132]

b. First Amendment Implications of Imposing Liability for Environmentally Harassing Speech

It seems even clearer after *Harris* that speech alone may violate Title VII. That is to say, sexually offensive, demeaning or obscene speech or pictorial displays may alone adversely alter the conditions of the plaintiff's employment.[133] Few courts have addressed the constitutional problems that arise where the supervisor's or co-worker's allegedly harassing "conduct" consists entirely of speech or symbolic speech.[134] When that is so, federal or state regulation in the form of mandated procedures and judicial sanctions implicates the First Amendment.[135]

allegedly defamatory statements made by accuser because statements were not made within scope of employment).

130. *Williams v. Garraghty*, 249 Va. 224, 455 S.E.2d 209 (Va.), *cert. denied*, 516 U.S. 814, 116 S.Ct. 66, 133 L.Ed.2d 28 (1995).

131. *Duffy v. Leading Edge Products, Inc.*, 44 F.3d 308 (5th Cir.1995). *Accord Deutsch v. Chesapeake Ctr.*, 27 F.Supp.2d 642 (D.Md.1998) (employer's dissemination of references shielded by conditional privilege not overcome by evidence of malice).

132. *Chalmers v. Quaker Oats Co.*, 61 F.3d 1340 (7th Cir.1995). *See also Malik v. Carrier Corp.*, 202 F.3d 97 (2d Cir.2000) (state law claim for negligent infliction of emotional distress arising out of sexual harassment charge is overridden by federal law requiring employers to investigate and remediate sexual harassment).

133. *See, e.g., Robinson v. Jacksonville Shipyards*, 760 F.Supp. 1486 (M.D.Fla. 1991) (liability predicated on displays of pornographic pinups and explicit sexual comments directed towards the plaintiff and other women).

134. *But see Aguilar v. Avis Rent A Car System, Inc.*, 21 Cal.4th 121, 87 Cal.Rptr.2d 132, 980 P.2d 846 (Cal.1999), *cert. denied*, ___ U.S. ___, 120 S.Ct. 2029, 146 L.Ed.2d 971 (2000) (injunction against supervisor's use of racial epithets that violated state fair employment law not violation of supervisor's First Amendment rights). Distinguishable from this situation is quid pro quo harassment, where the employment-related threat or benefit that hinges on compliance with a superior's sexual demand may be regarded as a form of conduct that violates Title VII, *see NLRB v. Gissel Packing Co.*, 395 U.S. 575, 89 S.Ct. 1918, 23 L.Ed.2d 547 (1969) (decision under National Labor Relations Act). Also less likely to raise First Amendment problems is gender-demeaning or stereotypical speech that the plaintiff cites as evidence that a distinct employment decision—a failure to promote, for instance—was based on a prohibited ground, as in *Price Waterhouse*.

135. *Cf. Baliko v. Stecker*, 275 N.J.Super. 182, 645 A.2d 1218 (N.J.Super.Ct.App.Div.1994) (under state discrimination law). A district court in Minnesota considered and rejected the argument that Title VII's regulation of speech infringed on the First Amendment. *Jenson v. Eveleth Taconite Co.*, 824 F.Supp. 847, 884 n. 89 (D.Minn.1993), *aff'd in part and vacated and remanded in part*, 130 F.3d 1287 (8th

The situation is aggravated by the reality that employers have an incentive to overregulate the speech of their employees by taking the "prompt and effective corrective action" that the courts have held will absolve them of liability for the sins of co-workers and sometimes even supervisors.[136]

Two features of emerging harassment law fuel that incentive. First, as the *Harris* language underscores, the contours of the violation are vague. Generally courts have found that a plaintiff states a prima facie case under Title VII when the environment is pervasively disrespectful to women or minorities.[137] Similarly, sexual propositions in the workplace can create a hostile environment.[138] The only guidance given employers is that, "verbal conduct of a sexual nature [that] has the purpose or effect of unreasonably interfering with an individual's work performance or creating an intimidating, hostile, or offensive work environment" is harassment.[139] Moreover, the existence of a hostile environment is determined by a totality of the circumstances test. The employer is uncertain as to whether a hostile environment exists until the court makes that determination.

Second, an effective policy and procedure against sexual harassment may avoid employer liability for harassment by subordinate employees and for environmental harassment by supervisors. Accordingly, when, as will frequently be the case, the employer is in doubt, it has the incentive, in order to avoid the vagaries of liability for uncertain workplace speech and pictorial displays, to overregulate and overpunish. Nevertheless, fired managers have generally had difficulty persuading courts that their discipline or discharge as the result of an internal investigation violates federal or state law.[140] Still, while an employer may discipline supervi-

---

Cir.1997), *cert. denied sub nom. Oglebay Norton Co. v. Jenson,* 524 U.S. 953, 118 S.Ct. 2370, 141 L.Ed.2d 738 (1998). This court determined that Title VII could proscribe conduct, including expression, occurring in the workplace when the same conduct could not be regulated outside the workplace. *Id.*

136. *See* Kingsley R. Browne, *Title VII as Censorship: Hostile–Environment Harassment and the First Amendment,* 52 Ohio St.L.J. 481 (1991); *see also,* Jules B. Gerard, *The First Amendment in a Hostile Environment: A Primer on Free Speech and Sexual Harassment,* 68 Notre Dame L.Rev. 1003 (1993).

137. *See State v. Human Rights Comm'n,* 178 Ill.App.3d 1033, 128 Ill.Dec. 141, 534 N.E.2d 161 (Ill.App.Ct.1989); *Lipsett v. University of Puerto Rico,* 864 F.2d 881 (1st Cir.1988); *EEOC v. Murphy Motor Freight Lines, Inc.,* 488 F.Supp. 381 (D.Minn.1980).

138. *See Continental Can Co. v. State,* 297 N.W.2d 241 (Minn.1980); *Ellison v. Brady,* 924 F.2d 872 (9th Cir.1991).

139. 29 C.F.R. § 1604.11(a).

140. *See, e.g., Malone v. Eaton Corp.,* 187 F.3d 960 (8th Cir.1999) (company enjoys qualified privilege to defamation claim by supervisor respecting manager's statement in meeting held to implement company's anti-harassment policy that supervisor had been fired for "a form of" sexual harassment); *Silva v. Lucky Stores Inc.,* 65 Cal.App.4th 256, 76 Cal.Rptr.2d 382 (Cal. Ct.App.1998) (male manager has no wrongful termination claim after being fired because he harassed subordinate; court sets out three part test to determine if employer had good cause); *Knabe v. The Boury Corp.,* 114 F.3d 407 (3d Cir.1997) (remedial action adequate to avoid liability even though investigation that produced it was flawed); *McDonnell v. Cisneros,* 84 F.3d 256 (7th Cir.1996) (insulating defendant from liability for conducting sexual harassment investigation even when court considered that investigation harsh and abusive). One court has further protected employers who investigate and act on complaints of sexual harassment by declining to find a per se

sors for engaging in sexual harassment, it may not discipline them for their speech or conduct in participating in an investigation of that harassment.[141]

§ 2.23 The Special Statutory Concept of "Religion"

Employers not qualifying for immunity from liability for religious discrimination under § 702 or § 703(e)(2), or for the BFOQ defense with respect to religiously-based hiring decisions (see Part A., above) are subject to a special affirmative obligation somewhat distinct from the normal duty not to discriminate. Section 703(a)(1) forbids an employer from discriminating because of "religion"; and § 701(j), added in 1972, in turn defines "religion" to include "all aspects of religious observance and practice as well as belief, unless an employer demonstrates that he is unable to reasonably accommodate to an employee's . . . religious observance or practice without undue hardship. . . ."

At the threshold, when does an employer rule discriminate because of "religion"? Circuit courts have assumed that employer rules excluding all but "Protestants" (no particular denomination required)[1] and preferring "Jesuits" (members of a Catholic order)[2] do draw distinctions on that prohibited statutory ground. In the latter case, the panel rejected the approach suggested by a concurring judge who argued that rejection of the Jewish plaintiff was not on an unlawful ground. Judge Posner wrote that plaintiff's rejection because he was not a Jesuit was *not* tantamount to a rejection for not being a Catholic, since a non-Jesuit Catholic would also have been denied the job. Implicitly Posner's position was that adverse distinctions drawn on the basis of being or not being Jesuit are not actionable, while those relating to Catholicism are, even though only Catholics can be Jesuit. This position could be rephrased as an argument that discrimination on the basis of "religion-plus" (being Catholic *plus* being a Jesuit) is not prima facie unlawful while discrimination on the basis of religion alone is. As such, it seems discredited by the Supreme Court's rejection in *Phillips*[3] of the employ-

---

sexual harassment violation just because a complainant is ordered to return to a position where she must work in proximity with co-workers or a supervisor who had harassed or arguably harassed her previously. *But cf. Cortes v. Maxus Exploration Co.*, 977 F.2d 195 (5th Cir.1992) (violation to order employee to return to work where a recurrence of sexual harassment was highly likely and employer took no precautionary or remedial measures); *Simpson v. Mars, Inc.*, 113 Nev. 188, 929 P.2d 966 (Nev.1997) (manager fired for sexually harassing co-worker has state law defamation claim even though communications about her conduct were only intracorporate and not communicated to third parties). *See also Vice v. Conoco Inc.*, 150 F.3d 1286 (10th Cir.1998) (rejecting sexual harasser's contention that employer's disciplinary letter created an

employment contract which abrogated Oklahoma's employment at will doctrine; letters contained only "general platitudes" and "vague assurances").

141. *See* discussion in § 2.22(a)(6) *supra*, and *Merritt v. Dillard Paper Co.*, 120 F.3d 1181 (11th Cir.1997). *See generally* § 2.40 *infra* on the Title VII protection against retaliation.

§ 2.23

1. *Kamehameha*, 990 F.2d 458.

2. *Pime v. Loyola Univ. of Chicago*, 803 F.2d 351.

3. *Phillips v. Martin Marietta Corp.*, 400 U.S. 542, 91 S.Ct. 496, 27 L.Ed.2d 613 (1971), *discussed supra* § 2.22.

er's assertion that its rule was not unlawful sex discrimination because it excluded not women alone but only those who shared the "plus" factor of having pre-school-aged children.[4]

On facts that sharpened the distinction between a religion and one of its orders, a later panel of the Seventh Circuit grappled with a Catholic plaintiff's claim that she was denied employment by another university because of sex and the school's Jesuit preference policy. The court rejected her claims, finding that she was denied an academic appointment not because of her gender but because her views did not conform to Catholic doctrine.[5] But if that were so, and if "religion" includes "all aspects of religious ... belief," why was she not held to have been discriminated against on the basis of religion, as she apparently claimed?[6] Did the court perhaps place a sub rosa interpretive gloss on the statute to the effect that a defendant may lawfully discriminate against a Catholic on the basis of non-adherence to Catholic belief?[7]

More typically, the plaintiff complains of a particular employer practice that burdens the practice of his religion. The prima facie case consists of evidence that an employer practice conflicts with the employee's exercise of a sincerely held religious belief,[8] that the employee has put the employer on notice of the conflict, and the employer has nevertheless imposed an employment detriment.[9] The employer then

4. This discussion is based on textual notes in Zimmer, Sullivan, Richards and Calloway, *Cases and Materials On Employment Discrimination* 647 (3d ed. Little Brown 1994).

5. *Maguire v. Marquette Univ.*, 814 F.2d 1213, 1216–1217 (7th Cir.1987).

6. Regarding the protection afforded "all aspects" of religious belief, see the case of the second grade teacher who sent home end-of-the-school-year gifts with her students. She gave each student a "magic rock" with a letter instructing the students that the rock had magical qualities; all they had to do was to rub the rock, close their eyes, and say to themselves "I am a special and terrific person, with talents of my own!" The children were then to think of three good things about themselves. On the recommendation of the principal, the school district fired the teacher because they perceived that she was teaching New Ageism and feared she had offended the religious sensibilities of the local community. The court found that the school acted out of religious concerns and awarded the teacher $18,000 but denied her reinstatement because the principal-teacher relationship was "badly damaged." *Cowan v. Strafford R–VI Sch. Dist.*, 140 F.3d 1153 (8th Cir.1998).

7. The authors of a noted casebook wonder further if in fact plaintiff *could* be considered a Catholic if her views conflicted with the established Catholic Church posi-

tion. *Cases and Materials on Employment Discrimination, supra,* at 649.

8. Personal preferences of the employee that do not constitute bona fide religious needs will not support employer liability. *See, e.g., Tiano v. Dillard Dep't Stores,* 139 F.3d 679 (9th Cir.1998) (timing of an employee's pilgrimage during employer's busy season was a matter of personal preference not a bone fide religious need).

9. *See Ansonia Bd. of Educ. v. Philbrook,* 479 U.S. 60, 107 S.Ct. 367, 93 L.Ed.2d 305 (1986). *Cf. Chalmers v. Tulon Co. of Richmond,* 101 F.3d 1012 (4th Cir. 1996), *cert. denied,* 522 U.S. 813, 118 S.Ct. 58, 139 L.Ed.2d 21 (1997) (evangelical employee who was terminated for sending letters to co-workers' homes that accused them of immorality failed to state a prima facie claim for failing to give her employer advance notice that sending such mail was a religious imperative). The court in *Chalmers* listed the plaintiff's prima facie elements as follows: (1) a bona fide religious belief that conflicts with an employer's requirement (2) notice to the employer of that belief and, despite that notice, (3) discipline for violating the work requirement. The employer could affirmatively defend, the court indicated, by showing its inability to accommodate the religious need without undue hardship. The dissent complained that the majority had "grafted a claim-

defends by showing either that it fulfilled its obligation to reasonably accommodate or that any accommodation of the plaintiff's religious needs would work an undue hardship.[10] But two Supreme Court decisions have greatly eased the resulting employer obligation to reasonably accommodate the religious practice.

In *Ansonia Bd. of Education v. Philbrook*,[11] the Court suggested that if an employer's schedule conflicts with the plaintiff's religious need to refrain from secular employment on holy days, the employer could ordinarily satisfy its accommodation obligation by offering the employee additional unpaid leave rather than affording additional paid leave. In particular, the employer was not required to accept the plaintiff's proffered fuller accommodation if the employer's own accommodation is "reasonable."[12] The Court wrote that the employer there would violate

defeating notice requirement" that "would preclude liability for every adverse employment action taken because of a religious practice if the employer did not know in advance that the practice would take place" even where the employer does recognize the practice as religiously motivated. It has been held that whether a circumstance or permission the plaintiff seeks is, as he claims, part of his religious "practice" or is instead a matter of his personal preference is a fact question for the jury. *Vetter v. Farmland Indus.*, 120 F.3d 749 (8th Cir. 1997) (upholding jury determination that plaintiff's desire to live in a particular town that had an active Jewish community and synagogue was a personal preference, so that employer's refusal to re-transfer him did not unlawfully interfere with his religious practice or observance).

Until the Court struck down the Religious Freedom Restoration Act of 1993, 42 U.S.C.A. § 2000bb et seq., last Term as an impermissible exercise of Congress' power to legislate under § 5 of the 14th Amendment, *City of Boerne, Texas v. Flores*, 521 U.S. 507, 117 S.Ct. 2157, 138 L.Ed.2d 624 (1997), it appeared that the prima facie showing could be made more easily by governmental employees. RFRA required government defendants to demonstrate that burdens on the exercise of religion were the least restrictive means to further a compelling governmental interest.

10. *See Balint v. Carson City, Nevada*, 180 F.3d 1047 (9th Cir.1999); *Chalmers v. Tulon Co. of Richmond*, 101 F.3d 1012 (4th Cir.1996), *cert. denied*, 522 U.S. 813, 118 S.Ct. 58, 139 L.Ed.2d 21 (1997). Several circuits have required the employer to prove more than hypothetical hardship. *See Smith v. Pyro Mining Co.*, 827 F.2d 1081, 1086 (6th Cir.1987), *cert. denied*, 485 U.S. 989, 108 S.Ct. 1293, 99 L.Ed.2d 503 (1988) (defendant must present evidence of undue

hardship; it cannot rely merely on speculation; *Draper v. United States Pipe & Foundry Co.*, 527 F.2d 515, 520 (6th Cir.1975) (expressing skepticism of hypothetical hardships that an employer thinks might be caused by an accommodation that has never been put into practice); *Toledo v. Nobel–Sysco Inc.*, 892 F.2d 1481, 1490, 1492 (10th Cir.1989), *cert. denied*, 495 U.S. 948, 110 S.Ct. 2208, 109 L.Ed.2d 535 (1990) (finding Defendant's argument that it would incur increased risk of tort liability for hiring a driver who uses peyote in religious ceremonies too speculative); *Brown v. Polk County*, 61 F.3d 650, 655 (8th Cir.1995), *cert. denied*, 516 U.S. 1158, 116 S.Ct. 1042, 134 L.Ed.2d 189 (1996) (finding that the defendants' examples of the burden they would have to bear due to the Plaintiff's spontaneous prayers and isolated references to Christian belief were insufficiently real and too hypothetical to satisfy the standard required to show undue hardship); *Burns v. Southern Pac. Transp. Co.*, 589 F.2d 403, 406–07 (9th Cir.1978), *cert. denied*, 439 U.S. 1072, 99 S.Ct. 843, 59 L.Ed.2d 38 (1979) (finding the defendant's unofficial and unscientific polls regarding employee dissatisfaction with persons who received different treatment speculative); *Anderson v. General Dynamics Convair Aerospace Div.*, 589 F.2d 397, 402 (9th Cir.1978), *cert. denied*, 442 U.S. 921, 99 S.Ct. 2848, 61 L.Ed.2d 290 (1979) (stating that undue hardship requires more than proof of co-worker's unhappiness with a particular accommodation; the defendant must show an actual imposition on co-workers or disruption of the work routine).

11. 479 U.S. 60, 107 S.Ct. 367, 93 L.Ed.2d 305 (1986).

12. For example, an accommodation that eliminates the religious conflict by offering an employee a job transfer or shift

Title VII only if it overtly discriminated against a religiously-necessitated employee absence—for example, if under similar circumstances it would provide paid leave for a non-religious reason. The Court therefore requires little more of an employer to meet this special statutory accretion to the definition of religion than to refrain from the ordinary kinds of disparate treatment or neutral-practice/disproportionate adverse impact.[13] (Contrast the far more substantial duty to accommodate disabilities under the ADA of 1990).

Second, the Court held in *Trans World Airlines, Inc. v. Hardison*[14] that an employer's reasonable accommodation, even as alleviated by *Ansonia*, works "undue hardship" whenever it results "in more than a *de minimis* cost." An accommodation that requires the employer to hire an additional worker in order to permit the plaintiff to observe his religion every Saturday works undue hardship.[15] So do accommodations that permit a religious observer to skip assignments that would have to be picked up by others,[16] or that allow the observer to work less than others, even if he reimburses the employer for the resulting additional costs.[17] Nor will a court likely require the employer to accommodate in a

change, particularly where there is no loss of pay or benefits, satisfies the duty even if it entails other undesirable features from the plaintiff's point of view. *See, e.g., Rodriguez v. City of Chicago, Ill.*, 156 F.3d 771 (7th Cir.1998), *cert. denied*, 525 U.S. 1144, 119 S.Ct. 1038, 143 L.Ed.2d 46 (1999); *Cook v. Lindsay Olive Growers*, 911 F.2d 233 (9th Cir.1990); *Brener v. Diagnostic Ctr. Hosp.*, 671 F.2d 141 (5th Cir.1982); *United States v. City of Albuquerque*, 545 F.2d 110 (10th Cir.1976), *cert. denied*, 433 U.S. 909, 97 S.Ct. 2974, 53 L.Ed.2d 1092 (1977). *See also* 29 C.F.R. § 1605.2(d)(1)(iii). *Cf. Ryan v. United States Dep't of Justice*, 950 F.2d 458 (7th Cir.1991), *cert. denied*, 504 U.S. 958, 112 S.Ct. 2309, 119 L.Ed.2d 230 (1992); *Beadle v. City of Tampa*, 42 F.3d 633 (11th Cir.), *cert. denied*, 515 U.S. 1152, 115 S.Ct. 2600, 132 L.Ed.2d 846 (1995).

13. *See, e.g., EEOC v. United Parcel Serv.*, 94 F.3d 314 (7th Cir.1996) (directing trial court to consider whether permitting employee to wear beard in accordance with dictates of his religion, notwithstanding employer's beard ban for public contact positions, would work an undue hardship).

14. 432 U.S. 63, 74 n. 9, 97 S.Ct. 2264, 2272 n. 9, 53 L.Ed.2d 113 (1977). *But see Brown v. Polk Co., Iowa*, 61 F.3d 650 (8th Cir.1995), *cert. denied*, 516 U.S. 1158, 116 S.Ct. 1042, 134 L.Ed.2d 189 (1996) (the hardship must be "real," not speculative, and employer had only shown that a supervisor's spontaneous prayers and affirmations of Christian belief would potentially polarize staff or make them fearful or uncomfortable).

15. *Cooper v. Oak Rubber Co.*, 15 F.3d 1375 (6th Cir.1994).

16. *But see Weber v. Roadway Exp., Inc.*, 199 F.3d 270, 274 (5th Cir.2000); *Lee v. ABF Freight System, Inc.*, 22 F.3d 1019 (10th Cir.1994) (holding that the plaintiff's "voluntary runaround" proposal of skipping over his position on the drivers' dispatch board was unreasonable as a matter of law); *Eversley v. MBank Dallas*, 843 F.2d 172, 175 (5th Cir.1988); *Brener v. Diagnostic Center Hosp.*, 671 F.2d 141, 146 (5th Cir.1982) (finding that an employer is not required to rearrange its neutral scheduling practices to accommodate an employee).

17. *Lee v. ABF Freight Sys., Inc.*, 22 F.3d 1019 (10th Cir.1994); *Stevenson v. Southport, Inc.*, 1997 WL 129389 (E.D.La. 1997) (accommodating Seventh Day Adventist's refusal to work Saturdays would cause undue hardship where employer that operated 7 days per week showed that failure to replace plaintiff would have resulted in a production loss and replacement would result in a greater than de minimis cost, even without evidence that voluntary shift swaps would be infeasible or that involuntary rescheduling would unduly burden co-workers). The Fourth Circuit has held that where a proposed accommodation would result in the religious adherent's imposing burdens on co-employees directly and personally—in that case, permitting him to write letters to their homes accusing them of immorality—no employer accommodation is possible because otherwise the employer would be serving as the government's agent in interfering with the co-employees' own

way that requires it to violate a collective bargaining agreement, in view of the separate command of Title VII Section 703(h), 42 U.S.C.A. § 2000e–2(h), that "Notwithstanding any other provision of this subchapter, it shall not be an unlawful employment practice for an employer to apply different ... terms, conditions, or privileges of employment pursuant to a bona fide seniority ... system."[18] But a transfer with no cut in pay or benefits that does not violate a collective bargaining agreement is a reasonable accommodation that does not constitute an undue hardship.[19] On the other hand, when an employee's religious vow commanded her to wear an anti-abortion button that contained a graphic photograph, an employer was held to have adequately accommodated by permitting her to wear the button so long as the photograph was covered.[20] Largely because the duty to accommodate has thus been substantially diluted by judicial construction, § 701(j) has survived challenge under the First Amendment's Establishment Clause.[21]

rights to religious freedom. *Chalmers v. Tulon Co., of Richmond*, 101 F.3d 1012 (4th Cir.1996), *cert. denied*, 522 U.S. 813, 118 S.Ct. 58, 139 L.Ed.2d 21 (1997). *But cf. Opuku–Boateng v. California*, 95 F.3d 1461 (9th Cir.1996), *cert. denied*, 520 U.S. 1228, 117 S.Ct. 1819, 137 L.Ed.2d 1027 (1997) (alternative holding) (district court erred in determining that employer would experience undue hardship in accommodating request of Seventh Day Adventist to observe Saturday sabbath, where state employer failed to prove either that an arrangement scheduling plaintiff for other shifts as undesirable as Saturdays would discriminate against co-workers, or that voluntary trading of shifts by co-employees would be infeasible).

18. *See Trans World Airlines, Inc. v. Hardison*, 432 U.S. 63, 97 S.Ct. 2264, 53 L.Ed.2d 113 (1977) and *Lee v. ABF Freight Sys., Inc.*, 22 F.3d 1019 (10th Cir.1994). There is some circuit conflict concerning whether an employer meets its obligations when it refuses to alter a shift system even where no premium pay or significant efficiency loss would be entailed. *Compare Weber v. Roadway Exp., Inc.*, 199 F.3d 270, 274 (5th Cir.2000); *Lee v. ABF Freight System, Inc.*, 22 F.3d 1019 (10th Cir.1994) (holding that the plaintiff's "voluntary runaround" proposal of skipping over his position on the drivers' dispatch board was unreasonable as a matter of law); *Eversley v. MBank Dallas*, 843 F.2d 172, 175 (5th Cir.1988); *Brener v. Diagnostic Center Hosp.*, 671 F.2d 141, 146 (5th Cir.1982) (finding that an employer is not required to rearrange its neutral scheduling practices to accommodate an employee) and *Beadle v. City of Tampa, Fla.*, 42 F.3d 633 (11th Cir.1995), *cert. denied*, 515 U.S. 1152, 115

S.Ct. 2600, 132 L.Ed.2d 846 (1995) (refusing to force defendant police department to alter its training and scheduling protocols) *with Brown v. General Motors Corp.*, 601 F.2d 956 (8th Cir.1979) (requiring defendant to allow plaintiff Fridays off for religious reasons). One circuit reads *Hardison* to mean that a bona fide seniority system does not altogether relieve an employer of the duty to make reasonable accommodation, provided the accommodation can be accomplished "without modification of" the system and with no more than de minimis cost. *Balint v. Carson City, Nevada*, 180 F.3d 1047 (9th Cir.1999) (to accommodate new employee, public safety employer had to consider "split shifts"—nonconsecutive days off—contrary to the long-established custom that formed the background of its seniority system for bidding on shifts). The judges were sharply divided, however, over the weight to be given the Section 703(h) seniority system defense in determining whether a proposed accommodation conflicts with such a system and, if not, whether the accommodation would entail more than de minimis cost and therefore undue hardship.

19. *Rodriguez v. City of Chicago*, 156 F.3d 771 (7th Cir.1998), *cert. denied*, 525 U.S. 1144, 119 S.Ct. 1038, 143 L.Ed.2d 46 (1999) (city transferred a police officer so he did not have to guard an abortion clinic).

20. *Wilson v. U.S. West Communications*, 58 F.3d 1337 (8th Cir.1995).

21. *Protos v. Volkswagen of America, Inc.*, 797 F.2d 129 (3d Cir.), *cert. denied*, 479 U.S. 972, 107 S.Ct. 474, 93 L.Ed.2d 418 (1986). As so diluted, the duty to reasonably accommodate without undue hardship reflects the minimum religious liberty demanded by the Free Exercise Clause; a pub-

§§ 2.24–5.29 [Reserved]

E. PARTICULAR PRACTICES GIVEN SPECIAL STATUTORY TREATMENT

§ 2.30 Wage Discrimination and the Interrelationship With EPA

As discussed below in Chapter 8, the EPA prohibits only sex-based pay differentials for "equal work," defined to mean jobs involving substantially the same skill, effort, and responsibility. EPA also contains four listed affirmative defenses to a claim of unequal pay for equal work.

The "Bennett Amendment" to Title VII, the last sentence of § 703(h), attempts to harmonize the two statutes' treatment of sex-based wage discrimination. It provides that a successful affirmative defense to an EPA claim does double duty as a defense to liability under Title VII. Lower courts are divided, however, on the converse question, whether EPA liability automatically means Title VII liability as well.[1]

On the other hand, intentional sex-based wage discrimination may violate Title VII even if no member of the opposite sex performs "equal work" within the meaning of EPA.[2] But the related "comparable worth" theory has generally been rejected. An employer does not violate Title VII merely by observing market norms that result in its paying more for male-dominated jobs than for female-dominated jobs that have similar value to the employer but would not be considered "equal" under EPA.[3] Nor can the Equal Pay Act be used to assert a claim for equal benefits based on the alleged "comparable worth" of male- and female-dominated jobs when those jobs do not entail the substantially equal skill, effort and responsibility that EPA claims require.[4] See Chapter 8 for a fuller discussion of the theory of comparable worth.

Even without explicit authorizing text in EPA, the circuit courts have held unlawful employer retaliation against employees for asserting an EPA claim or protesting an EPA violation.[5]

lic employer who violates the former also violates the latter. *Brown*, 61 F.3d 650.

§ 2.30

1. *Compare EEOC v. White and Son Enters.*, 881 F.2d 1006 (11th Cir.1989) *and Kouba v. Allstate Ins. Co.*, 691 F.2d 873, 875 (9th Cir.1982) (automatic Title VII liability) *with Tidwell v. Fort Howard Corp.*, 989 F.2d 406 (10th Cir.1993) (Equal Pay Act evidence did not show intentional discrimination violative of Title VII) *and Fallon v. Illinois*, 882 F.2d 1206 (7th Cir.1989) (Title VII liability standard is higher, since plaintiff bears burden of persuasion throughout).

2. *Washington County v. Gunther*, 452 U.S. 161, 101 S.Ct. 2242, 68 L.Ed.2d 751 (1981); *EEOC v. Reichhold Chems., Inc.*, 988 F.2d 1564 (11th Cir.1993).

3. *See American Federation of State, County and Mun. Employees v. Washington*, 770 F.2d 1401 (9th Cir.1985). A circuit court has expressly approved use of the neutral practice/disproportionate adverse impact proof mode in a case under PDA. *Garcia v. Woman's Hosp. of Texas*, 97 F.3d 810 (5th Cir.1996) (weight lifting requirement). *See* Chapter 4 on the required "adverse impact" proof.

4. *Beavers v. American Cast Iron Pipe Co.*, 975 F.2d 792 (11th Cir.1992).

5. *See, e.g., EEOC v. White and Son Enters.*, 881 F.2d 1006 (11th Cir.1989).

§ 2.31 Restrictions Relative to Pregnancy and Abortion

The Pregnancy Discrimination Act of 1978, or "PDA," added to Title VII a new § 701(k). This amendment defines the sex discrimination prohibited by § 703 to include distinctions "on the basis of pregnancy, childbirth or related medical conditions...." The PDA, in other words, effectively equates pregnancy discrimination with discrimination "because of sex" within the meaning of § 703. Refusing to hire or firing someone because she is pregnant therefore violates § 703, and such a violation is a form of facial or express gender discrimination, defensible only if the employer establishes a BFOQ. The PDA thus accomplishes the objective that principally motivated its enactment, overturning the Court's conclusion in *General Electric Co. v. Gilbert*[1] that discrimination based on pregnancy is not based on gender.

The PDA does not require an employer to provide leaves or benefits for pregnancy that it does not provide to male employees for "comparable" conditions; as the Court wrote in *California Federal Savings & Loan Ass'n v. Guerra*,[2] the amendment's dominant principle is nondiscrimination, rather than preference.[3] PDA does not even require an employer to provide *any* leaves or benefits for pregnancy if it treats similar disabilities the same.[4] For the same reason, the Act does not require

§ 2.31

1. 429 U.S. 125, 97 S.Ct. 401, 50 L.Ed.2d 343 (1976). *See* discussion of *Gilbert* earlier in this chapter, at § 2.22 *supra*.

2. 479 U.S. 272, 286–87, 107 S.Ct. 683, 692–93, 93 L.Ed.2d 613 (1987).

3. *See, e.g., Piraino v. International Orientation Resources*, 137 F.3d 987 (7th Cir. 1998) (employer's leave policy did not violate PDA even though it resulted in the discharge of employee on pregnancy leave because leave policy treated all employees—pregnant and nonpregnant—similarly).

4. *See, e.g., Armindo v. Padlocker, Inc.*, 209 F.3d 1319 (11th Cir.2000) (per curiam) (PDA does not require employer to treat pregnant employee who misses work more favorable than non-pregnant employee who misses work); *Spivey v. Beverly Enterprises*, 196 F.3d 1309, 1312–1313 (11th Cir.1999); *Urbano v. Continental Airlines* Inc., 138 F.3d 204 (5th Cir.), *cert. denied*, 525 U.S. 1000, 119 S.Ct. 509, 142 L.Ed.2d 422 (1998) (the PDA bars employers from treating pregnant employees differently from similarly situated employees but does not guarantee light duty assignments or other preferential treatment); *Barrash v. Bowen*, 846 F.2d 927 (4th Cir.1988) (per curiam). *See also Hishon v. King & Spalding*, 467 U.S. 69, 75, 104 S.Ct. 2229, 2233, 81 L.Ed.2d 59 (1984) (Title VII only requires equal treatment of employees if and after an employer has decided to provide a benefit). *See* "EEOC: Policy Guidance On Parental Leave," 405 FEP Man. 6885 (8/27/90) (acknowledging that Title VII does not require an employer to provide a parental or child care leave but cautioning that conditioning such a leave on a facially neutral criterion—for example, authorizing the leave only for working spouses—may constitute an unlawful employment practice if it results in a disproportionate adverse impact on one or another gender).

The Supreme Court has also construed the provision of the Federal Unemployment Tax Act that forbids states from denying benefits because of pregnancy not to require a state to treat pregnancy more favorably than other disabilities. In *Wimberly v. Labor & Indus. Relations Comm.*, 479 U.S. 511, 107 S.Ct. 821, 93 L.Ed.2d 909 (1987), the Court upheld a state unemployment compensation statute that deemed all disability leaves unsupported by good cause, with no exception for maternity. It is clear that neither *Guerra* nor *Wimberly* would permit an employer to treat pregnancy disadvantageously relative to other disabilities. But while *Guerra* holds that the PDA does not prohibit preferential employer treatment of pregnancy mandated by state law, at least in the limited sphere of actual physical disability, it does not hold that PDA itself mandates such treatment; and *Wimberly* makes it clear that in any event no such preferential treatment is mandated by FUTA.

more indulgence for absence[5] or tardiness[6] occasioned by pregnancy than for absences or tardiness attributable to any other ailment or medical condition.

On the other hand, as *Guerra* held, the Act does not preempt state legislation that preferentially treats pregnant employees by affirmatively requiring employers to offer leave benefits to pregnancy-disabled employees that the employer does not offer to others.[7] The Court has since explained that the state statute in question was not preempted because it "was not inconsistent with the purposes of the ... [PDA] and did not require an act that was unlawful under Title VII."[8] Similarly, an employer is not forbidden from offering greater health insurance benefits for pregnancy than for other medical conditions as a matter of contract.[9] On the other hand, an employer may not give female parents child care leaves, keyed to childbirth rather than to pregnancy disability, if fathers are denied leave under similar circumstances.[10]

There are some tensions and apparent contradictions in the patchwork of holdings under the PDA. How, for example, could *Guerra* affirm that the PDA enacts a nondiscrimination principle but then sustain state-mandated preferential employer treatment of pregnancy-related disabilities as not inconsistent with PDA's purposes? Why should a woman asserting a PDA violation be relieved of showing that a man received better treatment, if PDA enshrines only a principle of nondiscrimination?[11] If, on the other hand, PDA contemplates preferential han-

5. *In re Carnegie Ctr. Assocs.*, 129 F.3d 290 (3d Cir.1997), *cert. denied sub nom Rhett v. Carnegie Ctr. Assocs.*, 524 U.S. 938, 118 S.Ct. 2342, 141 L.Ed.2d 714 (1998); *Bush v. Commonwealth Edison Co.*, 990 F.2d 928, 931 (7th Cir.1993), *cert. denied*, 511 U.S. 1071, 114 S.Ct. 1648, 128 L.Ed.2d 367 (1994); *Rush v. McDonald's Corp.*, 966 F.2d 1104, 1107 (7th Cir.1992).

6. *Troupe v. May Dep't Stores Co.*, 20 F.3d 734 (7th Cir.1994).

7. *California Fed. Sav. & Loan Ass'n v. Guerra*, 479 U.S. 272, 107 S.Ct. 683, 93 L.Ed.2d 613 (1987).

8. *Johnson Controls*, 499 U.S. at 209, 111 S.Ct. at 1209 (distinguishing the possible tort liability that might be imposed on an employer who obeys *Johnson Controls'* interpretation of the PDA by permitting a fertile employee to work at a job that might endanger the health of her fetus; such tort liability would be preempted because it would "punish employers for *complying* with Title VII's clear command") (citing *Florida Lime & Avocado Growers, Inc. v. Paul*, 373 U.S. 132, 142–43, 83 S.Ct. 1210, 1217–18, 10 L.Ed.2d 248 (1963)). *See* Grover, *The Employer's Fetal Injury Quandary After Johnson Controls*, 81 Ky.L.J. 639 (1992–93).

9. *Aubrey v. Aetna Life Ins. Co.*, 886 F.2d 119 (6th Cir.1989).

10. *Schafer v. Board of Pub. Educ.*, 903 F.2d 243 (3d Cir.1990); *Barnes v. Hewlett–Packard Co.*, 846 F.Supp. 442 (D.Md.1994).

11. Where an employer terminated an employee who, as the result of pregnancy complications, took an amount of sick leave that was within the limitations of the employer's stated leave policy, a circuit court held that she was not required to show that a nonpregnant employee was treated more favorably under similar circumstances. Rather, it was the employer's burden to show the "unusual scenario" that it had discharged others for using their allotted leave. *Byrd v. Lakeshore Hosp.*, 30 F.3d 1380 (11th Cir.1994). *Cf. Ensley–Gaines v. Runyon*, 100 F.3d 1220 (6th Cir.1996) (plaintiff need only show that she was similar to comparator with respect to ability or inability to work, not, as with other Title VII cases, that she was similarly situated in all respects). *But see Geier v. Medtronic, Inc.*, 99 F.3d 238 (7th Cir.1996) (insufficient for plaintiff to show that she was discharged because of her absences from work absent evidence that non-pregnant employees' absences were treated less harshly); *In re Carnegie Ctr. Assocs.*, 129 F.3d 290 (3d

dling of pregnancy, why have EEOC and lower courts limited the permissible preference to periods of actual physical disability, and not to subsequent child-rearing leaves? The answers reside in the awkward construction of PDA's text and the history antedating its enactment.

The legislative history reflects PDA's principal purposes: not only to overturn the result of *Gilbert*, which dealt with leaves for still-disabled pregnant workers, but also to assure that working women would not be treated adversely respecting pregnancy disability or benefits relative to employees with other disabilities. The two clauses of the first sentence of § 701(k) attempt to implement these purposes, the first clause by addressing *Gilbert*, the second by enshrining a broad principle of nondiscrimination:

> The terms "because of sex" or "on the basis of sex" include, but are not limited to, because of on or on the basis of pregnancy, childbirth, or related medical conditions; and women affected by pregnancy, childbirth, or related medical conditions shall be treated the same for all employment-related purposes ... as other persons not so affected but similar in their ability or inability to work.

The second clause, which the Court has read as merely illustrative of and not exhausting the reach of the first,[12] asserts the standard equal treatment or nondiscrimination principle characteristic of Title VII liability. Women affected by pregnancy-related medical conditions "shall be treated the same" as, but not better than, other employees with similarly disabling conditions. The definition in the first clause, by clarifying that the § 703(a) prohibition on discrimination against an individual "because of sex" includes discrimination based on "medical conditions" related to pregnancy or childbirth, takes care of the holding of *Gilbert*. But considered in isolation that clause may also be read to accord special treatment, at least for pregnancy-related *medical conditions*, since it requires no similarly situated male employee comparator.[13] Hence *Guerra* could plausibly assert, by reference to the second clause, that PDA does not by its own force require covered employers to offer pregnant workers better leaves than those offered others for similarly disabling conditions, and at the same time assert, by reference to the first clause, that PDA's "purposes" are not offended by state laws that mandate (or apparently by voluntary employer policies that offer) preferential treatment of pregnancy during a "period of *actual physical disability*."[14]

Cir.1997), *cert. denied sub nom Rhett v. Carnegie Ctr. Assocs.*, 524 U.S. 938, 118 S.Ct. 2342, 141 L.Ed.2d 714 (1998); *Piraino*, 137 F.3d 987. More recently, the Seventh Circuit has even more plainly insisted that a comparator be similarly situated in more ways than ability or inability to work. *Ilhardt v. Sara Lee Corp.*, 118 F.3d 1151 (7th Cir.1997) (PDA claim fails because there was no "part-time member of the law department ... with whom to compare her").

12. *Newport News Shipbuilding & Dry Dock Co. v. EEOC*, 462 U.S. 669, 679 n. 14,

103 S.Ct. 2622, 2629 n. 14, 77 L.Ed.2d 89 (1983). *Accord Guerra*, 479 U.S. at 284, 107 S.Ct. at 691.

13. *See, e.g., Newport News*, 462 U.S. at 684–685, 103 S.Ct. at 2631–2632 (asserting that PDA "has now made clear that, for all Title VII purposes, discrimination based on a woman's pregnancy is, on its face [and without more?], discrimination because of her sex.").

14. 479 U.S. at 290, 107 S.Ct. at 694 (emphasis in original).

By thus conferring somewhat schizoid protection, Congress has left the courts to unravel a number of related interpretive difficulties. Suppose an employer acknowledges that the plaintiff's pregnancy played a part in its decision not to hire her,[15] to place her on involuntary disability leave,[16] or even to terminate her,[17] but also demonstrates that the adverse action was taken in accordance with a neutral, evenly applied disability rule that would have disqualified similarly disabled men or other women. Here the equal treatment approach has prevailed and liability rejected. Indeed the pure equal treatment approach proceeds with the same 3–stage *McDonnell Douglas* order of proof as any other gender, race, national origin or religious discrimination claim. Under that mode of proof, it is the plaintiff that bears the ultimate burden of persuasion, in rebutting a legitimate, nondiscriminatory reason offered by the employer, to prove that the defendant's explanation was a pretext or, more directly, that pregnancy was a significant factor in the challenged decision.[18]

Where, on the other hand, the plaintiff simply produces evidence that the adverse action was based on pregnancy,[19] and the employer fails to offer comparative evidence involving the disabilities of other employees, the first clause of the PDA has supported the per se equation of distinctions based on pregnancy with discrimination "because of sex."[20]

15. *See Marafino v. St. Louis County Circuit Court*, 707 F.2d 1005 (8th Cir.1983). *Cf. Piantanida v. Wyman Ctr., Inc.*, 116 F.3d 340 (8th Cir.1997) (discrimination against plaintiff because she was a "new mom" was based on her choice to adopt the social role of child rearer, a choice also made by men and not based on a medical condition).

16. *EEOC v. Detroit–Macomb Hosp. Ctr.*, 952 F.2d 403 (6th Cir.1992).

17. *See Morrocco v. Goodwill Indus.*, 1993 WL 268625 (M.D.N.C.1993). *Cf. Boyd v. Harding Acad. of Memphis, Inc.*, 88 F.3d 410 (6th Cir.1996) (employer's termination of pregnant teacher held on basis of her extramarital sexual relationship, rather than her pregnancy, and hence not violative of Title VII, even though she was fired only when she became pregnant and not a year earlier when she had miscarried). The authors are indebted to Professors Zimmer and his colleagues for these three examples, set forth at Zimmer, Sullivan, Richards and Calloway's *Cases and Materials On Employment Discrimination* 540 (3d ed. Little Brown 1994).

18. *See, e.g. Cone v. Longmont United Hosp. Ass'n*, 14 F.3d 526, 529 (10th Cir. 1994).

19. It is not always self-evident if the employer took the challenged action "because" of pregnancy even when pregnancy is the visible trigger for invocation of a broader employer rule. *See, e.g., Marshall v. American Hosp. Ass'n*, 157 F.3d 520 (7th Cir.1998) (employee failed to show she was terminated due to her pregnancy and not because she planned an extended leave during the busiest time of her first year as director of organization); *Fleming v. Ayers & Assocs.*, 948 F.2d 993 (6th Cir.1991) (discharge of plaintiff because of the high medical costs of caring for her hydrocephalic child held not because of her pregnancy and indeed unrelated to the fact that plaintiff was a woman); *Marafino v. St. Louis County Circuit Court*, 707 F.2d 1005 (8th Cir. 1983) (employer demonstrated its practice not to hire anyone, including the pregnant plaintiff, who would require a leave soon after starting work). And plaintiff has the burden of showing the employer's knowledge of her pregnant status. *Geraci v. Moody–Tottrup Int'l, Inc.*, 82 F.3d 578 (3d Cir.1996).

20. *See, e.g., Byrd v. Lakeshore Hosp.*, 30 F.3d 1380 (11th Cir.1994); *Tamimi v. Howard Johnson Co.*, 807 F.2d 1550 (11th Cir.1987) (court found requirement that plaintiff wear makeup was attributable to her pregnancy and employer's view that she was "less attractive when pregnant"); *Maddox v. Grandview Care Ctr.*, 780 F.2d 987 (11th Cir.1986) (maternity leave, and none other, limited to three months).

In effect this was the path the Supreme Court followed in *International Union, U.A.W. v. Johnson Controls,*[21] where an employer rule denying women jobs in positions where they would encounter special levels of lead was applied only to fertile, not all women. Finally, the permission for employers to accord pregnancy preferential treatment that is inferable from the first clause is sharply circumscribed. *Guerra* is reasonably clear that PDA does not mandate such treatment, and so does not require an employer to afford reasonable accommodation to pregnancy by offering *any* leaves, benefits or relaxed work assignments that it does not offer to employees with other disabilities.[22] And *Guerra* also suggests that voluntary preferential treatment of pregnancy is probably offensive to the overarching Title VII principle of nondiscrimination when it relates to pregnancy-related circumstances other than associated medical conditions. Viewed this way, PDA eases proof of liability for pregnancy-based intentional discrimination, but carves out only a very limited arena for preferential treatment.

Although the legislative history of PDA focused on the health and medical requirements of female employees, a majority of the Court has held that the amendment also prohibits employer-sponsored health insurance provisions that exclude spousal pregnancies and thereby offer male employees inferior total coverage than their female co-workers.[23] PDA also proscribes discriminating against an employee for undergoing an abortion, either by terminating her employment or, apparently, denying her sick leave available for other medical disabilities. But PDA

---

21. 499 U.S. 187, 111 S.Ct. 1196, 113 L.Ed.2d 158 (1991).

22. *See, e.g., Armstrong v. Flowers Hosp., Inc.,* 33 F.3d 1308 (11th Cir.1994) (PDA did not require a hospital to accommodate a pregnant nurse's request that she be reassigned so as not to have to treat a patient with AIDS, because PDA does not require preferential treatment). Similarly, the PDA does not confer immunity on a pregnant employee from the ordinary consequences of employer decisions taken for reasons unrelated to her pregnancy. *Smith v. F.W. Morse & Co.,* 76 F.3d 413 (1st Cir.1996) (plaintiff's position eliminated during her pregnancy because manager concluded position was redundant; fact that this decision coincided with pregnancy and followed manager's questions about the plaintiff's plans to have more children generated inference of discriminatory animus for trier of fact to resolve but did not suffice to establish a per se violation of PDA). *But cf. Atchley v. Nordam Group, Inc.,* 180 F.3d 1143, 1148 (10th Cir.1999) (corporate reorganization defense rejected where evidence showed that similarly situated but nonpregnant employees were granted leave and reinstated, with plaintiff the sole employee displaced by an alleged "restructuring"); *Quaratino v. Tiffany & Co.,* 71 F.3d 58 (2d Cir.1995) (position-elimination defense may

be overcome by evidence that management considered replacing plaintiff well before her leave commenced and interviewed a non-pregnant woman for her job).

23. *Newport News Shipbuilding and Dry Dock Co. v. EEOC,* 462 U.S. 669, 103 S.Ct. 2622, 77 L.Ed.2d 89 (1983). This result is also somewhat strange in view of the text and history of PDA. The first clause, defining "because of sex," works in tandem with the § 703(a) prohibition on discrimination against an individual concerning "his" (or, where appropriate, "her") terms or conditions of employment because of "such individual's" gender. That clause doesn't easily fit the facts of *Newport News,* where the employer deprived male employees of a benefit not by reference to their own gender but because of the pregnant condition, and hence under § 701(k) the gender, of their spouses. The second clause is no more easily adapted to *Newport News.* The "women affected by pregnancy" there were the plaintiffs' spouses, not employees of the defendant employer. How, then, could they have been treated differently from "other persons not so affected but similar in their ability or inability to work"?

explicitly relieves employers from subsidizing abortions through health insurance benefits, except in cases of "medical complications" or "where the life of the mother would be endangered if the fetus were carried to term."

Courts are still exploring the full reaches of the medical conditions related to pregnancy with respect to which the PDA applies. In *International Union, U.A.W. v. Johnson Controls*,[24] the Supreme Court held prima facie violative of PDA employer policies precluding fertile women from holding certain jobs in which their fetuses would be exposed to workplace environment health risks. Employers justified these rules as necessary to protect employees' fetuses or offspring from health risks, or to protect the employer from tort liability in the event employees' fetuses or children suffered injury that could be traced to the workplace. In effect the Court treated a woman's potential *capacity* to become pregnant as pregnancy itself or one of her[25] "related medical conditions" that triggers PDA protection. Presumably, then, *Johnson Controls* also provides support for the preexisting lower court decisions that have treated childrearing within the broad concept of "related medical conditions." Citing *Johnson Controls*, a district court has recently swept within PDA's embrace discrimination against a woman who was absent from work because of treatments for infertility. The opinion reasoned that she, too, was discriminated against because of "potential or intended pregnancy"; her inability to become pregnant without medical intervention was akin to the natural ability of fertile women to become pregnant that was protected in *Johnson Controls*.[26] But under the compromise course the courts have steered between the two key clauses of § 701(k), medical or physical conditions on the fore or aft periphery of pregnancy should be handled under the nondiscrimination principle, with voluntary employer preference reserved for the sphere of the plaintiff's own actual physical disability.[27]

24. 499 U.S. 187, 111 S.Ct. 1196, 113 L.Ed.2d 158 (1991).

25. Where an employer discharged a woman because of the high medical costs of caring for her child, however, no liability was found because, the court reasoned, "related medical conditions" as used in PDA refers to conditions of "pregnant women, not conditions of the resulting offspring." *Fleming v. Ayers & Assocs.*, 948 F.2d at 996–97. Similarly, the Supreme Court observed in passing in *Newport News* that an employer's exclusion of benefits for the pregnancy-related medical expenses of relatives, as distinct from spouses, would not violate PDA. Denying benefits to those relatives—daughters or mothers, for example—would adversely affect the terms and conditions of female as well as male employees, whereas denial of benefits for the pregnancy-related expenses of spouses adversely affects male employees only.

26. *Pacourek v. Inland Steel Co.*, 858 F.Supp. 1393 (N.D.Ill.1994). And a circuit court has held that PDA protects employees from termination not only for exercising the right to have an abortion, but, by analogous extension from *Johnson Controls*, also for contemplating an abortion. *Turic v. Holland Hospitality, Inc.*, 85 F.3d 1211 (6th Cir.1996).

27. Thus a circuit court has rejected the reasoning of *Pacourek*, 858 F.Supp. 1393, reasoning that infertility (unlike potential pregnancy) is not related to sex, at least where the policy is or might be applied to exclude health care benefits to infertile males as well as females. *Krauel v. Iowa Methodist Med. Ctr.*, 95 F.3d 674 (8th Cir. 1996). *See also Piantanida v. Wyman Ctr., Inc.*, 116 F.3d 340 (8th Cir.1997) (discrimination against plaintiff based on her choice to care for her newly born child is not a "medical condition" related to pregnancy or childbirth).

While PDA thus does not compel employers covered by Title VII to afford maternity leaves or benefits not provided for other disabilities, the Family & Medical Leave Act of 1993[28] requires employers with 50 or more employees to permit eligible employees, female and male alike, to take up to twelve weeks of unpaid leave per year after the birth or adoption of a child, as well as for serious health emergencies affecting the employee or his close relatives.[29]

§ 2.32 Fetal Vulnerability Rules

Because, as just observed, fetal vulnerability rules are prima facie subject to PDA, they must be treated as a form of express gender discrimination that can survive scrutiny only if they pass muster under the BFOQ defense. That, however, is unlikely under traditional BFOQ standards, since protection of employees' offspring would not normally be essential to the operation of an employer's business. In order to uphold these rules as a matter of public policy or personal morality, courts sometimes modified the BFOQ requirements or permitted the policies to be defended as though they were neutral practices.[1] EEOC also took the position that even though the discrimination resulting from fetal protection policies is expressly gender based, employers should not be restricted to the BFOQ defense but should be permitted to justify those policies under the somewhat less stringent standard of "business necessity."[2]

The Supreme Court has since definitively rejected these end-runs around the PDA, ruling that fetal protection policies exclude fertile women from employment opportunities on the basis of gender and are accordingly defensible only as BFOQs. Further, the Court stringently applied the BFOQ defense. In attempting to prove that fertile employees lacked essential job qualifications, employers had sought to justify their exclusion by invoking protection of the fetus. The Court held that the safety of an employee's fetus, as distinct from the safety of plant visitors or customers, is not essential to the operation of the employer's business in the sense meant by the BFOQ defense.[3] Perhaps the broadest significance of *Johnson Controls* is its explication of dual requirements for any BFOQ. Not only must the employer's gender-, religion- or national origin-based exclusion substantially relate to the plaintiff's ability to

---

28. Pub.L.No. 103–3, 29 U.S.C.A. §§ 2601–2654.

29. For details about the eligibility requirements and ancillary protections surrounding the leaves mandated by FMLA, as well as funding provisions, see Malin, *Fathers and Parental Leave,* 72 Tex.L.Rev. 1047, 1079 et seq. (1994).

§ 2.32

1. *See International Union, UAW v. Johnson Controls,* 886 F.2d 871 (7th Cir. 1989), *reversed by,* 499 U.S. 187, 111 S.Ct. 1196, 113 L.Ed.2d 158 (1991); *cf. Hayes v.*

Shelby Memorial Hosp., 726 F.2d 1543 (11th Cir.1984) (invalidating employer policy despite relaxed standards).

2. *EEOC: Policy Statement of Reproductive and Fetal Hazards Under Title VII,* (10/7/88). *But cf. EEOC: Policy Guide on Supreme Court's Johnson Controls Decision,* 405 FEP Man. 6941 (6/28/91) (reinstating BFOQ standard after *Johnson Controls*).

3. *International Union, UAW v. Johnson Controls, Inc.,* 499 U.S. 187, 111 S.Ct. 1196, 113 L.Ed.2d 158 (1991).

perform her particular job; it must also go to the "essence" or "central mission" of the employer's business.[4]

§ 2.33 Seniority Systems

Two unarguably neutral practices are singled out for special treatment by the text of Title VII. Section 703(h) provides that "notwithstanding any other provision" of Title VII, an employer does not commit an unlawful employment practice by imposing different terms or conditions of employment pursuant to a bona fide seniority or merit system. The employer is immune from liability even if the effect or impact of these systems falls more heavily on the plaintiff's protected group. Judicial construction of these provisions, however, has afforded far greater protection for seniority and merit systems than for professionally developed ability tests.

Unless the plaintiff is able to prove that a seniority system was initially adopted or maintained with a specific discriminatory purpose, and is thus not "bona fide," a seniority system cannot be the basis of employer liability.[1] And such a system is lawful even though it was first *adopted* after the enactment of Title VII.[2] Absent proof of discriminatory purpose by the employer and union in adopting or maintaining such a system, § 703(h) insulates a bona fide seniority system from being declared an unlawful employment practice notwithstanding that it perpetuates underlying hiring, assignment or promotion discrimination that took place before or even after the effective date of Title VII.[3] Thus a bona fide system may not be dismantled wholesale by declaratory judgment or injunction. But where other, primary unlawful employment practices are proved—hiring, assignment, or promotion discrimination, for example—courts have the remedial authority in effect to adjust the system's seniority ladder incrementally by awarding retroactive seniority for bidding or other competitive purposes to proven victims of discrimination.[4]

A system will not forfeit its status as bona fide merely because it has the effect of disproportionately "locking in" minority employees to lower paying or less skilled positions—for example, by discouraging them from transferring to better jobs in separate bargaining units where they might forfeit accumulated seniority with the company. The mere impact of the system does not standing alone demonstrate the requisite discriminatory

4. 499 U.S. at 201, 111 S.Ct. at 1204. *Johnson Controls* is discussed in greater detail in connection with the § 703(e)(2) exemption for religious institutions treated above and, especially, the defense of "bona fide occupational qualification" in Chapter 3.

§ 2.33

1. *International Bhd. of Teamsters v. United States*, 431 U.S. 324, 97 S.Ct. 1843, 52 L.Ed.2d 396 (1977).

2. *American Tobacco Co. v. Patterson*, 456 U.S. 63, 102 S.Ct. 1534, 71 L.Ed.2d 748 (1982); *United Air Lines, Inc. v. Evans*, 431 U.S. 553, 97 S.Ct. 1885, 52 L.Ed.2d 571 (1977).

3. *Teamsters*, 431 U.S. 324, 97 S.Ct. 1843, 52 L.Ed.2d 396.

4. *See* the discussion in Chapter 4 of *Franks v. Bowman Transp. Company*, 424 U.S. 747, 96 S.Ct. 1251, 47 L.Ed.2d 444 (1976), as modified by the remedial portion of the *Teamsters* opinion.

purpose.[5] Factors in assessing a system's bona fides include whether it discourages different protected groups equally from transferring between units; whether, if the seniority units are in separate bargaining units, the bargaining unit structure is rational and conforms to industry practice; whether the system has its "genesis" in prohibited discrimination; and whether subsequent negotiations that have maintained the system were tainted by unlawful motivation.[6]

The Court has broadly interpreted the kinds of collectively bargained arrangements that qualify as "seniority systems" entitled to the special protection of § 703(h). For example, a requirement that an employee work for a specified time *before* entering the permanent employee seniority ladder has itself been held to constitute part of a protected seniority system.[7] On occasion, however, a plaintiff has succeeded in sidestepping § 703(h) by framing a challenge to an employer decision that is related to but distinct from the functioning of a seniority system.[8]

The seniority system defense is bolstered in procedural ways as well. First, even though the structure and text of § 703(h) appear to create a true affirmative defense, the employer does not have to persuade the court that the system is bona fide. The employer is well advised to plead the defense affirmatively in its answer. But in response to a plaintiff's prima facie evidence that a facially neutral system had disproportionate adverse impact, the employer need only prove that the personnel decision in question was made pursuant to that system.[9] To overcome the defense the *plaintiff* must then prove by a preponderance that the system is *not* bona fide.[10] Second, the Supreme Court has held that trial court determinations about the adopters' intent—the ultimate issue on the bona fides of a seniority system—are unmixed findings of fact, reversible under Federal Rule of Civil Procedure 52(a) only if "clearly erroneous."[11]

5. *Teamsters*, 431 U.S. 324, 97 S.Ct. 1843, 52 L.Ed.2d 396; *James v. Stockham Valves & Fittings*, 559 F.2d 310, 352 (5th Cir.1977), *cert. denied*, 434 U.S. 1034, 98 S.Ct. 767, 54 L.Ed.2d 781 (1978). An apparent exception is represented by *EEOC v. E.I. Du Pont de Nemours & Co.*, 1992 WL 465707 (W.D.Ky.1992), where the court relied heavily on the fact that more than 98% of the higher paying jobs were held by white employees in condemning as nonbona fide a seniority system that had been in operation for fifteen years, including eight years after the effective date of Title VII.

6. *James*, 559 F.2d at 352.

7. *California Brewers Ass'n v. Bryant*, 444 U.S. 598, 100 S.Ct. 814, 63 L.Ed.2d 55 (1980). *But see Mitchell v. Jefferson County Bd. of Educ.*, 936 F.2d 539 (11th Cir.1991) (salary schedule that called for annual step increase held not part of a seniority system).

8. *See, e.g., Council 31, American Federation of State, County and Mun. Employees v. Ward*, 978 F.2d 373 (7th Cir.1992) (challenge to employer's decision to lay off employees in a particular office held not to constitute a challenge to the seniority system that governed how those layoffs were implemented).

9. In this respect the seniority system defense is treated procedurally much like the affirmative action plan "defense." See Chapter 4, *infra*.

10. *See Firefighters, Inc. for Racial Equality v. Bach*, 611 F.Supp. 166 (D.Colo. 1985); Hillman, *Teamsters, California Brewers and Beyond: Seniority Systems and Allocations of the Burden of Proving Bona Fides*, 54 St. Johns L.Rev. 706 (1980).

11. *Pullman–Standard v. Swint*, 456 U.S. 273, 102 S.Ct. 1781, 72 L.Ed.2d 66 (1982).

The intensity of the Supreme Court's commitment to insulate seniority systems from injunction was most recently evidenced by a decision, *Lorance v. AT & T Technologies*,[12] that the limitations period for a claim attacking the bona fides of a seniority system runs from the date a system is adopted, even if the plaintiff could not then have anticipated harm from the system or for that matter first became employed thereafter. Section 112 of the Civil Rights Act of 1991 overrules *Lorance* by providing statute of limitations accrual dates later than the original adoption of an intentionally discriminatory, collectively bargained seniority system. Where applicable, the limitations period on such a claim will now begin to run only when the plaintiff became subject to the system's challenged provision or, later still, when that provision was first applied to the plaintiff.[13] This change aids attacks on seniority systems, but only on those that discriminate intentionally; the legislation leaves undisturbed the Court's holdings[14] that a system's mere adverse effect on a group is immune from Title VII challenge.

§ 2.34   Professionally Developed Ability Tests

Section 703(h) also permits employers to act upon the results of a "professionally developed ability test." But in sharp contrast to the great deference shown seniority systems, the judicial protection accorded these tests has been inconsistent. In many cases it has proven even *more* difficult for an employer to defend the adverse impact of a paper-and-pencil test than to avoid liability for other neutral practices. This is because, soon after Title VII became effective, the EEOC issued "guidelines" on employee selection procedures that require employers to conduct highly technical and demanding "validation" studies of ability tests to demonstrate that they reliably pinpoint desired employee traits essential to a particular job. The Supreme Court's deferral to those guidelines in *Albemarle Paper Co. v. Moody*[1] required employers to incur considerable expense in validation efforts before they could safely hinge employment decisions on the results of tests having significant differential adverse impact.

Lower courts have since somewhat eased validation requirements, holding that employers need not slavishly adhere to the difficult and complex EEOC guidelines. Instead employers may defend more generally with evidence that tests are "predictive of or significantly correlated with important elements of work behavior ... relevant to the job ... for which candidates are being evaluated."[2] Nevertheless, even this version

12. 490 U.S. 900, 109 S.Ct. 2261, 104 L.Ed.2d 961 (1989).

13. Section 112 (amending Title VII § 706(e), 42 U.S.C.A. § 2000e–5(e) (1988)).

14. *Pullman–Standard v. Swint*, 456 U.S. 273, 102 S.Ct. 1781, 72 L.Ed.2d 66 (1982); *California Brewers Ass'n v. Bryant*, 444 U.S. 598, 100 S.Ct. 814, 63 L.Ed.2d 55 (1980); *United Air Lines, Inc. v. Evans*, 431 U.S. 553, 97 S.Ct. 1885, 52 L.Ed.2d 571 (1977); *International Bhd. of Teamsters v. United States*, 431 U.S. 324, 97 S.Ct. 1843, 52 L.Ed.2d 396 (1977).

§ 2.34

1. 422 U.S. 405, 430, 95 S.Ct. 2362, 2378, 45 L.Ed.2d 280 (1975).

2. *Contreras v. City of Los Angeles*, 656 F.2d 1267 (9th Cir.1981), *cert. denied*, 455 U.S. 1021, 102 S.Ct. 1719, 72 L.Ed.2d 140

of the validation defense places a considerably greater burden on an employer than merely producing evidence that "a challenged practice serves, in a significant way," one of many possible "legitimate employment goals."[3]

By its terms the Civil Rights Act of 1991, in an effort to restore the rigor of the defense, requires employers to justify the adverse impact of a particularly identified neutral practice by demonstrating the practice to be "job related for the position in question and consistent with business necessity...."[4] If the courts should abandon the relaxed scrutiny delineated by *Contreras* and hold professionally developed ability tests either to the new statutory standard or to strict compliance with the EEOC guidelines, employers would once again find it considerably more difficult to justify those tests than § 703(h) apparently intended. The 1991 amendments do not address validation standards in particular, but add a prohibition against the practice known as "race norming." The Act makes it unlawful in selecting, referring, or promoting employees to adjust or use different cutoff scores or otherwise alter test results because of race, color, religion, sex or national origin.

The Civil Rights Act of 1991 specifically forbids employers to use the employment related test in a way that would expand employment opportunities for minorities. Such tests have long been held unlawful when they disproportionately screen out applicants or employees on the basis of race, sex, religion or national origin and the employer cannot justify their use through a job-relatedness or business necessity defense. As a remedy for such violations, courts sometimes ordered employers not to fill vacancies on a rank-order basis but instead to fill them from among candidates with examination scores that fell within specified "bands" or ranges, in order to minimize the differential impact.[5] The new legislation does not directly attack this judicial remedy, and indeed one section specifically reaffirms "court-ordered remedies, affirmative action, or conciliation agreements, that are in accordance with the law."[6] Yet it adds a provision that makes it an unlawful employment practice for an employer itself "to adjust the scores of, use different cutoff scores

(1982). This formulation is quite similar to the Supreme Court's description of the business necessity defense to a neutral practice in *New York City Transit Auth. v. Beazer*, 440 U.S. 568, 99 S.Ct. 1355, 59 L.Ed.2d 587 (1979). *See* § 3.35, *infra*. Other moderate applications of the defense to disproportionately adversely impacting tests include *Williams v. Ford Motor Co.*, 187 F.3d 533 (6th Cir.1999) (pre-employment test used to screen for unskilled hourly workers held both content-and criterion-related and hence valid under EEOC's testing Guidelines, 29 C.F.R. § 1607.5(A)); *Allen v. Entergy Corp.*, 181 F.3d 902 (8th Cir.), *cert. denied*, 528 U.S. 1068, 120 S.Ct. 618, 145 L.Ed.2d 512 (1999) (aptitude tests used to select employees for layoff in RIF job-related, valid and consistent with Guidelines).

But cf. Lanning v. Southeastern Pa. Transp. Auth., 181 F.3d 478 (3d Cir.1999), *cert. denied*, 528 U.S. 1131, 120 S.Ct. 970, 145 L.Ed.2d 840 (2000) (discriminatory cutoff score on entry-level exams must be validated to measure the minimal qualifications of the jobs for which they screen).

3. *Wards Cove Packing Co. v. Atonio*, 490 U.S. 642, 109 S.Ct. 2115, 104 L.Ed.2d 733 (1989).

4. *See* Chapter 3, below.

5. *See, e.g., Bridgeport Guardians, Inc. v. City of Bridgeport*, 933 F.2d 1140 (2d Cir.), *cert. denied*, 502 U.S. 924, 112 S.Ct. 337, 116 L.Ed.2d 277 (1991).

6. Section 116.

for, or otherwise alter the results of, employment related tests'' on any of the prohibited grounds of discrimination.[7] Apparently, then, it is now specifically unlawful for an employer to do directly what a court may order it to do in order to offset the discriminatory effects of an employment related test.[8]

§§ 2.35–5.39 [Reserved]

F. RETALIATION

§ 2.40 In General

To protect employees who seek to vindicate their rights under § 703, a separate provision, § 704(a), broadly prohibits retaliation. Two basic species of conduct are protected: 1) participation in any administrative or judicial investigation, proceeding, or hearing to enforce Title VII rights; and 2) less formal, but good faith opposition to practices that an employee reasonably believes to be prohibited by the Act.

Once conduct is characterized as protected, the prima facie case is straightforward. The plaintiff must produce evidence of (1) her voluntary or involuntary[1] participation in proceedings authorized by Title VII,[2] or her opposition to what she reasonably and in good faith believes is one or more *apparently* prohibited practices (the practice opposed must be one

---

7. Section 106 (amending § 703 of Title VII, 42 U.S.C.A. § 2000e–2).

8. In between are cases where an employer adopts banding on its own initiative but does so in order to achieve goals set forth in a consent decree. *See Officers for Justice v. Civil Serv. Comm'n of San Francisco*, 979 F.2d 721 (9th Cir.1992), *cert. denied*, 507 U.S. 1004, 113 S.Ct. 1645, 123 L.Ed.2d 267 (1993) (banding upheld, without regard to § 106 of the 1991 Act, as a measure that did not violate Title VII or the Equal Protection Clause because of the city's past discrimination).

If employers can band when ordered to do so by a court, but not on their own, § 106 represents a reverse twist on the respective roles of employers and courts with respect to affirmative action. With certain constraints, an employer is generally free to favor black or female applicants or employees on grounds of race or gender under the terms of a voluntary affirmative action plan adopted despite the absence of any past employer violation of Title VII; put otherwise, the employer can act where the court would be without any authority to order any remedy. *See United Steelworkers of America v. Weber*, 443 U.S. 193, 99 S.Ct. 2721, 61 L.Ed.2d 480 (1979) and *Johnson v. Transportation Agency*, 480 U.S. 616, 107 S.Ct. 1442, 94 L.Ed.2d 615 (1987).

It is possible, however, that although the language of the new ban on race norming or score adjustment defines only an "unlawful employment practice" that might be committed by a "respondent," it will ultimately be held to ban such measures as part of a court-ordered remedy. Dole Interpretive Memorandum, *supra*, § 2.22, "Section 9. Discriminatory Use of Test Scores."

§ 2.40

1. *See Merritt v. Dillard Paper Co.*, 120 F.3d 1181, 1185 (11th Cir.1997) (plaintiff protected from retaliation for giving testimony damaging to employer defending sexual harassment case where he testified involuntarily with no intention to help the victim).

2. And under the participation clause, it apparently does not matter whether the allegations in the original charge were invalid or unreasonable. *See, e.g., Wyatt v. Boston*, 35 F.3d 13 (1st Cir.1994); *Sias v. City Demonstration Agency*, 588 F.2d 692, 695 (9th Cir.1978) (it is "well settled" that participation clause protects an employee regardless of the merit of his or her EEOC charge); *Pettway v. American Cast Iron Pipe Co.*, 411 F.2d 998, 1007 (5th Cir.1969) (fact that employee made false and malicious statements in his EEOC charge is irrelevant).

"made an unlawful employment practice by" Title VII,[3] although the plaintiff may prevail even if the employer was not in fact violating the statute);[4] (2) her employer's awareness of her[5] protected participation or

3. Thus, for example, there is no Title VII claim for age-based retaliation. *Lennon v. Rubin*, 166 F.3d 6 (1st Cir.1999). *See also Artis v. Francis Howell N. Band Booster Ass'n, Inc.*, 161 F.3d 1178, 1183 (8th Cir. 1998) (Title VII's retaliation provisions do not protect plaintiff who complains of a potential Title IX violation involving the harassment of an African–American student). And where the practice a police officer plaintiff opposed was discrimination directed by other officers against citizens, his retaliation claim was not cognizable because he could not have reasonably believed that discrimination against non-employees was a practice prohibited by Title VII. *Wimmer v. Suffolk County*, 176 F.3d 125 (2d Cir.), *cert. denied*, 528 U.S. 964, 120 S.Ct. 398, 145 L.Ed.2d 310 (1999).

4. It is settled that the practice the § 704 plaintiff opposed need not have violated Title VII in order for her opposition to it to be protected. *See, e.g., Taylor v. Runyon*, 175 F.3d 861 (11th Cir.1999) (a reasonable good faith belief that the alleged conduct was actionable is sufficient); *Jennings v. Tinley Park Community Consolidated Sch. Dist. No. 146*, 864 F.2d 1368 (7th Cir.1988); *Sias v. City Demonstration Agency*, 588 F.2d 692 (9th Cir.1978). But the requirement that opposition be to a practice "made an unlawful employment practice" by Title VII probably means that a retaliation claim cannot succeed if it is based on opposition to conduct that generically is not even arguably prohibited by Title VII or took place when the employer was not subject to its regulation. *See Winsey v. Pace College*, 394 F.Supp. 1324 (S.D.N.Y.1975) (opposition claim fails because conduct plaintiff opposed occurred before employer became subject to Title VII and therefore could not have been made unlawful by the statute). *See also* Schlei and Grossman, *Employment Discrimination Law* 543 n.38, 547 (describing *Winsey* as involving a plaintiff mistake of law rather than fact) (2d ed. 1983). Some courts require only that plaintiff protested with a good faith, but not necessarily reasonable belief that the practices she opposed were unlawful. *Monteiro v. Poole Silver Co.*, 615 F.2d 4 (1st Cir.1980) Others require that while the plaintiff need not demonstrate that the conduct she protested was an unlawful employment practice, her belief that the conduct was unlawful must be reasonable. *Berg v. La Crosse Cooler Co.*, 612 F.2d 1041 (7th Cir.1980). *Accord Trent v. Valley Elec. Ass'n Inc.*, 41

F.3d 524 (9th Cir.1994); *Folkerson v. Circus Circus Enters. Inc.*, 107 F.3d 754 (9th Cir. 1997) (even though sexual harassment of plaintiff by casino patron was arguably actionable, she lacked sufficient provocation to hit him and could not reasonably have believed that his advances were condoned by management, dooming her claim that her termination after hitting him was retaliatory). Some courts require both good faith and reasonableness. In the Eleventh Circuit, for activity to be protected within the meaning of the opposition clause, the plaintiff must have been reasonable in her belief that the activity she opposed is unlawful, a test that "must be measured against existing substantive law." *Clover v. Total System Servs., Inc.*, 176 F.3d 1346, 1351 (11th Cir.1999) (opposition not protected where plaintiff opposed intersexual flirtation directed against third party that court deemed an innocuous, routine exchange not sufficiently severe or pervasive to rise to the hostile or abusive level required for actionable sexual harassment) (citing *Harper v. Blockbuster Entertainment Corp.*, 139 F.3d 1385, 1388 n. 2 (11th Cir.), *cert. denied*, 525 U.S. 1000, 119 S.Ct. 509, 142 L.Ed.2d 422 (1998)). This means that the conduct the plaintiff opposes must be "close enough" to conduct that Title VII in fact condemns to support an objectively reasonable belief about its unlawfulness. Thus this standard charges a lay plaintiff with a degree of knowledge of the substantive law, and deprives her of protection if her understanding of Title VII departs substantially from a court's post hoc understanding of its requirements. And plaintiff's conduct, to be protected, can be founded only on what he knew occurred in the workplace, not also on what may in fact have happened of which plaintiff was unaware. *See also Little v. United Technologies*, 103 F.3d 956 (11th Cir.1997) (plaintiff must have good faith and reasonable belief that the employer was engaged in an unlawful employment practice); *Tipton v. Canadian Imperial Bank of Commerce*, 872 F.2d 1491 (11th Cir.1989); *Rucker v. Higher Educational Aids Bd.*, 669 F.2d 1179 (7th Cir.1982).

5. It appears that the plaintiff is protected even if she was not the person opposing or participating, as long as the participating or opposing person is closely related to the plaintiff. *See, e.g., EEOC Guidance on Investigating, Analyzing Retaliation Claims*, May 20, 1998; *Murphy v. Cadillac*

opposition;[6] (3) an adverse employment decision thereafter; and (4) a causal connection between the adverse employment action and the protected opposition or participation.[7] Evidence that the adverse action was taken shortly after the protected participation or opposition fortifies[8] or perhaps suffices to show the required causal link;[9] the passage of several years between the protected conduct and the act of alleged retaliation may defeat the inference of retaliatory motive;[10] but the passage of a substantial period of time does not conclusively refute the possibility of the required causation.[11] A plaintiff creates a jury question

Rubber & Plastics, Inc., 946 F.Supp. 1108 (W.D.N.Y.1996) (husband protected when wife is participating or opposing); *EEOC v. Ohio Edison Co.,* 7 F.3d 541 (6th Cir.1993) (plaintiff protected when representative of employee engaged in opposition); *McDonnell v. Cisneros,* 84 F.3d 256 (7th Cir.1996) (male employee stated cause of action for retaliation, when he alleged that employer retaliated against him for failing to prevent subordinate from filing sexual harassment complaint). *Cf. Karcher v. Emerson Elec. Co.,* 94 F.3d 502 (8th Cir.1996), *cert. denied* 520 U.S. 1210, 117 S.Ct. 1692, 137 L.Ed.2d 820 (1997) (employee-plaintiff may maintain action for retaliation directed against her because of the protected activity she engaged in to protest ill treatment of her co-employee husband). *But see Holt v. JTM Indus., Inc.,* 89 F.3d 1224 (5th Cir.1996), *cert. denied,* 520 U.S. 1229, 117 S.Ct. 1821, 137 L.Ed.2d 1029 (1997) (employee-spouse lacks standing to complain about retaliation he suffered solely in respect of protected activity engaged in by his co-employee wife).

6. *But see Cross v. Cleaver,* 142 F.3d 1059 (8th Cir.1998) (liability may lie against an employer whenever a supervisory employee uses that authority to retaliate even if the employee cannot prove the employer knew of the supervisor's retaliatory motive; thus, an employer is automatically vicariously liable for retaliation by an agent with authority to affect the plaintiff's tangible work environment).

7. *See, e.g., Mattern v. Eastman Kodak Co.,* 104 F.3d 702 (5th Cir.), *cert. denied,* 522 U.S. 932, 118 S.Ct. 336, 139 L.Ed.2d 260 (1997); *Little v. United Technologies,* 103 F.3d 956 (11th Cir.1997) (requiring protected activity, adverse action, and a causal link between the two); *Simmons v. Camden County Bd. of Educ.,* 757 F.2d 1187 (11th Cir.), *cert. denied,* 474 U.S. 981, 106 S.Ct. 385, 88 L.Ed.2d 338 (1985); *EEOC v. Crown Zellerbach Corp.,* 720 F.2d 1008, 1012 (9th Cir.1983). *But see Azzaro v. County of Allegheny,* 110 F.3d 968, 972 (3d Cir.1997) (eliminating "adverse term" element in a discharge case, and subsuming

"employer awareness" element within causal link requirement). *See also Aviles v. Cornell Forge Co.,* 183 F.3d 598 (7th Cir.1999) (retaliation against plaintiff for filing EEOC charge actionable even where no adverse employment action taken but employer falsely told police plaintiff was armed and threatening harm near the workplace).

8. *See, e.g., Farrell v. Planters Lifesavers Co.,* 206 F.3d 271, 283–84 (3d Cir.2000); *EEOC v. L.B. Foster Co.,* 123 F.3d 746, 753–55 (3d Cir.1997), *cert. denied,* 522 U.S. 1147, 118 S.Ct. 1163, 140 L.Ed.2d 174 (1998) (noting that the plaintiff had established a prima facie case of retaliation based on temporal proximity between the events plus inconsistencies in the defendant's testimony, certain conduct towards others, and refusals to provide a reference for the plaintiff).

9. *See Berman v. Orkin Exterminating Co., Inc.,* 160 F.3d 697 (11th Cir.1998) (causal link found where employee was transferred and his sales territory was reduced within two months of filing EEOC charge of religious discrimination).

10. *See Caudillo v. Continental Bank/ Bank of America Illinois,* 191 F.3d 455 (7th Cir.), *cert. denied,* 528 U.S. 1048, 120 S.Ct. 584, 145 L.Ed.2d 485 (1999) (fifteen months period is too long to raise an inference of retaliation); *Chavez v. Arvada,* 88 F.3d 861 (10th Cir.1996), *cert. denied,* 519 U.S. 1056, 117 S.Ct. 684, 136 L.Ed.2d 608 (1997) (ten year interval between filing of charge and nonpromotion excessive, absent evidence tying employer action to the protected activity); *Candelaria v. EG & G Energy Measurements, Inc.,* 33 F.3d 1259 (10th Cir.1994).

11. *Shirley v. Chrysler First, Inc.,* 970 F.2d 39 (5th Cir.1992). *Cf. Smith v. St. Louis Univ.,* 109 F.3d 1261 (8th Cir.1997) (passage of six months between protected activity and imposition of adverse term of employment may weaken inference of retaliation, but does not by itself foreclose claim); *Causey v. Balog,* 162 F.3d 795 (4th Cir.1998) (thirteen month interval between the charge and termination is too long to

on causation with evidence, including circumstantial evidence, that an employer decisionmaker was aware of the protected activity or expression at the time it took the adverse action;[12] and temporal proximity between the protected activity and the adverse action may permit the jury to find the required causal link.[13] It is thus critical for the plaintiff to offer evidence that one or more employer representatives whom the court will recognize as an ultimate decisionmaker had actual or constructive awareness of the protected opposition or participation, not merely of the conduct the plaintiff opposed.

Once the employee satisfies her prima facie burden, the resulting presumption of retaliation must be rebutted by the employer by producing evidence of a legitimate nondiscriminatory reason for the adverse employment action. If the employer meets this burden, the presumption of retaliation disappears, and the plaintiff must present evidence sufficient to prove to the fact finder that the reason proffered by the employer was a pretext for unlawful retaliation.[14] Section 703(m), the "mixed motives" provision that relieves an employer of retroactive relief when it demonstrates that it would have taken the same action apart from an unlawful ground, includes among such grounds only "race, color, religion, sex, or national origin," with no mention of retaliation. Nevertheless, as discussed below, an employer may mount a mixed-motive defense to retaliation on the terms provided by § 703(m) or under pre-existing law.

The "opposition" right has been subject to a number of fact-sensitive qualifications, developed case by case, concerning the lawful-

establish causation absent other evidence of retaliation). The Third Circuit commented that its own case law is "seemingly split" as to whether temporal proximity between the protected activity and the alleged retaliatory act can be sufficient in itself to create an inference of a causal connection for the purposes of a prima facie case of retaliation. This split, the court stated, is not an inconsistency in the analysis but demonstrates that the analysis is essentially fact-based. *See Farrell v. Planters Lifesavers Co.,* 206 F.3d 271, 279 (3d Cir.2000).

12. The burden is on the plaintiff to show that the decisionmaker knew of the protected activity. *See Sullivan v. National R.R. Passenger Corp.,* 170 F.3d 1056 (11th Cir.), *cert. denied,* 528 U.S. 966, 120 S.Ct. 402, 145 L.Ed.2d 314 (1999) (reversing jury verdict in the absence of evidence that decisionmaker knew of protected activity at time of adverse employment action). *See also Haynes v. Pennzoil Co.,* 207 F.3d 296 (5th Cir.2000) (no proof defendant knew of EEOC charge when plaintiff was terminated).

13. *Clover v. Total System Servs., Inc.,* 176 F.3d 1346 (11th Cir.1999), reaffirming (but factually distinguishing) *Goldsmith v.* *City of Atmore,* 996 F.2d 1155, 1163 (11th Cir.1993). In *Goldsmith,* the fact that the decisionmaker who imposed the adverse employment action on the plaintiff was aware of the protected conduct, coupled with the proximity of the adverse action to the protected conduct, sufficed to create a factual issue on the required causal link. In *Clover,* while the court found circumstantial evidence sufficient to support a finding that the decisionmaker was aware that another employee was being investigated, there was insufficient evidence to permit a jury reasonably to find that he was aware of the plaintiff's own participation in that investigation.

14. *See, e.g., Montgomery v. John Deere & Co.,* 169 F.3d 556 (8th Cir.1999); *McCue v. Kansas Dep't of Human Resources,* 165 F.3d 784 (10th Cir.1999); *Medlock v. Ortho Biotech, Inc.,* 164 F.3d 545 (10th Cir.), *cert denied,* 528 U.S. 813, 120 S.Ct. 48, 145 L.Ed.2d 42 (1999); *Parkins v. Civil Constructors of Ill., Inc.,* 163 F.3d 1027, (7th Cir.1998); *Causey v. Balog,* 162 F.3d 795 (4th Cir.1998); *Berman v. Orkin Exterminating Co., Inc.,* 160 F.3d 697 (11th Cir. 1998); *Zanders v. National R.R. Passenger Corp.,* 898 F.2d 1127 (6th Cir.1990).

ness or reasonableness of the manner and means of opposition. In *McDonnell Douglas Corp. v. Green*, the Supreme Court wrote that employers are not required to "absolve" employees who engage in "unlawful activity against it."[15] Employee protests that constitute both opposition to practices made unlawful by Title VII as well as violations of established, legitimate work rules have posed especially difficult problems. The linchpin is the "reasonableness" of the opposition. When a court adjudges an employee's manner of opposition to have gone beyond what is necessary for effective protest—when, for example, she gratuitously embarrasses a superior—employee discipline will likely be upheld.[16] The court balances the legislative purpose to protect reasonable opposition to arguably discriminatory employer conduct against the everpresent Congressional desire to preserve managerial control.[17] At the same time, however, an employer's unilateral sense of diminished loyalty resulting from the opposition will not by itself be considered a legitimate, nondiscriminatory reason for discipline.[18] The Fifth Circuit has declared a somewhat different balance that strips opposition of protection when the plaintiff's manner of protest "so interferes with the performance of his job that it renders him ineffective in the position for which he is employed."[19]

15.　411 U.S. 792, 803, 93 S.Ct. 1817, 1825, 36 L.Ed.2d 668 (1973). The Court did not actually decide the validity of the plaintiff's claim under § 704, but its language seems to extend to any claim under Title VII. *See also Hochstadt v. Worcester Found. for Experimental Biology*, 545 F.2d 222, 229–234 (1st Cir.1976) (conduct with the potential to disrupt work excessively held unreasonable and hence unprotected). *But cf. Folkerson v. Circus Circus Enters. Inc.*, 107 F.3d 754 (9th Cir.1997) (assumes that physical violence may constitute protected opposition if proportionate to threat of physical harm directed at plaintiff, but finds the contrary on the facts at bar).

16.　*See, e.g., Robbins v. Jefferson County Sch. Dist. R–1*, 186 F.3d 1253 (10th Cir. 1999) (frequent, voluminous, antagonistic, and inflammatory protests to immediate, and at times, ultimate supervisors forfeited the protection); *Kubicko v. Ogden Logistics Servs.*, 181 F.3d 544, 551 (4th Cir.1999) (to be protected, protests must be made "in an orderly and nondisruptive manner"); *Kiel v. Select Artificials, Inc.*, 169 F.3d 1131, 1136 (8th Cir.), *cert. denied*, 528 U.S. 818, 120 S.Ct. 59, 145 L.Ed.2d 51 (1999) (under ADA); *Laughlin v. Metropolitan Washington Airports Auth.*, 149 F.3d 253, 260 (4th Cir.1998) (employee removed and copied documents from boss's desk and mailed them to coworker for potential use in coworker's discrimination claim); *Evans v. Kansas City, Mo. Sch. Dist.*, 65 F.3d 98, 102 (8th Cir.1995), *cert. denied*, 517 U.S. 1104,

116 S.Ct. 1319, 134 L.Ed.2d 472 (1996); *Booker v. Brown & Williamson Tobacco Co.*, 879 F.2d 1304, 1312 (6th Cir.1989); *Jennings v. Tinley Park Cmty. Consol. Sch. Dist. No. 146*, 864 F.2d 1368 (7th Cir.1988); *Pettway v. American Cast Iron Pipe Co.*, 411 F.2d 998 (5th Cir.1969).

17.　*Wrighten v. Metropolitan Hosp., Inc.*, 726 F.2d 1346 (9th Cir.1984); *Hochstadt*, 545 F.2d at 231. *See also O'Day v. McDonnell Douglas Helicopter Co.*, 79 F.3d 756 (9th Cir.1996) (standard under ADEA). *See Kubicko v. Ogden Logistics Servs.*, 181 F.3d 544, 554 (4th Cir.1999) (noting but not deciding question whether plaintiff protected when decisionmaker took adverse action in the actual and well founded belief that plaintiff fabricated the content of his opposition activity).

18.　*See Jennings v. Tinley Park Cmty. Consol. Sch. Dist. No. 146*, 864 F.2d 1368 (7th Cir.1988); *EEOC v. Crown Zellerbach Corp.*, 720 F.2d 1008, 1014 (9th Cir.1983) (if the test were mere disloyalty, even reasonable opposition would be unprotected, since all opposition may be considered disloyal).

19.　*Douglas v. DynMcDermott Petroleum Operations Co.*, 144 F.3d 364 (5th Cir. 1998), *cert. denied*, 525 U.S. 1068, 119 S.Ct. 798, 142 L.Ed.2d 660 (1999). *See also Cruz v. Coach Stores, Inc.*, 202 F.3d 560, 566 (2d Cir.2000) (slapping the sexual harasser is not protected activity).

By contrast, the "participation" protection, designed to assure free access to the administrative and judicial bodies empowered to investigate and adjudicate Title VII violations, is virtually unlimited in scope.[20] Just as an "opposing" plaintiff's underlying informal complaint need not have been in fact well founded[21] under § 703 to support a claim of unlawful retaliation under § 704, so a "participating" plaintiff need not have prevailed in the proceeding initiated by her formal charge or lawsuit. Indeed it has been held that an employer's unilateral view that an employee lied in the EEOC charge documents cannot justify retaliatory action against him.[22] In *Clover v. Total System Services, Inc.*, the Eleventh Circuit announced a traditionally broad standard for the activity constituting protected "participation."[23] Plaintiff's responses to questions directed at her during an employer internal investigation prompted by a co-employee's filing of a charge with EEOC was recognized as participation "in any manner in an investigation . . . under this subchapter." The employer knows, according to the court, that information it gathers and submits to EEOC will be considered by that agency in its own investigation. Accordingly, the court swept the employer's own investigation under the umbrella of an investigation by EEOC, "at least where an employer conducts its investigation in response to a notice of charge of discrimination, and is thus aware that the evidence gathered will be considered by the EEOC as part of its investigation." The court's rule is permissive, since the pertinent regulations do not require the employer to submit all information it gathers to EEOC, only evidence that it "wishes to submit."[24]

Further, a plaintiff asserting that he was retaliated against for having filed an EEOC charge generally need not file a distinct retaliation charge with EEOC or otherwise exhaust administrative remedies before suing for retaliation in federal court. Such retaliation is actionable even if it occurs after dismissal of the plaintiff's EEOC charge.[25] At least one

---

20. All testimony, even if unreasonable, is protected. *Glover v. South Carolina Law Enforcement Div.*, 170 F.3d 411 (4th Cir. 1999). *Accord Kubicko v. Ogden Logistics Servs.*, 181 F.3d 544, 553–54 (4th Cir.1999). And that includes testimony given to a state and local deferral agency designated under 29 CFR § 1601.74, as well as testimony given to EEOC. *Id.* But an employee's refusal of her employer's demand that she file discrimination charges against coworkers was not deemed protected "participation." *Williams v. West*, 172 F.3d 54 (7th Cir. 1998).

21. Although it must have attacked a practice "made unlawful by" the statute.

22. *Pettway v. American Cast Iron Pipe Co.*, 411 F.2d 998 (5th Cir.1969); *EEOC v. Snyder Doors*, 844 F.Supp. 1020 (E.D.Pa. 1994).

23. 176 F.3d 1346 (11th Cir.1999).

24. 29 C.F.R.§ 1601.15(a).

25. *Malarkey v. Texaco, Inc.*, 983 F.2d 1204 (2d Cir.1993); *cf. Cornwell v. Robinson*, 23 F.3d 694 (2d Cir.1994) (same principle applied when subsequent charge alleges "harassment"). Within the federal government, merely contacting an agency's equal employment opportunity counselor, even without filing a charge, constitutes protected "participation," since that step is part of the machinery Title VII requires a federal employee to invoke as a precondition to suit. *Hashimoto v. Dalton*, 118 F.3d 671 (9th Cir.1997), *cert. denied*, 523 U.S. 1122, 118 S.Ct. 1803, 140 L.Ed.2d 943 (1998); *Eastland v. Tennessee Valley Auth.*, 704 F.2d 613, 627 (11th Cir.1983), *cert. denied*, 465 U.S. 1066, 104 S.Ct. 1415, 79 L.Ed.2d 741 (1984). Outside the federal sector, the Second Circuit has upheld as an exercise of managerial discretion an employer's decision to refer internal complaints that may result in the filing of formal discrimination charges before administrative agencies or

circuit reads a reasonableness requirement into the participation clause as well as the opposition clause.[26]

Section 704 in terms protects only "employees or applicants," unlike § 703's embrace of "any individual." Most courts that have considered the question have nevertheless concluded that even a former employee may maintain a claim of retaliation, and even for post-employment conduct. The classic example would be negative references of blacklisting by a former employer advising a prospective employer that she had filed an EEOC charge against it.[27] The Supreme Court has now confirmed that former employees do enjoy protection against retaliation.[28] But the retaliation against the ex-employee must usually impair an existing or subsequent prospective employment relationship.[29]

Another example of the breadth of the protection for participation is found in *Womack v. Munson*.[30] The plaintiff had formerly worked for a county sheriff. After he was hired by the state prosecutor, he filed a Title VII suit against the sheriff, alleging unlawful termination on the basis of race. After learning of the suit, the plaintiff's new boss questioned him regarding the allegations against the sheriff, and fired him shortly after. The court found that plaintiff had been unlawfully fired by his *current* employer for filing the suit against his *former* employer.[31]

Retaliation charges may be based on the manner in which an employer defends a charge or complaint of discrimination. Employer investigations of sexual or racial harassment undertaken to claim the

courts to its law department instead of its equal employment opportunity unit. *United States v. New York City Transit Auth.*, 97 F.3d 672 (2d Cir.1996).

26. *See Barnes v. Small*, 840 F.2d 972 (D.C.Cir.1988); *Parker v. Baltimore & Ohio R.R.*, 652 F.2d 1012 (D.C.Cir.1981) (excessively forceful opposition, including malicious accusations, may forfeit protection); *Pendleton v. Rumsfeld*, 628 F.2d 102 (D.C.Cir.1980) (if employee is fired for improper manner of opposition to racial discrimination, rather than for the opposition itself, § 704 is not violated).

27. *See, e.g., Berry v. Stevinson Chevrolet*, 74 F.3d 980 (10th Cir.1996) (filing criminal charge against former employee constitutes actionable retaliation); *Charlton v. Paramus Bd. of Educ.*, 25 F.3d 194 (3d Cir.1994), *cert. denied*, 513 U.S. 1022, 115 S.Ct. 590, 130 L.Ed.2d 503 (1994); *Bailey v. USX Corp.*, 850 F.2d 1506 (11th Cir.1988); *O'Brien v. Sky Chefs, Inc.*, 670 F.2d 864, 869 (9th Cir.1982), *overruled on other grounds by Atonio v. Wards Cove Packing Co.*, 810 F.2d 1477, 1481–82 (9th Cir.1987) (en banc); *Pantchenko v. C.B. Dolge Co.*, 581 F.2d 1052, 1055 (2d Cir.1978); *Rutherford v. American Bank of Commerce*, 565 F.2d 1162, 1165 (10th Cir.1977); *EEOC v. Metzger*, 824 F.Supp. 1 (D.D.C.1993) (hold-

ing retaliation against former employee actionable).

28. *Robinson v. Shell Oil Co.*, 519 U.S. 337, 117 S.Ct. 843, 136 L.Ed.2d 808 (1997), discussed in § 2.2, *supra*.

29. *Nelson v. Upsala College*, 51 F.3d 383 (3d Cir.1995). *But see Hashimoto v. Dalton*, 118 F.3d 671 (9th Cir.1997), *cert. denied*, 523 U.S. 1122, 118 S.Ct. 1803, 140 L.Ed.2d 943 (1998) (retaliation in the dissemination of a negative reference actionable even though plaintiff not entitled to reinstatement and did not lose prospective position because of the reference); *Veprinsky v. Fluor Daniel, Inc.*, 87 F.3d 881 (7th Cir.1996) (current employee may state claim for retaliatory act that does not affect terms or conditions of employment); *Aviles*, 183 F.3d 598.

30. 619 F.2d 1292 (8th Cir.1980), *cert. denied*, 450 U.S. 979, 101 S.Ct. 1513, 67 L.Ed.2d 814 (1981).

31. *See also Christopher v. Stouder Mem'l Hosp.*, 936 F.2d 870 (6th Cir.), *cert. denied*, 502 U.S. 1013, 112 S.Ct. 658, 116 L.Ed.2d 749 (1991) (defendant's frequent reference to applicant's charge against prior employer warranted inference that defendant's failure to hire was retaliatory).

affirmative defense authorized by *Faragher* and *Burlington* may also be "an investigation ... under this subchapter" in which participants are protected from retaliation.[32] Similarly, the "after-acquired evidence" doctrine that limits a plaintiff's relief when an employer discovers after-the-fact information that would have led it to terminate the plaintiff on lawful grounds[33] encourages employers to investigate plaintiff misconduct that occurred during employment after a charge or complaint has been filed.

Despite language in § 704 that appears to limit protection to those who have opposed or participated personally, the Sixth Circuit has recently upheld the legal sufficiency of a retaliation claim by an employee whose co-employee protested on his behalf.[34] In any event the plaintiff may state a claim for retaliation based on his own association with members of racial minorities[35] or because he was required by his employer to discriminate against others.[36] Courts are divided over the standing of plaintiffs to complain of retaliation based on discrimination practiced against other employees with whom the plaintiffs are associated or wish to associate.[37]

In the past several years the circuits have more critically scrutinized the element of a material adverse employment action. The views on this question are far from consistent. There are no brightline rules, and the courts must assess in each case if plaintiff suffered a material adverse change in the terms or conditions of employment. The decisions range from an apparent insistence that pay itself be diminished to the sugges-

32. *See, e.g., EEOC v. United Ass'n of Journeymen and Apprentices of Plumbing and Pipe Fitting Industry of U.S. and Canada, Local Union No. 189*, 311 F.Supp. 464 (S.D.Ohio 1970) (defense lawyer's questioning held retaliatory). But in order to encourage employers to take prompt and effective remedial action in cases of hostile environment sex or race discrimination, the courts have afforded them wide latitude in conducting investigations of underlying charges. *See Steffes v. Stepan Co.*, 144 F.3d 1070 (7th Cir.1998) (rejecting an absolute litigation privilege but stating that it will be a rare case when litigation conduct will be found to constitute unlawful retaliation).

33. *See McKennon v. Nashville Banner Pub. Co.*, 513 U.S. 352, 115 S.Ct. 879, 130 L.Ed.2d 852 (1995) discussed in Chapter 3.

34. EEOC v. Ohio Edison Co., 7 F.3d 541 (6th Cir.1993). Cf. *McDonnell v. Cisneros*, 84 F.3d 256 (7th Cir.1996) (finding actionable the retaliation claim of a manager who had not protested himself but who was punished for having failed to prevent the protests of subordinates). *But see* the even more recent cases cited *supra*, which reinforce the suggestion that the plaintiff herself must have protested to maintain a § 704 claim.

35. *Maynard v. City of San Jose*, 37 F.3d 1396 (9th Cir.1994). *But cf. Little v. United Technologies*, 103 F.3d 956 (11th Cir.1997) (white plaintiff allegedly punished for protesting racially derogatory remarks uttered by nonsupervisory co-worker concerning unspecified African–American co-workers cannot state claim against employer unless plaintiff brought the comments to the attention of supervisory or management employees who then failed to take prompt remedial action) (alternative holding); *Silver v. KCA, Inc.*, 586 F.2d 138 (9th Cir.1978) (plaintiff's opposition to co-worker's individual act of discrimination, unattributed to employer, not protected activity).

36. *Moyo v. Gomez*, 40 F.3d 982 (9th Cir.1994), *cert. denied*, 513 U.S. 1081, 115 S.Ct. 732, 130 L.Ed.2d 635 (1995).

37. *Compare Maynard v. City of San Jose*, 37 F.3d 1396 (9th Cir.1994) *with Childress v. City of Richmond*, 134 F.3d 1205 (4th Cir.) (en banc), *cert. denied*, 524 U.S. 927, 118 S.Ct. 2322, 141 L.Ed.2d 696 (1998) (affirming district court's ruling that white male police officers cannot maintain Title VII claims of hostile work environment directed against black and women officers by an equally divided en banc vote).

tion at the other extreme that a transfer to a higher paying position could constitute unlawful retaliation. It is widely accepted that purely lateral transfers do not constitute an adverse employment action;[38] if, however, the court perceives the transfer as equivalent to a demotion, the court will find actionable retaliation.[39] The circuits are split on whether negative employment evaluations alone constitute an adverse employment action sufficient to support a claim of retaliation.[40] In

38. *See Spears v. Missouri Dep't of Corr. and Human Resources*, 210 F.3d 850 (8th Cir.2000); *Boone v. Goldin*, 178 F.3d 253 (4th Cir.1999) (transfer was clearly not adverse where the new job commanded a higher salary and more responsibility even though there was greater stress); *Burger v. Central Apartment Mgmt., Inc.*, 168 F.3d 875 (5th Cir.1999) (denial of a request for a purely lateral transfer cannot support retaliation claim); *Sanchez v. Denver Pub. Schs.*, 164 F.3d 527, 532 (10th Cir.1998) (where the transfer merely increased the employee's commute and did not alter her salary, benefits, or elementary school teaching responsibilities); *Doe v. Dekalb County Sch. Dist.*, 145 F.3d 1441, 1452 (11th Cir.1998) (transfer was not a demotion; transfer had same salary, benefits, seniority, and relative level of prestige); *Ledergerber v. Stangler*, 122 F.3d 1142, 1144 (8th Cir.1997) (same); *Montandon v. Farmland Indus., Inc.*, 116 F.3d 355 (8th Cir.1997) (transfer to another town that required employee to relocate not a sufficient adverse employment action to support retaliation claim, as it did not affect his salary, title, or other term of employment); *Kocsis v. Multi–Care Mgmt., Inc.*, 97 F.3d 876, 886 (6th Cir.1996) (transfer that did not entail a loss of pay, benefits, duties, or prestige was not adverse action); *Williams v. Bristol–Myers Squibb Co.*, 85 F.3d 270, 274 (7th Cir.1996) (purely lateral transfer which does not involve demotion in form or substance was not adverse action); *Crady v. Liberty Nat'l Bank & Trust Co.*, 993 F.2d 132, 136 (7th Cir.1993) (lateral transfer with semantic change in title and alteration of job responsibilities not adverse employment action).

Similarly, the Eighth Circuit held that the refusal of a lateral transfer following an employee's filing of an EEOC charge did not rise to the level of an adverse employment action. *LePique v. Hove*, 217 F.3d 1012 (8th Cir.2000).

39. *See Trujillo v. New Mexico Dep't of Corrections*, 182 F.3d 933 (10th Cir.1999); *DiIenno v. Goodwill Indus. of Mid–Eastern Pa.*, 162 F.3d 235 (3d Cir.1998) (lateral transfer can constitute adverse employment action when new job involves tasks employer knew employee could not do); *Randlett v. Shalala*, 118 F.3d 857, 862 (1st Cir.1997)

(an employer's refusal to grant an employee's requested transfer could be an adverse employment action in a Title VII retaliation claim where the employee presented evidence showing that similar transfers for hardship reasons were so customary that they are a "privilege" of employment); *Davis v. City of Sioux City*, 115 F.3d 1365 (8th Cir.1997) (transfer after complaint of sexual harassment sufficiently adverse for retaliation claim where new position, despite higher salary, lacked supervisory status and offered less opportunity for promotion or salary increases); *de la Cruz v. New York City Human Resources Admin. Dep't of Social Servs.*, 82 F.3d 16, 21 (2d Cir.1996) (transfer to a less prestigious job with little opportunity for professional growth arguably altered the terms and conditions of employment and was an adverse employment action in a Title VII discrimination action); *Torre v. Casio, Inc.*, 42 F.3d 825, 831 n. 7 (3d Cir.1994) (allegation of transfer to dead-end job sufficient to create material fact issue of adverse employment action); *Collins v. Illinois*, 830 F.2d 692, 704 (7th Cir.1987) (transfer an adverse employment action where the transfer was really a demotion; employee lost her office and her professional listing as a library consultant).

40. *Compare Spears v. Missouri Dep't of Corrections and Human Resources*, 210 F.3d 850 (8th Cir.2000) (lowering of performance evaluation not actionable where evaluation was not sued to plaintiff's detriment); *Morris v. Oldham County Fiscal Court*, 201 F.3d 784 (6th Cir.2000) (same); *Hollins v. Atlantic Co., Inc.*, 188 F.3d 652 (6th Cir.1999); *Montandon v. Farmland Indus., Inc.* 116 F.3d 355 (8th Cir.1997); *Smart v. Ball State Univ.*, 89 F.3d 437 (7th Cir.1996); *Wyatt v. City of Boston*, 35 F.3d 13, 15–16 (1st Cir.1994); and *Yartzoff v. Thomas*, 809 F.2d 1371, 1375 (9th Cir.1987) (no) *with Wideman v. Wal–Mart Stores, Inc.*, 141 F.3d 1453 (11th Cir.1998) and *Hoeppner v. Crotched Mountain Rehab. Ctr., Inc.*, 31 F.3d 9 (1st Cir.1994) (yes). *See also Cullom v. Brown*, 209 F.3d 1035 (7th Cir.2000) (no adverse employment action where Department of Veterans Affairs "ov-

general, EEOC interprets the relevant statutory language as prohibiting any adverse treatment that rises above petty slights or trivial annoyances. The degree of harm, EEOC believes, goes to the issue of damages, not liability.[41] But in the circuit opinions, the authors are unable to discern any clear line dividing employer actions deemed sufficiently adverse,[42] and those that are not.[43] In the majority of the circuits,

errated" employee, making him ineligible for remedial program that might have accelerated plaintiff's advancement, but could also have led to his dismissal).

41. *See EEOC Guidance on Investigating, Analyzing Retaliation Claims*, May 20, 1998. EEOC explains that the qualifier "terms and conditions of employment" is not contained in the retaliation provision of Title VII and therefore, does not restrict the actions that can be challenged. And this latter point of view can find support in Supreme Court decisions in *Oncale, Burlington*, and *Faragher* where the Court reaffirmed earlier cases that sexual harassment is actionable even when it does not affect a tangible term or condition of employment. See also *Ray v. Henderson*, 217 F.3d 1234 (9th Cir.2000) (the severity of an action's ultimate impact goes to the issue of damages, not liability) (citing *Hashimoto v. Dalton*, 118 F.3d 671, 676 (9th Cir.1997), cert. denied, 523 U.S. 1122, 118 S.Ct. 1803, 140 L.Ed.2d 943 (1998)).

42. *Richardson v. New York State Dep't of Correctional Serv.*, 180 F.3d 426 (2d Cir. 1999); *Gunnell v. Utah Valley State College*, 152 F.3d 1253 (10th Cir.1998); *Knox v. Indiana*, 93 F.3d 1327, 1334 (7th Cir.1996) (co-worker hostility or retaliatory harassment, if sufficiently severe, may support retaliation claim); *Jeffries v. Kansas Dep't of Soc. and Rehabilitative Servs.*, 147 F.3d 1220 (10th Cir.1998) (denial of education benefits can support retaliation claim); *Wideman v. Wal–Mart Stores, Inc.*, 141 F.3d 1453 (11th Cir.1998) (holding that Title VII's protection against retaliation extends to adverse actions falling short of ultimate employment decisions; two reprimands, a one day suspension, being listed as absent on a scheduled day off and threatening remarks were sufficient to serve as grounds for a claim); *Berry v. Stevinson Chevrolet*, 74 F.3d 980, 986–87 (10th Cir.1996) (where management caused plaintiff's co-worker to initiate a criminal complaint against plaintiff, malicious prosecution may constitute an adverse employment action).

43. *Miller v. American Family Mut. Ins. Co.*, 203 F.3d 997, 1006 (7th Cir.2000) (denial of a bonus was not a sufficient adverse employment action within the meaning of Title VII); *Scusa v. Nestle U.S.A. Co., Inc.*, 181 F.3d 958 (8th Cir.1999) (employer's failure to stop plaintiff's ostracism by co-workers not sufficiently adverse); *Workman v. Frito–Lay, Inc.*, 165 F.3d 460 (6th Cir. 1999) (employer's continuing to refuse to return plaintiff to work, as it did before she filed charge, not an incremental adverse action) (case under ADA); *Hernandez-Torres v. Intercontinental Trading, Inc.*, 158 F.3d 43 (1st Cir.1998) (onerous assignments and critical reports of performance did not rise to level of adverse employment action); *Sweeney v. West*, 149 F.3d 550 (7th Cir. 1998) (two counseling reports placed in plaintiff's personnel file did not rise to level of adverse employment action); *Watts v. Kroger Co.*, 170 F.3d 505 (5th Cir.1999) (reneging on promise to arrange plaintiff's work schedule to her liking not an adverse employment action); *Greaser v. Missouri Dep't of Corr.*, 145 F.3d 979 (8th Cir.), cert. denied, 525 U.S. 1056, 119 S.Ct. 620, 142 L.Ed.2d 559 (1998) (threats made by supervisor that plaintiff should quit "before someone gets hurt" do not constitute adverse employment action); *Manning v. Metropolitan Life Ins. Co.*, 127 F.3d 686 (8th Cir.1997) (hostility and personal animus directed at plaintiffs by supervisors insufficient to show retaliation "[a]bsent evidence of some more tangible change in duties or working conditions that constituted a material employment disadvantage"); *Munday v. Waste Mgmt. of N. Am.*, 126 F.3d 239 (4th Cir.1997), cert. denied, 522 U.S. 1116, 118 S.Ct. 1053, 140 L.Ed.2d 116 (1998) (yelling at employee, telling others to ignore the employee, and asking others to spy on employee insufficient to constitute adverse employment action); *Ledergerber v. Stangler*, 122 F.3d 1142 (8th Cir.1997) (where employer replaced a supervisor's subordinate staff and placed a statement in supervisor's file that discrimination would not be tolerated, supervisor did not suffer an adverse employment action); *Chock v. Northwest Airlines, Inc.*, 113 F.3d 861 (8th Cir.1997) (retaliatory interference with plaintiff's pursuit of graduate education and his living arrangement with his direct supervisor not actionable because neither constituted a benefit of employment); *Wanamaker v. Columbian Rope Co.*, 108 F.3d 462 (2d Cir. 1997) (denying office facilities to employee about to be terminated so he could conduct

adverse employment actions are not, however, merely limited to ultimate employment decisions, and retaliatory harassment or co-worker hostility may, if sufficiently severe, support a retaliation claim.[44]

Some circuits treat the "mixed motive" provisions of § 107 of the Civil Rights Act of 1991 as inapplicable to retaliation, with the consequence that a retaliation plaintiff may have no remedy whatsoever. These opinions note that on its face § 107 amends only § 703, the main Title VII discrimination prohibition, and not § 704. Consequently, in these circuits, an employer shown to have acted against the plaintiff in part from a retaliatory motive can avoid liability altogether—even for prospective relief and attorney's fees—if it can carry the burden of demonstrating that it would have imposed the same employment detriment for one or more lawful reasons.[45] Other circuits, without analysis, have assumed that a retaliation plaintiff may take advantage of § 107 and hence subject the defendant to prospective relief and attorney's fees liability, even if the defendant carries the "same-decision" showing.[46]

job hunt not actionable because it did not worsen his already dismal employment circumstances and did not interfere with tangible future employment opportunities); *Mattern v. Eastman Kodak Co.*, 104 F.3d 702 (5th Cir.), *cert. denied*, 522 U.S. 932, 118 S.Ct. 336, 139 L.Ed.2d 260 (1997) (§ 704 retaliation protection extends only to employer "discrimination" affecting "ultimate employment decisions" of the kind prohibited by Section 703(a)(1), not to the broader proscription of Section 703(a)(2) against tangential interference with employment "opportunities"; accordingly, retaliation claim fails when adverse action was limited to co-employee hostility; a visit to plaintiff's home by two supervisors directing her to employer's medical department if her illness were work related; a verbal threat of termination; a missed pay increase; and being placed on final warning). *Nelson v. Upsala College*, 51 F.3d 383 (3d Cir.1995) (barring plaintiff from defendant's premises not sufficiently adverse to job opportunities).

44. The Second and Tenth Circuits have both held that an employer can be liable for co-workers' retaliatory harassment. *See Richardson v. New York State Dep't of Corr. Serv.*, 180 F.3d 426, 446 (2d Cir.1999) ("an employer [can] be held accountable for allowing retaliatory co-worker harassment to occur if it knows about that harassment but fails to act to stop it"); *Gunnell v. Utah Valley State Coll.*, 152 F.3d 1253, 1265 (10th Cir.1998).

In addition, the Seventh and Ninth Circuits have held that retaliatory harassment by a supervisor can be actionable in a Title VII case. *See Ray v. Henderson*, 217 F.3d 1234 (9th Cir.2000) (employee suffered cognizable adverse employment actions when em-

ployer, in alleged retaliation for employee's complaints concerning management's treatment of women employees, eliminated flexible start-time policy and instituted workplace "lockdown"); *Morris v. Oldham County Fiscal Ct.*, 201 F.3d 784, 791 (7th Cir.2000) (following complaint, supervisor stalked plaintiff, made obscene gestures at plaintiff and threw roofing nails in her driveway). *See also Knox v. Indiana*, 93 F.3d 1327, 1334 (7th Cir.1996) ("Nothing indicates why a different form of retaliation—namely, retaliating against a complainant by permitting her fellow employees to punish her for invoking her rights under Title VII—does not fall within the statute.").

But see Mattern v. Eastman Kodak Co., 104 F.3d 702, 707 (5th Cir.), *cert. denied*, 522 U.S. 932, 118 S.Ct. 336, 139 L.Ed.2d 260 (1997) (only "ultimate employment decisions" can be adverse employment decisions).

45. *Kubicko v. Ogden Logistics Servs.*, 181 F.3d 544, 552 n. 7 (4th Cir.1999); *McNutt v. Board of Trustees*, 141 F.3d 706 (7th Cir.1998); *Woodson v. Scott Paper Co.*, 109 F.3d 913, 933–935 (3d Cir.), *cert. denied*, 522 U.S. 914, 118 S.Ct. 299, 139 L.Ed.2d 230 (1997); *Tanca v. Nordberg*, 98 F.3d 680 (1st Cir.1996), *cert. denied*, 520 U.S. 1119, 117 S.Ct. 1253, 137 L.Ed.2d 333 (1997). *See also Provencher v. CVS Pharmacy, Div. of Melville Corp.*, 145 F.3d 5 (1st Cir.1998) (liability can be imposed only if the discrimination was the determinative factor in terminating plaintiff).

46. *See Merritt v. Dillard Paper Co.*, 120 F.3d 1181 (11th Cir.1997); *Veprinsky v. Fluor Daniel, Inc.*, 87 F.3d 881, 893 (7th

EEOC has concluded that § 107 should apply to retaliation claims in order to effectuate the purpose of maintaining "unfettered access to the statutory remedial mechanism."[47] Even circuits rejecting the application of § 107 scheme to retaliation claims recognize the "same decision" framework of *Price Waterhouse v. Hopkins.*[48] In these circuits, plaintiffs must have "direct" or "strong" prima facie evidence of retaliation to cast on defendant the burden of persuading that it would have reached the same decision plaintiff challenges for lawful reasons independent of retaliation; and if a defendant carries that burden, it is absolved of all liability.[49]

§§ 2.41–5.49   [Reserved]

G.   CONSTRUCTIVE DISCHARGE

§ 2.50   In General

Closely related to but distinguishable from environmental harassment and retaliation is the doctrine of constructive discharge. In essence, the claim avails an employee whose departure is in form voluntary but who in fact was virtually compelled to quit as the result of discriminatory job terms or harassment extreme in significance, duration or offensiveness. The consequence of establishing the claim is a broader remedy: the plaintiff who succeeds will be eligible for an order directing reinstatement as well as available monetary relief.[1]

At a minimum the claim requires the standard showing that the plaintiff's involuntary resignation[2] was caused[3] by differential treatment

Cir.1996); *Beinlich v. Curry Dev., Inc.,* 54 F.3d 772 (4th Cir.1995).

47. *See EEOC Guidance on Investigating, Analyzing Retaliation Claims,* May 20, 1998.

48. 490 U.S. 228, 109 S.Ct. 1775, 104 L.Ed.2d 268 (1989) (plurality opinion).

49. *See Kubicko,* 181 F.3d at 553 n.8; *Medlock v. Ortho Biotech, Inc.,* 164 F.3d 545, 549–551 (10th Cir.), *cert. denied,* 528 U.S. 813, 120 S.Ct. 48, 145 L.Ed.2d 42 (1999); *Thomas v. National Football League Players Ass'n,* 131 F.3d 198, 202–203 (D.C.Cir.1997); *Cosgrove v. Sears, Roebuck & Co.,* 9 F.3d 1033, 1039–41 (2d Cir.1993); *Griffiths v. CIGNA Corp.,* 988 F.2d 457, 468 (3d Cir.), *cert. denied,* 510 U.S. 865, 114 S.Ct. 186, 126 L.Ed.2d 145 (1993), *overruled on other grounds, Miller v. CIGNA Corp.,* 47 F.3d 586 (3d Cir.1995).

§ 2.50

1. *See, e.g., Coffman v. Tracker Marine,* 141 F.3d 1241 (8th Cir.1998) (where appellate court upheld jury finding of retaliation but reversed verdict of constructive discharge, plaintiff was entitled to emotional

distress and medical damages, but not for back pay).

2. Typically constructive discharge cases involve an outright resignation by the plaintiff. But an employee forced into an unpaid leave will also be considered to be constructively discharged. *White v. Honeywell, Inc.,* 141 F.3d 1270 (8th Cir.1998). Similarly, a plaintiff forced to accept early retirement following the elimination of his position in a restructuring was able to maintain a claim of constructive discharge. *Scott v. Goodyear Tire & Rubber Co.,* 160 F.3d 1121 (6th Cir.1998).

"Constructive demotion" is apparently a cognizable claim as well. In *Simpson v. Borg–Warner Auto., Inc.,* 196 F.3d 873 (7th Cir.1999), the Seventh Circuit established the prima facie case: a plaintiff must show that his or her working conditions were so intolerable that a reasonable person would have been compelled to take a demotion. *Id.* at 876–77. The court recognized one analytical difference, however; when a constructively discharged plaintiff resigns, she is removed completely from the intolerable working conditions. When a plaintiff is con-

unlawful because based on her race, sex, religion, national origin or age. Evidence that the plaintiff would have resigned for independent personal reasons or work-related reasons unconnected with substantial, aggravated discrimination[4] breaks the causal connection and therefore defeats the constructive discharge claim.[5] This is akin to the same-decision showing which, under *Price Waterhouse*, sufficed to avoid employer liability altogether and today, under the Civil Rights Act of 1991, still limits available relief.[6] The date of the forced resignation triggers the running of the applicable 180–or 300–day administrative charge filing period.[7]

The element that has generated the most litigation centers on the reasonableness of the employee's decision to quit in relation to particular unlawful employer conduct. The decisions are uniform that an employee has been constructively discharged when the termination results from intolerable working conditions that the employer created with the specific intent of forcing the employee to resign.[8] Some circuits consider evidence of subjective intent,[9] or of "aggravating circumstances,"[10] indis-

structively demoted, a close proximity to the intolerable working environment "might tend to tend to offset evidence that prior conditions were "intolerable." *Id.* at 876 n.2. The plaintiff in *Simpson* failed to establish that she was subjected to working conditions that a reasonable person would find intolerable. *Id.* at 877–78. The Fifth Circuit has recognized the claim of constructive demotion. *See Sharp v. City of Houston*, 164 F.3d 923, 934 (5th Cir.1999). In *Sharp*, the female plaintiff requested transfer from the elite Mounted Patrol unit of the Houston Police Department after responding to an Internal Affairs Division probe into sexual harassment at the unit. *Id.* at 928. After cooperating with the probe, the plaintiff's equipment was sabotaged in a way that jeopardized her safety on the job, she was excluded from required job functions, and was socially ostracized. *See id.* at 927. The court in *Sharp* affirmed a jury's finding that the "voluntary" transfer request was in fact an adverse employment action. *Id.* at 934.

3. Absence of a temporal nexus between the offensive conduct and the constructive discharge can defeat a claim. *See, e.g., Landrau–Romero v. Banco Popular De Puerto Rico*, 212 F.3d 607 (1st Cir.2000) (seven months between alleged sexual harassment and constructive discharge too long); *Smith v. Bath Iron Works Corp.*, 943 F.2d 164, 167 (1st Cir.1991) (no constructive discharge found where plaintiff quit six months after last reported incident of sexual harassment).

4. The conditions must be more than intolerable; they must have resulted from discrimination on an unlawful ground.

Chambers v. American Trans Air, Inc., 17 F.3d 998 (7th Cir.), *cert. denied*, 513 U.S. 1001, 115 S.Ct. 512, 130 L.Ed.2d 419 (1994).

5. *See Henson v. Dundee*, 682 F.2d 897 (11th Cir.1982).

6. *See* Chapter 3, below.

7. *Draper v. Coeur Rochester, Inc.*, 147 F.3d 1104 (9th Cir.1998).

8. *See, e.g., Bergstrom–Ek v. Best Oil Co.*, 153 F.3d 851 (8th Cir.1998); *Doe v. Dekalb County Sch. Dist.*, 145 F.3d 1441 (11th Cir.1998); *Kirsch v. Fleet Street, Ltd.*, 148 F.3d 149 (2d Cir.1998); *Munday v. Waste Mgmt. of N. Am., Inc.*, 126 F.3d 239 (4th Cir.1997), *cert. denied*, 522 U.S. 1116, 118 S.Ct. 1053, 140 L.Ed.2d 116 (1998); *Mungin v. Katten Muchin & Zavis*, 116 F.3d 1549 (D.C.Cir.1997).

9. *See Allen v. Bridgestone/Firestone, Inc.*, 81 F.3d 793 (8th Cir.1996); *Kader v. Paper Software, Inc.*, 111 F.3d 337 (2d Cir. 1997) (under New York law, plaintiff must prove that adverse employment condition was created with the aim of imposing unbearable working conditions that would force plaintiff's resignation). *Cf. Martin v. Cavalier Hotel Corp.*, 48 F.3d 1343, 1354 (4th Cir.1995) (permitting the required "intent" element to be shown by evidence demonstrating that the resignation was "the 'reasonable foreseeable consequence' of the employer's conduct," 48 F.3d at 1356). *See Bristow v. Daily Press, Inc.*, 770 F.2d 1251 (4th Cir.1985), *cert. denied*, 475 U.S. 1082, 106 S.Ct. 1461, 89 L.Ed.2d 718 (1986); *Coe v. Yellow Freight Sys., Inc.*, 646 F.2d 444 (10th Cir.1981). *Cf. Johnson v.*

pensable to constructive discharge. More, however, subscribe to an "objective" test,[11] requiring only a finding that the complained of conduct would have the foreseeable result of creating working conditions sufficiently unpleasant or difficult that a reasonable person in the employee's position would feel compelled to resign.[12] Because the employer conduct that gives rise to colorable claims of constructive discharge is usually extreme or persistent, those claims are often joined with companion claims under state law for such torts as outrage or intentional infliction of emotional distress.[13]

Most acts of discrimination are such that a "reasonable" employee should stay on the job; oppose the employer practice informally or by filing a charge; and trust in the efficacy of the separate § 704 protection against retaliation. Classic instances include wage discrimination, nonpromotion, or assignment to less attractive or lucrative (but not intolerably demeaning) positions.[14] At the other end of the spectrum, where the

Shalala, 991 F.2d 126 (4th Cir.1993), *cert. denied,* 513 U.S. 806, 115 S.Ct. 52, 130 L.Ed.2d 12 (1994) (under Rehabilitation Act of 1973). The Tenth Circuit may have changed course with the panel opinion in *Rupp v. Purolator Courier Corp.,* 45 F.3d 440 (10th Cir.1994), which requires only "working conditions so difficult that a reasonable person in the employee's position would feel compelled to resign." *See also Burks v. Oklahoma Publ'g Co.,* 81 F.3d 975 (10th Cir.), *cert. denied,* 519 U.S. 931, 117 S.Ct. 302, 136 L.Ed.2d 220 (1996).

10. *Dashnaw v. Pena,* 12 F.3d 1112 (D.C.Cir.1994), *cert. denied,* 513 U.S. 959, 115 S.Ct. 417, 130 L.Ed.2d 333 (1994) (case under ADEA holding failure to promote does not amount to required aggravated circumstances).

11. The reasonableness inquiry places this determination within the province of the jury. *See, e.g., Maschka v. Genuine Parts Co.,* 122 F.3d 566 (8th Cir.1997) (holding that whether the conditions of employment were so intolerable that they amounted to constructive discharge is for the jury to decide).

12. *See, e.g., Rupp v. Purolator Courier Corp.,* 45 F.3d 440 (10th Cir.1994); *Morgan v. Ford,* 6 F.3d 750 (11th Cir.1993), *cert. denied,* 512 U.S. 1221, 114 S.Ct. 2708, 129 L.Ed.2d 836 (1994); *Hukkanen v. International Union of Operating Eng'rs Local No. 101,* 3 F.3d 281 (8th Cir.1993); *Stephens v. C.I.T. Group/Equipment Financing, Inc.,* 955 F.2d 1023 (5th Cir.1992) *Schafer v. Board of Pub. Educ.,* 903 F.2d 243 (3d Cir.1990); *Brooms v. Regal Tube Co.,* 881 F.2d 412 (7th Cir.1989); *Watson v. Nationwide Ins. Co.,* 823 F.2d 360 (9th Cir.1987); *Bruhwiler v. University of Tenn.,* 859 F.2d 419 (6th Cir.1988); *Calhoun v. Acme Cleve-*

land Corp., 798 F.2d 559 (1st Cir.1986); *Wardwell v. School Bd. of Palm Beach County,* 786 F.2d 1554 (11th Cir.1986); *Meyer v. Brown & Root Const. Co.,* 661 F.2d 369 (5th Cir.1981).

In *Hukkanen,* the Court dispensed with an express finding that resignation was a reasonably foreseeable consequence of the defendant's agent's sexual harassment, deeming that finding implicit in the lower court's finding that a reasonable person in plaintiff's position would have felt compelled to quit.

13. *Rupp v. Purolator Courier Corp.,* 45 F.3d 440 (10th Cir.1994), illustrates that the same employer conduct may constitute constructive discharge for Title VII purposes yet not be sufficiently aggravated, indecent or shocking to amount to tortious wrongdoing under state law.

14. *See Lindale v. Tokheim Corp.,* 145 F.3d 953 (7th Cir.1998) (nonpromotion and "boorish" male colleagues fail to justify plaintiff's voluntary resignation); *Drake v. Minnesota Min. & Mfg. Co.,* 134 F.3d 878 (7th Cir.1998) (the voluntary termination of two white employees as a result of being shunned by white co-workers for being friends with black co-workers was not reasonable and could not support claim of constructive discharge); *Gartman v. Gencorp, Inc.,* 120 F.3d 127 (8th Cir.1997) (forced transfer with moving expenses and no loss in salary or benefits not sufficiently intolerable to justify resignation, even though future of new plant was uncertain); *Mungin v. Katten Muchin & Zavis,* 116 F.3d 1549 (D.C.Cir.1997) (relocation option not sufficient to trigger constructive discharge, even though that option was not advanced by prospective supervisor in new location) (al-

prospects of proving constructive discharge are much improved, lie the "aggravating circumstances" sometimes required to meet the objective test of "intolerable" working conditions. These include subjecting the plaintiff to repeated slurs,[15] assigning him especially demeaning work for unlawful discriminatory reasons, or subjecting him to egregious, unrelenting, and unremedied harassment. Sexual harassment in particular has served as a predicate for constructive discharge[16] but is not necessarily sufficiently severe to meet a particular circuit's test.[17] In one decision,[18] an employee who was subjected to shift changes, public berating, and demeaning job assignments for reporting apparent sexual harassment directed against a co-employee established constructive discharge, even though the retaliation lasted only three weeks. On occasion, "objective test" courts have dispensed with the necessity of aggravating circumstances, ruling that a "single non-trivial incident of discrimination" may suffice to make resignation reasonable.[19] Between the polar extremes are situations where the plaintiff is subjected to "unreasonably exacting standards of job performance"; one court announced a virtual presumption that an employee with this complaint cannot reasonably resign, or else the courts would be undermining employer insistence on high standards.[20]

The employee must therefore make a critical decision, usually without benefit of counsel, concerning how to respond to varied employer actions. If racial slurs are so offensive or repeated that an employee who quit over them would later be deemed by a court to have acted reasonably, the employee could safely quit or take the lesser measure of remaining on the job and demanding an apology. If he keeps working but

ternative holding); *Serrano-Cruz v. DFI Puerto Rico*, 109 F.3d 23 (1st Cir.1997) (transfer to new position with same benefits and salary insufficient to show constructive discharge); *Ward v. Bechtel Corp.*, 102 F.3d 199 (5th Cir.1997) (reasonable person in position of female African–American engineer would not have felt compelled to resign as a result of being placed with a subordinate who allegedly threatened her because of his reluctance to be supervised by an African–American woman); *Bourque v. Powell Elec. Mfg. Co.*, 617 F.2d 61 (5th Cir.1980) (unequal pay); *Cazzola v. Codman & Shurtleff, Inc.*, 751 F.2d 53 (1st Cir.1984) (reassignment); *cf. King v. AC&R Adver., Inc.*, 1994 WL 88998 (C.D.Cal.1994), *aff'd*, 65 F.3d 764 (9th Cir.1995) (salary reduction, other benefits cuts, and demotion did not amount to constructive discharge under California law.)

15. *But see Ugalde v. W.A. McKenzie Asphalt Co.*, 990 F.2d 239 (5th Cir.1993) (supervisor's ethnic slurs not sufficient to lead a reasonable person in plaintiff's position to resign where employer had agreed to transfer employee to another job).

16. *See, e.g., Hukkanen*, 3 F.3d 281; *Snider v. Consolidation Coal Co.*, 973 F.2d 555 (7th Cir.1992), *cert. denied*, 506 U.S. 1054, 113 S.Ct. 981, 122 L.Ed.2d 134 (1993). The Ninth Circuit suggested that a constructive discharge claim could be established entirely on the basis of crude and abusive sexual epithets. *Steiner v. Showboat Operating Co.*, 25 F.3d 1459 (9th Cir.1994), *cert. denied*, 513 U.S. 1082, 115 S.Ct. 733, 130 L.Ed.2d 636 (1995).

17. *See Landgraf v. USI Film Prods.*, 968 F.2d 427 (5th Cir.1992), *aff'd*, 511 U.S. 244, 114 S.Ct. 1483, 128 L.Ed.2d 229 (1994); *Yates v. Avco Corp.*, 819 F.2d 630 (6th Cir.1987).

18. *Rupp v. Purolator Courier Corp.*, 45 F.3d 440 (10th Cir.1994).

19. *Schafer*, 903 F.2d 243 (male resigned after being denied pregnancy leave to care for his child in violation of Title VII as amended by Pregnancy Disability Act).

20. *Clowes v. Allegheny Valley Hosp.*, 991 F.2d 1159, 1162 (3d Cir.), *cert. denied*, 510 U.S. 964, 114 S.Ct. 441, 126 L.Ed.2d 374 (1993) (case under ADEA).

his demand leads to his discharge, he might well have a claim for retaliation in violation of § 704.[21] But if he overestimates the seriousness or offensiveness of the employer's discrimination and quits, he may find that his only remedy is back pay from the time of the underlying discrimination until the date of his "voluntary" termination.[22]

Employers in constructive discharge cases growing out of sexual harassment may have the *Burlington/Faragher* defense available. That is, the employer may avoid liability if by a preponderance of the evidence it carries *both* elements of the following affirmative defense: "(a) that the employer exercised reasonable care to prevent and correct promptly any sexually harassing behavior, and (b) that the plaintiff employee unreasonably failed to take advantage of any corrective opportunities provided by the employer or to avoid harm otherwise." In a recent Eighth Circuit case, the court overturned a jury verdict for the plaintiff on constructive discharge because the employee failed to pursue the employer's posted policy for reporting incidents of sexual harassment. The evidence showed that the employee knew of the policy because she threatened her immediate supervisor that she would report him to the corporate headquarters. The court held that if an employee quits without giving her employer a chance to respond to her complaints, the plaintiff cannot maintain a constructive discharge claim.[23]

§§ 2.51–5.59   [Reserved]

H.   UNION LIABILITY

§ 2.60   In General

Labor unions are not excluded from the general definition of "employer," and consequently may be liable for violations of § 703(a) on the same terms as any other employer. In addition, § 703(c) declares distinct unlawful practices applicable to labor organizations alone. One, found in § 703(c)(3), is to "cause or attempt to cause an employer" to discriminate in violation of § 703. Another, declared by § 703(c)(2), is to rely on prohibited grounds in segregating or classifying union members or applicants, or in failing to refer individuals for employment, so as to deprive them of employment opportunities. Finally, wholly apart from any effect on employment opportunities, labor organizations are prohibited by § 703(c)(1) from excluding applicants from membership or otherwise discriminating against them. Construing this last prohibition quite broadly, the Supreme Court has held that a union commits an unlawful

---

21.   The example is suggested by Player, *Employment Discrimination Law* (West 1988), at 401 (*citing Walker v. Ford Motor Co.*, 684 F.2d 1355 (11th Cir.1982)).

22.   *See Coffman,* 141 F.3d 1241. Or worse. The Eighth Circuit stated that an employee has an obligation not to assume the worst and not to jump to conclusions too quickly to be reasonable, for purposes of

showing in Title VII constructive discharge action that a reasonable person would find his working conditions intolerable. *Phillips v. Taco Bell Corp.*, 156 F.3d 884 (8th Cir. 1998).

23.   *Howard v. Burns Bros., Inc.*, 149 F.3d 835 (8th Cir.1998). *See also West v. Marion Merrell Dow Inc.*, 54 F.3d 493 (8th Cir.1995).

employment practice by refusing to file race-bias grievances presented by black members, even when it does so in order to avoid antagonizing the employer and in turn to improve its chances of success on other collective bargaining issues, and even though the percentage of all types of grievances filed on behalf of black members is proportional to their representation in the union.[1]

Unions may also be liable for retaliation under § 704. For example, a union that refused to process race discrimination grievances under a collective bargaining contract whenever the would-be grievant had a charge pending against the union with a state or federal antidiscrimination agency was found to have violated Title VII. Liability attached even though the union processed other grievances as fairly for black as for white members and claimed that its policy was compelled by the employer.[2]

§ 2.60

1. *Goodman v. Lukens Steel Co.*, 482 U.S. 656, 107 S.Ct. 2617, 96 L.Ed.2d 572 (1987). *But see Carter v. Chrysler Corp.*, 173 F.3d 693 (8th Cir.1999) (union not liable under Title VII for not filing grievance where employee did not request it to do so).

2. *Johnson v. Palma*, 931 F.2d 203 (2d Cir.1991). *Cf. EEOC v. Board of Governors*, 957 F.2d 424 (7th Cir.), *cert. denied*, 506 U.S. 906, 113 S.Ct. 299, 121 L.Ed.2d 223 (1992) (collective bargaining agreement which provided that grievances could not proceed to arbitration if employee brought age discrimination claim violated the ADEA).

Chapter Three

MODES OF PROOF FOR A TITLE VII CLAIM

Analysis

---

§ 3.1 In General

The most critical and frequently litigated questions under Title VII concern the theories on which liability may be predicated and the corresponding modes of proof. When, in brief, does a distinction drawn by an employer to regulate terms and conditions of employment discriminate because or on the basis of race, gender, religion or national origin?

Broadly speaking, it may be said that there are two generic forms of employer conduct actionable under Title VII. First there are a variety of forms of intentional discrimination or "disparate treatment"; a broad legislative and social consensus supports imposing liability on employers when such conduct can be proved.[1] More controversial is employer liability for "neutral," that is facially nondiscriminatory, work practices that have greater adverse statistical impact on members of the plaintiff's protected group (and therefore, inferentially, on the plaintiff) than on others. The rubric under which liability is imposed in such circumstances is denoted by the terms "disproportionate adverse impact" or "disparate impact." Distinct proof modes have been developed to provide guidance to judges and now juries in determining liability under each of these theories. Each mode presents its own conceptual and practical difficulties, and these in turn have generated a burgeoning body of judicial decisions. It bears emphasis that these categories are not analytically airtight and that particular employer practices, in the hands of capable advocates, may implicate two or more modes of proof.

A. INDIVIDUAL DISPARATE TREATMENT— "DIRECT" EVIDENCE

§ 3.2 In General

The most obvious way of showing an unlawful employment practice is to offer "evidence that can be interpreted as an acknowledgment of discriminatory intent by the defendant or its agents...."[1] Examples include epithets or slurs uttered by an authorized agent of the employer, a decisionmaker's admission that he would or did act against the plaintiff because of his or her protected characteristic, or, even more clearly, an employer policy framed squarely in terms of race, sex, religion, or national origin.[2] When produced, such "direct" evidence will without more ordinarily suffice to show that an adverse employment condition, or limitation on an employment opportunity, was imposed "because of" the plaintiff's protected group characteristic—that is discrimination is presumed from the admission of evidence deemed "direct." Circuit opinions sometimes define direct evidence as evidence that, if believed, would prove the existence of the fact without inferences or presumption.[3] Others subscribe to an "animus" position that deems any

---

§ 3.1

1. *See* Blumoff & Lewis, *The Reagan Court and Title VII: A Common–Law Outlook On a Statutory Task*, 69 N.C.L.Rev. 1 (1990). It bears emphasis that these categories are not analytically airtight and that particular employer practices, in the hands of capable advocates, may implicate two or more modes of proof.

§ 3.2

1. *Troupe v. May Dep't Stores Co.*, 20 F.3d 734 (7th Cir.1994).

2. But even in the case of express, racially discriminatory hiring barriers, plaintiff must show that his particular harm was experienced as a result of an application of the policy. *Perry v. Woodward*, 199 F.3d 1126, 1134 (10th Cir.1999), *cert. denied*, ___ U.S. ___, 120 S.Ct. 1964, 146 L.Ed.2d 796 (2000) (case under § 1981).

3. *See Laderach v. U–Haul of Northwestern Ohio*, 207 F.3d 825, 829 (6th Cir. 2000) (testimony that supervisor twice said he would not promote plaintiff to position in question is direct evidence of discriminatory animus even though same manager

kind of evidence "direct" if it is tied to, that is directly reflects, the alleged discriminatory animus.[4] This approach is hospitable to circumstantial evidence, but excludes evidence of "stray" remarks not sufficiently tied to the challenged decision as to shed light on the employer agent's intention in making it. Still other circuits, the "animus plus" courts, have insisted not just on evidence of animus but also that the statements reflecting the animus bear squarely on the contested employment decision.[5] Under any of these formulations, it appears that statements weakly proved or inherently ambiguous cannot be considered "direct" either for purposes of enabling plaintiff to avoid the elements of inferential, *McDonnell Douglas* proof[6] or to place the "same-decision" persuasion burden on defendant in mixed-motive cases.[7]

Even if courts refuse to characterize evidence as direct, thereby relieving plaintiff of proving the *McDonnell Douglas/Burdine/St. Mary's* elements, the same evidence may sometimes fortify the inferential *McDonnell Douglas* prima facie case and rebuttal evidence when plaintiff

had promoted her only one month earlier); *Perry v. Woodward,* 199 F.3d 1126, 1134 (10th Cir.1999), *cert. denied,* ___ U.S. ___, 120 S.Ct. 1964, 146 L.Ed.2d 796 (2000) (racist statements not direct evidence absent nexus between them and the decision to terminate) (case under § 1981); *Shorter v. ICG Holdings, Inc.,* 188 F.3d 1204, 1207 (10th Cir.1999); *Haas v. ADVO Sys., Inc.,* 168 F.3d 732, 734 n. 2 (5th Cir.1999); *Jones v. Bessemer Carraway Med. Ctr.,* 151 F.3d 1321, 1323 n. 11 (11th Cir.1998); *Carter v. Three Springs Residential Treatment,* 132 F.3d 635, 641–42 (11th Cir.1998); *Evans v. McClain of Ga., Inc.,* 131 F.3d 957, 962 (11th Cir.1997); *Troupe v. May Dep't Stores Co.,* 20 F.3d 734 (7th Cir.1994). *But see Wright v. Southland Corp.,* 187 F.3d 1287 (11th Cir.1999) (direct evidence is simply evidence from which reasonable factfinder could find causal link between protected characteristic and adverse action by a preponderance) (opinion of Tjoflat, J. alone).

4. *See Lightfoot v. Union Carbide Corp.,* 110 F.3d 898, 913 (2d Cir.1997); *Kerns v. Capital Graphics, Inc.,* 178 F.3d 1011, 1017–18 (8th Cir.1999); *Hennessy v. Penril Datacomm Networks, Inc.* 69 F.3d 1344, 1348–50 (7th Cir.1995).

5. *See Taylor v. Virginia Union Univ.,* 193 F.3d 219, 232 (4th Cir.1999) (en banc), *cert. denied,* ___ U.S. ___, 120 S.Ct. 1243, 146 L.Ed.2d 101 (2000) (statement that decisionmaker said he would never send another female to academy not direct evidence that his refusal to send plaintiff there was gender based for purposes of triggering "mixed motive" analysis); *Thomas v. National Football League Players Ass'n,* 131 F.3d 198, 204 (D.C.Cir.1997); *Lambert v. Ackerley,* 180 F.3d 997, 1008–09 (9th Cir.

1999) (en banc), *cert. denied,* 528 U.S. 1116, 120 S.Ct. 936, 145 L.Ed.2d 814 (2000); *Sheehan v. Donlen Corp.,* 173 F.3d 1039, 1044 (7th Cir.1999); *Deneen v. Northwest Airlines, Inc.,* 132 F.3d 431, 436 (8th Cir. 1998). *See also Holbrook v. Reno,* 196 F.3d 255 (D.C.Cir.1999) (evidence not "direct" because supervisor not shown to have harbored the forbidden animus or to have participated in challenged decision).

6. *See Damon v. Fleming Supermarkets of Florida, Inc.,* 196 F.3d 1354, 1358–59 (11th Cir.1999), *cert. denied,* ___ U.S. ___, 120 S.Ct. 1962, 146 L.Ed.2d 793 (2000) (supervisor's statement expressing preference for promoting young men, made right after supervisor had terminated plaintiff, not direct evidence that ageist animus motivated decision to terminate) (case under ADEA); *Hopkins v. Electronic Data Systems Corp.,* 196 F.3d 655 (6th Cir.1999) (case under Americans With Disabilities Act); *Carter v. Three Springs Residential Treatment,* 132 F.3d 635, 641 (11th Cir.1998).

7. *See Fernandes v. Costa Brothers Masonry, Inc.,* 199 F.3d 572, 583–84 (1st Cir. 1999); *Taylor v. Virginia Union Univ.,* 193 F.3d 219, 232 (4th Cir.1999) (en banc), *cert. denied,* ___ U.S. ___, 120 S.Ct. 1243, 146 L.Ed.2d 101 (2000) (statement that decisionmaker said he would never send another female to academy not direct evidence that his refusal to send plaintiff there was gender based for purposes of triggering "mixed motive" analysis); *Thomas,* 131 F.3d at 204; *Fields v. New York State Office of Mental Retardation and Developmental Disab.,* 115 F.3d 116, 122 (2d Cir.1997); *Fuller v. Phipps,* 67 F.3d 1137, 1142–43 (4th Cir.1995).

proceeds to prove discrimination under those decisions.[8] The definitional debate is critical for two reasons. First, as suggested, adequate "direct" evidence means the plaintiff need not prevail on the particular hire, promotion, discipline or discharge variant of the *McDonnell Douglas* elements. Second, as discussed in § 3.11 below, in mixed motive cases, an increasing number of appellate courts are placing the burden of persuasion on a defendant to show it would have reached the challenged decision for an independent, lawful reason only where the plaintiff's evidence of a concurrent, unlawful reason is "direct."

Despite the importance of the question, there remains rampant disagreement and confusion in the appellate decisional understanding of what evidence is "direct." It is even sometimes difficult to determine whether an employer policy may be said to discriminate expressly or facially on the basis of race, color, sex, religion or national origin. In the notorious *Gilbert*[9] decision that prompted Congress to spank the Court by enacting the Pregnancy Discrimination Act of 1978, the Court held that an employer rule that denied disability benefits for pregnancy but no other physical conditions did not discriminate "because of gender" within the meaning of § 703. The rule, the Court explained, treated pregnant women differently, relative to benefits, not only from men but also from nonpregnant women. The rule therefore did not draw a distinction on the basis of gender, even though its sting was felt only by women.

By the same reasoning, the practice of excluding fertile women from working in areas where they will encounter sufficient lead exposure to endanger a fetus or potential fetus might be conceived of as not predicated on gender: it, too, treats fertile women differently not only from all men but also from nonfertile women. Yet the Supreme Court, evidently chastened by the legislative overruling of the result in *Gilbert*, viewed such a practice as expressly gender discriminatory, observing that the adverse effects of the practice fell 100% on women.[10] Similarly, an employer or union requirement that a new applicant be related by blood or marriage to an existing employee or union member, while neutral in form, may result in the absolute exclusion of members of a protected group that historically was systematically excluded through intentional discrimination. Such practices have been viewed on occasion as instances of express, egregious discrimination.[11] In other words, practices that are formally neutral may be analyzed as intentional disparate treatment

---

8. *But cf. Montgomery v. John Deere & Co.*, 169 F.3d 556 (8th Cir.1999) (given weakness of prima facie case and absent evidence of pretext, references by supervisors and others to plaintiff as "old fart" not sufficient to raise inference of discrimination) (case under ADEA).

9. *General Elec. Co. v. Gilbert*, 429 U.S. 125, 97 S.Ct. 401, 50 L.Ed.2d 343 (1976).

10. *International Union, UAW v. Johnson Controls, Inc.*, 499 U.S. 187, 111 S.Ct. 1196, 113 L.Ed.2d 158 (1991). The Court

also relied for this conclusion on § 701(k) of Title VII, added by the Pregnancy Discrimination Act of 1978, which equates any discrimination concerning pregnancy or, as the Court held in *Johnson Controls*, the *capacity* to become pregnant, with express gender discrimination for purposes of § 703(a).

11. *See, e.g., EEOC v. Enterprise Ass'n Steamfitters Local No. 638*, 542 F.2d 579 (2d Cir.1976), *cert. denied*, 430 U.S. 911, 97 S.Ct. 1186, 51 L.Ed.2d 588 (1977).

when their adverse impact is not merely substantial but absolute, or put otherwise, when they correlate to a very high degree with exclusion of a group protected by Title VII.[12]

Unsurprisingly, outside the realm of policies that discriminate by their clear terms on the basis of a protected characteristic, cases presenting smoking-gun exemplars of "direct," "express" or "facial" evidence are relative rarities.[13] Three decades after the effective date of Title VII employers are familiar with the requirements and penalties of the statute and consequently more apt to comply or better skilled in disguising noncompliance. In *Price Waterhouse v. Hopkins*,[14] the Supreme Court has treated employers' agents' statements reflecting stereotypical views of women as direct evidence of gender discrimination, even when the views expressed bear somewhat tangentially on the plaintiff's capacity to perform the core elements of the position.[15]

Justice O'Connor's concurring opinion sets out three prerequisites for employer speech to constitute "direct" evidence: the remarks must be by the applicable decision maker, be related to the decision process, and not "stray."[16] In practice, however, this standard gives rise to multiple, interrelated issues. At a minimum, for plaintiff's evidence to be deemed "direct"—thus enabling her to avoid the difficult evidentiary requirements of the inferential *McDonnell Douglas/St. Mary's* mode of proof—the statements she relies on must have been made by the person

---

12. *Compare Hazen Paper Co. v. Biggins*, 507 U.S. 604, 113 S.Ct. 1701, 123 L.Ed.2d 338 (1993) (discrimination that correlates to some degree with age is not unlawful disparate treatment under ADEA, discussed in Chapter 7).

13. *But see Caban–Wheeler v. Elsea*, 71 F.3d 837 (11th Cir.1996) (black decisionmaker told white plaintiff he wanted a black person in that job; the white employee was subsequently fired).

14. 490 U.S. 228, 109 S.Ct. 1775, 104 L.Ed.2d 268 (1989) (plurality opinion and opinion of O'Connor, J.). Expressing doubt whether evidence of supervisory speech reflecting negative stereotypes is in fact "direct" evidence, one court has read *Price Waterhouse* as not requiring direct evidence to set in motion the mixed-motive burden shifting endorsed by that decision. *Tyler v. Bethlehem Steel Corp.*, 958 F.2d 1176 (2d Cir.1992), *cert. denied*, 506 U.S. 826, 113 S.Ct. 82, 121 L.Ed.2d 46 (1992).

15. *But see Galdieri–Ambrosini v. National Realty & Dev. Corp.*, 136 F.3d 276, 290 (2d Cir.1998) (assigning woman stereotypical women's tasks like personal work for boss, absent inference that assignments would not have been given to male secretary, not unlawful); *Tyler v. Bethlehem Steel Corp.*, 958 F.2d 1176 (2d Cir.), *cert. denied*, 506 U.S. 826, 113 S.Ct. 82, 121 L.Ed.2d 46 (1992) (expressing doubt whether evidence of supervisory speech reflecting negative stereotypes is in fact "direct" evidence and reading *Price Waterhouse* as not requiring direct evidence to set in motion the mixed-motive burden shifting endorsed by that decision).

16. 490 U.S. at 277, 109 S.Ct. at 1804. One court has expanded Justice O'Connor's concept to include circumstantial evidence that relates to the question of discrimination in the particular challenged employment decision, as opposed to more generalized workplace discrimination. *See Thomas v. National Football League Players Ass'n*, 131 F.3d 198, 204 (D.C.Cir.1997). But if the remarks were made by someone only partially responsible for an adverse employment decision, liability may not ensue. Further, the requirement that the speech be by a decision maker will sometimes encounter crosscurrents from the "same actor" doctrine. This rule of evidence favorable to the defendant permits the inference that the employer did not discriminate when the same employer agent hired as well as fired the plaintiff. *Buhrmaster v. Overnite Transp. Co.*, 61 F.3d 461 (6th Cir.1995), *cert. denied*, 516 U.S. 1078, 116 S.Ct. 785, 133 L.Ed.2d 736 (1996) (sex discrimination). This doctrine is discussed more fully in § 7.1, *infra*.

who made the adverse employment decision of which she complains, by someone with power to make effective recommendations to that decision-maker, or by someone in the control group to which that decisionmaker belongs.[17] Second, the content of the statement or statements, together with the context in which they were made, must suggest to the trier of fact that the decisionmaker in fact relied on the bias those statements reflect in making the decision in question. For this reason statements made by or to the decisionmaker in connection with the making of the decision at issue are treated as far more probative of prohibited discrimination[18] than those made by the decisionmaker or others at times remote or on matters unrelated to the employment decision plaintiff is challenging.[19] And evidence of the bias of a subordinate is relevant where the

17. *See Kennedy v. Schoenberg, Fisher & Newman Ltd.*, 140 F.3d 716 (7th Cir.), *cert. denied*, 525 U.S. 870, 119 S.Ct. 167, 142 L.Ed.2d 136 (1998) (slur must be uttered by a decisionmaker and made in connection with the challenged decision); *Trotter v. Board of Trustees*, 91 F.3d 1449 (11th Cir.1996); *Bruno v. City of Crown Point*, 950 F.2d 355 (7th Cir.1991), *cert. denied* 505 U.S. 1207, 112 S.Ct. 2998, 120 L.Ed.2d 874 (1992).

18. *See Wichmann v. Board of Trustees*, 180 F.3d 791 (7th Cir.1999), *vacated in light of Kimel v. Florida Bd. of Regents*, 528 U.S. 62, 120 S.Ct. 631, 145 L.Ed.2d 522 (2000) (supervisor's explanation of termination that "you have to cut down the old big trees so that the little trees can grow underneath" direct evidence of age discrimination); *Deneen v. Northwest Airlines, Inc.*, 132 F.3d 431 (8th Cir.1998) (decisionmaker's statement that plaintiff could not return to work without doctor's note direct evidence of pregnancy discrimination because context showed he relied only on her assumed pregnancy condition, even though he did not refer to pregnancy). *But see Radabaugh v. Zip Feed Mills, Inc.*, 997 F.2d 444 (8th Cir.1993) (corporate documents citing as an advantage that "top and middle level managers are mostly young, well educated and results oriented" cannot be discounted as stray remarks even though the documents did not directly concern the employment decision at issue).

19. *See, e.g., Shorter v. ICG Holdings, Inc.*, 188 F.3d 1204 (10th Cir.1999) (race-based comments made by decisionmaker about plaintiff contemporaneous with her termination deemed not direct evidence because not linked to the reasons for the decision to terminate her); *Simmons v. Oce–USA, Inc.*, 174 F.3d 913 (8th Cir.1999) (supervisor's telling of racially offensive joke and reference to African–American plaintiff as "Buckwheat" not direct because two years before and not linked to his deci-

sion to terminate); *Walton v. McDonnell Douglas Corp.*, 167 F.3d 423 (8th Cir.1999) (supervisor's statements two years before he implemented reduction in force lacked required nexus to challenged conduct); *Standard v. A.B.E.L. Servs., Inc.*, 161 F.3d 1318 (11th Cir.1998) (comments by management employees who were not part of hiring process did not constitute direct evidence of discrimination); *Fortier v. Ameritech Mobile Communications Inc.*, 161 F.3d 1106 (7th Cir.1998) (comments reflecting desire to put a woman in a management job were not direct evidence of discrimination because the comments were not temporally or logically related to much later decision to terminate the male who occupied that job); *Lynn v. Deaconess Med. Ctr.-West Campus*, 160 F.3d 484, 489 (8th Cir.1998); *Boyd v. State Farm Ins. Cos.*, 158 F.3d 326 (5th Cir.1998), *cert. denied*, 526 U.S. 1051, 119 S.Ct. 1357, 143 L.Ed.2d 518 (1999) (absent a causal link between decision not to promote and comments referring to a black employee as "Porch Monkey" comments are stray remarks insufficient to support jury verdict); *Indurante v. Local 705, Int'l Bhd. of Teamsters*, 160 F.3d 364 (7th Cir. 1998) (statement that all Italians will be fired accompanied by slur made 16 months before plaintiff's firing not direct because not referring to the termination of the particular plaintiff); *Eiland v. Trinity Hosp.*, 150 F.3d 747 (7th Cir.1998) (racist comments made by staff physician did not constitute direct evidence that race was a determining factor in hospital's discharge of nurse); *McKnight v. Kimberly Clark Corp.*, 149 F.3d 1125 (10th Cir.1998) (disparaging remarks by coworkers who lacked decision-making authority were insufficient to establish hostile work environment); *Stopka v. Alliance of Am. Insurers*, 141 F.3d 681 (7th Cir.1998) (statement by corporate general counsel that paying women less was justified because women do not work as hard

ultimate decisionmaker is not insulated from the subordinate's influence.[20]

There remains considerable uncertainty about how to differentiate those gender-or age-related comments or conduct that amount to "direct" evidence of discrimination and therefore, standing alone, create a

inadmissible absent causal link); *Sattar v. Motorola, Inc.*, 138 F.3d 1164 (7th Cir.1998) (evidence of egregious behavior not admissible absent nexus to adverse employment decision); *Jones v. Bessemer Carraway Med. Ctr.*, 151 F.3d 1321, 1323 (11th Cir.1998) (evidence of supervisor's racial animus does not establish prima facie case where remarks not connected to events prompting plaintiff's discharge for insubordination by upper management); *O'Connor v. Consolidated Coin Caterers Corp.*, 56 F.3d 542, 549 (4th Cir.1995), *rev'd on other grounds*, 517 U.S. 308, 116 S.Ct. 1307, 134 L.Ed.2d 433 (1996) (supervisor's statements, two weeks and two days, respectively, before ADEA plaintiff's discharge, that plaintiff was "too damn old" and that the company needed "young blood," held not tantamount to direct evidence of age discrimination because not immediately connected with termination decision).

20. *See, e.g., Lam v. University of Haw.*, 164 F.3d 1186 (9th Cir.1998) (evidence of comments made by female professor regarding the discriminatory attitudes of faculty members on the hiring committee was probative of alleged discrimination by that committee in a failure to hire case); *Kramer v. Logan County Sch. Dist. No. R-1*, 157 F.3d 620 (8th Cir.1998) (bias of nondecisionmakers imputed to decisionmaker when decisionmaker is infected by the bias); *Carey v. Mount Desert Island Hosp.*, 156 F.3d 31 (1st Cir.1998) (seemingly stray remarks by members of management group may show corporate state of mind despite not correlating precisely with the "particular actors or time frame involved in the specific events that generated" the claim); *Danzer v. Norden Systems, Inc.*, 151 F.3d 50 (2d Cir.1998) (jury could believe that speaker's derogatory remarks reflected company policy even though speaker was not the officer who fired plaintiff and comments were made more than a year before termination); *Fast v. Southern Union Co., Inc.*, 149 F.3d 885 (8th Cir.1998) (employee satisfied prima facie case where company executive made age disparaging remarks unrelated to plaintiff, but terminating supervisor testified that these remarks gave her "insight" into executive's expectations); *Robinson v. Runyon*, 149 F.3d 507 (6th Cir.1998) (a particularly offensive document relating to qualifica-

tions for hire deemed relevant in discharge case because it came to the attention of upper level management); *Griffin v. Washington Convention Ctr.*, 142 F.3d 1308 (D.C.Cir.1998) (evidence of subordinate's bias is relevant where ultimate decision maker is not insulated from subordinate's influence); *Ryther v. KARE 11*, 108 F.3d 832 (8th Cir.1997) (en banc), *cert. denied*, 521 U.S. 1119, 117 S.Ct. 2510, 138 L.Ed.2d 1013 (1997); *Stacks v. Southwestern Bell Yellow Pages, Inc.*, 27 F.3d 1316, 1323 (8th Cir.1994) ("an employer cannot escape responsibility for ... discrimination ... when the facts on which the reviewers rely have been filtered by a manager determined to purge the labor force of [a protected class of] workers"); *Simpson v. Diversitech General, Inc.*, 945 F.2d 156, 160 (6th Cir.1991); *Shager v. Upjohn Co.*, 913 F.2d 398, 405 (7th Cir.1990).

The decisions differ, however, over such factors as whether a negative stereotype uttered by a decisionmaker has to focus upon the alleged disqualification of plaintiff in particular, or only her group. *Compare Taylor v. Virginia Union Univ.*, 193 F.3d 219, 232 (4th Cir.1999) (en banc), *cert. denied*, ___ U.S. ___, 120 S.Ct. 1243, 146 L.Ed.2d 101 (2000) (statement that decisionmaker said he would never send another female to academy not direct evidence that his refusal to send plaintiff there was gender based for purposes of triggering "mixed motive" analysis); *Indurante v. Local 705, Int'l Bhd. of Teamsters, AFL-CIO*, 160 F.3d 364 (7th Cir.1998) (stray remarks do not constitute direct evidence where remarks by decisionmakers were temporally remote and did not refer to plaintiff directly) *and Burrell v. Board of Trustees of Ga. Military College*, 125 F.3d 1390 (11th Cir. 1997) (evidence that supervisor said he wanted a man for one position was not direct evidence that he would fire a woman in a different job because of her gender) *with Haynes v. W.C. Caye & Co.*, 52 F.3d 928 (11th Cir.1995) (statement about the incompetence of women in general to do the kind of job in question sufficient). Decisions also differ as to the requisite proximity in time between the decisionmaker's utterance and his imposition of an adverse term and condition of employment.

prima facie case, from merely "isolated" incidents or "stray" remarks.[21] Even though slurs and stereotypes are sometimes treated as "direct" evidence of discriminatory intent, their real meaning or purpose may be equivocal.[22] The frequent ambiguity of language and intent lends support to Judge Posner's observation that perhaps the "only true direct evidence of intent that will ever be available" consists of outright litigation admissions or policies that discriminate by their own terms on grounds prohibited by the statute.[23]

Even if such comments are accepted as "direct" evidence of discrimination, the plaintiff may also have to prove that the attitudes they reflect played at least a motivating part in the employment decision under challenge.[24] Discrimination "in the air," that is, must be brought

21. *See, e.g., Eilam v. Children's Hosp. Ass'n*, 173 F.3d 863 (10th Cir.1999) (supervisor's demand that Jewish worker provide rabbi's note to support worker's request for religious holiday leave and stray pro-Christian remarks unrelated to the challenged action were insufficient to rise jury issue on religious discrimination claim); *Blackwell v. Cole Taylor Bank*, 152 F.3d 666, 671 (7th Cir.1998) (stating that employer's concern that certain employees were not "flexible" or "energetic" is not evidence of age discrimination); *O'Connor v. DePaul Univ.*, 123 F.3d 665 (7th Cir.1997) (stray age-based remarks cannot by themselves establish pretext); *Woodson v. Scott Paper Co.*, 109 F.3d 913 (3d Cir.), *cert. denied*, 522 U.S. 914, 118 S.Ct. 299, 139 L.Ed.2d 230 (1997) (merely "permitting" racist graffiti in the workplace cannot be considered direct evidence of the employer's own attitudes); *Davis v. Chevron U.S.A., Inc.* 14 F.3d 1082 (5th Cir.1994) (testimony that interviewer stared at plaintiff "from neck down" is not direct evidence of gender discrimination); *Merrick v. Farmers Ins. Group*, 892 F.2d 1434 (9th Cir.1990) (calling the selectee preferred to plaintiff a "bright, knowledgeable young man" only a stray comment).

22. *See Smith v. Firestone Tire & Rubber Co.*, 875 F.2d 1325 (7th Cir.1989) (a manager's expression of dislike for plaintiff's "type" too ambiguous to be definitively linked to plaintiff's race); *Gray v. University of Ark.*, 883 F.2d 1394 (8th Cir.1989) (doubting that supervisor meant what he said because he was then suffering from mental illness). The author is indebted to Professors Zimmer, Sullivan, Richards and Calloway who have collected several of the foregoing examples in the third edition of their fine casebook, *Cases and Materials on Employment Discrimination* (Little Brown 1994).

23. *Troupe v. May Dep't Stores*, 20 F.3d 734 (7th Cir.1994). *See, e.g., Miles v. M.N.C. Corp.*, 750 F.2d 867 (11th Cir.1985) (evidence that decisionmaker said he didn't hire blacks because "half of them weren't worth a shit" constituted direct evidence of discrimination so as to relieve plaintiff of the burden of the inferential proof more). Terming the task of distinguishing direct from indirect evidence "hopeless," the Second Circuit has similarly observed: "Even a highly probative statement like 'You're fired, old man' still requires the factfinder to draw the inference that the plaintiff's age had a causal relationship to the decision." *Tyler v. Bethlehem Steel*, 958 F.2d at 1185–1187. For example, the Seventh Circuit declined to find that a police chief's statement to an officer "nigger, you're suspended" constituted direct evidence sufficient to create a triable issue of fact even though, as the dissent observed, the epithet was uttered in the same sentence as the suspension order. *Sanders v. Village of Dixmoor*, 178 F.3d 869 (7th Cir.), *cert. denied*, 528 U.S. 1020, 120 S.Ct. 529, 145 L.Ed.2d 410 (1999).

24. *See Price Waterhouse* (liability turns on whether the unlawful factor or factors among two or more "mixed" motives played a motivating part in the challenged decision). *See also Carter v. Three Springs Residential Treatment*, 132 F.3d 635, 643 (11th Cir.1998) (conclusory allegations of racial animus do not constitute direct evidence); *Oates v. Discovery Zone*, 116 F.3d 1161 (7th Cir.1997) (a supervisor's refusal to remove a workplace depiction of an African–American employee as a monkey may have reflected prejudice, but did not suffice to show that African–American employees suffered disparate treatment in terms and conditions of employment). In some of its evolving variations, "environmental" sexual harassment has the potential of punishing pure speech or expression and hence running afoul of the First Amendment. See § 2.22.

to ground, lest Title VII be used as a mechanism for controlling pure thought or speech. To do so the plaintiff must show first that a discriminatory attitude was to some degree actually relied on by the relevant decisionmaker. In one decision,[25] for example, Chief Judge Posner wrote for a panel, "Discrimination is not preference or aversion; it is acting on the preference or aversion." For this reason, he concluded, an employer who would prefer to exclude members of national origin groups other than his own does not violate Title VII even if the employment practice in question (there, word-of-mouth hiring) brings about that result, so long as the practice is motivated only by other reasons, e.g., efficiency.[26] Similarly, a statement attributable to management or even a sign on the employer's premises expressing a disinclination to hire members of a protected group probably does not by itself violate Title VII, although it would violate the fair employment laws of some states and municipalities.[27] Of course, to bring a prejudicial statement to actionable territory the plaintiff must also show that the difference in treatment adversely affected a term or condition of the plaintiff's employment.[28]

The tendency of recent appellate court decisions to strain against labeling evidence "direct" may be moderated by a recent Supreme Court decision that should substantially aid plaintiffs in surviving motions for summary judgment or judgment as a matter of law in cases presenting evidence of slurs or other derogatory references to the abilities or characteristics of the members of plaintiff's protected group. In *Reeves v. Sanderson Plumbing Products, Inc.*,[29] the Court, in reversing an appellate court's grant of judgment as a matter of law pursuant to Federal Rule of Civil Procedure 50, wrote that the lower court impermissibly supplanted the jury's judgment about the weight of the evidence. In particular, it criticized the appellate court for failing to draw all reasonable inferences in plaintiff's favor on the question of whether the slur utterer was the actual decisionmaker and for discounting his age-related comments on the ground that they were not made directly in the context of plaintiff's termination. Rather, it described the manager's remarks as

---

25. *EEOC v. Consolidated Serv. Systems*, 989 F.2d 233, 236 (7th Cir.1993).

26. *Id.* at 236. *See also Chambers v. American Trans Air Inc.*, 17 F.3d 998 (7th Cir.), *cert. denied*, 513 U.S. 1001, 115 S.Ct. 512, 130 L.Ed.2d 419 (1994) (verbal expressions of bigotry aimed at women insufficient for plaintiff to resist summary judgment absent evidence of how sexism translated into lesser wage increases for her than for similarly situated males).

27. Title VII's only express pure-speech prohibition is found in § 704(b), which bans "any notice or advertisement relating to employment" that indicates a preference or limitation based on one of the prohibited grounds. But certain forms of "environmental" sexual harassment based on employer

or co-worker speech alone might be seen as another exception to Judge Posner's general observation. That is precisely why such regulation has raised First Amendment concerns. See Chapter 2.

28. *See Sanchez v. Denver Public Sch.*, 164 F.3d 527 (10th Cir.1998) (transfer at same pay not materially adverse despite longer commute); *Bragg v. Navistar Int'l Transp. Corp.*, 164 F.3d 373 (7th Cir.1998); *Crady v. Liberty Nat'l Bank & Trust Co.*, 993 F.2d 132 (7th Cir.1993) (ADEA case finding no violation because transfer did not diminish plaintiff's compensation or responsibilities).

29. 530 U.S. 133, 120 S.Ct. 2097, 147 L.Ed.2d 105 (2000).

"potentially damning" evidence of age-related bias, "critical" support for plaintiff's prima facie case, and "additional evidence that . . . [the manager] was motivated by age-based animus."[30]

The Court's deference to jury determinations was fortified more generally by its insistence that a reviewing court (presumably trial or appellate) assessing a Rule 50 motion "must disregard all evidence favorable to the moving party that the jury is not required to believe. . . . That is, the court should give credence to [all] the evidence favoring the nonmovant as well as [only] that 'evidence supporting the moving party that is uncontradicted and unimpeached, at least to the extent that that evidence comes from disinterested witnesses.' "[31] Moreover, since the Court reaffirmed in *Reeves* that the standards governing Rule 56 summary judgment motions are identical to those applicable to Rule 50 motions for judgment as a matter of law, these directives should also aid the plaintiff in resisting summary judgment motions based on the asserted inadequacy of evidence of slurs and similar evidence that is arguably "direct."

An employer's use of a facially unlawful classification like race or gender is treated as a form of express evidence, which has different legal significance than the "direct" evidence of discrimination that a court may find in a non-stray slur. Where an express classification is adopted by an employer representative informally—as where a supervisor decides that no women may hold a certain job—the employer's only defense is to establish that being male is a bona fide occupational qualification for the particular position, as discussed in the subsection that follows. By contrast, the Supreme Court has devised a special set of justificatory factors an employer must meet to sustain formal "benign," "voluntary" employer affirmative action programs.[32]

§ 3.3   The "BFOQ" Affirmative Defense

Section 703(e)(1) affords an employer a defense—the only defense—to policies or work rules that expressly or facially discriminate on the basis of gender, religion or national origin. It authorizes the employer to "hire and employ" (and a labor organization or joint labor management committee to "admit or employ" to membership or apprenticeship or retraining programs) on the basis of gender, religion or national origin when any of those characteristics is a "bona fide occupational qualification ['BFOQ'] reasonably necessary to the normal operation" of the enterprise. It does not excuse discrimination in post-hire terms and conditions of employment—compensation, promotion, discipline, harassment or discharge[1]—or any discrimination on the basis of race. ADEA contains a similarly worded BFOQ defense, and the Court has construed

30. Slip opinion at 16–18.

31. Slip opinion at 16–18.

32. *Johnson v. Transportation Agency,* 480 U.S. 616, 107 S.Ct. 1442, 94 L.Ed.2d 615 (1987). See Chapter 4 on the conditions that make such programs permissible.

§ 3.3

1. *See EEOC v. Fremont Christian Sch.,* 781 F.2d 1362, 1367 (9th Cir.1986).

the corresponding provisions of the two statutes virtually identically.[2] Perhaps because BFOQ serves as a defense to intentional, facial discrimination, the form most disfavored by the public and the Congress, the federal courts have given the defense very limited sway.

As its text would suggest, BFOQ is a true affirmative defense which the employer therefore has the burden of pleading and proving by a preponderance of the evidence. But the bare language of § 703(e)(1) would appear satisfied if an employer can show that a refusal to hire based on religion, sex, or national origin is reasonably necessary to the normal operation of the defendant's overall "enterprise." The text, that is, would not seem to require the employer to show that its discriminatory exclusion is conducive to the sound performance of the particular plaintiff's job, only that it is necessary to further general business goals. Nor does the text suggest that the discriminatory job qualification must relate to the heart of employer's business, only to its "normal operation." Yet in order to prevent the exception from virtually eliminating an applicant's protection against these forms of express discrimination, the Supreme Court has required the employer to show that its discriminatory rule relates to a trait that goes to the "essence" of the enterprise *and* bears a "high correlation" to the plaintiff's ability to perform her particular job.[3]

The two basic elements of the defense derive from a pair of decisions of the former Fifth Circuit, *Diaz v. Pan American World Airways, Inc.*,[4] and *Weeks v. Southern Bell Telephone & Telegraph Company.*[5] *Diaz* insisted that the job qualification or employee trait for which the employer's practice or policy screens must be closely related to the "essence" of the business. In that case, for example, the psychological reassurance or sexual titillation ostensibly afforded airline passengers by a requirement that flight attendants be female could not justify the exclusion of males once the court defined the essence of the business as safe transportation rather than maximum profit. Federal judges have since steadfastly refused to permit employers to define the essence of their business as maximizing profit, because then customer preference—often the embodiment of the very kind of accumulated prejudice or stereotype Title VII seeks to overcome—could be invoked to justify a vast range of absolute exclusions of women, minorities, and adherents of particular religions.[6] Despite the stringency of the *Diaz* "essence of the business" test, it remained uncertain until recently whether the trait for which the discriminatory employment rule selects must also relate to the duties of the particular jobs to which the rule is applied.

2. *See, e.g., Western Air Lines, Inc. v. Criswell*, 472 U.S. 400, 105 S.Ct. 2743, 86 L.Ed.2d 321 (1985).

3. *Criswell*, 472 U.S. 400, 105 S.Ct. 2743, 86 L.Ed.2d 321; *Johnson Controls*, 499 U.S. 187, 111 S.Ct. 1196, 113 L.Ed.2d 158.

4. 442 F.2d 385 (5th Cir.), *cert. denied*, 404 U.S. 950, 92 S.Ct. 275, 30 L.Ed.2d 267 (1971).

5. 408 F.2d 228 (5th Cir.1969).

6. *See Fernandez v. Wynn Oil Co.*, 653 F.2d 1273 (9th Cir.1981).

Weeks added the second layer. Even if an exclusion of members of a particular protected group is designed to enhance execution of a function critical to the business, the employer's evidence must demonstrate that "all or substantially all" members of the excluded group lack the required trait and would therefore be unable adequately to perform that function. This test is not quite as rigorous as the rule once prevalent in the Ninth Circuit[7] that the BFOQ defense could exclude members of a particular gender only from jobs they were biologically incapable of performing—male wet nurse or female sperm donor. But the *Weeks* test nevertheless defeats most assertions of the defense. By putting employers to their proof, it will doom most BFOQ defenses rooted in the assertion that only members of a particular gender have the strength or endurance required by the job.

Purporting to apply the *Weeks* test, the Supreme Court a decade ago appeared to endorse an alternative, less stringent version of the defense. The employer could prevail by proving that some, rather than "substantially all," members of the excluded gender, religion or national origin lack the critical ability to perform the trait essential to the business and that it would be highly impracticable to determine by individualized testing which ones could.[8] Casting further doubt on the Court's commitment to the *Weeks* "substantially all" test was an early decision, *Dothard v. Rawlinson*,[9] that upheld the exclusion of women from contact positions as guards in unusually dangerous maximum security prisons in Alabama. The exigent circumstances there that threatened the physical safety of employees and inmates salvaged the BFOQ defense even though Alabama had failed to offer any evidence that substantially all of the women who would seek those jobs would be incapable of maintaining order and safety. The Court merely hypothesized that women guards would be attacked (by sex offender inmates and others deprived of regular heterosexual contact) because they were women, skipping over the fact, stressed by Justice Marshall in dissent, that *all* guards in the Alabama maximum security system were targets simply because they were despised authority symbols.

The Supreme Court's decision in *International Union, U.A.W. v. Johnson Controls*[10] confirms the narrowness of the BFOQ defense, and appears to have closed to employers the doors it had left ajar in previous decisions. The employer's rule barred all still-fertile women of any age, marital status, or child-bearing inclination from holding a job in which they would likely be exposed to levels of lead that endangered the health of a fetus they might be carrying. First, the Court made clear, as it had in an ADEA case,[11] that in applying the *Diaz* prong of the defense, the trait the employer seeks to ensure with its discriminatory rule must not

---

7. *Rosenfeld v. Southern Pacific*, 519 F.2d 527 (9th Cir.1975).

8. *Criswell*, 472 U.S. 400, 105 S.Ct. 2743, 86 L.Ed.2d 321 (1985).

9. 433 U.S. 321, 97 S.Ct. 2720, 53 L.Ed.2d 786 (1977).

10. 499 U.S. 187, 111 S.Ct. 1196, 113 L.Ed.2d 158 (1991).

11. *Trans World Airlines, Inc. v. Thurston*, 469 U.S. 111, 105 S.Ct. 613, 83 L.Ed.2d 523 (1985).

only be essential to the business as a whole but must also pertain to the particular position in question. It stressed the "occupational" limitation in § 703(e)(1), concluding that the defense fails unless the employer demonstrates objectively that the exclusion is not only "reasonably necessary" to the "normal operation"[12] of the "particular"[13] business but also relates to "job-related skills and aptitudes." The Court rejected the defense because, so far as the record revealed, "Fertile women ... participate in the manufacture of batteries as efficiently as anyone else."[14] In this connection the Court distinguished *Dothard* and *Western Air Lines, Inc. v. Criswell*,[15] writing that third-party safety concerns were allowed to figure into the BFOQ analyses there only because inmate or customer safety "went to the core of the employee's job performance"—something demonstrably not the case with batterymaking.

Johnson Controls appears also to have restricted or eliminated the employer's option to skirt *Weeks* by showing only that some, rather than "substantially all" members of the excluded group lack traits essential to the job and business and that it is "impracticable" to ascertain the ones who do. The employer contended that it had to exclude all fertile women from the jobs in question because it could not feasibly determine which of them would become pregnant and thus endanger their fetuses and, in turn, subject the company to the risk of tort liability. The Supreme Court responded by reaffirming *Weeks*. Even assuming, it wrote, that the company had shown sufficient job-and business-related justification for excluding fertile women, it had not shown that "substantially all of its fertile women employees" presented the risk on which the company relied.[16] When the two requirements, re-refined by *Johnson Controls*, are combined, the defendant faces a formidable task: "An employer must direct its concerns about a woman's ability to perform her job safely and efficiently to those aspects of the woman's job-related activities that fall within the 'essence' of the particular business."[17]

Johnson Controls also squarely rejected arguments to expand the scope of the defense to embrace the employer's economic concerns

---

12. As Justice Marshall had observed in his dissent in *Dothard*, it is doubtful whether the exclusion of women would have been essential to the "normal" operation of Alabama's maximum security prisons, and as such could not be justified by the rampant violence, unconstitutional conditions of confinement, and other exceptional circumstances that then prevailed.

13. The statutory requirement of evidence that the rule is needed to meet the needs of a "particular" business also helps explain why general definitions of business essence in terms of profit or customer preference have not carried the day.

14. The Court also dismissed as "word play" an argument that the essence of *Johnson Controls'* business was "to make batteries without risk to fetuses." 499 U.S. at 207, 111 S.Ct. at 1208.

15. 472 U.S. 400, 105 S.Ct. 2743, 86 L.Ed.2d 321 (1985) (considering but ultimately rejecting a BFOQ defense based on alleged increased safety concerns related to the deteriorating health of flight engineers retained after age 60).

16. The Court found that *Johnson Controls* had fallen short of that showing because so few fertile women become pregnant in any one year and none of the babies born to its pregnant employees had birth defects or abnormalities.

17. *Johnson Controls*, 499 U.S. at 205, 111 S.Ct. at 1206.

associated with hiring members of a particular gender, religion, or national origin. The argument was generated by the employer's "fear that hiring fertile women will cost more" as the result of "the spectre of an award of damages" in tort actions that might be brought for prenatal injury or wrongful death. "The extra cost of employing members of one sex ... does not provide an affirmative Title VII defense for a[n express] discriminatory refusal to hire members of that gender."[18] Here it is important to remember, however, that BFOQ is a defense to intentional, disparate treatment discrimination. By contrast, cost savings are in effect available as a defense to claims that an employer's neutral practice disproportionately adversely impacted the plaintiff's group.[19]

Given the stringency of the BFOQ defense, its principal remaining utility may lie in resisting claims of age discrimination, especially in cases where an employee's deteriorating physical capabilities correlate strongly with aging and would impair safe hands-on performance.[20] It is scarcely conceivable, moreover, that the BFOQ defense could ever justify a slur, as opposed to an employer policy. Lower courts have, however, upheld relaxed applications of the defense to accommodate a legitimate business need to assure customer privacy.[21] Moreover, EEOC guidelines

18. *Johnson Controls, Inc.*, (individual disparate treatment case); *see also City of Los Angeles, Dep't of Water and Power v. Manhart*, 435 U.S. 702, 98 S.Ct. 1370, 55 L.Ed.2d 657 (1978) (systemic disparate treatment case).

19. *See* discussion below of the plaintiff's "less discriminatory alternative" rebuttal to the defendant's job relatedness/business necessity defense in disproportionate adverse impact cases. The statute as amended in 1991 may be construed to carry forward the Supreme Court's observations in the 1988 *Watson* case that a plaintiff's proposed less discriminatory alternative to the defendant's challenged practice must be "equally as effective" as the defendant's neutral practice under challenge, and that cost is a factor in equal effectiveness. *See* § 3.35 *infra*.

20. *See Usery v. Tamiami Trail Tours, Inc.*, 531 F.2d 224 (5th Cir.1976), cited with approval in *Criswell*, 472 U.S. at 412, 105 S.Ct. at 2750.

21. *Robino v. Iranon*, 145 F.3d 1109 (9th Cir.1998) (BFOQ for gender where correctional facility post required guard to accompany female prisoners to bathroom); *Healey v. Southwood Psychiatric Hosp.*, 78 F.3d 128 (3d Cir.1996) (gender a BFOQ justifying assignment of female hospital employee to night shift to further the privacy interests and therapeutic needs of patients); *Tharp v. Iowa Dep't of Corrections*, 68 F.3d 223 (8th Cir.1995), *cert. denied*, 517 U.S. 1135, 116 S.Ct. 1420, 134 L.Ed.2d 545

(1996) (rule precluding male employees from working certain shifts in women's prison unit justified by inmates' privacy interests in having only women conduct body searches); *Moteles v. University of Pa.*, 730 F.2d 913 (3d Cir.), *cert. denied*, 469 U.S. 855, 105 S.Ct. 179, 83 L.Ed.2d 114 (1984); *Local 567 Am. Fed'n of State, County, and Mun. Employees, AFL–CIO v. Michigan Council 25, Am. Fed'n of State, County, and Mun. Employees, AFL–CIO*, 635 F.Supp. 1010, 1012 (E.D.Mich.1986) (allowing sex BFOQ to protect privacy rights of mental health patients); *Backus v. Baptist Med. Ctr.*, 510 F.Supp. 1191 (E.D.Ark. 1981), *vacated as moot*, 671 F.2d 1100 (8th Cir.1982) (essential to hospital's business to safeguard patient concerns about privacy in the assignment of nurses) noted by the Supreme Court in *Johnson Controls*, 499 U.S. at 205, 111 S.Ct. at 1206, *Fesel v. Masonic Home of Delaware, Inc.*, 447 F.Supp. 1346 (D.Del.1978) (nursing home attendants), *aff'd*, 591 F.2d 1334 (3d Cir.1979). *Cf. Hodgson v. Robert Hall Clothes, Inc.*, 473 F.2d 589 (3d Cir.1973), *cert. denied*, 414 U.S. 866, 94 S.Ct. 50, 38 L.Ed.2d 85 (1973) (not challenging assignment of men only as salespersons in men's clothing department in case under EPA). *But see U.S. EEOC v. Sedita*, 755 F.Supp. 808, 810 (N.D.Ill.1991) (defense to a hiring rule that excluded men rejected for failure of proof that the privacy interests of health club customers were "entitled to protection under the law" and that no less discriminatory alternatives existed), *vacated on reconsideration*, 816

relax the rules where employers have an interest in the gender-authenticity of such employees as actresses, actors, strippers, and food and drink servers at restaurants or bars where a primary job and business function is the projection of a sexually provocative display.[22]

The Seventh Circuit has adopted a narrow, judicially-crafted racial BFOQ,[23] but subsequently limited its utility to the areas of law enforcement and corrections.[24] The Eleventh Circuit has rejected the application of the BFOQ defense to race-based discrimination.[25]

§§ 3.4–6.9 [Reserved]

B. INDIVIDUAL DISPARATE TREATMENT—
INFERENTIAL PROOF

§ 3.10 In General

Because direct evidence of intent has, at least before the Supreme Court's recent decision in *Reeves* discussed in § 3.2 , supra, been so rarely accepted, courts have recognized alternative ways of establishing unlawful discrimination. Circumstantial evidence may be classified into three types which, alone or in reinforcing combination, may suffice to show intentional discrimination forbidden by Title VII. First there is suspicious timing, ambiguous statements, or other behavior toward or comments directed at other employees in the protected group from which an inference of discriminatory intent might be drawn.

Second is evidence, statistical or anecdotal, that persons outside the plaintiff's protected group, otherwise similarly situated to the plaintiff, were treated differently with respect to the relevant terms and condi-

---

F.Supp. 1291 (1993) (evidence indicated men might invade privacy interests). *But cf. Johnson v. Phelan,* 69 F.3d 144 (7th Cir. 1995), *cert. denied sub nom. Johnson v. Sheahan,* 519 U.S. 1006, 117 S.Ct. 506, 136 L.Ed.2d 397 (1996) (naked male detainee's due process and Eighth Amendment rights not violated when he was monitored by female guards absent allegation that monitoring was designed to embarrass or humiliate him); *United States v. Gregory,* 818 F.2d 1114, 1114 (4th Cir.), *cert. denied,* 484 U.S. 847, 108 S.Ct. 143, 98 L.Ed.2d 99 (1987) (sheriff failed to establish that sex was a BFOQ in positions at an all-male jail). *But see Reed v. County of Casey,* 184 F.3d 597 (6th Cir.1999) (upholding as BFOQ reassignment of female deputy to graveyard shift to oversee and transport female prisoners as required by state law). *Contra Garrett v. Okaloosa County,* 734 F.2d 621, 624 (11th Cir.1984) (refusing to recognize BFOQ to justify regulation that prohibited female correctional officers from guarding male inmates).

22. *See* 29 C.F.R. § 1604.2 (1979) (actors and actresses).

23. *Wittmer v. Peters,* 87 F.3d 916 (7th Cir.1996), *cert. denied,* 519 U.S. 1111, 117 S.Ct. 949, 136 L.Ed.2d 837 (1997) (upholding "role model" theory as adequate constitutional justification for preferring African-American correctional officers for promotion based on expert testimony that African-American lieutenants were "needed because the black inmates are believed unlikely to play the correctional game of brutal drill sergeant and brutalized recruit unless there are some blacks in authority" in quasi-military "boot camp" setting).

24. *See McNamara v. City of Chicago,* 138 F.3d 1219 (7th Cir.), *cert. denied,* 525 U.S. 981, 119 S.Ct. 444, 142 L.Ed.2d 398 (1998) (declining to extend racial BFOQ to firefighters).

25. *See Ferrill v. Parker Group,* 168 F.3d 468, 475 (11th Cir.1999) (no BFOQ defense to race-matched telemarketing or polling).

tions of employment. This of course is the essence of disparate treatment, but plaintiffs should take care that their "comparator" is in fact similarly situated from the standpoint of status or conduct.[1] In one appellate decision, the court in effect viewed the Hispanic plaintiff laid off in a force reduction as a member of a (white) racial group, rather than as representing a particular national origin. Accordingly, it compared him not to non-Hispanics, who fared well in the force reduction, but to African–American employees, none of whom was terminated.[2] A pair of contemporaneous circuit decisions illustrate through comparator evidence the unlawfulness of differential race-based job assignments—in one case driven by actual customer preference,[3] in the other by stereotypical assumptions about managerial effectiveness.[4]

The third, or "pretext" mode, is perhaps most easily understood as an even more indirect way of showing the second, or "comparative" mode.

§ 3.10

1. *See, e.g., Lynn v. Deaconess Med. Ctr.-West Campus*, 160 F.3d 484 (8th Cir. 1998) (where plaintiff proceeds on a theory that he was disciplined more harshly than coworkers, plaintiff can establish that he was similarly situated by showing that he was treated differently than other employees whose work rule violations were comparable); *Hargett v. National Westminster Bank, USA*, 78 F.3d 836 (2d Cir.1996), *cert. denied*, 519 U.S. 824, 117 S.Ct. 84, 136 L.Ed.2d 41 (1996) (African–American employee could be subjected to harsher discipline than ostensible white comparators because he held position of higher rank and authority and accordingly could be held to higher standard of judgment and behavior). On the other hand, employees of different ranks may be "similarly situated" for the purpose of assessing the disparate discipline they received if both violated the same or substantially similar work rule. *Lathem v. Department of Children and Youth Servs.*, 172 F.3d 786, 793 (11th Cir.1999). "The relevant inquiry is not whether the employees hold the same job titles, but whether the employer subjected them to different employment policies." Thus, "when an individual proves that he was fired but one outside his class was retained although both violated the same work rule, this raises an inference that the rule was discriminatorily applied." *Nix v. WLCY Radio/Rahall Communications*, 738 F.2d 1181, 1186 (11th Cir. 1984). In this analysis, the most important factors "are the nature of the offenses committed and the punishments imposed." *Lathem*, 172 F.3d at 793. Thus an employer was permitted to exact harsher discipline (termination) on a fire department's clerical employee for her inadequate typing skills, mistakes in correspondence, and managing time than on three other employees for

verbal abuse, sleeping on the job and violating the fire code, and reading a co-employee's e-mail. *Kline v. City of Kansas City, Mo.*, 175 F.3d 660 (8th Cir.1999), *cert. denied*, ___ U.S. ___, 120 S.Ct. 1160, 145 L.Ed.2d 1072 (2000). Applying the same factors, another circuit upheld the discharge of a bank branch manager for failing to prevent further theft by a teller because the manager had greater responsibility respecting that task than another managerial employee who had also failed to prevent the theft but was retained. *Cardona Jimenez v. Bancomercio de Puerto Rico*, 174 F.3d 36 (1st Cir.1999). *See also Ricks v. Riverwood Int'l Corp.*, 38 F.3d 1016 (8th Cir.1994) (plaintiff could be discharged for felony drug conviction even though white coworker not discharged for the felony of armed false imprisonment because drugs were a particular workplace hazard and employer had drug use and testing policy); *Harvey v. Anheuser–Busch, Inc.*, 38 F.3d 968 (8th Cir. 1994) (discharge upheld because less severely disciplined employees had not engaged in same offense); *Polanco v. City of Austin*, 78 F.3d 968 (5th Cir.1996).

2. *Jackson v. E.J. Brach Corp.*, 176 F.3d 971 (7th Cir.1999).

3. *Ferrill v. Parker Group, Inc.*, 168 F.3d 468 (11th Cir.1999) (at the request of political candidates, telemarketing company engaged in get-out-the-vote pre-election calling required white employees to use a "white" script to call white voters and black employees to use a "black" script to call black voters). (case under § 1981).

4. *Johnson v. Zema Sys. Corp.*, 170 F.3d 734 (7th Cir.1999) (black supervisor fired for varying from race-based restrictions on the subordinate salespersons with whom he was permitted to have working relationships and friendships).

This method of proving "individual disparate treatment" owes its origin to *McDonnell Douglas Corp. v. Green*,[5] and was later elaborated in several other Supreme Court decisions culminating in *Texas Dep't of Community Affairs v. Burdine*,[6] and, most recently, *St. Mary's Honor Ctr. v. Hicks*.[7] The plaintiff makes a *McDonnell Douglas prima facie* showing in a failure to hire case—and thereby survives a Federal Rule of Civil Procedure 41(b) involuntary dismissal motion, or, in the jury trials authorized by the Civil Rights Act of 1991, a Rule 50(a)(1) motion for judgment as a matter of law at the close of her case in chief—by offering evidence that she (1) belongs to a protected group; (2) applied for or continued to desire the position in question; (3) met minimum uniform qualifications to receive or retain the position; and (4) was rejected, and thereafter the employer continued to receive applications from persons having the complainant's qualifications. This evidence, the Court has explained, eliminates several of the most common nondiscriminatory reasons for the plaintiff's failure to be hired (or other rejection, nonpromotion, discipline or discharge) and thus makes it more likely that the employer's real reason, or one of them, was a status protected by Title VII. In brief, when a qualified employee who is a member of a racial minority traditionally victimized by workplace discrimination is not hired for a vacant job, the failure to hire alone suffices to raise an inference of discrimination, which the employer must then rebut by producing evidence of a legitimate, nondiscriminatory reason.[8]

The elements, as the Court in *McDonnell Douglas* noted, are flexibly adapted to the facts of a given case. For example, the first of the numbered prima facie elements is *pro forma*—anyone, even a white male, can claim protected group status by contrasting himself in racial, religious, national origin, or gender terms to the group he claims was preferred.[9] Further, an employee complaining of promotion denial need

5. 411 U.S. 792, 93 S.Ct. 1817, 36 L.Ed.2d 668 (1973).

6. 450 U.S. 248, 101 S.Ct. 1089, 67 L.Ed.2d 207 (1981).

7. 509 U.S. 502, 113 S.Ct. 2742, 125 L.Ed.2d 407 (1993).

8. *See International Brotherhood of Teamsters v. United States*, 431 U.S. 324, 358 n. 44, 97 S.Ct. 1843, 52 L.Ed.2d 396 (1977) (Title VII claims of failure to hire and failure to promote).

9. *See McDonald*, 427 U.S. 273, 96 S.Ct. 2544. But some circuits have required in cases alleging discrimination against white plaintiffs additional evidence of "background circumstances" tending to prove that the defendant is the "unusual employer who discriminates against the majority." *See, e.g., Mills v. Health Care Serv. Corp.*, 171 F.3d 450 (7th Cir.1999); *Taken v. Oklahoma Corp. Comm'n*, 125 F.3d 1366, 1369 (10th Cir.1997); *Duffy v. Wolle*, 123 F.3d 1026, 1037 (8th Cir.1997), *cert. denied*, 523

U.S. 1137, 118 S.Ct. 1839, 140 L.Ed.2d 1090 (1998); *Reynolds v. School Dist. No. 1.* 69 F.3d 1523, 1534 (10th Cir.1995) (in failure to promote claims based on *McDonnell Douglas* evidence, requiring white plaintiffs, and those only, to show as part of prima facie case that person of another race received the promotion); *Murray v. Thistledown Racing Club, Inc.*, 770 F.2d 63, 66–67 (6th Cir.1985); *Parker v. Baltimore & Ohio R.R.*, 652 F.2d 1012, 1017 (D.C.Cir.1981); *Notari v. Denver Water Dep't*, 971 F.2d 585 (10th Cir.1992). But *see Pierce v. Commonwealth Life Ins. Co.*, 40 F.3d 796, 801 n. 7 (6th Cir.1994) (questioning additional requirement). In a failure to promote situation, the white or male plaintiff can meet this burden by proving that the plaintiff's qualifications were superior to those of the successful minority applicant, *Harding v. Gray*, 9 F.3d 150, 154 (D.C.Cir.1993)—a showing the Supreme Court has specifically ruled is not required in the ordinary Title VII case. *Patterson v. McLean Credit Union*,

not show element (2), that she applied for the higher position, if it was the employer's routine practice to offer promotions to persons with her seniority and position.[10] In general, however, courts read *McDonnell Douglas* to require a plaintiff to allege that she applied for a specific position for which she was rejected, rather than merely asserting that from time to time she requested promotion at large.[11] But a number of circuits have relieved plaintiffs of submitting a formal application for a particular position where the position was not posted, there was no formal application mechanism, and the employee had no knowledge of the position[12] or applied informally for a specific position in a manner endorsed by the employer.[13] The third element, qualifications for the position sought, has the greatest practical importance, as it eliminates the most common nondiscriminatory reason for rejection where an application for hire or promotion has been made. The Court has now declared relatively clearly that this showing refers to minimal or absolute rather than relative or comparative qualifications.[14] The final ele-

491 U.S. 164, 109 S.Ct. 2363, 105 L.Ed.2d 132 (1989). The same skepticism about anti-white animus under current social conditions has led one circuit to doubt that the inferential mode of proving intentional discrimination under *McDonnell Douglas* is available at all in cases of reverse discrimination. *See, e.g., Hill v. Burrell Communications Group, Inc.,* 67 F.3d 665, 668 n. 2 (7th Cir.1995). By contrast, the Third and Eleventh Circuits apply the ordinary *McDonnell Douglas/Burdine* formula to a white plaintiff's claim of race discrimination, with no mention of any required "background circumstances." *Iadimarco v. Runyon,* 190 F.3d 151 (3d Cir.1999); *Schoenfeld v. Babbitt,* 168 F.3d 1257, 1267–68 (11th Cir.1999). Direct evidence, of course, will support a reverse discrimination claim. *See McGarry v. Bd. of County Comm'rs of County of Pitkin,* 175 F.3d 1193 (10th Cir. 1999).

10. *Loyd v. Phillips Bros., Inc.,* 25 F.3d 518 (7th Cir.1994). *Cf. Lyoch v. Anheuser–Busch Cos.,* 139 F.3d 612 (8th Cir.1998) (describing plaintiff's lighter burden in prima facie case for nonpromotion where employers have a subjective and informal promotion policy).

11. *Brown v. Coach Stores, Inc.,* 163 F.3d 706, 710 (2d Cir.1998). The majority opinion in *Brown* also strongly suggests that an individual plaintiff cannot avoid the specific application requirement by relying on the "futility" doctrine of *International Bhd. of Teamsters v. United States,* 431 U.S. 324, 97 S.Ct. 1843, 52 L.Ed.2d 396 (1977), which permits class members at remedial phase of a systemic disparate treatment case to excuse their nonapplication by reference to the defendant's notorious practice of discriminating against her group.

12. *See Mauro v. Southern New England Telecomm., Inc.,* 208 F.3d 384, 386–387 (2d Cir.2000) (plaintiff alleging failure to promote need not show application for job in question where he had indicated interest in being promoted to relevant class of positions but was unaware of specific vacancies because employer did not post them); *Lyoch v. Anheuser–Busch Cos.,* 139 F.3d 612 (8th Cir.1998) (failure to post, coupled with subjective promotion criteria, raises suspicion of discrimination where non-minority members were solicited to apply); *Kehoe v. Anheuser–Busch, Inc.,* 96 F.3d 1095, 1105 n. 13 (8th Cir.1996); *Bernard v. Gulf Oil Corp.,* 841 F.2d 547, 570 (5th Cir. 1988); *Carmichael v. Birmingham Saw Works,* 738 F.2d 1126, 1132–33 (11th Cir. 1984); *Paxton v. Union Nat'l Bank,* 688 F.2d 552, 568 (8th Cir.1982), *cert. denied,* 460 U.S. 1083, 103 S.Ct. 1772, 76 L.Ed.2d 345 (1983) (plaintiff did not hear of unposted vacancy until after position filled); *cf. Chambers v. Wynne Sch. Dist.,* 909 F.2d 1214, 1217 (8th Cir.1990) (prima facie case fails because plaintiff had notice of position yet failed to apply).

13. *See Dews v. A.B. Dick Co.,* 231 F.3d 1016 (6th Cir. 2000); *EEOC v. Metal Serv. Co.,* 892 F.2d 341, 349 (3d Cir.1990); *Holsey v. Armour & Co.,* 743 F.2d 199, 208–09 (4th Cir.1984), *cert. denied,* 470 U.S. 1028, 105 S.Ct. 1395, 84 L.Ed.2d 784 (1985).

14. *Patterson v. McLean Credit Union,* 491 U.S. 164, 109 S.Ct. 2363, 105 L.Ed.2d 132 (1989) (plaintiff need not prove that she was better qualified than the white employee who received the contested promotion). *See also Walker v. Mortham,* 158 F.3d 1177 (11th Cir.1998), *cert. denied,* 528

ment, sometimes relaxed or waived by lower courts, is evidence that the employer, after rejecting the plaintiff, continued to seek applicants with her general qualifications and/or selected a person from outside her protected group.[15] In rehiring cases, the plaintiff need not show that he was identically situated with others of a different race who were initially terminated[16] or who resigned[17] at the same time; it suffices that the plaintiff's former position was filled by a member of a different race or simply that he was qualified for the new job for which he was rejected.

Accepting the Supreme Court's invitation to modify the basic template for differing circumstances, the circuit courts have adapted the *McDonnell Douglas* failure-to-hire elements to meet the realities of claims alleging unlawful discharge, promotion, discipline, and unequal pay. In an age discrimination case, the Court itself held unanimously that a terminated plaintiff need not invariably show that he was replaced by someone outside the protected class—there, someone younger than 40—so long as he was replaced by someone sufficiently younger as to generate a plausible inference that age was a determinative factor.[18] This

U.S. 809, 120 S.Ct. 39, 145 L.Ed.2d 36 (1999) (prima facie case need only address plaintiff's minimum or absolute, not relative, qualifications, and need not even show she was equally qualified as selectee); *McCullough v. Real Foods, Inc.*, 140 F.3d 1123 (8th Cir.1998) (subjective criteria for promotions are particularly easy for an employer to invent in an effort to sabotage a plaintiff's prima facie case and mask discrimination): *Lyoch v. Anheuser–Busch Cos., Inc.*, 139 F.3d 612 (8th Cir.1998) (describing nonpromotion prima facie case as less rigorous where employer had subjective, informal promotion policy); *Thomas v. Denny's*, 111 F.3d 1506 (10th Cir.), *cert. denied*, 522 U.S. 1028, 118 S.Ct. 626, 139 L.Ed.2d 607 (1997) (erroneously instructing jury that it must find plaintiff at least as qualified as successful candidates for promotion improperly enables jury to reject plaintiff's case at prima facie stage, thereby depriving plaintiff of opportunity to challenge defendant's proffered legitimate reason (relative qualifications) as pretextual); *MacDonald v. Eastern Wyoming Mental Health Ctr.*, 941 F.2d 1115 (10th Cir.1991); *Denison v. Swaco Geolograph Co.*, 941 F.2d 1416 (10th Cir.1991); *Siegel v. Alpha Wire Corp.*, 894 F.2d 50 (3d Cir.1990), *cert. denied*, 496 U.S. 906, 110 S.Ct. 2588, 110 L.Ed.2d 269 (1990). *Cf. Coco v. Elmwood Care, Inc.*, 128 F.3d 1177 (7th Cir.1997) (in termination case, employee must show that he was meeting employer's legitimate or bona fide expectations; otherwise, inference of discrimination is weak). *See St. Mary's Honor Ctr. v. Hicks*, 509 U.S. 502, 113 S.Ct. 2742, 125 L.Ed.2d 407 (1993) (referring to the "minimal requirements" of plaintiff's

prima facie individual disparate treatment case). But one court has held that plaintiff's prima facie case need only show that she was a member of a protected class and treated differently from similarly situated employees, and not also show a causal connection between defendant's challenged act and her protected group characteristic or statute. *Hollins v. Atlantic Co., Inc.*, 188 F.3d 652 (6th Cir.1999).

15. *See Patterson v. McLean Credit Union*, 491 U.S. at 186, 109 S.Ct. at 2377 (1989) (adapting Title VII's individual disparate treatment mode of proof to race discrimination claim under 42 U.S.C.A. § 1981). *See Walker v. Mortham*, 158 F.3d 1177 (11th Cir.1998), *cert. denied*, 528 U.S. 809, 120 S.Ct. 39, 145 L.Ed.2d 36 (1999) (plaintiff in promotion case need not show that the position remained open when someone else was promoted simultaneous with her rejection, or show that the selectee had equal or lesser qualifications). It should be stressed, however, that the plaintiff's replacement by a member of the same race does not prevent her from establishing prima facie that the initial decision to discharge her was unlawfully race based. *Carson v. Bethlehem Steel Corp.*, 82 F.3d 157 (7th Cir.1996).

16. *Talley v. Bravo Pitino Restaurant, Ltd.*, 61 F.3d 1241 (6th Cir.1995).

17. *Richardson v. Leeds Police Dep't*, 71 F.3d 801 (11th Cir.1995).

18. *O'Connor v. Consolidated Coin Caterers Corp.*, 517 U.S. 308, 312, 116 S.Ct. 1307, 134 L.Ed.2d 433 (1996).

is consistent with the approach *McDonnell Douglas* itself took in failure-to-hire situations, where the Court never described element (4)—the employer continued to seek applications from qualified persons after plaintiff's rejection—as requiring evidence that the employer hired, or by implication replaced plaintiff with, someone outside plaintiff's protected class. Such a requirement would preclude otherwise meritorious claims by a woman or minority deemed too feminist or assertive, provided their replacement was another woman or minority member; it would also doom claims against employers who replace the plaintiff with another member of her group solely in order to avoid the consequences of threatened or actual litigation.

Circuit courts have followed suit, generally listing the required prima facie elements in a termination case as follows: (1) plaintiff belongs to a protected class (a requirement that can be met under the right circumstances by anyone, even a white male); (2) plaintiff possessed the absolute, or minimum uniformly required qualifications for the job she held;[19] (3) despite those qualifications, she was discharged; and (4) the job was not eliminated after the discharge. Significantly, element (4) does not require the plaintiff, except perhaps a non-white plaintiff alleging race discrimination,[20] to show that her job was filled by a person outside her protected group.[21] Thus the termination plaintiff

19. In a termination case, this "existing qualifications" requirement has been waived where the plaintiff had long tenure in the job lost, as the court will "infer that he or she is qualified to hold that particular position." *Damon v. Fleming Supermarkets of Florida, Inc.*, 196 F.3d 1354, 1360 (11th Cir.1999), *cert. denied,* ___ U.S. ___, 120 S.Ct. 1962, 146 L.Ed.2d 793 (2000) (case under ADEA); *Young v. General Foods Corp.*, 840 F.2d 825, 830 n. 3 (11th Cir. 1988), *cert. denied*, 488 U.S. 1004, 109 S.Ct. 782, 102 L.Ed.2d 774 (1989). Alternatively, the qualifications requirement may be met by evidence that the plaintiff, before termination, was meeting the employer's "legitimate expectations." *See Cline v. Catholic Diocese of Toledo*, 206 F.3d 651, 658 (6th Cir.2000).

20. See note, *supra* this subsection, on the additional proof of "background circumstances" that some circuits impose on white plaintiffs alleging race discrimination.

21. *Compare Perry v. Woodward*, 199 F.3d 1126, 1135–1141 (10th Cir.1999), *cert. denied,* ___ U.S. ___, 120 S.Ct. 1964, 146 L.Ed.2d 796 (2000) (case under § 1981); *Cline v. Catholic Diocese of Toledo*, 206 F.3d 651, 658 (6th Cir.2000) (in Title VII pregnancy termination case, plaintiff required to show (1) she was pregnant (2) she was qualified for the job she had held, provable by evidence of performance at a level

that met her employer's legitimate expectations (3) she suffered an adverse employment consequence and (4) a nexus between her pregnancy and that adverse employment decision); *Cumpiano v. Banco Santander Puerto Rico*, 902 F.2d 148, 155 (1st Cir.1990) (pregnancy case) and *Meiri v. Dacon*, 759 F.2d 989, 995–96 (2d Cir.), *cert. denied*, 474 U.S. 829, 106 S.Ct. 91, 88 L.Ed.2d 74 (1985) (unequivocally holding that terminated plaintiff, to meet element (4), need not show replacement by someone outside her protected class) *with Pivirotto v. Innovative Sys., Inc.*, 191 F.3d 344, 352–54 & n. 6 (3d Cir.1999); *Nieto v. L. & H. Packing Co.*, 108 F.3d 621, 624 n. 7 (5th Cir.1997); *Carson v. Bethlehem Steel Corp.*, 82 F.3d 157, 159 (7th Cir.1996); *Williams v. Ford Motor Co.*, 14 F.3d 1305, 1308 (8th Cir.1994); *Nesbit v. Pepsico, Inc.*, 994 F.2d 703, 705 (9th Cir.1993); *Jackson v. Richards*, 961 F.2d 575, 587n.12 (6th Cir.1992); *Howard v. Roadway Express, Inc.*, 726 F.2d 1529, 1534 (11th Cir.1984) (holding that plaintiff not precluded, or necessarily precluded, from establishing prima facie termination case by inability to prove replacement by person of another group). *But see Brown v. McLean*, 159 F.3d 898, 904 (4th Cir.1998), *cert. denied sub nom. Brown v. Mayor and City Council of Baltimore*, 526 U.S. 1099, 119 S.Ct. 1577, 143 L.Ed.2d 672 (1999) (plaintiff claiming termination must "ordinarily" show position filled by some-

usually satisfies element (4) simply by producing evidence that the employer had a continuing need for someone to perform the plaintiff's work, or, even more clearly, that the employer in fact filled plaintiff's former position, but not necessarily with someone from another protected class.

On the other hand, in cases where an employer alleges and the court agrees[22] that plaintiff's termination was part of a classic, true reduction in force ("RIF"), i.e, where the plaintiff was not replaced, "it would make no sense to require a plaintiff to show the position from which she had been terminated 'remained open'...." One circuit modifies plaintiff's burden in that situation by substituting for the "remain open" requirement a showing that similarly situated employees not members of plaintiff's protected class were treated more favorably.[23] A plaintiff might carry that burden, in turn, with evidence that a non-protected class member was given plaintiff's work or a purportedly "riffed" non-protected class member was moved to another job with the employer.[24] But a replacement employee's work performance following a RIF is irrelevant to the critical question whether management had an economic or unlawful discriminatory motive at the time of terminating the plaintiff.[25] For more detail on RIFs in the context of the Age Discrimination in Employment Act, see § 9.1.

In failure to promote cases, the circuit opinions more often insist than in termination cases that plaintiff prove as part of the prima facie case that the successful promotee is not a member of plaintiff's protected class. Typical formulations of the prima facie elements require plaintiff to adduce evidence that (1) he is a protected group member; (2) he was qualified and applied for[26] the promotion; (3) he was then rejected despite those qualifications; and (4) equally or less qualified employees,

one not a member of plaintiff's protected class).

22. *But see Bellaver v. Quanex Corp.*, 200 F.3d 485, 494–495 (7th Cir.2000) (doubting that employer conducted true RIF, which court said typically involves "the layoff of many employees at once," and adding, "employers will not be allowed cynically to avoid liability by terming a decision to fire an employee with a unique job description as a 'RIF' when the decision in fact was nothing more than a decision to fire that particular employee"). Such single-discharge cases are sometimes termed "mini-RIFs," and in such circumstances the employee may generate the inference of unlawful discrimination by showing that after his termination his duties were absorbed by an employee or employees not part of his protected class. *See Wichmann v. Board of Trustees of Southern Ill. Univ.*, 180 F.3d 791, 802 (7th Cir.1999), *vacated in light of Kimel v. Florida Bd. of Regents*, 528 U.S. 62, 120 S.Ct. 631, 145 L.Ed.2d 522 (2000);

Gadsby v. Norwalk Furniture Corp., 71 F.3d 1324, 1331–32 (7th Cir.1995).

23. *Bellaver v. Quanex Corp.*, 200 F.3d 485, 494–495 (7th Cir.2000) (part of alternative holding).

24. *Thorn v. Sunstrand Aerospace Corp.*, 207 F.3d 383 (7th Cir.2000) (reinstating age discrimination claims of employee fired in reduction in force who proved he had been performing up to his employer's expectations and that his work was given to a substantially younger employee).

25. *Cullen v. Olin Corp.*, 195 F.3d 317 (7th Cir.1999), *cert. denied*, ___ U.S. ___, 120 S.Ct. 1423, 146 L.Ed.2d 315 (2000).

26. But see the text and footnotes, *supra* this section, that excuse the application requirement where the position is not posted and plaintiff has expressed an interest in the class of positions at issue, especially where non-protected group members are solicited to apply.

not members of plaintiff's protected class, were promoted.[27] Some opinions purport to trace the requirement that the promotee be outside plaintiff's protected group to the Supreme Court's opinion in *McDonnell Douglas*[28]; in fact, as at least one court has noted,[29] the High Court's actual language merely demands evidence that after the rejection, "the position remained open and the employer continued to seek applicants from persons of complainant's qualifications."[30] Recognizing this, a minority of the circuits treating the question streamline the prima facie promotion denial case, requiring evidence only that the plaintiff be a protected group member, an unsuccessful applicant for a position for which he was qualified, and thereafter the employer continued to seek applicants.[31]

The Title VII prima facie case of sex-based wage or salary discrimination is in most circuits more exacting than the required counterpart demonstration under the Equal Pay Act. Like the EPA plaintiff, the Title VII plaintiff must show that she is paid less for performing substantially comparable work to that performed by one or more members of the opposite gender. That showing suffices for a form of strict prima facie liability under EPA. In a Title VII action, however, the plaintiff must also offer at least inferential evidence, per *McDonnell Douglas*, that the salary shortfall is a product of the employer's intentional discrimination against her because of her or his gender. Thus she must first show, as under EPA, that (1) she is a member of a protected class and (2) that she was paid less than non-members of that class for work requiring substantially the same skill, effort and responsibility. Then she must also show, to establish a claim under Title VII, that the underpayment occurred under circumstances raising an inference of discrimination.[32]

Claims of disparate treatment in discipline present fewer complications. The plaintiff must show prima facie that (1) he belongs to a class

27. *See, e.g., Alexander v. Fulton County,* 207 F.3d 1303, 1339 (11th Cir.2000); *Cones v. Shalala,* 199 F.3d 512, 516–517 (D.C.Cir.2000) (distinguishing between "non-selection" promotion claims and "denial of increase in pay or grade" promotion claims, upholding a non-selection claim even though the selectee received the position in question through lateral transfer rather than promotion, but requiring for each claim proof that the employer selected someone outside plaintiff's group); *Sprague v. Thorn Americas, Inc.,* 129 F.3d 1355, 1362 (10th Cir.1997) (stating the requirement in a case not turning on it); *Brown v. State of Tennessee,* 693 F.2d 600, 603 (6th Cir.1982).

28. *See, e.g., Laderach v. U–Haul of Northwestern Ohio,* 207 F.3d 825, 828 (6th Cir.2000).

29. *Perry v. Woodward,* 199 F.3d 1126, 1137 n. 6 (10th Cir.1999), *cert. denied,* ___

U.S. ___, 120 S.Ct. 1964, 146 L.Ed.2d 796 (2000).

30. *McDonnell Douglas,* 411 U.S. at 802.

31. *Mauro v. Southern New England Telecommunications, Inc.* 208 F.3d 384, 386 (2d Cir.2000) (citing *Brown v. Coach Stores, Inc.,* 163 F.3d 706, 709 (2d Cir. 1998)). *See also Taylor v. Virginia Union Univ.,* 193 F.3d 219, 230 (4th Cir.1999) (en banc), *cert. denied,* ___ U.S. ___, 120 S.Ct. 1243, 146 L.Ed.2d 101 (2000) (in dictum, reciting that the failure-to-promote plaintiff's final prima facie element is to show that "(4) she was rejected under circumstances giving rise to an inference of unlawful discrimination.")

32. *See Belfi v. Prendergast,* 191 F.3d 129, 136, 139–140 (2d Cir.1999). A more detailed, multi-circuit comparison of EPA and Title VII requirements in such cases is set out in Chapter 8.

protected by Title VII; (2) that he was qualified for the job he holds or held; and (3) that a similarly situated employee engaged in identical or similar misconduct but received lesser or no discipline.[33]

The Supreme Court has made some seemingly contradictory pronouncements about the quantum of evidence the plaintiff must adduce to survive the prima facie stage of the case. On the one hand, when Title VII claims were entirely equitable and triable only to a judge, the Court wrote that the plaintiff must satisfy the trier of fact that the required elements are established by a preponderance of the evidence produced to that point in the trial.[34] More recently, however, after the Civil Rights Act of 1991 paved the way for jury trials and legal relief in disparate treatment cases, the Court has indicated that the requisite quantum is "infinitely less than what a directed verdict demands."[35] Taken literally, the latter statement suggests that the case should advance to the next stage even if reasonable jurors could not find plaintiff's way by a preponderance of the evidence on one or more of the elements that the plaintiff must ultimately prove.

If the plaintiff establishes the prima facie case, a judicially created presumption declares the resulting inference of discrimination conclusive unless the defendant offers evidence that it had one or more "legitimate, nondiscriminatory reasons" for an employment decision.[36] The defendant must set forth this reason "clearly" and through "admissible evidence."[37] Moreover, the reason must relate to what the defendant knew and relied on at the time of the challenged decision. "The defendant cannot testify in abstract terms as to what might have motivated the decision-maker; it must present specific evidence regarding the decision-maker's actual motivations with regard to each challenged employment decision."[38] Thus, for example, where the defendant has offered no such testimony, a court may not assume from its own perusal of the record that the decision-maker was motivated by a legitimate reason.[39] Similarly, a selectee's superior relative qualifications cannot be a legitimate nondiscriminatory reason absent evidence that the decision-maker knew of the applicants' relative qualifications at the time of the decision in question.[40] And a court should not seize on the employer's legitimate nondiscriminatory reason as a way of finding that a plaintiff

---

33. *See Alexander v. Fulton County*, 207 F.3d 1303, 1336 (11th Cir.2000).

34. *Burdine*, 450 U.S. 248, 101 S.Ct. 1089, 67 L.Ed.2d 207.

35. *St. Mary's Honor Ctr.*, 509 U.S. 502, 113 S.Ct. 2742, 125 L.Ed.2d 407.

36. *McDonnell Douglas*, 411 U.S. 792, 93 S.Ct. 1817, 36 L.Ed.2d 668.

37. *Burdine*, 450 U.S. 248, 101 S.Ct. 1089, 67 L.Ed.2d 207. But because the burden of persuasion on the ultimate issue of the employer's motivation remains with the plaintiff throughout, the employer's evidence may be offered entirely through cross-examination of plaintiff's witnesses;

an employer may meet it, that is, without calling any witnesses of its own. *Diehl v. Tele–Solutions*, 57 F.3d 482 (6th Cir.1995).

38. *Walker*, 158 F.3d at 1182 n.8.

39. *Increase Minority Participation by Affirmative Change Today of Northwest Florida, Inc. (IMPACT) v. Firestone*, 893 F.2d 1189, 1193–94 (11th Cir.1990).

40. *See Eastland v. Tennessee Valley Auth.*, 704 F.2d 613 (11th Cir.1983), *cert. denied sub nom. James v. TVA*, 465 U.S. 1066, 104 S.Ct. 1415, 79 L.Ed.2d 741 (1984).

failed to produce submissible evidence on an element of her prima facie case. Thus in deciding whether a plaintiff met the prima facie element in a termination case of showing that she had met her employer's standard, minimum legitimate expectations, a trial court improperly concluded "no" by reference to the employer's asserted reason for firing her. [41]

The preliminary question whether plaintiff established a *prima facie* case loses all significance once defendant presents its proof. Put otherwise, the definition of the prima facie case merely aids the court in determining whether to grant a defendant's motion for judgment as a matter of law under FRCP 50(a) at the close of plaintiff's case (or "directed verdict" as it is still known in most state courts). Once both sides rest, the trier of fact must evaluate all admitted evidence, including but not limited to the plaintiff's *prima facie* evidence, to decide if plaintiff has carried the ultimate burden of demonstrating intentional discrimination. [42] Thus jury instructions in an age discrimination case that in effect permitted the jurors to find that age was a determining factor in the plaintiff's termination if they believed his prima facie evidence that younger employees were treated more favorably during a reduction in force have been held harmfully prejudicial to the employer. [43] A trial judge's ultimate determination about discriminatory intent— whether shown through direct or indirect evidence—is one of fact and may therefore be overturned on appeal only if "clearly erroneous." [44]

Traditionally, most courts have viewed as "legitimate" virtually any reason [45] the employer shows it relied on [46] that can be distinguished from

41. *Cline v. Catholic Diocese of Toledo,* 206 F.3d 651, 660–664 (6th Cir.2000) (applying *United States Postal Serv. Bd. of Governors v. Aikens,* 460 U.S. 711, 103 S.Ct. 1478, 75 L.Ed.2d 403 (1983), discussed immediately below.

42. Once the defendant fails to persuade the court to grant a Rule 50(a) motion for judgment as a matter of law at the close of plaintiff's case, and defendant has offered evidence of a legitimate nondiscriminatory reason, the court should address the ultimate question of intentional discrimination *vel non,* and the question whether plaintiff established a prima facie case is no longer relevant. *United States Postal Serv. Bd. of Governors v. Aikens,* 460 U.S. 711, 103 S.Ct. 1478, 75 L.Ed.2d 403 (1983); *Alexander v. Fulton County,* 207 F.3d 1303, 1335 (11th Cir.2000); *Cline v. Catholic Diocese of Toledo,* 206 F.3d 651, 660–664 (6th Cir.2000); *Hopp v. City of Pittsburgh,* 194 F.3d 434 (3d Cir.1999); *Beaver v. Rayonier, Inc.,* 200 F.3d 723 (11th Cir.1999); *Thomas v. Denny's,* 111 F.3d 1506 (10th Cir.), *cert. denied,* 522 U.S. 1028, 118 S.Ct. 626, 139 L.Ed.2d 607 (1997). But note that *McDonnell Douglas* production questions are for the court; only pretext and ultimate discrimination questions are for the jury. *See Greenway v.*

Buffalo Hilton Hotel, 143 F.3d 47 (2d Cir. 1998).

43. *Seman v. Coplay Cement Co.,* 26 F.3d 428 (3d Cir.1994).

44. *Anderson v. City of Bessemer,* 470 U.S. 564, 105 S.Ct. 1504, 84 L.Ed.2d 518 (1985); Federal Rule of Civil Procedure 52(a).

45. Even a reason that turns out to be "mistaken, foolish, trivial, or baseless" is acceptable, as long as the employer honestly believed in its proffered reason. *Smith v. Chrysler Corp.,* 155 F.3d 799 (6th Cir.1998). *See also Kariotis v. Navistar Int'l Transp. Corp.,* 131 F.3d 672 (7th Cir.1997) (honest, but mistaken belief). See text *infra* this subsection.

46. When an employer did not know about an applicant's poor credit history when it decided not to hire him, its proffered reason that it relied on that history was held not "legitimate." *Turnes v. AmSouth Bank,* 36 F.3d 1057 (11th Cir.1994). There is also authority, however, that the employer may assert as a defense in court a reason that in fact commanded only minority support on the key employer committee responsible for the adverse employment decision in question. *Bina v. Providence Col-*

the five group characteristics protected by statute and from the few "proxy" factors that perfectly correspond with one of those groups. Thus personality conflicts between the plaintiff and a supervisor, or management's genuine perception, accurate or not, that a plaintiff is adversarial, are classic "legitimate, nondiscriminatory reasons" that will absolve the employer of liability unless plaintiff proves them to have been offered as a pretext for unlawful discrimination.[47] This view is evidently driven by deference to the employer's superior knowledge of its own productivity, safety and efficiency requirements.[48] It is fortified by the Court's decision in *Hazen Paper Co. v. Biggins*,[49] that factors highly but incompletely correlating with age, e.g., pension status or years of service, are factors other than age not expressly prohibited by the Age Discrimination in Employment Act (even if unlawful under ERISA), rather than unlawful proxies for intentional age discrimination. If a practice or policy, the terms of which are not expressly geared to a prohibited factor, nevertheless has a substantial (but not exclusive)[50] adverse impact on the plaintiff's protected group, that practice will violate Title VII or ADEA not as disparate treatment but only, if at all, on the "neutral practice/disproportionate adverse impact" theory of proof discussed below.

Indeed, at least with the hindsight of *Biggins*, it appears that several circuit decisions that had condemned word-of-mouth hiring as intentionally discriminatory (because it was highly, although not perfectly, correlated with carrying forward past racial or national origin imbalances in the employer's work force) are better justified as resting on showings that the effects of that neutral practice fell far more harshly on the plaintiffs' protected groups.[51] Of course if the practice is conceptualized as neutral, the employer will be called on only to produce and persuade about the "business necessity/job relatedness" defense that pertains to the neutral practice proof mode; and although the issue is not free from doubt, even after the legislative overhaul of the neutral practice defense by the 1991 Civil Rights Act, that defense remains arguably easier to carry than the "bona fide occupational qualification" defense that alone will overcome a plaintiff's showing of express or facial intentional discrimination.[52]

lege, 39 F.3d 21 (1st Cir.1994), *cert. denied*, 514 U.S. 1038, 115 S.Ct. 1406, 131 L.Ed.2d 292 (1995).

47. *See, e.g., Stewart v. Henderson*, 207 F.3d 374, 377–78 (7th Cir.2000).

48. *See Furnco Construction Corp. v. Waters*, 438 U.S. 567, 98 S.Ct. 2943, 57 L.Ed.2d 957 (1978).

49. 507 U.S. 604, 113 S.Ct. 1701, 123 L.Ed.2d 338 (1993).

50. *See* discussion at text *supra*, § 3.2.

51. *Compare EEOC v. Metal Serv. Co.*, 892 F.2d 341, 350–351 (3d Cir.1990); *Barnett v. W.T. Grant Co.*, 518 F.2d 543, 549 (4th Cir.1975); *Parham v. Southwestern Bell Tel. Co.*, 433 F.2d 421, 426–27 (8th Cir.1970) (word-of-mouth hiring that perpetuated such imbalances viewed as circumstantial evidence of disparate treatment) *with EEOC v. Consolidated Serv. Sys.*, 989 F.2d 233, 235 (7th Cir.1993) (same practice not intentionally discriminatory despite strong tendency to extend the dominance of national origin group in employer's workforce to the exclusion of others).

52. *See also EEOC v. Chicago Miniature Lamp Works*, 947 F.2d 292 (7th Cir.1991) (employer reliance on word-of-mouth hiring too passive to be a defined practice challengeable via disparate impact proof mode).

There is one apparent exception to the rule that a reason must not be grounded in one of the five prohibited characteristics to be a "legitimate" one that will rebut the *McDonnell Douglas* prima facie case. When whites or males mount "reverse discrimination" attacks on employment practices, employers will sometimes respond that the decision in question was made pursuant to an agreement settling a minority member or woman's claim of discrimination. There is no doubt here that the employment decision now challenged was taken on the basis of race or gender; but that is precisely what the settlement agreement called for. There is federal circuit court authority that reliance on a settlement in good faith of a claim of discrimination constitutes a legitimate business reason for the discriminatory employment practice that defeats the requisite showing of intent. Further, the employer's agreement to the settlement has been held not to constitute an independent act of unlawful discrimination.[53]

Although the opinion in *McDonnell Douglas* suggested that the employer need only "articulate" a legitimate, nondiscriminatory reason, perhaps simply in an argument or brief, the Court, after a couple of false starts, definitively determined in *Burdine* that the employer's burden, while not onerous, may be discharged only through evidence that clearly explains its proffered reason or reasons.[54] But the Court has insisted that the defendant's burden is one of production only and that the burden of persuading about intentional discrimination resides with the plaintiff throughout.[55] Accordingly, like the presumptions described in Federal Rule of Evidence 301, the *McDonnell Douglas* presumption of unlawful discriminatory motive that arises from a successful prima facie case disappears and has no further force in the litigation if the employer discharges its relatively modest burden of producing evidence of a legitimate, nondiscriminatory reason for the challenged employment action—the bubble bursts.[56]

A plaintiff can nevertheless prevail on rebuttal. To do so the plaintiff must persuade the court that the defendant's purported legitimate

---

53. *Marcantel v. Louisiana*, 37 F.3d 197 (5th Cir.1994); *Carey v. U.S. Postal Serv.*, 812 F.2d 621 (10th Cir.1987). *But see In re Birmingham Reverse Discrimination Employment Litig.*, 20 F.3d 1525, 1534 (11th Cir.1994), *cert. denied sub nom. Arrington v. Wilks*, 514 U.S. 1065, 115 S.Ct. 1695, 131 L.Ed.2d 558 (1995) (reverse discrimination not meeting strict requirements of Equal Protection Clause unlawful despite being directed by a consent decree settling employment discrimination litigation).

54. *Id.* and *EEOC v. McCall Printing Corp.*, 633 F.2d 1232 (6th Cir.1980).

55. But because the burden of persuasion on the ultimate issue of the employer's motivation remains with the plaintiff throughout, the employer's evidence may be offered entirely through cross-examination of plaintiff's witnesses; an employer may

meet it, that is, without calling any witnesses of its own. *Diehl v. Tele–Solutions*, 57 F.3d 482 (6th Cir.1995).

56. In *Walker*, 158 F.3d 1177, the court wrote that because the prima facie creates only a presumption, not an inference, of intentional discrimination, it acts as a procedural device that forces the defendant to produce evidence regarding why the plaintiff suffered an employment detriment. The opinion observed, however, that not only does the prima facie evidence not disappear, but in some cases it may be relied on by the plaintiff later in the case to cast doubt on the defendant's stated nondiscriminatory reason for the employment decision in question. *Accord, Danzer v. Norden Sys., Inc.*, 151 F.3d 50 at n. 4 (2d Cir.1998).

reason is a smokescreen or "pretext" for intentional discrimination. It bears emphasis, however, that the plaintiff does not encounter this burden until after the defendant has produced evidence of one or more specific legitimate nondiscriminatory reasons. Thus in making the prima facie case the plaintiff need only show that she possessed the base, minimum qualifications the employer uniformly required for attaining or retaining a job. She need not do more at that stage of the case—for example, rebut employer assertions that she engaged in misconduct or possessed qualifications equal to or superior to the employee retained or selected in her stead.[57] Such a requirement would in effect prematurely demand that she prove that the employer's reason is pretextual before the employer is called on clearly to identify, through evidence, its legitimate nondiscriminatory reason. That, in turn, would prematurely force the plaintiff to turn to the ultimate issue in the case, intentional discrimination.[58]

The Court had written that the plaintiff could make the pretext showing, by the standard preponderance of the evidence quantum, in either of two generic ways: by demonstrating through plaintiff's own affirmative evidence, *including* that previously adduced prima facie, that the employer, in reaching its decision, explicitly relied on plaintiff's protected group status, rather than on its proffered legitimate reason; or, less directly, simply by convincing the judge or jury that the proffered reason is an implausible explanation for the challenged decision.[59] The Supreme Court held, in *St. Mary's Honor Ctr.*, that the latter showing merely permits but does not mandate a judgment for the plaintiff.[60] In jury-triable intentional discrimination cases authorized by the Civil Rights Act of 1991, therefore, the jury should be charged accordingly.[61] But the Court reaffirmed that evidence of the falsity of the employer's proffered legitimate reason could suffice for liability. Thus the court rejected a "pretext-plus" rule that had evolved in some of the circuit courts which had required plaintiffs to prove discriminatory intent not only by establishing the falsity of the employer's explanation but also through affirmative independent evidence.[62]

57. *See Patterson v. McLean Credit Union*, 491 U.S. 164, 109 S.Ct. 2363, 105 L.Ed.2d 132; *Walker*, 158 F.3d 1177.

58. *See, e.g., Patterson v. McLean Credit Union*, 491 U.S. 164, 109 S.Ct. 2363, 105 L.Ed.2d 132; *Davenport v. Riverview Gardens Sch. Dist.*, 30 F.3d 940 (8th Cir.1994).

59. *Burdine*, 450 U.S. 248, 101 S.Ct. 1089, 67 L.Ed.2d 207; *Aikens*, 460 U.S. 711, 103 S.Ct. 1478, 75 L.Ed.2d 403.

60. *St. Mary's Honor Ctr.*, 509 U.S. 502, 113 S.Ct. 2742, 125 L.Ed.2d 407.

61. The Court alluded to the availability of jury trials. It mentioned judgment under Federal Rule of Civil Procedure 50(a)(1), which by its terms applies "during a trial by jury," and it referred broadly to decisions by the "trier of fact."

62. *See, e.g., Mesnick v. General Elec. Co.*, 950 F.2d 816 (1st Cir.1991), *cert. denied*, 504 U.S. 985, 112 S.Ct. 2965, 119 L.Ed.2d 586 (1992); *Galbraith v. Northern Telecom*, 944 F.2d 275 (6th Cir.1991), *cert. denied*, 503 U.S. 945, 112 S.Ct. 1497, 117 L.Ed.2d 637 (1992). Even after *St. Mary's*, however, the plaintiff who does not attempt to discredit the employer's nondiscriminatory explanation may bear in some circuits the burden of producing affirmative evidence of unlawful motivation going beyond the prima facie case. *Burns v. AAF-McQuay*, 96 F.3d 728 (4th Cir.1996), *cert. denied*, 520 U.S. 1116, 117 S.Ct. 1247, 137 L.Ed.2d 329 (1997).

The *St. Mary's* dissent expressed concern that plaintiffs' discovery and trial burdens will be unjustly magnified and employers more often erroneously exculpated if the fact finder's determination that the employer's reason is unworthy of belief does not compel the conclusion that its false reason is a pretext for prohibited discrimination. The majority, however, was fearful of erroneously inculpating the employer every time an employer witness testifies to a reason for the challenged employment action that is not in fact the employer's real reason, which may happen where the real reason is embarrassing[63] or even illegal[64] but not violative of Title VII.[65] The Court has shown somewhat less understanding about prevarication by plaintiffs who have proven unlawful employment discrimination but after termination are discovered by the former employers to have committed resume fraud. This "after-acquired evidence" defense is discussed below.

Despite some language in the *St. Mary's* majority opinion to the contrary, it appears that convincing evidence of the implausibility of the employer's proffered nondiscriminatory explanation, while not compelling a conclusion that the plaintiff has shown unlawful pretext, should continue to suffice to meet that burden if the factfinder further determines that the disbelieved reason was offered to mask prohibited race, gender, religious or national origin discrimination rather than something else.[66] An EEOC Enforcement Guidance explicitly confirms this conclusion.[67]

Post-*St. Mary's* decisions reflect the raft of interpretive problems the Court left in the wake of its contrapuntal opinion. On remand from the Supreme Court in *Biggins*, for example, the First Circuit, obedient to the Court's decision there, did not treat evidence that the company terminated plaintiff to deprive him of pension vesting as evidence of intentional unlawful age discrimination. Nevertheless, it upheld the verdict for plaintiff principally because it determined that the jury disbelieved the employer's assertion that plaintiff was terminated because of disloyal-

---

63. *See, e.g., Winder v. Wickes Lumber Co.,* 51 F.3d 1051 (11th Cir.1995) (per curiam) (manager falsely asserted that he had terminated African–American plaintiff during force reduction for receiving a less than satisfactory performance evaluation that manager in fact had not read before terminating plaintiff instead of white employee, but manager's real reason—his personal acquaintance with the white subordinate's work—held not based on discrimination because of race) (unpublished opinion); *Bell v. AT & T*, 946 F.2d 1507 (10th Cir.1991) (false reason apparently offered to hide nepotism); *Shager v. Upjohn Co.,* 913 F.2d 398 (7th Cir.1990).

64. One can imagine an employer that, for reasons of public relations, produces evidence of a false reason where the real reason was that the plaintiff had committed a felony related to employment, *e.g.,* arson on the premises. *Cf. Hazen Paper Company v. Biggins,* 507 U.S. 604, 113 S.Ct. 1701, 123 L.Ed.2d 338 (1993) (employer decision violating ERISA not unlawful under ADEA); *Carter v. Maloney Trucking & Storage, Inc.,* 631 F.2d 40 (5th Cir.1980) (plaintiff murdered another employee).

65. *See Hollander v. American Cyanamid Co.,* 172 F.3d 192 (2d Cir.), *cert. denied,* 528 U.S. 965, 120 S.Ct. 399, 145 L.Ed.2d 311 (1999) (that plaintiff's alleged interpersonal problems were a pretext for an employer's actual reason does not suggest that actual reason was plaintiff's age).

66. *See* 113 S.Ct. at 2749 & n.4. *Binder v. Long Island Lighting Co.,* 57 F.3d 193 (2d Cir.1995).

67. *EEOC Enforcement Guidance on St. Mary's Honor Ctr. v. Hicks,* 509 U.S. 502, 113 S.Ct. 2742, 125 L.Ed.2d 407 (1993).

ty.[68] That reason may have been offered only to mask pension discrimination that the Supreme Court had found *not* unlawful under ADEA. But evidence that only older employees were required to sign confidentiality agreements persuaded the court that the jury could properly assign age discrimination as "the real reason" for the termination.[69] Some circuit opinions squarely read *St. Mary's* as requiring the plaintiff to "do more than merely prove the articulated reasons false"[70]—that is, offer independent, affirmative evidence that the defendant's agents discriminated against plaintiff at least in part because of her protected group status.[71] While it is submitted that this more demanding approach misreads *St. Mary's* as a blueprint for Title VII cases, it may represent a sensible adaptation of the Supreme Court's opinion to cases under ADEA. This is because, as discussed in Chapter 7 below, *Biggins* now imposes on the age discrimination plaintiff the ultimate burden of demonstrating that age played a "determinative" role in the employer's decision, not, as with race or gender under the amended Title VII, merely a "motivating" factor.

Still other post-*St. Mary's* circuit opinions display understandable uncertainty about how to apply its teachings to motions for summary judgment or directed verdict. Certainly it is clear that judgment for the employer is consistent with *St. Mary's* where the employee fails to offer any kind of "pretext" evidence refuting the employer's evidence of a legitimate, nondiscriminatory reason. Where the employer proffers such a reason, the plaintiff may not be entitled to a trial, or to have a case go to the jury, based solely on evidence presented pretrial or during its case in chief that satisfies the minimal elements of the *McDonnell Douglas* prima facie case.[72] This is so even though, under *St. Mary's*, the trier of

68. *Biggins v. Hazen Paper Co.*, 1993 WL 406515 (1st Cir.1993), *withdrawn in part*, 1994 WL 398013 (1994).

69. *See also Anderson v. Baxter Healthcare Corp.*, 13 F.3d 1120 (7th Cir.1994) (observing that *St. Mary's* rejected the "pretext-plus" approach and instead permitted fact finder to infer intentional discrimination on a prohibited ground from the prima facie case coupled with disbelief of employer's proffered reason).

70. *Howard v. BP Oil Co., Inc.*, 32 F.3d 520, 525 (11th Cir.1994).

71. *See, e.g., Hidalgo v. Overseas Condado Ins. Agencies, Inc.*, 120 F.3d 328 (1st Cir.1997) (even if employee produces evidence that proffered legitimate reason was false, summary judgment for employer proper where employee did not show evidence of age based animus); *King v. Town of Hanover*, 116 F.3d 965 (1st Cir.1997); *Jiminez v. Mary Washington College*, 57 F.3d 369 (4th Cir.), *cert. denied*, 516 U.S. 944, 116 S.Ct. 380, 133 L.Ed.2d 304 (1995); *Smith v. Stratus Computer, Inc.*, 40 F.3d 11, 16 (1st Cir.1994), *cert. denied*, 514 U.S.

1108, 115 S.Ct. 1958, 131 L.Ed.2d 850 (1995) (even at summary judgment, requiring evidence of unlawful discrimination in addition to evidence enabling factfinder to disbelieve defendant's proffered legitimate nondiscriminatory reason); *Meeks v. Computer Assoc. Int'l*, 15 F.3d 1013, 1019 n. 1 (11th Cir.1994).

72. *Ruiz v. Posadas de San Juan Assoc.*, 124 F.3d 243 (1st Cir.1997) (employee must do more than cast doubt on employer's rationale; employee must produce evidence of such strength and quality as to permit a reasonable jury finding that the adverse employment decision was manifestly unsupported); *Pritchard v. Southern Co. Servs.*, 92 F.3d 1130 (11th Cir.), *amended on rehearing in part*, 102 F.3d 1118 (11th Cir. 1996), *cert. denied*, 520 U.S. 1274, 117 S.Ct. 2453, 138 L.Ed.2d 211 (1997); *Wallis v. J.R. Simplot Company*, 26 F.3d 885 (9th Cir. 1994) (so holding under ADEA as well as Title VII); *Davis v. Chevron U.S.A.*, 14 F.3d 1082 (5th Cir.1994). *See generally Durham v. Xerox Corp.*, 18 F.3d 836 (10th Cir.1994), *cert. denied*, 513 U.S. 819, 115 S.Ct. 80, 130

fact may take the prima facie evidence into account in assessing whether plaintiff has shown the falsity of defendant's asserted legitimate reason or has otherwise proven that the employer's reason was a pretext for discrimination on a prohibited ground.

But what if the plaintiff, in resisting summary judgment or before resting at trial, does offer evidence tending to refute the employer's proffered reason, failing, however, to offer "affirmative" evidence that the employer's real or motivating reason was discrimination on a ground prohibited by Title VII or ADEA? The *St. Mary's* majority observed, if only in passing, that "it is not enough to disbelieve the employer." Citing this language, a number of circuits required the plaintiff to produce independent evidence of unlawful motivation in order to survive defendant's motion for summary judgment or, before or after verdict, for judgment as a matter of law.[73] One opinion of a divided Fifth Circuit panel, for example, labeled as "dictum" the statement in *St. Mary's* that a factfinder's disbelief of the ostensibly legitimate reasons advanced by the employer, coupled with plaintiff's prima facie evidence, may "suffice to show intentional discrimination."[74] The opinion appears to rest on the assumption that the standard *McDonnell Douglas* prima facie case is not by itself sufficient evidence of discriminatory animus.[75] Subsequently the Fifth Circuit en banc concluded that although *St. Mary's* may not require independent evidence of discriminatory intent beyond the falsity of the proffered reason, a plaintiff's verdict may be searchingly scrutinized for "substantial evidence" of that falsity.[76] Most circuits,[77] howev-

L.Ed.2d 33 (1994); *Anderson v. Baxter Healthcare Corp.*, 13 F.3d 1120 (7th Cir. 1994); *Mitchell v. Data Gen. Corp.*, 12 F.3d 1310 (4th Cir.1993); *Geary v. Visitation of the Blessed Virgin Mary*, 7 F.3d 324 (3d Cir.1993); *LeBlanc v. Great Am. Ins. Co.*, 6 F.3d 836 (1st Cir.1993), *cert. denied*, 511 U.S. 1018, 114 S.Ct. 1398, 128 L.Ed.2d 72 (1994).

73. *See Hollander v. American Cyanamid Co.*, 172 F.3d 192 (2d Cir.), *cert. denied*, 528 U.S. 965, 120 S.Ct. 399, 145 L.Ed.2d 311 (1999) (Title VII plaintiff at summary judgment must show not only falsity of proffered reason but also that the false reason was advanced to disguise unlawful discrimination); *Vaughan v. MetraHealth Companies, Inc.*, 145 F.3d 197 (4th Cir. 1998) (to survive summary judgment, employee must adduce sufficient evidence both that the legitimate nondiscriminatory reason offered by employer was false, and that unlawful discrimination was the real reason for adverse employment action); *Hoeppner v. Crotched Mountain Rehabilitation Ctr.*, 31 F.3d 9, 17 (1st Cir.1994); *Manzer v. Diamond Shamrock Chemicals Co.*, 29 F.3d 1078, 1084 (6th Cir.1994); *Wolenski v. Manville Corp.*, 19 F.3d 34 (10th Cir.1994); *LeBlanc v. Great American Ins. Co.* 6 F.3d 836, 841 (1st Cir.1993), *cert. denied*, 511

U.S. 1018, 114 S.Ct. 1398, 128 L.Ed.2d 72 (1994); *Bodenheimer v. PPG Indus.*, 5 F.3d 955 (5th Cir.1993) (ADEA). *Cf. Hardin v. Hussmann Corp.*, 45 F.3d 262, 264 (8th Cir.1995) (where employer defends ADEA prima facie case by asserting that plaintiff was terminated as part of a reduction in force, plaintiff must produce "additional" evidence that age played a role). *See, e.g., Lennon v. Rubin*, 166 F.3d 6 (1st Cir.1999) (summary judgment for defendant affirmed where reasonable jury could disbelieve proffered reason but could not find discrimination animus).

74. *Rhodes v. Guiberson Oil Tools*, 39 F.3d 537 (5th Cir.1994).

75. In this vein the two judges in the majority assert that under the reading of *St. Mary's* offered here, an employer could be found liable on a "trial record ... absolutely devoid of any evidence or testimony that relates to discriminatory actions or animus." 39 F.3d at 545.

76. *Rhodes v. Guiberson Oil Tools*, 75 F.3d 989 (5th Cir.1996) (en banc). Alternatively, *Rhodes* could have been read to permit summary judgment for the employer even if the plaintiff adduces evidence adequate under F.R.C.P. 56 concerning her pri-

er, rejected the argument that the plaintiff must produce affirmative, independent evidence of discriminatory animus in addition to the prima facie case and evidence that the employer's proffered explanation was false. For these courts, evidence raising a genuine question about falsity, coupled with the still surviving (but no longer presumption raising) prima facie *McDonnell Douglas* proof, sufficed to warrant a trial, submit a case to the jury, or support a jury verdict under instructions consistent with *St. Mary's*.[78]

prima facie elements and the falsity of the employer's proffered reasons, if the court itself finds the evidence insufficient to support a reasonable inference that the challenged decision was impelled by unlawful discriminatory animus. *See id.* at 994. The Second Circuit similarly subjected to close examination under the "clearly erroneous" standard of FRCP 52(a) a district judge's factual finding that an employer's proffered reasons were a pretext for sex discrimination. *Fisher v. Vassar College*, 114 F.3d 1332 (2d Cir.1997) (en banc), *cert. denied*, 522 U.S. 1075, 118 S.Ct. 851, 139 L.Ed.2d 752 (1998). In a similar vein, the Eleventh Circuit upheld judgment for defendant as a matter of law because plaintiff's evidence tending to undermine the employer's reasons for terminating her did not suggest any suspicion of mendacity. *Walker v. Nations–Bank,* 53 F.3d 1548, 1557 (11th Cir.1995). The Supreme Court in *St. Mary's* did recognize that a factfinder might disbelieve a reason honestly or dishonestly presented by an employer witness. But the opinion did not appear to require that a plaintiff proceeding solely on the basis of the prima facie case, together with evidence that the employer's reason is unworthy of credence, must also cast doubt on the employer's veracity or present any direct evidence that the employer acted with an unlawful motive. The Supreme Court has provided definitive guidance on these issues in *Reeves v. Sanderson Plumbing Prods., Inc.,* discussed in text immediately below. The stakes were especially high because the High Court had just reaffirmed, in *Weisgram v. Marley Company*, 528 U.S. 440, 120 S.Ct. 1011, 145 L.Ed.2d 958 (2000), that a federal appellate court may itself enter judgment as a matter of law, without remanding for a new trial, either where it views the evidence presented at trial as originally insufficient to support a verdict, as in *Neely v. Martin K. Eby Construction Co.*, 386 U.S. 317, 87 S.Ct. 1072, 18 L.Ed.2d 75 (1967), or, as in *Weisgram* itself, where the jury's verdict becomes insufficient only after the appellate court rules that evidence supporting the verdict was improperly admitted.

77. *See Barber v. CSX Distribution Servs.,* 68 F.3d 694 (3d Cir.1995) (summary judgment); *Binder v. Long Island Lighting Co.,* 57 F.3d 193, 200 (2d Cir.1995) (reversing judgment as a matter of law, or "JNOV," in case under ADEA); *Barbour v. Merrill,* 48 F.3d 1270, 1277 (D.C.Cir.1995) (Rule 50(a) judgment as a matter of law properly denied where plaintiff introduced evidence sufficient for jury to accept the prima facie case and disbelieve the employer's legitimate nondiscriminatory reasons). See also cases cited in the next footnote.

78. *See Bogle v. Orange County Bd. of County Comm'rs,* 162 F.3d 653, 658 (11th Cir.1998) (but finding no such evidence in case under ADEA); *Aka v. Washington Hosp. Ctr.,* 156 F.3d 1284 (D.C.Cir.1998) (en banc) (plaintiff's discrediting of an employer's stated reason for its employment decision is entitled to considerable weight; plaintiffs should not be routinely required to submit evidence over and above rebutting the employer's stated explanation to survive summary judgment) (case under ADA); *Arrington v. Cobb County,* 139 F.3d 865 (11th Cir.1998) (plaintiff can survive summary judgment simply by presenting evidence sufficient to demonstrate a genuine issue of material fact as to the truth or falsity of the employer's legitimate nondiscriminatory reason); *Carter v. Three Springs Residential Treatment,* 132 F.3d 635, 641–42 (11th Cir.1998); *Evans v. McClain of Ga., Inc.,* 131 F.3d 957, 962 (11th Cir.1997); *Kline v. Tennessee Valley Auth.,* 128 F.3d 337 (6th Cir.1997) (after bench trial, court found that employee satisfied prima facie case and proved employer's reason pretextual; this was sufficient for judgment for plaintiff); *Carter v. DecisionOne Corp.,* 122 F.3d 997 (11th Cir. 1997); *Fisher v. Vassar College,* 114 F.3d 1332 (2d Cir.1997) (en banc), *cert. denied,* 522 U.S. 1075, 118 S.Ct. 851, 139 L.Ed.2d 752 (1998) (but subjecting the verdict to normal appellate review); *Ryther v. KARE 11,* 108 F.3d 832 (8th Cir.1997) (en banc), *cert. denied,* 521 U.S. 1119, 117 S.Ct. 2510, 138 L.Ed.2d 1013 (1997); *Kolstad v. American Dental Ass'n,* 108 F.3d 1431 (D.C.Cir.

The Supreme Court, in perhaps its most significant plaintiff-friendly employment discrimination opinion in decades, has resolved the post-*St. Mary's* debate favorably to plaintiffs, consistent with the approach taken by the majority of the circuit courts. In *Reeves v. Sanderson Plumbing Products, Inc.*,[79] a case under the Age Discrimination in Employment Act ("ADEA"), the Court, taking note of the differing *St. Mary's* passages, wrote that the jury may find the ultimate fact of discrimination on a prohibited ground simply from (1) evidence establishing a prima facie case, coupled with (2) "sufficient" evidence that the employer's asserted legitimate nondiscriminatory explanation is false. The Court considered this approach consistent with general evidence law: "the factfinder is entitled to consider a party's dishonesty about a material fact as 'affirmative evidence of guilt;' " and once the employer's asserted reason is rejected, unlawful discrimination "may well be the most likely alternative explanation." Of course, as *St. Mary's* had held, the jury may properly find liability in such a case only if properly charged that it must, from these two kinds of evidence, make dual findings :(1) that the reason or reasons offered by the employer for taking the adverse action against plaintiff were not its real reasons, and (2) that the employer's real reason was in fact the unlawful ground. But the Court disapproved the circuit cases that had required plaintiffs to adduce evidence not only that the employer's asserted legitimate reason was false but also sufficient, independent evidence that the employer's actual reason was an unlawful one.

That of course still left the Court to explain what it meant by the required "sufficient" or "enough" evidence that an employer's proffered legitimate reason is false. On this point the Court was refreshingly precise. Resolving a long-standing uncertainty as to the general standard for directed verdict (now the Federal Rule of Civil Procedure 50 motion

1997), *opinion vacated on other grounds*, 139 F.3d 958 (1998), *vacated on other grounds*, 527 U.S. 526, 119 S.Ct. 2118, 144 L.Ed.2d 494 (1999); *EEOC v. Yenkin–Majestic Paint Corp.*, 112 F.3d 831 (6th Cir. 1997); *Combs v. Plantation Patterns*, 106 F.3d 1519, 1529 (11th Cir.1997), *cert. denied sub nom. Combs v. Meadowcraft Co.*, 522 U.S. 1045, 118 S.Ct. 685, 139 L.Ed.2d 632 (1998); *Sheridan v. E.I. DuPont de Nemours and Co.*, 100 F.3d 1061 (3d Cir. 1996) (en banc), *cert. denied*, 521 U.S. 1129, 117 S.Ct. 2532, 138 L.Ed.2d 1031 (1997); *Cole v. Ruidoso Mun. Sch.*, 43 F.3d 1373 (10th Cir.1994) (summary judgment improper where material issue of fact remained as to whether disbelief of defendant's proffered reason complied with plaintiff's prima facie case, showed sex discrimination); *Torre v. Casio, Inc.*, 42 F.3d 825 (3d Cir.1994) (ADEA) and *Fuentes v. Perskie*, 32 F.3d 759 (3d Cir.1994) (ADEA) (to withstand summary judgment plaintiff need only have evidence from which the trier of fact could reasonably believe that an unlawful discriminatory reason was a motivating cause *or* could reasonably disbelieve the reason proffered by the employer); *Gaworski v. ITT Commercial Fin. Corp.*, 17 F.3d 1104 (8th Cir.), *cert. denied*, 513 U.S. 946, 115 S.Ct. 355, 130 L.Ed.2d 310 (1994); *Anderson v. Baxter Healthcare Corp.*, 13 F.3d 1120 (7th Cir.1994); *Mitchell v. Data General Corp.*, 12 F.3d 1310 (4th Cir.1993); *Washington v. Garrett*, 10 F.3d 1421 (9th Cir.1993); *Hairston v. Gainesville Sun Publ'g Co.*, 9 F.3d 913 (11th Cir.1993); *Kline v. Tennessee Valley Auth.*, 1 F.3d 1241 (6th Cir.1993). *See also Ellis v. NCNB Texas National Bank*, 842 F.Supp. 243 (N.D.Tex.1994). *Cf. EEOC v. Ethan Allen, Inc.*, 44 F.3d 116 (2d Cir.1994) (employer's inconsistent explanations of its ostensibly legitimate nondiscriminatory reasons warrant denying summary judgment in ADEA case).

79.   530 U.S. 133, 120 S.Ct. 2097, 147 L.Ed.2d 105 (2000).

for "judgment as a matter of law") in the federal courts, the Court wrote that a trial or appellate court should consider the entire record, not merely evidence favoring the non-moving party—i.e., in the *St. Mary's* context, the plaintiff. But it stressed that the deciding court must draw all reasonable inferences in favor of the nonmovant, refraining from making credibility determinations itself or weighing the evidence. And it clarified that in order to avoid intruding on that jury function, the court "must disregard all evidence favorable to the moving party [the defendant, in the *St. Mary's* setting] that the jury is not required to believe.... That is, the court should give credence to [all] the evidence favoring the nonmovant [plaintiff] as well as [only] that 'evidence supporting the moving party that is uncontradicted and unimpeached, at least to the extent that that evidence comes from disinterested witnesses.' "

Accordingly, as long as plaintiff's counsel substantially impeaches or contradicts defendant-favorable evidence, a court should not consider that evidence in determining whether to uphold a plaintiff's verdict. In effect *Reeves* not only affirms the approach of most of the lower courts that uncorroborated evidence of the decisionmaker may not be taken into account in the face of plaintiff's contradicting evidence; it rules the same way when plaintiff's evidence merely impeaches the decisionmaker's statement of legitimate, nondiscriminatory reasons.

In elaborating these Rule 50 standards, the Court relied heavily on *Anderson v. Liberty Lobby*,[80] its most recent principal guidance on deciding motions for summary judgment. Indeed the Court repeated the *Liberty Lobby* observation that the inquiry under the summary judgment and directed verdict (judgment as a matter of law) motions is "the same."[80A] So it now appears settled in cases under ADEA (and, as discussed below, under Title VII) that it is possible for a disparate treatment plaintiff to survive summary judgment and proceed to trial, or to survive a motion for judgment as a matter of law during trial or after a favorable verdict, provided only it has offered evidence establishing the minimal, *McDonnell Douglas* prima facie case and "sufficient," that is significant impeaching or contradicting, evidence tending to show the falsity of the employer's asserted legitimate nondiscriminatory reason. The plaintiff need not also have presented evidence of an employer decisionmaker's ageist, racist or sexist remarks, or evidence that a similarly situated comparator who was younger or of a different race, sex, religion, or national origin received more favorable treatment. (Although such additional evidence had been presented in *Sanderson*, the opinion made clear that only *McDonnell Douglas* prima facie evidence, plus "sufficient" evidence that the employer's stated reason is false, is necessary to permit a jury to reach the ultimate conclusion that the employer relied on an unlawful factor.) And in considering when

80. 477 U.S. 242, 106 S.Ct. 2505, 91 L.Ed.2d 202 (1986).

80A. *See Schnabel v. Abramson*, 232 F.3d 83 (2d Cir.2000) (*Reeves* applies with equal force to summary judgment motion). (see under ADEA); *Hinson v. Clinch County*, 231 F.3d 821 (11th Cir.2000) (under Title VII)

evidence of falsity suffices, the trial court should take into account only evidence favoring the plaintiff and unimpeached, uncontradicted testimony favoring the defendant.

Judgment as a matter of law should accordingly now be granted only in the presumably rare case that a court—considering all of the plaintiff's evidence and the uncontradicted, unimpeached evidence favoring the defendant—determines that a jury could not rationally find (or, after verdict, could not have rationally found) by a preponderance of that evidence the ultimate fact of unlawful race, sex, religious, national origin, or age discrimination, even assuming it believes the plaintiff's prima facie case and the falsity of the employer's stated legitimate, nondiscriminatory reason. The Court observed that this could happen where, for example, the record "conclusively revealed" affirmative evidence that the employer's challenged decision was taken for a different nondiscriminatory reason—as where the employer gave the false, nondiscriminatory explanation to conceal a lawful but embarrassing reason, or a reason unlawful under some law other than Title VII or ADEA. Or, the Court added, judgment as a matter of law may be warranted where the employer presents "abundant and uncontroverted independent evidence" that it did not act on an unlawful ground and the plaintiff "created only a weak issue of fact as to whether the employer's reason was untrue."[80B] As Justice Ginsburg observed in her concurring opinion, conclusive demonstrations by unimpeached and uncontradicted evidence that discrimination could not have been the employer's actual motivation will be "atypical." Accordingly, in her words, a plaintiff will have to produce evidence beyond the two minimally required categories–the *McDonnell Douglas* prima facie showing and evidence that the employer's stated nondiscriminatory reason is false–only in "uncommon" circumstances. Consequently, "the ultimate question of liability ordinarily should not be taken from the jury once the plaintiff has introduced" the two minimally required categories of evidence.

It seems apparent from the *Sanderson* opinion that the Supreme Court intends these rules to apply to cases under Title VII, not just to cases under ADEA. Citing and adopting the approach taken by the courts of appeals, the Court assumed arguendo that the Title VII, *McDonnell Douglas* evidentiary framework for cases based on "circumstantial," as opposed to "direct" evidence, as that framework was elaborated in *St. Mary's*, was "fully applicable" to the ADEA case at hand.[80C] This conclusion follows logically as well. The Court repeated its statement from *Hazen Paper Co. v. Biggins*,[81] that in ADEA actions, the plaintiff must show that his age played not just a role but had a

---

80B. *See* e.g., *Schnabel supra* note 80A; *Vadie v. Mississippi State Univ.*, 218 F.3d 365, 374 n.23 (5th Cir.2000) (ADEA cases observing that evidence of falsity may not suffice to resist summary judgment or judgment as a material law unless the evidence as a whole creates a reasonable inference that age was determinative).

80C. *Reeves* has in fact applied to Title VII actions. *See* e.g., *Hinson, supra* note 80A.

81. 507 U.S. 604, 610, 113 S.Ct. 1701, ——, 123 L.Ed.2d 338 (1993).

"determinative influence" on the outcome of the employer's decision-making process. In Title VII cases, by contrast, the statute as amended in 1991 provides that a plaintiff need only prove that race, sex, religion or national origin was a "motivating" factor in the employer's decision. It is therefore to be expected that Title VII plaintiffs should be able to survive Rule 56 summary judgment motions and Rule 50 motions for judgment as a matter of law at least as readily as ADEA plaintiffs will be able to under the standards announced in *Sanderson*.

At least three circuits have at one time or another proposed applying different standards to govern pretrial versus trial proceedings. One example is requiring the lesser showing of mere disbelief of the employer's stated reason to survive summary judgment, but affirmative and possibly even independent evidence of intentional discrimination at trial when defendant moves before or after judgment for judgment as a matter of law under FRCP 50(a).[82] Such decisions reflect a common sense appreciation that summary judgment is typically decided upon evidence presented only through papers, while at trial plaintiff's live witnesses might have a more effective or fuller opportunity to develop evidence persuasive on the ultimate issue of intentional discrimination. Yet they are somewhat inconsistent with the Supreme Court's *equation* of the summary judgment and directed verdict standards in *Anderson v. Liberty Lobby, Inc.*[83] Moreover, the recent opinions insist that courts do and should apply the same standards on summary judgment as on Rule 50 motions before or after verdict.[84] In any event, this movement towards procedurally bifurcated tests appears superseded by the predominant recognition of the circuits that liability may rest on a factually sufficient finding of the plaintiff's prima facie elements, a factually sufficient rejection of the defendant's proffered legitimate reasons, plus the reasonable inferences drawn therefrom that a prohibited factor played a motivating part in the challenged decision.[85]

There remains the possibility, of course, that the courts preferring a stricter approach have been swayed more by the relative weakness of the plaintiffs' prima facie evidence in particular cases than by the belief that she must produce affirmative evidence of unlawful motive in all cases. This may be only a particular instance of a more general question about the power of the presumption accorded the plaintiff based upon the bare prima facie evidence of inferential disparate treatment. Notwithstanding *McDonnell Douglas* and *Burdine*, some prima facie evidence may only be strong enough to *threaten* the defendant with an adverse judgment if it fails to produce evidence of a legitimate nondiscriminatory reason but insufficiently strong to *entitle* plaintiff to such a judgment. This could

82. *See Randle v. City of Aurora*, 69 F.3d 441, 452 (10th Cir.1995); *Howard v. BP Oil Co.*, 32 F.3d 520, 525 (11th Cir. 1994); *Anderson v. Baxter Healthcare Corp.*, 13 F.3d 1120, 1124 (7th Cir.1994).

83. 477 U.S. 242, 106 S.Ct. 2505, 91 L.Ed.2d 202 (1986).

84. *See, e.g., Combs v. Plantation Patterns*, 106 F.3d 1519, 1529 (11th Cir.1997), *cert. denied sub nom Combs v. Meadowcraft Co.*, 522 U.S. 1045, 118 S.Ct. 685, 139 L.Ed.2d 632 (1998); *Rhodes v. Guiberson Oil Tools*, 75 F.3d 989 n. 4 (5th Cir.1996) (en banc).

85. See § 3.11, *infra*.

happen "if plaintiff's prima facie case is held to be inadequate in law or fails [by a preponderance of the evidence] to convince the factfinder."[86] In other words, there will always be a question about "the strength of the inference of discrimination based on the prima facie case,"[87] and sometimes the inference may be so slight that the Federal Rule 301 presumption may not be invoked.

On the other hand, a defendant is not necessarily well advised to throw in a kitchen sink of legitimate, nondiscriminatory reasons. It is true that the general rule is "that the employee has the burden of demonstrating that each proffered nondiscriminatory reason is pretextual."[88] But where an employer's multiple reasons are intertwined, or the "pretextual character of one of them" is markedly "fishy and suspicious," the factfinder has been held entitled to reject supplementary, alternative reasons if it rejects one of them.[89] Thus it has been written that the plaintiff "need not disprove all possible reasons for his discharge," but "only offer sufficient evidence to support a reasonable inference that he was terminated for" an unlawful reason.[90] All the more, if plaintiff casts substantial doubt on a "fair number of" or "some" of the defendant's proffered reasons, its credibility may be sufficiently impaired as to authorize the factfinder to reject its remaining reasons.[91] And in determining whether to apply this exception, a court may consider not only the strength of the evidence undermining one or more of defendant's reasons, but also the plaintiff's prima facie case.[92]

Alternatively, special factors favoring the defendant may make it less likely, or perhaps even impermissible, for the jury to draw the ultimate conclusion of discrimination from the bare fact that defendant's stated legitimate nondiscriminatory reason was false. A frequently recurring example is the "same actor" situation, where the alleged discriminator hired, promoted, or otherwise preferred the plaintiff at some time prior to the alleged unlawful conduct. This doctrine, most widely applied in age discrimination cases,[93] has also been embraced as a defensive factor in cases under Title VII and ADA.[94] Where the doctrine is

---

86. Zimmer, Sullivan, Richards and Calloway, *Cases and Materials on Employment Discrimination* 150 n.4 and accompanying text (3d ed. Little Brown 1994).

87. *Mardell v. Harleysville Life Ins. Co.*, 31 F.3d 1221 (3d Cir.1994), *vacated on other grounds*, 514 U.S. 1034, 115 S.Ct. 1397, 131 L.Ed.2d 286 (1995).

88. *Chapman v. AI Transport*, 229 F.3d 1012 (11th Cir.2000) (en banc); *Wilson v. AM General Corp.*, 167 F.3d 1114, 1120 (7th Cir.1999).

89. *Id.* (citing Seventh Circuit authority). By negative implication or in dictum, this proposition is supported by statements in other circuit opinions as well. *Smith v. Chrysler Corp.*, 155 F.3d 799, 809 (6th Cir. 1998); *Bennett v. Total Minatome Corp.*, 138 F.3d 1053, 1060 (5th Cir.1998).

90. *EEOC v. HBE Corp.*, 135 F.3d 543, 555 (8th Cir.1998).

91. Quoting, respectively, *Stephens v. Kerrigan*, 122 F.3d 171, 182 (3d Cir.1997) and *Fuentes v. Perskie*, 32 F.3d 759, 764 n. 7 (3d Cir.1994).

92. *Burns v. AAF-McQuay, Inc.*, 96 F.3d 728, 733 (4th Cir.1996), *cert. denied*, 520 U.S. 1116, 117 S.Ct. 1247, 137 L.Ed.2d 329 (1997).

93. See § 7.1 for discussion of same actor doctrine in ADEA cases. Most recently, see *Schnabel v. Abramson*, 232 F.3d 83 (2d Cir.2000).

94. *Bradley v. Harcourt, Brace & Co.*, 104 F.3d 267 (9th Cir.1996) (sex); *Evans v. Technologies Applications & Serv. Co.*, 80 F.3d 954 (4th Cir.1996) (sex); *E.E.O.C. v.*

recognized, it creates only a permissible inference of nondiscrimination to be weighed by the jury in determining whether an employer's stated reason, even if false, is a pretext for unlawful discrimination. The strength of that inference depends in large part on how soon before the challenged decision the same actor preferred the plaintiff.[95] At least one circuit holds that an identity between hirer and firer is simply evidence that should not be accorded any special value.[96] And in any event no same-actor inference is appropriate where the plaintiff's evidence of discrimination is express or direct.[97]

In contrast, there may be unusual factors suggesting the employer acted against plaintiff because of his protected group status that will relieve plaintiff of the ordinary necessity of demonstrating that the employer's stated reason was false. For example, if the defendant has applied an arguably unconstitutional affirmative action plan to disadvantage other members of plaintiff's group, plaintiff raises a factual issue concerning unlawful discrimination without having to rebut the employer's proffered legitimate reasons for the employment action she challenges.[98] In that case, however, plaintiff may have to prove that the particular affirmative action program exceeds the permissible limits under Title VII, the Constitution, or both.[99]

Because under *St. Mary's* as elucidated by *Reeves* the fact finder will continue to be permitted to infer unlawful age discrimination in most cases where the "legitimate nondiscriminatory reason" proffered by the employer is disbelieved, one may imagine a fairly complex, sequential series of decisions to be made by the judge, or instructions to be followed by the jury, in post–1991 Act intentional discrimination actions. First, in rare cases the trial judge must at the close of defendant's case grant the plaintiff judgment as a matter of law under FRCP 50(a)(1). This would happen only if any rational jury would have to find by a preponderance

Our Lady of Resurrection Med. Ctr., 77 F.3d 145 (7th Cir.1996) (race); *Buhrmaster v. Overnite Transp. Co.*, 61 F.3d 461 (6th Cir. 1995), *cert. denied*, 516 U.S. 1078, 116 S.Ct. 785, 133 L.Ed.2d 736 (1996) (sex); *Jacques v. Clean–Up Group, Inc.*, 96 F.3d 506 (1st Cir.1996) (disability); *Jiminez v. Mary Washington College*, 57 F.3d 369 (4th Cir.), *cert. denied*, 516 U.S. 944, 116 S.Ct. 380, 133 L.Ed.2d 304 (1995) (race and national origin).

95. *See, e.g., Taylor v. Virginia Union Univ.*, 193 F.3d 219, 231 (4th Cir.1999) (en banc), *cert. denied*, ___ U.S. ___, 120 S.Ct. 1243, 146 L.Ed.2d 101 (2000) (applying doctrine to a failure to promote claim); *Bradley*, 104 F.3d 267. *Cf. Buhrmaster*, 61 F.3d 461 (a short period of time is not indispensable to the doctrine).

96. *See Waldron v. SL Industries, Inc.*, 56 F.3d 491 (3d Cir.1995).

97. *See Laderach v. U–Haul of Northwestern* Ohio, 207 F.3d 825, 829 (6th Cir.

2000) (testimony that supervisor twice said he would not promote plaintiff to position in question is direct evidence of discriminatory animus even though same manager had promoted her only one month earlier); *Madel v. FCI Mktg., Inc.*, 116 F.3d 1247 (8th Cir.1997).

98. *See Thigpen v. Bibb County, Ga. Sheriff's Dep't*, 223 F.3d 1231, 2000 WL 1277600, at *6 (11th Cir.2000) (where discrimination is express, as under a consent decree or affirmative action program, plaintiff need not meet the *McDonnell Douglas/St. Mary's* elements) (case under § 1983); *Messer v. Meno*, 130 F.3d 130 (5th Cir.1997), *cert. denied sub nom. Texas Educ. Agency v. Messer*, 525 U.S. 1067, 119 S.Ct. 794, 142 L.Ed.2d 657 (1999). One of the co-authors was co-counsel for the plaintiffs-appellants in *Thigpen*.

99. *See §§ 4.40 and 4.45 infra.*

the existence of the facts constituting the plaintiff's prima facie case and the defendant failed even to produce evidence recognized as a nondiscriminatory reason for the challenged action.

Second, far more commonly, the judge at the close of all the evidence may, at the employer's request, have to charge the members of the jury that if the plaintiff has persuaded them not to believe the evidence the employer produced about a purported legitimate nondiscriminatory reason, they nevertheless *need not* conclude that the employer relied on that reason as a pretext for unlawful discrimination. Third, the judge may also have to charge, at plaintiff's request, that the jury members *may* find unlawful pretext, and hence the ultimate fact of intentional discrimination, based solely on their disbelief of defendant's proffered legitimate reason, together with the prima facie evidence earlier presented by plaintiff during her case in chief, even absent other more "direct" or "affirmative" evidence of unlawful pretext.[100]

It should be remembered that even after *St. Mary*'s a plaintiff *may* prevail on pretext by buttressing its case about the falsity of the employer's stated reason with more direct or affirmative evidence that the employer relied on a group characteristic prohibited by statute. That in fact occurred in *Reeves*. Alternatively, such evidence may suffice by itself to show intentional discrimination, as it does in the cases of "express" or "facial" discrimination mentioned above—e.g., cases involving slurs by employer agents or explicit employer prohibitions against the hire or placement of members of a particular protected group. Moreover, the Court has placed no categorical limitations on the types of affirmative evidence that may establish pretext in the *McDonnell Douglas/Burdine/St. Mary's* indirect disparate treatment case. For example, a plaintiff is not required to demonstrate that she was better qualified than a successful applicant, but may alternatively or additionally present evidence, including statistical evidence, that the employer had previously practiced unlawful discrimination against her or her group.[101] This is true even where the employer's asserted legitimate nondiscriminatory reason is that the selectee was better qualified than the plaintiff.[102]

On the other hand, a plaintiff's demonstration in a non-promotion case that he was in fact the most qualified applicant is not necessarily tantamount to a showing that the employer understood or agreed with that assessment and promoted another as a pretext for discrimination. The employer's explanation, in other words, may be erroneous in fact but sincerely believed by the decision-maker and therefore nonpretextual in the sense intended by *St. Mary's*.[103] An employer's decision may be subjective, mistaken, unwise, erroneous, or reflect a misjudging of relevant credentials, without necessarily being motivated by a consideration

100. *See Smith v. Borough of Wilkinsburg*, 147 F.3d 272 (3d Cir.1998) (harmful error to deny plaintiff that instruction even though jury was properly instructed as to plaintiff's ultimate burden in case) (case under ADEA).

101. *See McDonnell Douglas*, 411 U.S. at 804–805, 93 S.Ct. at 1825–1826; *Patter-*

son, 491 U.S. at 185–188, 109 S.Ct. at 2377–2379.

102. *See Walker*, 158 F.3d 1177.

103. *Hughes v. Brown*, 20 F.3d 745 (7th Cir.1994).

prohibited by Title VII or ADEA.[104] For example, only if a disparity between the credentials of the plaintiff and a comparator "jump off the page and slap you in the face"[105] and thus warrant a jury's conclusion that the employer based its decision on something other than qualifications[106] can employer error furnish the foundation for liability. The employment decision based on arguably innocent employer inaccuracy, plain error or even foolishness may be one example of what EEOC apparently had in mind when it noted, in an enforcement guidance, that "[w]hile *Hicks* does not, as a matter of law, require a plaintiff to produce additional evidence of intent to discriminate where the employer's explanation for its actions is found not to be credible, it does, as a practical matter, permit a fact finder to require such affirmative evidence."[107] This substantive law principle has enormous impact on the admissibility and weight accorded evidence introduced on motions for summary judgment and at trial. For example, evidence that others evaluated plaintiff's work as deficient will not be hearsay even if attested to only by the supervisor-decisionmaker who relied on that evaluation; the testimony will not be offered for the truth of the matter asserted by only as evidence of what motivated the supervisor to take adverse action against the plaintiff.[108]

---

104. *See Coleman v. Quaker Oats Company*, 232 F.3d 1271 (9th Cir.2000); *Alexander v. Fulton County*, 207 F.3d 1303, 1339–1340 (11th Cir.2000) (merely questioning wisdom of employer decision will not suffice); *Damon v. Fleming Supermarkets of Florida, Inc.*, 196 F.3d 1354, 1361 (11th Cir.1999), *cert. denied*, ___ U.S. ___, 120 S.Ct. 1962, 146 L.Ed.2d 793 (2000) (declining to assess whether employer decision is "prudent or fair"); *Walker v. Mortham*, 158 F.3d 1177 (11th Cir.1998), *cert. denied*, 528 U.S. 809, 120 S.Ct. 39, 145 L.Ed.2d 36 (1999) (misjudging qualifications does not by itself expose employer to liability); *Simms v. Oklahoma ex. rel. Dep't of Mental Health and Substance Abuse Servs.*, 165 F.3d 1321, 1329 (10th Cir.), *cert. denied*, 528 U.S. 815, 120 S.Ct. 53, 145 L.Ed.2d 46 (1999) (court eschews role as "personnel department" that "second-guesses employers' business judgments.") *See Hawkins v. PepsiCo, Inc.* 203 F.3d 274, 280 (4th Cir.), *cert. denied*, ___ U.S. ___, 121 S.Ct. 181, 148 L.Ed.2d 125 (2000) (plaintiff must show that evaluation of her work was "dishonest or not the real reason for her termination," because the court does not sit to appraise the employer's appraisal of plaintiff). One circuit takes the plaintiff's proof requirement even further in this situation, specifying that a plaintiff can succeed in showing pretext in the relevant sense only with evidence that the defendant's proffered legitimate reason "is a lie or completely lacks a factual basis." *Jordan v. Summers*, 205 F.3d 337, 343 (7th Cir.2000). *See also Stewart v. Henderson*, 207 F.3d 374, 378 (7th Cir.2000) ("The focus of a pretext inquiry is whether the employer's stated reason was honest, not whether it was accurate, wise, or well-considered.... Our only concern is whether the legitimate nondiscriminatory reason provided by the employer is in fact the true one" (internal citations omitted). This statement appears at odds with the Supreme Court's approach in *St. Mary's* on two counts. It demands too much because even an honest, factually based reason may be offered to mask an unlawful one. It demands too little because a lie might be offered to mask a lawful, but embarrassing reason. Of course subjective reasons, while not in themselves unlawful, may be a ready mechanism to cover up an unlawful discriminatory intent. *See Rowe v. General Motors Corp.*, 457 F.2d 348 (5th Cir. 1972).

105. *Deines v. Texas Dep't of Protective and Regulatory Servs.*, 164 F.3d 277, 280 (5th Cir.1999).

106. *Simms v. Oklahoma ex. rel. Dep't of Mental Health and Substance Abuse Servs.*, 165 F.3d 1321, 1329–30 (10th Cir.), *cert. denied*, 528 U.S. 815, 120 S.Ct. 53, 145 L.Ed.2d 46 (1999).

107. *EEOC Enforcement Guidance on St. Mary's, supra*, at n. 6.

108. *See Stewart v. Henderson*, 207 F.3d 374, 377–378 (7th Cir.2000), discussed in Chapter 12.

A standard legitimate nondiscriminatory reason, of course, is that plaintiff violated a customary work rule of the employer. The decisions outline a number of specific ways in which a plaintiff may show such a reason pretextual. First, a plaintiff may persuade a jury that she did not violate the rule in question if the testimony about many of her alleged deficiencies does not accurately reflect the work situation.[109] Of course evidence that the plaintiff did not in fact violate the rule does not preclude the possibility that the employer honestly believed she did, but nevertheless has been held to preclude summary judgment; more clearly still, summary judgment is improper if a plaintiff who concededly did violate a work rule offers evidence that other employees outside her protected class were not similarly disciplined for committing a similar infraction.[110] Evidence that the decisionmaker herself engaged in the same policy violation as the plaintiff is "especially compelling" evidence of pretext.[111]

McDonnell Douglas, in describing the variety of evidence the plaintiff may use to rebut a proffered legitimate, nondiscriminatory reason, makes clear that the individual disparate treatment plaintiff who sues alone may fortify the inference of discrimination arising from his use of direct or indirect evidence with anecdotal evidence that one or more similarly situated members of his protected group experienced discriminatory treatment at the hands of the same employer.[112] Statistical evidence of the adverse differential treatment of the plaintiff's group may also fortify the case of the solo disparate treatment plaintiff.[113] On a similar premise, the Supreme Court held in *Bazemore v. Friday*,[114] that "proof that an employer engaged in racial discrimination prior to the effective date of Title VII might in some circumstances support the inference that such discrimination continued, particularly where relevant aspects of the decision making process had undergone little change." Thus, in the words of a circuit decision, "[a] discriminatory act which is not made the basis for a timely charge ... may constitute relevant background evidence in a proceeding in which the status of a current practice is at issue."[115] Testimony of prior discriminatory acts

109. *See, e.g., Bassett v. City of Minneapolis*, 211 F.3d 1097, 1107–08 (8th Cir. 2000) (inconsistent explanations of alleged misconduct coupled with employer attempts to "paper" plaintiff's personnel file, sometimes without notice to her) (Title VII retaliation case).

110. *See Damon v. Fleming Supermarkets of Florida, Inc.*, 196 F.3d 1354, 1363 (11th Cir.1999), *cert. denied*, ___ U.S. ___, 120 S.Ct. 1962, 146 L.Ed.2d 793 (2000) (citing cases).

111. *Ross v. Rhodes Furniture, Inc.*, 146 F.3d 1286, 1291 (11th Cir.1998).

112. *See, e.g., Damon v. Fleming Supermarkets of Florida, Inc.*, 196 F.3d 1354, 1361–1362 (11th Cir.1999), *cert. denied*, ___ U.S. ___, 120 S.Ct. 1962, 146 L.Ed.2d 793 (2000).

113. *See Cooper v. Federal Reserve Bank of Richmond*, 467 U.S. 867, 876, 104 S.Ct. 2794, 2799, 81 L.Ed.2d 718 (1984) ("evidence of pervasive discrimination against others is admissible if such evidence is similar to the complainant's experience and tends to establish" that unlawful discrimination was the defendant's "standard operating procedure.... " (quoting *International Brotherhood of Teamsters v. United States*, 431 U.S. 324, 336, 97 S.Ct. 1843, 1855, 52 L.Ed.2d 396 (1977)).

114. 478 U.S. 385, 402, 106 S.Ct. 3000, ___, 92 L.Ed.2d 315 (1986).

115. *Thigpen v. Bibb County, Georgia*, 223 F.3d 1231, 2000 WL 1277600, at *10 n. 19 (11th Cir.2000) (*citing United Air Lines v. Evans*, 431 U.S. 553, 558, 97 S.Ct. 1885, 52 L.Ed.2d 571 (1977)).

against members of plaintiff's protected group by the particular employer agent alleged to have discriminated against plaintiff is particularly probative of that agent's state of mind.[116] Of course the assertedly comparable evidence must reflect discrimination under similar circumstances to be admissible on the question whether the particular plaintiff was also the victim of unlawful discrimination.[117]

It should be stressed that all these modes of intentional discrimination are designed to ferret out and penalize only employer conduct that adversely differentiates on the basis of one or more[118] of Title VII's prohibited grounds; they are not designed to assure workplace norms or mores that are fair in other respects. Thus any reason for the employer's challenged decision deemed not "because of" race, gender, religion or national origin (or a proxy for one of those grounds) is likely to be viewed as legitimate, even if the trier of fact also considers that reason unfair, unreasonable or unenlightened.[119] In particular, courts express great reluctance to substitute their own judgment for the standards of proficiency or competence assertedly relied on by academic employers.[120] This question must be sharply distinguished, however, from the question whether the academic employer actually relied on the standards it professed to follow; *St. Mary's* implicitly leaves that question for the jury.[121]

116. *See Heyne v. Caruso*, 69 F.3d 1475, 1479 (9th Cir.1995). But the discrimination must of course evince hostility towards "a well-defined and protected group such as persons of a particular race" gender, national origin, religion, age or disability, and because of that group's status. An employer agent's irritation with or hostility to such persons based solely on their work habits is not probative of unlawful discriminatory animus. *Beachy v. Boise Cascade Corporation*, 191 F.3d 1010, 1014 (9th Cir.1999), cert. denied, ___ U.S. ___, 120 S.Ct. 1425, 146 L.Ed.2d 316 (2000).

117. *See Palmer v. Bd. of Regents*, 208 F.3d 969, 972 (11th Cir.2000) (affirming trial court's ruling that evidence of discriminatory acts by other decisionmakers in other departments was too remote to be relevant to motive of the decisionmaker at bar and accordingly was properly excludable as having greater prejudicial effect than probative value); *Roy v. The Austin Company*, 194 F.3d 840, 843 (7th Cir.1999) (approving trial court's use of general proposition "that showing disparate treatment by a different supervisor does not normally further a plaintiff's ability to make out a discrimination claim under Title VII.").

118. There is authority that a plaintiff complaining about discrimination on a "compound" basis—race and gender, for example, or gender and national origin—must demonstrate that the employer discriminates on those grounds in combination, not

merely on one or the other. *Lam v. University of Haw.*, 40 F.3d 1551 (9th Cir.1994). This suggests that the plaintiff's counsel in such a case should take care to plead unlawful grounds in the alternative if it is possible to do so consistent with the rules governing ethics in pleading. On the other hand, some courts consider that proof of discrimination on the compound basis only fails to show discrimination based on either of the separate grounds. *See Hardin v. S.C. Johnson & Son, Inc.*, 167 F.3d 340 (7th Cir.1999), cert. denied, 528 U.S. 874, 120 S.Ct. 178, 145 L.Ed.2d 150 (1999).

119. Consider, for example, Judge Posner's observation in *Troupe*, that "Employers can treat pregnant women as badly as they treat similarly affected but nonpregnant employees" so long as the adverse treatment is predicated on a feature of the workplace or of employee behavior that is distinct from pregnancy or gender.

120. *See Scott v. University of Miss.*, 148 F.3d 493 (5th Cir.1998); *Stern v. Trustees of Columbia Univ.*, 131 F.3d 305 (2d Cir.1997); *Fisher v. Vassar College*, 114 F.3d 1332 (2d Cir.1997) (en banc), cert. denied, 522 U.S. 1075, 118 S.Ct. 851, 139 L.Ed.2d 752 (1998).

121. *See Stern*, 131 F.3d 305. *But see Scott*, 148 F.3d 493 (confusing those questions and substituting appellate review for the jury's determination that the employer

Even before *Sanderson*, circuits agreed that when a jury concludes that an employer has not relied on the neutral ground it advanced, *St. Mary's* permits but does not compel the jury to reach the ultimate conclusion that the employer made the challenged decision for an unlawful discriminatory reason.[122] But the appellate opinions varied widely in the degree of deference due verdicts reaching that ultimate conclusion. Some indulge, at least formally, a mild presumption that adequate evidence of falsity alone entitles the jury to conclude that the employer unlawfully discriminated.[123] Others acknowledge that they conduct a searching review of the record in cases where the jury verdict for plaintiff rested entirely on evidence of falsity, or in fact apply that standard.[124] Special factors in particular cases may account for the divergent outcomes. Where, for example, the court regards the plaintiff's prima facie evidence as particularly strong, it may relax its review of plaintiff's falsity evidence.[125] Where, on the other hand, the person who terminated plaintiff had hired her only a few days before, the court insisted on affirmative evidence of age discrimination in addition to evidence of falsity.[126]

While the employment discrimination statutes do not require just cause for discipline,[127] the Title VII theory of disparate treatment does punish employer conduct that would otherwise be manifestly just or even legally mandated except for having been tainted, in whole or significant part, by discrimination on one of the prohibited grounds. Where, for example, a white plaintiff was discharged for conduct that apparently constituted felonious theft, the Supreme Court nevertheless found that the employer had violated Title VII because African–American employees who had engaged in the same conduct were subjected to lesser discipline.[128] Finally, a claim may fail even where relevant evidence of

relied on something other than its stated reason).

122. *But see Alvarez–Fonseca v. Pepsi Cola of Puerto Rico Bottling Co.*, 152 F.3d 17 (1st Cir.1998), *cert. denied*, 526 U.S. 1123, 119 S.Ct. 1778, 143 L.Ed.2d 806 (1999) (declining to sustain jury's ultimate conclusion of discrimination despite agreeing that there was sufficient evidence to doubt whether company in fact relied on the neutral reason it proffered). *See also Grady v. Affiliated Cent., Inc.*, 130 F.3d 553 (2d Cir.1997), *cert. denied*, 525 U.S. 936, 119 S.Ct. 349, 142 L.Ed.2d 288 (1998) (requiring, in addition to evidence raising a genuine question about falsity of the employer's asserted legitimate nondiscriminatory reason, evidence from which a jury could find more directly that employer was motivated by an impermissible consideration).

123. *See Aka v. Washington Hosp. Ctr.*, 156 F.3d 1284 (D.C.Cir.1998) (en banc) (case under ADA); *Scott*, 148 F.3d 493 (declaring that evidence of falsity standing alone will often, if not usually, suffice, but

overturning verdict by applying a more stringent standard).

124. *See, e.g., Fisher v. Vassar College*, 114 F.3d 1332 (2d Cir.1997) (en banc), *cert. denied*, 522 U.S. 1075, 118 S.Ct. 851, 139 L.Ed.2d 752 (1998). *See also Scott*, 148 F.3d 493.

125. *See, e.g., Danzer v. Norden Systems, Inc.*, 151 F.3d 50 (2d Cir.1998) (reversing summary judgment in ADEA case); *Stern*, 131 F.3d 305.

126. *See, e.g., Grady v. Affiliated Cent., Inc.*, 130 F.3d 553 (2d Cir.1997), *cert. denied*, 525 U.S. 936, 119 S.Ct. 349, 142 L.Ed.2d 288 (1998) (case under ADEA).

127. See *Hazen Paper Co. v. Biggins*, 507 U.S. 604, 113 S.Ct. 1701, 123 L.Ed.2d 338 (1993) (case under ADEA). *But see* Blumrosen, *Strangers No More: All Workers Are Entitled To "Just Cause" Protection Under Title VII*, 2 Ind. Rel. L.J. 519 (1978).

128. *McDonald v. Santa Fe Trail, Transp. Co.*, 427 U.S. 273, 96 S.Ct. 2574, 49 L.Ed.2d 493 (1976). The same principle was

discriminatory intent was improperly excluded if the appellate court deems the error harmless.[129]

§ 3.11   The Problem of "Mixed Motives"

The classic evidentiary structure erected by *McDonnell Douglas* and *Burdine*, while furnishing a workable matrix for inferentially ferreting out intentional discrimination, does not fully come to grips with the complexities of many cases because it assumes that an employer's motivation was grounded *entirely* on a prohibited reason *or* a legitimate one. In fact, employers commonly advance more than one asserted legitimate reason for a challenged employment decision, and courts often conclude that an employer relied on one or more of those reasons as well as a reason condemned by Title VII.

In *Price Waterhouse v. Hopkins*,[1] a Supreme Court plurality concluded that when an employer undertakes a challenged employment decision for more than one reason, and the reason that is unlawful under Title VII is a "motivating," or "substantial motivating" factor in the employer's decision, liability will attach unless the employer can prove by a preponderance of the evidence that it would have reached the same decision for one or more independent, lawful reasons. The plurality rejected the dissenters' suggestion that an employer should also be nonliable if the court finds such an independent reason existed at the time of the challenged decision, regardless of whether the employer relied on it. The plurality insisted that the employer, to be relieved of liability, must have *acted* on the basis of a lawful reason, of which it necessarily had knowledge.

If an employer carries that persuasion burden, the plurality wrote, it should be found not to have committed an unlawful employment practice, despite the evidence of partial unlawful motive.[2] If on the other hand the employer cannot carry by a preponderance of the evidence the "same-decision" showing, it will be liable. Indeed, even a plaintiff using evidence of indirect disparate treatment who fails its burden of persuading that a lawful reason proffered by the employer at trial is a pretext for prohibited discrimination (see the *McDonnell Douglas/Burdine/St. Mary's Honor Ctr.* mode of proof discussed above) can still prevail under *Price Waterhouse* by showing another employer motive that was unlawful and motivated the challenged decision.[3]

applied in favor of an African–American former state trooper who, unlike his similarly situated white officers, was not reinstated after having been acquitted of felony charges. *Johnson v. Arkansas State Police*, 10 F.3d 547 (8th Cir.1993).

129. *See Taylor v. Virginia Union Univ.*, 193 F.3d 219 (4th Cir.1999) (en banc), *cert. denied*, ___ U.S. ___, 120 S.Ct. 1243, 146 L.Ed.2d 101 (2000) (affirming jury verdict for defendant on failure to promote claim).

§ 3.11

1. 490 U.S. 228, 109 S.Ct. 1775, 104 L.Ed.2d 268 (1989).

2. *Id.* at 245 n.10.

3. *See Stacks v. Southwestern Bell Yellow Pages, Inc.*, 996 F.2d 200 (8th Cir. 1993).

A critical fifth vote for saddling the employer with the burden of persuasion on this "same decision" issue was cast by Justice O'Connor. She, however, would have imposed that burden only where the plaintiff proffers "direct evidence" that the discriminatory factor played a substantial role in the employer's decision.[4] Justice White, who wrote the other concurrence, took no position on whether the plaintiff's prima facie evidence must be "direct" to trigger the employer's burden of persuasion, but he agreed that plaintiff's case must be "substantial."[5]

The three dissenting justices would not have compelled the employer to persuade on any issue. They relied primarily on decisions of the Court that had imposed the persuasion burden on the plaintiff through all stages of an "individual disparate treatment" or *McDonnell Douglas* case, in which the plaintiff seeks to prove discrimination inferentially.[6] As a matter of principle, the dissenters wrote, cases where the plaintiff's prima facie evidence may be characterized as "direct" or "substantial" are indistinguishable from those where her showing is inferential. In each situation, the sole statutory question is whether the employer has made an adverse employment decision "because of" a prohibited characteristic, and on that question the plaintiff must produce evidence of, and persuade about, "but-for" causation.[7]

Much has been written about the *Price Waterhouse* decision.[8] Observers differ on whether affording the employer an escape from liability when it makes the "same-decision" showing but saddling it with the persuasion burden on that question, a development favorable to plaintiffs or defendants.[9]

In any event the Civil Rights Act of 1991 substantially incorporates and in one respect enhances the plurality's pro-plaintiff perspective in defining the circumstances that impose the "same decision" persuasion

---

4. 490 U.S. at 276, 109 S.Ct. at 1804 (O'Connor, J., concurring).

5. *Id.* at 259, 109 S.Ct. at 1795 (White, J., concurring).

6. *See Texas Dep't of Community Affairs v. Burdine*, 450 U.S. 248, 101 S.Ct. 1089, 67 L.Ed.2d 207 (1981); *McDonnell Douglas Corp. v. Green*, 411 U.S. 792, 93 S.Ct. 1817, 36 L.Ed.2d 668 (1973).

7. *Price Waterhouse*, 490 U.S. at 280–282, 109 S.Ct. at 1806–1807 (Kennedy, J., dissenting).

8. *See* Blumoff & Lewis, *The Reagan Court and Title VII: A Common–Law Outlook On a Statutory Task*, 69 N.C.L.Rev. 1 (1990); Blumrosen, *Society in Transition II: Price Waterhouse and the Individual Employment Discrimination Case*, 42 Rutgers L.Rev. 1023 (1990).

9. *Compare* Justice Department Memorandum for the Attorney General, prepared by the Civil Rights Division (February 7, 1991) (arguing that the decision has worked favorably for plaintiffs, since they have prevailed in fifteen (15) of nineteen (19) subsequent reported lower court decisions applying *Price Waterhouse* and that the plurality approach was as or more favorable to plaintiffs than the approach taken by eight of the eleven courts of appeals to address the issue) with Blumoff & Lewis, 69 N.C.L.Rev. at 56, 66 (observing that *Price Waterhouse* shifts no burden to the employer on the threshold question of unlawful motivation, since the "same decision" phase of the case arises only after the plaintiff, through direct or inferential evidence, has shown such motivation; further observing that the plurality's position had previously been adopted by most federal appellate courts that had addressed the issue). *See also* Blumrosen, 42 Rutgers L.Rev. at 1052 (*Price Waterhouse* affords defendants an additional opportunity to evade liability because the "mixed motive cases presuppose that the plaintiff has [already] persuaded the court that the illicit factor did influence the employment decision.").

burden on the employer. Section 107 declares that an unlawful employment practice is established when the plaintiff demonstrates that employer reliance on protected group status was a "motivating factor" for "any" employment practice, "even though other factors also motivated the practice."[10] The language requiring a "motivating" factor, derived from *Price Waterhouse*, evolved in the legislative process from the less stringent "contributing." It first surfaced in a Democratic substitute bill passed June 5, 1991 that was designed to allay business and Administration concerns. The resulting linguistic connotation, against the background of existing appellate jurisprudence about mixed motive, suggests that at least this change should marginally improve the litigation prospects of defendant employers.[11] And the "motivating" requirement also appears less burdensome than the counterpart demonstration of a "determinative" factor that has evolved in cases under the ADEA.[12]

On the other hand, by omitting any reference to the kind of "direct" or "substantial" evidence of unlawful discrimination that the *Price Waterhouse* concurrers would have required, the Act can easily be read to require the employer to bear, or at least give it the option of bearing, the same-decision burden regardless of the kind or strength of the plaintiff's prima facie case, so long as she has shown in some fashion that discrimination was a motivating factor.[13] Whether plaintiff's initial

---

10. (Adding Title VII § 703(m), 42 U.S.C.A. § 2000e–2(m) (1988)).

11. *See* Blumoff and Lewis, 69 N.C.L.Rev. at 66 (seven federal circuit courts before *Price Waterhouse* required the employer to make the same-decision showing to avoid liability when impermissible motivation played *any* part in the adverse decision or when that motive was either a "substantial" *or* a "motivating" one.) *But see EEOC v. Our Lady of Resurrection Medical Ctr.*, 77 F.3d 145 (7th Cir.1996) (using "determining factor" language in Title VII race case; this resembles the arguably more stringent standard used in actions under ADEA). *See* Chapter 7, *infra*.

12. See Chapter 7, *infra*.

13. Although the subject is still one of debate among the circuits, the absence of any reference in the text of § 107 of the 1991 Act, Section 703(m) of Title VII, to "direct" or "substantial" evidence as a prerequisite to placing the "same-decision" persuasion burden on the defendant suggests that in Title VII, if not ADEA cases, this defense is available regardless of whether plaintiff's prima facie case showing *one* unlawful motivation rests on direct or indirect evidence. *See Pulliam v. Tallapoosa County Jail*, 185 F.3d 1182, 1184 (11th Cir. 1999) (assuming the mixed-motives defense is an affirmative defense on which defendant has burden of proof, but declining to decide whether defense must be pleaded under Federal Rule of Civil Procedure 8(c)

or included in pretrial order to be preserved); *Thomas v. National Football League Players Ass'n*, 131 F.3d 198 (D.C.Cir.1997) ("[u]nder *Price Waterhouse*, the burden of persuasion shifts to the defendant when the plaintiff has shown by a preponderance of any sufficiently probative direct or indirect evidence that unlawful discrimination was a substantial factor in the employment decision"); *Thomas v. Denny's*, 111 F.3d 1506 (10th Cir.1997), *cert. denied*, 522 U.S. 1028, 118 S.Ct. 626, 139 L.Ed.2d 607 (1997); *Harris v. Shelby County Bd. of Educ.*, 99 F.3d 1078 (11th Cir.1996); *Kerr-Selgas v. American Airlines, Inc.*, 69 F.3d 1205, 1210 (1st Cir.1995); (stating or assuming plaintiff may establish liability through § 107 of the 1991 Civil Rights Act, Section 703(m) of Title VII, even when plaintiff's prima facie case rests only on indirect or "pretext" and not "direct" or "mixed motive" evidence); *Woodson v. Scott Paper Co.*, 109 F.3d 913, 935 n. 29 (3d Cir.), *cert. denied*, 522 U.S. 914, 118 S.Ct. 299, 139 L.Ed.2d 230 (1997) (suggesting, without reaching the issue, that "there is considerable force to [the] view" that § 107 should apply to "pretext" and "mixed motive" cases alike). *Cf. Deneen v. Northwest Airlines, Inc.*, 132 F.3d 431, 436 (8th Cir. 1998) (defining direct evidence liberally, thereby increasing the possible number of applications of § 703(m) and its placing of the burden of persuasion on defendant on the "same-decision" issue).

proof takes the form of "direct" anecdotal testimony of discriminatory motive, substantial (or for that matter insubstantial) evidence that a decision, practice or policy treats her less favorably by reference to a prohibited characteristic, or simply the more common "inferential" formula,[14] she will now on this reading, have demonstrated intentional discrimination forbidden by Title VII.[15] But an increasing number of circuit opinions, relying predominantly on Justice O'Connor's concurring opinion in *Price Waterhouse* and concluding that § 107 was enacted solely to overrule that part of the opinion that absolves the employer who carries the same-decision showing of all liability, take the position that the § 107(a) burden shift on that showing is triggered by "direct" evidence only.[16]

14. Blumoff & Lewis, 69 N.C.L.Rev. at 9–10, 58. *Cf.* Blumrosen, 42 Rutgers L.Rev. at 1057–59 (observing that intentional discrimination may consist either of "evil motive" or simply unequal treatment).

15. This conclusion that plaintiff's mode of proof is irrelevant is supported by the absence of any discussion of these different modes of proof in *Mt. Healthy City Sch. Dist. Bd. of Educ. v. Doyle*, 429 U.S. 274, 97 S.Ct. 568, 50 L.Ed.2d 471 (1977), the § 1983 counterpart to *Price Waterhouse*. And again in *McKennon v. Nashville Banner Publ'g Co.*, 513 U.S. 352, 115 S.Ct. 879, 130 L.Ed.2d 852 (1995), the Court failed to distinguish among the various proof modes.

16. *See Fields v. New York State Office of Mental Retardation and Developmental Disab.*, 115 F.3d 116 (2d Cir.1997) (plaintiff, to insist on a dual motivation charge to jury, must have presented "direct" evidence of discrimination or "circumstantial-plus" evidence like slurs tied directly to the alleged animus; therefore, plaintiff who presented only statistical and other circumstantial evidence of unlawful animus not entitled to mixed-motive instruction that defendant did not request, although defendant entitled to that instruction regardless of nature of plaintiff's evidence that a discriminatory reason was a motivating factor in challenged employment decision); *Kubicko v. Ogden Logistics Servs.*, 181 F.3d 544, 553 (4th Cir.1999) (retaliation plaintiff must have "direct" evidence, or at least strong evidence, to trigger mixed motive proof scheme under Title VII); *Fuller v. Phipps*, 67 F.3d 1137, 1142 (4th Cir.1995) (only the plaintiff who adduces "direct evidence" or a "mixed motive" case can establish liability and obtain limited relief under § 703(m) and 706(g)(2)(B); when the plaintiff relies on "inferential disparate treatment" or "pretext" evidence per *McDonnell Douglas*, defendant's same-decision showing defeats liability altogether). The First Circuit has not decided the issue, but has

"dropped inconclusive hints" that seem to favor the O'Connor position that only where the plaintiff offers "direct" evidence of discrimination violating Title VII does the defendant bear the burden of persuading that it would have reached the same decision for independent, lawful reasons. *Fernandes v. Costa Brothers Masonry, Inc.*, 199 F.3d 572, 580–582 (1st Cir.1999). *See also Carey v. Mt. Desert Island Hosp.*, 156 F.3d 31 (1st Cir.1998) (dissenting judge argues that the burden shift should be allowed only in cases of direct evidence). *Id.* (Stahl, J., dissenting).

The Third and Fourth Circuits, harkening back to the concurring opinions of Justices O'Connor and White in *Price Waterhouse*, have squarely insisted on *"direct"* plaintiff's evidence that the employer *substantially* relied on an unlawful factor before a plaintiff is entitled to an instruction placing the burden on defendant to show that it would have reached the same decision independent of such reliance. *Watson v. Southeastern Pa. Transp. Auth.*, 207 F.3d 207 (3d Cir.2000) (case under Title VII); *Walden v. Georgia–Pacific Corp.*, 126 F.3d 506, 513–14 (3d Cir.1997), *cert. denied*, 523 U.S. 1074, 118 S.Ct. 1516, 140 L.Ed.2d 669 (1998); *Miller v. CIGNA Corporation*, 47 F.3d 586 (3d Cir.1995) (en banc) (case under ADEA); *Fuller v. Phipps*, 67 F.3d 1137, 1142 (4th Cir.1995). Although this view draws little support from the text of § 107 of the 1991 amendments, which added Section 703(m) to Title VII, it is true that the legislation did not amend the ADEA. Accordingly, a same-decision showing in an ADEA case may still defeat liability altogether. *See Lewis v. Young Men's Christian Ass'n*, 208 F.3d 1303 (11th Cir.2000) (no liability at all where defendant in ADEA retaliation case carries same-decision showing); *DeMarco v. Holy Cross High Sch.*, 4 F.3d 166, 172 (2d Cir.1993). *But see Fast v. Southern Union Co.*, 149 F.3d 885, 889 (8th

To avoid monetary liability, the employer must then demonstrate "that it would have taken the same action in the absence of the impermissible motivating factor"[17]—even if there is evidence that at the time of the adverse employment action the employer knew that the employee had disobeyed work rules or lied.[18] The Act codifies the *Price Waterhouse* requirement that the required employer "demonstration," once triggered, extends to the burden of persuasion as well as production on this question.[19]

In fact the legislation goes somewhat beyond the *Price Waterhouse* plurality in providing that even the defendant who makes the required demonstration is relieved only of monetary liability. If unlawful discrimination was a "motivating" factor in the challenged employment decision, the employer has committed a law violation remediable by prospective

Cir.1998); *Miller v. Illinois Dep't of Corrections*, 107 F.3d 483, 484 (7th Cir.1997); and *Gonzagowski v. Widnall*, 115 F.3d 744, 749 (10th Cir.1997) (assuming or deciding that § 107 applies to ADEA claims, relying on the interchangeability of many Title VII and ADEA proof requirements in disparate treatment cases). Moreover, the Supreme Court has written that in ADEA cases the plaintiff's ultimate burden is to show that age played not merely a motivating but a "determinative" role in the challenged employment decision. *See Hazen Paper Co. v. Biggins*, 507 U.S. 604, 113 S.Ct. 1701, 123 L.Ed.2d 338 (1993). Although "determinative" clearly does not mean "sole" factor, *Miller v. CIGNA*, 47 F.3d at 597, or even a "predominant" factor in the sense of one that outweighs all others, it may suggest a "but-for" factor without which the challenged decision would not have been made. If so, a "same-decision" aspect of an ADEA case would make no sense, for it would negate what the plaintiff is required to prove; thus ADEA plaintiffs required to prove that age was a "but-for" or determinative factor should not be eligible for any "same-decision" instruction placing the reverse burden on the employer. *See id.* (ADEA plaintiff who proceeds with *McDonnell Douglas* formula, in contrast to "direct" evidence of age discrimination, has "but-for" burden and therefore gets no "same-decision" instruction.) Even if "determinative" means only a somewhat weightier factor than a merely motivating one, there may be some horse sense, reflecting that Congress explicitly eased plaintiff's burden only under Title VII, in demanding that the prima facie evidence of the ADEA, as distinguished from the Title VII, plaintiff, be of a more probative nature or magnitude (e.g., "direct" or "substantial" or both) before he is entitled to that instruction. But none of this is any reason why the Title VII plaintiff, in either a "direct"/ "*Price Waterhouse*" or "indirect"/ *McDonnell Douglas* "pretext" case, should have to show that discrimination was anything more than a motivating factor, among others. *See Fields, supra,* 115 F.3d at 121. *But see Watson, supra* (because 703(m)'s burden shift does not apply in indirect evidence or "pretext" cases, plaintiffs in such Title VII cases, not just in ADEA cases, must show that discrimination was the "determinative," not merely a "motivating" factor); *Woodson v. Scott Paper Co.,* 109 F.3d 913 (3d Cir.), *cert. denied,* 522 U.S. 914, 118 S.Ct. 299, 139 L.Ed.2d 230 (1997) (unless Title VII § 703(m) applies to indirect evidence "pretext" cases of discrimination, a question the court did not then decide, defendant liable only if unlawful conduct had "determinative" effect on the challenged employment decision).

17. Section 107(b) (amending Title VII § 706(g), 42 U.S.C.A. § 2000e–5(g) (1972)).

18. *Stacks v. Southwestern Bell Yellow Pages, Inc.,* 27 F.3d 1316 (8th Cir.1994).

19. Section 104 (adding subsection 701(m) to Title VII, 42 U.S.C.A. § 2000e–m). Although the same-decision showing under § 703(m) and § 706(g)(2)(B) is a partial affirmative defense in the sense that it limits relief but does not defeat all liability, a defendant has been allowed to offer evidence on the defense by raising it in the pretrial order even without having pled it in the answer in accordance with Federal Rule of Civil Procedure 8(a). *See Pulliam v. Tallapoosa County Jail.,* 185 F.3d 1182, 1185 and n. 4 (11th Cir.1999). And in *Pulliam,* the court also found harmless the trial judge's failure to instruct that defendant bears the burden of persuasion on the defense in the absence of timely objection by plaintiff. *Id.* at 1188–89.

relief and attorney's fees.[20]

Price Waterhouse, reflecting the law prevailing before the effective date of the 1991 Act, illustrates the potential significance of this and another change worked by the Act. The court of appeals there viewed the evidence as showing that all three employer decisionmakers admitted relying on a reason that would constitute retaliation under Title VII § 704. But it also found that they had relied as well on several lawful reasons for not promoting the plaintiff, and that she had failed to persuade that the unlawful reason was "substantial" as well as "motivating." It therefore agreed with the district court that the plaintiff's evidence did not cast on the employer the burden of making the *Price Waterhouse* "same-decision" showing.[21] The new statutory text, by contrast, would have permitted the plaintiff to cast the "same-decision" showing on the defendant upon proof that unlawful discrimination was a "motivating," even if not a "substantial motivating" reason for the challenged action.

Further, let us suppose that the employer could then have shown that when it acted its lawful reasons, independent of the unlawful one, would have led it to decline to promote the plaintiff. Under the 1991 Act, but not *Price Waterhouse*, the employer would nevertheless be adjudged to have committed a Title VII violation for which it could be saddled with injunctive relief and attorney's fees. Its showing would relieve it only of monetary liability. These liberalizations of the mixed-motive case manifest Congress' resolve to facilitate proof of individual, intentional discrimination on the grounds prohibited by Title VII.[22] In doing so,

20. Section 107(b)(3) (adding paragraph (2)(B) to § 706(g) of Title VII, 42 U.S.C.A. § 2000e–5(g)). A circuit that requires "direct" plaintiff's evidence before placing the same-decision burden on the defendant may encounter difficulty applying the concept because there is so much uncertainty whether certain kinds of employer speech constitute "direct" evidence of discriminatory intent. See § 3.2 *supra*. It may therefore be tempting for such a court to pretermit the problem by turning immediately to see if the employer has carried the same-decision defense, and then limiting plaintiff's relief under Section 706(g)(2)(B) if it answers that question "Yes" but not if it answers that question "No." See *Kerr–Selgas,* 69 F.3d 1205. But in light of *St. Mary's,* it may not be fair to the defendant to avoid characterizing the prima facie case. If plaintiff's prima facie evidence is in fact the weaker, inferential "indirect" variety authorized by *McDonnell Douglas/Burdine,* and she offers no "affirmative" evidence of unlawful discrimination, *St. Mary's* requires her to persuade the trier of fact not only that defendant's proffered legitimate reason is false, but also that the defendant acted with unlawful discriminatory intent.

If the court skips over the details of plaintiff's threshold burden of demonstrating at least one unlawful motivation and instead proceeds directly to the employer's "same-decision" defense that merely limits relief, it may well overlook that fundamental liability prerequisite and improperly require the defendant to pay at least attorney's fees and maybe full monetary relief.

21. *Price Waterhouse*, 825 F.2d at 471.

22. In *Patterson v. McLean Credit Union*, 491 U.S. 164, 109 S.Ct. 2363, 105 L.Ed.2d 132 (1989), the Supreme Court assimilated the *McDonnell Douglas/Burdine* mode of inferential proof into the trial of claims under § 1981. Nevertheless, the Civil Rights Act of 1991 contains no amendment to § 1981 or the ADEA similar to § 703(m) or § 706(g)(2)(B), even though it does amplify § 1981 remedies and modify ADEA procedures. In mixed-motive situations, therefore, § 1981 and § 1983 may ultimately be construed as subject to the pre-existing *Mt. Healthy* regime, in which there lingers at least an argument that a plaintiff may recover punitive damages even when the employer carries the "same-decision" burden. See *Mabra v. United Food &*

Congress reflects the public's widespread agreement not to tolerate intentional discrimination in the realm of private employment.[23]

Price Waterhouse aggravates the problem of complicated instructions. At some point before instructing the jury, the trial judge must decide if there is sufficient evidence that the challenged employment action was motivated by both lawful and unlawful factors to warrant a *Price Waterhouse* instruction.[24] If so, she will have to issue an intricate, additional set of instructions concerning whether, if the jury finds (using, for example, the complex *McDonnell Douglas* framework) at least one unlawful employer motivation, the employer has persuaded that it would have reached the same decision for independent lawful reasons. This instruction must apparently be given, at the employer's request, even if the employer takes the primary position that the prohibited reason played no part in its challenged action.[25] But the defendant,

Commercial Workers, 176 F.3d 1357, 1357–58 (11th Cir.1999) and *Harris v. Shelby County Bd. of Educ.*, 99 F.3d 1078 (11th Cir.1996) (the 1991 amendments to § 703 do not apply to claims under § 1981 and § 1983, respectively). *See also* Chapter 5 concerning remedies under § 1981. Similarly, in ADEA mixed-motive cases, plaintiffs may remain under the pre–1991 Act *Price Waterhouse* regime, which would foreclose them from receiving even the limited prospective relief available under § 706(g)(2)(B) where the employer makes the kind of showing required by § 703(m). *See Lewis v. Young Men's Christian Ass'n*, 208 F.3d 1303 (11th Cir.2000) (no liability at all where defendant in ADEA retaliation case carries same-decision showing); *DeMarco v. Holy Cross High Sch.*, 4 F.3d 166, 172 (2d Cir.1993). *But see Fast v. Southern Union Co.*, 149 F.3d 885, 889 (8th Cir. 1998); *Miller v. Illinois Dep't of Corrections*, 107 F.3d 483, 484 (7th Cir.1997); and *Gonzagowski v. Widnall*, 115 F.3d 744, 749 (10th Cir.1997) (assuming or deciding that § 107 applies to ADEA claims, relying on the interchangeability of many Title VII and ADEA proof requirements in disparate treatment cases). *See* the pertinent discussion of that issue in Chapter 7 which treats ADEA. Nor do Title VII's mixed-motive amendments apply textually to claims under the Americans with Disabilities Act. *See* Chapter 10. Indeed, in terms, §§ 703(m) and 706(g)(2)(b) do not even apply to retaliation claims under Title VII itself, only to claims of discrimination. The resulting circuit court uncertainty as to whether to apply the *Price Waterhouse* or 1991 Act Amendments approach to mixed-motive retaliation claims is discussed in § 2.40, *supra*. And courts have also contended with the issue whether the 1991 amendments, in particular § 706(g), by authorizing an

award of attorneys' fees where plaintiffs prevail in mixed-motive cases , effectively mandate or, as the circuits have so far held, merely permit fees in the court's discretion. That issue is addressed in § 11.5, *infra*.

23. Blumoff & Lewis, 69 N.C.L.Rev. at 8–9. A poll-taker recently summarized his conclusions as follows: "If civil rights is defined as quotas, it's a losing hand. If it's defined as protection against discrimination and efforts to promote opportunity, then it will remain a mainstream value in American life." *Rights–Bill Backers Issue Call To More Transcendent Battle*, New York Times, April 3, 1991, at A18 (quoting Geoffrey Garin).

24. *See Radabaugh v. Zip Feed Mills Inc.*, 997 F.2d 444 (8th Cir.1993) (case under ADEA).

25. *Cf. Gooden v. Neal*, 17 F.3d 925, 929 (7th Cir.), *cert. denied*, 513 U.S. 816, 115 S.Ct. 73, 130 L.Ed.2d 28 (1994) (action under 42 U.S.C.A. § 1983, with employer relying on doctrine of *Mt. Healthy City Sch. Dist. Bd. of Educ. v. Doyle*, 429 U.S. 274, 97 S.Ct. 568, 50 L.Ed.2d 471 (1977), the counterpart to *Price Waterhouse* for mixed-motive constitutional cases). But a circuit decision warns defendant's counsel that special jury interrogatories raising the same-decision defense should be drafted with extreme care when the plaintiff presses multiple grounds of discrimination. In *Kerr–Selgas v. American Airlines, Inc.*, 69 F.3d 1205 (1st Cir.1995), the jury's special verdicts reflected that it had found both gender discrimination and retaliation to be motivating factors in plaintiff's termination. Yet on each issue the jury also found, in separate responses, that the employer would more likely than not have made the same employment decisions even absent, respectively,

fearful that the jury might then be more likely to find a forbidden motive, or hopeful that it might believe the "same-decision" burden is on the plaintiff, is often unwilling to ask for a *Price Waterhouse*/Section 703(m) instruction.[26] Presumably the plaintiff might then seek the instruction, on the theory that half a loaf (prospective relief and attorney's fees) is better than none. The plaintiff has been held entitled to the burden-shifting instruction on this "defense" where the evidence could support a finding of unlawful as well as lawful motives.[27]

Loose language in one decision suggests that plaintiffs must stake out early in the lawsuit whether they are seeking to prove a "pretext" case or a "mixed motive" case. Only in the latter event, this opinion asserts, would the plaintiff be entitled to an instruction allowing it to prevail by demonstrating that the unlawful motive was "significant," "determinative," "substantial," or "motivating." Otherwise, the plaintiff must prove that the adverse employment action was the product of a discriminatory motive alone.[28] This conclusion appears to conflict with the Supreme Court's recognition in *Price Waterhouse* that the full range of questions for the jury may not be apparent until all the evidence is in, as well as its observation that Congress rejected an amendment that would have limited the ban of Title VII to discrimination "solely" on one of its prohibited grounds.[29]

A more fluid approach is reflected in a circuit opinion which recognizes that the ordinary *McDonnell–Douglas/St. Mary's* inferential disparate treatment case, together with its *Price Waterhouse*/Section 703(m) overlay, operate on a continuum. This view starts from the premise that, as *Hazen Paper* instructs, "because of" does not mean "solely because of." It means rather that the unlawful factor is a "but-for" or "motivating" (in a Title VII case) or "determinative" (in an ADEA case) cause of the employer's adverse action. *St. Mary's*, then, is significant because it illustrates that the trier of fact need not choose between finding that the

gender discrimination and retaliation (the jury also found, concerning a pendent wrongful discharge claim, that the defendant did not have just cause for plaintiff's dismissal). Nevertheless, the court upheld a plaintiff's verdict because the form of the special interrogatories did not exclude the possibility, with respect to the gender claim, that defendant acted from an unlawful *retaliatory* motive. Similarly, the jury might have found, respecting the retaliation claim, that the defendants acted unlawfully based on *gender*!

26. *See Ostrowski v. Atlantic Mut. Ins. Cos.*, 968 F.2d 171, 181 (2d Cir.1992).

27. *Id.* But the circuits do not agree if the plaintiff is entitled to the dual-motivation instruction in an "indirect evidence" or "pretext" case if the defendant does not request it. *Contrast Thomas v. Denny's*, 111 F.3d 1506 (10th Cir.1997), *cert. denied*, 522 U.S. 1028, 118 S.Ct. 626, 139 L.Ed.2d 607

(1997) (yes) *with Fields v. New York State Office of Mental Retardation and Developmental Disab.*, 115 F.3d 116 (2d Cir.1997) (no).

28. *Griffiths v. CIGNA Corp.*, 988 F.2d 457 (3d Cir.), *cert. denied*, 510 U.S. 865, 114 S.Ct. 186, 126 L.Ed.2d 145 (1993).

29. *See Price Waterhouse*, 490 U.S. at 241 n.7, 109 S.Ct. at 1786 n.7. The Fourth Circuit has explicitly recognized that sorting out whether the evidence supports instructions or verdicts under the *McDonnell Douglas* approach (which assumes a unitary employer motive), the *Price Waterhouse* or § 703(m) approach (which assume mixed employer motives in ADEA and Title VII cases, respectively), or under both such approaches is an analytical task for the court and factfinder after the evidence is in, not a subject of advance mandatory election by plaintiff's counsel. *Russell v. Microdyne Corp.*, 65 F.3d 1229 (4th Cir.1995).

alleged discriminatory motive or the employer's proffered nondiscriminatory explanation was the sole cause of the challenged action. Alternatively, the trier may conclude that the employer acted only for lawful reasons not advanced by either party—in which case it should not find unlawful discrimination. Or it may conclude that a discriminatory motive and some nondiscriminatory explanation, whether or not it is the one advanced by the employer, both played a role. In that event the trier must decide if the discriminatory component of the overall complex of employer reasons was "motivating," and, if so, whether the employer has demonstrated under Section 706(g)(2)(B) that it "would have taken the same action in the absence of the impermissible motivating factor...." Therefore in most cases the charge to the jury should allow for the possibility that the employer's decision was the product of more than one consideration, and should instruct that at a minimum the plaintiff has the burden of demonstrating that a prohibited consideration had a motivating (Title VII) or determinative (ADEA) influence on the outcome.[30] This analysis is useful because it points up that all the complexities of mixed-motive analysis may but need not arise in a case where the parties have previously confronted all the complexities of inferential evidence analysis, including *St. Mary's*.

After several years of more fundamental disagreement about the meaning and application of *St. Mary's*, the 1997 and late–1996 circuit decisions have arrived at substantial consensus. First, with the exception of one or possibly two circuits,[31] these federal appellate opinions have converged on a common conception of "legal sufficiency" in a Title VII indirect evidence case. The jury should be instructed that it is permitted to impose liability for unlawful discrimination when it (1) finds by a preponderance of the evidence that the plaintiff has established the elements of his prima facie inferential disparate treatment case and that each of defendant's proffered legitimate nondiscriminatory reasons is false, provided it also (2) determines, as it may from no more than this same evidence, that the employer acted against the plaintiff in motivating part on the basis of a ground forbidden by Title VII.[32] Second, closely read, each of these circuit opinions contemplates that trial judges, subject to normal appellate review, may and should assess the "factual sufficiency" of *at least* the item (1) components of "legal sufficiency" (and, in a smaller number of circuits, the item (2) determination as well) on motions for summary judgment or motions during trial or after verdict for judgment as a matter of law under Federal Rule of Civil Procedure 50(a) and 50(b). Thus the major remaining area of disagreement centers on whether a factually supportable showing of falsity or "pretext" *suffices* to support a verdict for the plaintiff, where the jury was properly instructed that a plaintiff's verdict also required it to

30. *Miller v. CIGNA Corp.,* 47 F.3d 586 (3d Cir.1995) (en banc) (case under ADEA).

31. A definite exception is *LeBlanc v. Great Am. Ins. Co.,* 6 F.3d 836 (1st Cir. 1993), *cert. denied,* 511 U.S. 1018, 114 S.Ct. 1398, 128 L.Ed.2d 72 (1994). A possible

exception is *Rhodes v. Guiberson Oil Tools,* 75 F.3d 989 (5th Cir.1996) (en banc), discussed *supra* § 3.10.

32. See cases cited § 3.10.

conclude that the employer was motivated in part by an unlawful reason.[33]

We can now see the full significance of the addition to Title VII of Sections 703(m) and 706(g)(2)(B), and, in contrast, the significance of their omission from the ADEA. First, thanks to Section 703(m), the plaintiff's ultimate burden in establishing Title VII liability is only to demonstrate that an unlawful ground motivated, rather than determined, the imposition of an employment detriment or denial of an employment benefit. Second, correlatively, where the Title VII plaintiff attempts to meet this burden through the indirect *McDonnell Douglas* formula, judges ruling on summary judgment and FRCP 50 motions will apply the *St. Mary's* requirements for "pretext" less stringently than in similar litigation under ADEA. Third, a Title VII plaintiff who takes the *McDonnell Douglas* path and presents evidence sufficient under *St. Mary's* to survive a Rule 50 motion at the close of all the evidence will, like the Title VII plaintiff who uses "direct" evidence, usually be entitled to a Section 703(m) instruction imposing on the employer the burden of demonstrating that it would have reached the same decision independent of the unlawful reason. It is not at all clear that the counterpart ADEA plaintiff who presents only indirect evidence of age discrimination is eligible for such an instruction under *Price Waterhouse*.[34] Fourth, under Section 706(g)(2)(B), the Title VII defendant who carries the "same-

---

33. Most circuits addressing the issue have written that neither summary judgment nor judgment as a matter of law may be granted if the plaintiff has evidence raising a genuine factual issue about, or enabling a reasonable jury to find, that the plaintiff had a prima facie case and that the employer's proffered nondiscriminatory reasons were not credible—evidence, that is, about the item (1) components alone. *See, e.g., Aka v. Washington Hosp. Ctr.*, 156 F.3d 1284 (D.C.Cir.1998) (en banc) (case under ADA); *Combs v. Plantation Patterns*, 106 F.3d 1519, 1529 (11th Cir.1997), *cert. denied sub nom. Combs v. Meadowcraft Co.*, 522 U.S. 1045, 118 S.Ct. 685, 139 L.Ed.2d 632 (1998); *Randle v. City of Aurora*, 69 F.3d 441, 451 (10th Cir.1995); *Perdomo v. Browner*, 67 F.3d 140, 145 (7th Cir.1995); *Manzer v. Diamond Shamrock Chem. Co.*, 29 F.3d 1078, 1083 (6th Cir.1994); *Mitchell v. Data Gen. Corp.*, 12 F.3d 1310, 1316 (4th Cir.1993); *Washington v. Garrett*, 10 F.3d 1421, 1433 (9th Cir.1993). Others would deny trial or set aside a verdict not only for a factually insufficient showing of the item (1) components, but alternatively for an unreasonable jury inference respecting item (2) that the employer relied on a prohibited factor. *See, e.g., Rothmeier v. Investment Advisers, Inc.*, 85 F.3d 1328, 1335 (8th Cir. 1996) ("Intentional discrimination *vel non* is like any other ultimate question of fact: either the evidence is sufficient to support

a finding that the fact has been proven, or it is not."). The *en banc* Eighth Circuit subsequently construed the quoted language to authorize judicial review of determination (2) as well as factual sufficiency review of the item (1) components. *Ryther v. KARE 11*, 108 F.3d 832 (8th Cir.1997) (en banc), *cert. denied*, 521 U.S. 1119, 117 S.Ct. 2510, 138 L.Ed.2d 1013 (1997). *See also Rhodes v. Guiberson Oil Tools*, 75 F.3d 989 (5th Cir.1996) (en banc); *Woods v. Friction Materials, Inc.*, 30 F.3d 255 (1st Cir.1994). Similarly, on appeal from a liability determination after a bench trial, another circuit reserves the right to reverse for clear error in the trial judge's ruling on determination (2). *Fisher v. Vassar College*, 114 F.3d 1332 (2d Cir.1997) (en banc), *cert. denied*, 522 U.S. 1075, 118 S.Ct. 851, 139 L.Ed.2d 752 (1998). For these latter courts, the question is not simply whether a reasonable factfinder could disbelieve the employer's proffered reasons, but whether a reasonable fact-finder could believe that a reason actually motivating the employer was discriminatory.

34. *See Miller v. CIGNA Corporation*, 47 F.3d 586 (3d Cir.1995) (en banc), discussed in Chapter 7 concerning the ADEA. *See also Lewis v. Young Men's Christian Ass'n*, 208 F.3d 1303 (11th Cir.2000) (no liability at all where defendant in ADEA retaliation case carries same-decision showing).

decision" showing is nevertheless liable and subject to limited declaratory and injunctive relief and attorney's fees; the ADEA defendant who carries that showing per *Price Waterhouse* is relieved of liability altogether.

§ 3.12 The Defense or Mitigation of "After–Acquired Evidence"

Suppose an the employer can produce evidence it discovered during a post-termination investigation or litigation of a legitimate nondiscriminatory reason that would have induced it to take the same action against the plaintiff had the facts come to light before the adverse action. Should it be relieved of liability altogether, enjoy a limitation on liability, or be subject to full relief?

In *McKennon v. Nashville Banner Publ'g Company*,[1] the Court steered a middle course among these alternatives. To capitalize on employee misconduct discovered only after the employer discriminatorily imposed an employment detriment, the employer bears the burden of proving[2] "that the wrongdoing was of such severity that the employee *in fact would* have been *terminated* on those grounds alone if the employer had known of it at the time of the discharge."[3] It appears from this standard that it is unnecessary for the court to agree with the employer's assessment that the employee's misconduct is "serious" or "pervasive" as long as the employer can prove that under its established rules, applied without discrimination, it would have discharged the employee had it known of such conduct when it occurred.[4]

---

§ 3.12

1. 513 U.S. 352, 115 S.Ct. 879, 130 L.Ed.2d 852 (1995).

2. The employer must carry this burden by the normal "preponderance of the evidence" quantum. *O'Day v. McDonnell Douglas Helicopter Co.*, 79 F.3d 756 (9th Cir.1996).

3. *McKennon*, 115 S.Ct. at 882 (emphases added). Thus the mere *possibility* that the employer could have terminated the plaintiff under its usual work rules does not suffice to meet the employer's burden. *Shearin v. IBM Corp.*, 1995 WL 133761 (S.D.N.Y.1995). And the employer must show that had it known of plaintiff's misconduct at the relevant time, it would, applying general neutral rules, have *fired* her, not merely failed to *hire* her. *Shattuck v. Kinetic Concepts, Inc.*, 49 F.3d 1106 (5th Cir.1995) (post-*McKennon* ADEA case). The employer must show that it would have discharged the plaintiff had it known of the misconduct. *Ricky v. Mapco, Inc.*, 50 F.3d 874, 876 (10th Cir.1995). The EEOC, to decide whether the employer would have discharged the plaintiff, first looks to the employer's handling of past comparable incidents. Failing those, it considers such criteria as whether the misconduct is criminal or "compromised the integrity of the employer's business." *EEOC Enforcement Guidance on After Acquired Evidence*, No. 915.002 (12/14/95).

Although *McKennon* involved misconduct during employment, one circuit court has clarified that its limitation on liability applies equally to an employee misrepresentation in the application process—provided the employer proves that under its normal work rules it would have fired the plaintiff had it discovered the misrepresentation before it discharged the plaintiff on other, unlawful grounds. *Wallace v. Dunn Constr. Co.*, 62 F.3d 374 (11th Cir.1995) (en banc). By contrast, *post*-employment misconduct cannot serve as the predicate for the *McKennon* limitation. *Sigmon v. Parker Chapin Flattau & Klimpl*, 901 F.Supp. 667 (S.D.N.Y.1995); *Carr v. Woodbury County Juvenile Detention Ctr.*, 905 F.Supp. 619 (N.D.Iowa 1995).

4. *See, e.g. O'Driscoll v. Hercules, Inc.*, 12 F.3d 176 (10th Cir.1994), *vacated in light of McKennon v. Nashville Banner Publ'g Co.*, 513 U.S. 352, 115 S.Ct. 879, 130 L.Ed.2d 852 (1995).

Still, the employer demonstration of such misconduct serves only to limit liability, not as a complete defense. The Supreme Court observed that under ADEA as well as Title VII, remedies serve the twin objectives of deterring violations and compensating past injuries. The plaintiff advances those objectives, the Court wrote, by demonstrating the employer's discrimination. Allowing after-acquired evidence to serve as a complete bar to liability would unjustifiably undermine the statutes' remedial goals. In reaching this conclusion, the Supreme Court specifically distinguished mixed-motive situations; after-acquired evidence does not even figure in the decisional calculus until the factfinder has determined that the employer's sole or motivating basis for the challenged employment decision was unlawful (and that the employer would not have reached the same decision independent of its pure or partial unlawful motivation).[5]

But the Court was equally insistent that the employer's wrongdoing could not simply be disregarded in the formulation of an appropriate remedy. In this connection the Court read ADEA's authorization of legal or equitable relief as a mandate for the trial court to take the employee's wrongdoing into account as a way of recognizing the significant managerial prerogatives that ADEA, like Title VII, preserves to the employer. While acknowledging that the relevant equitable considerations will vary from case to case, the Court nevertheless concluded that "here, and as a general rule in cases of this type, neither reinstatement nor front pay is an appropriate remedy. It would be both inequitable and pointless to order the reinstatement of someone the employer would have terminated, and will terminate, in any event and upon lawful grounds."[6]

The Court considered the "proper measure of back pay" to present "a more difficult problem." Ordinarily, the compensatory objective of ADEA remedies would require a back pay award that would make the employee whole—restore her to the position she would have occupied absent the unlawful discrimination. The justices were unwilling to implement that objective fully in the face of evidence of employee wrongdoing that, had the employer known about it, would have led to her lawful termination. Moreover, parting company to this degree with the approach taken by the Eleventh Circuit, the Court wrote that it could not "require the employer to ignore the information, even if it is acquired during the course of discovery in a suit against the employer and even if the information might have gone undiscovered absent the suit."[7]

Declining to formulate an across-the-board back pay rule, the Court did conclude, however, that the "beginning point" in the trial court's formulation of a monetary remedy" should be calculation of back pay from the date of the unlawful discharge to the date the new information was discovered."[8] On the other hand, unlike the "mixed-motive" em-

5. *McKennon,* 513 U.S. 352 at 359, 115 S.Ct. 879 at 885, 130 L.Ed.2d 852.

6. *Id.* at ___, 115 S.Ct. at 886.

7. *Id.*

8. *Id.*

ployer who establishes that it would have taken the challenged action at the time even absent reliance on a motivating factor forbidden by Title VII,[9] the employer who carries the persuasion burden on after-acquired evidence will almost surely sustain some monetary liability, even if that liability terminates as of the date of discovery of employee wrongdoing. This is because after-acquired evidence presupposes that the employer committed an unlawful employment practice; the tardily discovered legitimate reason was not any part of its motivation when it demoted or terminated the plaintiff.[10]

In a somewhat vague afterthought the Court in *McKennon* added that the trial judge could "consider taking into further account extraordinary equitable circumstances that affect the legitimate interests of either party."[11] Further, because the Court in *McKennon* remanded for further consistent proceedings concerning remedy, the Court had no occasion to consider whether a back pay award in any amount could be doubled to provide the "liquidated" damages that ADEA authorizes in the case of "willful" violations. Nor did the Court discuss whether the employer who prevails on a showing of after-acquired evidence may thereby avoid the two species of monetary relief provided for Title VII cases by the 1991 Civil Rights Act, but unavailable in cases under ADEA: compensatory and punitive damages.

In principle, the line drawn by the Court for back pay—presumptively available before but not after the date of the employer's discovery of the information that would have led to termination independent of the unlawful employment practice—should apply to ADEA "liquidated" damages and Title VII compensatory and punitive damages as well. As

---

9. *See* Section 107(b) of the 1991 Civil Rights Act, discussed in § 3.11 *supra*.

10. Only if the employer acted on, and hence knew about the facts underlying its legitimate reason at the time it made the challenged decision could it rely on the *Price Waterhouse* "same-decision" rule. As now codified by sections 703(m) and 706(g)(2)(B) of the 1991 Civil Rights Act, the rule relieves the employer of monetary liability but subjects it to prospective relief and attorney's fees.

11. 513 U.S. at ___, 115 S.Ct. at 886. It is the EEOC's position that one extraordinary circumstance warranting additional relief is presented whenever the employee misconduct is discovered during an investigation launched by the employer, after a formal or informal charge of discrimination, to discredit a complaining party or discourage other charges or opposition to unlawful activity. In that case EEOC would extend back pay beyond the date of discovery of employee wrongdoing until the underlying charge is resolved. *See EEOC Enforcement Guidance on After Acquired Evidence*, No. 915.002. It is commonplace for employee misconduct to be discovered as the result of

an investigation prompted by a charge or complaint of discrimination. Discovery of misconduct during ordinary discovery is not an "extraordinary" circumstance; if it were the *McKennon* back pay end date would become a practical nullity. Instead, discovery after investigation should void the *McKennon* back pay reduction only where the employer acts with subjective retaliatory purpose rather than merely to limit relief. At least one circuit has permitted cross-examining the plaintiff, a former employee, on his alleged receipt of kickbacks while employed, even though the employer learned about those kickbacks only during discovery in the plaintiff's Title VII action. *Vichare v. AMBAC Inc.*, 106 F.3d 457 (2d Cir.1996) (holding that the allegation that he had been secretly accepting the kickbacks was relevant to his credibility). And the *McKennon* rule implicitly recognizes that the search during litigation or prelitigation proceedings for evidence of plaintiff wrongdoing is not by itself retaliation prohibited by Title VII § 704 or ADEA § 623(d).

the Court wrote about back pay, an absolute rule barring these remedies "would undermine the ADEA's objective of forcing employers to consider and examine their motivations, and of penalizing them for employment decisions that spring from age discrimination."[12] On this reasoning, only "extraordinary equitable circumstances" would defeat claims under Title VII for compensatory, punitive damages or both through that date of discovery. Neither type of damages would constrain significant managerial prerogatives or discretions, the sole equitable consideration the Court identified as a reason for restricting plaintiff's recovery.

The EEOC and at least one circuit court have since opined that Title VII compensatory and punitive damages and ADEA liquidated damages are available notwithstanding after-acquired evidence.[13] Further, EEOC does not view the *McKennon* concern of protecting the employer's interest in severing the employment relationship as a warrant to place a time limit on compensatory damages for emotional harm. Rather, the after-acquired showing limits only those out-of-pocket losses that are analogous to back pay. Nor does EEOC see in *McKennon* a ban or limitation on punitive damages, provided the plaintiff proves the employer's malice or reckless indifference.[14]

The after-acquired evidence defense has practical potency well beyond its limitation on relief. Defense counsel will routinely pursue discovery on the issue, which should raise the costs to plaintiff and intimidate some serious wrongdoers. And at trial even defendants who fail in their burden of proving misconduct so serious as to warrant discharge may nevertheless succeed in damaging the plaintiff's credibility, with a consequent loss of jury sympathy and potential reduction of compensatory and punitive awards.[15] Plaintiffs may counter these tactics with motions to limit discovery, or with motions *in limine* to exclude misconduct evidence unless the employer makes a threshold showing that under established policies or practices it would have fired employees for the misconduct in question.

Now that the Supreme Court has recognized after-acquired evidence as a factor that lessens relief, trial judges in Title VII[16] jury actions will have to issue still another set of instructions on top of the many already required in even the simplest cases of individual disparate treatment. Presumably these would be the last in the series, following any required instructions on mixed motive. For example, the jury might be charged that if it finds the employer would have made the challenged decision for lawful reasons independent of other, unlawful reasons that the jury finds the employer also took into account, the employer is presumptively liable only for prospective relief and attorney's fees under the Civil Rights Act

12. *Id.* at ___, 115 S.Ct. at 886.

13. *Russell v. Microdyne,* 65 F.3d 1229 (4th Cir.1995) (Title VII); *EEOC Enforcement Guidance on After Acquired Evidence,* No. 915.002.

14. *EEOC Guidance on After Acquired Evidence, supra.*

15. *See, e.g. Vichare v. AMBAC,* 106 F.3d 457 (2d Cir.1996) (permitting defendant to cross examine at trial).

16. *McKennon,* decided under ADEA, has been held fully applicable to cases under Title VII. *Wehr v. Ryan's Family Steak Houses,* 49 F.3d 1150 (6th Cir.1995).

of 1991's modification of *Price Waterhouse. If, however,* the jury also finds after-acquired evidence of employee misconduct sufficiently serious that the employer would have terminated the plaintiff upon discovery during the plaintiff's employment, the court would not order the plaintiff reinstated either. The only potential relief remaining in that situation would be a declaratory judgment, an injunction, or nominal damages, and perhaps attorney's fees to the extent of the plaintiff's limited success.[17] The mind-bending possible permutations will surely tax the capacities of the typical jury.

§§ 3.13–6.19 [Reserved]

C. SYSTEMIC DISPARATE TREATMENT

§ 3.20 In General

Intentional discriminatory treatment may also be demonstrated in the aggregate. "Systemic disparate treatment" proof depends primarily upon statistical evidence of gross disparities between the actual and expected representation of the plaintiff's group in one or more levels of an employer's workforce. According to the underlying theory, articulated in *International Brotherhood of Teamsters v. United States,*[1] an employer that does not routinely discriminate should over time achieve within its employee complement an incidence of protected group representation not significantly less than the group's representation in an available pool of qualified applicants.[2]

Systemic disparate treatment, the residue of a number of individually discriminatory decisions, is evidenced by a significant workforce underrepresentation of a protected group relative to the incidence one would expect based on its members' interest, availability and qualifications. Unlike the impact case, it is predicated on a showing of intentional discrimination. Further, the systemic treatment case is typically brought by several joined plaintiffs or a plaintiff class,[3] and endeavors to prove

---

17. Fees were recently awarded where a plaintiff recovered only nominal damages after defendant carried the "same decision" showing under Section 706(g)(2)(B), which authorizes such fees expressly in those circumstances. *Sheppard v. Riverview Nursing Ctr., Inc.,* 88 F.3d 1332 (4th Cir.), *cert. denied,* 519 U.S. 993, 117 S.Ct. 483, 136 L.Ed.2d 377 (1996). For considerations bearing on the availability and calculation of attorney's fees in such pyrrhic victory settings, see Chapter 11.

§ 3.20

1. 431 U.S. 324, 97 S.Ct. 1843, 52 L.Ed.2d 396 (1977).

2. *Id.* at 335, n.15, 97 S.Ct. at 1854, n. 15.

3. Statistical evidence of the adverse differential treatment of the plaintiff's group

may, however, fortify the case the single disparate treatment plaintiff who sues alone. *See Cooper v. Federal Reserve Bank of Richmond,* 467 U.S. 867, 876, 104 S.Ct. 2794, 2799, 81 L.Ed.2d 718 (1984) ("evidence of pervasive discrimination against others is admissible if such evidence is similar to the complainant's experience and tends to establish" that unlawful discrimination was the defendant's "standard operating procedure...." (quoting *International Brotherhood of Teamsters v. United States,* 431 U.S. 324, 336, 97 S.Ct. 1843, 1855, 52 L.Ed.2d 396 (1977)). On a similar premise, the Supreme Court held in *Bazemore v. Friday,* 478 U.S. 385, 402, 106 S.Ct. 3000, 92 L.Ed.2d 315 (1986) that "proof that an employer engaged in racial discrimination prior to the effective date of Title VII might in some circumstances support

that the defendant, as the result of an unspecified variety of policies, practices, and individual decisions by employer agents, discriminated against members of the protected group in general. In the systemic treatment case all members of the protected group denied hire or promotion to the job level during the period when the protected group was found to be grossly underrepresented are presumptively entitled to remedies, regardless of which particular employer policies or decisions by employer agents led to their rejection.[4] By contrast, relief in the "impact" case is limited to those plaintiffs, sometimes as few as one, who suffered an employment detriment as the result of a particular practice shown to have had disproportionate adverse impact on the plaintiff's group.

Occasionally, an employer's policy will on its face draw a distinction on the basis of a prohibited characteristic; a group of plaintiffs suing as a class or joined under Federal Rule 20 could then establish systemic disparate treatment on the basis of the policy alone.[5]

More typically, the plaintiffs will offer statistical evidence in an attempt to show a raw, substantial underrepresentation of their protected group relative to the numbers of their members that might have been expected had the employer hired or promoted randomly. This prima facie statistical case of systemic disparate treatment compares the employer's actual or "observed" number of protected group members hired for or promoted to the job in question against a hypothetical number of protected group members that an employer who hired or promoted randomly might have been "expected" to select. The theoretical underpinning of statistically-premised judicial findings of systemic disparate treatment is that, "absent explanation, it is ordinarily to be expected that nondiscriminatory hiring practices will in time result in a work force more or less representative of the racial and ethnic composition of the" relevant pool.[6] Although anecdotal evidence of instances of individ-

the inference that such discrimination continued, particularly where relevant aspects of the decision making process had undergone little change." Thus "[a] discriminatory act which is not made the basis for a timely charge ... may constitute relevant background evidence in a proceeding in which the status of a current practice is at issue." *Thigpen v. Bibb County, Georgia,* 223 F.3d 1231, 2000 WL 1277600, at *10 n. 19 (11th Cir.2000) (*citing United Air Lines v. Evans,* 431 U.S. 553, 558, 97 S.Ct. 1885, 52 L.Ed.2d 571 (1977)). Even non-statistical, anecdotal evidence concerning the discriminatory treatment of similarly situated co-plaintiffs or nonparties who are members of plaintiff's protected group "undoubtedly are relevant to every other plaintiff's core allegation of systemic discrimination." *Alexander v. Fulton County,* 207 F.3d 1303, 1325 (11th Cir.2000). And such anecdotal evidence is also relevant in cases of solo plaintiffs alleging individual disparate treat-

ment. *Damon v. Fleming Supermarkets of Florida, Inc.,* 196 F.3d 1354, 1361 (11th Cir.1999), *cert. denied,* ___ U.S. ___, 120 S.Ct. 1962, 146 L.Ed.2d 793 (2000).

4. *Franks v. Bowman Transp. Co.,* 424 U.S. 747, 96 S.Ct. 1251, 47 L.Ed.2d 444 (1976).

5. *See, e.g., Los Angeles Dep't of Water & Power v. Manhart,* 435 U.S. 702, 98 S.Ct. 1370, 55 L.Ed.2d 657 (1978), and *Arizona Governing Committee v. Norris,* 463 U.S. 1073, 103 S.Ct. 3492, 77 L.Ed.2d 1236 (1983) (policies that, respectively, required greater contributions from female than male employees for the same periodic pension benefits and provided women lesser periodic pension benefits than men for equal amounts contributed).

6. *Teamsters,* 431 U.S. at 339 n.20, 97 S.Ct. at 1856 n.20.

ual disparate treatment certainly fortifies the inference of systemic disparate treatment raised by statistical disparities, it has been held that statistical disparities alone may prove intentional discrimination, at least where the disparities are gross.[7]

In undertaking a showing of gross underrepresentation of the protected group the plaintiff must take care to calculate the "expected" number by reference to the relevant pool from which the selection will be made; and that pool must be refined to account for the minimum qualifications, including geographic proximity, requisite for the job in question.[8] In an order that ascends with the complexity of the skill level at issue, this pool may range from general population (*Teamsters*) or workforce (*Hazelwood*) statistics within an actual or feasible recruiting zone,[9] to a nationwide pool of candidates with the key educational or experience credentials. In the case of promotions that the employer has historically made exclusively or primarily from within, the pool would consist of lower-level employees in the employer's own workforce who meet the base requirements for promotion. Statistical analyses may also compare employees who are competing against one another to be retained notwithstanding a reduction in force, but in such cases comparisons of protected group members with others must be strictly limited to the pool of persons evaluated by the same decisionmaker.[10]

Defining the pool from which the expected percentage of minority representation should be calculated is often keenly contested. While protected group representation in a recruiting-zone population or local workforce may suffice where the jobs in question are largely unskilled,[11] or from the percentage of protected group members employed by other area employers for jobs that are moderately skilled,[12] the fair measure-

---

7. *Equal Employment Opportunity Commission v. O & G Spring and Wire Forms Specialty Co.*, 38 F.3d 872 (7th Cir.1994), *cert. denied*, 513 U.S. 1198, 115 S.Ct. 1270, 131 L.Ed.2d 148 (1995).

8. *See Hazelwood Sch. Dist. v. United States*, 433 U.S. 299, 97 S.Ct. 2736, 53 L.Ed.2d 768 (1977) (where special qualifications are at issue, the relevant statistical pool must refer to the number of members of the plaintiff class qualified for, interested in, and able to commute to the particular task); *Alexander v. Fulton County*, 207 F.3d 1303, 1327–28 (11th Cir.2000) (holding that the general population is not "readily qualified" for the law enforcement positions in question, and observing that evidence of a minority's underrepresentation in an employer's workforce by reference to the general population is probative of discrimination only in the rare case "involving jobs with low skill levels where the applicant pool can be considered roughly coextensive with the general population.")

9. *See Abron v. Black & Decker Mfg. Co.*, 439 F.Supp. 1095, 1105 (D.Md.1977)

(identifying the availability pool from which potential protected group member "expectation" percentage will be drawn as the "appropriate labor force ... encompassed in the area within which the employer can reasonably expect people to commute"), *affirmed in part, vacated in part*, 654 F.2d 951 (4th Cir.1981). A strong indication that an employer can reasonably be expected to recruit from a particular area is evidence that the defendant itself, see *Abron*, or neighboring employers in the same business, see *Hazelwood*, have in fact hired from that area in the past.

10. *Smith v. Xerox Corp.*, 196 F.3d 358, 370–71 (2d Cir.1999).

11. *Teamsters*, 431 U.S. 324, 97 S.Ct. 1843, 52 L.Ed.2d 396. *See United States v. City of Miami, Fla.*, 115 F.3d 870 (11th Cir.1997) (insisting that relevant labor market, rather than census data, forms baseline of qualified, interested minority applicants for promotion).

12. This was the availability pool used in *Hazelwood*, where the position in question was that of public school teacher.

ment of disparities in highly skilled positions demands refinement not just for availability and interest but, above all, for specialized qualifications.[13] Courts have on occasion dispensed with refined evidence of the characteristics of the pool from which applicants are drawn when the disparities presented are extreme. The classic example is where the protected group in question constitutes what has been termed the "inexorable zero"—no representation at all in the employer's workforce.[14]

Whatever comparison is used, plaintiff must establish a statistically significant "gross" disparity between observed and expected protected group representation. The magnitude of this disparity must be sufficient to show that discrimination was an employer's routine operating procedure such that relief should be granted to the entire underrepresented class. This generally requires expert testimony concerning the statistical technique of binomial distribution and its key measure, standard deviation. The actual and expected numbers of protected group members, together with the total number of persons hired for or promoted to the job during the liability period alleged in the complaint, are fed into the binomial distribution formula, which is designed to gauge the degree to which an "underrepresentation" departs from hypothetical "random" or "chance" hiring or promotion. Statisticians have conventionally ruled out chance as the likely cause of a negative deviation from the norm when the formula shows that the observed number falls more than 1.95 standard deviations below the expected number; this convention holds that there is then less than a 5% chance that the underrepresentation is itself the result of chance.[15] Apparently determined to avoid "false positives"—implicating an innocent employer—the Supreme Court has written somewhat vaguely that unlawful discrimination may be suspected as the cause of an underrepresentation only "if the difference between the expected value and the observed number is 'greater than two or three [negative] standard deviations' "[16]—a level at which statisti-

---

13. *See Hazelwood Sch. Dist. v. United States*, 433 U.S. 299, 97 S.Ct. 2736, 53 L.Ed.2d 768 (1977); *cf. Wards Cove Packing Co., Inc. v. Atonio*, 490 U.S. 642, 109 S.Ct. 2115, 104 L.Ed.2d 733 (1989). *See United States v. City of Miami, Fla.*, 115 F.3d 870 (11th Cir.1997) (pool from which expected percentage of promotions that might randomly be expected to go to minorities must account for interest and qualifications in city fire department).

14. *Teamsters*; *EEOC v. O & G Spring & Wire Forms Specialty Co.*, 38 F.3d 872 (7th Cir.1994), *cert. denied*, 513 U.S. 1198, 115 S.Ct. 1270, 131 L.Ed.2d 148 (1995). *But see Carter v. Ball*, 33 F.3d 450 (4th Cir. 1994) (unless protected group's representation is compared with its representation in a labor pool from which qualified applicants are drawn, even an "inexorable zero" is not probative).

15. *But see* Kingsley Browne, *Statistical Proof of Discrimination: Beyond "Damned Lies"*, 68 Wash.L.Rev. 477 (1993) (disputing the assumption that such statistical showings can realistically demonstrate that an "underrepresentation" is the product of chance, and therefore challenging statistically based judicial conclusions that exclude chance as the explanation for workforce disparities).

16. *Hazelwood*, 433 U.S. at 309 n.14, 97 S.Ct. at 2742 n.14 (quoting *Castaneda v. Partida*, 430 U.S. 482, 497 n. 17, 97 S.Ct. 1272, 1281 n. 17, 51 L.Ed.2d 498 (1977)); *Benson v. Tocco, Inc.*, 113 F.3d 1203 (11th Cir.1997) (negative standard deviations of 3.04 and 2.66, representing chance or randomness probabilities of, respectively, .0002 and .0008, met "2 or 3" standard deviation test to support an inference of systemic

cians would exclude chance as the explanation with overwhelming confidence.

It is because the law requires an underrepresentation of this magnitude that a court may rely solely on statistical evidence to indict an employer for systemic disparate treatment discrimination in violation of § 703(a) without running afoul of a distinct provision of Title VII, § 703(j). Section 703(j) provides that Title VII shall not be

> "interpreted to require any employer to grant preferential treatment ... because of race, color, religion, sex, or national origin ... on account of an imbalance which may exist with respect to the total number or percentage of persons of any race, color, religion, sex or national origin employed by any employer ... in comparison with the total number or percentage of persons of such race, color, religion, sex, or national origin in any community ... or in the available work force in any community...."

The Court in *Teamsters* could plausibly deny that holding an employer liable for systemic treatment discrimination upon proof of a gross statistical underrepresentation was tantamount to a requirement, condemned by § 703(j), "that a work force *mirror* the general population."[17] Many employee complements will fail to mirror the protected group's percentage in a surrounding population or work force without falling short *enough* to violate the "two or three standard deviation" test or therefore to violate § 703(a).

A more sophisticated statistical technique, multiple regression analysis,[18] will usually be required to establish the requisite disparity when variations in the particular term and condition of employment at issue— for example, compensation—are explainable by reference to a large number of factors.[19] Regression analysis has also been held mandatory when the employer's measure of which employees will receive a scarce benefit–say, performance evaluations used to decide who will be retained during a reduction in force–are a product of multiple causes.[20] The Court

discrimination in ADEA reduction-in-force case).

17. *Teamsters*, 431 U.S. at 339 n.20, 97 S.Ct. at 1856 n.20 (emphasis added).

18. *See generally* Barbara A. Norris, *A Structural Approach to Evaluation of Multiple Regression Analysis as Used to Prove Employment Discrimination: The Plaintiff's Answer to Defense Attacks of "Missing Factors" and "Pre–Act Discrimination"*, 49 Law & Contemp. Probs. 65 (1986); Thomas J. Campbell, *Regression Analysis in Title VII Cases: Minimum Standards, Comparable Worth, and Other Issues Where Law and Statistics Meet*, 36 Stan.L.Rev. 1299 (1984); Note, *Beyond the Prima Facie Case in Employment Discrimination Law: Statistical Proof and Rebuttal*, 89 Harv.L.Rev. 387 (1975).

19. *See Munoz v. Orr*, 200 F.3d 291, 301–302 (5th Cir.), *cert. denied*, ___ U.S. ___, 121 S.Ct. 45, 148 L.Ed.2d 15 (2000) (no abuse of discretion to exclude testimony of expert who failed "to consider other variables such as education and experience as explanations for any observed discrepancy between promotion rates" or to conduct multiple regression analysis to sort out the influence of those factors). *See Tagatz v. Marquette Univ.*, 861 F.2d 1040, 1045 (7th Cir.1988) (deeming "worthless" expert testimony that failed to control for other variables).

20. *Smith v. Xerox Corp.*, 196 F.3d 358, 370–71 (2d Cir.1999). *See also Hollander v. American Cyanamid Co.*, 172 F.3d 192, 203 (2d Cir.), *cert. denied*, 528 U.S. 965, 120 S.Ct. 399, 145 L.Ed.2d 311 (1999); *Raskin v. Wyatt Co.*, 125 F.3d 55, 67–68 (2d Cir.

has indicated, however, that a plaintiff's multiple regression analysis need not eliminate all potential nondiscriminatory explanations of disparity, only the most significant.[21]

Once the plaintiff group adduces express or statistical evidence of systemic disparate treatment, the employer has an opportunity to offer what *Teamsters* termed a nondiscriminatory "explanation" by way of rebuttal. Absent a defense, liability will be deemed established and the case moves to a second, bifurcated remedy phase.[22] The employer's principal defense in these cases is to present evidence that casts doubt on the logical, statistical, or legal probative value of plaintiff's evidence. For example, an employer may avoid the force of evidence of disparity by showing infirmities in the plaintiff-defined pool that exaggerate the availability of qualified members of the protected group;[23] by challenging the validity of the statistical conclusions drawn by plaintiff's expert, including objections to insufficient sample size;[24] or by demonstrating (as will seldom be the case twenty-five years after the effective date of the Act) that a protected group's underrepresentation is attributable largely to then-lawful, even if discriminatory, hiring that took place before the employer became subject to Title VII.[25]

In the alternative, the employer may affirmatively present counter-comparative statistics. A more restrictively refined availability pool, for example, may generate negative disparities of a magnitude (less than two or three standard deviations) that judges will deem insignificant to alter the status quo and impose liability on an employer. Indeed, the employer may refute the existence of any negative disparity by offering data suggesting that it hired or promoted a *greater* number of protected group members than their availability in the employer-advocated pool would

1997) (underrepresentation statistics insufficient for failure to account for other causes of age-related disparity).

21. *Bazemore v. Friday*, 478 U.S. 385, 106 S.Ct. 3000, 92 L.Ed.2d 315 (1986). *But see Smith v. Virginia Commonwealth Univ.*, 84 F.3d 672 (4th Cir.1996) (en banc) (defendant unlawfully relied on multiple regression analysis to justify increase in female faculty members' salaries where analysis left out key performance, productivity, and merit factors that university considered in determining prior pay increases).

22. This presumption of liability must be modified in a systemic sexual harassment case because a prima facie case of sexual harassment requires a showing of subjective unwelcomeness. *See Harris* and *Meritor*, § 2.22. One district court held that liability for sexual harassment can be established by a pattern or practice of discrimination, but individual recovery hinges on an individual showing of subjective unwelcomeness. *See EEOC v. Mitsubishi Motor Mfg. of Am., Inc.*, 990 F.Supp. 1059, 1072 (C.D.Ill.1998).

23. Thus, where the employment is in the typical American metropolitan area in which minority groups are more heavily concentrated in the urban core, the defendant would usually assert that the entire "Standard Metropolitan Statistical Area" defined by the federal government, rather than the central city alone, is the proper measure of applicant, and hence protected group, availability. *See Hazelwood*, 433 U.S. 299, 97 S.Ct. 2736, 53 L.Ed.2d 768.

24. *See Mayor of Philadelphia v. Educational Equality League*, 415 U.S. 605, 620–621, 94 S.Ct. 1323, 1333–1334, 39 L.Ed.2d 630 (1974), cited in *Teamsters*, 431 U.S. at 339 n.20, 97 S.Ct. at 1856 n.20; *Birkbeck v. Marvel Lighting Corp.*, 30 F.3d 507 (4th Cir.1994), *cert. denied* 513 U.S. 1058, 115 S.Ct. 666, 130 L.Ed.2d 600 (1994) (case under ADEA holding sample size of four laid-off employees too small to serve as predicate for a statistically significant conclusion that employer practiced age discrimination).

25. *See Hazelwood*, 433 U.S. 299, 97 S.Ct. 2736, 53 L.Ed.2d 768.

predict: in that instance, the standard deviation would be positive.[26] Most powerfully, an employer that has maintained records differentiating its applicants by race, national origin or gender[27] may be able to offer "applicant flow" statistics to establish that it hired at least as great a percentage of protected group members as of others.[28] Such evidence tends to show the particular defendant's comparative treatment of actual members of the protected group and others who had the requisite interest to offer themselves for hire or promotion. Applicant flow evidence is therefore generally credited with greater probative value than standard deviation evidence drawn from the number of hires or promotions that might theoretically have been expected based on protected group availability in an appropriately defined pool of persons none of whom may have actually sought employment with the defendant.

In the face of a showing of gross underrepresentation of the protected group, as evidenced by substantially unimpeached standard deviation data, applicant flow data could nevertheless point in favor of the employer. When the employer treated fairly or even favorably a relatively small number of protected group members applied. But why did so few protected group members apply, given their significant representation in the underlying pool? One possibility is a self-selected lack of interest in the particular employment, despite presumptive minimum qualifications and availability.[29] That argument appears to have lesser force when the court views the statistical underrepresentation as overwhelming, and particularly when there are no protected group members in the job in

26. *Cf. Hollander v. American Cyanamid Co.*, 172 F.3d 192 (2d Cir.), *cert. denied*, 528 U.S. 965, 120 S.Ct. 399, 145 L.Ed.2d 311 (1999) (underrepresentation in the 50–59 year old group to which plaintiff belonged rebutted by inference drawn from increase in the number of managers aged 60–79; decrease in 55–69 group to which plaintiff belonged explained by similar disproportionate decrease in group aged 60–69).

27. The EEOC's record keeping regulations do not require employers to keep records differentiating applicants by their protected group status, and indeed many state fair employment laws prohibit employers from asking applicants to indicate their race or gender. The regulations only require employers to keep applications for one year. 29 C.F.R. § 1602.14 (1994).

28. *Hazelwood*, 433 U.S. 299, 97 S.Ct. 2736, 53 L.Ed.2d 768. The employer demonstrates that conclusion by presenting evidence of simple arithmetic proportions. The percentage of protected group members selected (from among protected group members who applied) is compared with the corresponding percentage of nonprotected group members selected (from among non-

protected group members who applied). *See also Anderson v. Douglas & Lomason Co.*, 26 F.3d 1277 (5th Cir.1994), *cert. denied*, 513 U.S. 1149, 115 S.Ct. 1099, 130 L.Ed.2d 1066 (1995) (deferring to district court decision to credit employer expert's analysis of applicant flow figures). *But see EEOC v. American Nat'l Bank*, 652 F.2d 1176, 1193–97 (4th Cir.1981), *cert. denied*, 459 U.S. 923, 103 S.Ct. 235, 74 L.Ed.2d 186 (1982) (employer's applicant flow figures, to be probative, must correspond to the same time periods and kinds of workers whose availability is reflected in the plaintiff's statistics that the applicant flow data is designed to refute). And of course applicant flow figures may reinforce the *plaintiff's* showing of gross statistical underrepresentation if employer records show that it hired a significantly lower percentage of qualified protected group applicants than of others. *See EEOC v. Olson's Dairy Queens, Inc.*, 989 F.2d 165 (5th Cir.1993).

29. *See EEOC v. Sears, Roebuck & Co.*, 839 F.2d 302 (7th Cir.1988) (upholding women's lesser interest in commissions sales jobs as an explanation that serves to rebut systemic disparate treatment evidence of gender discrimination in hiring, promotion, and compensation).

question.[30]

Another explanation of underapplication by the protected group is a well-developed, notorious employer reputation for discrimination against the group in question, a reputation so extreme as to render it "futile" for a member of that group to apply. If the plaintiffs can prove that more protected group members would have applied during the period of the alleged discrimination but for the employer's discriminatory practices, they may persuade a court to disregard or discount the employer's applicant flow evidence.[31] An employer unable to impeach or counter a finding of gross statistical underrepresentation must nevertheless be permitted to attempt to offer some other nondiscriminatory "explanation" for the disparity.[32] A controversial defense accepted by some courts is that, relative to others, the particular protected group lacked interest in or qualifications for the job in question. A highly publicized Seventh Circuit decision so held with respect to women seeking positions as commissioned salespersons.[33] The court seemed to consider it irrelevant whether, assuming the validity of the key fact findings, the relative lack of interest in or qualifications to hold those positions was "inherent" in women or a product of stereotyping long rooted in American history or culture. In particular, the court did not consider it important to examine the "employer's [own] role in shaping the interest of applicants."[34]

An employer may also explain an unimpeached, prima facie gross statistical underrepresentation by offering evidence that one of its own neutral practices had disproportionate adverse impact on the protected group.[35] This puts the employer in the odd position of becoming its own accuser, since such a practice may independently give rise to Title VII liability even without proof of discriminatory intent.[36] In effect, the employer argues that an unlawful employment practice (a facially neutral test or experience requirement that disproportionately affects the protected group) explains the significant bottom-line underrepresentation of the protected group in the job level for which the test or experience requirement screens. Courts before the 1991 Civil Rights Act that permitted employers to defend a gross underrepresentation by pointing to such a neutral practice required them to bear the burden of

---

30. *EEOC v. O & G Spring and Wire Forms Specialty* 38 F.3d 872 (7th Cir.1994), *cert. denied*, 513 U.S. 1198, 115 S.Ct. 1270, 131 L.Ed.2d 148 (1995) (rejecting employer argument that blacks had "self-selected" themselves out of the applicant pool for low-skilled jobs held predominantly by Polish-and Spanish-speaking employees, many of whom did not speak English).

31. *Cf. International Bhd. of Teamsters v. United States*, 431 U.S. 324, 97 S.Ct. 1843, 52 L.Ed.2d 396 (1977) (permitting individual nonapplicants to obtain relief at the remedy stage of a systemic disparate treatment case if they can make such a showing of futility).

32. *Teamsters*, 431 U.S. at 340 n.20, 97 S.Ct. at 1857 n.20.

33. *EEOC v. Sears, Roebuck & Co.*, 839 F.2d 302 (7th Cir.1988).

34. *Id.* (Cudahy, J., concurring in part and dissenting in part).

35. *See, e.g., Griffin v. Carlin*, 755 F.2d 1516 (11th Cir.1985); *Segar v. Smith*, 738 F.2d 1249 (D.C.Cir.1984), *cert. denied sub nom. Meese v. Segar*, 471 U.S. 1115, 105 S.Ct. 2357, 86 L.Ed.2d 258 (1985). *See also Powers v. Alabama Dep't of Educ.*, 854 F.2d 1285 (11th Cir.1988), *cert. denied*, 490 U.S. 1107, 109 S.Ct. 3158, 104 L.Ed.2d 1021 (1989).

36. See Part F, this chapter.

persuasion on the neutral practice justification.[37] By undertaking this showing the employer may limit its liability to those members of the protected group who were personally affected by the neutral practice. Even if the employer cannot persuade the trier of fact that the neutral practice that caused the systemic underrepresentation was justified, the employer will be exposed only to back pay liability for an unlawful neutral practice, and not for the compensatory and punitive damages available since 1991 for intentional discrimination. Better yet for the employer, the court may conclude that the neutral practice which accounts for an underrepresentation is justified because "job related for the position in question and consistent with business necessity" within the meaning of § 703(k)(1)(A)(i), added by § 105(a) of the Civil Rights Act of 1991; then the employer would not be liable to anyone for anything.

It is unclear whether these decisions will survive an amendment to Title VII, also added by § 105(a) of the Civil Rights Act of 1991, that provides: "A demonstration that an employment practice is required by business necessity may not be used as a defense against a claim of intentional discrimination under this title."[38] At a minimum this provision confirms the Supreme Court's position in *International Union, UAW v. Johnson Controls, Inc.*,[39] that a facially discriminatory practice may be excused, if at all, only under the stringent BFOQ defense, and not merely by a showing of job relatedness and business necessity. Read broadly, however, the new § 703(k)(2) could also be applied to cases where the prima facie evidence of intentional discrimination consists of gross statistical disparities sufficient to establish systemic disparate treatment of the plaintiff class. If so, Section 703(k)(2) would appear to deny the employer the last-chance defense discussed in *Griffin* and *Segar*.[40]

The sounder view, however, is that new Section 703(k)(2) should be limited to the context that gave rise to its enactment: express or facial, as contrasted to statistically proven systemic disparate treatment. Part of the fundamental underpinning of the systemic disparate treatment theory is that an employer should not be exposed to classwide liability if it has a nondiscriminatory explanation for the gross statistical underrepresentation of the plaintiff's protected group. A neutral practice that the employer can prove was the real cause of a systemic disparity proven by the plaintiff is precisely such a nondiscriminatory explanation. While the employer who can carry that explanation should still have to defend the adverse impact of its neutral practice on specific protected group members disadvantaged by it, it should not face the more far-reaching liability to every member of that group who was denied a job or promotion during the period of systemic underrepresentation.

37. *Griffin v. Carlin*, 755 F.2d 1516; *Segar v. Smith*, 738 F.2d 1249.

38. Title VII, § 703(k)(2).

39. 499 U.S. 187, 111 S.Ct. 1196, 113 L.Ed.2d 158 (1991).

40. These decisions are discussed in the preceding paragraph of text.

§§ 3.21–6.24 [Reserved]

D. THE RELIEF STAGE OF THE BIFURCATED SYSTEMIC DISPARATE TREATMENT ACTION

§ 3.25 In General

Systemic treatment trials are conducted in distinct liability and remedial phases. First, from evidence of a facially discriminatory policy, from statistics alone, from anecdotal evidence, or some combination of the above, the court determines whether the employer has intentionally discriminated against the plaintiff's protected group. If so, individual members of the plaintiff class who reapply (or, in certain cases, apply for the first time) for a position or promotion at this stage of the action may thus become eligible to receive the full panoply of all otherwise appropriate Title VII remedies: not only declaratory and injunctive relief but reinstatement, back pay, retroactive seniority and, since the violation involves intentional discrimination, the capped compensatory and punitive damages made available by the Civil Rights Act of 1991.

The Supreme Court has substantially eased the individual plaintiff's burden of demonstrating entitlement to relief at the remedy stage of the systemic treatment case. Even if the prima facie case consists only of statistical evidence, that evidence, if believed by the factfinder and not successfully rebutted with a nondiscriminatory explanation, gives rise to a presumption that each plaintiff who unsuccessfully sought hire, promotion, or retention during the established liability period was rejected because of his or her protected group status.[1] So long as the individual applied for the position in question during the established liability period, she need not even produce evidence of her minimum qualifications. Proof of a broad-based policy of unlawful discrimination, in other words, generates "reasonable grounds to infer that individual hiring decisions were made in pursuit of the discriminatory policy and to require the employer to come forth with evidence dispelling that inference."[2] Although the prima facie case does not "conclusively demonstrate that all of the employer's decisions were part of the proven discriminatory pattern and practice," it creates "a greater likelihood that any single decision was a component of the overall pattern."[3] The employer is now a "proven wrongdoer," and must bear the burden of showing nondiscriminatory reasons for rejecting any individual plaintiff.[4] But individual plaintiffs have been denied this automatic inference at the relief stage, and required to prove the *McDonnell Douglas* elements (especially that they were qualified at the time they were denied a

---

§ 3.25

1. *Franks v. Bowman Transp. Co.*, 424 U.S. 747, 772, 96 S.Ct. 1251, 1268, 47 L.Ed.2d 444 (1976), § 3.20. *See also Pettway v. American Cast Iron Pipe Co.*, 494 F.2d 211, 260 (5th Cir.1974).

2. *Teamsters*, 431 U.S. at 359 & n.45, 97 S.Ct. at 1866 & n.45.

3. *Id.*

4. *Id.*

position), where the classwide finding of liability is the product of a settlement and consent decree, rather than trial.[5] And it has been suggested that even after trial the inference of discrimination as to each individual should not be drawn where the evidence of classwide liability, instead of showing that the plaintiffs' protected group was absolutely excluded from the positions at issue, revealed that significant numbers of plaintiffs' group obtained (and unlawfully were denied) those positions.[6]

To rebut the presumption, the employer may avoid liability to individual plaintiffs or plaintiff class members by persuading a court that they were not in fact victims of discrimination. For example, the employer may demonstrate that there were no vacancies in the pertinent position at the time a particular class member applied, that the plaintiff lacked minimum qualifications that the employer insisted upon at the time of the plaintiff's rejection, or that a successful applicant was better qualified.[7] Even class members who did not apply for a position during the proven liability period may sometimes receive individual relief; but they carry the heavy burden of persuading that it was futile for them to apply because of an employer's notorious reputation for egregious discrimination against their protected group and that they would have applied otherwise.[8] It does not suffice for nonapplicants to show only that they are interested in obtaining a job at the time of judgment; discriminatees may be awarded retroactive seniority for the period they would have accrued seniority had the employer not discriminated, so the job available through court order may be far more attractive than it was originally. Further, they, unlike "applicant" plaintiff class members, bear the burden of showing their own minimum qualifications at the time that, but for futility, they prove they would have applied.[9]

§§ 3.26–6.29 [Reserved]

E. HOW THE INDIVIDUAL AND SYSTEMIC DISPARATE TREATMENT CASES INTERRELATE

§ 3.30 In General

Given the relative ease of establishing a *prima facie* case of individual disparate treatment under *McDonnell Douglas/Burdine*, and the expense and difficulty of gathering and analyzing the data necessary to establish a case of systemic disparate treatment, solo plaintiffs usually proceed with "direct" or inferential evidence alone. Nevertheless, there is a complementary relationship between evidence of individual and systemic disparate treatment. A well financed individual plaintiff may

---

5. *Reynolds v. Roberts*, 202 F.3d 1303, 1319 n. 26 (11th Cir.2000).

6. *Id.* at 1319 n.27 (dictum).

7. *Franks*, 424 U.S. at 773 n.32, 96 S.Ct. at 1268 n.32 (1976); *Teamsters*, 431 U.S. at 359 n.45, 97 S.Ct. at 1866 n.45.

8. *Teamsters*, 431 U.S. at 365, 97 S.Ct. at 1870, text § 3.20 *supra*.

9. *Id.* at 369 n.53, 97 S.Ct. at 1872 n.53.

fortify the individual disparate treatment case with evidence of statistically discriminatory patterns. Similarly, a plaintiff class may, and as a practical matter is well advised, to bolster a case of systemic discriminatory treatment with anecdotal evidence of discrimination against its individual members. The advocate should bear in mind that statistical systemic treatment evidence merely suggests that the employer routinely discriminated, but by itself does not suggest how. Counsel may fill the gap for skeptical judges by offering "direct" or inferential evidence that individual plaintiffs were discriminatorily treated. In both *Teamsters* and *Hazelwood* the Supreme Court observed that the plaintiffs had breathed life in the statistical evidence by offering evidence of individual disparate treatment.

On the other hand, the failure of a systemic treatment class action—or of the government plaintiff equivalent, a "pattern or practice" action by the U.S. Attorney General under Section 707—does not imply lack of merit to the individual disparate treatment case of any particular member of the plaintiff class.[1] Nor, as we shall see shortly, does that failure negate the employer's potential liability to an individual member of a plaintiff class for harm caused by a neutral employment practice. A given practice may have disproportionately adversely impacted those members of the plaintiff group who encountered it even though the group fared well at the "bottom line" that registers the aggregate of all employer policies, practices and discrete decisions by employer agents.[2]

§§ 3.31–6.34   [Reserved]

F. NEUTRAL PRACTICES WITH DISPROPORTIONATE ADVERSE IMPACT

§ 3.35   In General

The federal courts have at times struggled to clarify the evidentiary frameworks for proving individual and systemic disparate treatment, but there has been no real question that such intentional conduct constitutes unlawful discrimination. By contrast, neutral employer practices that in operation fall with disproportionate adverse impact on the plaintiff's protected group have proven far more troublesome.

Initially a strong judicial consensus emerged that Congress intended to eradicate such practices on much the same terms as intentional acts of discrimination. Writing for a unanimous Court in *Griggs v. Duke Power Co.*,[1] Chief Justice Burger wrote that practices fair in form but discrimi-

§ 3.30

1. *See* discussion of *Cooper v. Federal Reserve Bank of Richmond*, 467 U.S. 867, 104 S.Ct. 2794, 81 L.Ed.2d 718 (1984), in §§ 4.9 and Chapter 12.

2. *Connecticut v. Teal*, 457 U.S. 440, 102 S.Ct. 2525, 73 L.Ed.2d 130 (1982).

§ 3.35

1. 401 U.S. 424, 91 S.Ct. 849, 28 L.Ed.2d 158 (1971).

natory in effect may violate Title VII even though the employer's motivation in adopting the practice is neutral or benign. The early cases developing this theory considered the lawfulness of "objective" (really, specific or concrete or readily identifiable) employer practices such as educational requirements or standardized aptitude or psychological tests.[2] The classic example is a labor union's requirement that an applicant for membership had to be sponsored by one of the existing members, all of whom were white. When none of the 30 members admitted under this policy during a six-year period were African–Americans or Hispanic, the plaintiff had proven prima facie that this "neutral" practice had a disproportionate adverse impact on members of the protected group.[3]

Occasionally, however, disproportionate adverse impact analysis was applied to a "subjective" employer process such as the unstructured evaluation of black employees by white foremen.[4] The Supreme Court approved the use of impact analysis to scrutinize these "subjective" promotion decisions,[5] a decision not addressed and therefore apparently left undisturbed by the Civil Rights Act of 1991. Even a single employer practice—for example, a one-time layoff—may trigger disproportionate adverse impact analysis; the practice need not be a repeated or customary method of operation to be subject to impact scrutiny.[6] Yet even after the 1991 Act, there are decisions ruling out the use of disparate impact proof when, in the court's view, the plaintiff fails to specify a particular aspect of an employer's subjective decisionmaking process that is allegedly responsible for an underrepresentation of the plaintiff class.[7] And a court has held that an employer's reliance on interviews to screen subjectively for such traits as empathy and caring in the selection of social workers does not in and of itself reflect gender bias, even if those

2. See Griggs and Albemarle Paper Co. v. Moody, 422 U.S. 405, 95 S.Ct. 2362, 45 L.Ed.2d 280, (1975); height and weight requirements, Dothard, 433 U.S. 321, 97 S.Ct. 2720, 53 L.Ed.2d 786; or rules prohibiting the employment of drug addicts, New York City Transit Auth. v. Beazer, 440 U.S. 568, 99 S.Ct. 1355, 59 L.Ed.2d 587 (1979); arrestees, Gregory v. Litton Systems, Inc., 472 F.2d 631 (9th Cir.1972); convicts, Green v. Missouri Pacific R.R. Co., 523 F.2d 1290 (8th Cir.1975); or debtors whose wages have been frequently garnished, Wallace v. Debron Corp., 494 F.2d 674 (8th Cir.1974).

3. E.E.O.C. v. Steamship Clerks Union, Local 1066, 48 F.3d 594 (1st Cir.), cert. denied, 516 U.S. 814, 116 S.Ct. 65, 133 L.Ed.2d 27 (1995).

4. Rowe v. General Motors Corp., 457 F.2d 348 (5th Cir.1972).

5. Watson v. Fort Worth Bank and Trust, 487 U.S. 977, 108 S.Ct. 2777, 101 L.Ed.2d 827 (1988).

6. Council 31, Am. Fed'n of State, County and Mun. Employees v. Ward, 978 F.2d 373 (7th Cir.1992). But see EEOC v. Chicago Miniature Lamp Works, 947 F.2d 292, 304–05 (7th Cir.1991) (word-of-mouth recruiting not an employer "practice" subject to scrutiny under disparate impact theory). Contra, Thomas v. Washington County Sch. Bd., 915 F.2d 922, 924–26 (4th Cir.1990).

7. See, e.g., Ilhardt v. Sara Lee Corp., 118 F.3d 1151 (7th Cir.1997) (layoff of pregnant employee was one-time event, not a "practice" that could serve as predicate for neutral practice liability) (alternative holding); Anderson v. Douglas & Lomason Co., 26 F.3d 1277 (5th Cir.1994), cert. denied, 513 U.S. 1149, 115 S.Ct. 1099, 130 L.Ed.2d 1066 (1995) (employer policy requiring individuals to fill out applications at the plant insufficiently specific).

traits are disproportionately evident in women, because one may assume the traits are present in all candidates for the position of social worker.[8]

In *Connecticut v. Teal,*[9] the Supreme Court clarified that a single component of an employer's multi-stage selection process may have unlawfully discriminatory adverse impact on the particular protected group members it screens out even if the protected group as a whole fares better than a non-minority group in the overall process. The Court explained that the "principal focus" of Title VII is "the protection of the individual employee," rather than of minority groups. It rooted the disproportionate adverse impact theory in the language of § 703(a)(2): even though a plaintiff is not "discriminated against" in the disparate treatment sense intended by § 703(a)(1), neutral practices may, in the language of § 703(a)(2), "deprive or tend to deprive . . . [the] individual of employment opportunities. . . ." Section 703(a)(2) is accordingly not concerned solely with how the plaintiff's group fares at the statistical "bottom line" of jobs or promotions, but also with "limitations" or "classifications" that deprive individual members of that group of the chance to advance. In sum, a racially balanced workforce—even one that results from affirmative action in favor of the plaintiff's protected group—does not immunize an employer from liability for a specific act of discrimination, whether intentional or neutral.

How to measure whether an employer's neutral practice has a "disproportionate" adverse impact on a protected group is a question that is addressed only vaguely by the Court's cases and remains unresolved by the 1991 Act. Some courts have adopted as a measure of disproportion the "eighty percent rule" from EEOC's Uniform Guidelines on Employee Selection Procedures.[10] These provide that a protected group's selection rate which is less than 80 percent of the rate for the group with the greatest success will be regarded by the Commission for enforcement purposes as evidence of adverse impact.[11]

8. *Scott v. Parkview Mem'l Hosp.,* 175 F.3d 523 (7th Cir.1999).

9. 457 U.S. 440, 102 S.Ct. 2525, 73 L.Ed.2d 130 (1982); *Williams v. Ford Motor Co.,* 187 F.3d 533 (6th Cir.1999) (plaintiff established prima facie case that test had disproportionate adverse impact despite fact that defendant had hired a greater percentage of plaintiff's protected group than were represented in local labor pool). *Teal* has been applied to the interview component of the selection process for a firefighter position. *Thomas v. City of Omaha,* 63 F.3d 763 (8th Cir.1995). *Cf. Cronin v. Aetna Life Ins. Co.,* 46 F.3d 196 (2d Cir.1995) (statistical evidence that overall impact of reduction in force was not age discriminatory does not negate possibility of employer disparate treatment liability for discriminating against the plaintiff in the way in which the RIF was conducted). *But cf. District Council 37, Am. Fed'n of State, County & Mun. Employees v. New York City Dep't of Parks*

and Recreation, 113 F.3d 347 (2d Cir.1997) (*Teal* instruction need only be given affirmatively, as an alternative way for plaintiff to prevail; the jury need not be told that lack of impact at the bottom line does not preclude liability respecting a step of the process) (ADEA layoff case).

10. *Smith v. Xerox Corp.,* 196 F.3d 358, 365 (2d Cir.1999); *Waisome v. Port Auth. of New York & New Jersey,* 948 F.2d 1370, 1376 (2d Cir.1991). *See In Re Employment Discrimination Litigation Against The State of Alabama,* 198 F.3d 1305, 1312 (11th Cir. 1999). *See also* Blumoff & Lewis, 69 N.C.L.Rev. at 21–22.

11. 29 C.F.R. § 1607.4. *See Connecticut v. Teal,* 457 U.S. 440, 444 n. 4, 102 S.Ct. 2525, 2528 n. 4, 73 L.Ed.2d 130 (1982); *Pietras v. Board of Fire Comm'rs,* 180 F.3d 468 (2d Cir.1999).

But the 80% rule has come under increasing attack from academic and court critics alike. It does not take sample size into account and thus may fail to detect statistically significant adverse impact on large samples,[12] and its comparison of group pass rates may not measure the magnitude (as opposed to mere statistical significance) of a disparity as well as other techniques.[13] Justice O'Connor, writing for a plurality in *Watson v. Fort Worth Bank & Trust.*,[14] observed that EEOC's 80% test, while perhaps appropriate as a rough administrative guide for allocating agency prosecutorial resources, was not binding on judges. Insisting that the plaintiff should have to produce evidence that the challenged practice had a "significantly discriminatory impact," Justice O'Connor alluded to the need for a more rigorous and reliable measure of intergroup disparity. Justice O'Connor hinted that a better measure of whether a practice has legally and not just statistically significant adverse impact is the binomial distribution analysis approved by the Court for cases of systemic disparate treatment.[15]

A year later, a majority of the court in *Wards Cove Packing Co. v. Atonio* appeared to agree with this approach when it required a prima facie demonstration that the challenged practice has a "significantly disparate impact" on the protected group.[16] Further, the Court in *Wards Cove* appeared to demand prima facie evidence virtually indistinguishable from the statistical showing it had required for systemic *treatment* cases. Consistent with the Court's concerns, circuit decisions, too, have approved or even required standard deviation analysis[17] or multiple regression analysis[18] These developments leave a lingering question. Why would a plaintiff undertake an impact challenge to a neutral practice—a proof mode the Court devised in *Griggs* precisely as an alternative to proof of intentional discrimination—if she must develop the same data and proffer the same expert statistical testimony that a class must adduce when it undertakes to show across-the-board intentional discrimination?

But several recent decisions emphasize that regardless of the particular measure of the magnitude of disparate impact created by an employer's neutral practice, the disparity will have no significance unless

---

12. *See* Shoben, *Differential Pass–Fail Rates in Employment Testing: Statistical Proof Under Title VII*, 91 Harv.L.Rev. 793 (1978). Professor Shoben proposes instead that courts use an "independent proportions" test to measure disparities between the success and failure of two protected groups with respect to a particular employer practice or a "chi square" test suitable for comparing the success/failure frequencies of more than two groups.

13. David C. Baldus & James W. L. Cole, *Statistical Proof of Discrimination* (1989).

14. 487 U.S. 977, 108 S.Ct. 2777, 101 L.Ed.2d 827 (1988).

15. *Id.* at 984 n.1, 108 S.Ct. at 2783 n.1, and accompanying text.

16. 490 U.S. 642, 657, 109 S.Ct. 2115, 2125, 104 L.Ed.2d 733 (1989).

17. *See Smith v. Xerox Corp.*, 196 F.3d 358, 365–367 (2d Cir.1999) (but observing that "two" standard deviations suffice for this purposes, somewhat less of a disparity than the "two or three" standard deviations that the Supreme Court in *Hazelwood* wrote would be necessary to show systemic disparate treatment.)

18. *See Eastland v. TVA*, 704 F.2d 613, 621 (11th Cir.1983), *cert. denied sub nom. James v. TVA*, 465 U.S. 1066, 104 S.Ct. 1415, 79 L.Ed.2d 741 (1984).

it is based on a fair and logical comparison. Thus, "what the plaintiff must attempt to do is show that there is a legally significant disparity between (a) the racial composition, caused by the challenged employment practice, of the pool of those enjoying a job or benefit; and (b) the racial composition of the qualified applicant pool."[19] These decisions reject the probative value of disparities derived from populations that fail to reflect the employment realities of the relevant applicant pool or employer practice.[20]

The seeds of a coming collapse in the Court's commitment to the neutral practice theory were unwittingly planted in *Griggs* itself. The Court wrestled with inventing a judge-made defense to the judge-made *prima facie* case and produced several different verbal formulations of notably different stringency. In later years a Court less enamored of the disparate impact theory would exploit the resulting confusion. If, as *Teal* later explained, balanced "bottom line" hiring or deployment of the work force does not serve as a defense to a practice's disproportionate adverse impact, what does? The Court wrote in *Griggs* that an employer could avoid liability if it could show that the challenged requirement "related" to the job in question. But related to what degree? Elsewhere in *Griggs* the Court described the defense, in increasing order of rigor, as requiring evidence that the employer practice be "demonstrably" or "manifestly" related to the job in question or that the practice be a matter of business "necessity".

This last suggestion, that an employer must show a neutral practice to be necessary or essential to its business, rather than just desirable, was inconsistent with an emerging third phase of the "neutral practice" case. In *Albemarle Paper Co. v. Moody*,[21] the Court explained in dictum that even if an employer (by whatever standard) justifies the adverse effect of its practice by reference to a business reason, the plaintiff may still prevail by demonstrating that the employer could have met its needs with a "less discriminatory alternative." If the plaintiff does show such an alternative, however, it necessarily demonstrates that the employer's chosen practice could not have been a matter of strict necessity. By the same token, if the employer's own, second-stage evidence must show genuine business "necessity," the third stage becomes superfluous: how could a less discriminatory alternative fully meet the employer's needs if the employer's original, chosen practice was essential?

19. *In Re Employment Discrimination Litigation Against The State of Alabama,* 198 F.3d 1305, 1312 (11th Cir.1999).

20. *See In Re Employment Discrimination Litigation Against The State of Alabama,* 198 F.3d 1305, 1312–1314 (11th Cir. 1999) (plaintiffs failed to tailor the qualified applicant pool so that it reflected only applicants or potential applicants qualified but for their failure to meet the challenged employment requirement) (citing *New York City Transit Auth. v. Beazer,* 440 U.S. 568, 585, 99 S.Ct. 1355, 1366, 59 L.Ed.2d 587 (1979); *Smith v. Xerox Corp.,* 196 F.3d 358, 365–368–370 (2d Cir.1999) (the base measuring population in a reduction-in force situation consists of all, and only, the workers subject to termination according to the criteria of the RIF).

21. 422 U.S. 405, 95 S.Ct. 2362, 45 L.Ed.2d 280 (1975).

After *Griggs* the Court also waffled on whether the plaintiff or defendant bears the burden of persuading on the justification issue (whatever its content) once a plaintiff carries the day on the prima facie case. The Court more often wrote that the employer defense is an affirmative one on which the employer bears the burden of persuasion[22] but on occasion implied otherwise.[23]

In 1989 the Court resolved both these questions—the nature of the employer defense and the allocation of the burden of persuasion—so as to undermine severely the *Griggs* neutral practice mode of proof. Ironically, this resolution began the year before with *Watson*, the case which extended the application of disproportionate adverse impact analysis to subjective employer practices. A plurality there also wrote that an employer may defend adverse impact merely by producing evidence that its practice is "based on legitimate business reasons." As the dissent complained, this description renders the employer defense to a neutral practice case virtually indistinguishable from the easily established "legitimate non-discrimination reason" defense to a *McDonnell Douglas/Burdine* case of individual disparate treatment.

This position of the *Watson* plurality then commanded a majority in *Wards Cove*, which also apparently extends the holding to cases that challenge the more traditional "objective" neutral practices.[24] A neutral practice that disproportionately adversely affects the plaintiff's protected group could survive Title VII challenge, the Court held, if it simply "serves, in a significant way, the legitimate employment goals of the employer." The practice need not be " 'essential' or 'indispensable' to the employer's business. . . ." The *Wards Cove* opinion is equally explicit that the employer carries only the burden of producing evidence, the burden of persuasion remaining with the plaintiff.

Finally, as though to confirm the *Watson* dissent's lament that the Court was improperly equating the disproportionate adverse impact case with a case of individual disparate treatment, the *Wards Cove* majority wrote that by showing a lesser discriminatory alternative the plaintiff demonstrates that the employer's chosen practice was merely a "pretext" for discrimination. In this way the Court suggests that a method of demonstrating unlawful discrimination which *Griggs* developed for cases where discriminatory intent could *not* be shown still turns, in the end, on employer intent. This approach echoes Justice O'Connor's suggestion in *Watson* the year before that the prima facie impact case may demand statistical evidence of the same reliability and magnitude as the Court had required for cases of systemic disparate treatment.

22. *See, e.g., Dothard*, 433 U.S. 321, 97 S.Ct. 2720, 53 L.Ed.2d 786.

23. *See, e.g., New York City Transit Auth. v. Beazer*, 440 U.S. 568, 99 S.Ct. 1355, 59 L.Ed.2d 587 (1979).

24. For a fuller discussion of the *Wards Cove* decision, see Blumoff and Lewis, *The Reagan Court and Title VII: A Common-Law Outlook On a Statutory Task*, 69 N.C.L.Rev. 1 (1990). Among other points, the authors assert that most of the restrictions on the disproportionate adverse impact case announced in that decision were unnecessary, because the only issue remaining on appeal concerned plaintiffs' plainly deficient statistical evidence of systemic disparate treatment.

Removing any doubt about its hostility to the neutral practice case, the Court then cautioned the judiciary against too readily accepting a plaintiff's proposed lesser discriminatory alternative. The alternative must be "equally effective" as the employer's chosen practice, and "cost or other burdens" are "relevant in determining whether they would be equally as effective...." The Court added that if a plaintiff could demonstrate the existence of a less discriminatory alternative so defined, in essence it would be showing that the employer's reliance on its original, challenged practice would be a "pretext" for discrimination. By thus implying that impact proof ultimately shows an employer's state of mind that is prohibited in any event by individual or systemic treatment evidence, the Court leaves us to wonder about the independent utility of the impact case so resoundingly supported by the unanimous decision in *Griggs* less than two decades before.

The Civil Rights Act of 1991 attempted to overrule significant aspects of the *Wards Cove* decision—just how effectively remains to be seen. As we consider the specifics, it is important to keep in mind that *Wards Cove* enfeebled group attacks on neutral practices by altering preexisting understandings about the three major phases of the disparate impact case: (1) plaintiff's prima facie evidence that a particular employment practice caused a specified disproportionate adverse impact on plaintiff's group; (2) the nature and quantum of the employer's defense to disproportionate impact; and (3) the plaintiff's rebuttal that an alternative practice would have largely, rather than perfectly, served the employer's legitimate goals, with lesser adverse impact on the group.

The legislation unequivocally declares that the employer's justification to a prima facie case is an affirmative defense on which the employer must persuade as well as produce evidence. In most other respects, though, the Act reflects Congress' inability to reach a unitary understanding about any of the three previously declared stages of the disproportionate adverse impact case. It fails to clarify the magnitude of the required prima facie case of disproportionate impact; it procedurally complicates the prima facie showing by requiring that the plaintiff ordinarily disentangle the effects of bundled employer practices; it declares that the defense consists of separate elements of job relatedness and business necessity, but offers only a calculatedly ambiguous understanding of what business necessity means; and it carries forward the seemingly unworkable *Wards Cove* innovation that the employer may avoid liability by adopting an alternative practice, perhaps even at the eleventh hour in the middle of a trial. On balance, therefore, the legislation falls well short of restoring the impact case to its pre-*Wards Cove* state.

The central provision, § 703(k)(1)(A), declares that an impact-based unlawful employment practice is proved when:

> (i) a complaining party demonstrates that a respondent uses a particular employment practice that causes a disparate impact on the basis of race, color, religion, sex, or national origin and the

respondent fails to demonstrate that the challenged practice is job related for the position in question and consistent with business necessity; or

(ii) the complaining party makes the demonstration described in subparagraph (C) with respect to an alternative employment practice and the respondent refuses to adopt such alternative employment practice.

The legislation sheds no light on the required magnitude of prima facie differential impact. In the hands of a Court that has proven resolutely hostile to borderline Title VII evidentiary showings,[25] the legislative void on this question may well be filled by restrictive new mathematical requirements that could be justified on the authority of *Watson* and *Wards Cove*, which in this respect remain untouched.

Wards Cove, again furnishing a majority for a proposition that a plurality had endorsed in *Watson*, also required the plaintiff to isolate the single practice among several that produces an alleged adverse impact.[26] New § 701(k)(1)(B)(i) relieves the plaintiff who is attempting to demonstrate adverse impact under § 703(k)(1)(A)(i) from having to disentangle bundled practices, but only if she can "demonstrate" (again a burden of persuasion as well as production) "that the elements of a respondent's decisionmaking process [a 'process' is apparently a package of 'practices'] are not capable of separation for analysis."[27] Otherwise she must show that "each particular challenged employment practice causes a disparate impact...."[28] These provisions invite satellite litigation over the extent to which the plaintiff has taken advantage of discovery and the employer has forthrightly responded. Employer initiated motions on the issue are more than a remote possibility.[29]

A related provision, § 703(k)(1)(B)(ii), is apparently intended to apply when the plaintiff has been allowed, by virtue of § 703(*l*), to attack an entire selection process without demonstrating the adverse impact of each particular component practice. Subdivision (ii) relieves the employer of showing the business necessity[30] of any particular practice that *it* can demonstrate does not cause a disparate impact on plaintiff's group. In tandem, subdivisions (i) and (ii) of § 703(k)(1)(B) seem to assume that sometimes the employer will be able to disentangle the effects of bundled practices even after the plaintiff has satisfied the court that, after discovery, she cannot.

25. *See* Blumoff & Lewis, 69 N.C.L.Rev. 1; Blumrosen, 42 Rutgers L.Rev. 1023.

26. *Wards Cove*, 490 U.S. at 657, 109 S.Ct. at 2125; *see also id.* at 672 (Stevens, J., dissenting).

27. Section 105(a) (adding Title VII § 703(k)(1)(B)(i)).

28. *Id.*

29. Unlike plaintiffs' counsel, who typically depend on recovering attorney's fees from the defendant, but who can recover them under § 701(k) only if their clients prevail, counsel for defendant employers are typically compensated by the hour regardless of the outcome of the litigation.

30. For reasons unexplained, the text does not in terms relieve the employer of showing the job-relatedness of such a practice.

The Court's most publicized and excoriated innovation in *Wards Cove* was to relax both the nature and quantum of an employer's defensive evidence required to justify practices shown to have had a disproportionate adverse impact. Eschewing earlier appellate formulations that sometimes required the employer to demonstrate that its practice was essential to the safe and efficient conduct of its business, the Court wrote that the prima facie case is countered if the defendant merely produces some evidence that the challenged practice serves, "in a significant way, the legitimate goals of the employer."[31] An intricate legislative compromise appears in the end to stiffen the easily satisfied *Wards Cove* version of the defense only slightly insofar as it relates to the overall enterprise, yet also to require the employer to show some link between its chosen practice and the needs of the particular job.

Once the plaintiff demonstrates that a specific practice causes a disparate impact (of still unquantified magnitude), the employer must, after the effective date of the 1991 Act, "demonstrate that the challenged practice is job-related for the position in question and consistent with business necessity...."[32] Further, the obligation to "demonstrate" these elements imposes on the employer, as was generally held before *Wards Cove*, the burden of persuasion on this defense.[33] The net result is that the text of the legislatively overhauled impact defense closely resembles the two-pronged *Diaz/Weeks* BFOQ defense to an expressly discriminatory policy after *Johnson Controls*. The employer bears the compound burden of showing that a neutral practice is necessary for the business (probably a less demanding showing than the *Diaz* "essence of the business" requirement) and is keyed to the particular occupation it screens for (although only "related" to that job, a showing considerably less demanding than the required *Weeks* proof that "all or substantially all" protected group members could not perform it). It is true that requiring the employer to link its practice to requirements of the job, and not just to unspecified "legitimate goals" of the business as a whole, seems to place the plaintiff in a somewhat better posture than she was in after *Wards Cove*. But what do job-relatedness and business necessity now mean? Congress tell us in a preliminary provision on legislative purpose, Section 3, that it seeks to codify those concepts as they were defined by *Griggs* and in subsequent Supreme Court disparate impact decisions before *Wards Cove*.[34] In an unusual attempt to control the judicial interpretive process in advance, Congress adds in § 105(b) that only one specified interpretive memorandum may be "relied upon in any

31. *Wards Cove*, 490 U.S. at 659 n.9, 109 S.Ct. at 2126 n.9.

32. Section 105(a) (adding Title VII § 703(k)(1)(A)(i), 42 U.S.C.A. § 2000e–2(k)(1)(A)(i)) (emphasis added). This compound requirement of a job link and an overall business justification is similar to the defense provided by § 103(a) of the ADA, 42 U.S.C.A. § 12113, for employer screening devices that have adverse impact on disabled individuals. Such practices will not violate that statute if they are "shown to be job-related and consistent with business necessity...."

33. *See supra* text this section.

34. In contrast, predecessor versions of the legislation had "purposes" sections that expressed the intention to overrule the *Wards Cove* business necessity definition. *See, e.g.*, HR 1, Section (o)(2).

way as legislative history in construing or applying ... any provision of this Act that relates to *Wards Cove*—Business necessity/cumulation/alternate business practice." Unfortunately, the referenced memorandum, dated October 25, 1991, rather unhelpfully repeats virtually verbatim Section 3's statement that the business necessity and job relatedness concepts in the Act are akin to those developed by the Supreme Court before *Wards Cove*.

Leaving the definition of the defense for decision by the federal bench could result in a formulation markedly less stringent than the consensus approach of the intermediate appellate courts during the years preceding *Wards Cove*.[35] There is even some possibility that the Supreme Court will return to a definition that approximates the lax *Wards Cove* standard: whether the challenged practice serves to some unspecified degree unspecified general business goals. The Court's latitude to do so arises from the opposing directions, pointed to by its pre-*Wards Cove* decisions, the new benchmark mandated by the 1991 Act.

The Court's early post-*Griggs*, pre-*Wards Cove* impact opinions contained language announcing a stringent standard. In *Albemarle Paper Co. v. Moody*,[36] the Court fastened on the *Griggs* formulation that demanded a "manifest relation" between the neutral practice and requirements of the job in question. In *Dothard v. Rawlinson*,[37] the Court's language was even more exacting. It borrowed the *Griggs* assertion that "the touchstone is business necessity," which it proceeded to equate with a showing that the disparately impacting neutral practice be "necessary to safe and efficient job performance...." Taken literally, almost no practices could be justified under the latter standard, since safety and efficiency are generally tradeoffs; a practice necessary to safety would scarcely ever be necessary to efficiency. But these statements seem the sheerest dictum in each case. In *Albemarle*, the employer's attempted validation of a battery of tests failed to show that they predicted superior job performance for many of the jobs for which the

35. *See* Blumoff & Lewis, 69 N.C.L.Rev. at 16–17 (discussing judicial descriptions of the defense that required the employer to show a "demonstrable" or "manifest" relationship between the challenged practice and important elements of the job). *See, e.g., Contreras v. City of Los Angeles*, 656 F.2d 1267 (9th Cir.1981), *cert. denied*, 455 U.S. 1021, 102 S.Ct. 1719, 72 L.Ed.2d 140 (1982). Somewhat surprisingly, considering its purpose to allay employer concerns, the Democratic substitute measure that the House passed on June 5, 1991 appeared to strengthen the required job-related link, describing it as a "substantial and manifest relationship" between the challenged practice and "requirements for effective job performance." That language has disappeared from the legislation enacted into law.

It should be noted, moreover, that under Senator Dole's interpretive memorandum on the Civil Rights Act of 1991, 137 Cong. Rec. S15472–S15478 (daily ed. October 30, 1991), which President Bush has directed executive branch officials to respect as "authoritative interpretive guidance," President's Statement on Signing the Act, November 21, 1991, DLR No. 226, p. D–1, November 22, 1991, the job-related prong of the defense—"job-related for the position in question"—is, in the Senator's words, "to be read broadly, to include any legitimate business purpose, even those that may not be strictly required for the actual day-to-day activities of an entry level job." Dole Memorandum Section–By–Section Analysis concerning section 8.

36. 422 U.S. 405, 425, 95 S.Ct. 2362, 2375, 45 L.Ed.2d 280 (1975).

37. 433 U.S. 321, 331 n. 14, 97 S.Ct. 2720, 2728 n. 14, 53 L.Ed.2d 786 (1977).

tests were administered; because, by the employer's own reckoning, the tests bore no relation to those jobs, the question whether they had to have a "manifest" relation to them was never presented. And in *Dothard*, the Court observed that the state had not produced any evidence attempting to link height and weight requirements with the strength required for the jobs in question. Once again, therefore, the Court's footnoted mention of a "business necessity" test under which the practice could be justified only if necessary to safety and efficiency went well beyond the needs of the case.

The Court's later post-*Griggs*, pre-*Wards Cove* decisions have used much looser language. The opinion in *Teal* wrote mildly that to defend a test the employer need only show that it measures "skills related to effective performance" of the job in question.[38] No dimension of performance was specified, nor any degree of linkage between the employer's requirement and "effective" performance. In *New York City Transit Auth. v. Beazer*,[39] the Court again referred to a "manifest relationship" standard but deemed it met if the employer's general "legitimate employment goals of safety and efficiency" are "significantly served by— even if they do not require" the practice in question.[40] While this statement, too, might be dismissed as dictum—the Court also criticized weaknesses in the plaintiff's prima facie evidence, so there may have been no prima facie showing against which to defend—in context it looks more like an alternative holding. Then in *Watson*, the most immediate *Wards Cove* precursor, a plurality cited *Beazer* in asserting that the employer could meet a manifest relationship standard if its challenged practice "significantly served" "legitimate business purposes."[41]

Set against this chronology, of course, is the simple fact that Congress advertently did *not* permit reference to *Wards Cove* itself, the opinion that manifests in full flower the lax standards for job relatedness and business necessity earlier enunciated by *Beazer* and *Watson*. Further, the purposes section "would be superfluous if Congress did not believe that the Court had changed the concepts of business necessity and job relatedness in *Wards Cove*," and it rejects that change.[42] In

---

38.   457 U.S. at 451, 102 S.Ct. at 2533.

39.   440 U.S. 568, 99 S.Ct. 1355, 59 L.Ed.2d 587 (1979).

40.   *Id.* at 587 n. 31, 99 S.Ct. at 1366, n. 31. If this analysis is right, and a *Beazer* or *Watson* formulation of business necessity ultimately prevails, that prong of the defense to a disproportionately impacting neutral practice will remain significantly less stringent than the bona fide occupational qualification (BFOQ) defense to a practice, policy or rule that expressly discriminates on the basis of sex, religion, or national origin. *International Union, UAW v. Johnson Controls*, 499 U.S. 187, 111 S.Ct. 1196, 113 L.Ed.2d 158 (1991) (Congress narrowed the BFOQ defense "to qualifications that

affect an employee's ability to do the job"). Under the position taken by Senator Dole's interpretive memorandum, *see supra*, even the job-relatedness prong of the impact defense would not require a strict relationship between the challenged practice and the requirements of the job in question.

41.   487 U.S. at 998, 108 S.Ct. at 2791. Admittedly, because *Watson* was only a plurality opinion, it may not qualify as one of the opinions of the Supreme "Court" to which Section 3 authorizes judges to refer in fleshing out job relatedness and business necessity.

42.   Note, *The Civil Rights Act of 1991: The Business Necessity Standard*, 106 Harv. L.Rev. 896, 911, (1993) (noting that Title

addition, because Congress restored the burden of proof concerning the impact defense to the employer, in contrast to the disparate treatment model, it makes "no sense to apply the loose definition of 'business necessity' [which was] derived from [*Wards Cove*'s] analogizing disparate impact to disparate treatment...."[43] Given the vague terms of the Congressional reprise on *Wards Cove*, it is scarcely surprising that commentators have taken diametrically opposed positions about the likely ultimate interpretation of these concepts.[44]

Two decisions subsequent to the 1991 Act, in reaching different conclusions about the validity of a no-beard rule, illustrate how application of the new job relatedness and business necessity defense may vary depending upon the requirements of the job. In September 1993 the Eleventh Circuit, on the assumption that the standards of the 1991 Act applied, upheld a fire department's beard ban despite its acknowledged disproportionate adverse impact on black men. The evidence established that black males who shave are far more likely than whites to suffer from the bacterial disorder pseudofolliculitis barbae, or PFB. The court found the practice justified as a matter of business necessity, citing expert testimony that any amount of facial hair could prevent a secure seal between the face and self contained breathing apparatuses, thereby jeopardizing a firefighter's safety.[45] Interestingly, it made no mention of job relatedness, even though the statute now expressly requires the adverse impact to be justified by both business necessity and the requirements of the job in question.

Only a month later, by contrast, the Eighth Circuit struck down Domino's Pizza's no-beard rule as it was enforced against black males suffering from PFB. In general, the court wrote, the company could establish any grooming or dress standards it chose. But when those standards have a disproportionate adverse impact on a group defined by race (though apparently not sex),[46] the justification must rise to the level of a true business necessity. In the court's view, even strong evidence that customers preferred clean-shaven deliverymen would not suffice as

VII's new definition of the compound defense is identical to the language in the ADA, which requires employers to show a "close connection between a challenged practice and an employee's ability to perform the job," and thus declares a standard far more stringent than *Wards Cove*'s "legitimate goals of the employer") (citing 137 Cong.Rec. S13,582 (daily ed. Sept. 24, 1991); comments of Sen. Durenburger on ADA).

43. *Id.* at 913.

44. *Compare* Kingsley Browne, *The Civil Rights Act of 1991: A "Quota Bill," A Codification of Griggs, a Partial Return to Wards Cove, or All of the Above?*, 43 Case Western L.Rev. 287, 348–63 (1993) (interpreting "business necessity" as used in the legislation to mean no more than "job related," or at most to mean the same thing as

the *Wards Cove* standard "serves, in a significant way") *with* Note, *The Civil Rights Act of 1991: The Business Necessity Standard*, 106 Harv.L.Rev. 896.

45. *Fitzpatrick v. City of Atlanta*, 2 F.3d 1112 (11th Cir.1993). The opposite conclusion was reached on a different record in *Kennedy v. District of Columbia*, 654 A.2d 847 (D.C.App.1994) (decision under Washington, D.C. Human Rights Act).

46. *See* discussion of grooming and dress standards in Chapter 2 above. *Cf. Fraternal Order of Police Newark Lodge No. 12 v. City of Newark*, 170 F.3d 359 (3d Cir.), *cert. denied*, 528 U.S. 817, 120 S.Ct. 56, 145 L.Ed.2d 49 (1999) (affirming permanent injunction against city policy prohibiting police officers from wearing beards because rule interfered with tenet of plaintiff's religion).

a business justification, because the employer had failed to show "that customers would order less pizza in the absence of a strictly enforced no-beard rule."[47] Perhaps the Eleventh Circuit employed a more flexible business necessity standard for positions, like firefighters, that entail greater responsibility or special risks to the public.[48] By contrast, another circuit has concluded that the 1991 Amendments exalt the stringent *Griggs/Dothard* formulation of the defense over the laxer *Beazer/Wards Cove* approach. It held accordingly that an employer can defend a discriminatory cutoff score on an entry level examination only if the score validly measures the minimum qualifications necessary for successful performance of the job in question.[49] See § 2.34, *supra,* on defending the adverse impact of tests.

Even more curious is the Act's treatment of the plaintiff's rebuttal. At first blush the Act appears to ameliorate the obstacles *Wards Cove* had placed in the plaintiff's path when she tries to surmount the employer's defense by proving the existence of a less discriminatory alternative. But then it also appears to give the employer a trump card that lets it escape liability altogether simply by adopting that alternative when all else fails. The rebuttal phase of the impact case is of potentially enormous significance. Employers often succeeded with the business justification defense in the eighteen years between *Griggs* and *Wards Cove,* and the new legislation's compound but dubiously rigorous defensive standard—job-relatedness and business necessity—may prove no more demanding than it was then. It may therefore be predicted that the outcome of many impact cases will ultimately hang on the fate of the plaintiff's rebuttal.

Before *Wards Cove,* the plaintiff could rebut the employer's defense of business justification by establishing that an alternative practice would serve the employer's job-related needs with less discriminatory impact on the protected group.[50] *Wards Cove* tightened the concept by insisting that the plaintiff's identified alternative be "equally" effective as the employer's chosen practice, cautioning that the "cost or other burdens of proposed alternative selection devices are relevant"[51] in

47. *Bradley v. Pizzaco of Neb., Inc.,* 7 F.3d 795 (8th Cir.1993).

48. *See* Andrew C. Spiropoulos, *Defining the Business Necessity Defense to the Disparate Impact Cause of Action: Finding the Golden Mean,* 74 N.C.L.Rev. 1479, 1485 (1996) (arguing that the Supreme Court opinions articulate two different versions of the business necessity defense).

49. *Lanning v. Southeastern Pa. Transp. Auth.,* 181 F.3d 478 (3d Cir.1999), *cert. denied,* 528 U.S. 1131, 120 S.Ct. 970, 145 L.Ed.2d 840 (2000).

50. *Albemarle Paper Co. v. Moody,* 422 U.S. 405, 425, 95 S.Ct. 2362, 2375, 45 L.Ed.2d 280 (1975). Placing the burden on the plaintiff to rebut the defense by identifying an alternative practice that would still

meet the goals sought to be served by the employer's original, challenged practice made it logically inconsistent to require the employer to have shown previously that its challenged practice was a matter of strict "necessity." *See Contreras v. City of Los Angeles,* 656 F.2d 1267 (9th Cir.1981), *cert. denied,* 455 U.S. 1021, 102 S.Ct. 1719, 72 L.Ed.2d 140 (1982).

51. *Wards Cove,* 490 U.S. at 661, 109 S.Ct. at 2127 (quoting *Watson,* 487 U.S. at 998, 108 S.Ct. at 2791). The Justice Department has evidently appreciated this point. Its "fact sheet" on an Administration version of the 1991 legislation observes that a rebutting plaintiff must demonstrate the existence of an alternative employment practice that is "comparable in cost and

making that determination. It so concluded even though cost defenses ordinarily have not avoided Title VII violations predicated on disparate treatment.[52]

The Act responds to the *Wards Cove* requirement that an alternative practice be "equally effective" by returning to "the law as it existed on June 4, 1989, [the day before the *Wards Cove* decision] with respect to the concept of 'alternative employment practice.' "[53] Of course this still leaves the possibility that the courts will continue to adhere to the *Wards Cove* insistence on equal effectiveness, with its focus on avoiding additional cost to the employer, because that notion had earlier surfaced in the plurality opinion in *Watson*.[54] In any event, even if the Act is construed to allow the plaintiff to rebut with a less effective, somewhat more expensive alternative, it is doubtful that the Court will read it to require an employer to bear as much additional expense as the Americans With Disabilities Act requires employers to bear in making "reasonable accommodations" to individuals with disabilities.[55]

Finally, even if the plaintiff meets whatever new standards the Court may demand for demonstrating a less discriminatory alternative, the rebuttal may ultimately fail because the Act also carries forward another innovation of *Wards Cove* that first surfaced in *Watson*: there will be no law violation unless in addition "the respondent refuses to adopt such alternative employment practice."[56] Section 703(k)(1)(A)(ii) provides that an unlawful employment practice is established if the plaintiff "makes the demonstration described in subparagraph (C) with

equally effective in measuring job performance or achieving the respondence's [sic] legitimate employment goals."

52. *International Union, UAW v. Johnson Controls*, 499 U.S. 187, 111 S.Ct. 1196, 113 L.Ed.2d 158 (1991). *See* Blumoff & Lewis, 69 N.C.L.Rev. at 42.

53. Section 105(a) (adding subparagraph (k)(1)(C) to § 703 of Title VII, 42 U.S.C.A. § 2000e–2).

54. In this connection it may be significant that courts are free when they try to pour content into the less restrictive alternative concept to look to the whole of "the law" that preceded *Wards Cove*, not just to the decisions of "the Supreme Court" that Congress in Section 3 and the Interpretive Memorandum made the sole source of reference for elucidating the "business necessity" and "job relatedness" standards. Presumably, therefore, judges will be free to borrow the equal effectiveness restriction enunciated by *Watson*, despite the fact that Justice O'Connor there wrote only for a plurality.

55. Section 102(b)(5)(A) of the ADA effective as to private employment on July 26, 1992, defines unlawful discrimination to include a failure to make "reasonable ac-

commodations to the known physical or mental limitations of an otherwise qualified individual with a disability ... unless [the employer] ... can demonstrate that the accommodation would impose an undue hardship on the operation of the business...." 42 U.S.C.A. § 12112(b)(5). "Undue hardship," in turn, is defined to mean "an action requiring significant difficulty or expense...." Section 101(10) of ADA, 42 U.S.C.A. § 12111(10). Thus a covered employer must incur all expenses short of those deemed "significant" in order to avoid discriminating in violation of ADA. Even if the Court, in construing the Civil Rights Act of 1991, rejects the *Watson* plurality's statement that the plaintiff's less discriminatory alternative must be "equally" as effective, cost considered, as the employer's original chosen practice, it is unlikely to require the employer to bear the full range of additional expense mandated by ADA "reasonable accommodation."

56. Section 105(a)(ii) (adding subsection (k)(1)(A)(ii) to § 703 of Title VII, 42 U.S.C.A. § 2000e–2). The *Watson* plurality opinion would appear to be part of the "the law" to which courts may recur when they adumbrate the meaning of the less restrictive alternative concept.

respect to an alternative employment practice [the subparagraph that returns to the pre-*Wards Cove* law] *and* the respondent refuses to adopt such alternative practice."

When must such a refusal take place to pin liability on the employer under this provision? "Respondent" and "complaining party" rather than "defendant" and "plaintiff" are the words used here, which might suggest that the employer's last chance to trump a showing of violation is during state, local or EEOC proceedings rather than at trial. But the section in which the refusal-to-adopt provision is found prescribes for the entire "title" how to establish an "unlawful employment practice" based on disparate impact. This implies that an employer may defeat the plaintiff's newly relaxed showing of a lesser discriminatory alternative as late as the latter stages of a trial on the merits.[57] That construction is supported by the present-tense verbs in Section 703(k)(1)(A)(ii): the violation is established if the respondent "refuses to adopt" an alternative practice, but that happens only after the complaining party "makes the demonstration" of such a practice. A "demonstration," in turn, probably cannot be made until judicial trial; "demonstrates" is defined by new § 701(m) to refer to satisfying burdens of production and persuasion.

In any event, whether it refers to agency or court proceedings, § 703(k)(1)(A)(ii) is set in *some* sort of adversary context. This casts doubt on the assertion of one scholar that the 1991 Act imposes on employers an independent duty, arising before any charge is filed, to ascertain whether a less discriminatory alternative exists before they select a neutral employment practice and that they are therefore liable even for practices justified by business necessity "when the risk of . . . a discriminatory result could have been avoided by using a less harmful selection device."[58]

If a Supreme Court majority holds that a last-minute employer adoption of the plaintiff's proffered alternative avoids all liability (because, in the words of the Act, there would then be no "unlawful employment practice"), the named plaintiffs, who successfully attacked the employer's original practice through all three phases of the impact case, will be deprived of any relief and, in turn, eligibility for attorney's fees. Although protected group members who work for that employer will enjoy the benefits of the adopted lesser discriminatory practice in futuro, what incentive would prospective plaintiffs have to sue (or prospective plaintiffs' counsel to take the case)? The problem is particularly acute because in the end Congress failed to overturn Supreme Court decisions approving of defendants' procedural maneuvers that avoid or diminish their liability for attorney's fees to prevailing plaintiffs.[59]

57. See Blumoff & Lewis, 69 N.C.L.Rev. at 43–44.

58. Oppenheimer, *Negligent Discrimination*, 141 U.Pa.L.Rev. 899, 933, 935 (1993).

59. H.R. 1 had proposed overruling

The structure of new § 703(k)(1)(A), added by the 1991 Act, has suggested to some commentators[60] that the plaintiff now may follow two independent paths to proving disproportionate adverse impact. She can prevail under subdivision (i), they contend, by demonstrating the adverse impact of a discrete practice if the defendant "fails to demonstrate" job relatedness and business necessity; or under subdivision (ii) if she "makes the demonstration described in subparagraph (C)[61] with respect to an alternative employment practice and the respondent refuses to adopt such alternative practice." The commentators' reading is supported as a formal matter by the punctuation in subparagraph (k)(1)(A), where a semicolon precedes "or (ii)." But in practice the less restrictive alternative approach of subdivision (ii) may become pertinent only when it always has, that is when a fact finder concludes that the employer prevails rather than "fails" on its defense. How, after all, can a plaintiff show under subdivision (ii) that a proposed alternative practice has *less* adverse impact except by contrast to the adverse impact of the employer's original, challenged practice that the plaintiff had to prove prima facie under subdivision (i)?

Put otherwise, subdivision (ii) does not identify separate real-life employer conduct that gives rise to liability, only a different way of showing the unlawfulness of the employer practice challenged by the complaint.[62] If the subdivisions are thus read together as creating only one, unified multi-stage mode of proof, subdivision (ii) perpetuates the logical conundrum of prior law by predicating employer liability on an alternative practice assumed to be available even when the employer's challenged practice has been shown, at least in theory, a matter of strict business "necessity." Of course the Court could resolve the conundrum by reading its pre-*Wards Cove* cases, referenced by Section 3 and the Interpretive Memorandum, to require something less than strict necessity.

In sum, the Civil Rights Act of 1991 reflects Congressional equivocation about the group protection theory advanced by the disproportionate adverse impact mode of proof. Although it describes a defensive standard likely to be somewhat more rigorous than that declared by *Wards Cove*, it leaves the prima facie case vulnerable not only to ad hoc statistical requirements but also to unrealistic trial court conclusions that discovery devices suffice to enable the plaintiff to disentangle the effects of

---

those decisions. Section 9, for example, struck statutory text that the Court had construed to allow a defendant's offer of judgment under the Federal Rules of Civil Procedure to relieve it of liability to a prevailing plaintiff for subsequently accruing attorney's fees. H.R. 1 § 9 (amending Title VII § 706(k) and effectively overruling *Marek v. Chesny*, 473 U.S. 1, 105 S.Ct. 3012, 87 L.Ed.2d 1 (1985)). It also required parties or their counsel to attest, before entry of a consent order or judgment, that a waiver of statutory attorney's fees was not compelled as a condition of settlement. *Id.* (effectively overruling *Evans v. Jeff D.*, 475 U.S. 717, 106 S.Ct. 1531, 89 L.Ed.2d 747 (1986)).

60. Zimmer, Sullivan, Richards and Calloway, *Cases on Employment Discrimination* 443–445 (3d ed. Little, Brown 1994); Oppenheimer, 141 U.Pa.L.Rev. at 935–36.

61. Subdivision (C) refers to a showing of an "alternative employment practice" that is "in accordance with the law as it existed on June 4, 1989," the day before *Wards Cove* was decided.

62. See text *supra*.

compound employer practices. More clearly still, the Act fails in the end to restore the pre-*Wards Cove* status of the plaintiff's rebuttal, by affording the employer a last-ditch means of avoiding liability altogether.

It may now be timely to return to the caution at the beginning of this chapter that the modes of proof under Title VII or ADEA often overlap. A recent appellate decision considered a "dual status" rule that required civilian security guards of a state's national guard to be active members of the Guard as well. But because federal military regulations, in turn, terminate eligibility for National Guard duty at age 60, the plaintiff civilian security guard argued that his termination at that age on the basis of the employer's "dual status" rule violated ADEA. Two members of the panel concluded that the dual status rule was discriminatory on its face, since all civilian guards would be separated at age 60 in compliance with the federal military requirement. Consequently, only a BFOQ defense could avail the defendant—it was insufficient for the state to offer, as a "legitimate, nondiscriminatory reason" for the rule, that civilian security guards might be better trained and prepared if they were also active members of the Air National Guard. The dissent, on the other hand, would have found that the plaintiff had established a prima facie case only under the inferential approach of *McDonnell Douglas*. Observing that over–60 security guards with sufficient seniority could obtain a waiver from the dual status rule, and that guards younger than 60, not eligible for the waiver, would also lose their jobs if they did not maintain active weekend guard status, the dissent concluded that the state's reliance on the rule was not inextricably linked to age but merely correlated with it.[63] For the dissent, therefore, the defendant's proffer of legitimate, nondiscriminatory reasons relating to training and preparedness rebutted the inferential *McDonnell Douglas* prima facie case; and since the plaintiff had failed to show that those reasons were a pretext for age discrimination, ADEA was not violated. Alternatively, the court might have viewed the plaintiff's prima facie case as based on the showing of a facially neutral practice that, despite the waiver possibility, might have had a statistically disproportionate adverse impact on members of the protected group over 60. In that event the state would have borne the burden of showing that the dual status rule is justified by job relatedness and business necessity.

63. *See Hazen Paper Co. v. Biggins,* 507 U.S. 604, 113 S.Ct. 1701, 123 L.Ed.2d 338 (1993) (employer does not expressly discriminate on the basis of age within the meaning of ADEA when it relies on a factor merely statistically correlated with age).

Chapter Four

TITLE VII ADMINISTRATIVE PRE-REQUISITES, PROCEDURES AND REMEDIES

Analysis

---

§ 4.1 In General

Title VII sets out federal and state agency prerequisites to suit. In general, the private sector applicant or employee need only comply with two such prerequisites: (1) timely filing of a charge with the U.S. Equal Employment Opportunity Commission ("EEOC"), either in the first instance or, in the majority of states that have parallel state or local antidiscrimination legislation and agencies, after filing with those agencies; and (2) timely filing of a federal or state court action within 90 days after receipt from EEOC of a "notice of right to sue." Failure to follow the specified procedures and meet the charge-filing and suit-commencement deadlines usually results in dismissal of the administrative charge or ensuing judicial action.

This chapter identifies the agency and court procedures and the relationship between them, discusses the possible retroactivity of particular sections of the Civil Rights Act of 1991, and outlines the remedies available under Title VII as amended by the 1991 Act.

A. ADMINISTRATIVE PREREQUISITES AND PROCEDURES

§ 4.2 In General

Although 1972 amendments to Title VII gave EEOC the right to seek judicial relief in the first instance, most judicial action takes the form of private suits in federal district court. The path to court is strewn with a series of intricate and time-consuming administrative procedures at the state and federal levels. These requirements are designed to give state or local antidiscrimination agencies and EEOC opportunities to obtain voluntary resolution of discrimination disputes, as well as to promote federal-state comity.

The complainant must first file a written charge with the EEOC,[1] "sufficiently precise to identify the parties and to describe generally the

---

§ 4.2

1. Section § 706(b), 42 U.S.C.A. § 2003–5(b).

action or practice complained of.''[2] In addition, however, the statute requires "deferral" to a state or local agency where local law prohibits the unlawful employment practice alleged and establishes an agency with authority to grant or seek relief concerning that practice.[3] In the few states that do not have such fair employment practices legislation and enforcement agencies, or where the local law does not provide its authority jurisdiction over a particular violation, a charge must be filed with EEOC within 180 days of an alleged unlawful employment practice.[4] In the great majority of states that do have such laws and agencies, the charge must be filed with EEOC within the earlier of 300 days of the alleged violation, or 30 days after the charging party receives "notice that the state or local antidiscrimination agency has terminated" proceedings under state or local law.[5] But unless it dismisses a charge earlier, this state or local "deferral" agency must be given 60 days in which to attempt to resolve the dispute before EEOC may proceed.[6] This latter requirement suggests not only that the state filing must precede a filing with EEOC,[7] but also, by subtracting 60 from 300, that the charge must ordinarily be filed with the state or local "deferral" agency within 240 days of the alleged unlawful employment practice.[8] However, a state

2.   29 C.F.R. § 1601.12(b) (1992). This EEOC regulation has been construed liberally to require only the bare minimum there specified. *Waiters v. Robert Bosch Corp.*, 683 F.2d 89, 92 (4th Cir.1982). For example, an EEOC intake questionnaire was held tantamount to a formal charge of age discrimination where the interview notes of the agency's intake officer referred to the plaintiff as a "charging party" and the questionnaire itself identified both the plaintiff and the employer as well as the alleged discriminatory conduct. *Downes v. Volkswagen of Am., Inc.*, 41 F.3d 1132 (7th Cir.1994). *But see Novitsky v. American Consulting Engineers, L.L.C.*, 196 F.3d 699 (7th Cir.1999) (intake form is not sent to employer and cannot give notice of grounds of complaint); *Whitmore v. O'Connor Mgmt., Inc.*, 156 F.3d 796, 799 (8th Cir. 1998) (no evidence that intake form is intended to function as a formal charge); *Shempert v. Harwick Chemical Corp.*, 151 F.3d 793 (8th Cir.1998), *cert. denied*, 525 U.S. 1139, 119 S.Ct. 1028, 143 L.Ed.2d 38 (1999) (intake questionnaire not a "charge" where it was neither signed under oath or verified); *Diez v. Minnesota Mining and Manufacturing Co.*, 88 F.3d 672 (8th Cir. 1996). *Cf. Schlueter v. Anheuser–Busch, Inc.*, 132 F.3d 455 (8th Cir.1998) (EEOC intake questionnaire containing allegations of sex discrimination did not function as charge of discrimination under ADEA or Title VII, but actions taken by EEOC worker excused employee's neglect in filing late Title VII charge); *Lawrence v. Cooper Communities, Inc.*, 132 F.3d 447 (8th Cir.1998)

(employee mailed written allegations to EEOC within time limit but EEOC delayed in preparing the charge and sending it to employee to sign).

3.   Section 706(c), 42 U.S.C.A. § 2000e–5(c).

4.   Section 706(e), 42 U.S.C.A. § 2000e–5(e).

5.   Section 706(e), 42 U.S.C.A. § 2000e–5(e).

6.   *See generally* § 706 of Title VII. *See Zugay v. Progressive Care*, 180 F.3d 901 (7th Cir.1999) (plaintiff's cooperation with state deferral agency for 60 days met exhaustion requirement notwithstanding she withdrew her state charge thereafter).

7.   *See Mohasco Corp. v. Silver*, 447 U.S. 807, 100 S.Ct. 2486, 65 L.Ed.2d 532 (1980). One circuit has accordingly held that a federal action may not be stayed pending state agency deferral because prior resort to the state agency is a jurisdictional prerequisite to a timely filing with EEOC and, in turn, to the commencement of an action in federal court. *Citicorp Person-to-Person Financial Corp. v. Brazell*, 658 F.2d 232 (4th Cir.1981). In this respect the Title VII scheme differs from that under ADEA, where the state agency and EEOC filings may be simultaneous. *Oscar Mayer & Co. v. Evans*, 441 U.S. 750, 755, 99 S.Ct. 2066, 2071, 60 L.Ed.2d 609 (1979).

8.   The Court so held in *Mohasco. See Anderson v. Board of Regents*, 140 F.3d 704 (7th Cir.1998) (ADEA claim time-barred

or local filing later than 240 but still within 300 days of the alleged unlawful practice will be considered timely if the state or local agency terminates its proceedings before day 300.[9] Moreover, the plaintiff gets the benefit of the 300-day period for filing with EEOC, and may use the 240-day "plus" schedule approved by *Mohasco* for filing with the state or local agency, even if the latter filing is untimely under the state or local antidiscrimination law to which the EEOC is deferring.[10] These time constraints apply, however, even if the plaintiff seeks only declaratory relief.[11]

It will be noted that the foregoing time limitations specified by statute refer to filing directly "with" the state or local agency and then "with" EEOC. In fact, informal administrative agreements between EEOC and many state and local deferral agencies, now sanctioned by case law, have altered these requirement so that a filing with one can constitute a filing with the other; the EEOC filing may even precede the local one. For example, the state or local administrative filing will be considered adequate even where the complainant has filed a charge only or initially with EEOC, if EEOC itself refers the charge to the local agency and suspends its proceedings for the required 60 days or until local proceedings terminate.[12] Conversely, a "worksharing" agreement may specify that where the complainant files first with a state or local agency, that agency becomes EEOC's agent for receiving the charge even if it never forwards the charge to EEOC.[13]

Where a state or local agency waives the right to process the charge initially, or to proceed if the charge is filed more than a specified time after the occurrence of the alleged unlawful employment practice, the circuit courts have extended the Supreme Court's approval of worksharing agreements by holding that the state's waiver is a "termination" of state or local proceedings that authorizes the EEOC to begin its

---

and not subject to equitable tolling where plaintiff filed with state agency but not EEOC on day 300 because late filing denied state agency opportunity to consider charge).

9. *Mohasco*, 447 U.S. 807, 100 S.Ct. 2486, 65 L.Ed.2d 532.

10. *EEOC v. Commercial Office Prods.*, 486 U.S. 107, 108 S.Ct. 1666, 100 L.Ed.2d 96 (1988). *Cf. Ashley v. Boyle's Famous Corned Beef Co.*, 66 F.3d 164 (8th Cir.1995) (en banc) (no laches defense to monetary relief under Title VII for unreasonable delay, provided charge filed within 300 days).

11. *See Algrant v. Evergreen Valley Nurseries Ltd. Partnership*, 126 F.3d 178 (3d Cir.1997); *International Ass'n of Machinists & Aerospace Workers v. Tennessee Valley Auth.*, 108 F.3d 658, 668 (6th Cir. 1997); *Levald, Inc. v. City of Palm Desert*, 998 F.2d 680, 688–89 (9th Cir.1993), *cert. denied*, 510 U.S. 1093, 114 S.Ct. 924, 127

L.Ed.2d 217 (1994); *Gilbert v. City of Cambridge*, 932 F.2d 51, 57–58 (1st Cir.), *cert. denied*, 502 U.S. 866, 112 S.Ct. 192, 116 L.Ed.2d 153 (1991); *Clulow v. Oklahoma*, 700 F.2d 1291, 1302 (10th Cir.1983). *Cf. Town of Orangetown v. Gorsuch*, 718 F.2d 29, 41–42 (2d Cir.1983), *cert. denied sub nom. Town of Orangetown v. Ruckelshaus*, 465 U.S. 1099, 104 S.Ct. 1592, 80 L.Ed.2d 124 (1984) (when a "claim for declaratory relief could have been resolved through another form of action which has a specific limitations period, the specific period of time will govern.")

12. This practice was devised by EEOC regulations, 29 C.F.R. § 1601.13 (1993), and approved by the Supreme Court in *Love v. Pullman*, 404 U.S. 522, 92 S.Ct. 616, 30 L.Ed.2d 679 (1972).

13. *See, e.g., Williams v. Washington Metro. Area Transit Auth.*, 721 F.2d 1412 (D.C.Cir.1983).

investigation without waiting 60 days.[14] In such a jurisdiction the complainant need never file with a state or local agency and need file a charge with EEOC only within 300 days of the alleged unlawful employment practice, instead of the 240 days that would govern if there were no work-sharing agreement. The state or local agency may retain jurisdiction, however, to process the charge thereafter if it chooses.[15]

In brief, although § 706 appears to require that the state or local filing precede the filing of a charge with EEOC, it is apparent from the Court's approval of deferral and work-sharing agreements that in practice EEOC is often the first, and sometimes the only agency to investigate and conciliate charges, even in deferral states. Nevertheless, where the state or local agency has made a prior determination, the statute directs EEOC to give its findings "substantial weight" in determining whether there is reasonable cause to support the charge.[16] Nevertheless, it is not a prerequisite to suit that EEOC find reasonable cause to believe the Act violated, and even an EEOC determination to the contrary will not bar suit in court.[17]

The 180–day or 300–day charge-filing deadline periods are triggered only when the alleged unlawful employment practice is complete and when the applicant or employee knows or should know of the facts that support a claim under the statute. For this purpose the date of an alleged unlawful employment practice is usually the date on which the complaining applicant or employee should be aware of the consequences and unlawfulness of employer conduct, not when those consequences become manifest.[18] This approach can cut both ways: starting the

14. *See Laquaglia v. Rio Hotel & Casino, Inc.,* 186 F.3d 1172 (9th Cir.1999); *Ford v. Bernard Fineson Dev. Ctr.,* 81 F.3d 304 (2d Cir.1996); *Griffin v. City of Dallas,* 26 F.3d 610 (5th Cir.1994) (Texas Commission on Human Rights ("TCHR") waiver of right to proceed if charge filed more than 180 days after alleged Title VII violation held to authorize EEOC, as TCHR's agent, to initiate charges immediately after it received a charge, without waiting 60 days); *Worthington v. Union Pac. R.R.,* 948 F.2d 477 (8th Cir.1991).

15. *EEOC v. Commercial Office Prods.,* 486 U.S. 107, 108 S.Ct. 1666, 100 L.Ed.2d 96 (1988).

16. Section 706(b), 42 U.S.C.A. § 2000e–5(b).

17. *See McDonnell Douglas Corp. v. Green,* 411 U.S. 792, 93 S.Ct. 1817, 36 L.Ed.2d 668 (1973). On the admissibility of EEOC determinations of "cause" or "no cause" in subsequent Title VII judicial proceedings, see Chapter 12 below.

18. *Delaware State College v. Ricks,* 449 U.S. 250, 101 S.Ct. 498, 66 L.Ed.2d 431 (1980) (an employer that expresses an "official position" and simultaneously "indicate[s] a willingness to change its [official position]" based on the outcome of a pending grievance proceeding does not thereby render that "official position" a "tentative" decision. *See Iglesias v. Mutual Life Ins. Co.,* 156 F.3d 237 (1st Cir.1998), *cert. denied,* 528 U.S. 812, 120 S.Ct. 45, 145 L.Ed.2d 41 (1999) (letter to plaintiff from employer advising him he would no longer serve as agency manager triggered 300–day EEOC charge filing period). But where an authoritative voice expressly disavowed the finality of the initial determination, the clock does not begin to run when the "final decision" was communicated to employee). *Currier v. Radio Free Europe/Radio Liberty, Inc.,* 159 F.3d 1363 (D.C.Cir.1998).

This timeliness rule may have harsh consequences for the plaintiff alleging a denial of promotion that can be traced back to a denial of training. The Eleventh Circuit has held that the accrual date was the date that the training was denied, not the date the employee was denied a promotion or job transfer. *Turlington v. Atlanta Gas Light Co.,* 135 F.3d 1428 (11th Cir.), *cert. denied,* 525 U.S. 962, 119 S.Ct. 405, 142 L.Ed.2d 329 (1998). But if the employee had filed

charge-filing clock well before a termination is consummated[19] or stopping the clock from running until, after termination, the employee learns the facts that suggest the termination was unlawful.[20] Pursuing a grievance under a collective bargaining agreement will not toll the time to file a charge with EEOC.[21] But the 180–day and 300–day EEOC charge-filing deadlines, although critical, are not technically jurisdictional. Rather they are procedural preconditions to suit, analogous to statutes of limitations, and thus may be waived, estopped, or equitably tolled.[22]

A recent Third Circuit opinion illustrates both the accrual date definition problem and the doctrine of equitable tolling. A law firm employee asserted a claim of discriminatory dismissal in her EEOC charge, later amending that charge to complain of a subsequent failure to rehire. These claims would have been untimely under the applicable 300–day charge-filing period if they accrued on the date of her dismissal.

the charge on the denial of training, he may well have lost on the issue of whether he suffered an adverse employment action. *See* discussion of what constitutes an adverse employment action in Chapter 2, *supra*.

19. *See Ricks*, 449 U.S. 250, 101 S.Ct. 498, 66 L.Ed.2d 431 (charge-filing clock began to run when university professor was notified that his contract would come to an end a year later, even though that decision was subject to change through internal grievance proceedings).

20. *See, e.g., EEOC v. City of Norfolk Police Dep't*, 45 F.3d 80 (4th Cir.1995) (claim that white officers suspended because of pending criminal charges were immediately reinstated when charges dismissed while plaintiff was not accrued only on date plaintiff learned or should have learned of their reinstatement). *Sturniolo v. Sheaffer, Eaton, Inc.*, 15 F.3d 1023 (11th Cir.1994) (180–day period under ADEA did not begin to run until plaintiff knew or should have known that he had been replaced by a younger person). *But see Hulsey v. Kmart, Inc.*, 43 F.3d 555 (10th Cir.1994) (claim accrued when plaintiffs learned of their demotions and transfers, rather than at later dates they suspected those actions were taken because of their age).

21. *International Union of Electrical Workers v. Robbins & Myers*, 429 U.S. 229, 97 S.Ct. 441, 50 L.Ed.2d 427 (1976).

22. *Zipes v. Trans World Airlines, Inc.*, 455 U.S. 385, 102 S.Ct. 1127, 71 L.Ed.2d 234 (1982); *Gibson v. West*, 201 F.3d 990 (7th Cir.2000) (on remand). *See Schlueter v. Anheuser–Busch, Inc.*, 132 F.3d 455 (8th Cir.1998) (EEOC intake questionnaire containing allegations of sex discrimination did not function as charge of discrimination under ADEA or Title VII, but actions taken by EEOC worker excused employee's neglect in filing late Title VII charge); *Lawrence v. Cooper Communities, Inc.*, 132 F.3d 447 (8th Cir.1998) (written allegations mailed to EEOC within time limit sufficed as "charge" notwithstanding EEOC delay in preparing formal charge and sending it to employee to sign).

Employer conduct, too, can equitably toll the statute of limitations. *Currier v. Radio Free Europe/Radio Liberty, Inc.*, 159 F.3d 1363 (D.C.Cir.1998) (an employer's affirmatively misleading statements that a grievance will be resolved in the employee's favor can establish an equitable estoppel); *Miranda v. B & B Cash Grocery Store, Inc.*, 975 F.2d 1518, 1532 (11th Cir.1992) (sex discrimination plaintiff was given "repeated assurances" that her salary would be raised to the level that other workers were receiving); *Coke v. General Adjustment Bureau*, 640 F.2d 584, 595 (5th Cir.1981) (employer misrepresented to employee that it would reinstate him). But an employer has no duty to apprise plaintiff of similar alleged violations respecting co-workers, so the plaintiff may not invoke tolling based on the lack of that information. *Hentosh v. Herman M. Finch Univ. of Health Sciences/Chicago Med. Sch.*, 167 F.3d 1170 (7th Cir.1999).

In a Second Circuit case, an ADEA claimant withdrew his EEOC charge in exchange for an additional year of employment as part of an OWBPA waiver of his ADEA claim. When the waiver was later found to be invalid, the court tolled the statute of limitations for the one year period of his continued employment. *See Hodge v. New York College of Podiatric Medicine*, 157 F.3d 164 (2d Cir.1998).

But the plaintiff claimed in addition that the firm had actively misled her about the reason for termination, misrepresenting that there was insufficient work for her to do when in fact there was. The court held that under the "discovery" rule, which marks the running of a claim when the plaintiff learns of an injury, both claims were barred. Plaintiff knew of the termination when it occurred, making her dismissal claim untimely, and the failure to [re-]hire claim was therefore simply an amendment to an untimely charge. By contrast, if her claim of misrepresentation proved well founded, the court held, the plaintiff could benefit from equitable tolling. It explained that active deception will toll the running of the charge-filing period until the facts that would support a charging party's allegations become apparent or should be apparent to a person having a reasonably prudent regard for her rights.[23]

Tolling does not necessarily require positive misconduct on the part of the employer. Some courts have equitably tolled the 300–day EEOC filing deadline when an unrepresented claimant receives misleading advice about filing from a state deferral agency, even when the advice is only ambiguous rather than false.[24] But equitable tolling will not save the untimely filing of a claimant who simply waits until others similarly situated complete a successful challenge to the policy affecting them all.[25] Further, there is no general doctrine that allegations of constructive discharge will equitably toll the relevant deadlines.[26]

§ 4.3 Continuing Violations

The judicially created continuing violations doctrine allows a court to find liability for a discriminatory act that occurred "outside," that is, before the beginning of, the statute of limitations period. Unlike the generous acceptance afforded the doctrine in cases brought under the Equal Pay Act,[1] the courts have sometimes severely restricted the doctrine's application in Title VII cases. With most employment practices challenged under Title VII, courts limit the employer's liability to discriminatory *acts* that occur within the limitations period; adverse *effects* of pre-period discriminatory conduct do not ordinarily revive the statute on that conduct even when those effects are felt within the period. As we shall see, however, the difference between the judicial

23. *Oshiver v. Levin, Fishbein, Sedran & Berman,* 38 F.3d 1380 (3d Cir.1994).

24. *See, e.g., Anderson v. Unisys Corp.,* 47 F.3d 302 (8th Cir.), *cert. denied,* 516 U.S. 913, 116 S.Ct. 299, 133 L.Ed.2d 205 (1995) (letter from state agency informed claimant that he had one year from the alleged discriminatory act to file an administrative charge with that agency, but also advised that the agency would file the charge with EEOC if the charge alleged federal law violations, with no mention that the EEOC filing deadline was 300 days).

25. *Chakonas v. City of Chicago,* 42 F.3d 1132 (7th Cir.1994). *But cf.* the "sin-

gle-filing" rule, discussed in Section 4.9, *infra.*

26. In constructive discharge cases, the clock begins to run on the date of the employee's allegedly forced resignation. *Draper v. Coeur Rochester, Inc.,* 147 F.3d 1104 (9th Cir.1998). *See also Hulsey v. Kmart, Inc.,* 43 F.3d 555 (10th Cir.1994) (case under ADEA) (constructive discharge, being the discriminatory act itself that gives rise to an age discrimination claim, should not be treated differently from any other adverse employment decision).

§ 4.3

1. *See* § 10.22.

acceptance of the doctrine in Title VII and EPA cases is perhaps ultimately explained by the differing conduct reached by each. The sole violation under EPA, discrimination in compensation, is by its nature continuing; Title VII, by contrast, reaches in addition a variety of other employer conduct, much of which can be conceived of as one-time or static.

In considering potentially "continuing" violations of Title VII, courts have made it clear that the timing of the specific discriminatory act identified in the complaint is crucial. At least with regard to most employment practices, it is the unlawful employment practice, not its later effects, that triggers the statute. But this apparently simple principle is complicated in circumstances where the plaintiff becomes aware or suffers the consequences of such a one-time act only later. Early commentators wrote that "[w]here the initial invasion is of an 'inherently unknowable' type the period should be postponed until the plaintiff should reasonably learn of the cause of action, whether the defendant's conduct ceases before or after the manifestation of harm."[2] The Fifth Circuit wrote in a similar vein that the EEOC charge-filing period does not begin to run "until the facts that would support a charge of discrimination under Title VII were apparent or should have been apparent to a person with a reasonably prudent regard for his rights similarly situated to the plaintiff."[3] Another important variable is the special substantive law treatment of bona fide seniority systems. A seniority systems violates Title VII only if the complainant proves intentional discrimination in its adoption or maintenance.[4]

Title VII's provision permitting back pay to accrue as far back as two years (i.e., roughly 730 days) before the filing of a charge with EEOC,[5] considered together with its 180–or at most 300–day EEOC

---

2. *Developments in the Law, Statutes of Limitations,* 63 Harv.L.Rev. 1177, 1207 (1950) (citations omitted).

3. *Reeb v. Economic Opportunity Atlanta, Inc.,* 516 F.2d 924, 931 (5th Cir.1975) (employee learned that she had been terminated on the basis of sex discrimination after the Title VII limitations period had run). *See also Anderson v. Reno,* 190 F.3d 930 (9th Cir.1999); *Galloway v. General Motors Serv. Parts Operations,* 78 F.3d 1164 (7th Cir.1996) (applying principle to environmental sexual harassment claims to discourage initiation of formal legal proceedings until harassing conduct is sufficiently continuous or aggravated that a plaintiff should be expected to recognize the conduct as actionable). For an appraisal that hostile environment claims often stem from ongoing, episodic conduct rather than one-time triggers, see *infra* this section, and § 2.22, *supra.* Another recent circuit decision endorses treating sexual harassment as a continuing violation where it consists of such continual, intermittent, and substance-re-

lated episodes rather than unrelated, isolated incidents or flagrant one-time violations. *Rush v. Scott Specialty Gases,* 113 F.3d 476 (3d Cir.1997). *See also Huckabay v. Moore,* 142 F.3d 233 (5th Cir.1998) (allowing plaintiff to rely on continuing violation doctrine for sexual harassment claim but barring claims of demotion and failure to promote as discrete instances of discriminatory conduct).

4. *See* § 703(h) of Title VII (codified at 42 U.S.C.A. § 2000e–2(h) (1994)), as construed by *International Brotherhood of Teamsters v. United States,* 431 U.S. 324, 97 S.Ct. 1843, 52 L.Ed.2d 396 (1977), *California Brewers Ass'n v. Bryant,* 444 U.S. 598, 100 S.Ct. 814, 63 L.Ed.2d 55 (1980), and *American Tobacco Co. v. Patterson,* 456 U.S. 63, 102 S.Ct. 1534, 71 L.Ed.2d 748 (1982).

5. Section 706(g), 42 U.S.C.A. § 2000e–5(g).

charge-filing deadline,[6] may obliquely support the continuing violations theory, by suggesting that Congress "envisioned continuing remediable violations that existed prior to the running of the period."[7] The argument is that unless Congress had continuing violations in mind, it would have limited relief to acts occurring no more than 180 or 300 days before the filing of the EEOC charge.[8] But this textual support is equivocal, because it is also possible to limit the 2–year relief period to cases of fraudulent concealment or estoppel.[9]

The first important Supreme Court case addressing the continuing violations doctrine is *United Air Lines, Inc. v. Evans*.[10] Evans was fired from her job as a flight attendant in 1968 because of an employment practice that required female attendants to be single. She was rehired in 1972 after the policy was terminated, but United refused to credit her with seniority for the time she worked prior to 1968. Evans would have been eligible for greater benefits, including higher pay, had she been credited for the earlier time worked. Her complaint alleged that United discriminated against her, first, by firing her in 1968 and, second, by rehiring her without seniority in 1972. She brought suit under Title VII after Title VII's statute of limitations for filing administrative charges with EEOC and local agencies had run on both claims. She argued, however, that United was guilty of a continuing violation of Title VII because the seniority system gave "present effect to a past act of discrimination."[11]

The Supreme Court affirmed a dismissal of her complaint as time barred. Writing for the majority, Justice Stevens rejected the plaintiff's argument based on the effects created by the seniority system, asserting that the "critical question is whether any present *violation* exists."[12] In short, the Court held that actionable discriminatory conduct must occur within the limitations period. Of the three possible unlawful acts— termination, rehiring without seniority, and application of the current seniority system to her terms and conditions of employment—only the last was within the period. Unfortunately for Evans, the statute had run on the 1968 firing; and the rehire claim could not be saved by a

---

6. Section 706(e)(1), 42 U.S.C.A. § 2000e–5(e)(1).

7. Zimmer, Sullivan, Richards, Calloway, *Cases and Materials On Employment Discrimination* (Little, Brown, 3d ed. 1994) 965.

8. For example, an appellate court approved the district court's awarding backpay to individuals who had applied to work earlier than two years before the filing of an EEOC charge, on the theory that, absent discriminatory hiring, they might have been employed during that two-year period. The court added, however, that any backpay recovery for those individuals would be limited to the time beginning two years before the filing of the charge. *EEOC v. O & G Spring and Wire Forms Specialty Co.*, 38

F.3d 872 (7th Cir.1994), *cert. denied*, 513 U.S. 1198, 115 S.Ct. 1270, 131 L.Ed.2d 148 (1995). *See also Kline v. City of Kansas City*, 175 F.3d 660, 666–67 (8th Cir.1999), *cert. denied*, ___ U.S. ___, 120 S.Ct. 1160, 145 L.Ed.2d 1072 (2000) (damages limited to statutory time period even where pre-limitations period evidence is admissible to establish claim).

9. Laycock, *Continuing Violations, Disparate Impact in Compensation and Other Title VII Issues*, 49 Law & Contemporary Problems 53, 58 (Autumn 1986).

10. 431 U.S. 553, 97 S.Ct. 1885, 52 L.Ed.2d 571 (1977).

11. *Id.* at 558, 97 S.Ct. at 1889.

12. *Id.* (emphasis added).

continuing violations theory predicated on the effects of the seniority system because § 703(h) was construed to immunize such systems unless they were adopted with intentionally discriminatory purpose.

Three years later, the Court applied the *Evans* principles to an alleged discriminatory discharge. In *Delaware State College v. Ricks*,[13] the College, after deciding to deny Ricks tenure in March, 1974, offered Ricks a one-year contract that would expire on June 30, 1975. On April 4, 1975, he filed a complaint with the EEOC alleging that the College had discriminated against him on the basis of race when it decided to deny him tenure. The district court dismissed the complaint as untimely, concluding that the statute of limitations had begun to run on June 26, 1974, the date the school notified Ricks of the tenure decision. Ricks argued that the statute did not begin to run until the contract expired in June 1975, because the termination was a delayed effect of the discrimination he alleged the College had committed by denying him tenure.

Quoting *Evans*, the Court reaffirmed that present effects of past discrimination are insufficient to extend the limitations period. The *Ricks* opinion specifically held that Title VII violations occur when discriminatory decisions are made, not thereafter when their effects are felt.[14] The discrimination occurred in 1974 when the tenure decision was made, and accordingly, the district court's dismissal was upheld.

Nine years later, the Court returned to the continuing violations doctrine in a seniority system context somewhat different from that presented in *Evans*. In *Lorance v. AT & T Technologies, Inc.*,[15] the plaintiffs mounted a primary challenge to a seniority system itself, alleging that it intentionally discriminated against women. The allegation of intent was necessary to sidestep the special protection afforded seniority systems by § 703(h). The system in question had been adopted in 1979, but its effects were not felt until 1982. Traditionally, male workers had predominated in the position described as "tester." Under the defendant's old seniority system, time worked at any position transferred upon an employee's promotion to the tester position. Under a new system, however, seniority as a tester included only the time spent in that position. Thus, most incumbent testers, predominantly men, had a distinct seniority advantage over women; when the company decided to decrease the number of employees in the position, the plaintiffs, women who had been promoted under the new system, were the first to be demoted.

The plaintiffs filed a complaint with the EEOC in 1983. The district court dismissed the complaint as untimely, and the Supreme Court affirmed the dismissal, relying on both *Evans* and *Ricks*. *Lorance* held

13. 449 U.S. 250, 101 S.Ct. 498, 66 L.Ed.2d 431 (1980).

14. *Id.* at 258, 101 S.Ct. at 504 (citing *Abramson v. University of Hawaii*, 594 F.2d 202, 209 (9th Cir.1979)). *See Ashley v. Boyle's Famous Corned Beef Co.*, 66 F.3d 164 (8th Cir.1995) (en banc) (applying *Ricks* to hold that claim about initial job assignment, like most hiring or firing claims, cannot benefit from continuing violation theory, but holding contra regarding ongoing pay discrimination practice).

15. 490 U.S. 900, 109 S.Ct. 2261, 104 L.Ed.2d 961 (1989).

that a plaintiff may challenge the application of a facially neutral seniority system, adopted with discriminatory intent, only when the system is applied *to her* within the limitations period, although it acknowledged that "a *facially* discriminatory ... system can be challenged anytime."[16] The Civil Rights Act of 1991 overruled *Lorance* by providing that a violation of Title VII occurs, with respect to a seniority system, not only when the system is adopted, but also when a person is injured by it.[17] Of course the current, Congressional approach does not really revive the continuing violations doctrine in the case of seniority systems; by late dating the occurrence of the unlawful employment practice, Congress made resort to the doctrine unnecessary.[18]

It is clear, however, that some Title VII violations are subject to the continuing violations doctrine. In *Bazemore v. Friday*,[19] plaintiffs challenged a public employer's pay system. Title VII became applicable to public employers, like the Service in 1972. Prior to 1965, the North Carolina Agricultural Extension Service had been divided into white and "Negro" branches. Responding to the Civil Rights Act of 1964, the Service merged the two branches, but salaries paid to the black workers, which were lower than those paid to similarly situated white workers, remained the same. The plaintiffs alleged, among other things, that the Service discriminated in pay on the basis of race, in violation of Title VII, even though the statute's charge-filing period would have run on allegations that the Service discriminated when it adopted and first applied the system. The Court held that "[e]ach week's pay check that delivers less to a black than to a similarly situated white is a wrong actionable under Title VII."[20] The Court reasoned that the Service was responsible for discriminatory payments made after Title VII was enacted even though the discrimination had begun before the defendant was subject to the statute.

This decision applies the continuing violations doctrine under Title VII, although the Court was careful to distinguish and reaffirm *Evans*. Whereas the plaintiff in *Evans* failed to challenge any present discrimination, the defendant in *Bazemore* had not "made all ... [its within-time] employment decisions in a wholly nondiscriminatory way."[21] The Court noted that evidence of past discrimination "might in some circumstances support the inference that such discrimination continued, particularly where relevant aspects of the [discriminatory] decisionmaking

---

16. 490 U.S. at 912, 109 S.Ct. at 2269 (emphasis added).

17. Section 706(e)(2).

18. Notwithstanding this provision in the Civil Rights Act, the Court may still apply its reasoning in *Lorance* in other situations. *See, e.g., Newport News Shipbuilding & Dry Dock Co. v. EEOC*, 462 U.S. 669, 686, 103 S.Ct. 2622, 2632, 77 L.Ed.2d 89 (1983) (Rehnquist, J., dissenting) (Pregnancy Discrimination Act of 1978 overturned only the holding, not the reasoning of an

earlier Court decision). The dissenters in *Newport News* now hold a majority on the Court, and thus this approach to Congressional overruling of the Court's prior construction of Title VII may now find more support.

19. 478 U.S. 385, 106 S.Ct. 3000, 92 L.Ed.2d 315 (1986).

20. *Id.* at 396, 106 S.Ct. at 3006.

21. *Id.* at 397 n.6, 106 S.Ct. at 3006 n.6.

process had undergone little change."[22] The *Lorance* majority later described *Bazemore* as involving an intentional violation that occurred within the relevant Title VII time period.

In grappling with these mixed signals from the Supreme Court, the lower federal courts have described two contrasting idealized types of claims. First is the claim, typified by a case like *Bazemore*, that an employer continuously maintains an unlawful employment practice. In such a case the "continuation of the violation into the present"[23] means that the employee may file her EEOC charge within 300 (or, in the relatively few states that do not have local antidiscrimination laws and "deferral" agencies, 180) days "after the last occurrence of an instance of that practice."[24] Second is the claim, typified by cases like *Ricks* and *Lorance*, "where the employer engaged in a discrete act of discrimination,"[25] the effects of which continue. In such a case the "present consequence of a one-time violation" does not extend the period, and so the EEOC charge must be filed within 300 (or 180) days of that discrete act.[26]

Practices falling within the first category, that are considered to continue in and of themselves rather than simply through their effects, include, in addition to the salary discrimination discussed in *Bazemore*, ongoing denials of promotion[27] or union membership[28] and nonstriking, repeated episodes of "hostile environment" or "nontangible" racial or sexual harassment. Thus so long as at least one alleged act of harassment occurred within the 300–day charge-filing period, courts will admit related evidence, antedating the beginning of that period, that constitutes part of the same general pattern of conduct that altered the plaintiff's conditions of employment or created an abusive work environment.[29] Decisions differ, however, in the degree of nexus they require

22. *Id.* at 402, 106 S.Ct. at 3010 (Brennan, J., concurring) (quoting *Hazelwood Sch. Dist. v. United States*, 433 U.S. 299, 309–10, 97 S.Ct. 2736, 2742–43, 53 L.Ed.2d 768 (1977)). *Cf. Stewart v. Rutgers*, 120 F.3d 426 (3d Cir.1997) (previous acts of discrimination, though time barred, are relevant to show subsequent discrimination).

23. *Webb v. Indiana Nat'l Bank*, 931 F.2d 434, 438 (7th Cir.1991).

24. *Beavers v. American Cast Iron Pipe Co.*, 975 F.2d 792, 796 (11th Cir.1992).

25. *Id.*

26. *Webb*, 931 F.2d at 438. For other decisions recognizing this distinction, see *EEOC v. Westinghouse Elec. Corp.*, 725 F.2d 211, 219 (3d Cir.1983), *cert. denied*, 469 U.S. 820, 105 S.Ct. 92, 83 L.Ed.2d 38 (1984); *Williams v. Owens–Illinois, Inc.*, 665 F.2d 918, 925 n. 3 (9th Cir.), *cert. denied*, 459 U.S. 971, 103 S.Ct. 302, 74 L.Ed.2d 283 (1982); and *Association Against Discrimination in Employment, Inc. v. Bridgeport*, 647 F.2d 256, 274 (2d Cir.1981), *cert. denied*, 455 U.S. 988, 102 S.Ct. 1611, 71 L.Ed.2d 847 (1982).

27. *Gonzalez v. Firestone Tire & Rubber Co.*, 610 F.2d 241, 249 (5th Cir.1980). *See also Thigpen v. Bibb County*, 223 F.3d 1231, 2000 WL 1277600, at *10 (11th Cir.2000) (distinguishing ongoing violations and a series of repeated violations, and finding that a series of discriminatory promotion denials was not subject to the continuing violations doctrine) (case under § 1983).

28. *See Alexander v. Local 496, Laborers' Int'l Union*, 177 F.3d 394 (6th Cir. 1999), *cert. denied*, ___ U.S. ___, 120 S.Ct. 1158, 145 L.Ed.2d 1070 (2000) (union practice of refusing membership to African–Americans based on "working-in-the-calling" rule was ongoing and actionable even though some denials occurred before the beginning of the charge-filing period).

29. *See Thigpen v. Bibb County*, 223 F.3d 1231, 2000 WL 1277600, at *10 n. 19 (11th Cir.2000) (evidence of an act of discrimination which is not made the basis for

between the harassing conduct occurring before and that occurring within the charge-filing period. One decision holds, for example, that there is no requirement that the discriminatory conduct of each co-worker who participated in creating the hostile environment must have taken place both before and during that period, so long as there was evidence of employer awareness of a hostile work environment both before the period began and thereafter.[30] A later opinion, however, found the nexus between the harassment allegedly occurring before and that allegedly occurring within that period insufficient to permit the introduction of evidence concerning the former conduct.[31] Environmental sexual harassment is eligible for continuing violation treatment when it consists of an ongoing series of non-outrageous, not physically invasive incidents that in the aggregate nevertheless unreasonably interfere with the plaintiff's work environment, with the claim accruing only after several such incidents occur.[32] But the continuing violation theory generally fails where the harassment consists of a "discrete trigger event and the discrimination is overt,"[33] or where the pre-limitations periods acts are different in kind or temporally isolated.[34]

In one recent Eleventh Circuit decision, the male plaintiff alleged that his employer's facially neutral practice of providing insurance coverage only to those employees' children who resided full time with an employee-parent had a disproportionate adverse impact on the benefits package of male employees, as they were awarded custody significantly less frequently than female employees. The court treated the violation as continuing, rejecting the defendant's argument that the lack of coverage

a timely charge is admissible as relevant background); *Hawkins v. PepsiCo, Inc.*, 203 F.3d 274, 281 n. 2 (4th Cir.), *cert. denied*, __ U.S. __, __ S.Ct. __, 121 S.Ct. 181, 148 L.Ed.2d 125 (2000); *Kline v. City of Kansas City*, 175 F.3d 660 (8th Cir.1999), *cert. denied*, __ U.S. __, 120 S.Ct. 1160, 145 L.Ed.2d 1072 (2000) (allowing plaintiff to establish hostile work environment claim with evidence well before limitations period but denying the same with respect to her disparate treatment claim); *Tinsley v. First Union Nat'l Bank*, 155 F.3d 435, 442–43 (4th Cir.1998); *Draper v. Coeur Rochester, Inc.*, 147 F.3d 1104 (9th Cir.1998). *But see Quinn v. Green Tree Credit Corp.*, 159 F.3d 759 (2d Cir.1998) (when alleged acts of sexual harassment are not continuous in nature, continuing violation doctrine is not available); *DeNovellis v. Shalala*, 124 F.3d 298 (1st Cir.1997) (where scattered derogatory remarks are not pervasive enough to constitute a hostile work environment, employee could not rely on continuing violation doctrine).

30. *West v. Philadelphia Elec. Co.*, 45 F.3d 744 (3d Cir.1995).

31. *Annis v. County of Westchester*, 136 F.3d 239 (2d Cir.1998) (although evidence of prior bad acts was probative, potential prejudice justified exclusion even when plaintiff asserts a continuing violation); *Koelsch v. Beltone Electronics Corp.*, 46 F.3d 705 (7th Cir.1995).

32. See cases cited *supra* § 2.22.

33. *See Garrison v. Burke*, 165 F.3d 565 (7th Cir.1999) (where harasser allegedly forcibly and painfully touched plaintiff's breasts and kissed her on lips, she did not require subsequent events to put her on notice of the potential unlawfulness of his conduct); *Webb v. Cardiothoracic Surgery Associates of N. Texas*, 139 F.3d 532 (5th Cir.1998). *Cf. West*, 45 F.3d 744. *But cf. Stoll v. Runyon*, 165 F.3d 1238 (9th Cir. 1999) (where sexual harassment so severe that it renders plaintiff psychologically disabled from assisting or even communicating directly with her attorney, equitable tolling appropriate).

34. *See, e.g., Anderson v. Reno*, 190 F.3d 930 (9th Cir.1999) (incidents occurring outside time period should be considered by factfinder in establishing hostile work environment when acts show a pattern unless the acts are isolated or different in kind.)

is merely the "residual effect of a single discriminatory act," namely, the company's first implementation of the policy. Rather, "each week in which divorced men are denied insurance coverage for their nonresident children ... constitutes a wrong arguably actionable under Title VII."[35]

Such decisions reflect that, notwithstanding *Lorance*, most neutral practices with allegedly unlawful discriminatory effects may be challenged as continuing violations. The *Lorance* plaintiffs were out of time to challenge the facially neutral seniority system there as having been originally adopted with discriminatory intent; and it was only the special, substantive insulation that § 703(h) affords bona fide, facially neutral seniority systems that prevented them from attacking the system's ongoing consequences.[36] Other courts have similarly cabined *Lorance* to the seniority system context.[37]

Despite this general agreement on which kinds of claims are susceptible to continuing violation treatment, there remain differences in application. It is not always easy to distinguish between an ongoing unlawful practice and "the delayed consequence of a single discriminatory act" that took place long before an EEOC charge is filed.[38] The circuits are split, for example, on when the limitations period begins to run on challenges to hiring lists compiled from discriminatory test results. The Ninth Circuit, reasoning that no one on such a list would be *certain* of a discriminatory impact until the list was no longer in use, concluded that an EEOC complaint was timely if filed within a limitations period marked from the date the hiring list expired.[39] But the Third Circuit, following the *Ricks* holding that the discriminatory decision puts the complainant on notice of *likely* adverse effect, requires that the complaint be filed within a limitations period that runs from the date the hiring list was compiled.[40] And while the First Circuit holds that a challenge to a subjective employment evaluation is not time barred if filed within a limitations period that runs from the date the evaluation resulted in adverse effect,[41] the Seventh Circuit holds that it is an actual denial of training, not a later layoff based on the lack of training, that triggers the statute.[42]

35. *Beavers,* 975 F.2d at 798.

36. *Id.,* (describing the Supreme Court in *Lorance* as acknowledging that the allegations of the plaintiffs there "normally would have been sufficient to state a [timely] cause of action for discrimination under the disparate impact theory.")

37. *See, e.g., Webb v. Indiana Nat'l Bank,* 931 F.2d at 438; *Hendrix v. Yazoo City,* 911 F.2d 1102, 1104 (5th Cir.1990).

38. *See Beavers,* 975 F.2d at 799.

39. *Bouman v. Block,* 940 F.2d 1211 (9th Cir.1991), *cert. denied,* 502 U.S. 1005, 112 S.Ct. 640, 116 L.Ed.2d 658 (1991).

40. *Bronze Shields, Inc. v. New Jersey Dep't of Civil Serv.,* 667 F.2d 1074 (3d Cir.

1981), *cert. denied,* 458 U.S. 1122, 102 S.Ct. 3510, 73 L.Ed.2d 1384 (1982).

41. *See Thomas v. Eastman Kodak Co.,* 183 F.3d 38 (1st Cir.1999), *cert. denied,* ___ U.S. ___, 120 S.Ct. 1174, 145 L.Ed.2d 1082 (2000); *Johnson v. General Elec.,* 840 F.2d 132 (1st Cir.1988).

42. *Hamilton v. Komatsu Dresser Indus., Inc.,* 964 F.2d 600 (7th Cir.), *cert. denied,* 506 U.S. 916, 113 S.Ct. 324, 121 L.Ed.2d 244 (1992). *See also Turlington v. Atlanta Gas Light Co.,* 135 F.3d 1428 (11th Cir.), *cert. denied,* 525 U.S. 962, 119 S.Ct. 405, 142 L.Ed.2d 329 (1998).

As noted above, the courts have manifested widespread acceptance of the continuing violations theory in cases brought under the Equal Pay Act. *Ross v. Buckeye Cellulose Corp.*,[43] illustrates that the same liberality may not be accorded if a compensation discrimination claim is pursued under Title VII. Ross brought his action four years after he was subjected to a wage determination program that allegedly discriminated on the basis of race. Because the statute of limitations had tolled on the discrimination allegedly perpetrated when the program was first applied to him, Ross argued that paychecks he received later "continued" the violation into the limitations period. But the Eleventh Circuit, relying on *Evans*, *Ricks*, and *Lorance*, rejected Ross's attempt to cure Title VII untimeliness via the continuing violations doctrine. The Court distinguished *Bazemore* by noting that the pay system in that case was facially discriminatory, while the system in the case at bar was not.[44] The consensus in EPA cases, however, is that an actionable violation occurs each time an employee receives an "unequal" paycheck.[45] Had someone in Ross' situation filed a claim under the Equal Pay Act, any "unequal" paycheck within the limitations period would have avoided the limitations problem, because each paycheck would be recognized as a separate actionable violation regardless of the underlying cause that produced the unequal amount. So although compensation discrimination based on sex can serve as the basis of a claim under both EPA and Title VII, an EPA claim may offer late filing plaintiffs a critical procedural advantage.[46]

§ 4.4   Charge–Filing Procedure

Within the 180– or 300–day period described above, a charge may be filed either by an aggrieved individual or a commissioner of EEOC.[1] It need only be in writing, be subscribed to by oath or affirmation, and contain "such information and be in such form as the Commission [by regulation] requires;[2] and Commission regulations require only that the charge include" a clear and concise statement of the facts, including the pertinent dates, constituting the alleged unlawful employment practices.[3] Nevertheless, the complainant, to protect her ability to commence a

---

43. 980 F.2d 648 (11th Cir.1993), *cert. denied*, 513 U.S. 814, 115 S.Ct. 69, 130 L.Ed.2d 24 (1994).

44. *See also Miller v. American Family Mut. Ins. Co.*, 203 F.3d 997, 1003–04 (7th Cir.2000) (rejecting continuing violation theory for unequal pay claim under the PDA, reasoning that if the plaintiff knew, or with the exercise of reasonable diligence would have known after each act that it was discriminatory and had harmed her, she must sue over that act within the relevant statute of limitations).

45. *See, e.g., Gandy v. Sullivan County*, 24 F.3d 861 (6th Cir.1994). *See also* § 8.22, *infra*.

46. It is not clear how the reasoning of this opinion squares with that of another

Eleventh Circuit panel the year before in *Beavers*, 975 F.2d at 796, discussed *supra*.

§ 4.4

1. Title VII § 706(b), 42 U.S.C.A. § 2000e–5(b).

2. Section 706(b), 42 U.S.C.A. § 2000e–5(b). Some courts require that a charge information form be verified to qualify as a "charge" meeting the statutory requirement. *See Lawrence v. Cooper Communities, Inc.*, 132 F.3d 447 (8th Cir.1998); *Schlueter v. Anheuser–Busch, Inc.*, 132 F.3d 455 (8th Cir.1998) (EEOC intake questionnaire did not suffice as "charge" under ADEA or Title VII).

3. 29 CFR § 1601.12(a)(3) (1994).

judicial action should she remain aggrieved after the relief if any is afforded through the EEOC proceedings, must provide the defendant notice of the ground or grounds of prohibited discrimination alleged as well as the circumstances giving rise to the charge through a timely filed charge.[4]

EEOC regulations provide that certain amendments to charges may relate back to the filing date of the original charge, and if so would be deemed timely although the amendment was not made until after the applicable 180– or 300–day deadline. Under the regulations, an amendment, to be eligible for relation back, must correct technical defects or omissions, clarify or amplify the allegations in the original charge, or add new allegations "related to or growing out of the subject matter of the original charge."[5] The last category is naturally the most controversial, and the lower federal courts have devised a variety of formulations to gauge whether allegations in amendment meet the quoted requirement.[6]

Regardless of who files a charge, EEOC is required to serve a notice of the charge on the respondent or respondents, setting forth the "date, place and circumstances of the alleged unlawful employment practice," within ten days after its filing.[7] The statute protects the confidentiality of Commission proceedings by stipulating criminal penalties if a Commission employee, prior to the institution of a judicial proceeding, makes public information obtained by the Commission.[8] This prohibition, however, does not apply to the charging party.[9] To protect the Commission's role as a guardian of the public interest, courts have regularly invalidated private agreements, usually entered into to settle an ongoing dispute,

---

4. See 42 U.S.C.A. § 2000e–5(e)(1); 29 C.F.R. § 1601.13 (1998).

5. 29 C.F.R. § 1601.12(b).

6. Compare the permissive test that allows relation back of claims based on different legal theories, so long as each derives from the same operative facts described in the original charge, *Hornsby v. Conoco, Inc.*, 777 F.2d 243, 247 (5th Cir.1985); *Washington v. Kroger Co.*, 671 F.2d 1072, 1075–76 (8th Cir.1982); *Alexander v. Precision Machining, Inc.*, 990 F.Supp. 1304, 1310 (D.Kan.1997); *Conroy v. Boston Edison Co.*, 758 F.Supp. 54, 58 (D.Mass.1991) with the more restrictive one that will not permit relation back of an amendment advancing a new theory of recovery, even when the new allegations arise out of the same events described in the timely filed charge. *See Simms v. Oklahoma ex rel. Dep't of Mental Health and Substance Abuse Servs.*, 165 F.3d 1321, 1326–27 (10th Cir.), *cert. denied*, 528 U.S. 815, 120 S.Ct. 53, 145 L.Ed.2d 46 (1999) (no relation back of retaliation claim based on events antedating the filing of race discrimination claim); *Gunnell v. Utah Valley State College*, 152 F.3d 1253, 1260 n. 3 (10th Cir.1998) (sexual harassment claim

in amended charge could not relate back to original charge, which alleged only retaliation); *Fairchild v. Forma*, 147 F.3d 567, 575 (7th Cir.1998) (untimely amendment alleging entirely new theory does not relate back); *Evans v. Technologies Applications & Serv. Co.*, 80 F.3d 954, 963 (4th Cir.1996) (denying relation back of age discrimination to underlying sex discrimination claim); *Pejic v. Hughes Helicopters, Inc.*, 840 F.2d 667, 675 (9th Cir.1988) (same); *Hopkins v. Digital Equip. Corp.*, 1998 WL 702339, at *2 (S.D.N.Y.1998) (denying the relation back of retaliation and disability claims asserted in amended charge because neither claim flowed from underlying claim of race discrimination). *Cf. Conroy*, 758 F.Supp. at 58, permitting relation back where the protected categories relied on in the original and amended charges are related, as with race and national origin.

7. *Id.*

8. Section 709(e), 42 U.S.C.A. § 2000e–8(e).

9. *See EEOC v. Associated Dry Goods Corp.*, 449 U.S. 590, 598–604, 101 S.Ct. 817, 822–25, 66 L.Ed.2d 762 (1981).

whereby an employee or former employee agrees not to file a charge with EEOC or not to assist in an EEOC investigation.[10]

The Agency is entitled to examine and copy evidence of any person under investigation that is "relevant to the charge under investigation."[11] The Supreme Court has construed the statute to give the Commission administrative subpoena power to enforce its right of access to evidence in the possession of an investigated person that is relevant to a prohibited unlawful employment practice and the charge in question.[12] The charge must meet the minimal statutory requirements before an EEOC subpoena warrants judicial enforcement,[13] but no greater detail is required for a "pattern or practice" charge than for charges alleging individual instances of discrimination.[14] In addition, compliance with the notice requirement is apparently a jurisdictional prerequisite to judicial enforcement of the subpoena,[15] but the notice, like the detail concerning the objects of the subpoena, need be no more elaborate in a pattern or practice case.[16] The Court has fortified the Commission's subpoena authority by refusing to recognize a common-law privilege for academic institutions that would have required the Commission to show particularized need for subpoenaed documents, rather than mere relevance.[17] Similarly, the Seventh Circuit, observing that under Federal Rule of Evidence 501 state law privileges do not apply in federal litigation, has upheld on federal supremacy grounds an EEOC subpoena for a tran-

10. EEOC has categorically refused to enforce employee agreements not to file a charge or participate in an EEOC proceeding. The agency treats such agreements as "null and void" regardless of whether they are contained in employee handbooks, individual contracts, or waiver agreements entered into as part of a settlement agreement. *EEOC Guidance on Waivers Under Civil Rights Laws*, No. 915.002 (April 10, 1997). *See also EEOC v. Astra USA, Inc.*, 94 F.3d 738, 744 (1st Cir.1996) (affirming injunction prohibiting employer from enforcing settlement agreement provisions that purported to bar employees from assisting EEOC in investigating charges); *EEOC v. Cosmair, Inc.*, 821 F.2d 1085, 1090 (5th Cir.1987) (invalidating employee promise not to file EEOC charge). The Supreme Court has recognized the invalidity of such an agreement even where the employee has also agreed to arbitrate a statutory discrimination claim and is accordingly required to arbitrate on the employer's demand before pursuing (or perhaps in lieu of pursuing) a judicial action. *See Gilmer v. Interstate/Johnson Lane Corp.*, 500 U.S. 20, 28, 111 S.Ct. 1647, 1653, 114 L.Ed.2d 26 (1991), discussed in § 4.6, *infra*. On the other hand, the Commission and the courts recognize that an employer who has secured an otherwise valid *settlement* waiver agreement can effectively shield itself from *fur-*

ther recovery sought by an employee filing an employment discrimination charge. *EEOC Guidance, supra*; *EEOC v. Astra USA*, 94 F.3d at 744.

11. Section 709(a), 42 U.S.C.A. § 2000e–8.

12. *See generally EEOC v. Shell Oil Co.*, 466 U.S. 54, 104 S.Ct. 1621, 80 L.Ed.2d 41 (1984).

13. *Id.* at 65, 104 S.Ct. at 1629.

14. *Id.* at 67–68 n. 19, 104 S.Ct. at 1630–31 n. 19. For an example of the generous judicial attitude toward enforcement of EEOC subpoenas, especially in "pattern" cases, *see EEOC v. Lockheed Martin Corp.*, 116 F.3d 110 (4th Cir.1997) (requiring employer to turn over computerized personnel files to enable agency to "better focus its investigation" and enhance the "efficient search for information" where it was investigating more than 20 charges).

15. *Id.* at 66–67, 104 S.Ct. at 1629–31.

16. *Id.* at 79, 81, 104 S.Ct. at 1636, 1637.

17. *University of Pa. v. EEOC*, 493 U.S. 182, 110 S.Ct. 577, 107 L.Ed.2d 571 (1990). But the agency's subpoena power is limited by the attorney-client and work product privileges. *EEOC v. Lutheran Soc. Servs.*, 186 F.3d 959 (D.C.Cir.1999).

script of a state unemployment compensation hearing.[18] The 300–day charge-filing deadline does not serve as a temporal limit on the scope of EEOC's subpoena, which may reach records dating from three years or more before the alleged unlawful employment practice.[19] While no statute of limitations applies to an EEOC pattern or practice suit, employers have on rare occasions successfully argued laches.[20]

Recognizing the Agency's public function, the Supreme Court has declined to limit the EEOC's ability, after investigation, to seek judicial enforcement in its own name to the 180–day period in which it alone, to the exclusion of a private party, may file suit.[21] But a circuit court has held that once private parties have initiated litigation by requesting right to sue notices from the Agency and filing a civil complaint based on the events described in their EEOC charges, EEOC, whatever its independent power to file suit in its own name, may no longer continue to investigate.[22]

§ 4.5 From EEOC to Action in Federal or State Court

The EEOC investigation ultimately arrives at one of two basic conclusions. After investigation, the Agency may find "reasonable cause" to believe that the Act has been violated, and must then undertake conciliation; or it may find "no reasonable cause" and issue a notice of dismissal.[1] In either event, a complainant is entitled upon demand to receive a "right-to-sue" letter from EEOC no later than 180 days after the effective date of the filing of a charge with the agency.[2] Since EEOC has not uncommonly taken many months or even years to process charges, the question has arisen how long a prospective Title VII plaintiff may wait beyond 180 days before demanding a right-to-sue letter. Courts have occasionally barred Title VII actions in these circumstances on grounds of laches, when a delay of several years in demanding a suit letter was deemed unreasonable and caused tangible prejudice to the defendant.[3] An appellate court has reached the opposite conclusion

---

18. *EEOC v. Illinois Dep't of Employment Sec.*, 995 F.2d 106 (7th Cir.1993).

19. *EEOC v. Ford Motor Credit Co.*, 26 F.3d 44 (6th Cir.1994).

20. See § 4.8, *infra*.

21. *Occidental Life Ins. Co. v. EEOC*, 432 U.S. 355, 97 S.Ct. 2447, 53 L.Ed.2d 402 (1977). For a discussion of the several limits on a private party's judicial action, see § 4.2, *supra*.

22. *EEOC v. Hearst Corp.*, 103 F.3d 462 (5th Cir.1997) (denying enforcement of EEOC subpoenas because Agency lacked continuing authority to investigate).

§ 4.5

1. 42 U.S.C.A. § 2000e–5.

2. *Id. McDonnell Douglas Corp. v. Green*, 411 U.S. 792, 93 S.Ct. 1817, 36 L.Ed.2d 668 (1973), holds *inter alia* that an

EEOC finding of no reasonable cause does not impair the charging party's ability to proceed against the respondent in court.

3. *See, e.g., National Ass'n of Gov't Employees v. San Antonio City Public Serv. Bd.*, 40 F.3d 698 (5th Cir.1994) (invoking doctrine to bar suit brought nine years after termination of EEOC conciliation efforts, during which period Department of Justice failed to issue plaintiffs right to sue letter or notify them of intent to prosecute and plaintiffs' counsel made no inquiry of either agency as to status of charges). The Fifth Circuit applied the standard elements of common law laches, an unexcused delay by plaintiff in initiating suit that causes the defendant undue prejudice in its ability to defend. *Cf. Ashley v. Boyle's Famous Corned Beef Co.*, 48 F.3d 1051 (8th Cir. 1995) (laches based on delay in filing charge with EEOC). *But see Springer v. Partners*

under ADEA, reasoning that laches cannot be a bar under a federal statute that contains a statute of limitations, as ADEA did until its recent amendment in 1991.[4] And what if EEOC, recognizing that its backlog prevents it from promptly addressing the charge, is willing to issue the right to sue notice *before* the end of its 180–day period of presumptive exclusive jurisdiction specified by 42 U.S.C.A. § 2000e–5(f)(1)? Two of three circuits to address the question squarely have held that the plaintiff may proceed to court, provided she files within 90 days of receiving the notice.[5]

Title VII affords plaintiffs a liberal federal venue choice among the districts where the alleged unlawful employment practice occurred; where records pertaining to the practice are maintained; or where the plaintiff allegedly would have worked but for the unlawful practice.[6] When the prospective defendant cannot be "found" in any of the above districts, the statute provides as a default the district where it has its principal office.[7] The text also indicates that each of these districts is a suitable place for the action to be transferred under 28 U.S.C.A. §§ 1404 and 1406.[8] It has recently been held that in considering a motion for transfer under Title VII, the court should apply the same considerations of party and witness convenience that ordinarily apply under those sections, rejecting the argument that the special Title VII venue choices are intended to give plaintiff the last word on forum selection.[9]

Although the vast majority of Title VII actions have been brought in federal court, it is settled that state courts have concurrent jurisdiction.[10] The reasons a plaintiff may opt for state over federal court are similar to

---

in Care, 17 F.Supp.2d 133 (E.D.N.Y.1998) (allowing pro se plaintiff to proceed despite 13 year delay; EEOC allowed charge to languish for 10 years with no action and employer failed to make specific showing of prejudice).

4. *Miller v. Maxwell's Int'l, Inc.,* 991 F.2d 583 (9th Cir.1993), *cert. denied,* 510 U.S. 1109, 114 S.Ct. 1049, 127 L.Ed.2d 372 (1994).

5. *Sims v. Trus Joist MacMillan,* 22 F.3d 1059 (11th Cir.1994) (EEOC's use of its full 180 days of exclusive jurisdiction is not a prerequisite to the subject matter jurisdiction of a court); *Brown v. Puget Sound Elec. Apprenticeship & Training Trust,* 732 F.2d 726, 729 (9th Cir.1984), *cert. denied,* 469 U.S. 1108, 105 S.Ct. 784, 83 L.Ed.2d 778 (1985). *Cf. Weise v. Syracuse Univ.,* 522 F.2d 397, 412 (2d Cir.1975) (allowing early issuance of notice of right to sue on ad hoc basis). But the District of Columbia Circuit disagrees, reasoning that early issue will often pretermit EEOC's fulfillment of its independent, mandatory statutory obligation to investigate the charge and make a reasonable cause determination "as promptly as possible and, so far as

practicable, not later than one hundred and twenty days from the filing of the charge." *Martini v. Federal Nat'l Mortgage Ass'n,* 178 F.3d 1336 (D.C.Cir.1999), *cert. denied,* ___ U.S. ___, 120 S.Ct. 1155, 145 L.Ed.2d 1065 (2000) (quoting 42 U.S.C.A. § 2000e–5(b)). District court decisions from other circuits are about equally divided on the issue. *See* cases cited in *Martini.*

6. Title VII § 706(f)(3), 42 U.S.C.A. § 2000e–5(f)(3).

7. *Id.*

8. *See id.,* providing that the "principal office" district shall be considered one in which the action "might have been brought," a designation that makes it a suitable transferee district under the Supreme Court's decision in *Hoffman v. Blaski,* 363 U.S. 335, 80 S.Ct. 1084, 4 L.Ed.2d 1254 (1960).

9. *Ross v. Buckeye Cellulose Corp.,* 980 F.2d 648, 655 (11th Cir.1993), *cert. denied,* 513 U.S. 814, 115 S.Ct. 69, 130 L.Ed.2d 24 (1994).

10. *Yellow Freight Sys., Inc. v. Donnelly,* 494 U.S. 820, 110 S.Ct. 1566, 108 L.Ed.2d 834 (1990).

the choice-influencing considerations pertaining to claims under § 1983.[11] For example, a political read of the state court judge, as compared to the counterpart federal judge who is significantly insulated from popular reaction to her decisions by life tenure during good behavior, may attract the plaintiff. So might less congested state court calendars. Differences in evidentiary and procedural rules may also influence decision. And the plaintiff's interest in interim or injunctive relief may be better served by filing in state court.[12]

In any event, a complainant who wishes to sue in either state or federal court must commence an action (by filing a complaint with the court)[13] within 90 days after *receipt* of the EEOC "right-to-sue" letter or notice of dismissal.[14] That deadline is generally strictly enforced, although it, like the administrative charge-filing deadline, is amenable to equitable tolling,[15] estoppel, or waiver.[16] To benefit from tolling, howev-

11. These are discussed more fully in Chapter 12 on Procedure.

12. Of course a putative plaintiff with intentional race discrimination claims and a need for immediate injunctive relief will in that respect be better served by proceeding under § 1981 than under Title VII, because no administrative exhaustion is required under the Reconstruction-era statutes.

13. Federal Rule 3, which equates commencement with the timely filing of the complaint, rather than with subsequent service, provides the guide for measuring compliance with the 90–day requirement. *See West v. Conrail*, discussed in Chapter 12.

14. The statute in terms calls for the civil action to be brought "within ninety days after the *giving* of such notice" 42 U.S.C.A. § 2000e–5(f)(1) (emphasis supplied). But the courts have consistently equated the "giving" of notice with the date when notice is constructively "received" upon its delivery to the address the charging party left with EEOC. *See, e.g., Graham–Humphreys v. Memphis Brooks Museum of Art*, 209 F.3d 552 (6th Cir.2000) (plaintiff constructively received right-to-sue notice when the letter carrier deposited the first of two certified-letter notifications at plaintiff's last known address); *Scholar v. Pacific Bell*, 963 F.2d 264, 267 (9th Cir.), *cert. denied*, 506 U.S. 868, 113 S.Ct. 196, 121 L.Ed.2d 139 (1992); *Harvey v. City of New Bern Police Dep't*, 813 F.2d 652, 654 (4th Cir.1987) (no equitable tolling where plaintiff knew of right to sue letter within six days after it arrived and therefore still had 84 days to file from the date of constructive receipt). The claimant may not secure a suspension of the 90–day deadline for the time between constructive and actual receipt, however, where she has failed to retrieve a notice that presumably identified

EEOC as sender, to notify EEOC of a change of address, or to take steps to check on mail at a former address. *See Zillyette v. Capital One Fin. Corp.*, 179 F.3d 1337 (11th Cir.1999) (duty to retrieve letter when post office notice apparently identifies EEOC as sender); *Nelmida v. Shelly Eurocars, Inc.*, 112 F.3d 380 (9th Cir.), *cert. denied*, 522 U.S. 858, 118 S.Ct. 158, 139 L.Ed.2d 103 (1997); *Hill v. John Chezik Imports*, 869 F.2d 1122 (8th Cir.1989) (denying equitable tolling where claimant failed to inform EEOC of change of address); *Banks v. Rockwell Int'l N. Am. Aircraft Operations*, 855 F.2d 324, 325 (6th Cir.1988) (90 days begins to run 5 days after EEOC mailed the notice to address of record); *St. Louis v. Alverno College*, 744 F.2d 1314, 1315 (7th Cir.1984). Where, on the other hand, the charging party does take reasonable steps to ensure his receipt of mail delivered to the address he provided EEOC, the 90 days may not begin to run until actual receipt. *Jackson v. Continental Cargo–Denver*, 183 F.3d 1186 (10th Cir.1999); *Houston v. Sidley & Austin*, 185 F.3d 837 (7th Cir.1999); *Archie v. Chicago Truck Drivers Union*, 585 F.2d 210 (7th Cir.1978). Tolling may be found where EEOC misinformed plaintiff of timeliness obligations. *Browning v. AT&T Paradyne*, 120 F.3d 222 (11th Cir.1997) (per curiam). In the case of federal employees, the plaintiff must commence the civil action within 90 days after the administrative complaint is dismissed. *Robbins v. Bentsen*, 41 F.3d 1195 (7th Cir.1994).

15. Where the employer's own outrageous acts leave plaintiff traumatized to the point of incapacity, the limitations period may be tolled, even if plaintiff is represented by counsel. *See Stoll v. Runyon*, 165 F.3d 1238 (9th Cir.1999). *But see Biester v. Midwest Health Servs., Inc.*, 77 F.3d 1264 (10th

er, the plaintiff may have to show her own due diligence;[17] and if she asserts that she was misled into failing to file within 90 days, she may have to show active deception on the part of the defendant or that she was lulled into inaction in reliance on pending state or federal agency proceedings or advice.[18] Related actions under the Reconstruction Civil Rights Acts may be commenced even before Title VII charges have been administratively processed, but the limitations periods and administrative deadlines of the respective statutes must be satisfied independently.[19]

Because the only two prerequisites for Title VII private party[20] actions are a timely filed EEOC charge (i.e., within 180 or, in a deferral state, 300 days after the alleged unlawful employment practice) followed by commencement of a judicial action within 90 days after the charging

Cir.1996) (depression of plaintiff, represented by counsel, insufficient to justify tolling).

16. *See Baldwin County Welcome Ctr. v. Brown*, 466 U.S. 147, 104 S.Ct. 1723, 80 L.Ed.2d 196 (1984). The requirement that a putative plaintiff receive a right-to-sue letter before, rather than after, commencing a civil action is a statutory precondition subject to equitable modification, rather than an inflexible jurisdictional prerequisite, *see Pietras v. Board of Fire Comm'rs*, 180 F.3d 468 (2d Cir.1999) and *Rivers v. Barberton Bd. of Educ.*, 143 F.3d 1029, 1032 (6th Cir.1998); nevertheless, a plaintiff's lack of cooperation with EEOC has been held to disentitle her to such equitable relief. *Forehand v. Florida State Hosp.*, 89 F.3d 1562 (11th Cir.1996). For examples of the sparing use of equitable tolling to extend the suit-filing period beyond 90 days after the date of constructive receipt, see the cases cited *supra*.

17. *See South v. Saab Cars USA, Inc.*, 28 F.3d 9 (2d Cir.1994) (mailing complaint to the sheriff, rather than the court, one day before the deadline not sufficient diligence to permit plaintiff to invoke equitable tolling). And the employer's display of a poster notifying employees of the applicable limitations period for bringing a Title VII claim as required by law precludes tolling based on the plaintiff's asserted ignorance of statutory filing requirements. *Clark v. Runyon*, 116 F.3d 275 (7th Cir.1997). *See also Washington v. Washington Metro. Area Transit Auth.*, 160 F.3d 750 (D.C.Cir.1998), *cert. denied*, 527 U.S. 1038, 119 S.Ct. 2399, 144 L.Ed.2d 798 (1999) (employer's touting of own internal grievance procedure as appropriate forum does not equitably toll time limits where employer included non-misleading information about EEOC and complaint procedure); *Belhomme v. Widnall*, 127 F.3d 1214 (10th Cir.1997), *cert. denied*, 523 U.S. 1100, 118 S.Ct. 1569, 140 L.Ed.2d

803 (1998) (a timely petition submitted to EEOC for reconsideration of EEOC decision will toll the filing deadline for a suit in district court, but an untimely petition will have no tolling effect).

Generally, an attorney's delinquency is chargeable to the client and, at all events, is not a basis for equitable tolling. However, fraudulent conduct by plaintiff's own counsel may equitably toll the limitations period. *See Seitzinger v. Reading Hosp. and Med. Ctr.*, 165 F.3d 236 (3d Cir.1999) (where counsel repeatedly misrepresented to client that he had filed her Title VII complaint, statute is tolled).

18. *See Simons v. Southwest Petro-Chem, Inc.*, 28 F.3d 1029 (10th Cir.1994) (defense counsel's mere acknowledgment that employee would file a second suit after taking a voluntary dismissal without prejudice not sufficiently deceptive to trigger equitable tolling).

19. *Johnson v. Railway Express Agency, Inc.*, 421 U.S. 454, 95 S.Ct. 1716, 44 L.Ed.2d 295 (1975). *See* text § 1.2.

20. There is authority that federal employees, apparently unlike employees of either private or state or local government employers, must actually *exhaust* their administrative remedies, and so may lose the right to sue if they reject what a court later determines to have been an offer of full relief at the agency level. *Francis v. Brown*, 58 F.3d 191 (5th Cir.1995); *Wrenn v. Secretary, Dep't of Veterans Affairs*, 918 F.2d 1073 (2d Cir.1990), *cert. denied*, 499 U.S. 977, 111 S.Ct. 1625, 113 L.Ed.2d 721 (1991). *But see Greenlaw v. Garrett*, 59 F.3d 994 (9th Cir.1995), *cert. denied sub nom. Greenlaw v. Dalton*, 519 U.S. 836, 117 S.Ct. 110, 136 L.Ed.2d 63 (1996) (pro se federal Title VII plaintiff need not assess if administrative relief is full in order to exhaust remedies). See § 4.7 *infra* on federal employees.

party receives EEOC's notice of right to sue, the right to bring a judicial lawsuit does not turn on EEOC's evaluation of the probable merits of a charge. The judicial action may be commenced even if EEOC concludes that there is no reasonable cause to believe that the employer has violated Title VII,[21] and probably even if it believes that a settlement offer it has procured from the employer affords the charging party full relief.[22] An EEOC determination that there was no reasonable cause to believe that race discrimination allegations were true may be admissible under the public record exception to the hearsay rule in a private action for employment discrimination.[23] Similarly, an EEOC or state agency determination that there is reasonable cause may also be admissible.[24] But the agency's determination of "reasonable cause" or "no reasonable cause" will be given only such weight at trial as the federal court believes it deserves. If EEOC certifies to the court that a case initiated by a private party is of "general public importance," it may intervene as of right in the proceeding.[25]

Title VII also provides that a district court may appoint counsel "[u]pon application by the complainant and in such circumstances as the court may deem just."[26] The circuits are split on the issue of whether a court order denying the appointment of counsel is immediately appealable under the collateral order exception to the "final decision" rule of 28 U.S.C.A. § 1291.[27]

21. *McDonnell Douglas*, 411 U.S. 792, 93 S.Ct. 1817, 36 L.Ed.2d 668.

22. *Long v. Ringling Brothers–Barnum & Bailey Combined Shows Inc.*, 9 F.3d 340 (4th Cir.1993) (reversing a summary judgment entered against plaintiff who had rejected employer's settlement offer during EEOC conciliation, even where trial court viewed settlement as affording maximum relief then available under Title VII); *cf. Wrenn v. Secretary, Dep't of Veterans Affairs*, 918 F.2d 1073 (2d Cir.1990), *cert. denied*, 499 U.S. 977, 111 S.Ct. 1625, 113 L.Ed.2d 721 (1991) (holding otherwise where settlement offer made during federal employee administrative complaints process under ADEA that the court held claimant had duty to exhaust in good faith).

23. *Barfield v. Orange County*, 911 F.2d 644 (11th Cir.1990), *cert. denied sub nom. Barfield v. Lamar*, 500 U.S. 954, 111 S.Ct. 2263, 114 L.Ed.2d 715 (1991).

24. *Heyne v. Caruso*, 69 F.3d 1475 (9th Cir.1995); *Gilchrist v. Jim Slemons Imports*, 803 F.2d 1488, 1500 (9th Cir.1986); *Plummer v. Western Int'l Hotels Co.*, 656 F.2d 502, 504 (9th Cir.1981) (reversible error to exclude EEOC reasonable cause determination because probative value outweighs prejudicial effect). *But cf. Gilchrist*, 803 F.2d 1488 (district court should exercise discretion whether to admit EEOC letter of violation, which represents a determi-

nation that a violation has occurred). *But see Walker v. NationsBank*, 53 F.3d 1548 (11th Cir.1995) (categorically declining to admit EEOC determinations in jury trials because their variable detail and quality create potential for unfair prejudice).

25. Section 706(f)(1), 42 U.S.C.A. § 2000e–5(f)(1). See Federal Rule of Civil Procedure 24(a) (authorizing intervention as of right when so provided by federal statute).

26. 42 U.S.C.A. § 2000e–5(f)(1).

27. The Third, Fifth, Eighth, and Ninth Circuits allow interlocutory appeal of such orders. *See Spanos v. Penn Cent. Transp. Co.*, 470 F.2d 806, 807 n. 3 (3d Cir.1972); *Caston v. Sears, Roebuck & Co.*, 556 F.2d 1305, 1308 (5th Cir.1977); *Slaughter v. City of Maplewood*, 731 F.2d 587, 588–89 (8th Cir.1984); *Bradshaw v. Zoological Soc'y*, 662 F.2d 1301, 1305–18 (9th Cir.1981). The Sixth, Seventh, Eleventh Circuit, and District of Columbia Circuits reach the opposite conclusion. *See Henry v. City of Detroit Manpower Dep't*, 763 F.2d 757, 761–64 (6th Cir.) (en banc), *cert. denied*, 474 U.S. 1036, 106 S.Ct. 604, 88 L.Ed.2d 582 (1985); *Randle v. Victor Welding Supply Co.*, 664 F.2d 1064, 1065–67 (7th Cir.1981) (per curiam); *Hodges v. Department of Corr.*, 895 F.2d 1360, 1361–62 (11th Cir.1990) (per curiam); *Ficken v. Alvarez*, 146 F.3d 978, 980 (D.C.Cir.1998).

§ 4.6 Arbitration as Precluding the Civil Lawsuit: The Potential of the Gilmer Decision

Until 1991, it was settled that a putative plaintiff's resort to a grievance or *arbitration* procedure, prosecuted by her union, would not bar her later judicial action under Title VII, even after an unfavorable arbitral disposition.[1] That was the message of *Alexander v. Gardner–Denver Co.*,[2] a 1974 decision of the Supreme Court.[3] Today, however, the judicial avenue of redress may be altogether foreclosed to an uncertain number of potential plaintiffs who, individually or perhaps even through their union's agreement in collective bargaining, have agreed to arbitrate claims of employment discrimination.

The entering wedge posing this possibility is a 1991 decision by the Supreme Court that arose from an arbitration requirement contained in a securities exchange's rules that a brokerage house employee agreed to abide by in his application with a member firm. In *Gilmer v. Interstate/Johnson Lane Corp.*,[4] the Court ruled that an employee who made such an agreement could be compelled to arbitrate his statutory discrimination claim—there, under the Age Discrimination in Employment Act—by virtue of the Federal Arbitration Act ("FAA"). The Court also strongly implied, although it did not hold, that an adverse arbitration award would bar the plaintiff's subsequent ADEA action (although not a classwide enforcement action by EEOC).[5] In so suggesting the Court distinguished *Gardner–Denver* as a case where the agreement to arbitrate (1) was collectively bargained and (2) required arbitration of claims concerning the interpretation and application of the terms of the union contract, rather than claims of statutory employment discrimination. The majority's opinion reflected some sensitivity to the risk that a union's agreement to arbitrate might effectively bargain away the statutory rights of union members.[6]

§ 4.6

1. *Alexander v. Gardner–Denver Co.*, 415 U.S. 36, 94 S.Ct. 1011, 39 L.Ed.2d 147 (1974). *Cf. Bell v. Conopco, Inc.*, 186 F.3d 1099 (arbitrator's decision that employer had not violated nondiscrimination clause may be admitted in subsequent Title VII suit but accorded only such weight as court or jury deems appropriate; award may therefore not be predicate for summary judgment); *Alexander* and subsequent circuit authority also permit the grievant who prevails in arbitration to pursue any additional applicable relief available under Title VII in a later judicial action, subject to the traditional ban on duplicative recovery. *Id.* at 51 n. 14, 94 S.Ct. at 1021 n. 14; *Cooper v. Asplundh Tree Expert Co.*, 836 F.2d 1544, 1553–54 (10th Cir.1988).

2. *Alexander*, 415 U.S. 36, 94 S.Ct. 1011, 39 L.Ed.2d 147.

3. The Court has applied *Alexander*'s holding that there can be no prospective waiver of an employee's statutory rights to both § 1983 and the FLSA. *See McDonald v. West Branch*, 466 U.S. 284, 104 S.Ct. 1799, 80 L.Ed.2d 302 (1984) (§ 1983); *Barrentine v. Arkansas–Best Freight System, Inc.*, 450 U.S. 728, 101 S.Ct. 1437, 67 L.Ed.2d 641 (1981) (FLSA).

4. 500 U.S. 20, 111 S.Ct. 1647, 114 L.Ed.2d 26 (1991).

5. But such an award does bar an EEOC suit brought on behalf of an individual. *See EEOC v. Kidder, Peabody & Co., Inc.*, 156 F.3d 298 (2d Cir.1998). *See also New Orleans S.S. Ass'n v. EEOC*, 680 F.2d 23, 25 (5th Cir.1982) (reaching that conclusion because of res judicata); *EEOC v. Goodyear Aerospace Corp.*, 813 F.2d 1539, 1543 (9th Cir.1987) (same conclusion because of mootness).

6. The Fifth Circuit has since distinguished *Alexander*, and followed *Gilmer*, in ordering the submission of a Title VII sexu-

Thus when a pre-dispute agreement to arbitrate is contained in a collectively bargained agreement, most post-*Gilmer* decisions have continued to apply *Gardner–Denver*, excusing the plaintiff from arbitrating a statutory claim and permitting him to pursue it in court, unless he agrees to arbitrate after a dispute has arisen.[7] But the Fourth Circuit construed *Gilmer* as overriding *Gardner-Denver* even when an arbitration clause is contained in a collective agreement. It upheld arbitration under a collective bargaining agreement that specifically required the employer to comply with federal civil rights laws. The court dismissed *Gardner–Denver* as "old law" superseded by *Gilmer* and relied on changes in legal culture that have increasingly favored arbitration as a means to resolve statutory discrimination claims, including *Gilmer* itself

al harassment claim to arbitration under the authority of the Railway Labor Act ("RLA"). *Hirras v. National R.R. Passenger Corp.*, 10 F.3d 1142 (5th Cir.1994), *vacated,* 512 U.S. 1231, 114 S.Ct. 2732, 129 L.Ed.2d 855 (1994). Unlike the general national labor statutes at issue in *Alexander* that allow the employer and union to agree upon the scope of grievance arbitration and give the union wide discretion whether to prosecute an individual grievance within that scope, the RLA mandated the arbitration of so-called "minor disputes" arising from claims "founded upon some incident of the employment relationship . . . independent of those covered by the collective bargaining agreement." That circuit also treats claims under *state* anti-discrimination law as preempted by § 301 of the Taft–Hartley Act where their resolution turns on interpreting the terms of a collective bargaining agreement. *Reece v. Houston Lighting & Power Co.*, 79 F.3d 485 (5th Cir.), *cert. denied,* 519 U.S. 864, 117 S.Ct. 171, 136 L.Ed.2d 112 (1996); *but cf. Ramirez v. Fox Television Station, Inc.*, 998 F.2d 743 (9th Cir.1993) (state law claim not preempted by § 301 where its resolution does not turn on the meaning of collective bargaining agreement). *Cf. Chaulk Servs., Inc. v. Massachusetts Comm'n Against Discrimination*, 70 F.3d 1361 (1st Cir.1995), *cert. denied,* 518 U.S. 1005, 116 S.Ct. 2525, 135 L.Ed.2d 1049 (1996) (state sex discrimination proceedings preempted by earlier filed unfair labor practice charges before National Labor Relations Board where state law claim and unfair labor practice charge brought by union are founded upon identical facts).

7. *See Doyle v. Raley's Inc.*, 158 F.3d 1012 (9th Cir.1998); *Johnson v. Bodine Elec. Co.*, 142 F.3d 363, 367 (7th Cir.1998) (Title VII); *Peterson v. BMI Refractories*, 132 F.3d 1405 (11th Cir.1998) (§ 1981); *Harrison v. Eddy Potash, Inc.*, 112 F.3d 1437, 1453 (10th Cir.1997), *vacated on other grounds,* 524 U.S. 947, 118 S.Ct. 2364, 141 L.Ed.2d 732 (1998) (Title VII); *Brisentine v. Stone & Webster Eng'g Corp.*, 117 F.3d 519, 526 (11th Cir.1997) (ADA); *Penny v. United Parcel Serv.*, 128 F.3d 408, 414 (6th Cir. 1997) (ADA); *Pryner v. Tractor Supply Co.*, 109 F.3d 354 (7th Cir.), *cert. denied,* 522 U.S. 912, 118 S.Ct. 294, 139 L.Ed.2d 227 (1997); *Varner v. National Super Markets, Inc.*, 94 F.3d 1209 (8th Cir.1996), *cert. denied,* 519 U.S. 1110, 117 S.Ct. 946, 136 L.Ed.2d 835 (1997) (Title VII); *Tran v. Tran*, 54 F.3d 115, 117 (2d Cir.1995), *cert. denied,* 517 U.S. 1134, 116 S.Ct. 1417, 134 L.Ed.2d 542 (1996) (FLSA); *EEOC v. Board of Governors*, 957 F.2d 424 (7th Cir.), *cert. denied,* 506 U.S. 906, 113 S.Ct. 299, 121 L.Ed.2d 223 (1992).

On the other hand, the Supreme Court has held that an employer must honor its obligations under a collective bargaining agreement even though that agreement conflicts with its obligations under a Title VII consent decree. *W.R. Grace & Co. v. Local Union 759*, 461 U.S. 757, 103 S.Ct. 2177, 76 L.Ed.2d 298 (1983).

Because under *Gardner-Denver* a union cannot waive the right of the employees it represents to bring suit in a judicial forum, arbitration clauses are not mandatory subjects of collective bargaining. In *Air Line Pilots Ass'n v. Northwest Airlines, Inc.*, 199 F.3d 477, 485–86 (D.C.Cir.1999), *judgment reinstated,* 211 F.3d 1312 (D.C.Cir.2000), *petition for cert. filed,* Aug. 16, 2000, the defendant airline individually negotiated arbitration agreements with newly hired pilots who were not yet eligible for union representation. The union argued that arbitration clauses were a mandatory subject of bargaining. Explaining that *Gilmer* did not abrogate *Gardner-Denver*, the court found that because an individual can agree to arbitrate statutory claims and unions cannot, arbitration clauses cannot be mandatory subjects of bargaining because the union cannot bargain away a right that is not the union's to give. *Id.* at 486.

and § 118 of Title VII, an encouragement to voluntary alternative dispute resolution added by the Civil Rights Act of 1991.[8] The court wrote broadly that as long as an agreement to arbitrate is voluntary, it is valid whether contained in "a securities registration application, a simple employment contract, or a collective bargaining agreement."[9] The EEOC takes the extreme opposite position: pre-dispute agreements entered into as a condition of employment that mandate arbitration of discrimination claims are by their nature presumptively involuntary or coercive. EEOC will therefore process a charge of statutory discrimination regardless of whether the charging party's pre-dispute agreement to arbitrate is contained in an individual or collectively bargained contract.[10] A circuit split has developed as to whether EEOC in its role as public representative is bound by an agreement to arbitrate when it seeks classwide injunctive relief, or even monetary relief for the individual who agreed to arbitrate and others similarly situated.[11]

The Supreme Court agreed to review the Fourth Circuit's idiosyncratic approach, but in the end dodged the major issue. In *Wright v. Universal Maritime Service Corp.*,[12] the Court declined to decide if a union-negotiated, pre-dispute waiver of a judicial forum for the resolution of federal statutory employment discrimination rights could ever be validly enforced against the individual union member. Instead it held that such a waiver was not entitled to any presumption of arbitrability and must at a minimum be clear and unmistakable. Because the collective bargaining agreement at issue did not specifically require the employer to adhere to the ADA, and the arbitration clause did not specifically refer to claims under the ADA (or any other federal employment discrimination statute), the Court's "clear statement" requirement was not met and the grievant accordingly could not be required to arbitrate as a precondition of filing suit.

Intermediate views about the compulsory arbitrability of statutory employment claims pursuant to collectively bargained agreements are

---

8. *Austin v. Owens–Brockway Glass Container, Inc.*, 78 F.3d 875 (4th Cir.), *cert. denied*, 519 U.S. 980, 117 S.Ct. 432, 136 L.Ed.2d 330 (1996).

9. *Austin*, 78 F.3d 875.

10. *EEOC Policy Statement on Mandatory Arbitration*, No. 915.002 (7/10/97).

11. *Compare EEOC v. Frank's Nursery & Crafts, Inc.*, 177 F.3d 448 (6th Cir.1999) (EEOC not bound, even from pursuing monetary relief on behalf of all class members, including individual who agreed to arbitrate) *with EEOC v. Kidder, Peabody & Co.*, 156 F.3d 298 (2d Cir.1998) (EEOC bound and thus barred from pursuing monetary relief on individual's behalf). The Fourth Circuit, recognizing EEOC's authority to vindicate the public's interest in ending discrimination, has in effect, split the baby, holding that the EEOC cannot be

compelled, by reason of an arbitration agreement between the charging party and his employer, to arbitrate its claims, but that, to the extent that the EEOC seeks to obtain "make-whole" relief on behalf of a charging party who is subject to an arbitration agreement, it is precluded from seeking such relief in a judicial forum. See *EEOC v. Waffle House, Inc.*, 193 F.3d 805, 806–07 (4th Cir.1999), *petition for cert. filed*, May 15, 2000.

12. 525 U.S. 70, 119 S.Ct. 391, 142 L.Ed.2d 361 (1998). *Wright* has been applied in *Bratten v. SSI Servs., Inc.*, 185 F.3d 625 (6th Cir.1999); *Brown v. ABF Freight Sys., Inc.*, 183 F.3d 319 (4th Cir.1999) and *Carson v. Giant Food, Inc.*, 175 F.3d 325 (4th Cir.1999). In each case, the court found that the demanding *Wright* standard of unmistakable waiver of judicial forum to litigate statutory claims was not met.

discernible in opinions of the lower federal courts. In *Pryner v. Tractor Supply Co.*,[13] the panel sought to reconcile *Gardner-Denver* with *Gilmer* by observing that statutory rights are arbitrable whenever the facts demonstrate that the plaintiff himself has consented to arbitrate them. That consent would be evident, for example, in a post-dispute side agreement to arbitrate that was not expressly precluded by a collective agreement. But the court held that the union cannot supply such consent "by signing a collective bargaining agreement that consigns the enforcement of statutory rights to the union-controlled grievance and arbitration machinery created by the agreement." Another circuit would allow *Gilmer* to trump *Alexander* in the collective bargaining setting only if (a) the employee individually agreed to the arbitration clause or the collective agreement in which it is contained; (b) the agreement authorizes the arbitrator to decide federal statutory, and not just contract claims; and (c) the employee is empowered to compel arbitration if dissatisfied by the outcome of the internal grievance process, independent of the will of the union.[14]

Another post-*Gilmer* decision observes that even if an antidiscrimination clause in the collective agreement tracks the language of a statutory guarantee, the clause confers a separate right rooted in contract and may be interpreted by an arbitrator to have its own distinctive meaning. In that light the plaintiff's statutory claims asserted in court are not subject to the standard arbitration clause because they do not concern the interpretation or application of the collective agreement. Accordingly, the court hewed to *Gardner–Denver* by holding that the arbitrator's decision did not foreclose the right to sue.[15] In an effort to harmonize *Gilmer* with *Gardner–Denver*, another district court has held *Gilmer* limited to front-end enforceability: the question whether a lawsuit may be stayed and the plaintiff ordered to submit her claim to arbitration. Under this view *Gardner–Denver* still governs the question whether the post-arbitration award precludes litigation of statutory employment discrimination claims under a doctrine akin to res judicata or claim preclusion; and *Gardner–Denver* holds it does not.[16]

Outside the collective bargaining context, in the continuing absence of controlling Supreme Court guidance, federal appellate courts have incrementally extended *Gilmer* beyond ADEA by enforcing individual employees' agreements to arbitrate. The circuit decisions began by

---

13. *Pryner v. Tractor Supply Co.*, 109 F.3d 354 (7th Cir.), *cert. denied*, 522 U.S. 912, 118 S.Ct. 294, 139 L.Ed.2d 227 (1997). *Cf. Almonte v. Coca–Cola Bottling Co. of N.Y.*, 959 F.Supp. 569 (D.Conn.1997) (requiring pre-suit arbitration of employment discrimination claims brought under 42 U.S.C.A. § 1981 because collective bargaining arbitration provision specifically encompassed claims "under any federal, state or local fair employment practice law," even though it appeared that only the union could invoke arbitration). Both the cited decisions relied heavily on the spur that

§ 118 of the Civil Rights Act of 1991 provides for voluntary arbitration of statutory discrimination claims.

14. *Brisentine v. Stone & Webster Eng'g Corp.*, 117 F.3d 519 (11th Cir.1997).

15. *Greene v. United Parcel Serv.*, 864 F.Supp. 48 (N.D.Ill.1994).

16. *Hillding v. McDonnell Douglas Helicopter Co.*, 59 FEP Cases 869, 1992 WL 443421 (D.Ariz.1992), *aff'd*, 985 F.2d 573 (9th Cir.1993).

compelling arbitration, in the same securities industry setting, of claims asserted under Title VII.[17] These courts have found that *Gilmer* can coexist with *Gardner–Denver* because the latter simply holds that an employee has not waived the right to pursue the Title VII statutory remedy merely by permitting his union to arbitrate a grievance procedure contractually agreed to and controlled by his employer and his union. By contrast, these courts have ruled, the individual employee's acquiescence in the arbitration clause, manifested by her signing a registration application such as the one that the New York Stock Exchange[18] requires of applicants for employment with member firms, evidenced a voluntary personal commitment to arbitrate all claims related to that employment. These agreements to arbitrate statutory discrimination claims have therefore been deemed enforceable under the FAA when contained in contracts which, like most, touch interstate commerce.

Whether the federal judiciary will in the end enforce individual employees' agreements to arbitrate discrimination claims when those agreements are contained in a plaintiff's own employment contract— that is, outside the securities industry where the agreement is formally obtained by an applicant's agreement to abide by rules of an exchange of which the prospective employer is a member—may depend on the resolution of several related issues. A threshold question is how broadly the courts will interpret an exception to FAA's enforcement powers contained in FAA § 1. That provision excludes from FAA's reach arbitration agreements in "contracts of employment of seamen, railroad employees, or any other class of workers engaged in foreign or interstate commerce." In *Gilmer* the majority found it unnecessary to construe the quoted language because the agreement to arbitrate was contained not in an employment contract as such but in the rules of a securities exchange.

Pre-*Gilmer* decisions often interpreted § 1 narrowly, thereby expanding the reach of FAA. These decisions declined to stretch the "other class of workers" language of the exception beyond transportation industries to include all collectively bargained agreements to arbitrate, or arbitration agreements by other workers actually engaged in or even merely affecting interstate commerce.[19] Similarly, since *Gilmer*, eleven

17. *Koveleskie v. SBC Capital Markets, Inc.*, 167 F.3d 361, 365 (7th Cir.), cert. denied, 528 U.S. 811, 120 S.Ct. 44, 145 L.Ed.2d 40 (1999); *Seus v. John Nuveen & Co., Inc.*, 146 F.3d 175 (3d Cir.1998), cert. denied, 525 U.S. 1139, 119 S.Ct. 1028, 143 L.Ed.2d 38 (1999); *Metz v. Merrill Lynch, Pierce, Fenner & Smith, Inc.*, 39 F.3d 1482, 1487 (10th Cir.1994); *Hurst v. Prudential Securities, Inc.*, 21 F.3d 1113 (9th Cir. 1994); *Bender v. A.G. Edwards & Sons, Inc.*, 971 F.2d 698 (11th Cir.1992) (sexual harassment claim); *Mago v. Shearson Lehman Hutton Inc.*, 956 F.2d 932 (9th Cir. 1992); *Willis v. Dean Witter Reynolds, Inc.*, 948 F.2d 305 (6th Cir.1991); *Alford v. Dean Witter Reynolds, Inc.* 939 F.2d 229 (5th Cir.1991).

18. *See Williams v. Cigna Financial Advisors, Inc.*, 56 F.3d 656 (5th Cir.1995) (arbitration clause held to encompass age discrimination claim, and plaintiff's agreement to arbitrate held knowing and voluntary waiver of right to judicial forum consistent with Older Workers Benefits Protection Act and ADEA.).

19. *See, e.g., Miller Brewing Co. v. Brewery Workers Local Union No. 9*, 739 F.2d 1159 (7th Cir.1984), cert. denied, 469

circuit courts have embraced the narrow, "transportation-only" interpretation of § 1, enforcing agreements to arbitrate Title VII, ADEA, and ADA claims where those agreements are found in the individual employment contracts of a wide variety of nontransportation employees.[20] These courts have construed the § 1 exclusionary clause to apply only to employment contracts of seamen, railroad workers, and other classes of workers similarly engaged in moving goods through interstate commerce, with no general exclusion from FAA coverage for collectively bargained agreements to arbitrate. But most have also recognized the continuing force of *Gardner-Denver*, refusing to bar pre-or post-arbitration resort to court by claimants alleging discrimination prohibited by Federal law if their agreement to arbitrate those claims was collectively granted on their behalf by a union. And the Ninth Circuit, alone among the circuits, has categorically denied employers the ability to compel arbitration of statutory discrimination claims, holding that the FAA does not apply to any employment contracts or collective bargaining agreements.[21] Construing the § 1 exception broadly in light of § 2, the court concluded that the Act was meant to apply to contracts between merchants buying and selling goods, and not to employment or labor

U.S. 1160, 105 S.Ct. 912, 83 L.Ed.2d 926 (1985); *See, e.g., Stokes v. Merrill Lynch, Pierce, Fenner & Smith*, 523 F.2d 433 (6th Cir.1975); *Erving v. Virginia Squires Basketball Club*, 468 F.2d 1064 (2d Cir.1972); *Dickstein v. duPont*, 443 F.2d 783 (1st Cir. 1971); *Tenney Eng'g, Inc. v. United Elec. Radio & Machine Workers*, 207 F.2d 450 (3d Cir.1953). *But see American Postal Workers Union v. U.S. Postal Serv.*, 823 F.2d 466 (11th Cir.1987) (extending the exclusion to postal workers many of whom were not involved in transportation).

20. *Koveleskie*, 167 F.3d 361; *Rosenberg v. Merrill Lynch, Pierce, Fenner & Smith, Inc.*, 170 F.3d 1 (1st Cir.1999) (ADEA); *Johnson v. Circuit City Stores*, 148 F.3d 373 (4th Cir.1998) (§ 1981 and Title VII); *Mouton v. Metropolitan Life Ins. Co.*, 147 F.3d 453 (5th Cir.1998) (even where agreement did not specifically mandate arbitration of employment disputes) (Title VII); *Seus v. John Nuveen & Co.*, 146 F.3d 175, 179, 182–83 (3d Cir.1998), *cert. denied*, 525 U.S. 1139, 119 S.Ct. 1028, 143 L.Ed.2d 38 (1999) (Title VII and ADEA); *McWilliams v. Logicon, Inc.*, 143 F.3d 573, 576 (10th Cir.1998) (ADA); *Paladino v. Avnet Computer Techs., Inc.*, 134 F.3d 1054, 1062 (11th Cir.1998) (Title VII); *Bercovitch v. Baldwin Sch., Inc.*, 133 F.3d 141 (1st Cir.1998) (ADA); *Gibson v. Neighborhood Health Clinics, Inc.*, 121 F.3d 1126, 1130 (7th Cir.1997); *Miller v. Public Storage Mgmt., Inc.*, 121 F.3d 215 (5th Cir.1997) (ADA); *O'Neil v. Hilton Head Hosp.*, 115 F.3d 272, 274 (4th Cir.1997); *Patterson v. Tenet Healthcare, Inc.*, 113

F.3d 832 (8th Cir.1997) (Title VII); *Great Western Mortgage Corp.v. Peacock*, 110 F.3d 222 (3d Cir.), *cert. denied*, 522 U.S. 915, 118 S.Ct. 299, 139 L.Ed.2d 230 (1997); *Pryner v. Tractor Supply Co.*, 109 F.3d 354, 358 (7th Cir.1997), *cert. denied*, 522 U.S. 912, 118 S.Ct. 295, 139 L.Ed.2d 227 (1997); *Cole v. Burns Int'l Sec. Servs.*, 105 F.3d 1465 (D.C.Cir.1997); *Rojas v. TK Communications, Inc.*, 87 F.3d 745, 747–748 (5th Cir. 1996); *Asplundh Tree Expert Co. v. Bates*, 71 F.3d 592, 596–601 (6th Cir.1995); *Metz v. Merrill Lynch, Pierce, Fenner & Smith, Inc.*, 39 F.3d 1482, 1487 (10th Cir.1994); *Willis v. Dean Witter Reynolds, Inc.*, 948 F.2d 305, 308, 312 (6th Cir.1991); *Alford v. Dean Witter Reynolds, Inc.*, 939 F.2d 229, 230 (5th Cir.1991); *Erving v. Virginia Squires Basketball Club*, 468 F.2d 1064, 1069 (2d Cir.1972); *Dickstein v. duPont*, 443 F.2d 783, 785 (1st Cir.1971). *See also Crawford v. West Jersey Health Systems*, 847 F.Supp. 1232 (D.N.J.1994); *cf. Williams v. Katten, Muchin & Zavis*, 837 F.Supp. 1430 (N.D.Ill.1993) (discrimination claim was by former law partner, raising a question whether the agreement could even be considered a contract of "employment" within the meaning of § 1).

21. *Craft v. Campbell Soup Co.*,161 F.3d 1199 (9th Cir.1998); *Circuit City Stores, Inc. v. Adams*, 194 F.3d 1070 (9th Cir.1999), *cert. granted*, ___ U.S. ___, 120 S.Ct. 2004, 146 L.Ed.2d 955 (2000); *Circuit City Stores, Inc. v. Ahmed*, 195 F.3d 1131 (9th Cir. 1999), *petition for cert. filed*, February 16, 2000.

contracts of any kind.[22] The Supreme Court has granted certiorari to review the Ninth Circuit's position.[23]

Regardless of the ultimate outcome of the § 1 issue, the Supreme Court may reaffirm the holding of *Gardner–Denver* by permitting Title VII or ADEA plaintiffs to pursue their statutory discrimination claims in court even after an adverse arbitration award, issued pursuant to the authority of the FAA, determines their rights under a *collective* bargaining agreement. To conform *Gilmer* to the broadest implications of *Gardner–Denver*, the Court might go further still and deny even front-end enforceability under the FAA to arbitration promises contained in agreements that are collectively bargained. Even then, *non-union* employers subject to Title VII, the ADEA, and the Americans with Disabilities Act will have an incentive to "negotiate"—more realistically, at least where jobs are scarce, to insert unilaterally—agreements to arbitrate statutory discrimination claims in *individual* employment contracts. Even if *Gardner-Denver* is reaffirmed, those agreements would presumably be enforceable, unless the Supreme Court ultimately construes the § 1 exclusion to apply to industries other than those specifically listed in that section.

Finally, even if the § 1 exception to enforceability is construed broadly, or *Gilmer* is construed to require only front-end enforceability of promises to arbitrate, rather than deference to rendered arbitration awards, *Gilmer* may spur enforcement under *state* law of promises to arbitrate claims under the federal employment discrimination statutes.[24] *Gilmer* declares that nothing in the history or purposes of ADEA, or presumably Title VII, opposes the resolution of discrimination claims by the procedures of modern arbitration. This relatively recent judicial receptiveness to arbitration contrasts markedly with the traditional hostility towards that process reflected in *McDonald v. City of West Branch*,[25] and *Barrentine v. Arkansas–Best Freight System*,[26] which held arbitration procedures inadequate to resolve claims under, respectively, § 1983 and the Fair Labor Standards Act. The Court has gone out of its way to reverse the ancient judicial hostility to the arbitration of statutory rights,[27] a development that has emboldened federal judges to order

---

22. *Id.*

23. *Circuit City Stores, Inc. v. Adams,* 194 F.3d 1070 (9th Cir.1999), *cert. granted,* ___ U.S. ___, 120 S.Ct. 2004, 146 L.Ed.2d 955 (2000).

24. The Supreme Court has held that state laws imposing special restrictions on the enforceability of arbitration clauses are pre-empted by the FAA. *Doctor's Assocs., Inc. v. Casarotto,* 517 U.S. 681, 116 S.Ct. 1652, 134 L.Ed.2d 902 (1996) (Montana law that conditioned enforceability of arbitration clause on compliance with special notice requirements was pre-empted). *See also Southland Corp. v. Keating,* 465 U.S. 1, 10, 104 S.Ct. 852, 858, 79 L.Ed.2d 1 (1984) (the

enactment of the FAA "withdrew the power of the states to require a judicial forum for the resolution of claims which the contracting parties agreed to resolve by arbitration").

25. 466 U.S. 284, 104 S.Ct. 1799, 80 L.Ed.2d 302 (1984).

26. 450 U.S. 728, 101 S.Ct. 1437, 67 L.Ed.2d 641 (1981).

27. *See, e.g., Mitsubishi Motors Corp. v. Soler Chrysler–Plymouth, Inc.,* 473 U.S. 614, 105 S.Ct. 3346, 87 L.Ed.2d 444 (1985) (action under the Sherman Act); *Shearson/American Express, Inc. v. McMahon,* 482 U.S. 220, 107 S.Ct. 2332, 96 L.Ed.2d 185 (1987) (action under the Securities Ex-

the arbitration of employment discrimination claims in the years since *Gilmer*.

With the 1991 Act's addition of § 118 to Title VII, most circuits that have confronted the issue have extended *Gilmer* to enforce individual employees' agreements to arbitrate Title VII and other statutory employment discrimination claims against employers outside the securities industry. Although the Civil Rights Act of 1991 is silent about *Gilmer*, § 118 provides additional impetus for the arbitration of several kinds of statutory discrimination claims. Section 118 provides: "Where appropriate and to the extent authorized by law, the use of alternative means of dispute resolution, including settlement negotiations, conciliation, facilitation, mediation, fact-finding, minitrials, and arbitration, is encouraged to resolve disputes arising under the Acts or provisions of Federal law amended by this title." This includes Title VII, ADEA, § 1981, and ADA. Several federal circuit courts have relied *inter alia* on § 118 in holding that claims under the ADA and Title VII may not proceed in court where the plaintiff had failed to invoke a grievance or arbitration forum contemplated by a pre-dispute agreement to arbitrate. And at least nine circuits now hold that Congress did not intend to prohibit the use of predispute arbitration agreements for resolving claims under Title VII and other statutes prohibiting employment discrimination.[28] Some of these decisions cite the Supreme Court's directive to resolve all doubts concerning arbitrability in favor of arbitration,[29] even when the agree-

change Act of 1934 and the Racketeer Influenced and Corrupt Organization Act); *Rodriguez de Quijas v. Shearson/American Express, Inc.*, 490 U.S. 477, 109 S.Ct. 1917, 104 L.Ed.2d 526 (1989) (action under Securities Act of 1933 and the Securities and Exchange Act of 1934); *Gilmer v. Interstate/Johnson Lane Corp.*, 500 U.S. 20, 111 S.Ct. 1647, 114 L.Ed.2d 26 (1991) (action under Age Discrimination in Employment Act). In *Gilmer* the Court expressly repudiated the "mistrust of the arbitral process" reflected in its earlier decisions about the arbitration of statutory claims.

28. *Desiderio v. National Ass'n of Securities Dealers*, 191 F.3d 198 (2d Cir.1999), *petition for cert. filed*, January 31, 2000 (§ 118's phrase "to the extent authorized by law" refers to FAA's scope of enforceability); *Hooters of Am. v. Phillips*, 173 F.3d 933 (4th Cir.1999); *Koveleskie v. SBC Capital Markets, Inc.*, 167 F.3d 361, 365 (7th Cir.), *cert. denied*, 528 U.S. 811, 120 S.Ct. 44, 145 L.Ed.2d 40 (1999); *Seus v. John Nuveen & Co.*, 146 F.3d 175, 182 (3d Cir. 1998), *cert. denied*, 525 U.S. 1139, 119 S.Ct. 1028, 143 L.Ed.2d 38 (1999) (Title VII and ADEA); *McWilliams v. Logicon, Inc.*, 143 F.3d 573 (10th Cir.1998) (ADA); *Paladino v. Avnet Computer Techs., Inc.*, 134 F.3d

1054 (11th Cir.1998) (Title VII) (but finding clause too ambiguous to include Title VII claims and in any event unenforceable because of degree to which arbitration agreement limited damages); *Miller v. Public Storage Mgmt., Inc.*, 121 F.3d 215 (5th Cir. 1997) (ADA); *Patterson v. Tenet Healthcare, Inc.*, 113 F.3d 832 (8th Cir.1997) (Title VII); *Cole v. Burns Int'l Sec. Servs.*, 105 F.3d 1465 (D.C.Cir.1997) (insisting, however, that the arbitration tribunal meet certain minimal procedural and remedial characteristics); *Metz v. Merrill Lynch, Pierce, Fenner & Smith, Inc.*, 39 F.3d 1482 (10th Cir. 1994); *Bender v. A.G. Edwards & Sons, Inc.*, 971 F.2d 698 (11th Cir.1992); *Willis v. Dean Witter Reynolds, Inc.*, 948 F.2d 305 (6th Cir.1991); *Alford v. Dean Witter Reynolds, Inc.*, 939 F.2d 229 (5th Cir.1991). But the enforceability of an individual employee's agreement to arbitrate will not prevent EEOC from suing on behalf of that employee and others, at least for injunctive relief. See *EEOC v. Waffle House, Inc.*, 193 F.3d 805 (4th Cir.1999), *petition for cert. filed*, May 15, 2000; *EEOC v. Northwest Airlines, Inc.*, 188 F.3d 695, 701–02 (6th Cir.1999).

29. See *Moses H. Cone Mem. Hosp. v. Mercury Constr. Corp.*, 460 U.S. 1, 23, 103 S.Ct. 927, 941, 74 L.Ed.2d 765 (1983).

ment to arbitrate was made before the dispute arose and as a condition of employment.[30]

But the Ninth Circuit, again alone among circuits addressing the issue, has held that the Civil Rights Act of 1991, enacted to expand employees' rights and increase the possible remedies available to civil rights plaintiffs, *precludes* such arbitration because the kind of "voluntary" alternative dispute resolution encouraged by § 118 impliedly prohibits employers from requiring their employees, as a condition of employment, to agree to arbitrate Title VII claims.[31] The opinion illustrates the full range of the arguments available to plaintiffs seeking to avoid arbitration clauses exacted as a condition of employment. First, *Duffield* holds that the text and legislative history of Section 118 of the Civil Rights Act of 1991, while encouraging the voluntary submission of Title VII disputes to arbitration, preclude the compulsory arbitration of such disputes based on agreements to arbitrate in noncollectively bargained as well as collectively bargained settings. It concludes that Congress, after the drafting but before the enactment of the 1991 Act, incorporated into that section the principle of *Gardner–Denver* precluding "compulsory" arbitration of claims under Title VII; and that it either did not consider or rejected the approach taken by the Supreme Court in *Gilmer* that approves re-dispute agreements to arbitrate claims under ADEA. Second, *Duffield* reads the *Gardner-Denver* principle as not only allowing a putative plaintiff to resort to court despite a completed, adverse arbitration award, but as preventing a pre-dispute arbitration agreement from interfering with a putative Title VII plaintiff's immediate, direct access to court before arbitration proceedings have been demanded or initiated.[32] The Ninth Circuit did acknowledge in *Duffield* that an agreement to arbitrate statutory discrimination claims entered into *after* a dispute arises may be voluntary and enforceable within the meaning of § 118.

Even in circuits that enforce agreements whereby the plaintiff is required, as a condition of initial or continued employment, to waive prospectively her right to resort to federal court, she can argue, as EEOC has done in some twenty five amicus briefs in the past few years, that her particular "compulsory" arbitration agreement is involuntary and violative of Congress's intent to make available to plaintiffs the full platter of rights, remedies, and procedural protections embodied in the antidiscrimination statutes. For example, a panel of the Ninth Circuit rejected a securities industry employer's demand to arbitrate when it found that the waiver by the particular employees in question was not fully knowing. In so holding the court relied on legislative history underlying § 118 to the effect that alternative dispute resolution mecha-

30. *See Koveleskie*, 167 F.3d 361 (Title VII claim); *Armijo v. Prudential Ins. Co. of Am.*, 72 F.3d 793 (10th Cir.1995) (Title VII claims); *Matthews v. Rollins Hudig Hall Co.*, 72 F.3d 50 (7th Cir.1995) (ADEA claim).

31. *Duffield v. Robertson Stephens & Co.*, 144 F.3d 1182 (9th Cir.), *cert. denied*, 525 U.S. 982, 119 S.Ct. 445, 142 L.Ed.2d 399 (1998).

32. 144 F.3d at 1197 n.14.

nisms were "intended to supplement, not supplant, the remedies provided by Title VII," H.R.Rep.No. 40 (I), 102nd Cong. 1st Sess., reprinted in 1991 U.S.C.C.A.N. 549, 635, and that the provision is designed to encourage arbitration only "where the parties knowingly and voluntarily elect to use these methods," 137 Cong.Rec. S. 15472, S. 15478 (Daily Ed. October 30, 1991), statement of Senator Dole. This opinion,[33] and others that have followed, require a case-by-case inquiry into whether the pre-dispute agreement to arbitrate specifically addresses disputes arising from statutory discrimination claims,[34] whether it covers the particular type of employer and employment dispute at issue, and whether plaintiff's acceptance of it was knowing and voluntary.[35] Circuit opinions involving alleged agreements by securities industry employees to arbitrate discrimination claims under the rules of the National Association of Securities Dealers ("NASD") have scrutinized especially carefully whether the agreement to arbitrate statutory rights was knowing and voluntary.[36] More recently, circuits have begun to assess whether the

---

33. *See Prudential Ins. Co. of Am. v. Lai*, 42 F.3d 1299 (9th Cir.1994), *cert. denied*, 516 U.S. 812, 116 S.Ct. 61, 133 L.Ed.2d 24 (1995).

34. *See Paladino v. Avnet Computer*, 134 F.3d 1054 (11th Cir.1998) and *Brisentine v. Stone & Webster Eng'g*, 117 F.3d 519 (11th Cir.1997) (agreement must distinctly authorize the arbitrator to resolve federal statutory claims, although not every statute need be listed).

35. *See Burns v. New York Life Ins. Co.*, 202 F.3d 616 (2d Cir.2000) (employer which was the sole parent of a "member" of the National Association of Securities Dealers could not force plaintiff to arbitration because it could not avail itself of the broader definition of a "person associated with a member" in the Securities Exchange Act); *Bailey v. Federal Nat'l Mortgage Ass'n*, 209 F.3d 740, 744–45 (D.C.Cir.2000) (employer cannot compel arbitration where arbitration agreement was unilaterally imposed on employees already working for company); *Gardner v. Benefits Communications Corp.*, 175 F.3d 155 (D.C.Cir.1999) (arbitration not required because corporate employer not an "associated person" construed to refer only to natural person); *Doyle v. Raley's, Inc.*, 158 F.3d 1012 (9th Cir.1998); *Gibson v. Neighborhood Health Clinics*, 121 F.3d 1126, 1129 (7th Cir.1997); *Nelson v. Cyprus Bagdad Copper Corp.*, 119 F.3d 756 (9th Cir.1997), *cert. denied*, 523 U.S. 1072, 118 S.Ct. 1511, 140 L.Ed.2d 665 (1998) (applying same strict interpretation to ADA claim). *See also Keymer v. Management Recruiters Int'l, Inc.*, 169 F.3d 501 (8th Cir. 1999) (agreement's arbitration procedure specifically excluded controversies about employer's right to terminate plaintiff); *Brennan v. King*, 139 F.3d 258 (1st Cir.

1998) (where arbitration agreement limited arbitrator's authority to procedural matters in tenure disputes, employee was not required to arbitrate tenure denial). *Cf. Brown v. Trans World Airlines*, 127 F.3d 337 (4th Cir.1997) (employee not required to arbitrate statutory claims where clause in collective bargaining agreement only refers to contract terms). *See also Floss v. Ryan's Family Steak Houses, Inc.*, 211 F.3d 306 (6th Cir.2000) (refusing to compel arbitration where arbitration agreement did not run to the employer but was between employee and a third-party arbitration service).

36. In *Farrand v. Lutheran Brotherhood*, 993 F.2d 1253 (7th Cir.1993), the Court ruled that the scope of arbitration to which employees agree by agreeing to arbitrate disputes under the rules of the NASD does not include employment disputes because the NASD rules themselves were not specific on that point. In *Prudential Ins. Co. of Am. v. Lai*, 42 F.3d 1299 (9th Cir.1994), *cert. denied*, 516 U.S. 812, 116 S.Ct. 61, 133 L.Ed.2d 24 (1995), the Ninth Circuit reached the same conclusion but also rested decision on its own determination that the plaintiffs in that case did not knowingly waive rights to the judicial determination of Title VII claims in forms they signed when employed by Prudential. The Ninth Circuit decision is potentially more far reaching because it requires a discrete, case-by-case inquiry into whether a plaintiff knowingly and voluntarily waived the right to litigate a statutory employment claim. *Renteria v. Prudential Insurance Co. of Am.*, 113 F.3d 1104 (9th Cir.1997); *Thomas James Assocs., Inc. v. Jameson*, 102 F.3d 60, 64 (2d Cir. 1996). *See Seus v. John Nuveen & Co., Inc.*,

employer, under the standards of applicable state law, supplies adequate consideration in exchange for the employee's promise to arbitrate.[37]

Yet some circuits, relying on the judicially crafted FAA presumption of arbitrability, have found even general language in individual employment contracts (whereby the parties agree to resolve all contract-related disputes) adequate to embrace statutory discrimination claims.[38] On the other hand, courts have not been nearly so ready to infer a knowing, voluntary waiver of substantive statutory rights when the employer relies on a complete release of those rights contained in an ad hoc agreement entered into at the time of a termination.[39] Perhaps the difference is that in the arbitration setting the employee is not waiving the statutory right altogether, but "merely" the judicial forum and perhaps some of the remedies that Congress provided for its vindication.[40]

Alternatively, a plaintiff may argue that the arbitral forum she agreed to (1) lacks sufficient procedural protections; (2) fails to afford remedies adequate to meet the standards a particular statute might require as prerequisite to final arbitral resolution of a controversy; or (3) features arbitrators who are unable or unwilling to enforce statutory rights.[41] Still, most reported circuit decisions uphold the arbitration

146 F.3d 175 (3d Cir.1998), *cert. denied*, 525 U.S. 1139, 119 S.Ct. 1028, 143 L.Ed.2d 38 (1999) (NASD arbitration code encompassed employment disputes, but particular waiver not knowing and voluntary).

37. *Gibson v. Neighborhood Health Clinics, Inc.*, 121 F.3d 1126, 1131 (7th Cir. 1997) (manual stated that Title VII claims, among other disputes, were subject to arbitration but that manual itself "does not constitute a contract or promise of any kind"; court finds no consideration for plaintiff's promise to be bound either in manual or in employer's promise to hire or continue to hire her). *But cf. Michalski v. Circuit City Stores*, 177 F.3d 634 (7th Cir. 1999) (information given to plaintiff contemporaneously with her agreement to arbitrate expressed employer's promise to be bound, which was adequate consideration even though employer did not agree to submit to arbitration its claims against her); *Koveleskie v. SBC Capital Markets*, 167 F.3d 361, 366 (7th Cir.), *cert. denied*, 528 U.S. 811, 120 S.Ct. 44, 145 L.Ed.2d 40 (1999) (consideration in employer's agreement to be bound and to hire plaintiff); *Johnson v. Circuit City*, 148 F.3d 373, 378 (4th Cir.1998) (same as *Michalski* except employee's agreement to arbitrate her disputes and employer's agreement to be bound by result of arbitration were contained in the same document).

38. *See Seus v. John Nuveen & Co., Inc.*, 146 F.3d 175 (3d Cir.1998), *cert. de-*

nied, 525 U.S. 1139, 119 S.Ct. 1028, 143 L.Ed.2d 38 (1999); *Patterson v. Tenet Healthcare, Inc.*, 113 F.3d 832 (8th Cir. 1997); *Rojas v. TK Communications, Inc.*, 87 F.3d 745, 749 (5th Cir.1996); *Matthews v. Rollins Hudig Hall Co.*, 72 F.3d 50, 55 (7th Cir.1995); *Asplundh Tree Expert Co. v. Bates*, 71 F.3d 592, 595 (6th Cir.1995); *Kidd v. Equitable Life Assurance Soc'y*, 32 F.3d 516 (11th Cir.1994); *Bender v. A.G. Edwards & Sons, Inc.*, 971 F.2d 698 (11th Cir.1992).

39. *See Puentes v. United Parcel Serv., Inc.*, 86 F.3d 196 (11th Cir.1996); *Beadle v. City of Tampa*, 42 F.3d 633 (11th Cir.), *cert. denied*, 515 U.S. 1152, 115 S.Ct. 2600, 132 L.Ed.2d 846 (1995).

40. *See DeGaetano v. Smith Barney, Inc.*, 1996 WL 44226 (S.D.N.Y.1996) (because § 118 of the 1991 Civil Rights Act evinces legislative receptiveness to alternative methods of dispute resolution, arbitration of Title VII claims is not necessarily inconsistent with Congressional intent merely because a particular arbitration agreement precludes certain statutory remedies like punitive damages or attorney's fees).

41. *See Cole v. Burns Int'l Sec. Servs.*, 105 F.3d 1465 (D.C.Cir.1997) (emphasizing the necessity of adequate review in enforcing a mandatory, pre-dispute agreement to arbitrate Title VII discrimination claims; also holding that arbitration agreements

agreements in question. Adequate judicial review of the arbitration award may be an additional prerequisite to barring plaintiff from commencing a de novo judicial action.[42] Last, a plaintiff might contend that the contract in which an agreement to arbitrate is contained is a contract of adhesion, a circumstance the Supreme Court in *Gilmer* recognized as possibly precluding enforcement.[43] These arguments have largely failed, too, even when the agreement is extracted on a "take it or leave it" basis as a condition of initial hire.[44]

are valid only if employer pays all costs). *See also Hooters of Am., Inc. v. Phillips*, 173 F.3d 933 (4th Cir.1999) (where employer does not have to respond to employee's notice of the claim and acts or omissions at issue, only employee must provide witness list and outline of witness testimony, employer entirely controls list of potential arbitrators, only employer may record the proceedings or move for summary judgment, only employer can sue to vacate or modify award, and employer may alter the arbitration rules at any time, agreement is so one-sided as to violate employer's implicit agreement to establish a neutral forum and may be revoked by employee); *Shankle v. B–G Maintenance Mgmt. of Colo., Inc.*,163 F.3d 1230 (10th Cir.1999) (striking down agreement to arbitrate statutory claim because it required plaintiff to pay half of arbitrator's fee, thereby depriving plaintiff of an effective, accessible alternative forum); *Paladino*, 134 F.3d 1054 (agreement to arbitrate unenforceable if employee required to pay fees of arbitration). *But cf. Koveleskie*, 167 F.3d 361 and *Rosenberg*, 170 F.3d 1 (agreement enforceable despite possibility that plaintiff may bear arbitration fees). To the extent that these decisions preclude arbitration on the mere possibility that the claimant might bear substantial arbitration fees, they have probably been eclipsed by the Supreme Court's decision in *Green Tree Fin. Corp. v. Randolph*, __ U.S. __, 121 S.Ct. 513, 148 L.Ed.2d 373 (2000).

42. *See Cole*, 105 F.3d 1465. Courts generally adhere to the normal deferential review of arbitration awards under the Federal Arbitration Act, which in practice means that awards are often upheld despite their inconsistency with the principles of the underlying employment discrimination statutes unless the arbitrator knew of a defined, explicit, and clearly applicable legal principle yet ignored or refused to apply it. *See DiRussa v. Dean Witter Reynolds Inc.*, 121 F.3d 818 (2d Cir.1997), *cert. denied*, 522 U.S. 1049, 118 S.Ct. 695, 139 L.Ed.2d 639 (1998) (upholding award despite arbitrator's failure to award attorney's fees that would be mandatory in an action under ADEA, because the arbitra-

tors did not state their reasons for denying fees and therefore could not be said to have known of but intentionally disregarded the ADEA provision). But some judges are beginning to treat awards determining federal statutory employment discrimination claims less deferentially. *See Williams v. Cigna Fin. Advisors, Inc.*, 197 F.3d 752, 759 (5th Cir.1999), *cert. denied*, __ U.S. __, 120 S.Ct. 1833, 146 L.Ed.2d 777 (2000) (when reviewing the arbitration of federal statutory employment claims, an arbitrator's award may be vacated for manifest disregard of the law, a standard necessary, in the court's view, to ensure compliance with the requirements of the federal antidiscrimination statutes but finding that plaintiff had not met the standard in this case); *Halligan v. Piper Jaffray, Inc.*, 148 F.3d 197 (2d Cir.1998), *cert. denied*, 526 U.S. 1034, 119 S.Ct. 1286, 143 L.Ed.2d 378 (1999) (overturning arbitration award based on manifest disregard of the applicable law, because, even though the arbitrator had issued no accompanying opinion, evidence of unlawful discrimination was overwhelming; court stressed the necessity after *Gilmer* of adequate judicial review of arbitration awards deciding statutory rights) (citing cases).

43. *See Doctor's Assocs., Inc. v. Casarotto*, 517 U.S. 681, 686, 116 S.Ct. 1652, 1656, 134 L.Ed.2d 902 (1996); *Prudential Ins. Co. v. Lai*, 42 F.3d 1299, 1304 (9th Cir.1994), *cert. denied*, 516 U.S. 812, 116 S.Ct. 61, 133 L.Ed.2d 24 (1995).

44. *See Koveleskie*, 167 F.3d at 367 (holding that only fraud would void the agreement under Illinois law); *Alford v. Dean Witter Reynolds, Inc.*, 975 F.2d 1161, 1163 (5th Cir.1992); *Beauchamp v. Great W. Life Assurance Co.*, 918 F.Supp. 1091 (D.Mich.1996), *Lockhart v. A.G. Edwards & Sons, Inc.*, 1994 WL 34870, at *2 (D.Kan. 1994); *Feinberg v. Bear, Stearns & Co.*, 1991 WL 79309, at *3 (S.D.N.Y.1991); *and Neubrander v. Dean Witter Reynolds, Inc.*, 81 Ohio App.3d 308, 610 N.E.2d 1089, 1091 (Ohio App.1992) (all rejecting unconscionability challenges to arbitration agreements).

The Supreme Court may resolve the questions regarding interpretation of § 118 of Title VII and § 1 of the FAA in a number of distinct ways. It might reject the dominant view of the circuit courts by construing § 1 of FAA broadly; then *Gilmer* would remain as authority for ordering pre-suit arbitration only in the rare situation where the agreement to arbitrate is not contained in a § 1 "contract of employment" but, say, in an ancillary agreement to abide by the rules of a securities exchange. At the other extreme, the Court might overrule *Gardner–Denver* by asserting that its numerous recent decisions facilitating arbitration, coupled with § 118, have completely sapped the vitality of its earlier decisions that denied preclusive effect to arbitration awards in actions under other labor and civil rights statutes.[45]

But there are a number of more moderate possibilities. For all FAA-covered enterprises (i.e., all except those in the transportation industries specifically mentioned in § 1), the Court could follow the lower courts by extending *Gilmer* beyond ADEA to reach Title VII claims, without overruling or limiting *Gardner–Denver*. This could mean that the putative plaintiff who has agreed to arbitrate grievances or disputes related to statutory discrimination prohibitions must first submit to arbitration procedures, but would not be bound by the arbitral award. Or the Court might limit *Gardner–Denver*'s insistence that the plaintiff may sue after an unfavorable arbitration award to the collective bargaining setting, where the plaintiff is not in control of the grievance and arbitration process and thus can less plausibly be said to have waived a judicial forum. Then all potential plaintiffs (outside the transportation industries) who have agreed to arbitrate the controversy at hand (or perhaps only those whose agreements to arbitrate specifically refer precisely to the claims of *statutory* employment discrimination at issue) would be remitted to pre-suit arbitration per *Gilmer*, but only those whose promises to arbitrate are contained in collectively bargained agreements could sue in court after an adverse award.

There are still other possible possibilities. Suppose the Court, in the spirit of § 118 and the new solicitude for arbitration, departs from the civil rights analogue, modifies *Gardner–Denver* by holding that while awards resulting from a "quasi-judicial" arbitration process[46] do not inevitably bar a judicial claim under a federal anti-discrimination statute, they do have ordinary issue preclusive effect in subsequent judicial actions under Title VII and ADEA. Then presumably the plaintiff who prevailed in arbitration but seeks greater remedies could use preclusion offensively in a subsequent federal statutory action, just as a victorious employer could issue preclude the plaintiff defensively.[47] Questions

45. See text *supra*, this section.

46. See also the discussion in Chapter 12 on *University of Tennessee v. Elliott*, which holds that a prior administrative decision may have preclusive effect in federal litigation if it is "quasi-judicial" in character.

47. See discussion of preclusion principles in Chapter 12; *cf. Meredith v. Beech Aircraft Corp.*, 18 F.3d 890 (10th Cir.1994) (judgment in favor of plaintiff in prior Title VII action has collateral estoppel or "issue preclusion" effect in second Title VII action brought by different employee against same employer).

would nevertheless remain as to the scope of such preclusion in any individual case.

For example, if the plaintiff prevailed in arbitration but then sought some of the greater Title VII remedies made available by the Civil Rights Act of 1991, her lawsuit would ordinarily be precluded if her judicial "claim" is deemed to be the same as that advanced in arbitration. Under the modern, expansive approach to res judicata (or, as it is now most commonly known, "claim preclusion") the fact that the plaintiff's legal theory is different—in court she alleges a violation of Title VII, at the arbitration she sought to show a violation of the individual employment contract or collective agreement—or that she seeks additional relief would not necessarily prevent a finding that the claims are the same. It would be enough for preclusion to apply if they arose from the same real-life transaction, defined in spatial and temporal terms.[48]

Yet § 26(1)(c) of the Second Restatement of Conflicts of Laws, to which the federal courts usually refer in shaping the contours of federal preclusion law, provides an exception to claim preclusion where the first forum lacked subject matter jurisdiction to entertain, or remedial authority to award the subsequently asserted claim or remedy.[49] Most arbitrators, in accord with some of the post-*Gilmer* judicial decisions as well as long-standing Supreme Court authority, have concluded that under the typical collective agreement, their authority is limited to interpreting, applying and rendering a decision about the terms of the parties' bargain as opposed to a distinct statutory norm.[50] Further, many arbitrators conclude that a particular contract or collective agreement places limits on the remedies they may direct, with compensatory and punitive damages among the most common exclusions.[51] In such circumstances the plaintiff may escape claim preclusion by convincing the court that she seeks in litigation to prevail on claims or obtain remedies beyond the authority of the arbitrator.

Another argument that achieves the same result is that the arbitration proceeding did not afford the plaintiff a "full and fair" opportunity to litigate key questions requiring resolution in the judicial forum.[52] But the Supreme Court has now held that where contracting parties explicitly authorize the arbitrator to award punitive damages, the FAA demands

---

48. See discussion of claim preclusion under § 24 of the Restatement (Second) of Conflicts of Laws in Chapter 12.

49. See Chapter 12 concerning this exception.

50. Even though many arbitrators feel free to refer to the statutory standards in an effort to flesh out the meaning the parties had in mind when they agreed to an ambiguous contract provision, they are clear that in the end it is the contract, rather than the referenced statute, that they are construing. *See* Elkouri and El-

kouri, *How Arbitration Works* (4th ed. (1985)).

51. *See Koveleskie*, 167 F.3d 361, and *Cole*, 105 F.3d 1465 (noting especially reluctance or lack of contract authority to award punitive damages).

52. *Cf. Ryan v. City of Shawnee*, 13 F.3d 345 (10th Cir.1993) (federal courts not bound to accord preclusive effect to prior state court judgment that reviewed arbitration award because state limitations on judicial review prevented litigation of the key issue presented).

enforcement of such an award even if state law is to the contrary.[53] And the Court construed the terms of the parties' agreement respecting remedies quite liberally in order to find an "explicit" authorization for punitive damages.[54] Indeed the Court's opinion itself would not plainly preclude interpreting the FAA to *require* arbitration agreements affecting interstate commerce to authorize punitive awards, although such an interpretation would violate the tradition that the parties fashion the scope of the arbitration agreement to suit their particular needs.

Suppose, on the other hand, that the employer prevails in arbitration and asserts claim preclusion defensively in court. The "same claim" requirement is again a prerequisite to preclusion. If, because of one of the jurisdictional or remedial limitations just mentioned, a judge determines that the Restatement exception to claim preclusion applies, the award—even though it is sufficiently "quasi-judicial" to have potential preclusive effect in federal litigation—could not preclude the plaintiff's claim; at most it would be accorded collateral estoppel or "issue preclusive" effect. In that event specific arbitral fact findings may bind the court in its conduct of the ensuing Title VII or ADEA action, while in other respects the action would proceed without regard to the arbitral award. But issue preclusion might be of limited utility to either party seeking to ease its proof burden in the judicial action. Arbitrators, precisely in order to provide a less expensive and more expeditious alternative to litigation, often issue only a terse decision ("award," in arbitral parlance) that declares the disposition of the grievance submitted, dispensing with any accompanying opinion. In other cases the opinion is less complete or thorough than, for example, the judicial findings required by Federal Rule of Civil Procedure 52.

The Supreme Court has not decided whether *Gardner–Denver* permits a court to entertain a Title VII claim following confirmation of an arbitral award in state court. Some circuits have denied preclusion in this situation, finding that the state court's limited scope of review did not constitute a final judgment on the merits and in any event did not involve the same "claim" as that afforded by Title VII.[55] Another circuit, however, invoked collateral estoppel or "issue preclusion" in a Title VII action after finding that the state court that had confirmed the arbitration award had ruled not just on plaintiffs' collective bargaining rights but also on the merits of their Title VII claims.[56]

53. *Mastrobuono v. Shearson/Lehman Hutton, Inc.,* 514 U.S. 52, 115 S.Ct. 1212, 131 L.Ed.2d 76 (1995).

54. *Id.*

55. *Ryan v. City of Shawnee,* 13 F.3d 345 (10th Cir.1993); *Kirk v. Board of Educ. of Bremen Cmty. High Sch.,* 811 F.2d 347 (7th Cir.1987); *Bottini v. Sadore Mgmt. Corp.,* 764 F.2d 116 (2d Cir.1985). To similar effect is *Aleem v. General Felt Indus. Inc.,* 661 F.2d 135, 137 (9th Cir.1981).

56. *Rider v. Pennsylvania,* 850 F.2d 982 (3d Cir.), *cert. denied,* 488 U.S. 993, 109 S.Ct. 556, 102 L.Ed.2d 582 (1988). *Cf. Caldeira v. County of Kauai,* 866 F.2d 1175 (9th Cir.), *cert. denied,* 493 U.S. 817, 110 S.Ct. 69, 107 L.Ed.2d 36 (1989) (precluding § 1983 action in deference to state court confirmation in which plaintiff had opportunity to challenge the merits of the arbitrator's decision).

How does the Older Workers Benefit Protection Act (OWBPA) coexist with *Gilmer*? Shortly after *Gilmer* was decided, commentators suggested an apparent conflict between the OWBPA and *Gilmer*, in actions arising under the ADEA. The OWBPA requires that any waiver of ADEA "rights or claims" be "knowing and voluntary."[57] If a waiver of ADEA "rights" includes a waiver of a right to a jury trial or access to federal court, the OWBPA could be interpreted to invalidate many agreements to arbitrate exacted as a condition of initial or continued employment.[58] But the federal courts to consider the issue have uniformly held that the OWBPA does not undermine the holding of *Gilmer*.[59]

§ 4.7 Federal Employee Lawsuits

In 1972, Congress expanded Title VII's coverage to federal employees in the executive branch and those units in the legislative and judicial branch having positions in the competitive civil service. The 1991 Civil Rights Act and the Government Employee Rights Act (GERA) further amended Title VII to extend its *substantive* provisions to Congressional employees, employees of the agencies of the legislative branch, and presidential appointees. The enforcement procedure for these newly covered federal employees is internal. Title VII's procedure applies only to those federal employees covered by the 1972 amendments to Title VII.[1]

57. 29 U.S.C.A. § 626(f).

58. *See generally* Christine Godsil Cooper, *Where Are We Going with Gilmer? Some Ruminations on the Arbitration of Discrimination Claims*, 11 St. Louis U.Pub. L.Rev. 203, 235–36 (1992).

59. *See, e.g., Rosenberg v. Merrill Lynch, Pierce, Fenner & Smith, Inc.*, 170 F.3d 1 (1st Cir.1999) (interpreting ADEA "rights" protected by OWBPA as referring only to substantive rights); *Seus v. John Nuveen & Co.*, 146 F.3d 175, 181–82 (3d Cir.1998)), *cert. denied*, 525 U.S. 1139, 119 S.Ct. 1028, 143 L.Ed.2d 38 (1999); *Williams v. Cigna Fin. Advisors, Inc.*, 56 F.3d 656, 660–61 (5th Cir.1995).

§ 4.7

1. In addition to executive agency employees, Title VII applies to "those units of the legislative and judicial branches of the Federal Government having positions in the competitive service." 42 U.S.C.A. § 2000e–16(a). Section 2102 of Title 5 of the United States Code states:

The competitive service consists of:

(1) all civil service positions in the executive branch, except—

(A) positions which are specifically excepted from the competitive service by or under statute;

(B) positions to which appointments are made by nomination for confirmation by the Senate, unless the Senate otherwise directs; and

(C) positions in the Senior Executive Service;

(2) civil service positions not in the executive branch *which are specifically included in the competitive service by statute*; and

(3) positions in the government of the District of Columbia which are specifically included in the competitive service by statute (emphasis added).

For legislative and judicial branch employees not covered by Title VII, such as federal probation officers (judicial branch employees not "specifically included in the competitive service by statute," *see* 5 U.S.C.A. § 2102), the only remedial scheme afforded by statute is that of the Civil Service Reform Act ("CSRA"). (Perhaps also available is the Back Pay Act, 5 U.S.C.A. § 5596, which affords certain federal employees a monetary remedy for "unjustified or unwarranted personnel action—presumably including discrimination on the grounds prohibited by Title VII—that has resulted in the withdrawal or reduction" of the employees' pay.) The CSRA classifies employees and provides various remedial schemes dependent on the civil service employee's

The ADEA was amended in 1974 to require most federal personnel decisions to be made free from discrimination based on age.[2] Title VII's § 717 procedural requirements do not apply to the ADEA, however, and a federal ADEA plaintiff may proceed to federal court without a formal administrative process.[3] Timely notice to EEOC is all that is required.[4] The ADA does not generally reach federal employees, but these employees receive comparable protection from the Rehabilitation Act, which expressly incorporates § 717's remedies, procedures and rights.[5]

As amended, § 717 of Title VII provides that "[a]ll personnel actions affecting employees or applicants for employment ... [in executive branch agencies and other specifically listed federal employers] shall be made free from any discrimination based on race, color, religion, sex, or national origin." A covered federal employee may ultimately bring suit with de novo review in federal court.[6] However, the employee first must exhaust stringent administrative remedies.[7] This comprehensive scheme has persuaded the Supreme Court that Congress impliedly intended to

classification. *See, e.g.,* 5 U.S.C.A. §§ 2108, 7511; *see generally United States v. Fausto,* 484 U.S. 439, 445–49, 108 S.Ct. 668, 672–75, 98 L.Ed.2d 830 (1988).

Some employees covered by the CSRA have a right to appeal adverse personnel actions to the Merit Systems Protection Board (MSPB), followed by a right to judicial review in the Federal Circuit. *See Fausto,* 484 U.S. at 444–47. Other employees such as federal probation officers, *see Lee v. Hughes,* 145 F.3d 1272 (11th Cir.1998), *cert. denied,* 525 U.S. 1138, 119 S.Ct. 1026, 143 L.Ed.2d 37 (1999), and certain Fish and Wildlife employees, *see Fausto,* 484 U.S. at 441 n.1, are classified as "nonpreference eligible" members of the excepted service who, under the CSRA, are not afforded any administrative or judicial review of adverse personnel actions, including appeal to the MSPB. In *Fausto,* the Supreme held that such employees are barred from seeking judicial review under the Tucker Act, 28 U.S.C.A. § 1419, which grants jurisdiction to the United States Court of Federal Claims for certain tort and contract claims against the federal government. In *Lee v. Hughes,* the Eleventh Circuit held that such employees are also precluded from resort to a *Bivens* action to seek judicial review because the CSRA's comprehensive remedial scheme is a "special factor" counseling against recognition of a *Bivens* suit. *See Bivens,* 403 U.S. at 396. *Accord Saul v. United States,* 928 F.2d 829, 836 (9th Cir.1991) (holding that the CSRA is a special factor counseling against recognition of a *Bivens* remedy); *Lombardi v. Small Business Admin.,* 889 F.2d 959, 961 (10th Cir.1989); *Volk v. Hobson,* 866 F.2d 1398, 1403–04 (Fed.Cir.), *cert. denied,* 490 U.S. 1092, 109 S.Ct. 2435, 104 L.Ed.2d 991

(1989). *See generally* § 2.48, *supra,* on CSRA as precluding federal employee *Bivens* actions. In 1999, the Administrative Office of the U.S. Courts directed local courts and probation officers to provide a more uniform review and hearing process, available even to nonpreference eligible employees, that would reach claims of discrimination in employment.

2. 29 U.S.C.A. § 633a. But the very fact of this separate protection prevents a plaintiff from pursuing under Title VII a claim alleging retaliation on a complaint of age discrimination. *See Lennon v. Rubin,* 166 F.3d 6 (1st Cir.1999).

3. *See Stevens v. Department of Treas.,* 500 U.S. 1, 111 S.Ct. 1562, 114 L.Ed.2d 1 (1991) (federal employee complaining of age discrimination does not have to seek relief from employing agency or Equal Employment Opportunity Commission (EEOC); employee can decide to present merits of claim to federal court in first instance).

4. "[N]o civil action may be commenced by any individual under this section until the individual has given the Commission not less than thirty days' notice of an intent to file such action. Such notice shall be filed within one hundred and eighty days after the alleged unlawful practice occurred." 29 U.S.C.A. § 633a.

5. 29 U.S.C.A. § 794(a).

6. *See* 42 U.S.C.A. § 2000e–16(c); *Chandler v. Roudebush,* 425 U.S. 840, 96 S.Ct. 1949, 48 L.Ed.2d 416 (1976) (de novo review).

7. *See Brown v. General Servs. Admin.,* 425 U.S. 820, 832–33, 96 S.Ct. 1961, 1967–68, 48 L.Ed.2d 402 (1976).

make Title VII the sole remedy for discrimination in federal employment, when Title VII is available to covered employees with respect to covered claims, to the exclusion of the Reconstruction Civil Rights Acts.[8]

a. Exhaustion of Administrative Remedies

In 42 U.S.C.A. § 2000e–16(b), Congress delegated to EEOC the authority to enforce § 2000e–16(a) and to promulgate "such rules, regulations, orders, and instructions as it deems necessary and appropriate to carry out its responsibilities under this section." Pursuant to those regulations, a federal employee who believes she has been discriminated against in violation of Title VII must, within 45 days of the discriminatory act, consult an Equal Employment Opportunity ("EEO") counselor within the employing agency to try to resolve the matter informally.[9] If the effort at informal resolution is unsuccessful, the EEO counselor notifies the employee of her right to file a formal administrative complaint with the employing agency itself.[10] The complaint to the employing agency must be filed with 15 days of this notice,[11] and is expressly limited to those "matter(s) raised in precomplaint counseling (or issues like or related to issues raised in pre-complaint counseling)."[12]

Upon receiving the complaint, the employing federal agency is directed to conduct an investigation to "develop a complete and impartial factual record upon which to make findings on the matters raised by the written complaint."[13] The agency is afforded 180 days to complete the investigation, but this can be extended by agreement for an additional 90 days, or the agency can unilaterally extend the time frame an additional 30 days in certain circumstances.[14] After completing the investigation, the agency gives the complaining employee a copy of the investigative file. At this point, the agency can make the employee an offer of "full relief."[15] If the employee rejects the offer of "full relief," the agency is required to dismiss the complaint.[16] The employee can then

---

8. *See Brown* (Title VII precludes federal employee claim under § 1981). *Cf. Great Am. Fed. Savings & Loan v. Novotny*, 442 U.S. 366, 99 S.Ct. 2345, 60 L.Ed.2d 957 (1979) (availability of Title VII to any employee precludes claim under 42 U.S.C.A. § 1985(3)). The Fifth Circuit has held that Title VII also preempts state law and other non-Title VII remedies for federal employees. *Pfau v. Reed*, 167 F.3d 228 (5th Cir.), *cert. denied*, 528 U.S. 813, 120 S.Ct. 49, 145 L.Ed.2d 43 (1999).

9. *See* 29 C.F.R. § 1614.105(a). But the regulations also allow an "ignorance of the law" defense: an aggrieved employee is absolved from complying with the filing period if he can show "that he . . . was not notified of the time limits and was not otherwise aware of them." 29 C.F.R. S 1614(a)(2). *See Pauling v. Secretary of Dep't of Interior*, 160 F.3d 133 (2d Cir.1998) (discussing actual

and constructive notice of the 45 day time limit).

10. *See* 29 C.F.R. § 1614.105(d).

11. *See* 29 C.F.R. § 1614.106(b)

12. 29 C.F.R. § 1614.105(b). *See also Artis v. Greenspan*, 158 F.3d 1301 (D.C.Cir. 1998) (failure to present class claim to EEO Counselor waives claim for class action status).

13. 29 C.F.R. § 1614.108(b). An employee's failure to respond to an agency's request for information relative to claimed damages has been held a failure to exhaust administrative remedies. *Crawford v. Babbitt*, 186 F.3d 1322 (11th Cir.1999).

14. *See* 29 C.F.R. § 1614.108(e).

15. *See* 29 C.F.R. § 1614.107(h). "Full relief" is discussed *infra*.

16. *See id.*

appeal to the EEOC or file a civil action in federal district court.[17]

If an appeal is taken to the EEOC, and the EEOC agrees that the agency's offer constituted "full relief," then the appeal must be dismissed.[18] (There is no counterpart duty on the part of a charging party alleging discrimination by a private or state or local government employer.) But if the EEOC concludes that the offer did not constitute "full relief," it issues a final written decision.[19] "If the decision contains a finding of discrimination, appropriate remedies shall be included."[20] This may include interest, costs, and attorney's fees.[21] The employee, but not the employing agency,[22] may appeal the EEOC's final decision by filing an action in federal district court.[23]

If, however, the employing agency decides not to make an offer of "full relief" at the conclusion of its investigation, the agency must notify the employee that she has a right to either (1) request a administrative hearing, or (2) receive an immediate final decision on the claim from the employing agency.[24]

If the employee elects to request a hearing, the administrative judge conducts the hearing and, within 180 days of the request for the hearing (unless good cause exists to extend the time), issues findings of fact and conclusions of law, and, if unlawful discrimination is found, orders appropriate remedies.[25] The administrative judge has no authority to hear issues which the employing agency has not had an opportunity to address.[26] The employing agency has sixty days to reject or modify the administrative judge's findings or relief ordered and issue its own "final decision."[27] The "final decision" must "consist of findings by the agency on the merits of each issue in the complaint and, when discrimination is found, appropriate remedies and relief."[28] If the employing agency fails to issue a final decision, then the conclusions of the administrative judge and the relief ordered become the agency's final decision.[29]

If the employee chooses, she may appeal the agency's final decision to the EEOC or file a civil action in federal district court.[30] If the employee appeals to the EEOC, the Office of Federal Operations ("OFO") handles the appeal on behalf of the EEOC,[31] and it must issue a final written decision.[32] If the OFO finds discrimination, its final

---

17. *See* 29 C.F.R. § 1614.401(a).

18. *See* 29 C.F.R. § 1614.405. *See also Francis v. Brown*, 58 F.3d 191 (5th Cir. 1995); *Wrenn v. Secretary, Dep't of Veterans Affairs*, 918 F.2d 1073 (2d Cir.1990), *cert. denied*, 499 U.S. 977, 111 S.Ct. 1625, 113 L.Ed.2d 721 (1991).

19. *See id.*

20. *Id.*

21. *Id.*

22. *See* 29 C.F.R. § 1614.504(a).

23. *See* 42 U.S.C.A. 2000e–16(c).

24. *See* 29 C.F.R. § 1614.108(f). If the employee decides not to request a hearing, the employing agency must issue a "final decision" within sixty days. *See* 29 C.F.R. § 1614.110.

25. *See* 29 C.F.R. § 1614.109(g).

26. *See* 29 C.F.R. § 1614.109(a).

27. *See* 29 C.F.R. § 1614.109(g).

28. 29 C.F.R. § 1614.110.

29. *See* 29 C.F.R. § 1614.109(g).

30. *See* 42 U.S.C.A. § 2000e–16(c); 29 C.F.R. § 1614.408.

31. 1*See* 29 C.F.R. § 1614.404.

32. *See* 29 C.F.R. § 1614.405.

decision must include appropriate remedies.[33] The employee, but not the agency,[34] can opt to have the OFO's final decision reviewed in federal court.[35] The head of the agency is the only proper defendant in the suit.[36] By whatever route the employee obtains the right to sue in federal court, the suit must be commenced within 90 days of the final decision the employee receives.[37]

Recognizing that this rather elaborate remedial scheme can break down, causing delays in processing a complaint, § 717 contains an escape hatch: "after one hundred and eighty days from the filing of the initial charge with the department, agency, or unit or with the [EEOC] on appeal . . . an employee or applicant for employment, if aggrieved . . . by the failure to take final action on his complaint, may file a civil action. . . ." In this respect, then, the federal employee is on a par with the private plaintiff; true administrative exhaustion is not required, but the agency and EEOC must be given an opportunity, for at least 180 days, to consider the complaint. On the other hand, when an employing agency was held to have made a reasonable request of the claimant for evidence connecting the alleged discrimination was her damages, her refusal to comply with the request was deemed a failure to exhaust.[38] The same equitable tolling rules apply to federal employees as are available to private defendants.[39]

b. Remedies

When either the employing agency or the EEOC finds unlawful discrimination by the employing agency, the employing agency must provide the employee "full relief."[40] For a current employee, full relief includes nondiscriminatory placement with back pay and interest, cancellation of any unwarranted personnel action, full opportunity to participate in any employee benefit denied because of discrimination, and attorney's fees and costs.[41] Some but not all circuits hold that a federal

---

33. *See id.*

34. *See* 29 C.F.R. § 1614.504(a).

35. *See* 29 C.F.R. § 1614.408; 42 U.S.C.A. § 2000e–16(c).

36. *See* 42 U.S.C.A. § 2000e–16(c). Plaintiffs who name the agency itself as the defendant, or commit some other error in styling the case, can resort to Federal Rule of Civil Procedure 15(c)(3). It serves to ensure that an amended complaint will relate back to the original filing when, "within the period provided by Rule 4(m) for service of the summons and complaint, the party to be brought in by amendment (A) has received such notice of the institution of the action that the party will not be prejudiced in maintaining a defense on the merits, and (B) knew or should have known that, but for a mistake concerning the identity of the proper party, the action would have been brought against the party." *See also* Fed. R. Civ. P. 15(c)(3) advisory committee notes (1991).

37. *See* 42 U.S.C.A. S 2000e–16(c). Circuit opinions divide over whether a request for reconsideration or a petition to reopen EEOC's final decision tolls the ninety-day filing deadline applicable under Title VII. *See Holley v. Department of Veterans Affairs*, 165 F.3d 244 (3d Cir.1999) (yes); *Belhomme v. Widnall*, 127 F.3d 1214 (10th Cir.1997), *cert. denied*, 523 U.S. 1100, 118 S.Ct. 1569, 140 L.Ed.2d 803 (1998) (no).

38. *Briley v. Carlin*, 172 F.3d 567 (8th Cir.1999).

39. *See Irwin v. Department of Veterans Affairs*, 498 U.S. 89, 95–96, 111 S.Ct. 453, 457–58, 112 L.Ed.2d 435 (1990).

40. *See* 29 C.F.R. § 1614.501(a).

41. *See* 29 C.F.R. § 1614.501(c). Full relief for an applicant to a federal agency is described in 29 C.F.R. § 1614.501(b).

employee forfeits the right to sue by rejecting an agency offer that a court later deems "full relief."[42]

Compensatory damages are available against a federal agency that engaged in intentional discrimination,[43] but if the employee seeks compensatory damages, either party may demand a trial by jury.[44] This availability of damages, at least in court, led to a split among the circuits that the Supreme Court has resolved. The Court held that the EEOC, and not just a court, can award compensatory damages against a federal agency without denying the agency's right to a jury trial.[45] The Court rejected the assertion that because EEOC's determinations are binding against the federal agency, and thus nonappealable, an EEOC award of compensatory damages would deny the agency the statutory right to a jury trial. It found that the jury trial right could be read to obtain only if the proceedings eventuated in an "action" in court. The Court was principally persuaded that the EEOC may award compensatory damages in the administrative process by virtue of the text of the enabling statute,[46] which empowers EEOC to provide a remedy that is "appropriate," which the Court held could include a remedy like compensatory damages that was not available until the 1991 Amendments to Title VII. Because it is now settled that EEOC may award such damages, a claimant seeking them must exhaust the administrative process with EEOC to the full extent generally required.[47]

§ 4.8 Suit by EEOC

The EEOC has an option other than issuing a determination of reasonable or no reasonable cause and a notice of right to sue. It may initiate suit in its own name against private[1] employers.[2] Unlike individual plaintiffs, the agency faces no fixed deadlines within which it must file suit, and there is even authority that it may commence an action based on a charge filed by an employee whose own judicial action was dismissed as untimely.[3] Thus only a delay long enough to invoke the

42. See authority cited supra § 4.5.

43. See 42 U.S.C.A. § 1981a(a).

44. See 42 U.S.C.A. § 1981a(c).

45. West v. Gibson, 527 U.S. 212, 119 S.Ct. 1906, 144 L.Ed.2d 196 (1999)(reversing Gibson v. Brown, 137 F.3d 992 (7th Cir.1998)).

46. 42 U.S.C.A. § 2000e–16(b).

47. West, 527 U.S. 212, 119 S.Ct. 1906, 144 L.Ed.2d 196. Exhaustion thus apparently requires the claimant to seek compensatory damages before the employing agency. See, e.g., Crawford v. Babbitt, 186 F.3d 1322 (11th Cir.1999).

§ 4.8

1. Suits against a state or local "government, governmental agency, or political subdivision" named in a charge filed with EEOC may be brought only by the Attorney General. See §§ 706(f)(1) and 707, 42 U.S.C.A. §§ 2000e–5(f)(1) and 2000e–6.

2. Id.

3. See EEOC v. Harris Chernin, Inc., 10 F.3d 1286 (7th Cir.1993) (upholding EEOC's right to sue independent of the individual plaintiff's rights, but limiting it to injunctive relief). Indeed it has been held that EEOC has authority to sue even when all the protected group members for whom it purports to speak have signed affidavits disclaiming their personal interest in pursuing a claim. EEOC v. Johnson & Higgins, Inc., 91 F.3d 1529 (2d Cir.1996), cert. denied, 522 U.S. 808, 118 S.Ct. 47, 139 L.Ed.2d 13 (1997) (case under ADEA). And EEOC may proceed on behalf of an employee who has waived the right to a judicial forum in an agreement to arbitrate, at least to obtain injunctive relief. EEOC v. Waffle

defense of laches serves as a check on EEOC's promptness in bringing suit.[4]

But unlike private litigants, who need satisfy *only* charge-filing and action-commencement time requirements in order to sue, EEOC, freed of those fetters, has other pre-suit responsibilities. It must comply with the statutory requirements of notifying the charged party within 10 days after it receives a charge[5] and attempting during the administrative process to eliminate unlawful employment practices through "conference, conciliation, and persuasion."[6]

If EEOC files suit before one can be commenced by a private charging party, the private party is limited to intervention in EEOC's action and may not file her own.[7] And EEOC may attempt to preserve its suit priority by rescinding a previously issued notice of right to sue before the private action is commenced.[8] If, however, the charging party commences an action under Title VII before EEOC does, some courts have held that EEOC may not commence its own action but may only exercise its statutory right to intervene in the private party's suit.[9]

If EEOC wins the race to the courthouse, there is authority suggesting that the charging party, to avoid being bound by an adverse judgment and to preserve a right to appeal a judgment against EEOC, must intervene.[10] It is unclear whether this authority survives *Martin v. Wilks*[11] or is affected by the provision of the 1991 Act that bars challenges to employment practices authorized or commanded by litigated judgments or consent decrees only if the challenger received notice of the proceedings or was adequately represented in them by another

House, Inc., 193 F.3d 805 (4th Cir.1999)), *petition for cert. filed,* May 15, 2000; *EEOC v. Northwest Airlines, Inc.,* 188 F.3d 695, 701–02 (6th Cir.1999).

4. *See Occidental Life Ins. Co. of Cal. v. EEOC,* 432 U.S. 355, 97 S.Ct. 2447, 53 L.Ed.2d 402 (1977).

5. 42 U.S.C.A. § 2000e–5(b); *see EEOC v. Burlington Northern, Inc.,* 644 F.2d 717, 720–21 (8th Cir.1981).

6. *Id. See EEOC v. Klingler Elec. Corp.,* 636 F.2d 104 (5th Cir.1981).

7. *See Behlar v. Smith,* 719 F.2d 950 (8th Cir.1983), *cert. denied sub nom. University of Arkansas Bd. of Trustees v. Greer,* 466 U.S. 958, 104 S.Ct. 2169, 80 L.Ed.2d 552 (1984).

8. *Lute v. Singer Co.,* 678 F.2d 844 (9th Cir.1982), *amended,* 696 F.2d 1266 (9th Cir. 1983).

9. *EEOC v. Continental Oil Co.,* 548 F.2d 884 (10th Cir.1977); *Johnson v. Nekoosa–Edwards Paper Co.,* 558 F.2d 841 (8th Cir.), *cert. denied sub nom. Nekoosa Papers, Inc. v. EEOC,* 434 U.S. 920, 98 S.Ct. 394, 54 L.Ed.2d 276 (1977); *EEOC v. Missouri Pa-*

cific R.R. Co., 493 F.2d 71 (8th Cir.1974). *But see EEOC v. North Hills Passavant Hosp.,* 544 F.2d 664 (3d Cir.1976); *EEOC v. McLean Trucking Co.,* 525 F.2d 1007 (6th Cir.1975); *EEOC v. Huttig Sash & Door Co.,* 511 F.2d 453, 455 (5th Cir.1975) (EEOC limited to intervention if it raises issues pertaining and seeks relief only on behalf of the private plaintiff, but may seek broader relief in spite of previously filed individual action). There is authority under the ADEA, however, that EEOC may either intervene *or* commence an independent action even if the complainant has filed first. *EEOC v. G–K–G, Inc.,* 39 F.3d 740 (7th Cir.1994); *EEOC v. Wackenhut Corp.,* 939 F.2d 241 (5th Cir.1991) (authorizing suit by EEOC filed after action by individual plaintiff).

10. *Adams v. Proctor & Gamble Mfg. Co.,* 697 F.2d 582 (4th Cir.1983) (en banc), *cert. denied,* 465 U.S. 1041, 104 S.Ct. 1318, 79 L.Ed.2d 714 (1984).

11. 490 U.S. 755, 109 S.Ct. 2180, 104 L.Ed.2d 835 (1989). *Wilks* is discussed in § 4.45, *infra.*

party—e.g., EEOC.[12]

§ 4.9 Plaintiff Joinder and Class Actions; Identity of Defendants

Title VII actions in federal court are limited by statutory requirements concerning parties and allegations. The EEOC charge which forms the predicate for a Title VII action may be filed either "by or on behalf of" a person who is "aggrieved."[1] Thus named plaintiffs who have filed charges may prosecute the action on behalf of class members in a Federal Rule 23 class action, and those class members need not themselves have filed individual EEOC or state agency charges if the class is certified.[2] But the Supreme Court, with its 1980 decision in *General Telephone Co. of Southwest v. Falcon*,[3] has strictly applied the Rule 23 requirements for class certification.

Rule 23, applicable also to class actions under the ADA and § 1981, has the following four threshold requirements:

(1) a sufficient number of class members that ordinary joinder under Rule 20 would be impracticable;

(2) questions of law or fact common to the class;

(3) claims (or, in a defendant class action, defenses) of the representative parties that are "typical" of those of the class as a whole; and

(4) a likelihood that the representative parties will fairly and adequately protect the interests of the class.

The first two requirements are usually easily met in employment discrimination class actions, which characteristically involve a plaintiff class. Numerosity is seldom a problem, with classes containing as few as 18 members having been certified.[4] And so long as the named plaintiffs assert that disparate treatment on a prohibited ground is classwide, or that one or more neutral practices has classwide impact on a protected group, the commonality requirement is also rarely a barrier. Employment discrimination by its very nature partakes of classwide discrimination.

The third and fourth factors, typicality and representativeness, have proven most difficult to surmount. For a putative class to comply with Rule 23's requirement that the claims of the named plaintiffs be "typical" of those of the class, *Falcon* insists that in most cases the complement of named plaintiffs in a private Title VII class action include at

---

12. Section 108 (adding subsection 703(n)(1) to Title VII, 42 U.S.C.A. § 2000e–2(n)(1)). Section 108 is discussed in more detail below and in Chapter 12.

§ 4.9

1. Section 706(f)(1). Standing under Title VII and related statutes is discussed in Chapter 12.

2. *Albemarle Paper Co. v. Moody*, 422 U.S. 405, 95 S.Ct. 2362, 45 L.Ed.2d 280 (1975).

3. 457 U.S. 147, 102 S.Ct. 2364, 72 L.Ed.2d 740 (1982).

4. *Cypress v. Newport News Gen. & Nonsectarian Hosp. Ass'n*, 375 F.2d 648 (4th Cir.1967).

least one representative who complains not only on the same prohibited ground of discrimination (e.g., race or sex) as the putative class, but also of each particular discriminatory practice the class proposes to attack. In a famous footnote 15, the court recognized an exception that permits certification despite diversity in the practices challenged by the representative plaintiffs and class members where those practices are the product of a common device (e.g. a test) or common decisionmaker applying the same subjective criteria.[5] Indeed, defendants have argued that *Falcon* also demands that at least one of the named plaintiffs must have allegedly suffered the same detrimental term or condition of employment—failure to hire, unequal pay or discipline, nonpromotion, on-the-job harassment, discharge—as the members of each class or subclass sought to be represented. Thus, unless the named plaintiff or plaintiffs who originally retained class counsel happen to embody all the characteristics of the putative class members, share all their same grievances and suffer their same injuries, *Falcon* effectively compels class counsel to try to assemble a wider group of named plaintiffs. Then some, but not all of the wider group can individually assert that they, as applicants or employees, were aggrieved by the particular employment practices, and affected in the same terms and conditions of employment, as other members of the class.

Falcon has had at least two distinct consequences. First, by effectively requiring the formation of a large and diverse plaintiff group, it has more sharply put into focus the ethical concerns associated with the solicitation of additional named plaintiffs. The Court has been rather lenient about permitting plaintiff class counsel, directly or through the original clients, to encourage others similarly situated to join the named plaintiff group, particularly when the class action is serving a "private attorney general" function in combating race discrimination.[6] But there are limits to solicitation even after *Falcon*. For example, the Eleventh Circuit vacated two class communications and a certification order because plaintiffs' counsel's efforts to communicate with class members caused serious irreparable injury to the defendant.[7]

Second, defendants have been resourceful in responding to the larger named plaintiff complements that *Falcon* in effect compels. *Falcon* has spurred more elaborate and expensive motion practice about the propriety of class certification and limitations on precertification discov-

5. See, e.g., *Carpenter v. Stephen F. Austin State Univ.*, 706 F.2d 608 (5th Cir.1983) (applying note 15 to certify class of current, past and future employees respecting varied job positions). *See also Caridad v. Metro–North Commuter R.R.*, 191 F.3d 283 (2d Cir.1999), *cert. denied sub nom. Metro–North Commuter R.R. Co. v. Norris*, ___ U.S. ___, 120 S.Ct. 1959, 146 L.Ed.2d 791 (2000) (commonality requirement could be met by alleging that company-wide policies delegate substantial authority to departmental supervisors who operate without

sufficient oversight even though plaintiffs challenged a subjective practice that would be applied differently to different plaintiffs).

6. *Gulf Oil Co. v. Bernard*, 452 U.S. 89, 101 S.Ct. 2193, 68 L.Ed.2d 693 (1981).

7. *See Jackson v. Motel 6 Multipurpose, Inc.*, 130 F.3d 999 (11th Cir.1997) (nationwide 800 number, mass mailings, and nationally published notices preceded certification by almost six months).

ery. Defendants commonly assert, frequently with success,[8] that the resulting diverse named plaintiff group—representing, for example, applicants, employees, and former employees; subordinates and superiors; unsuccessful test takers and victims of discriminatory discipline; women sexually harassed, and those suffering unequal pay; persons discharged, and persons not promoted—is rife with internal conflicts, so that, in Rule 23's terms, the named plaintiffs are not fairly "representative" of the class members whose fate will ride with them if the class is certified. To alleviate such conflicts, plaintiffs or district courts have sometimes proposed that the class be subdivided into "subclasses" that one or more of the named plaintiffs can fairly represent. On occasion, however, the result of forming subclasses is that each is fewer than the approximately 30 or so that the courts have generally required before a plaintiff group is sufficiently numerous to warrant class action certification. In this way a defendant's Rule 23 objections snowball: a challenge to typicality generates a challenge to representativeness that in turn generates a challenge to numerosity. By their nature these challenges invite early consideration of the merits of the class members' claims, although the court is formally prohibited from considering those merits in determining whether to certify.[9]

A December 1, 1998 amendment to Rule 23 of the Federal Rules of Civil Procedure overturns the result of a Supreme Court decision that had denied plaintiffs interlocutory review of decisions denying class certification. The new provision permits an appeal within 10 days of a district court's decision granting or denying certification or decertifying a previously certified class.[10] The court of appeals' discretion to grant or deny permission to appeal should help prevent the new rule from becoming a delaying tactic in the case of employer appeals from decisions granting certification.[11]

Sections 706(f)(1) and 707(e) of Title VII authorize the EEOC to initiate a civil suit on behalf of victims of discrimination and to bring a pattern or practice suit against private employers that engage in systemic discrimination.[12] A district court has addressed whether and how EEOC can bring a pattern or practice case of sexual harassment,

---

8. *See, e.g., Robinson v. Sheriff of Cook County,* 167 F.3d 1155 (7th Cir.), *cert. denied,* 528 U.S. 824, 120 S.Ct. 71, 145 L.Ed.2d 60 (1999). *Watson v. Fort Worth Bank & Trust,* 798 F.2d 791 (5th Cir.1986), *vacated on other grounds,* 487 U.S. 977, 108 S.Ct. 2777, 101 L.Ed.2d 827 (1988) (application and promotion discrimination); *Briggs v. Anderson,* 796 F.2d 1009 (8th Cir.1986) (current and terminated employees); *Walker v. Jim Dandy Co.,* 747 F.2d 1360 (11th Cir.1984) (employee and applicant classes).

9. *Eisen v. Carlisle & Jacquelin,* 417 U.S. 156, 177, 94 S.Ct. 2140, 2152, 40 L.Ed.2d 732 (1974). That caution from *Eisen* was applied in *Wagner v. The Nutra-Sweet Co.,* 170 F.R.D. 448 (N.D.Ill.1997).

10. FRCP 23(f), in part overruling *Coopers & Lybrand v. Livesay,* 437 U.S. 463, 98 S.Ct. 2454, 57 L.Ed.2d 351 (1978).

11. *See, e.g., Blair v. Equifax Check Servs., Inc.,* 181 F.3d 832 (7th Cir.1999) (granting company's request for review under Rule 23(f)).

12. 42 U.S.C.A. §§ 2000e–5(f)(1) and 2000e–6. EEOC need not satisfy the Rule 23 class action requirements to bring such pattern or practice suits. *See Falcon,* 446 U.S. at 323; *General Tel. Co. of the Northwest, Inc. v. EEOC,* 446 U.S. 318, 100 S.Ct. 1698, 64 L.Ed.2d 319 (1980); *EEOC v. Northwest Airlines, Inc.,* 188 F.3d 695, 702 (6th Cir.1999).

inherently problematic due to the subjective elements of the prima facie case.[13] The court employed a bifurcated liability phase, focusing in part one on a pattern or practice of the existence of a hostile environment of sexual harassment that the employer had notice of and was negligent in not preventing or correcting it. The second phase, the individual relief phase, incorporates the *Meritor* subjective standard that the complained-of conduct was unwelcome and that it affected the work environment of the individual.

Requests for monetary damages can also pose problems in seeking certification. In *Allison v. Citgo Petroleum Corp.*,[14] the Fifth Circuit rejected a bifurcated liability-damages trial and affirmed the denial of class status because monetary claims require individualized proof. The court rejected a Federal Rule of Civil Procedure Rule 23(b)(2)[15] certification because the court found that claims for monetary relief dominated claims for injunctive or declaratory relief.[16] A Rule 23(b)(3)[17] certification was also found to be inappropriate on grounds of manageability due to the large number (over 1,000) of plaintiffs, the individual-specific issues, and the problem of a bifurcated trial. In addition, plaintiffs pressed claims regarding hiring, firing, training, compensation and promotion practices.

The Seventh Circuit has likewise vacated class certification in a pattern and practice Rule 23(b)(2) class where money damages were sought.[18] Although it declined to set out a blanket rule that 23(b)(2) certification was unattainable where monetary damages were sought, the court warned that where the monetary damages were more than merely incidental to the equitable remedy, 23(b)(2) status was unlikely. The court did however suggest alternatives for the district court. First, the court could divide the claims, and certify a 213(b)(2) class for injunctive relief and a 23(b)(3) class for damages, while trying the damages claims first to preserve the right to a jury trial. Alternatively, the district court, under the authority granted it by Rule 23 to issue appropriate orders, could treat the 23(b)(2) class as if it were a 23(b)(3) class and provide notice and opt-out rights.

---

13.   *EEOC v. Mitsubishi Motor Manufacturing of Am., Inc.*, 990 F.Supp. 1059 (C.D.Ill.1998). *See also Warnell v. Ford Motor Co.*, 189 F.R.D. 383 (N.D.Ill.1999) (certifying private sexual harassment class action under Fed.R.Civ.P. 23).

14.   151 F.3d 402 (5th Cir.1998).

15.   "An action may be maintained as a class action if . . . the party opposing the class has acted or refused to act on grounds generally applicable to the class, thereby making appropriate final injunctive relief or corresponding declaratory relief with respect to the class as a whole."

16.   *But see Warnell v. Ford Motor Co.*, 189 F.R.D. 383(N.D.Ill.1999) (certifying a 23(b)(2) class alleging classwide sexual harassment and seeking compensatory and punitive damages as well as injunctive relief). *See also Zachery v. Texaco Exploration & Prod., Inc.*, 185 F.R.D. 230 (W.D.Tex. 1999) (plaintiffs sought only injunctive relief and back pay to circumvent *Allison* and Fifth Circuit precedent).

17.   "An action may be maintained as a class action if . . . the court finds that the questions of law or fact common to the members of the class predominate over any questions affecting only individual members, and that a class action is superior to other available methods for the fair and efficient adjudication of the controversy."

18.   *Jefferson v. Ingersoll Int'l Inc.*, 195 F.3d 894 (7th Cir.1999).

Where, as is unusual in an employment discrimination action, injunctive relief is unavailable and certification is therefore not possible under Rule 23(b)(2), there is authority permitting certification under Rule 23(b)(3) where the plaintiffs can satisfy the court that issues common to class members predominate over those affecting only individuals, and that a class action is a more efficient means of proceeding than multiple actions or Rule 20 joinder.[19] However, plaintiffs seeking to certify disparate treatment class actions under the inferential proof mode of *McDonnell Douglas* may face significant problems because defendants can defeat such claims by articulating a nondiscriminatory, nonpretextual reason for the adverse employment action–an inquiry that courts view as highly individualized.[20]

ADEA suits are not subject to Rule 23. Instead, these "collective actions" are governed under § 216 of the Fair Labor Standards Act.[21] There are some substantial differences between the ADEA class action and a Rule 23 class action. First, the only prerequisite for a § 216 action is that all putative class members must be "similarly situated." This is, of course, a fact-based inquiry, but courts have held that the standard is lower than that imposed by Rule 23(a).[22] Second, all ADEA § 216 actions are opt-in actions; that is no potential plaintiff is part of the collective action unless that plaintiff affirmatively consents in writing to be part of the action.[23] Third, plaintiffs who do opt-in to an ADEA collective action are granted full party status.

The rejection on the merits of class claims of systemic treatment does not bar the claims of individual class members alleging disparate treatment à la *McDonnell Douglas/Burdine*.[24] Moreover, when a court denies class action certification, the claims of individual class members who have not filed a charge with EEOC or commenced a judicial action may still be timely. This is because the filing of a class action has been held to toll, until the denial of certification,[25] both the 90–day period for

19. *But see Zapata v. IBP, Inc.,* 167 F.R.D. 147 (D.Kan.1996) (denying class certification because of lack of commonality).

20. *See, e.g., Ardrey v. United Parcel Serv., Inc.,* 798 F.2d 679, 683–84 (4th Cir. 1986), *cert. denied,* 480 U.S. 934, 107 S.Ct. 1575, 94 L.Ed.2d 766 (1987); *Coates v. Johnson & Johnson,* 756 F.2d 524, 548 (7th Cir.1985).

21. "An action to recover the liability ... may be maintained against any employer (including a public agency) in any Federal or State court of competent jurisdiction by any one or more employees for and in behalf of himself or themselves and other employees similarly situated." 29 U.S.C.A. § 216(b).

22. *See, e.g., Jackson v. New York Tel. Co.,* 163 F.R.D. 429, 432 (S.D.N.Y.1995); *Church v. Consolidated Freightways, Inc.,* 137 F.R.D. 294, 306 (N.D.Cal.1991). *But see Shushan v. University of Colo.,* 132 F.R.D.

263 (D.Colo.1990) (requiring ADEA collective action plaintiffs to satisfy Rule 23).

23. Rule 23(b)(3) actions are opt-out classes; 23(b)(1) and (b)(2) classes are mandatory. *See* FRCP 23.

24. *Cooper v. Federal Reserve Bank of Richmond,* 467 U.S. 867, 104 S.Ct. 2794, 81 L.Ed.2d 718 (1984). But members of a decertified class may not pursue a pattern or practice case under the *Teamster* proof mode; individuals possessing only circumstantial evidence of discrimination must negotiate the inferential proof mode of *McDonnell Douglas/Burdine. Lowery v. Circuit City Stores, Inc.,* 158 F.3d 742 (4th Cir.1998), *judgment vacated on other grounds,* 527 U.S. 1031, 119 S.Ct. 2388, 144 L.Ed.2d 790 (1999).

25. *Armstrong v. Martin Marietta Corp.,* 138 F.3d 1374 (11th Cir.), *cert. denied,* 525 U.S. 1019, 119 S.Ct. 545, 142 L.Ed.2d 453

filing suit[26] and the applicable deadline (180 or 300 days) for filing a charge with EEOC.[27] Even when a class was decertified because no class representative had standing to assert the claim subsequently brought by individual plaintiffs, those plaintiffs have been allowed to "piggyback" on the timely filed EEOC charges of the class action plaintiffs.[28] But rejection of class claims on the merits has preclusive effect under federal common law in subsequent actions asserting the same pattern claims.[29] And the pendency of a class action in which class status was denied or a class decertified does not toll the charge-filing or action-commencement deadlines for class members who bring a subsequent *class* action— otherwise there would be "endless rounds of litigation ... over the adequacy of successive named plaintiffs to serve as class representatives."[30]

A "single-filing" rule recognized by most federal circuits outside the class action context permits plaintiffs who have not filed their own EEOC charge, or in some circuits, plaintiffs who have filed an invalid charge, to piggyback on a charge or charges filed by coplaintiffs. The plaintiffs are relieved of filing their own valid charges if the claims of all parties are based on a common employer practice or practices during the same rough time frame and the filed charge or charges timely[31] and adequately alerted the employer to the alleged illegality of all the practices ultimately challenged in court.[32] It is not a prerequisite to

(1998) (pendency of class action tolls applicable statute of limitations, but statute begins to run again immediately upon district court's entry of interlocutory order denying class certification).

26. *Crown, Cork & Seal Co. v. Parker*, 462 U.S. 345, 103 S.Ct. 2392, 76 L.Ed.2d 628 (1983).

27. *Griffin v. Singletary*, 17 F.3d 356 (11th Cir.1994), *cert. denied sub nom. Florida v. Platt*, 513 U.S. 1077, 115 S.Ct. 723, 130 L.Ed.2d 628 (1995). *But see Basch v. Ground Round, Inc.*, 139 F.3d 6 (1st Cir.), *cert. denied*, 525 U.S. 870, 119 S.Ct. 165, 142 L.Ed.2d 135 (1998) (rule that the commencement of a class action tolls the statute of limitations as to successive claims of class members does not apply to toll limitations period on ADEA claim based on the stacking of two sequential claims).

28. *Griffin v. Singletary*, 17 F.3d 356 (11th Cir.1994), *cert. denied sub nom. Florida v. Platt*, 513 U.S. 1077, 115 S.Ct. 723, 130 L.Ed.2d 628 (1995).

29. *See* Chapter 12.

30. *Griffin v. Singletary*, 17 F.3d 356, 359 (11th Cir.1994), *cert. denied sub nom. Florida v. Platt*, 513 U.S. 1077, 115 S.Ct. 723, 130 L.Ed.2d 628 (1995).

31. *See Levy v. U.S. Gen. Accounting Office*, 175 F.3d 254 (2d Cir.), *cert. denied*, 528 U.S. 876, 120 S.Ct. 183, 145 L.Ed.2d 154 (1999) (single filing rule not applicable

where employees filed timely charges against federal agency but judicial complaint not filed within the required 90 days after agency's final decision). *See generally Griffin v. Dugger*, 823 F.2d 1476, 1492 (11th Cir.1987), *cert. denied*, 486 U.S. 1005, 108 S.Ct. 1729, 100 L.Ed.2d 193 (1988) (it is not necessary for all class members to have filed EEOC charges or to have received notices of the right to sue in order to be represented by the class) (citing *Oatis v. Crown Zellerbach Corp.*, 398 F.2d 496, 498–99 (5th Cir.1968)). As long as one named plaintiff timely files an EEOC charge, "the precondition to a Title VII action is met for all other named Plaintiffs and class members," *id.* (citing Oatis, 398 F.2d at 498–99), and under the so-called "single-filing rule," if one plaintiff, in a multi-plaintiff, nonclass action suit, " 'has filed a timely EEOC complaint as to that plaintiff's individual claim, then co-plaintiffs with individual claims arising out of similar discriminatory treatment in the same time frame need not have satisfied the filing requirement.' " *Forehand v. Florida State Hosp.*, 89 F.3d 1562, 1566 n. 8 (11th Cir.1996) (quoting *Jackson v. Seaboard Coast Line R.R.*, 678 F.2d 992, 1011 (11th Cir.1982)).

32. *Howlett v. Holiday Inns, Inc.*, 49 F.3d 189 (6th Cir.), *cert. denied sub nom. Holiday Inns, Inc. v. McNeely*, 516 U.S. 943, 116 S.Ct. 379, 133 L.Ed.2d 302 (1995)

single filing that the foundation claim allege classwide discrimination.[33] The rule has also been applied to permit the plaintiff who has not filed an EEOC charge to intervene in an action brought by the plaintiff who has,[34] or to join that action as coplaintiff after an unsuccessful attempt at intervention.[35]

Another requirement, that the action be brought "against the respondent named in the charge,"[36] has sometimes been construed to authorize jurisdiction over a successor employer[37] or even over a defendant improperly named, or not formally named in the charge at all, if its identity is sufficiently revealed in the substance of the charge or if that employer is closely related to a named respondent.[38] In some circuits the civil action has even been allowed to reach defendants not likely to have received notice of the original EEOC charge if the agency's investigation, reasonably confined to the facts alleged in the charge, would have focused on them.[39]

§ 4.10   Relation of Federal Lawsuit to EEOC Investigation

Since the EEOC charge is the necessary foundation for a Title VII action, the issues that may be litigated in federal court will be tied to some degree to the contents of the charge. But recognizing that EEOC charges are often drafted by unrepresented employees ill-equipped to craft them with care, courts following the leading case of *Sanchez v. Standard Brands, Inc.*[1] have permitted Title VII plaintiffs to try claims

---

(allowing age discrimination plaintiff who filed untimely charge with EEOC to invoke the rule even though timely foundation charge did not allege classwide discrimination); *EEOC v. Wilson Metal Casket Co.,* 24 F.3d 836 (6th Cir.1994) (citing cases); *Calloway v. Partners Nat'l Health Plans,* 986 F.2d 446, 449 (11th Cir.1993) (nonfiling plaintiff can piggyback); *Kloos v. Carter–Day Co.,* 799 F.2d 397, 400 (8th Cir.1986) (nonfiling plaintiffs). *But see Washington v. Brown & Williamson Tobacco Corp.,* 756 F.Supp. 1547 (M.D.Ga.1991), *aff'd,* 959 F.2d 1566 (11th Cir.1992) (no piggybacking by applicant challenging failure to hire where plaintiff who did file charge was current employee who therefore lacked standing to complain about hiring).

The Fifth, Eighth and Eleventh Circuits agree that only nonfiling plaintiffs can piggyback; plaintiffs who do file are bound by the parameters of their own charge and cannot subsequently use the single filing rule to avoid the statute of limitations. *See Gitlitz v. Compagnie Nationale Air France,* 129 F.3d 554, 557–58 (11th Cir.1997); *Mooney v. Aramco Servs. Co.,* 54 F.3d 1207, 1223–24 (5th Cir.1995); *Anderson v. Unisys Corp.,* 47 F.3d 302, 308–09 (8th Cir.), *cert. denied,* 516 U.S. 913, 116 S.Ct. 299, 133 L.Ed.2d 205 (1995).

33. *Howlett v. Holiday Inns Inc.,* 49 F.3d 189 (6th Cir.1995), *cert. denied sub nom. Holiday Inns, Inc. v. McNeely,* 516 U.S. 943, 116 S.Ct. 379, 133 L.Ed.2d 302 (1995).

34. *See Wheeler v. American Home Prods. Corp.,* 582 F.2d 891 (5th Cir.1977).

35. *Calloway v. Partners Nat'l Health Plans,* 986 F.2d 446 (11th Cir.1993).

36. Section 706(f)(1).

37. *See, e.g., EEOC v. MacMillan Bloedel Containers, Inc.,* 503 F.2d 1086 (6th Cir.1974).

38. *See, e.g., Evans v. Sheraton Park Hotel,* 503 F.2d 177 (D.C.Cir.1974) (international union must defend when charge named two of its locals). For the standing of "testers" to prosecute violations of the employment discrimination laws, see the Procedure chapter below.

39. *See, e.g., Tillman v. Milwaukee,* 715 F.2d 354 (7th Cir.1983); *Tillman v. Boaz,* 548 F.2d 592 (5th Cir.1977).

§ 4.10

1. 431 F.2d 455, 466 (5th Cir.1970); *Cornwell v. Robinson,* 23 F.3d 694 (2d Cir. 1994) (harassment allegations were reason-

"like or related to allegations contained in the charge and growing out of such allegations during the pendency of the case before the Commission."

The widespread adoption of the *Sanchez* rule puts a premium on defendants' efforts to limit the scope of EEOC proceedings. Generalizations about the meaning of "like or related" are particularly hazardous. But it may be ventured that allegations in a Title VII judicial complaint that add a new ground of discrimination (race or sex, for instance) are less likely to be entertained than are allegations that touch on additional terms or conditions of employment or implicate other potential plaintiffs in different departments or divisions.[2] Even then, plaintiffs whose administrative charges complained of adverse treatment respecting limited terms and conditions of employment will be permitted to target in court only those other terms and conditions of employment that EEOC could reasonably have been expected to investigate based on the charge.[3] The

ably related to discrimination charges concerning a previous tour of duty and therefore need not be separately charged before EEOC but may be added by amended complaint in the district court).

2. See, for example, the Second Circuit's framework recognizing only three types of situations where claims not included in an EEOC charge may be sufficiently related to the EEOC charge to sustain jurisdiction over a Title VII claim: (1) where the conduct complained of would fall within the scope of the EEOC investigation which can reasonably be expected to grow out of the charge of discrimination; (2) where the reasonably related claim is one alleging retaliation in response to the filing of an EEOC charge; and (3) where the plaintiff alleges further incidents of discrimination carried out in precisely the same manner as the conduct complained of in the EEOC charge. *Butts v. City of N.Y. Dep't of Hous. Preservation and Dev.*, 990 F.2d 1397, 1402–03 (2d Cir.1993). *See Alonzo v. Chase Manhattan Bank N.A.*, 25 F.Supp.2d 455, 457–58 (S.D.N.Y.1998) (race claim sufficiently like and reasonably related to national origin charge); *Chambers v. American Trans. Air, Inc.*, 17 F.3d 998 (7th Cir.), *cert. denied*, 513 U.S. 1001, 115 S.Ct. 512, 130 L.Ed.2d 419 (1994) (promotion denial allegations not sufficiently encompassed by allegations in EEOC charge of unequal compensation).

3. *Compare Ang v. Procter & Gamble Co.*, 932 F.2d 540 (6th Cir.1991) (holding that a race discrimination charge was precluded where plaintiff failed to check the appropriate box on the EEOC charge and failed to allege race discrimination in the factual statement); *Jones v. Sumser Retirement Village*, 209 F.3d 851, 853–54 (6th Cir.2000)(where a plaintiff filed an ADA

termination claim, she failed to exhaust her administrative remedies for an ADA failure to accommodate claim because the accommodation claim did not reasonably grow out of the termination claim); *Park v. Howard Univ.*, 71 F.3d 904 (D.C.Cir.1995), *cert. denied* 519 U.S. 811, 117 S.Ct. 57, 136 L.Ed.2d 20 (1996) (hostile work environment sex discrimination claim cannot proceed based on EEOC charge limited to sex and national origin discrimination concerning a selection process); *Griffin v. Dugger*, 823 F.2d 1476, 1493 (11th Cir.1987), *cert. denied*, 486 U.S. 1005, 108 S.Ct. 1729, 100 L.Ed.2d 193 (1988) (holding as dissimilar for the purposes of the single-filing rule non-filing plaintiff's objective testing claim and plaintiff's subjective promotion and discipline claims); *Hill v. AT & T Technologies, Inc.*, 731 F.2d 175, 181 (4th Cir.1984) (holding as dissimilar EEOC charges alleging discrimination in the conditions of employment and plaintiff's allegations of discrimination in hiring); *with Alexander v. Fulton County*, 207 F.3d 1303, 1333 (11th Cir.2000) (charges of discriminatory denial of access to promotional exams, reclassifications, and transfers that were not specifically mentioned in the EEOC charges were sufficiently similar to the promotions and job assignment claims that were included in the EEOC charge as all involve the allegedly race-based rejection of plaintiffs for desired positions); *Duggins v. Steak 'N Shake, Inc.*, 195 F.3d 828 (6th Cir.1999) (allowing claim of retaliation where plaintiff filed an internal affidavit with the EEOC contemporaneously with initial charge); *Taylor v. Virginia Union Univ.*, 193 F.3d 219 (4th Cir. 1999), *cert. denied*, ___ U.S. ___, 120 S.Ct. 1243, 146 L.Ed.2d 101 (2000) (plaintiff who alleged sex discrimination in promotion

Seventh Circuit appears to be moving to an alternative, and apparently stricter, standard: whether the claims in the judicial action are "fairly encompassed" within or "implied" by the charge the plaintiff filed with EEOC. Decisions applying the new standard have precluded allegations by the same plaintiff on the same prohibited ground of discrimination that attack different terms and conditions of employment or implicate different individuals from those targeted by the EEOC charge.[4] At least where the additional practices sought to be challenged in court are plausibly asserted to arise out of the practices cited in the EEOC charge,[5] it would appear that this standard bars the litigation of claims that would be heard under the *Sanchez* "like or related" test.

An especially liberal application of the charge-filing requirement generally permits a plaintiff to press a retaliation claim under § 704, without first filing a separate EEOC charge of retaliation, where that claim grows out of a properly and timely filed predicate charge of discrimination under § 703.[6] But that liberality is usually extended only when the underlying charge of primary discrimination was itself administratively exhausted and timely, or added by an amendment to the original charge that the court permits to relate back to the original.[7]

could pursue sexual harassment claim in court because her affidavit to EEOC identified incidents of alleged harassment).

4. *See, e.g., Vela v. Village of Sauk Village*, 218 F.3d 661 (7th Cir.2000) (plaintiff's claim of sexual harassment, stated in her complaint, was "wholly diverse" from the claim of disparate treatment described in EEOC charge, it was not reasonably related, and the charge is therefore not an adequate predicate for it); *Sauzek v. Exxon Coal USA, Inc.*, 202 F.3d 913, 920 (7th Cir.2000) (employer's decision to terminate worker not reasonably related to subsequent decision not to rehire worker during a recall); *Novitsky v. American Consulting Engineers, L.L.C.*, 196 F.3d 699, 701–02 (7th Cir.1999) (claim of failure to accommodate plaintiff's religion not reasonably related to EEOC charge discussing discrimination on bases of age and religion, even where plaintiff described in intake form an incident that supported her failure to accommodate theory); *Chambers v. American Trans Air, Inc.*, 17 F.3d 998 (7th Cir.), *cert. denied*, 513 U.S. 1001, 115 S.Ct. 512, 130 L.Ed.2d 419 (1994) (gender-based pay discrimination alleged in EEOC charge cannot support judicial claim of gender-based promotion denials, even though plaintiff asserted that the promotion denials caused the pay differentials); *Kirk v. FPM Corp.*, 22 F.3d 135 (7th Cir.1994) (race-based failure to promote allegation in EEOC charge cannot support judicial claim of race-based discriminatory denial of educational opportunities, despite plaintiff's assertion that the latter arose from the former). *Cf. Cheek*

v. Western & Southern Life Ins. Co., 31 F.3d 497 (7th Cir.1994) (gender discrimination complaint based on different events and implicating different individuals not like and related even in the *Sanchez* sense to EEOC charge also alleging discrimination based on gender); *Jenkins v. Blue Cross Mut. Hosp. Ins., Inc.*, 538 F.2d 164, 167–69 (7th Cir.) (en banc), *cert. denied*, 429 U.S. 986, 97 S.Ct. 506, 50 L.Ed.2d 598 (1976) (plaintiff sufficiently alleged facts supporting claim of sex discrimination in EEOC charge to proceed with sex discrimination claim in court, despite plaintiff's failure to check the box for sex discrimination on the charge).

5. This would appear to be the case in *Kirk*, but perhaps not *Chambers*, both cited in the note immediately preceding.

6. *See, e.g., Duggins v. Steak 'N Shake*, 195 F.3d 828 (6th Cir.1999); *Shah v. New York State Dep't of Civil Serv.*, 168 F.3d 610 (2d Cir.1999); *Malarkey v. Texaco, Inc.*, 983 F.2d 1204 (2d Cir.1993). The reverse is not true: a primary discrimination claim may not be tacked onto a claim of retaliation, where only the latter was administratively charged. *Noreuil v. Peabody Coal Co.*, 96 F.3d 254 (7th Cir.1996).

7. *Jones v. Runyon*, 91 F.3d 1398 (10th Cir.1996), *cert. denied*, 520 U.S. 1115, 117 S.Ct. 1243, 137 L.Ed.2d 326 (1997) (no subject matter jurisdiction under "piggybacking" approach over retaliation charge sought to be heard in conjunction with underlying Title VII claim that itself was not

Some circuits have limited the federal court's ancillary jurisdiction in such cases to charges of alleged retaliation occurring after, and not before, the filing of the underlying charge;[8] this position is consistent with the applicable EEOC regulations, discussed above,[9] that require the filing of an original charge within the applicable 180–or 300–day period after a claim accrues.

§ 4.11   Employer Recordkeeping Requirements

Pursuant to statutory authority,[1] EEOC has promulgated regulations requiring employers to maintain records pertinent to a wide range of employment decisions. These require employers to retain all personnel records for six months after they are created and, when a charge is filed, to retain all records relevant to that charge "until final disposition of the charge or action."[2] In employment discrimination actions, the employer has custody of virtually all records critical to resolution of the disputed claim; hence in the reported decisions it is the employer that allegedly violated the Title VII recordkeeping requirements.

But judicial enforcement of employer recordkeeping violations has generally been conspicuously lenient. Typically the courts of appeals that have found employers to have destroyed documents in violation of the EEOC regulation give the plaintiff the benefit of a "presumption that the destroyed documents would have bolstered her case."[3] But then they

exhausted before EEOC); *Hargett v. Valley Fed. Sav. Bank*, 60 F.3d 754 (11th Cir.1995) (plaintiff's underlying charge of discrimination must be timely before plaintiff may have related retaliation claim, not the subject of an EEOC charge, heard in court case under ADEA). On the requirements for "relation back" of amended EEOC charges, see *supra* § 4.4.

8. *See Heuer v. Weil–McLain*, 203 F.3d 1021, 1023 (7th Cir.2000) (a complaint that charges discrimination is deemed not to place the employer on notice that he is being charged with retaliation); *Sloop v. Memorial Mission Hosp., Inc.*, 198 F.3d 147, 149 (4th Cir.1999) (employee failed to raise Title VII retaliation claim where she mentioned only age discrimination in EEOC charge, and, although she later sent EEOC a letter stating she needed to add charge of retaliation, she reiterated her view in letter that age was the real reason for her dismissal and nothing in letter indicated she wanted to raise Title VII retaliation claim as opposed to ADEA retaliation claim); *Simms v. Oklahoma ex rel. Dep't of Mental Health and Substance Abuse Servs.*, 165 F.3d 1321, 1327–28 (10th Cir.), *cert. denied*, 528 U.S. 815, 120 S.Ct. 53, 145 L.Ed.2d 46 (1999); *Wallin v. Minnesota Dep't of Corr.*, 153 F.3d 681 (8th Cir.1998), *cert. denied*, 526 U.S. 1004, 119 S.Ct. 1141, 143 L.Ed.2d 209 (1999) (if facts supporting claim of re-

taliation are known at time of filing charge but the charge does not mention retaliation, plaintiff cannot maintain retaliation claim due to failure to exhaust administrative remedies); *Seymore v. Shawver & Sons, Inc.*, 111 F.3d 794, 799 (10th Cir.), *cert. denied*, 522 U.S. 935, 118 S.Ct. 342, 139 L.Ed.2d 266 (1997) (no amendment permitted where retaliatory act occurred before the EEOC charge was filed, and the plaintiff had failed to allege retaliation either in the original EEOC charge or a timely amendment thereto); *Mosley v. Pena*, 100 F.3d 1515 (10th Cir.1996) (the exception that excuses filing separate charge of retaliation applies only to employer conduct occurring after the filing of an original charge with EEOC); *McKenzie v. Illinois Dep't of Transp.*, 92 F.3d 473 (7th Cir.1996); *Ang v. Procter & Gamble Co.*, 932 F.2d 540 (6th Cir.1991).

9. See § 4.4, *supra*.

§ 4.11

1. Section 709(c), 42 U.S.C.A. § 2000e–8(c).

2. 29 CFR § 1602.14 (1994).

3. *See, e.g., Favors v. Fisher*, 13 F.3d 1235, 1239 (8th Cir.1994); *Hicks v. Gates Rubber Co.*, 833 F.2d 1406, 1419 (10th Cir. 1987); *Capaci v. Katz & Besthoff, Inc.*, 711

either assume[4] or conclude[5] that the presumption was "overcome"—the evidence for which may simply be an innocent explanation by an authorized employer agent, coupled with his assertion that he had not been instructed to preserve records in accordance with the government regulation. Alternatively, these decisions often find that other employer evidence either supports a proposition that the destroyed records might have negated, or undermines a proposition they might have established, so the recordkeeping violation of Title VII should simply be overlooked.[6] And those courts that impose sanctions have denied substantial sanctions, preferring instead such milder measures as requiring the defendant to bear the costs of record reconstruction; limiting its production of evidence on the matters reflected in the destroyed documents; or invoking the presumption that the records would have supported plaintiff's case.[7] Default, it is said, requires bad faith resistance to discovery orders; it is not enough that the violation is technically "willful" because the records were destroyed after defendant's receipt of the EEOC notice of charge that contained an admonition about the employer's recordkeeping obligations under the EEOC regulation.[8] Yet even a court that imposed sanctions after finding "outrageous" and "deliberate, willful and contumacious" violations designed to "make forever unavailable" pertinent records and documents and which in fact prejudiced the plaintiffs[9] drew back from default or dismissal. In that court's view, it would also have to be shown that alternative sanctions would fail adequately to punish and deter. Until such a showing could be made, the court ordered the defendant to pay the plaintiffs twice the amount of all attorney's fees and costs associated with presenting motions relative to the recordkeeping violations and possible record reconstruction, together with a fine to be paid into the court. The court observed that these steps would probably not fully compensate plaintiffs for the harm they sustained but that "plaintiffs have not been wholly deprived of the means to attempt their proof."[10]

§§ 4.12–7.19   [Reserved]

F.2d 647, 661 n. 7 (5th Cir.1983), *cert. denied*, 466 U.S. 927, 104 S.Ct. 1709, 80 L.Ed.2d 182 (1984). *Cf. EEOC v. American Nat'l Bank*, 652 F.2d 1176, 1195–96 (4th Cir.1981), *cert. denied*, 459 U.S. 923, 103 S.Ct. 235, 74 L.Ed.2d 186 (1982) (employer not relieved of ordinary litigation inferences drawn from its not possessing data merely because EEOC regulations did not affirmatively require retention of that data at relevant time).

   4. *Capaci*, 711 F.2d 647.

   5. *Favors v. Fisher*, 13 F.3d at 1239.

   6. *Id.*; see generally the terms of the proposed remand in *Hicks v. Gates Rubber Co.*, 833 F.2d 1406.

   7. *Webb v. District of Columbia*, 146 F.3d 964 (D.C.Cir.1998) (reversing district court's entry of default judgment with instructions to consider less onerous sanctions); *EEOC v. Jacksonville Shipyards, Inc.*, 690 F.Supp. 995, 998–999 (M.D.Fla. 1988).

   8. *Jacksonville Shipyards*, 690 F.Supp. at 998.

   9. *See, e.g., Capellupo v. FMC Corp.*, 126 F.R.D. 545, 551–52 (D.Minn.1989).

   10. *Id.* at 553.

B. RETROACTIVITY OF THE CIVIL RIGHTS ACT OF 1991

§ 4.20 In General

A raging controversy raising intricate arguments about statutory construction centers on whether the Civil Rights Act of 1991, or parts thereof, may be applied retroactively to cases pending or conduct occurring prior to the November 21, 1991 date of enactment. Specific prohibitions in the Act against retroactive application to the particular employer charged in the *Wards Cove v. Atonio*[1] case and against retroactivity of the amendment providing for the extraterritorial reach of Title VII led a number of district courts to conclude that Congress must have intended the statute to apply retroactively in other respects.[2] But most federal circuit courts concluded that the Civil Rights Act is ambiguous on retroactive application and decided the other way.[3] The circuit opinions resolved the ambiguity in Congressional intent by relying on the presumption against applying statutes retroactively enunciated most recently in *Bowen v. Georgetown University Hospital*[4] despite the tension between the *Bowen* canon and the "general rule" announced in *Bradley v. Richmond School Board*[5] that a court should apply the law in effect at the time of decision.

The Supreme Court has put some of this confusion to rest. It ruled in *Landgraf v. USI Film Products*[6] that §§ 102(a) and (c) of the 1991 Act—providing, respectively, for compensatory and punitive damages and for trials by jury with respect to Title VII claims of intentional discrimination—do not apply to cases pending on the 1991 Act's date of enactment. In a companion case, *Rivers v. Roadway Express, Inc.*,[7] the Court ruled against retroactive application of § 101, which restored the full scope of § 1981 as it was uniformly construed before *Patterson* to embrace all phases of the contractual or employment relationship, including discriminatory on-the-job harassment and terminations.

In *Landgraf*, the Court began by agreeing with the courts of appeals that the 1991 Act did not unambiguously prescribe retroactive application of the provisions in question. It then attempted to harmonize *Bradley* with *Bowen* and to choose between them for a default rule. The

§ 4.20

1. 490 U.S. 642, 109 S.Ct. 2115, 104 L.Ed.2d 733 (1989).

2. *See, e.g., Stender v. Lucky Stores, Inc.*, 780 F.Supp. 1302 (N.D.Cal.1992).

3. *See, e.g., Johnson v. Uncle Ben's, Inc.*, 965 F.2d 1363 (5th Cir.1992), *cert. denied*, 511 U.S. 1068, 114 S.Ct. 1641, 128 L.Ed.2d 362 (1994); *Luddington v. Indiana Bell Telephone Co.*, 966 F.2d 225 (7th Cir. 1992), *cert. denied*, 511 U.S. 1068, 114 S.Ct. 1641, 128 L.Ed.2d 362 (1994); *Mozee v. American Commercial Marine Serv. Co.*, 963 F.2d 929 (7th Cir.), *cert. denied*, 506 U.S. 872, 113 S.Ct. 207, 121 L.Ed.2d 148 (1992); *Fray v. Omaha World Herald Co.*,

960 F.2d 1370 (8th Cir.1992); *Vogel v. City of Cincinnati*, 959 F.2d 594 (6th Cir.), *cert. denied*, 506 U.S. 827, 113 S.Ct. 86, 121 L.Ed.2d 49 (1992); *Baynes v. AT & T Technologies, Inc.*, 976 F.2d 1370 (11th Cir. 1992).

4. 488 U.S. 204, 109 S.Ct. 468, 102 L.Ed.2d 493 (1988).

5. 416 U.S. 696, 94 S.Ct. 2006, 40 L.Ed.2d 476 (1974).

6. 511 U.S. 244, 114 S.Ct. 1483, 128 L.Ed.2d 229 (1994).

7. 511 U.S. 298, 114 S.Ct. 1510, 128 L.Ed.2d 274 (1994).

Court acknowledged that some language in *Bradley* suggested a categorical presumption favoring the retroactive application of all new rules of law, but argued that in fact it "did not alter the well-settled presumption [as articulated in *Bowen*] against application of the class of new statutes that ... have genuinely retroactive effect." And a statute that either impaired the rights a party possessed when it acted, increased its liability for past conduct, or imposed new duties concerning completed transactions would be a statute that had a "genuinely retroactive effect."

The question, then, was which of the challenged provisions had "genuinely retroactive effect." The Court described punitive damages as sharing the key attributes of criminal sanctions because they are designed to sanction wrongdoers; as such, retroactive application of § 102(b)(1) would present a potential ex post facto constitutional problem that the Court declined to reach absent statutory language explicitly authorizing punitive damages for preenactment conduct. Although calling the question considerably closer, the Court also viewed the compensatory damages authorized by § 102(a)(1) as having retroactive effect because it is a "backward-looking" mechanism that affects defendants' liabilities. And § 102 as a whole, the Court noted, imposed monetary liability in circumstances where none had been previously been provided for the very same cause of action—in the case at bar, unlawful harassment that did not erode the plaintiff's tangible employment compensation, status, or benefits.[8]

The Court did assume that the right to jury trial accorded by § 102(c)(1) was "plainly a procedural change" that, standing alone, could be applied to trials after the Act's effective date. But since that section provides for jury trial only where compensatory or punitive damages are sought, the jury trial right washed out with the decision that the damages provisions could not be retroactively applied.[9]

Section 101 of the 1991 Act, it will be recalled, restored the broad interpretation of 42 U.S.C.A. § 1981 shared by the federal courts of appeals before the Supreme Court, in its 1989 *Patterson* decision, held that statute to forbid race discrimination only in the formation of a contract and not in its implementation or breach. In *Rivers*, the Court refused to use § 101 as the measure of the employer's conduct even though the defendant had terminated the plaintiffs before *Patterson* had been decided and thus was fairly on notice that it might be liable for a racially based discharge from employment.

---

8. *See also Joseph v. New York City Bd. of Educ.*, 171 F.3d 87 (2d Cir.), *cert. denied*, 528 U.S. 876, 120 S.Ct. 182, 145 L.Ed.2d 154 (1999) (applying *Landgraf* to bar action filed after November 21, 1991, but based on alleged unlawful employment decision deemed final before that date).

9. *See Tomasello v. Rubin*, 167 F.3d 612 (D.C.Cir.1999) (federal employee not eligible for jury trial on pre-November 1991 Title VII claims because that right was tied to the 1991 Act's allowance of damages and an award of the latter would have impermissible retroactive effect). To the same effect is *Joseph v. New York City Bd. of Educ.*, 171 F.3d 87 (2d Cir.), *cert. denied*, 528 U.S. 876, 120 S.Ct. 182, 145 L.Ed.2d 154 (1999).

From the plaintiffs' perspective, there could be no unfairness in applying § 101 to conduct that preceded November 21, 1991, the general effective date of the 1991 Act, because § 101 simply restored the liability rule that the employer should have known of when it acted. Applying the pre-legal realist maxim that judicial common law decisions operate retrospectively because they merely declare what was always a correct interpretation of the law, the Court took *Patterson*, rather than the pre-*Patterson* court of appeals decisions, as its baseline. In this light the Court saw § 101 as changing the preexisting legal landscape—i.e., *Patterson*—in a way that enlarged the category of conduct for which the employer could be liable under § 1981 and thereby implicated the key concern identified in *Landgraf* as animating the *Bowen* presumption favoring prospective application of statutes.

The Court followed that presumption because it could no more find in § 101 than it had found in § 102 a clear Congressional statement directing retroactivity. For the plaintiffs, the opinion must have read as heads you lose, tails you lose as well. The canon mandating retrospective application of judicial decisions meant that the lower courts had correctly applied the restrictive *Patterson* interpretation to employer conduct that had antedated that decision by several years; the canon presuming prospective application of statutes absent clear contrary Congressional directive deprived them of relief from the *Patterson* interpretation via § 101.

Will the other provisions of the 1991 Act similarly be denied retroactive effect? Before *Landgraf* and *Rivers*, one district court had held that § 115 of the 1991 Civil Rights Act (which relieves ADEA plaintiffs of compliance with the 2–year statute of limitations under the Portal-to-Portal Act; see Chapter 7 on the ADEA) should, unlike most others, be applied retroactively, as it treats a matter that is merely "procedural."[10] In *Landgraf*, the Supreme Court observed that matters of procedure usually involve "diminished reliance interests," but cautioned that "the mere fact that a new rule is procedural does not mean that it applies to every pending case."[11] And in fact it has not: the 1991 Act's extension from 30 to 90 days of the time in which federal employees must file Rehabilitation Act suits[12] has been held not to revive a claim barred under the former limit.[13] *Landgraf* provides slim direct guidance for predicting the vitality of the foregoing decisions or how the Court itself will rule on the retroactive application of 1991 Act provisions that might reasonably be branded "procedural": Section 108, which responds to *Martin v. Wilks* by making somewhat more difficult collateral attacks on

10. *Cf. Vernon v. Cassadaga Central Sch. Dist.*, 49 F.3d 886 (2d Cir.1995) (Section 115 may be applied, nonretroactively, so as to bar an action filed after the effective date of the new limitations statute based on a claim that accrued before that date). *But see Banas v. American Airlines*, 969 F.2d 477 (7th Cir.1992) (a generous limitations rule of the 1991 Act held unavailing to a sex discrimination plaintiff whose action was on appeal when the Act was enacted).

11. *Landgraf*, 511 U.S. 244, 114 S.Ct. 1483, 128 L.Ed.2d 229.

12. Section 114(1) of the Act.

13. *Chenault v. U.S. Postal Serv.*, 37 F.3d 535 (9th Cir.1994).

race-conscious consent decrees;[14] Section 112, which overrules *Lorance* and facilitates challenges to discriminatory seniority systems; and § 115, which substantially conforms the ADEA pre-suit procedures with those under Title VII.[15] But *Landgraf,* by distinguishing *Bradley's* approval of retroactive application of statutory law in effect at the time of appellate decision on the ground that the issue there, attorney's fees, was collateral to and separable from the main action, may suggest that § 113, providing for the recovery by prevailing parties of expert witness fees, may also be permitted to apply retroactively.[16] On the other hand, the strong presumption against legislative retroactivity to which the Court gave voice in *Landgraf* and *Rivers* makes retroactive application rather unlikely with respect to the 1991 Act's other more evidently "substantive" provisions: Section 105, which overruled *Wards Cove Packing Co.* by explicitly placing the burden of persuasion on defendants concerning the defense to a prima face case of disproportionate adverse impact; and § 107, which fine-tuned *Price Waterhouse* by imposing limited employer liability even where the employer carries the "same-decision" showing.[17]

§§ 4.21–7.24 [Reserved]

C. TITLE VII REMEDIES

§ 4.25 Reinstatement and Back and Front Pay

The range of judicial remedial authority is prescribed by § 706(g). This section provides for injunctions and "such affirmative action as may be appropriate," including orders directing reinstatement or hire, back pay, and other equitable relief. It also "limits" a defendant's back pay liability retrospectively to no earlier than two years before the filing of a charge with EEOC. "Limits" is placed in quotation marks because the statute's deadlines for filing a charge with EEOC are only 180 days, in the handful of states that do not have their own local antidiscrimination laws and agencies, or 300 days in the majority of states that do. Thus in

---

14. An Eighth Circuit decision has held that § 108 does not apply where the underlying proceedings challenging primary discrimination were completed before the November 1991 effective date of the Act. In such cases the "reverse discrimination" challenge to an affirmative action consent decree may therefore proceed whether or not the plaintiff had received notice and an opportunity to participate in the underlying action. Relying on *Landgraf,* the court reasoned that § 108 impairs pre-existing rights of the putative challenger and attaches new legal consequences to events fully completed before the effective date of the 1991 Act. *Maitland v. University of Minnesota,* 43 F.3d 357 (8th Cir.1994). *Accord, Rafferty v. City of Youngstown,* 54 F.3d 278 (6th Cir.), *cert. denied,* 516 U.S. 931, 116 S.Ct. 338, 133 L.Ed.2d 236 (1995).

15. Perhaps, however, if, as the Court in *Landgraf* asserted, the right to jury trial is merely procedural and hence susceptible to retroactive application, the same might be said at least § 115.

16. *But cf. Shipes v. Trinity Indus.,* 31 F.3d 347 (5th Cir.1994) (denying expert witness fees under new § 113 to plaintiffs where fee request was properly denied under prior law by a district court decision issued before November 21, 1991, but leaving open possibility that such fees should be awarded for in cases arising from preenactment conduct when ruled upon after that date).

17. *See Hook v. Ernst & Young,* 28 F.3d 366 (3d Cir.1994) (holding § 107 has no retroactive application).

effect the 2–year "limit" on back pay authorizes its award *earlier* than the "trigger" date that starts the running of Title VII's administrative charge-filing deadlines.

Prevailing plaintiffs are routinely awarded injunctions against ongoing violations, and, where disparate treatment has been proved,[1] reinstatement or, if there is no position available at the time of judgment, priority in filling vacancies.[2] As with the systemic disparate treatment case, discussed above,[3] reinstatement may be denied, however, where the discriminatee, although qualified when unlawfully rejected, is no longer qualified for the position in question at the time of judgment.[4]

Back pay is also awarded almost as a matter of course. This is because, as the Supreme Court has explained, back pay serves both of the Act's remedial goals: to restore discrimination victims to the approximate status they would have enjoyed absent discrimination (the "make whole" purpose), and to deter employer violations. Accordingly, the Court, while recognizing that federal judges enjoy some discretion to withhold any Title VII remedy in particular circumstances, held in *Albemarle Paper Co. v. Moody*[5] that back pay may be denied only for unusual reasons which, if applied generally, would not impede those remedial objectives.[6] For example, the "neutral practice/disproportionate adverse impact" case dispenses with evidence of discriminatory intent, and a general good faith exception to back pay liability would therefore seriously erode the advantages of that mode of proof. The Court has consequently rejected such an exception.[7] It has also held that the

---

§ 4.25

1. Where the plaintiff has proven only that she was denied employment by virtue of a neutral practice that disproportionately adversely impacted her group, the court has less assurance than in a case of proven disparate treatment that she is otherwise qualified for the position she seeks. In such cases the court may direct the employer to reconsider the plaintiff's application under standards that meet the applicable defense to a neutral practice case. *Young v. Edgcomb Steel Co.*, 499 F.2d 97 (4th Cir. 1974).

2. *Anderson v. Phillips Petroleum Co.*, 861 F.2d 631 (10th Cir.1988).

3. See the discussion of the remedy stage of a bifurcated systemic disparate treatment action in Chapter 3. *See EEOC v. Ilona of Hungary*, 108 F.3d 1569 (7th Cir. 1997) (where employer revoked its religious accommodation policy and insisted that it never discriminated, injunction prohibiting further discrimination required). But plaintiffs are not ordinarily entitled to a preliminary injunction, because monetary relief after trial will be an adequate remedy at law. *Adam–Mellang v. Apartment Search, Inc.*, 96 F.3d 297 (8th Cir.1996).

4. *See, e.g., Kamberos v. GTE Automatic Elec., Inc.*, 603 F.2d 598 (7th Cir.1979), *cert. denied*, 454 U.S. 1060, 102 S.Ct. 612, 70 L.Ed.2d 599 (1981).

5. 422 U.S. 405, 95 S.Ct. 2362, 45 L.Ed.2d 280 (1975).

6. The circuits continue to recognize that successful Title VII claimants are "presumptively" entitled to back pay. *Lathem v. Dep't of Children & Youth Servs.*, 172 F.3d 786, 794 (11th Cir.1999) (back pay awarded where defendant's unlawful conduct caused plaintiff's disability).

7. *Albemarle*, 422 U.S. 405, 95 S.Ct. 2362, 45 L.Ed.2d 280. On occasion, the presumption in favor of back pay has been overcome. In *Los Angeles Dep't of Water and Power v. Manhart*, 435 U.S. 702, 98 S.Ct. 1370, 55 L.Ed.2d 657 (1978), discussed in Chapter 2, the Court held unlawful as express gender discrimination the City's requirement that women contribute greater amounts than men to purchase a pension benefit of the same monthly amount. The Court nevertheless declined to order it to refund excess contributions. It referred to its ruling as a "marked departure from past practice" and expressed concern that the brunt of the requested remedy would fall on

ordinary Eleventh Amendment immunity of states from federal court monetary awards is overridden in Title VII actions because Congress enacted the statute in at least partial reliance on its powers under the Fourteenth Amendment to enforce the Equal Protection Clause.[8]

Back pay is defined as the total compensation the employee would have earned absent the unlawful conduct,[9] reduced by any compensation the employee actually received and any additional amount the employee would have received through reasonable efforts to mitigate the damages. It is awarded only for a period in which plaintiff is "available and willing to accept substantially equivalent employment," with periods of disability usually excluded from the award.[10] The employer bears the burden of proof on the issue of mitigation, which is itself a jury issue.[11] An employer's "unconditional" offer of reinstatement that is refused by the plaintiff ends the defendant's ongoing responsibility for back pay.[12]

Rejected applicants seeking back pay are not required to prove they

innocent third parties—pensioners or current employees participating in the fund. 435 U.S. at 719–721, 98 S.Ct. at 1380–1382.

Presumably, under the reasoning in *Albemarle*, the mere fact that liability may not have been anticipated should not have sufficed to relieve the defendant of retroactive monetary liability, for if good faith were a generally applied defense it would eviscerate the compensatory goal of Title VII remedies. (Among other things, there could never be monetary liability in a neutral practice/disproportionate adverse impact case.) The concern for innocent third parties is also a bit peculiar, since the burden of sizeable monetary awards against private employers is also felt by innocent third parties, their shareholders, yet courts have not hesitated too make such awards against private corporations. Perhaps there lurks here a tacit public-private distinction, an underlying awareness that the ultimate payors in *Manhart* may have been the city's taxpayers. See dissenting opinion of Marshall, J.

8. *Fitzpatrick v. Bitzer*, 427 U.S. 445, 96 S.Ct. 2666, 49 L.Ed.2d 614 (1976). It remains to be seen if the Supreme Court will conclude that this exercise of Congressional authority is proportionate to the 14th Amendment evil it aims to combat and is otherwise valid under the Court's subsequent decision in *City of Boerne v. Flores*, 521 U.S. 507, 117 S.Ct. 2157, 138 L.Ed.2d 624 (1997).

9. That issue may be relatively straightforward if a plaintiff was paid a straight salary by the former employer. But where the plaintiff is paid on the basis of commission, the determination is fraught with subjective and speculative factors. *See, e.g, Kirsch v. Fleet Street, Ltd.*, 148 F.3d 149 (2d Cir.1998) (plaintiff salesman not permitted

to introduce evidence about the compensation paid after his termination to other salespersons or sales managers, absent evidence that plaintiff's compensation would have been tied to theirs). And any appreciation on unrealized stock options is awardable as well. In *Greene v. Safeway Stores, Inc.*, 210 F.3d 1237 (10th Cir.2000), the court calculated the amount as the difference in the value of the stock options at the time the employee was forced to exercise them due to his unlawful termination and their value at the time he would have otherwise exercised them. *Id.* at 1243–44.

10. *Miller v. Marsh*, 766 F.2d 490, 492 (11th Cir.1985). But where plaintiff's disability was caused by defendant's unlawful discriminatory conduct, back pay is proper. *Lathem v. Dep't of Children & Youth Servs.*, 172 F.3d 786, 794 (11th Cir.1999).

11. *See Deffenbaugh–Williams v. Wal-Mart Stores, Inc.*, 156 F.3d 581, 588–89 (5th Cir.1998), *vacated on grant of reh'g en banc*, 169 F.3d 215 (5th Cir.1999), *reinstated in relevant part*, 182 F.3d 333 (5th Cir.1999).

12. *Ford Motor Co. v. EEOC*, 458 U.S. 219, 102 S.Ct. 3057, 73 L.Ed.2d 721 (1982) (Title VII); *Hogan v. Bangor and Aroostook R.R. Co.*, 61 F.3d 1034 (1st Cir.1995) (holding employer's conditioning reinstatement on employee's passing of a Functional Capacity Evaluation Test did not toll employer's back pay liability because there was no evidence that employee's passing of test would lead to reinstatement unless employee met other requirements) (ADA case); *Clarke v. Frank*, 960 F.2d 1146 (2d Cir. 1992) (holding that plaintiff's right to back pay in Title VII case ended on day he rejected and requested deferral of employer's unconditional offer).

would have been hired absent the unlawful discrimination.[13] But any plaintiff seeking back pay must have made reasonable efforts to mitigate her losses.[14] Back pay awards are reduced by amounts the plaintiff earned, or with reasonable diligence could have earned, since the date of a discharge or failure or refusal to hire; but a failure to mitigate may not

13. *EEOC v. Joint Apprenticeship Committee of Joint Industry Bd. of Elec. Industry,* 164 F.3d 89 (2d Cir.1998) (rejecting defendant's argument that *Wards Cove's* holding that the ultimate burden of proof remains at all times with the plaintiff applies not only to the liability phase of a Title VII claim, but also to the determination of back pay). Similarly, an employee is not required to reapply with employers who have previously rejected them. *See United States v. City of Warren, Mich.,* 138 F.3d 1083 (6th Cir.1998) (a Title VII claimant who was not hired because of discriminatory employment practices is not precluded from a back pay award because he did not reapply for work with the same employer when it eliminated its discriminatory practices).

14. The usual requirement for proving failure to mitigate requires the employer to prove that suitable work exists and that the employee has not made reasonable efforts to find it. *See Carey v. Mt. Desert Island Hosp.,* 156 F.3d 31 (1st Cir.1998). Some courts have fashioned an exception of sorts: if the employer proves the employee made no reasonable efforts to secure subsequent employment, the employer need not also prove that comparable work was available. *See Greenway v. Buffalo Hilton Hotel,* 143 F.3d 47 (2d Cir.1998); *Weaver v. Casa Gallardo, Inc.,* 922 F.2d 1515, 1527 (11th Cir. 1991); *Sellers v. Delgado College,* 902 F.2d 1189, 1193 (5th Cir.), *cert. denied,* 498 U.S. 987, 111 S.Ct. 525, 112 L.Ed.2d 536 (1990). *See also Dailey v. Societe Generale,* 108 F.3d 451 (2d Cir.1997) (holding that plaintiff who choose to attend school only when diligent efforts to find work proved fruitless, may satisfy her duty to mitigate) (Title VII case); *Thurman v. Yellow Freight Sys., Inc.,* 90 F.3d 1160 (6th Cir.)), *amended on denial of rehearing,* 97 F.3d 833 (6th Cir.1996) (holding that there must be evidence that plaintiff acted intentionally to constitute a "wilful loss of earnings" for purposes of tolling back pay in Title VII and § 1981 cases); *Dominguez v. Tom James Co.,* 113 F.3d 1188 (11th Cir.1997) (court did not "foreclose the possibility that receipt of Social Security benefits may be evidence that a plaintiff failed to use his best efforts to mitigate damages" in ADEA case). The plaintiff of course cannot recover duplicative damages, so where instructions to the jury could be read to permit the jury to

award back pay, the court cannot award back pay itself. *Collins v. Kibort,* 143 F.3d 331 (7th Cir.1998). *See Hawkins v. 1115 Legal Serv. Care,* 163 F.3d 684 (2d Cir. 1998) (employee must use reasonable diligence but is not obligated to be successful; burden on defendant to prove a failure to mitigate); *Pierce v. F.R. Tripler & Co.,* 955 F.2d 820, 830 (2d Cir.1992) (ultimate question is whether the plaintiff acted reasonably in attempting to gain other employment or in rejecting proffered employment); *EEOC v. Manville Sales Corp.,* 27 F.3d 1089 (5th Cir.1994), *cert. denied,* 513 U.S. 1190, 115 S.Ct. 1252, 131 L.Ed.2d 133 (1995) (finding that "[a]n offer of an interview is not tantamount to an unconditional job offer and therefore the plaintiff's refusal to interview does not automatically toll" accrual of damages); *Morris v. American Nat'l Can Corp.,* 952 F.2d 200 (8th Cir. 1991) (holding that conditioning reinstatement on employee's taking physical exam was reasonable where employee quit for medical reasons, was bound by a collective bargaining agreement allowing physicals, and had received worker's compensation benefits) (Title VII) (distinguishing *Orzel v. City of Wauwatosa Fire Dep't,* 697 F.2d 743 (7th Cir.), *cert. denied,* 464 U.S. 992, 104 S.Ct. 484, 78 L.Ed.2d 680 (1983) (where conditioning offer of reinstatement on passing physical did not toll back pay damages); *Giandonato v. Sybron Corp.,* 804 F.2d 120 (10th Cir.1986) (holding that employee's wife's illness, his not wanting to work under a certain supervisor, and his view that the offer had too many "uncertainties" were not valid reasons for refusing employer's offer of reinstatement under ADEA); *Lewis v. Federal Prison Indus., Inc.,* 953 F.2d 1277 (11th Cir.1992) (finding employee's refusal to accept offer of reinstatement reasonable given evidence of antagonistic relationship with supervisors and fact that employee was only four years from retirement) (ADEA); *Ford Motor Co. v. EEOC,* 458 U.S. 219, 231, 102 S.Ct. 3057, 3065, 73 L.Ed.2d 721 (1982) (although an unemployed claimant would generally forfeit her right to back pay if she refused a job substantially equivalent to the one she was denied, she need not go into another line of work, accept a demotion, or take a demeaning position).

absolutely forfeit the right to recovery for back pay.[15] In those courts
where an employer is relieved of the burden to prove there was comparable work available after it proves that the employee made no reasonable
efforts to seek subsequent work, the employee must prove that comparable compensation was not available to save any part of a back pay
award.[16] Several circuits have held that self-employment is an acceptable
form of mitigation for this purpose.[17] The back pay clock should stop
when "the sting" of discriminatory conduct has ended.[18] There is considerable division in the circuit opinions as to whether "collateral sources"
of income may be deducted from the back pay award, and if so which
ones.[19]

15. *Booker v. Taylor Milk Co.,* 64 F.3d
860 (3d Cir.1995).

16. *See Greenway v. Buffalo Hilton Hotel,* 143 F.3d 47 (2d Cir.1998).

17. *Smith v. Great American Rests.,
Inc.,* 969 F.2d 430 (7th Cir.1992) (ADEA
case) (plaintiff opened own restaurant);
Carden v. Westinghouse Elec. Corp., 850
F.2d 996, 1005 (3d Cir.1988). *But see Hansard v. Pepsi–Cola Metro. Bottling Co.,* 865
F.2d 1461, 1468 (5th Cir.), *cert. denied,* 493
U.S. 842, 110 S.Ct. 129, 107 L.Ed.2d 89
(1989) (ADEA plaintiff's opening of part-
time flea market booth did not constitute
self-employment sufficient to satisfy obligation to attempt to mitigate damages). *See
also Boehms v. Crowell,* 139 F.3d 452 (5th
Cir.1998), *cert. denied,* 525 U.S. 1102, 119
S.Ct. 866, 142 L.Ed.2d 768 (1999) (employee's participation in employer's transition
program satisfied employee's duty to mitigate); *Dailey v. Societe Generale,* 108 F.3d
451 (2d Cir.1997) (plaintiff did not fail to
mitigate damages by attending school full
time after an unsuccessful job search).

18. *Syvock v. Milwaukee Boiler Mfg.
Co.,* 665 F.2d 149, 160 n. 14 (7th Cir.1981),
overruled on other grounds, 860 F.2d 834
(7th Cir.1988).

19. *Compare Swanks v. Washington
Metro. Area Transit Auth.,* 116 F.3d 582
(D.C.Cir.1997) (successful plaintiff in an
ADA suit may have any backpay award
reduced to the extent necessary to prevent
double recovery) (Social Security case);
*EEOC v. Enterprise Ass'n Steamfitters Lo-
cal No. 638,* 542 F.2d 579, 591–92 (2d Cir.
1976), *cert. denied sub nom. Rios v. Enterprise Ass'n Steamfitters, Local No. 638,* 430
U.S. 911, 97 S.Ct. 1186, 51 L.Ed.2d 588
(1977) (allowing district courts to offset
public assistance payment against Title VII
back pay award); *Merriweather v. Hercules,
Inc.,* 631 F.2d 1161, 1168 (5th Cir.1980)
(deductions for unemployment compensation avoids possibility of double payment to
plaintiff and such decision is within the
discretion of the trial court) (Title VII);

Carey v. Mt. Desert Island Hosp., 156 F.3d
31 (1st Cir.1998) (holding employee entitled
to recover back pay, reduced by any compensation actually received and any amount
he would have received through reasonable
efforts to mitigate) (Title VII and Maine
Human Rights Act); *Orzel v. City of Wauwatosa Fire Dep't,* 697 F.2d 743, 756 (7th
Cir.), *cert. denied,* 464 U.S. 992, 104 S.Ct.
484, 78 L.Ed.2d 680 (1983) (magistrate did
not abuse his discretion in deducting unemployment and pension benefits in an ADEA
case); *EEOC v. Wyoming Retirement Sys.,*
771 F.2d 1425, 1431 (10th Cir.1985) (holding under ADEA that "deduction of collateral sources of income from a back pay
award is a matter within the trial court's
discretion") (Social Security) *with Craig v.
Y & Y Snacks, Inc.,* 721 F.2d 77, 81–85 (3d
Cir.1983) (holding that unemployment compensation should not be deducted from a
Title VII back pay award); *EEOC v. Ford
Motor Co.,* 688 F.2d 951, 952 (4th Cir.1982)
(similar) (Title VII and state unemployment
benefits); *Brown v. A.J. Gerrard Mfg. Co.,*
715 F.2d 1549, 1550–51 (11th Cir.1983)
(holding that unemployment compensation
benefits should not be deducted from Title
VII back pay awards) (applies to ADEA
also); *Dominguez v. Tom James Co.,* 113
F.3d 1188 (11th Cir.1997) (extending
Brown and holding that Social Security
benefits are not to be deducted from ADEA
award). Several circuits have apparently
conflicting opinions on the subject. *Compare Thurman v. Yellow Freight Sys. Inc.,*
90 F.3d 1160 (6th Cir.), *amended on denial
of reh'g,* 97 F.3d 833 (6th Cir.1996) (citing
Hawley v. Dresser Indus., Inc., 958 F.2d
720, 726 (6th Cir.1992) and approving deduction of pension benefits from an ADEA
back pay award) *with Rasimas v. Michigan
Dep't of Mental Health,* 714 F.2d 614, 627
(6th Cir.1983), *cert. denied,* 466 U.S. 950,
104 S.Ct. 2151, 80 L.Ed.2d 537 (1984)
(holding that "unemployment benefits ...
should not be deducted from back pay
awards" under Title VII). *Compare Glover*

Title VII authorizes the award of back pay to a date as early as two years before the filing of the required EEOC charge—as distinct from the later date on which the complaint is filed in a judicial action. In states without their own anti-discrimination laws and agencies, EEOC may immediately assert jurisdiction over a plaintiff's initial charge; and any charging party may demand a notice of right to sue from EEOC after it has exercised that jurisdiction for 180 days. Even in the majority of states, where the charging party must, at least in theory, exhaust administrative remedies before state or local "deferral" agencies, the plaintiff may be able to invoke EEOC's jurisdiction promptly if the state or local agency waives its right to proceed either in the individual case or by a "work-sharing" agreement with EEOC. And at the outside the plaintiff has 300 days from the latest alleged unlawful employment practice to file with EEOC, which then can be compelled to authorize suit 180 days later. Thus as a practical matter most Title VII judicial actions will be commenced well before two years have expired after the filing of the EEOC charge. The two-year back pay accrual rule nevertheless permits back pay for violations that occurred up to two years before that charge was filed. That is to say, back pay may be recovered for "continuing violations"[20] that began before the last event that triggers Title VII's "statute of limitations."[21]

Although, as the next section considers, the 1991 Act adds compensatory and punitive damages as "legal" remedies to the Title VII plaintiff's arsenal, it does not change the "equitable" character of the pre-existing remedies like back pay or restoration of lost pension benefits.[22] Determination of eligibility for back pay, although virtually automatic under the *Albemarle* presumption, is therefore formally for the court, not the jury, as is the critical calculation of the back pay amount.[23]

---

v. McDonnell Douglas Corp., 12 F.3d 845, 848 (8th Cir.), *cert. denied*, 511 U.S. 1070, 114 S.Ct. 1647, 128 L.Ed.2d 366 (1994) (holding that district court erred in refusing to offset pension payments from an ADEA award of back pay) *with Doyne v. Union Elec. Co.*, 953 F.2d 447, 451–52 (8th Cir. 1992) (holding that pension benefits should not be considered in fashioning an ADEA front pay award). *Compare Naton v. Bank of Cal.*, 649 F.2d 691, 700 (9th Cir.1981) (holding district court has discretion to deduct collateral benefits from ADEA back pay awards) *with Kauffman v. Sidereal Corp.*, 695 F.2d 343, 347 (9th Cir.1982) (holding in a Title VII case that unemployment benefits received by a successful plaintiff in an employment discrimination action are not offsets against a backpay award). *See also Lussier v. Runyon*, 50 F.3d 1103 (1st Cir.), *cert. denied*, 516 U.S. 815, 116 S.Ct. 69, 133 L.Ed.2d 30 (1995) (tends to agree with those courts that have held offsetting collateral benefits against back pay to be a matter within the district court's discretion, but question left open) (VA benefits) (Rehabilitation Act of 1973).

20. For a closer look at the intricacies of the "continuing violation" theory, see § 4.3, *supra*, and § 8.22, *infra*.

21. *See, e.g., Palmer v. Kelly*, 17 F.3d 1490 (D.C.Cir.1994) (plaintiff who retired only 9 days after discriminatory promotion denial, and who was thus arguably eligible only for 9 days of back pay, nevertheless received back pay for the full two years before he filed with EEOC, when court determined that the employer had continually denied promotions because of race).

22. *See Banks v. Travelers Companies*, 180 F.3d 358 (2d Cir.1999) (restoration of lost pension benefits a claim for equitable relief that judge could award) (case under ADEA).

23. *Simpson v. Lucky Stores*, 1993 WL 414668 (N.D.Cal.1993). Thus one court has recently suggested a rule of law based on the "lost-chance" concept used in tort cases to calculate back pay where it is less than

Yet at least one circuit has held that "the issue of reasonable mitigation is ultimately a question of fact for the jury."[24]

Front pay is a discretionary remedy granted by the court as a substitute for reinstatement if reinstatement is impossible, impracticable or inequitable. It may be the only feasible way to make a victim of discrimination whole where there is no available position in which to reinstate her, or where, as in a constructive discharge or other harassment case, reinstatement would be unsuccessful or unproductive because of the workplace hostility that either prompted the claim or resulted from its prosecution.[25] It is awarded in an amount that estimates the total future salary, pension and other benefits the plaintiff, absent an unlawful discriminatory discharge, would have earned with the employer from date of judgment until probable loss of job or date of retirement; and prospective losses of post-retirement benefits may be measured until actuarially predicted date of death. Because it is awarded and calculated on the basis of highly speculative assumptions about the health of the business, the health of the plaintiff, and the plaintiff's future satisfactory work performance and prospects for advancement, front pay is devilishly difficult to measure. That difficulty suggests that front pay may be a form of future nonpecuniary, rather than pecuniary loss. Yet there is an irreducible element of speculation in almost every front pay award—e.g., trying to determine if the plaintiff, after termination, would have survived a subsequent reduction in force and otherwise performed well enough to resist termination—and speculation alone should not render front pay unavailable, unless it is excessive.[26]

Squarely endorsed by only one member of the Supreme Court,[27] the lower federal courts have come to presume the front pay award appropri-

certain that the plaintiff would have been hired or promoted even absent discrimination—as where two or more candidates seek only one available position. The court suggested that the plaintiff be awarded the same percentage of back pay as his percentage chance of being promoted. *Doll v. Brown*, 75 F.3d 1200 (7th Cir.1996) (case under Rehabilitation Act). EEOC Guidelines recognize a "no-injury" defense but require the employer to prove by "clear and convincing" evidence that, despite its discriminatory conduct, the plaintiff suffered no harm as a result. 29 C.F.R. §§ 1614.203, 1614.501(b), (c).

24. *Smith v. Great American Rests., Inc.*, 969 F.2d 430, 439 (7th Cir.1992).

25. *See, e.g., Farley v. Nationwide Mut. Ins. Co.*, 197 F.3d 1322, 1338–39 (11th Cir. 1999) (although recognizing the usual remedy is reinstatement, court declined to reinstate plaintiff due to pervasive and severe verbal abuse plaintiff suffered on the job); *Robinson v. Southeastern Pa. Transp. Auth.*, 982 F.2d 892 (3d Cir.1993) (court declined to reinstate victorious plaintiff who

had characterized his supervisors as "South African dogs"); *Ellis v. Ringgold Sch. Dist.*, 832 F.2d 27 (3d Cir.1987), *cert. denied*, 494 U.S. 1005, 110 S.Ct. 1298, 108 L.Ed.2d 475 (1990); *Sanchez v. Philip Morris Inc.*, 774 F.Supp. 626 (W.D.Okl.1991), *reversed on other grounds*, 992 F.2d 244 (10th Cir.1993) (front pay preferable to reinstatement where plaintiff would have to work with employees who testified against him). Traditionally, it has been thought that front pay is a substitute for, not a supplement to, reinstatement; remedies may not be cumulative. *Suggs v. ServiceMaster Educ. Food Mgmt.*, 72 F.3d 1228 (6th Cir.1996). *But cf. Selgas v. American Airlines, Inc.*, 104 F.3d 9 (1st Cir.1997) (where reinstatement issue not decided until after intervening appeal, during which plaintiff received front pay, trial court could subsequently order reinstatement to commence upon expiration of front pay).

26. *See, e.g., Banks v. Travelers Companies*, 180 F.3d 358 (2d Cir.1999).

27. *See Franks* (Burger, C.J., concurring).

ate where reinstatement is infeasible or ill advised.[28] Most but not all circuit courts, in decisions before the 1991 Act, held front pay available under Title VII.[29] The principal argument against front pay revolved around the fact that all Title VII remedies were then equitable, and some judges characterized front pay as "legal."[30] Now that the 1991 Act adds legal remedies to the menu of relief under Title VII, the Supreme Court, in dictum, has noted the availability of front pay with approval.[31]

Front pay leaves the incumbent in place and, beginning as of final judgment, orders the employer to pay the discriminatee an amount equivalent to what he would earn if actually reinstated.[32] Because of the uncertain duration of the period during which the victim of discrimination would have remained employed after judgment, or at what level and pay, the front pay remedy is fraught with computational difficulties. Given its purpose to restore an injured party to the position she would have occupied absent the employer's unlawful discrimination, determining the appropriateness, duration and amount of front pay is an exercise that entails "predicting the future":

> [S]uch an exercise involves an attempt to determine the degree to which a plaintiff possesses qualities that would make plaintiff successful in attaining career advancement. For advancements that come simply with longevity, courts have uniformly assumed that such advancement would occur, in the absence of specific disqualifying information.

> On the other hand, courts will not automatically assume that a person discriminated against possesses characteristics so sterling as to receive every advancement not made illegal or logically impossible under the employer's rules.[33]

The circuit opinions grapple with a host of circumstances governing

---

28. *See, e.g., Williams v. Pharmacia, Inc.,* 137 F.3d 944, 951 (7th Cir.1998); *Reed v. A.W. Lawrence & Co., Inc.,* 95 F.3d 1170, 1177 n. 7 (2d Cir.1996); *Winsor v. Hinckley Dodge, Inc.,* 79 F.3d 996, 1002 (10th Cir. 1996); *Carter v. Sedgwick County, Kansas,* 36 F.3d 952 (10th Cir.1994); *Weaver v. Casa Gallardo,* 922 F.2d 1515, 1528 (11th Cir. 1991); *Farber v. Massillon Bd. of Educ.,* 917 F.2d 1391 (6th Cir.1990), *cert. denied,* 498 U.S. 1082, 111 S.Ct. 952, 112 L.Ed.2d 1041 (1991); *Shore v. Federal Express Corp.,* 777 F.2d 1155, 1159 (6th Cir.1985).

29. *Compare Weaver v. Casa Gallardo, Inc.,* 922 F.2d 1515, 1528 (11th Cir.1991); *Green v. USX Corp.* 843 F.2d 1511, 1531–32 (3d Cir.1988), *reinstated in relevant part,* 896 F.2d 801 (3d Cir.), *cert. denied,* 498 U.S. 814, 111 S.Ct. 53, 112 L.Ed.2d 29 (1990); *Pitre v. Western Elec. Co.,* 843 F.2d 1262, 1278–79 (10th Cir.1988); and *Shore v. Federal Express Corp.,* 777 F.2d 1155, 1159 (6th Cir.1985); *Goss v. Exxon Office Sys-*

tems Co., 747 F.2d 885, 889 (3d Cir.1984) (acknowledging the remedy) *with McKnight v. General Motors Corp.,* 908 F.2d 104, 117 (7th Cir.1990), *cert. denied,* 499 U.S. 919, 111 S.Ct. 1306, 113 L.Ed.2d 241 (1991) (expressing doubt whether Title VII authorizes front pay, but asserting that the ADEA does). *See* Belton, *Remedies in Employment Discrimination Law* § 10.3 (John Wiley, 1992) (citing cases).

30. *McKnight v. General Motors Corp.,* 908 F.2d at 116–117.

31. *United States v. Burke,* 504 U.S. 229, 239 n. 9, 112 S.Ct. 1867, 1873 n. 9, 119 L.Ed.2d 34 (1992).

32. *See Patterson v. American Tobacco Co.,* 535 F.2d 257 (4th Cir.), *cert. denied,* 429 U.S. 920, 97 S.Ct. 314, 50 L.Ed.2d 286 (1976).

33. *Griffin v. Michigan Dep't of Corr.,* 5 F.3d 186, 189 (6th Cir.1993).

the appropriateness and duration of front pay awards.[34] The award will

34. 1. *General Prerequisites*

a) *Whittlesey v. Union Carbide Corp.*, 742 F.2d 724, 729 (2d Cir.1984) (upholding award of back pay until plaintiff reached 70 because the time period was relatively short (4 years) and the award did not involve undue speculation either as to: 1) the possibility of mitigation or 2) the amount plaintiff would have made had he not been fired from employer.) (ADEA)

b) *Griffin v. Michigan Dep't of Corr.*, 5 F.3d 186 (6th Cir.1993) (in considering whether to award expected advancements as front pay, the court determined that "the average worker with the basic qualifications possessed by the injured party" was the measuring stick. The defendant would thus bear the burden of showing that the plaintiff would not have performed as well as the average employee, while plaintiff would bear the burden of proving that she would have performed better than that average.) (Title VII)

c) *Roush v. KFC Nat'l Mgmt. Co.*, 10 F.3d 392 (6th Cir.1993), *cert. denied*, 513 U.S. 808, 115 S.Ct. 56, 130 L.Ed.2d 15 (1994) (factors in awarding front pay include: a) an employee's duty to mitigate, b) the availability of employment opportunities, c) the period within which one by reasonable efforts might be re-employed, d) the employee's work and life expectancy, e) the discount tables to determine the present value of future damages, and f) other factors pertinent to any award of future damages.) (ADEA)

d) *Barbour v. Merrill*, 48 F.3d 1270 (C.A.D.C.1995) (factors include: plaintiff's age, plaintiff's intention to remain at the job until retirement, length of time people held that same position, how long plaintiff had held that position, length of time others in other companies hold these positions, and other contentions that plaintiff would not have remained at his job until retirement.) (§ 1981)

e) *Scarfo v. Cabletron Systems, Inc.*, 54 F.3d 931 (1st Cir.1995) (error to award both back pay and front pay when the two awards overlapped for over three years. The appellate court reduced the back pay award, deeming it preferable to reduce the smaller amount in accord with the goal of modifying only to avoid duplication.) (Title VII)

f) *Suggs v. ServiceMaster Educ. Food Mgmt.*, 72 F.3d 1228, 1234 (6th Cir.1996) (stressing necessity to consider "the employee's future in the position from which she was terminated." Also, this case is remanded because the issue whether front pay could be awarded could not be answered without determining if the plaintiff could be reinstated—reinstatement and front pay thus being treated as alternative rather than cumulative remedies.) (Title VII)

2. *No Job Remaining*

a) *Selgas v. American Airlines*, 104 F.3d 9 (1st Cir.1997) (front pay an available alternative to compensate a plaintiff when there are conditions that preclude the employee's return such as hostility in the workplace or the need for an innocent employee to be "bumped" from a job. Observes that front pay merely takes the employee back to the point of employability while reinstatement "perfect[s]" the remedy.) (Title VII)

b) *Williams v. Pharmacia*, 137 F.3d 944 (7th Cir.1998) (upholding award of one year of front pay in lieu of reinstatement because plaintiff's division was eliminated by a subsequent merger.) (Title VII)

3. *Hostility in the Workplace*

a) *Whittlesey v. Union Carbide Corp.*, 742 F.2d 724, 729 (2d Cir.1984) (upholding district court's award of front pay because reinstatement was impossible because of defendant's "hostility and outrage" and plaintiff would be "ostracized" due to his suit, where defendant had no justification for degree of hostility.) (ADEA)

b) *Lewis v. Federal Prison Indus.*, 953 F.2d 1277, 1281 (11th Cir.1992) (front pay available only in "egregious" circumstances, but particular plaintiff eligible for front pay when he would not return to an antagonistic, discriminatory work place with an emotional disturbance and he had only four years to retirement.) (ADEA)

c) *Newhouse v. McCormick & Co.*, 110 F.3d 635 (8th Cir.1997) (while reinstatement is the preferred remedy absent some evidence of hostility, no abuse of discretion to allow front pay in lieu of reinstatement in view of strained relationship between plaintiff and his manager and fact that plaintiff was already collecting social security benefits which made reinstatement impractical.) (ADEA)

d) *Kelley v. Airborne Freight Corp.*, 140 F.3d 335, 353–354 (1st Cir.), *cert. denied*, 525 U.S. 932, 119 S.Ct. 341, 142 L.Ed.2d 281 (1998) (upholding district court's refusal to grant reinstatement due to animosity that extended beyond litigation as exhibited by plaintiff's supervisor and a management staff that had "vilified Kelley, which completely undermined his value as a manager." Further, the court did not trust the

not necessarily terminate when plaintiff quits subsequent, substitute employment; on the other hand, in recognition of the duty to mitigate, the employer need only pay such a plaintiff the difference between the amount she would have received had she remained employed (or secured substantially equivalent employment) and the amount she could have continued to receive in the *lesser*-paying substitute job that she quit.[35] Almost invariably when front pay is awarded, there are numerous considerations counseling the reduction or termination of the award, including mitigation, unclean hands, speculation about the duration of plaintiff's position or personal retention, collateral sources, and the kinds and amounts of other relief awarded for the unlawful discrimination.[36] Because front pay awards are replacing anticipated compensation

defendant when it came to reinstatement intentions.) (ADEA and Massachusetts law)

e) *Cowan v. Strafford R–VI Sch. Dist.*, 140 F.3d 1153, 1160 (8th Cir.1998) (although reinstatement is preferred to front pay, front pay allowed when reinstatement would create an "extreme burden" on a teacher-principal relationship so badly damaged that no functioning rapport could be reestablished.) (Title VII)

4. *Available Absent a Special Request for Reinstatement*

a) *Roush v. KFC Nat'l Mgmt. Co.*, 10 F.3d 392, 398 (6th Cir.1993)), *cert. denied*, 513 U.S. 808, 115 S.Ct. 56, 130 L.Ed.2d 15 (1994) ("We have never held that a plaintiff must request reinstatement as a prerequisite to recovering front pay, and we decline to so hold in this case") (also noting that front pay is not automatically awarded if plaintiff does not seek reinstatement.) (ADEA)

b) *Reneau v. Wayne Griffin & Sons, Inc.*, 945 F.2d 869 (5th Cir.1991).

c) *Williams v. Valentec Kisco, Inc.*, 964 F.2d 723 (8th Cir.), *cert. denied*, 506 U.S. 1014, 113 S.Ct. 635, 121 L.Ed.2d 566 (1992).

5. *Plaintiff Refuses Unconditional Offer of Reinstatement*

The rule of *Ford Motor Co. v. EEOC*, 458 U.S. 219, 102 S.Ct. 3057, 73 L.Ed.2d 721 (1982), that plaintiff's refusal of an unconditional offer for reinstatement which ends the defendant's liability for back pay applies to front pay as well. So while the plaintiff need not request reinstatement as a condition of front pay, a plaintiff's failure to accept unconditional reinstatement will terminate its right to front as well as back pay.

35. *Shore v. Federal Express Corp.*, 42 F.3d 373 (6th Cir.1994). *See Suggs v. ServiceMaster Educ. Food Mgmt.*, 72 F.3d 1228 (directing district court to specify the duration, amount and end date of award, and to

deduct amounts plaintiff could earn during front pay period through reasonable efforts to secure comparable substitute employment). *See also Boehms v. Crowell*, 139 F.3d 452 (5th Cir.1998), *cert. denied*, 525 U.S. 1102, 119 S.Ct. 866, 142 L.Ed.2d 768 (1999) (employee's participation in employer's transition program satisfied employee's duty to mitigate).

36.   a) *Duty to Mitigate*

1) *Dominic v. Consolidated Edison Co. of N.Y., Inc.*, 822 F.2d 1249 (2d Cir.1987) (holding that defendant's failure to show that plaintiff had not mitigated damages does not entitle plaintiff to a lifetime front-pay award because the court should take into account the plaintiff's ability to mitigate in the future by finding a similar job. Thus an award of two years of front pay is upheld because there was no abuse of discretion.) (ADEA) The fact that the two-year award did not take into account raises was also upheld because the defendant could show its dissatisfaction with the plaintiff's work apart from any discrimination.

2) *Shore v. Federal Express Corp.*, 42 F.3d 373 (6th Cir.1994) (citing *Ford Motor Co. v. EEOC*, 458 U.S. 219, 102 S.Ct. 3057, 73 L.Ed.2d 721 (1982), and *Rasimas v. Michigan Dep't of Mental Health*, 714 F.2d 614, 624 (6th Cir.1983), *cert. denied*, 466 U.S. 950, 104 S.Ct. 2151, 80 L.Ed.2d 537 (1984) (applying back pay duty to mitigate to front pay, thus holding that a plaintiff has the duty to mitigate damages by looking for a "substantially equivalent" job, meaning "virtually identical promotional opportunities, compensation, job responsibilities, working conditions, and status.") (Title VII)

3) *Barbour v. Merrill*, 48 F.3d 1270 (C.A.D.C.1995) (factors to consider in mitigation were current job market and industry conditions, as well as the amount of time reasonably required for plaintiff to secure comparable employment.) (§ 1981)

4) *Padilla v. Metro–North Commuter R.R.*, 92 F.3d 117 (2d Cir.1996), *cert. denied*, 520 U.S. 1274, 117 S.Ct. 2453, 138 L.Ed.2d 211 (1997) (plaintiff did not fail to mitigate even when he did not look for a job because: 1) his job of superintendent of train operations was functionally unique, 2) he only had a high-school education, 3) plaintiff had worked only for the railroad since the age of twenty-two, and 4) defendant failed to carry burden of showing an available job.) (ADEA)

5) *Kehoe v. Anheuser–Busch, Inc.*, 96 F.3d 1095 (8th Cir.1996) (the court rules that while the plaintiff has the reasonable duty to mitigate, the defendant has the burden to show that the plaintiff failed to do so.) (ADEA)

6) *Newhouse v. McCormick & Co.*, 110 F.3d 635, 641 (8th Cir.1997) (the plaintiff must show an attempt to mitigate damages or face a reduction in the damage award. Plaintiff can mitigate by using "reasonable diligence in finding other suitable employment and not to refuse a job that is substantially equivalent to the one at issue." But the duty "is not onerous and does not require success. All that is required by law is an honest, good faith effort." Here, plaintiff successfully mitigated by applying for comparable work and seeking help from Nebraska job services. Also, plaintiff testified that even though he started accepting social security, he would have given this up to keep his job.) (ADEA)

7) *EEOC v. Pape Lift, Inc.*, 115 F.3d 676 (9th Cir.1997) (holding that plaintiff need only look for a "substantially equivalent" job in order to fulfill his duty to mitigate. Still, the position of parts manager at a warehouse was not similar to an animal health manager, sound effects manager or music librarian. The jury charge of "like kind, status and pay" as "substantially equivalent" was upheld. Also, the court rejected the defendant's argument that the plaintiff should have lowered his sights in looking for a similar job after a long period of unsuccessful searching, at least where defendant did not ask for such a charge to the jury.) (ADEA)

8) *Migis v. Pearle Vision*, 135 F.3d 1041 (5th Cir.1998) (plaintiff's duty to mitigate was fulfilled even though she delayed finding a job because she first had to find adequate child care for her daughter.) (Title VII)

9) *Carey v. Mt. Desert Island Hosp.*, 156 F.3d 31 (1st Cir.1998) (trial court did not abuse discretion in accepting expert witness' testimony as to the number of applications made relative to the number of positions available that plaintiff did not use

reasonable diligence to seek. This finding allowed a reduction in back pay of $100,000 to $110,070 for failure to properly mitigate.) (Title VII and Maine Human Rights Act)

b) *Unclean Hands*

1) *Kama Rippa Music, Inc. v. Schekeryk*, 510 F.2d 837, 844 (2d Cir.1975) ("equity's distaste for forfeitures is almost certainly matched by its repugnance for petitioners beseeching its aid with unclean hands.")

c) *Challenging Speculative Assumptions Underlying Request*

1) *Williams v. Pharmacia*, 137 F.3d 944 (7th Cir.1998) (front pay limited to one year because plaintiff would have lost job due to a subsequent merger.) (Title VII)

2) *Cowan v. Strafford R–VI Sch. Dist.*, 140 F.3d 1153 (8th Cir.1998) (two-year award of front pay to a probationary teacher with a one-year contract upheld where no guarantee that she would continue living in the school district because she might move to a different job or because her contract might not be renewed for legitimate reasons.) (Title VII, religious discrimination)

d) *Deductions for Collateral Sources*

1) *Roush v. KFC Nat'l Mgmt. Co.*, 10 F.3d 392 (6th Cir.1993), *cert. denied*, 513 U.S. 808, 115 S.Ct. 56, 130 L.Ed.2d 15 (1994) (plaintiff's "intentional limitation of her income in order to continue receiving social security benefits terminates any entitlement to front pay which she may otherwise have had.") (ADEA)

2) *Lussier v. Runyon*, 50 F.3d 1103 (1st Cir.1995), *cert. denied*, 516 U.S. 815, 116 S.Ct. 69, 133 L.Ed.2d 30 (1995) (in determining front pay, court has equitable discretion to take into account collateral benefits "received by the plaintiff as a traceable consequence of the defendant's statutory violation.") (Rehabilitation Act) *Compare Newhouse v. McCormick & Co.*, 110 F.3d 635 (8th Cir.1997), *Dominguez v. Tom James Co.*, 113 F.3d 1188 (11th Cir.1997), and *Maxfield v. Sinclair Int'l*, 766 F.2d 788 (3d Cir.1985), *cert. denied*, 474 U.S. 1057, 106 S.Ct. 796, 88 L.Ed.2d 773 (1986) (award under ADEA should not be reduced by Social Security benefits received during pendency of suit) *with Guthrie v. J.C.Penney Co., Inc.*, 803 F.2d 202 (5th Cir.1986) and *EEOC v. Wyoming Retirement System*, 771 F.2d 1425 (10th Cir.1985) (leaving that question for decision by the trial court, case by case.)

e) *Loss of Front Pay Due to Awards of Other Relief*

1) *Graefenhain v. Pabst Brewing Co.*, 870 F.2d 1198 (7th Cir.1989) (plaintiff could not receive an award of lost pension benefits

after judgment that is not yet due, they must be discounted to present value;[37] and there are numerous other technical issues that must be faced in calculating the award.[38] All that can be said with confidence is that purely arbitrary limits on front pay may be overturned as an abuse of the trial court's discretion.[39] On occasion, awards of as long as 25 years have been made when that represents plaintiff's first eligibility for a full pension.[40] Perhaps the most significant unsettled issue is whether

where a subsequent job had a greater pension than the one from which he was fired, consistent with make-whole remedial policy.) (ADEA)

2) *Barbano v. Madison County*, 922 F.2d 139 (2d Cir.1990) (district court acted within its discretion in denying front pay entirely because other relief, including back pay, prejudgment interest, and attorney's fees sufficed to make the plaintiff whole.) (Title VII)

3) *Weaver v. Casa Gallardo*, 922 F.2d 1515 (11th Cir.1991) (front pay award is appropriate "only when the other damages awarded will not fully compensate the plaintiff for his injury.") (Title VII and U.S.C.A. 1981)

4) *Hadley v. VAM P T S*, 44 F.3d 372, 376 (5th Cir.1995) (holding that "a substantial liquidated damage award may indicate that an additional award of front pay is inappropriate or excessive.") (Title VII)

5) *Lussier v. Runyon*, 50 F.3d 1103 (1st Cir.1995), *cert. denied*, 516 U.S. 815, 116 S.Ct. 69, 133 L.Ed.2d 30 (1995) (trial court properly tailored front pay award to take into account the VA benefits plaintiff received as a result of the unlawful discharge.) (Rehabilitation Act)

6) *Suggs v. ServiceMaster Educ. Food Mgmt.*, 72 F.3d 1228 (6th Cir.1996) (employee who was discriminatorily discharged must be made whole, but is not entitled to a windfall, consistent with Title VII's purpose of restoring the injured party to the same position they would have occupied but for the discrimination.) (Title VII)

7) *Newhouse v. McCormick & Co.*, 110 F.3d 635 (8th Cir.1997) (liquidated damages do not cut off the plaintiff's eligibility for front pay because the former are punitive while the latter are equitable, citing *Thurston*, 469 U.S. at 12.) (ADEA)

37. *See Williams v. Pharmacia*, 137 F.3d 944 (7th Cir.1998) (front pay award gives the employee the present value of the earnings from former job less any earnings from new or anticipated positions).

38. *See, e.g. Kelley v. Airborne Freight Corp.*, 140 F.3d 335, 354 n. 12 (1st Cir.), *cert. denied*, 525 U.S. 932, 119 S.Ct. 341, 142 L.Ed.2d 281 (1998) (upholding a jury

award of front pay of $1,000,000, reasoning that plaintiff would never again attain his former salary of $100,000 because of his lack of education) (ADEA and Massachusetts Law); *Williams v. Pharmacia*, 137 F.3d 944 (7th Cir.1998) (front pay award gives the employee the present value of the earnings from former job less the earnings from new (or expected) job) (Title VII); *Kim v. Nash Finch Co.*, 123 F.3d 1046 (8th Cir. 1997) (upholding jury award of $477/month, even though plaintiff's highest salary in the position he lost was $360/month) (Title VII & Section 1981); *Padilla v. Metro–North Commuter R.R.*, 92 F.3d 117 (2d Cir.1996), *cert. denied*, 520 U.S. 1274, 117 S.Ct. 2453, 138 L.Ed.2d 211 (1997) (upholding front pay award of more than 20 years, until plaintiff turned 67, based on the lesser pay plaintiff received in the new job he held at time of judgment, because the old position was unique and court believed plaintiff would not be able to find a similar position) (ADEA); *Dominic v. Consolidated Edison Co. of N.Y., Inc.*, 822 F.2d 1249 (2d Cir. 1987) (upholding an award of front pay granting the plaintiff $17,000 per year for two years based on the difference between his present job and the one he was discharged from, but not included assumed subsequent raises because the employer was dissatisfied with plaintiff's performance) (ADEA); *Marcing v. Fluor Daniel, Inc.*, 826 F.Supp. 1128 (N.D.Ill.1993), *rev'd on other grounds*, 36 F.3d 1099 (7th Cir. 1994) (discussing present value discount rates, and observing that front pay represented the present value of the future income that plaintiff would have earned if she had remained employed by the defendant) (ADEA).

39. *See, e.g., Carter v. Sedgwick County, Kansas*, 36 F.3d 952 (10th Cir.1994) (reversing a six-month limit on front pay and directing trial court to fashion a front pay award that would compensate the victim "for the continuing future effects of discrimination until the victim can be made whole.") (quoting its prior decision in *Carter v. Sedgwick County*, 929 F.2d 1501, 1505 (10th Cir.1991)).

40. *Padilla v. Metro–North Commuter R.R.*, 92 F.3d 117 (2d Cir.1996), *cert. de-*

front pay is a species of recovery that is subject to the dollar caps placed by the Civil Rights Act of 1991 on the sum of compensatory and punitive damages, an issue discussed in detail in § 4.26 immediately following.

Lower courts have divided over how to allocate front pay issues between judge and jury. The First Circuit, for example, appears to allow juries to determine not only the amount of front pay but the threshold question of its availability.[41] By contrast, the Sixth Circuit insists that the propriety of front pay in any amount is an equitable question for the court that "must ordinarily precede ... submission of the case to the jury."[42] The Tenth Circuit allocates the determination of both the availability and amount of front pay to the judge.[43] A Ninth Circuit opinion articulates the same position, holding that the jury decides only the appropriate amount.[44] A circuit-wide line-up on the question is catalogued in the footnote that follows.[45] Where the jury does compute

nied, 520 U.S. 1274, 117 S.Ct. 2453, 138 L.Ed.2d 211 (1997) (upholding front pay award of more than 20 years, until plaintiff turned 67, based on the lesser pay plaintiff received in the new job he held at time of judgment, because the old position was unique and court believed plaintiff would not be able to find a similar position) (ADEA); *Tyler v. Bethlehem Steel*, 958 F.2d 1176 (2d Cir.), *cert. denied*, 506 U.S. 826, 113 S.Ct. 82, 121 L.Ed.2d 46 (1992) (17 years of front pay in ADEA case).

41. *Sinai v. New England Tel. & Tel. Co.*, 3 F.3d 471 (1st Cir.1993), *cert. denied*, 513 U.S. 1025, 115 S.Ct. 597, 130 L.Ed.2d 509 (1994). *Sinai* appears to be at variance with the consistent understanding in ADEA cases that the court determines eligibility. *See, e.g., Smith v. World Ins. Co.*, 38 F.3d 1456, 1466 (8th Cir.1994) (district court in its discretion may award whatever equitable relief, including front pay, is appropriate to make the victorious ADEA plaintiff whole). But in those cases the circuits are sharply divided as to whether, once a judge determines the appropriateness of front pay in lieu of reinstatement, a jury may then decide the amount of the award. *Contrast Hansard v. Pepsi–Cola Metro. Bottling Co.*, 865 F.2d 1461, 1470 (5th Cir.), *cert. denied*, 493 U.S. 842, 110 S.Ct. 129, 107 L.Ed.2d 89 (1989); *Fite v. First Tennessee Prod. Credit Ass'n*, 861 F.2d 884, 893 (6th Cir.1988); *Cassino v. Reichhold Chem., Inc.*, 817 F.2d 1338, 1347 (9th Cir.1987), *cert. denied*, 484 U.S. 1047, 108 S.Ct. 785, 98 L.Ed.2d 870 (1988); and *Maxfield v. Sinclair Int'l*, 766 F.2d 788, 796 (3d Cir.1985), *cert. denied*, 474 U.S. 1057, 106 S.Ct. 796, 88 L.Ed.2d 773 (1986) (jury may determine amount) *with Newhouse v. McCormick & Co.*, 110 F.3d 635 (8th Cir.1997); *Fortino v. Quasar Co.*, 950 F.2d 389, 398 (7th Cir.1991); *Denison v. Swaco Geolograph Co.*, 941 F.2d

1416, 1426 (10th Cir.1991); *Duke v. Uniroyal, Inc.*, 928 F.2d 1413,1424 (4th Cir.), *cert. denied*, 502 U.S. 963, 112 S.Ct. 429, 116 L.Ed.2d 449 (1991); and *Dominic v. Consolidated Edison Co. of N.Y., Inc.*, 822 F.2d 1249, 1257 (2d Cir.1987) (judge determines amount as well as eligibility). The latter courts have reasoned that the ADEA's jury trial provision is limited to those fact issues that underlie claims for legal, rather than equitable, relief.

42. *Roush v. KFC Nat'l Mgmt. Co.*, 10 F.3d 392 (6th Cir.1993), *cert. denied*, 513 U.S. 808, 115 S.Ct. 56, 130 L.Ed.2d 15 (1994). The Seventh Circuit appears to agree. *Williams v. Pharmacia, Inc.*, 137 F.3d 944 (7th Cir.1998).

43. *McCue v. Kansas Dep't of Human Resources*, 165 F.3d 784 (10th Cir.1999).

44. *Cassino v. Reichhold Chemicals, Inc.*, 817 F.2d 1338 (9th Cir.1987), *cert. denied*, 484 U.S. 1047, 108 S.Ct. 785, 98 L.Ed.2d 870 (1988) (case under ADEA). The Court also held that the jury must reduce the amount of a front pay award to the extent it finds the plaintiff failed reasonably to mitigate damages.

45. a) Decisions holding the *jury* decides the award *amount* after the district court decides whether the plaintiff can be awarded front pay in lieu of reinstatement:

1) *Maxfield v. Sinclair Int'l*, 766 F.2d 788 (3d Cir.1985), *cert. denied*, 474 U.S. 1057, 106 S.Ct. 796, 88 L.Ed.2d 773 (1986)

2) *Hansard v. Pepsi–Cola Metro. Bottling Co.*, 865 F.2d 1461 (5th Cir.), *cert. denied*, 493 U.S. 842, 110 S.Ct. 129, 107 L.Ed.2d 89 (1989)

3) *Roush v. KFC Nat'l Mgmt. Co.*, 10 F.3d 392 (6th Cir.1993), *cert. denied*, 513 U.S.

the amount, the dominant view is that it may rely on lay testimony about future earnings and other compensation, as well as appropriate inflation and discount rates.[46]

At least one circuit allows a distinct award for lost future earnings in addition to a limited front pay award.[47] The reasoning is that front pay is functionally equivalent to reinstatement and hence compensates for losses in the particular job, while an award for lost future earnings relates to potential losses during the remainder of a career even if reinstatement to the particular job were possible. To recover for such career loss in addition to front pay the plaintiff should be required to prove reputational harm that would impair her ability to advance in the relevant industry or field. In any event, defense counsel should argue for a reduction in the front pay award to the extent the separate award for lost earnings includes future pay in the particular lost job.

Because each species of Title VII relief before the 1991 Civil Rights Act was considered equitable, jury trials were not available unless a Title VII claim was joined with a claim for legal relief—for instance, a claim under § 1981. Although the Supreme Court strongly suggested that there was no right to jury trial under Title VII, it never actually ruled on the question.[48] Section 102 of the Civil Rights Act of 1991, codified at 42 U.S.C.A. § 1981a, now specifically authorizes jury trials for claimants alleging intentional discrimination in actions under, among other statutes, Title VII and the Americans With Disabilities Act. In addition, there is clearly a jury trial right under § 1981,[49] and where an action presents claims under both statutes, the right to jury trial under § 1981 may not be estopped by the prior bench trial of an equitable claim. Rather, prior jury determinations of facts reached in deciding the legal, § 1981 claims should be adopted by the trial court when it later

808, 115 S.Ct. 56, 130 L.Ed.2d 15 (1994) (ADEA)

4) *Cassino v. Reichhold Chem., Inc.*, 817 F.2d 1338 (9th Cir.1987), *cert. denied*, 484 U.S. 1047, 108 S.Ct. 785, 98 L.Ed.2d 870 (1988)

  b) Decisions holding the *judge* determines the *amount* as well as the appropriateness of any award

1) *Dominic v. Consol. Edison Co. of N.Y., Inc.*, 822 F.2d 1249 (2d Cir.1987)

2) *Duke v. Uniroyal, Inc.*, 928 F.2d 1413 (4th Cir.), *cert. denied*, 502 U.S. 963, 112 S.Ct. 429, 116 L.Ed.2d 449 (1991)

3) *Fortino v. Quasar Co.*, 950 F.2d 389 (7th Cir.1991)

4) *Denison v. Swaco Geolograph Co.*, 941 F.2d 1416 (10th Cir.1991)

5) *Bevan v. Honeywell, Inc.*, 118 F.3d 603, 613 (8th Cir.1997) (submitting the amount of front pay award to the jury for conclusive determination was in violation of circuit rule established in *Newhouse*, but the district court "may, in its equitable discretion submit the issue to a jury in an advisory capacity.") (ADEA and Minnesota Statute)

6) *Allison v. Citgo Petroleum Corp.*, 151 F.3d 402, 422 n. 19 (5th Cir.1998) (front pay and back pay are equitable remedies under Title VII, as amended in 1991, and thus the jury does not have the right to determine these issues.)

46. *Cassino v. Reichhold Chemicals, Inc.*, 817 F.2d at 1345 (citing cases).

47. *Williams v. Pharmacia*, 137 F.3d 944 (7th Cir.1998) (Title VII).

48. *United States v. Burke*, 504 U.S. 229, 112 S.Ct. 1867, 119 L.Ed.2d 34 (1992); *Chauffeurs, Teamsters and Helpers Local No. 391 v. Terry*, 494 U.S. 558, 110 S.Ct. 1339, 108 L.Ed.2d 519 (1990).

49. *Johnson v. Railway Express Agency, Inc.*, 421 U.S. 454, 95 S.Ct. 1716, 44 L.Ed.2d 295 (1975).

determines any equitable claims under Title VII.[50] But a district court has ruled that it is not precluded from granting back pay as a remedy additional to whatever damages remedies may have been awarded by the jury.[51]

The "equity" characterization has also limited the available monetary relief under Title VII (before the 1991 amendments) to an award of back pay, precluding more generous measures such as compensation for emotional distress or punitive damages.[52] The equitable nature of all Title VII awards before the new Act also led some courts to deny nominal damages, viewing them as compensatory in nature.[53] While nominal damages now appear available, some courts insist that the plaintiff demand them as early as the Rule 16 pretrial order; under that view a plaintiff could not wait until after verdict, or even shortly before, to seek nominal damages as a way of obtaining at least the minimal economic recovery that may be needed to support an award of punitive damages.[54] But prejudgment, as well as the standard post-judgment, interest is an ordinary item of compensation integrally related to back pay,[55] routinely awarded in Title VII actions.[56] It may even be an abuse of discretion to deny it,[57] absent unusual reasons.[58]

Any prevailing party, plaintiff or defendant, is of course eligible for an award of "costs" under Federal Rule of Civil Procedure 54(d). These are limited, however, to items specified by 28 U.S.C.A. § 1920: clerk and marshal fees, fees by court reporters for transcripts "necessarily obtained for use in the case"; printing disbursements and witness fees; specified docket fees; and fees for court-appointed experts and certain interpreters. Most important, "costs" as used in Rule 54(d) do *not* include the prevailing party's attorney's fees. This is consistent with the

50. *Cf. Lytle v. Household Mfg., Inc.*, 494 U.S. 545, 110 S.Ct. 1331, 108 L.Ed.2d 504 (1990), esp. n.4.

51. *Hennessy v. Penril Datacomm Networks*, 864 F.Supp. 759 (N.D.Ill.1994), *aff'd in part, vacated in part*, 69 F.3d 1344 (7th Cir.1995).

52. *See Cumpiano v. Banco Santander Puerto Rico*, 902 F.2d 148 (1st Cir.1990).

53. *See Kerr–Selgas v. American Airlines, Inc.*, 69 F.3d 1205, 1210 n. 6 (1st Cir.1995); *Griffith v. Colorado, Div. of Youth Servs.*, 17 F.3d 1323 (10th Cir.1994); *Walker v. Anderson Electrical Connectors*, 944 F.2d 841 (11th Cir.1991), *cert. denied*, 506 U.S. 1078, 113 S.Ct. 1043, 122 L.Ed.2d 352 (1993).

54. *See Walker v. Anderson Elec. Connectors*, 944 F.2d 841, 844 (11th Cir.1991), *cert. denied*, 506 U.S. 1078, 113 S.Ct. 1043, 122 L.Ed.2d 352 (1993) (case before 1991 Amendments to Title VII first expressly provided for legal relief). *But cf. Campos–Orrego v. Rivera*, F.3d (1st Cir.1999) (plaintiff in action under 42 U.S.C.A. § 1983 could demand nominal damages after a jury

verdict that awarded her punitive but not compensatory damages on due process claim, by asking that $1 of the punitives be reallocated as nominal damages).

55. *Donnelly v. Yellow Freight System, Inc.*, 874 F.2d 402 (7th Cir.1989), *aff'd on other grounds*, 494 U.S. 820, 110 S.Ct. 1566, 108 L.Ed.2d 834 (1990). *Cf. Barbour v. Merrill* 48 F.3d 1270 (D.C.Cir.1995) (same holding under § 1981).

56. *Loeffler v. Frank*, 486 U.S. 549, 108 S.Ct. 1965, 100 L.Ed.2d 549 (1988) (available even against Federal government, notwithstanding sovereign immunity); *Clarke v. Frank*, 960 F.2d 1146 (2d Cir.1992).

57. *Sellers v. Delgado Cmty. College*, 839 F.2d 1132 (5th Cir.), *cert. denied*, 498 U.S. 987, 111 S.Ct. 525, 112 L.Ed.2d 536 (1990).

58. *Hutchison v. Amateur Electronic Supply, Inc.*, 42 F.3d 1037 (7th Cir.1994); *EEOC v. Delight Wholesale Co.*, 973 F.2d 664 (8th Cir.1992).

ordinary "American rule" which, absent express statutory authorization, calls for each side to pay its own attorney's fees.[59] Section 706(k) of Title VII is one such statute. It provides that a prevailing party may recover a reasonable attorney's fee as part of "costs."[60] And for purposes of calculating the postjudgment interest allowed by 28 U.S.C.A. § 1961 "on any money judgment in a civil case recovered in a district court," these statutorily shifted attorney's fees shall be included as part of the judgment.[61]

Section 113 of the Act authorizes the court to include the fees of experts, without a specific cap, as part of the award of attorney's fees to prevailing Title VII plaintiffs, contrary to the thrust of two recent decisions of the Court.[62] This change facilitates the neutral practice case as well as the case of intentional discrimination. But the Act's authorization of prospective relief, and hence attorney's fees, despite the defendant's discharge of the "same decision" burden in the intentional "mixed motive" situation,[63] affords greater relative inducement to bring intentional discrimination claims.

§ 4.26 Compensatory and Punitive Damages for Title VII and Americans With Disabilities Act Violations After November 20, 1991

Section 102 of the Civil Rights Act of 1991, codified at 42 U.S.C.A. § 1981a, authorizes jury trials and compensatory and punitive damages for claimants alleging intentional discrimination in actions under, among other statutes, Title VII and the Americans With Disabilities Act. These remedies are "in addition to any relief authorized by" § 706(g) of Title VII,[1] and the compensatory portion of an award "shall not include back pay, interest on back pay, or any other type of relief authorized under" § 706(g) of Title VII—in other words, the equitable relief available before the Civil Rights Act of 1991.[2] But compensatory and punitive damages are available only if the "complaining party cannot recover under 42 U.S.C.A. 1981."[3] Citing applicable legislative history, however, the EEOC has interpreted the latter restriction only to bar double

59. *Alyeska Pipeline Serv. Co. v. Wilderness Soc'y*, 421 U.S. 240, 95 S.Ct. 1612, 44 L.Ed.2d 141 (1975).

60. See Chapter 11 on Civil Rights Attorney's Fee Act of 1988. Of course, the suit must be an "action or proceeding" under Title VII. Thus, a prevailing plaintiff in a state-law discrimination case cannot recover attorney's fees under § 706(k). *Paz v. Long Island R. Co.*, 128 F.3d 121 (2d Cir. 1997).

61. *Carter v. Sedgwick County, Kansas*, 36 F.3d 952 (10th Cir.1994).

62. Section 113(b) (amending § 706(k) of Title VII, 42 U.S.C.A. § 2000e–5(k)). *See Crawford Fitting Co. v. J. T. Gibbons, Inc.*, 482 U.S. 437, 107 S.Ct. 2494, 96 L.Ed.2d 385 (1987) ($30 per day witness fee limit of

28 U.S.C.A. § 1821(b) defines full extent of a federal court's power to shift litigation costs); *West Virginia Univ. Hosps., Inc. v. Casey*, 499 U.S. 83, 111 S.Ct. 1138, 113 L.Ed.2d 68 (1991) (applying *Crawford* limits to expert witness fees recoverable under 42 U.S.C.A. § 1988, the counterpart for civil rights actions to the attorney's fee provision of Title VII § 706(k)).

63. *See* § 6.11.

§ 4.26

1. Section 102 (adding § 1977A(1) to the Revised Statutes, 42 U.S.C.A. § 1977A(1)), 42 U.S.C.A. § 1981a(a)(1).

2. 42 U.S.C.A. § 1981a(b)(2).

3. *Id.*

recovery under Title VII and § 1981, not to interfere with administrative or judicial processing of claims under either statute prior to judgment.[4]

The Act expressly denies either form of damages–compensatory or punitive–to challengers of facially neutral practices. Title VII plaintiffs who prevail only by demonstrating the disproportionate adverse impact of neutral practices,[5] or ADA plaintiffs who demonstrate only a failure to reasonably accommodate by an employer who "demonstrates good faith efforts,"[6] are still limited to the traditional, equitable Title VII remedies of prospective relief and back pay. Perhaps more than any other, these provisions manifest the congressional view that intentional discrimination deserves more serious legal sanctions.

Section 1981a also makes compensatory, but not punitive, damages available to plaintiffs who prosecute intentional discrimination claims successfully against a government agency or subdivision.[7] The Supreme Court held in *West v. Gibson*[8] that the EEOC may award compensatory damages to federal employees (for intentional discrimination) during the federal administrative complaints process.

Punitive damages are authorized against nongovernmental defendants who are proven to have engaged in an unlawful discriminatory practice "with malice or with reckless indifference to the federally protected rights of an aggrieved individual."[9] Although the precise standards governing jury awards of punitive damages will require considerable case law explication by analogy to punitive damages in tort,[10] it has already been held that, as under §§ 1981 and 1983,[11] compensatory damages are not a prerequisite to a punitive award.[12] This is particularly

---

4. *EEOC Policy Guide on Compensatory and Punitive Damages Under 1991 Civil Rights Act,* July 7, 1992. BNA Fair Employment Manual 405:7091, 7092 (1992) (hereinafter, *"EEOC Damages Guidance"*). *See Bradshaw v. University of Me.,* 870 F.Supp. 406 (D.Me.1994) (plaintiff not required to elect an available claim under § 1981 when allegations also state claim under Title VII for the relief provided by new § 1981a). *See also Passantino v. Johnson & Johnson Consumer Prods., Inc.,* 212 F.3d 493, 509–10 (9th Cir.2000) (allocating all of plaintiff's compensatory damages to state law claim and avoiding Title VII cap); *Pavon v. Swift Transp. Co.,* 192 F.3d 902 (9th Cir.1999) (court allocated recovery in excess of the $300,000 Title VII cap to plaintiff's companion claim under § 1981, which does not impose a ceiling on damages).

5. 42 U.S.C.A. § 1981a(a)(1).

6. 42 U.S.C.A. § 1981a(a)(3).

7. *Compare* § 102(b)(2) with § 102(b)(1). And the quasi-governmental U.S. Postal Service has been held a "government agency" exempt from punitive

damages under 42 U.S.C.A. § 1981a(b)(1). *Baker v. Runyon,* 114 F.3d 668 (7th Cir. 1997), *cert. denied,* 525 U.S. 929, 119 S.Ct. 335, 142 L.Ed.2d 277 (1998).

8. 527 U.S. 212, 119 S.Ct. 1906, 144 L.Ed.2d 196 (1999).

9. 42 U.S.C.A. § 1981a(b)(1).

10. *See* discussion *infra,* this section.

11. *See Smith v. Wade,* 461 U.S. 30, 55 n. 21, 103 S.Ct. 1625, 1639, 75 L.Ed.2d 632 (1983).

12. *See Greenway v. Buffalo Hilton Hotel,* 143 F.3d 47 (2d Cir.1998); *Provencher v. CVS Pharmacy,* 145 F.3d 5 (1st Cir.1998) (punitive award upheld despite no award of compensatory damages); *Timm v. Progressive Steel Treating, Inc.,* 137 F.3d 1008 (7th Cir.1998); *Hennessy v. Penril Datacomm Networks,* 69 F.3d 1344 (7th Cir.1995). *But cf. Kerr–Selgas v. American Airlines, Inc.,* 69 F.3d 1205 (1st Cir.1995) (punitives unavailable absent either compensatory or nominal damages for employment discrimination claim not under federal law).

important in environmental harassment claims, as victims may not incur always compensatory damages.[13]

Section 1981a(b)(3) places dollar caps that vary with employer size on the *sum* of compensatory and punitive damages "for each complaining party."[14] For this purpose, compensatory damages are defined by § 1981a(b)(2) to include monetary relief for "future pecuniary losses, emotional pain, suffering, inconvenience, mental anguish,[15] loss of enjoyment of life, and other nonpecuniary losses."[16] These caps are set at $50,000 for businesses that employ between 15 and 100 persons;[17] $100,000 where the employer has between 101 and 200 employees; $200,000 where the employer has between 201 and 500 employees; and $300,000 for all employers with 501 or more employees.[18] Because these damages are "in addition to" traditional, pre-November 1991 Title VII equitable relief, complaining parties' recoveries of back pay, interest on back pay, and other relief formerly available under Title VII before the

13. *See, e.g., Timm,* 137 F.3d 1008. When employers take prompt and appropriate corrective action in response to complaints of racial or sexual harassment, as the Supreme Court's decisions in *Faragher* and *Burlington* encourage, any emotional distress or compensatory damages may be minimized. See Chapter 2 on the *Faragher/Burlington* affirmative defense.

14. *Hudson v. Reno,* 130 F.3d 1193 (6th Cir.1997), *cert. denied,* 525 U.S. 822, 119 S.Ct. 64, 142 L.Ed.2d 50 (1998) (cap applies to all claims by a party); *Hall v. Stormont Trice Corp.,* 976 F.Supp. 383 (E.D.Va.1997) (cap applies to aggregate of all counts). A plaintiff's argument for recovering up to the cap separately for compensatory and punitive damages has been rejected; the cap defines the maximum amount available for *both* kinds of harm defined. *Hogan v. Bangor and Aroostook R.R.,* 61 F.3d 1034 (1st Cir.1995). On the other hand, it seems clear that where there are multiple parties who have joined together under FRCP 20 or 23 to assert common claims, "Each complaining party may receive (to the extent appropriate) up to the cap amount." *EEOC Memorandum on Computation of Compensatory and Punitive Damages* (April 18, 1995). § 1981a(c)(2) further provides that "the court shall not inform the jury" about the statutory damages caps. This stricture has been held also to preclude counsel from referring to the caps, for example during closing argument. *Sasaki v. Class,* 92 F.3d 232 (4th Cir.1996).

15. When employees seek compensatory damages for mental anguish, the burden is on the employer to prove apportionment. Apportionment is an affirmative defense applicable only where the damage is divisible and employees bear no evidentiary burdens

on the issue. *Jenson v. Eveleth Taconite Co.,* 130 F.3d 1287 (8th Cir.1997), *cert. denied sub nom. Oglebay Norton Co. v. Jenson,* 524 U.S. 953, 118 S.Ct. 2370, 141 L.Ed.2d 738 (1998).

16. 42 U.S.C.A. § 1981a(b)(2). The Seventh Circuit has described future nonpecuniary damages as analogous to injury to professional standing, injury to character or reputation, or the loss to a plaintiff of economic opportunities. These injuries are distinct from front pay because front pay is a pecuniary loss, i.e., what the plaintiff would have earned absent the unlawful conduct, while future nonpecuniary damages compensate for a lifetime of diminished earning resulting from reputation harms. The court allocated future nonpecuniary loss to the jury, reserving the front pay decision for the court. *Williams v. Pharmacia, Inc.,* 137 F.3d 944 (7th Cir.1998).

17. Certain entities having fewer than 15 employees are nevertheless subject to Title VII—e.g., labor organizations and employment agencies. *See EEOC Compliance Manual,* Vol. II, Sec. 605. BNA FEP Manual 405:6607. Thus the damages caps, applicable in terms only to employers with 15 or more employees, could be read by negative implication to impose unlimited damages liability on those smaller entities, or, alternatively, to free them from damages liability altogether. EEOC has rejected "both interpretations and concludes that all covered employment agencies and labor organizations with 100 or fewer employees are subject to the $50,000 cap on damages." *EEOC Damages Guidance,* at 405:7093.

18. Section 102(b)(3), 42 U.S.C.A. § 1981a(b)(3).

1991 amendments are not restricted by the caps.[19] Moreover, despite the somewhat uncertain status of front pay under the pre–1991 Act case law,[20] EEOC considers it a type of relief previously authorized by Title VII and hence excluded from the § 1981a(b)(2) definition of compensatory damages and in turn not subject to a § 1981a(b)(3) cap.[21] In any event, a plaintiff with a state law claim that authorizes unlimited damages may avoid the Title VII and ADA damages caps altogether, and in some circumstances may assert that claim in the same federal court action.[22]

Two principal interpretive questions are raised about the application of these caps. First, which components of a compensatory damages award—front pay is particularly important—are subject to the caps? Second, when multiple plaintiffs join together under Federal Rule 20 or, in class form, Rule 23, do the caps limit the total recovery of the group or only of each individual member?

On the first question, EEOC has concluded that the general category of compensatory damages encompasses all of the following species of relief: "past pecuniary loss (out-of-pocket loss), future pecuniary loss,[23] and nonpecuniary loss (emotional harm)." Included within pecuniary losses, past or future, are such "quantifiable" losses caused by discriminatory conduct as moving and job search expenses and psychiatric, physical therapy, and other medical expenses.[24] Nonpecuniary losses include damages for "intangible injuries of emotional harm such as emotional pain, suffering, inconvenience, mental anguish, and loss of enjoyment of life," as well as injury to professional standing, character, reputation, credit standing, or health.[25] Section 1981a(b)(3) throws only

19. *EEOC Damages Guidance,* 405:7094.

20. *See* text § 4.35, *infra.*

21. *EEOC Damages Guidance,* at 405:7094. But see text *infra,* for the varying circuit court views on this question.

22. *See, e.g., Passantino v. Johnson & Johnson Consumer Prods., Inc.,* 212 F.3d 493 (9th Cir.2000) (allocating all of plaintiff's $3.1 million compensatory verdict to state law claims, but allocating the $8.6 million punitive award to Title VII claim and subjecting it to the cap where the state law did not allow for punitive award). See the section on Supplemental Jurisdiction in Chapter 12.

23. *See Fitzgerald v. Mountain States Tel. & Tel. Co.,* 46 F.3d 1034 (10th Cir.), *vacated on rehearing in part,* 60 F.3d 837 (10th Cir.1995) (compensatories extended to plaintiff's loss of future business opportunities with defendant).

24. *EEOC Damages Guidance,* at 405:7095. *See also Malloy v. Monahan,* 73 F.3d 1012 (10th Cir.1996) (permitting re-

covery of lost profits in Reconstruction Civil Rights Act case).

25. *Id.* at 405:7096. Traditional authority to the effect that an award for emotional distress might rest on the plaintiff's own testimony, without specific evidence of the economic value of that loss, *see, e.g., Atchley v. The Nordam Group,* 180 F.3d 1143, 1149–50 (10th Cir.1999); *Ferrill v. The Parker Group,* 168 F.3d 468, 476 (11th Cir. 1999); *Bolden v. SEPTA,* 21 F.3d 29 (3d Cir.1994) (collecting cases); *H.C. by Hewett v. Jarrard,* 786 F.2d 1080, 1088 (11th Cir. 1986); *Stallworth v. Shuler,* 777 F.2d 1431, 1435 (11th Cir.1985); and *Marable v. Walker,* 704 F.2d 1219, 1220 (11th Cir.1983), is being tested by decisions that insist at least where the injury is not severe on corroborating testimony by a spouse, co-workers, friends, relatives and perhaps even treating or other medical experts. *See Forshee v. Waterloo Indus., Inc.,* 178 F.3d 527, 531 (8th Cir.1999); *Price v. City of Charlotte, N.C.,* 93 F.3d 1241 (4th Cir.1996), *cert. denied,* 520 U.S. 1116, 117 S.Ct. 1246, 137 L.Ed.2d 328 (1997); *Patterson v. P.H.P. Healthcare Corp.,* 90 F.3d 927 (5th Cir.

future pecuniary, as well as *all nonpecuniary*, losses into the compensatory-cum-punitive damages pot that is subject to a cap. In other words, past pecuniary losses are uncapped. And in the Commission's view the line that divides past from future pecuniary losses is "the date of the resolution of the damage claim, i.e., conciliation, settlement, or the conclusion of litigation."[26]

Read in isolation, Section *1981a(b)(3)* caps as "compensatory damages" not only future pecuniary losses but all "claims that typically do not lend themselves to precise quantification, i.e., punitive damages ... and [past or future] nonpecuniary losses."[27] In other words, only *past pecuniary* losses like backpay and interest on backpay appear to be uncapped by *§ 1981a(b)(3)*. But the immediately preceding subsection, *§ 1981a(b)(2)* provides, *"Compensatory damages* awarded under this section *shall not include* backpay, interest on backpay, or *any other type of relief authorized under section 706(g) of the Civil Rights Act of 1964."* The EEOC believes that this final phrase of subsection (2), excluding any kind of pre–1991 relief from the "compensatory damages" capped by 1981a(b)(3), encompasses front pay. It observes that front pay was a type of Title VII relief that was generally available before the 1991 amendments. On this view, front pay, not just backpay, is excepted from the caps.[28]

In sum, it is EEOC's view that the caps limit "only claims that typically do not lend themselves to precise quantification, i.e., punitive damages, future pecuniary losses, and [all] nonpecuniary losses."[29] Because front pay is so hard to measure,[30] it might be classified as a form of future nonpecuniary loss as reasonably as a form of future pecuniary loss. In any event front pay is clearly not a form of *past* pecuniary loss; and it would therefore apparently be capped by 1981a(b)(3) standing alone, at least if a traditionally equitable remedy like front pay can be considered a species of compensatory "damages." But regardless of whether front pay fits within the taxonomy of § 1981a(b)(3), EEOC views it as removed from that subsection's capped compensatory-punitive pot as an equitable remedy available before the 1991 Amendments and therefore excluded at the outset from the subsection *(b)(2)* definition of compensatory damages.

1996), *cert. denied*, 519 U.S. 1091, 117 S.Ct. 767, 136 L.Ed.2d 713 (1997); *Fitzgerald v. Mountain States Telephone and Telegraph Co.*, 68 F.3d 1257 (10th Cir.), *vacated on rehearing in part*, 60 F.3d 837 (10th Cir. 1995). *But see Smith v. Norwest Financial Acceptance, Inc.*, 129 F.3d 1408 (10th Cir. 1997) (allowing corroboration from the circumstances of public humiliation and degradation). Further, it has been held that the emotional distress must be linked to the defendant's unlawful conduct, not just to the loss of job. *See Forshee*, 178 F.3d at 531. But if a plaintiff's claim for damages is limited to humiliation, embarrassment and other negative emotions caused by defendant's unlawful conduct, and does not ex-tend to the cost of subsequent psychiatric treatment or symptoms or conditions, she preserves her patient-psychotherapist privilege and need not disclose her medical records. *Santelli v. Electro–Motive*, 188 F.R.D. 306 (N.D.Ill.1999).

26. *Id.* at 405:7095.

27. *EEOC   Damages   Guidance*   at 405:7094.

28. *EEOC   Damages   Guidance*, 405:7094.

29. *Id.* at 405:7094.

30. *See* § 4.25, *supra*.

The Sixth Circuit disagrees with EEOC, holding instead that front pay is a legal remedy subject to the cap.[31] The court reasons that the common, ordinary meaning of the term "future pecuniary loss" is "an amount of money which will be lost at a later time." Thus, front pay, by both its definition and purpose in the law, is a "future pecuniary loss" because it is a monetary award for the salary that the employee would have received in the future but for the discrimination. The Sixth Circuit observes that because only backpay, not front pay, was *expressly* provided for by Section 706(g) as enacted in 1964, the § 1981a(b)(2) exception to capped "damages" pertains only to back, not front pay.[32] The majority of the circuits, however, agree with EEOC that front pay is not capped.[33] These circuits view front pay in equitable terms, "not so much a monetary award for the salary that the employee would have received but for the discrimination, but rather the monetary equivalent of reinstatement, to be given in situations where reinstatement is impracticable or impossible."[34] Accordingly, front pay amounts to equitable relief of the kind available before November 21, 1991, and hence is not "damages" within the meaning of § 1981a(b)(2).

EEOC has also determined that in a multiple joinder or class action situation, "each complaining employee may receive" all otherwise appropriate relief up to the full value of the pertinent cap.[35] The employer's aggregate liability, in other words, is the sum of the total proven compensatory damages (other than past pecuniary losses) and punitive damages of all plaintiffs (the applicable cap limiting each employee's damages recovery), plus the full amount of all proven back pay, front pay, past pecuniary losses, interest, and attorney's fees. Circuit courts, disagreeing with EEOC, have held that where a single plaintiff prevails on multiple claims (for example discrimination and retaliation) under the same capped statute (e.g. Title VII, or ADA), the compensatory-cum-

31. See Hudson v. Reno, 130 F.3d 1193, 1202–04 (6th Cir.1997), cert. denied, 525 U.S. 822, 119 S.Ct. 64, 142 L.Ed.2d 50 (1998). A different Sixth Circuit panel recently expressed doubt about the decision in Hudson, and stated that although it agreed with the plaintiff that front pay should not be subjected to the cap, it was bound by Hudson. Pollard v. E.I. Dupont de Nemours Co., 213 F.3d 933 (6th Cir.2000), cert. granted, 2001 WL 12416 (2001).

32. But front pay was frequently, although not invariably, see McKnight v. General Motors, 908 F.2d 104, 117 (7th Cir.1990), cert. denied, 499 U.S. 919, 111 S.Ct. 1306, 113 L.Ed.2d 241 (1991), held available under Title VII before the 1991 Civil Rights Act amendments first authorized legal relief in the form of compensatory and punitive damages.

33. See e.g., Pals v. Schepel Buick & GMC Truck, Inc., 220 F.3d 495 (7th Cir. 2000); Kramer v. Logan County Sch. Dist. No. R-1, 157 F.3d 620, 626, (8th Cir.1998); Passantino v. Johnson & Johnson Consumer Prods., Inc., 212 F.3d 493, 510 n. 14 (9th Cir.2000); Gotthardt v. National R.R. Pas-

senger Corp., 191 F.3d 1148, 1154 (9th Cir. 1999); McCue v. Kansas Dep't of Human Resources, 165 F.3d 784, 792 (10th Cir. 1999); Medlock v. Ortho Biotech, Inc., 164 F.3d 545, 556 (10th Cir.), cert. denied, 528 U.S. 813, 120 S.Ct. 48,145 L.Ed.2d 42 (1999); U.S. EEOC v. W&O, Inc., 213 F.3d 600, 618–19 & n.10; Martini v. Federal Nat'l Mortgage Ass'n, 178 F.3d 1336 (D.C.Cir.1999), cert. denied, ___ U.S. ___, 120 S.Ct. 1155, 145 L.Ed.2d 1065 (2000). see also Allison v. Citgo Petroleum Corp., 151 F.3d 402, 423 n.19 (5th Cir.1998) (holding that front pay is an equitable remedy, but not specifically holding that front pay is not subject to the cap). The Supreme Court has agreed to review the issue. See Pollard v. E.I. Dupont de Nemours Co., 213 F.3d 933 (6th Cir.2000), cert. granted, 2001 WL 12416 (2001).

34. Kramer, 157 F.3d 620, 626 (8th Cir. 1998). See also Newhouse v. McCormick & Co., 110 F.3d 635, 641 (8th Cir.1997); Philipp v. ANR Freight System, Inc., 61 F.3d 669, 674 (8th Cir.1995).

35. EEOC Damages Guidance, at 405:7093–7094.

punitive-damages cap applies to both claims combined.[36]

Left unanswered by the text of the new damages provision and the EEOC's Damages Guidance is whether the plaintiff who joins in one action claims under both Title VII *and* ADA for distinct, independently unlawful employer practices may recover more than the applicable cap pertaining to each statute alone. Suppose for instance that an employer denies plaintiff a promotion because of his race and a few weeks later discharges him because of a disability recognized under ADA. From a substantive law standpoint, plaintiff could bring two civil actions, one based on Title VII (or Section 1981), the other on ADA. But as a practical matter he is more likely to join both claims in one action to achieve an efficient, consistent resolution of the controversy, and he will be permitted to do so by Federal Rule of Civil Procedure 18(a) and the similar joinder rules of most state courts. Indeed, although the employer conduct consists of two separate acts on two separate occasions, plaintiff might be *compelled* to join both claims in the same action under the broad transactional definition of "same claim" that the Restatement (Second) of Judgments[37] adopts as the referent for res judicata on, as it is now known, claim preclusion.

If that plaintiff had brought separate actions, he would be eligible for the appropriately capped amount of compensatory and punitive damages in each proceeding. 42 U.S.C.A. § 1977A(b) stipulates the amount of the cap corresponding to the size of the employer; and subsections (a)(1) and (2) provide for damages up to the subsection (b) cap "in an action" under Title VII and ADA, respectively. Yet a single lawsuit combining these claims could be pigeonholed as "an action" under either Title VII or ADA, with the employer arguing accordingly that the maximum compensatory-punitive recovery is limited to the amount of the single cap pertaining to an action under either statute. This seems a strained reading that ignores the possible compulsion to join claims flowing from the law of claim preclusion and assumes that the Civil Rights Act of 1991 impliedly repeals F.R.C.P. 18(a)'s authorization for joinder of claims. The better reading would limit plaintiff's recovery concerning the conduct violative of *Title VII* to the Title VII cap referenced in Section 1977A(a)(1), and his recovery for the conduct violative of *ADA* to the cap of the same amount referenced in Section 1977A(a)(2), subject of course to standard instructions forbidding the jury from authorizing greater damages for the combination of these unlawful employment practices than plaintiff actually suffered.

The Commission also assumes that, as with back and front pay, the complaining party has a duty to mitigate pecuniary losses, with the burden of proof on the employer to demonstrate a failure to exercise reasonable diligence.[38] On claims for nonpecuniary loss such as emotional distress, it expects the complainant to bear the usual burdens devel-

---

36. *Baty v. Willamette Indus., Inc.*, 172 F.3d 1232 (10th Cir.1999) (citing similar rulings by the Sixth and Seventh Circuit Courts of Appeals).

37. For discussion of this test, *see* § 17.118 *et seq.*

38. *EEOC Damages Guidance* at 405:7095 (citing *Weaver v. Casa Gallardo,*

Inc., 922 F.2d 1515 (11th Cir.1991)); *Wooldridge v. Marlene Indus. Corp.*, 875 F.2d 540 (6th Cir.1989).

See also infra § 4.35 (reduction where plaintiff has a "collateral source" of income).

oped by tort law concerning causation. Thus the claim "will be seriously undermined if the onset of symptoms ... preceded the discrimination"; but the fact that an unusually sensitive complainant resembles the classical "eggshell plaintiff" of tort law "will not absolve the respondent from responsibility for the greater emotional harm."[39] Expert testimony that stress resulted from discriminatory working conditions is an adequate basis for an award,[40] and sometimes even plaintiff's own testimony about loss of sleep, marital strain, humiliation and the like will suffice.[41]

The circuit decisions are divided over whether an emotional distress award is adequately supported by plaintiff's own testimony standing alone, or whether that testimony requires corroboration by fact witnesses like family and friends, or even by medical experts. A breakdown of the several approaches taken to this problem appears in the footnote that follows.[42]

---

39. *Id.* at 405:7096–7097.

40. *Id.* at 405:7098–99 (citing *Rowlett v. Anheuser–Busch, Inc.*, 832 F.2d 194 (1st Cir.1987), decided under § 1981).

41. *Id.* at 405:7098 (citing *Stallworth v. Shuler*, 777 F.2d 1431 (11th Cir.1985), another decision under § 1981).

42. 1) *Plaintiff's Own Testimony Is Sufficient*

a) *Migis v. Pearle Vision*, 135 F.3d 1041 (5th Cir.1998) (upholding award based on plaintiff's lone testimony of anxiety, stress, sleeplessness, marital hardship and loss of self esteem.) (Title VII)

b) *Bolden v. SEPTA*, 21 F.3d 29 (3d Cir. 1994) (given other corroborating testimony, no need for medical testimony to recover for emotional distress.) (civil rights claim)

c) H.C. by *Hewett v. Jarrard*, 786 F.2d 1080 (11th Cir.1986)

d) *Stallworth v. Shuler*, 777 F.2d 1431 (11th Cir.1985)

e) *Marable v. Walker*, 704 F.2d 1219 (11th Cir.1983)

f) *Ferrill v. Parker Group, Inc.*, 168 F.3d 468 (11th Cir.1999) (no particular kind of evidence is indispensable, and plaintiff's testimony alone may suffice.) (citing *Stallworth v. Shuler*)

2) *Plaintiff's Own Testimony Will Not Suffice, At Least To Support Large Awards*

a) *Hetzel v. County of Prince William*, 89 F.3d 169, 173 (4th Cir.), *cert. denied*, 519 U.S. 1028, 117 S.Ct. 584, 136 L.Ed.2d 514 (1996). (The jury awarded plaintiff $500,000 for emotional distress, based "almost entirely on [the plaintiff's] own testimony." The court reversed, holding that such scant evidence was "grossly excessive" when compared to the limited evidence of harm presented at trial and would result in

a serious "miscarriage of justice" if upheld.) (Title VII and § 1983).

b) *Delph v. Dr. Pepper Bottling Co. of Paragould, Inc.*, 130 F.3d 349 (8th Cir.1997) (follows *Kim v. Nash Finch Co.*, 123 F.3d 1046 (8th Cir.1997), in holding that "medical or other expert evidence is not required to prove emotional distress," but that testimony of the plaintiff and his spouse alone could not support an award of $150,000 because the emotional and physical complaints were ill-defined, vague, and not especially intense. The court reduced the award to $50,000.) (Title VII)

3) *Corroborating Testimony Desirable*

a) *Fitzgerald v. Mountain States Telephone and Telegraph Co.*, 68 F.3d 1257 (10th Cir.), *vacated on rehearing in part*, 60 F.3d 837 (10th Cir.1995) (evaluation of the following factors supports an emotional distress award for a constitutional violation: 1) the degree of emotional distress; 2) the context of the events surrounding the emotional distress; 3) the evidence tending to corroborate the plaintiff's testimony; 4) the nexus between the challenged conduct and the emotional distress; and 5) any mitigating circumstances.)

b) *Price v. City of Charlotte, N.C.*, 93 F.3d 1241, 1254–56 (4th Cir.1996), *cert. denied*, 520 U.S. 1116, 117 S.Ct. 1246, 137 L.Ed.2d 328 (1997) (because emotional distress must be based upon "genuine injury," a plaintiff's testimony alone may suffice in proving damages if the evidence is demonstrable and sufficiently articulated; but "neither conclusory statements that the plaintiff suffered emotional distress nor the mere fact that a constitutional violation occurred supports an award of compensatory damages." In case at hand, court rejects award because there was no evidence of: 1)

As observed above, in cases of intentional Title VII and ADA violations, 42 U.S.C.A. § 1981a(b)(1) authorizes punitive damages where the plaintiff also shows the defendant acted with "malice or with reckless indifference to the federally protected rights of an aggrieved individual." The Supreme Court has borrowed, in adapted form, standards for awarding these damages from the principles it has applied under the Reconstruction Civil Rights Acts. Textually, the "malice or . . . reckless indifference" required by § 1981a(b)(1) seems in substance indistinguishable from the standard the Supreme Court announced in *Smith v. Wade*[43] for punitive damages under § 1983: juries may assess punitive damages "when the defendant's conduct is shown to be motivated by evil motive or intent, or when it involves reckless or callous indifference to the federally protected rights of others."[44] Indeed the Report of the House Judiciary Committee explained that the Title VII punitive damages standard is "taken directly from civil rights law," and it quoted and cited with approval the page in the *Smith* opinion that announced the "evil motive or intent" or "reckless or callous indifference" formulations.[45] Accordingly, the use in the 1991 Act of "malice"

the need for medicine; 2) physical symptoms; 3) psychological disturbance or counseling; 4) loss of income or pecuniary expense; 5) a description of their emotional distress; or 6) how plaintiff's conduct changed.) (Equal Protection Case)

c) *Patterson v. P.H.P. Healthcare Corp.*, 90 F.3d 927, 939 (5th Cir.1996), *cert. denied*, 519 U.S. 1091, 117 S.Ct. 767, 136 L.Ed.2d 713 (1997) (disallowing emotional distress claim because the plaintiff presented no corroborating testimony nor did he offer expert medical or psychological damages caused by his alleged distress. Also, no evidence of type that EEOC Damages Guidance recommends suggesting that plaintiff suffered from sleeplessness, anxiety or depression. Opinion cites *Carey* for proposition that emotional damages require a high degree of specificity, which "may include corroborating testimony or medical or psychological evidence.") (§ 1981 and Title VII)

d) *Farpella-Crosby v. Horizon Health Care*, 97 F.3d 803, 809 (5th Cir.1996) (upholding award of $150,000 for mental anguish even though there was no corroborating medical testimony because there was sufficient other evidence to conclude the plaintiff's emotional harm manifested itself as humiliation and stress.) (Title VII)

e) *Kim v. Nash Finch Co.*, 123 F.3d 1046, 1065 (8th Cir.1997) ("medical or other expert evidence is not required to prove emotional distress" under U.S.C.A. § 1981 where there is other corroborating testimony. But court resists per se ruling that corroboration is needed, saying a "plaintiff's own testimony, along with the circum-stances of a particular case, can suffice to sustain the plaintiff's burden.") (Title VII and § 1983)

4) *Corroboration Indispensable*

a) *Koopman v. Water Dist. No. 1 of Johnson Cnty., Kansas*, 41 F.3d 1417 (10th Cir. 1994), *cert. denied*, 516 U.S. 965, 116 S.Ct. 420, 133 L.Ed.2d 337 (1995) (insufficient evidence of emotional distress under *Carey v. Piphus* because there were no other witnesses to corroborate plaintiff's testimony.) (Due Process)

b) *Dill v. City of Edmond, Okl.*, 155 F.3d 1193, 1209 (10th Cir.1998) (plaintiff's uncorroborated testimony of his emotional or mental state is insufficient to prove emotional distress.) (citing *Koopman*) (U.S.C.A. § 1983)

43. 461 U.S. 30, 103 S.Ct. 1625, 75 L.Ed.2d 632 (1983).

44. *Id.* at 56, 103 S.Ct. at 1640. *See also Lowery v. Circuit City Stores, Inc.*, 206 F.3d 431, 441 (4th Cir.), *cert. denied*, ___ U.S. ___, 121 S.Ct. 66, 148 L.Ed.2d 31 (2000) (Congress intended passage of the Civil Rights Act of 1991 to permit the imposition of punitive damages with respect to an intentional discrimination claim under Title VII to the same extent and under the same standards that they are available to plaintiffs under § 1981); *Barbour v. Merrill*, 48 F.3d 1270 (D.C.Cir.1995).

45. H.R.Rep.No. 102–40, pt. 2, p. 29 (1991). The Report of the House Education and Labor Committee echoes this approach. H.R.Rep.No. 102–40, p. 74 (1991).

instead of "evil motive or intent," the phrase used in *Smith*, is inconsequential, particularly because in *Smith* itself the Court wrote that " 'malice' ... may be an appropriate term to denote ill will or an intent to injure."[46] Nevertheless, the circuit courts, reflecting a similar uncertainty that surfaced in the § 1983 decisions in the wake of *Smith*, were divided over whether the same evidence of employer misconduct that establishes an intentional Title VII violation makes the plaintiff eligible for a punitive award, or whether an employer's conduct potentially warranting punitive damages must be "egregious."[47]

The Supreme Court has clarified the dispute in *Kolstad v. American Dental Association.*[48] Plaintiff's case of promotion discrimination based on gender was based in part on testimony that the stated reasons for the selection of another candidate were pretextual, that the high employer officials who participated in the decision had pre-selected the other candidate, and indeed that the entire process had been constructed ad hoc as a sham. The Court held that the statutory requirements of "malice" or "reckless indifference" focus solely on the defendant's state of mind. Accordingly, while evidence of an employer's egregious conduct may enable the plaintiff to persuade[49] a judge or jury that the defendant, through its agent or agents, acted with the requisite "malice" or "reckless indifference," Section 1981a(b)(1) "does not require a showing of egregious or outrageous discrimination independent of the employer's state of mind." Accordingly, if the employer's agents could be shown on remand to have acted with malice or reckless indifference to plaintiff's rights, and the employer shown to be responsible for their actions undertaken with that state of mind, the employer might be liable for punitive damages even if its agents' conduct could not be characterized as "egregious" or "outrageous."

46. 461 U.S. at 37, n.6, 103 S.Ct. at 1630 n.6.

47. *Compare Luciano v. Olsten Corp.*, 110 F.3d 210, 219–220 (2d Cir.1997) (no additional finding required that employer's conduct was egregious) *with Dudley v. Wal-Mart Stores, Inc.*, 166 F.3d 1317 (11th Cir. 1999) (egregious conduct required); *Ngo v. Reno Hilton Resort Corp.*, 140 F.3d 1299 (9th Cir.1998) (requiring "evidence of conduct more egregious than intentional discrimination to support an award of punitive damages in Title VII cases"); *Kolstad v. American Dental Ass'n*, 139 F.3d 958, 968 (D.C.Cir.1998) (en banc) (holding that punitive damages can be imposed only upon a showing of egregious conduct), *vacated*, 527 U.S. 526, 119 S.Ct. 2118, 144 L.Ed.2d 494 (1999). *See also Harris v. L & L Wings, Inc.*, 132 F.3d 978, 982 (4th Cir.1997) (punitive damages are extraordinary remedy); *Emmel v. Coca-Cola Bottling Co. of Chicago*, 95 F.3d 627, 636 (7th Cir.1996) (characterizing standard for punitive damages as a "higher hurdle" than that for proving the underlying discrimination); *Karcher v. Emerson Elec. Co.*, 94 F.3d 502, 509 (8th Cir. 1996), *cert. denied*, 520 U.S. 1210, 117 S.Ct. 1692, 137 L.Ed.2d 820 (1997) (beyond the evidence establishing an intentional sex discrimination and retaliation violation, plaintiff must produce an uncertain "something extra" to warrant punitive damages); *Turic v. Holland Hospitality, Inc.*, 85 F.3d 1211, 1216 (6th Cir.1996); and *McKinnon v. Kwong Wah Rest.*, 83 F.3d 498, 508 (1st Cir.1996) (endorsing concept of a higher standard for punitive damages).

48. 527 U.S. 526, 119 S.Ct. 2118, 144 L.Ed.2d 494 (1999).

49. *Id.* at 2124. The burden of proof on punitive damages is governed by the usual rule of civil litigation that damages must be proven by a preponderance of the evidence. *Karnes v. SCI Colorado Funeral Servs., Inc.*, 162 F.3d 1077 (10th Cir.1998); *Community Hosp. v. Fail*, 969 P.2d 667 (Colo. 1998).

The Court summarized on this point that § 1981a(a)(1) requires proof of an intentional violation to subject the defendant to the possibility of compensatory or punitive damages; § 1981a(b)(1) further qualifies the availability of punitive damages, limiting them to situations where the employer has carried out intentional discrimination with " 'malice or with reckless indifference to [the plaintiff's] federally protected rights.' " It then examined the nature of the evidence that can demonstrate the requisite "malice" or "reckless indifference." From *Smith* the Court borrowed the requirement that the evidence must reflect the defendant's subjective consciousness of the risk of illegality. "Applying this standard in the context of § 1981a, an employer must at least discriminate in the face of a perceived risk that its actions will violate federal law to be liable in punitive damages." Thus where the intentional violation is founded on egregious or outrageous conduct, the fact finder may infer the requisite "evil motive" from that evidence alone. Alternatively, a punitive award may rest on evidence showing the "employer's knowledge that it may be acting in violation of federal law."[50] Justice Stevens, writing for four members of the Court who concurred on this point, observed that while the standard does not require employer knowledge of the law, "he must know that his acts violate the law or must 'carelessly disregard whether or not one has the right so to act' in order to act 'wilfully.' " He suggested that a jury might find a willful violation authorizing punitive damages from evidence that an employer expressed "hostility toward employment discrimination laws" or concealed its actual selection procedures "because it knows they violate federal law." How frequently juries are able to appraise such evidence, of course, depends in part on how stringently federal district judges apply summary judgment standards to the evidence of willfulness or reckless indifference that *Kolstad* deems indispensable to a punitive award.

In any event, the *Kolstad* majority insists that an employer's mere awareness "that it is engaging in discrimination" will not, standing alone, support the award.[51] It identified a number of circumstances in which a violation, while intentional in the sense that the defendant intends to harm the plaintiff, or to discriminate in a generic sense, or to subject the plaintiff to "disparate treatment" within the meaning of Title VII or ADA, should not expose the defendant to punitive damages. "[T]he employer may simply be unaware of the relevant federal prohibition. There will be cases, moreover, in which the employer discriminates

50. *See, e.g., Alexander v. Fulton County*, 207 F.3d 1303, 1337–38 (11th Cir.2000) (allowing punitive damages where evidence showed that sheriff knew that disparate treatment on the basis of race was unlawful); *Lowery v. Circuit City Stores, Inc.*, 206 F.3d 431, 443 (4th Cir.), *cert. denied*, ___ U.S. ___, 121 S.Ct. 66, 148 L.Ed.2d 31 (2000) (punitive damages upheld where manager who intentionally refused to promote plaintiff knew that race discrimination was unlawful and had attended week-long seminar that included education on federal discrimination law).

51. *See, e.g., Dhyne v. Meiners Thriftway, Inc.*, 184 F.3d 983, 988 (8th Cir. 1999) (affirming lower court's rejection of plaintiff's requested punitive damages instruction where, in response to sexual harassment complaint, defendant delayed but ultimately investigated and took remedial action).

with the distinct belief that its discrimination is lawful. The underlying theory of discrimination may be novel or otherwise poorly recognized, or an employer may reasonably believe that its discrimination satisfies a bona fide occupational qualification defense or other statutory exception to liability." Evidence that an employer knowingly relied on a ground prohibited by statute, in short, does not in itself translate into evidence that the employer knew it was acting in violation of federal law.

The majority then announced standards for imputing liability for punitive damages to an employer for the willful or recklessly indifferent acts of its agents—a question that Justice Stevens, dissenting on this point, said that neither of the parties had addressed and employer counsel had disavowed. It accepted the Restatement (Second) of Agency (1957) as a "useful starting point" for defining the extent to which agents' misconduct may be imputed to an employer for purposes of a punitive damages award. Indeed, while these circumstances were not presented by the facts of *Kolstad*, the majority appeared to adopt wholesale for purposes of § 1981a(b)(1) the Restatement's imputation of punitive damages against a master for the acts of an agent where: "(a) the principal authorized the doing and the manner of the act, or (b) the agent was unfit and the principal was reckless in employing him, or ... (d) the principal or a managerial agent of the principal ratified or approved the act."[52]

The Restatement principle the majority found more troublesome—implicated by the facts of *Kolstad*—was the imputation of punitive damages liability where "(c) the agent was employed in a managerial capacity and was acting in the scope of employment, ..."[53] It cautioned that courts, in defining "managerial capacity," " 'should review the type of authority that the employer has given to the employee, the amount of discretion that the employee has ... and how it is accomplished.' "[54] The majority was even more concerned by an ancillary Restatement principle that even intentional torts are considered within the scope of employment, for purposes of § 217C(c), *supra*, provided the conduct is the kind the employee is expected to perform, takes place substantially within the authorized spatial and temporal limits of the employment, and is even in part actuated by a purpose of serving the employer.[55] Even "specifically forbidden" acts and means could fall within the Restatement's concept of scope of employment for this purpose.[56] Thus the Court feared that "even an employer who makes every effort to comply with Title VII would be held liable for the discriminatory acts of agents acting in a 'managerial capacity.' " That, in turn, would create "perverse incentives" for employers who implement antidiscrimination programs, in

---

52. *Kolstad*, 527 U.S. at ___, 119 S.Ct. at 2128 (citing Restatement (Second) of Agency (1957) § 217C). *See, e.g., Lowery*, 206 F.3d at 444–45.

53. *Id.* at ___, 119 S.Ct. at 2128.

54. *Id.* at ___, 119 S.Ct. at 2128 (citing 1 L. Schlueter & K. Redden, Punitive Damages, § 4.4(B)(2)(a), p. 182 (3d ed. 1995)).

The *Kolstad* "managerial" factor was applied in *EEOC v. Wal–Mart Stores, Inc.*, 187 F.3d 1241 (10th Cir.1999) (case under ADA).

55. Restatement (Second) of Agency, § 228(1), at 504.

56. *Id.* at § 230, at 511.

particular, sexual harassment policies and grievance mechanisms: the more they educate themselves and their employees about Title VII and ADA statutory duties, the more likely it could be inferred in court that any violations were committed with malice or with reckless indifference, with their efforts to comply not shielding them from punitive liability. Accordingly, the Court "adapted" subsection "c" to the employment discrimination setting by engrafting on to it the following caveat: "an employer may not be vicariously liable for the discriminatory employment decisions of managerial agents where these decisions are contrary to the employer's 'good faith efforts to comply with Title VII.' "[57] In this way, by making indirect deterrence in the form of punitive damages less generally available, the Court seeks to further Title VII's deterrence objective directly.

In applying the *Kolstad* pronouncements on "malice," "reckless indifference," and imputation of punitive damages liability, lower courts will also be guided by pre-*Kolstad* decisions and agency guidance. The key threshold inquiry in deciding the availability and appropriate amount of punitive damages still focuses on what mental state, in addition to that inherent in any intentional violation of Title VII or ADA, is requisite for the award. Malice is readily found when there is proof of ill will accompanying the defendant's conduct.[58] Malice will also normally be found where there is proof of retaliation for opposing at least well founded complaints of unlawful activity.[59] EEOC, in a damages guidance cited by the majority in *Kolstad*, suggests that the following additional unweighted factors should be taken into account: egregiousness of the conduct, as where it shocks or offends the conscience; the nature, extent and severity of the harm suffered by the complaining party; duration of the discriminatory conduct; whether the respondent engaged in similar conduct in the past; evidence of conspiracy or cover-up;[60] and the employer's response after notice to discriminatory conduct by its agents.[61] Factors in an environmental sexual harassment case that

57. *Kolstad*, 527 U.S. at ___, 119 S.Ct. at 2128 (quoting *Kolstad*, 139 F.3d 958, 974 (D.C.Cir.1998) (en banc) (Tatel, J., dissenting)). *See, e.g., Lowery*, 206 F.3d at 445–46 (sincerity of defendant's commitment to a company-wide policy against racial discrimination is called into question with evidence that two top executives acted with racial animus and that a subjective promotional system instituted by those executives had the capacity to mask race discrimination in promotional decisions). *But see Deters v. Equifax Credit Info. Servs., Inc.*, 202 F.3d 1262, 1270–71 (10th Cir.2000) (good faith defense unavailable where corporate defendant directly liable for punitive damages).

58. *See, e.g., Soderbeck v. Burnett County*, 752 F.2d 285, 289 (7th Cir.), *cert. denied*, 471 U.S. 1117, 105 S.Ct. 2360, 86 L.Ed.2d 261 (1985).

59. *See, e.g., Blackmon v. Pinkerton Sec. & Investigative Servs.*, 182 F.3d 629, 635–

36 (8th Cir.1999) (post-*Kolstad* sexual harassment case upholding punitive award where employer retaliated after plaintiff complained); *Hunter v. Allis–Chalmers Corp.* 797 F.2d 1417, 1425 (7th Cir.1986); *Erebia v. Chrysler Plastic Prods. Corp.*, 772 F.2d 1250, 1260 (6th Cir.1985), *cert. denied*, 475 U.S. 1015, 106 S.Ct. 1197, 89 L.Ed.2d 311 (1986). *But see Karcher v. Emerson Elec. Co.*, 94 F.3d 502 (8th Cir.1996), *cert. denied*, 520 U.S. 1210, 117 S.Ct. 1692, 137 L.Ed.2d 820 (1997) (evidence beyond retaliation required).

60. *EEOC v. Wal–Mart Stores, Inc.*, 156 F.3d 989 (9th Cir.1998) (cover up of discrimination on the basis of pregnancy warrants punitives).

61. EEOC Damages Guidance, at 405: 7100–7101. *See Preston v. Income Producing Mgmt., Inc.*, 871 F.Supp. 411 (D.Kan. 1994) (employer inaction after sexual

may support a punitive damages award include the lack of or failure to implement a sexual harassment prevention policy or grievance procedure, failure to respond to complaints, and the nature of the harassment.[62] Courts have been particularly reluctant to assess punitive damages against an employer for an employee-agent's conduct that it neither fostered nor countenanced.[63] The most common example is a hostile work environment case, where the intentional discrimination is a "frolic and detour" undertaken for the harasser's own reasons and outside the scope of the normal agency relationship.[64] Perhaps an additional reason for denying damages in such circumstances is the unavailability of contribution in Title VII actions.[65]

There is a wide range of circumstances in which the propriety of punitives is uncertain. At one extreme, it seems clear that mere proof of an intentional violation does not warrant a punitive award in a variety of situations analogous to the ADA defendant that is expressly exempt from punitives if it makes a good-faith but ultimately inadequate effort to reasonably accommodate an employee's disability. For example, the employer may have been unaware of a statutory prohibition or reasonably believed that its conduct was not reached by the prohibition or relied plausibly on an affirmative defense that privileged its conduct.[66] At the other extreme, a trial court's instructions were held to authorize punitive damages in a Reconstruction Act case when, in addition to proof of an intentional wrong, it merely advised the jury that such awards were designed to punish the defendant for "outrageous conduct" and "to deter him and others like him from similar conduct in the future."[67]

harassment complaint, coupled with manager's contribution to harassing environment, warrant punitives).

62. *See Harris v. L & L Wings, Inc.,* 132 F.3d 978 (4th Cir.1997); *EEOC v. Wal-Mart Stores, Inc.,* 187 F.3d 1241 (10th Cir.1999) (applying *Kolstad* to affirm punitive damages award in part because defendant had not made good faith effort to educate employees about ADA prohibitions); *Knowlton v. Teltrust Phones, Inc.,* 189 F.3d 1177 (10th Cir.1999) (unresponsiveness to plaintiff's complaints of sexual harassment supports punitive award).

63. *See Passantino v. Johnson & Johnson Consumer Prods., Inc.,* 212 F.3d 493 (9th Cir.2000) (remanding for consideration of *Kolstad* principles where the court found the record lacking as to the status of the decisionmakers); *Tincher v. Wal-Mart Stores, Inc.,* 118 F.3d 1125 (7th Cir.1997) (manager's disparaging remark about plaintiff's observance of Saturday sabbath insufficient to show the callous or reckless disregard that supports punitive award); *Reynolds v. CSX Transp., Inc.,* 115 F.3d 860, 869 (11th Cir.1997), *vacated,* 524 U.S. 947, 118 S.Ct. 2364, 141 L.Ed.2d 732 (1998) (no punitives may be assessed against employer for retaliation by supervi-

sor found not to be part of "higher management"). *See also Patterson v. P.H.P. Healthcare Corp.,* 90 F.3d 927 (5th Cir. 1996), *cert. denied,* 519 U.S. 1091, 117 S.Ct. 767, 136 L.Ed.2d 713 (1997); *Fitzgerald v. Mountain States Telephone and Telegraph Co.,* 68 F.3d 1257, 1263 (10th Cir.), *vacated on rehearing in part,* 60 F.3d 837 (10th Cir.1995).

64. *See Farpella-Crosby v. Horizon Health Care,* 97 F.3d 803, 809–810 (5th Cir.1996).

65. *Northwest Airlines, Inc. v. Transport Workers Union of Am.,* 451 U.S. 77, 101 S.Ct. 1571, 67 L.Ed.2d 750 (1981); *Atchley v. The Nordam Group, Inc.,* 180 F.3d 1143, 1999 WL 374241 *8 (10th Cir. 1999) (in Title VII actions, no statutory or common law right of contribution).

66. *See, e.g., Hazen Paper Co. v. Biggins,* 507 U.S. 604, 113 S.Ct. 1701, 123 L.Ed.2d 338 (1993) employer not liable even for ADEA liquidated damages if it "incorrectly but in good faith and nonrecklessly believes that the statute permits a particular age-based decision."

67. *Rowlett v. Anheuser-Busch, Inc.,* 832 F.2d 194, 205 (1st Cir.1987).

Courts have particularly struggled with establishing reasonable limits on the amount of a punitive award. In general, the award should "bear some relation" to the nature of defendant's conduct and the harm it caused;[68] and taking defendant's resources into account, it should "sting" rather than "destroy."[69] But the EEOC takes the position that in general punitive awards under Title VII and ADA should rarely be grossly excessive, because the sum of punitive damages together with future pecuniary losses and all nonpecuniary losses must stay within the caps of § 1981a(b)(3).[70]

Consistent with this position, the Supreme Court's recently announced Due Process limits on punitive damages,[71] or similar state law limits, will most often constrain punitive awards where there is no statutory cap on the plaintiff's claim like the $300,000 maximum combined compensatory-punitive award available under those statutes. Examples include punitive awards under state law or under § 1981, § 1983 or the other Reconstruction Acts.[72] If the amount of a punitive damages award is reduced pursuant to these rather rarely invoked Due Process

---

68. *Rowlett*, 832 F.2d at 207. One circuit, for example, has held that a punitive award may not be given in the maximum amount permitted by an applicable statutory cap unless the violation was egregious. *Hennessy v. Penril Datacomm Networks, Inc.*, 69 F.3d 1344 (7th Cir.1995). *Compare Emmel v. Coca–Cola Bottling Co. of Chicago*, 95 F.3d 627 (7th Cir.1996) (affirming maximum punitive award because defendant intentionally disregarded statutory rights).

69. *Keenan v. City of Phila.*, 1991 WL 40355 (E.D.Pa.1991), *aff'd in part, vacated in part*, 983 F.2d 459 (3d Cir.1992). EEOC has summarized a number of factors relevant to ascertaining the defendant's financial position for this purpose. *EEOC Damages Guidance*, at 405:7101–7102. *See Chavez v. Keat*, 34 Cal.App.4th 1406, 41 Cal.Rptr.2d 72 (Cal.Ct.App.1995), *cert. denied*, 516 U.S. 1115, 116 S.Ct. 918, 133 L.Ed.2d 848 (1996) (citing federal rule that places burden of producing evidence of defendant's financial condition on defendant). But the Supreme Court indicated in *BMW of N. Am. v. Gore*, 517 U.S. 559, 116 S.Ct. 1589, 134 L.Ed.2d 809 (1996), that Due Process would be offended by a punitive award that exceeded 10% of a defendant's net worth.

70. *EEOC Damages Guidance*, at 405:7101 n.18. *See, e.g., Deters v. Equifax Credit Info. Servs., Inc.*, 202 F.3d 1262, 1273 (10th Cir.2000) (allowing punitive award up to statutory cap; "only when an award would shock the judicial conscience, and constitute a denial of justice, for example because it would result in the financial ruin of the defendant or constitute a dispro-

portionately large percentage of a defendant's net worth, will we reduce the award below the statutory cap") (citations omitted).

71. *BMW of N. Am. v. Gore*, 517 U.S. 559, 116 S.Ct. 1589, 134 L.Ed.2d 809 (1996) measures the excessiveness of punitive damage awards by the guideposts of (1) degree of reprehensibility; (2) ratio of punitive to compensatory damages; and (3) relation between damages in the instant and comparable cases. *See Kimzey v. Wal–Mart Stores, Inc.*, 107 F.3d 568 (8th Cir.1997) (applying Missouri law to reduce $5 million punitive award to $350,000 because the hostile environment sexual harassment, although serious enough to lead to plaintiff's constructive discharge, involved no physical touching or assault, and because the award was excessive in light of awards in similar cases).

72. *See Kim v. Nash Finch Co.*, 123 F.3d 1046 (8th Cir.1997) (apparently applying *BMW* and Title VII caps to § 1981 case; with $100,000 in compensatory damages, the jury's award of $7 million was grossly excessive, but the trial court's reduction to $300,000, which resulted in a 3:1 ratio, was not); *Lee v. Edwards*, 101 F.3d 805 (2d Cir.1996) (applying *BMW v. Gore*'s Due Process limits to reduce $200,000 punitive award in § 1983 police misconduct action, relying on awards in comparable cases). *But see Pavon v. Swift Transp. Co., Inc.*, 192 F.3d 902 (9th Cir.1999) ($300,000 punitive award for racial and ancestry discrimination in violation of § 1981 not excessive under *BMW* although exceeding out-of-pocket damages by 250 to 1).

limits, it is unsettled if the question is one of law or of judicial discretion. If it is a question of law, then, notwithstanding the Seventh Amendment's "reexamination clause," the trial or appellate court may enter final judgment for the amount as reduced to comply with Due Process, without giving the plaintiff the option of a new trial.[73] If the determination is considered discretionary, the plaintiff whose verdict has been ruled constitutionally excessive must be given the choice between a reduced verdict and a new trial so as not to violate the Seventh Amendment.[74]

But a trial court may also conclude in its discretion that either a compensatory or punitive award is simply excessive on the evidence, and may then order a new trial unless the plaintiff agrees to remit a portion of the jury's award.[75] When a judge exercises the discretion to reduce either a compensatory or punitive award for ordinary excessiveness,[76] the Amendment requires that the plaintiff be afforded the option of a new trial under Federal Rule of Civil Procedure 59(a) in lieu of the court's remittitur of a portion of the jury's award.[77] But if, by contrast, damages are reduced as the result of a defendant's successfully moving after verdict under Federal Rule 50(b) for partial summary judgment as a matter of law—for example, if the evidence was insufficient to support a reasonable jury award of *any* damages respecting a particular incident or period of time—the trial court may enter final judgment on a reduced verdict and is not required by the Seventh Amendment to grant a plaintiff's motion for new trial.[78]

§ 4.26A Defense Checklist: Reducing Remedial Exposure

The following outline lists, in alphabetical sequence, issues that defense counsel should consider raising to limit available remedies. It

73. *Johansen v. Combustion Eng'g, Inc.,* 170 F.3d 1320, 1330–1332 (11th Cir.), *cert. denied sub nom. Combustion Eng'g, Inc. v. McGill,* 528 U.S. 931, 120 S.Ct. 329, 145 L.Ed.2d 256 (1999) (court may enter judgment to the extent it reduces the jury's verdict to the constitutionally permitted maximum; to the extent there is any further, discretionary reduction, the verdict is "reexamined" and the plaintiff must be afforded the option to elect new trial).

74. *Continental Trend Resources, Inc. v. OXY USA Inc.,* 101 F.3d 634, 643 (10th Cir.1996), *cert. denied,* 520 U.S. 1241, 117 S.Ct. 1846, 137 L.Ed.2d 1049 (1997). *See Lee v. Edwards,* 101 F.3d 805, 813 (2d Cir.1996) (court offered plaintiff new trial, but it was not entirely clear if the court's reduction of the verdict was grounded in unconstitutional excessiveness pursuant to *BMW of N. Am. v. Gore,* 517 U.S. 559, 116

S.Ct. 1589, 134 L.Ed.2d 809 (1996)). See also text *infra* this section.

75. *Dimick v. Schiedt,* 293 U.S. 474, 486–87, 55 S.Ct. 296, 301, 79 L.Ed. 603 (1935).

76. *See Gasperini v. Center for Humanities, Inc.,* 518 U.S. 415, 116 S.Ct. 2211, 135 L.Ed.2d 659 (1996) (elaborating the limits on that discretion dictated by state law when federal court hears claim under state law, and specifying that Seventh Amendment restricts federal appellate review of such state law remittiturs to an abuse of discretion standard, *id.* at 435).

77. *Hetzel v. Prince William County, Va.,* 523 U.S. 208, 118 S.Ct. 1210, 140 L.Ed.2d 336 (1998).

78. *Central Office Tel., Inc. v. American Tel. & Tel. Co.,* 108 F.3d 981 (9th Cir.1997), *rev'd on other grounds,* 524 U.S. 214, 118 S.Ct. 1956, 141 L.Ed.2d 222 (1998).

takes into account the liability standards of Chapter 3, the Remedies listed immediately above in Chapter 4, and the discussion of attorney's fees for prevailing parties in Chapter 11. Of course, plaintiffs' counsel will try to anticipate and blunt these tactics in their pleadings, the witnesses they call, and the way they maintain specific, defensible time records.

a. The "Same–Decision" Defense in Mixed–Motive Cases: Barring All Remedies Under ADEA, and All Remedies Except Injunctive Relief and Attorney's Fees Under Title VII

Under Sections 703(m) and 706(g)(2)(B) of Title VII, as amended in 1991, the employer who demonstrates that it would have reached the same challenged employment decision for a lawful reason, independent of any reliance on an unlawful reason the plaintiff has proven, is relieved of all monetary remedies and of the duty to reinstate. The ADEA defendant who carries that showing is probably relieved of all liability, under the authority of *Price Waterhouse v. Hopkins*, 490 U.S. 228, 109 S.Ct. 1775, 104 L.Ed.2d 268 (1989). *See* §§ 3.11, 7.5.

Exception: Economic loss and emotional distress damages are arguably available in race discrimination cases under § 1983 or § 1981, even if the employer *does* demonstrate that despite its unlawful discrimination, someone other than plaintiff would have gotten the job or promotion in question. Here the employer has in effect made the "same decision" showing about the job, contract or school admission in question. Accordingly, the law recognizes that, in equity and logic, the employer should not be ordered to hire or promote the plaintiff or suffer a judgment for back or front pay. But courts have also recognized that the violation in such cases, and some damage, is complete upon proof that plaintiff was denied a race-neutral right to compete. Those courts will award plaintiffs who demonstrate that they were unconstitutionally denied a race-free right to compete damages for any economic loss not predicated on their obtaining or retaining the job, contract, or school admission, and possibly also emotional distress damages, as well as fees. *See, e.g., Price v. City of Charlotte, N.C.,* 93 F.3d 1241 (4th Cir.1996), *cert. denied,* 520 U.S. 1116, 117 S.Ct. 1246, 137 L.Ed.2d 328 (1997) (recognizing the availability of emotional distress damages for plaintiffs who had been excluded from consideration for promotion, even if they would not have otherwise received the promotions); *Hopwood v. Texas,* 78 F.3d 932 (5th Cir.), *cert. denied,* 518 U.S. 1033, 116 S.Ct. 2581, 135 L.Ed.2d 1095 (1996) (denial of admission to state's law school). Other courts, by contrast, deem a plaintiff's failure to prove that she would have been selected so fundamental as to deprive her of standing, at least if she falls short of minimum eligibility requirements. *See, e.g., Grahek v. City of St. Paul, Mn.,* 84 F.3d 296 (8th Cir.1996) (city hiring).

b. The "After–Acquired Evidence" Defense: Relieving the Employer of Liability for Reinstatement and Front Pay, and Limiting Back Pay to the Period Preceding Employer's Discovery of Evidence of Plaintiff's Severe Misconduct Warranting Discharge

An employer who is found liable and cannot carry the "same-decision" burden respecting its employment decision challenged in the lawsuit may nevertheless substantially reduce its exposure to remedies by developing and proving subsequently discovered evidence of employee misconduct. In *McKennon v. Nashville Banner Publishing Co.*, 513 U.S. 352, 115 S.Ct. 879, 130 L.Ed.2d 852 (1995), the Supreme Court granted the employer that demonstrates sufficient plaintiff misconduct relief from forward-looking remedies. While acknowledging that the relevant equitable considerations will vary from case to case, the Court nevertheless concluded that "here, and as a general rule in cases of this type, neither reinstatement nor front pay is an appropriate remedy. It would be both inequitable and pointless to order the reinstatement of someone the employer would have terminated, and will terminate, in any event and upon lawful grounds." While *McKennon* was an ADEA case, it has subsequently been applied by lower courts to actions under Title VII. *Russell v. Microdyne*, 65 F.3d 1229 (4th Cir.1995); *Wallace v. Dunn Constr. Co.*, 62 F.3d 374 (11th Cir.1995) (en banc); *Wehr v. Ryan's Family Steak Houses, Inc.*, 49 F.3d 1150 (6th Cir.1995).

In after-acquired evidence cases, while the defendant will be liable for fees to the extent the plaintiff prevails, the only normal monetary remedy should be backpay, calculated from the date of an unlawful discharge to the date the information about plaintiff misconduct was discovered. *See Russell*, 65 F.3d 1229. *Cf. Ricky v. Mapco*, 50 F.3d 874, 876 (10th Cir.1995) (jury may award back pay past the date of the employer's discovery of the plaintiff's misconduct, through the date the employer proves it would have fired him). So unlike the "mixed-motive" employer—who establishes that it would have made the challenged decision without any reliance on an unlawful motivating factor—the employer who cannot make that showing but carries the persuasion burden on after-acquired evidence will likely sustain some monetary liability. Indeed the after-acquired evidence limitation on remedies becomes relevant only after the factfinder has determined not only that the sole, motivating (Title VII), or determinative (ADEA) basis for the challenged employment decision was unlawful, but also that the employer would not have reached the same decision at that time on lawful grounds.

To avail itself of the after-acquired evidence remedy limitation, the employer bears the burden of proving "that the wrongdoing was of such severity that the employee *in fact would* have been *terminated* on those grounds alone if the employer had known of it at the time of the discharge." A mere possibility or speculation that the employer would have terminated the plaintiff based on the subsequently discovered evidence will not suffice; the employer must show that it would have discharged the plaintiff had it known of the misconduct. *Ricky,* 50 F.3d 874. On the other hand, the court need not agree that the employee's misconduct is "serious" or "pervasive," so long as the employer can prove that under its own established rules, applied without discrimination, it would have discharged the employee had it known of such conduct when it occurred. *See, e.g. O'Driscoll v. Hercules, Inc.,* 12 F.3d 176 (10th Cir.1994), *vacated in light of McKennon v. Nashville Banner Publ'g,* 513 U.S. 352, 115 S.Ct. 879, 130 L.Ed.2d 852 (1995).

The employer must carry this burden by the normal "preponderance of the evidence" quantum. *O'Day v. McDonnell Douglas Helicopter Co.,* 79 F.3d 756 (9th Cir.1996). The employer must show that had it known of plaintiff's misconduct at the relevant time, it would have *fired* her, not merely failed to *hire* her. *Shattuck v. Kinetic Concepts, Inc.,* 49 F.3d 1106 (5th Cir.1995) (post-*McKennon* ADEA case).

EEOC and circuit court decisions after *McKennon* have opined that Title VII *compensatory* and *punitive damages,* or ADEA *liquidated* damages, are available (if otherwise appropriate) notwithstanding after-acquired evidence. *Russell,* 65 F.3d 1229; *Wallace,* 62 F.3d 374; *EEOC Enforcement Guidance on After–Acquired Evidence.* According to EEOC, the after-acquired showing limits only those out-of-pocket losses that are analogous to backpay. Other decisions applying *McKennon* include *Padilla v. Metro–North Commuter R.R.,* 92 F.3d 117 (2d Cir.1996), *cert. denied,* 520 U.S. 1274, 117 S.Ct. 2453, 138 L.Ed.2d 211 (1997) (front pay allowed upon employer's failure to prove it would have denied plaintiff a promotion for a misstatement in the plaintiff's affidavit to the EEOC); *Thurman v. Yellow Freight Systems, Inc.,* 90 F.3d 1160 (6th Cir.)), *amended on denial of rehearing,* 97 F.3d 833 (6th Cir.1996) (employer did not carry its burden in Title VII case); *Castle v. Rubin,* 78 F.3d 654 (D.C.Cir.1996) (denying front pay in Title VII action based upon after-acquired evidence "of such severity that the employee in fact would have been terminated on those grounds alone if the employer had known of it at the time of the discharge").

c. Taking Prompt, Appropriate Corrective Action Will Avoid or Limit Employer Liability for a Co–Worker's or Supervisor's Creation of a Hostile Work Environment in Sexual or Racial Harassment Cases

Co-worker hostile environment harassment: Employer liable only if upon notice it fails to take prompt, appropriate corrective action reasonably calculated to end the harassment. *Burlington Indus., Inc. v. Ellerth,* 524 U.S. 742, 118 S.Ct. 2257, 141 L.Ed.2d 633 (1998) (dictum) and *Faragher v. City of Boca Raton,* 524 U.S. 775, 118 S.Ct. 2275, 141 L.Ed.2d 662 (1998).

Hostile environment created by supervisor, manager or other high official: Affirmative defense declared by Supreme Court avoids any employer liability if plaintiff unreasonably fails to utilize fair, specific, well disseminated, evenly applied policy and procedure to prevent unlawful harassment, provided employer takes prompt appropriate corrective action upon receiving informal notice of actionable harassing conduct. *Burlington, Faragher.* If plaintiff does utilize established complaints procedure, employer probably is liable but may still substantially limit its exposure for emotional distress damages by investigating thoroughly and taking prompt, appropriate corrective action. *See id.*

d. *General Back Pay Limiting Tactics*

—The employer should consider making an unconditional offer of reinstatement to limit back pay liability to the date plaintiff unreasonably fails to accept offer. *Ford Motor Co. v. EEOC*, 458 U.S. 219, 102 S.Ct. 3057, 73 L.Ed.2d 721 (1982).

—Avoid or limit back pay by demonstrating that plaintiff was unavailable for work; that plaintiff's position would have been eliminated or plaintiff himself laid off before date of judgment; and that plaintiff breached his duty to mitigate damages.

—Challenge the qualifications of any plaintiff's expert and the assumptions underlying plaintiff's back pay testimony—e.g., the number of hours per week plaintiff would have worked, how plaintiff's compensation might have varied over time.

—Challenge fringe benefit claims as speculative.

—Contend for lowest prejudgment interest rate allowable under circuit authority.

e. *General Front Pay Limiting Tactics*

—As with back pay, the employer should consider making an unconditional offer of reinstatement to limit back pay liability to the date plaintiff unreasonably fails to accept offer. *Ford Motor Co. v. EEOC*, 458 U.S. 219, 102 S.Ct. 3057, 73 L.Ed.2d 721 (1982).

—Argue that judge rather than jury determines appropriateness of any award.

—Where the hostility generated by termination and litigation not excessive, consider taking position that reinstatement is not infeasible, so front pay award unnecessary.

—Argue that other remedies—especially back pay, prejudgment interest, and, in ADEA cases, liquidated damages—render a front pay award unnecessary to make plaintiff whole.

—Object to unreasonably speculative evidence about probable duration of plaintiff's job and level of his future salary and benefits.

—Seek denial or offset of front pay claim for plaintiff's failure to mitigate by seeking comparable employment or self-employment.

—Argue in Title VII, and ADA (but not § 1981 or ADEA) cases that front pay is one of the components of relief that, together with emotional distress damages and punitives, are capped according to employer size at

$50,000 to a maximum of $300,000. Circuit authority is divided on this argument.

—Be sure that front pay award is discounted to present value.

—Offset front pay claim by amounts plaintiff has earned or is likely to earn, including projected benefits increases.

—Consider expert testimony to combat plaintiff's use of a low rate for discounting to present value the ultimate award of front pay, including benefits.

f. Collateral Source Offsets to Back and Front Pay

Depending on circuit approach, try to reduce back and front pay award by amounts plaintiff received for unemployment insurance, private or public disability payments, social security, pension benefits, workers' compensation, etc.

g. General Emotional Distress Limiting Tactics

—Insist on corroboration of plaintiff's own testimony, preferably by medical witnesses and in any event by family members, friends, co-workers, neighbors. Argue that plaintiff's own testimony insufficient standing alone.

—Offer evidence tending to show any such damages are attributable to pre-existing or concurrent causes, rather than the challenged employment decision.

—Argue in Title VII and ADA (but not § 1981 or ADEA) cases that the sum of emotional distress damages and punitive damages are capped according to employer size at $50,000 to a maximum of $300,000.

—Move for reduction as excessive; plaintiff may accept remittitur, or decline and insist on new trial. *Hetzel v. Prince William County*, 523 U.S. 208, 118 S.Ct. 1210, 140 L.Ed.2d 336 (1998).

h. Punitive Damages Limitations

—Never against governmental entities, either under Reconstruction Act or contemporary employment discrimination statutes.

—Argue that they are available at all only if plaintiff recovers compensatory or nominal damages (more fruitful under Title VII than under § 1983).

—In any event, punitives are available only under the *Kolstad* standards (U.S.1999).

—Argue in Title VII and ADA (but not § 1981 or ADEA) cases that the sum of emotional distress damages and punitive damages are capped according to employer size at $50,000 to a maximum of $300,000.

—Move for reduction as excessive; plaintiff may accept remittitur, or decline and insist on new trial. *Hetzel v. Prince William County*, 523 U.S. 208, 118 S.Ct. 1210, 140 L.Ed.2d 336 (1998).

—In Reconstruction Act litigation, move to reduce under loose Due Process limits as to proportionality (*BMW of N. Am., Inc. v. Gore,* 517 U.S. 559, 116 S.Ct. 1589, 134 L.Ed.2d 809 (1996)).

i. Prejudgment Interest

—Available only for back (not front) pay.

—Search authority of circuit where action pending for lowest possible standard rate.

j. Limiting Recoverable Attorney's Fees

—Argue if appropriate that plaintiff not prevailing party because the relief obtained did not require defendant tangibly to change its position.

—Argue if appropriate that plaintiff, although technically prevailing because she recovered nominal damages, is reasonably entitled to an award of $0 because relief obtained (e.g., nominal damages) is trivial in relation to relief sought in complaint (*Farrar v. Hobby,* 506 U.S. 103, 113 S.Ct. 566, 121 L.Ed.2d 494 (1992)).

—Argue that plaintiff's counsel's work on unsuccessful issues was distinct from and not essential to work on successful issues, with recovery limited to latter.

—Argue that some hours devoted (by plaintiff's counsel, paraprofessionals and others) even to successful issues were unnecessary and violated standard "billing judgment".

—Develop evidence of low market hourly rate for work of the kind in question.

For several of the suggestions in the above list, the authors are indebted to Mason and Ekman, *Defending Against Damages Claims In Discrimination Cases,* 13 Lab.Law. 471 (Winter/Spring 1998).

§ 4.27 1996 Legislation Treats Virtually All Settlement or Judgment Proceeds in Employment Discrimination and Civil Rights Actions As Includable In Gross Income, Except In Cases of Physical Injury

Plaintiffs are of course more inclined to settle for less if they are persuaded that the proceeds of a settlement will not be taxed. Until August 20, when President Clinton signed the Small Business Job Protection Act of 1996, Section 104(a)(2) of the Internal Revenue Code, 26 U.S.C.A. § 104(a)(2), excluded from gross income "the amount of any *damages* received (whether by suit or agreement . . .) *on account of personal injuries* or sickness. . . ."[1] An elaborate and confusing jurisprudence developed separately under ADEA and Title VII concerning the

§ 4.27

1. 26 U.S.C.A. § 104(a)(2) (emphasis added).

extent to which various elements of recovery under those statutes could be excludable under Section 104(a)(2) as "damages" received by a taxpayer plaintiff "on account of personal injuries or sickness."[2]

The "personal injuries or sickness" requirement was acutely raised by employment discrimination, and to a lesser degree civil rights, claims. In most such cases the plaintiff's immediate injuries, while arguably "personal," and commonly resulting in emotional distress that is sometimes medically treated, are nonphysical. In 1995 the Supreme Court held that in the typical, nonphysical situation, neither the back pay nor the liquidated damages recoverable in an action under the Age Discrimination in Employment Act could ordinarily be considered "damages" on account of "personal injuries."[3] That decision rested uncomfortably with the Court's strong suggestion three years earlier that the back pay and emotional distress damages recoverable under Title VII, as amended by the 1991 Civil Rights Acts, would be excludable from the plaintiff's income under Section 104(a)(2).[4] At the same time, text added to Section 104 in 1989 rendered punitive damages, available since November 1991 in Title VII actions, non-excludable in a case—like most employment discrimination and many civil rights cases—that did "not involv[e] physical injury or physical sickness." (The Supreme Court has since rejected the negative pregnant that punitive damages were excludable in cases that did involve physical injury or sickness!)[5]

Except for the nonexcludability of punitive damages, most of this landscape was altered by a stroke of President Clinton's pen in August 1996. Two additions to the text of Section 104(a)(2), underlined for the reader's convenience, tell most of the tale:

> (a).... gross income does not include—
>
> > (2) the amount of any damages (other than punitive damages) received (whether by suit or agreement ...) on account of personal physical injuries or physical sickness;

The rest of the tale is told by an addendum to Section 104(a):

> For purposes of paragraph (2), emotional distress shall not be treated as a physical injury or physical sickness. The preceding sentence shall not apply to an amount of damages not in excess of the amount paid for medical care ... attributable to emotional distress.

2. The case law and Treasury regulations implementing Section 104(a)(2) still govern the excludability of amounts received under binding written agreements, court decrees, or mediation awards in effect on, or issued on or before, September 13, 1995, or of amounts actually received by the taxpayer (under agreements executed after September 13, 1995) on or before August 20, 1996, the effective date of the amendments.

3. *Commissioner v. Schleier,* 515 U.S. 323, 115 S.Ct. 2159, 132 L.Ed.2d 294 (1995).

4. *United States v. Burke,* 504 U.S. 229, 112 S.Ct. 1867, 119 L.Ed.2d 34 (1992).

5. *O'Gilvie v. United States,* 519 U.S. 79, 117 S.Ct. 452, 136 L.Ed.2d 454 (1996).

The English translation? The most important change from current law, particularly for Title VII cases, is the requirement of physical injury as a precondition for exclusion under Section 104(a)(2). In the usual Title VII or ADEA case, where the employer's conduct does not result in "physical" injury or sickness, no part of any judgment or settlement for back or front pay will be eligible for exclusion under Section 104(a)(2).[6] Second, because the first sentence of the addendum excludes emotional distress from the Section 104(a)(2) definition of "physical" injury or sickness, the part of any settlement or judgment representing recovery for the intangible harms of emotional distress will also be nonexcludable in non-physical cases.[7] Third, however, where a civil rights (or, more rarely, employment discrimination) plaintiff does suffer some actual "physical" injury as the result of the defendant's conduct—police abuse cases may be the paradigm, with the rape and invasive touching variants of sexual harassment strong possibilities—she may exclude "any damages" (other than punitive) received in respect of those injuries. Accordingly, the pertinent House Committee Report indicates that such a plaintiff may exclude not just the part of a settlement or judgment received on account of lost income, but also the part received on account of emotional distress. Fourth, because of the "(other than punitive damages)" language, punitive damages will now almost never[8] be eligible for exclusion, even when they are awarded in cases of *physical* injury. It therefore becomes critical from the plaintiff's perspective to seek settlement agreements that label as "compensatory" rather than "punitive" as much of the total monetary recovery as may plausibly be so characterized in view of the underlying facts and the allegations of any previously

---

6. And an EEOC Memorandum states that federal employment taxes, including income tax and social security, must be withheld from that amount considered to be wages under the tax code. Withholding then is required on back and front pay amounts, but not on compensatory damages, attorney's fees, or interest. *See EEOC Memorandum, Whether Remedies Under the Anti–Discrimination Laws are Taxable as Wages,* Nov. 6. 1998. *But see Newhouse v. McCormick & Co.,* 157 F.3d 582 (8th Cir.1998) (front and back pay awards in job applicant's ADEA action were not "wages" triggering a withholding requirement on part of defendant company, and, thus, company had no authority to withhold payroll taxes on the awards, since plaintiff was an applicant and not an employee at time of the discrimination from which judgment arose).

7. The second sentence of the addendum offers a tiny consolation to the employment discrimination or civil rights plaintiff who suffers no actual physical injury but incurs medical expenses attributable to emotional distress. That sentence *treats* the portion of any settlement or judgment representing reimbursement for those expenses as a "physical" injury and therefore excludable. (Those who have taken a course in basic income taxation will know that this exclusion for medical expenses should result in better tax treatment than a mere deduction.) But of course the portion of a recovery attributable to nonpecuniary, intangible emotional distress will usually be much greater than the medical expenses for that distress; and intangible emotional distress is defined as something other than physical injury or sickness, and therefore as nonexcludable, by the first sentence of the addendum. Accordingly, except for medical expense reimbursement, recoveries for emotional distress will be nonexcludable under amended Section 104(a)(2), provided the defendant's conduct did not cause some *actual* physical injury.

8. In certain wrongful death actions resulting from the infliction of physical injury or sickness, punitive damages will continue to be excludable where the applicable state law authorizes *only* punitive awards for wrongful death. 26 U.S.C.A. § 104(c). This exception should have little or no application to employment discrimination or civil rights claims under federal law.

asserted demand letters, pleadings, and subsequent litigation documents. A recent Tax Court decision, warns, however, that an allocation negotiated by the parties will not be respected if they never bargained over the allocation before arriving at an overall settlement or if an allocation is "patently inconsistent" with the underlying claims.[9]

The essence of these changes, as applicable to claimants under federal employment discrimination and civil rights laws, may be summarized as follows: (1) At least some "physical" (probably bodily) injury or sickness is necessary for the taxpayer to exclude from gross income *any* settlement or judgment proceeds, except the relatively minor portion representing reimbursement for medical expenses attributable to emotional distress; (2) where the settlement or judgment resolves a claim involving *some* "physical" injury or sickness, the taxpayer may exclude all back pay, front pay, or compensatory damages that are received "on account of" that injury or sickness, including *all* emotional distress damages, not just those that reimburse for medical expenses; but (3), even in cases of actual physical injury or sickness, punitive damages will not be excludable.

The new legislation apparently leaves unaffected the treatment of a plaintiff's attorney's fees expense as a miscellaneous itemized deduction; as such, it remains available only to the extent it exceeds 2% of a plaintiff's adjusted gross income. Some plaintiff's lawyers have sought to eliminate the amount of their attorney's fees from the taxable portion of their clients' award by inducing defense lawyers to write a separate check to the lawyer to cover fees, reducing the check to the plaintiff accordingly. But while this gambit may reduce the risk of an audit concerning taxes owed on those fees, the IRS if it does challenge the return will likely argue that the lawyer's check was income to the client, who was thereby relieved of a debt. There is a more confident way to reduce a claimant's or plaintiff's tax bill if she has filed a parallel workers' compensation claim. Then a reasonable portion of the discrimination claim settlement might fairly be allocated as a settlement of the workers' compensation case. These payments, while still deductible expenses for the employer, would be considered nontaxable payments to the employee-claimant.

The threshold requirement for excludability is whether, assuming the plaintiff obtains the kind of "damages" for "personal injuries" that § 104(a)(2) makes excludable, she receives them "by suit or agreement." A recent appellate decision holds that the receipt by an employee of a lump sum termination payment that the company increased because of his willingness to waive all claims relating to his employment or termination, including claims related to age discrimination, could not be considered "damages," or therefore the result of a "settlement," so defined. The court reasoned that a "claim must be asserted before it can be settled; plaintiff waived all claims before asserting them...."[10] This

9. *Lefleur v. Commissioner*, T.C. Memo 1997–312 (Tax Ct.1997).

10. *Taggi v. United States*, 35 F.3d 93 (2d Cir.1994).

ruling is apparently in some tension with Tax Court practice, the waiver procedure approved for ADEA claims by the OWBPA, as well as the expressed preference of § 118 of the 1991 Civil Rights Act for alternative means of dispute resolution.[11] Its lesson to older employees in a circuit subscribing to this view and facing a reduction in force would appear to be not to enter into a valid agreement waiving ADEA rights under the terms of OWBPA, but instead to have a lawyer assert a formal charge or claim before settling with the employer. This seems an unnecessary expense and formality, since it is well established that sums paid to settle a previously asserted ADEA claim may be excludable if they meet the (now stringent) requirements of § 104(a)(2).[12]

Employer counsel should seek to reduce the payroll tax due on settlements of statutory discrimination claims, by specifying in the settlement agreement which components of recovery are non-wage items. Likely candidates include reimbursements for medical expenses and payments allocated for future medical expenses and health insurance premiums.

§§ 4.28–7.29 [Reserved]

D. TITLE VII AND ADEA REMEDIES COMPARED

§ 4.30 In General

Before the 1991 legislation, Title VII plaintiffs were limited to actual out of pocket loss in the form of back or front pay. By contrast, plaintiffs under the Age Discrimination in Employment Act of 1967 (ADEA) could also recover, in willful cases, an equal additional amount of liquidated damages.[1] It is true that after the amendments, the recovery by the Title VII intentional discrimination plaintiff of compensatory or punitive damages or both may exceed the liquidated double damages available to the willful violation plaintiff under ADEA; and that ADEA plaintiffs, even after the 1991 amendments, may not recover compensatory or punitive damages.[2] In practice, however, many ADEA plaintiffs will still

---

11. *See* §§ 7.15 to 7.17, *infra.*

12. *Downey v. Commissioner*, 33 F.3d 836 (7th Cir.1994), *cert. denied*, 515 U.S. 1141, 115 S.Ct. 2576, 132 L.Ed.2d 827 (1995); *Bennett v. United States*, 30 Fed.Cl. 396 (1994), *rev'd*, 60 F.3d 843 (Fed.Cir. 1995); *Rickel v. Commissioner*, 900 F.2d 655 (3d Cir.1990).

§ 4.30

1. Age Discrimination in Employment Act of 1967, § 7(d), 29 U.S.C.A. § 626(b) (1982), incorporates by reference the remedies authorized under the Fair Labor Standards Act (FLSA), 29 U.S.C.A. §§ 216–17 (1982). The liquidated damages authorized in turn by § 216(b) of FLSA are defined as an additional amount equal to the amount of unlawfully withheld unpaid minimum wages. The Supreme Court has held that liquidated damages are appropriate when an employer knows that, or recklessly disregards whether, its conduct violates the ADEA. *McLaughlin v. Richland Shoe Co.*, 486 U.S. 128, 108 S.Ct. 1677, 100 L.Ed.2d 115 (1988). See Chapter 7.3 for a discussion of ADEA remedies.

2. *Capparell v. National Health Mgmt., Inc.*, 1993 WL 516399 (E.D.Pa.1993). For more on the effects of the 1991 Act on ADEA, see Eglit, *The Age Discrimination In Employment Act, Title VII, And The Civil Rights Act of 1991: Three Acts And A Dog That Didn't Bark*, 39 Wayne L.Rev. 1093 (1993).

recover more. Long-tenured older workers typically receive far higher base compensation than most Title VII plaintiffs, and ADEA juries have been notoriously willing to deem the circumstances of an older worker's discharge "willful."

ADEA plaintiffs are even more likely to maintain their remedial edge with respect to smaller employers. The Title VII cap on the sum of compensatory damages (defined to include all monetary relief for future pecuniary and past and future nonpecuniary losses) and punitive damages is $100,000 where the employer has between 101 and 200 employees; $200,000 where the employer has between 201 and 500 employees; $300,000 for larger employers; but only $50,000 for the 98% of all businesses that employ 100 or fewer persons.[3] But the EEOC has taken the position that in Commission-initiated litigation on behalf of multiple plaintiffs, the caps limit only each aggrieved individual's relief, and not the relief available to the group. The Commission will thus seek relief up to the applicable cap on behalf of each aggrieved individual.[4]

Another surviving advantage for ADEA plaintiffs, at least textually, is the availability of jury trials in any kind of action where legal relief is sought, even where the plaintiff complains only of a facially neutral practice.[5] In reality, however, although the new Act in terms authorizes Title VII jury trials only for claims that authorize compensatory or punitive damages, which in turn means claims of intentional discrimination, most Title VII plaintiffs assert only such claims; they should therefore gain the advantages of jury trial to the same extent as their ADEA counterparts. In view of the Act's provisions easing the proof under Title VII of intentional discrimination in mixed-motive situations, and its incentives to assert intentional claims to obtain compensatory and punitive damages, most Title VII plaintiffs may be expected to assert at least one claim alleging discriminatory intent. Further, as discussed in Chapter 7, they are more likely to prevail in indirect evidence and mixed-motive cases than their ADEA counterparts. To the extent that facts found by the jury on the intent claim may be relevant to a separate neutral practice/adverse impact claim, the jury's findings on the intent claim should bind the trial court in reaching its determination about the neutral practice.[6] Moreover, since relatively few age discrimination

---

3. Section 102(b)(3). The 98% estimate comes from the Dole interpretive memorandum, supra § 3.35. The memorandum does not state if the 98% estimate includes the many employers too small to be covered by Title VII at all, i.e., those employing fewer than 15 employees during at least 20 calendar weeks in the current or preceding calendar year. Title VII § 701(b), 42 U.S.C.A. § 2000e(b).

4. *EEOC Policy Guide on Compensatory and Punitive Damages Under 1991 Civil Rights Act,* July 7, 1992; *EEOC General Counsel's Revised Litigation Guidance on the Civil Rights Act of 1991 and Related Matters,* March 1, 1993.

5. *Lowe v. Commack Union Free Sch. Dist.,* 886 F.2d 1364 (2d Cir.1989), *cert. denied,* 494 U.S. 1026, 110 S.Ct. 1470, 108 L.Ed.2d 608 (1990), is an example of a neutral practice case under ADEA. Whether the theory survives the Supreme Court's decision in *Hazen Paper Co. v. Biggins,* 507 U.S. 604, 113 S.Ct. 1701, 123 L.Ed.2d 338 (1993), is discussed in Chapter 7.

6. Where mixed legal and equitable claims are intertwined by common questions of fact, the Supreme Court has required that the legal claims be tried first to the jury. When the trial court thereafter determines the equitable claims, it will be

claims proceed on the neutral practice theory, and indeed there is a serious question after *Hazen Paper Co. v. Biggins* whether that theory continues to be viable under ADEA,[7] both Title VII and ADEA plaintiffs will in practice enjoy the right to demand a jury trial with respect to the vast majority of claims each asserts.

§§ 4.31–7.34 [Reserved]

E. RETROACTIVE SENIORITY FOR PROVEN VICTIMS OF DISCRIMINATION—A FIRST LOOK AT THE PROBLEM OF "REVERSE DISCRIMINATION"

§ 4.35 In General

More complex and controversial than the availability of back pay in Title VII actions are awards of retroactive "remedial" seniority to victorious discriminatees who secure orders directing their hire, promotion or reinstatement. These are awards of seniority that enhance the measure of employer-paid compensation or benefits. Because remedial seniority restores discriminatees to their "rightful place"—the rung on the ladder to which they likely would have climbed between the date of discrimination and date of judgment—and produces benefits that are paid by the adjudicated wrongdoer (the employer), it serves both Title VII remedial objectives, deterrence as well as compensation. Accordingly, in *Franks v. Bowman Transportation Co.*,[1] the Supreme Court held that retroactive remedial seniority for those economic purposes is presumptively available on the same terms as back pay. In doing so the Court rejected the argument that § 703(h)—which insulates bona fide seniority systems from being declared unlawful, and therefore protects them from *wholesale* dismantling by injunction—also prohibits the *incremental* adjustment of places on the seniority ladder that results when judges award discriminatees fictional, retroactive seniority as a remedy for an underlying discrimination in hiring, assignment or promotions.

On the other hand, retroactive seniority also serves an alternative or additional purpose: improving the discriminatee's position relative to other employees in competing for scarce job resources like better-paying positions, more favorable hours, or, most critically, protection against demotion or layoff. Unlike seniority for benefits purposes, retroactive "competitive" seniority furthers only the goal of compensation, not employer deterrence. In *Franks*, the Court recognized that such protec-

---

bound by the jury's explicit or implicit fact findings on the common questions. This order of trial preserves the seventh amendment rights of the party demanding jury trial on legal claims. See *Lytle v. Household Mfg. Inc.*, 494 U.S. 545, 110 S.Ct. 1331, 108 L.Ed.2d 504 (1990) (applying *Beacon Theatres, Inc. v. Westover*, 359 U.S. 500, 79 S.Ct. 948, 3 L.Ed.2d 988 (1959) to an action

presenting intertwined claims under Title VII and 42 U.S.C.A. § 1981).

7. See Chapter 7 on the neutral practice/disproportionate adverse impact theory, which is problematic under ADEA.

§ 4.35

1. 424 U.S. 747, 96 S.Ct. 1251, 47 L.Ed.2d 444 (1976).

tion is necessary to make a proven victim of discrimination whole; without it, she is vulnerable to layoff, termination or simply poorer job assignments without any of the seniority protection that she would almost surely have earned absent the employer's unlawful conduct.[2] It therefore held, following *Albemarle Paper Co. v. Moody*,[3] that the "competitive" as well as the "benefits" brand of retroactive fictional seniority is presumptively available.

A year later, in *International Brotherhood of Teamsters v. United States*,[4] the Court also agreed that an award of retroactive seniority, because it is essential to redress proven discrimination, is also not a "preference" prohibited by § 703(j).[5] But there, in contrast to the situation in *Franks*, immediate implementation of retroactive seniority for competitive purposes would have visited highly visible harm on incumbent employees already out on layoff: restoring the discriminatees to "their" rung on the seniority ladder would have delayed the incumbents' day of recall. On those facts the Court drew back from authorizing the automatic or immediate implementation of retroactive seniority for competitive purposes. Rather, to decide "when" and "the rate at which" discriminatees may be made whole by such awards, it directed the district courts to exercise their "qualities of mercy and practicality"[6] in balancing several unweighted equities. These include the number of protected group and non-protected group persons interested in the scarce resource, the number of current vacancies, and the economic prospects of the industry.[7] *Teamsters* left undisturbed the *Franks* holding that seniority for benefits purposes should be implemented presumptively, unequivocally and immediately after issuance of a judgment.

Although the Supreme Court has implied that § 706(g) provides limited discretion to "bump" an incumbent employee in order to reinstate a proven victim or "discriminatee," lower courts have displayed great reluctance to do so,[8] even when the order protects the displaced employee's former level of compensation.[9] They have instead sometimes awarded the discriminatee "front pay," discussed in § 4.25, *supra*.

§§ 4.36–7.39 [Reserved]

2. *Franks v. Bowman Transp. Co.*, 424 U.S. 747, 96 S.Ct. 1251, 47 L.Ed.2d 444 (1976).

3. 422 U.S. 405, 95 S.Ct. 2362, 45 L.Ed.2d 280 (1975). See text § 4.25, *supra*.

4. 431 U.S. 324, 97 S.Ct. 1843, 52 L.Ed.2d 396 (1977).

5. *Teamsters*, 431 U.S. at 375 n.61, 97 S.Ct. at 1975 n.61.

6. *Teamsters*, 431 U.S. at 375, 97 S.Ct. at 1875 (quoting *Hecht Co. v. Bowles*, 321 U.S. 321, 329–330, 64 S.Ct. 587, 591–592, 88 L.Ed. 754 (1944)).

7. *Teamsters; see also Franks*, 424 U.S. 747, 96 S.Ct. 1251, 47 L.Ed.2d 444 (Powell, J., concurring).

8. *See, e.g., Walsdorf v. Board of Comm'rs*, 857 F.2d 1047 (5th Cir.1988); *Harper v. General Grocers Co.*, 590 F.2d 713 (8th Cir.1979).

9. *Patterson v. American Tobacco Co.*, 535 F.2d 257 (4th Cir.), *cert. denied*, 429 U.S. 920, 97 S.Ct. 314, 50 L.Ed.2d 286 (1976).

F. AFFIRMATIVE ACTION BY "VOLUNTARY" PROGRAMS AND JUDICIAL DECREES

§ 4.40 In General

"Voluntary," "benign" employer affirmative action, and reverse discriminatory remedies imposed by court order or consent decree, raise similar yet legally distinct questions of fairness as between minority and majority group employees. Strictly speaking, employer affirmative action in the form of self-imposed quotas or goals does not really implicate the judiciary's remedial authority under § 706(g) at all. An employer simply institutes racial or gender preferences, without court compulsion, typically to avoid lawsuits by the group benefitting from the preference or to preserve federal contracts that require affirmative action.[1] Rather, such a plan is unlawful, if at all, because it operates to prefer members of defined minority or female groups or classes, rather than individuals proven to have suffered discrimination at the hands of the defendant employer. As a result, these preferences are suspect under § 703 as ordinary unlawful employment practices directed against any majority group members or males who are denied employment opportunities by the plan.[2] The jeopardy would seem considerable because the Court has regularly emphasized that the statute seeks to protect individuals from discrimination on the basis of group characteristics, rather than groups as such.[3]

But the Supreme Court, in a landmark 1979 opinion, *United Steelworkers of America v. Weber*,[4] that expressly elevated a supposed legislative "spirit" over statutory text, gave qualified approval to "voluntary," "benign" racial preferences. A majority held that the employer there had lawfully taken race into account in preferring black employees as a group for admission to an on-the-job training program—a preference that on its face violated the specific terms of § 703(d). The Court acknowledged that the white race of Brian Weber was the factor that resulted in his denial of the employment benefit, in apparent violation of that section. But it concluded from the spirit animating Title VII's enactment that Congress would not have intended § 703 to apply in the context of the

---

§ 4.40

1. Thus challenges by white or male plaintiffs to voluntary affirmative action plans have been distinguished from reverse discrimination claims based on the employer's implementation of an agreement settling charges of discrimination already pending before EEOC or in court. In the latter setting, employers almost always prevail with the argument that a settlement in good faith of a charge of discrimination is a legitimate, nondiscriminatory reason for the hiring or promotion decision under challenge. *See Marcantel v. State of La., Dep't of Transp.*, 37 F.3d 197 (5th Cir. 1994), discussed in Chapter 2, above.

2. *See, e.g., Billish v. City of Chicago*, 962 F.2d 1269 (7th Cir.1992), *cert. denied*, 510 U.S. 908, 114 S.Ct. 290, 126 L.Ed.2d 240 (1993); *Baker v. Elmwood Distrib. Inc.*,

940 F.2d 1013 (7th Cir.1991); *United States v. City of Chicago*, 870 F.2d 1256 (7th Cir. 1989). But in an individual disparate treatment case not brought on behalf of a class, it is the plaintiff's burden to show how the defendant used or applied the plan to adversely affect his terms or conditions of employment. Absent such use, the plan's mere existence does not constitute evidence of unlawful discrimination. *Whalen v. Rubin*, 91 F.3d 1041 (7th Cir.1996).

3. *See, e.g., Connecticut v. Teal*, 457 U.S. 440, 455, 102 S.Ct. 2525, 2535, 73 L.Ed.2d 130 (1982); *City of Los Angeles Dep't of Water & Power v. Manhart*, 435 U.S. 702, 710, 98 S.Ct. 1370, 1376, 55 L.Ed.2d 657 (1978).

4. 443 U.S. 193, 99 S.Ct. 2721, 61 L.Ed.2d 480 (1979).

"benign" program at issue. The Court relied instead on a weak negative pregnant from § 703(j), which provides that nothing in Title VII shall "require" employers with work forces racially imbalanced vis-a-vis surrounding local population percentages to grant minorities preferential treatment in order to redress such imbalances. Section 703(j), however, was not at all on point, for Brian Weber was certainly not arguing that the defendants were required to discriminate against him. Rather, he was claiming that § 703(d)—so directly implicated by the training program opportunity in question that, as the dissent observed, it might have been written with him in mind—plainly prohibited that discrimination.

Further, it appeared from the *Weber* opinion that an employer could justifiably adopt race-conscious programs of this type whenever it found a manifest underrepresentation of blacks in a traditionally segregated job category; the employer need not first uncover evidence of its *own* prior discrimination in filling those positions.[5] Finally, the employer plan in *Weber* was approved despite being arguably involuntary: the plan was adopted after the Office of Federal Contract Compliance Programs had threatened the employer with debarment from federal contracts under Executive Order 11246 if it did not increase its skilled minority representation.[6]

---

5. The Court confirmed this reading of *Weber* in *Johnson v. Transportation Agency*, 480 U.S. 616, 633 n. 10, 107 S.Ct. 1442, 1453 n. 10, 94 L.Ed.2d 615 (1987). A recent circuit decision extends the Supreme Court's *Johnson* rationale by permitting ad hoc gender discrimination against males in the assignment of shifts at a state prison, even absent any formal affirmative action plan. The court reasoned that it could employ the limiting factors of *Weber* and *Johnson* instead of finding the gender discrimination per se unlawful because the discriminating assignments favored women, whom it deemed a specially protected Title VII class. It concluded that the "minimal restriction" on male employment opportunities was justified by legitimate penological and privacy concerns furthered by the gender based assignment policy. *Tharp v. Iowa Dep't of Corr.*, 68 F.3d 223 (8th Cir. 1995), *cert. denied*, 517 U.S. 1135, 116 S.Ct. 1420, 134 L.Ed.2d 545 (1996). In effect this approach permits an employer to defend express discrimination without having to establish a BFOQ. *But see Smith v. Virginia Commonwealth Univ.*, 84 F.3d 672 (4th Cir.1996) (en banc) (female-preferential salary increases informally instituted in response to salary equity study not necessarily a defense to Title VII and Equal Pay Act reverse discrimination claims by male employees).

6. Executive Order 11246 prohibits race, color, religion, sex or national origin discrimination by federal contractors holding contracts exceeding $50,000. It contains no statute of limitations and a district court rejected a statute of limitations defense when the administrative proceeding was instituted six years after the unlawful conduct. *See Lawrence Aviation Indus., Inc. v. Reich*, 28 F.Supp.2d 728, 737 (E.D.N.Y. 1998), *aff'd in relevant part*, 182 F.3d 900 (2d Cir.1999), *cert. denied*, ___ U.S. ___, 120 S.Ct. 1157, 145 L.Ed.2d 1069 (2000). It also requires them to conduct "utilization analyses" of minorities in its workforce to determine if they are underrepresented in relation to the relevant potential pool of minority applicants holding at least minimal qualifications for particular jobs. The Order, which is administered by the Department of Labor's Office of Federal Contract Compliance Programs ("OFCCP"), also requires the contractor to take "affirmative action" in hiring and promotion to correct any perceived utilization deficiencies.

OFCCP's chief enforcement weapon is the ultimate threat of debarment from future contracts, but in practice it usually threatens or imposes a number of lesser measures even when debarment is proposed.

An April 12, 1999 Memorandum of Understanding between EEOC and OFCCP, delegates to OFCCP, as EEOC's "agent," authority to process and resolve the Title VII component of charges that include vio-

Perhaps to ease its misgivings about approving a form of race discrimination that the text of § 703(d) expressly prohibited, the *Weber* majority listed a number of sanitizing factors to circumscribe the scope of lawful "benign" discrimination. It observed that the employer plan before it did not require white employees to be discharged and therefore did not "unnecessarily trammel" their interests; that it did not absolutely bar white employees from the skilled positions, but merely limited their numbers; and that it was a temporary measure, intended not to maintain a racial balance but to eliminate a manifest imbalance in the skilled job categories. The Court satisfied itself on these points again in *Johnson v. Transportation Agency of Santa Clara County*,[7] when it extended the *Weber* principle by upholding an explicit *gender* preference for *promotions*, this time in the face of the apparently plain prohibition of § 703(a). But it has been held that where race is used as a tie-breaker to choose which employee will be subject to *layoff,* the minority preference plan violates Title VII because it is "overly intrusive to the rights of nonminorities."[8] In the cited highly-publicized reverse-discrimination case, a public school system's desire for racial diversity among its faculty as a whole was held not adequate to justify such a severe harm to a nonminority employee who worked in a department where there was no demonstrated minority underrepresentation. The appellate court so ruled even on the assumption that Title VII permits more race-conscious preferential treatment than does the Supreme Court's current race-neutral concept of equal protection.[9] Moreover, even when the sting of an affirmative action program is felt only by an applicant for employment—that is, affects initial hire rather than promotion, layoff, or discharge—a program that absolutely excludes members of one race violates Title VII.[10]

More forthrightly in *Johnson* than in *Weber,* Justice Brennan for the majority acknowledged that the employer need not itself have firm or indeed any evidence of its own prior discrimination against the group that benefits from the program. Instead, it is a sufficient predicate for instituting a race-or gender-based affirmative action program that the beneficiary group is merely underrepresented in a traditionally segregated job category for any reason—societal prejudice, self selection, discrimination by other businesses or unions. Further, "underrepresentation"

---

lations of Title VII as well as E.O. 11246. The delegation includes the authority to seek monetary damages to resolve Title VII allegations against federal contractors.

7. 480 U.S. 616, 107 S.Ct. 1442, 94 L.Ed.2d 615 (1987).

8. *United States v. Board of Educ. of Piscataway,* 832 F.Supp. 836, 850 (D.N.J. 1993), *aff'd, Taxman v. Piscataway Township Bd. of Ed.,* 91 F.3d 1547 (3d Cir.1996) (en banc).

9. *Id.* The Justice Department brought suit, during the Bush Administration, in the name of the United States on behalf of the plaintiff, a white teacher. During the

Clinton Administration it sought to advocate the position of the defendant school board, but was halted in that effort by the Third Circuit Court of Appeals. It then, at the Supreme Court's request, filed an amicus brief which argued that affirmative action measures in education could generally be justified solely on a rationale of "diversity," but which also unsuccessfully urged the Court to deny review of the Third Circuit's decision on behalf of the plaintiff.

10. That is the position advanced by the Department of Justice in *United States v. Board of Trustees of Illinois State Univ.,* 944 F.Supp. 714 (C.D.Ill.1996).

may be measured in relation to that group's representation in the surrounding labor market, unrefined for interest[11] or qualifications.[12] And the Court even dispensed with the necessity of a specific end date for the program because no specific number of slots were set aside for members of the beneficiary group. But race-conscious affirmative action under *Johnson* must not use race or gender as a dispositive factor, must be narrowly tailored to the discrimination it purports to remedy, and must have the purpose of remedying the effects of past discrimination against a group that was in fact the victim of unlawful discrimination.[13]

Affirmative action plans have fared less well when challenged as violations of equal protection. For example, the Court concluded in *Wygant v. Jackson Board of Education*[14] that a public employer, before instituting such a program, must have "convincing evidence" of its own prior discrimination and must employ means narrowly tailored to rectify that conduct. The collective bargaining agreement in *Wygant* required the layoff of non-minority teachers with greater seniority than minority teachers who were retained, a feature that might also have offended the *Weber* sanitizing factor of "unnecessary trammeling." In any event, the *Wygant* plurality's broader approach commanded a majority of the Court in *City of Richmond v. J.A. Croson Co.*,[15] where the Court struck down a municipal program to set aside a minimum amount of subcontracting work for minority business enterprises. The Court insisted that the Equal Protection Clause is violated whenever government takes race into account unless (1) it has a compelling justification and (2) the means adopted are narrowly tailored to go only so far as that justification requires. *Croson*, then, supplies the framework for evaluating the constitutionality of a current plan.[16] A circuit court, taking note of the first of the *Croson* requirements, has observed that a local government will now be hard pressed to justify a race-based set-aside program unless it can offer current statistical evidence demonstrating its own prior discriminatory practices and their ongoing effects.[17] A common circuit reformulation of those requirements takes into account four factors: (1) the necessity for the relief and efficacy of alternative means; (2) the flexibili-

11. *See EEOC v. Sears, Roebuck & Co.*, 839 F.2d 302 (7th Cir.1988).

12. *See Hazelwood Sch. Dist. v. United States*, 433 U.S. 299, 97 S.Ct. 2736, 53 L.Ed.2d 768 (1977).

13. *See Schurr v. Resorts Int'l Hotel, Inc.*, 196 F.3d 486 (3d Cir.1999) (plaintiff's failure to hire claim successful where plan lacked remedial purpose and was not based on any historic or current discrimination); *Hill v. Ross*, 183 F.3d 586 (7th Cir.1999) (sex played a larger role than *Johnson* permitted and goal that each department mirror gender composition of those with minimum qualifications not narrowly tailored to any past sex discrimination); *Cunico v. Pueblo Sch. Dist. No. 60*, 917 F.2d 431, 437 (10th Cir.1990) (group benefitted not discriminated against in past).

14. 476 U.S. 267, 106 S.Ct. 1842, 90 L.Ed.2d 260 (1986).

15. 488 U.S. 469, 109 S.Ct. 706, 102 L.Ed.2d 854 (1989).

16. *See Thigpen v. Bibb County*, 223 F.3d 1231, 2000 WL 1277600, at *6–8 (11th Cir.2000); *Engineering Contractors Ass'n of S. Fla., Inc. v. Metropolitan Dade County*, 122 F.3d 895, 906 (11th Cir.1997), *cert. denied*, 523 U.S. 1004, 118 S.Ct. 1186, 140 L.Ed.2d 317 (1998) (evaluating programs that created preferences based on race and ethnicity pursuant to *Croson*).

17. *Associated Gen. Contractors of Conn., Inc. v. New Haven, Conn.*, 41 F.3d 62 (2d Cir.1994).

ty and duration of the relief; (3) the the fit between the plan's numerical goals and the relevant labor market; and (4) the degree to which the relief adversely affects third parties, e.g., nonminority employees or applicants.[18] Under these strict standards, most such equal protection challenges to current plans have succeeded.[19]

18. *Black Fire Fighters Ass'n of Dallas v. City of Dallas*, 19 F.3d 992 (5th Cir.1994) (citing plurality opinion in *United States v. Paradise*, 480 U.S. 149, 107 S.Ct. 1053, 94 L.Ed.2d 203 (1987)).

19. *See Dallas Fire Fighters Ass'n v. City of Dallas, Tx.*, 150 F.3d 438, 440 (5th Cir.1998), *cert. denied*, 526 U.S. 1038, 119 S.Ct. 1333, 143 L.Ed.2d 498 (1999) (invalidating promotions of black, Hispanic and female firefighters before nonminority firefighters who had higher scores on validated promotion examinations, made pursuant to plan adopted by city council after U.S. Department of Justice finding that city had engaged in practices inconsistent with Title VII and that minorities were underrepresented in firefighter workforce, for lack of "proof of a history of egregious and pervasive discrimination or resistance to affirmative action that has warranted more serious measures in other cases"; in any event, the city failed to show that the principal alternative measure employed, the use of validated promotion examinations, had been ineffective merely because it did not advance minorities "as quickly" as out-of-rank promotions); *Engineering Contractors Ass'n of S. Fla., Inc. v. Metropolitan Dade County*, 122 F.3d 895 (11th Cir. 1997), *cert. denied*, 523 U.S. 1004, 118 S.Ct. 1186, 140 L.Ed.2d 317 (1998) (a government cannot as a matter of law establish that a racial preference program is narrowly tailored where it has not made a serious good faith effort to use race neutral means); *Alexander v. Estepp*, 95 F.3d 312 (4th Cir.1996), *cert. denied sub nom. Prince George's Co. v. Alexander*, 520 U.S. 1165, 117 S.Ct. 1425, 137 L.Ed.2d 535 (1997) (striking down county's affirmative action program that set caps on the number of white, male firefighters to be hired because less drastic means were available to counteract alleged prior discriminatory attitudes and because plan benefitted other minorities not shown to have been discriminated against at all); *Middleton v. City of Flint, Mich.*, 92 F.3d 396 (6th Cir.1996), *cert. denied*, 520 U.S. 1196, 117 S.Ct. 1552, 137 L.Ed.2d 700 (1997) (voluntary plan reserving half of all police promotions for the position of sergeant to minority group members unlawful because geared to black population of city's general labor force rather than previously hired, lower-ranking officers, and in any event because not

narrowly tailored to any accurately assessed discrimination); *Associated Gen. Contractors of Conn., Inc. v. New Haven, Conn.*, 41 F.3d 62 (2d Cir.1994); *Black Fire Fighters Ass'n of Dallas v. City of Dallas*, 19 F.3d 992 (5th Cir.1994) (striking down race-conscious promotion plan as overinclusively benefitting black nonvictims of discrimination). *But see Majeske v. City of Chicago*, 218 F.3d 816 (7th Cir.2000) (ten year old affirmative action plan that admittedly promoted African–American and Hispanic police officers over white officers was remedial in purpose and narrowly tailored to meet that purpose); *Boston Police Superior Officers Fed'n v. City of Boston*, 147 F.3d 13 (1st Cir.1998) (one-time promotion of minority officer just slightly out of rank order on promotion test held narrowly tailored and justified by long history of discrimination not fully remedied by implementation of 1972 consent decree); *McNamara v. City of Chicago*, 138 F.3d 1219 (7th Cir.), *cert. denied*, 525 U.S. 981, 119 S.Ct. 444, 142 L.Ed.2d 398 (1998) (upholding Chicago's affirmative action plan for promoting firefighters where evidence plan was narrowly tailored to remedy history of past discrimination); *Wittmer v. Peters*, 87 F.3d 916 (7th Cir.1996), *cert. denied*, 519 U.S. 1111, 117 S.Ct. 949, 136 L.Ed.2d 837 (1997) (upholding "role model" theory as adequate constitutional justification for preferring African–American correctional officers for promotion based on expert testimony that African–American lieutenants were "needed because the black inmates are believed unlikely to play the correctional game of brutal drill sergeant and brutalized recruit unless there are some blacks in authority" in quasimilitary "boot camp" setting); *Peightal v. Metropolitan Dade County*, 26 F.3d 1545 (11th Cir.1994), *cert. denied*, 502 U.S. 1073, 112 S.Ct. 969, 117 L.Ed.2d 134 (1992) (plan narrowly tailored to EEOC definition of "Hispanic" and to past discrimination against that group).

On the issue of qualified immunity for officials acting pursuant to an affirmative action plan, see *Moniz v. City of Fort Lauderdale*, 145 F.3d 1278, 1282–83 (11th Cir. 1998) (individual local officials implementing the requirements of a federal court consent decree entitled to qualified immunity

In public contracting and employment settings, it is not a sufficiently compelling justification for the government to offer a purportedly "benign" preference designed to redress general societal or historical discrimination against African–Americans; in general, race has been accepted as a lawful factor in doling out benefits only to redress the governmental unit's own prior discrimination, and only as long as and to the extent necessary to remedy the discriminatory injury the government inflicted.[20] No formal, judicial determination of past discrimination by the governmental unit in question is necessary to show the requisite compelling governmental interest.[21] But the evidence of such discrimination must be "strong" or "convincing."[22] For this purpose the defendant resisting a reverse-discrimination action may use reliable statistical evidence of the kind that establishes a prima facie case of systemic disparate treatment under Title VII—evidence reflecting a gross disparity between, on one hand, the percentage of protected group members one would "expect" to see selected based on their percentage representation in a qualified labor pool, and, on the other, the actual percentage of

where constitutionality of its requirements had not been challenged in court); *Wolfe v. City of Pittsburgh*, 140 F.3d 236, 240 (3d Cir.1998) (individual local officials implementing the requirements of a federal court-ordered affirmative action plan entitled to both qualified and absolute immunity where constitutionality had not been challenged in court); *Erwin v. Daley*, 92 F.3d 521 (7th Cir.1996), *cert. denied*, 519 U.S. 1116, 117 S.Ct. 958, 136 L.Ed.2d 845 (1997) (local officials granted qualified immunity for reverse-discriminatory employment decisions exceeding scope of court-ordered affirmative action plan because constitutional principles suggesting the unlawfulness of their actions were too confusing and recent for the defendants to be expected to have conformed to them); *Wilson v. Bailey*, 934 F.2d 301, 304 (11th Cir. 1991) (personnel board members acting pursuant to federal court consent decree in making race-conscious employment decisions eligible for qualified immunity. *But cf. Maitland v. University of Minnesota*, 155 F.3d 1013, 1019 (8th Cir.1998) (in case where plaintiff challenged lawfulness of consent decree ordering preference for female academic employees in salaries, university officials denied qualified immunity for agreeing to and implementing that plan because it was not objectively reasonable under established law for them to agree to plan given uncertainty whether there had been a conspicuous prior gender-based salary imbalance favoring men that would justify the decree's female preference).

In contrast, the Eleventh Circuit's doctrine in the *Birmingham* cases deals not with an individual's qualified immunity, but rather with a government entity's liability when it blindly implements unconstitutional consent decrees. In *In re Birmingham Reverse Discrimination Employment Litig.*, 20 F.3d 1525 (11th Cir.1994), *cert. denied sub nom. Arrington v. Wilks*, 514 U.S. 1065, 115 S.Ct. 1695, 131 L.Ed.2d 558 (1995), the court found that the city itself could not be sheltered from liability because of the evolvement of the law. The court thus charged the city with the duty, at least implicitly, to recognize that an earlier decree may become unconstitutional and to take the steps necessary—including suing to dissolve the decree—when the unlawfulness of the decree becomes apparent.

20. *See, e.g.,* the dicta to that effect in *City of Richmond v. J.A. Croson*, 488 U.S. at 493, 109 S.Ct. at 721 (plurality opinion) (government contracting); *cf. Hopwood v. Texas*, 78 F.3d 932, 944 (5th Cir.), *cert. denied*, 518 U.S. 1033, 116 S.Ct. 2581, 135 L.Ed.2d 1095 (1996) (law school admissions).

21. *See Croson*, 488 U.S. 469, 109 S.Ct. 706, 102 L.Ed.2d 854; *Brunet v. City of Columbus*, 1 F.3d 390, 406 (6th Cir.1993), *cert. denied sub nom. Brunet v. Tucker*, 510 U.S. 1164, 114 S.Ct. 1190, 127 L.Ed.2d 540 (1994) (holding, however, that plaintiff challengers of gender-preference program rebutted an inference of past discrimination, thereby destroying the predicate for preference, by tracing the statistical underrepresentation of women firefighters to a lawful, job-related test).

22. *United Black Firefighters Ass'n v. City of Akron*, 976 F.2d 999 (6th Cir.1992) (relying on *Croson*).

those persons selected.[23] For example, one circuit court has held that the litigant defending governmental contract set asides must demonstrate a strong evidentiary basis of discrimination. Where a disparity in percentage of contracting dollars awarded to minority businesses can be explained by evidence that these businesses are smaller and are thus awarded smaller contracts, the set asides program will be found to violate equal protection.[24] On the other hand, racial preference provisions not justified by sufficient evidence of such underrepresentation as is required to show a remedial necessity for the preference, or not narrowly tailored to that underrepresentation, may be no better able to survive equal protection strict scrutiny merely because they are court-ordered as part of a consent decree settling litigation.[25]

There nevertheless lingers even after these decisions authority for the proposition that in the context of public education racial diversity of the student body is a compelling governmental interest distinct from any government interest in providing a remedy for its own prior discrimination.[26] In a closely watched reverse discrimination challenge to features of the University of Texas Law School's admissions process that gave preferential consideration to racial and ethnic minorities, the Fifth Circuit has squarely rejected that proposition. The law school used an "index" that represented a weighted composite of the undergraduate grade point averages and law school aptitude scores of its applicants. Race or ethnic status functioned as a "plus" factor in admissions because the school maintained separate presumptive index levels for minorities and whites such that some minority candidates would almost certainly be admitted with indices considerably lower than the indices of white candidates who would almost certainly be rejected. Even within a nonpresumptive, discretionary selection range, the files of minority ap-

23. *Id.* at 1011. *See also Majeske v. City of Chicago*, 218 F.3d 816 (7th Cir.2000) (city produced persuasive statistical evidence that past discrimination in the hiring and promotion of African–American and Hispanic police officers reduced the number of black and Hispanic detectives on the police force).

24. *See Engineering Contractors Ass'n of S. Fla., Inc. v. Metropolitan Dade County*, 122 F.3d 895 (11th Cir.1997), *cert. denied*, 523 U.S. 1004, 118 S.Ct. 1186, 140 L.Ed.2d 317 (1998).

25. *Dallas Fire Fighters Ass'n v. Dallas*, 150 F.3d 438 (5th Cir.1998), *cert. denied*, 526 U.S. 1038, 119 S.Ct. 1333, 143 L.Ed.2d 498 (1999) (striking down city fire department's affirmative action plan as violative of, inter alia, equal protection where the only evidence of racial discrimination was a 1976 consent decree that rested on a finding of a Title VII violation and an analysis that showed minorities underrepresented in higher ranks); *In re Birmingham Reverse*

Discrimination Employment Litig., 833 F.2d 1492, 1501 (11th Cir.1987), *aff'd sub nom. Martin v. Wilks*, 490 U.S. 755, 109 S.Ct. 2180, 104 L.Ed.2d 835 (1989); *In re Birmingham Reverse Discrimination Employment Litig.*, 20 F.3d 1525, 1534 (11th Cir. 1994), *cert. denied sub nom. Arrington v. Wilks*, 514 U.S. 1065, 115 S.Ct. 1695, 131 L.Ed.2d 558 (1995). *Cf. Wolfe v. City of Pittsburgh*, 140 F.3d 236 (3d Cir.1998) (§ 1983 relief unavailable to white officers denied promotions by public officials acting pursuant to court order that imposed race preferences, reasoning that public officials enjoy absolute § 1983 immunity from liability for any damages caused by their compliance with a facially valid court order).

26. *Regents of Univ. of Cal. v. Bakke*, 438 U.S. 265, 98 S.Ct. 2733, 57 L.Ed.2d 750 (1978) (plurality opinion by Powell, J.); *Smith v. University of Washington* (D.Wash. 1999) (law school affirmative action admissions program may be lawful if narrowly tailored to genuine educational goal of diversity).

plicants were separately and in practice preferentially reviewed by a minority subcommittee whose decisions were "virtually final." And as a consequence of segregated waiting lists, even minority applicants not initially admitted received preferential treatment.

Unsuccessful white applicants challenged this scheme principally as a violation of equal protection, as well as of Title VI. Relying heavily on recent Supreme Court authority surveyed elsewhere in this section that subjects all governmental racial classifications, whether or not characterized as "benign," to strict scrutiny, the Fifth Circuit ruled these preferential features unconstitutional. It noted at the outset that in *Wygant* the Supreme Court had already rejected as "compelling" justifications the goals of counteracting "societal" discrimination and of increasing minority role models. It then rejected the view advanced by Justice Powell in *Bakke* that attaining a diverse student body is a sufficiently important goal in the context of higher education to warrant the use of race—either per se or as a proxy for other constitutional factors like cultural, economic or educational disadvantage—as one of several factors that a state-run professional school may permissibly consider. The problem for the Fifth Circuit was that even if the reliance on race is restricted to the margins, race is then the factor that ultimately may tip the scales among minimally qualified applicants.

Instead, the Fifth Circuit viewed the residue of modern equal protection jurisprudence as recognizing only one state interest sufficiently compelling to justify even narrowly tailored race-preferential programs: remedying the current effects of past racial discrimination practiced by the particular governmental unit defendant that is taking race into account. Texas' law school, in other words, could not defend on the basis of even strong evidence of past racial discrimination in Texas public education as a whole, or even in Texas higher education; it could rely only on as yet unremedied discrimination against the minority group members benefitted by the plan and recently practiced by the law school itself. The record did not support such a finding in the view of the Fifth Circuit, still less that the Law School's several admissions preferences were "narrowly tailored" to redress only any lingering effects of its own recent prior discrimination against the preferentially treated groups. In particular, the court declined to recognize the school's awareness of its prior history of race discrimination or its still subsisting reputation for discrimination among members of the beneficiary groups as the kind of continuing effects of past discrimination that are constitutionally remediable through race-conscious means.[27]

Unlike "voluntary" affirmative action, judgments directing preferential treatment for a minority or gender group, issued after litigated findings of discrimination or upon the parties' consent, squarely test the

27. *Hopwood v. Texas*, 78 F.3d 932 (5th Cir.), *cert. denied*, 518 U.S. 1033, 116 S.Ct. 2581, 135 L.Ed.2d 1095 (1996). Another circuit, using similar rationales, has struck down a state university's race-based schol- arship program. *Podberesky v. Kirwan*, 46 F.3d 5 (4th Cir.1994), *cert. denied*, 514 U.S. 1128, 115 S.Ct. 2001, 131 L.Ed.2d 1002 (1995).

limits of a court's remedial authority under § 706(g) to "order such affirmative action as may be appropriate." In the case of public employers, these judgments may also deny the disfavored racial or gender groups equal protection. The justices have been deeply divided over the equitable propriety under § 706(g) of consent judgments that afford relief to minority group members who are not themselves proven victims of discrimination. The degree of "trammelling" appears important. An opinion that in dictum declared such relief beyond a court's authority concerned a consent judgment modification that would have required more senior non-minority firefighters to be laid off before their more junior minority counterparts.[28] Yet the Court subsequently upheld a district judge's authority to approve a consent judgment that established firefighters' promotion quotas but did not compel layoffs or terminations.[29]

Although formal, judicial findings of past discrimination are not indispensable to the approval of group-based remedies, the Supreme Court has more often upheld programs that were judicially ordered after litigated findings of persistent, egregious discrimination.[30] One judgment, for example, would have absolutely excluded certain whites from union membership, in turn precluding their employment. But the goal was upheld in part because there was evidence of long-standing intentional discrimination and contumacious defiance of prior judicial orders.[31] Moreover, as the Supreme Court had stressed in *Wygant,* the burdens of a hiring goal are "diffused to a considerable extent among society generally" and do not "impose the same kind of injury" as layoffs or even promotions. It remains unclear, however, just *why* the animus or stubborn litigiousness of an employer or union justifies a race-based remedy the burden of which is felt principally not by the adjudicated wrongdoer but by an applicant for employment or union membership, even if it "only" costs the remedy's victim a chance at employment or a promotion rather than an existing job.

The strict scrutiny approach to "benign" racial preferences reflected in the Supreme Court's recent equal protection decisions,[32] notably *Wygant* and *Croson,* has since been applied to employment discrimination consent decrees involving government employers.[33] And circuit

---

28. *Firefighters Local Union No. 1784 v. Stotts,* 467 U.S. 561, 104 S.Ct. 2576, 81 L.Ed.2d 483 (1984).

29. *Local No. 93, Int'l Ass'n of Firefighters v. City of Cleveland,* 478 U.S. 501, 106 S.Ct. 3063, 92 L.Ed.2d 405 (1986). *Cf. United States v. City of Hialeah,* 140 F.3d 968 (11th Cir.1998) (affirming district court refusal to approve consent decree that adversely affected seniority rights of objecting intervenors; dissent argues that consenting parties may demonstrate necessity of relief at hearing or trial). *But see In re Birmingham Reverse Discrimination Employment Litig.,* 20 F.3d 1525 (11th Cir.1994), *cert. denied sub nom. Arrington v. Wilks,* 514

U.S. 1065, 115 S.Ct. 1695, 131 L.Ed.2d 558 (1995).

30. *Local 28, Sheet Metal Workers' Int'l Ass'n v. EEOC,* 478 U.S. 421, 106 S.Ct. 3019, 92 L.Ed.2d 344 (1986) (membership goal for defendant union); *United States v. Paradise,* 480 U.S. 149, 107 S.Ct. 1053, 94 L.Ed.2d 203 (1987) (quota promotion plan).

31. *Local 28, Sheet Metal Workers' Int'l Ass'n v. EEOC,* 478 U.S. 421, 106 S.Ct. 3019, 92 L.Ed.2d 344.

32. See text *supra,* this section.

33. *See, e.g., Aiken v. City of Memphis,* 37 F.3d 1155 (6th Cir.1994); *United Black*

decisions have held that a preference enjoys no greater protection because it is embodied in a judicial decree than when it is part of an employer's "voluntary" affirmative action plan.[34] It is therefore quite likely, if not logically compelled,[35] that an affirmative action plan or consent decree affecting a state or local government employer[36] may pass

Firefighters Ass'n v. City of Akron, 976 F.2d 999 (6th Cir.1992).

34. *See, e.g., Engineering Contractors Ass'n of S. Fla., Inc. v. Metropolitan Dade County*, 122 F.3d 895 (11th Cir.1997), *cert. denied*, 523 U.S. 1004, 118 S.Ct. 1186, 140 L.Ed.2d 317 (1998) (finding no reason to treat a consent decree entered into pursuant to a voluntary settlement differently from a voluntary affirmative action plan); *United Black Firefighters Ass'n v. Akron*, 976 F.2d 999, 1008 (6th Cir.1992) (citing *Croson*); *In re Birmingham Reverse Discrimination Employment Litig.*, 833 F.2d 1492, 1501 (11th Cir.1987), *aff'd sub nom. Martin v. Wilks*, 490 U.S. 755, 109 S.Ct. 2180, 104 L.Ed.2d 835 (1989).

35. See text *infra.*

36. The Court upheld a *federal* contracting minority set-aside program similar in relevant respects to the one struck down in *Croson* in reliance on Congress' special enforcement powers under § 5 of the 14th Amendment. *Fullilove v. Klutznick*, 448 U.S. 448, 100 S.Ct. 2758, 65 L.Ed.2d 902 (1980). Expanding on the *Fullilove* doctrine, the Court in *Metro Broadcasting, Inc. v. F.C.C.*, 497 U.S. 547, 110 S.Ct. 2997, 111 L.Ed.2d 445 (1990), held that "benign, race-conscious measures mandated by Congress" do not violate the constitution so long as they are substantially related to important governmental objectives, even though they do not seek to remedy prior discrimination. There the "important governmental objective" was to enhance broadcast programming diversity. *Adarand Constructors, Inc. v. Pena*, 515 U.S. 200, 115 S.Ct. 2097, 132 L.Ed.2d 158 (1995) affords the four dissenting justices in *Metro Broadcasting* an opportunity to overturn *Fullilove* by insisting that congressional preference programs meet the same "strict scrutiny" equal protection standards that the Court imposes on state and local governments under *Croson*. The program at issue in *Adarand* provides prime contracts in federal highway construction projects bonuses if they award subcontracts to "disadvantaged business enterprises." Implementing regulations establish a presumption "that socially and economically disadvantaged individuals include" a number of designated racial and ethnic minorities.

The Court has since decided *Adarand*, holding that "all racial classifications, im-

posed by whatever federal, state, or local governmental actor, must be analyzed ... under strict scrutiny." Any such classification must therefore be "narrowly tailored" or "necessary" to "further compelling governmental interests." The opinion endorses the *Wygant* conclusion that the level of equal protection scrutiny of a racial classification does not change just because it operates to disadvantage a group that historically has not been the target of government discrimination; and it specifically rejects the *Metro Broadcasting* conclusion that racial classifications adopted for ostensibly "benign" purposes by the *federal* government need only satisfy "intermediate" scrutiny—that is, need only "substantially" relate to "important" governmental objectives. Even *Fullilove* was branded "no longer controlling" to the uncertain extent that it departed from strict scrutiny and held federal racial classifications to a less rigorous standard. This holding discounts a principal underpinning of the *Fullilove* decision: that Congress has special authority under § 5 of the Fourteenth Amendment to enact legislation to effectuate the Amendment's guarantees. *But see City of Boerne v. P.F. Flores*, 521 U.S. 507, 117 S.Ct. 2157, 138 L.Ed.2d 624 (1997) (striking down the Religious Freedom Restoration Act as exceeding the proper limits of Congressional § 5 authority).

The Court remanded for a determination, first, whether the lowbidding nonminority subcontractor plaintiff in fact was denied a subcontract as the result of an irrebuttable racial preference or, for example, as the result of an individualized assessment of economic or social disadvantage. If the former, the lower courts were directed to decide if any interests served by the federal subcontractor compensation clauses at issue were "compelling." Finally, the majority cautioned that any racial preference implemented through the application of the federal regulations and purportedly justified by the goal of eliminating the effects of prior discrimination must be narrowly tailored to serve such a compelling interest—at a minimum, that is, the lower court must decide whether the government had considered race-neutral means to increase minority business participation and whether the program of racial preference would last no

muster under Title VII's *Weber/Johnson* standards as not constituting impermissible reverse discrimination, yet still run afoul of the Constitution.[37] Now the flow is beginning to run the other way. The new "race-neutral" constitutional guideposts seem to have heightened the circuit courts' scrutiny *under Title VII* of government employer affirmative action and consent decrees; the previously prevailing permissiveness appears to be waning.[38] Indeed the Eleventh Circuit has frankly ac-

longer than necessary to eliminate those effects.

What state or governmental interests may suffice as "compelling" after *Adarand* is significantly less clear. Only Justice Scalia, concurring in part, asserts that there is never a compelling interest justifying race discrimination "in order to 'make up' for past racial discrimination in the opposite direction." But the majority's opinion suggests that such a remedial justification will be applied strictly. It observes that the *Wygant* plurality not only rejected the minority role model justification for a government affirmative action program in employment, but in particular required as a predicate convincing evidence of the government employer's own prior race discrimination. Justice Souter, dissenting, explicitly offered Congress' special authority under Section 5 of the 14th Amendment, deferred to by the *Fullilove* plurality, "as the source of an interest of the national government sufficiently important to satisfy ... strict scrutiny." In effect this is an argument that the federal government, though held to the same formal strict scrutiny standard as state and local governments, nevertheless may more easily meet the requirement of a compelling interest for affirmative action. Justice O'Connor for the majority was noncommittal on that point, content to observe "that various Members of this Court have taken different views of the authority § 5 of the Fourteenth Amendment confers upon Congress to deal with the problem of racial discrimination, and the extent to which courts should defer to Congress' exercise of that authority."

37. *See, e.g., Brunet v. City of Columbus,* 1 F.3d 390 (6th Cir.1993), *cert. denied sub nom. Brunet v. Tucker,* 510 U.S. 1164, 114 S.Ct. 1190, 127 L.Ed.2d 540 (1994) (upholding constitutional challenge under § 1983 to fire department's consent decree that gave hiring preference to women); *Peightal v. Metropolitan Dade County,* 940 F.2d 1394 (11th Cir.1991), *cert. denied,* 502 U.S. 1073, 112 S.Ct. 969, 117 L.Ed.2d 134 (1992).

38. *See, e.g., In re Birmingham Reverse Discrimination Employment Litig.,* 20 F.3d 1525 (11th Cir.1994), *cert. denied sub nom.*

Arrington v. Wilks, 514 U.S. 1065, 115 S.Ct. 1695, 131 L.Ed.2d 558 (1995); *Ensley Branch v. Seibels,* 20 F.3d 1489 (11th Cir. 1994), *withdrawn and superseded,* 31 F.3d 1548 (11th Cir.1994). Justice Scalia, dissenting in *Johnson v. Transportation Agency of Santa Clara County,* 480 U.S. 616, 107 S.Ct. 1442, 94 L.Ed.2d 615 (1987), foreshadowed this approach by proposing that *Weber* be reevaluated in light of the Court's Fourteenth Amendment jurisprudence. This same phenomenon was at work in *United States v. Board of Educ. of Piscataway,* 832 F.Supp. 836, 844–848 (D.N.J.1993), *aff'd, Taxman v. Piscataway Township Bd. of Ed.,* 91 F.3d 1547 (3d Cir.1996) (en banc), where the court rejected the educational goal of promoting racial diversity among faculty as an adequate justification under Title VII for race-conscious affirmative action. The court's construction of Title VII was heavily influenced by the Supreme Court's recent Fourteenth Amendment decisions that reject general societal discrimination and a "role model" theory as justifications for affirmative action, notwithstanding the indication of *Regents of Univ. of Cal. v. Bakke,* 438 U.S. 265, 98 S.Ct. 2733, 57 L.Ed.2d 750 (1978), that the attainment of a diverse *student* body in an institution of higher education is such a constitutionally permissible goal. By limiting the justification for race-based decisionmaking under Title VII to the only justification that reliably survives Equal Protection scrutiny—providing a remedy for the defendant's own unlawful discrimination—the Third Circuit opinion may have restricted the latitude afforded Title VII employers by *Weber* and *Johnson.*

That approach may be in some tension with § 116 of the Civil Rights Act of 1991, which provides that nothing in the 1991 amendments "shall be construed to affect court-ordered remedies, affirmative action, or conciliation agreements, that are in accordance with the law." Section § 116 has been read by commentators as manifesting, at least indirectly, a Congressional intent not to disturb the *Weber* and *Johnson* interpretations of Title VII. See Zimmer, *Taxman: Affirmative Action Dodges Five Bul-*

knowledged that its "application of the *Johnson* [i.e., Title VII] manifest imbalance test ... is informed by *Croson's* discussion of the necessity [under the Equal Protection Clause] for a government entity to identify with specificity the discrimination it seeks to remedy through race conscious measures."[39] The decisions have been particularly critical of promotion preferences when they are not narrowly tailored to remedy prior discrimination by the government defendant.[40]

These decisions are curious. First, it is difficult to see why the Title VII test adumbrated in *Johnson* should be "informed" by the requirement of a finding that the particular defendant discriminated against the preferred group, when the Court in *Johnson* expressly rejected the argument that such a finding was essential to justify affirmative action under Title VII. Second, why equate the recently declared strict scrutiny constitutional standard for judging classifications burdening majority groups with the longer-standing, distinctly laxer statutory standard? Perhaps the assumption is that, in the case of a public employer, the statutory permissiveness on affirmative action must give way to the stricter equal protection standard announced in cases like *Wygant* and

lets, 1 U.Pa.J.Lab. & Emp. L. 229, 235 (1998). As a textual matter, if the "court-ordered" modifier extends to the entire list of vehicles for race-based decisionmaking that follows, it is difficult to see how § 116 validates *Weber* and *Johnson*, cases that concerned voluntary employer programs undertaken without judicial compulsion. If, however, that modifier refers only to the vehicle listed immediately after it, "remedies," then the "affirmative action" vehicle that is next on the list may indeed include voluntary measures of the type approved in *Weber* and *Johnson*. There is some awkwardness to this latter reading, however, in that "court-ordered" would then presumably also not refer to the last listed vehicle, "conciliation agreements," which typically do become court ordered.

39. *In re Birmingham Reverse Discrimination Employment Litig.*, 20 F.3d 1525 (11th Cir.1994), *cert. denied sub nom. Arrington v. Wilks*, 514 U.S. 1065, 115 S.Ct. 1695, 131 L.Ed.2d 558 (1995). *Cf. Hill v. Ross*, 183 F.3d 586 (7th Cir.1999) (declining to decide if the permissive *Johnson* approach applicable to Title VII claims survives stricter constitutional standards enunciated in *Adarand*.

40. *Dallas Fire Fighters Ass'n v. Dallas*, 150 F.3d 438 (5th Cir.1998), *cert. denied*, 526 U.S. 1038, 119 S.Ct. 1333, 143 L.Ed.2d 498 (1999) (striking down city fire department's affirmative action plan as violative of, inter alia, equal protection, but upholding promotion under the affirmative action plan where the plan rested on an analysis that showed minorities underrepresented in

higher ranks); *Aiken v. City of Memphis*, 37 F.3d 1155 (6th Cir.1994); *In re Birmingham Reverse Discrimination Employment Litig.*, 20 F.3d 1525 (11th Cir.1994), *cert. denied sub nom. Arrington v. Wilks*, 514 U.S. 1065, 115 S.Ct. 1695, 131 L.Ed.2d 558 (1995); *Black Fire Fighters Ass'n of Dallas v. City of Dallas*, 19 F.3d 992 (5th Cir.1994). *Aiken* and *Birmingham* do differ, however, in the way they apply the "narrowly tailored" prong. The Eleventh Circuit, in *Birmingham*, held that an interim 50% minority promotion goal was impermissible as a means of reaching an ultimate goal of 28% minority representation because the 50% goal bore no relation to the minorities' past underrepresentation or therefore to remediable injury. By contrast, the Sixth Circuit in *Aiken* read the Supreme Court's plurality opinion in *United States v. Paradise*, 480 U.S. 149, 179–180, 107 S.Ct. 1053, 1071, 94 L.Ed.2d 203 (1987) to authorize such interim goals so long as the ultimate percentage goal is tied to the pool of qualified minority applicants. On that point the Sixth Circuit struck down a city's plan because the ultimate minority promotion goals were keyed to minority hiring goals which in turn were based on local labor force statistics that were undifferentiated by the requisite qualifications for initial hire. The Fifth Circuit has upheld consent decree provisions calling for police department promotions where the remedial promotions were offered on a one-time-only basis for no longer than five years and where the decree did not call for the discharge of nonminority officers. *Edwards v. City of Houston*, 37 F.3d 1097 (5th Cir. 1994).

Croson. But is this necessarily so? In relation to discrimination *against* minorities and women, Title VII was Congress' attempt to provide protection, first in the private and then in the public sector, that was *not* afforded by the Constitution. Thus the Supreme Court has traditionally defended the permissive Title VII standards it has devised to facilitate "benign" reverse discrimination against whites and men as consonant with the *statute's* imperative to end discrimination against minorities and women. It is unclear why that permissive construction of Title VII (however mistaken or misguided it may be)[41] should suddenly fail affirmatively acting state and local government employers when their racial or gender preferences are challenged under Title VII, merely because it is now settled that such conduct would violate the Constitution in settings not reached by Title VII.[42]

Somewhat different questions are presented by a controversial California constitutional amendment prohibiting the state from according preferential treatment based on race or gender in public employment, education or contracting. Proposition 209, which implemented the change, was challenged as violating equal protection by impeding the political access of minorities who could otherwise petition local government for race-preferential legislation. The Ninth Circuit has rejected the challenge, reasoning that equal protection is violated only when political access is denied in a racially discriminatory manner, and not when, as the court asserted was the case with Proposition 209, it does so neutrally by *prohibiting* legislative distinctions based on race. Moreover, "that the Constitution permits [but does not require] the rare race-based or gender-based preference hardly implies that the state cannot ban them altogether."[43]

Similarly, by viewing Title VII as flatly prohibiting discriminatory preference for any group, the court declined to find Proposition 209 preempted by that statute; Proposition 209, that is, neither requires the kind of discriminatory preference forbidden by Title VII nor, thought the court, is inconsistent with any of its purposes. Of course this view of Title VII to some degree discounts Supreme Court voluntary affirmative action decisions like *Weber* and *Johnson* that treat the preferential advancement of minority group interests as an implicit goal of that statute.[44]

41. We have argued that *Weber* and *Johnson* rely on a weak negative pregnant in § 703(j), a provision not in point, in preference to the apparently plain prohibitions of §§ 703(d) and 703(a), the provisions directly at issue in *Weber* and *Johnson*, respectively. See text *supra*, this section.

42. The majority in *Johnson v. Transportation Agency of Santa Clara County*, 480 U.S. 616, 628 n. 6, 107 S.Ct. 1442, 1450 n. 6, 94 L.Ed.2d 615 (1987), for example, rejected the notion that a public employer's obligations under Title VII were coextensive with its obligations under the Constitution.

43. *Coalition for Economic Equity v. Wilson*, 122 F.3d 692, 708 (9th Cir.), *cert. denied*, 522 U.S. 963, 118 S.Ct. 397, 139 L.Ed.2d 310 (1997).

44. *Id.* Legislation mirroring Proposition 209 has been introduced on the federal level. See the "Anti–Discrimination Act of 1997," HR 1909, that would ban any officer or agent of the federal government from granting race-, sex-, or national origin-based preference in federal contracting, employment, or any other federal program.

Indeed, it is even plausible that the tail, Title VII, can wag the dog, Equal Protection, when a government employer's conduct is challenged *under the Constitution*. Put otherwise, the Court's permissive construction of Title VII as respects "benign" affirmative action might actually trump the Court's own interpretation of the demands of Equal Protection as elaborated in *Wygant*. After all, in authorizing federal courts to award monetary relief against state and local government defendants notwithstanding the Eleventh Amendment, the Supreme Court relied on the fact that Congress' authority to enact Title VII derived from § 5 of the Fourteenth Amendment.[45] Title VII might thus be viewed as a particularized expression of the Fourteenth Amendment's mandate for the employment setting, one that arguably prevails over the more general Fourteenth Amendment understanding that governs in, say, the government contract setting of *Croson*. Although the Court also applied its strict scrutiny approach in *Wygant*, an employment case, the argument advanced here was not squarely presented. The Court considered only a general equal protection challenge to the layoffs; it did not consider whether its prevailing interpretation of Title VII, and hence, through § 5, of the Fourteenth Amendment, should "inform" its more general view of what the Fourteenth Amendment demands. Stated baldly, the argument here asserts that Congress may by statute (as interpreted, in this case, by the Court) authoritatively construe the equal protection clause to permit state and local government employers to engage in the kind of broad, "benign" affirmative action that Title VII encourages and permits—so authoritatively as to foreclose a later determination by the Court (e.g., in *Wygant*) that those same governments are subject to a considerably stricter, race-blind conception of equal protection[46]

Of course this argument rests at bottom on the assumption that Congress, by the exercise of its § 5 powers, may effectively construe the Fourteenth Amendment *contrary* to the strict scrutiny construction placed on it by the Court. It thus raises a stark challenge to the American principle of judicial review enunciated in *Marbury v. Madison*[47] under which the Court ultimately decides what the Constitution commands.[48] Even more modest propositions—for example, that Con-

45. *Fitzpatrick v. Bitzer*, 427 U.S. 445, 96 S.Ct. 2666, 49 L.Ed.2d 614 (1976). *But see United Steelworkers of Am. v. Weber*, 443 U.S. 193, 206 n. 6, 99 S.Ct. 2721, 2729 n. 6, 61 L.Ed.2d 480 (1979), quoted in *Johnson v. Transportation Agency, Santa Clara County*, 480 U.S. 616, 107 S.Ct. 1442, 94 L.Ed.2d 615 (1987) ("Title VII ... was enacted pursuant to the commerce power to regulate purely private decisionmaking and was not intended to incorporate and particularize the commands of the Fifth and Fourteenth Amendments.")

46. The *Fitzpatrick* holding has not yet been successfully challenged as an impermissible exercise of Congress' § 5 authority

under the standards the Court elaborated in *City of Boerne v. Flores*, 521 U.S. 507, 117 S.Ct. 2157, 138 L.Ed.2d 624 (1997).

47. 5 U.S. (1 Cranch) 137, 2 L.Ed. 60 (1803).

48. *See City of Boerne v. Flores*, 521 U.S. 507, 117 S.Ct. 2157, 138 L.Ed.2d 624 (1997) (striking down Religious Freedom Restoration Act as contrary to the Court's prior construction of the Free Exercise Clause and therefore as an impermissible exercise of § 5 authority to implement the First Amendment as selectively incorporated through the Fourteenth). *See generally* R. Bork, *Constitutionality of the President's*

gress through § 5 may add to substantive rights the courts have previously found in the Fourteenth Amendment—are highly controversial in constitutional jurisprudence.[49] The particular challenge posed here is further complicated by two factors. First, and cutting against the argument, the permissive approach to affirmative action taken by the statute, and hence by "Congress," really only emerged from a judicial gloss placed on it by *Weber* and *Johnson*, i.e., by the Court. But second, and cutting somewhat in favor of the contention, that gloss—and hence the § 5 determination of "Congress"—was in place *before* the Court's recent equal protection decisions that insist on strict scrutiny even of "benign" racial discrimination. Further, the Court until recently recognized that Congress may use its § 5 authority to require minority set-asides in federal contracting that would be infirm if adopted by a state or locality[50] ; might Congress then not also be empowered through Title VII to

Busing Proposals 10 (1972) (commenting on *Katzenbach v. Morgan*, 384 U.S. 641, 86 S.Ct. 1717, 16 L.Ed.2d 828 (1966)), discussed *infra*. But see Gordon, *The Nature and Uses of Congressional Power Under Section Five of the Fourteenth Amendment to Overcome Decisions of the Supreme Court*, 72 Nw. U.L.Rev. 656 (1977) (asserting that Court retains ultimate interpretive primacy where decision turns on "normative" rather than "empirical" matters concerning the assembling of legislative facts). *See also* Nathanson, *Congressional Power to Contradict the Supreme Court's Constitutional Decisions. Accommodation of Rights in Conflict*, 27 Wm. & M.L.Rev. 331 (1986).

49. For example, in *Katzenbach v. Morgan*, 384 U.S. 641, 86 S.Ct. 1717, 16 L.Ed.2d 828 (1966), a majority of the Court, over a dissent that would have limited Congress' § 5 role to providing remedies for conduct elsewhere proscribed by the Amendment, found in § 5 "a positive grant of legislative power authorizing Congress to exercise its discretion in determining whether and what legislation is needed to secure the guarantees of [the Equal Protection Clause of Section 1] of the Fourteenth Amendment." A second rationale in the majority's opinion is still more pertinent to the argument in text. Justice Brennan asserted that Congress through § 5 may authoritatively interpret conduct as violative of the primary Fourteenth Amendment guarantees, notwithstanding a prior holding of the Court to the contrary. See Barron, Dienes, McCormack, and Redish *Constitutional Law: Principles and Policy* 174 (Michie 4th ed. 1992). To an uncertain degree, however, that rationale has been undercut by the Court's decision in *Oregon v. Mitchell*, 400 U.S. 112, 91 S.Ct. 260, 27 L.Ed.2d 272 (1970), which struck down provisions of the 1970 Voting Rights Act that purported to lower the voting age to 18 in state elections.

One reason for the Court's hesitancy to embrace fully a Congressional interpretive power under § 5 (aside from preserving its own institutional prerogatives) is undoubtedly the difficulty of limiting the sphere of Congressional interpretive primacy in light of the renowned, grand vagueness of the § 1 clauses—due process and equal protection—that § 5 permits Congress to implement. See Note, *Congressional Power to Enforce Due Process Rights*, 80 Colum.L.Rev. 1265 (1980).

It is not much of a stretch to argue, for example, that because § 2 of the Voting Rights Act is also an exercise of Congress' Fourteenth Amendment powers, it can constitutionally authorize precisely the kind of race-based congressional redistricting designed to assure or expand minority representation that the Supreme Court, in *Shaw v. Reno*, 509 U.S. 630, 113 S.Ct. 2816, 125 L.Ed.2d 511 (1993), recently condemned as offensive to a "general," race-neutral understanding of equal protection, at least when the new district shapes are so "bizarre" as to leave no other reasonable conclusion but that the shape was dictated by considerations of race. (That argument was apparently not made and was not discussed in the *Shaw* opinion.) But could Congress then mandate application of all federal procedural rules in state courts if it thought that necessary to secure due process to litigants? And does § 5 authorize Congress, in an effort to secure the due process right to life, to define life as existing from conception? *See* S. 158 and H.R. 900, 97th Cong., 1st Sess. (1981).

50. *Compare Fullilove v. Klutznick*, 448 U.S. 448, 100 S.Ct. 2758, 65 L.Ed.2d 902 (1980) *with Croson. But see Adarand Constructors, Inc. v. Pena*, 512 U.S. 1288, 115 S.Ct. 41, 129 L.Ed.2d 936.

permit states and localities to engage in employment affirmative action that would otherwise violate the Court's strict scrutiny interpretation of the Fourteenth Amendment?[51]

After *Croson*, the Court, left to its own devices, might be inclined to overrule *Weber* itself, as one justice has urged.[52] Indeed even an affirmative action plan valid under *Weber* might be held unlawful under § 703(m) of Title VII, as amended by the 1991 CRA. That section provides that an unlawful employment practice is "established" when race or gender is shown to be "a motivating factor . . . even though other [e.g., benign, compensatory] factors motivated the practice." The preface to § 703(m), though, reads "Except as otherwise provided in this title. . . ."; and part of that title, § 116 of the Civil Rights Act of 1991, provides that its amendments shall not be construed to affect "court-ordered remedies, affirmative action, or conciliation agreements, that are in accordance with the law."

Does this "savings" clause protect only affirmative action plans that are "court-ordered"? It might if that compound adjective were construed to modify "affirmative action" as well as "remedies," for then only "court-ordered," as distinct from voluntary *Weber/Johnson*-type affirmative action would be saved. That would leave the Court free to overturn the rather lenient *Weber/Johnson* standards in place before the CRA of 1991. But how could "court-ordered" modify both "remedies" and "affirmative action" without also modifying "conciliation agreements," the third remedy source in the statutory list? And since conciliation agreements are understood, by their nature, not to be court ordered, then perhaps "court-ordered" modifies only the first item on the list, "remedies." Even non-court-ordered, i.e., "voluntary" affirmative action plans would then be saved, provided they are in accordance with the standards of pre-November 1991 law. EEOC has given § 116 this latter reading.[53] Without even wrestling with the text, which it found "clear" as applied to a court-ordered consent decree, the Ninth Circuit has concluded that § 116 modifies the general prohibition of § 703(m) to uphold the continued validity of an affirmative action plan designed to comply with that decree.[54]

51. *See* Note, *City of Richmond v. J.A. Croson Co: A Federal Legislative Answer*, 100 *Yale L.J.* 451, 468 (1990) ("The court's determination that a state's race-based program is unconstitutional does not preclude congress from independently sanctioning a similar race-based program under its section 5 enforcement powers."). *But see Adarand Constructors, Inc. v. Pena*, 512 U.S. 1288, 115 S.Ct. 41, 129 L.Ed.2d 936.

52. *Johnson*, 480 U.S. 616, 107 S.Ct. 1442, 94 L.Ed.2d 615 (Scalia, J., dissenting). Further support for the suggestion in text may be gleaned from the Court's opinions in *Martin v. Wilks*, 490 U.S. 755, 109 S.Ct. 2180, 104 L.Ed.2d 835 (1989) and *Independent Fed'n of Flight Attendants v. Zipes*,

491 U.S. 754, 109 S.Ct. 2732, 105 L.Ed.2d 639 (1989), discussed in the section that follows.

53. *EEOC Enforcement Guidance* dated July 7, 1992, Part IV.

54. *Officers for Justice v. Civil Serv. Comm'n of San Francisco*, 979 F.2d 721 (9th Cir.1992), *cert. denied*, 507 U.S. 1004, 113 S.Ct. 1645, 123 L.Ed.2d 267 (1993). The Sixth Circuit has even upheld an affirmative action program designed to meet the requirements of a conciliation agreement when the employer overshot the target requirements for women apprentices but did so as part of a good faith attempt to comply with the agreement. *Plott v. General Motors*

§§ 4.41–7.44 [Reserved]

G. PROCEDURES FOR CHALLENGING AFFIRMATIVE ACTION

§ 4.45 In General

The Court's early support for "voluntary" affirmative action by Title VII employers, both private[1] and public,[2] was expressed in a parallel procedural holding. When a white or male plaintiff challenges an employment practice as a form of intentional discrimination, the employer may assert that the practice was dictated by the provisions of a valid affirmative action plan. The Court might have treated the employer justification as a true affirmative defense, thereby casting on it burdens of both production and persuasion. Instead, it treated the plaintiff's prima facie case as resting essentially on the inferential *McDonnell Douglas* mode of proof, and accordingly held that the employer may justify simply by producing evidence that its challenged decision was made pursuant to an affirmative action plan. In contrast to the BFOQ defense to express discrimination, the employer does not have to bear the burden of persuasion in defending an expressly discriminatory individual employment decision made pursuant to a valid affirmative action plan; rather, the plaintiff must prove either that the decision was not made pursuant to the plan, or that the plan is invalid.[3] The Court has similarly held that when race-based government action is challenged under the Equal Protection Clause, "the ultimate burden remains with the employees to demonstrate the unconstitutionality of an affirmative-action program."[4] Some courts have modified the equal protection burdens by placing on the defendant the burden of producing evidence of the plan's constitutionality, still leaving the plaintiff with the "ultimate burden of proving its unconstitutionality."[5]

Corp., 71 F.3d 1190 (6th Cir.1995), *cert. denied,* 517 U.S. 1157, 116 S.Ct. 1546, 134 L.Ed.2d 649 (1996).

§ 4.45

1. *See United Steelworkers of Am. v. Weber,* 443 U.S. 193, 99 S.Ct. 2721, 61 L.Ed.2d 480 (1979).

2. *See Johnson v. Transportation Agency, Santa Clara County,* 480 U.S. 616, 107 S.Ct. 1442, 94 L.Ed.2d 615 (1987).

3. *Johnson,* 480 U.S. 616, 107 S.Ct. 1442, 94 L.Ed.2d 615; *Smith v. Virginia Commonwealth Univ.,* 62 F.3d 659 (4th Cir. 1995). *Cf. Maitland v. University of Minn.,* 155 F.3d 1013 (8th Cir.1998) (reversing grant of summary judgment against challenger because a genuine issue of fact existed as to whether a manifest imbalance existed when consent order was entered).

4. *Wygant v. Jackson Bd. of Educ.,* 476 U.S. 267, 277–78, 106 S.Ct. 1842, 1848–50,

90 L.Ed.2d 260 (1986). *Cf. Maitland v. University of Minn.,* 155 F.3d 1013 (8th Cir. 1998) (reversing grant of summary judgment against challenger because a genuine issue of fact existed as to whether a conspicuous gender imbalance existed when consent order was entered).

5. *Aiken v. City of Memphis,* 37 F.3d 1155 (6th Cir.1994) (citing *Brunet v. City of Columbus,* 1 F.3d 390, 404–05 (6th Cir. 1993), *cert. denied sub nom. Brunet v. Tucker,* 510 U.S. 1164, 114 S.Ct. 1190, 127 L.Ed.2d 540 (1994)). A consent decree is a contract, and must be enforced through the court's civil contempt power. *See, e.g., Reynolds v. Roberts,* 207 F.3d 1288, 1298 (11th Cir.2000). The party seeking to enforce the consent decree must move the court to issue a show cause order why the violator should not be adjudged in civil contempt and sanctioned. *Id.* A consent decree is akin to an injunction, and the party seeking a modification of a consent decree must

But there is less consensus about the remedies appropriately award-ed nonminority plaintiffs when they succeed in demonstrating the un-constitutionality of a voluntary or court-ordered affirmative action plan. A growing number of federal courts have taken the position, for example, that white plaintiffs who demonstrate that they were denied the right to compete on an equal basis because of their race[6] are entitled to damages to the extent of any demonstrated economic loss or emotional distress, even if they fail to demonstrate that, but for the race-based preference, they would have been selected.[7] These decisions build on the Supreme Court's decision in *Northeastern Florida Chapter of the Associated General Contractors of America v. City of Jacksonville,*[8] which held, in the setting of a government contract "set aside" program for minorities, that when "government erects a barrier that makes it more difficult for members of one group to obtain a benefit than it is for members of another group, a member of the former group seeking to challenge the barrier need not allege that he would have obtained the benefit but for the barrier...." It is enough if the plaintiff asserts that the barrier has denied him the right to be considered or compete for the benefit in question.[9] In this view, the equal protection violation is complete when the plaintiff cannot fairly compete. It consists of a denial of the right to compete "on a level playing field," which in itself produces the "ignomi-ny and illegality of ..." erecting a racial bar to promotions.[10]

initiate suit to dissolve or modify the de-cree. *Id.* at 1300 & n.22.

6. Plaintiffs claiming they were denied equal opportunity must prove either that they were disadvantaged or that they were excluded from full consideration. *Byers v. City of Albuquerque,* 150 F.3d 1271 (10th Cir.1998).

7. *See, e.g., Price v. City of Charlotte, N.C.,* 93 F.3d 1241 (4th Cir.1996), *cert. de-nied,* 520 U.S. 1116, 117 S.Ct. 1246, 137 L.Ed.2d 328 (1997) (promotion denial in city employment; plaintiff denied promotion but accorded standing, prevailed on liabili-ty, and held eligible for all monetary reme-dies despite city's showing that even absent its reliance on race it would not have pro-moted plaintiff); *cf. Salter v. Douglas Mac-Arthur State Technical College,* 929 F.Supp. 1470, 1477–78 (M.D.Ala.1996) (employer li-able for reverse discrimination under Title VII, because white plaintiff was denied an equal right to compete, although he would not have been hired in any event). *But see United States v. City of Miami,* 195 F.3d 1292, 1301–02 (11th Cir.1999), *cert. denied,* __ U.S. __, 121 S.Ct. 52, 148 L.Ed.2d 20 (2000) (pro-rata relief where only two of multiple plaintiffs could have obtained a job benefit even absent unlawful discrimina-tion). *See also Hopwood v. Texas,* 78 F.3d 932 (5th Cir.), cert. denied, 518 U.S. 1033, 116 S.Ct. 2581, 135 L.Ed.2d 1095 (1996)

(denial of admission to state's law school). The opinion in *Hopwood* went further to provide that the adjudicated law violator, and not the plaintiff, bears the burden of persuasion on that issue. *Id.* at 956–57.

8. 508 U.S. 656, 113 S.Ct. 2297, 124 L.Ed.2d 586 (1993). *See also Engineering Contractors Ass'n of S. Fla. Inc. v. Metro-politan Dade County,* 122 F.3d 895 (11th Cir.1997), *cert. denied,* 523 U.S. 1004, 118 S.Ct. 1186, 140 L.Ed.2d 317 (1998) (ex-pressly relying on *Northeastern Fla. Chap-ter*); *Cone Corp. v. Hillsborough County,* 5 F.3d 1397 (11th Cir.1993) (applying *North-eastern Fla. Chapter*). This liberalized standing approach to equal protection chal-lenges traces to *Regents of the Univ. of Cal. v. Bakke,* 438 U.S. 265 nn.14, 54, 98 S.Ct. 2733, 57 L.Ed.2d 750 (1978).

9. *Northwestern Fla. Chapter,* 508 U.S. at 663, 113 S.Ct. at 2302.

10. *Price,* 93 F.3d at 1248. *But cf. Byers v. City of Albuquerque,* 150 F.3d 1271 (10th Cir.1998) (plaintiffs lack standing because they could not show a causal relationship between their failure to be promoted and the challenged affirmative action plan); *Grahek v. City of St. Paul, Mn.,* 84 F.3d 296 (8th Cir.1996) (plaintiff who, even absent use of affirmative action plan, would not have even advanced through the first-stage minimal screen of a city hiring process has

The Court's apparent retreat from the approval of consent judgments that embody group-based or quota remedies, and perhaps ultimately from voluntary employer affirmative action programs, is signalled by a different procedural development. A 5–4 majority held in *Martin v. Wilks*,[11] that non-minority employees who object to a consent judgment adverse to their interests are not required to intervene in a Title VII action but instead may collaterally attack the judgment in independent actions. Since the Court had several times recognized that employers are principally motivated to adopt "voluntary" affirmative action programs, or settle pending lawsuits by consent agreements, in order to avoid the costs of extended litigation, the *Wilks* decision appears designed to remove much of the incentive for these arrangements.[12]

The Civil Rights Act of 1991 substantially overrules *Wilks* by foreclosing many collateral challenges, typically by whites or males, to employment practices adopted under the authority of litigated or consent judgments. These attacks customarily assert that the underlying judgment unlawfully provides group-based, reverse-discriminatory relief to minority or female applicants or employees, including those not shown to have suffered discrimination at the hands of the defendant employer. The Court in *Wilks*, in permitting such attacks even where attackers know about the underlying litigation but do not try to intervene, relied on the familiar due process principle that a judgment cannot bind a litigant who was not a party or privy and therefore lacked an opportunity to be heard.[13] Under the new provision, the white or male challengers generally will be barred if they had a reasonable opportunity, after adequate notice, to raise their objections during the primary proceedings or were adequately represented in them by a similarly situated litigant.[14]

On the other hand, this provision of the Act also makes it more difficult for the parties to the primary lawsuit—the minority or female plaintiffs and the defendant employer—to achieve assurance that a judgment in their litigation will effectively end the controversy among all relevant parties. They will have to give actual notice to identifiable incumbent employees who might be adversely affected by a proposed judgment—one, for example, that directs group-based goals or quotas for a training program, promotion, or adjustments to seniority. And when

not shown injury in fact and so lacks standing).

11. 490 U.S. 755, 109 S.Ct. 2180, 104 L.Ed.2d 835 (1989).

12. Indeed, on remand from the Supreme Court's decision in *Wilks*, the Eleventh Circuit has ruled that the underlying consent decree, which indefinitely reserved 50% of a city fire department's promotions to lieutenant for African–Americans, violates Title VII as well as the Equal Protection Clause. *Bennett v. Arrington*, 20 F.3d 1525 (11th Cir.1994), *cert. denied* 514 U.S. 1065, 115 S.Ct. 1695, 131 L.Ed.2d 558 (1995).

13. *See, e.g., Parklane Hosiery v. Shore*, 439 U.S. 322, 327 n. 7, 99 S.Ct. 645, 649 n. 7, 58 L.Ed.2d 552 (1979); *Hansberry v. Lee*, 311 U.S. 32, 40–41, 61 S.Ct. 115, 117–118, 85 L.Ed. 22 (1940). *See also Rutherford v. City of Cleveland*, 137 F.3d 905 (6th Cir. 1998) (non-minority applicants seeking hiring opportunities could challenge consent decree governing hiring practices because fraternal police organization that was a party to a consent decree lacked commonality of interest with non-minority applicants).

14. Section 108 (adding subsection 703(n)(1) to Title VII, 42 U.S.C.A. § 2000e–2(n)(1)).

such notice is given, the Act, unlike its predecessor versions,[15] leaves intact another of the Court's 1988 Term decisions[16] that generally[17] relieves intervening challengers from liability for the attorney's fees incurred by the primary parties in defending the group protection features of the proposed underlying judgment.

The difficulties faced by the primary parties are even greater with respect to contemplated relief—goals or quotas concerning hiring or, in the case of a union defendant, membership—that will affect nonminority employees who are not readily identifiable and accordingly cannot be given actual notice. In those situations the primary parties, if they seek a durable, comprehensive judgment, will have to join as additional parties persons or groups who will be deemed adequate representatives of the absentees likely to be affected by the judgment.

On balance, then, the Act makes it riskier for a putative challenger to wait to attack such a judgment until after it is entered and he is denied hire or promotion pursuant to its terms. To this degree it affords indirect support for group protection remedies in the context of completed or, in the case of a consent judgment, partial litigation. On the other hand, since challengers are unlikely to face liability for their adversaries' attorney's fees, they have no substantial financial disincentive to intervene to attack proposed group-based judgments. And in cases that involve proposed group-based hiring or membership remedies, the primary parties may still be reluctant to enter into consent judgments for fear that they cannot locate or join adequate representatives of all the absent nonincumbents, who would then remain free to attack the judgment collaterally.

In a parallel procedural decision that similarly has the potential to limit Title VII affirmative action along constitutional lines, the Second Circuit has held that employment discrimination consent decrees involving a private employer may be modified before their full implementation upon the same relaxed standards the Supreme Court has applied to decrees affecting instrumentalities of government. In such "public issues litigation not involving a governmental entity," the Second Circuit wrote, it is appropriate for a court to entertain modification or termination either for "changed circumstances or substantial attainment of the decree's objective."[18]

§§ 4.46–7.49 [Reserved]

15. H.R. 1 § 9 (amending Title VII § 6(k), 42 U.S.C.A. § 2000e–5(k) (1988)).

16. *Independent Fed'n of Flight Attendants v. Zipes*, 491 U.S. 754, 109 S.Ct. 2732, 105 L.Ed.2d 639 (1989).

17. The Court had saddled such a challenger with liability only when its position was "frivolous, unreasonable, or without foundation." *Zipes*, 491 U.S. at 768, 109 S.Ct. at 2740 (Blackmun, J., concurring) (quoting *Christiansburg Garment Co. v. EEOC*, 434 U.S. 412, 98 S.Ct. 694, 54 L.Ed.2d 648 (1978)).

18. *Patterson v. Newspaper & Mail Deliverers' Union of N.Y.*, 13 F.3d 33 (2d Cir. 1993), *cert. denied*, 513 U.S. 809, 115 S.Ct. 58, 130 L.Ed.2d 16 (1994).

H. AGGREGATE EFFECTS OF THE 1991 ACT ON CLAIMS ASSERTING GROUP AND INDIVIDUAL RIGHTS, INTENTIONAL AND "IMPACT" DISCRIMINATION

§ 4.50 In General

Despite the Act's tendency to tilt toward the intentional model, it offers no comfort to multiple plaintiffs seeking to assert those claims together. For one thing, it does not disturb the Court's decision in *Falcon* that pressures several representative plaintiffs to band together to assert claims on behalf of differently situated employees with differing grievances and thereby exposes the resulting patchwork plaintiff class to the charge of internal conflicts of interest.

Moreover, the legislation ignores other procedural features that make class proceedings cumbersome. Adverse rulings on class certification are not appealable when made, because they are not "final decisions" within the meaning of 28 U.S.C.A. § 1291.[1] Accordingly, after a class certification denial, counsel for the plaintiffs must litigate the claims of individual, named, class representatives alone; appeal regardless of the outcome; and then return to trial on claims of the class should the court of appeals reverse the certification denial.

The legislation also overlooks the limitations on remedies available to joined or class action plaintiffs who surmount these obstacles and demonstrate "systemic disparate treatment." This theory requires the plaintiffs to prove that discrimination was the employer's standard operating procedure. It is typically established by statistical evidence that persuades the court of an overwhelming or "gross" disparity between the availability of qualified members of the protected group and their actual, lesser representation on the employer's staff.[2]

As discussed above, the Court held in *International Bhd. of Teamsters v. United States*[3] that an individual systemic treatment class member is not necessarily entitled to immediate implementation of retroactive seniority of the "competitive type"—seniority used to ration scarce resources like jobs or preferred routes—and therefore will not necessarily receive full, make-whole relief. This is true even when she demonstrates that her application for a relevant position was denied during the period of proven, routine discrimination, and the employer fails to prove a nondiscriminatory reason for her rejection. Although each such plaintiff is presumptively entitled to receive back pay and

§ 4.50

1. This contrasts strikingly with the Court's willingness to create a "collateral order" exception to the final decision rule that enables public officials charged with civil rights violations to take an immediate interlocutory appeal from orders denying their defense of qualified immunity. *See Mitchell v. Forsyth*, 472 U.S. 511, 105 S.Ct. 2806, 86 L.Ed.2d 411 (1985).

2. *See, e.g., Hazelwood Sch. Dist. v. United States*, 433 U.S. 299, 97 S.Ct. 2736, 53 L.Ed.2d 768 (1977); *International Bhd. of Teamsters v. United States*, 431 U.S. 324, 97 S.Ct. 1843, 52 L.Ed.2d 396 (1977).

3. 431 U.S. 324, 97 S.Ct. 1843, 52 L.Ed.2d 396 (1977).

retroactive seniority for benefits purposes immediately upon issuance of a judgment,[4] the Court found no similar entitlement to an award of retroactive seniority that the plaintiff needs to compete for scarce employment resources. Rather, the Court instructed trial judges that they might refuse to order competitive seniority, if implementing the award would result in the inequitable promotion or retention of the discriminatee at the expense of an incumbent employee with greater earned seniority.[5] In weighing those equities, the trial courts were told only to exercise their qualities of "mercy and practicality."[6]

A common consequence of denying a discriminatee retroactive, competitive seniority, under these amorphous standards, is to deprive him of an order directing his promotion, reinstatement, or recall from layoff—relief that is essential if he is to be restored to the place he would have held absent the original act of discrimination. This injustice is compounded by the Court's refusal, notwithstanding the recommendation of Chief Justice Burger,[7] to declare proven victims eligible for postjudgment "front pay" in lieu of orders restoring them to that "rightful place." Following the Court's uncertain lead, the lower courts, which awarded front pay in age discrimination cases almost as a matter of course,[8] were at times been unsure about its availability under Title VII.[9] Now front pay is clearly available under the 1991 Title VII amendments allowing compensatory relief. See § 4.25, *supra*.

The 1991 Civil Rights Act therefore lends substantial implicit support to the far more controversial concept of group-based affirmative action. As observed above,[10] the amendments substantially insulate from collateral attack judgments that incorporate group-enhancement goals favoring minorities and women who may never have encountered discrimination at the hands of the defendant. Still more significant, the amendments omit explicit mention of—and thereby will probably be held to acquiesce in—the Supreme Court decisions[11] that have permitted employers to take such affirmative action, on their own, with little fear of liability to whites or males for a primary violation of Title VII. Indeed Congress indirectly lends support to those decisions by proclaiming that the legislation should not be "construed to affect court-ordered remedies,

4. *Franks v. Bowman Transp. Co.*, 424 U.S. 747, 96 S.Ct. 1251, 47 L.Ed.2d 444 (1976).

5. *International Bhd. of Teamsters v. United States*, 431 U.S. 324, 97 S.Ct. 1843, 52 L.Ed.2d 396 (1977).

6. *Id.*

7. *Id.* at 781, 96 S.Ct. at 1272 (Burger, C.J., concurring in part and dissenting in part).

8. *See, e.g., Bartek v. Urban Redev. Auth. of Pittsburgh*, 882 F.2d 739, 746–47 (3d Cir.1989); *McNeil v. Economics Laboratory, Inc.*, 800 F.2d 111, 118 (7th Cir.1986), *cert. denied*, 481 U.S. 1041, 107 S.Ct. 1983, 95 L.Ed.2d 823 (1987).

9. *See McKnight v. General Motors Corp.*, 908 F.2d 104, 117 (7th Cir.1990), *cert. denied*, 499 U.S. 919, 111 S.Ct. 1306, 113 L.Ed.2d 241 (1991). The trend, however, was to award front pay in Title VII cases on the same terms as in actions under ADEA. *See, e.g., Carter v. Sedgwick County*, 929 F.2d 1501, 1504 (10th Cir.1991) (Title VII front pay available subject to specified limitations).

10. *See* § 4.45, *supra*.

11. *Johnson v. Transportation Agency*, 480 U.S. 616, 107 S.Ct. 1442, 94 L.Ed.2d 615 (1987); *United Steelworkers of Am. v. Weber*, 443 U.S. 193, 99 S.Ct. 2721, 61 L.Ed.2d 480 (1979).

affirmative action, or conciliation agreements, that are in accordance with the law."[12]

In leaving undisturbed the Court's approval of "voluntary" employer initiated affirmative action, while stiffening the penalties for intentional discrimination, Congress supplies considerable incentive for employers to dispense aggregate group justice by resorting to reverse discrimination that would otherwise be condemned as a violation of Title VII.[13] The amendments thus straddle but fail to resolve this fundamental tension between protecting the individual and fostering opportunities for a disadvantaged group.

On the other hand, the Court's increasing solicitude for the innocent white or male incumbent who is harmed by a preferential, group-based remedy is reflected in its decision that nonminority intervenors who unsuccessfully oppose Title VII consent decrees that threaten them with personal injury will ordinarily not be liable for the fees incurred by plaintiffs in resisting their objections.[14]

The Civil Rights Act of 1991 concentrates its formal attack on intentional employer conduct. The legislation, thus, acts on the teaching of conventional economic wisdom that this type of discrimination is inefficient. On the other hand, since legislation is a classic form of government interference, eradicating discrimination by means of the Act conflicts with the dominant economic dictum that market forces are the cure. In some respects, though, the legislation is only modestly intrusive. For example, it creates incentives for private employers to fashion group-based preferences (although only for minority groups and women) calculated to reduce the incidence of litigation. When lawsuits cannot be avoided, the legislation will in some cases permit the parties to secure more reliable and durable judgments upon consent, although only after the conclusion of proceedings made somewhat more cumbersome and expensive by additional requirements of notice and joinder. Viewed this way, the legislation generally takes the "efficient" route, both in targeting the more inefficient kind of discrimination (intentional), and in permitting private, relatively consensual means to combat it.

To the extent that Congress explicitly addressed the question whether corrective mechanisms should be public or private, it again chose a relatively unintrusive course. Section 118 encourages "the use of alternative means of dispute resolution, including settlement negotiations, conciliation, facilitation, mediation, factfinding, minitrials, and arbitration...." Yet no funds are appropriated for the purpose and no specific incentives are provided. The section may therefore prove little more than hortatory, a nod to the fashion of alternative dispute resolution.[15]

---

12. Section 116 of the Civil Rights Act of 1991.

13. *See McDonald v. Santa Fe Trail Transp. Co.,* 427 U.S. 273, 96 S.Ct. 2574, 49 L.Ed.2d 493 (1976) (the Title VII ban on race discrimination includes discrimination against whites).

14. *Independent Fed'n of Flight Attendants v. Zipes,* 491 U.S. 754, 109 S.Ct. 2732, 105 L.Ed.2d 639 (1989).

15. It is possible, however, that this section will have some real impact as interpretive guidance to the courts to permit binding arbitration of Title VII claims where the

Of course Congress also authorized compensatory and punitive damages for intentional violations. It can therefore be argued that the amendments provide greater incentive to employers to avoid the risks of litigation by complying with Title VII. But the availability of damages also undercuts Title VII's long-standing emphasis on conciliation by an administrative agency whose processes must be exhausted before litigation is commenced.

Similarly, Congress could have done more to stimulate private sector antidiscrimination initiatives than simply continuing to countenance affirmative action. It might have approved direct incentives, like tax relief, for employers whose minority or women employees are significantly better represented in the employer's workforce than would be predicted from their qualified availability. Congress might also have fostered the recruitment and training necessary to attain these favorable bottom lines by establishing more lenient liability standards for qualifying employers.[16]

The piebald picture that emerges from these developments may be summed up as follows. The legislation aims its heaviest guns against intentional discrimination—the kind most disfavored philosophically, politically, and economically. It does so, however, largely through a haphazard litigation strategy that impedes efficient joinder devices and fails to assure full make-whole relief even to proven victims of this paradigm discrimination. At the same time, in overturning only ambiguously the restrictions of the *Wards Cove* decision, the legislation makes only a faint stab at eradicating group impact discrimination resulting

parties have agreed to that process in an employment contract. Following the lead of the Supreme Court in an age discrimination case, *Gilmer v. Interstate/Johnson Lane Corp.*, 500 U.S. 20, 111 S.Ct. 1647, 114 L.Ed.2d 26 (1991), at least one circuit court has stayed federal statutory discrimination actions and compelled arbitration under authority of the Federal Arbitration Act, 9 U.S.C.A. §§ 1–15 (1988) (hereafter, "FAA"). *See, e.g., Willis v. Dean Witter Reynolds, Inc.*, 948 F.2d 305 (6th Cir.1991). But the court stressed that the New York Stock Exchange's securities registration form in which each brokerage house employee's agreement to arbitrate was contained was not among the "contracts of employment" excluded from the scope of FAA by § 1 thereof, 9 U.S.C.A. § 1. By contrast, collective bargaining agreements have been held to constitute such "contracts of employment," *cf. United Paperworkers Int'l Union v. Misco*, 484 U.S. 29, 40 n. 9, 108 S.Ct. 364, 372 n. 9, 98 L.Ed.2d 286 (1987), and perhaps in part for that reason the Supreme Court, well before *Gilmer*, refused to preclude litigation under Title VII of previously arbitrated claims under a collective bargaining agreement. *Alex-*

ander v. Gardner–Denver Co., 415 U.S. 36, 94 S.Ct. 1011, 39 L.Ed.2d 147 (1974).

In light of § 118's encouragement of, inter alia, arbitration, federal judges would now have some warrant for finding a Title VII exception to the FAA's exclusion of "contracts of employment." They might therefore be more inclined to stay (usually on motion of the employer) Title VII actions in favor of arbitration, provided of course the parties agreed to arbitrate such claims in an individual or collective employment agreement. Particularly in tight labor markets, employers would likely be able to extract that agreement in individual employment contracts; and unions would perhaps sacrifice what would otherwise be their members' right to a judicial forum for redress of a Title VII injury if they acceded to an employer demand to arbitrate such claims. A fuller discussion of *Gilmer* and its effect, if any, on *Alexander* will be found in § 4.6, *supra*.

16. *See* Blumrosen, 42 Rutgers L.Rev. at 271–72 (urging that employers with good "bottom lines" should benefit from legal rules that make it easier for them to defend against disparate impact claims).

from facially neutral practices, a type of discrimination economists consider efficient and society views as less clearly unfair. Further, employers remain free to indulge in group preference affirmative action that discriminates against individual whites and males but tends to obviate lawsuits by minorities and women. And when minorities and women do sue, the legislation assists them as groups by offering employers the settlement incentive of a consent judgment that is better shielded from collateral attack.

Chapter Five

SECTIONS 1981 AND 1983

§ 5.1 The Civil War Era Reconstruction Acts in General

The Civil Rights Acts of 1866, 1870, and 1871 are generally referred to as the Reconstruction Civil Rights Acts, and they were originally intended to enforce the 13th and 14th Amendments in the post-Civil War era. The most frequently invoked provisions are codified at 42 U.S.C.A. §§ 1981, 1983, and 1985(3). These acts remained dormant for many years but were resurrected in the 1960's.[1]

What is now § 1981 was first enacted in 1866 under authority of the 13th Amendment, and re-enacted in 1870, two years after ratification of the 14th Amendment. This history has spawned doctrinal schisms and jurisprudential inconsistencies. On one hand, the Supreme Court has relied on the 13th Amendment origins of § 1981 (and § 1982, its legislative companion that bars discrimination in the acquiring, holding and disposing of property) to apply these statutes to purely private defendants, at least with respect to transactions held open to the public.[2] On the other, the court has relied on the 14th Amendment origins of § 1981 to limit its reach to violations that reflect race discrimination that is intentional in character.[3] And while the Court has insisted that it is the intent of the enacting Congress that controls the breadth of the §§ 1981 and 1982 definitions of "race,"[4] its reliance on the 13th Amendment origins of these statutes seemingly caused it to depart from the norms of that Congress by holding the statutes to bar purely private discrimination, subject only to possible First Amendment limitations related to freedom of association.[5]

§ 5.1

1. See Jones v. Alfred H. Mayer Co., 392 U.S. 409, 88 S.Ct. 2186, 20 L.Ed.2d 1189 (1968).

2. Jones, 392 U.S. 409, 88 S.Ct. 2186, 20 L.Ed.2d 1189 (§ 1982); Runyon v. McCrary, 427 U.S. 160, 96 S.Ct. 2586, 49 L.Ed.2d 415 (1976) and Patterson v. McLean Credit Union, 491 U.S. 164, 109 S.Ct. 2363, 105 L.Ed.2d 132 (1989) (§ 1981).

3. General Building Contractors Ass'n v. Pennsylvania, 458 U.S. 375, 102 S.Ct. 3141, 73 L.Ed.2d 835 (1982).

4. McDonald v. Santa Fe Trail Transp. Co., 427 U.S. 273, 96 S.Ct. 2574, 49 L.Ed.2d 493 (1976) and St. Francis College v. Al-Khazraji, 481 U.S. 604, 107 S.Ct. 2022, 95 L.Ed.2d 582 (1987) (§ 1981) and Shaare Tefila Congregation v. Cobb, 481 U.S. 615, 107 S.Ct. 2019, 95 L.Ed.2d 594 (1987) (§ 1982).

5. See, e.g., Runyon, 427 U.S. at 186, 96 S.Ct. at 2602 (Powell, J., concurring).

§ 5.2 Section 1981

Section 1981 secures equal contracting rights without regard to race. It affords "all persons" in the United States "the same right . . . to make and enforce contracts . . . and to the full and equal benefit of all laws . . . as is enjoyed by white citizens." By its terms § 1981 reaches a host of contracting relationships—with private schools, to name just one—not reached by Title VII.[1] And § 1981, unlike Title VII, has no minimum-employee numerical threshold for employer liability. Section 1981 has also been interpreted to provide a civil damages remedy for racial discrimination arising from contracts of employment, even though Congress has comprehensively addressed employment discrimination much more recently in Title VII.[2] Moreover, the Court has held, *Runyon v. McCrary*,[3] and reaffirmed, *Patterson v. McLean Credit Union*,[4] that § 1981, long assumed to reach only state action, also reaches purely private conduct.

A contract for § 1981 purposes is not necessarily the legalistic agreement that the word conjures up in one's mind. In *Patterson*, the Supreme Court impliedly acknowledged that an at-will employee may bring an action under § 1981. The Court stated that Patterson, an at-will employee, might have a cause of action against her employer for failure to promote: "the question whether a promotion claim is actionable under § 1981 depends upon whether the nature of the change in position was such that it involved the opportunity to enter into a new contract with the employer. If so, then the employer's refusal to enter the new contract is actionable under § 1981."[5] Justice Stevens, writing separately in *Patterson*, explained that an "at-will employee . . . is not merely performing an existing contract; she is constantly remaking that contract."[6] As noted by the Fifth Circuit, early federal decisions on the issue were few, and were not unanimous.[7] The 1998 Supreme Court

---

§ 5.2

1. The First Circuit has written that a § 1981 defendant can be liable to an independent contractor for a racially hostile work environment. In *Danco, Inc. v. Wal-Mart Stores, Inc.*, 178 F.3d 8 (1st Cir.1999), *cert. denied*, 528 U.S. 1105, 120 S.Ct. 843, 145 L.Ed.2d 712 (2000), Wal-Mart contracted with Danco, solely owned by Benjamin Guiliani, to maintain a Wal-Mart store's parking lot. Racist graffiti was spray painted in the area near Guiliani's truck and a Wal-Mart employee made racist remarks to Guiliani. These incidents were reported to Wal-Mart management, who subsequently fired Danco. Guiliani could have pursued a § 1981 hostile work environment claim, despite his status as an independent contractor, the court wrote, if he (other than his company) had been a party to the contract with Wal-Mart.

2. *See Johnson v. Railway Express Agency*, 421 U.S. 454, 95 S.Ct. 1716, 44

L.Ed.2d 295 (1975); *McDonald v. Santa Fe Trail Transp. Co.*, 427 U.S. 273, 96 S.Ct. 2574, 49 L.Ed.2d 493 (1976).

3. 427 U.S. 160, 96 S.Ct. 2586, 49 L.Ed.2d 415 (1976).

4. 491 U.S. 164, 109 S.Ct. 2363, 105 L.Ed.2d 132 (1989).

5. *Id.* at 185, 109 S.Ct. at 2363.

6. *Id.* at 221, 109 S.Ct. at 2363 (Stevens, J., concurring in part).

7. *Compare, e.g., Fadeyi v. Planned Parenthood of Lubbock, Inc.*, 160 F.3d 1048, 1049 n. 11 (5th Cir.1998) (allowing at-will to proceed under § 1981) and cases cited therein *with Gonzalez v. Ingersoll Milling Mach. Co.*, 133 F.3d 1025 (7th Cir.1998) (suggesting that no contract exists in an at-will employment relationship to support a cause of action under § 1981).

decision in *Haddle v. Garrison*[8] wherein the Court held that an at-will employee can state a claim under § 1985(2) apparently has put this issue to rest. Every circuit to consider the issue since *Haddle* has held that at-will employees can state a claim under § 1981.[9]

The Supreme Court has construed the language that secures to all the same contracting rights as "white citizens" to refer only to the racial (as opposed to, say, gender-based or religious) character of the prohibited discrimination, rather than to limit the class of appropriate plaintiffs to non-whites. Accordingly, while the lower courts are in agreement that the statute does not prohibit discrimination because of gender, it is also settled that whites as well as blacks may assert contract denial claims under § 1981 on the basis of race.[10]

The Supreme Court has construed § 1981's ban on "race" discrimination to include also discrimination on the basis of ancestry. The Court has understood ancestry, in turn, to mean membership in an "ethnically and physiognomically distinctive sub-grouping."[11] This somewhat vague formulation has generated predictable confusion among the lower federal courts. We do know that § 1981 "ancestry" does not mean national origin, religion, or alienage status as such.[12] On the other hand, these latter characteristics are often statistically correlated with an individual's descendence from a particular ancestry. For example, in one recent case, a hiring supervisor disparaged the plaintiff's Israeli background and in particular his prior sales experience in Israel, saying "Israel doesn't count." The appellate court ruled that the jury was entitled to treat these comments not just as discrimination on the basis of national origin—actionable under Title VII—but also as discrimination based on the plaintiff's Israeli ancestry, and thus "race" within the meaning of § 1981.[13] It reasoned that the Israeli population was composed primarily of members of a particular ancestry and therefore the jury might have

8. 525 U.S. 121, 119 S.Ct. 489, 142 L.Ed.2d 502 (1998).

9. *See Lauture v. International Business Machines Corp.*, 216 F.3d 258 (2d Cir.2000); *Fadeyi*, 160 F.3d 1048; *Spriggs v. Diamond Auto Glass*, 165 F.3d 1015 (4th Cir.1999) (at will employment relationship is contractual); *Perry v. Woodward*, 199 F.3d 1126, 1133–34 (10th Cir.1999), *cert. denied*, ___ U.S. ___, 120 S.Ct. 1964, 146 L.Ed.2d 796 (2000). *See also Faulk v. Home Oil Co., Inc.*, 184 F.R.D. 645 (M.D.Ala.1999). *But cf. Bishop v. Avera*, 177 F.3d 1233 (11th Cir. 1999) (granting § 1981 defendant qualified immunity in light of the unsettled law governing availability of § 1981 claim to at will employee). The Eleventh Circuit did not mention *Haddle* in its decision.

10. *McDonald*, 427 U.S. 273, 96 S.Ct. 2574, 49 L.Ed.2d 493. But race, rather than mere discipline, must be the subject matter of the complaint. *Hughes v. Ortho Pharmaceutical Corp.*, 177 F.3d 701 (8th Cir.1999). The Fifth Circuit has held that discrimination on the basis of the plaintiff's interracial relationship constituted actionable race discrimination under § 1981. *See Deffenbaugh–Williams v. Wal–Mart Stores, Inc.*, 156 F.3d 581, 588–89 (5th Cir.1998), *vacated on grant of reh'g en banc*, 169 F.3d 215 (5th Cir.1999), *reinstated in relevant part*, 182 F.3d 333 (5th Cir.1999).

11. *St. Francis College v. Al–Khazraji*, 481 U.S. 604, 107 S.Ct. 2022, 95 L.Ed.2d 582 (1987) and *Shaare Tefila Congregation v. Cobb*, 481 U.S. 615, 107 S.Ct. 2019, 95 L.Ed.2d 594 (1987) (protection against ancestry, as opposed to religious, discrimination available to, respectively, Arabs and Jews).

12. *See id.*

13. *Sinai v. New England Tel. & Tel. Co.*, 3 F.3d 471 (1st Cir.1993), *cert. denied* 513 U.S. 1025, 115 S.Ct. 597, 130 L.Ed.2d 509 (1994).

concluded that by disparaging Israel the defendant was really, or also, discriminating against plaintiff because of his "race"—in the nineteenth century sense approved by the Supreme Court.

Although § 1981, like Title VII, does not prohibit discrimination on the basis of alienage *per se*, a limited protection from employment discrimination on the basis of non-citizenship status is now provided by the Immigration Reform and Control Act of 1986, discussed in Chapter 2. But aliens, like other "persons within the jurisdiction of the United States," may complain of race or ancestry and possibly citizenship[14] discrimination under § 1981, or of race, gender, religious, or national origin, but not ancestry or citizenship discrimination under Title VII.[15] None of the Reconstruction Civil Rights Acts reaches gender or religious discrimination as such, although discrimination on those grounds might violate Equal Protection and accordingly would be redressable under § 1983.

The federal judiciary began to place significant limitations on the utility of § 1981 in *General Building Contractors Association v. Pennsylvania*.[16] There the Supreme Court held that a showing of disparate impact does not suffice to prove a § 1981 employment violation, which requires instead a direct or inferential demonstration of discriminatory intent. Consistent with this ruling, the Court in *Patterson* approved for use in § 1981 actions the Title VII intentional disparate treatment mode of proof first outlined in *McDonnell Douglas Corporation v. Green*.[17] Yet at times one encounters some suggestion in the cases that the showing of intent required in § 1981 cases by *General Building Contractors* in practice demands somewhat more "direct" evidence of discrimination

14. *Contrast Anderson v. Conboy*, 156 F.3d 167 (2d Cir.1998) (allowing § 1981 alienage discrimination claim against a private defendant and noting that all circuits recognize a § 1981 claim for alienage discrimination by government defendants); *Duane v. GEICO*, 37 F.3d 1036 (4th Cir. 1994) (§ 1981 prohibits private defendant alienage discrimination against a lawfully admitted, permanent resident alien) *and Bhandari v. First Nat'l Bank of Commerce*, 829 F.2d 1343 (5th Cir.1987) (*en banc*), *vacated on other grounds*, 492 U.S. 901, 109 S.Ct. 3207, 106 L.Ed.2d 558 (1989) (§ 1981 does not prohibit private alienage discrimination). The Fifth Circuit's position was based largely on its unwillingness to "extend" to discrimination based on alienage the application of § 1981's race discrimination ban to private defendants, which the Supreme Court had upheld in *Runyon v. McCrary*, 427 U.S. 160, 96 S.Ct. 2586, 49 L.Ed.2d 415 (1976). The Court's reaffirmation of *Runyon* in *Patterson v. McLean Credit Union*, 491 U.S. 164, 109 S.Ct. 2363, 105 L.Ed.2d 132 (1989) may have eroded the continuing vitality of *Bhandari*, although on remand the Fifth Circuit held that *Patterson* did not affect its holding in *Bhandari v. First Nat'l Bank of Commerce*, 887 F.2d 609 (5th Cir.1989), *cert. denied*, 494 U.S. 1061, 110 S.Ct. 1539, 108 L.Ed.2d 778 (1990). The Fourth Circuit in *Duane* stressed that even undocumented aliens are among the "persons" granted rights by § 1981.

15. *Espinoza v. Farah Mfg. Co.*, 414 U.S. 86, 94 S.Ct. 334, 38 L.Ed.2d 287 (1973) (Title VII); *Bhandari v. First Nat'l Bank of Commerce*, 829 F.2d 1343 (5th Cir.1987) (*en banc*), *vacated on other grounds by* 492 U.S. 901, 109 S.Ct. 3207, 106 L.Ed.2d 558 (1989), *opinion reinstated on remand*, 887 F.2d 609 (5th Cir.1989), *cert. denied*, 494 U.S. 1061, 110 S.Ct. 1539, 108 L.Ed.2d 778 (1990) (§ 1981).

16. 458 U.S. 375, 102 S.Ct. 3141, 73 L.Ed.2d 835 (1982).

17. 411 U.S. 792, 93 S.Ct. 1817, 36 L.Ed.2d 668 (1973). *Patterson*, 491 U.S. at 186, 109 S.Ct. at 2377.

than would usually be required under Title VII.[18] And it remains uncertain whether, in § 1981 "mixed motive" situations, the courts will hew to the complete-defense approach mandated for at least some constitutional violations in actions under § 1983;[19] to the more limited defense mandated by the 1991 Civil Rights Act for post-November 21, 1991 employment practices that violate Title VII;[20] or to the rules laid down by the Supreme Court in *Price Waterhouse v. Hopkins,* which governed Title VII violations before they were modified by the 1991 Act.[21] The uncertainty is fueled by the fact that the 1991 Act, which in other respects expressly and materially modifies § 1981, refers only to Title VII in the provisions that modify *Price Waterhouse.*[22]

Section 1981 has also been read more narrowly than Title VII with respect to the ability of plaintiffs to assert the rights of third parties. The problem has recently arisen in connection with suits by "testers" to

---

18. *See Durham v. Xerox Corp.,* 18 F.3d 836 (10th Cir.1994), *cert. denied,* 513 U.S. 819, 115 S.Ct. 80, 130 L.Ed.2d 33 (1994). Compare the standards the Tenth Circuit applied in *Durham* in upholding district court's grant of summary judgment to the employer on the § 1981 claim with the lower court decisions after *St. Mary's Honor Ctr. v. Hicks,* 509 U.S. 502, 113 S.Ct. 2742, 125 L.Ed.2d 407 (1993) that deem it inappropriate to grant the defendant summary judgment when the plaintiff produces sufficient prima facie evidence of race discrimination under Title VII. *See* Chapter 3 concerning *St. Mary's* and its progeny.

19. *See Mt. Healthy City Sch. Dist. Bd. of Educ. v. Doyle,* 429 U.S. 274, 97 S.Ct. 568, 50 L.Ed.2d 471 (1977). *Mt. Healthy* itself involved a First Amendment violation. A circuit decision applies the *Mt. Healthy* approach—which altogether relieves the defendant of liability upon its showing that it would have reached the same challenged decision even had it not considered an unconstitutional factor—to a § 1983 claim alleging a violation of equal protection based on race discrimination. *See Harris v. Shelby County Bd. of Educ.,* 99 F.3d 1078 (11th Cir.1996). This extension of *Mt. Healthy* is in tension with a line of Supreme Court and circuit decisions beginning with *Regents of Univ. of Cal. v. Bakke,* 438 U.S. 265, 98 S.Ct. 2733, 57 L.Ed.2d 750 (1978), that permits plaintiffs who challenge racial preferences as equal protection violations to retain standing and obtain limited remedies despite a defendant's "same decision" showing. This tension was noted neither in *Harris* nor in a subsequent decision of the same circuit that extends the *Mt. Healthy* complete defense approach to race discrimination claims under § 1981. *Mabra v. United Food & Commercial Workers Local Union No. 1996,* 176 F.3d 1357 (11th Cir.

1999). The two Eleventh Circuit decisions correctly contrast §§ 1983 and 1981 with the 1991 Civil Rights Act amendments to Title VII, which, unlike those Reconstruction-era statutes, limit the force of the mixed-motive defense by expressly providing that the Title VII plaintiff may establish liability and recover prospective relief and attorneys' fees notwithstanding a "same decision" showing. But the decisions then assume that a same-decision showing constitutes a complete defense to *all* actions under the Reconstruction Acts, without considering whether § 1983 actions based on Equal Protection violations represent an exception because of the contrary implications of the *Bakke* line of cases. The issue is also acute in actions under § 1981. To prevail under that statute, the plaintiff must show intentional race discrimination, see *General Building Contractors, supra,* similar to the kind that generated the *Bakke* exception which permits the plaintiff to establish liability and obtain limited relief despite the defendant's "same decision" showing. It remains unresolved, in other words, whether the consequence that *Mt. Healthy* attaches to a mixed-motive showing (a judgment of nonliability) serves as an across-the-board defense to all actions under §§ 1983 and 1981, or only to those constitutional and statutory claims under § 1983 (like the First Amendment claim in *Mt. Healthy* itself) whose policies may not be offended by a complete judgment for defendant.

20. *See* § 3.11, *infra.*

21. *Id.*

22. For a discussion of the liability and remedy differences that depend on whether the original *Price Waterhouse* approach or its legislative codification prevails, *see* § 3.11.

challenge discriminatory referrals by employment agencies. Testers have been defined as persons of the opposite race "equipped with fake credentials intended to be comparable" who apply for employment to an agency or employer without an intention to accept an offer if one is forthcoming.[23] The typical ensuing claim is that the employment agency, on grounds of race, failed to refer the African–American (or female) tester but did refer the other (white or male) tester. Title VII provides that any "person claiming to be aggrieved" by an unlawful employment practice may, after exhausting administrative remedies, sue such an agency in court.[24] Consequently, testers may be able to state a Title VII claim despite their own lack of a bona fide interest in employment.[25]

By contrast, the text of § 1981 suggests that only a person deprived of what is otherwise a legal right to make or enforce a contract has standing. Reasoning that testers could not have enforced an employment contract offer because of the material misrepresentations of fact they made to the defendant employment agency about their intentions to secure employment, several appellate courts have held that tester plaintiffs cannot state a claim for damages under § 1981: "the loss of the opportunity to enter into a *void* contract—i.e., a contract that *neither* party can enforce—is not an injury cognizable under § 1981, for a void contract is a legal nullity."[26] In *Kyles*, the Seventh Circuit explained that Congress creates "a substantive right, the denial of which alone gives rise to a cognizable injury and the right to sue."[27] By its terms, § 1981 protect only the contractual relationship and the class of persons who can sue is therefore limited to those wishing to enter in, or remain in, that relationship.[28]

This standing problem, however, should be distinguished from the question of how broadly a violation of the plaintiff's own rights under § 1981 may be defined in relation to discriminatory actions immediately directed against another. Here the courts have shown considerable flexibility, permitting the assertion of § 1981 claims where intimate or

---

23. *See Fair Employment Council of Greater Wash., Inc. v. BMC Mktg. Corp.*, 28 F.3d 1268 (D.C.Cir.1994).

24. 42 U.S.C.A. §§ 2000e–5(b), (c), (f)(1).

25. *Fair Employment Council of Greater Wash.*, 28 F.3d 1268; *but see* n.1 of that decision, which reserves decision on the question whether the lack of a bona fide interest in employment defeats standing.

26. *Fair Employment Council of Greater Wash.*, 28 F.3d 1268. *See also Kyles v. J.K. Guardian Sec. Servs., Inc.*, 222 F.3d 289 (7th Cir.2000) (finding that testers lack standing to sue under § 1981 for employment discrimination, but can pursue a Title VII claim); *Evans v. Kansas City, Mo. Sch. Dist.*, 65 F.3d 98 (8th Cir.1995), *cert. denied*, 517 U.S. 1104, 116 S.Ct. 1319, 134 L.Ed.2d 472 (1996) (holding that only stu-

dents or parents, not a teacher, have standing to challenge segregation order). *But cf. Watts v. Boyd Properties*, 758 F.2d 1482 (11th Cir.1985) and *Meyers v. Pennypack Woods Home Ownership Ass'n*, 559 F.2d 894 (3d Cir.1977), *overruled on other grounds by Goodman v. Lukens Steel Co.*, 777 F.2d 113 (3d Cir.1985), *aff'd*, 482 U.S. 656, 107 S.Ct. 2617, 96 L.Ed.2d 572 (1987) (according fair-housing testers standing to sue under §§ 1982 and 1981, respectively, although not squarely addressing question whether the testers had suffered legal injury within the meaning of those statutes).

27. 222 F.3d at 303.

28. *Id.* The court distinguished Title VII, finding that a tester can sue for employment discrimination because Congress created in Title VII "a broad substantive right that extends far beyond the simple refusal or failure to hire." *Id.* at 298.

associational rights of the plaintiff are allegedly invaded by a defendant whose conduct was aimed at third parties.[29] A related, but distinct question is whether the defendant must be the party with whom the plaintiff contracts or seeks to contract. Courts have answered this question in the negative, holding § 1981 is violated by a racially motivated interference with a plaintiff's right to enter into contracts with nonwhites[30] and by third parties' attempts to punish the plaintiff for making such contracts.[31]

When a customer complains of racial discrimination by an employee of a retailer, the employer can be held vicariously liable for the acts of the employee if the employee was acting within the scope of the employment.[32] Unlike sexual harassment employment cases,[33] in these public accommodation § 1981 cases, it is no defense to respondeat superior liability that the customer suffered the discrimination at the hands of a low-level clerk. "[A] rule that only actions by supervisors are imputed to the employer would result, in most cases, in a no liability rule."[34]

Recent additional restrictions on the use of § 1981 in actions against government defendants, and a short-lived restriction on the availability of § 1981 to attack post-hire conditions of employment, are described below.

The Supreme Court has directed the lower federal courts to borrow analogous state statutes of limitations in actions under § 1981, and has held that pursuing Title VII administrative procedures does not toll the § 1981 statute of limitations.[35] The Court has since clarified that in actions under any of the Reconstruction Civil Rights Acts, the forum state's "personal injury" statute of limitations should apply;[36] and the particular period the court should borrow is the state's general or residual statute on personal injury claims rather than, for example, a

---

29. *See, e.g., Alizadeh v. Safeway Stores, Inc.,* 802 F.2d 111, 114 (5th Cir.1986) and *Parr v. Woodmen of the World Life Ins. Co.,* 791 F.2d 888, 890 (11th Cir.1986) (upholding § 1981 claims where defendant employer allegedly fired (*Alizadeh*) or refused to hire (*Parr*) the plaintiff because of a spouse's race); *Fiedler v. Marumsco Christian Sch.,* 631 F.2d 1144, 1149 (4th Cir. 1980) (§ 1981 claim stated on claim by white students that private school expelled them because they had associated with blacks).

30. *See, e.g., Des Vergnes v. Seekonk Water Dist.,* 601 F.2d 9 (1st Cir.1979).

31. *See, e.g., Winston v. Lear–Siegler, Inc.,* 558 F.2d 1266, 1270 (6th Cir.1977); *DeMatteis v. Eastman Kodak Co.,* 511 F.2d 306, 312, *modified,* 520 F.2d 409 (2d Cir. 1975); *cf. Sullivan v. Little Hunting Park,* 396 U.S. 229, 237, 90 S.Ct. 400, 404, 24 L.Ed.2d 386 (1969) (same result under § 1982).

32. *See, e.g., Arguello v. Conoco, Inc.,* 207 F.3d 803, 809–12 (5th Cir.), *cert. denied sub nom. Escobedo v. Conoco, Inc.,* ___ U.S. ___, 121 S.Ct. 177, 148 L.Ed.2d 121 (2000). *Cf. City of Chicago v. Matchmaker Real Estate Sales Ctr., Inc.,* 982 F.2d 1086, 1089 (7th Cir.1992), *cert. denied sub nom. Ernst v. Leadership Council for Metro. Open Cmtys.,* 508 U.S. 972, 113 S.Ct. 2961, 125 L.Ed.2d 662 (1993) (arising under the Fair Housing Act and § 1982).

33. *See* discussion of vicarious liability in sexual harassment cases in § 2.22(a)(2) and (4).

34. *Arguello,* 207 F.3d at 810.

35. *Johnson v. Railway Express Agency,* 421 U.S. 454, 95 S.Ct. 1716, 44 L.Ed.2d 295 (1975).

36. *See Wilson v. Garcia,* 471 U.S. 261, 105 S.Ct. 1938, 85 L.Ed.2d 254 (1985) (§ 1983); *Goodman v. Lukens Steel Co.,* 482 U.S. 656, 107 S.Ct. 2617, 96 L.Ed.2d 572 (1987) (§ 1981).

statute geared specifically to intentional torts.[37] A more detailed discussion of the selection and application of statutes of limitations under the Reconstruction Civil Rights Acts may be found in the Chapter 12.

Title 42 U.S.C.A. § 1977A(a)(1), added by § 102 of the Civil Rights Act of 1991, provides that damages under Title VII are recoverable only if the complainant "cannot recover" under § 1981. But the EEOC, relying on the Sponsors' Interpretive Memorandum,[38] has interpreted that language to bar only double recovery for the same injury, not parallel proceedings under the two statutes. Putative plaintiffs with intentional race discrimination claims against employers large enough to be covered by and not exempt from Title VII can therefore apparently choose whether to proceed under Title VII or § 1981 or both.

That choice will be heavily influenced by the availability of unlimited compensatory and punitive damages under § 1981, free of Title VII's variable caps, and by the immediate access to court under § 1981, free of the Title VII state and federal administrative prerequisite requirements with their rather early filing deadlines. Some such claimants, however, who, despite the availability of attorneys' fees, are unable to attract counsel might nevertheless prefer the Title VII route, because by statute the EEOC is expected to assist with investigation and conciliation.

In practice, however, § 1981 will usually look more attractive. Procedurally and remedially, the Reconstruction Civil Rights Acts, § 1981 in particular, may hold several attractions over Title VII. For one, no administrative exhaustion is required.[39] Second, the applicable limitation periods borrowed from state law are normally longer than the usual 180–day or 240/300–day Title VII deadline for filing charges with federal or state agencies. Third, although jury trials are now available under either statute with respect to claims of intentional discrimination, the nineteenth-century statutes offer compensatory and punitive damages unlimited in amount;[40] while, even after the Civil Rights Act of 1991, Title VII plaintiffs who prove intentional discrimination are subject to caps on those damages that vary with the number of employees working for the defendant employer.[41] In one respect, Title VII lines up precisely with § 1983 and § 1981: punitive damages are not available

37. *Owens v. Okure,* 488 U.S. 235, 109 S.Ct. 573, 102 L.Ed.2d 594 (1989).

38. 137 Cong. Rec. S15484 (Oct. 30, 1991).

39. *See Patsy v. Board of Regents,* 457 U.S. 496, 102 S.Ct. 2557, 73 L.Ed.2d 172 (1982) (§ 1983). *But see* § 17.121 on newer, more stringent administrative exhaustion requirements applicable to state and federal prisoners under the Prison Litigation Reform Act of 1996.

40. The Eleventh Circuit has held that a punitive damage award under § 1981 is available only when the plaintiff proves that the defendant acted with "malice or

reckless disregard" of the plaintiff's rights. *Ferrill v. Parker Group, Inc.,* 168 F.3d 468, 476 (11th Cir.1999). The court vacated an award of punitive damages because the lower court had specifically found no evidence of animus or malice.

41. *See Olmsted v. Taco Bell Corp.,* 141 F.3d 1457 (11th Cir.1998) (affirming lower court's decision to reduce damage awards of $450,000 in compensatory and $3 million in punitive damages to Title VII's cap of $300,000 because plaintiff had abandoned his § 1981 claim in a pre-trial stipulation).

against a defendant government entity.[42]

But what if the § 1981 defendant is able to prove something akin to what the Supreme Court's *Mt. Healthy City School Dist. Bd. of Educ. v. Doyle*[43] decision encourages § 1983 defendants to prove: that the challenged employment action would have been taken for lawful reasons independent of the racial component of the employer's overall motivation? The effect of this showing under § 1983 appears to be (except with respect to procedural due process and certain express or facial equal protection violations) that no federal law violation is established and the defendant may not be mulcted in damages. Under Title VII, as amended in 1991, however, the defendant who makes this "same-decision" showing is relieved only of retroactive, monetary relief; she is still considered to have violated the law and is therefore subject to prospective relief and attorneys' fees.[44] The 1991 amendments to Title VII did not, however, make the same amendment to § 1981 or the ADEA, although it amended those statutes in other respects. Consequently, the post–*Mt. Healthy*, pre–1991 regime governing § 1981 defendants who carry the showing is therefore likely to prevail in most circuits.[45] And under that regime the § 1981 defendant may escape without liability, whereas the Title VII plaintiff will establish a violation and thereby have an opportunity to receive declaratory and injunctive relief and, in turn, attorney's fees as a "prevailing party."[46] Indeed, even if the Section 1981 defendant fails to plead the defense affirmatively, it may be preserved if mentioned in the

42. Section 1981(b)(1) authorizes punitive damages when intentional Title VII discrimination is proved (and other, traditional requirements for punitive damages are satisfied) except against "a government, government agency, or political subdivision." The Supreme Court has held punitive damages generally unavailable in § 1983 actions against government in *City of Newport v. Fact Concerts, Inc.*, 453 U.S. 247, 101 S.Ct. 2748, 69 L.Ed.2d 616 (1981). And lower courts have extended the *City of Newport* ruling to actions under § 1981. *See Walters v. City of Atlanta*, 803 F.2d 1135 (11th Cir.1986) and cases there cited.

43. 429 U.S. 274, 97 S.Ct. 568, 50 L.Ed.2d 471 (1977).

44. *See* Chapter 3 on Title VII proof modes.

45. *Pulliam v. Tallapoosa County Jail*, 185 F.3d 1182, 1184 (11th Cir.1999); *Mabra v. United Food & Commercial Workers Local Union*, 176 F.3d 1357 (11th Cir.1999). The Eighth Circuit, purporting to distinguish § 1981 from Section 1983 in this respect, upheld a jury award of damages for a violation of Section 1981 even though the defendant had carried the showing described (for § 1983 cases) by *Mt. Healthy. See Edwards v. Jewish Hosp.*, 855 F.2d

1345 (8th Cir.1988). The court asserted that § 1981 aims to deter as well as compensate, while § 1983 has only a compensation rationale. Some support may have been drawn for the proposition that § 1983 seeks only to compensate from the Supreme Court's decisions in *Mt. Healthy* and *Carey v. Piphus*, 435 U.S. 247, 98 S.Ct. 1042, 55 L.Ed.2d 252 (1978). But well before *Edwards* was decided, the Court had made clear that § 1983 has a distinct deterrent rationale, and that punitive damages are sometimes necessary to fulfill it. *Smith v. Wade*, 461 U.S. 30, 103 S.Ct. 1625, 75 L.Ed.2d 632 (1983). *But see* § 4.45, *infra.* This section discusses recent authority to the effect that the § 1983 defendant found to have violated *equal protection* is liable, and subject to declaratory and injunctive relief and attorneys' fees, and possibly also emotional distress and punitive damages (but not to a hiring or promotion order or economic compensation like back or front pay), even when he carries the "same decision" showing that ordinarily negates any liability altogether.

46. But see text *supra. See* Chapter 11 on Attorney's Fees under § 706(k) of Title VII and 42 U.S.C.A. § 1988 with respect to actions under all of the Reconstruction Civil Rights Acts.

pretrial order.[47]

A potential plaintiff with an intentional race discrimination claim actionable under both statutes may prefer Title VII if she cannot afford counsel and believes that state or federal agency administrative processing of her charge will induce her employer to settle. In addition, it remains possible, to an as yet uncertain extent, for a plaintiff who cannot prove intentional discrimination and would therefore fail under § 1981 to succeed under Title VII by establishing that an employer's neutral practice had a disproportionate adverse impact on her group and that the employer cannot justify the practice as a matter of job relatedness and business necessity.

In actions against state and local government employers, there is considerable doubt, as discussed in detail in the *"Jett"* sections that follow,[48] whether § 1981 is available on its own terms, or whether the plaintiff must also surmount the additional proof requirements and defenses available under § 1983. If the latter, then Title VII once again would become a more attractive option. And Title VII would appear to be the *only* remedy for race discrimination in federal employment, which has been held outside the reach of § 1981.[49]

In its 1988 Term, the Court held in *Patterson v. McLean Credit Union*[50] that discriminatory conduct directed against an employee after her initial hiring falls outside the right granted by § 1981 to "make" a contract free from racial discrimination. The 1991 legislation overturns this decision and thereby restores 42 U.S.C.A. § 1981 as a forceful supplementary vehicle for redressing race or ancestry discrimination in contracting, although only when the defendant's conduct is shown, by direct or indirect evidence, to be *intentional*.[51] The legislation provides that the right to "make" a contract extends beyond initial formation to include "performance, modification and termination" and thus reaches not only dismissal but also ongoing terms and conditions of employment, including retaliation.[52]

The 1991 legislation, then, arguably restores § 1981 post-hiring retaliation claims by overturning *Patterson*.[53] The contours of such a

---

47. *Pulliam v. Tallapoosa County*, 185 F.3d at 1185, n.4.

48. §§ 5.2A and 5.2B.

49. *Lee v. Hughes*, No. 5:96–CV–316–3 (M.D.Ga.1997), *aff'd on other grounds*, 145 F.3d 1272 (11th Cir.1998); *cert. denied*, 119 S.Ct. 1026, 143 L.Ed.2d 37 (1999); *Williams v. Glickman*, 936 F.Supp. 1, 5 (D.D.C.1996); *Gallardo v. Board of County Comm'rs*, 857 F.Supp. 783 (D.Kan.1994). *See Martin v. Heckler*, 773 F.2d 1145, 1152 (11th Cir. 1985).

50. 491 U.S. 164, 109 S.Ct. 2363, 105 L.Ed.2d 132 (1989).

51. *See General Bldg. Contractors Ass'n. v. Pennsylvania*, 458 U.S. 375, 102 S.Ct. 3141, 73 L.Ed.2d 835 (1982).

52. Section 101(b) (amending 42 U.S.C.A. § 1981 (1988)); *Hawkins v. 1115 Legal Service Care*, 163 F.3d 684 (2d Cir. 1998) (§ 1981 as amended in 1991 reaches claims of unlawful retaliation, harassment and discrimination in hiring, discharge, demotion, promotion, and transfer); *Andrews v. Lakeshore Rehab. Hosp.*, 140 F.3d 1405, 1412–13 (11th Cir.1998) (same); *Kim v. Nash Finch Co.*, 123 F.3d 1046, 1059 (8th Cir.1997); *Barge v. Anheuser–Busch, Inc.*, 87 F.3d 256, 259 (8th Cir.1996) (same).

53. *Cf.* EEOC Guidance on Investigating, Analyzing Retaliation Claims, EEOC Compliance Manual § 8–1 (1998).

claim, however, remain unclear.[54] The Eleventh Circuit, for example, revived a § 1981 post-hiring retaliation claim by a black plaintiff alleging that she was terminated for filing an EEOC charge for race discrimination,[55] but rejected a claim by a white plaintiff fired for complaining of racial slurs about blacks.[56] The Seventh Circuit also requires this type of double causation: in order for retaliation to be actionable under § 1981, the plaintiff must show that the defendant interfered with his right to enforce the contract on account of race, and the plaintiff must then show that the retaliation itself had a racial motivation.[57] However, this double causation requirement is suspect; the party complaining of retaliation need not also be a member of a protected group.[58]

The Eleventh Circuit has held that neither the BFOQ nor business necessity defense, available in some circumstances under Title VII, will prevail in a § 1981 claim.[59] The court stated that the business necessity defense is available only to claims of disparate impact, a claim not cognizable under § 1981, which requires proof of intentional discrimination.[60] And a BFOQ defense, the court noted, is not available to a charge of racial discrimination.[61]

Section 1981 contains no threshold numerical requirement for employer coverage. In the course of considering the amendments, Congress observed that § 1981 constitutes the only protection against race or ancestry discrimination for those millions of applicants or employees whose employers are too small to be covered by Title VII. Despite this understanding, the amendments make no attempt to protect those applicants or employees against the other forms of discrimination prohibited by Title VII, that is, sex, religion, or national origin, or against race discrimination resulting solely from the effects of a neutral practice.[62] Indeed, by capping Title VII damages, while leaving uncapped the

---

54. *See Olmsted v. Taco Bell Corp.*, 141 F.3d 1457 (11th Cir.1998).

55. *Andrews v. Lakeshore Rehab. Hosp.*, 140 F.3d 1405 (11th Cir.1998).

56. *Little v. United Tech.*, 103 F.3d 956 (11th Cir.1997).

57. *Daniels v. Pipefitters' Ass'n Local Union No. 597*, 945 F.2d 906 (7th Cir.1991), *cert. denied*, 503 U.S. 951, 112 S.Ct. 1514, 117 L.Ed.2d 651 (1992) (for retaliation to be actionable under § 1981, the retaliation itself must be racially motivated). *See also Kim v. Nash Finch Co.*, 123 F.3d 1046 (8th Cir.1997) (allowing § 1981 claim by Korean plaintiff retaliated against because he filed EEOC complaint).

58. *See, e.g., Anderson v. Phillips Petroleum Co.*, 722 F.Supp. 668, 671–72 (D.Kan. 1989).

59. *See Ferrill v. Parker Group, Inc.*, 168 F.3d 468, 473–74 (11th Cir.1999).

60. *Id. See* the discussion of the "business necessity" defense in § 3.35, *infra*.

61. *Id.* This holding by the Eleventh Circuit arguably conflicts with a Seventh Circuit case, *Wittmer v. Peters*, 87 F.3d 916 (7th Cir.1996), *cert. denied*, 519 U.S. 1111, 117 S.Ct. 949, 136 L.Ed.2d 837 (1997), in which the court crafted a narrow racial BFOQ. *See* the discussion of the BFOQ defense in § 3.3, *infra*.

62. It is well settled that § 1981 affords no protection against discrimination based on gender. *See McDonald v. Santa Fe Trail Transp. Co.*, 427 U.S. 273, 96 S.Ct. 2574, 49 L.Ed.2d 493 (1976). *See also Runyon v. McCrary*, 427 U.S. 160, 96 S.Ct. 2586, 49 L.Ed.2d 415 (1976) (applying § 1981 to purely private conduct and affirmed in that respect by *Patterson v. McLean Credit Union*, 491 U.S. 164, 109 S.Ct. 2363, 105 L.Ed.2d 132 (1989)). While it is also clear that § 1981 does prohibit discrimination based on ancestry (ethnic or physiognomic characteristic), *St. Francis College v. Al-Khazraji*, 481 U.S. 604, 107 S.Ct. 2022, 95 L.Ed.2d 582 (1987); *Shaare Tefila Congre-*

compensatory and punitive damages recoverable under § 1981, Congress rather pointedly expresses greater concern with intentional race discrimination than with unintentional discrimination or intentional discrimination based on Title VII's other prohibited grounds.

Courts commonly permit the showing of intent requisite under the Reconstruction Acts to be made inferentially, that is, through the *McDonnell Douglas/Burdine/St. Mary's* formula of shifting evidentiary burdens that is paradigmatic under Title VII.[63] Nevertheless, there are rumblings of discontent with the dominant view that treats such inferential evidence as an adequate foundation not only for liability but also for punitive damages.[64] The Supreme Court's decision in *Kolstad v. American Dental Association,*[65] should put and end to these rumblings.

As observed above, while the damages caps in 42 U.S.C.A. § 1981a limit the recovery of compensatory and punitive damages available under Title VII,[66] they do not limit the recovery available to plaintiffs who prevail under the amended § 1981.[67] For this reason, plaintiffs complaining under both Title VII and § 1981 of underlying intentional race or ancestry discrimination may be well advised to pursue a related retaliation claim under § 1981, as well as Title VII. But to prevail under § 1981, the retaliation plaintiff must show that the defendant took action against him in reprisal for plaintiff's assertion of one of the rights protected by § 1981—i.e., the right to be free of interference in the making or enforcement of contracts because of race or ancestry, and not, for example, gender, a prohibited ground only under Title VII.[68] And the

gation v. Cobb, 481 U.S. 615, 107 S.Ct. 2019, 95 L.Ed.2d 594 (1987), those opinions also suggest that it provides no protection against religious discrimination as such. The circuits are split on whether § 1981 reaches private sector discrimination because of alienage. *See Anderson v. Conboy,* 156 F.3d 167 (2d Cir.1998) (holding yes; relying especially on 1991 amendments' confirmation that the statute reaches private interference with contracting); *Duane v. GEICO,* 37 F.3d 1036 (4th Cir.1994) (holding yes); *Bhandari v. First Nat'l Bank of Commerce,* 829 F.2d 1343 (5th Cir.1987) (*en banc*), *vacated on other grounds,* 492 U.S. 901, 109 S.Ct. 3207, 106 L.Ed.2d 558 (1989), *opinion reinstated on remand,* 887 F.2d 609 (5th Cir.1989), *cert. denied,* 494 U.S. 1061, 110 S.Ct. 1539, 108 L.Ed.2d 778 (1990) (holding no). Appellate decisions are in accord that governmental alienage discrimination is actionable under § 1981.

63. *See, e.g., St. Mary's Honor Ctr. v. Hicks,* 509 U.S. 502, 506 n. 1, 113 S.Ct. 2742, 2746, 125 L.Ed.2d 407 (1993), *Patterson v. McLean Credit Union,* 491 U.S. 164, 109 S.Ct. 2363, 105 L.Ed.2d 132 (1989); *Barbour v. Merrill,* 48 F.3d 1270 (D.C.Cir. 1995). The Tenth Circuit recently applied this analytical framework in *Perry v. Woodward,* 199 F.3d 1126, 1135–41 (10th Cir.

1999), *cert. denied,* ___ U.S. ___, 120 S.Ct. 1964, 146 L.Ed.2d 796 (2000). In *Perry,* the defendant argued that a Hispanic plaintiff could not meet the prima facie burden because she could not prove her replacement was a non-Hispanic. In rejecting this argument, the court noted its disagreement with those circuits that require some additional fact from which an inference of discrimination can arise whenever the plaintiff is replaced with a person possessing the same attributes. See the discussion in Chapter 3 on plaintiff's burdens of proof.

64. On the general Reconstruction Act standard for punitive damages, *see Smith v. Wade,* 461 U.S. 30, 103 S.Ct. 1625, 75 L.Ed.2d 632 (1983). For the recent rumblings, see the petition for writ of certiorari in *Barbour v. Merrill,* 48 F.3d 1270 (D.C.Cir.1995).

65. 527 U.S. 526, 119 S.Ct. 2118, 144 L.Ed.2d 494 (1999).

66. *See* 42 U.S.C.A. § 1981a(b)(3).

67. 42 U.S.C.A. § 1981a(b)(4).

68. *Hawkins,* 163 F.3d 684; *Manning v. Metropolitan Life Ins. Co.,* 127 F.3d 686, 689 n. 1 (8th Cir.1997) (retaliation for opposing gender discrimination not actionable under § 1981).

plaintiff who has tried primary discrimination or retaliation claims under both Title VII and § 1981 and receives a favorable jury verdict may bear the additional burden of demonstrating to the court that the jury accepted her § 1981 claim in particular if she hopes to avoid the Title VII cap on damages.[69]

§ 5.2A   *Jett, Will,* and the Civil Rights Act Of 1991: Proving Section 1981 Violations In Actions Against State Or Local Governments

With its decisions in *Will v. Michigan Department of State Police,*[1] and *Jett v. Dallas Independent School Dist.,*[2] the Supreme Court imposed significant restrictions on plaintiffs alleging intentional race discrimination and seeking redress against state and local governments under, respectively, 42 U.S.C.A. § 1983 and 42 U.S.C.A. § 1981. The Civil Rights Act of 1991 casts some doubt on the continued vitality of *Jett.* How the federal courts interpret the 1991 Act as applied to *Jett* will determine whether and to what degree such a plaintiff can pursue remedies against government under § 1981, or only under or subject to the restrictions of § 1983.

§ 1.11   Claims Arising From Acts of Discrimination in Employment on or Before Nov. 21, 1991

The Supreme Court has held that the Civil Rights Act of 1991 does not apply retroactively. It prohibits acts of employment discrimination that occur after its enactment on November 21, 1991.[3] As a result, our analysis begins with the interplay of §§ 1981 and 1983 after *Will* and *Jett,* but before Nov. 21, 1991, and without regard to the 1991 Civil Rights Act.

In *Will v. Michigan Department of State Police,*[4] the Supreme Court held that "neither a state or its officials acting in their official capacities are 'persons' under Section 1983."[5] Hence, the Court concluded that under § 1983 states are not suable at all in their own name and state officials sued in their official capacities are subject only to prospective relief.[6]

In that same term, the Court also decided *Jett v. Dallas Independent School Dist.*[7] In *Jett,* the Court severely limited the applicability of § 1981. The Court stated,

> We think the history of the 1866 Act and the 1871 Act ... indicates that Congress intended that the explicit remedial provisions of

---

69. *See Hawkins*, 163 F.3d 684.

§ 5.2A

1. 491 U.S. 58, 109 S.Ct. 2304, 105 L.Ed.2d 45 (1989).

2. 491 U.S. 701, 109 S.Ct. 2702, 105 L.Ed.2d 598 (1989).

3. *Landgraf v. USI Film Products,* 511 U.S. 244, 114 S.Ct. 1483, 128 L.Ed.2d 229 (1994); *Rivers v. Roadway Express,* 511 U.S.

298, 114 S.Ct. 1510, 128 L.Ed.2d 274 (1994).

4. 491 U.S. 58, 109 S.Ct. 2304, 105 L.Ed.2d 45, (1989).

5. *Id.* at 71, 109 S.Ct. at 2312.

6. *Id.* at 63, 109 S.Ct. at 2308.

7. 491 U.S. 701, 109 S.Ct. 2702, 105 L.Ed.2d 598 (1989).

Section 1983 be controlling in the context of damages actions brought against state actors alleging violation of the rights declared in Section 1981.[8]

Consequently, "the express 'action at law' provided by Section *1983* ... provides the exclusive federal damages *remedy* for the violation of the *rights* guaranteed by Section 1981 when the claim is pressed against a state actor."[9] The Court explained the effect of this holding:

> [T]o prevail on his [Section 1981] claim for damages against the school district, [plaintiff] must show that the violation of his 'right to make contracts' protected by Section 1981 was caused by a custom or policy within the meaning of Monell and subsequent [Section 1983] cases.[10]

The language of the *Jett* opinion broadly applies the § 1983 limitations to any § 1981 claim against a "state actor." A plaintiff seeking redress for deprivations of the rights guaranteed by § 1981 must therefore also satisfy the additional prima facie proof element of § 1983—a showing of official policy or custom.

Accordingly, after *Will* and *Jett* but before the 1991 Act, an employee with a claim of intentional discrimination faced several potential roadblocks to redress under §§ 1981 and 1983. The Supreme Court, in *Brown v. GSA*,[11] had held Title VII to preempt § 1981 claims against *federal* employers. Under *Jett*, the plaintiff clearly couldn't win a suit under § 1981 against a *municipality* or *local* government unless he could show a policy or custom as required by § 1983. Because of *Will*, she couldn't sue the *state* as such, under § 1983. And perhaps her § 1981 claim against a *state* would falter as well. After all, the language of *Jett* apparently required the plaintiff to meet all § 1983 requirements in order to perfect a § 1981 claim against a state actor, and under *Will* a state was no longer a § 1983 "person."

On the other hand, under the logic of *Jett*, a plaintiff possibly *could* recover against a state under § 1981. The Court in *Jett* was primarily concerned with preventing a plaintiff from using § 1981 as an "end-around" § 1983's requirements for bringing suit against a state or local governmental actor. But, since the Court had just held in *Will* that states could *not* be sued under § 1983, § 1981 claims against states could no longer be viewed as circumventing § 1983 requirements. That is, allowing a plaintiff to proceed against a state under the less rigorous standards of § 1981 would not have been circumventing the stricter standards of § 1983, since states were no longer suable under § 1983 at all. On this reasoning, a plaintiff could still sue a state under § 1981 without meeting the "policy" hurdle of § 1983.

The Civil Rights Act of 1991 amended Section 1981 by designating the former text—the substantive protection against intentionally race-

---

8. *Id.* at 731, 109 S.Ct. at 2720.

9. *Id.* at 735, 109 S.Ct. at 2723 (emphasis added).

10. *Id.* at 735–736, 109 S.Ct. at 2723.

11. 425 U.S. 820, 96 S.Ct. 1961, 48 L.Ed.2d 402 (1976).

based interference with the right to make and enforce contracts—as Section 1981(a). [The plaintiff seeking relief under this provision must take pains to plead the claim as arising under "42 U.S.C. Section *1981(a)," with* parentheses, in order to receive the *uncapped* damages this Reconstruction-era statute affords. A complaint designating a desire to recover only under "42 U.S.C. Section *1981a,"* without parentheses, may be understood to refer to the provision the same 1991 Congress added to *Title VII,* see § 4.26, *supra,*—a provision that for the first time authorized compensatory and punitive damages for intentional violations of that 1964 statute, *but capped them.*[12]] Congress also amended the former Section 1981 by adding a subsection (b) that overturned *Patterson* and thus restored the application of the section to all pre- or post-hire aspects of a contract or employment relationship.

Finally, Congress added a new subparagraph, Section 1981(c). In § 101(c) of the 1991 Act, Congress provided:

(c) The rights protected by this section are protected against impairment by nongovernmental discrimination *and impairment under color of state law.*[13]

The crucial inquiry raised by the italicized text is whether Congress intended to overrule *Jett.* We now turn to that question.

§ 5.2B Claims of Section 1981 Violations Asserted Against Local or State Government After the Effective Date of the 1991 Amendments to Section 1981

Early reported *district* court cases addressing the issue held or implied that the 1991 Act overrules *Jett.* For example, in *Arnett v. Davis County School District,*[1] the court wrote,

In the Civil Rights Act of 1991, however, Congress amended § 1981 to make clear its intent that § 1981's protections be extended to impairment of that section's rights "under color of State law."[2]

Similarly, in *Morris v. State of Kansas Department of Revenue,*[3] a United States District Court observed,

The Civil Rights Act of 1991 amended s 1981 to clarify that "[t]he rights protected by this section are protected against ... impairment under color of State law." 42 U.S.C.A. § 1981(c). In effect, this amendment overrules *Jett.* (emphasis added).[4]

12. *Olmsted v. Taco Bell Corp.,* 141 F.3d 1457 (11th Cir. 1998)(upholding a cap on plaintiff's damages where pretrial order referred to claims only under "1981a," rather than "1981(a)").

13. Pub.L. 102–166, § 101 (1991) (codified at 42 U.S.C.A. § 1981(c)) (emphasis added).

§ 5.2A

1. 1993 WL 434053 at 5 & n. 8 (D.Utah 1993).

2. Codified at 42 U.S.C.A. § 1981(c) (*overruling Jett v. Dallas Indep. Sch. Dist.,* 491 U.S. 701, 109 S.Ct. 2702, 105 L.Ed.2d 598 (1989)).

3. 849 F.Supp. 1421 (D.Kan.1994).

4. *Morris,* 849 F.Supp. at 1426 (citing *Arnett,* 1993 WL 434053 at 5).

In *Ford v. City of Rockford*,[5] another district court concluded that *Jett* had been overruled. The district court stated, "Congress ... *overruled* the Jett holding in its enactment of the Civil Rights Act of 1991,[6] by extending the ambit of Section 1981 to state action."[7]

Vakharia v. Swedish Covenant Hospital,[8] implicitly reached the same conclusion. The district court stated,

> [W]hen a municipal agency is involved, the municipal employee's isolated acts will not subject the municipal employer to liability under Section 1981—*at least as Section 1981* existed prior to the Civil Rights Act of 1991—unless the employee was following established policy.[9]

By emphasizing that its decision was based on the law before the 1991 Act, the district court suggested that the 1991 Act had overruled *Jett.*

Nevertheless, at least as strong an argument can be made—an argument the more recent *circuit* court opinions explicitly or implicitly accept—that the 1991 Act did *not* overrule *Jett*. For example, the Act nowhere expressly contravenes the *Jett* holding, e.g., by authorizing a § 1981 claim against a state or local government employee to proceed without regard to the limitations of § 1983. The simple statement in new § 1981(c) that § 1981 protects against "impairment under color of state law" does not contradict the holding in *Jett*. In fact, the whole premise of *Jett* was that a plaintiff suing a state or local government employer was not limited to a claim under § 1983 but could assert a claim, albeit a peculiarly limited one, under § 1981 as well. *Jett* demanded only that the plaintiff bringing a § 1981 claim against a government entity satisfy the requirements of § 1983 for entity liability. Viewed this way, the language of new § 1981(c) arguably codifies, rather than overrules, *Jett*.

The argument that the *Jett* limitation survives the 1991 Act is fortified by the way a Supreme Court that takes a "plain-text" approach to statutory interpretation is likely to view subsection (c). Even if the Court resorts to legislative history it would find only a Congressional determination to codify *Runyon*. There is no stated intention to overrule *Jett*, despite the express stated intention found elsewhere in the 1991 legislation to overrule other specifically named Supreme Court decisions. Accordingly, more recent *circuit* court decisions have held that *Jett* enjoys continuing vitality notwithstanding § 1981(c) and accordingly that Section 1983 affords the only claim against state actor defendants— or at least cities and counties, because states as such are not after *Will* suable "persons" under Section 1983[10]—for vindicating a violation of the rights protected by Section 1981(a).[11] In effect, then, in these circuits

---

5. 1992 WL 309603 at 2 (N.D.Ill.1992).

6. 42 U.S.C.A. § 1981(c)(2).

7. 1992 WL 309603 at 2 (emphasis added).

8. 824 F.Supp. 769 (N.D.Ill.1993). *See also La Compania Ocho, Inc. v. United States Forest Serv.*, 874 F.Supp. 1242, 1251 (D.N.M.1995) (same conclusion in dictum).

9. *Id.* at 785 & n. 1 (emphasis added).

10. *Will v. Michigan Dept of State Police*, 491 U.S. 58, 109 S.Ct. 2304, 105 L.Ed.2d 45 (1989).

11. *Butts v. County of Volusia* , 222 F.3d 891 (11th Cir. 2000); *Dennis v. County of Fairfax*, 55 F.3d 151, 156 n. 1 (4th Cir. 1995). *See Williams v. Little Rock Mun.*

Section 1983's "and laws" clause, discussed in Section 5.3 immediately following, is the sole Reconstruction-era remedy against local government for violations of the Section 1981(a) right to be free of intentional race discrimination in employment and other contracts. Of course Title VII remains available to remedy intentional race discrimination in local (and state) government employment; claims under that statute are provable without regard to the "official policy" proof requirement that encumbers Section 1983 actions against government entities, but compensatory damages will be capped.

Other circuit decisions have suggested an intermediate position. These courts treat § 1981(c) as overruling the *Jett* holding that § 1981 violations can be remedied only under § 1983. Thus § 1981 stands on its own as the source of a remedy, not just a right, so that a Section 1981 claim against state or local government remains cognizable for pleading purposes. Nevertheless, these courts also observe that nothing about the 1991 amendment implies that local governments should be liable *vicariously* under § 1981, any more than they are under § 1983. Rather, "municipal liability for public officials' violations of Section 1981" must be determined by reference to the principles applicable "under sec. 1983 using the *Monell* analysis."[12] Thus under either approach taken by the circuit courts, a claim against local government for violating Section 1981 rights, whether asserted via the "and laws" clause of Section 1983 or under Section 1981 itself, can succeed only if the plaintiff establishes that the violation occurred under circumstances satisfying the "official policy or custom" requirement of Section 1983. And there is authority that Section 1983 defenses are also available to the individual government official sued for a violation of Section 1981 rights.[13]

§ 1.13   The Practical Significance of the *Jett*–Related Language in the Civil Rights Act of 1991

If, contrary to the extant circuit court holdings, the 1991 Act is ultimately construed to overrule *Jett*, a plaintiff with an intentional race employment discrimination claim against a state or local government employer could supplement his Title VII claim with a claim under

---

Water Works, 21 F.3d 218 (8th Cir.1994); *Cotterell v. New York City Transit Police Dep't*, 1995 WL 604700 (E.D.N.Y.1995) (reaching that conclusion after but without reference to the 1991 amendments to Section 1981).

   12. *Federation of African American Contractors v. City of Oakland*, 96 F.3d 1204 (9th Cir.1996). *See also Smith v. Chicago Sch. Reform Bd. of Trustees*, 165 F.3d 1142, 1148–49 (7th Cir.1999) (reversing plaintiff's verdict where the only defendant was a municipal government agency, explaining that respondeat superior was not available even if a high-ranking official committed the discrimination, and remanding to allow plaintiff to try to prove that the agency's official policy or custom was dis-

criminatory); *Hopp v. City of Pittsburgh*, 1999 WL 825457 (3d Cir.1999) (§ 1981 claim lies against local government entity, but plaintiff must prove the "policy" element required to establish a § 1983 claim). *See also Philippeaux v. North Central Bronx Hosp.*, 871 F.Supp. 640, 655 (S.D.N.Y.1994). *Gallardo v. Board of County Comm'rs*, 857 F.Supp. 783, 786 (D.Kan.1994). For a discussion of vicarious governmental entity liability under § 1983 as elaborated in *Monell v. Dep't of Social Servs.*, 436 U.S. 658, 98 S.Ct. 2018, 56 L.Ed.2d 611 (1978), see Chapter 2.

   13. *Bishop v. Avera*, 177 F.3d 1233 (11th Cir.1999) (using the § 1983 qualified immunity defense to defend a § 1981 damages claim).

§ 1981, unencumbered by the "policy" proof demanded by § 1983. This § 1981 claim would be against all "state action" defendants, local governmental entities as well as the states themselves. The availability of § 1981 gives the plaintiff several advantages as compared to a claim under Title VII. She avoids the administrative exhaustion requirements of Title VII (as well as the prima facie elements of § 1983). She will have a probably longer statute of limitations provided by state law and will be able to recover unlimited compensatory damages, free of the Title VII caps.

On the other hand, if, as the circuit decisions hold, *Jett* is held not overruled by the 1991 Act and is extended to claims against state employers, a plaintiff with an intentional race discrimination claim against any state or local government defendant will be significantly hamstrung. She can still supplement her Title VII claim with a claim under § 1981, probably even against the state. At a minimum, the 1991 Act confirms that § 1981 furnishes a *right* to be free of racial discrimination in contracting that may not be impaired "under color of state law," including presumably by the state itself. But to recover, the plaintiff would have to satisfy the proof requirements of § 1983 by showing that her injury was inflicted by a formal government policy, a local policy-making official, or through "deliberate indifference."

A modified version of this last scenario will result if *Jett* is definitively held not to have been overruled by the 1991 Act, but is held to apply only to local government defendants. *Will v. Michigan Dept of State Police*[14], decided earlier in the same week as *Jett*, clearly precluded § 1983 claims against state governments sued in their own names. A post-*Jett* court might accordingly conclude, following *Jett's* broad language, that if there can be no Section 1983 claim against a state, and if all violations of Section 1981 rights must be prosecuted as claims under Section 1983, there can be no claim against a state for violating rights secured by Section 1981. But suppose *Jett's* language is subordinated to *Jett's* logic: the concern that Section 1981 claims against government should be subject to the same proof requirements that restrict the reach of the contemporaneously enacted Section 1983. If, as *Will* holds, there *is* no parallel Section 1983 claim against states, then § 1981 claims against state, as opposed to local governments could perhaps proceed free of the restrictions of Section 1983. Under this interpretation, an employee with an intentional race discrimination claim could use § 1981 "neat" in actions against *state* governments but would remain obliged to meet § 1983's "policy" requirement when seeking redress under § 1981 from *local* government defendants.

Title VII, where applicable, displaces preexisting discrimination remedies relating to federal employment, *Brown*, and to conspiracies affecting employment, *Novotny*. As a result, unless Congress acts to overrule *Will* or to clarify that it intended to overrule *Jett*, only plaintiffs challenging the conduct of municipal or other local, as opposed to state

14. 491 U.S. 58, 109 S.Ct. 2304, 105 L.Ed.2d 45 (1989).

or federal, governments may now be able to take advantage of the immediate court access and uncapped remedies afforded by the Reconstruction Civil Rights Acts; and even those plaintiffs may have to meet the formidable new requirements of § 1983. Yet when a *private* defendant intentionally refuses, because of race or ancestry, to execute or perform an employment contract, the unsuccessful applicant will clearly still have a claim under § 1981, in accordance with new paragraph (c), which codifies the result in *Runyon*; and after the overruling of *Patterson* by new paragraph (b), the Section 1981 claim will once again secure the right to make and enforce contracts without discrimination or retaliation across the entire spectrum of the contractual relationship, including post-hire terms and conditions of employment. The ironic residue is that § 1981 claims against government defendants are less clearly (in the case of states) or not at all (in the case of the federal government) actionable, and may (in the case of local governments) succeed only on stricter terms, than claims against private sector defendants—this despite that fact that, until *Runyon* was decided in 1976, private defendants were not thought subject to suit under § 1981 at all!

§ 5.3 Section 1983 as a Remedy for Federal Statutory Violations

In *Maine v. Thiboutot*,[1] the Court, fully cognizant of the enormous resulting potential increase of § 1983 "filings in our already overburdened courts,"[2] nevertheless charted a course conspicuously hospitable to the assertion of these historically tangential claims.

Section 1983 got off to an uncertain start as a remedy for federal statutory violations. In *Pennhurst State School and Hospital v. Halderman*,[3] Justice Rehnquist articulated two related but distinct potential limitations on the use of § 1983 to remedy violations of other federal statutes. The first was a substantive rights restriction, corresponding to the *Paul* or *Parratt* restrictions in due process cases, that inquires whether the particular § 1983 plaintiff has a private right of action to enforce the predicate statute. The second was a more general limitation that would oust § 1983 even when the plaintiff has standing to enforce the underlying federal statutory guarantee if that statute could be read to provide the " 'exclusive remedy for violations of its terms.' "[4]In

§ 5.3

1. 448 U.S. 1, 100 S.Ct. 2502, 65 L.Ed.2d 555 (1980).

2. *Id.* at 23, 100 S.Ct. at 2514 (Powell, J., dissenting).

3. 451 U.S. 1, 101 S.Ct. 1531, 67 L.Ed.2d 694 (1981) [hereinafter *Pennhurst* I].

4. *Id.* at 28, 101 S.Ct. at 1545 (quoting *Thiboutot*, 448 U.S. at 22 n.11, 100 S.Ct. at 2514 n.11 (Powell, J., dissenting)).

The second limitation was applied soon thereafter, but has since waned. Justice Powell found the "exclusive remedy" standard met in *Middlesex County Sewerage Auth. v. Nat'l Sea Clammers Ass'n*, 453 U.S. 1, 13, 101 S.Ct. 2615, 2622, 69 L.Ed.2d 435 (1981) (finding that Congress had provided "unusually elaborate [judicial] enforcement provisions" in two environmental statutes that should oust § 1983). Similarly, in *Smith v. Robinson*, 468 U.S. 992, 1009, 104 S.Ct. 3457, 3467, 82 L.Ed.2d 746 (1984), the Court held that the remedy formulated by Congress for the violation of the Education of the Handicapped Act was exclusive avenue of redress.

Golden State Transit Corp. v. City of Los Angeles,[5] the Court clarified that the plaintiff has the burden of proving that her claim under Section 1983 involves the violation of a federal right of action, of which she is the beneficiary, as opposed to a mere violation of federal law. By contrast, respecting the second limitation sketched in *Pennhurst,* it is the defendant who bears the burden of demonstrating that Congress, by providing a comprehensive, detailed remedial scheme for enforcement of the predicate statute, has expressly or impliedly foreclosed the possibility of enforcement under Section 1983.

a. The Substantive Rights Restriction

The first limitation Justice Rehnquist articulated in *Pennhurst,* a narrow definition of the "rights secured by" a predicate federal statute, until recently also garnered little support.[6] After *Golden State,* a § 1983 plaintiff ordinarily will have an enforceable "right" of action for local governmental violations of other federal statutes whenever the statutory provision in question can be said to have been intended to benefit that plaintiff. The § 1983 right of action is defeasible only if the predicate provision reflects a mere "congressional preference" rather than a binding governmental obligation or if the plaintiff's interest is so "vague and amorphous" that the judiciary cannot enforce it.[7]

Only twice since *Pennhurst* has the Court found a federal statutory mandate too generalized to give rise to a "right" enforceable through § 1983. In *Suter v. Artist M.,*[8] the Court considered a claim based on alleged violations of a statutory provision that conditioned federal funding for state child welfare, foster care and adoption programs upon a state's submission of a plan approved by the Secretary of Health and Human Services. To be approved the plan had to contain assurances that

---

5. 493 U.S. 103, 106, 110 S.Ct. 444, 448, 107 L.Ed.2d 420 (1989).

6. In *Wright v. City of Roanoke*, 479 U.S. 418, 107 S.Ct. 766, 93 L.Ed.2d 781 (1987), the Court held that low-income tenants had a right, enforceable through § 1983, to sue a housing authority for utility charges that allegedly exceeded ceilings established by administrative regulations issued under federal housing legislation, where the regulations defined the "reasonable amount" allowed. Justice Kennedy raised the "rights" objection again in *Golden State Transit Corp. v. City of Los Angeles*, 493 U.S. 103, 110 S.Ct. 444, 107 L.Ed.2d 420 (1989), but was joined only by Chief Justice Rehnquist and Justice O'Connor. *See id.* at 114–19, 110 S.Ct. at 452–55 (Kennedy, J., dissenting). The Court permitted a private cab company in *Golden State* to maintain a § 1983 damages action against Los Angeles after the city conditioned renewal of its franchise on the company's reaching agreement with a union on a new labor contract. The Court viewed the company as having an enforceable "right" to a remedy for conduct by the city that the National Labor Relations Act in terms prohibited only as between employers and unions.

The Court continued to reject the "rights" argument in its 1990 term. In *Wilder*, the Court permitted Medicaid providers to sue under § 1983 for reimbursement at rates that federal law demanded be "reasonable and adequate," where the predicate statute and implementing regulations at least identified the "factors to be considered" in determining the required rates. *See Suter v. Artist M.*, 503 U.S. 347, 355, 112 S.Ct. 1360, 1366, 118 L.Ed.2d 1 (1992) (citing *Wilder*); *cf. Dennis v. Higgins*, 498 U.S. 439, 111 S.Ct. 865, 112 L.Ed.2d 969 (1991) (giving similar broad meaning to the constitutional "rights" enforceable through § 1983).

7. *Wilder*, 496 U.S. at 509, 110 S.Ct. at 2517 (quoting, respectively, *Pennhurst* and *Golden State*).

8. 503 U.S. 347, 112 S.Ct. 1360, 118 L.Ed.2d 1 (1992).

the state would make "reasonable efforts" to avoid removing children from their homes and reasonable efforts, if they were removed, to reunify their families. The Court observed that, in contrast to the provisions at issue in *Wright* and *Wilder*, neither the statute nor its implementing regulations offered the states concrete guidance about the required "reasonable efforts," other than that they must be described in a plan to be approved by the Secretary. It concluded that the term therefore imposed a mere "generalized duty" unenforceable through an action under § 1983 action or, for the same reason, through a private right of action implied directly under the adoption statute.[9] But whenever Congress does specify the state's duties in a regulatory statute, a plaintiff who is an intended beneficiary of the statute will have a "right" to enforce it against local governments and officials and state officials.[10]

In *Blessing v. Freestone*,[11] the Court held that § 1983 could not be used to enforce Title IV–D of the Social Security Act against a state's child support services program and achieve substantial compliance with the statute's requirements. In a narrow holding, the Court stated that the plaintiffs failed to "identify with particularity the rights they claimed, since it is impossible to determine whether Title IV–D, as an undifferentiated whole, gives rise to undefined rights."[12] Justices Scalia and Kennedy concurred, stating that it was unnecessary for the Court to decide whether third party beneficiaries to a spending clause statute could ever be successful in pressing a right to sue to enforce such statutes.[13] This concurrence casts doubt on the Court's holdings in *Wilder* and *Wright*, two other spending clause "and laws" cases, and highlights the change in the Court's composition since those cases. What remains unclear is whether the statutes in *Suter* and *Blessing* simply failed the vagueness test or represent a fundamental change in the availability of § 1983 to enforce federal statutes.

Some federal circuit courts seem to have mounted something of a rear-guard action against *Suter*, distinguishing it with regularity. Although these courts have sometimes noted that the court in *Suter* did not reverse *Golden State*, *Wilder*, or *Wright*, it also did not follow the two-part paradigm set out in *Golden State*.[14] Instead, these courts have

9. In turn, an authoritative judicial determination that there is no implied private right of action under a particular statute may mean that federal courts will lack subject matter jurisdiction to revisit that issue in a subsequent case, at least for a period of time sufficiently long to respect a later court's conception of stare decisis. *See Bell v. Hood*, 327 U.S. 678, 682, 66 S.Ct. 773, 776, 90 L.Ed. 939 (1946).

10. Because of *Will v. Michigan Dep't of State Police*, 491 U.S. 58, 109 S.Ct. 2304, 105 L.Ed.2d 45 (1989), and the vapors of the Eleventh Amendment, the entitlement suit must take the form of an action against an individual state official. Yet in substance, it is a suit against a state entity charged with a violation in implementing a federal statute or regulation. Thus, there is no "settled law" defense; in any case the settled nature of the right exists a priori in the federal enactment. Additionally, there is no doubt about the existence of state "policy" for purposes of entity liability, because the policy resides in the challenged regulation.

11. 520 U.S. 329, 117 S.Ct. 1353, 137 L.Ed.2d 569 (1997).

12. *Id.* at 1360.

13. *Id.* at 1364.

14. *Miller v. Whitburn*, 10 F.3d 1315, 1319 (7th Cir.1993); *Arkansas Med. Soc'y, Inc. v. Reynolds*, 6 F.3d 519, 524 (8th Cir. 1993).

read *Suter* as simply reemphasizing the point made in *Pennhurst* that conditions imposed on the grant of federal monies under the Congressional spending power "must be imposed unambiguously."[15] In finding that Section 1983 may be used to vindicate other relatively vague, statutory provisions—not all that different from the "reasonable efforts" requirement of the Child Welfare Act that *Suter* held too vague to be enforced under Section 1983—these courts have stressed that in *Wilder* the court authorized the use of Section 1983 to enforce the "reasonable and adequate" reimbursement rates standard in the Boren Amendment to the Medicaid Act. What distinguishes cases like *Wilder* from cases like *Suter* and *Blessing,* these courts have concluded, is a detailed specification, either in the predicate statute alone or in its implementing regulations, of factors that aid judges in determining whether the state has complied with a federal mandate or followed specific directions for executing a generalized state plan.[16]

Thus in *Lampkin v. District of Columbia,*[17] the court held the right to educate homeless children, created by the McKinney Homeless Assistance Act, enforceable through Section 1983. While its description of the contents of the required state plan was no more elaborate than that contained in the adoption statute at issue in *Suter,* "the McKinney Act provides specific directions for the plan's execution," as well as "obligations that are independent of the plan." Similarly, in *Miller v. Whitburn,*[18] a child was permitted to enforce a right to "necessary ... treatment" under the Medicaid Act because the statute, together with its implementing regulations, specified "in copious detail, those services for which a Medicaid-participating state must provide payment in order to discharge its obligation to make ... services available to all qualified individuals." Although the state agency administering the program had substantial discretion to choose how to comply with the federal mandate to pay for necessary treatment, and in particular could exclude "experimental" treatment, federal courts could review under Section 1983 whether the agency's definitions of "experimental" comported with relevant federal definitions of that term.[19] And in *Arkansas Medical Society v. Reynolds,*[20] a Medicaid Act provision requiring a state plan to provide for care and services "to the extent that such care and services are available to the general population in the geographic area" was held sufficiently definite to be enforceable under Section 1983. The court found this "equal access" provision arguably more specific than the language of the Boren Amendment found enforceable in *Wilder,* because its legislative history and implementing regulations in effect defined

15. *Arkansas Medical Soc'y., Inc.,* 6 F.3d 519, citing *Suter,* 503 U.S. at 355, 112 S.Ct. at 1366.

16. *But see City of Chicago v. Lindley,* 66 F.3d 819 (7th Cir.1995) (Older Americans Act provision that agencies "take into account" geographical and social factors in erecting formula for distributing funds too amorphous to create rights enforceable under § 1983).

17. 27 F.3d 605, 610–612 (D.C.Cir.), *cert. denied,* 513 U.S. 1016, 115 S.Ct. 578, 130 L.Ed.2d 493 (1994).

18. 10 F.3d 1315, 1319–1320 (7th Cir. 1993).

19. *Id.* at 1320.

20. 6 F.3d 519 (8th Cir.1993).

"general population" to require a comparison of Medicaid recipients' access with that of the insured population, rather than the entire population of the surrounding geographic area.

Not all circuits have taken aim on *Suter*, however. The First Circuit, in *Stowell v. Ives*[21] rejected plaintiff's attempt to enforce a provision of the Medicare Catastrophic Coverage Act that required the Secretary of Health and Human Services to disapprove any state plan for medical assistance if payment levels were less than payment levels in effect under plan on May 1, 1988. The court held that this spending clause statute did not impose any direct obligation on the state so as to give rise to cause of action cognizable under § 1983. Similarly, in *City of Chicago v. Lindley*,[22] the Seventh Circuit held that the Older Americans Act, which required states to use "the best available data" to develop a funds-distribution formula "that takes into account" the geographical distribution of older individuals within the state with "particular attention" to low-income minority older individuals, did not create any rights enforceable under § 1983. The court found that this statute was too vague and imposed no specific obligations on the state, thus precluding the plaintiff's claim.[23]

The Sixth Circuit offers an approach that reconciles these cases. In *Tony L. v. Childers*,[24] the court proposed that there are two kinds of "and laws" cases—those like *Wilder* in which the statutes or implementing regulations provide certain and enforceable criteria and those like *Suter* that lack the specificity needed for judicial enforcement. Statutes that require the payment of specified sums of money,[25] that require the recognition of tribal adoptions,[26] that mandate the institution of individualized rehabilitation programs,[27] or that require a public agency to comply with a grievance award[28] can be enforced through a § 1983 claim because the courts can have confidence in crafting a judicial remedy.[29]

21. 976 F.2d 65 (1st Cir.1992).

22. 66 F.3d 819 (7th Cir.1995).

23. *See also King v. Town of Hempstead*, 161 F.3d 112 (2d Cir.1998) (no § 1983 cause of action for town's allegedly negligent administration of Housing and Community Development Act); *White v. Chambliss*, 112 F.3d 731 (4th Cir.), *cert. denied*, 522 U.S. 913, 118 S.Ct. 296, 139 L.Ed.2d 228 (1997) (rejecting plaintiff's § 1983 claim to enforce the Adoption Assistance and Child Welfare Act); *Clifton v. Schafer*, 969 F.2d 278 (7th Cir.1992) (AFDC program not enforceable by § 1983 private right of action).

24. 71 F.3d 1182 (6th Cir.1995), *cert. denied*, 517 U.S. 1212, 116 S.Ct. 1834, 134 L.Ed.2d 938 (1996).

25. *Buckley v. City of Redding*, 66 F.3d 188 (9th Cir.1995) (allowing § 1983 claim to enforce a statute requiring a certain sum of money to be spent on recreational boat-

ing); *Albiston v. Maine Comm'r of Human Servs.*, 7 F.3d 258 (1st Cir.1993).

26. *Native Village of Venetie IRA Council v. State of Alaska*, 155 F.3d 1150 (9th Cir.1998) (Indian Child Welfare Act created an enforceable right and contained no specific enforcement scheme).

27. *Mallett v. Wisconsin Div. of Vocational Rehab.*, 130 F.3d 1245 (7th Cir.1997); *Marshall v. Switzer*, 10 F.3d 925 (2d Cir. 1993).

28. *Farley v. Philadelphia Hous. Auth.*, 102 F.3d 697 (3d Cir.1996).

29. *See also Doe v. Chiles*, 136 F.3d 709 (11th Cir.1998) (statute requiring state Medicaid plan to provide medical assistance with reasonable promptness created federal right enforceable under § 1983 by developmentally disabled persons who had been placed on a waiting list for entry into intermediate care facility).

Statutes that fail to specifically define the content of a right cannot be judicially enforced through § 1983.[30]

b.   *The Remedies Restriction*

On this second issue, Justice White dissenting in *Pennhurst*, argued that the Court should read *Thiboutot* as erecting the "presumption that a federal statute creating federal rights may be enforced in a Section 1983 action," rebuttable only by an express indication in the underlying statute that Congress considered its stated remedies to be exclusive.[31]

In three decisions that presumption has apparently carried the day. The Court has found § 1983 available if the predicate statute provides either no remedy, as in *Golden State Transit Corp.*, or only an administrative remedy, as in *Wilder* and *Wright*, for the kind of violation alleged. Only when the entitlement statute created its own judicial remedy[32] or a "carefully tailored administrative and judicial mechanism"[33] was § 1983 held displaced as a matter of congressional intent. The cases therefore seem to hold that § 1983 is supplanted only when Congress has provided a carefully considered federal[34] *judicial* remedy for the predicate statutory violation. The circuit decisions reach varying conclusions as to when such a remedy is sufficiently comprehensive to preclude the action under § 1983.[35]

30. *See, e.g., Harris v. James*, 127 F.3d 993 (11th Cir.1997).

31. *Pennhurst I*, 451 U.S. at 51, 101 S.Ct. at 1557 (White, J., dissenting in part); *cf. Bush v. Lucas*, 462 U.S. 367, 390, 103 S.Ct. 2404, 2417, 76 L.Ed.2d 648 (1983) (Marshall, J., concurring in unanimous decision) (precluding *Bivens* recovery for a government employee if Congress provided a comprehensive administrative and judicial remedy that was "substantially as effective as a damages action").

32. *See Middlesex County Sewerage Auth. v. National Sea Clammers*, 453 U.S. 1, 101 S.Ct. 2615, 69 L.Ed.2d 435 (1981).

33. *Smith v. Robinson*, 468 U.S. 992, 1009, 104 S.Ct. 3457, 3467, 82 L.Ed.2d 746 (1984). *But see* Handicapped Children's Protection Act of 1986, 20 U.S.C.A. § 1415 (1988) (overruling *Smith* and authorizing attorney's fees pursuant to 42 U.S.C.A. § 1988 in connection with successful constitutional or federal statutory claims even when the same relief, with an express fee authorization, is available under the Education of the Handicapped Act, 20 U.S.C.A. §§ 1401–1485 (1988)).

34. *Wilder* provided support for a "federal" qualification by rejecting the argument that the availability of state judicial review of Virginia's implementation of the Medicaid amendment was relevant to the availability of relief under § 1983. *See Wil-*

der v. Virginia Hosp. Ass'n, 496 U.S. at 524 n.20, 110 S.Ct. at 2525 n.20.

35. *Compare Murrell v. School Dist. No. 1*, 186 F.3d 1238, 1249 (10th Cir.1999); *Seamons v. Snow*, 84 F.3d 1226, 1233 (10th Cir.1996); *Doe v. Petaluma City Sch. Dist.*, 54 F.3d 1447 (9th Cir.1995) (holding or assuming that Title IX claim gives rise to § 1983 "and laws" claim); and *Lillard v. Shelby County Bd. of Educ.*, 76 F.3d 716 (6th Cir.1996) (Title IX enforcement scheme, even including implied judicial cause of action, insufficiently comprehensive to foreclose § 1983 action based on independent due process rights) *with Lollar v. Baker*, 196 F.3d 603, 608–610 (5th Cir. 1999) (available Rehabilitation Act claim against employing agency, but not individual state actor, forecloses § 1983 claim against individual state actor where only alleged deprivation of rights is under Rehabilitation Act); *Alsbrook v. City of Maumelle*, 184 F.3d 999, 1010–11 (8th Cir.1999), *cert. dismissed sub nom Alsbrook v. Arkansas*, ___ U.S. ___, 120 S.Ct. 1265, 146 L.Ed.2d 215 (2000) (Americans With Disabilities Act judicial remedial scheme providing monetary compensation against entity sufficiently comprehensive to bar § 1983 individual capacity claims); *Kendall v. City of Chesapeake, Va.*, 174 F.3d 437 (4th Cir. 1999) (detailed criminal penalties, private right of action for unpaid wages, overtime, liquidated damages and ancillary relief im-

When there is an express judicial remedy provided in the predicate statute, the circuit courts have uniformly disallowed § 1983 claims to enforce the statute.[36] At the other extreme, where only state administrative grievance procedures (or less) are available, the courts permit § 1983 enforcement.[37] There is less agreement when the statute provides only for federal administrative procedures[38] or when there exists an implied private right of action to enforce the predicate statute.[39]

Why would the Court assiduously nick away at § 1983 jurisdiction in its primary sphere, the vindication of constitutional rights, yet open the doors to an acknowledged potential onslaught of litigation whenever any of a multitude of federal statutes, mostly *not* providing for civil rights, is violated under color of state law? Particularly inexplicable is this embrace of federal statutory claims under § 1983 after the Court had just announced a notably more restrictive approach to implying judicial rights of action directly under other federal statutes.[40] The Court's open-ended receptiveness to § 1983 statutory claims is even more baffling because this result is not compelled. For example, there is

pliedly preclude relief based on FLSA rights under § 1983); *Holbrook v. City of Alpharetta, Ga.*, 112 F.3d 1522 (11th Cir.1997) (the remedial frameworks under the Rehabilitation Act and the Americans with Disabilities Act sufficiently extensive and comprehensive to displace separate judicial remedy under § 1983); *Pfeiffer v. Marion Ctr. Area School Dist.*, 917 F.2d 779 (3d Cir.1990) (Title IX administrative enforcement scheme, coupled with implied judicial cause of action, comprehensive enough to foreclose all § 1983 claims); *Hobbs v. Hawkins*, 968 F.2d 471 (5th Cir.1992) (civil rights claim for damages for a violation of right to a free election under Labor Management Relations Act held preempted by a comprehensive administrative enforcement mechanism); and *Mennone v. Gordon*, 889 F.Supp. 53 (D.Conn.1995) (rejecting use of § 1983 as vehicle for Title IX claim). For the possible expansion of remedial preclusion of "and laws" claims that may follow in the wake of *Seminole Tribe of Fla. v. Florida*, 517 U.S. 44, 116 S.Ct. 1114, 134 L.Ed.2d 252 (1996) (overruling *Pennsylvania v. Union Gas Co.*, 491 U.S. 1, 109 S.Ct. 2273, 105 L.Ed.2d 1 (1989)), see the discussion in Chapter 12, *infra*.

36. *See, e.g., Sellers v. School Bd. of Manassas, Va.*, 141 F.3d 524 (4th Cir.1998), *cert. denied*, 525 U.S. 871, 119 S.Ct. 168, 142 L.Ed.2d 137 (1998) (Individuals with Disabilities Education Act); *Mattoon v. City of Pittsfield*, 980 F.2d 1 (1st Cir.1992) (Safe Water Drinking Act included administrative fines and allowed private right of action to establish drinking water regulations and obtain injunctions); *Garcia v. Cecos Inter-*

nat'l, Inc., 761 F.2d 76 (1st Cir.1985) (Resource Conservation and Recovery Act).

37. *See, e.g., Native Village of Venetie IRA Council v. State of Alaska*, 155 F.3d 1150 (9th Cir.1998) (Indian Child Welfare Act); *Wright v. Roanoke*, 479 U.S. 418, 107 S.Ct. 766, 93 L.Ed.2d 781 (1987) (Brooke Amendment to the Fair Housing Act); *Victorian v. Miller*, 813 F.2d 718 (5th Cir.1987) (Food Stamp Act).

38. *See, e.g., Chan v. New York*, 1 F.3d 96 (2d Cir.), *cert. denied*, 510 U.S. 978, 114 S.Ct. 472, 126 L.Ed.2d 423 (1993) (allowing a § 1983 suit to enforce the Housing and Community Development Act).

39. *Compare Lakoski v. James*, 66 F.3d 751 (5th Cir.1995), *cert. denied sub nom Lakoski v. University of Tex.*, 519 U.S. 947, 117 S.Ct. 357, 136 L.Ed.2d 249 (1996) (§ 1983 unavailable in Title IX) *with Crawford v. Davis*, 109 F.3d 1281 (8th Cir.1997) (allowing § 1983 claim to enforce Title IX).

40. *See, e.g., Transamerica Mortgage Advisors, Inc. v. Lewis*, 444 U.S. 11, 24, 100 S.Ct. 242, 249, 62 L.Ed.2d 146 (1979) (holding that there is "a limited private remedy under the Investment Advisors Act of 1940" despite no express provision for a private cause of action); *Touche Ross & Co. v. Redington*, 442 U.S. 560, 576–77, 99 S.Ct. 2479, 2489–90, 61 L.Ed.2d 82 (1979) (refusing to find a private cause of action under § 17(a) of the Securities Exchange Act of 1934, 15 U.S.C.A. § 78g(a) (1988), despite having previously found one under § 14(a), 15 U.S.C.A. § 78n(a) (1988)). This curiosity is elaborated by Monaghan, 91 Colum.L.Rev. 233.

a more than respectable historical argument that the addition in 1874 of the words "and laws" to § 1983 was intended merely to parallel the subject matter jurisdiction conferred by the forerunner of 28 U.S.C.A. § 1343(3), a section limited to claims arising under "any law providing for equal rights."[41] On that reading, the Court might have restricted "and laws" claims to statutes forbidding discrimination, rather than embracing violations of all manner of ordinary federal commerce and welfare laws.

Most § 1983 "and laws" claims are brought against local governmental entities for alleged failures to implement faithfully welfare or benefits programs as prescribed by federal law. On occasion, however, an "and laws" damages claim will be brought against an individual state or local official. And it has been held in such cases that public officials may assert qualified immunity against damages liability for violations of federal statutory rights , just as they may claim that immunity in cases alleging violations of federal constitutional rights.[42]

SUMMARY OF THE "AND LAWS" BRANCH OF § 1983

Section 1983 claim can be predicated on violation of *any* federal statute (*Thiboutot*), subject to the following "rights" and "remedies" caveats:

IF	UNLESS
Plaintiff shows she is an intended beneficiary of the federal statutory standard and thus has an enforceable "*right*";	*Defendant shows* that comprehensive *remedies* (perhaps only judicial remedies) provided by the predicate statute impliedly preclude a civil claim under Section 1983.
and	x *National Sea Clammers* x *Smith v. Robinson* (predicate statutes provided limited but detailed *judicial* remedies)
That right, as elaborated by the statute, its legislative history, and federal implementing regulations, is sufficiently definite for judicial enforcement.	
	√ *Wright v. Roanoke* (predicate statute provided only *administrative* remedies)
√ *Wilder* x *Suter*	
Post-*Suter* circuit decisions mostly distinguish *Suter*, follow *Wilder*	

√ =	Claim recognized
x =	Claim rejected

---

41. *See Maine v. Thiboutot*, 448 U.S. 1, 14–19, 100 S.Ct. 2502, 2509–2512, 65 L.Ed.2d 555 (1980) (Powell, J., dissenting) (reviewing the historical argument); *cf.* John C. Jeffries, Jr., *Damages for Constitutional Violations: The Relation of Risk to Injury in Constitutional Torts*, 75 Va.L.Rev. 1461, 1485 n.60 (1989) (discussing the Supreme Court's efforts to except particular statutes from its general rule that § 1983 provides a private damages action for all federal statutes).

42. *Blake v. Wright*, 179 F.3d 1003 (6th Cir.1999), *cert. denied*, ___ U.S. ___, 120 S.Ct. 980, 145 L.Ed.2d 930 (2000).

Chapter Six

THE COMBINED USE OF SECTIONS 1983, 1985(3), OR 1981 WITH TITLE VII FOR DISCRIMINATION CLAIMS AGAINST STATE AND LOCAL GOVERNMENT EMPLOYERS

Analysis

---

§ 6.1   Introduction

With the enactment of Title VII of the Civil Rights Act of 1964 and the resurgence of 42 U.S.C.A. § 1983, employment discrimination plaintiffs have been provided several vehicles through which to remedy the injuries they have suffered. The interrelation between them has provided a great deal of controversy. Much of this controversy surrounds the issue of whether Title VII provides the exclusive remedy for employment discrimination, thereby impliedly preempting § 1983. The United States Supreme Court has yet to directly address this issue. Nonetheless, its resolution will have far reaching effects. Specifically, a decision on this issue will determine whether plaintiffs suing "state action" employers will be allowed access to the uncapped compensatory damages under § 1983, as opposed to the capped compensatory damages under Title VII, either by proving a parallel constitutional predicate violation or simply by fitting the Title VII violation under the "and laws" language of § 1983—i.e., showing a federal statutory violation under color of state law.

§§ 6.2–8.4   [Reserved]

A.   TO WHAT EXTENT, IF ANY, DOES A TITLE VII CLAIM PREEMPT A CONSTITUTIONAL OR FEDERAL STATUTORY CLAIM UNDER SECTION 1983?

§ 6.5   In General

There are several sources of possible Title VII/§ 1983 preemption authority even apart from doctrine developed in deciding employment discrimination claims "under color of state law."

One line of cases has focused on the "and laws" language of 42 U.S.C.A. § 1983. In *Maine v. Thiboutot*,[1] the Supreme Court held that the § 1983 remedy "broadly encompasses violations of federal statutory as well as constitutional law."

In *Pennhurst State Sch. & Hosp. v. Halderman*,[2] however, the Court limited the availability of the "and laws" language as a source of relief. Relying on a statement in Justice Powell's dissent in *Thiboutot*, the Court reasoned that "Section 1983 would not be available where the 'governing statute provides an exclusive remedy for violations of its terms.' "[3]Consequently, because the Court of Appeals had failed to address whether the express remedy contained in the Developmentally Disabled Assistance and Bill of Rights Act provided the exclusive remedy for violations of the Act, the Court remanded the case for further consideration.[4]

Similarly, in *Middlesex County. Sewerage Auth. v. National Sea Clammers Ass'n.*,[5] the Court considered whether § 1983's "and laws" language could be invoked to redress violations of the Federal Water Pollution Control Act (FWPCA) and the Marine Protection, Research, and Sanctuaries Act of 1972 (MPRSA). The Court relied on the *Pennhurst* limitation to hold that a § 1983 claim was unavailable.[6] The Court concluded,

§ 6.5

1. 448 U.S. 1, 4, 100 S.Ct. 2502, 2504, 65 L.Ed.2d 555 (1980).

2. 451 U.S. 1, 101 S.Ct. 1531, 67 L.Ed.2d 694 (1981).

3. *Id.* at 28, 101 S.Ct. at 1545 (quoting *Thiboutot,* 448 U.S. at 22, 100 S.Ct. at 2513).

4. *Pennhurst,* 451 U.S. at 30, 101 S.Ct. at 1546.

5. 453 U.S. 1, 101 S.Ct. 2615, 69 L.Ed.2d 435 (1981).

6. *Id.* at 19, 101 S.Ct. at 2626.

[T]he existence of these express remedies [contained in the FWPCA and the MPRSA] demonstrates not only that Congress intended to foreclose implied private actions but also that it intended to supplant any remedy that otherwise would be available under Section 1983.[7]

In *Smith v. Robinson*,[8] the Court considered whether the comprehensive remedial structure of the Education of the Handicapped Act (EHA) precluded bringing a claim under § 1983.[9] The Court held that "[w]e have little difficulty concluding that Congress intended the EHA to be the exclusive avenue through which a plaintiff may assert an equal protection claim to a publicly financed special education."[10] In support of its conclusion, the Court emphasized,

> In light of the comprehensive nature of the procedures and guarantees set out in the EHA and Congress' express efforts to place on local and state educational agencies the primary responsibility for developing a plan to accommodate the needs of each individual handicapped child, we find it difficult to believe that Congress also meant to leave undisturbed the ability of a handicapped child to go directly to court with an equal protection claim to a free appropriate public education [under Section 1983].[11]

In these "and laws" cases, the Court seems to focus on whether the federal statute under consideration provides its own comprehensive remedial scheme. The more comprehensive the remedial scheme, the more willing the Court has been to find preemption. For example, in *National Sea Clammers*, the Court emphasized, "When the remedial devices provided in a particular Act are 'sufficiently comprehensive,' they may suffice to demonstrate congressional intent to preclude the remedy of suits under Section 1983."[12] Moreover, in *Smith*, the Court wrote, "Allowing a plaintiff to circumvent the EHA administrative remedies would be inconsistent with Congress' 'carefully tailored scheme.' "[13] Consequently, the comprehensiveness of the federal statute that provides the substantive cause of action likely will play a major role in whether a claim under § 1983 will be precluded. And Title VII is widely viewed as extremely comprehensive in its detailing of state and federal administrative and judicial procedures and remedies.[14]

Another line of cases addresses the preemptive effect of Title VII on Reconstruction-era statutes other than § 1983. *Great American Fed. S & L Ass'n v. Novotny*,[15] analyzed "[w]hether the rights created by Title VII

7. *Id.* at 21, 101 S.Ct. at 2627.

8. 468 U.S. 992, 104 S.Ct. 3457, 82 L.Ed.2d 746 (1984).

9. *Id.* at 1002–1003, 104 S.Ct. at 3463–3464.

10. *Id.* at 1009, 104 S.Ct. at 3467.

11. *Id.* at 1011, 104 S.Ct. at 3468.

12. 453 U.S. at 20, 101 S.Ct. at 2626 (emphasis added).

13. 468 U.S. at 1012, 104 S.Ct. at 3468 (emphasis added).

14. *See, e.g., Rivers v. Roadway Express*, 511 U.S. 298, 114 S.Ct. 1510, 128 LEd.2d 274 (1994).

15. 442 U.S. 366, 99 S.Ct. 2345, 60 L.Ed.2d 957 (1979).

may be asserted within the remedial framework of Section 1985(3)." In concluding that Title VII preempts § 1985(3) claims challenging conspiratorial deprivations of Title VII rights, the Court noted,

> [Section] 1985(3) may not be invoked to redress violations of Title VII.... Unimpaired effectiveness can be given to the plan put together by Congress in Title VII only by holding that deprivation of a right created by Title VII cannot be the basis of a cause of action under Section 1985(3).[16]

In *Novotny*, the Court found persuasive the reasoning of *Brown v. General Services Administration*.[17] The Court in *Brown* considered [w]hether § 717 of the Civil Rights Act of 1964 provided the exclusive judicial remedy for a claim of employment discrimination in the federal sector, thereby preempting a claim under § 1981. In answering affirmatively, the Court explained

> The balance, completeness, and structural integrity of § 717 are inconsistent with the petitioner's contention that the judicial remedy afforded by § 717(c) was designed merely to supplement other putative judicial relief. His view fails, in our estimation, to accord due weight to the fact that unlike these other supposed remedies, § 717 does not contemplate merely judicial relief. Rather, it provides for careful blend of administrative and judicial enforcement powers.[18]

The Court concluded that it "would require the suspension of disbelief to ascribe to Congress the design to allow its careful and thorough [Title VII] remedial scheme to be circumvented by artful pleading."[19] Lower courts have held otherwise, however, with respect to employment discrimination claims by state and municipal employees.

Although both *Novotny* and *Brown* relied to a certain extent on the comprehensive nature of the remedy provided in the federal statute under consideration, both cases also focused on additional elements. In *Novotny*, for example, the Court paid particular attention to the fact that § 1985(3) is a purely remedial statute that itself confers no independent rights.[20] Because Title VII provides both substantive rights and a remedy, the Court concluded that § 1985(3) was preempted where Title VII covered the defendant's conduct.[21] In *Brown*, the Court could not make the same point, for § 1981, unlike § 1985(3), does provide a right independent of Title VII, the right to make and enforce contracts. So the

16. *Id.* at 378, 99 S.Ct. at 2352.

17. 425 U.S. 820, 96 S.Ct. 1961, 48 L.Ed.2d 402 (1976).

18. *Id.* at 832–33, 96 S.Ct. at 1967–68. *See also Perez v. FBI*, 71 F.3d 513 (5th Cir.), *cert. denied*, 517 U.S. 1234, 116 S.Ct. 1877, 135 L.Ed.2d 173 (1996) (extending *Brown* by holding that the exclusive Title VII remedy for federal employment discrimination also ousts constitutional claims under *Bivens v. Six Unknown Named Agents of Fed. Bureau of Narcotics*, 403 U.S. 388, 91 S.Ct. 1999, 29 L.Ed.2d 619 (1971)).

19. *Id.* at 833, 104 S.Ct. at 1968. *See also Rowe v. Sullivan*, 967 F.2d 186 (5th Cir.1992). *See* § 11.19 on whether Title VII's detailed enforcement scheme forecloses a judicial remedy for the violation of a subsequently enacted civil rights statute, Title IX of the Education Amendments of 1992.

20. 442 U.S. at 376, 99 S.Ct. at 2351.

21. *Id.* at 376–78, 99 S.Ct. at 2351–52.

Court observed more generally, "In a variety of contexts the Court has held that a precisely drawn detailed statute preempts more general remedies."[22] By concluding that Title VII is a more precisely drawn statute than the general Civil Rights statutes, the Court was able to hold that "§ 717 of the Civil Rights Act of 1964, as amended, provides the exclusive judicial remedy for claims of employment discrimination in federal employment."[23]

Brown is in considerable tension with *Johnson v. Railway Express Agency*,[24] decided a year earlier. There the Court approached the preemption issue in terms of congressional intent. In deciding that Title VII does not preempt § 1981 where the claim does not concern federal employment, the Court reiterated the conclusion of *Alexander v. Gardner–Denver Co.*[25] that

> " '[T]he legislative history of Title VII manifests a congressional intent to allow an individual to pursue independently his rights under both Title VII and other applicable state and federal statutes.' "[26]

The Court added,

> Despite Title VII's range and its design as a comprehensive solution for the problem of invidious discrimination in employment the aggrieved individual clearly is not deprived of other remedies he possesses and is not limited to Title VII in his search for relief.[27]

Relying on the legislative history of the Civil Rights Act of 1972 to the effect that Title VII and § 1981 "augment each other and are not mutually exclusive,"[28] the Court concluded that the "remedies available under Title VII and under § 1981, although related, and although directed to most of the same ends, are separate, distinct, and independent."[29] Evidently the Court must have viewed § 717 of Title VII as providing an even *more* detailed blend of administrative and judicial remedies for claims by federal employees than does Title VII's § 706, governing claims against private and state and local government employers.

The cases that follow the reasoning of *Johnson* also turn on the Court's view of Congressional intent. For example, in *Novotny*, in the course of finding Title VII preemption of § 1985(3), the Court explained that because 42 U.S.C.A. § 1981 and § 1983 were mentioned in the legislative debates preceding passage of the Civil Rights Act of 1968 and the 1972 amendments to the Civil Rights Act of 1964. Those sections

22. 425 U.S. at 834, 96 S.Ct. at 1968.

23. *Id.* at 835, 96 S.Ct. at 1969.

24. 421 U.S. 454, 95 S.Ct. 1716, 44 L.Ed.2d 295 (1975).

25. 415 U.S. 36, 94 S.Ct. 1011, 39 L.Ed.2d 147 (1974).

26. *Johnson v. Railway Express Agency,* 421 U.S. at 459, 95 S.Ct. at 1720 (quoting *Alexander v. Gardner–Denver Co.,* 415 U.S. 36, 48, 94 S.Ct. 1011, 1020, 39 L.Ed.2d 147 (1974)).

27. *Id.* at 459, 95 S.Ct. at 1720.

28. 421 U.S. at 459, 95 S.Ct. at 1720 (citing H.R.Rep.No. 92–238, p. 19 (1971)).

29. *Id.* at 461, 95 S.Ct. at 1720.

could not have been impliedly repealed.[30] Similarly, in *Smith v. Robinson*,[31] the Court emphasized,

> We do not lightly conclude that Congress intended to preclude reliance on § 1983 as a remedy for a substantial equal protection claim. Since 1871, when it was passed by Congress, § 1983 has stood as an independent safeguard against deprivations of federal constitutional and statutory rights. Nevertheless, § 1983 is a statutory remedy; and Congress retains the authority to repeal it or replace it with an alternative remedy. The crucial consideration is what Congress intended.

Several dominant factors may be distilled from these decisions, despite their not entirely consistent results. First, does the later statute provide a comprehensive and precisely tailored remedial structure? Second, is the earlier statute purely remedial, or does it provide substantive rights as well? Third, does the legislative history of the modern statute suggest that Congress intended to repeal the earlier statute?

The first two factors suggest that Title VII should preempt § 1983 employment discrimination claims for which both statutes provide a remedy. Not only is Title VII a comprehensive and carefully tailored remedial scheme, but § 1983, like § 1985(3), is a purely remedial statute that declares no substantive rights of its own. On the other hand, because § 1983 was discussed in the debates surrounding the Civil Rights Act of 1964 and the 1972 amendments to the 1964 Act, yet not expressly preempted, the legislative history of Title VII suggests that Congress did not intend to preempt § 1983. Although these factors push in different directions, the decisions of the courts of appeals on the issue are surprisingly uniform.

§§ 6.6–8.9   [Reserved]

B.   SECTION 1983 CLAIMS GENERALLY NOT PREEMPTED BY TITLE VII

§ 6.10   In General

The federal Courts of Appeals are in accord that the mere availability of a Title VII claim does not altogether preempt a § 1983 constitutional claim based on the same circumstances.[1] All but one of these courts,[2]

30. *Id.* at 377 n.21, 99 S.Ct. at 2315 n.21.

31. 468 U.S. at 1012, 104 S.Ct. at 3468.

§ 6.10

1. Thus, for example, a § 1983 claim may be maintained standing alone by a government employee who need not also assert an available companion claim under Title VII. *See, e.g., Thigpen v. Bibb County*, 223 F.3d 1231, 2000 WL 1277600, at *6 (11th Cir.2000) (one of the co-authors was

co-counsel for plaintiffs in *Thigpen*); *Annis v. County of Westchester*, 36 F.3d 251, 254 (2d Cir.1994); *Ratliff v. City of Milwaukee*, 795 F.2d 612, 623–24 (7th Cir.1986). And when both claims are brought, the failure of the Title VII claim does not necessarily impair the § 1983 claim. *See Arrington v. Cobb County*, 139 F.3d 865, 871–72 (11th Cir.1998). But it appears, at least in two circuits, that the ADEA may preempt § 1983 claims for age discrimination. *See e.g., Lafleur v. Texas Dep't of Health*, 126 F.3d 758 (5th Cir.1997); *Zombro v. Balti-*

however, also hold that such a plaintiff cannot rest simply on the "and laws" language of § 1983, that is cannot use § 1983 to challenge conduct that violates Title VII but not the constitution.[3] Rather, to proceed under § 1983, these courts require the plaintiff to prove an independent *constitutional* violation, typically of the Fourteenth Amendment, to serve as the predicate for his § 1983 claim. The significance of the distinction is illustrated by a Title VII "neutral practice/disparate impact" claim, which may violate Title VII, as amended by the Civil Rights Act of 1991, but fails to show the intentional discrimination requisite for a violation of the Equal Protection Clause.[4]

In *Pontarelli v. Stone*,[5] the plaintiffs brought claims for sex discrimination and retaliation under 42 U.S.C.A. § 1983 and Title VII. The First Circuit wrote that

> Section 1983 expressly embraces actions to redress 'deprivation[s, under color of state law,] of ... rights, privileges, or immunities

more City Police Dep't, 868 F.2d 1364 (4th Cir.), *cert. denied*, 493 U.S. 850, 110 S.Ct. 147, 107 L.Ed.2d 106 (1989) (holding that plaintiff could not maintain an action for age discrimination under § 1983 because the claim fell within scope of the ADEA); *Paterson v. Weinberger*, 644 F.2d 521 (5th Cir.1981) (holding that a federal employee's Fifth Amendment age discrimination claim was preempted by § 633a of the ADEA, as the ADEA was intended to provide the exclusive remedy for age discrimination).

2. *See Cross v. State of Alabama*, 49 F.3d 1490, 1507 (11th Cir.1995); *Wu v. Thomas*, 863 F.2d 1543 (11th Cir.1989) (allowing the plaintiff to state a claim under the "and laws" language of § 1983 by relying solely on a violation of Title VII, i.e., proving only the Title VII "elements"). *But see Johnson v. City of Ft. Lauderdale*, 148 F.3d 1228 (11th Cir.1998) (Civil Rights Act of 1991 does not impliedly oust § 1983 as a discrimination remedy for municipal employees if the § 1983 claim asserts a constitutional violation). *But cf. Dickerson v. Alachua County Comm'n*, 200 F.3d 761, 765–767 (11th Cir.), *cert. denied*, ___ U.S. ___, 121 S.Ct. 1, 147 L.Ed.2d 1025 (2000) (distinguishing *Novotny* and holding that Title VII did not preempt a § 1985(3) claim but only because the latter was based on an alleged deprivation of constitutional, as distinct from Title VII rights).

3. *Pontarelli v. Stone*, 930 F.2d 104 (1st Cir.1991); *Carrero v. New York City Housing Auth.*, 890 F.2d 569 (2d Cir.1989); *Bradley v. Pittsburgh Bd. of Educ.*, 913 F.2d 1064 (3d Cir.1990); *Keller v. Prince George's County*, 827 F.2d 952, 957 (4th Cir.1987); *Southard v. Texas Bd. of Criminal Justice*, 114 F.3d 539 (5th Cir.1997);

Johnston v. Harris County Flood Control Dist., 869 F.2d 1565 (5th Cir.1989), *cert. denied*, 493 U.S. 1019, 110 S.Ct. 718, 107 L.Ed.2d 738 (1990); *Day v. Wayne County Bd. of Auditors*, 749 F.2d 1199 (6th Cir. 1984); *Alexander v. Chicago Park Dist.*, 773 F.2d 850 (7th Cir.1985), *cert. denied*, 475 U.S. 1095, 106 S.Ct. 1492, 89 L.Ed.2d 894 (1986); *Hicks v. St. Mary's Honor Ctr.*, 970 F.2d 487 (8th Cir.1992), *rev'd on other grounds*, 509 U.S. 502, 113 S.Ct. 2742, 125 L.Ed.2d 407 (1993); *Roberts v. College of the Desert*, 870 F.2d 1411 (9th Cir.1988); *Notari v. Denver Water Dep't*, 971 F.2d 585, 587 (10th Cir.1992). *Cf. Jackson v. City of Atlanta, Texas*, 73 F.3d 60, 63 n. 13 (5th Cir.), *cert. denied*, 519 U.S. 818, 117 S.Ct. 70, 136 L.Ed.2d 30 (1996) (insisting that complaint clearly identify a distinct constitutional right allegedly violated before allegations actionable under Title VII may also state claim under Section 1983). *But see Hughes v. Bedsole*, 48 F.3d 1376, 1383 n. 6 (4th Cir.), *cert. denied*, 516 U.S. 870, 116 S.Ct. 190, 133 L.Ed.2d 126 (1995) (holding, in reliance on *Novotny* and without citing the Fourth Circuit's decisions in *Keller*, 827 F.2d 952, or *Beardsley*, 30 F.3d 524 (4th Cir.1994), that *no* § 1983 claim for sex discrimination lies, even for a Fourteenth Amendment violation, where a plaintiff could have sued under Title VII). The Eleventh Circuit has since repudiated the Fourth Circuit's holding in *Hughes*. *See Thigpen v. Bibb County*, 223 F.3d 1231, 2000 WL 1277600, at *5 (11th Cir.2000).

4. *Compare* § 105 of the Civil Rights Act of 1991 codifying the Title VII "impact" on "effects" case *with Washington v. Davis*, (only intentional discrimination violates equal protection) 426 U.S. 229, 96 S.Ct. 2040, 48 L.Ed.2d 597 (1976).

5. 930 F.2d 104 (1st Cir.1991).

secured by the Constitution,' 42 U.S.C. Section 1983; this necessarily includes a deprivation of the right to equal protection of the law.[6]

Thus, the First Circuit reasoned that § 1983 provided a cause of action for sex discrimination, despite the fact that Title VII also covered such actions. But, the opinion appeared to assume that plaintiff had to establish all the elements of an equal protection violation to state the § 1983 claim.[7]

Likewise, in *Carrero v. New York City Housing Authority*,[8] the plaintiff sought relief from a hostile work environment by bringing claims under both § 1983 and Title VII. The Second Circuit held that Title VII did not offer the exclusive remedy for employment discrimination against state or local government employees.[9] In reaching its decision, the Second Circuit observed that "it has been assumed in this Circuit that a § 1983 claim is not precluded by a concurrent Title VII claim, when the former is based on substantive rights distinct from Title VII."[10] "In the instant case, plaintiff has sufficiently distinguished her Section 1983 claims from Title VII to permit suit on both."[11] More recently a Second Circuit panel has written that in amending Title VII in 1972 to extend it to state and local government entities, Congress "repeatedly considered the exclusivity question and, in the end, resolved not to make Title VII the sole statutory remedy for employment discrimination by state and municipal employers that amounts to a constitutional tort."[12] In particular, the court held, aggravated forms of sexual harassment may violate the equal protection clause and therefore punishable under § 1983 despite the parallel, but more limited remedy under Title VII.[13]

In *Bradley v. Pittsburgh Board of Education*,[14] the plaintiff claimed racial discrimination in violation of both Title VII and § 1983. The Third Circuit observed,

> Although Bradley does not explicitly identify in the complaint or briefs the substantive basis for his race discrimination claim under section 1983, that claim must be grounded on the equal protection clause of the Fourteenth Amendment.[15]

---

6. *Id.* at 114.

7. *See also Azzaro v. County of Allegheny,* 110 F.3d 968, 975 (3d Cir.1997) (permitting § 1983 retaliatory discharge claim founded on a First Amendment violation but growing out of same facts supporting plaintiff's retaliation claim under Title VII).

8. 890 F.2d 569 (2d Cir.1989).

9. *See Vulcan Soc'y of the New York City Fire Dep't, Inc. v. Civil Serv. Comm'n,* 490 F.2d 387, 390 (2d Cir.1973).

10. *Carrero,* 890 F.2d at 576 (*citing Vulcan Soc'y of the New York City Fire Dep't, Inc. v. Civil Serv. Comm'n,* 490 F.2d 387

(2d Cir.1973)). *Accord, Gierlinger v. New York State Police,* 15 F.3d 32 (2d Cir.1994).

11. *Carrero,* 890 F.2d at 576.

12. *Annis v. County of Westchester, N.Y.,* 36 F.3d 251 (2d Cir.1994).

13. *Id.* at 254 (citing *Davis v. Passman,* 442 U.S. 228, 99 S.Ct. 2264, 60 L.Ed.2d 846 (1979), which sustained a *Bivens* claim of sex discrimination against a U.S. congressman under the equal protection component of the Fifth Amendment's due process clause).

14. 913 F.2d 1064 (3d Cir.1990).

15. *Id.* at 1079.

Consequently, the Third Circuit found that Title VII did not preempt § 1983.

In *Keller v. Prince George's County*,[16] the Fourth Circuit also was faced with deciding "whether Congress intended in adopting § 2 of the Equal Employment Opportunity Act of 1972 to make Title VII the exclusive remedy for public sector [nonfederal] employment discrimination in violation of constitutional safeguards." In concluding that the legislative history of the 1972 amendments to Title VII did not evince a congressional intent to repeal § 1983, the Fourth Circuit stated, "[T]hat history clearly indicates that § 2 of the Act was not intended to preempt the preexisting remedy under Section 1983 for violations of the fourteenth amendment by state employers."[17]

The Fifth Circuit addressed the preemption issue in *Johnston v. Harris County Flood Control Dist.*[18] In holding that the plaintiff could pursue employment discrimination claims under § 1983 as well as Title VII,[19] the Fifth Circuit stressed that conduct violating Title VII alone would not be actionable under § 1983: "Title VII is the *exclusive* remedy for a violation of its *own* terms. But when a public employer's conduct violates both Title VII and a *separate* constitutional or statutory right, the injured employee may pursue a remedy under Section 1983 as well as under Title VII."[20] Referring to the "and laws" clause of § 1983, the Fifth Circuit acknowledged that Title VII creates rights secured by the "laws" of the United States, "Section 1983, however, is not an available remedy for deprivation of a statutory right when the statute, itself, provides an exclusive remedy for violations of its own terms. (citations omitted). Consequently, a violation of sec. 704(a) of Title VII, alone, will not constitute an underlying statutory violation for purposes of imposing liability under Section 1983."[21]

In concluding that plaintiff could maintain both causes of action, the Fifth Circuit explained,

> When, however, unlawful employment practices encroach, not only on rights created by Title VII, but also on rights that are independent of Title VII, Title VII ceases to be exclusive. At this point, Section 1983 and Title VII overlap, providing supplemental remedies.[22]

In *Day v. Wayne County Board of Auditors*,[23] the plaintiff alleged that he had been retaliated against for filing a claim of discrimination with the EEOC. Although the Sixth Circuit reasoned that "Title VII provides the exclusive remedy when the only Section 1983 cause of action is based on a violation of Title VII," the court recognized that a

---

16. 827 F.2d 952, 957 (4th Cir.1987).

17. *Id.* at 958.

18. 869 F.2d 1565 (5th Cir.1989), *cert. denied*, 493 U.S. 1019, 110 S.Ct. 718, 107 L.Ed.2d 738 (1990).

19. *Id.* at 1568.

20. *Id.* at 1573 (emphasis added).

21. *Id.* at 1574.

22. *Id.* at 1576.

23. 749 F.2d 1199 (6th Cir.1984).

claim under both Title VII and § 1983 may be maintained when the § 1983 claim is based on a violation of the constitution.[24]

> Where an employee establishes employer conduct which violates both Title VII and rights derived from another source—the constitution or a federal statute—which existed at the time of the enactment of Title VII, the claim based on the other source is independent of the Title VII claim, and the plaintiff may seek the remedies provided by Section 1983 in addition to those created by Title VII.[25]

In *Alexander v. Chicago Park District*,[26] the Seventh Circuit tackled the "and laws" problem directly:

> Generally, where a statute provides its own comprehensive enforcement scheme, that scheme may not be bypassed by pleading an underlying violation of the statute and bringing suit directly under [the "and laws" language of] Section 1983. (cits. omitted). "Title VII is one of those statutes that may not be bypassed."[27]

In the case at hand, however, the Seventh Circuit permitted claims under both statutes to proceed. "Only if the right asserted [under § 1983] was created by Title VII must it be vindicated through the procedural system set up in that Act."[28] Thus, the Seventh Circuit concluded, "Title VII is not the sole remedy for employment discrimination claims of state employees [having claims under other statutes or the Constitution]. Congress intended to retain preexisting remedies."[29]

The Eighth Circuit addressed the relationship between Title VII and § 1983 in *Hicks v. St. Mary's Honor Center*.[30] In *Hicks*, the plaintiff brought an intentional racial discrimination claim under Title VII and an equal protection claim under § 1983. That is, plaintiff's Title VII claim alleged intentional discrimination on a ground also considered "suspect" for equal protection purposes. Accordingly, the court reasoned, "[U]nder the circumstances of this case, to the extent plaintiff prevails on his Title VII claim against St. Mary's, he is equally entitled to relief ... under Section 1983."[31]

Roberts v. College of the Desert, C.A.,[32] plaintiff brought claims for sex discrimination under both Title VII and § 1983. In considering whether Title VII provides the exclusive remedy for sex discrimination, the Ninth Circuit cautioned, "The Supreme Court has stated generally that Title VII does not deprive aggrieved parties of other remedies."[33]

24. *Id.* at 1204–1205.

25. *Id.* at 1205. *See also Grano v. Department of Dev.*, 637 F.2d 1073 (6th Cir. 1980).

26. 773 F.2d 850 (7th Cir.1985), *cert. denied,* 475 U.S. 1095, 106 S.Ct. 1492, 89 L.Ed.2d 894 (1986).

27. *Id.* at 856 (quoting *Novotny*, 442 U.S. at 375–378, 99 S.Ct. at 2350–3752).

28. *Id.* at 855.

29. *Id.* at 855. *See also Trigg v. Fort Wayne Community Schools*, 766 F.2d 299 (7th Cir.1985).

30. 970 F.2d 487 (8th Cir.1992) *reversed on other grounds,* 509 U.S. 502, 113 S.Ct. 2742, 125 L.Ed.2d 407 (1993).

31. *Id.* at 491.

32. 870 F.2d 1411 (9th Cir.1988).

33. *Id.* at 1415 (citing *Johnson v. Railway Express*, 421 U.S. at 459, 95 S.Ct. at 1720).

The court concluded that Title VII did not preempt § 1983, when the § 1983 claim was based on an independent constitutional violation. "We agree with the reasoning of those courts that have held that Title VII does not preempt an action under section 1983 for a violation of the fourteenth amendment."[34]

In *Notari v. Denver Water Department*,[35] the Tenth Circuit, too, concluded that claims under both Title VII and § 1983 could be maintained, again where the § 1983 claim was based on an "independent" constitutional or statutory violation.[36] Like the Seventh Circuit in *Alexander*, the Tenth Circuit reasoned that "[o]nly those Section 1983 claims that rely upon Title VII's provisions as the substantive basis for their validity are foreclosed under this analysis."[37] In explaining the requirements for showing an "independent" basis for a § 1983 claim, the court stated,

> [T]he basis for a Section 1983 claim is independent from Title VII when it rests on substantive rights provisions outside Title VII— that is, when it rests on a constitutional right or a federal statutory right other than those created by Title VII. We emphasize that the basis of a Section 1983 claim may be independent of Title VII even if the claims arise from the same factual allegations and even if the conduct alleged in the Section 1983 claim also violated Title VII. For example, a Section 1983 claim of racial discrimination is independent of a statutory disparate treatment claim arising out of the same set of facts because the Section 1983 claim is substantively grounded in the Equal Protection Clause of the Fourteenth Amendment, whereas the disparate treatment claim flows from Title VII. Because the substantive legal standards emanate from different sources, as long as the substantive legal bases for these claims are distinct, our 'independence' requirement is satisfied and Title VII does not foreclose and employment discriminatory plaintiff's Section 1983 claim.[38]

It is significant that the court used the example of a Title VII "disparate treatment" claim (conduct violating only the statute's prohibition against employer use of practices having disproportionate adverse *impact*) because it would not also violate the Equal Protection Clause, and therefore could not amount to an independent constitutional violation actionable under § 1983.

One reported decision, *Marrero–Rivera v. Department of Justice of the Commonwealth of Puerto Rico*[39] goes the other way, concluding that Title VII completely preempts § 1983. The district court held:

---

34. *Id.*

35. 971 F.2d 585, 587 (10th Cir.1992).

36. *Id.* at 587–588.

37. *Id.* at 587–588.

38. *Id.* at 587. *See also Brown v. Hartshorne Pub. School Dist. No. 1*, 864 F.2d 680 (10th Cir.1988).

39. 800 F.Supp. 1024 (D.P.R.1992), *aff'd without opinion*, 36 F.3d 1089 (1st Cir.1994).

Following the reasoning of Novotny and Brown, and given the remedial parity of Title VII and section 1981 after the Civil Rights Act of 1991, we find that the amended statutory structure indicates an intent on the part of Congress to make Title VII whole to the exclusion of section 1983.[40]

Marrero–Rivera seemingly contradicts the ruling of its own circuit's court of appeals in *Pontarelli*.[41] *Marrero–Rivera*'s conclusion has been specifically rejected by recent decisions, which find nothing in the expansion of Title VII remedies in the Civil Rights Act of 1991 to suggest a Congressional intent to supplant § 1983. The Fourth Circuit, for example, starts with the proposition from *Alexander v. Gardner–Denver* that Congress intended an employment discrimination claimant to be free to "pursue independently his rights under both Title VII and other applicable state and federal statutes."[42] The circuit court also observes that even as amended by the 1991 Act, Title VII is not coextensive with § 1983 because it does not apply to employers with fewer than fifteen employees.[43] Indeed even when both statutes apply, Title VII still does not provide all of the relief available under § 1983, because the Title VII plaintiff must pursue administrative remedies and file suit more quickly. In addition, § 1983 does not contain the 1991 Act's caps on compensatory and punitive damages.[44] Citing the declaration in § 2 of the 1991 Act that "additional remedies under Federal law are needed to deter unlawful harassment and intentional discrimination in the workplace," the Fourth Circuit termed it "perverse to conclude that the Congress that provided additional remedies simultaneously intended silently to extinguish the remedy that Section 1983 has provided for many years."[45]

The Eleventh Circuit has on occasion also departed from the majority view but in a more expansive direction. In *Wu v. Thomas*,[46] the Eleventh Circuit approved two distinct kinds of § 1983 claims based on employment discrimination. After clarifying that the plaintiffs had not invoked § 1983 to remedy a violation of the fourteenth amendment, the court explained, "By pleading section 1983, the appellants only seek the additional remedies that the section affords for the appellee's alleged

40. *Id.* at 1032.

41. 930 F.2d 104.

42. *Beardsley v. Webb,* 30 F.3d 524, 527 (4th Cir.1994) (quoting *Alexander,* 415 U.S. at 48–49, 94 S.Ct. at 1020). Other circuits agree. *See Southard v. Texas Bd. of Criminal Justice,* 114 F.3d 539, 550 (5th Cir. 1997); *Whitney v. State of New Mexico,* 113 F.3d 1170, 1174 (10th Cir.1997); *Kern v. City of Rochester,* 93 F.3d 38, 43 (2d Cir. 1996), *cert. denied,* 520 U.S. 1155, 117 S.Ct. 1335, 137 L.Ed.2d 494 (1997); *Annis v. County of Westchester, N.Y.,* 36 F.3d 251 (2d Cir.1994); *Bohen v. City of East Chicago,* 799 F.2d 1180, 1185 (7th Cir.1986). *See also Dickerson v. Alachua County Comm'n,* 200 F.3d 761, 765 (11th Cir.), *cert. denied,* ___ U.S. ___, 121 S.Ct. 1, 147 L.Ed.2d 1025

(2000) (allowing a § 1985(3) employment discrimination conspiracy claim despite the availability of Title VII where the plaintiff claims a violation of his Constitutional rights, and not rights protected only by Title VII); *Johnson v. City of Ft. Lauderdale,* 148 F.3d 1228 (11th Cir.1998) (Civil Rights Act of 1991 does not impliedly oust § 1983 as a discrimination remedy for municipal employees, but § 1983 remedy supplements those under Title VII or § 1981).

43. *Beardsley,* 30 F.3d at 527.

44. *See Stoner v. Department of Agriculture,* 846 F.Supp. 738 (W.D.Wis.1994).

45. *Beardsley,* 30 F.3d at 527.

46. 863 F.2d 1543 (11th Cir.1989).

violation of 42 U.S.C. Section 2000e."[47] In context, the Eleventh Circuit was approving the use of a violation of Title VII alone as the sole predicate for an "and laws" claim under § 1983.[48] This conclusion was reaffirmed in the Eleventh Circuit's subsequent consideration of this case. The court stated,

> But the plaintiffs relied on more than the fourteenth amendment. They also sought damages under section 1983 for a Title VII violation. 42 U.S.C. § 2000e–3(a) prohibits discriminating against an employee for pursuing Title VII claims. Earlier in this case, we held that plaintiffs might recover under section 1983 if they proved a violation of this Title VII provision.[49]

Thus, in the Eleventh Circuit, it appears that a plaintiff may state a claim under the "and laws" language of § 1983 by relying solely on a violation of Title VII itself.

§§ 6.11–8.14   [Reserved]

C. WHAT ELEMENTS MUST BE PROVEN UNDER SECTION 1983 AND TITLE VII IN CIRCUITS THAT PERMIT ACTIONS PURSUING BOTH

§ 6.15   In General

Many courts have concluded that the purposeful discrimination element of a § 1983 claim based on an equal protection violation is the same as a showing of purposeful discrimination under Title VII. The standard formula under Title VII for showing purposeful discrimination inferentially was set out in *McDonnell Douglas Corp. v. Green*,[1] and later reaffirmed in *Texas Dept. of Community Affairs v. Burdine*.[2]

The *McDonnell Douglas* framework "establishe[s] an allocation of the burden of production and an order for the presentation of proof in Title VII discriminatory treatment cases."[3] First, the plaintiff must establish by a preponderance of the evidence a prima facie case of racial discrimination.[4] The plaintiff can satisfy this burden by showing (1) that

47. *Id.* at 1549 n.9.

48. *But see Johnson v. City of Fort Lauderdale*, 148 F.3d 1228, 1230–31 (11th Cir.1998) (implying that the conduct complained of must be unconstitutional to violate § 1983, not merely an "and laws" violation of, for example, Title VII). *Cf. Dickerson v. Alachua County Comm'n*, 200 F.3d 761, 765 (11th Cir.), *cert. denied*, ___ U.S. ___, 121 S.Ct. 1, 147 L.Ed.2d 1025 (2000) (allowing a § 1985(3) employment discrimination conspiracy claim despite the availability of Title VII where the plaintiff claims a violation of his Constitutional rights, and not rights protected only by Title VII).

49. *Wu v. Thomas*, 996 F.2d 271, 273 (11th Cir.1993) (citing *Wu v. Thomas*, 863 F.2d at 1549 n. 9), *cert. denied*, 511 U.S. 1033, 114 S.Ct. 1543, 128 L.Ed.2d 195 (1994).

§ 6.15

1. 411 U.S. 792, 93 S.Ct. 1817, 36 L.Ed.2d 668 (1973).

2. 450 U.S. 248, 101 S.Ct. 1089, 67 L.Ed.2d 207 (1981).

3. *St. Mary's Honor Center v. Hicks*, 509 U.S. 502, 504, 113 S.Ct. 2742, 2746, 125 L.Ed.2d 407 (1993).

4. *McDonnell Douglas Corp.*, 411 U.S. at 802, 93 S.Ct. at 1824.

he belongs to a racial minority, (2) that he applied for and was qualified for a job for which the employer was taking applications, (3) that, despite his qualifications, he was rejected, and (4) that, after his rejection, the job remained open, and the employer continued to take applications from people with plaintiff's same qualifications.[5] Second, if the plaintiff makes out a prima facie case, the defendant has the burden to produce evidence of some non-discriminatory reason for the plaintiff's rejection.[6] Last, if the defendant rebuts by producing that evidence, the plaintiff can prevail nevertheless by proving by a preponderance of the evidence that the defendant's proffered reason was in fact a pretext for discrimination on a ground prohibited by the statute.[7]

In the context of a § 1983 claim, the Supreme Court has assumed that "the McDonnell Douglas framework is fully applicable to racial-discrimination-in-employment claims under 42 U.S.C.A. § 1983."[8] The Eighth Circuit has concluded likewise. In *Richmond v. Board of Regents of the University of Minnesota*,[9] the court observed.

> To meet her burden of showing a prima facie case of discrimination under *Title VII*, section 1981, section *1983*, or the ADEA, Richmond must show: that she belongs to a protected class; that she was qualified for the job from which she was discharged; that she was discharged; and that after her discharge, the employer sought people with her qualifications to fill the job. (emphasis added).[10]

Similarly, in *Boutros v. Canton Regional Transit Authority*,[11] the Sixth Circuit observed that "the required elements of prima facie proof necessary for a plaintiff charging a racially hostile work environment under both Title VII and 42 U.S.C. Section 1983 are the same." In other words, by satisfying the *McDonnell Douglas* formula for showing intentional discrimination under Title VII, or by showing intentional discrimination more directly, a plaintiff also establishes a Fourteenth Amendment violation and therefore is eligible to recover under § 1983. The Eleventh Circuit has also approved the use of a violation of Title VII alone as the sole predicate for an "and laws" claim under § 1983.[12]

But this only establishes a predicate violation—the plaintiff still must contend with the distinct additional requirements and defenses of

---

5. *Id.*

6. *Id.*

7. *Id.*

8. *St. Mary's Honor Center v. Hicks,* 509 U.S. 502, 503–508 n. 1, 113 S.Ct. 2742, 2746–2747 n. 1, 125 L.Ed.2d 407 (1993).

9. 957 F.2d 595, 598 (8th Cir.1992).

10. *Citing McDonnell Douglas Corp.,* 411 U.S. at 802, 93 S.Ct. at 1824. *See also Duffy v. Wolle,* 123 F.3d 1026 (8th Cir. 1997), *cert. denied,* 523 U.S. 1137, 118 S.Ct. 1839, 140 L.Ed.2d 1090 (1998) (using the inferential Title VII framework for a claim against a federal employer under *Bivens* and relying on § 1983 precedent).

11. 997 F.2d 198, 202 (6th Cir.1993).

12. *See Wu,* 863 F.2d 1543. *But see Johnson v. City of Fort Lauderdale,* 148 F.3d 1228, 1230–31 (11th Cir.1998) (implying that the conduct complained of must be unconstitutional to violate § 1983, not merely an "and laws" violation of, for example, Title VII); *Dickerson v. Alachua County Comm'n,* 200 F.3d 761, 765 (11th Cir.), *cert. denied,* ___ U.S. ___, 121 S.Ct. 1, 147 L.Ed.2d 1025 (2000) (allowing a § 1985(3) employment discrimination conspiracy claim despite the availability of Title VII where the plaintiff claims a violation of his Constitutional rights, and not rights protected only by Title VII)

§ 1983. Whether, as in most circuits, the plaintiff has to show a separate constitutional predicate violation or, as in the Eleventh, can proceed under § 1983 merely by proving the discrimination elements of a Title VII violation, the plaintiff also must show the other elements of a § 1983 prima facie case and contend with its defenses. In particular, the plaintiff must show that the employment discrimination occurred "under color of state law," and, in the case of municipalities and other local governments, that the discrimination occurred as result of an "official policy or custom" or "deliberate indifference." Further, even if the plaintiff makes out his prima facie case, the plaintiff must overcome an individual defendant's assertion of qualified immunity.[13]

13. *See Wu*, 863 F.2d 1543.

Chapter Seven

THE AGE DISCRIMINATION IN EMPLOYMENT ACT OF 1967, AS AMENDED ("ADEA")

Analysis

---

§ 7.1 Introduction

There is a paradox about age discrimination. Age of course differs from race, sex, religion and national origin in that it more clearly lies on a continuum, and everyone who lives to be 40 crosses into the federally protected category. The universal vulnerability to age discrimination and consequent identification with its victims generated widespread political support for protection. This support found expression in ADEA remedies that, as originally enacted in 1967, were more generous than those afforded by Title VII as originally enacted in 1964. Indeed, in the 1960's Congress decided it could trust juries to fairly consider claims of age, but not the Title VII grounds of discrimination, and at least in part this is a reflection of the universality of aging.[1] Initially, these factors also appeared to have engendered sympathetic handling of age claims not only by juries but by the federal judiciary as well.

On the other hand, perhaps because of its very universality, age is a ground of discrimination that is subject to less social stigma than those banned by Title VII.[2] There is a greater general willingness to acknowledge that some types of performance decline with advancing age than that work-related capabilities vary by gender, national origin, or race. Age discrimination is therefore seen as a less invidious form of discrimination; protection is needed more from exaggerated than from statistically supportable stereotypes, from "arbitrary"[3] rather than all discrimination.

In recent years, these latter attributes have come to the fore, with consequent alteration of the legislative and legal landscape. Age discrimination protection remains at a 20–employee threshold for employer coverage, while Title VII and the Americans with Disabilities Act apply to employers with only 15 or more employees. And, as we shall see, when Congress in the Civil Rights Act of 1991 eased the Title VII plaintiff's burden of proving disparate treatment discrimination, especially for the common case where employer motives are mixed, it did not make any comparable amendment to ADEA. Soon thereafter, the Supreme Court declared in *Hazen Paper Co. v. Biggins* that the plaintiff's ultimate burden in an ADEA disparate treatment case is to demonstrate that the employer's reliance on age had a "determinative influence on the outcome,"[4] a requirement more onerous than the Title VII plaintiff's

§ 7.1

1. There is also authority to the effect that Congress could not then conceive that all or largely white juries, particularly in the deep South, could fairly entertain claims of discrimination because of race. The Civil Rights Act of 1991 does authorize trial by jury for Title VII claims of intentional (or "disparate treatment") race, as well as sex, religion, and national origin discrimination accruing after November 21, 1991.

2. Indeed, age-biased firings do not qualify under Georgia law as wrongful terminations in violation of the state's public policy exception to Georgia's at-will employment law. *See Reilly v. Alcan Aluminum*

Corp., 272 Ga. 279, 528 S.E.2d 238 (Ga. 2000).

3. Age Discrimination in Employment Act, 29 U.S.C.A. § 621, *Statement of Findings and Purpose*.

4. 507 U.S. 604, 113 S.Ct. 1701, 123 L.Ed.2d 338 (1993). *See Madel v. FCI Mktg., Inc.*, 116 F.3d 1247 (8th Cir.1997) (applying "determinative" factor); *Owen v. Thermatool Corp.*, 155 F.3d 137, 139 (2d Cir.1998) (holding that use of the phrase "substantial factor" rather than "motivating factor" was not misleading and adequately informed the jury of the law; "substantial" and "motivating" are reasonably interchangeable). *But see Renz v. Grey Adver., Inc.*, 135 F.3d 217 (2d Cir.1997) (stating that ADEA plaintiff need only show

burden, after the 1991 amendments, to show that race, sex, religion or national origin was a "motivating factor." Some language in the opinion even suggested that ADEA does not bar all age-based disparate treatment, only instances motivated by ageist animus or perhaps predicated on overbroad stereotypes about aging.

Following suit, some federal courts, taking note of the 1991 amendments to Title VII and of *Hazen,* have announced more difficult standards for ADEA than for Title VII plaintiffs who try to disparate treatment discrimination inferentially. Some have required that the plaintiff suing under ADEA, unlike her Title VII counterpart after 1991, must present prima facie evidence of disparate treatment that is "direct," "substantial" or both before the defendant bears the burden of persuading that it would have reached the same decision in reliance on lawful factors alone. Similarly, the ADEA defendant who carries the "same-decision" burden apparently defeats liability altogether, whereas the 1991 Civil Rights Act subjects the Title VII defendant who carries that burden to potential liability for declaratory relief and attorney's fees. Still other lower federal courts have explicitly permitted employers to defend ADEA claims by relying on the high cost of employing, and the asserted declining productivity of older workers; the similar Title VII BFOQ defenses have been in distinctly bad odor since the *Johnson Controls* decision and new § 703(k)(2) added in 1991. Moreover, shortly after Congress took steps in 1991 to revive the judicially eroded disproportionate adverse impact theory under Title VII, federal judges, again taking their cues from *Hazen,* are looking skeptically at the entire concept of disproportionate adverse impact under ADEA. Finally, while the 1991 amendments gave the Title VII plaintiff virtual parity with the ADEA plaintiff with respect to a right to trial by jury, the ADEA monetary remedies originally authorized in 1970 (back pay and, for willful violations, an equal additional amount of "liquidated" damages) remain unchanged and have arguably been eclipsed by the more generous compensatory and punitive damages now available under Title VII per the 1991 amendments.

The ADEA prohibits age discrimination against employees or job applicants who are 40 years of age or older. It is therefore clear that the plaintiff must be 40 at the time of the alleged unlawful employment practice.[5] In view of the principal purposes underlying its enactment, ADEA has also been held not to prohibit "reverse" age discrimination in *favor* of an older worker.[6] On the other hand, ADEA is a traditional anti-

---

that age contributed to or played a motivating part, so that instruction that age must be "the real reason" is erroneous) (dictum, because instruction ultimately held harmless error).

5. *See, e.g., Doyle v. Suffolk County,* 786 F.2d 523 (2d Cir.), *cert. denied,* 479 U.S. 825, 107 S.Ct. 98, 93 L.Ed.2d 49 (1986).

6. *See Hamilton v. Caterpillar, Inc.,* 966 F.2d 1226 (7th Cir.1992) (upholding em-

ployer provision of early retirement benefits only to workers over 50 with specified years of service). EEOC Interpretive Rules, 29 C.F.R. § 1625.2(b) (1986), contemplate limited preferential treatment of older workers (i.e., vis-a-vis an over–40 plaintiff) with respect to benefits like severance pay. *But see Zanni v. Medaphis Physician Servs. Corp.,* 240 Mich.App. 472, 612 N.W.2d 845 (Mich. App.2000) (Michigan state law protects

discrimination statute, and as such does not require an employer to grant preferential treatment or affirmative action on the basis of age.[7] But the fact that age lies along a continuum has created definitional confusion about prohibited discrimination when the plaintiff compares himself to another, younger member of the protected group who allegedly received more favorable treatment than or replaced the plaintiff. The circuits were split as to whether this "comparator" must be under forty. The Supreme Court has resolved this dispute by rejecting the position that the ADEA plaintiff must show she was replaced by someone younger than forty.[8] Prima facie she need only produce evidence that generates an inference that the employer relied on age in making the challenged decision. The Court added, however, that "such an inference cannot be drawn from the replacement of one worker with another worker *insignificantly younger*."[9] The opinion nevertheless implies that in rare circumstances a plaintiff may be able to prove an employer's reliance on age even if a replacement is not substantially younger than she.[10]

Indeed, an over-forty plaintiff did not have prima facie evidence that he was replaced at all where younger, otherwise similarly situated employees were retained after plaintiff was let go and assumed plaintiff's duties once the employer decided it could not afford a replacement.[11] On the other hand, it has been held that a claim lies when the employer,

against age bias against younger employees).

7. *See Bryan v. East Stroudsburg Univ.*, 101 F.3d 689 (3d Cir.1996), *cert. denied*, 520 U.S. 1118, 117 S.Ct. 1251, 137 L.Ed.2d 332 (1997) (university not liable for rejecting committee recommendation that applicant be hired because of his experience and age).

8. *O'Connor v. Consolidated Coin Caterers Corp.*, 517 U.S. 308, 116 S.Ct. 1307, 134 L.Ed.2d 433 (1996).

9. *Id.* at 313, 116 S.Ct. at 1310 (emphasis added).

10. *O'Connor*, 517 U.S. 308, 116 S.Ct. 1307, 134 L.Ed.2d 433. The circuits vary in their analysis of the "substantially younger" language. *Compare, e.g., Hoffmann v. Primedia Special Interest Pubs.*, 217 F.3d 522 (7th Cir.2000) (three year age difference insufficient); *Bush v. Dictaphone Corp.*, 161 F.3d 363, 368 (6th Cir.1998) (five year age difference too small); *Richter v. Hook–SuperRx, Inc.*, 142 F.3d 1024 (7th Cir. 1998) (holding as a matter of law that a 7 year age gap between plaintiff and his replacement was insufficient to state a claim for age discrimination); *Schiltz v. Burlington N. R.R.*, 115 F.3d 1407 (8th Cir.1997) (five years too small) *with Damon v. Fleming Supermarkets of Florida, Inc.*, 196 F.3d 1354, 1359–60 (11th Cir.1999), *cert. denied*,

___ U.S. ___, 120 S.Ct. 1962, 146 L.Ed.2d 793 (2000) (finding five years sufficient); *Miller v. Borden, Inc.* 168 F.3d 308, 313 (7th Cir.1999) (10 years is presumptively substantial); *Hartley v. Wisconsin Bell, Inc.*, 124 F.3d 887, 892–893 (7th Cir.1997) (10 year gap held to be presumptively substantial); *Carter v. DecisionOne Corp.*, 122 F.3d 997, 1003 (11th Cir.1997) (holding that plaintiff aged 42, who was replaced by employee aged 39, met the "substantially younger" replacement requirement). *See also Carlton v. Mystic Transp., Inc.*, 202 F.3d 129 (2d Cir.), *cert. denied*, ___ U.S. ___, 120 S.Ct. 2718, 147 L.Ed.2d 983 (2000) (evidence that some of plaintiff's job duties were transferred to a person 18 years younger and that the remaining job duties were transferred to an even younger employee hired three months after plaintiff's termination was sufficient evidence to give rise to an inference of unlawful age discrimination).

11. *Torre v. Casio, Inc.*, 42 F.3d 825 (3d Cir.1994). The Eleventh Circuit established the circumstantial evidence prima facie discharge case in *Damon*, 196 F.3d at 1359. The plaintiff must show (1) that she is a member of the protected class (over 40); (2) that she suffered an adverse employment action; (3) that a substantially younger person filled the position; and (4) the plaintiff was qualified to perform the job.

after rejecting the plaintiff, hires, promotes or retains an older employee.[12] It would seem that plaintiff's difficult proof problems in this last setting are best overcome by evidence that favorable treatment of the older comparator was either an afterthought, unrelated to intentional age discrimination against the plaintiff, or an after-the-fact ploy to mask the unlawful treatment of plaintiff.

A related issue is whether over–40 employees, although clearly within the group protected from discrimination on the ground that they are too old, state a cognizable claim when they complain that they suffered discrimination because they are too young. In a case of first impression at the appellate level, the Seventh Circuit rejected an attempt by workers aged 40–50 to assert that a special early retirement program made available only to workers at least 50 years old amounted to unlawful reverse discrimination against the plaintiff class. In effect the court construed the statutory phrase prohibiting discrimination against an employee "because of his age" as a one-way street banning only discrimination *against* an individual who is older. The court relied on what it took to be Congress' desire in enacting ADEA to protect older persons from discrimination rooted in stereotypes that ability and productivity diminish with age.[13]

An emerging and as yet unsettled question is whether the ADEA prohibits harassment on the basis of age. Several Tenth Circuit decisions discuss the issue without specifically addressing the viability of such a claim.[14] At least three other circuits have explicitly recognized such a claim.[15] And the Fourth Circuit assumes the existence of a hostile environment claim under ADEA and explicates the prima facie case: "employee seeking to establish such claim was required to show that: (1) she was at least 40 years old; (2) she was harassed based on her age; (3) the harassment had the effect of unreasonably interfering with her work, creating an environment that was both objectively and subjectively

12. *See Greene v. Safeway Stores, Inc.*, 98 F.3d 554 (10th Cir.1996); *Walther v. Lone Star Gas Co.*, 952 F.2d 119 (5th Cir. 1992).

13. *Hamilton v. Caterpillar, Inc.*, 966 F.2d 1226, 1227 (7th Cir.1992) (citing *Wehrly v. American Motors Sales Corp.*, 678 F.Supp. 1366 (N.D.Ind.1988)).

14. *See Holmes v. Regents of Univ. of Colo.*, 176 F.3d 488 (10th Cir.1999); *McKnight v. Kimberly Clark Corp.*, 149 F.3d 1125, 1129 (10th Cir.1998) (considering and deciding a hostile work environment claim under the ADEA, but not addressing the apparent lack of authority for the theory).

15. *See Montgomery v. John Deere & Co.*, 169 F.3d 556 (8th Cir.1999) (otherwise reasonable inquiries into the retirement plans of its employees can sometimes be so unnecessary and excessive as to constitute evidence of discriminatory harassment); *Breeding v. Arthur J. Gallagher and Co.*, 164 F.3d 1151, 1158–59 (8th Cir.1999); *Peecook v. Northwestern Nat'l Ins. Group*, 156 F.3d 1231 (6th Cir.1998) ("In order to prove a prima facie case of a hostile work environment, a plaintiff must show: (1) the employee is 40 years or older; (2) the employee was subjected to harassment, either through words or actions, based on age; (3) the harassment had the effect of unreasonably interfering with the employee's work performance and creating an objectively intimidating, hostile, or offensive work environment; and (4) the existence of some basis for liability on the part of the employer"); *U.S. EEOC v. Massey Yardley Chrysler Plymouth, Inc.*, 117 F.3d 1244 (11th Cir.1997); *Crawford v. Medina General Hosp.*, 96 F.3d 830 (6th Cir.1996).

hostile or offensive; and (4) she had some basis for imputing liability to her employer."[16]

ADEA was amended in 1986 to remove the then current upper age limitation, 70, for the vast majority of covered employees. Thus, in general, ADEA prohibits mandatory retirement because of age at any age for covered employers. The most important surviving exception authorizes the mandatory retirement at age 65 of a highly compensated person "employed in a bona fide executive or a high policy making position" who has an "immediate, nonforfeitable annual retirement benefit" aggregating $44,000.[17] But to be "entitled" to that nonforfeitable benefit within the meaning of the exemption, and hence denied protection, it may not suffice that the executive is actually receiving in excess of $44,000. Two circuits have divided on whether payments in the requisite amount must be due and owing *at retirement* under the terms of a pension, profit-sharing, savings, or deferred compensation plan, or whether an employer may, on an ad hoc basis, purchase the right to discriminate by inflating the plaintiff's *post*-retirement income to push it over the $44,000 threshold.[18]

Until recently, other exceptions permitted the mandatory retirement of tenured college-and university-level professors and law enforcement officers and firefighters. They were subject to involuntary retirement at age 70 (professors) or, in the case of public safety officers, younger, at the local governments' discretion.[19] Those exceptions expired December 31, 1993. The President has since signed legislation re-establishing a retirement exemption with respect to the public safety officers.[20] Similarly, in October 1998, a "safe harbor" provision was added to the ADEA under which institutions of higher education may offer to tenured faculty members, upon their voluntary retirement, supplemental benefits that are reduced or eliminated as employees age, subject to three conditions: (1) the institution must not implement any age-based reduction or cessation of benefits other than these supplemental benefits; (2) these supplemental benefits must be in addition to any retirement or

16. *Burns v. AAF–McQuay, Inc.*, 166 F.3d 292, 294 (4th Cir.1999); *Causey v. Balog*, 162 F.3d 795, 801 (4th Cir.1998).

17. ADEA § 12(c)(1), 29 U.S.C.A. § 631(c)(1).

18. *Compare Passer v. American Chem. Soc'y*, 935 F.2d 322, 328–330 (D.C.Cir.1991) (arrangement must be fixed before retirement) *with Morrissey v. Boston Five Cents Sav. Bank*, 54 F.3d 27 (1st Cir.1995) (permitting an age-based mandatory retirement under the policymaker exemption by an employer that, after a forced retirement decision, declared "nonforfeitable" just enough of the forfeitable portion of a pension benefit so that the total nonforfeitable benefit exceeded $44,000).

19. *See* Act of October 31, 1986, Pub.L. No. 99–592.

20. ADEA § 4(j), 29 U.S.C.A. § 623(j), as reenacted and amended by the Age Discrimination in Employment Amendments of 1996, Pub.L. 104–208, effective September 30, 1996. After approximately four years, however, a state or local government seeking to continue to rely on the retirement exemption must provide individual firefighters or law enforcement officers who have reached that government's mandatory retirement age an annual opportunity to demonstrate their continued physical and mental fitness by passing valid, nondiscriminatory job performance tests that are to be identified by federal regulations. Within certain limits, these amendments also permit state and local governments to establish maximum ages for hiring firefighters and law enforcement officers.

severance benefits that have been available to tenured faculty members generally, independent of any early retirement or exit-incentive plan, within the preceding 365 days; and (3) any tenured faculty member who attains the minimum age and satisfies all non-age-based conditions for receiving such a supplemental benefit has an opportunity for at least 180 days to elect to retire and receive the maximum supplemental benefit that could then be elected by a younger but otherwise similarly situated employee, and must have the ability to delay retirement for at least 180 days after making that election.[21]

ADEA covers "employers"[22] who have 20 or more employees for each working day in each of 20 weeks in the current or preceding calendar year;[23] labor unions having 25 members; and employment agencies.[24] As of July 1994, the numerical coverage threshold under the 1990 Americans with Disabilities Act has been coextensive with that under Title VII, namely 15 employees; this will mean that fewer persons will be protected from age than from the other major forms of discrimination, an irony given the previously broader scope of the prohibition against age discrimination. The Older American Act Amendments of 1984 specifically protect U.S. citizens "employed by an employer in a workplace in a foreign country." At a minimum this covers overseas employees of American corporations,[25] and may also cover employees

21. Higher Education Amendments of 1998, Pub.L. 105–244, § 941, 112 Stat. 1581 (1998). *But cf. Solon v. Gary Community Sch.*, 180 F.3d 844 (7th Cir.1999) (early retirement incentive plan in local school district that provided higher benefits to those retiring at younger age discriminated solely on basis of age and prima facie violated ADEA).

22. A determination that a particular plaintiff is not an "employee" but, in fact, an "independent contractor" will also mean that the defendant is not a Title VII "employer" of that plaintiff. For decisions elaborating the same common-law employee-independent contractor distinction under Title VII, see *supra* § 2.2. One circuit has ruled in an ADEA case that where, as is usually the case, the "employer" question turns on disputed questions of fact, decision on that issue should be made by the jury rather than by a pretrial motion to dismiss for lack of subject matter jurisdiction. *Garcia v. Copenhaver, Bell & Assocs.*, 104 F.3d 1256 (11th Cir.1997) (plaintiff must show that defendant is an "employer" as an element of her prima facie case, so the issue goes to the merits and should be decided at trial unless defendant can undermine the plaintiff's factual foundation on that question sufficiently for summary judgment).

As under Title VII, the appellate courts have held that an individual supervisor of the corporate employer is not himself an "employer" liable under ADEA. *See, e.g., Birkbeck v. Marvel Lighting Corp.*, 30 F.3d 507 (4th Cir.), *cert. denied*, 513 U.S. 1058, 115 S.Ct. 666, 130 L.Ed.2d 600 (1994).

23. *Hoekel v. Plumbing Planning Corp.*, 20 F.3d 839 (8th Cir.), *cert. denied*, 513 U.S. 974, 115 S.Ct. 448, 130 L.Ed.2d 358 (1994).

24. The scope of the term "employer" under both Title VII and ADEA is discussed at the outset of Chapter 2.

Section 623(i)(1) of the ADEA also prohibits "an employer, an employment agency, a labor organization, or any combination thereof ... to establish or maintain an employee pension plan which requires or permits ... in the case of a defined benefit plan, the cessation of an employee's benefit accrual, or the reduction of the rate of an employee's benefit accrual, because of age." *See Lee v. California Butchers' Pension Trust Fund*, 154 F.3d 1075 (9th Cir.1998) (extending ADEA coverage to trusts established by employers and unions).

25. See references to ADEA overseas coverage in Chapter 2 concerning Title VII. *But see Brownlee v. Lear Siegler Management Servs. Corp.*, 15 F.3d 976, 978 (10th Cir.), *cert. denied*, 512 U.S. 1237, 114 S.Ct. 2743, 129 L.Ed.2d 862 (1994) (no ADEA violation where employees hired to work in Saudi Arabia under employer's contract with Saudi air force were terminated at Saudi officials' insistence because Saudis

working at U.S. branches of foreign employers with more than 20 workers *worldwide*.[26] State and local governments were included in the term "employer" by amendments in 1974, but the Supreme Court has since held that Congress lacked the authority under § 5 of the Fourteenth Amendment to abrogate the states' immunity from ADEA suits in federal court.[27]

But elected officers of state and local government are excluded from the "employee" definitions and thus enjoy no protection under Title VII or ADEA.[28] Moreover, until recently, these definitions also excluded from protection members of such officers' personal staffs, immediate advisors, and other appointees responsible for setting policy, unless they were subject to state or local civil service laws. Reasoning that Congress did not exclude judges from the class of excluded policymaking appointees with the specificity required to overcome the presumption of state sovereignty implicit in the Tenth Amendment, the Supreme Court held that they, like elected judges, were outside the protection of ADEA.[29] The Civil Rights Act of 1991 overturns the result of *Gregory* and more generally protects the other, previously exempt appointees of elected officials by extending to them all "rights" and "protections" of both Title VII and ADEA, together with the "remedies" that would ordinarily be available in actions against state or local government—that is, all but punitive damages.[30] But unlike other state or local government (or private) employees, whose charges are simply investigated and perhaps conciliated by EEOC and who are therefore entitled to a de novo hearing in state or federal court, these newly-covered government appointees are remitted to an adjudicatory hearing before EEOC, subject only to limited judicial review.[31]

Although the Act does not include the federal government within the definition of "employer," a separate provision requires that personnel actions affecting most federal employees 40 or older shall be made "free from any discrimination based on age."[32] Specific provisions in other statutes authorize mandatory separation of federal air traffic controllers and law enforcement officers and firefighters at various specified ages,[33] and it appears that only civilian members of the military

---

considered them too old; age-discriminatory animus of air force cannot be imputed to its "agent," the plaintiffs' employer).

26. *See Morelli v. Cedel*, 141 F.3d 39 (2d Cir.1998).

27. *Kimel v. Florida Bd. of Regents*, 528 U.S. 62, 120 S.Ct. 631, 145 L.Ed.2d 522 (2000). The Eleventh Amendment is discussed in Chapter 12.

28. See Title VII § 701(f), 42 U.S.C.A. § 701(f), and ADEA § 11(f), 29 U.S.C.A. § 630(f).

29. *Gregory v. Ashcroft*, 501 U.S. 452, 111 S.Ct. 2395, 115 L.Ed.2d 410 (1991).

30. *See* § 321(a), incorporating § 302(1) (Title VII rights), § 302(2) (ADEA rights),

and § 307(h) (Title VII and ADEA remedies).

31. Section 321(c) and (d).

32. ADEA § 15, 29 U.S.C.A. § 633a.

33. See 5 U.S.C.A. § 8335. Because they express bona fide occupational qualifications, federal regulations setting age limits on particular jobs to protect public safety or health shield employers who rely on them from ADEA liability. *Coupe v. Federal Express Corp.*, 121 F.3d 1022 (6th Cir.1997), *cert. denied*, 523 U.S. 1020, 118 S.Ct. 1300, 140 L.Ed.2d 467 (1998); *Western Air Lines, Inc. v. Criswell*, 472 U.S. 400, 105 S.Ct. 2743, 86 L.Ed.2d 321 (1985). Further, the ADEA does not restrict the regulatory authority of federal agencies to adopt or retain

departments are covered.[34] EEOC has adjudicatory authority to resolve federal employees' age discrimination complaints. In contrast to federal employee complaints under Title VII, the age discrimination complainant may bypass any process available from his employing agency as well as from EEOC and proceed directly to federal court for a de novo hearing.[35] A complainant making this choice need only give EEOC, within 180 days after the alleged unlawful employment practice, 30 days' notice of its intent to sue.[36] The federal age discrimination complainant who chooses to initiate administrative review of the challenged decision will be deemed to have exhausted those remedies if the employing agency or EEOC has taken no action on a charge within 180 days of its filing. Alternatively, if the agency or EEOC reaches a decision, the complainant has 90 days within which to file a judicial action.[37]

ADEA forbids age discrimination in hiring, firing or classifying employees or job applicants and in other "terms, conditions, or privileges of employment."[38] It also bars age-related bias in employment advertisements or referrals. The prima facie theories of liability under ADEA parallel those of Title VII, from which its language was derived. Many cases involve express or direct evidence, such as statements attributed to management agents that the employer needs "new blood," strives to become "young, lean, and mean," or needs to purge itself of "old farts" or "dead wood." A supervisor's reference in the context of plaintiff's termination to cutting down "old, big trees so the little trees underneath can grow" qualified as direct evidence despite its metaphorical nature.[39] Liability may not be predicated on such statements when they are merely "stray remarks in the workplace," by which courts usually mean that they are uttered by co-employees or low-level supervisors or are divorced from the decisional process affecting the particular plaintiff.[40]

such rules. *Professional Pilots Fed'n v. F.A.A.*, 118 F.3d 758 (D.C.Cir.1997), *cert. denied*, 523 U.S. 1117, 118 S.Ct. 1794, 140 L.Ed.2d 936 (1998) (upholding Federal Aviation Administration's regulatory authority to retain a rule requiring commercial airline pilots to retire when they reach age 60). And an airline could decline to hire pilots approaching the FAA's age—60 mandatory retirement age when its motivation was economic and not based on age-based assumptions about abilities. *Criley v. Delta Air Lines, Inc.*, 119 F.3d 102 (2d Cir.), *cert. denied*, 522 U.S. 1028, 118 S.Ct. 626, 139 L.Ed.2d 607 (1997).

34. *Helm v. California*, 722 F.2d 507 (9th Cir.1983).

35. *See* Chapter 4, Section A for a discussion of the procedural requirements of Title VII.

36. ADEA § 15(c), (d), 29 U.S.C.A. § 633a(c), (d).

37. *See Adler v. Espy*, 35 F.3d 263 (7th Cir.1994).

38. 29 U.S.C.A. § 623(a)(1). Citing the quoted language and relying on the common purposes of ADEA and Title VII, a circuit court has held that ADEA also prohibits the creation of an age-hostile environment. *Crawford v. Medina Gen. Hosp.*, 96 F.3d 830 (6th Cir.1996).

39. *Wichmann v. Bd. of Trustees of Southern Illinois University*, 180 F.3d 791 (7th Cir.1999), *judgment vacated on other grounds*, 528 U.S. 1111, 120 S.Ct. 929, 145 L.Ed.2d 807 (2000).

40. *See, e.g., Stone v. Autoliv ASP, Inc.*, 210 F.3d 1132, 1140–41 (10th Cir.), *cert. denied*, ___ U.S. ___, 121 S.Ct. 182, 148 L.Ed.2d 125 (2000) (stray remark was isolated and lacked necessary nexus to adverse employment decision); *Standard v. A.B.E.L. Services, Inc.*, 161 F.3d 1318, 1329–30 (11th Cir.1998) (supervisor whose statement indicated doubt about older workers' competence not discrimination respecting plaintiff); *Krumwiede v. Mercer County Ambulance Serv.*, 116 F.3d 361 (8th

But express statements reflecting preference for youth or animus toward age lose their "stray" character and become actionable when announced by top executives or incorporated into official company planning documents[41] or when uttered by a representative of management with decisionmaking authority with respect to the plaintiff.[42] And the fact that such comments were made over a long period of time argues for rather than against their admissibility; while any particular comment may be remote in time from the alleged violation, as a whole the comments may show a pattern of age-based animus.[43] Moreover, age-related remarks that can be linked to managers responsible for overseeing the implementation of a layoff are relevant as tending to show that the layoffs themselves were tainted by unlawful motivation.[44] Even if the slur or stray remark does not arise to the level of direct evidence necessary to allow the plaintiff to avoid the inferential proof mode, such evidence can support a determination that the employer's proffered legitimate nondiscriminatory reason for the adverse employment action was an unlawful pretext for age discrimination.[45]

Cir.1997) (co-worker's references to plaintiff insufficient to support ADEA claim absent evidence that employer was aware of them). Even a supervisor's comment that the plaintiff was an "old fart" did not demonstrate that the employer's stated reason for not rehiring plaintiff was pretextual absent a nexus between the supervisor's state of mind and the employer's reason for its decision; *Bolton v. Scrivner, Inc.*, 36 F.3d 939 (10th Cir.1994), *cert. denied*, 513 U.S. 1152, 115 S.Ct. 1104, 130 L.Ed.2d 1071 (1995); *Thomure v. Phillips Furniture Co.*, 30 F.3d 1020 (8th Cir.1994), *cert. denied*, 513 U.S. 1191, 115 S.Ct. 1255, 131 L.Ed.2d 135 (1995) (employer comment that plaintiff might want to consider retirement "stray" when made in response to plaintiff's complaints about deeper wage cuts for older employees); *Cone v. Longmont United Hosp. Ass'n*, 14 F.3d 526, 531 (10th Cir. 1994) ("isolated comments, unrelated to the challenged action, are insufficient to show discriminatory animus in termination decisions").

41. *See generally supra* § 3.2 for decisions attempting to delineate which remarks are "stray." *See also Madel v. FCI Mktg., Inc.*, 116 F.3d 1247 (8th Cir.1997) (manager's age-related epithets not "stray" as a matter of law and might be attributed to employer, even though he was not ultimately responsible for plaintiffs' discharge, since a jury could reasonably find that he played a role in that decision); *Bevan v. Honeywell, Inc.*, 118 F.3d 603 (8th Cir. 1997); *Radabaugh v. Zip Feed Mills, Inc.*, 997 F.2d 444 (8th Cir.1993).

42. *EEOC v. Manville Sales Corp.*, 27 F.3d 1089 (5th Cir.1994), *cert. denied*, 513

U.S. 1190, 115 S.Ct. 1252, 131 L.Ed.2d 133 (1995).

43. *Id.*

44. *Armbruster v. Unisys Corp.*, 32 F.3d 768 (3d Cir.1994).

45. *See, e.g., Damon v. Fleming Supermarkets of Florida, Inc.*, 196 F.3d 1354, 1358–59 (11th Cir.1999), *cert. denied*, ___ U.S. ___, 120 S.Ct. 1962, 146 L.Ed.2d 793 (2000) (statement by decisionmaker immediately after plaintiff's termination that "what the company needed was aggressive young men" does not amount to direct evidence of discrimination but is probative circumstantial evidence); *Beaver v. Rayonier Inc.*, 200 F.3d 723 (11th Cir.1999) (finding that decisionmaker's comment that he wanted to attract "younger, engineer-type employees or supervisors" in reduction-in-force case did not rise to level of direct evidence of discrimination); *Hindman v. Transkrit Corp.*, 145 F.3d 986 (8th Cir. 1998) (stray remarks by supervisors three years prior to adverse employment action are relevant as background evidence, helpful in proving ultimate issue of age discrimination); *Kelley v. Airborne Freight Corp.*, 140 F.3d 335, 353 (1st Cir.), *cert. denied*, 525 U.S. 932, 119 S.Ct. 341, 142 L.Ed.2d 281 (1998) (ageist remarks by nondecisionmaker admissible in inferential proof mode); *Carter v. DecisionOne Corp.*, 122 F.3d 997 (11th Cir.1997) (manager's remark that he preferred "nubile young women" as sales persons and an executive's comment that he had gotten rid of all the "sleazy old people" supported a finding of pretext). For a discussion of the inferential proof mode, *see infra*, this section.

One defense that seems to have particular potency in ADEA claims, perhaps even more than in actions under Title VII,[46] is that the supervisor who imposed the employment detriment (e.g. firing) on the plaintiff is the same person who had hired him; the "same actor" doctrine.[47] Thus it may be difficult to believe that the employer developed a certain aversion to older people only two years after hiring one.[48] In such circumstances, the plaintiff must show that this proffered justification is a pretext for age discrimination.[49] Similarly, if the decisionmaker is also a member of the protected group, an inference of age discrimination is weakened.[50]

A common mode of proof tracks the individual *"McDonnell Douglas"*disparate treatment case of the kind that also predominates under Title VII.[51] In these cases employers have enjoyed particular success when the plaintiff's termination can be shown to have taken place as

---

46. See discussion of the application of the same actor doctrine in cases arising under Title VII (and the ADA) in § 3.10. *See, e.g., Bradley v. Harcourt, Brace & Co.,* 104 F.3d 267 (9th Cir.1996) (sex); *Evans v. Technologies Applications & Service Co.,* 80 F.3d 954 (4th Cir.1996) (sex); *EEOC v. Our Lady of Resurrection Med. Ctr.,* 77 F.3d 145 (7th Cir.1996) (race); *Buhrmaster v. Overnite Transp. Co.,* 61 F.3d 461 (6th Cir. 1995), *cert. denied,* 516 U.S. 1078, 116 S.Ct. 785, 133 L.Ed.2d 736 (1996) (sex); *Jacques v. Clean–Up Group, Inc.,* 96 F.3d 506 (1st Cir.1996) (disability); *Jiminez v. Mary Washington College,* 57 F.3d 369 (4th Cir.), *cert. denied,* 516 U.S. 944, 116 S.Ct. 380, 133 L.Ed.2d 304 (1995) (race and national origin).

47. *See, e.g., Schnabel v. Abramson,* 232 F.3d 83, 91 (2d Cir.2000); *Roberts v. Separators, Inc.,* 172 F.3d 448 (7th Cir.1999); *Williams v. Vitro Services Corp.,* 144 F.3d 1438 (11th Cir.1998); *Grady v. Affiliated Ctr., Inc.,* 130 F.3d 553 (2d Cir.1997), *cert. denied,* 525 U.S. 936, 119 S.Ct. 349, 142 L.Ed.2d 288 (1998); *Renz v. Grey Advertising, Inc.,* 135 F.3d 217 (2d Cir.1997); *Chiaramonte v. Fashion Bed Group, Inc.,* 129 F.3d 391 (7th Cir.1997), *cert. denied,* 523 U.S. 1118, 118 S.Ct. 1795, 140 L.Ed.2d 936 (1998); *Brown v. CSC Logic, Inc.,* 82 F.3d 651 (5th Cir.1996); *Hartsel v. Keys,* 87 F.3d 795 (6th Cir.1996), *cert. denied,* 519 U.S. 1055, 117 S.Ct. 683, 136 L.Ed.2d 608 (1997); *Rand v. CF Indus., Inc.,* 42 F.3d 1139, 1147 (7th Cir.1994); *LeBlanc v. Great Am. Ins. Co.,* 6 F.3d 836, 847 (1st Cir.1993), *cert. denied,* 511 U.S. 1018, 114 S.Ct. 1398, 128 L.Ed.2d 72 (1994); *Lowe v. J.B. Hunt Transp., Inc.,* 963 F.2d 173, 175 (8th Cir. 1992); *Proud v. Stone,* 945 F.2d 796, 797–98 (4th Cir.1991). *But cf. Banks v. Travelers Cos.,* 180 F.3d 358 (2d Cir.1999) (declining

to hold that trial judges are required to give the same actor instruction).

48. *Rand v. C.F. Indus., Inc.,* 42 F.3d 1139 (7th Cir.1994). *See also Roberts v. Separators, Inc.,* 172 F.3d 448 (7th Cir. 1999) (only one year between hire and fire bars plaintiff's age claim).

49. *Roper v. Peabody Coal Co.,* 47 F.3d 925 (7th Cir.1995).

50. *See Richter v. Hook–SupeRx, Inc.,* 142 F.3d 1024 (7th Cir.1998) (calling evidence that decisionmakers were 46, 53, and 60 years old "significant").

51. *See O'Connor v. Consolidated Coin Caterers Corp.,* 517 U.S. 308, 116 S.Ct. 1307, 134 L.Ed.2d 433 (1996) (accepting parties' assumption and extensive circuit court authority that the basic Title VII *McDonnell Douglas* evidentiary framework applies to ADEA claims); *Bellaver v. Quanex Corp.,* 200 F.3d 485 (7th Cir.2000); *Roper v. Peabody Coal Co.,* 47 F.3d 925 (7th Cir.1995); *Rinehart v. City of Independence,* 35 F.3d 1263 (8th Cir.1994), *cert. denied,* 514 U.S. 1096, 115 S.Ct. 1822, 131 L.Ed.2d 744 (1995); *Seman v. Coplay Cement Co.,* 26 F.3d 428 (3d Cir.1994); *Roush v. KFC Nat. Mgt. Co.,* 10 F.3d 392 (6th Cir.1993), *cert. denied,* 513 U.S. 808, 115 S.Ct. 56, 130 L.Ed.2d 15 (1994); *Lindsey v. Prive Corp.,* 987 F.2d 324 (5th Cir.1993); *Goldstein v. Manhattan Indus., Inc.,* 758 F.2d 1435 (11th Cir.), *cert. denied,* 474 U.S. 1005, 106 S.Ct. 525, 88 L.Ed.2d 457 (1985); *Haskell v. Kaman Corp.,* 743 F.2d 113 (2d Cir.1984); *Cuddy v. Carmen,* 694 F.2d 853 (D.C.Cir. 1982); *Douglas v. Anderson,* 656 F.2d 528 (9th Cir.1981); *Loeb v. Textron, Inc.,* 600 F.2d 1003 (1st Cir.1979); *Schwager v. Sun Oil Co. of Pa.,* 591 F.2d 58 (10th Cir.1979). See Chapter 3, Section B for a complete discussion of the disparate treatment claim under Title VII.

part of a comprehensive, economically motivated reduction in force. Because such a force reduction is itself a legitimate reason for termination, courts typically require plaintiffs discharged in those circumstances to produce "plus" evidence beyond the prima facie case tending to show that age was a factor in the challenged termination.[52] In appellate decisions, one plaintiff carried that burden by offering evidence of two age-related comments by company officials in connection with the transfer of two younger employees into the department from which plaintiff had been downsized.[53] Another succeeded by showing half-hearted efforts to place him in alternative positions for which he was qualified.[54] In the latter case, the company's statistical evidence tending to show that the organization as a whole was not age-discriminatory failed to conclusively negate the inference plaintiff's evidence raised that he individually had been treated unfavorably because of his age. If the plaintiff makes that showing, the employer must then come forward with an age-neutral justification for the discharge of the particular plaintiff— a neutral justification, that is, separate and apart from the fact that the termination took place as part of a reduction in force.[55]

Indeed in some circuits the "RIFFed" plaintiff enjoys an easier burden than the "single-discharge" plaintiff. For example, she need only show that younger employees received more favorable treatment during a RIF, and not that her particular replacement was younger.[56] The inference of discriminatory treatment is not drawn so lightly in a single-discharge case, in which there can be no assumption that job requirements are fungible, unless the single plaintiff's responsibilities are absorbed by others.[57] In RIF cases the plaintiff's prima facie case may be similarly eased on the element of comparative qualifications.[58]

52. *See, e.g., Regel v. K–Mart Corp.*, 190 F.3d 876 (8th Cir.1999); *Hardin v. Hussmann Corp.*, 45 F.3d 262 (8th Cir.1995); *Healy v. New York Life Ins. Co.*, 860 F.2d 1209 (3d Cir.1988), *cert. denied*, 490 U.S. 1098, 109 S.Ct. 2449, 104 L.Ed.2d 1004 (1989). Evidence of a replacement employee's unsatisfactory performance following a RIF is irrelevant to a determination of whether the RIFFed employee was fired in violation of ADEA. *See Cullen v. Olin Corp.*, 195 F.3d 317 (7th Cir.), *cert. denied*, ___ U.S. ___, 120 S.Ct. 1423, 146 L.Ed.2d 315 (2000). *See also Thorn v. Sundstrand Aerospace Corp.*, 207 F.3d 383 (7th Cir.2000) (distinguishing proof elements for two kinds of RIFs: (1) where the plaintiff was replaced and (2) the presumably more common situation where she is not).

53. *Hardin*, 45 F.3d at 266.

54. *Cronin v. Aetna Life Ins. Co.*, 46 F.3d 196 (2d Cir.1995).

55. *Viola v. Philips Med. Sys. of N. Am. & N. Am. Philips Corp.*, 42 F.3d 712 (2d Cir.1994).

56. *See, e.g., Bellaver v. Quanex Corp.*, 200 F.3d 485 (7th Cir.2000); *Collier v. Budd Co.*, 66 F.3d 886 (7th Cir.1995).

57. *Gadsby v. Norwalk Furniture Corp.*, 71 F.3d 1324 (7th Cir.1995). In such "single-discharge" or "mini-RIF" cases, the inference of discrimination arises where the terminated employee's duties are absorbed by other employees not in the protected class. *See Bellaver*, 200 F.3d at 495.

58. *Cf. O'Connor v. Consolidated Coin Caterers Corp.*, 84 F.3d 718 (4th Cir.), *cert. denied*, 519 U.S. 1040, 117 S.Ct. 608, 136 L.Ed.2d 533 (1996) (in RIF case, employee need not meet standard *McDonnell Douglas* prima facie element that his work met employer's legitimate expectations, but only lesser burden of showing that he was performing at level substantially equivalent to that of the lowest-performing retained employees).

The RIFFed plaintiff must show prima facie that one or more similarly situated persons below the age of 40, or at least younger than herself, were retained or hired shortly after plaintiff's layoff while she was dismissed despite having met the employer's legitimate performance expectations.[59] Even then, the employer can avoid liability by offering evidence of a legitimate nondiscriminatory reason for retaining the younger workers, thereby casting on the plaintiff the final burden of demonstrating the pretextual nature of that justification.[60] When an employer reduces its force for economic reasons, it generally incurs no duty to transfer laid off workers to other positions. However, if a job is currently available for which the plaintiff is qualified and the employer fills that job with a person outside the protected group, an inference of discrimination is permitted.[61] Similarly, the inconsistent application of RIF criteria can suffice to show pretext.[62] One circuit court has stressed that in analyzing RIF cases "the similarity of the jobs held by an older and younger employee is the touchstone for determining whether a layoff of the older may be found to be an ADEA violation by a trier of fact."[63] That same circuit delineates two types of actionable RIFs: cases that center on "who took the place of the covered employee," and those center on whether the selection of RIFFed employees was influenced by an impermissible ground.[64]

As under Title VII, the more generalized and subjective the employer justification in response to a *McDonnell Douglas* prima facie case, the more vulnerable it is to a finding of "pretext."[65] The Supreme Court's

---

59. Circuit courts have applied *O'Connor* to RIFs so that plaintiffs need only show that employees "sufficiently younger" than they, not necessarily under 40, were retained or newly hired. *Showalter v. University of Pittsburgh Med. Ctr.*, 190 F.3d 231 (3d Cir.1999). *Cf. Pitasi v. Gartner Group, Inc.*, 184 F.3d 709 (7th Cir.1999) (applying "substantially younger standard but finding newly hired younger employee not similarly situated). At least one circuit has utilized the doctrine of equitable (or judicial) estoppel to defeat an ADEA employee's prima facie element that he was qualified for his job. The employee had applied for and received Social Security disability benefits. On his application, the employee made statements under penalty of perjury that he was "unable to work." Because that statement was "patently and admittedly contrary to his central claim" that "he is able to work," the employee was estopped from prosecuting his ADEA claim. *Simon v. Safelite Glass Corp.*, 128 F.3d 68, 73 (2d Cir.1997). See Chapter 10 for a discussion of judicial estoppel as applied to the ADA.

60. *See Beaver v. Rayonier, Inc.*, 200 F.3d 723 (11th Cir.1999) (reliance on cost-savings pretextual where plaintiff told company he would take any job available); *King*

v. General Elec. Co., 960 F.2d 617 (7th Cir.1992); *Oxman v. WLS–TV*, 846 F.2d 448 (7th Cir.1988). In two cases, one circuit concluded the plaintiff failed to carry the burden of pretext for want of evidence showing that the average age of the relevant employee complement had decreased after the RIF. *Watkins v. Sverdrup Tech., Inc.*, 153 F.3d 1308, 1315 (11th Cir.1998); *Tidwell v. Carter Products*, 135 F.3d 1422, 1427 (11th Cir.1998).

61. *See Jameson v. Arrow Co.*, 75 F.3d 1528 (11th Cir.1996).

62. *See Beaird v. Seagate Tech., Inc.*, 145 F.3d 1159, 1169 (10th Cir.), *cert. denied*, 525 U.S. 1054, 119 S.Ct. 617, 142 L.Ed.2d 556 (1998)..

63. *Burger v. New York Inst. of Tech.*, 94 F.3d 830, 833 (2d Cir.1996).

64. *Danzer v. Norden Sys., Inc.*, 151 F.3d 50, 55 (2d Cir.1998).

65. *Compare Taggart v. Time, Inc.*, 924 F.2d 43 (2d Cir.1991) (employer's rejection of plaintiff as "overqualified" held pretextual) *with EEOC v. Insurance Co. of N. Am.*, 49 F.3d 1418 (9th Cir.1995) (plaintiff's rejection as overqualified not pretextual) *and Stein v. National City Bank*, 942 F.2d 1062 (6th Cir.1991) (upholding as objective-

refinement of the Title VII "pretext" concept in the *St. Mary's Honor Center* decision[66] has been adapted to actions under ADEA. Thus even though the employer's stated reason for its conduct is refuted by the evidence, the employer may be absolved of liability if the factfinder determines that the false explanation was not a cover for discrimination because of age.[67]

Relative to cases under Title VII, ADEA plaintiffs who attempt to show pretext solely by attempting to undermine the employer's stated legitimate reason may have anticipated even more exacting scrutiny under the *St. Mary's* standard, because their burden after *Hazen* is to demonstrate that age is not merely a "motivating" but rather a "determinative" factor in the employer's decision.[68] Perhaps because of this complicating consideration, the lower courts experienced at least as much difficulty in applying *St. Mary's* to ADEA cases as to actions under Title VII.[69]

But the Supreme Court, in perhaps its most significant plaintiff-friendly employment discrimination opinion in decades, has resolved the post-*St. Mary's* debate favorably to plaintiffs, consistent with the approach taken by the majority of the circuit courts. In *Reeves v. Sanderson Plumbing Products, Inc.,*[70] an ADEA case, the Court, taking note of the differing *St. Mary's* passages, wrote that the jury may find the ultimate fact of discrimination on a prohibited ground simply from (1)

ly related to the goal of reducing turnover the rejection of plaintiff for a non-exempt position because he was a college graduate; employer could rationally believe that a non-graduate would less likely become bored with the work and would have fewer market alternatives). *See* Chapter 3, Section B for a discussion of "pretext."

66. See Chapter 3 on Title VII modes of proof for a discussion of the *St. Mary's* decision.

67. *See, e.g., Keller v. Orix Credit Alliance, Inc.,* 130 F.3d 1101 (3d Cir.1997) (en banc); *Miller v. CIGNA Corp.,* 47 F.3d 586 (3d Cir.1995) (en banc); *Rea v. Martin Marietta Corp.,* 29 F.3d 1450 (10th Cir.1994); *Biggins v. Hazen Paper Co.,* 30 F.3d 126 (1st Cir.1994) (on remand from Supreme Court). Other ADEA cases that turn on the *St. Mary's* decision are included in a discussion in Chapter 3 of the Title VII proof requirements at issue in that opinion.

68. *See, e.g., Rhodes v. Guiberson Oil Tools,* 75 F.3d 989 (5th Cir.1996) (en banc) (holding that ADEA plaintiff's evidence of the *McDonnell Douglas* prima facie elements and of the falsity of the employer's reason must be "substantial," "not overwhelmed by contrary proof," and "adequate to enable a reasonable factfinder to infer that the intentional age-based discrimination was a determinative factor in the ad-

verse employer action" to survive summary judgment or Rule 50 judgment as a matter of law). *See also Hidalgo v. Overseas Condado Ins. Agencies, Inc.,* 120 F.3d 328 (1st Cir.1997) (requiring proof not only of pretext but also evidence sufficient for the factfinder reasonably to conclude that the employer's decision was wrongfully based on age); *Miller v. CIGNA Corp.,* 47 F.3d 586 (3d Cir.1995) (en banc) (referring to high hurdle facing the "indirect pretext" ADEA plaintiff after *St. Mary's* due to the requirement of showing that age was a "determinative" factor).

69. *Compare Bogle v. Orange County Bd. of County Comm'rs,* 162 F.3d 653, 658 (11th Cir.1998); *Sempier v. Johnson & Higgins,* 45 F.3d 724 (3d Cir.1995), *cert. denied,* 515 U.S. 1159, 115 S.Ct. 2611, 132 L.Ed.2d 854 (1995); *Waldron v. SL Indus.,* 56 F.3d 491 (3d Cir.1995); and *E.E.O.C. v. Ethan Allen, Inc.,* 44 F.3d 116 (2d Cir.1994) (inconsistent employer explanations for action enough to send case to jury concerning ultimate issue of pretext) *with Ingels v. Thiokol Corp.,* 42 F.3d 616 (10th Cir.1994) (inconsistencies in employer explanation do not suffice to show that employer practice was a pretext for age discrimination).

70. 530 U.S. 133, 120 S.Ct. 2097, 147 L.Ed.2d 105 (2000).

evidence establishing a prima facie case, coupled with (2) "sufficient" evidence that the employer's asserted legitimate nondiscriminatory explanation is false.[71] The Court considered this approach consistent with general evidence law: "the factfinder is entitled to consider a party's dishonesty about a material fact as 'affirmative evidence of guilt' "; and once the employer's asserted reason is rejected, unlawful discrimination "may well be the most likely alternative explanation."[72] Of course, as *St. Mary's* had held, the jury may properly find liability in such a case only if properly charged that it must, from these two kinds of evidence, make dual findings :(1) that the reason or reasons offered by the employer for taking the adverse action against plaintiff were not its real reasons, and (2) that the employer's real reason was in fact the unlawful ground. To that extent the Court disapproved the circuit cases that had required plaintiffs to adduce evidence not only that the employer's asserted legitimate reason was false but also sufficient, independent evidence that the employer's actual reason was an unlawful one.

§§ 7.2–9.4 [Reserved]

A. AGE AS A "DETERMINATIVE" FACTOR: "MIXED MOTIVES" IN ADEA CASES; STRICTER DISPARATE TREATMENT PROOF REQUIREMENTS AFTER *HAZEN*?; THE POST-*HAZEN* DECLINE OF THE NEUTRAL PRACTICE/ADVERSE TREATMENT THEORY; ADEA RETALIATION; ADEA BFOQ DEFENSE

§ 7.5 Age as a "Determinative" Factor: "Mixed Motives"

Where the evidence shows lawful as well as unlawful factors for the employer's conduct, ADEA plaintiffs must show that age was a determinative factor in the challenged employment decision; the employer must then carry the burden of persuading that it would have taken the same employment action independent of the unlawful component of its aggregate complex of reasons.[1] Where there is no employer admission of unlawfulness, and the evidence does not reveal an obviously unlawful motivation, the Supreme Court held in *Hazen Paper Co. v. Biggins*[2] that

---

71. The plaintiff must impeach or contradict every legitimate, nondiscriminatory reason offered by the defendant. *See, e.g., Chapman v. AI Transport,* 229 F.3d 1012 (11th Cir.2000).

72. *See also Vadie v. Mississippi State Univ.,* 218 F.3d 365, 374 n.23 (5th Cir.2000) (summary judgment will not always be denied where plaintiff shows pretext because the ultimate burden borne by plaintiff is whether, based on the whole record, age was a *determinative* factor for the adverse job action); *Schnabel v. Abramson,* 232 F.3d 83, 90–91 (2d Cir.2000).

§ 7.5

1. *See, e.g., Rose v. National Cash Register Corp.,* 703 F.2d 225 (6th Cir.), *cert. denied,* 464 U.S. 939, 104 S.Ct. 352, 78 L.Ed.2d 317 (1983). *See* Chapter 3, Section B(1) for a fuller discussion of the *Price Waterhouse* burden shifting scheme and its modification by the Civil Rights Act of 1991.

2. 507 U.S. 604, 113 S.Ct. 1701, 123 L.Ed.2d 338 (1993). *See also Miller v. CIGNA Corp.,* 47 F.3d 586 (3d Cir.1995) (en banc).

the jury should be charged that the plaintiff must prove that age played a "determinative" role in the challenged decision.

"Determinative" represents a middle ground that requires a showing, where the challenged decision proceeds from more than one motive, that age was a "but-for" cause of the decision, yet does not require a showing that the unlawful factor was predominant.[3] Still, in practice, the "determinative" standard demands that the unlawful age-related factor represents a greater proportion of the employer's overall complex of reasons than the Title VII counterpart term, "motivating." Although the phrase "determining factor" is frequently used in the ADEA opinions of the lower federal courts, it appears nowhere in the statute and has not been squarely endorsed by the Supreme Court.[4] Nevertheless, the ADEA "determinative influence" language of *Hazen* connotes a more stringent proof requirement than the "motivating factor" counterpart language under Title VII. The term is really only another attempt to wrestle with the intractable question that must be answered to resolve any claim of intentional employment discrimination, whether under ADEA or Title VII: was the adverse term or condition of employment imposed "because of" a prohibited factor. The Seventh Circuit's recommendation for jury instructions on this issue convey a but-for requirement by asking the jury to decide "whether age accounts for the decision—in other words, whether the same events would have transpired if the employee had been younger than 40 and everything else had been the same."[5]

Before the Civil Rights Act of 1991, the Supreme Court addressed the "mixed motive" problem under Title VII. In *Price Waterhouse v. Hopkins*,[6] a plurality concluded that when an employer undertakes a challenged employment decision for more than one reason, and the conduct that is unlawful under Title VII is a "motivating," or "substantial motivating" factor in the employer's decision, liability will attach unless the employer can persuade that it would have reached the same decision for one or more independent, lawful reasons. If an employer carries that persuasion burden, the plurality wrote, it should be found not to have committed an unlawful employment practice, despite the evidence of partial unlawful motive.[7]

The Civil Rights Act of 1991 substantially incorporates and even enhances the *Price Waterhouse* plurality's pro-plaintiff perspective in defining the circumstances that impose the "same decision" persuasion burden on the employer. Section 107 declares that an unlawful employment practice is established when the plaintiff demonstrates that employer reliance on protected group status was a "motivating factor" for "any" employment practice, "even though other factors also motivated

3. *Miller,* 47 F.3d 586.

4. *See Gehring v. Case Corp.,* 43 F.3d 340 (7th Cir.1994), *cert. denied,* 515 U.S. 1159, 115 S.Ct. 2612, 132 L.Ed.2d 855 (1995).

5. *Id.*

6. 490 U.S. 228, 109 S.Ct. 1775, 104 L.Ed.2d 268 (1989).

7. *Id.* at 245 n.10, 109 S.Ct. at 1788 n.10.

the practice."[8] And the statute makes no reference to the kind of "direct" or "substantial" prima facie evidence of unlawful discrimination that the *Price Waterhouse* concurrers would have required as prerequisite to a shift of burden to the defendant.[9] Section 107 therefore apparently requires the defendant employer in a Title VII action to bear the same decision burden regardless of the kind or strength of the plaintiff's prima facie case, so long as the plaintiff has shown in some fashion that discrimination was a motivating factor.[10] In Title VII cases, then, "direct" anecdotal testimony of discriminatory motive; substantial or less than substantial evidence that an employer decision, practice or policy treated the plaintiff adversely on a prohibited ground; or simply the more common *McDonnell Douglas/Burdine* "inferential" evidence that the plaintiff applied, was minimally qualified and was rejected–now *all* apparently suffice to require the employer to demonstrate "that it would have taken the same action in the absence of the impermissible motivating factor."[11]

Section 107 of the 1991 Act amendments to Title VII also codify the *Price Waterhouse* requirement that the required employer "demonstration," once triggered, entails a burden of persuasion as well as production.[12] Importantly, the legislation goes somewhat beyond the *Price Waterhouse* plurality by providing that even the defendant who makes the required "same-decision" showing has committed an unlawful employment practice and is relieved only of monetary liability. If the employer was properly required to make that showing—that is if unlawful discrimination was a "motivating" factor in the challenged employment decision—the employer does not completely escape liability but is deemed to have committed a law violation remediable by prospective relief and attorney's fees.[13]

It is unclear whether these key modifications to Title VII mixed-motive cases will ultimately be held to apply to ADEA actions. Although other parts of the 1991 Act refer directly to ADEA,[14] § 107 does not. If the omission is ultimately regarded as legislative oversight, the ADEA

---

8. Adding Title VII § 703(m), 42 U.S.C.A. § 2000e–2(m) (1988).

9. See Chapter 3 on Title VII modes of proof.

10. *See* § 3.11, *supra.* That appears to be the dominant conclusion of the lower courts even in cases decided under *Price Waterhouse* itself rather than under the 1991 Act. *See Tyler v. Bethlehem Steel Corp.*, 958 F.2d 1176 (2d Cir.), *cert. denied*, 506 U.S. 826, 113 S.Ct. 82, 121 L.Ed.2d 46 (1992); *but cf. Griffiths v. CIGNA Corp.*, 988 F.2d 457, 470 (3d Cir.1993), *cert. denied*, 510 U.S. 865, 114 S.Ct. 186, 126 L.Ed.2d 145 (1993) (to trigger the mixed motive burden shifting, the plaintiff must produce "circumstantial evidence" of conduct or comments by decisionmakers that "directly" reflect their discriminatory attitude).

The authors are unsure what the Third Circuit has in mind by "circumstantial" evidence that reflects a state of mind "directly." Perhaps it means that the testimony must relate "directly" to the decisionmaker's state of mind but need not come in the form of an admission by the decisionmaker herself.

11. Section 107(b) (amending Title VII § 706(g), 42 U.S.C.A. § 2000e–5(g) (1972)). See Chapter 3.

12. Section 104 (adding subsection 701(m) to Title VII, 42 U.S.C.A. § 2000e(m)).

13. Section 107(b)(3) (adding paragraph (2)(B) to § 706(g) of Title VII, 42 U.S.C.A. § 2000e–5(g)).

14. *See, e.g.*, § 115.

defendant, like the Title VII one, will be forced to carry the same-decision burden regardless of how the plaintiff establishes prima facie that age was a "determinative" factor. Moreover, the employer who carries the "same-decision" burden, because he still was found to have acted in part because of the plaintiff's age, will have violated ADEA and be liable for prospective relief and attorney's fees. But the lower federal courts have instead generally given the 1991 Act a "plain text" reading, thereby treating the absence of any reference to ADEA in § 107 as advertent.[15] Accordingly, they consider ADEA mixed-motive cases to be governed by the former Title VII regime of the *Price Waterhouse* plurality, as tightened up by concurring Justices White or O'Connor. Under that composite approach the employer does not bear a "same-decision" burden in ADEA cases unless the plaintiff's prima facie evidence of age-based motivation is "direct" (per Justice O'Connor), "substantial" (per Justice White), or both.[16] Moreover, the ADEA defendant who carries that burden will not be exposed to declaratory relief or attorney's fees as under the amended Title VII, but will, per the assumption of all the justices participating in *Price Waterhouse*, escape liability completely.[17]

The prevailing understanding that "determinative" means age was a "but for" factor[18] presents a more fundamental logical conundrum. If the ADEA plaintiff is required to show prima facie that "but-for" the employer's reliance on age it would not have taken the challenged action, then the employer who carries the "same decision" defense is asked to negate exactly what the plaintiff just proved! In other words, the employer mounts the "same decision" defense only if and after the plaintiff first has presented an adequate prima facie case—that is, has shown that age was a "but for" or determinative factor. To give both the "determinative" and "same decision" concepts independent, internally consistent significance, then, perhaps a "determinative" factor should be viewed as something less weighty than a "but for" factor, although more substantial in an employer's total calculus than a Title VII "motivating" factor.[19]

15. The Eleventh Circuit has held that the modifications to *Price Waterhouse* do not apply to ADEA retaliation claims because § 2000e–5(g)(2)(B) applies by its terms to only claims arising under § 2000e–2(m), and ADEA retaliation claims are not among those unlawful employment practices listed in § 2000e–2(m). *See Lewis v. Young Men's Christian Ass'n*, 208 F.3d 1303 (11th Cir.2000).

16. *See, e.g., Miller v. CIGNA Corp.*, 47 F.3d 586 (3d Cir.1995) (en banc) (ADEA plaintiff who presents no "direct" evidence of age discrimination, relying instead on *McDonnell Douglas/St. Mary's*-type circumstantial evidence tending to discredit the employer's asserted legitimate reasons for the challenged employer conduct, is not en-

titled to a "same-decision" burden-shifting instruction).

17. *Id.*

18. *See Arnett v. California Public Employees Retirement System*, 179 F.3d 690 (9th Cir.1999), *vacated on other grounds*, 528 U.S. 1111, 120 S.Ct. 930, 145 L.Ed.2d 807 (2000); *Huff v. UARCO, Inc.*, 122 F.3d 374, 388 (7th Cir.1997).

19. Title VII does not present the same logical difficulty. It is perfectly consistent for the employer to show it would have reached the same decision for a lawful reason even though the plaintiff has already shown the employer was "motivated," in an unspecified degree, by an unlawful one.

The plaintiff's individual disparate treatment evidence of age discrimination, whether direct or inferential, may be buttressed, as under Title VII, by statistical or anecdotal evidence or both that the employer systemically discriminates on a widespread, routine basis.[20] But courts have required refined and technically significant statistical evidence and sometimes also anecdotal testimony by multiple individuals before they will conclude that the employer is responsible for a pattern or practice of discrimination.[21]

§ 7.6 Stricter Disparate Treatment Proof Requirements After *Hazen*?

Hazen Paper Co. v. Biggins, discussed also in the next section, holds that an employer does not intentionally discriminate in violation of ADEA simply by making a decision based on a factor other than age—there, the fact that plaintiff was nearing pension eligibility—even if that factor strongly correlates with age. Thus firing an older worker to reduce high current salaries or future benefits,[1] making employment decisions based on employees' bad backs,[2] choosing an older worker for termination because his eligibility for a pension would lessen the blow of the termination,[3] or distinguishing on the basis of seniority[4] do not violate the Act even though in each case the distinguishing neutral feature may be more prevalent in older workers.[5]

But the *Hazen* opinion added qualifiers that have perplexed the circuit courts in deciding similar cases. On one hand, the Court observed that an employer might be liable if independent evidence shows that the employer relied on the ostensibly neutral factor (e.g., pension status or years of service) as a proxy for age, or if the employer was subjectively motivated not only by the neutral factor but also by the plaintiff's age as such.[6] On the other, broad language in the opinion could be read to

20. See EEOC v. Western Electric, 713 F.2d 1011 (4th Cir.1983); EEOC v. Sandia, 639 F.2d 600 (10th Cir.1980).

21. King, 960 F.2d 617.

§ 7.6

1. Dilla v. West, 179 F.3d 1348 (11th Cir.1999); Broaddus v. Florida Power Corp., 145 F.3d 1283, 1287 (11th Cir.1998); Anderson v. Baxter Healthcare Corp., 13 F.3d 1120 (7th Cir.1994).

2. Beith v. Nitrogen Products, Inc., 7 F.3d 701, 703 (8th Cir.1993).

3. Cruz-Ramos v. Puerto Rico Sun Oil Co., 202 F.3d 381 (1st Cir.2000).

4. Williams v. General Motors Corp., 656 F.2d 120, 130 n. 17 (5th Cir.1981), cert. denied, 455 U.S. 943, 102 S.Ct. 1439, 71 L.Ed.2d 655 (1982).

5. See also Thorn v. Sundstrand Aerospace Corp., 207 F.3d 383 (7th Cir.2000) (no ADEA claim where employer selected employees for reduction in force based on their "longest-term potential" because in making RIF decisions an employer is free to decide which employees are likeliest to contribute most to the company over the long haul); Furr v. Seagate Technology, Inc., 82 F.3d 980, 987 (10th Cir.1996), cert. denied sub nom. Doan v. Seagate Technology, Inc., 519 U.S. 1056, 117 S.Ct. 684, 136 L.Ed.2d 608 (1997); Watkins v. Sverdrup Technology, Inc., 153 F.3d 1308, 1317 (11th Cir.1998); Brocklehurst v. PPG Industries, Inc., 123 F.3d 890, 896 (6th Cir.1997).

6. See Arnett v. California Public Employees Retirement System, 179 F.3d 690 (9th Cir.1999), vacated on other grounds, 528 U.S. 1111, 120 S.Ct. 930, 145 L.Ed.2d 807 (2000) (the factor determining public safety officers' disability benefits, potential years of service calculated by reference to age at hire, is a "strict function of age" and hence possibly violative of ADEA; opinion distinguishes actual length of service, se-

suggest that an ADEA plaintiff attempting to prove intentional discrimination must prove not only age-based differences in treatment, but a subjective, age-ist cast of mind on the part of the employer decisionmaker, or perhaps even animus against those over 40. The Court wrote that "[p]roof of discriminatory motive is critical" to establish disparate treatment under ADEA, adding:

> [T]he very essence of age discrimination [is] for an older employee to be fired because the employer believes that productivity and competence decline with age. Congress' promulgation of the ADEA was prompted by its concern that older workers were being deprived of employment on the basis of inaccurate and stigmatizing stereotypes.[7]

Relying on this language, circuit opinions sometimes insist that the plaintiff prove not only that the challenged practice denies benefits or imposes burdens because of age, but also an age-related "intent"[8] or "discriminatory motive" or even "discriminatory animus" underlying the defendant's adoption of that practice.[9] They differ sharply, however, over the kind of evidence that meets this state of mind requirement.[10] More broadly, it is arguable that the "motive" language in *Hazen* requires no distinct state of mind evidence whatsoever. The Supreme Court's observation about the importance of evidence about motive in disparate treatment cases traces to *International Brotherhood of Teamsters v. United States*,[11] where the Court's observed:

> Proof of discriminatory motive is critical, *although it can in some situations be inferred from the mere fact of differences in treatment....*[12]

§ 7.7 The Post-*Hazen* Decline of the Neutral Practice/Adverse Impact Theory

Although the Supreme Court has not yet decided the issue,[1] the neutral practice theory derived from the *Griggs v. Duke Power* interpretation of Title VII has until recently been widely recognized to be

---

niority, or other factors that are merely "empirically correlated" with age and therefore permissible under *Hazen*).

7. *Hazen,* 507 U.S. at 609.

8. *See, e.g., Arnett,* 179 F.3d at 696.

9. *Lyon v. Ohio Educ. Ass'n and Professional Staff Union,* 53 F.3d 135, 138, 140 (6th Cir.1995).

10. *Compare Lyon,* 53 F.3d at 138–140 (plaintiff must produce evidence suggesting defendant acted with a specific, subjective purpose to harm protected group employees, as opposed, for example, to saving money) *with EEOC v. Borden's, Inc.,* 724 F.2d 1390, 1393 (9th Cir.1984) (discrimination is intentional in the sense required to prove ADEA disparate treatment if the drafter of

the challenged policy simply knows of and intends the policy's discriminatory effects).

11. 431 U.S. 324, 97 S.Ct. 1843, 52 L.Ed.2d 396 (1977).

12. *Id.* at 335 n.15 (emphasis added). Ironically, both the Ninth Circuit in *Arnett* and the Sixth Circuit in *Lyon* cited to or included the relevant quotation from *Teamsters,* but without further discussion assumed that independent evidence of age-based intent or motive was required in addition to the fact of age-related differences in treatment.

§ 7.7

1. *See Hazen Paper Co. v. Biggins,* 507 U.S. 604, 113 S.Ct. 1701, 123 L.Ed.2d 338 (1993).

available to prove claims under ADEA.[2] As we shall see, the continued utility of neutral practice/adverse impact proof in ADEA actions has been undermined by a recent Supreme Court decision technically limited to defining age-based disparate treatment.[3] In any event, courts have not been sympathetic to showings of disparate impact measured by reference to subsets of the over–40 protected group. Rather, the plaintiff must show that the employer's practice has significant adverse impact on protected group members vis-a-vis similarly situated employees younger than 40.[4] More generally, ADEA complainants face the defense that apparently neutral requirements or benefits limitations that have disproportionate adverse impact on the basis of age are motivated by and in fact conducive to cost reduction or productive efficiency. Where cost has proven to be a limited defense in Title VII impact cases, employers have enjoyed greater latitude in citing cost to defend the adverse impact of neutral practices on older workers. And one court has precluded use of the disparate impact theory to prove age discrimination resulting from across-the-board cost-cutting measures implemented by a company in an effort to avoid bankruptcy.[5] The problem is particularly acute where employment compensation is geared to years of service, which in turn is usually strongly correlated with age. The employer thus incurs a higher average cost in employing older than younger workers. When the employer then lays off higher-paid employees or those with greater seniority because of the greater cost reductions it thereby achieves, is it unlawfully discriminating because of age? If so, is the form of discrimination express or simply the disparate effect of a neutral practice?

Where the covariance between compensation or seniority and age is overwhelming, most courts initially treated a practice that selects employees for termination or forced early retirement on the basis of higher salary or greater service as a variety of express discrimination. Further, unless the circumstances showed the company to be teetering on the brink of bankruptcy,[6] these courts followed the EEOC's administrative interpretation,[7] and rejected the defense that cost savings is a "reasonable factor other than age" that justifies such a discrimination under § 4(f)(1) of the Act.[8] Even viewing such practices as neutral, some courts

---

2. See, e.g., Abbott v. Federal Forge, Inc., 912 F.2d 867 (6th Cir.1990); EEOC v. Borden's, Inc., 724 F.2d 1390 (9th Cir.1984); Geller v. Markham, 635 F.2d 1027 (2d Cir. 1980), cert. denied, 451 U.S. 945, 101 S.Ct. 2028, 68 L.Ed.2d 332 (1981). See Chapter 3 for a discussion of the neutral practice theory under Title VII.

3. See discussion of Hazen Paper Co. v. Biggins, 507 U.S. 604, 113 S.Ct. 1701, 123 L.Ed.2d 338 (1993), at text infra.

4. EEOC v. McDonnell Douglas Corp., 191 F.3d 948 (8th Cir.1999); Lowe v. Commack Union Free Sch. Dist., 886 F.2d 1364 (2d Cir.1989), cert. denied, 494 U.S. 1026, 110 S.Ct. 1470, 108 L.Ed.2d 608 (1990).

5. Finnegan v. Trans World Airlines, Inc., 967 F.2d 1161 (7th Cir.1992).

6. EEOC v. Chrysler Corp., 733 F.2d 1183 (6th Cir.1984).

7. 29 C.F.R. § 1625.7(f) (1986).

8. 29 U.S.C.A. § 623(f). See, e.g., Metz v. Transit Mix, Inc., 828 F.2d 1202 (7th Cir. 1987); Dace v. ACF Indus., Inc., 722 F.2d 374 (8th Cir.1983), aff'd on reh'g, 728 F.2d 976 (8th Cir.1984); Geller v. Markham, 635 F.2d 1027 (2d Cir.1980), cert. denied, 451 U.S. 945, 101 S.Ct. 2028, 68 L.Ed.2d 332 (1981) (regarding disparate treatment claims by individual plaintiffs). See also Leftwich v. Harris–Stowe State College, 702 F.2d 686 (8th Cir.1983) (similar conclusions

held the cost savings rationale insufficient to justify the resulting adverse impact on protected group members under the defense of business necessity.[9] Alternatively, they concluded that the defense, even if adequate on its own terms, ultimately failed because the employer bypassed available less restrictive means—for example reducing the salaries of senior workers—to effect the desired savings.[10]

But the Supreme Court has rendered much of this law obsolete by holding that discrimination on the basis of a factor merely correlated with age—for example pension status, years of service or seniority—is not unlawful disparate *treatment* under the ADEA.[11] The employer in *Hazen Paper Co. v. Biggins* allegedly fired the plaintiff to prevent his pension benefits from vesting, which the Court of Appeals found, and the Supreme Court agreed, violated ERISA. But the same conduct, standing alone, does not violate ADEA, the Court concluded, unless, for example, a particular employer is dually motivated by the employee's age as well as pension status or is shown to have treated pension status as a proxy for age. And to guide courts in determining whether the employer was motivated by the plaintiff's age, the Court described the "essence of what Congress sought to prohibit in the ADEA" as inaccurate, stigmatizing stereotyping based on beliefs that older workers are less productive or efficient.[12] It follows that if an employer fires an employee solely in order to reduce salary costs it is not intentionally discriminating on the basis of age, even if being older correlates to some degree—usually a high degree—with higher compensation.[13]

There is an instructive contrast here with Title VII's approach to disparate treatment based on factors correlated with a prohibited factor.

regarding systemic treatment or disparate impact claims by plaintiff groups).

9. *Leftwich*, 702 F.2d 686; *Geller*, 635 F.2d 1027.

10. *See Metz*, 828 F.2d 1202.

11. *Hazen Paper Co. v. Biggins,* 507 U.S. 604, 113 S.Ct. 1701, 123 L.Ed.2d 338 (1993).

12. *Id.* at 610, 113 S.Ct. at 1707. Addressing a question expressly left open by Hazen, one circuit has held that an employer may also gear hiring decisions to retirement status in the rare circumstance where date of retirement is lawfully dictated by age. *See Criley v. Delta Air Lines, Inc.*, 119 F.3d 102 (2d Cir.), *cert. denied*, 522 U.S. 1028, 118 S.Ct. 626, 139 L.Ed.2d 607 (1997) (airline could decline to hire pilots approaching the age–60 mandatory retirement age set by the Federal Aviation Administration when evidence showed its motivation to be economic and not based on age-based assumptions about abilities). Further, that the plaintiff perceives an employer's reason for an adverse action as stereotypical does not necessarily mean a court will impute

the stereotype to the employer. *See Grossmann v. Dillard Dep't Stores*, 109 F.3d 457 (8th Cir.1997) (supervisor's assertion that plaintiff was fired because he was not mobile and therefore not transferable not reflective of age-biased stereotype, even though plaintiff interpreted statement to refer to his age).

13. *Chiaramonte v. Fashion Bed Group, Inc.*, 129 F.3d 391 (7th Cir.1997), *cert. denied*, 523 U.S. 1118, 118 S.Ct. 1795, 140 L.Ed.2d 936 (1998) (evidence that employer retained consultants and hired two new workers after plaintiff was terminated did not suffice to show pretext; management has discretion to determine how and where to save costs); *Snow v. Ridgeview Med. Ctr.*, 128 F.3d 1201 (8th Cir.1997) (evidence that employee was terminated because she had been employed longer than her coworkers, and thus earned comparatively higher salary, was insufficient to show that termination was based upon age); *Anderson v. Baxter Healthcare Corp.*, 13 F.3d 1120 (7th Cir.1994) (concluding that *Hazen* eroded the rationale of *Metz v. Transit Mix, Inc.*, 828 F.2d 1202).

In *Los Angeles Dep't of Water & Power v. Manhart*,[14] an employer defended its requirement that female employees contribute more than their male counterparts to a pension fund on the ground that women have greater longevity and would therefore enjoy greater aggregate benefits. The Court observed that the case involved "a generalization that the parties accept as unquestionably true: Women, as a class, do live longer than men."[15] It nevertheless rejected the employer's defense that the discrimination was based not on gender but merely on a factor, longevity, that highly correlates with gender: "Even a true generalization about the class is an insufficient reason for disqualifying an individual to whom the generalization does not apply."[16] And while the Court once treated discrimination because of pregnancy as lawfully based on a neutral factor merely correlated, indeed perfectly correlated, with gender,[17] Congress replied in effect that discrimination on a ground so highly correlated with gender is indistinguishable from gender discrimination itself.[18]

The Court in *Hazen* had no occasion to decide whether employer reliance on years of service or pension status, as distinct from age as such, could violate ADEA through evidence of disparate impact, for no disparate impact claim was made there. It is now more doubtful, however, that the current Court would answer that question affirmatively. As it wrote in *Hazen*, the Court continues to view disparate treatment, as distinct from disproportionate adverse impact, "the essence of what Congress sought to prohibit...." Three justices alluded to "substantial arguments that it is improper to carry over ... impact analysis from Title VII to the ADEA."[19] The logic here seems to be that allowing the impact theory would illegitimately undermine the Court's conclusion that employer reliance on factors correlated with age is not unlawful disparate *treatment*. After all, disproportionate adverse impact results because the neutral factor on which an employer relied has had exactly that correlation.[20]

Moreover, the absence of any reference to age discrimination in the provision of the 1991 Civil Rights Act that identifies the range of permissible impact-theory claims may imply a Congressional understand-

---

14. 435 U.S. 702, 98 S.Ct. 1370, 55 L.Ed.2d 657 (1978).

15. *Id.* at 707, 98 S.Ct. at 1374.

16. *Id.* at 708, 98 S.Ct. at 1375.

17. *General Elec. Co. v. Gilbert*, 429 U.S. 125, 97 S.Ct. 401, 50 L.Ed.2d 343 (1976).

18. *See* discussion of the Pregnancy Discrimination Act of 1978 in Chapter 2, above.

19. *Hazen*, 507 U.S. at 618, 113 S.Ct. at 1710 (Kennedy, J., concurring, joined by Chief Justice Rehnquist and Justice Thomas).

20. This argument mirrors appellate court refusals to permit homosexuals to attack anti-homosexual practices—neutral on their face because Title VII does not prohibit sexual orientation discrimination—because those practices may have a disproportionate adverse impact on one or another gender. *See DeSantis v. Pacific Tel. & Tel.*, 608 F.2d 327 (9th Cir.1979), discussed in Chapter 2. It is also reminiscent of the Seventh Circuit's conclusion that foreign employers privileged by treaty to discriminate against Americans because of their citizenship cannot be held liable when the same practice has the effect of discriminating on the basis of national origin. *See Fortino v. Quasar*, 950 F.2d 389 (7th Cir. 1991).

ing that the impact proof mode is unavailable under ADEA.[21] There is also no mention of the ADEA in the section of the 1991 Act that modifies the *Wards Cove* decision by easing to some extent the plaintiff's burden of proving a practice's disproportionate adverse impact. Even if these omissions were only oversights, the 1991 Act's tepid overturning of *Wards Cove* with respect to (1) the plaintiff's required prima facie statistical showing that a specifically identifiable practice caused a given level of disproportionate adverse impact, (2) the nature of the employer's defense, and (3) the plaintiff's less discriminatory alternative rebuttal leaves federal judges ample room to manifest their skepticism about the use of impact proof in cases under ADEA.[22] A cost savings defense to an ADEA disproportionate adverse impact claim may well be treated as "job related for the position in question and consistent with business necessity,"[23] or an employer may be able to avoid liability by agreeing to salary reduction as a less discriminatory alternative to termination. Alternatively, the Court may craft a more limited exclusion of disparate impact liability based on pension status or years of service. If, per *Hazen*, reliance on those grounds is not unlawful age discrimination of the disparate treatment variety, still less could it constitute unlawful discrimination through the distinctly less favored proof mode of disproportionate adverse impact.

Some of these possibilities are emerging in the post-*Hazen* lower court decisions. One disparate treatment claim challenged the employer's downsizing of operations in one state followed by the hiring of younger, less expensive, non-union employees in two others as part of an effort to increase profitability by reducing labor costs. The plaintiffs' systemic disparate treatment evidence consisted of statistics showing that 80% of

21. *Martincic v. Urban Redevelopment Auth. of Pittsburgh*, 844 F.Supp. 1073 (W.D.Pa.1994), *aff'd*, 43 F.3d 1461 (3d Cir. 1994) (discussing § 105 of the 1991 Act).

22. See, for example. the Eighth Circuit's opinion in *Allen v. Entergy Corp., Inc.*, 193 F.3d 1010, 1014–15 (8th Cir.1999), wherein the appellate refused to find the district court committed plain error when it declined to tailor jury instructions to reflect that the 1991 Civil Rights Act overturned *Wards Cove*'s business-justification analysis. The appellate court stated that the district court could have chosen either way; as it did, to follow *Wards Cove* because the 1991 Civil Rights Act did not explicitly state that *Wards Cove* was overruled in the ADEA context, or alternatively, the district court could have chosen not to apply *Wards Cove* by reasoning that the current statement of Title VII disparate-impact analysis, as reflected in the 1991 Civil Rights Act, should apply. See Chapter 3 for a discussion of how the 1991 Civil Rights Act responds to the *Wards Cove* decision.

23. *See Jones v. Unisys Corp.*, 54 F.3d 624 (10th Cir.1995) (reduction in force as attempt to halt high economic losses). *But*

see *EEOC v. Crown Point Community Sch. Corp.*, 1997 WL 54747 (N.D.Ind.1997) (costs savings could be a potential defense to early retirement plan that decreased benefits for each year an employee waited to retire, and that therefore had age-related adverse impact, only if there were a "very close correlation" between age and cost savings). It is admittedly hard to see how cost savings is related to the capability of an individual to perform a particular job. But there is some possibility that judicial interpretations of the new defense to prima facie impact proof may read that requirement out of existence, leaving only the "business necessity" prong to which costs savings manifestly does pertain. See discussion of the legislative modification of *Wards Cove Packing Co.* in Chapter 3 concerning Title VII. In any event, that approach may be justifiable under ADEA because *Wards Cove*, untouched by the 1991 Act insofar as ADEA is concerned, declared a new, modest "business justification" defense, with no distinct job relatedness requirement.

the workers at the old plants were over the age of 40, while 83% of the new hires were under 40. Describing *Hazen* as a reflection of "our capitalistic system, Darwinian though it may be," the court of appeals affirmed a grant of summary judgment for the employer. After *Hazen*, the court observed, ADEA "does not constrain an employer who acts on the basis of ... factors ... that are empirically correlated with age," absent proof that the employer is using such a factor as a pure proxy for age. Among such factors that are permissible, because they do not involve stigmatizing or inaccurate stereotypes about older workers, are "the costs frequently associated with experienced, skilled, pensioned, high wage workers." Therefore not only did the plaintiffs have to prove a significant age disparity between those discharged and those retained as a result of the reduction in force, they also were obliged to eliminate the most common nondiscriminatory explanations for that disparity. That second burden, of course, is one that the *defendant* must shoulder in a systemic disparate treatment action under Title VII.[24] This plaintiffs could not do. It "was to be expected" that most of those laid off at the former facilities were over 40, because the employer had followed seniority in making previous layoffs. Nor did it surprise the court that 83% of those hired in the new locations were under 40, where the plaintiffs had not shown any disproportion between that figure and the relevant hiring pool in those areas. In brief, reduced labor costs, the principal reason both sides acknowledged as motivating the move, was not tantamount to unlawful discrimination despite its high correlation with age.[25]

24. *See* discussion of the employer's burden at the remedy stage of a statistically grounded systemic treatment case as established by *Franks v. Bowman Transp. Co.*, 424 U.S. 747, 96 S.Ct. 1251, 47 L.Ed.2d 444 (1976), and *International Bhd. of Teamsters v. United States*, 431 U.S. 324, 97 S.Ct. 1843, 52 L.Ed.2d 396 (1977), in Chapter 3 above.

25. *Allen v. Diebold, Inc.*, 33 F.3d 674 (6th Cir.1994). The furtherance of the free-market premise underlying the anti-discrimination laws—management prerogatives should be preserved and respected whenever they don't draw an unlawful distinction—is also evident in *Thornley v. Penton Publishing, Inc.*, 104 F.3d 26 (2d Cir. 1997). There the court vacated a plaintiff's jury verdict because instructions permitted the jury to reject the employer's legitimate nondiscriminatory reason defense of unsatisfactory job performance by reference to the standards of "an employer," rather than the specific standards of the particular defendant employer. *See also Lyon v. Ohio Educ. Ass'n*, 53 F.3d 135 (6th Cir.1995) (early retirement plan that had effect of producing higher benefits for younger persons with equivalent service not violation because its purpose was to buy out expensive workers—a neutral reason after *Hazen*—and accomplishing that goal may have required employer to pay more to younger workers); *EEOC v. Insurance Co. of N. Am.*, 49 F.3d 1418 (9th Cir.1995) (rejecting applicant on ground of "overqualification" lawful even though that factor might be strongly correlated with advanced age, but opinion warns of different result where that ground functions as a proxy for age discrimination, as where "overqualification" is defined subjectively); *Thomure v. Phillips Furniture Co.*, 30 F.3d 1020 (8th Cir.1994), *cert. denied* 513 U.S. 1191, 115 S.Ct. 1255, 131 L.Ed.2d 135 (1995) (during general wage reduction, employer decision to cut more deeply the wages of senior, higher-paid employees not tantamount to age discrimination even though years of service and wage rate may correlate with age). *But see Johnson v. New York*, 49 F.3d 75 (2d Cir.1995) (discharging civilian security guard at age 60 because he could not under federal law remain on active duty status with the National Guard after that age discriminates on its face, even though some guards over 60 could obtain a waiver of the requirement to remain on active National Guard duty and even though rule requiring active duty status in National Guard applied to guards under 60 as well).

Does this mean, however, that employers may base employment decisions even on certain age-correlated factors that *do* perpetuate age-based stigma or stereotype? Perhaps. There are "true" or at least partially true stereotypes, and one of them, according to a district court decision, is that job performance declines with age. In other words, it is precisely because of such correlations that a neutral employment practice that disproportionately falls on older workers should not, standing alone, yield an inference of unlawful age-based discrimination. According to the opinion, the neutral practice-disproportionate adverse impact theory should therefore be confined to situations involving race or gender.[26]

Before *Hazen*, employers who cited poorer performance ratings as the nondiscriminatory explanation for layoffs that disproportionately affected older workers nevertheless shied away from relying on the stereotype that in general performance declines with age.[27] *Hazen* would seem to provide two positive boosts to such defendants. First, they need not fear that their "performance" defense to systemic disparate treatment will be condemned as itself age based simply because a court finds a performance-age correlation. Second, they have less reason to fear plaintiffs' arguments that the performance defense to age-based disparate treatment discrimination identifies an actionable, disproportionately impacting neutral practice.

The long shadows cast by *Hazen* have led circuit courts to refuse to apply the neutral practice/impact theory to the ADEA claim of a rejected applicant. In *EEOC v. Francis W. Parker School*,[28] the employer linked salary to work experience and also declared a salary cap on the teaching position for which plaintiff, a 63-year-old with thirty years' experience, applied. Expert testimony, not questioned by the court, showed that this policy would exclude over-40 applicants at 4.2 times the rate of younger applicants.[29] Although plaintiff would have worked for a salary within the cap, the school rejected him because, under its policy, plaintiff's experience would have yielded a salary above the cap. Relying principally on *Hazen*, the court wrote that although the school's years-of-service factor was age-correlated, its salary policy was "economically defensible and reasonable"; plaintiff therefore had the burden to "demonstrate that the reason given was a pretext for a stereotype-based rationale." Although the court branded "the belief that older employees are less efficient or less productive" as one of the "inaccurate and stigmatizing stereotypes," it found no such belief embedded in the school's policy that linked wages to experience. It fortified its conclusion by reference to two ADEA defenses allowing differential treatment of employees "based on

26. *Hiatt v. Union Pacific R.R. Co.*, 859 F.Supp. 1416 (D.Wyo.1994), *aff'd*, 65 F.3d 838 (10th Cir.1995), *cert. denied*, 516 U.S. 1115, 116 S.Ct. 917, 133 L.Ed.2d 847 (1996).

27. *See EEOC v. Sandia Corp.*, 639 F.2d 600, 614 (10th Cir.1980).

28. 41 F.3d 1073 (7th Cir.1994), *cert. denied* 515 U.S. 1142, 115 S.Ct. 2577, 132 L.Ed.2d 828 (1995).

29. *Id.* at 1076 n.1.

reasonable factors other than age"[30] and observance of "the terms of a bona fide seniority system."[31] And it observed that § 703(a)(2) of Title VII, in which the Supreme Court in *Griggs v. Duke Power* first located the neutral practice proof mode, bans employer conduct that would limit the employment opportunities of "employees or applicants," whereas ADEA's counterpart provision refers only to "employees."[32]

None of these rationales for the decision is entirely satisfactory. In *Hazen* the Supreme Court accepted that the employer's actual motivation was cost avoidance. In contrast, the Parker School's insistence on applying its salary policy linked to years of service was not calculated to reduce costs, because plaintiff would have worked for less. The court mentioned no other economic or business justification for the policy. The court's reliance on the "reasonable factors other than age" defense simply begs the question whether there was *any* factor other than age that supported application of the policy to the plaintiff. And the court mentioned no evidence from which it might be inferred that the school's policy, applied to plaintiff on an ad hoc basis (the policy normally applied only to incumbents), was part of a "bona fide seniority system." Finally, the court's suggestion, by contrast with § 703(a)(2) of Title VII, that Congress may have advertently limited use of the ADEA impact proof mode to incumbents rather than applicants ignores the fact that the ADEA provision was enacted in 1967 and it wasn't until four years later that the Supreme Court in *Griggs* identified § 703(a)(2) as the source of the impact proof mode under Title VII. Further, as the dissenting judge in *Parker* pointed out, even if the omission of a reference to applicants in the ADEA counterpart to § 703(a)(2) is significant, there is authority finding an alternative basis for the Title VII impact proof mode in § 703(a)(1), and therefore in ADEA's counterpart subsection 623(a)(1).[33]

In any event, if the decision rests on the contrast between ADEA's § 623(a)(2) and Title VII's § 703(a)(2), *Parker* may come to be limited to a holding that applicants cannot state a cognizable impact claim under ADEA. Other circuits have launched broad attacks on the ADEA impact claim, relying not just on *Hazen* but on Congress' failure, when it codified and reinvigorated the Title VII impact theory in the 1991 Civil Rights Act, to add a parallel provision to the ADEA.[34] EEOC, however,

---

30. *Id.* at 1076–77, quoting 29 U.S.C.A. § 623(f)(1). There is justification for the court's reliance on § 623(f) as revealing a defect in plaintiff's proof, even though in form § 623(f) is an affirmative defense. The Supreme Court has indicated that in ADEA, like Title VII trials it is the plaintiff's burden throughout to prove discrimination because of age; in this light the "reasonable factors other than age" provision is better viewed as merely underscoring the plaintiff's burden than as a true affirmative defense. Contrast the similar language in the Equal Pay Act that authorizes gender-based unequal pay for equal work where the differentiation is based on "any other factor

other than sex," 29 U.S.C.A. § 206(d)(iv), which the Court has treated as an affirmative defense on which the employer bears all pleading and proof burdens. *Corning Glass Works v. Brennan,* 417 U.S. 188, 94 S.Ct. 2223, 41 L.Ed.2d 1 (1974).

31. *Francis W. Parker,* 41 F.3d at 1078, quoting 29 U.S.C.A. § 623(f)(2).

32. *Id.* at 1077, citing 29 U.S.C.A. § 623(a).

33. *Id.* at 1080 n.3 (Cudahy, J., dissenting).

34. *Mullin v. Raytheon Co.,* 164 F.3d 696, 703 (1st Cir.), *cert. denied,* 528 U.S. 811, 120 S.Ct. 44, 145 L.Ed.2d 40 (1999);

has indicated it will prosecute ADEA disparate impact claims unless the case arises in a circuit that bars such claims.[35]

§ 7.8   ADEA Retaliation

Section 623(d) of ADEA provides protection against retaliation in the same terms as § 704(a) of Title VII. Former employees, in particular those who have been discharged, are among the "employees" shielded by § 623(d).[1] Further, the employer need not have affected the terms or conditions of the former employment; withholding letters of recommendation or providing negative information to prospective employers may also constitute forbidden retaliation.[2] The ADEA provision, like the Title VII counterpart, has been construed to shield a wide range of on-the-job "opposition" in addition to formal participation in ADEA proceedings.[3] One circuit court has held, however, that retaliation against a plaintiff who filed an age discrimination claim is not cognizable under Title VII.[4] See generally § 5.40 for the elements of an emerging exceptions to a claim of retaliation.

§ 7.9   ADEA BFOQ Defense

The BFOQ defense declared by § 4(f)(1) was delimited stringently

Ellis v. United Airlines, Inc., 73 F.3d 999, 1007 (10th Cir.), *cert. denied,* 517 U.S. 1245, 116 S.Ct. 2500, 135 L.Ed.2d 191 (1996); *Lyon v. Ohio Educ. Ass'n & Professional Staff Union,* 53 F.3d 135, 139 n. 5 (6th Cir.1995) (casting doubt on viability of impact proof mode after under ADEA after *Hazen* but noting pre-*Hazen* circuit authority approving possibility of theory); *DiBiase v. SmithKline Beecham Corp.,* 48 F.3d 719 (3d Cir.), *cert. denied,* 516 U.S. 916, 116 S.Ct. 306, 133 L.Ed.2d 210 (1995); *Martincic v. Urban Redev. Auth.,* 844 F.Supp. 1073, 1078 (W.D.Pa.1994), *aff'd,* 43 F.3d 1461 (3d Cir.1994) (disparate impact not applicable under ADEA). *But see Frank v. United Airlines, Inc.,* 216 F.3d 845, 856 (9th Cir.2000) (acknowledging *Hazen,* but limiting it to barring ADEA claims only where plaintiff relies on a factor that is merely empirically correlated with age); *EEOC v. McDonnell Douglas Corp.,* 191 F.3d 948, 950 (8th Cir.1999) (acknowledging that the circuit allowed disparate impact theory refusing to recognize the theory where plaintiff alleged that a RIF had a disparate impact on a subgroup of those aged 55 and older because to allow the claim would require the employer to achieve statistical parity among an infinite number of age subgroups); *Criley v. Delta Air Lines,* 119 F.3d 102, 105 (2d Cir.), *cert. denied,* 522 U.S. 1028, 118 S.Ct. 626, 139 L.Ed.2d 607 (1997); *District Council 37 v. New York City Dep't of Parks and Recreation,* 113 F.3d 347, 351 (2d Cir.1997) (relying on pre-*Hazen* circuit precedent); *Smith v. City of Des Moines, Iowa.,* 99 F.3d 1466 (8th Cir.1996) (declaring that the ADEA neutral practice/disproportionate adverse impact case survives, yet upholding annual stress test requirement as bearing a "manifest relation" to plaintiff's job despite fire department's admission that plaintiff would "very seldom" have to perform the tasks for which the test was required); *Mangold v. California Pub. Utils. Comm'n,* 67 F.3d 1470 (9th Cir.1995); *Houghton v. SIPCO, Inc.,* 38 F.3d 953, 958–59 (8th Cir.1994) (recognizing a disparate impact theory under the ADEA without explanation and without discussion of *Hazen*); *EEOC v. Local 350, Plumbers and Pipefitters,* 998 F.2d 641, 648 (9th Cir.1992) (reaffirming viability of impact theory under ADEA after and despite *Hazen*).

35. *See EEOC Enforcement Guidance No. 915.002,* Sept. 18, 1996. *See, e.g., EEOC v. McDonnell Douglas Corp.,* 191 F.3d 948, 950 (8th Cir.1999).

§ 7.8

1. *Passer v. American Chem. Soc'y,* 935 F.2d 322, 330–31 (D.C.Cir.1991); *EEOC v. Cosmair, Inc.,* 821 F.2d 1085, 1088–89 (5th Cir.1987).

2. *Passer,* 935 F.2d at 331.

3. *See, e.g., Grant v. Hazelett Strip-Casting Corp.,* 880 F.2d 1564 (2d Cir.1989).

4. *Lennon v. Rubin,* 166 F.3d 6 (1st Cir.1999).

by the Supreme Court in *Criswell*.[1] BFOQ is now the employer's only real defense to an age-based forced retirement, since § 4(f)(2), after its amendment in 1978, no longer countenances use of benefit plans to compel retirement at any age.[2] But § 4(f)(2) also provides that an employer does not violate the Act merely by observing the terms of an age-discriminatory "bona fide seniority system or any bona fide employee benefit plan such as a retirement, pension, or insurance plan, which is not a subterfuge to evade the purposes of this chapter...." In *Betts*, the Supreme Court, rejecting the unanimous position of the courts of appeals and the EEOC, gave this exemption an expansive reading. First, the Court held that the exemption pertains to plans that regulate any fringe benefit (for example, disability plans) and not just to retirement, pension, or insurance plans. Second, as a matter of law, a plan provision adopted before an employer becomes subject to ADEA cannot be deemed a "subterfuge" to evade the Act's purposes. Third, even a plan provision adopted thereafter will not be considered a subterfuge except in the unlikely event that the plaintiff is able to prove that it was "intended to serve the purpose of discriminating in some nonfringe-benefit aspect of the employment relation," such as discrimination in hiring or compensation. As the following section explains, *Betts* has now been legislatively overruled.

B. THE OLDER WORKERS BENEFIT PROTECTION ACT

§ 7.10 Background

The Age Discrimination in Employment Act of 1967 ("ADEA") prohibits age discrimination against employees or job applicants in "compensation, terms, conditions or privileges of employment." Prior to the 1990 enactment of the Older Workers Benefit Protection Act ("OWBPA"), § 4(f)(2) of the ADEA exempted "a bona fide employee benefit plan such as retirement, pension, or insurance plan, which is not a subterfuge to evade the purpose of [the ADEA]."[1] The EEOC had interpreted this exemption to require an age-based, cost justification for any age discriminatory provision in an employee benefit plan. The EEOC interpretation required that any reduction in fringe benefits for older employees would be lawful only if the employer's actual cost of providing that benefit was higher for older employees than younger ones and the employer was spending the same amount for its older employees as its younger ones. Thus, an employer was permitted to reduce the health insurance coverage of an older employee only if the premiums for covering the worker were not lower than those of covering a younger

§ 7.9

1. *Western Air Lines, Inc. v. Criswell,* 472 U.S. 400, 105 S.Ct. 2743, 86 L.Ed.2d 321 (1985).

2. *Public Employees Retirement System of Ohio v. Betts,* 492 U.S. 158, 165 n. 2, 109

S.Ct. 2854, 2860 n. 2, 106 L.Ed.2d 134 (1989).

§ 7.10

1. 29 U.S.C.A. § 623(f)(2).

worker. Applying this requirement stringently, a district court has limited the costs savings defense to situations where the correlation between age and cost savings is "very close."[2]

§ 7.11 The Supreme Court's *Betts* Decision and the Enactment of OWBPA

In *Public Employees Retirement System of Ohio v. Betts*,[1] the Supreme Court rejected the EEOC's "equal cost or equal benefit" rule. The Court held that § 4(f)(2) of the ADEA broadly exempted employee benefit plans from coverage of the ADEA. The Court further held that in order to violate the ADEA the benefit plan must be truly designed as a subterfuge to disguise age discrimination in employment. Thus, if the employer reduced salaries for all employees while substantially increasing the fringe benefits for younger employees, the benefit plan might be held to be a subterfuge to evade the purposes of the ADEA.

On October 16, 1990, the OWBPA was signed into law, amending the ADEA to overturn *Betts*. It reinstates the EEOC interpretation and clarifies that the ADEA prohibits age discrimination in both the design and administration of employee benefit plans.

The OWBPA applies immediately to any employee benefit established or modified on or after the date of enactment (October 16, 1990). For plans which pre-date the enactment, employers were given 180 days after enactment (until April 14, 1991) to bring their plans in compliance with the Act. Benefit payments that began prior to October 16, 1990 and continue thereafter are not affected by the passage of the OWBPA. Additionally, the legislative history of the Act indicates that the Act does not apply to current retirees' benefits or to subsequent changes in those benefits.

For plans which are part of collective bargaining agreements in effect on the date of enactment, the OWBPA amendments do not apply until the earlier of June 1, 1992 or the termination of the agreement. Finally, the OWBPA applies to States and its subdivisions. But, if the plan can be modified only through a change in applicable State or local law, the OWBPA's provisions do not apply for two years after the date of enactment.

§ 7.12 OWBPA Provisions

The OWBPA repeals the § 4(f)(2) exemption, reinstates the EEOC cost justification rule, and declares that employee benefit plans are covered by the ADEA's general prohibition against age discrimination. Specifically, the Act requires that "for each benefit or benefit package,

2. *EEOC v. Crown Point Community Sch. Corp.*, 1997 WL 54747 (N.D.Ind.1997) (holding invalid an early retirement plan that decreased benefits for each year an employee waited to retire and denied plan benefits altogether for retirements after age 65).

§ 7.11

1. 492 U.S. 158, 109 S.Ct. 2854, 106 L.Ed.2d 134 (1989).

the actual amount of payment made or cost incurred on behalf of an older worker [shall be] no less than that made or incurred on behalf of a younger worker."

The OWBPA also expressly permits employers to follow the terms of a bona fide seniority system, provide for the attainment of a specified age as a condition of eligibility for a pension plan, and provide bona fide voluntary early retirement incentive plans.

§§ 7.13–9.14 [Reserved]

C. WAIVER OF RIGHTS OR CLAIMS UNDER THE ADEA AFTER OWBPA

§ 7.15 Background

Some employers have required employees to sign a release waiving all rights and claims, if any, under the ADEA as a condition to receiving enhanced severance benefits.[1] Prior to the enactment of OWBPA, the ADEA did not state whether an employee could release her rights under the ADEA without supervision by the EEOC. Courts of Appeals, however, generally uphold the validity of private releases so long as the waiver was "knowing and voluntary."

§ 7.16 OWBPA Resolution

The OWBPA resolves this question by specifically permitting unsupervised releases,[1] provided that the following minimum standards are met:

(1) the waiver is in writing and written in terms likely to be understood by the average individual eligible to participate in the plan (or by the individual herself);

(2) the waiver specifically refers to the rights or claims arising under the ADEA;

(3) the individual does not waive rights or claims that may arise *after* the waiver is executed;[2]

(4) the individual waives rights or claims only in exchange for additional consideration (that is, consideration in addition to anything of value to which the individual is already entitled to receive);

(5) the individual is advised in writing to consult with an attorney prior to executing the waiver;

§ 7.15

1. Unenhanced severance packages lack adequate consideration for the waiver of the ADEA claims.

§ 7.16

1. That is, releases not supervised by the EEOC.

2. *Cf. Adams v. Philip Morris, Inc.,* 67 F.3d 580 (6th Cir.1995) (observing in ADEA and reverse discrimination case that public policy may preclude agreements—other than possibly agreements to arbitrate, *see* § 4.6 *supra*—that resolve prospective employment discrimination claims). See generally text § 3.2 *supra*.

(6) the individual is give at least 21 days in which to consider the agreement (the individual must be given 45 days if the waiver is requested in connection with an exit incentive or group termination program);[3]

(7) the agreement provides for a period of at least seven (7) days following execution to revoke the agreement and does not become effective until this period has expired;

(8) if the waiver is requested as part of an exit incentive or group termination program, the employer must inform the individual in writing (in understandable language), as to:

    (a) any class or group of individuals covered by the program and any eligibility factors and time limits for the program; and

    (b) the job titles and ages of all individual eligible or selected for the program and those within the same job classification or organization unit not eligible or selected for the program.

Compliance with these minimum standards, however, does not prevent a later attack that the waiver was not "knowing and voluntary."[4] The OWBPA imposes the burden of proof upon the proponent of the release to prove that the minimum statutory requirements for ADEA release have been satisfied. The OWBPA, however, does not change the minimum requirements or burden of proof of the "knowing and voluntary" standards. Furthermore, no waiver or settlement of an EEOC or court action is considered "knowing or voluntary" unless the above requirements have been met and the individual is given a "reasonable period" in which to consider the settlement.[5] Finally, no waiver agreement affects the EEOC's ability to enforce the ADEA or an individual's right to file a charge or participate in an EEOC investigation or proceeding.

The Supreme Court, in *Oubre v. Entergy Operations, Inc.,*[6] resolved a circuit conflict as to the effect of a plaintiff's failure to tender back benefits received through a severance or retirement plan or agreement. Prior to *Oubre*, some circuits held that failure to tender back should be deemed to ratify releases exacted in exchange for those benefits and hence bar claims that the releases did not conform to OWBPA require-

---

3. But the twenty-one-day review period provided by the OWBPA does not give the employee an irrevocable power of acceptance for twenty-one days; the employer may withdraw the offer within that period before it is accepted. *See Ellison v. Premier Salons Int'l, Inc.,* 164 F.3d 1111, 1112 (8th Cir.1999).

4. *See Griffin v. Kraft General Foods, Inc.,* 62 F.3d 368 (11th Cir.1995) (waiver not "knowing and voluntary" unless employees of closed plant given information about other employees outside of that plant). *See also Bennett v. Coors Brewing Co.,* 189 F.3d 1221 (10th Cir.1999) (in the face of allegations of fraud in the procurement of ADEA claim waivers, the waivers do not automatically bar the claim) (remanding).

5. But where the OWBPA requirements are met, even if plaintiff believes he was terminated because of his age, the waiver will be enforced: the plaintiff chose enhanced severance benefits in exchange for the knowingly and voluntary waiver of the ADEA claim. *See Lloyd v. Brunswick Corp.,* 180 F.3d 893 (7th Cir.1999).

6. 522 U.S. 422, 118 S.Ct. 838, 139 L.Ed.2d 849 (1998).

ments.[7] This position was rejected by the Court, which relied on the OWBPA's language that a waiver cannot effectively release ADEA claims unless it satisfies the OWBPA's requirements.[8] Thus, the employer who obtains a waiver through a nonconforming release cannot defeat an ADEA claim simply because the plaintiff did not tender back consideration paid in exchange for the waiver. But parsing the various opinions in the case also leads to the conclusion that a nonconforming release is not void, only voidable.[9] Thus, employees should be protected from employer threats to cancel the obligations it incurred to obtain the invalid release.[10] On the other hand, treating a nonconforming release as voidable may allow the employer who is ultimately sued to recover any benefits paid out between the termination and the commencement of the suit.[11] And after *Oubre*, a circuit court has held that an invalid waiver agreement that required plaintiff to withdraw his then pending ADEA suit nevertheless tolled the ninety day period for filing suit.[12]

The "knowing and voluntary" requirement is also implicated by employer policies that require all employees who are terminated, whatever their age, to sign a general release of all claims to be eligible for enhanced severance benefits.[13] Such a policy has been held not to discriminate expressly, even though it pressures only members of the

7. *Contrast Oubre v. Entergy Operations*, 112 F.3d 787 (5th Cir.1996), *rev'd*, 522 U.S. 422, 118 S.Ct. 838, 139 L.Ed.2d 849 (1998); *Blakeney v. Lomas Info.*, 65 F.3d 482 (5th Cir.1995), *cert. denied*, 516 U.S. 1158, 116 S.Ct. 1042, 134 L.Ed.2d 189 (1996); *Blistein v. St. John's College*, 74 F.3d 1459 (4th Cir.1996) (accepting benefits under early retirement agreement that plaintiff knew did not comply with OWBPA ratified agreement and thus forfeited ADEA claim); *Wamsley v. Champlin Refining and Chems., Inc.*, 11 F.3d 534 (5th Cir.1993), *cert. denied*, 514 U.S. 1037, 115 S.Ct. 1403, 131 L.Ed.2d 290 (1995) (even a release not complying with OWBPA is ratified if employees accept severance payments and refuse to tender them back); *and O'Shea v. Commercial Credit Corp.*, 930 F.2d 358 (4th Cir.), *cert. denied*, 502 U.S. 859, 112 S.Ct. 177, 116 L.Ed.2d 139 (1991) (allowing ratification of pre-OWBPA releases) *with Long v. Sears Roebuck & Co.*, 105 F.3d 1529 (3d Cir.1997), *cert. denied*, 522 U.S. 1107, 118 S.Ct. 1033, 140 L.Ed.2d 100 (1998) (employee need not tender back to pursue ADEA claim where release is noncompliant with OWBPA); *Howlett v. Holiday Inns, Inc.*, 49 F.3d 189 (6th Cir.), *cert. denied*, 516 U.S. 943, 116 S.Ct. 379, 133 L.Ed.2d 302 (1995); *Raczak v. Ameritech Corp.*, 103 F.3d 1257 (6th Cir.1997), *cert. denied*, 522 U.S. 1107, 118 S.Ct. 1033, 140 L.Ed.2d 101 (1998) (same); *Smith v. World Ins. Co.*, 38 F.3d 1456 (8th Cir.1994) (plaintiff could accept early retirement benefits and sue for constructive discharge, lest he be forced to

remain on the job and face what he alleged were intolerable discriminatory conditions); *Oberg v. Allied Van Lines, Inc.*, 11 F.3d 679 (7th Cir.1993), *cert. denied*, 511 U.S. 1108, 114 S.Ct. 2104, 128 L.Ed.2d 665 (1994) (rejecting tender-back requirement as permitting employers to circumvent OWBPA guidelines governing releases) *and Forbus v. Sears Roebuck & Co.*, 958 F.2d 1036 (11th Cir.), *cert. denied*, 506 U.S. 955, 113 S.Ct. 412, 121 L.Ed.2d 336 (1992) (plaintiff not required to tender benefits under pre-OWBPA release in order to proceed with litigation).

8. *Oubre*, 118 S.Ct. at 842.

9. The three dissenting justices, Scalia, Thomas and Rehnquist, plus the two concurring justices, Breyer and O'Connor, seem to support this conclusion.

10. *Oubre*, 118 S.Ct. at 844 (Breyer, J., concurring).

11. *Id.*

12. *Hodge v. New York College of Podiatric Med.*, 157 F.3d 164 (2d Cir.1998).

13. *EEOC v. Sears Roebuck & Co.*, 857 F.Supp. 1233 (N.D.Ill.1994), *modified in part by* 883 F.Supp. 211 (D.Ill.1995) (suggesting that the mandatory OWBPA period for employee to consider an "agreement" may apply to a proposed severance package as a whole, not just the part in which the employee trades rights under ADEA for additional benefits).

over–40 protected group to waive rights under ADEA. Rather, the court concluded, that policy is facially nondiscriminatory because it requires all employees, as a condition of enhanced benefits, to waive whatever rights they may (or may not) have under the same group of statutes. Thus the bundle of accrued claims that an over–40 employee would have to release would not necessarily be worth more than the bundle released by any particular employee under 40. This would be true, for example, if more of the younger employees were members of minority groups or women, who as such enjoyed separate protection under other of the statutes with respect to which waiver was required.[14]

EEOC regulations make it clear that the OWBPA covers voluntary retirees as well as involuntary terminations.[15] The regulations also clarify what information the employer is required to provide to workers who are asked to sign a waiver, and elaborate on issues regarding consideration, arbitrability, wording, and time limits.[16]

§§ 7.17–9.19   [Reserved]

D. ADEA PROCEDURES

§ 7.20   In General

EEOC is charged with enforcement of the Act, and ADEA provides criminal penalties for intentional or willful interference with its processes. It investigates claims of age discrimination, attempts conciliation, and has the power to file civil actions. But individual actions are the major means of enforcement, and procedures and remedies are borrowed from the Fair Labor Standards Act.[1]

The standards for administrative charge filing under ADEA are more relaxed than those under Title VII.[2] The major superficial similarities are the twin requirements that a complainant file a charge of discrimination (1) with EEOC, within 180 days of an alleged violation, or within 300 days in a deferral state; and (2) with an appropriately empowered state agency, if one exists, which then must be deferred to for a maximum of 60 days or until it dismisses or surrenders jurisdiction. But EEOC itself is given only 60 days of deferral, in contrast to the 180 days specified by Title VII, and plaintiffs may proceed to federal court without demanding or receiving a "right to sue" letter from that agency.[3] If, however, the plaintiff awaits EEOC's right to sue notice, the

14. *DiBiase v. SmithKline Beecham Corp.*, 48 F.3d 719 (3d Cir.), *cert. denied*, 516 U.S. 916, 116 S.Ct. 306, 133 L.Ed.2d 210 (1995).

15. *See* 29 C.F.R. § 1625.22.

16. *Id.*

§ 7.20

1. *See, e.g., U.S. EEOC v. Tire Kingdom, Inc.*, 80 F.3d 449 (11th Cir.1996) (the ADEA § 7(d) timeliness requirements apply only to individual plaintiffs; therefore a timely charge by an individual is not a prerequisite to investigation and suit by EEOC).

2. See Chapter 4, Section A for a discussion of Title VII's administrative prerequisites.

3. *Adams v. Burlington N. R.R. Co.*, 838 F.Supp. 1461 (D.Kan.1993).

action must be commenced, as under Title VII, within 90 days after the plaintiff receives it. The ADEA time limitations are procedural preconditions to suit, analogous to statutes of limitations, and thus may be waived, estopped, or equitably tolled.[4]

In addition, the Supreme Court has leniently construed the ADEA's apparent requirement that a state filing precede the filing of an ADEA action in federal court. A complainant's failure to file a state agency charge before commencing a federal action is not fatal; the federal court will simply stay its proceedings until a state charge is filed and the state deferral period elapses.[5] For this reason lower courts in ADEA cases have also not followed the Supreme Court's Title VII approach of subtracting the 60–day state deferral period from the 300 EEOC filing deadline;[6] the 300 days to file with EEOC in ADEA actions remains 300, rather than 240 days.[7]

Securities industry employees who have agreed to arbitrate statutory discrimination claims have been held precluded by the Federal Arbitration Act ("FAA") from instituting judicial actions under ADEA without first exhausting the agreed upon arbitration procedures.[8] It is likely but not definitely settled that those employees will also be precluded from resuming such stayed lawsuits after the issuance of an adverse arbitration award. Most circuits agree that employees in other industries may have to honor agreements to arbitrate statutory discrimination claims and be bound by an adverse award, but it remains uncertain whether the same compulsion attaches where the arbitration promise is contained in a collectively bargained agreement negotiated not by the putative plaintiff but by her union. For a discussion of these issues, refer to § 4.6.

Until the Civil Rights Act of 1991, the plaintiff was required to initiate an ADEA action within the 2– or 3–year limitations period applicable under the Portal-to-Portal Act.[9] But an amendment made by the Act eliminates the Portal-to-Portal Act limitations periods. Section 115 instead requires EEOC, when it dismisses or otherwise terminates a proceeding, to notify the charging party, who may then bring a private action against the respondent within 90 days of receipt of that notice.[10]

4. *See Anderson v. Board of Regents,* 140 F.3d 704 (7th Cir.1998) (ADEA claim time-barred and not subject to equitable tolling where plaintiff filed with state agency but not EEOC on day 300 because late filing denied state agency opportunity to consider charge).

5. *Oscar Mayer & Co. v. Evans,* 441 U.S. 750, 99 S.Ct. 2066, 60 L.Ed.2d 609 (1979). *See Brodsky v. City Univ. of New York,* 56 F.3d 8 (2d Cir.1995) (ADEA complainant may file simultaneously with state agency and EEOC, because statute requires no 60–day deferral period for state on local processing).

6. See Chapter 4.

7. *Thelen v. Marc's Big Boy Corp.,* 64 F.3d 264 (7th Cir.1995); *Aronson v. Gressly,* 961 F.2d 907 (10th Cir.1992).

8. *Gilmer v. Interstate/Johnson Lane Corp.,* 500 U.S. 20, 111 S.Ct. 1647, 114 L.Ed.2d 26 (1991).

9. See discussion of limitations periods under the EPA in Chapter 4 above. (The complainant did not, however, have to not comply with state limitations rules. *Oscar Mayer,* 441 U.S. 750, 99 S.Ct. 2066, 60 L.Ed.2d 609).

10. *See Littell v. Aid Ass'n for Lutherans,* 62 F.3d 257 (8th Cir.1995); *Sperling v. Hoffmann–La Roche, Inc.,* 145 F.R.D. 357

That amendment was not made to shorten the statute of limitations on ADEA claims but rather to preserve them: EEOC had proven incapable of acting on many age discrimination claims before the former 2– or 3–year statutes expired.[11] Nevertheless circuit courts, regarding the new 90–day private plaintiff court filing deadline as "procedural," have applied it to bar claims filed after the effective date of the 1991 Civil Rights Act even on claims accruing before that date.[12]

ADEA may be somewhat more restrictive than Title VII in one procedural respect, although probably largely in form. No ADEA class action may be maintained under Federal Rule 23, which in appropriate circumstances permits class members to be bound without their specific consent. But multiple plaintiffs may join together under Federal Rule 20, and "representative" actions are permitted under ADEA § 7(b), which incorporates by reference, among other provisions, § 16(b) of FLSA, 29 U.S.C.A. § 216(b). The class representatives must frame their complaint so as to notify the employer that it will have to defend an opt-in representative action.[13] Section 16(b) then allows a would-be "class member" who has not filed a charge affirmatively to "opt in" the action by giving a written consent to joinder as a party plaintiff. The Supreme Court has authorized district courts to facilitate this process by ordering employers to produce the names and addresses of employees similarly situated to the representative and to issue a consent document approved in form by the court itself.[14] Further, paralleling the practice followed under Title VII in the case of true Rule 23 class actions, most circuit courts have adopted a "single-filing" rule that rather liberally permits would-be ADEA representees who have not filed timely charges with EEOC to piggyback on the timely filed charges of their co-joined individual plaintiffs or "representatives."[15] Membership in a pending class

(D.N.J.1992), *aff'd*, 24 F.3d 463 (3d Cir. 1994). For a discussion of the relationship between state agency determinations and ADEA court actions, see Chapter 12.

11. *Sperling*, 145 F.R.D. at 360.

12. *Garfield v. J.C. Nichols Real Estate*, 57 F.3d 662 (8th Cir.), *cert. denied*, 516 U.S. 944, 116 S.Ct. 380, 133 L.Ed.2d 303 (1995); *St. Louis v. Texas Worker's Compensation Comm'n*, 65 F.3d 43 (5th Cir.1995), *cert. denied*, 518 U.S. 1024, 116 S.Ct. 2563, 135 L.Ed.2d 1080 (1996).

13. *Sperling v. Hoffmann–La Roche, Inc.*, 145 F.R.D. 357. The Third Circuit has also insisted, as a prerequisite to an ADEA representative action, that the class representatives must have included a similar notice in their administrative charge filed with EEOC. *Lusardi v. Lechner*, 855 F.2d 1062, 1077–78 (3d Cir.1988).

14. *Hoffmann–La Roche, Inc. v. Sperling*, 493 U.S. 165, 110 S.Ct. 482, 107 L.Ed.2d 480 (1989). And the required degree of substantial similarity between the allegations of the putative joiner and those

of the named plaintiff is less than is required for FRCP 20(a) permissive joinder. *Helton v. K Mart Corp.*, 79 F.3d 1086 (11th Cir.), *cert. denied*, 519 U.S. 987, 117 S.Ct. 447, 136 L.Ed.2d 342 (1996).

15. *See, e.g., Howlett v. Holiday Inns, Inc.*, 49 F.3d 189 (6th Cir.), *cert. denied*, 516 U.S. 943, 116 S.Ct. 379, 133 L.Ed.2d 302 (1995); *Sperling v. Hoffmann–La Roche, Inc.*, 145 F.R.D. 357; *Tolliver v. Xerox Corp.*, 918 F.2d 1052 (2d Cir.1990), *cert. denied*, 499 U.S. 983, 111 S.Ct. 1641, 113 L.Ed.2d 736 (1991); *Anderson v. Montgomery Ward & Co., Inc.*, 852 F.2d 1008 (7th Cir.1988); *Kloos v. Carter–Day Co.*, 799 F.2d 397 (8th Cir.1986); *Naton v. Bank of Cal.*, 649 F.2d 691 (9th Cir.1981); *Mistretta v. Sandia Corp.*, 639 F.2d 588 (10th Cir. 1980). *Cf. Grayson v. K Mart Corp.*, 79 F.3d 1086 (11th Cir.1996) *cert. denied*, 519 U.S. 987, 117 S.Ct. 447, 136 L.Ed.2d 342 (1996) (permitting piggybacking into ADEA representative action by plaintiff who did not file EEOC charge but requiring her to opt into that action before applicable limitations pe-

action tolls the ninety day period for filing an individual suit,[16] but the statute begins to run again when the district court enters an interlocutory order denying class certification.[17]

§§ 7.21–9.24 [Reserved]

E. ADEA REMEDIES

§ 7.25 In General

An individual may be awarded injunctive relief, back wages, statutory "liquidated" damages equal to the amount of back wages, attorney's fees, and costs.[1] Although, as under Title VII, back pay is routinely available as a remedy for a proven ADEA violation, similar limitations on its scope apply. For example back pay will be denied for the period beginning after an employer eliminates the position from which plaintiff was terminated, provided it has not created a comparable position.[2]

The circuits universally approve front pay as an ADEA remedy that is routinely available when needed.[3] Its duration extends until the plaintiff fails to make reasonable efforts to secure substantially equivalent employment or obtains or is offered such employment.[4] The circuit decisions are in accord that ADEA front pay is a form of equitable relief, so that a plaintiff's eligibility for a front pay award is a decision for the trial judge.[5] But they are sharply divided as to whether, once a judge determines the appropriateness of ADEA front pay in lieu of reinstate-

riod on her individual claim has expired). *But see Whalen v. W.R. Grace & Co.,* 56 F.3d 504 (3d Cir.1995) (rejecting use of single-filing rule under ADEA).

16. *See Crown, Cork & Seal Co., Inc. v. Parker,* 462 U.S. 345, 354–55, 103 S.Ct. 2392, 2397–98, 76 L.Ed.2d 628 (1983); *Armstrong v. Martin Marietta Corp.,* 138 F.3d 1374, 1380 (11th Cir.), *cert. denied,* 525 U.S. 1019, 119 S.Ct. 545, 142 L.Ed.2d 453 (1998).

17. *Armstrong,* 138 F.3d at 1380.

§ 7.25

1. 29 U.S.C.A. § 626(b) incorporates by reference the remedies authorized under the Fair Labor Standards Act, 29 U.S.C.A. §§ 216–17.

2. *Bartek v. Urban Redevelopment Auth. of Pittsburgh,* 882 F.2d 739, 746–747 (3d Cir.1989). See Chapter 4 concerning detailed standards for and computation of front pay.

3. *See, e.g., McKnight v. General Motors Corp.,* 908 F.2d 104, 117 (7th Cir.1990), *cert. denied,* 499 U.S. 919, 111 S.Ct. 1306, 113 L.Ed.2d 241 (1991). *But see Wells v. New Cherokee Corp.,* 58 F.3d 233 (6th Cir.

1995) (awarding of front pay when reinstatement denied is not automatic, but should be determined by trial court before jury assesses amount).

4. *See Dominic v. Consolidated Edison Co. of N.Y., Inc.,* 822 F.2d 1249 (2d Cir. 1987); *Green v. USX Corp.,* 843 F.2d 1511 (3d Cir.1988), *vacated,* 490 U.S. 1103, 109 S.Ct. 3151, 104 L.Ed.2d 1015 (1989), *reinstated in part,* 896 F.2d 801 (3d Cir.1990), *cert. denied,* 498 U.S. 814, 111 S.Ct. 53, 112 L.Ed.2d 29 (1990).

5. *See, e.g., Smith v. World Ins. Co.,* 38 F.3d 1456, 1466 (8th Cir.1994) (district court in its discretion may award whatever equitable relief is appropriate to make the victorious ADEA plaintiff whole). Courts divide, however, on whether the amount of front pay should be reduced by such collateral sources as veterans disability benefits, unemployment compensation, or social security. *Compare Hamlin v. Charter Township,* 165 F.3d 426 (6th Cir.1999) (yes) *with Lussier v. Runyon,* 50 F.3d 1103 (1st Cir.), *cert. denied,* 516 U.S. 815, 116 S.Ct. 69, 133 L.Ed.2d 30 (1995) (no). See generally § 4.25 for ADEA and Title VII decisions on offsetting back and front pay awards by the amount of collateral benefits.

ment, a jury may then decide the amount of the award.[6]

Even in jurisdictions that recognize front pay, the employer's abolition of plaintiff's former position limits the amount of front pay the plaintiff may recover.[7] Since the age 70 cap on the class protected by ADEA was removed effective January 1, 1987, it is theoretically possible for front pay to continue indefinitely, or at least for the duration of an employee's lifetime as predicted by a standard mortality table. But an employer's normal retirement age may well serve as a practical cap on the duration of what would otherwise be an astronomical total amount of front pay.[8] Plaintiffs customarily also seek as part of the award any loss of future retirement pay attributable to lower earnings following an age-based termination.

Liquidated damages are available under ADEA in the same circumstances as they are available under the EPA, i.e., when the violation is "willful" within the meaning of the FLSA. This means that the double award is available only if the employer knows that its employment practice violates ADEA or recklessly disregards that its conduct will violate the Act; it is not enough that the employer knows that the Act is potentially applicable to the practice in question.[9] The Supreme Court further explained that while an employer need not have knowledge of the law to act "willfully," he must know that his acts violate the law or carelessly disregard whether the law gives him a right so to act.[10] An employer reference to the possibility that the employee's age might create an equal opportunity problem was held an adequate basis for a jury to infer that the employer took steps to hide an ageist intent and knew or at least recklessly disregarded whether its acts violated ADEA.[11] After *Thurston*, the Third Circuit has held that liquidated damages are available in an intentional disparate treatment case only when the plaintiff produces evidence of "outrageous" employer conduct beyond that minimally necessary to establish age discrimination.[12] Other circuits

6. *Contrast Hansard v. Pepsi–Cola Metro. Bottling Co.*, 865 F.2d 1461, 1470 (5th Cir.), *cert. denied*, 493 U.S. 842, 110 S.Ct. 129, 107 L.Ed.2d 89 (1989); *Fite v. First Tenn. Prod. Credit Ass'n*, 861 F.2d 884, 893 (6th Cir.1988); *Cassino v. Reichhold Chem., Inc.*, 817 F.2d 1338, 1347 (9th Cir.1987), *cert. denied*, 484 U.S. 1047, 108 S.Ct. 785, 98 L.Ed.2d 870 (1988); *Maxfield v. Sinclair Int'l*, 766 F.2d 788, 796 (3d Cir.1985), *cert. denied*, 474 U.S. 1057, 106 S.Ct. 796, 88 L.Ed.2d 773 (1986) (jury may determine amount) *with Newhouse v. McCormick & Co.*, 110 F.3d 635 (8th Cir.1997); *Fortino v. Quasar Co.*, 950 F.2d 389, 398 (7th Cir. 1991); *Denison v. Swaco Geolograph Co.*, 941 F.2d 1416, 1426 (10th Cir.1991); *Duke v. Uniroyal, Inc.*, 928 F.2d 1413,1424 (4th Cir.), *cert. denied*, 502 U.S. 963, 112 S.Ct. 429, 116 L.Ed.2d 449 (1991); *Dominic v. Consolidated Edison Co. of New York, Inc.*, 822 F.2d 1249, 1257 (2d Cir.1987) (judge determines amount as well as eligibility).

The latter courts have reasoned that the ADEA's jury trial provision is limited to those fact issues that underlie claims for legal, rather than equitable, relief, and front pay is purely equitable.

7. *Bartek*, 882 F.2d 739.

8. *Olitsky v. Spencer Gifts, Inc.*, 964 F.2d 1471 (5th Cir.1992), *cert. denied*, 507 U.S. 909, 113 S.Ct. 1253, 122 L.Ed.2d 652 (1993).

9. *Trans World Airlines Inc. v. Thurston*, 469 U.S. 111, 105 S.Ct. 613, 83 L.Ed.2d 523 (1985).

10. *Thurston*, 469 U.S. at 127.

11. *See Spencer v. Stuart Hall Co., Inc.* 173 F.3d 1124 (8th Cir.1999).

12. *Dreyer v. Arco Chem. Co.*, 801 F.2d 651 (3d Cir.1986), *cert. denied*, 480 U.S. 906, 107 S.Ct. 1348, 94 L.Ed.2d 519 (1987); *Anastasio v. Schering Corp.*, 838 F.2d 701

have rejected the requirement that the defendant's conduct be outrageous but required as a prerequisite for liquidated damages that the underlying evidence of discrimination be "direct."[13] This latter view seems more in accord with the Supreme Court's holding in *Kolstad v. American Dental Association.*[14] In *Thurston* the Supreme Court wrote that ADEA liquidated damages are "punitive in nature,"[15] and in *Kolstad* the Court rejected the view that a showing of outrageous conduct is essential for punitive damages under Title VII.[16]

A Supreme Court reaffirmation of the *Thurston* test, *Hazen Paper Co. v. Biggins,*[17] has specifically rejected these additional requirements. *Hazen* also made it clear that the *Thurston* definition of willfulness applies to cases concerning alleged disparate treatment against an individual employee, as well as to alleged disparate treatment resulting from the kind of formal policy at issue in *Thurston*. But the Court reemphasized that employer conduct must be more than merely voluntary and negligent to constitute a willful violation. Indeed, the Court wrote, even an employer "who knowingly relies on age" does not "invariably" commit a knowing or reckless violation of the ADEA. This is because the Court's test finds willfulness only when the employer knows that or recklessly disregards whether it is violating the prohibitions of the statute, not simply when it knowingly takes age into account.[18] Specifically, the Court sought to preserve "two tiers of liability" in ADEA cases by finding liability for back pay whenever an intentional violation is established, but denying liquidated damages even for intentional violations when "an employer incorrectly but in good faith and nonrecklessly" believes that its conduct is not prohibited or is affirmatively authorized by the statute.[19] Thus although conduct constituting a constructive discharge is by its nature serious, aggravated and almost surely inten-

---

(3d Cir.1988). Courts in that circuit have struggled to develop a consistent definition of outrageous conduct. *Compare Bartek*, 882 F.2d at 744–746 (comment by superior that plaintiff might "look around for another job" if not happy at work insufficient to show outrageous conduct) *with Bruno v. W.B. Saunders Co.*, 882 F.2d 760, 771 (3d Cir.1989), *cert. denied sub nom. CBS Inc. v. Bruno*, 493 U.S. 1062, 110 S.Ct. 880, 107 L.Ed.2d 962 (1990) (custom-tailored job description designed to fit qualifications of younger selectee rather than plaintiff sufficiently outrageous to support liquidated damages).

13. *See, e.g., Neufeld v. Searle Laboratories*, 884 F.2d 335 (8th Cir.1989).

14. 527 U.S. 526, 119 S.Ct. 2118, 144 L.Ed.2d 494 (1999).

15. *Thurston*, 469 U.S. at 125.

16. Indeed four Justices, concurring on this point, equated the *Kolstad* interpretation of the Title VII punitive damages section with the *Thurston* holding on the willfulness required for liquidated damages under ADEA.

17. 507 U.S. 604, 113 S.Ct. 1701, 123 L.Ed.2d 338 (1993).

18. *Brown v. Stites Concrete, Inc.*, 994 F.2d 553, 561 (8th Cir.1993) (Loken, J., dissenting). *But see Starceski v. Westinghouse Elec.*, 54 F.3d 1089 (3d Cir.1995), discussed *infra*.

19. *Hazen Paper Co.*, 507 U.S. at 616, 113 S.Ct. at 1709. For the same reason, double liquidated damages may seldom if ever be available for ADEA violations predicated solely on disparate impact evidence, assuming, as is unclear, that ADEA liability may be predicated at all on that mode of proof. How often could a trier of fact logically conclude that an employer knowingly violated ADEA or recklessly disregarded its liability under that statute when it adopts a practice that by hypothesis does not refer to age at all? Perhaps that conclusion would have merit in the rare case where the employer's adoption of the practice followed a recent, dispositive judicial decision condemning the neutral practice in question.

tional, it does not follow that every such violation is willful.[20] Some violations, however—unlawful retaliation is an example—may inherently involve knowledge or reckless disregard of the prohibitions of the statute so that liquidated damages should follow as a matter of course from a finding of liability.[21] In any event, it appears that the same evidence that establishes intentional discrimination in violation of ADEA may suffice to support a jury's finding of willfulness and hence liquidated damages, provided that evidence satisfies the distinct *Hazen* legal standard.[22] Accordingly, where a jury could reasonably find that the employer's agent took action to disguise what he understood to be an ADEA violation, the "good faith, nonreckless" situation was inapplicable and the jury's determination of willfulness upheld.[23]

The circuits are in agreement that front pay is excludable from the liquidated damages award.[24] However, there is some disagreement whether the doubling should be based on the full compensatory award, including replacement of lost pension income and other fringe benefits,[25] or should be limited to the amount of lost wages.[26] There is also there is a conflict in the circuits concerning whether, when liquidated damages

20. *Peterson v. Insurance Co. of N. Am.*, 40 F.3d 26 (2d Cir.1994).

21. *Compare Edwards v. Board of Regents*, 2 F.3d 382, 383–84 (11th Cir.1993) (declining to decide whether retaliation under ADEA necessarily entails willfulness) *with Grant v. Hazelett Strip–Casting Corp.*, 880 F.2d 1564 (2d Cir.1989) (stating that it does). This appears to be the view relied on in *Starceski v. Westinghouse Elec.*, 54 F.3d 1089 (3d Cir.1995) (upholding finding of willfulness because particular older employees were specifically targeted for layoff, so that company's decisions were not in that sense merely negligent, notwithstanding evidence that company's managers were counseled to select layoff candidates only for business reasons and that legal counsel reviewed managers' asserted justifications—in other words, despite evidence which suggested that defendant did not know it was violating ADEA). But see Title VII decisions holding evidence demonstrating retaliation does not necessarily suffice for punitive award, cited in § 4.26, *supra*.

22. *EEOC v. Pape Lift, Inc.*, 115 F.3d 676 (9th Cir.1997).

23. *Newhouse v. McCormick & Co.*, 110 F.3d 635 (8th Cir.1997).

24. *See Farley v. Nationwide Mut. Ins. Co.*, 197 F.3d 1322, 1340 (11th Cir.1999); *Olitsky v. Spencer Gifts, Inc.*, 964 F.2d 1471, 1479 (5th Cir.1992), *cert. denied*, 507 U.S. 909, 113 S.Ct. 1253, 122 L.Ed.2d 652 (1993); *Wheeler v. McKinley Enters.*, 937 F.2d 1158, 1163 n. 2 (6th Cir.1991); *Powers v. Grinnell Corp.*, 915 F.2d 34, 35 (1st Cir. 1990); *Graefenhain v. Pabst Brewing Co.*,

870 F.2d 1198, 1210 (7th Cir.1989); *Cooper v. Asplundh Tree Expert Co.*, 836 F.2d 1544, 1556–57 (10th Cir.1988); *Blum v. Witco Chemical Corp.*, 829 F.2d 367, 382–83 (3d Cir.1987); *Dominic v. Consolidated Edison Co.*, 822 F.2d 1249, 1258–59 (2d Cir.1987); *Cassino v. Reichhold Chems., Inc.*, 817 F.2d 1338, 1348 (9th Cir.1987), *cert. denied*, 484 U.S. 1047, 108 S.Ct. 785, 98 L.Ed.2d 870 (1988).

25. Although stock options, a common type of fringe benefit, have been held excludable from the liquidated damages award, they can amount to a large damages award given the proper expert testimony. For example, in *Greene v. Safeway Stores, Inc.*, 210 F.3d 1237, 1243–44 (10th Cir. 2000), the plaintiff was forced to exercise his vested stock options within three months of his discriminatory termination or the options would have expired. Through expert testimony, the plaintiff showed that had he been permitted to work until he was eligible for retirement three years later, his stock options would have been worth $3 million more, a gain attributable to the rise in company stock price. The court upheld a jury verdict of more than $6 million including some $4.4 million for both vested and unvested stock options.

26. *Compare Greene v. Safeway Stores, Inc.*, 210 F.3d 1237, 1246–47 (10th Cir. 2000) (doubling salary, bonuses, and employee and retirement benefits); *Kossman v. Calumet County*, 849 F.2d 1027, 1032–33 (7th Cir.1988) (including health insurance benefits in liquidated damages award);and *Fariss v. Lynchburg Foundry*, 769 F.2d 958,

are awarded, the court may additionally award front pay[27] or prejudgment interest.[28]

Despite *Hazen*'s confirmation that ADEA authorizes "legal remedies," the Civil Rights Act of 1991 gives Title VII plaintiffs alleging disparate treatment (not disproportionate adverse impact) important remedies that the circuit courts have uniformly held *unavailable* under ADEA: compensatory and punitive damages.[29] (Those damages are allowed in ADEA retaliation cases; the exception is made because both types of damages are allowed for retaliation claims under FLSA, the remedial scheme adopted by reference in the ADEA.)[30] State law claims authorizing compensatory or punitive damages may often be joined with ADEA claims, however, and care must then be taken to distinguish the respective authorizing standards.[31]

Accordingly, while it could be said categorically before the 1991 Act that an ADEA plaintiff was remedially better situated than a claimant

964–67 (4th Cir.1985) (including life insurance premiums in calculation) *with Blum v. Witco*, 829 F.2d 367, 382–383 (3d Cir.1987) (excluding lost pension benefits); *Blackwell v. Sun Elec. Corp.*, 696 F.2d 1176 (6th Cir. 1983) (excluding health insurance benefits from the calculation).

27. *Compare Walther v. Lone Star Gas Co.*, 952 F.2d 119 (5th Cir.1992) and *Brooks v. Hilton Casinos, Inc.*, 959 F.2d 757 (9th Cir.), *cert. denied*, 506 U.S. 906, 113 S.Ct. 300, 121 L.Ed.2d 224 (1992) (holding no); *Price v. Marshall Erdman & Assocs., Inc.*, 966 F.2d 320 (7th Cir.1992); *Castle v. Sangamo Weston, Inc.*, 837 F.2d 1550 (11th Cir.1988) (holding yes).

28. Courts that, despite *Thurston*, view liquidated damages as at least partly compensatory reject prejudgment interest, holding that the plaintiff who receives both would be overcompensated. *See, e.g., Powers v. Grinnell Corp.*, 915 F.2d 34, 40–42 (1st Cir.1990); *McCann v. Texas City Refining, Inc.*, 984 F.2d 667 (5th Cir.1993); *Fortino v. Quasar Co.*, 950 F.2d 389 (7th Cir. 1991); *Hamilton v. 1st Source Bank*, 895 F.2d 159, 165–66 (4th Cir.1990). Courts that consider liquidated damages as the ADEA's substitute for punitive damages allow prejudgment interest. *See, e.g., Starceski v. Westinghouse Elec.*, 54 F.3d 1089 (3d Cir.1995); *Reichman v. Bonsignore, Brignati and Mazzotta*, 818 F.2d 278 (2d Cir.1987); *Lindsey v. American Cast Iron Pipe Co.*, 810 F.2d 1094 (11th Cir.1987); *Kelly v. American Standard, Inc.*, 640 F.2d 974 (9th Cir. 1981). The latter view is fortified by the Supreme Court's reaffirmation that ADEA liquidated damages are designed to be punitive. *See Commissioner v. Schleier*, 513 U.S. 998, 115 S.Ct. 507, 130 L.Ed.2d 415 (1994).

29. For decisions denying ADEA plaintiffs compensatory and punitive damages, including damages for pain and suffering and emotional distress, *see Moskowitz v. Trustees of Purdue Univ.*, 5 F.3d 279 (7th Cir.1993); *Wilson v. Monarch Paper Co.*, 939 F.2d 1138, 1144 (5th Cir.1991); *Haskell v. Kaman Corp.*, 743 F.2d 113, 120–121 n. 2 (2d Cir.1984) and cases cited therein; *Pfeiffer v. Essex Wire Corp.*, 682 F.2d 684 (7th Cir.), *cert. denied*, 459 U.S. 1039, 103 S.Ct. 453, 74 L.Ed.2d 606 (1982); *Naton v. Bank of California*, 649 F.2d 691 (9th Cir.1981); *Frith v. Eastern Air Lines, Inc.*, 611 F.2d 950 (4th Cir.1979); *Vazquez v. Eastern Air Lines, Inc.*, 579 F.2d 107 (1st Cir.1978); *Dean v. American Sec. Ins. Co.*, 559 F.2d 1036 (5th Cir.1977), *cert. denied*, 434 U.S. 1066, 98 S.Ct. 1243, 55 L.Ed.2d 767 (1978); *Rogers v. Exxon Research & Engineering Co.*, 550 F.2d 834 (3d Cir.1977), *cert. denied*, 434 U.S. 1022, 98 S.Ct. 749, 54 L.Ed.2d 770 (1978). Congress' silence about ADEA in the provisions of the 1991 Act that authorized those damages for Title VII disparate treatment plaintiffs shows an intent to continue to withhold those remedies in actions under ADEA. *Capparell v. National Health Management, Inc.*, 1993 WL 516399 (E.D.Pa.1993).

30. *Moskowitz*, 5 F.3d 279.

31. *See Sanchez v. Puerto Rico Oil Co.*, 37 F.3d 712 (1st Cir.1994) (plaintiff could recover separate award of punitive damages under Puerto Rico law); *Ryther v. KARE 11*, 864 F.Supp. 1525 (D.Minn.1994) (court finds ADEA wilfulness, and thus doubles jury's back pay award as ADEA liquidated damages, but does not find the deliberate disregard of plaintiff's rights required by state law for the award of punitive damages).

under Title VII, that is no longer necessarily true. To be awarded more than back and, with luck, front pay, the ADEA plaintiff must prove wilfulness; and even then she is likely to receive an award equal to only back pay doubled, or at best twice the amount of back and front pay combined. By contrast, the Title VII plaintiff may now recover, by showing no more than an intentional violation, significantly more than back and, probably, front pay: compensatory damages, capped in amounts that vary with the size of the defendant's employee complement. Only when she seeks punitive damages must the Title VII plaintiff show something akin to ADEA wilfulness. On the other hand, the 1991 Act caps the sum of compensatory and punitive damages available under Title VII, while there is no absolute cap on the size of ADEA liquidated damages. An ADEA plaintiff who recovers a very large award of back pay, front pay or both may accordingly still find that his liquidated damages exceed the amount a Title VII counterpart could recover by way of compensatory and punitive damages.

Further, it appears that the 1991 Act denies successful ADEA plaintiffs, unlike their Title VII counterparts, any recovery for the fees of expert witnesses.[32] But in contrast to § 706(k) of Title VII, the FLSA, and therefore ADEA, authorizes attorney's fees only to "plaintiffs," not "prevailing parties"; yet it authorizes that award as a supplement to "any judgment awarded to the plaintiff or plaintiffs."[33] Thus even a prevailing defendant who can make the extraordinary showing of frivolousness demanded by the *Christiansburg Garment* interpretation of § 706(k) may not be entitled to an award of attorney's fees from the plaintiff in an action under ADEA. But the plaintiff, to recover fees based on "any judgment" favorable on the merits, must also have achieved a sufficient change in defendant's position as a result of the judgment to be considered a "prevailing" party within the meaning of the fee-shifting provisions of Title VII and 42 U.S.C. § 1988(b).[34]

In considering whether to settle an ADEA claim, counsel for both parties should also take into account the employer's potential liability for pre-and post-judgment interest;[35] compelled waiver of statutory attorney's fees either by a successful offer of judgment under Federal Rule of Civil Procedure 68 or by provision of the settlement agreement;[36] Federal Rule of Civil Procedure 54(d) "costs," defined by 28 U.S.C.A. § 1920 to include clerks' and marshals' fees, fees of court reporters for tran-

---

32. *James v. Sears, Roebuck & Co.*, 21 F.3d 989 (10th Cir.1994); *Houghton v. Sipco, Inc.*, 828 F.Supp. 631 (D.Iowa 1993), *amended*, 38 F.3d 953 (8th Cir.1994).

33. 29 U.S.C. § 216(b).

34. *See Salvatori v. Westinghouse Elec. Corp.*, 190 F.3d 1244 (11th Cir.1999), *cert. denied*, ___ U.S. ___, 120 S.Ct. 1172, 145 L.Ed.2d 1081 (2000); *Nance v. Maxwell Fed. Credit Union*, 186 F.3d 1338 (11th Cir. 1999).

35. *See Gelof v. Papineau*, 829 F.2d 452 (3d Cir.1987).

36. *See* Chapter 11 on Attorney's Fees, in particular the discussion of *Evans v. Jeff D.*, 475 U.S. 717, 106 S.Ct. 1531, 89 L.Ed.2d 747 (1986). Note, however, that FLSA, unlike Title VII, does not describe attorney's fees as "costs." Under the logic of *Evans*, an EPA or ADEA defendant may still be at risk for plaintiff's fees (but not costs) that accrue after the plaintiff rejects a Rule 68 offer even if that offer turns out to exceed the amount of plaintiff's judgment.

scripts, printing and witness fees, copy costs, docket fees, and fees for court-appointed experts and interpreters; and the tax treatment of plaintiffs' settlement proceeds.[37]

37. See Chapter 4.

Chapter Eight

THE EQUAL PAY ACT OF 1963

Analysis

---

§ 8.1   Introduction

The Equal Pay Act of 1963[1] ("EPA") requires "equal pay for equal work" within the same establishment regardless of sex. The concept of

§ 8.1

1.   29 U.S.C.A. § 206(d). The Equal Pay

Act provides: No employer having employees subject to any provisions of this section

409

"equal work" lies at the heart of the Act. General comparisons between two jobs carrying unequal pay will not suffice to establish that work is "equal"; rather, demonstrating an EPA violation demands specific showings of equivalent skill, effort, and responsibility, as well as performance under similar working conditions. Once an inequality is found, however, it cannot be remedied by a reduction in the wages of the higher paid sex.

The EPA contains four affirmative defenses. Specifically, the EPA allows exceptions to the equal pay for equal work principle when differentials are pursuant to: (1) seniority systems; (2) merit systems; (3) systems which measure earnings by quantity or quality of production (incentive systems); or (4) factors other than sex.

After examining which employers are covered by the EPA, this chapter will discuss the elements of the plaintiff's prima facie case and the employer's defenses. Second, this chapter will address EPA's anti-retaliation provisions. Third, it will look at EPA enforcement and remedies. Fourth, this chapter will compare the EPA with Title VII. Finally, this chapter will examine the doctrine of comparable worth and its uncomfortable fit with either the EPA or Title VII.

A. EPA COVERAGE, THE PRIMA FACIE CASE AND AFFIRMATIVE DEFENSES

§ 8.2 Coverage

Why would a plaintiff resort to the Equal Pay Act when Title VII proscribes sex discrimination in *all* terms and conditions of employment, not just for compensation between persons of different genders holding "equal" jobs? For starters, it may be the only game in town. EPA looks primarily to the Fair Labor Standards Act[1] ("FLSA"), to which it is an amendment, for provisions on coverage, as well as enforcement. In sharp contrast to Title VII, EPA has no coverage threshold defined in terms of the employer's number of employees. Instead, it embraces in the first instance employees from employers of any size, unless the employer is in one of several specifically exempted industries.[2] These industries include certain fishing and agricultural businesses as well as small local newspapers.

An employee not in an exempted industry may assert an FLSA, and therefore an EPA claim if she has some contact with interstate com-

shall discriminate, within any establishment in which such employees are employed, between employees on the basis of sex by paying wages to employees in such establishment at a rate less than the rate at which he pays wages to employees of the opposite sex in such establishment for equal work on jobs the performance of which requires equal skill, effort, and responsibility, and which are performed under similar working conditions, except where such payment is made pursuant to (i) a seniority system; (ii) a merit system; (iii) a system which measures earnings by quantity or quality of production; or (iv) a differential based on any factor other than sex. *Provided*, That an employer who is paying a wage rate differential in violation of this subsection shall not, in order to comply with the provisions of this subsection, reduce the wage rate of any employee.

§ 8.2

1. 29 U.S.C.A. § 209 *et seq.*

2. 29 U.S.C.A. § 213.

merce. This contact may be established by satisfying one of two requirements. The first concerns the nature of the work implicated by the plaintiff's claim. If the employee is "engaged in commerce" or produces "goods for commerce," the work is covered, no matter what the employer's size.

An alternative FLSA avenue protects employees who, though not themselves engaged in or producing goods for interstate commerce, work for nonexempt businesses that are. This alternative measure of FLSA coverage extends EPA's protection to persons employed by "enterprises" engaged in commerce or producing goods for commerce. Such enterprises will be deemed to meet the interstate commerce test if they (1) achieved certain sales volumes or (2) were part of certain industries specifically mentioned in FLSA, provided in each case that other employees of such enterprises were engaged in or producing goods for commerce.

A third approach, based on text unique to EPA, arguably reaches more broadly than the FLSA alternatives. It focuses on the relation between other employees' production and interstate commerce, without regard to the commerce involvement of the plaintiff or the defendant employer. The EPA prohibits employers that have "employees subject to" EPA from engaging in unequal pay discrimination against "employees."[3] Read literally, the EPA would therefore appear to protect all employees of employers that have at least two employees of different genders who are engaged in or producing goods for commerce, even if those employers are not FLSA "enterprises."

The Act defines an employer as "any person acting directly or indirectly in the interest of an employer in relation to an employee. . . ."[4] Notwithstanding this definition, claims against supervisors or managers in their individual as distinct from official capacities are likely to be dismissed because in an individual capacity a defendant lacks control over the plaintiff's terms of employment.[5] State instrumentalities are included within the definition, and subject to suit in federal court notwithstanding Eleventh Amendment sovereign immunity, which Congress effectively abrogated pursuant to its Fourteenth Amendment, § 5 enforcement power.[6]

---

3. 29 U.S.C.A. § 206(d)(1).

4. 29 U.S.C.A. § 203(d).

5. *See Welch v. Laney,* 57 F.3d 1004 (11th Cir.1995).

6. *See Hundertmark v. Florida Dep't of Transp.,* 205 F.3d 1272, 1277 (11th Cir. 2000); *O'Sullivan v. Minnesota,* 191 F.3d 965, 967–68 (8th Cir.1999); *Anderson v. State Univ. of N.Y.,* 169 F.3d 117, 120 (2d Cir.1999) (per curiam), *judgment vacated and remanded for further consideration in light of Kimel,* 528 U.S. 1111, 120 S.Ct. 929, 145 L.Ed.2d 807 (2000) *Ussery v. Louisiana,* 150 F.3d 431, 437 (5th Cir.1998), cert. dismissed, 526 U.S. 1013, 119 S.Ct. 1161, 143 L.Ed.2d 225 (1999); *Ussery v. Louisiana,* 150 F.3d 431 (5th Cir.1998) (EPA contains express abrogation and Congress's Fourteenth Amendment § 5 authority clearly authorizes legislation aimed at ending gender discrimination); *Varner v. Illinois State Univ.,* 150 F.3d 706 (7th Cir.1998) (same), *judgment vacated and remanded for further consideration in light of Kimel,* 528 U.S. 1110, 120 S.Ct. 928, 145 L.Ed.2d 806 (2000); *Timmer v. Michigan Dep't of Commerce,* 104 F.3d 833 (6th Cir.1997); *Usery v. Charleston County Sch. Dist.,* 558 F.2d 1169, 1171 (4th Cir.1977); *Usery v. Allegheny County Inst. Dist.,* 544 F.2d 148, 155 (3d Cir.1976), *cert. denied sub nom. Allegheny County Inst. Dist. v. Marshall,* 430 U.S. 946, 97 S.Ct. 1582, 51 L.Ed.2d 793 (1977).

§ 8.3 Equal Work

The first step in the plaintiff's prima facie case is to establish that the plaintiff performed work equal to that of another of the opposite sex. *Corning Glass Works v. Brennan*[1] observes that job equivalence, as measured by skill, effort, responsibility, and working conditions, need not be precise, only substantial.[2] The circuit courts have consistently so held.[3] The Third Circuit, for example, has found that the EPA requires only that the jobs be substantially similar.[4] The court held that the disparity in rates of pay between female selector-packers and male selector-packers was discriminatory. Although the men were also available to perform physical labor, the jobs were substantially similar because other male employees who routinely performed physical labor were paid at wages close to those of the female selector-packers. There was, therefore, no appreciable economic benefit to the employer in having the male selector-packers perform these physical tasks.

The issue in *Corning Glass* was whether the employer violated the EPA by paying a higher base wage to male night shift inspectors than it paid to female day shift inspectors. Long before the advent of EPA, Corning, in order to fill the male night inspector positions, had paid the night inspectors more than the female day inspectors. After the enactment of the EPA, Corning opened both jobs to members of both genders and moved to eliminate the differential rates, but a collective-bargaining agreement perpetuated them.

In determining whether there was equal pay for equal work, the Supreme Court compared the working conditions of both the day and night inspectors.[5] Guided by legislative history, the Court defined "working conditions" by reference to its common meaning in the language of industrial relations, focusing on the job's "hazards" and "surroundings."[6] In that lexicon, "hazards" referred to the physical hazards regularly encountered by all employees and "surroundings" to constant workplace features or elements like dangerous chemicals or fumes.[7] The work performed by the Corning night and day inspectors was substantially similar, the Court found, with respect to hazards and surroundings

---

§ 8.3

1. 417 U.S. 188, 94 S.Ct. 2223, 41 L.Ed.2d 1 (1974).

2. *Id.* at 203 n.24, 94 S.Ct. at 2232 n.24.

3. *See, e.g., Hein v. Oregon College of Educ.*, 718 F.2d 910 (9th Cir.1983); *EEOC v. Kenosha Unified Sch. Dist. No. 1*, 620 F.2d 1220 (7th Cir.1980); *Horner v. Mary Inst.*, 613 F.2d 706 (8th Cir.1980); *Brennan v. South Davis Community Hosp.*, 538 F.2d 859 (10th Cir.1976); *Brennan v. Owensboro–Daviess County Hosp.*, 523 F.2d 1013 (6th Cir.1975), *cert. denied sub nom. Owensboro–Daviess County Hosp., Inc. v. Usery*, 425 U.S. 973, 96 S.Ct. 2170, 48 L.Ed.2d 796 (1976); *Hodgson v. Corning Glass Works*, 474 F.2d 226 (2d Cir.1973), *aff'd on* others grounds sub nom. *Corning Glass Works v. Brennan*, 417 U.S. 188, 94 S.Ct. 2223, 41 L.Ed.2d 1 (1974); *Hodgson v. Fairmont Supply Co.*, 454 F.2d 490 (4th Cir. 1972); *Hodgson v. Brookhaven Gen. Hosp.*, 436 F.2d 719 (5th Cir.1970); *Shultz v. Wheaton Glass Co.*, 421 F.2d 259 (3d Cir.), *cert. denied*, 398 U.S. 905, 90 S.Ct. 1696, 26 L.Ed.2d 64 (1970).

4. *Shultz*, 421 F.2d 259.

5. The EPA requires equal pay for equal work "performed under similar working conditions." 29 U.S.C.A. § 206(d)(1).

6. *Corning Glass*, 417 U.S. at 202.

7. *Id.*

so defined.[8] The only substantial difference between the two jobs was time of day.[9] The Court concluded that the different time of day worked did not render unequal otherwise substantially equal working conditions.[10] Accordingly, Corning had prima facie violated the EPA by paying women less than men for equal work. Whether time of day can constitute an affirmative defense for such a prima facie claim will be discussed below.

§ 8.4   Unequal Pay

Another element of the plaintiff's prima facie case is a showing that the plaintiff was paid less than another of the opposite sex. This element involves two distinct concepts. First, the plaintiff must be paid a lesser "rate" of pay.[1] Second, this rate must be compared with that of an individual of the opposite sex performing substantially similar work.

a.   Equal "Rate" of Pay

What constitutes an "equal rate of pay" was addressed by the Sixth Circuit in *Bence v. Detroit Health Corp.*[2] Plaintiff was a female manager at a health club. The club designated certain days as women's days and other days as men's. Only staff members and managers of the sex assigned to that day's customer gender worked any one day. The managers were paid commissions on the health club memberships they sold. There were, however, more women's than men's memberships to be sold.[3] The health club thus paid a higher percentage commission, per membership sold, to its male than to its female managers, although they received approximately equal aggregate compensation.[4]

Ms. Bence challenged the practice as a violation of the EPA because she was paid a lesser "rate" (percentage commission) than a male manager.[5] The court concluded that compensation on a "per sale" basis made it clear that the female managers were being paid less than their male counterparts.[6] If total compensation had been based upon total service to the employer's clientele, the court wrote, the total equal

8. *Id.* at 203.

9. The Court noted that Corning's own job evaluation plans had always treated the two positions as equal in all respects, including working conditions. *Id.* at 202–03.

10. *Id.*

§ 8.4

1. Where plaintiff provides no evidence of the payment received by a comparator, she fails to make out a prima facie case. *See Bragg v. Navistar Int'l Transp. Corp.*, 164 F.3d 373 (7th Cir.1998).

2. 712 F.2d 1024 (6th Cir.1983), *cert. denied*, 465 U.S. 1025, 104 S.Ct. 1282, 79 L.Ed.2d 685 (1984).

3. The ratio of women's memberships sold to men's memberships was 60:40. *Id.* at 1027.

4. The commissions paid by the employer were determined in a way that ensured equal compensation to both male and female managers. Female managers were paid 5% on the sale of memberships where male managers were paid 7½%. *Id.* at 1026. The employer argued unsuccessfully that there was no EPA violation because the men and women employees received substantially equal compensation for the equal work performed. *Id.* at 1027–28.

5. *Id.*

6. *Id.* at 1027.

compensation argument might have merit. But commissions worth less per sale to women than to men employees violated the EPA.[7]

b. The Necessity of a Comparator Within a Single "Establishment"

In order to show unequal pay, there must be some comparison between the complaining individual and one of the opposite sex in a substantially similar position. The plaintiff, therefore, must demonstrate that an individual of the opposite sex received greater compensation for substantially the same job. This task is accomplished through the use of a comparator. The comparator may be one who held the job before the plaintiff,[8] who replaced the plaintiff, or who held a substantially similar position contemporaneously with the plaintiff. Finally, the comparator must also be employed in the same establishment as the plaintiff. These requirements may be subdivided into four components.

First, the comparator may not be hypothetical but rather a specific and better paid individual performing a job of substantially equal skill, effort, and responsibility.[9] Where a plaintiff identified her male comparators in general terms as "any men who got any higher salary increases than [the plaintiff] did," the plaintiff failed to carry a prima facie case.[10]

Second, the comparator must perform a substantially similar job. The court analyzes the job, not the qualification or performance characteristics of individual employees holding the job, and only the skill and qualifications actually needed to perform the job in question are considered.[11] Additionally, the examination rests on the primary, not the incidental or insubstantial job duties. Where the plaintiff performs substantially similar tasks but the comparator also has significant additional primary duties, the plaintiff has not established a prima facie case.[12]

Third, the comparator may be a past, present or future employee in a substantially similar position. The Eleventh Circuit found a valid comparison between the plaintiff, a former "Vice–President, Administra-

---

7. *Id.* at 1027–28.

8. *Arrington v. Cobb County,* 139 F.3d 865 (11th Cir.1998). A female employee stated EPA and Title VII claims although her male comparators were no longer employed or were employed in equivalent positions within the applicable limitations periods. *Brinkley–Obu v. Hughes Training, Inc.,* 36 F.3d 336 (4th Cir.1994).

9. *EEOC v. Liggett & Myers, Inc.,* 690 F.2d 1072, 1076–78 (4th Cir.1982).

10. *Houck v. Virginia Polytechnic Inst. and State Univ.,* 10 F.3d 204, 206 (4th Cir.1993). *See also Berg v. Norand Corp.,* 169 F.3d 1140 (8th Cir.), *cert. denied,* 528 U.S. 872, 120 S.Ct. 174, 145 L.Ed.2d 147 (1999) (affirming summary judgment to defendant where plaintiff provided only conclusory affidavit testimony that male comparators had jobs "equal" to hers).

11. *Arrington v. Cobb County,* 139 F.3d 865 (11th Cir.1998); *Miranda v. B & B Cash Grocery Store, Inc.,* 975 F.2d 1518 (11th Cir.1992).

12. *See Stopka v. Alliance of Am. Insurers,* 141 F.3d 681 (7th Cir.1998) (comparators had responsibility for core policymaking that plaintiff did not have)*; Sprague v. Thorn Americas, Inc.,* 129 F.3d 1355 (10th Cir.1997) (male comparators had greater marketing experience and were given more discretion; plaintiff's department produced less than 10% of the revenue of the departments headed by men); *Mulhall v. Advance Sec., Inc.,* 19 F.3d 586, 593 (11th Cir.), *cert. denied,* 513 U.S. 919, 115 S.Ct. 298, 130 L.Ed.2d 212 (1994).

tion," and a current "Vice–President, Controller" because financial concerns were essential to both jobs.[13] But if the plaintiff cannot establish that the plaintiff's predecessor, successor, or contemporary was paid more for the same responsibilities, the plaintiff has failed to make a prima facie showing.[14]

Finally, the individual identified as the comparator must be an employee of the same "establishment" as the plaintiff. The Secretary of Labor has defined "establishment" to mean "a distinct physical place of business rather than ... an entire business or 'enterprise' which may include several separate places of business."[15] In "unusual circumstances," however, a single establishment may include more than one physical location.[16] When there is centralized control and administration, some courts have been willing to find a single EPA establishment though there are different physical locations.[17] If there is centralized control and a working relationship between the plaintiff and the comparator, a reasonable trier of fact could infer that a single establishment existed for purposes of the EPA. For example, a plaintiff comparing herself to subordinate project managers working in separate locations satisfied the "single establishment" requirement by demonstrating "centralized control of job descriptions, salary administration and job assignments."[18] The project managers reported to the plaintiff in a central office and sought her approval on significant situations. Further, the plaintiff approved all wage and benefit levels and exercised ultimate control over operations at the separate facilities.[19]

Courts have refused to extend the definition of "establishment" beyond the bounds of single physical location when the different offices are geographically and operationally distinct—with operational distinctiveness marked principally by degree of centralized control. For example, the Eleventh Circuit restricted the consideration of salaries to

---

13. *Mulhall,* 19 F.3d at 593–95. Plaintiff (who held the position of Vice–President, Administration from 1981 to 1991) offered as comparator an employee holding the position of Vice–President, Controller in 1994. The plaintiff's responsibilities had included, among other things, managing costs on contracts, handling risk management, and arranging leases for the corporate headquarters. *Id.* at 594 n.17. Responsibilities of the current Vice–President, Controller included direct control of corporate accounting and financial matters. *Id.* at 594. Although the duties of the Vice–President, Controller had changed significantly since the plaintiff resigned in 1991, the Court concluded that the plaintiff had established this element of the prima facie case because the "monetary concerns permeat[ing] all aspects of the plaintiff's position" and the proposed comparator's responsibility for corporate economic well-being were substantially similar.

14. *Weiss v. Coca–Cola Bottling Co. of Chicago,* 990 F.2d 333, 337–38 (7th Cir.

1993) (plaintiff's predecessor's starting salary was the same as the plaintiff's, and her successor's was higher because he had additional duties).

15. 29 C.F.R. § 1620.9(a) (1993).

16. 29 C.F.R. § 1620.9(b) (1993) provides, "[U]nusual circumstances may call for two or more distinct physical portions of a business enterprise being treated as a single establishment."

17. *See e.g., Brennan v. Goose Creek Consol. Indep. Sch. Dist.,* 519 F.2d 53 (5th Cir.1975).

18. *Mulhall,* 19 F.3d at 591. The district court ruled that the plaintiff and the project managers, subordinates of the plaintiff, occupied positions substantially similar for EPA purposes. The court of appeals reviewed only the district court's conclusion that the project managers and the plaintiff did not work in a single establishment.

19. *Id.*

employees in one physical location[20] when the local office made the ultimate hiring decision and, within a broad range set by the central office, set specific salaries.[21] Similarly, the Ninth Circuit refused to extend the "establishment" concept beyond the confines of one physical location[22] of a defense contractor that used independent management for different customers with different needs, maintained separate project budgets, and endowed managers at separate facilities with independent authority to make personnel decisions.[23]

§ 8.5 The Employer's Defenses

Once a plaintiff has established a prima facie case, the employer bears the burden of proving—producing evidence and persuading—that the employment practice fits within one or more of EPA's affirmative defenses. The EPA provides four specific defenses. "Unequal pay" for equal work is permitted when the payment is made pursuant to (i) a seniority system, (ii) a merit system; (iii) a system which measures earnings by quantity or quality of production; or (iv) a differential based on any factor other than sex.[1]

The burden of establishing one of the four affirmative defenses is "a heavy one,"[2] because the statutory exemptions are "narrowly construed."[3] Indeed, two recent circuit opinions demonstrate that the employers' burden in EPA cases is heavier than that in a Title VII case, and, in at least one sense, the plaintiff's burden is lighter. Unlike in Title VII, once the employer proffers one of the four affirmative defenses, the burden to prove the defense remains with the employer. Compare this to the burden shifting scheme of Title VII pretext inferential proof cases, which is more fully discussed in § 3.10, where the plaintiff must persuade that the proffered legitimate, nondiscriminatory reason for the adverse term or condition of employment is but a pretext for intentional discrimination. Moreover, under the EPA, the employer must "submit evidence from which a reasonable factfinder could conclude not merely that the employer's proffered reasons could explain the wage disparity [as under the Title VII burden-shifting paradigm], but that the proffered reasons do in fact explain the wage disparity."[4]

In *Stanziale v. Jargowsky*,[5] the Third Circuit reversed the trial court's grant of defendants' summary judgment motion because the defendant failed to show some evidence that its decision to give the male comparator a starting salary $2,000 more than plaintiff was in fact made

---

20. *Meeks v. Computer Assocs. Int'l*, 15 F.3d 1013, 1017 (11th Cir.1994).

21. *Id.* at 1017.

22. *Foster v. Arcata Assocs., Inc.*, 772 F.2d 1453, 1464 (9th Cir.1985), *cert. denied*, 475 U.S. 1048, 106 S.Ct. 1267, 89 L.Ed.2d 576 (1986).

23. *Id.* at 1464–65.

§ 8.5

1. 29 U.S.C.A. § 206(d)(1).

2. *Timmer v. Michigan Dep't of Commerce*, 104 F.3d 833, 843 (6th Cir.1997).

3. *EEOC v. Aetna Ins. Co.*, 616 F.2d 719, 724 (4th Cir.1980) (citing *Hodgson v. Colonnades, Inc.*, 472 F.2d 42, 47 (5th Cir. 1973)).

4. *Stanziale v. Jargowsky*, 200 F.3d 101, 107–08 (3d Cir.2000).

5. 200 F.3d 101 (3d Cir.2000).

pursuant to a factor other than sex. Because it was [defendants'] burden to establish this fact "so clearly that no rational jury could find to the contrary", the appellate court found that the grant of defendants' motion for summary judgment was error.[6]

Similarly, in *Ryduchowski v. Port Authority of N.Y. and N.J.*,[7] the Second Circuit reversed a trial court's grant of judgment as a matter of law after a plaintiff's verdict on her EPA claim. The appellate court found that the jury could have reasonably concluded that the defendant failed to meet its burden to establish that a valid merit system was in place and systematically administered.[8]

Affirmative defenses (i)-(iii) are rarely used. These three defenses specifically require a "system." This system must be an organized and structured procedure,[9] and employees must know about the system.[10] And a defendant asserting a seniority system affirmative defense must "be able to identify standards for measuring seniority which are systematically applied and observed."[11] Further, the system must be operated in good faith and not used as a way to maintain sex-based wage differences. The third defense of a system based on quality or quantity of production, however, has little independent vitality. First, if employees are paid the same "rate" for their work based on production, there is no EPA violation. Second, a quality or quantity system is so closely related to a merit system that it has no separate identity. The majority of litigation in the area of affirmative defenses, therefore, has centered around the rather ambiguous defense (iv), "any factor other than sex."

Examples of "factors other than sex" include salary retention policies, prior salary consideration, and economic benefit to the employer.[12] In determining that a salary retention policy qualified as a "factor other than sex," a district court noted that the policy was part of a company-

6. *Id.* at 108.

7. 203 F.3d 135 (2d Cir.), *cert. denied,* ___ U.S. ___, 120 S.Ct. 2743, 147 L.Ed.2d 1007 (2000).

8. *Id.* at 143–45.

9. *See Ryduchowski v. Port Authority of N.Y. and N.J.*, 203 F.3d 135, 142–43 (2d Cir.), *cert. denied,* ___ U.S. ___, 120 S.Ct. 2743, 147 L.Ed.2d 1007 (2000) (reinstating plaintiff's jury verdict and holding that defendant failed to prove it had formulated an organized and structured system based on predetermined criteria and also that it had systematically administered its plans for a merit system.; *Aetna Ins. Co.*, 616 F.2d at 725; *Maxwell v. City of Tucson*, 803 F.2d 444, 447 (9th Cir.1986); *Ottaviani v. SUNY at New Paltz*, 679 F.Supp. 288, 337 (S.D.N.Y.1988), *aff'd*, 875 F.2d 365 (2d Cir. 1989), *cert. denied*, 493 U.S. 1021, 110 S.Ct. 721, 107 L.Ed.2d 740 (1990).

10. *See Aetna Ins. Co.*, 616 F.2d at 725.

11. *Irby v. Bittick*, 44 F.3d 949, 954 (11th Cir.1995) (but "defined exceptions which are known and understood by the employees" do not invalidate a system). *See also Belfi v. Prendergast*, 191 F.3d 129 (2d Cir.1999) (seniority rules not applied adversely to 3 male comparators as to plaintiff).

12. *See, e.g., Stanley v. University of Southern Calif.*, 178 F.3d 1069 (9th Cir.), *cert. denied*, 528 U.S. 1022, 120 S.Ct. 533, 145 L.Ed.2d 413 (1999) (avoiding question of whether male coach of men's basketball team could be paid more than female coach of women's team by finding male coach's greater experience and better qualifications a "factor other than sex" that justifies a higher rate of pay); *Kouba v. Allstate Ins. Co.*, 691 F.2d 873 (9th Cir.1982); *Hodgson v. Robert Hall Clothes, Inc.*, 473 F.2d 589 (3d Cir.), *cert. denied*, 414 U.S. 866, 94 S.Ct. 50, 38 L.Ed.2d 85 (1973).

wide business strategy.[13] Employees were permitted to retain a previous salary after transfer to a lesser paid position. The court noted that the policy recognized length of service, improved employee morale, and avoided the additional expenses of searching for new employees.

A second factor that may fall within the "any factor other than sex" exception is the use of a prior salary to set a salary with a new company.[14] The Ninth Circuit held use of a prior salary was not flatly prohibited by the EPA because the "any other factor other than sex" defense (unlike the "job relatedness" component of the Title VII "business necessity" defense to disparate impact) is not limited to criteria pertaining to a particular job.[15] The key questions, the court wrote, concern the genuineness and significance of the employer's business reasons for the policy. The Eleventh Circuit also allows reliance on prior salary but only when other business considerations—such as the selectee's greater amount of experience in a closely related job—reasonably explain its utilization.[16]

Another factor that has been approved as something "other than sex" is reliance on differential economic benefit to the employer of otherwise equal "male" and "female" jobs.[17] A clothier could pay its salesmen more than its saleswomen where the men produced greater benefit to the employer because the men's clothing department generated higher profit margins and revenues. Further, the employer considered sex segregation in the jobs unavoidable (deploying only male salespersons in the men's clothing department) to prevent embarrassment to customers.[18]

Several circuits also recognize lesser experience, translating into a lower pay grade, as a factor other than sex.[19] The Ninth Circuit affirmed a district court's grant of summary judgment to the defendant, University of Southern California, in an EPA suit brought by the women's basketball coach, Marianne Stanley. The university justified Stanley's lower pay in comparison to the men's basketball coach based on the men's coach's greater experience, his experience as an Olympic coach, his garnering various national coaching awards, his greater marketing

---

13. *Christiana v. Metropolitan Life Ins. Co.*, 839 F.Supp. 248, 252–54 (S.D.N.Y. 1993).

14. *Kouba*, 691 F.2d 873.

15. *Id.* at 878.

16. *Irby*, 44 F.3d at 955. More experience in similar positions remains a neutral, nondiscriminatory reason even if the plaintiff has greater total service. *See EEOC v. Louisiana Office of Community Servs.*, 47 F.3d 1438 (5th Cir.1995) (case under ADEA). In *Irby*, for example, the male comparator employees were lawfully able to be paid at a higher rate than plaintiff based on their prior salary earned in other positions in the *same division* of the employer. The court acknowledged that prior salary *alone*

cannot justify unequal pay. But it considered its holding consistent with *Kouba* because in *Irby* the facts suggested that experience played only *a* role in setting the salary at the new job. *But see Peters v. City of Shreveport*, 818 F.2d 1148 (5th Cir.1987) (regardless of other factors, where sex is even a "but for" cause, the EPA is violated).

17. *Byrd v. Ronayne*, 61 F.3d 1026 (1st Cir.1995) (alternative holding); *Robert Hall*, 473 F.2d at 597.

18. *Robert Hall*, 473 F.2d at 597.

19. *See, e.g., Wollenburg v. Comtech Manufacturing Co.*, 201 F.3d 973, 976 (7th Cir.2000); *Lindale v. Tokheim Corp.*, 145 F.3d 953, 957–58 (7th Cir.1998).

and promotional experience, and the higher revenue generated for the university by the men's program. The court found that the record "convincingly support[ed]" the university's contention that Stanley was paid less based on "a factor other than sex."[20]

Some factors have been rejected by the courts as not within the "other than sex" exception. For example, compensation disparities keyed to gender-based actuarial differences unlawfully discriminate despite their link to longevity. In *City of Los Angeles, Department of Water and Power v. Manhart*,[21] female city employees were required to pay more into their pension fund than were male employees. The employer argued that the contribution differentials were based upon the statistical generalization that women live longer than men. Observing that longevity hinges on many factors other than gender that vary significantly by individual, the Supreme Court concluded that the longevity factor as applied by the defendant was itself based on gender alone and was not, therefore, a "factor other than sex."

The Court has also rejected time of day as an "other than sex" factor where time of day is the sole difference between the jobs. In *Corning Glass*, the Court determined that the time during which work is performed does not constitute the kind of difference in working conditions that renders jobs "unequal;" instead time of work should be analyzed as a possible "factor other than sex."[22] The Court acknowledged that a shift differential is permitted under the EPA provided that it is nondiscriminatory in origin and application. While Corning had paid men a higher wage for night work than for day work when women were not permitted to work at night, these differentials continued even after women were admitted to night work. Against this background, the Court found the shift differential discriminatory and not a "factor other than sex."

§§ 8.6–10.9 [Reserved]

B. RETALIATION

§ 8.10 In General

The FLSA anti-retaliation provision, applicable by reference to EPA, prohibits retaliation in language more cramped than § 704 of Title VII. By offering protection against reprisal only to those who have "filed any complaint" or "instituted any proceeding," it does not in terms protect those who have made an informal on-the-job protest. But the federal judiciary views access to available avenues of protest of such importance

20. *Stanley v. University of S. Cal.*, 178 F.3d 1069, 1075 (9th Cir.), *cert. denied*, 528 U.S. 1022, 120 S.Ct. 533, 145 L.Ed.2d 413 (1999).

21. 435 U.S. 702, 98 S.Ct. 1370, 55 L.Ed.2d 657 (1978). *Manhart* involved a Title VII claim. However, the Court concluded that the Bennett Amendment to Title VII

incorporated the EPA affirmative defenses into Title VII litigation. The Court therefore construed the "any factor other than sex" EPA defense and applied it to a claim under Title VII.

22. See text *supra*, § 8.3.

that at least five circuit courts have nevertheless extended such protection to informal protesters.[1] Indeed EPA has been held to authorize compensatory and punitive damages for unlawful retaliation.[2]

§§ 8.11–10.14 [Reserved]

C. UNEQUAL PAY FOR EQUAL WORK: EPA AND TITLE VII COMPARED

§ 8.15 In General

Why would some plaintiffs resort to the Equal Pay Act, with its narrow proscription of one limited kind of sex-based wage discrimination, when Title VII in addition prohibits other forms of sex-based wage discrimination as well as sex discrimination affecting different terms and conditions of employment? The answer lies in varying proof requirements and differences in enforcement and remedial schemes.

In an unequal pay for equal work situation, there are three possible ways of proving a claim under Title VII. A plaintiff may offer "direct" evidence of gender discriminatory intent, evidence from which such discriminatory intent may be inferred, or evidence that establishes an EPA violation. The federal circuit decisions are divided over which of these proof modes is permissible or indispensable. The Fifth Circuit, for example, requires direct evidence of discriminatory intent to show an "equal pay" violation of Title VII.[1] The court concluded from the Supreme Court's *County of Washington v. Gunther*[2] decision that only a transparently based sex-biased system for wage determination could state an unequal pay for equal work claim under Title VII. The Seventh Circuit has said the same.[3] For these courts, then, the *Gunther* facts represent the outer limit of Title VII liability for gender-based discrimination in compensation.

§ 8.10

1. *See EEOC v. Romeo Community Schs.*, 976 F.2d 985, 989 (6th Cir.1992); *EEOC v. White and Son Enters.*, 881 F.2d 1006, 1011 (11th Cir.1989); *Brock v. Richardson*, 812 F.2d 121, 124–25 (3d Cir.1987); *Love v. RE/Max of Am., Inc.*, 738 F.2d 383, 387 (10th Cir.1984); *Brennan v. Maxey's Yamaha, Inc.*, 513 F.2d 179, 181 (8th Cir. 1975). *But see Lambert v. Genesee Hosp.*, 10 F.3d 46 (2d Cir.1993), *cert. denied*, 511 U.S. 1052, 114 S.Ct. 1612, 128 L.Ed.2d 339 (1994) (construing language strictly to find no protection to informal protestor).

2. *Travis v. Gary Community Mental Health Ctr., Inc.*, 921 F.2d 108, 112 (7th Cir.1990), *cert. denied*, 502 U.S. 812, 112 S.Ct. 60, 116 L.Ed.2d 36 (1991). The court reasoned that in amending FLSA to include "legal" as well as "equitable" relief as ap-

propriate, Congress intended to include compensatory and punitive damages for intentional torts. *Id.* at 111–12.

§ 8.15

1. *Plemer v. Parsons–Gilbane*, 713 F.2d 1127, 1133–34 (5th Cir.1983).

2. 452 U.S. 161, 101 S.Ct. 2242, 68 L.Ed.2d 751 (1981). See Section E below for a thorough discussion of *Gunther*.

3. *EEOC v. Sears, Roebuck & Co.*, 839 F.2d 302, 340–342 (7th Cir.1988). Only a year later, however, another panel (with, however, only one different judge) strongly suggested that a plaintiff could prevail in a gender-based compensation action under Title VII by meeting the burdens of proof specified by *McDonnell Douglas* and *Burdine*. *Fallon v. Illinois*, 882 F.2d 1206, 1213–1217 (7th Cir.1989).

On the other hand, several circuits have decided that the *McDonnell Douglas/Burdine*[4] inferential evidence approach may be used in an unequal pay for equal work situation to prove a violation of Title VII.[5] These circuits, however, divide over whether the traditional Title VII allocation of burdens of proof, or the very different framework established by the EPA, controls. A slim majority consider Title VII and EPA claims completely independent; these courts require proof that meets the distinct elements and burden shifts of each statute.[6] Other circuits, however, hold that a violation of the EPA is *ipso facto* a violation of Title VII, so that the Title VII claim requires no additional proof.[7] Regulations promulgated by the EEOC support the latter view.[8]

The difference between these approaches can substantially affect outcome. The prima facie case for an EPA claim is that the employer pays different wages to employees of the opposite sex for "equal work"— work requiring equal skill, effort, and responsibility and performed under similar working conditions.[9] Once the plaintiff has made this showing, the defendant bears the burden of establishing—producing evidence and persuading by a preponderance—one of the affirmative defenses. There is no separate requirement under the EPA that the plaintiff offer evidence of intent to discriminate; in this sense the EPA has been called a "strict liability" statute.[10]

By contrast, the standard, inferential prima facie evidence required to establish a Title VII individual disparate treatment claim merely *begins* with a showing that the plaintiff occupies a job similar to that of a higher paid member of the opposite sex.[11] The defendant must then

4. See Chapter 3, Section B for a complete discussion of this inferential way of proving a Title VII claim.

5. *See, e.g., Miranda v. B & B Cash Grocery, Inc.,* 975 F.2d 1518, 1530–31 (11th Cir.1992) and cases cited *infra*.

6. *See Meeks v. Computer Assocs. Int'l,* 15 F.3d 1013, 1021 (11th Cir.1994); *Tidwell v. Fort Howard Corp.,* 989 F.2d 406, 410–12 (10th Cir.1993); *Fallon v. Illinois,* 882 F.2d 1206, 1213–1217 (7th Cir.1989); *Peters v. City of Shreveport,* 818 F.2d 1148, 1154–55 (5th Cir.1987), *cert. dismissed,* 485 U.S. 930, 108 S.Ct. 1101, 99 L.Ed.2d 264 (1988); *Brewster v. Barnes,* 788 F.2d 985, 992–93 (4th Cir.1986).

7. *See Korte v. Diemer,* 909 F.2d 954, 959 (6th Cir.1990); *Floyd v. Kellogg Sales Co.,* 841 F.2d 226, 229 n. 2 (8th Cir.), *cert. denied,* 488 U.S. 970, 109 S.Ct. 501, 102 L.Ed.2d 537 (1988); *McKee v. Bi–State Dev. Agency,* 801 F.2d 1014, 1019 (8th Cir.1986); *Kouba v. Allstate Ins. Co.,* 691 F.2d 873, 875 (9th Cir.1982).

8. 29 C.F.R. § 1620.27(a) (1993). The regulation states in relevant part,"[W]here the jurisdictional prerequisites of both the EPA and [T]itle VII ... are satisfied, any violation of the [EPA] is also a violation of Title VII."

9. *See Gunther,* 452 U.S. at 168, 101 S.Ct. at 2247.

10. *See Ryduchowski v. the Port Authority of N.Y. and N.J.,* 203 F.3d 135, 142 (2d Cir.), *cert. denied,* ___ U.S. ___, 120 S.Ct. 2743, 147 L.Ed.2d 1007 (2000); *Belfi v. Prendergast,* 191 F.3d 129 (2d Cir.1999); *Meeks v. Computer Assocs. Int'l,* 15 F.3d 1013, 1019 (11th Cir.1994); *Patkus v. Sangamon–Cass Consortium,* 769 F.2d 1251, 1260 n. 5 (7th Cir.1985); *Strecker v. Grand Forks County Social Service Bd.,* 640 F.2d 96, 99 n. 1 (8th Cir.1980).

11. The Eleventh Circuit recognized that Title VII incorporates a more "relaxed standard" of similarity between male and female occupied jobs. The plaintiff, therefore, is not required to meet the exacting standard of substantial equality of positions set forth in the EPA. The court, however, did not elaborate on what this "relaxed standard" was. The court explicitly stated that this "relaxed standard" applied only in "disparate treatment" cases. *Miranda v. B & B Cash Grocery Store, Inc.,* 975 F.2d 1518, 1526 & n. 11 (11th Cir.1992).

produce evidence of a legitimate nondiscriminatory reason for paying less. If the defendant does so, the plaintiff may still prevail by proving in a variety of ways that the employer intended to discriminate based on gender.[12] In sharp contrast to EPA, employer intent is critical, and it is the Title VII plaintiff who throughout the case bears the risk of nonpersuasion on the "ultimate" question of intentional disparate treatment because of sex.[13]

The Fourth, Fifth, Seventh, Tenth, and Eleventh Circuits view EPA and Title VII claims as entirely distinct, with the plaintiff bearing the respective burdens imposed by each statute.[14] To prevail under Title VII, the plaintiff must establish an intent to discriminate on the part of the employer, and the burden of persuasion rests with the plaintiff throughout. The employer is required merely to advance through evidence a legitimate justification once the plaintiff has made the prima facie showing. In virtually all litigated cases the employer should have little difficulty rebutting the prima facie case in this fashion. Thus the case will usually turn on whether the plaintiff persuades the factfinder by a preponderance of all the evidence that the defendant intended to discriminate.

The Sixth, Eighth, and Ninth Circuits, on the other hand, have viewed the distinction between EPA and Title VII claims as "overly technical"[15] and have accordingly melded the EPA proof structure into the trial of Title VII claims.[16] For example, the Sixth Circuit in *Korte v. Diemer* concluded, "A finding of 'sex discrimination in compensation' under one Act [EPA] is tantamount to a finding of 'pay discrimination on the basis of sex' under the other [Title VII]."[17] Put otherwise, gender based pay disparities found prima facie to be based on sex and not employer-justified by nondiscriminatory reasons cannot later be found to lack an underlying unlawful intent to discriminate within the meaning of Title VII.[18]

Ironically, these circuits, like those that take the opposite view and require distinct evidence of intent through the mode established under Title VII, have relied heavily on *County of Washington v. Gunther*.[19] The Supreme Court there held that Title VII's Bennett Amendment extended the four affirmative defenses of EPA to a defendant facing an unequal pay claim under Title VII, and left the door open for other kinds of Title

---

12. *See Texas Dept. of Community Affairs v. Burdine*, 450 U.S. 248, 101 S.Ct. 1089, 67 L.Ed.2d 207 (1981); *McDonnell Douglas Corp. v. Green*, 411 U.S. 792, 93 S.Ct. 1817, 36 L.Ed.2d 668 (1973).

13. *See St. Mary's Honor Center v. Hicks* and *Burdine*, discussed at length in Chapter 3.

14. *Meeks*, 15 F.3d 1013; *Tidwell*, 989 F.2d 406; *Fallon*, 882 F.2d 1206; *Peters*, 818 F.2d 1148; *Brewster*, 788 F.2d 985.

15. *See Korte v. Diemer*, 909 F.2d 954, 959 (6th Cir.1990).

16. *See Korte*, 909 F.2d 954; *Floyd*, 841 F.2d 226; *McKee*, 801 F.2d 1014; *Kouba*, 691 F.2d 873.

17. *Korte*, 909 F.2d at 959; *see also McKee*, 801 F.2d at 1019 ("Where a claim is for unequal pay for equal work based upon sex, the standards of the Equal Pay Act apply whether the suit alleges a violation of the Equal Pay Act or of Title VII.").

18. *Korte*, 909 F.2d 954.

19. 452 U.S. 161, 101 S.Ct. 2242, 68 L.Ed.2d 751.

VII prima facie claims of sex-based wage discrimination. In passing, the Court also observed that it was not addressing how the litigation of a Title VII claim of unequal pay for equal work should be structured to take into account the EPA affirmative defense that effectively requires the *employer* to show that wage discrimination is based on a "factor other than sex."[20] One inference that might be drawn from this passage is that only intentional discrimination is prima facie actionable under EPA.[21] But the "equating" circuits have read *Gunther* to imply that EPA is violated simply by a showing of unequal pay for equal work, without more, and that the Title VII plaintiff complaining of unequal pay need only satisfy the standards and burdens of the EPA. That is, the Title VII plaintiff with a claim of sex-based wage discrimination need not prove, as she might for similar Title VII claims, an intent to discriminate, and the employer must prove one of the statutory affirmative defenses by a preponderance of the evidence.

These circuit opinions express the desire to interpret the EPA and Title VII harmoniously, as well as the fear that distinguishing between the statutes in equal pay for equal work situations would produce inconsistent results depending solely on how the plaintiff states her claim. By relieving the plaintiff of her typical Title VII burden to prove intentional discrimination in unequal pay for equal work cases, these circuits have in effect permitted the plaintiff to prevail on claims under both the EPA and Title VII by prevailing under either. But the employer's failure to meet its burden of persuasion on the EPA "factor other than sex" affirmative defense may show only that "the trier of fact cannot conclusively decide"; that result is "not inconsistent with a finding that the employer did not intentionally discriminate [for Title VII purposes] because discriminatory intent is not an element of an Equal Pay Act claim."[22]

For a time, these different approaches in the circuits had minimal practical importance. The remedies under EPA were more congenial to the plaintiff than the remedies under Title VII, because EPA afforded the possibility of liquidated damages while Title VII often remitted the plaintiff to back pay. In that regime the plaintiff with only an equal pay claim usually took the EPA route, foregoing the separate remedy under Title VII. But the passage of the Civil Rights Act of 1991 has expanded the remedies under Title VII to include compensatory as well as punitive damages for intentional or "disparate treatment" violations; and most EPA violations fit that description, even if no direct evidence of intent is required. In the circuits that import the eased EPA standards into Title VII equal pay litigation, the plaintiff can now recover Title VII's potentially more generous remedies by carrying the lighter EPA burden.

20. *Id.* at 170, 101 S.Ct. at 2248.

21. A divided panel of the Seventh Circuit recently read *Gunther* that way. *EEOC v. Francis W. Parker Sch.*, 41 F.3d 1073, 1077 (7th Cir.1994), *cert. denied*, 515 U.S. 1142, 115 S.Ct. 2577, 132 L.Ed.2d 828 (1995).

22. *Fallon*, 882 F.2d at 1216.

Perhaps these circuits should therefore reassess their conclusion that the distinction between the two is merely "technical."

§§ 8.16–10.19 [Reserved]

D. ENFORCEMENT AND REMEDIES

§ 8.20 Enforcement

Although the EEOC has enforcement responsibility and may file civil actions under the EPA, a private plaintiff need not exhaust state or federal administrative remedies before proceeding to court. Under provisions of the FLSA that EPA incorporates by reference, the action may be brought in either state or federal court against either a private or public employer.[1] A suit may be brought under the EPA by either an employee or the EEOC. The EPA grants the authority to the Secretary of Labor to initiate suit against an employer for monetary damages or injunctive relief. In 1978, President Carter, under the authority of the Reorganization Act of 1977,[2] implemented a reorganization plan that transferred EPA enforcement authority from the Secretary of Labor to EEOC. The courts have upheld the constitutionality of this transfer.[3]

While under Title VII the EEOC must try to eliminate an unlawful practice through informal methods of conciliation,[4] the EPA contains no similar provision. The Court in *Gunther* noted that "the Equal Pay Act, unlike Title VII, has no requirement of filing administrative complaints and awaiting administrative conciliation efforts."[5] Accordingly, courts have found no requirement of prior administrative filing or informal conciliation.[6]

An employee may initiate suit against an employer seeking monetary damages up until the point the EEOC files a complaint against the employer. When the EEOC files against the employer, the employee's right to sue or become a party to an action brought by other employees is terminated. The EEOC's suit is deemed to commence from the date a complaint is filed that names EEOC as a party plaintiff or from the date the EEOC's name is added as a party plaintiff.

An employee may bring suit individually or on behalf of a class. As under ADEA, if the suit is brought as a class action, each class member

§ 8.20

1. 29 U.S.C.A. § 216(b).

2. 5 U.S.C.A. §§ 901–12.

3. *See, e.g., EEOC v. Hernando Bank, Inc.*, 724 F.2d 1188 (5th Cir.1984); *Muller Optical Co. v. EEOC*, 743 F.2d 380 (6th Cir.1984) (transfer of ADEA enforcement to EEOC constitutional).

4. 42 U.S.C.A. § 2000e–5(b) requires the EEOC to "endeavor to eliminate any ... alleged unlawful employment practice by informal methods of conference, conciliation, and persuasion" before it can bring a

Title VII action. See Chapter 4, Section A for discussion of the administrative prerequisites and procedural requirements under Title VII.

5. County of Washington v. Gunther, 452 U.S. 161, 175 n. 14, 101 S.Ct. 2242, 2251 n. 14, 68 L.Ed.2d 751 (1981).

6. *See Hernando Bank*, 724 F.2d at 1194; *Ososky v. Wick*, 704 F.2d 1264 (D.C.Cir.1983); *EEOC v. Home of Econ., Inc.*, 712 F.2d 356 (8th Cir.1983).

must consent in writing to become a party and the consent must be filed with the court.[7]

§ 8.21   Limitations

An EPA action is governed by the FLSA statute of limitations. The FLSA provides a two year statute of limitations for filing, three years in the case of a "willful" violation.[1] These statutes of limitations compare favorably from the plaintiff's perspective with the 180–day or 300–day administrative filing deadlines of Title VII, now also made applicable to ADEA. (See Chapter 4, Section A for further discussion of the Title VII time limitations and see Chapter 7, Section 3 for further discussion of ADEA time limitations).

The three-year limitations period for willful violations is available, under the terms of the Portal-to-Portal Act of 1947,[2] when an employer knows that, or recklessly disregards whether, its conduct violates the statute.[3] The Court observed in *McLaughlin v. Richland Shoe Co.* that willfulness under the FLSA refers to conduct that is more than merely negligent; yet it also held that the requisite willfulness may be found not just when the employer believes its conduct violates the statute but also when the employer is shown to have been merely indifferent to whether its conduct constitutes such a violation.[4]

§ 8.22   Continuing Violations

The judicially-created "continuing violations" doctrine provides certain plaintiffs an escape from the statute of limitations. The doctrine allows a court to take jurisdiction over a cause of action, or impose liability, for a discrete EPA violation that occurred outside the limitations period. Plaintiffs have invoked the doctrine under both the Equal Pay Act and Title VII, but the courts have afforded it a wider sweep in EPA cases. This is probably because of the nature of the sole EPA violation, which is predicated on unequal compensation, a fact of workplace life that continues from paycheck to paycheck.[1]

Two decisions of the Sixth Circuit illustrate how the continuing violations doctrine is applied to EPA claims.

---

7. 29 U.S.C.A. § 216(b). Under either ADEA or EPA, therefore, a class action may not be pursued under Federal Rule of Civil Procedure 23, only by those who have consented in writing. *See Lachapelle v. Owens–Illinois, Inc.*, 513 F.2d 286 (5th Cir.1975).

§ 8.21

1. 29 U.S.C. § 255(a).

2. 29 U.S.C.A. §§ 251 *et seq.*

3. *See McLaughlin v. Richland Shoe Co.*, 486 U.S. 128, 133, 108 S.Ct. 1677, 1681, 100 L.Ed.2d 115 (1988).

4. *Trans World Airlines, Inc. v. Thurston*, 469 U.S. 111, 125–29, 105 S.Ct. 613, 623–26, 83 L.Ed.2d 523 (1985) (ADEA case); *Walton v. United Consumers Club, Inc.*, 786 F.2d 303, 310–11 (7th Cir.1986); *EEOC v. Madison Community Unit Sch. Dist. No. 12*, 818 F.2d 577, 585 (7th Cir. 1987).

§ 8.22

1. *Brinkley-Obu v. Hughes Training, Inc.*, 36 F.3d 336 (4th Cir.1994). For a discussion of the continuing violations doctrine in Title VII cases, *see* Section 4.3.

In *EEOC v. Penton Industrial Publishing Co.*,[2] the defendant paid female workers less than a similarly-situated male worker. The plaintiff brought suit more than three years after the male worker was terminated. The employer argued that unequal pay ended when the male comparator was terminated and that the statute of limitations therefore barred the plaintiff's claim. Because the plaintiff could not show an "overarching policy of discrimination," the court, deeming the plaintiff's current unequal pay merely a "present effect to a past act of discrimination" rather than a "present violation," labeled the discrimination "isolated" and upheld the limitations defense.[3]

Six years after *Penton*, the same circuit announced that "because each unequal paycheck is considered a separate violation of the Equal Pay Act, a cause of action may be brought for any or all violations occurring within the limitations period...."[4] In *Gandy v. Sullivan County*,[5] the plaintiff took a position at a pay rate below that of her predecessor and was paid unequally for nine years before she filed suit. The defendant argued that the statute tolled three years after the first unequal paycheck. The court concluded that an equal pay violation occurred each time the plaintiff received an "unequal" paycheck. Further, an action was not time-barred as long as at least one discriminatory act occurred within the limitations period. The Court distinguished the holdings in *Penton* and *Gandy*,[6] but also questioned the *Penton* decision, noting that "the court in *Penton* [did] not suggest how the discrimination ceased since the female employees continued to be compensated at the discriminatory rate...."[7]

A majority of circuits concur with *Gandy* that an actionable EPA violation occurs each time an employee receives an "unequal" paycheck; the defendant will not usually succeed by arguing that the statute began to run on the date of the first such paycheck.[8] In contrast, the Supreme Court has severely limited the scope of the continuing violation concept in Title VII actions,[9] usually by the device of defining the alleged

---

2. 851 F.2d 835 (6th Cir.1988).

3. *Id.* at 838.

4. *Gandy v. Sullivan County*, 24 F.3d 861, 865 (6th Cir.1994).

5. *Id.*

6. *Id.* Although the court's distinction was somewhat different, it may fairly be said that in *Gandy*, but not *Penton*, all the elements of an unequal pay violation, including a comparator, were still in place within the limitations period.

7. *Id.*

8. *See, e.g., Pollis v. New Sch. for Soc. Research*, 132 F.3d 115 (2d Cir.1997) (but recovery is limited to the statutory period); *Ashley v. Boyle's Famous Corned Beef Co.*, 66 F.3d 164 (8th Cir.1995); *Gandy v. Sullivan County*, 24 F.3d 861 (6th Cir.1994); *Knight v. Columbus*, 19 F.3d 579 (11th Cir.), *cert. denied*, 513 U.S. 929, 115 S.Ct.

318, 130 L.Ed.2d 280 (1994); *Nealon v. Stone*, 958 F.2d 584 (4th Cir.1992); *Miller v. Beneficial Mgt. Corp.*, 977 F.2d 834 (3d Cir.1992); *Webb v. Indiana Nat'l Bank*, 931 F.2d 434 (7th Cir.1991); *Berry v. Bd. of Supervisors of La. State. Univ.*, 783 F.2d 1270 (5th Cir.), *cert. denied*, 479 U.S. 868, 107 S.Ct. 232, 93 L.Ed.2d 158 (1986); *Gibbs v. Pierce County Law Enforcement Support Agency*, 785 F.2d 1396 (9th Cir.1986); *EEOC v. McCarthy*, 768 F.2d 1 (1st Cir. 1985).

9. *See, e.g., United Air Lines, Inc. v. Evans*, 431 U.S. 553, 97 S.Ct. 1885, 52 L.Ed.2d 571 (1977); *Delaware State College v. Ricks*, 449 U.S. 250, 101 S.Ct. 498, 66 L.Ed.2d 431 (1980); and *Lorance v. AT & T Techs.*, 490 U.S. 900, 109 S.Ct. 2261, 104 L.Ed.2d 961 (1989).

unlawful employment practice as complete as of an early date more than 180 or 300 days before the plaintiff has filed a charge with EEOC. The circuits have followed suit.

In *Ross v. Buckeye Cellulose Corp.*,[10] for example, the plaintiff brought suit under Title VII four years after he was subjected to an allegedly discriminatory wage determination program. Plaintiff Ross argued that the paychecks he received immediately before he filed suit "continued" the discrimination into the limitations period. The court concluded that while a continuing present violation—such as reapplication of the program within the limitations period—extends the period, a mere lingering consequence of past discrimination—the recent "unequal" paycheck in *Ross*—does not.[11]

§ 8.23 Remedies

EPA remedies are governed by two provisions of FLSA, 29 U.S.C.A. §§ 216 and 217. These sections authorize recovery not only of unlawfully withheld wages (the rough equivalent of Title VII "back pay") but also of an equal amount denominated "liquidated damages." An employee plaintiff may then recover unlawfully withheld wages, liquidated damages and attorney fees plus costs. Unlawfully withheld wages accrue from no earlier than two years prior to the filing of the complaint and continue until a court order. The accrual period begins three years prior to the filing of a complaint if the employer is found to have acted "willfully." Timeliness of filing is measured as of the date an individual plaintiff files a suit, or in a class action, from the date the plaintiff is added as a named plaintiff.

Before the Portal-to-Portal Act of 1947, the imposition of liquidated damages was mandatory. After the passage of the Act, however, liquidated damages became discretionary with the trial judge.[1] She may not award liquidated damages when the employer proves "to the satisfaction of the court" that it acted in good faith and had a reasonable belief that its conduct did not violate FLSA. The burden is on the employer to show that it acted in the sincere and reasonable belief that its conduct was lawful.

Suppose a jury finds that the defendant acted willfully for purposes of the 2- or 3-year statute of limitations. Does this finding become the law of the case, so that the trial judge must then determine that the employer acted in bad faith for liquidated damages purposes? The Supreme Court has defined willful—the 3-year limitations trigger—to mean that the employer "knew or showed reckless disregard for the matter of whether its conduct was prohibited."[2] Good faith—which

10. 980 F.2d 648 (11th Cir.1993), *cert. denied*, 513 U.S. 814, 115 S.Ct. 69, 130 L.Ed.2d 24 (1994).

     11. *Id.* at 658.

§ 8.23

     1. 29 U.S.C.A. § 260.

2. *Thurston*, 469 U.S. at 128–29, 105 S.Ct. at 624 (case under ADEA, which, like EPA, borrows FLSA remedies). *See EEOC v. Cherry-Burrell Corp.*, 35 F.3d 356 (8th Cir.1994).

avoids liquidated damages—has been defined to mean "an honest intention to ascertain what the . . . Act requires and to act in accordance with it."[3] Under these definitions, wilfulness and good faith appear mutually exclusive, unless "reckless disregard" is somehow reconcilable with "an honest intention to ascertain what the . . . Act requires. . . ." The Fifth, Sixth, Eighth and Tenth Circuits accordingly conclude that a finding of willfulness by the jury mandates the imposition of liquidated damages by the judge.[4] But by giving full sway to the jury's determination on willfulness, these courts deprive the defendant of its statutory right to have the "court" determine its good faith for purposes of damages.[5] This interpretation nullifies the provision for judicial discretion to award liquidated damages whenever more than two years have elapsed between accrual of the claim and filing of the action.[6]

One circuit, treating the willfulness that lengthens the limitations period as signifying simply conscious or voluntary conduct, not bad purpose, has concluded that a practice may be deliberate or willful, notwithstanding that it is honestly motivated.[7] Under this view an action may proceed based on the three-year statute of limitations and the defendant still escape liquidated damages. This decision was rendered, however, before the Supreme Court's attempts to define the ADEA and FLSA concept of willfulness in, respectively, *Trans World Airlines, Inc. v. Thurston* and *McLaughlin v. Richland Shoe Co.*[8] The Fourth Circuit has nevertheless taken the same position after *Thurston* and *McLaughlin*: "We do not believe that . . . Congressional intent would be effectuated by a scheme in which, in every case, the trial court's discretion to award liquidated damages would be completely constrained by the jury's determination on 'willfulness' for the purposes of the statute of limitations."[9]

In 1974, FLSA was amended to extend the reach of EPA to state and local government employers. The constitutional validity of this extension was assured when the Supreme Court, overruling *National League of Cities v. Usery*,[10] rejected a Tenth Amendment challenge to the power of the federal government to regulate wages and hours of state and local government entities under the FLSA.[11]

3. *Laffey v. Northwest Airlines, Inc.*, 567 F.2d 429, 464 (D.C.Cir.1976), *cert. denied*, 434 U.S. 1086, 98 S.Ct. 1281, 55 L.Ed.2d 792 (1978).

4. *Brinkman v. Department of Corrections of Kansas*, 21 F.3d 370 (10th Cir.), *cert. denied*, 513 U.S. 927, 115 S.Ct. 315, 130 L.Ed.2d 277 (1994); *EEOC v. City of Detroit Health Dep't*, 920 F.2d 355 (6th Cir.1990); *Blackmon v. Brookshire Grocery Co.*, 835 F.2d 1135 (5th Cir.1988); *McKee v. Bi–State Dev. Agency*, 801 F.2d 1014 (8th Cir.1986).

5. The employer is given the opportunity to demonstrate "to the satisfaction of the court that the act or omission giving rise to such action was in good faith and that he had reasonable grounds for believing that his act or omission was not violative of the [Act]." 29 U.S.C.A. § 260.

6. The damages issues would be reached in such cases only if the limitations question was resolved favorably to the plaintiff.

7. *Laffey*, 567 F.2d at 463.

8. See respectively §§ 9.25 (ADEA) and 8.21 (EPA).

9. *Fowler v. Land Management Groupe, Inc.*, 978 F.2d 158, 163 (4th Cir.1992).

10. 426 U.S. 833, 96 S.Ct. 2465, 49 L.Ed.2d 245 (1976).

11. *Garcia v. San Antonio Metro. Transit Auth.*, 469 U.S. 528, 105 S.Ct. 1005, 83

§§ 8.24–10.29 [Reserved]

E. GENDER–BASED COMPENSATION DISCRIMI-NATION PROHIBITED BY TITLE VII AL-THOUGH NOT REACHED BY EPA

§ 8.30 In General

To better understand how Title VII's reach can sometimes exceed EPA's, we must start with the Supreme Court's attempt in *County of Washington v. Gunther*[1] to explain the relationship between the statutes in unequal pay situations. *Gunther* itself dealt with a situation in which the pay discrimination alleged did not implicate EPA because it was established that the male and female comparator jobs did not involve substantially equal work. Instead, the question raised was whether by virtue of the Bennett Amendment to Title VII,[2] part of § 703(h), all gender-based compensation discrimination not prohibited by EPA is by that fact alone insulated from regulation under Title VII. The Court's answer to that broad question was no.

The Court in *Gunther* was faced with the argument on one hand that the Bennett Amendment required that any Title VII claim for gender-based wage discrimination was prohibited unless there was unequal pay for equal work. On the other hand, the Court heard that the Amendment merely extended the four EPA affirmative defenses to a Title VII cause of action.

The majority opinion by Justice Brennan took the latter view. It focused on the meaning of "authorized" as used in the Amendment. The Court concluded that the only conduct affirmatively authorized by the EPA was that embraced by the affirmative defenses. It could not imagine that the Congress that wrote EPA could have intended by silence to authorize any kind of sex-based wage discrimination other than unequal pay for equal work that the employer has justified under one of the EPA affirmative defenses; apart from those defenses, the Court observed, EPA contained only prohibitory language. Looking to legislative history, the Court also concluded that the "technical" nature of the Bennett Amendment supported the reading that only the EPA affirmative defenses, and not the limited EPA prohibition, should be incorporated into Title VII.

L.Ed.2d 1016 (1985). *See also* cases cited in § 8.2 (rejecting Eleventh Amendment immunity of states in actions under EPA).

§ 8.30

1. 452 U.S. 161, 101 S.Ct. 2242, 68 L.Ed.2d 751 (1981).

2. 78 Stat. 257, 42 U.S.C.A. § 2000e-2(h). The Bennett Amendment provides:

It shall not be unlawful employment practice under this title [Title VII] to differentiate upon the basis of sex in determining the amount of the wages paid or to be paid to employees of such employer if such differentiation is *authorized by* the provisions of § 6(d) of the Fair Labor Standards Act of 1938, as amended.

29 U.S.C.A. § 206(d) [i.e., EPA] (emphasis supplied).

Finally, the Court considered the practical ramifications of requiring gender-based wage discrimination claim to be prohibited by the EPA before it could be actionable under Title VII. This interpretation would deprive a woman who suffered intentional discrimination of any remedy for compensation discrimination when she held a unique position, i.e. one that by hypothesis is not held by any comparator. Another example, furnished by *Manhart*, is that of a woman forced to pay more into a pension fund than male employees. If no male employee in that organization holds a position "equal" to that of a particular woman plaintiff, she might have no Title VII remedy; another female employee, with a job "equal" to that of a male counterpart, would. Thus the Court concluded that at least some Title VII sex-based wage discrimination claims could lie although they are not banned by EPA.

The dissent, authored by then-Justice Rehnquist, relied principally on the legislative history of EPA to support its conclusion. The dissent found a clear congressional consensus, only a year before Title VII was enacted, against recovery in the situation of unequal pay for merely "comparable" rather than "equal" work. Interpreting Title VII to allow for recovery in that situation would dramatically expand liability that Congress had rejected when it focused on the question more particularly and extensively in the debates over EPA; the dissenters could find no warrant for such an implied repeal of EPA. Finally, the dissent attacked the Court's reliance on the public policy rationale, finding that any such determination should be made by Congress not the Court. The dissent thus concluded that all unlawful gender-based wage discrimination, whether under Title VII or EPA, must be contained within the narrow "equal work" concept of EPA.

Gunther on its facts generates a limited holding: *intentional*, indeed virtually express sex discrimination in compensation states a Title VII claim even where jobs are "unequal" within the meaning of EPA. But what if, in a non-EPA situation, the intent to discriminate can be proved only inferentially, a la *McDonnell Douglas/Burdine*? What if the employer has dual intentions, one intentionally discriminatory and another benign, as in *Price Waterhouse*, the landmark Title VII "mixed motives" decision? What of compensation practices neutral on their face that have discriminatory impact by gender? And what of comparable worth? *Gunther* provides little guidance as to the viability of these claims under Title VII.

§§ 8.31–10.34   [Reserved]

F.   THE COMPARABLE WORTH THEORY

§ 8.35   In General

Women are disproportionately concentrated in lower-wage jobs. Because the principle of equal pay for equal work is limited to comparing the wages of individual women and men who perform substantially the same work, it does not address even significant wage disparities between groups of male and female employees holding different positions. The theory of comparable worth seeks to bridge this gap. It would mandate upward adjustment in the wage rates of all those who encumber jobs traditionally held predominantly by women, even without evidence of disparate wages between particular male and female employees whose work is "equal" and without evidence of intentional discrimination based on gender. Plaintiffs would prove simply that a "woman's" job (one held mainly but not exclusively by women) was of similar "worth" to the employer as a "man's" job (one held mainly but not exclusively by men) yet commanded lesser compensation. The revised wage level is supposed to represent a court's or legislature's evaluation of the job's "worth" to the employer.

A claim of equal pay for a job of equal economic "worth" to the employer can succeed, if at all, only under Title VII. By hypothesis, a plaintiff is driven to rely on comparable worth only when there is neither "equal work" or a comparator position, so EPA affords no relief. Under the comparable worth theory, the plaintiff and the higher paid employee are performing different jobs. The similarity is not in the job or the working conditions of the job but rather in the "worth" of the respective jobs to the employer. This line, while conceptually distinct, is in practice sometimes blurred. Suppose, for example, an employer hinges salary increases on employees' contributions to their respective profit centers. Is a court that finds EPA liability because the employer fails to raise a female plaintiff's pay to a level commensurate with her profit-generating capacity implicitly resting liability on the notion of comparable worth?[1]

The difficulty with a comparable worth challenge under Title VII is that the Title VII plaintiff must prove either that a neutral practice had disproportionate adverse impact on her group or that she herself suffered disparate treatment. The impact proof mode challenges a facially neutral practice, not justified by business necessity, that has a disproportionately adverse impact upon members of a group protected by Title VII.[2] The challenge must be to a specific, clearly delineated employment practice. But most compensation systems are heavily keyed to a complex of market factors responsive to supply and demand, factors that may not amount to a single, identifiable practice of the employer. The employer does not create the disparities in the market (at least not by itself), but only builds on them. Further, even if the plaintiff succeeds in establishing the Title VII prima facie impact case, courts typically regard the employer's reliance on market factors to be justified by important, business related reasons.

The other, more common mode of Title VII challenge is disparate treatment.[3] This claim requires proving the employer's intent to treat

§ 8.35

1. *See Mulhall*, 19 F.3d at 596.

2. For a more complete discussion of the disproportionate adverse impact proof mode see Chapter 3, Section D.

3. For complete discussion of disparate treatment, see Chapter 3, Section B.

employees of the opposite sex differently with respect to compensation. As suggested above, the principal Title VII paradigm for proving sex-based wage discrimination is disparate treatment. The Title VII plaintiff must usually[4] prove a gender specific intent to discriminate. That intent cannot be inferred from the bare fact that the employer pays different wages to mixed-gender groups who hold jobs that have similar worth to the employer, even if one gender predominantly holds the better paying job.

Attempts to secure judicial recognition of the comparable worth theory have been conspicuously unsuccessful.[5] In *American Federation of State, County, and Municipal Employees v. Washington,*[6] for example, a class of state employees in job categories at least 70% female brought a Title VII suit alleging sex discrimination. The Ninth Circuit rejected the challenge because the plaintiffs demonstrated neither disparate impact nor disparate treatment. The court concluded that a compensation system which resulted from surveys, hearings, budget proposals, executive actions, and legislative enactments did not constitute a specific, isolatable practice that could serve as the springboard for a claim of disparate impact.[7] The compensation system was the result of complex market factors, not a single practice. The court further concluded that there was no disparate treatment where the state set salaries based upon market rates and those salaries lead to an unintended disparity for jobs deemed of comparable worth. The state did not create the market disparity and was not shown to have been motivated by impermissible sex-based considerations in using the markets to set wages for male-or female-dominated classifications.[8]

In *Spaulding v. University of Washington,*[9] nursing faculty at the University of Washington challenged their compensation under Title VII. The plaintiffs asserted that they were paid less than the faculty in other schools within the University solely because of their participation in a traditionally woman's field. The Ninth Circuit rejected their claim, refusing to infer discriminatory intent from the existence of wage differences between "unequal" jobs. Similarly, the court rejected the disparate impact claim. Reliance on competitive market prices did not constitute an actionable discrete neutral practice or policy. According to the Ninth Circuit, the court should focus on "the substance of the employer's acts and whether those neutral acts are a non-job related pretext to shield an invidious judgment." The court deemed the employ-

---

4. We have already seen the exception, in some circuits, for Title VII unequal pay claims. See text *supra,* § 8.15.

5. The action on this front has been in the state legislatures; but most states, under severe budgetary pressure themselves and fearful of increasing private employers' costs in the midst of recession, continue to reject the notion that market-driven job wage rates equate to discrimination based on gender.

6. 770 F.2d 1401 (9th Cir.1985).

7. *Id.* at 1406. "[S]uch a compensation system [one responsive to supply and demand], the result of complex market forces, does not constitute a single practice that suffices to support a claim under disparate impact theory." *Id.*

8. *Id.* at 1406–07.

9. 740 F.2d 686 (9th Cir.), *cert. denied,* 469 U.S. 1036, 105 S.Ct. 511, 83 L.Ed.2d 401 (1984).

er's reliance on market factors inherently job-related and thus not subject to disparate impact analysis.

The Supreme Court has not addressed the issue of comparable worth. *County of Washington v. Gunther*[10] did not present the issue. The Court made it clear that the challenge was to the employer's practice of intentionally setting the wage scale for female, but not male guards at a lower level than recommended by its survey of outside markets. The employer's survey suggested paying female guards 95% of the salary of male guards, who performed more arduous and dangerous work. Instead, male guards were paid 100% of their determined worth to the employer, while female guards were paid only 70% of the amount paid to the male guards. The failure to pay the women guards in accordance with the employer's commissioned survey was held to be the result of intentional sex discrimination. The Court specifically noted that allowing the claim did not require it to make its own subjective assessment of the value of the male and female guard jobs, or to attempt by statistics or other methods to quantify the effect of sex discrimination. Thus *Gunther* addressed the unusual situation where a wage difference was the result of a "smoking gun" intentional reduction in wages.

Faint hope for the comparable worth theory was furnished by a pair of Supreme Court decisions that suggest the viability of disproportionate adverse impact challenges to "subjective" practices. A plurality in *Watson v. Fort Worth Bank and Trust*[11] held that a discretionary promotion system could be scrutinized under disparate impact analysis even though it could reasonably be termed a "subjective" practice. The Court recognized that a plaintiff can challenge a subjective neutral factor provided she can identify a specific practice and show its causal relationship to a negative impact on her protected group. A year later in *Wards Cove Packing Co v. Atonio*,[12] a Supreme Court majority confirmed that a plaintiff could mount a disparate impact challenge to either an "objective" or "subjective" employment practice. In context, "objective" and "subjective" appear to mean something different from their dictionary definitions. "Objective" means a specific practice particular to the defendant employer. Examples include written tests or education, height and weight requirements. "Subjective," on the other hand, includes general practices, or a complex of practices, that have their origins in society in general—for example, reliance on the market to determine wages. Either type of practice is now apparently susceptible to challenge on the impact theory if the plaintiff can meet the identification and causation requirements.

But the same decisions also substantially fortified the employer's defense to the neutral practice case. Not only did the Court dilute the required link between a practice and a job or business need, it also

---

10. 452 U.S. 161, 101 S.Ct. 2242, 68 L.Ed.2d 751 (1981).

11. 487 U.S. 977, 108 S.Ct. 2777, 101 L.Ed.2d 827 (1988).

12. 490 U.S. 642, 109 S.Ct. 2115, 104 L.Ed.2d 733 (1989).

explicitly relieved the employer of the burden of proof on the defense. The Civil Rights Act of 1991 left untouched the *Watson/Wards Cove* indication that plaintiffs may challenge not only specific, "objective" practices of the particular defendant employer but also general or "subjective" factors having more global or social origins.[13] Yet it also failed definitively to overturn the Court's permissive new formulations of the employer defense. Nominally, it is true, the Act provides, as was generally held before *Wards Cove*, that the employer bears the burden of persuasion. The Act also stiffens the content of the defense, requiring the employer to establish that the challenged practice is "job related" *and* "consistent with business necessity."[14] But the peculiar legislative history accompanying those provisions directs the courts to interpret these terms according to decisions of the Supreme Court that antedated *Wards Cove*. Included among those decisions are some that express an extremely pliable view of both quoted concepts—that effectively treat a practice as justified if it bears any plausible relation to *either* job relatedness *or* business necessity.[15]

Most comparable worth claims will therefore probably still fail. Even if the plaintiff can now establish a prima facie case of adverse impact for the "subjective" pay practice in question, the employer can assert a market-related justification still likely to be adjudged a matter of business necessity.[16] In the face of the case law that consistently rejected comparable worth claims, the silence of the Civil Rights Act of 1991 on the subject is a significant indication that Congress hews to the relatively narrow yardstick of nondiscrimination, eschewing preferential affirmative action or gender-based minimum standards.[17]

---

13. See § 3.35 *supra*.

14. 42 U.S.C.A. 2000e–2(k)(1)(A).

15. For additional discussion of the disproportionate adverse impact case and the changes brought about by the Civil Rights Act of 1991, see Chapter 3, Section D.

16. *See, e.g., Donnelly v. Rhode Island Bd. of Governors for Higher Educ.*, 110 F.3d 2 (1st Cir.1997) (even if salary plan providing different tiers of salaries for different disciplines had disparate impact on female faculty, any differences were attributable to their choice of academic field and the national market influencing salaries in those fields). Alternatively, the practice may be

justified on the theory, asserted in *Spaulding*, that a pay scale geared to the external market is "inherently" job related. The logic of this assertion is a bit elusive, however, since by definition a system that sets wages across the board is not driven by the essential requirements of any given job.

17. *See Smith v. Virginia Commonwealth Univ.*, 84 F.3d 672 (4th Cir.1996) (en banc) (female-preferential pay increases challengeable under EPA even though purportedly adopted as an informal "affirmative action program" in response to salary equity study).

Chapter Nine

PROHIBITIONS ON SEX DISCRIMINATION IN FEDERALLY FUNDED EDUCATION PROGRAMS: TITLE IX

Analysis

§ 9.1 In General

Title IX of the Education Amendments of 1972, modeled after Title VI,[1] prohibits sex discrimination in federally funded programs.[2] Title IX, however, is broader that Title VI because Title XI does not contain the same a general disclaimer of applicability to employment practices found in Title VI. Accordingly, to some degree Title IX redresses employment discrimination on the basis of sex, as well as in admissions and general educational activities, by federally funded education programs.[3]

Despite these differences, the statutes are mostly of similar design, and many of the issues arising under Title VI also arise under Title IX. Accordingly, in *Grove City College v. Bell*, the Supreme Court recognized

---

§ 9.1

1. Title VI of the Civil Rights Act of 1964, codified at 42 U.S.C.A. §§ 2000d—2000d–4a, prohibits discrimination based on race, color, or national origin in federally funded programs or activities. Notwithstanding this broad provision, the Title does not reach employment practices except where a primary objective of the federal assistance is to provide employment. Thus, except for federally funded employment programs, Title VI is unavailable to supplement Title VII of the 1964 Civil Rights Act as a remedy for race or national origin discrimination in employment.

2. Title IX is codified at 20 U.S.C.A. §§ 1681–1688.

3. *North Haven Bd. of Educ. v. Bell*, 456 U.S. 512, 520–35, 102 S.Ct. 1912, 1917–26, 72 L.Ed.2d 299 (1982).

the practice of looking to the substantial body of law developed under Title VI when examining Title IX questions.[4]

Title IX's primary prohibition provides that . . .

No person in the United States shall, on the basis of *sex*, be excluded from participation in, be denied the benefit of, or be subjected to discrimination under any *education* program or activity receiving Federal financial assistance. . . .[5]

Federal assistance includes grants, loans, or contracts other than those of insurance or guaranty.[6] The *Grove City College* holding that federal assistance funneled directly to students constitutes "assistance" to the students' educational institutions, thus triggering Title IX regulation of programs or of the institution itself, appears undisturbed either by subsequent decisions[7] or by the 1987 Restoration Act.

§ 9.2 Covered Programs or Activities

The "program or activity" language in Title IX has followed the same interpretive evolution as the same language in Title VI. Lower courts held that discrimination in any program within an institution receiving federal assistance was a violation of Title IX even though the particular discriminatory program was not the subject of the assistance. But in *Grove City College*, the Supreme Court interpreted the phrase "program or activity" narrowly, holding that Title IX prohibited discrimination only in the *particular* educational program or activity receiving the federal assistance, not in all the educational programs and activities conducted by the institution receiving such assistance.[1] The Civil Rights Restoration Act of 1987[2] overturned this holding by defining the "program or activity" covered by Title IX to include "all" of a recipient's operations.[3] So where federal aid is extended to any program within a college, university or other public system of elementary, secondary or higher education, the entire institution or system is covered by the prohibitions of Title IX.[4] Where a state and local government department (or agency) other than schools receives federal aid for an educational program or activity and the funds stay within that particular department, only that department is subject to Title IX sanctions; but if

---

4. 465 U.S. 555, 566, 104 S.Ct. 1211, 1218, 79 L.Ed.2d 516 (1984), overruled in another respect by the Civil Rights Restoration Act of 1987, discussed below (interpreting Education Amendments of 1972, Title IX, 20 U.S.C.A. §§ 1681–1693).

5. 20 U.S.C.A. § 1681. *See also* 20 U.S.C.A. § 1684 (prohibiting discrimination because of blindness or severe visual impairment).

6. 20 U.S.C.A. § 1682. *See* 20 U.S.C.A. § 1685 (contracts of insurance or guaranty).

7. *Cf. United States Dep't of Transp. v. Paralyzed Veterans of America*, 477 U.S. 597, 106 S.Ct. 2705, 91 L.Ed.2d 494 (1986).

§ 9.2

1. *Grove City College*, 465 U.S. at 566, 104 S.Ct. at 1218.

2. Pub.L.No. 100–259 (1988).

3. 20 U.S.C.A. § 1687.

4. 42 U.S.C.A. § 1687(2)(B). *See Yusuf v. Vassar College*, 35 F.3d 709 (2d Cir.1994) (because Vassar was an institution that receives Federal financial assistance, a claim for damages from sexual harassment could be made under Title IX).

the aid is distributed to other departments or agencies, all entities that receive it are covered.[5] Finally, a private corporation that receives aid as a whole or that provides a public service would fall under Title IX. But the entire corporation may not be covered if the federal funds are extended to only a geographically separate facility.[6]

As under Title VI, a government agency that provides funding has power to review all of a recipient's programs for discrimination. But denial or termination of funds is limited to the "particular program, or part thereof" in which the noncompliance is found.[7]

Are indirect beneficiaries of federal funds covered by Title IX? For example, the National Collegiate Athletic Association is funded by dues paid by federally-funded colleges and universities. Can it be sued pursuant to Title IX? In *NCAA v. Smith*,[8] the Court said no. A female graduate student athlete sued the NCAA under, inter alia, Title IX seeking a waiver of the rule that prohibits a graduate student from participating in intercollegiate athletics at any school except the student's undergraduate institution. The NCAA filed a motion to dismiss alleging that it could not be liable under Title IX because it did not receive federal funds. The plaintiff argued that it was an indirect recipient of federal funds under 34 C.F.R. § 106.2(h), which defines "recipient" as any entity "to whom Federal financial assistance is extended directly or through another recipient." The Court, however, interpreted this regulation to mean that only those entities that actually receive federal monies, either directly or through an intermediary, are covered by Title IX; those entities that merely benefit economically are not. The Court distinguished *Grove City College*, where the schools received federal funds through its students who receive federal grants and loans: those monies were earmarked for education and the money flowed directly from the federal government to the schools through the students. The NCAA merely benefitted by its members' receipt of the money.

§ 9.3 Exemptions

Title IX contains no counterpart to Title VI's general disclaimer on applicability to employment practices. Thus, Title IX redresses sex discrimination in employment by federally funded education institutions.[1] The Restoration Act exempts entities controlled by religious organizations from Title IX coverage if the application of Title IX's provisions would conflict with the organization's religious tenets.[2]

§ 9.4 Administrative Enforcement

Administrative enforcement provisions under Title IX mandate fed-

5. 42 U.S.C.A. § 1687(1)(B).
6. 42 U.S.C.A. § 1687(3)(B).
7. 42 U.S.C.A. § 1682.
8. 525 U.S. 459, 119 S.Ct. 924, 142 L.Ed.2d 929 (1999).

§ 9.3
1. *See North Haven Bd. of Educ.*, 456 U.S. 512, 102 S.Ct. 1912, 72 L.Ed.2d 299.
2. 20 U.S.C.A. § 1687(4).

eral agencies to issue regulations designed to effectuate Title IX's goals.[1] Applicants for and recipients of federal financial assistance must comply with those regulations. The agencies may enforce the regulations by refusing to grant or by terminating funds upon an administrative determination of non-compliance with the regulations.[2] Federal agencies are required to engage in coordinated enforcement efforts with the U.S. Attorney General. They may, for example, refuse to grant or continue assistance only after notice to the offending party and failure of attempts to secure voluntary compliance.[3]

§ 9.5 Elements of the Private Action Under Title IX

The Supreme Court has implied a private right of action under Title IX.[1] The right of action appears to extend to claims of sex discrimination in employment.[2] The preceding statement must be qualified, however, because the Supreme Court's decision holding Title IX applicable to employment practices did not specifically consider the private right of action question.[3] Thus a debate is emerging in the circuit decisions over whether the existence of a detailed judicial remedy for employment discrimination under Title VII of the 1964 Civil Rights Act (amended as of 1991 to permit compensatory and punitive damages subject to statutory caps) forecloses a judicially implied remedy under Title IX (which has no cap on such relief, *see* § 9.6, *infra*) with respect to gender discriminatory practices that are actionable under Title VII and committed by federally funded education institutions or their agents.[4]

Even if a federal education funds recipient may be subject to a private damages claim under Title IX for gender discrimination in employment, the scope of the liability is unclear. The Supreme Court

§ 9.4

1. 20 U.S.C.A. § 1682.

2. *Id.*

3. *Id.*

§ 9.5

1. *Cannon v. Univ. of Chicago,* 441 U.S. 677, 688, 99 S.Ct. 1946, 1953, 60 L.Ed.2d 560 (1979).

2. *Preston v. Virginia,* 31 F.3d 203 (4th Cir.1994); *Bowers v. Baylor Univ.,* 862 F.Supp. 142 (W.D.Tex.1994); *Henschke v. New York Hosp.–Cornell Med. Ctr.,* 821 F.Supp. 166 (S.D.N.Y.1993). Interestingly, education programs conducted by the federal government itself are not included. President Clinton has indicated interest in promulgating an executive order that would extend Title IX principles to those programs. BNA, 66 USLW No. 5, p. 2070 (August 5, 1997).

3. *See North Haven Bd. of Educ. v. Bell,* 456 U.S. 512, 102 S.Ct. 1912, 72 L.Ed.2d 299 (1982).

4. *Compare Lakoski v. James,* 66 F.3d 751 (5th Cir.1995), *cert. denied,* 519 U.S. 947, 117 S.Ct. 357, 136 L.Ed.2d 249 (1996) (Title IX claim foreclosed) *and Holt v. Lewis,* 955 F.Supp. 1385, 1388–89 (N.D.Ala. 1995), *aff'd without opinion,* 109 F.3d 771 (11th Cir.1997), *cert. denied,* 522 U.S. 817, 118 S.Ct. 67, 139 L.Ed.2d 29 (1997) (no Title IX private right of action for retaliatory discharge) *with Lipsett v. University of Puerto Rico,* 864 F.2d 881, 896–97 (1st Cir. 1988) *and O'Connor v. Peru State College,* 781 F.2d 632, 642 n. 8 (8th Cir.1986) (no foreclosure of Title IX claim) *and Mabry v. State Bd. of Community Colleges and Occupational Educ.,* 813 F.2d 311, 316–18 (10th Cir.), *cert. denied,* 484 U.S. 849, 108 S.Ct. 148, 98 L.Ed.2d 104 (1987) (assuming no foreclosure). *Cf. Lowrey v. Texas A & M Univ. Sys.,* 117 F.3d 242 (5th Cir.1997) (distinguishing *Lakoski* to permit Title IX retaliation claim based on employer reaction to plaintiff's participation in Title IX administrative investigation, reasoning that such a retaliation claim lies exclusively under Title IX).

held that a student claiming sexual harassment by a teacher has no claim unless an official with authority to end the discrimination had actual knowledge of the discrimination had actual knowledge and failed to act such that the failure amounted to deliberate indifference.[5] Presumably a small number of teachers with gender-based employment discrimination claims could meet this strict standard if the harassment was committed by or came to the attention of a principal or other high ranking administrative official. Liability would be considerably broader, and could more easily reach co-worker sexual harassment of teachers, if *Gebser* is limited to the student-plaintiff context and entity liability standards in employment cases are borrowed from those the Court has declared under Title VII.[6]

The administrative regulations promulgated under Title IX prohibit discrimination resulting from facially neutral policies that have gender-discriminatory effect as well as intentional discrimination based on gender.[7] Lower courts have applied the impact principle to Title IX actions when the plaintiff distinctly pleads a violation of the applicable implementing regulations, as distinct from the statute alone.[8] Use of the impact theory is fortified by the growing judicial receptiveness to transplanting Title VII liability principles to claims under Title IX.[9]

A related uncertain question is whether individual supervisors and managers, as distinct from institutional educational federal funds recipients, are separately subject to Title IX liability. A majority of the few decisions on point hold that they are not,[10] thus reaching a result

5. *Gebser v. Lago Vista Ind. Sch. Dist.*, 524 U.S. 274, 118 S.Ct. 1989, 141 L.Ed.2d 277 (1998).

6. *See* the discussion of sexual harassment liability standards under Title VII in § 2.22 *supra*.

7. One regulation, for example, bans "administer[ing] or operat[ing] any test or other criteria for admission which has a disproportionately adverse effect on persons on the basis of sex unless the use of such test is shown to predict validly success in the education program or activity in question and alternative tests or criteria which do not have such a disproportionate adverse effect are shown to be unavailable." 34 C.F.R. § 106.21(b)(2).

8. *See, e.g., Mabry*, 813 F.2d at 317 n.6; *Sharif v. New York State Educ. Dep't*, 709 F.Supp. at 361.

9. *See Murray v. New York Univ. College of Dentistry*, 57 F.3d 243 (2d Cir.1995); *Brown v. Hot, Sexy and Safer Productions, Inc.*, 68 F.3d 525 (1st Cir.1995), *cert. denied*, 516 U.S. 1159, 116 S.Ct. 1044, 134 L.Ed.2d 191 (1996) (applying Title VII hostile sexual environment standards to Title IX settings).

10. *Boulahanis v. Board of Regents*, 198 F.3d 633, 640 (7th Cir.1999), *cert. denied*, ___ U.S. ___, 120 S.Ct. 2762, 147 L.Ed.2d 1022 (2000); *Hartley v. Parnell*, 193 F.3d 1263, 1270 (11th Cir.1999); *Kinman v. Omaha Pub. Sch. Dist.*, 171 F.3d 607, 611 (8th Cir.1999); *Smith v. Metropolitan Sch. Dist. Perry Tp.*, 128 F.3d 1014, 1019 (7th Cir.1997), *cert. denied*, 524 U.S. 951, 118 S.Ct. 2367, 141 L.Ed.2d 736 (1998); *Lillard v. Shelby County Bd. of Educ.*, 76 F.3d 716, 730 (6th Cir.1996) (Nelson, J., concurring) (stating that only educational institutions may be found liable for Title IX violations); *Lipsett v. University of Puerto Rico*, 864 F.2d 881, 896–97 (1st Cir.1988); *Nelson v. Temple Univ.*, 920 F.Supp. 633 (E.D.Pa. 1996). *But see Murrell v. School Dist. No. 1*, 186 F.3d 1238 (10th Cir.1999) (implicitly accepting the notion of individual liability); *Mennone v. Gordon*, 889 F.Supp. 53 (D.Conn.1995) (holding individual defendant potentially liable under Title IX but according him a purported "qualified immunity" defense under that statute); *Oona R. v. McCaffrey*, 143 F.3d 473 (9th Cir. 1998), *cert. denied*, 526 U.S. 1154, 119 S.Ct. 2039, 143 L.Ed.2d 1047 (1999) (denying qualified immunity to school official because student's Title IX rights to be free

consistent with the weight of recent authority under Title VII.[11] Creative plaintiffs' counsel have attempted to skirt this obstacle by suing educational officials individually for Title IX statutory violations under the "and laws" branch of § 1983, with mixed success.[12] Section 1983 claims alleging that teachers and other individuals have committed constitutional violations, as opposed to Title IX violations, have enjoyed somewhat greater success.[13]

§ 9.6 Damages

In *Franklin v. Gwinnett County Public Schools*, the Supreme Court held that a successful Title IX plaintiff is eligible for all traditional legal and equitable relief that may be appropriate, damages as well as back pay and prospective relief.[1] Further, the Civil Rights Remedies Equalization Amendment of 1986[2] permits federal courts to award retrospective relief under, among other statutes, Titles IX, against a state or state agency, expressly abrogating what would otherwise be their immunity under the Eleventh Amendment.[3] Because *Franklin* concerned intention-

from sexual harassment law was clearly established without deciding if individuals are subject to suit under Title IX) ; *Doe v. Petaluma City Sch. Dist.*, 54 F.3d 1447 (9th Cir.1995) (on a motion to dismiss, discussing qualified immunity defense without deciding if individuals are subject to suit under Title IX).

11. *See supra* § 2.3.

12. *Compare Crawford v. Davis*, 109 F.3d 1281, 1284 (8th Cir.1997) (finding no preclusion) *and Lillard v. Shelby County Bd. of Educ.*, 76 F.3d 716, 722–24 (6th Cir.1996) (same) *with Boulahanis v. Board of Regents*, 198 F.3d 633, 639–40 (7th Cir. 1999), *cert. denied*, ___ U.S. ___, 120 S.Ct. 2762, 147 L.Ed.2d 1022 (2000) (finding preclusion); *Bruneau v. South Kortright Central Sch. Dist.*, 163 F.3d 749 (2d Cir.1998), *cert. denied*, 526 U.S. 1145, 119 S.Ct. 2020, 143 L.Ed.2d 1032 (1999) (Title IX precludes § 1983 suit to enforce rights arising under both Title IX and the equal protection clause); *Waid v. Merrill Area Pub. Schs.*, 91 F.3d 857, 862–63 (7th Cir.1996) (dicta); *Seamons v. Snow*, 84 F.3d 1226, 1234 n. 8 (10th Cir.1996) (allowing § 1983 claim for constitutional violations but not for Title IX statutory violations) *and Lakoski v. James*, 66 F.3d 751, 755 (5th Cir.1995), *cert. denied*, 519 U.S. 947, 117 S.Ct. 357, 136 L.Ed.2d 249 (1996).

13. *See Kinman v. Omaha Pub. Sch. Dist.*, 171 F.3d 607, 611 (8th Cir.1999); *Crawford v. Davis*, 109 F.3d 1281, 1284 (8th Cir.1997); *Seamons v. Snow*, 84 F.3d 1226, 1234 n. 8 (10th Cir.1996); *Lillard v. Shelby County Bd. of Educ.*, 76 F.3d 716,

722–24 (6th Cir.1996). *But see Bruneau v. South Kortright Central Sch. Dist.*, 163 F.3d 749 (2d Cir.1998), *cert. denied*, 526 U.S. 1145, 119 S.Ct. 2020, 143 L.Ed.2d 1032 (1999) (Title IX precludes § 1983 suit to enforce rights arising under both Title IX and the equal protection clause); *Waid v. Merrill Area Pub. Schs.*, 91 F.3d 857, 863 (7th Cir.1996) (Congress effectively superseded a cause of action under § 1983 that was based on constitutional principles of equal protection); *Williams v. Sch. Dist. of Bethlehem, Pa.*, 998 F.2d 168, 176 (3d Cir. 1993), *cert. denied*, 510 U.S. 1043, 114 S.Ct. 689, 126 L.Ed.2d 656 (1994); *Pfeiffer v. Marion Center Area Sch. Dist.*, 917 F.2d 779, 789 (3d Cir.1990).

§ 9.6

1. 503 U.S. 60, 112 S.Ct. 1028, 117 L.Ed.2d 208 (1992) (when Title IX was passed there was a presumption in favor of all available remedies, and Congress made no effort to alter that presumption).

2. 42 U.S.C.A. § 2000d–7(b).

3. *See also Franks v. Kentucky Sch. for the Deaf*, 142 F.3d 360, 363 (6th Cir.1998) (Congress validly abrogated states' Eleventh Amendment immunity in actions brought under Title IX); *Doe v. University of Ill.*, 200 F.3d 499 (7th Cir.1999) (abrogation valid with respect to Title IX); *Crawford v. Davis*, 109 F.3d 1281, 1283 (8th Cir.1997) (valid abrogation regarding Title IX). Alternatively, both the Fourth and Fifth Circuits have expressly held that the states waive their Eleventh Amendment immunity pursuant to Congressional sending

al discrimination, it is unclear what the effect of its broad language may be on damages in Title IX cases challenging neutral practices.

clause power by accepting federal funds under Title IX. *Pederson v. Louisiana State Univ.*, 213 F.3d 858, 875 (5th Cir.2000); *Litman v. George Mason Univ.*, 186 F.3d 544, 555 (4th Cir.1999), *cert. denied,* ___ U.S. ___, 120 S.Ct. 1220, 145 L.Ed.2d 1120 (2000). *Cf. Davis v. Monroe County Bd. of Ed.*, 526 U.S. 629, 119 S.Ct. 1661, 1669, 143 L.Ed.2d 839 (1999) (stating that "we have repeatedly treated Title IX as legislation enacted pursuant to Congress' authority under the Spending Clause").

Chapter Ten

DISABILITY DISCRIMINATION IN FEDERAL PROGRAMS AND THE PRIVATE SECTOR: THE REHABILITATION ACT OF 1973 AND THE AMERICANS WITH DISABILITIES ACT OF 1990

Analysis

A. INTRODUCTION

442

F.   "WITH A *DISABILITY*"

A.   INTRODUCTION

§ 10.1   Disability Discrimination in General

In deliberating on the Americans With Disabilities Act or "ADA,"[1] Congress observed in 1989 that there are approximately 43 million Americans with one or more physical or mental disabilities,[2] of whom an estimated 8.2 million want to work.[3] On July 26, 1990, the ADA became the first comprehensive federal mandate to non-government-affiliated private employers to provide equal employment opportunity to those individuals. The pre-ADA provision with the broadest reach in this area is the Rehabilitation Act of 1973 or "RHA."[4] RHA's § 504 applies, however, only to recipients of government funds and government contractors and subcontractors,[5] and § 501 applies only to the federal government as employer.[6] Thus the ADA is the first national comprehensive prohibition against handicap discrimination in the private sector.

§ 10.1

1.   Pub.L.No. 101–336, 104 Stat. 327, 42 U.S.C.A. §§ 12101–12213.

2.   42 U.S.C.A. § 12101(a)(1).

3.   S.Rep.No. 101–116, at 9 (1989); H.R.Rep.No. 101–485(II), at 32 (1990).

4.   29 U.S.C.A. §§ 701–794.

5.   Section 504 is codified at 29 U.S.C.A. § 794.

6.   Section 501 is codified at 29 U.S.C.A. § 791.

Nevertheless, because many of the principles developed in RHA litigation were incorporated into ADA,[7] it is still important to survey the general contours of the earlier statute.

§§ 10.2–15.4 [Reserved]

B. THE REHABILITATION ACT OF 1973

§ 10.5 Section 504: Discrimination by Federal Funds Recipients

Section 504 of the Rehabilitation Act prohibits federal funds recipients from excluding or discriminating against any "otherwise qualified handicapped individual" in "any program or activity receiving federal financial assistance."[1] The Civil Rights Restoration Act of 1987 overruled *Grove City College v. Bell*[2] with respect to § 504, thereby effectively banning handicap discrimination in all the recipient institution's operations, not merely in programs or activities for which federal assistance is granted.

Section 504 is enforced by the administrative procedures of Title VI, which may lead to termination of funding or refusal to extend future assistance. In addition, the Supreme Court, without expressly deciding whether § 504 gives rise to a private right of action, has approved the award of relief in such a case and held that employers violate the statute even if the federal aid they receive is not for the primary purpose of promoting employment.[3] By contrast, a private right of action has not been generally recognized under § 503 of the Act,[4] which requires federal government contractors to "take affirmative action to employ and advance in employment qualified handicapped individuals."

RHA provides that the "remedies, procedures, and rights" specified by Title VI of the 1964 Civil Rights Act shall be available under § 504.[5] It has not been definitively decided if full "legal" remedies, and therefore a constitutionally required jury trial right, are available under Title VI; but in *Franklin v. Gwinnett County Public Schools,*[6] the Court held

---

7. *See, e.g., Bolton v. Scrivner, Inc.,* 36 F.3d 939, 942–43 (10th Cir.1994), *cert. denied,* 513 U.S. 1152, 115 S.Ct. 1104, 130 L.Ed.2d 1071 (1995) (citing legislative history of ADA).

§ 10.5

1. 29 U.S.C.A. § 794. Only the federal funds recipients are liable under the RHA, and the Fifth Circuit has held that a public employee cannot avoid the bar against individual liability by suing under § 1983. *See Lollar v. Baker,* 196 F.3d 603 (5th Cir. 1999).

2. 465 U.S. 555, 563–570, 104 S.Ct. 1211, 1216–1220, 79 L.Ed.2d 516 (1984).

3. *See Consolidated Rail Corp. v. Darrone,* 465 U.S. 624, 104 S.Ct. 1248, 79 L.Ed.2d 568 (1984).

4. *See, e.g., Fisher v. City of Tucson,* 663 F.2d 861 (9th Cir.1981), *cert. denied,* 459 U.S. 881, 103 S.Ct. 178, 74 L.Ed.2d 146 (1982); *Davis v. United Air Lines, Inc.,* 662 F.2d 120 (2d Cir.1981), *cert. denied,* 456 U.S. 965, 102 S.Ct. 2045, 72 L.Ed.2d 490 (1982); *Simpson v. Reynolds Metals Co.,* 629 F.2d 1226 (7th Cir.1980); *Rogers v. Frito–Lay, Inc.,* 611 F.2d 1074 (5th Cir.), *cert. denied,* 449 U.S. 889, 101 S.Ct. 246, 66 L.Ed.2d 115 (1980).

5. 29 U.S.C.A. § 794(a)(2).

6. 503 U.S. 60, 112 S.Ct. 1028, 117 L.Ed.2d 208 (1992). *See* discussion of *Franklin* and Title IX in Chapter 9.

that monetary damages were available under Title IX of the 1964 Civil Rights Act, so they are probably available under Title VI as well. A circuit court, relying on the similarities between Title IX and § 504, has held that the full spectrum of legal remedies is therefore also available in § 504 cases, even classifying back pay under § 504 as a "legal" remedy.[7] To the extent legal relief is demanded, the court concluded, the Seventh Amendment secures a jury trial right in actions under § 504. Accordingly, since *Franklin,* courts have uniformly allowed compensatory damages for intentional discrimination under § 504,[8] and many courts have extended *Franklin* to allow for punitive damages as well.[9] No federal limitations period for such claims having been declared by Congress, federal courts have applied whichever forum state limitations period pertains to claims most closely analogous to claims of handicap discrimination. They have usually concluded that the state's general personal injury limitations period represents the closest analogy.[10]

In 1974, Congress amended the definition of "handicapped individual" for § 504 purposes to include not just those with actual physical impairments, "but also those who are regarded as impaired and who, as a result, are substantially limited in a major life activity."[11] Moreover, the Supreme Court held that a person suffering impairment of major life activities from tuberculosis is considered handicapped even though his disease is contagious.[12] But to be eligible for relief, a plaintiff must generally also be "otherwise qualified," or able to perform the "essential functions" of the particular job. And while inability to function may not be inferred simply from the fact of a handicap, a tuberculosis sufferer may not be "otherwise qualified" if his contagion poses "a serious health threat to others."[13] Lower courts after *Arline* have found that AIDS victims may qualify under RHA as handicapped individuals, at least where they experience a related physical impairment.[14]

---

7. *Waldrop v. Southern Co. Servs., Inc.,* 24 F.3d 152 (11th Cir.1994).

8. *See, e.g., W.B. v. Matula,* 67 F.3d 484, 494 (3d Cir.1995) (allowing mother of disabled child to recover monetary damages upon proof of intentional discrimination); *Rodgers v. Magnet Cove Pub. Schs.,* 34 F.3d 642, 645 (8th Cir.1994) (holding that money damages are available under § 504); *Waldrop,* 24 F.3d at 157 n. 5 (11th Cir.1994) (applying the holding of *Franklin* to § 504 claims); *Pandazides v. Virginia Bd. of Educ.,* 13 F.3d 823, 830–31 (4th Cir.1994) (same).

9. *See Filardi v. Loyola Univ.,* 1998 WL 111683 (N.D.Ill.1998); *Saylor v. Ridge,* 989 F.Supp. 680, (E.D.Pa.1998); *Burns-Vidlak v. Chandler,* 980 F.Supp. 1144 (D.Haw. 1997); *Kilroy v. Husson College,* 959 F.Supp. 22 (D.Me.1997); *Hernandez v. City of Hartford,* 959 F.Supp. 125 (D.Conn. 1997); *DeLeo v. City of Stamford,* 919 F.Supp. 70 (D.Conn.1995). *But see, e.g., Moreno v. Consolidated Rail Corp.,* 99 F.3d 782 (6th Cir.1996); *Winfrey v. City of Chica-*

go, 957 F.Supp. 1014 (N.D.Ill.1997); *Doe v. Marshall,* 882 F.Supp. 1504 (E.D.Pa.1995).

10. *See, e.g., Baker v. Board of Regents,* 991 F.2d 628, 632 (10th Cir.1993) (analogizing Rehabilitation Act claims to personal injury claims); *Morse v. University of Vt.,* 973 F.2d 122, 127 (2d Cir.1992) ("we now hold that actions under § 504 of the Rehabilitation Act are governed by the state statute of limitations applicable to personal injury actions"); *Hickey v. Irving Indep. Sch. Dist.,* 976 F.2d 980, 982–83 (5th Cir. 1992).

11. 29 U.S.C.A. § 705(20)(B).

12. *School Bd. of Nassau County v. Arline,* 480 U.S. 273, 107 S.Ct. 1123, 94 L.Ed.2d 307 (1987).

13. *Id.*

14. *See, e.g., Chalk v. United States Dist. Court, Cent. Dist. of Cal.,* 840 F.2d 701 (9th Cir.1988).

A circuit court decision implies that the Rehabilitation Act provides no claim of retaliation for advocating the rights of the handicapped, distinct from its basic prohibition against handicap discrimination.[15] On the other hand, RHA does contain a concept of constructive discharge, although it has been restrictively applied.[16]

§ 10.6 Section 501: Discrimination Against Federal Employees

Section 501 of RHA protects certain federal employees from discrimination on the basis of mental or physical disability.[1] Indeed, RHA provides the only protection for disabled federal workers because ADA specifically excludes the federal government from coverage.[2] Section 505 provides that the "remedies, procedures, and rights" of § 717 of Title VII apply to § 501 cases.[3] Like the ADA, § 501 imposes a duty on the federal government to provide reasonable accommodations to an individual "otherwise qualified" for employment.[4] The regulations also define a "qualified" handicapped person, for the purposes of § 501, as someone who "can perform the essential functions of the position in question without endangering the health and safety of the individual or others."[5] This requires a case-by-case determination that the person would create "a reasonable probability of substantial harm."[6]

Prior to filing a complaint of discrimination against a federal agency, an aggrieved federal employee must notify the employing agency's Equal Employment Opportunity counselor within 45 days of the alleged discriminatory act to allow an opportunity for an informal resolution of the matter.[7] The 45-day time limit may be extended for cause; if, for example, the individual shows that she was neither notified nor aware of the time limits, that she reasonably could not have known that the discriminatory action occurred, or that despite due diligence she was unable to notify the counselor within the time period.[8] This limitations period is considered a statute of limitations, not a jurisdictional prerequisite.[9]

15. *Smith v. Barton*, 914 F.2d 1330, 1338 (9th Cir.1990), *cert. denied*, 501 U.S. 1217, 111 S.Ct. 2825, 115 L.Ed.2d 995 (1991).

16. *Johnson v. Shalala*, 991 F.2d 126 (4th Cir.1993), *cert. denied*, 513 U.S. 806, 115 S.Ct. 52, 130 L.Ed.2d 12 (1994) (claim established only if plaintiff shows that employer knew of employee's handicap, failed to afford reasonable accommodation, and did so intending to cause plaintiff to quit).

§ 10.6

1. *See* 29 U.S.C.A. § 791.

2. *See* 42 U.S.C.A. § 12111(5).

3. *See* 29 U.S.C.A. § 794a(a)(1) and discussion of § 717 in Chapter 4.

4. *See* 29 C.F.R. § 1613.701 et seq. Under the RHA, federal employers face a high-er standard regarding reassignment. Once a reasonable accommodation is requested, the federal employer bears the burden of locating another job that the disabled employee can perform. *See Woodman v. Runyon*, 132 F.3d 1330, 1343 (10th Cir.1997). The EEOC proposed a rule on March 1, 2000 that would import the reasonable accommodation/undue hardship analysis of the ADA into § 501. 60 Fed. Reg. 11, 019–11023 (March 1,2000).

5. 29 C.F.R. § 1613.702(f).

6. *Mantolete v. Bolger*, 767 F.2d 1416, 1422 (9th Cir.1985).

7. *See* 29 C.F.R. § 1614.105(a)(1).

8. *See* 29 C.F.R. § 1614.105(a)(2).

9. *See, e.g., Johnson v. Runyon*, 47 F.3d 911, 917 (7th Cir.1995) (45–day limitations

The counselor has thirty days to attempt to achieve an informal resolution, but must in any case conduct a final interview with the aggrieved person within 30 days of the date the employee contacted the counselor.[10] If no resolution has been reached, the counselor must notify the employee in writing of the employee's right to file a discrimination complaint within 15 days of receipt of the notice.[11]

The employee must then file a written complaint of disability discrimination with the employing agency.[12] The agency shall conduct an investigation which must be completed within 180 days of the date of filing of the written complaint unless both parties agree to a longer period of time not to exceed 90 days.[13] At the end of 180 days, the agency must notify the complainant of the completion of the investigation, at which time the complainant has the right to receive an immediate final decision from the agency or request a hearing before an administrative law judge ("ALJ").[14]

If the employee requests a hearing, the EEOC appoints an ALJ to conduct the hearing.[15] EEOC regulations provide for a procedure similar to summary judgment.[16] Whether through this procedure or after a hearing, the ALJ must issue findings of fact and conclusions of law and recommend appropriate relief when warranted, within 180 days after the date the hearing was requested.[17] After receiving the ALJ's recommendation, the employing agency has 60 days to issue a final decision.[18] If the agency does not issue a decision within the 60 days, the ALJ's decision becomes final.[19] The complainant may appeal within 30 days the final decision of the agency to the Director, Office of Federal Operations, Equal Employment Opportunity Commission.[20]

The employee has the right to file a lawsuit in federal court within 90 days of receipt of final agency action; within 180 days after the date of filing of a complaint if no final agency decision has taken place; within 90 days after receipt of final action taken by the Commission; or within 180 days from the date of filing an appeal with the Commission if there has been no Commission decision.[21] Failure to file an administrative complaint will bar a private right of action.[22]

A § 501 plaintiff is entitled to the full panoply of Title VII remedies including back pay and other appropriate equitable relief. Under 29 U.S.C.A. § 794a(b), a prevailing party under § 501 is also entitled to attorney's fees.

---

period extended when posted notices of limitations period did not impart constructive notice to applicant).

10. *See* 29 C.F.R. § 1614.105(d).

11. *Id.*

12. *See* 29 C.F.R. § 1614.106(a).

13. *See* 29 C.F.R. § 1614.108(d), (e).

14. *See* 29 C.F.R. § 1614.108 (f).

15. *See* 29 C.F.R. § 1614.109(a).

16. *See* 29 C.F.R. § 1614.109(e).

17. *See* 29 C.F.R. § 1614.109(g).

18. *See* 29 C.F.R. § 1614.110.

19. *See* 29 C.F.R. § 1614.109(g).

20. *See* 29 C.F.R. §§ 1614.401(a), 1614.402, 1614.403(a).

21. *See* 29 C.F.R. § 1614.408.

22. *See* McGuinness v. United States Postal Serv., 744 F.2d 1318 (7th Cir.1984).

§§ 10.7–15.9   [Reserved]

C. THE AMERICANS WITH DISABILITIES ACT OF 1990

§ 10.10   In General

The ADA prohibits discrimination against a "qualified individual with a disability because of that disability." The ADA substantially replicates the language of the RHA, with the term "disability" substituted for "handicap."[1] Congress amended the § 504 definition of handicap in 1974, broadening it to include three protected groups: persons who have a physical or mental impairment that substantially limits a major life activity; those with a record of such an impairment; and those regarded as having such an impairment.[2] Apart from retaining these protected groups, however, the scope of the ADA is much broader than that of the RHA.

Despite this broadening of protection from disability discrimination, ADA has been described as a "windfall for defendants." Research of reported cases shows that at trial court level, defendants prevail in more than 93% of ADA employment discrimination cases (Title I) decided on the merits at the trial court level. On appeal, defendants prevail in eighty-four percent of reported cases. "These results are worse than results found in comparable areas of the law; only prisoner rights cases fare as poorly."[3]

The ADA is composed of five titles. Title I[4] generally prohibits disability discrimination by an employer, employment agency, labor organization, or joint labor-management committee against a qualified individual with a disability in hiring, promotion, termination, compensation, training and other terms, conditions and privileges of employment.[5] Title I does not simply prohibit disability discrimination; it requires employers to make reasonable accommodations for the known physical or mental disabilities of an otherwise qualified applicant or employee with a disability, unless the entity can show that the accommodation would create an undue hardship on the operation of its business.[6] Title I also significantly restricts the ability of a covered entity to conduct pre-offer medical examinations or inquiries and requires that all medical

---

§ 10.10

1. S.Rep.No. 101–116 states that the term has been modified to reflect the more up-to-date and currently accepted terminology.

2. See 29 U.S.C.A. § 705(20).

3. Ruth Colker, *The Americans with Disabilities Act: a Windfall for Defendants*, 34 Harv.C.R.–C.L.L.Rev. 99 (1999). The American Bar Association's Commission on Mental and Physical Disability Law reports that in 1999, employers prevailed on 291 cases decided in the federal courts, and

plaintiffs prevailed just 19 times, representing a win rate of 95.7% for defendants. Indeed, the vast majority of defendant wins come at summary judgment. Of the 291 wins, 257 were on summary judgment. These numbers do not, of course, include cases that settle out of court.

4. Implementing regulations for Title I are found in 29 C.F.R. pt. 1630.

5. See 42 U.S.C.A. § 12112(a).

6. See 42 U.S.C.A. § 12112(b)(5) and discussion *infra*.

example, in *Parker v. Metropolitan Life Ins. Co.*,[9] employees sued to force their employer's insurer to offer the same long-term disability benefits for employees disabled by a mental illness as the company offered to for employees disabled by a physical illness. The Sixth Circuit rejected the employees' claim, holding that a benefit plan offered by an employer is not a good offered by a place[10] of public accommodation;[11] employment discrimination, including the terms and conditions of an employee benefit plan, does not fall within the purview of Title III;[12] and the ADA prohibits discrimination only between disabled and nondisabled persons.[13] Similarly, the Third Circuit in *Ford v. Schering–Plough Corp.*,[14]

extended to all other categories of handicapped persons." In *Alexander*, the Court held that a state's Medicaid plan which disproportionately impacted disabled individuals did not violate RHA. *See also* 29 U.S.C.A. § 300gg–5, the Mental Health Parity Act of 1996, which prohibits group health plans from applying lower dollar limits on mental health benefits than on medical and surgical benefits under the same plan. One commentator argues that the passage of the Mental Health Parity Act demonstrates that Congress did not believe that ADA required equity in benefits plans. *See* Nicole Martinson, *Inequality Between Disabilities: the Different Treatment of Mental Versus Physical Disabilities in Long-term Disability Benefit Plans*, 50 Baylor L.Rev. 361, 376 (1998).

9. 121 F.3d 1006 (6th Cir.1997), *cert. denied*, 522 U.S. 1084, 118 S.Ct. 871, 139 L.Ed.2d 768 (1998).

10. A "place of public accommodation" is defined by the applicable regulations as "a facility, operated by a private entity, whose operations affect commerce" and fall within at least one of the twelve public accommodation categories listed in the statute. 28 C.F.R. § 36.104. "Facility" is defined as "all or any portion of buildings, structures, sites, complexes, equipment, rolling stock or other conveyances, roads, walks, passageways, parking lots, or other real or personal property, including the site where the building, property, structure, or equipment is located." *Id.*

11. *See also Weyer v. Twentieth Century Fox Film Corp.*, 198 F.3d 1104, 1115 (9th Cir.2000); *Stoutenborough v. National Football League, Inc.*, 59 F.3d 580 (6th Cir.), *cert. denied*, 516 U.S. 1028, 116 S.Ct. 674, 133 L.Ed.2d 523 (1995). In *Stoutenborough*, an association of hearing impaired persons filed suit against the National Football League and several television stations under Title III of the ADA alleging that the NFL's "blackout rule" discriminates against them because hearing impaired individuals have no other means of accessing

football games when live telecasts are prohibited. They cannot, for example, listen to the broadcast on the radio. *Id.* at 582. To place the blackout rule within the purview of Title III, the plaintiffs argued that they were denied substantially equal access to live television transmissions of football games which is a service of a public accommodation. *Id.* The Sixth Circuit rejected the plaintiffs' contention, holding that the defendants did not fall within any of the twelve categories enumerated in § 12181(7). *Id.* at 583.

The First and Second Circuits have held, however, that the ADA's prohibition on disability discrimination in the products and services of places of public accommodation is not limited to physical structures and may in some instances include insurance policies and underwriting practices. *See Pallozzi v. Allstate Life Ins. Co.*, 198 F.3d 28 (2d Cir.1999), *amended on denial of reh'g*, 204 F.3d 392 (2d Cir.2000); *Carparts Distrib. Ctr., Inc. v. Automotive Wholesaler's Ass'n of New England, Inc.*, 37 F.3d 12, 19 (1st Cir.1994).

12. "[D]iscrimination in the provision of fringe benefits during employment is governed strictly by Title I and the provision of a long-term disability plan is a fringe benefit of employment." *Parker*, 121 F.3d at 1015.

13. *But see Conners v. Maine Med. Ctr.*, 42 F.Supp.2d 34, 41 (D.Me.1999) (long term benefits plan administrator constituted a "public accommodation" whose insurance policies were a "good or service" under Title III of the ADA which proscribes denial, on basis of disability, of opportunity to benefit from goods, services, privileges, advantages, or accommodations of an entity; therefore, former employee whose long term disability benefits for mental disability were terminated could maintain action under Title III against employer and administrator for discrimination based on different treatment of mental and physical disabilities under plan).

---

information obtained regarding an applicant or employee be kept confidential.[7] Titles II and III of ADA are briefly discussed in the following sections. Title IV, not discussed in this text, covers telecommunications, and Title V's miscellaneous provisions cover retaliation, exemptions, attorney's fees, and amendments to the RHA. Most readers will encounter the ADA in actions concerning employment. The EEOC in early 1994 reported that ADA employment litigation constituted almost 20% of the charges it receives under all the statutes it enforces. The bulk of this chapter concentrates on Title I.

§ 10.11 Title II

Title II[1] of the ADA protects qualified disabled individuals against discrimination in the provision of services, programs, or activities of state and local governments and their affiliates,[2] including government contracting.[3] Public entities, defined as "any State or local government" and "any department, agency, special purpose district, or other instrumentality of a State or States or local government,"[4] are required to make programs accessible to qualified disabled individuals except when doing so would result in a fundamental alteration in the nature of the program.[5] Title II applies to a broad array of services including public education, transportation, recreation, health care, social services, law enforcement,[6] courts,[7] prisons,[8] voting, and town meetings. A circuit split exists on whether Title II protects against employment discrimination by public entities as well.[9] To qualify for Title II protection, an individual

7. *See* 42 U.S.C.A. § 12112 and discussion *infra*.

§ 10.11

1. A detailed discussion of Title II is beyond the scope of this book. This section is intended only to alert practitioners about the general scope of the Title. Title II implementing regulations are found in 28 C.F.R. pt. 35.

2. *See* 42 U.S.C.A. § 12132.

3. *See Johnson v. City of Saline*, 151 F.3d 564 (6th Cir.1998). *See also* implementing regulations found at 28 C.F.R. § 35.130(b)(5) ("[a] public entity, in the selection of procurement contractors, may not use criteria that subject qualified individuals with disabilities to discrimination on the basis of disability").

4. *See* 42 U.S.C.A. § 12131(1).

5. *See* 28 C.F.R. § 35.130(b)(7).

6. *See, e.g., Ferguson v. City of Phoenix*, 157 F.3d 668, 674–75 (9th Cir.1998), *cert. denied*, 526 U.S. 1159, 119 S.Ct. 2049, 144 L.Ed.2d 216 (1999) (suit alleging discrimination against persons dependent upon telecommunications devices for the deaf, or

TDDs, in municipality's operation of its 911 emergency service).

7. *See, e.g., Memmer v. Marin County Courts*, 169 F.3d 630 (9th Cir.1999); *Duffy v. Riveland*, 98 F.3d 447 (9th Cir.1996) (prison disciplinary hearing).

8. *See Pennsylvania Dep't of Corrections v. Yeskey*, 524 U.S. 206, 118 S.Ct. 1952, 141 L.Ed.2d 215 (1998). The Court held as a matter of statutory interpretation that Title II applies to inmates in state prisons, but the Court declined to reach the issue of states' Eleventh Amendment immunity to federal court actions for money damages. *See* § 10.20 for a discussion of this latter issue.

9. *Compare Bledsoe v. Palm Beach County Soil and Water Conservation Dist.*, 133 F.3d 816, 825 (11th Cir.1998), *cert. denied*, 525 U.S. 826, 119 S.Ct. 72, 142 L.Ed.2d 57 (1998), *and Doe v. University of Md. Med. Sys. Corp.*, 50 F.3d 1261 (4th Cir.1995) (Title II protection extends to employment) *with Zimmerman v. Oregon Dep't of Justice*, 170 F.3d 1169, 1178 (9th Cir.1999), *petition for cert. filed*, Aug. 10, 1999 (holding that Title II does not apply to employment). *See also Davoll v. Webb*, 194

must meet the essential eligibility requirements for the receipt of services or the participation in programs or activities provided by the public entity, with or without reasonable modifications to rules, policies, or practices; the removal of architectural, communication, or transportation barriers; or the provision of auxiliary aids and services.[10]

Title II, like Title IX, incorporates[11] the enforcement scheme of Title VI of the Civil Rights Act of 1964, which prohibits race discrimination in federally-funded programs.[12] Like Title VI and IX, then, Title II creates an implied private right of action, and this may mean that Title IX cases such as *Gebser v. Lago Vista Ind. Sch. Dist.*[13] have application in Title II cases. If so, compensatory damages under Title II may be available only where the entity has actual knowledge and is deliberately indifferent to the rights of disabled persons. At least one circuit has found that monetary damages are not available under Title II absent a showing of discriminatory intent or animus; plaintiffs would be limited, then, to injunctive relief and attorney's fees.[14] In Title II and III cases, because ADA does not contain its own statute of limitations, courts look to the most analogous state statute of limitations.[15] An ADA suit is essentially a claim to vindicate injuries to personal rights,[16] and in cases under these titles courts most often adopt the state statute of limitations for personal injury.[17]

F.3d 1116, 1130 (10th Cir.1999) (recognizing issue and assuming arguendo that Title II bars employment discrimination). Implementing regulations of the Justice Department interpret the section to ban discrimination in employment. *See* 28 C.F.R. § 35.140(a) (1992).

Section 203, codified at 42 U.S.C.A. § 12133, provides that Title II is enforced through "the remedies, procedures, and rights set forth in section 505 of the Rehabilitation Act," and legislative history clarifies that § 505(a)(2) is intended. This means that there is no administrative agency filing prerequisite to commencing the private right of action under Title II, unlike a suit brought under Title I against private employers which does require administrative exhaustion. *See* S.Rep.No. 116, at 57–58; *Bledsoe,* 133 F.3d at 825.

10. *See* 42 U.S.C.A. § 12131(2).

11. *See* 42 U.S.C.A. § 12133.

12. *See* discussion of Title IX in Chapter 9.

13. 524 U.S. 274, 118 S.Ct. 1989, 141 L.Ed.2d 277 (1998).

14. *See Ferguson v. City of Phoenix,* 157 F.3d 668, 674–75 (9th Cir.1998)), *cert. denied,* 526 U.S. 1159, 119 S.Ct. 2049, 144

L.Ed.2d 216 (1999). *But see Davoll v. Webb,* 194 F.3d 1116, 1142 (10th Cir.1999) (theorizing that because "Title II entities are not necessarily recipients of federal funds, and the arguments against liability for compensatory damages absent intent are arguably less relevant, ... [o]ne could ... contend that intent should not be required for [compensatory damages awards for] Title II violations.").

15. *See Wilson v. Garcia,* 471 U.S. 261, 266–67, 105 S.Ct. 1938, 1942, 85 L.Ed.2d 254 (1985) (case under § 1983).

16. *See Goodman v. Lukens Steel Co.,* 482 U.S. 656, 661, 107 S.Ct. 2617, 2621, 96 L.Ed.2d 572 (1987) (action for discrimination is one for "fundamental injury to the individual rights of a person"); *Wilson,* 471 U.S. at 276, 105 S.Ct. at 1947 (claims which allege discrimination are best characterized as personal injury actions).

17. *See, e.g., Everett v. Cobb County Sch. Dist.,* 138 F.3d 1407, 1409 (11th Cir.1998); *Soignier v. American Bd. of Plastic Surgery,* 92 F.3d 547, 551 (7th Cir.1996), *cert. denied,* 519 U.S. 1093, 117 S.Ct. 771, 136 L.Ed.2d 716 (1997) (district court correctly applied Illinois' two-year statute of limitations for personal injuries as the most analogous limitations period for an ADA claim).

§ 10.12   Title III

Title III[1] is perhaps best known as the section of the ADA that requires the removal of architectural barriers. Title III generally prohibits discrimination against "individuals"[2] on the basis of disability in the full and equal enjoyment of all the goods, services, facilities, privileges, advantages, or accommodations of any place of public accommodation by any person who owns, leases (or leases to), or operates a place of public accommodation.[3] "Public accommodations" are defined as including a broad range of businesses including hotels, restaurants, bars, theaters, concert halls, auditoriums, stadiums, retail stores, shopping malls, service establishments such as banks, offices of accountants, doctors or lawyers, hospitals, public transportation depots, museums, libraries, parks, schools, social service centers, gymnasiums, bowling alleys, and other places of exercise or recreation.[4] Title III prohibits public accommodations from utilizing eligibility criteria that screen out individuals with disabilities and it requires reasonable modifications to policies, practices, and procedures to ensure that no disabled individual is excluded, denied services or otherwise treated differently than nondisabled individuals.[5] Title III also specifically addresses barrier removal by places of public accommodation.[6]

Several courts have dismissed actions brought under Title III[7] by employees of private entities seeking equity in insurance benefits.[8] For

§ 10.12

1. A detailed discussion of Title III is beyond the scope of this book. This section is intended only to alert practitioners of the general scope of the Title. Title III implementing regulations are found in 28 C.F.R. pt. 36.

2. Because Title III refers to "individuals" and not customers or clients, the Third Circuit allowed a physician with attention deficit disorder who lost his staff privileges and was barred from utilizing the hospital's physical facilities to provide services to his patients to sue the hospital under Title III. *See Menkowitz v. Pottstown Memorial Med. Ctr.,* 154 F.3d 113, 123 (3d Cir.1998).

3. *See* 42 U.S.C.A. § 12182(a).

4. *See* 42 U.S.C.A. § 12181(7).

5. Perhaps the most well known Title III case involves disabled professional golfer Casey Martin. Martin sued the Professional Golf Association for the right to use a golf cart during PGA-sanctioned golf tournaments due to a disabling condition that makes it difficult for him to walk. The Ninth Circuit affirmed the district court's holding that use of golf cart, as a reasonable modification to accommodate the disabled professional golfer, would not frustrate the PGA's walking rule and would not alter the fundamental nature of professional golf tournament competition. *Martin v. PGA*

Tour, Inc., 204 F.3d 994 (9th Cir.2000), *petition for cert. filed,* July 5, 2000. In a nearly identical case, the Seventh Circuit held exactly the opposite, finding that the use of a cart would fundamentally alter the nature of competition. *See Olinger v. Unites States Golf Ass'n,* 205 F.3d 1001 (7th Cir. 2000).

6. *See* 42 U.S.C.A. §§ 12182, 12183. ADA's architectural barrier provisions of Title III are beyond the scope of this book.

7. Similar actions under Title II have also failed. *See, e.g., Rogers v. Department of Health and Environmental Control,* 174 F.3d 431 (4th Cir.1999) (long term disability plan for state employees that provides fewer benefits for mental disabilities than for physical disabilities does not violate ADA).

8. Support for this view can be found in two Supreme Court RHA cases: *Traynor v. Turnage,* 485 U.S. 535, 108 S.Ct. 1372, 99 L.Ed.2d 618 (1988), and *Alexander v. Choate,* 469 U.S. 287, 105 S.Ct. 712, 83 L.Ed.2d 661 (1985). In *Traynor,* the Supreme Court found that a distinction in the GI Bill between two groups of disabled veterans did not violate RHA because "(t)here is nothing in the Rehabilitation Act that requires that any benefit extended to one category of handicapped persons also be

held that disparities between benefits for mental and physical disabilities violates neither Title I nor Title III because ADA does not require equal coverage for every type of disability; as long as each employee, whether disabled or not, is offered the same plan, ADA is satisfied.[15] Other circuits are in accord.[16]

The District of Columbia Circuit analyzed a similar claim under the ADA safe-harbor provision for ERISA-governed employee benefits plans. The ADA's safe harbor appears in section 501(c): "Subchapters I through III of this chapter and title IV of this Act shall not be construed to prohibit or restrict ... a person or organization covered by this chapter from establishing, sponsoring, observing or administering the terms of a bona fide benefit plan that is not subject to State laws that regulate insurance."[17] This safe harbor "shall not be used as a subterfuge to evade the purposes" of Title I or Title III of the ADA.[18] In *EEOC v. Aramark Corp.*,[19] the parties had agreed that the defendant's benefit plan was bona fide and was not subject to state laws regulating insurance by virtue of ERISA preemption. Relying on precedent under the ADEA and RHA,[20] the Third Circuit found no subterfuge because Aramark's benefit plan containing the allegedly discriminatory term was adopted long before the ADA's 1990 enactment. Under the plain meaning of "subterfuge," a plan provision enacted before the ADA could not have been adopted in an effort to evade or circumvent a statutory purpose.[21]

§§ 10.13–15.19   [Reserved]

D.   TITLE I: "NO *COVERED ENTITY* SHALL *DISCRIMINATE* ..."

14. 145 F.3d 601 (3d Cir.1998), *cert. denied*, 525 U.S. 1093, 119 S.Ct. 850, 142 L.Ed.2d 704 (1999).

15. *Id.* at 608, 612 (stating that "[t]erms and conditions of employment are covered under Title I, not Title III.").

16. *See EEOC v. Staten Island Savings Bank*, 207 F.3d 144 (2d Cir.2000) (Title I does not require disability benefit plans to provide equal mental and physical disability benefits); *Weyer v. Twentieth Century Fox Film Corp.*, 198 F.3d 1104, 1109 (9th Cir. 2000); *Lewis v. Kmart Corp.*, 180 F.3d 166 (4th Cir.1999), *cert. denied*, ___ U.S. ___, 120 S.Ct. 978, 145 L.Ed.2d 929 (2000) (lower benefits for mental disabilities in long-term disability plan sponsored by private employer); *Rogers*, 174 F.3d at 436 (same holding respecting plan for state employees); *EEOC v. CNA Ins. Cos.*, 96 F.3d 1039, 1045 (7th Cir.1996) (no ADA violation in differentiating between mental illnesses and physical ailments in long-term disability plans).

17. 42 U.S.C. §§ 12201(c)(3).

18. 42 U.S.C.A. § 12201(c).

19. 208 F.3d 266, 268–72 (D.C.Cir. 2000).

20. *Modderno v. King*, 82 F.3d 1059 (D.C.Cir.1996), *cert. denied* 519 U.S. 1094, 117 S.Ct. 772, 136 L.Ed.2d 717 (1997) (holding that the plan challenged in that case could not be a subterfuge because the employer had adopted it prior to the Rehabilitation Act amendment that incorporated the subterfuge provision); *United Air Lines, Inc. v. McMann*, 434 U.S. 192, 98 S.Ct. 444, 54 L.Ed.2d 402 (1977) (similar holding under the ADEA); *Public Employees Retirement Sys. of Ohio v. Betts*, 492 U.S. 158, 166, 109 S.Ct. 2854, 106 L.Ed.2d 134 (1989) (same).

21. *Aramark*, 208 F.3d at 269–270. *See also Leonard F. v. Israel Discount Bank of New York*, 199 F.3d 99, 103–04 (2d Cir. 1999); *Weyer v. Twentieth Century Fox Film Corp.*, 198 F.3d 1104, 1109 (9th Cir.2000) (alternative holding); *Ford v. Schering-Plough Corp.*, 145 F.3d 601, 611 (3d Cir. 1998), *cert. denied*, 525 U.S. 1093, 119 S.Ct. 850, 142 L.Ed.2d 704 (1999); *Krauel v. Iowa Methodist Med. Ctr.*, 95 F.3d 674, 678–79 (8th Cir.1996).

§ 10.20 Coverage

Title I, effective July 26, 1992, prohibits discrimination by employers, unions, employment agencies and union-management committees.[1] "Employers" are persons engaged in an industry affecting commerce who have 15 or more employees for each working day in each of 20 or more calendar weeks in the current or preceding calendar year, and their agents.[2] The ADA excludes from coverage as employers the United States,[3] wholly owned United States corporations, Indian tribes,[4] and tax-exempt private membership clubs, but not labor organizations.[5] Following an interpretation of the word "employer" that has also commanded the support of most courts of appeals construing the same term under Title VII, the circuits limit the private cause of action to defendant employing entities, as distinct from individual supervisors, officers, or managers.[6]

Through its adoption of the procedures, powers and remedies of Title VII,[7] ADA's Title I also empowers the United States Attorney General to bring a pattern and practice claim whenever the "Attorney General has reasonable cause to believe that any person or group of persons is engaged in a pattern or practice of resistance to the full enjoyment of any of the rights secured by this subchapter, and that the pattern or practice is of such a nature and is intended to deny the full exercise of the rights herein described."[8] The framework for such a case is also borrowed from Title VII case law.[9]

Whether a state can be sued in federal court for money damages for violations of the ADA is disputed. Under post-*Seminole Tribe*[10] and *City of Boerne*[11] Eleventh Amendment jurisprudence, the issues are (1) whether Congress provided a clear legislative statement of its intent to abrogate states' immunity; and (2) whether the ADA is a legitimate

§ 10.20

1. 42 U.S.C.A. § 12111(2).

2. 42 U.S.C.A. § 12111 (5)(A).

3. An aggrieved federal employee must seek relief under the RHA. *See* § 10.6.

4. Although Indian tribes are not covered as employers, tribe-run businesses are "public accommodations" subject to coverage under Title III in suits brought by the United States Attorney General, but not by private plaintiffs, due to tribal sovereign immunity. For a comprehensive discussion of this issue, *see Florida Paraplegic, Ass'n, Inc. v. Miccosukee Tribe of Indians of Fla.,* 166 F.3d 1126 (11th Cir.1999).

5. 42 U.S.C.A. § 12111(5)(B).

6. *See Hiler v. Brown,* 177 F.3d 542 (6th Cir.1999) (retaliation case under RHA); *Butler v. City of Prairie Village, Kan.,* 172 F.3d 736, 744 (10th Cir.1999); *Pritchard v. Southern Co. Servs.,* 102 F.3d 1118 (11th Cir.1996) (per curiam), *cert. denied,* 520 U.S. 1274, 117 S.Ct. 2453, 138 L.Ed.2d 211 (1997); *Mason v. Stallings,* 82 F.3d 1007, 1009 (11th Cir.1996); *U.S. EEOC v. AIC Sec. Investigations, Ltd.,* 55 F.3d 1276, 1282 (7th Cir.1995). *See also* § 5.3 for similar Title VII authority.

7. 42 U.S.C.A. § 12117(a).

8. 42 U.S.C.A. § 2000e–6(a).

9. *See Davoll v. Webb,* 194 F.3d 1116, 1147–48 (10th Cir.1999) (importing the framework from *International Bhd. of Teamsters v. United States,* 431 U.S. 324, 97 S.Ct. 1843, 52 L.Ed.2d 396 (1977), a systemic disparate treatment Title VII case).

10. *Seminole Tribe v. Florida,* 517 U.S. 44, 116 S.Ct. 1114, 134 L.Ed.2d 252 (1996) .

11. *City of Bourne v. Flores,* 521 U.S. 507, 117 S.Ct. 2157, 138 L.Ed.2d 624 (1997).

exercise of Congressional power under § 5 of the Fourteenth Amendment.[12] The Supreme Court expressly reserved ruling on these issues in *Pennsylvania Dep't of Corrections v. Yeskey,*[13] where the Court held that ADA Title II applied to state prisons, because the issue had not been raised below. Most circuits considering states' immunity to ADA damages suits in federal court prior to the Supreme Court decision in *Kimel v. Florida Bd. of Regents,*[14] had found that Congress clearly and properly abrogated states' immunity.[15] However, after the Court decision in *Kimel* that in enacting the ADEA, Congress did not abrogate the States' Eleventh Amendment immunity pursuant to a valid exercise of its § 5 enforcement powers, circuit courts have consistently held that the ADA is similarly an invalid exercise of Congressional authority under the Fourteenth Amendment.[16] The Supreme Court has granted certiorari.[17]

§ 10.21   Former Employees

Several courts have dismissed ADA suits brought by former employees, finding that these plaintiffs do not meet the statutory definition of

12. *See* discussion of Eleventh Amendment in Chapter 12, *infra.*

13. 524 U.S. 206, ___, 118 S.Ct. 1952, 1956, 141 L.Ed.2d 215 (1998).

14. 528 U.S. 62, 120 S.Ct. 631, 145 L.Ed.2d 522 (2000).

15. *Garrett v. University of Ala. Bd. of Trustees,* 193 F.3d 1214 (11th Cir.1999); *Dare v. California,* 191 F.3d 1167, 1174 (9th Cir.1999), *petition for cert. filed,* Feb. 24, 2000 (holding that in enacting Title II of the ADA, Congress validly abrogated state sovereign immunity pursuant to its 14th Amendment Section 5 powers); *Martin v. Kansas,* 190 F.3d 1120, 1127 (10th Cir. 1999) (holding that Congress's statutory abrogation of 11th Amendment immunity in ADA was a valid exercise of its Section 5 power to enforce the 14th Amendment); *Muller v. Costello,* 187 F.3d 298, 307–11 (2d Cir.1999) (holding that Congress successfully abrogated the states' immunity under the ADA); *Kimel v. State Bd. of Regents,* 139 F.3d 1426 (11th Cir.1998), *cert. granted sub nom. Florida Dep't of Corrections v. Dickson,* ___ U.S. ___, 120 S.Ct. 976, 145 L.Ed.2d 926 (2000) and *cert. dismissed,* ___ U.S. ___, 120 S.Ct. 1236, 145 L.Ed.2d 1131 (2000); *Coolbaugh v. Louisiana,* 136 F.3d 430, 432–38 (5th Cir.), *cert. denied,* 525 U.S. 819, 119 S.Ct. 58, 142 L.Ed.2d 45 (1998) (holding that "the ADA represents a proper exercise of Congress's Section 5 enforcement power under the 14th Amendment"); *Clark v. California,* 123 F.3d 1267, 1270–71 (9th Cir.1997), *cert. denied sub nom. Wilson v. Armstrong,* 524 U.S. 937, 118 S.Ct. 2340, 141 L.Ed.2d 711 (1998). See also *Torres v. Puerto Rico Tourism Co.,* 175 F.3d 1, 6 n. 7 (1st Cir.1999) (declining to address issue but stating in dicta "we have considered the issue of Congress's authority sufficiently to conclude that, were we to confront the question head-on, we almost certainly would join the majority of courts upholding the [abrogation] provision"). *But see Alsbrook v. City of Maumelle,* 184 F.3d 999 (8th Cir.1999), *cert. dismissed,* ___ U.S. ___, 120 S.Ct. 1265, 146 L.Ed.2d 215 (2000) (holding that Title II of the ADA was not a valid exercise of Congress's 14th Amendment Section 5 powers); *Brown v. North Carolina Div. of Motor Vehicles,* 166 F.3d 698, 702–10 (4th Cir.1999), *petition for cert. filed,* Sep. 8, 1999 (holding that states' 11th Amendment immunity was not validly abrogated because Congress exceeded its Section 5 enforcement power in forbidding states, under the ADA, from charging a fee to disabled persons to cover the cost of accessibility programs).

16. *See Lavia v. Pennsylvania Dep't of Corrections,* 224 F.3d 190 (3d Cir.2000); *Stevens v. Illinois Dep't of Transp.,* 210 F.3d 732 (7th Cir.2000), *petition for cert. filed,* June 30, 2000; *Erickson v. Board of Governors,* 207 F.3d 945 (7th Cir.2000), *petition for cert. filed,* June 26, 2000 (abrogating *Crawford v. Indiana Dep't of Corrections,* 115 F.3d 481 (7th Cir.1997)).

17. *See Garrett,* ___ U.S. ___, 120 S.Ct. 1669, 146 L.Ed.2d 479 (2000). This is the third time the Court has granted certiorari on this issue, but certiorari was dismissed when the other two cases settled.

"qualified individual[s] with a disability."[1] Other courts, however, finding a contradiction between the statutory phrases "terms, conditions, and privileges of employment"[2] and "qualified individual with a disability," have allowed such suits to proceed, so long as the plaintiff is able to perform essential job requirements at the time of suit.[3] As the Third Circuit observed, Title I allows suit by those qualified individuals who can perform the essential functions of the job that the individual holds or desires.[4]

But when a former employee, now disabled such that she cannot perform essential job functions with or without accommodation, sues to receive disability benefits, the textual limitations on the proper plaintiff could operate to bar the suit. Title I explicitly prohibits discrimination by employers regarding the "terms, conditions, and privileges of employment," including fringe benefits.[5] The Third Circuit found that this contradiction creates an ambiguity as to whether "the ADA contains a temporal qualifier of the term 'qualified individual with a disability.' "[6] Finding support in *Robinson v. Shell Oil Co.*[7] where the Supreme Court held that the term "employees" as used in § 704(a) of Title VII encompassed former employees in order to provide former employees legal recourse against post-termination retaliation, the Third Circuit resolved the ADA ambiguity by allowing disabled former employees to sue their former employers regarding disability benefits.[8]

The Second Circuit came to same conclusion but followed a different route. In *Castellano v. City of New York*,[9] the court found an ambiguity in the ADA's failure to specify *when* a plaintiff must be a "qualified

---

§ 10.21

1. *See, e.g., Weyer v. Twentieth Century Fox Film* Corp., 198 F.3d 1104, 1110 (9th Cir.2000); *EEOC v. CNA Ins. Cos.*, 96 F.3d 1039, 1045 (7th Cir.1996) (former employee lacked standing to sue under Title I of the ADA); *Gonzales v. Garner Food Servs., Inc.*, 89 F.3d 1523, 1526–27 (11th Cir.1996), *cert. denied sub nom. Wood v. Garner Food Servs., Inc.*, 520 U.S. 1229, 117 S.Ct. 1822, 137 L.Ed.2d 1030 (1997) (employee failed to satisfy the "qualified individual with a disability" requirement because plaintiff was no longer an employee when alleged discriminatory act occurred); *Rogers v. International Marine Terminals*, 87 F.3d 755, 759 (5th Cir.1996) (plaintiff not a qualified individual because he could not work); *Fitts v. Federal Nat. Mortg. Ass'n*, 44 F.Supp.2d 317 (D.D.C.1999) (same); *Fennell v. Aetna Life Ins. Co.*, 37 F.Supp.2d 40, 43 (D.D.C. 1999) (same); *Fobar v. City of Dearborn Heights*, 994 F.Supp. 878, 884 (E.D.Mich. 1998) (same); *Dickey v. Peoples Energy Corp.*, 955 F.Supp. 886, 889–90 (N.D.Ill. 1996), *aff'd*, 182 F.3d 921 (7th Cir.1999) (plaintiff who cannot perform essential job functions lacks standing).

2. *See* 42 U.S.C.A. § 12112(a).

3. *See Ford v. Schering–Plough Corp.*, 145 F.3d 601, 606–07 (3d Cir.1998), *cert. denied*, 525 U.S. 1093, 119 S.Ct. 850, 142 L.Ed.2d 704 (1999) (finding ambiguity in definitions); *Castellano v. City of New York*, 142 F.3d 58, 69 (2d Cir.1998), *cert. denied*, 525 U.S. 820, 119 S.Ct. 60, 142 L.Ed.2d 47 (1998) (same).

4. *Ford*, 145 F.3d at 605 (citing 42 U.S.C.A. § 12111(8)).

5. Title I confers the right to sue if "a contractual or other arrangement or relationship ... has the effect of subjecting a covered entity's qualified applicant or employee with a disability to ... discrimination (such relationship includes a relationship with ... an organization providing fringe benefits to an employee of the covered entity"). *Ford*, 145 F.3d at 605 (quoting 42 U.S.C.A. § 12112(a)-(b)).

6. *Ford*, 145 F.3d at 606 (quoting 42 U.S.C.A. § 12112(a)).

7. 519 U.S. 337, 340, 117 S.Ct. 843, 846, 136 L.Ed.2d 808 (1997).

8. *Ford*, 145 F.3d at 606–07.

9. *Castellano*, 142 F.3d 58.

individual with a disability.''[10] Finding no satisfactory answers in the legislative history, the court relied on policy to conclude that ''[w]here the alleged discrimination relates to the provision of post-employment benefits, rather than to hiring, promotion, or firing, Congress's expressed concern about qualifications is no longer implicated ... Provided that retired employees were qualified ... while employed ... the purpose of the essential functions requirement has been met.''[11]

§ 10.22 The Three Principal Types of Prohibited Discrimination

Title I's broad anti-discrimination policy blends concepts of equal treatment and affirmative support. An employer may incur liability by (1) engaging in conduct that constitutes disparate treatment discrimination against a qualified disabled person; (2) adopting neutral practices that result in discrimination against a qualified individual or individuals because they screen or tend to screen them out;[1] or (3) by failing to provide a reasonable accommodation that would enable a qualified individual to perform the essential job functions of the position held or desired.[2] More comprehensively, an employer may not:

(1) limit, segregate, or classify a disabled applicant or employee in a way that adversely affects the opportunities or status of the person;

(2) participate in an arrangement with another organization that has the effect of discriminating against the disabled individual;

(3) utilize standards, criteria, or methods of administration which have the effect of discriminating on the basis of the disability or perpetuating discrimination by others subject to common administrative control;

(4) exclude or otherwise deny equal jobs or benefits to an individual because she has a relationship or is associated with a disabled individual;

10. *Id.* at 67.

11. *Id.* at 68.

§ 10.22

1. *See* 42 U.S.C.A. §§ 12112(b)(3)(A), 12112(b)(6); 29 C.F.R. pt. 1630 app. § 1630.10. *See also Gonzales v. City of New Braunfels*, 176 F.3d 834, 839 n. 26 (5th Cir.1999) (''the disparate impact theory has been adopted entirely by the ADA''); *Matthews v. Commonwealth Edison Co.*, 128 F.3d 1194, 1195–96 (7th Cir.1997) (acknowledging the option but refusing to consider the argument as it was not raised in the court below); *Crowder v. Kitagawa*, 81 F.3d 1480, 1483–84 (9th Cir.1996) (disparate impact ADA case under Title II). The ADA disparate impact proof mode is discussed in § 10.24. See also discussion of Title VII disparate impact theory in Chapter 3.

2. *See, e.g., Willis v. Conopco*, 108 F.3d 282 (11th Cir.1997) (per curiam). *Cf. Johnson v. Gambrinus Co.*, 116 F.3d 1052 (5th Cir.1997) (with respect to public accommodations, plaintiff has burden of proof on whether proposed modification is reasonable, but defendant has burden of proof on whether proposed modification would fundamentally alter nature of public accommodation at issue). *But cf. Benson v. Northwest Airlines, Inc.*, 62 F.3d 1108 (8th Cir.1995) (employer has burden of showing it is unable to accommodate without undue hardship once plaintiff identifies a purportedly reasonable accommodation). Sections 10.26 and 10.28, *infra*, discuss, respectively, reasonable accommodation and undue hardship.

(5) use standards or tests that screen out or tend to screen out an individual with disabilities (*unless* the standard is job-related and consistent with business necessity);

(6) use tests whose results reflect the impairment of the individual rather than the skills or aptitude of the test-taker; or

(7) fail to make reasonable accommodations to the known physical or mental limitations of an otherwise qualified individual (unless the accommodation would impose undue hardship.)[3]

§ 10.23 The Prima Facie Case of Disparate Treatment Discrimination

The discrimination concept has been held to mean that the plaintiff's disability played at least some role in the challenged decision. The plaintiff may prove that directly, or indirectly through the shifting evidentiary showings of the *McDonnell Douglas/Burdine* matrix used to show disparate treatment discrimination under Title VII of the 1964 Civil Rights Act.[1] Direct evidence usually consists of slurs or disability-based derogatory comments, but these typically qualify as direct evidence only where the comments are temporally linked to the decisionmaker[2] or high-ranking corporate officers.

Title I, 42 U.S.C.A. § 12112(a), bans discrimination "because of" the plaintiff's disability. Despite its text, several circuits have imported an implicit "solely" into the prohibition, although usually in dictum.[3]

3.   42 U.S.C.A. § 12112(b).

§ 10.23

1. *See, e.g., Martin v. Barnesville Exempted Village Sch. Dist. Bd. of Educ.,* 209 F.3d 931 (6th Cir.2000); *Rehling v. City of Chicago,* 207 F.3d 1009, 1017–18 (7th Cir. 2000); *Allen v. Rapides Parish Sch. Bd.,* 204 F.3d 619, 623 n. 3 (5th Cir.2000); *Shaner v. Synthes,* 204 F.3d 494, 500 (3d Cir. 2000); *Walsh v. United Parcel Service,* 201 F.3d 718, 725 (6th Cir.2000); *Taylor v. Pepsi-Cola Co.,* 196 F.3d 1106, 1109 (10th Cir. 1999); *Hardy v. S.F. Phosphates Ltd. Co.,* 185 F.3d 1076, 1079 (10th Cir.1999); *Young v. Warner–Jenkinson Co., Inc.,* 152 F.3d 1018, 1021 (8th Cir.1998); *EEOC v. Amego, Inc.,* 110 F.3d 135, 145 (1st Cir.1997); *Newman v. GHS Osteopathic, Inc., Parkview Hosp. Div.,* 60 F.3d 153 (3d Cir.1995). For the order of proof in cases under Title VII, *see McDonnell Douglas Corp. v. Green,* 411 U.S. 792, 802–03, 93 S.Ct. 1817, 1824–25, 36 L.Ed.2d 668 (1973); *St. Mary's Honor Ctr. v. Hicks,* 509 U.S. 502, 506–07, 113 S.Ct. 2742, 2746–47, 125 L.Ed.2d 407 (1993); *Texas Dep't of Community Affairs v. Burdine,* 450 U.S. 248, 252–56, 101 S.Ct. 1089, 1093–95, 67 L.Ed.2d 207 (1981). See Chapter 3 for a discussion of these cases

and the various proof modes in the Title VII context.

2. *See, e.g., Hopkins v. Electronic Data Sys. Corp.,* 196 F.3d 655, 661 (6th Cir.1999) (supervisor's comment calling plaintiff "the mentally ill guy on Prozac that's going to shoot the place up" was isolated and ambiguous and does not rise to the level of direct evidence).

3. The Sixth Circuit has consistently incorporated the term "solely" into the prima facie case for both reasonable accommodation and disparate treatment cases, and has likened the ADA plaintiff's ADA prima facie burden to that under the RHA. *See, e.g., Marcum v. Consolidated Freightways,* 225 F.3d 659 (6th Cir.2000); *Black v. Wayne Ctr.,* 225 F.3d 658 (6th Cir.2000); *Archer v. Mesaba Aviation Inc.,* 210 F.3d 371 (6th Cir.2000); *Jones v. Martin,* 205 F.3d 1340 (6th Cir.2000); *Walsh v. United Parcel Serv.,* 201 F.3d 718, 724 (6th Cir.2000); *Cain v. Airborne Express,* 188 F.3d 506 (6th Cir.1999); *Smith v. Ameritech,* 129 F.3d 857, 866 (6th Cir.1997); *Roush v. Weastec, Inc.,* 96 F.3d 840, 843 (6th Cir.1996). Other circuits have made passing references to "solely." *See, e.g., Deppe v. United Airlines,* 217 F.3d 1262 (9th Cir.2000) ("Title I of the

Perhaps these courts are using the RHA and ADA prima facie cases interchangeably–RHA prohibits discrimination against a person "solely by reason of her or his disability."[4] Nevertheless, the importing of "solely" into an ADA case is highly suspect,[5] and that interpretation has been squarely rejected by several circuit courts. These decisions hold that ADA requires nothing more than a showing that disability was a motivating, or in some cases, a "but-for" or determinative cause of the adverse term and condition of employment.[6] These courts have applied

ADA prohibits an employer from discharging a "qualified individual with a disability" solely on the basis of that employee's disability"); *Broussard v. University of Calif.*, 192 F.3d 1252, 1255 (9th Cir.1999); *Gonzales v. City of New Braunfels*, 176 F.3d 834 (5th Cir.1999); *Zukle v. Regents of Univ. of Cal.*, 166 F.3d 1041, 1045 (9th Cir.1999); *Turco v. Hoechst Celanese Corp.*, 101 F.3d 1090, 1092 (5th Cir.1996); *Siefken v. Village of Arlington Heights*, 65 F.3d 664 (7th Cir. 1995) (a decision that the immediate cause of the plaintiff police officer's diabetic reaction while on duty was his own failure to monitor his condition effectively implicitly rests on the assumption that in order to be actionable his disability had to be the sole cause of the predicament that led to his discharge *Despears v. Milwaukee County*, 63 F.3d 635 (7th Cir.1995) (holding); *White v. York Int'l Corp.* 45 F.3d 357, 363 (10th Cir.1995) (dictum). Other circuits have rejected importing the RHA's "solely" element into the ADA. *See, e.g., Parker v. Columbia Pictures Indus.*, 204 F.3d 326, 337 (2d Cir.2000) (the absence of "solely" in ADA's language "suggests forcefully that Congress intended the statute to reach beyond the Rehabilitation Act to cover situations in which discrimination on the basis of disability is one factor, but not the only factor, motivating an adverse employment action"); *Farley v. Nationwide Mutual Ins. Co.*, 197 F.3d 1322, 1334 (11th Cir.1999); *Baird v. Rose*, 192 F.3d 462, 469 (4th Cir. 1999) (abrogating all earlier cases that referenced a "solely" element); *McNely v. Ocala Star–Banner Corp.*, 99 F.3d 1068, 1077 (11th Cir.1996), *cert. denied*, 520 U.S. 1228, 117 S.Ct. 1819, 137 L.Ed.2d 1028 (1997) (in ADA context, "because of" does not mean "solely because of").

4. 29 U.S.C.A. § 794(a).

5. Just one year before the ADA's enactment, a plurality of the Supreme Court interpreted Title VII's "because of" language, the same language that is in ADA, to require a showing that the unlawful factor was merely a *motivating* factor. *Price Waterhouse v. Hopkins*, 490 U.S. 228, 244–45, 109 S.Ct. 1775, 1787–88, 104 L.Ed.2d 268 (1989). And just one year after the ADA

was enacted, Congress codified the *Price Waterhouse* holding in § 703(m), 42 U.S.C.A. § 2000e–2(m), of the Civil Rights Act of 1991, which states that an impermissible consideration must not be "a motivating factor" of an employment decision. While § 703(m) is not expressly incorporated into ADA, the ADA arguably does incorporate § 706(g)(2)(B), 42 U.S.C.A. § 2000e–5(g)(2)(B), the Title VII section that identifies limited, prospective remedies that are available even when a defendant carries the "same decision" showing. See ADA § 107, 42 U.S.C.A. § 12117.

6. *See, e.g., Weber v. Strippit, Inc.*, 186 F.3d 907, 918 (8th Cir.1999), *cert. denied*, 528 U.S. 1078, 120 S.Ct. 794, 145 L.Ed.2d 670 (2000) (where district court instructed jury that defendants should be found liable if plaintiff's disability was "a motivating factor" behind their actions, a more specific mixed-motive instruction was not required); *Kiel v. Select Artificials, Inc.*, 169 F.3d 1131, 1135 (8th Cir.), *cert. denied*, 528 U.S. 818, 120 S.Ct. 59, 145 L.Ed.2d 51 (1999) (requiring plaintiff to prove that his disability was a "motivating factor" in the employer's decision); *Foster v. Arthur Andersen, LLP*, 168 F.3d 1029, 1033 (7th Cir. 1999) (motivating factor); *Newberry v. East Texas State Univ.*, 161 F.3d 276, 279 (5th Cir.1998) (motivating factor); *Young v. Warner–Jenkinson Co., Inc.*, 152 F.3d 1018, 1022–23 (8th Cir.1998) ("determinative" factor); *Doane v. City of Omaha*, 115 F.3d 624, 629 (8th Cir.1997), *cert. denied*, 522 U.S. 1048, 118 S.Ct. 693, 139 L.Ed.2d 638 (1998) (motivating factor); *Morgan v. Hilti, Inc.*, 108 F.3d 1319, 1323 (10th Cir.1997) (determinative factor); *McNely v. Ocala Star–Banner Corp.*, 99 F.3d 1068, 1077 (11th Cir.1996), *cert. denied*, 520 U.S. 1228, 117 S.Ct. 1819, 137 L.Ed.2d 1028 (1997) (but using *Price Waterhouse*, rather than Title VII § 703(m)/706(g)(2)(B) framework for analyzing mixed motives); *Katz v. City Metal Co., Inc.*, 87 F.3d 26, 33 (1st Cir. 1996) (motivating factor); *Ennis v. National Ass'n of Bus. & Educ. Radio, Inc.*, 53 F.3d 55, 59 (4th Cir.1995) (determining factor); *Tyndall v. National Educ. Ctrs., Inc. of*

the Title VII mixed motive and same decision analysis to ADA cases.[7]

Circuit courts have formulated various versions of the inferential disparate treatment prima facie case. The Sixth Circuit has described a five prong prima facie case: plaintiff must show that "(1) he or she is disabled; (2) otherwise qualified for the position, with or without reasonable accommodation; (3) suffered an adverse employment decision;[8] (4) the employer knew or had reason to know of the plaintiff's disability; and (5) the position remained open while the employer sought other applicants or the disabled individual was replaced."[9] In contrast, the Eighth Circuit requires the plaintiff to show prima facie: "(1) that she was a disabled person within the meaning of the ADA, (2) that she was qualified to perform the essential functions of the job, and (3) that she suffered an adverse employment action under circumstances giving rise to an inference of unlawful discrimination."[10] Although facially these

Cal., 31 F.3d 209, 214 (4th Cir.1994) (motivating factor); *cf. Roth v. Lutheran Gen. Hosp.*, 57 F.3d 1446, 1457 n. 17 (7th Cir. 1995) (noting that the plaintiff's disability was not the factor motivating the adverse action).

7. *See, e.g., Parker v. Columbia Pictures Indus.*, 204 F.3d 326, 336–37 (2d Cir.2000) (holding that mixed motive analysis available in the Title VII context applies equally to cases brought under the ADA and vacating district court's dismissal of plaintiff's claim that his disability was an excuse for firing him); *Baird v. Rose*, 192 F.3d 462, 470 (4th Cir.1999) (holding that complaint stated a claim under the ADA even though it may be read to contain allegations that absenteeism also played a role in the adverse job action); *Foster v. Arthur Andersen, LLP*, 168 F.3d 1029, 1033–34 (7th Cir.1999) (relying on Civil Rights Act of 1991's Title VII language "a motivating factor" to hold that "a motivating factor . . . obviously means that the discriminatory factor, here the alleged disability, need not be the employer's only reason for termination"); *Doane v. City of Omaha*, 115 F.3d 624, 629 (8th Cir.1997) (recognizing that 42 U.S.C.A. §§ 2000e–2(m) & 2000e–5(g)(2)(B) apply in actions brought pursuant to the ADA); *McNely v. Ocala Star–Banner Corp.*, 99 F.3d 1068, 1076 (11th Cir.1996), *cert. denied*, 520 U.S. 1228, 117 S.Ct. 1819, 137 L.Ed.2d 1028 (1997); *Katz v. City Metal Co.*, 87 F.3d 26, 33 (1st Cir.1996); *Buchanan v. City of San Antonio*, 85 F.3d 196, 200 (5th Cir.1996); *Pedigo v. P.A.M. Transp., Inc.*, 60 F.3d 1300, 1301–02 (8th Cir.1995) (in a case where the employee's disability was a motivating factor in the employer's decision but the employer proves that it would have made the same decision absent consideration of the employee's disability, the remedies available are limited to a declaratory

judgment, an injunction that does not include an order for reinstatement or for back pay, and some attorney's fees and costs).

8. Exactly what constitutes an "adverse employment action" engenders much litigation under the ADA, as it does under Title VII and the ADEA. *See, e.g., Krocka v. City of Chicago*, 203 F.3d 507, 511 (7th Cir.2000) (district court holding as a matter of law that placement of a police officer in a special program due to his Prozac use constituted an adverse employment action because program participants were reputed to be disciplinary problems). As under Title VII and ADEA, lateral transfers are not considered adverse employment actions under ADA. *See, e.g., Hopkins v. Electronic Data Sys. Corp.*, 196 F.3d 655, 662 (6th Cir.1999) (no adverse action where plaintiff received the same pay and benefits after his transfer as he had before). *But see Duda v. Board of Educ.*, 133 F.3d 1054 (7th Cir. 1998) (forced transfer of bipolar school custodian to position that required him to work alone and he was prohibited from speaking with anyone was adverse employment action under § 12112(b)(10 prohibiting the segregation of a disabled person).

9. *Cehrs v. Northeast Ohio Alzheimer's Research Ctr.*, 155 F.3d 775, 779 (6th Cir. 1998) (citing *Monette v. Electronic Data Sys. Corp.*, 90 F.3d 1173, 1186 (6th Cir.1996)).

10. *Wallin v. Minnesota Dep't of Corrections*, 153 F.3d 681, 686 (8th Cir.1998), *cert. denied*, 526 U.S. 1004, 119 S.Ct. 1141, 143 L.Ed.2d 209 (1999). Other circuits have recited a similar prima facie case. *See Taylor v. Phoenixville Sch. Dist.*, 184 F.3d 296, 306 (3d Cir.1999) (the plaintiff must show: "(1) he is a disabled person within the meaning of the ADA; (2) he is otherwise qualified to perform the essential functions of the job,

formulations are different, in practice they appear to operate in a similar manner. For example, implicit in the Sixth Circuit's "otherwise qualified" prong is the requirement that the plaintiff be able to perform all the essential functions of the job, a requirement explicit in the Eighth Circuit's second prong.[11] Following the *McDonnell Douglas* order of proof, a plaintiff bears the burden of showing that an employer's neutral reason for an adverse decision is a pretext for disability discrimination.[12]

The Third Circuit held it was error to require an ADA inferential proof mode plaintiff to show prima facie that he met his employer's subjective "expectations" regarding plaintiff's work performance, or to require plaintiff to show that nondisabled persons were treated more favorably than plaintiff.[13] On the first point, the court explained that "while objective job qualifications should be considered in evaluating the plaintiff's prima facie case, the question of whether an employee possesses a subjective quality is better left to the later [pretext] stage of the *McDonnell Douglas* analysis."[14] The plaintiff need only prove prima facie that he was objectively qualified for his position by showing that he could perform the essential function of his job with or without reasonable accommodation. "At the prima facie stage, the district court should have made no further inquiry concerning [plaintiff's] qualifications."[15]

with or without reasonable accommodations by the employer; and (3) he has suffered an otherwise adverse employment decision as a result of discrimination"); *Gaul v. Lucent Technologies, Inc.*, 134 F.3d 576, 580 (3d Cir.1998); *Matczak v. Frankford Candy & Chocolate Co.*, 136 F.3d 933 (3d Cir.1997).

11. *See Cehrs*, 155 F.3d at 782 (discussing under prong two plaintiff's burden to prove she can perform the essential functions of the job).

12. Consider, for example, *Matthews v. Commonwealth Edison Co.*, 128 F.3d 1194 (7th Cir.1997). There, the employee was forced to reduce his work schedule while recovering from a heart attack, and his work output was correspondingly lower. Because the employer considered each employee's work output when deciding which employees would be laid off during a RIF, the employee was terminated. The Seventh Circuit rejected the plaintiff's ADA claim, finding that the termination was not "because of" the disability, but because of the legitimate nondiscriminatory reason of relatively poor work output. *See also Kells v. Sinclair Buick–GMC Truck. Inc.*, 210 F.3d 827 (8th Cir.2000) (reversing district court grant of summary judgment to defendant in part because of evidence that employer's nondiscriminatory reason may have been manufactured post-hoc to support a nondiscriminatory explanation for plaintiff's demotion; *Hopkins v. Electronic Data Sys. Corp.*, 196 F.3d 655, 662 (6th Cir.1999)

(outlining three ways a plaintiff may establish pretext: by showing (1) that the proffered reason had no basis in fact; (2) that the proffered reason did not actually motivate the actions; or (3) that the proffered reason was insufficient to motivate the actions; *Cehrs v. Northeast Ohio Alzheimer's Research Ctr.*, 155 F.3d 775, 779 (6th Cir. 1998) (interactive dialogue about leave as a reasonable accommodation belied employer's proffered nondiscriminatory reason that plaintiff failed to follow company procedures in seeking extended leave); *Morgan v. Hilti, Inc.*, 108 F.3d 1319 (10th Cir.1997) (granting summary judgment for employer where plaintiff failed to prove pretext); *Kocsis v. Multi–Care Management, Inc.*, 97 F.3d 876, 883 (6th Cir.1996) (an employee can show pretext by offering evidence that the employer's proffered reason had no basis in fact, did not actually motivate its decision, or was never used in the past to discharge an employee).

13. *See Matczak v. Frankford Candy & Chocolate Co.*, 136 F.3d 933, 938–39 (3d Cir.1997). *But see Ennis v. National Ass'n of Business and Educ. Radio, Inc.*, 53 F.3d 55 (4th Cir.1995) (under ADA a discharge claimant must show she was meeting the employer's legitimate expectations).

14. *Id.* at 938–39 (quoting *Weldon v. Kraft*, 896 F.2d 793, 798 (3d Cir.1990)).

15. *Id.* at 939.

On the court's second holding, that a plaintiff need not show that nondisabled persons were treated more favorably, the court explained that the *McDonnell Douglas* prima facie case is adaptable to the case at hand.[16] The goal of the prima facie case is simply to eliminate the more fundamental reasons why an employer may take an adverse employment action against an employee and to create an inference that the action was taken for an unlawful reason. Further, plaintiffs can satisfy this burden in a variety of ways: the plaintiff could show that the position was filled with a person not belonging to the protected category;[17] or that after the rejection or firing, the employer sought applicants with the plaintiff's qualifications; or by any other showing that raises an inference that the employer was motivated by the plaintiff's status as disabled.[18]

Presumably, courts will import into ADA litigation much of the body of case law developed under other antidiscrimination statutes. The Eleventh Circuit, for example, relied on both Title VII and ADEA case law in holding that whether an employment action is adverse under ADA must be determined objectively rather than subjectively.[19] Similarly, as observed above, courts have applied the "motivating factor" analysis from Title VII to disparate treatment cases under ADA. And under Title VII, practices that are facially neutral may nevertheless be treated as, and may be defended only as, intentional disparate treatment when their adverse impact is not merely substantial but absolute.[20]

§ 10.24 The Prima Facie Case of Disproportionate Adverse Impact (Neutral Practice) Discrimination

The ADA, in 42 U.S.C.A. § 12112(b)(3), (5), and (6), describes in detail the kinds of practices, neutral on their face, that are nevertheless

---

16. *See id.* at 938–39 (noting that the Court in *McDonnell Douglas* "cautioned that there is no rigid formulation of a prima facie case and the requirements may vary with differing factual situations" (citing *McDonnell Douglas*, 411 U.S. at 802 n. 13, 93 S.Ct. at 1824 n. 13)). The Supreme Court has held that a Title VII plaintiff need not show that his qualifications were superior to those of a selectee. *Patterson v. McLean Credit Union*, 491 U.S. 164, 109 S.Ct. 2363, 105 L.Ed.2d 132 (1989).

17. *See, e.g., Kells v. Sinclair Buick–GMC Truck. Inc.*, 210 F.3d 827 (8th Cir. 2000) reversing grant of summary judgment based on evidence of insensitive comments by supervisor, repeated denials of reasonable accommodation requests, and replacement by a non-disabled worker).

18. *See Matczak,* 136 F.3d at 938–39.

19. *See Doe v. Dekalb County Sch. Dist.*, 145 F.3d 1441, 1447–48 (11th Cir.1998) (citing *Maddow v. Procter & Gamble Co.*, 107 F.3d 846, 852–53 (11th Cir.1997) (discussing same under ADEA)); *Collins v. Illinois*, 830 F.2d 692, 702–704 (7th Cir.1987) (discussing same under Title VII).

20. *See, e.g., International Union, UAW v. Johnson Controls, Inc.*, 499 U.S. 187, 111 S.Ct. 1196, 113 L.Ed.2d 158 (1991) (finding that a practice that prohibited fertile women from holding certain jobs was expressly gender discriminatory, observing that the adverse effects of the practice fell 100% on women); *EEOC v. Enterprise Ass'n Steamfitters Local No. 638*, 542 F.2d 579 (2d Cir.1976), *cert. denied*, 430 U.S. 911, 97 S.Ct. 1186, 51 L.Ed.2d 588 (1977) (holding as intentionally discriminatory a union requirement that a new applicant be related by blood or marriage to an existing employee or union member because the policy, while neutral in form, may result in the absolute exclusion of qualified minorities).

prohibited because they fall with disproportionate adverse impact on the disabled. An employer may not:

"(3) utilize standards, criteria, or methods of administration which have the effect of discriminating on the basis of the disability or perpetuating discrimination by others subject to common administrative control;

(5) use standards or tests that screen out or tend to screen out an individual with disabilities (*unless* the standard is job-related and consistent with business necessity); or

(6) use tests whose results reflect the impairment of the individual rather than the skills or aptitude of the test-taker."

As under Title VII, the plaintiff must prove that any such practice has such an adverse impact on the class of disabled persons to which she belongs, and therefore inferentially on her.[1] The defendant then has the burden of proving that the standards, tests, or selection criteria that have that adverse impact are justified as "job related and consistent with business necessity," pursuant to Section 12113 discussed in § 10.25 immediately following. And at least one circuit has held that if the neutral practice is shown to have adverse impact on the basis of a disability, the employer could justify only by proving that it had no practicable alternative to the challenged practice that could meet its business objective.[2]

§ 10.25 Statutory Defenses To Disparate Treatment and Disproportionate Adverse Impact Discrimination

Section 12113 establishes several affirmative defenses available to the ADA defendant. Section 12113(a) is a defense to disproportionate adverse impact claims. It allows the use of "qualification standards, tests, or selection criteria" that have been to shown to be "job related and consistent with business necessity," even if they "screen out or tend to screen out" disabled individuals. Thus, employers bound by industry regulations, licensing requirements, or other administrative rules, or employers that impose physical, testing, experience or educational qualifications on applicants or employees, can defend an ADA suit by proving that the requirement imposed on the individual is both related to the job in question and necessary for the operation of the business.[1] By its terms, this defense also protects employers who require post-offer medi-

§ 10.24

1. *See, e.g., McWright v. Alexander*, 982 F.2d 222 (7th Cir.1992).

2. *See Stutts v. Freeman*, 694 F.2d 666 (11th Cir.1983).

§ 10.25

1. *See, e.g., Belk v. Southwestern Bell Tel. Co.*, 194 F.3d 946, 950 (8th Cir.1999)

(finding error where district court refused requested business necessity instruction); *Andrews v. Ohio*, 104 F.3d 803 (6th Cir. 1997) (weight restrictions for highway patrol officers).

cal examinations.[2] The phrase "job related and consistent with business necessity" is drawn from the provision in Title VII which, as amended in 1991, permits an employer to defend against the disproportionate adverse impact of a neutral practice if it demonstrates "that the challenged practice is job related for the position in question and consistent with business necessity."[3] Circuit courts have interpreted the Title VII provision with varying degrees of stringency.[4]

Although defendants have argued that plaintiffs must prove that they satisfy employment qualification standards as part of their prima facie case,[5] courts have generally followed the structure and language of the statute and considered these employment qualifications as defenses that the employer must justify as job related and consistent with business necessity once the plaintiff has established a prima facie case that the practice in question screens out or tends to screen out the disabled.[6] In *Albertson's, Inc. v. Kirkingburg*,[7] the Supreme Court held that an employer that requires its employees to satisfy a federal safety regulation as a precondition to employment can *defend* an ADA suit by relying on the federal regulation as job-related and necessary to the operation of the business.[8] In *Albertson's*, the defendant argued that

2. *See* 42 U.S.C.A. § 12112(d)(4)(A); *Watson v. City of Miami Beach*, 177 F.3d 932 (11th Cir.1999) (if the prohibition against pre-offer medical inquiries and examinations protects even nondisabled employees, a tuberculosis exam was related to the job of a police officer and consistent with business necessity and therefore not violative of ADA).

3. 42 U.S.C.A. § 2000e–2(k)(1)(A).

4. *Compare Lanning v. Southeastern Pa. Transp. Auth.*, 181 F.3d 478 (3d Cir. 1999), *cert. denied*, 528 U.S. 1131, 120 S.Ct. 970, 145 L.Ed.2d 840 (2000) (concluding that the 1991 Amendments exalt the stringent *Griggs/Dothard* formulation of the defense over the laxer *Beazer/Wards Cove* approach, and holding accordingly that an employer can defend a discriminatory cutoff score on an entry level examination only if the score validly measures the minimum qualifications necessary for successful performance of the job in question) *with Bradley v. Pizzaco of Neb., Inc.*, 7 F.3d 795, 797–798 (8th Cir.1993) (rigorously applying *Griggs* standard by insisting on evidence that customers would order less pizza from bearded delivery persons, not just that customers preferred delivery persons to be clean shaven) *with Fitzpatrick v. City of Atlanta*, 2 F.3d 1112, 1117–19 (11th Cir. 1993) (upholding defense by deeming practice necessary to an "important business goal" without separately examining whether the practice was related to performance of the job in question). *See* § 3.35, *supra*, for a detailed discussion of the application

of the defense to disparate impact cases under Title VII.

5. An ADA plaintiff must of course show prima facie that she is a "qualified individual with a disability." Defendants argue that because the ADA definition of "qualified" means an ability to perform essential job functions, plaintiffs who cannot meet a neutrally applied employment qualification cannot show they can perform an essential job function.

6. *See, e.g., Andrews v. Ohio*, 104 F.3d 803 (6th Cir.1997) (job-relatedness of employer's allegedly discriminatory policy is not element of prima facie case of handicap discrimination; rather, it is defense to be presented where plaintiff has set forth prima facie case); *Riel v. Electronic Data Sys. Corp.*, 99 F.3d 678 (5th Cir.1996) (under ADA, employer bears burden of proof of establishing both "undue burden" and "business necessity," because both are affirmative defenses under language of statute).

7. 527 U.S. 555, 119 S.Ct. 2162, 144 L.Ed.2d 518 (1999). In *Albertson's*, the defendant employer required all truck drivers to pass the Department of Transportation's basic visual acuity test and obtain certification. The plaintiff could not pass the test due to his monocular vision, but was able to get certified through a waiver program.

8. *Id.* at ___, 119 S.Ct. at 2169–70. Likewise, in *Murphy v. United Parcel Service, Inc.*, 527 U.S. 516, 119 S.Ct. 2133, 144

because the plaintiff failed to satisfy the federally mandated visual acuity standard for commercial truck drivers, the plaintiff could not perform an essential job function and was not a "qualified individual with a disability." In effect, the defendant sought to place a prima facie burden on the plaintiff to disprove the employer's position that the plaintiff was not qualified. Faithful to the statutory language, however, the Court treated the defendant's argument as a defense.[9] On the merits of that defense, however, it held that the existence of a governmental requirement suffices to show job-relatedness and business necessity. By contrast, employers who self-impose an employment qualification standard of their own devise must make a particularized showing that the requirement is related to successful performance of an essential function of the job in question and necessary to the employer's business.[10]

Section 12113(b) provides a second affirmative defense, applicable to cases of individual disparate treatment. It allows an employer to discriminate by applying a qualification standard insisting that the plaintiff not pose a "direct threat to the health or safety of other individuals in the work place."[11] "Direct threat" is defined to mean a "significant risk" to the health or safety of others that "cannot be eliminated by reasonable accommodation."[12] The existence of such a risk is determined from the perspective of the person charged with discrimination but must be "based on the objective, scientific information available to him and

L.Ed.2d 484 (1999) the Court characterized the § 12113(a) language as providing a "defense" for the employer.

9. *Albertson's,* 527 U.S. at ___, 119 S.Ct. at 2170 (absent the issue of a waiver program, "there would be no basis to question Albertson's unconditional obligation to follow the regulation and its consequent right to do so"). See also Thomas, J., concurring in the judgment based on the job relatedness and business necessity defense, but asserting, contrary to the majority, that in other cases the plaintiff should have to prove that he meets the employment standard or qualification in question in order to demonstrate prima facie that he is a qualified individual with a disability. *Id.* at ___, 119 S.Ct. at 2175.

10. *See id.* at ___, 119 S.Ct. at 2171 ("It is crucial to its position that [the defendant] was not insisting upon a job qualification merely of its own devising, subject to possible questions about genuine appropriateness and justifiable application to an individual for whom some accommodation may be reasonable."); *Hamlin v. Charter Township of Flint,* 165 F.3d 426, 431 (6th Cir. 1999) (burden on defendant to prove that firefighting was essential job function of being assistant fire chief).

11. 42 U.S.C.A. § 12113(b). *See, e.g., Kapche v. City of San Antonio,* 176 F.3d 840

(5th Cir.1999) and *Gonzales v. City of New Braunfels, Tex.,* 176 F.3d 834 (5th Cir.1999) (driving an essential function of police officer, and a driver with insulin-dependent diabetes posed direct threat to the health and safety of others); *Onishea v. Hopper,* 171 F.3d 1289 (11th Cir.1999), *cert. denied,* 528 U.S. 1114, 120 S.Ct. 931, 145 L.Ed.2d 811 (2000) (HIV+ prison inmates posed a direct threat to fellow inmates and could be segregated for recreational, religious, and educational programs) (case under RHA); *Montalvo v. Radcliffe,* 167 F.3d 873 (4th Cir.), *cert. denied* 528 U.S. 813, 120 S.Ct. 48, 145 L.Ed.2d 43 (1999) (HIV+ minor posed a substantial and direct threat to safety of others in a martial arts instructional program and no reasonable modification could sufficiently reduce this risk without fundamentally altering the nature of the program) (case under Title III); *Doe v. University of Md. Med. Sys. Corp.,* 50 F.3d 1261 (4th Cir.1995); *Bradley v. University of Texas M.D. Anderson Cancer Ctr.,* 3 F.3d 922 (5th Cir.1993), *cert. denied,* 510 U.S. 1119, 114 S.Ct. 1071, 127 L.Ed.2d 389 (1994) (HIV+ employee not "otherwise qualified" under RHA to remain in surgical technician position because risk of transmitting the disease during surgery, while small, would have "lethal consequences").

12. 42 U.S.C.A. § 12111(3).

others."[13] This defense is particularly important in ADA litigation involving AIDS as a disability,[14] but is certainly not limited to infectious diseases.[15] An individual cannot be disqualified under this provision if a reasonable accommodation neutralizes the threat.[16] The decision as to whether an individual (or someone she is associated with)[17] poses a direct threat to the health or safety of others[18] must be made on a case by case basis.[19]

In *School Board of Nassau County v. Arline*,[20] the Supreme Court, relying upon RHA regulations, held that a person afflicted with a contagious disease is not *automatically* excluded from § 504 protection. In *Arline*, the defendant admitted that the plaintiff, an elementary school teacher, had been fired solely because of her tuberculosis. The Court found, based on medical evidence, that the plaintiff was a "handicapped" individual, i.e., that she had a physical impairment that substantially limited a major life activity. The more difficult question was whether the legitimate concerns over the highly contagious nature of the disease posed a sufficiently significant threat that she was not "otherwise qualified" to be a teacher. The Court formulated what has come to be known as the significant risk test, a multi-factor test that balances the level of risk with the nature of the harm. The factors to be considered are "(a) the nature of the risk (how the disease is transmit-

13. *Bragdon v. Abbott*, 524 U.S. 624, 649, 118 S.Ct. 2196, 2210, 141 L.Ed.2d 540 (1998).

14. *See* discussion in § 10.41, *supra*.

15. *Nunes v. Wal–Mart Stores, Inc.*, 164 F.3d 1243, 1245 (9th Cir.1999) (plaintiff suffered from a fainting disorder); *LaChance v. Duffy's Draft House, Inc.*, 146 F.3d 832 (11th Cir.1998) (line cook with epilepsy was a direct threat to safety of himself and others and no reasonable accommodation could alleviate the risk).

16. *See* 42 U.S.C.A. § 12113(3).

17. *See Den Hartog v. Wasatch Academy*, 129 F.3d 1076, 1091 (10th Cir.1997) (resident teacher, fired because his son threatened headmaster's family, was not otherwise qualified).

18. A conflict is developing among the circuits whether the direct threat defense permits employers to refuse to hire an applicant on the ground that the individual, while posing no threat to the health and safety of others, poses a direct threat to his own health and safety. The Ninth Circuit holds that the employer may not refuse on that ground, while the Eleventh Circuit has held the opposite, but with no analysis of the issue. *Compare Echazabal v. Chevron USA, Inc.*, 213 F.3d 1098 (9th Cir.2000) (plaintiff with chronic liver condition working in a chemical plant) and *Kohnke v. Delta Airlines, Inc.* 932 F.Supp. 1110 (N.D.Ill.1996) (accident-prone baggage handler) *with Moses v. American Nonwovens, Inc.*, 97 F.3d 446, 447 (11th Cir.1996), *cert. denied*, 519 U.S. 1118, 117 S.Ct. 964, 136 L.Ed.2d 849 (1997) (with no analysis of the issue).

19. *Id. See also Nunes v. Wal–Mart Stores, Inc.*, 164 F.3d 1243 (9th Cir.1999) (whether cashier's occasional fainting episodes posed direct threat where she would seldom be carrying a heavy object over her head that could harm others if she suffered an attack a fact question precluding summary judgment); *Onishea*, 171 F.3d 1289; *Montalvo*, 167 F.3d 873; *Turco v. Hoechst Celanese Corp.*, 101 F.3d 1090 (5th Cir. 1996) (diabetic not qualified because disability rendered him unable to concentrate while working with complicated machinery and dangerous chemicals that had potential to harm himself or others; "implausible" that proposed accommodation of switch to day shift would eliminate that risk, and in any event switch would work undue hardship on employer that had no chemical operators working only during day); *Altman v. New York City Health and Hosps. Corp.*, 100 F.3d 1054 (2d Cir.1996) (alcoholic physician who drank while treating patients posed direct threat to health and safety of others).

20. 480 U.S. 273, 107 S.Ct. 1123, 94 L.Ed.2d 307 (1987).

ted); (b) the duration of the risk (how long is the carrier infectious); (c) the severity of the risk (what is the potential harm to third parties); and (d) the probabilities the disease will be transmitted and will cause varying degrees of harm."[21] The Court noted that when making these findings, "courts normally should defer to the reasonable medical judgments of public health officials."[22] The ADA codifies *Arline*'s significant risk test,[23] and the Court cited this portion of *Arline* with approval in *Bragdon v. Abbott*,[24] a case arising under ADA Title III involving an HIV + dental patient. Courts routinely apply *Arline*'s significant risk test in ADA "direct threat" cases.[25]

The government as amicus curiae in *Albertson's* argued that safety qualifications imposed by defendants must be justified not only as job related and consistent with business necessity, but also as a direct threat under § 12113(b).[26] Some lower courts have accepted this argument, which stems from an ambiguity in statutory language and implementing regulations.[27] The Fifth Circuit rejected the government's position in *EEOC v. Exxon Corp.*[28] After the 1989 Exxon Valdez oil tanker spill in the Pacific Northwest, an accident in part attributable to the tanker's chief officer's alcohol use, Exxon Corporation imposed a safety qualification that applies to approximately ten percent of its work force: any employee who has undergone treatment for substance abuse is permanently barred from certain safety-sensitive, little-supervised positions, including chief officer of an oil tanker. The EEOC brought suit, challenging the across-the-board ban, arguing that the only defense available to an employer who imposes a safety qualification standard is for the employer to prove that the *individual* poses a "direct threat" to the safety of others.[29] Exxon argued that an employer may defend a safety qualification under either the individual "direct threat" or general "business necessity" prong on § 12113.[30] The Fifth Circuit rejected the

21. *Id.* at 288, 107 S.Ct. at 1131.

22. *Id.*

23. *See* 28 C.F.R. pt. 36 app. B § 36.208(noting that the direct threat provision in Title III of the ADA codifies the Court's holding in *Arline*).

24. 524 U.S. at 649, 118 S.Ct. at 2210.

25. See, e.g., Montalvo, 167 F.3d at 877; *Nunes*, 164 F.3d at 1248; *Doe v. Dekalb County Sch. Dist.*, 145 F.3d 1441, 1445–46 (11th Cir.1998) (overturning district court for failing to make specific fact finding about an HIV + teacher's risk under *Arline*); *Mauro v. Borgess Med. Ctr.*, 137 F.3d 398, 400 (6th Cir.), *cert. denied*, 525 U.S. 815, 119 S.Ct. 51, 142 L.Ed.2d 39 (1998); *Den Hartog*, 129 F.3d at 1091; *EEOC v. Amego, Inc.*, 110 F.3d 135, 143 (1st Cir. 1997).

26. 527 U.S. at—, 119 S.Ct. at 2170.

27. *See* 42 U.S.C.A. § 12113(b) ("The term 'qualification standards' may include a requirement that an individual shall not

pose a direct threat to the health or safety of other individuals in the workplace."); 29 C.F.R. pt. 36 app. at § 1630.2(r) (requiring safety-related standards to be evaluated under the ADA's direct threat standard). *See also, e.g., Leverett v. City of Indianapolis*, 51 F.Supp.2d 949 (S.D.Ind.1999) (holding that a hearing acuity requirement imposed on firefighters "is job-related and consistent with business necessity insofar as it is related to a 'direct threat.' ").

28. 203 F.3d 871, 872 (5th Cir.2000).

29. In an Interpretive Guidance, the EEOC had asserted its position that only the "direct threat" defense was available when the employer instituted a safety requirement. *See* 29 C.F.R. pt. 1630, App. § 1630.15 (b) & (c).

30. Section 12113 provides, in relevant part:

    (a) In general. It may be a defense to a charge of discrimination under this chap-

EEOC's position, holding that an employer may impose a *general* safety qualification standard and need not individual justify the standard on the basis of the direct threat defense.[31] The Fifth Circuit also acknowledged, albeit in dicta, that an employer may assert potential tort liability as a defense.[32] The Supreme Court had found it unnecessary to resolve the general issue in *Albertson's*. There it simply did not insist that the employer meet the terms of the direct threat defense, because the particular safety requirement in question was imposed externally by the government. It was not an employer-devised requirement that required justification, as does the direct-threat provision, with reference to an "individual for whom some accommodation may be reasonable."[33] It is submitted, however, that even in other cases, compounding the job-related/business necessity defense with the direct threat defense appears to impose on employers a higher burden to justify safety-related qualification standards than other job requirements, contrary to the general thrust of *Albertson's*.

While the statute by its terms characterizes "direct threat" as a defense,[34] some courts have treated this issue as part of plaintiff's prima facie case, or have required the employee to carry the burden of proof once the defendant raises the defense. For example, courts have held that the plaintiff must show that she is not a direct threat to others as part of the prima facie requirement of showing she is "a qualified individual."[35] Other courts allocate the burden to the defendant.[36] The

ter that an alleged application of qualification standards ... that screen out or tend to screen out or otherwise deny a job or benefit to an individual with a disability has been shown to be job-related and consistent with business necessity....

(b) Qualification standards. The term "qualification standards" may include a requirement that an individual shall not pose a direct threat to the health or safety of other individuals in the workplace.

31. *Exxon*, 203 F.3d at 875.

32. Citing *International Union v. Johnson Controls, Inc.*, the court also stated that while it found Exxon's fear of massive tort liability like it suffered after the Valdez accident subsumed in the safety motivation, the Supreme Court had noted in *Johnson Controls* that tort liability might be a valid defense if the added cost would threaten the employing corporation's survival.

33. *Albertson's*, 527 U.S. at ___, 119 S.Ct. at 2171.

34. While the statute seems clear, the implementing regulations seem to ignore the statutory language. *See* 29 C.F.R. § 1630.2(r) ("An employer may require, as a qualification standard, that an individual not pose a direct threat to the health or safety of himself/herself or others"). Perhaps the apparent contradiction explains the Fifth Circuit's instructions regarding

burden of proof to a district court when remanding a "direct threat" case: "[a]n employee who is a direct threat is not a qualified individual with a disability. As with all affirmative defenses, the employer bears the burden of proving that the employee is a direct threat." *Rizzo v. Children's World Learning Ctrs., Inc.*, 84 F.3d 758, 764 (5th Cir.1996) (*Rizzo I*). On remand, the district court first instructed the jury that the plaintiff must prove that she is a qualified individual with a disability who "can perform the essential functions of the employment positions ... and who does not pose a direct threat to the health and safety of herself or others." *Rizzo v. Children's World Learning Ctrs., Inc.*, 213 F.3d 209, 212 (5th Cir.2000) (*Rizzo II*) (quoting the district court's instructions). The district court went on to instruct that the "defendant has the burden to prove by a preponderance of the evidence that a direct threat exists." *Id.* On appeal after remand, the circuit court declined to resolve the apparent conflict, stating that the "question of who bears the burden of establishing that an individual's disability poses a direct threat ... is not a simple one." *Id.* Apparently so!

35. *See, e.g., LaChance v. Duffy's Draft House, Inc.*, 146 F.3d at 836 ("the employee retains at all times the burden of persuad-

Court's discussion in *Albertson's* of the job qualification defense of § 12113(a) appears equally applicable to the direct threat defense of § 12113(b) and implies that courts should not front load the "direct threat" issue or burden of proof into the plaintiff's prima facie case.

§ 10.26   Discrimination By Failing to Make Reasonable Accommodation

Although an employer has no obligation to grant a preference to applicants with disabilities, this does not mean that an employer may treat disabled individuals exactly like other candidates. Apart from the duty not to discriminate by disparately treating disabled individuals or subjecting them to practices that screen them out and cannot be justified by job relatedness and business necessity, employers are required to make "reasonable accommodation" to the known physical or mental limitations of a otherwise qualified disabled person[1] unless to do so would impose "undue hardship."[2] Plaintiffs need not prove any discriminatory animus on the part of the defendant; any failure to provide reasonable accommodations for a disability is necessarily "because of a disability".[3] The duty to accommodate distinguishes ADA from the Civil Rights Act of 1964. Except in the case of religious beliefs and observance, which the employer does have a modest duty to accommodate, Title VII prohibits employers merely from discriminating on the ground of race, sex, or national origin.[4]

ing the jury either that he was not a direct threat or that reasonable accommodations were available"); *Moses v. American Nonwovens, Inc.*, 97 F.3d 446, 447 (11th Cir. 1996), *cert. denied*, 519 U.S. 1118, 117 S.Ct. 964, 136 L.Ed.2d 849 (1997) (same).

36. *See, e.g., Nunes v. Wal–Mart Stores, Inc.*, 164 F.3d 1243, 1247 (9th Cir.1999) (employer bears burden of proving employee is direct threat).

§ 10.26

1. As the Senate explained, the use of the term "qualified" in § 12112(b)(5) "does not refer to the definition of 'qualified individual with a disability' set forth in [§ 12111(7)] because such an interpretation would be circular and meaningless. Rather, as in section 504 regulations, the term 'qualified' in [§ 12112(b)(5)] means 'otherwise qualified' (See 45 C.F.R. 84.12(a)), i.e., a person with a disability who meets all of an employer's job-related selection criteria except such criteria he or she cannot meet because of a disability." S.Rep.No. 101–116, at 33.

2. 42 U.S.C.A. § 12112(b)(5). Thus reasonable accommodation obligation requires more than equal treatment; it is a duty to make special adjustments for individuals with disabilities. *See Davoll v. Webb*, 194 F.3d 1116, 1133–34 (10th Cir.1999) (district

court did not err by refusing to instruct the jury that the ADA simply requires equal treatment); *McAlindin v. County of San Diego*, 192 F.3d 1226 (9th Cir.1999), *amended*, 201 F.3d 1211 (9th Cir.), *cert. denied*, ___ U.S. ___, 120 S.Ct. 2689, 147 L.Ed.2d 961 (2000); *Shapiro v. Cadman Towers, Inc.*, 51 F.3d 328, 334–35 (2d Cir. 1995).

3. *See Higgins v. New Balance Athletic Shoe, Inc.*, 194 F.3d 252, 264 (1st Cir.1999). The First Circuit established the prima facie showing a plaintiff must make to survive summary judgment: a plaintiff ordinarily must furnish significantly probative evidence that he is a qualified individual with a disability within the meaning of the applicable statute; that he works (or worked) for an employer whom the ADA covers; that the employer, despite knowing of the employee's physical or mental limitations, did not reasonably accommodate those limitations; and that the employer's failure to do so affected the terms, conditions, or privileges of the plaintiff's employment.

4. Even the Pregnancy Disability Act of 1978, which amends the Title VII definition of discrimination because of sex to include all discriminations made on the ground of pregnancy or related medical condition,

The ADA definition of "reasonable accommodation" includes illustrations of accommodations that might be appropriate in certain circumstances, but is not intended to be exhaustive.[5] Ineffective modifications are not "reasonable accommodations."[6] Requests for stress-free or allergen-free workplaces have been held to be unreasonable as a matter of law.[7] Although Congress intended employers to discuss the possibilities of accommodation with employees, the employer is not required to follow the individual's preference.[8] Where there are two equally efficacious accommodations, the employer may choose the less expensive or easier alternative, as long as equal employment opportunity is provided.[9] If there is no reasonable accommodation that will enable the person to perform the essential functions of the job, the individual with a disability need not be given the job.[10]

Various illustrations of accommodations are provided in the ADA. For example, § 12111(9)(A) provides that existing facilities should be made readily accessible to and usable by disabled individuals,[11] unless making the facilities accessible would impose an undue hardship.[12]

does not demand preferential treatment of pregnant employees. *Cf. California Fed. Sav. & Loan Ass'n v. Guerra,* 479 U.S. 272, 286–87, 107 S.Ct. 683, 692–93, 93 L.Ed.2d 613 (1987). *See* § 5.31.

5. *See* 42 U.S.C.A. § 12111(9); S.Rep. No. 101–116, at 17.

6. *See Vollmert v. Wisconsin Dep't of Transp.,* 197 F.3d 293 (7th Cir.1999) (learned disabled employee was entitled to specialized training on new computer applications where she established that she could master new system with appropriate training despite her failure to learn with extra standard training). *See also* EEOC Policy Guidance on Reasonable Accommodation under the ADA, March 1, 1999; S.Rep.No. 101–116, at 35 ("reasonableness" of an accommodation is assessed in terms of "effectiveness and equal opportunity").

7. *See, e.g., Gaul v. Lucent Technologies, Inc.,* 134 F.3d 576, 581 (3d Cir.1998) (request for a stress-free workplace was a "wholly impractical obligation" that would entail "extraordinary administrative burdens" and was subject to "tremendous abuse"); *Cassidy v. Detroit Edison Co.,* 138 F.3d 629, 634 (6th Cir.1998) (request for allergen-free workplace was "too vague" to be considered reasonable).

8. S.Rep.No. 101–116, at 35.

9. *See Kiel v. Select Artificials, Inc.,* 169 F.3d 1131, 1136–37 (8th Cir.), *cert. denied,* 528 U.S. 818, 120 S.Ct. 59, 145 L.Ed.2d 51 (1999) (although deaf employee requested TDD to make necessary phone calls, employer may shift phone call responsibility to

another employee as a reasonable accommodation); *Malabarba v. Chicago Tribune Co.,* 149 F.3d 690, 699 (7th Cir.1998) ("An employer is not obligated to provide an employee the accommodation he requests or prefers, the employer need only provide some reasonable accommodation"). The Appendix to the ADA regulations explains that "the employer providing the accommodation has the ultimate discretion to choose between effective accommodations, and may choose the less expensive accommodation or the accommodation that is easier for it to provide." 29 C.F.R. pt. 1630 app. at 415. And as the Supreme Court has held in analogous circumstances, an employee cannot make his employer provide a specific accommodation if another reasonable accommodation is instead provided. *See Ansonia Bd. of Educ. v. Philbrook,* 479 U.S. 60, 68–69, 107 S.Ct. 367, 371–72, 93 L.Ed.2d 305 (1986).

10. S.Rep.No. 101–116, at 33–34. *See, e.g., Braunling v. Countrywide Home Loans, Inc.,* 220 F.3d 1154 (9th Cir.2000) (even with reasonable accommodation, plaintiff's performance was inadequate).

11. *See* 42 U.S.C.A. § 12111(9)(A).

12. S.Rep.No. 101–116, at 31; H.R.Rep. No. 101–485, at 65. *See Lyons v. Legal Aid Society,* 68 F.3d 1512 (2d Cir.1995) (whether providing parking space to employee whose disability makes walking difficult is reasonable depends on such factors as employer's location and financial resources) (relying on EEOC Interpretive Guidance on Title I of ADA, 29 C.F.R. pt. 1630 app. at 407).

Job restructuring, an accommodation specifically listed in the statute,[13] may include reallocating or redistributing marginal job functions or altering when and/or how an essential or nonessential function is performed. Essential job functions need not be eliminated,[14] but an employer may be required to remove nonessential elements that present barriers to performance preventing a disabled employee from satisfactorily performing a particular job.[15]

Paid and unpaid leave can also be a reasonable accommodation, particularly to enable substance abusing-employees to participate in a treatment program.[16] Some courts, however, have presumed that regular attendance is a job requirement, leading to the conclusion that an individual who requires medical leave is not "a qualified individual."[17] The Sixth Circuit rejected this presumption in favor of treating leave as any other accommodation; the employee proposes the leave as an accommodation and the burden shifts to the employer to show that leave is unreasonable and/or imposes an undue burden.[18] Extended leave may constitute an undue burden on smaller employers, but where the employer is large enough to allow other employees to perform the disabled employee's job, leave may be a required accommodation,[19] particularly

13.   42 U.S.C.A. § 12111(9)(B).

14.   *See Earl v. Mervyns, Inc.*, 207 F.3d 1361, 1366 (11th Cir.2000) (per curiam) (punctuality essential job function where employer has history of emphasizing punctuality, had counseled employees in the past where they were late, and plaintiff's specific job tasks must be performed at a particular time on a daily basis); *Davis v. Florida Power & Light Co.*, 205 F.3d 1301 (11th Cir.2000) (no need to accommodate a request for no overtime where overtime was an essential job function); *Feliciano v. Rhode Island*, 160 F.3d 780, 785–86 (1st Cir.1998) (lifting was an essential job function for nurses and request to remove that responsibility from the position was unreasonable); *Laurin v. Providence Hosp.*, 150 F.3d 52, 59 (1st Cir.1998) (1st Cir.1998) (employer need not permit nurse to work only day shifts to accommodate her fatigue-induced seizures because shift rotation requirement for nurses was an essential function of job); *Malabarba v. Chicago Tribune Co.*, 149 F.3d 690, 699 (7th Cir.1998) (request for employer to restructure a job by removing essential job functions from the position is unreasonable, and it was essential function of job of packager to rotate among all the "inserting" jobs performed by particular machine); *Foreman v. Babcock & Wilcox Co.*, 117 F.3d 800, 809 (5th Cir. 1997), *cert. denied*, 522 U.S. 1115, 118 S.Ct. 1050, 140 L.Ed.2d 113 (1998); *Cochrum v. Old Ben Coal Co.*, 102 F.3d 908, 913 (7th Cir.1996); *White v. York Int'l Corp.*, 45 F.3d 357, 362 (10th Cir.1995); *Smith v. Blue*

Cross Blue Shield of Kansas, Inc., 102 F.3d 1075 (10th Cir.1996), *cert. denied*, 522 U.S. 811, 118 S.Ct. 54, 139 L.Ed.2d 18 (1997).

15.   *See, e.g., Kiel*, 169 F.3d at 1136–37.

16.   *See Williams v. Widnall*, 79 F.3d 1003, 1006 (10th Cir.1996); *Fuller v. Frank*, 916 F.2d 558, 562 (9th Cir.1990). An employee who needs leave as a reasonable accommodation may be entitled to leave under the Family and Medical Leave Act, 29 U.S.C.A. § 2612(a)(1)(D).

17.   *See e.g., Dutton v. Johnson County Bd. of County Comm'rs*, 859 F.Supp. 498, 507 (D.Kan.1994) (collecting cases).

18.   *Cehrs v. Northeast Ohio Alzheimer's Research Ctr.*, 155 F.3d 775, 782 (6th Cir. 1998).

19.   *See, e.g., Criado v. IBM Corp.*, 145 F.3d 437 (1st Cir.1998); *Rascon v. US West Communications, Inc.*, 143 F.3d 1324, 1333–35 (10th Cir.1998) (five month leave for intensive treatment for post-traumatic stress disorder was a reasonable accommodation where company employed over 50,-000 and had a pre-existing leave policy that allowed up to six months leave with guaranteed reinstatement). *Cf. Milton v. Scrivner, Inc.*, 53 F.3d 1118, 1125 (10th Cir.1995) ("accommodation that would result in other employees having to worker harder or longer hours is not required"). *See* 29 C.F.R. § 1630.2(p)(2)(v) (impact on other employees respecting their ability to perform their duties is a relevant factor in determining the reasonableness of an accommodation).

where leave has routinely been granted in the past.[20] Employers may demand information regarding the expected duration of treatment,[21] and an *indefinite* unpaid leave may not be reasonable.[22]

Modified or part-time work schedules are another form of compliance with the reasonable accommodation requirement.[23] Although the modified work schedule may cause some inconvenience to the employer, the employer is obliged to bear this burden unless it amounts to undue hardship.[24] And a proposed accommodation is unreasonable if it calls for such a radical restructuring of plaintiff's job duties, work schedules, and supervision that it would alter the fundamental requirements of the job or transform the essence of the position.[25]

Offering qualified[26] disabled individuals reassignment[27] to pre-exist-

20. *See Cehrs*, 155 F.3d at 783; *Criado*, 145 F.3d 437.

21. *Id.*

22. *Walsh v. United Parcel Service*, 201 F.3d 718, 725–26 (6th Cir.2000) (request for indefinite leave following 18 months of leave is not a reasonable accommodation); *Taylor v. Pepsi–Cola Co.*, 196 F.3d 1106, 1110 (10th Cir.1999); *Nowak v. St. Rita High Sch.*, 142 F.3d 999, 1004 (7th Cir. 1998) (finding that, "[t]he ADA does not require an employer to accommodate an employee who suffers from a prolonged illness by allowing him an indefinite leave of absence."); *Ralph v. Lucent Technologies*, 135 F.3d 166, 172 (1st Cir.1998) (reviewing a preliminary injunction granted by the district court and agreeing with the court's decision that a very limited four weeks leave time might be required as a reasonable accommodation, even after plaintiff had been given 52 weeks of leave with pay); *Duckett v. Dunlop Tire Corp.*, 120 F.3d 1222, 1225–26 (11th Cir.1997) (stating that where plaintiff had been on salary continuation for 10 months already, defendant had no obligation to maintain this benefit for the remaining two months the company allowed when the defendant could not show that he would likely be able to return to work at the end of this period); *Monette v. Electronic Data Systems Corp.*, 90 F.3d 1173, 1187 (6th Cir.1996) (holding that it is not a reasonable accommodation to require employers to keep employees on medical leave indefinitely in the hope that a position that they can perform will come available); *Hudson v. MCI Telecommunications Corp.*, 87 F.3d 1167, 1169 (10th Cir.1996); *Rogers v. International Marine Terminals*, 87 F.3d 755 (5th Cir.1996) (plaintiff unqualified because unable to be available for work for indefinite period following elective surgery); *Myers v. Hose*, 50 F.3d 278, 283 (4th Cir. 1995) (holding that "reasonable accommodation does not require the [employer] to

wait indefinitely for [the plaintiff's] medical conditions to be corrected"). *Cf. McDonald v. Pennsylvania*, 62 F.3d 92 (3d Cir.1995) (employee unable to work for two months after surgery not even disabled because inability to work was of limited duration).

23. *See Stewart v. Happy Herman's Cheshire Bridge, Inc.*, 117 F.3d 1278 (11th Cir.1997) (longer breaks, unpaid break, shorter work shifts, and a leave of absence satisfied employer duty). But if the employer has previously eliminated all part-time positions, ADA does not require the employer to create such a position as an accommodation. *See Terrell v. USAir*, 132 F.3d 621 (11th Cir.1998).

24. *See, e.g., id.*

25. *See Hypes v. First Commerce Corp.*, 134 F.3d 721 (5th Cir.1998) (request to work at home was unreasonable considering the confidential nature of the documents plaintiff would need to accomplish his assignments); *Carrozza v. Howard County, Md.*, 45 F.3d 425 (4th Cir.1995).

26. And it is clear that a 'qualified individual with a disability' includes a disabled employee who desires and can perform with or without reasonable accommodation an available reassignment job within the company, though unable to perform his or her existing job. *See Smith v. Midland Brake, Inc.*, 180 F.3d 1154, 1161 (10th Cir.1999) (en banc) (noting that nearly every circuit addressing the issue has adopted this interpretation of "qualified individual with a disability").

27. The Second Circuit has established the plaintiff's burden when the employer has offered reassignment as a reasonable accommodation: the employee must offer evidence showing both that the position offered was inferior to her former job and that a comparable position, for which the

ing, vacant[28] positions in order to avoid terminating their employment is a key accommodation explicitly provided for in the statute.[29] Thus, an employee's inability to perform the essential functions of her current job does not automatically justify discharge. If a disabled employee can no longer perform the essential functions of her present job, and that inability cannot be cured by some other reasonable accommodation,[30] an employer must offer the employee a transfer to a vacant, existing position for which the employee is qualified.[31] But the employer is not

employee was qualified, was open. *See Norville v. Staten Island Univ. Hosp.*, 196 F.3d 89, 99 (2d Cir.1999).

28. It is not reasonable to require a private employer to create a new job for the purpose of reassigning an employee to that job. *See Hoskins v. Oakland County Sheriff's Dep't*, 227 F.3d 719 (6th Cir.2000) (permanent reassignment to a rotating position was not reasonable accommodation); *Willis v. Pacific Maritime Ass'n*, 162 F.3d 561, 567 (9th Cir.1998) ("In order for reassignment to a vacant position to be reasonable, an existing position must be vacant: there is no duty to create a new position for the disabled employee."); *Aka v. Washington Hosp. Ctr.*, 156 F.3d 1284, 1305 (D.C.Cir. 1998) ("[E]mployers are not required to . . . create a new position."); *Terrell v. USAir*, 132 F.3d 621, 626 (same); *Smith v. Ameritech*, 129 F.3d 857, 867 (6th Cir.1997) (same); *Gerdes v. Swift–Eckrich, Inc.*, 125 F.3d 634 (8th Cir.1997); *Still v. Freeport–McMoran, Inc.*, 120 F.3d 50, 53 (5th Cir. 1997); *White v. York Int'l Corp.*, 45 F.3d 357, 362 (10th Cir.1995); *Gile v. United Airlines, Inc.*, 95 F.3d 492, 499 (7th Cir. 1996); *Benson v. Northwest Airlines, Inc.*, 62 F.3d 1108, 1114 (8th Cir.1995).

29. *See* 42 U.S.C.A. § 12111(9)(B) (reasonable accommodation may include "reassignment to a vacant position"). Reassignment, however, "mean[s] something more than merely allowing a disabled person to compete equally with the rest of the world for a vacant position. . . . If reassignment is a reasonable accommodation under all of the circumstances, . . . then the disabled employee has a right in fact to the reassignment, and not just to the consideration process leading up to the potential reassignment." *Smith v. Midland Brake, Inc.*, 180 F.3d 1154, 1165–76 (10th Cir.1999) (en banc) (noting that "nearly every circuit" to consider the issue has found that reassignment is a reasonable accommodation). According to the EEOC guidelines, an employer who utilizes reassignment to meet the duty of reasonable accommodation for a current employee "should reassign the individual to an equivalent position in terms of pay, status, etc., if the individual is quali-

fied, and if the position is vacant within a reasonable amount of time." *EEOC Interpretive Guidance on Title I of the Americans with Disabilities Act*, 29 C.F.R. App. § 1630.2(o). *See also Norville v. Staten Island Univ. Hosp.*, 196 F.3d 89, 99–100 (2d Cir.1999) (reassignment does not constitute "reasonable accommodation" where a position comparable to the employee's former placement is available, for which the employee is qualified, but the employee instead is assigned to a position that would involve a significant diminution in salary, benefits, seniority or other advantages that she possessed in her former job); *Smith*, 180 F.3d at 1177 ("The employer should first consider lateral moves to positions that are regarded as equivalent. An employer may only consider lesser jobs that constitute a demotion if there are no such equivalent positions available."). *Cf. Allen v. Rapides Parish Sch. Bd.*, 204 F.3d 619 (5th Cir. 2000) (demotion is reasonable accommodation where employee was unqualified for any lateral vacant positions); *Cassidy v. Detroit Edison Co.*, 138 F.3d 629, 634 (6th Cir.1998) ("An employer may reassign an employee to a lower grade and paid position if the employee cannot be accommodated in the current position and a comparable position is not available.").

30. *See, e.g., Vollmert v. Wisconsin Dep't of Transp.*, 197 F.3d 293 (7th Cir.1999) (employer violated ADA by demoting learned disabled employee where she established that she could master new computer system used in her current job with appropriate training by a learning disability trainer despite her failure to learn with standard training).

31. *See, e.g., Burns v. Coca–Cola Enterprises, Inc.* 222 F.3d 247 (6th Cir.2000) (after employee requests transfer, employer is obligated to consider reassigning employee who is unable to perform current job); *Williams v. Toyota Motor Manufacturing, Kentucky, Inc.*, 218 F.3d 609 (6th Cir.2000) (plaintiff with carpal tunnel syndrome unable to perform repetitive manual tasks must be reassigned to another position); *Fjellestad v. Pizza Hut of America, Inc.*, 188

required to reassign the employee if the vacant job would entail a

F.3d 944, 950 (8th Cir.1999); *Bratten v. SSI Servs., Inc.,* 185 F.3d 625, 634 (6th Cir. 1999); *Smith v. Midland Brake, Inc.,* 180 F.3d 1154 (10th Cir.1999) (en banc); *Zukle v. Regents of Univ. of Cal.,* 166 F.3d 1041, 1046–47 (9th Cir.1999) ("In the employment context, '[o]nce the plaintiff has established the existence of a reasonable accommodation that would enable him or her to perform the essential functions of an available job, the burden switches to the defendant to show that this accommodation would constitute an undue hardship.' ") (quotations omitted); *Feliciano v. Rhode Island,* 160 F.3d 780, 785–86 (1st Cir.1998) ("The determination that [the employee] cannot perform the essential functions of her job ... does not end the analysis.... Section 12111(9)(B) of the ADA states that 'reasonable accommodation' may include 'reassignment to a vacant position.' "); *Aka v. Washington Hosp. Ctr.,* 156 F.3d 1284, 1301 (D.C.Cir.1998) (en banc) ("An employee seeking reassignment to a vacant position is thus within the definition [of an 'otherwise qualified individual with a disability'] if, with or without reasonable accommodation, she can perform the essential functions of the employment position to which she seeks reassignment."); *Malabarba v. Chicago Tribune Co.,* 149 F.3d 690, 699 (7th Cir.1998); *Baert v. Euclid Beverage, Ltd.,* 149 F.3d 626, 631 (7th Cir.1998) (plaintiff survives summary judgment on evidence that he was qualified for two other vacant jobs in company); *Aldrich v. Boeing Co.,* 146 F.3d 1265, 1271 (10th Cir.1998), *cert. denied,* 526 U.S. 1144, 119 S.Ct. 2018, 143 L.Ed.2d 1030 (1999) (finding evidentiary support for employee's argument that there existed two other positions to which he could have been reassigned as a reasonable accommodation); *Dalton v. Subaru–Isuzu Automotive, Inc.,* 141 F.3d 667, 677 (7th Cir.1998) ("It is well established that under the ADA, the employer's duty reasonably to accommodate a disabled employee includes reassignment of the employee to a vacant position for which she is qualified. The option of reassignment is particularly important when the employee is unable to perform the essential functions of his or her current job, either with or without accommodation or when accommodation would pose an undue hardship for the employer."); *Gaul v. Lucent Technologies, Inc.,* 134 F.3d 576, 578, 580 (3d Cir.1998) (employee who "cannot perform his former duties" must, if the required accommodation is a transfer to another department or supervisor, "demonstrate that there were vacant, funded positions whose essential duties he

was capable of performing, with or without reasonable accommodation") (quotations omitted); *Stone v. City of Mount Vernon,* 118 F.3d 92, 100 (2d Cir.1997), *cert. denied,* 522 U.S. 1112, 118 S.Ct. 1044, 140 L.Ed.2d 109 (1998) (refusing to hold unreasonable as a matter of law a requested reassignment of a partially paralyzed firefighter to the fire department's administrative bureau); *Mengine v. Runyon,* 114 F.3d 415, 418 (3d Cir.1997); *Williams v. Channel Master Satellite Sys., Inc.,* 101 F.3d 346, 350 (4th Cir.1996), *cert. denied sub nom. Williams v. Avnet, Inc.,* 520 U.S. 1240, 117 S.Ct. 1844, 137 L.Ed.2d 1048 (1997); *Gile v. United Airlines, Inc.,* 95 F.3d 492, 498 (7th Cir. 1996) ("Our review of the ADA, its regulations, and the EEOC's interpretive guidance leads us to the conclusion of the majority of courts that have addressed the issue that the ADA may require an employer to reassign a disabled employee to a different position as reasonable accommodation where the employee can no longer perform the essential functions of their current position."); *Monette v. Electronic Data Sys. Corp.,* 90 F.3d 1173, 1187 (6th Cir. 1996) ("it is true that employers may be required, as a reasonable accommodation, to transfer a disabled employee to a vacant position for which he or she is qualified"); *Benson v. Northwest Airlines, Inc.,* 62 F.3d 1108, 1112, 1114 (8th Cir.1995) (employee's previous job as a mechanic would be totally inappropriate given his condition, but if the employer "had a vacant, existing position for which [the employee] qualified, [the employee's] assignment to the position might have been a reasonable accommodation"); *White v. York Int'l Corp.,* 45 F.3d 357, 362 (10th Cir.1995) (after finding no "possible accommodations" enabling employee to continue working in his present position, rejected various reassignment accommodations because employee was either not qualified for vacant jobs, no vacancies existed, or reassignment would have been a promotion). *See* 29 C.F.R. § 1630.2(*o*)(2)(ii).

Under the RHA, federal employers face a higher standard regarding reassignment. Once a reasonable accommodation is requested, the federal employer bears the burden of locating another job that the disabled employee can perform. *See Woodman v. Runyon,* 132 F.3d 1330, 1343 (10th Cir. 1997). The EEOC proposed a rule on March 1, 2000 that would import the reasonable accommodation/undue hardship analysis of the ADA into § 501. 60 Fed. Reg. 11, 019–11023 (March 1,2000).

promotion,[32] or if the reassignment would bump an incumbent employee or violate a collective bargaining agreement or long-standing intracorporate transfer or seniority policy.[33] And when an employer has "committed significant time and effort" in a futile attempt to find another position for a disabled employee, the employer's obligation is met.[34]

Another accommodation provided for in the statute is the modification of examinations, training materials or methods[35] or employment policies.[36] A common policy is exemplified in the Senate Report regarding drivers' licenses.[37] Many employers require employees to have a driver's license on the theory that someone who drives will be on time for work or may run occasional errands. Such a policy must be modified when applied to persons with disabilities who can perform the essential functions of the job, but cannot drive.[38]

Finally, the provision of readers, interpreters, or other attendants may constitute a reasonable accommodation. Whether such assistance is required depends on the concept of undue hardship. To the extent that

---

32. *Malabarba v. Chicago Tribune Co.*, 149 F.3d 690, 699 (7th Cir.1998); *Shiring v. Runyon*, 90 F.3d 827, 832 (3d Cir.1996); *White v. York Int'l Corp.*, 45 F.3d 357, 362 (10th Cir.1995).

33. *See Pond v. Michelin North America*, 183 F.3d 592 (7th Cir.1999) (even where collective bargaining agreement allowed the more senior plaintiff to bump an incumbent in the position she sought, that job not "vacant" for ADA purposes because "Congress did not intend that other workers lose their positions in order to accommodate a disabled worker."); *Willis v. Pacific Maritime Ass'n*, 162 F.3d 561, 567 (9th Cir.1998) ("However, the positions [the employees] requested were not vacant. The CBA provided that those jobs should be assigned based on seniority. [The employees] could not transfer to these permanent light duty work positions because other employees with greater seniority were eligible for any opening ... before either of them."); *Malabarba v. Chicago Tribune Co.*, 149 F.3d 690, 699 (7th Cir.1998) (reassignment not required if it requires bumping more senior employees); *Dalton v. Subaru-Isuzu Automotive, Inc.*, 141 F.3d 667, 678 (7th Cir.1998) ("Nothing in the ADA requires an employer to abandon its legitimate, nondiscriminatory company policies defining job qualifications, prerequisites, and entitlements to intra-company transfers."); *Kralik v. Durbin*, 130 F.3d 76, 83 (3d Cir.1997); *Foreman v. Babcock & Wilcox Co.*, 117 F.3d 800 (5th Cir.1997), *cert. denied*, 522 U.S. 1115, 118 S.Ct. 1050, 140 L.Ed.2d 113 (1998) (citing cases); *Eckles v. Consolidated Rail Corp.*, 94 F.3d 1041 (7th Cir.1996), *cert. denied*, 520 U.S. 1146, 117

S.Ct. 1318, 137 L.Ed.2d 480 (1997); *Benson v. Northwest Airlines, Inc.*, 62 F.3d 1108, 1114 (8th Cir.1995); *Wooten v. Farmland Foods*, 58 F.3d 382, 386 (8th Cir.1995); *Milton v. Scrivner, Inc.*, 53 F.3d 1118, 1125 (10th Cir.1995) (recognizing that plaintiffs' collective bargaining agreement prohibits their transfer to any other job because plaintiffs lack the requisite seniority). This ruling transplants from Title VII religious discrimination cases the rule that an accommodation entails undue hardship if it requires a union to acquiesce in an alteration of existing collectively bargained rights of other employees. See § 2.23, *supra*. As such it appears inconsistent with the Congressional direction that the *de minimis* principles for determining reasonable accommodation under Title VII religious discrimination cases are inapplicable under the ADA, as discussed at § 10.28, *infra*. ADA is fundamentally different from Title VII (and ADEA) in another important respect: Title VII expressly exempts bona fide seniority systems and ADA does not.

34. *See Malabarba v. Chicago Tribune Co.*, 149 F.3d 690, 699 (7th Cir.1998).

35. *See, e.g., Vollmert v. Wisconsin Dep't of Transp.*, 197 F.3d 293 (7th Cir.1999) (learned disabled employee was entitled to specialized training on new computer applications where she established that she could master new system with appropriate training despite her failure to learn with standard training).

36. S.Rep.No. 101–116, at 31.

37. *Id.* at 33.

38. *Id.*

an attendant is needed for only a portion of the workday, the employer is less likely to satisfy the undue hardship standard.[39]

Employers should modify or acquire equipment that is adaptive to the needs of disabled employees, such as electronic visual aids, braille devices, talking calculators, magnifiers, and audio recordings. In the telecommunications field, employers should acquire telephones compatible with hearing aids, devices for the hearing impaired, gooseneck telephone headsets, mechanical pageturners, and raised or lowered furniture or equipment.[40] But an employer is not required to provide a disabled employee with the most technologically advanced equipment.[41]

§ 10.27 The Interactive Dialogue Prerequisite To Reasonable Accommodation: Burdens and Responsibilities

Accommodation by the employer is required only for "known" disabilities.[1] Therefore, employees and applicants must normally be given the opportunity and have a duty to request accommodation.[2] The plaintiff[3] bears the initial burden[4] of proposing a reasonable accommoda-

39. *Id.* at p. 33; H.R.Rep.No. 101–485, at 64.

40. *Id. Cf. McCauley v. Winegarden*, 60 F.3d 766 (11th Cir.1995) (per curiam), *cert. denied*, 517 U.S. 1149, 116 S.Ct. 1451, 134 L.Ed.2d 570 (1996) (Title II does not require a public entity to provide a chemically hypersensitive state court litigant with a filtration device).

41. *See* 29 C.F.R. pt. 1630 app. § 1630.9 ("[A]n employer would not have to provide an employee disabled by a back impairment with a state-of-the-art mechanical lifting device if it provided the employee with a less expensive or more readily available device that enabled the employee to perform the essential functions of the job.").

§ 10.27

1. *See, e.g., Burns v. Coca–Cola Enterprises, Inc.*, 222 F.3d 247 (6th Cir.2000) (plaintiff's failure to request transfer fatal to his reasonable accommodation claim); *Gaston v. Bellingrath Gardens & Home, Inc.*, 167 F.3d 1361 (11th Cir.1999) (duty to provide accommodation is not triggered unless a specific demand for accommodation is made).

2. *See Taylor v. Principal Fin. Group, Inc.*, 93 F.3d 155, 165 (5th Cir.), *cert. denied*, 519 U.S. 1029, 117 S.Ct. 586, 136 L.Ed.2d 515 (1996) ("If the employee fails to request accommodation, the employer cannot be liable for failing to provide one."); *Miller v. National Casualty Co.*, 61 F.3d 627 (8th Cir.1995) (failure to inform employer of mental impairment); *Hedberg*

v. Indiana Bell Tel. Co., Inc., 47 F.3d 928 (7th Cir.1995) (informing supervisor that plaintiff had a major health problem that he wished to be kept confidential did not communicate to employer the requisite knowledge of plaintiff's particular disability). *But see Bultemeyer v. Fort Wayne Community Schs.*, 100 F.3d 1281 (7th Cir.1996) (employer required to initiate interactive dialogue about disability with paranoid schizophrenic where employer from prior experience might have known that plaintiff's failure to do so himself was a product of his disability).

3. The EEOC compliance manual provides that "a family member, friend, health professional, or other representative may request a reasonable accommodation on behalf of an individual with a disability." 2 EEOC Compliance Manual, Enforcement Guidance for Psychiatric Disabilities, at 20–21. The Seventh Circuit has allowed an employee's psychiatrist to make a request for accommodations on behalf of an employee, *Bultemeyer v. Fort Wayne Community Schs.*, 100 F.3d 1281, 1286 (7th Cir.1996), and the Third Circuit allowed the plaintiff's son to make the request. *Taylor v. Phoenixville Sch. Dist.*, 184 F.3d 296, 313 (3d Cir. 1999).

4. But if a request for reassignment, for example, is futile because of a long-standing employer policy of refusing reassignments, the employee may be relieved of the responsibility of requesting a reassignment where reassignment is the only reasonable accommodation. *See Davoll v. Webb*, 194 F.3d

tion,[5] and the proposal must be reasonably specific and compatible with the particular workplace, at least where the employee is familiar with the job and job site.[6] But "[r]equests for reasonable accommodations do not need to be in writing,"[7] and "an individual may use 'plain English' and need not mention the ADA or use the phrase 'reasonable accommodation.' "[8] Once the plaintiff has established the existence of reasonable accommodation that would enable her to perform the essential functions of an available job, the burden switches to the defendant to show that this accommodation would constitute an undue hardship.[9] In *Borkowski v. Valley Central School District*,[10] the Second Circuit laid out a two-step

1116, 1132–33 (10th Cir.1999).*Cf. Beck v. University of Wisconsin Bd. of Regents*, 75 F.3d 1130, 1135 (7th Cir.1996) ("[N]either party should be able to cause a breakdown in the process for the purpose of either avoiding or inflicting liability.").

5. *See Flemmings v. Howard Univ.*, 198 F.3d 857, 861–62 (D.C.Cir.1999) (the request for accommodation must come during the time period when a reasonable accommodation could enable the employee to perform); *Terrell v. USAir*, 132 F.3d 621 (11th Cir.1998) (plaintiff has burden to identify an accommodation that permits her to perform essential functions and to establish that accommodation is reasonable); *Willis v. Conopco, Inc.*, 108 F.3d 282, 285 (11th Cir. 1997) (holding that the ADA places on the plaintiff the burden of "producing probative evidence that reasonable accommodations were available"); *Monette v. Electronic Data Sys. Corp.*, 90 F.3d 1173, 1183 (6th Cir. 1996) ("[T]he disabled individual bears the initial burden of proposing an accommodation and showing that accommodation is objectively reasonable."); *White v. York Int'l Corp.*, 45 F.3d 357, 361 (10th Cir.1995) (holding that the plaintiff must show that accommodation is possible, the employer must then show inability to accommodate, and the plaintiff must then produce concrete suggestions for possible accommodations); *Benson v. Northwest Airlines, Inc.*, 62 F.3d 1108 (8th Cir.1995) (employer has burden of showing it is unable to accommodate without undue hardship once plaintiff identifies a purportedly reasonable accommodation). *But see Stone v. City of Mount Vernon*, 118 F.3d 92, 98 (2d Cir.1997), *cert. denied*, 522 U.S. 1112, 118 S.Ct. 1044, 140 L.Ed.2d 109 (1998) (holding that plaintiff must merely " 'suggest the existence of a particular plausible accommodation,' " which the defendant must then show is unreasonable). *But cf. Beck v. University of Wis. Bd. of Regents*, 75 F.3d 1130 (7th Cir.1996) (once the employee identifies a disability, an employer has "at least some responsibility in determining the necessary accommodation") (citing 29 C.F.R.

§ 1630.2(*o*)(3), which calls for the employer to "initiate an informal interactive process . . . [to] identify the precise limitations resulting from the disability and potential reasonable accommodations. . . . ").

6. *See Cassidy v. Detroit Edison Co.*, 138 F.3d 629, 634 (6th Cir.1998) (request for allergen-free workplace was "too vague" to be considered reasonable).

7. 2 EEOC Compliance Manual, Enforcement Guidance for Psychiatric Disabilities, at 21.

8. *Id.* at 19. See *Taylor v. Phoenixville School District*, 184 F.3d 296, 313–14 (3d Cir.1999) (plaintiff need only request an accommodation and need not use the words reasonable accommodation).

9. But an employer does not violate the reasonable accommodation duty if it is unable to determine what would reasonably enable the employee despite her disability to perform the essential functions of the job because the employee frustrates or obstructs the dialogue by supplying misleading information or failing to provide information within her particular knowledge— e.g., information about her medical condition. *Beck*, 75 F.3d at 1135. *See also* 42 U.S.C.A. § 12112(b)(5)(A).

10. 63 F.3d 131, 137–38 (2d Cir.1995). Thus, the court found that the burden of establishing that a vacancy exists on the plaintiff-employee. When a plaintiff brings an action alleging that a defendant violated the ADA by failing to offer a reasonable accommodation, the claim fails unless the plaintiff establishes that an effective accommodation existed that would render her otherwise qualified. The burden of persuasion on the "existence" of an "effective accommodation" is not satisfied by mere speculation. A plaintiff seeking to hold the employer liable for failing to transfer her to a vacant position as a reasonable accommodation must demonstrate that there was a vacant position into which she might have been transferred. *See Jackan v. New York*

process to evaluate whether the failure to provide a proposed accommodation constitutes a violation of the ADA. First, "the plaintiff bears the burden of proving ... that an accommodation exists that permits her to perform the job's essential functions." If the plaintiff meets that burden, the analysis shifts to the question whether the proposed accommodation is reasonable; on this question the burden of persuasion lies with the defendant.[11]

Implementing regulations state that "[t]o determine the appropriate reasonable accommodation it may be necessary for the [employer] to initiate an informal, interactive process with the [employee] with a disability in need of the accommodation. This process should identify the precise limitations resulting from the disability and potential reasonable accommodations that could overcome those limitations."[12] The EEOC's interpretive guidelines also state that: "Once a qualified individual with a disability has requested provision of a reasonable accommodation, the employer must make a reasonable effort to determine the appropriate accommodation. The appropriate reasonable accommodation is best determined through a flexible, interactive process that involves both the employer and the [employee] with a disability."[13]

The Seventh Circuit has held that both parties have a responsibility to participate in an interactive process and that "courts should look for signs of failure to participate in good faith or failure by one of the parties to make reasonable efforts to help the other party determine what specific accommodations are necessary."[14] Moreover, where a plaintiff has caused a breakdown of the interactive process, summary judgment for the defendant is appropriate.[15] But several circuits have rejected plaintiffs' argument that a separate cause of action exists for an employer's failure to engage in an interactive process with the disabled employee.[16] Employers even in such circuits have some incentive to participate

State Dep't of Labor, 205 F.3d 562 (2d Cir. 2000).

11. *Id.* at 138.

12. 29 C.F.R. § 1630.2(*o*)(3).

13. 29 C.F.R. § 1630, App. § 1630.9.

14. *Beck*, 75 F.3d at 1135 ("Where the missing information is of the type that can only be provided by one of the parties, failure to provide the information may be the cause of the breakdown and the party withholding the information may be found to have obstructed the [interactive] process"). *See also Taylor v. Phoenixville Sch. Dist.*, 184 F.3d 296, 314 (3d Cir.1999) (employer is obligated to take some initiative in interactive process); *Taylor v. Principal Fin. Group, Inc.*, 93 F.3d 155, 165 (5th Cir.), *cert. denied*, 519 U.S. 1029, 117 S.Ct. 586, 136 L.Ed.2d 515 (1996) (The "employee's initial request for an accommodation ... triggers the employer's obligation to participate in the interactive process ...").

15. *See Loulseged v. Akzo Nobel, Inc.*, 178 F.3d 731 (5th Cir.1999) (judgment as a matter of law against plaintiff who abandoned interactive process before employer could evaluate the adequacy of proposed accommodation); *Hennenfent v. Mid Dakota Clinic*, 164 F.3d 419 (8th Cir.1998); *Templeton v. Neodata Servs., Inc.*, 162 F.3d 617 (10th Cir.1998) (employee's failure to provide medical information needed by employer to provide accommodation obstructed process and defeated employee's claim); *Steffes v. Stepan Co.*, 144 F.3d 1070, 1072–73 (7th Cir.1998) (plaintiff caused breakdown by failing to respond adequately to the defendant's offer of reassignment); *Beck*, 75 F.3d 1130. Employers, however, cannot escape ADA liability by making unreasonable requests for information. *See Langon v. Department of Health and Human Servs.*, 959 F.2d 1053 (D.C.Cir.1992).

16. *See Rehling v. City of Chicago*, 207 F.3d 1009, 1015–16 (7th Cir.2000); *Fjellestad v. Pizza Hut of America, Inc.*, 188 F.3d 944 (10th Cir.1999) (failure of employee to engage in process is prima facie evidence of

in the dialogue, because good faith participation in the interactive process may protect the employer from liability for punitive and certain compensatory damages.[17]

Where a lawyer negotiates with an employer about how to reasonably accommodate the client's disability, those negotiations do not make the lawyer a necessary witness, and do not therefore disqualify the lawyer from further representing the client in the suit.[18]

It is permissible in appropriate circumstances for an employer to initiate accommodation discussions with a particular employee who appears to be experiencing performance difficulties because of a known disability.[19] However, while an employer may invite a discussion of known disabilities, it is not permissible to compel an individual or employee to disclose or discuss an underlying disability. An invitation to discuss accommodation is all that should be made.

§ 10.28   The Undue Hardship Exception to the Duty to Make Reasonable Accommodation

Undue hardship is the employer's affirmative defense for failing to make a reasonable accommodation for an otherwise qualified individual once such accommodation is requested and feasible. Employers are not expected to make accommodations that are unduly costly, extensive, substantial or disruptive, or that will fundamentally alter the nature of the program.[1] In this view, the burden is on the plaintiff to show that

bad faith requiring a factual question or ultimate question of reasonable accommodation); *Willis v. Conopco, Inc.*, 108 F.3d 282, 285 (11th Cir.1997) (holding that the plaintiff has the burden of showing available accommodations and that the employer cannot be found liable "merely for failing to engage in the [interactive] process itself"). *But see Soto–Ocasio v. Federal Exp. Corp.*, 150 F.3d 14, 19 (1st Cir.1998) (holding employer did not breach duty to discuss because plaintiff failed to provide evidence that she could perform essential duties even with reasonable accommodation, but writing "[t]here may well be situations in which the employer's failure to engage in an informal interactive process would constitute a failure to provide reasonable accommodation that amounts to a violation of the ADA"); *Mengine v. Runyon*, 114 F.3d 415, 420 (3d Cir.1997) (citing ADA cases and holding that, under the Rehabilitation Act, "both parties have a duty to assist in the search for appropriate reasonable accommodation and to act in good faith," but stating that, in the absence of a reasonable accommodation, the employer cannot be liable under the ADA or the Rehabilitation Act); *Taylor v. Principal Fin. Group*, 93 F.3d 155, 165 (5th Cir.), *cert. denied*, 519 U.S. 1029, 117 S.Ct. 586, 136 L.Ed.2d 515 (1996) (holding that "the employee's initial re-

quest for an accommodation ... triggers the employer's obligation to participate in the interactive process of determining one").

17. *See* EEOC Policy Guidance on Reasonable Accommodation Under the ADA, March 1, 1999 at n. 22 (citing 42 U.S.C.A. § 1981a(a)(3)).

18. *See Harter v. University of Indianapolis*, 5 F.Supp.2d 657 (S.D.Ind.1998).

19. *See, e.g., Bultemeyer v. Fort Wayne Community Schs.*, 100 F.3d 1281 (7th Cir. 1996) ("if it appears that the employee may need an accommodation but doesn't know how to ask for it, the employer should do what it can to help").

§ 10.28

1. H.R.Rep.No. 101–485, at 67; S.Rep. No. 101–116, at 35. *See also Vande Zande v. Wisconsin Dep't of Admin.*, 44 F.3d 538 (7th Cir.1995) (the employer "is not required to expend enormous sums in order to bring about trivial improvements in the life of a disabled employee"); *Smith v. Blue Cross Blue Shield of Kansas, Inc.*, 102 F.3d 1075 (10th Cir.1996), *cert. denied*, 522 U.S. 811, 118 S.Ct. 54, 139 L.Ed.2d 18 (1997) (accommodation that required eliminating job's es-

the accommodation is reasonable in the sense that its likely benefits are proportional to the costs the employer must incur to implement it.

42 U.S.C.A. § 12111(10)(B)(i–iv) provides that the type of accommodation that is "reasonable" and does not cause "undue hardship" depends upon the type of business in question. For example, it may be impossible to make a construction site readily accessible to employees in wheelchairs, given the constantly changing boundaries.[2] The cost and nature of the needed accommodation is the umbrella under which all cost considerations can be placed.[3] Many accommodations involve local site factors, such as the overall financial resources of the facility involved, the number of persons employed there, and the impact the expenses will have on the operation of the facility.[4] Corporate factors to be considered include overall financial resources, overall size of the business and the impact on its business.[5] Finally, other relevant factors to be considered are number of people who will benefit, permanency of the affected worksite and availability of outside funding for the accommodations. If public funding for an accommodation is available, an employer is obligated to investigate and obtain that funding.[6] The weight attributed to each factor varies with the facts of the situation.[7] The definition of undue hardship is designed to be interpreted and applied consistently with its use under the RHA.[8]

The impact of the proposed accommodation on other employees has also been considered as a relevant factor by the courts. In *Turco v. Hoechst Celanese Corp.*, for example, the Fifth Circuit rejected an accommodation that would result in other employees having to work harder or longer.[9] And in *Mears v. Gulfstream Aerospace Corp.*, the court held that an accommodation was an undue burden on the employer if it adversely impacts other employees' ability to do their job.[10]

sential function would not be reasonable or would work undue hardship).

2. H.R.Rep.No. 101–485, at 69.

3. Some courts have engaged in a cost-benefit analysis, an approach suggested by Judge Posner, but the benefit of a proposed accommodation is not mentioned as a factor to be considered in the statute. *See, e.g., Borkowski v. Valley Cent. Sch. Dist.*, 63 F.3d 131, 142 (2d Cir.1995); *Vande Zande v. Wisconsin Dep't of Admin.*, 44 F.3d 538 (7th Cir.1995).

4. 42 U.S.C.A. § 12111(10)(b).

5. *See, e.g., Moritz v. Frontier Airlines, Inc.*, 147 F.3d 784, 788 (8th Cir.1998) (small start-up airline with a limited budget for staffing not required to provide assistant for employee to perform essential job function); *Haschmann v. Time Warner Entertainment Co., L.P.*, 151 F.3d 591 (7th Cir. 1998) (large entertainment company would not suffer undue hardship by allowing short-term medical leave to vice president

when position had been vacant for several months both before and after her occupancy and subordinates were able to handle her responsibilities during that time without disruption to the company); *EEOC v. Amego, Inc.*, 110 F.3d 135 (1st Cir.1997) (finding proposed accommodations would cause an undue hardship for the employer, a small not-for-profit organization which cares for severely disabled individuals).

6. H.R.Rep.No. 101–485, at 69.

7. *Id.*

8. *Id.* at p. 67.

9. 101 F.3d 1090, 1094 (5th Cir.1996).

10. 905 F.Supp. 1075, 1080 (S.D.Ga. 1995), *aff'd without opinion*, 87 F.3d 1331 (11th Cir.1996). *See also Jacques v. Clean-Up Group, Inc.*, 96 F.3d 506 (1st Cir.1996) (provision of transportation for epileptic cleaner to and from work-site may pose undue hardship where cleaning company showed: (1) all company vans were assigned to other crews and unavailable for trans-

Congress has expressly provided that the *de minimis* principles for determining reasonable accommodation under Title VII in religious discrimination cases,[11] are inapplicable under the ADA.[12] Under the *de minimis* standard, an accommodation which requires the employer to bear more than a de minimis cost creates an undue hardship. Instead, under the ADA, an accommodation must require significant difficulty or expense on the part of the employer before an undue hardship arises. The Court determined in *Hardison* that an accommodation causes undue hardship whenever that accommodation results in more "than a de minimis cost" to the employer.[13] The Court found that requiring TWA to bear more than a de minimis cost in order to give respondent Saturdays off for religious observances would be an undue hardship.[14]

In a case arising under the RHA, the Fifth Circuit explained the justification for giving the defendant the burden of demonstrating that the individual's disability could not be reasonably accommodated:

> The employer has greater knowledge of the essentials of the job than does the handicapped applicant. The employer can look to its own experience, or, if that is not helpful, to that of other employers who have provided jobs to individuals with handicaps similar to those of the applicant in question. Furthermore, the employer may be able to obtain advice concerning possible accommodations from private and government sources.[15]

§§ 10.29–15.34 [Reserved]

E. "... AGAINST A *QUALIFIED INDIVIDUAL* ..."

§ 10.35 Qualified Individual in General

Whether the plaintiff proceeds with a disparate treatment,[1] disproportionate adverse impact,[2] or reasonable accommodation[3] claim, the ADA protects only a "qualified individual with a disability."[4] A "quali-

porting epileptic cleaner; (2) no company employee was available to transport the cleaner daily; (3) given cleaning company's narrow profit margins, it would have been economically detrimental to hire someone to drive cleaner to the job-site); *Williams v. Widnall*, 79 F.3d 1003 (10th Cir.1996) (employer was not required to continue to accommodate an alcoholic employee who was making threats against his supervisor and coworkers because continuing to accommodate would result in an undue hardship in the form of potential harm to plaintiff's supervisor and coworkers); *Milton v. Scrivner, Inc.*, 53 F.3d 1118 (10th Cir.1995) (grocery order selectors who could not keep up with new, faster production standards because of their disability were not entitled to work at a slower pace because that accommodation would require other employees to work harder).

11. *Trans World Airlines, Inc. v. Hardison*, 432 U.S. 63, 97 S.Ct. 2264, 53 L.Ed.2d 113 (1977).

12. H.R.Rep.No. 101–485, at 40.

13. *Hardison*, 432 U.S. at 84, 97 S.Ct. at 2277.

14. *Id.* at 65, 97 S.Ct. at 2267.

15. *Prewitt v. United States Postal Serv.*, 662 F.2d 292, 308 (5th Cir.1981). The employer bears the burden of showing it cannot reasonably accommodate under the ADA as well. *See, e.g., Benson v. Northwest Airlines, Inc.*, 62 F.3d 1108 (8th Cir.1995).

§ 10.35

1. *See* § 10.23, *supra*.

2. *See* § 10.24, *supra*.

3. *See* § 10.26, *supra*.

4. 42 U.S.C.A. § 12112(a).

fied individual with a disability" is one who, with or without reasonable accommodation, can perform the essential functions of the job held or desired.[5] The ADA specifically ties "qualification" to reasonable accommodation. Therefore, an employer must take possible reasonable accommodations into account in considering whether an individual[6] has the ability to perform the essential functions of the job.[7] But a claim can founder if plaintiff fails to prove he could perform essential job functions even assuming a reasonable accommodation were granted; if plaintiff fails to prove that an accommodation he identifies as necessary to enable him to perform essential functions is reasonable; or if the employer proves a requested reasonable accommodation entails undue hardship.[8]

Some courts have held that employees who have a record of excessive absenteeism or tardiness are barred from claiming they are otherwise "qualified" because they cannot perform an essential function of the job, i.e., regular and prompt attendance at work.[9] According to the

5. 42 U.S.C.A. § 12111(8). This definition excludes from coverage persons who are totally disabled. See, e.g., Weyer v. Twentieth Century Fox Film Corp., 198 F.3d 1104, 1109–10 (9th Cir.2000); EEOC v. CNA Ins. Cos., 96 F.3d 1039 (7th Cir.1996).

6. And the inquiry must be individualized. See, e.g., Holiday v. Chattanooga, 206 F.3d 637, 643–44 (6th Cir.2000) (reversing district court grant of summary judgement where third party physician under contract to employer failed to make an individualized inquiry into whether HIV + applicant was otherwise qualified). The Supreme Court's 1999 trilogy of ADA cases all emphasize this individualized determination. See Sutton v. United Air Lines, Inc., 527 U.S. 471, 119 S.Ct. 2139, 2147, 144 L.Ed.2d 450 (1999) (holding that mitigating or corrective measures must be taken into account in judging whether an individual possesses a disability because doing otherwise would "run[ ] directly counter to the individualized inquiry mandated by the ADA"); Murphy v. United Parcel Serv., Inc., 527 U.S. 516, 119 S.Ct. 2133, 144 L.Ed.2d 484 (1999) (holding that a truck driver with high blood pressure did not suffer a "disability" under the ADA where the medication he took allowed him to perform major life activities without substantial limitation); Albertson's, Inc. v. Kirkingburg, 527 U.S. 555, 119 S.Ct. 2162, 144 L.Ed.2d 518 (1999) (holding that the ADA imposes a statutory obligation to determine the existence of disabilities on a case-by-case basis, based upon the actual effect of the impairment on the life of the individual in question).

7. Id.

8. See Cochrum v. Old Ben Coal Co., 102 F.3d 908 (7th Cir.1996) and Smith v. Blue Cross Blue Shield of Kansas, Inc., 102 F.3d 1075 (10th Cir.1996), cert. denied, 522 U.S. 811, 118 S.Ct. 54, 139 L.Ed.2d 18 (1997) (considering and rejecting possible accommodations as unreasonable before determining that plaintiffs' physical restrictions and panic disorder, respectively, prevented them from performing essential job functions).

9. See, e.g., Jovanovic v. In–Sink–Erator Division of Emerson Elec. Co., 201 F.3d 894, 899–900 (7th Cir.2000) (attendance is usually essential job function especially for factory or production workers); Buckles v. First Data Resources, Inc., 176 F.3d 1098 (8th Cir.1999) (regular and reliable attendance is a necessary element of most jobs); Nesser v. Trans World Airlines, Inc., 160 F.3d 442 (8th Cir.1998); Waggoner v. Olin Corp., 169 F.3d 481 (7th Cir.1999) (record of erratic absences but recognizing that a failure to accommodate reasonable requests for medical leave violates the ADA); Corder v. Lucent Technologies, Inc., 162 F.3d 924, 928 (7th Cir.1998) (history of absenteeism permits an inference of future absenteeism if no rebuttal evidence is produced); Nowak v. St. Rita High Sch., 142 F.3d 999, 1003 (7th Cir.1998) (regular attendance is an essential function of a job); Halperin v. Abacus Technology Corp., 128 F.3d 191 (4th Cir.1997); Rogers v. International Marine Terminals, 87 F.3d 755 (5th Cir.1996) (plaintiff unqualified because unable to be available for work for indefinite period following elective surgery); Vande Zande v. Wisconsin Dep't of Admin., 44 F.3d 538 (7th Cir.1995); Carr v. Reno, 23 F.3d 525, 529 (D.C.Cir.1994) ("coming to work regularly" an "essential function" requisite to being "otherwise qualified"). Cf. Dutton v. Johnson County Bd. of County Comm'rs, 859

Fourth Circuit, "[e]xcept in the unusual case where an employee can effectively perform all work-related duties at home, an employee 'who does not come to work cannot perform *any* of his job functions, essential or otherwise.' Therefore, a regular and reliable level of attendance is a necessary element of most jobs."[10] But the issue is muddled because medical leave is a key accommodation contemplated by the ADA[11] and is mandated in some cases by the Family Medical Leave Act.[12] Some courts have allowed the employer to use evidence of excessive absenteeism as a legitimate nondiscriminatory reason for the adverse employment action under the *McDonnell Douglas/Burdine* matrix.[13] An impairment necessitating only a brief absence may render a plaintiff not even "disabled."[14] Other courts analyze excessive absences as disqualifying the plaintiff from proving that she is a "qualified individual with a disability" because she cannot perform the essential function of regular attendance.[15] Others consider the issue as part of the reasonable accommodation/undue burden analysis.[16]

A plaintiff may forfeit "qualified individual" status because of deficient work performance or misconduct. An employer may insist that its employees meet new production standards that compel them to complete their work more quickly.[17] It may also require obedience to generally applied work rules or punish unacceptable behavior like the commission, or threat of committing, violent acts, even when such

F.Supp. 498, 507 (D.Kan.1994) (agreeing that "regular attendance is no doubt an essential part of almost every job, but the question is one of degree" and concluding that defendant had failed to show that plaintiff's requested scheduling accommodation to minimize absences caused by migraine headaches was unreasonable).

10. *Tyndall v. National Educ. Ctrs., Inc. of Cal.*, 31 F.3d 209 (4th Cir.1994) (quoting *Wimbley v. Bolger*, 642 F.Supp. 481, 485 (W.D.Tenn.1986), *aff'd*, 831 F.2d 298 (6th Cir.1987)). *But see Ward v. Massachusetts Health Research Inst..* 209 F.3d 29, 35 (1st Cir.2000) (finding that employer who regularly offered a flex-time schedule had failed to carry its burden of showing that prompt arrival at work was essential job function).

11. *See* § 10.26, *supra*. *See also Waggoner v. Olin Corp.*, 169 F.3d 481 (7th Cir. 1999) (upholding dismissal of ADA claim because plaintiff's record of erratic absences disqualified her, but recognizing that a failure to accommodate reasonable requests for medical leave violates the ADA).

12. *See* 29 U.S.C.A. § 2612. *See Churchill v. Star Enterprises*, 183 F.3d 184 (3d Cir.1999) (illustrating the interplay between accommodation required under the Family Medical Leave Act and ADA, and the potential of claim preclusion to bar a second action under one of those statutes

once a prior action under the other statute has come to judgment).

13. *See, e.g., Swanks v. Washington Metro. Area Transit Auth.*, 179 F.3d 929, 937 n. 9 (D.C.Cir.), *cert. denied*, 528 U.S. 1061, 120 S.Ct. 614, 145 L.Ed.2d 509 (1999) (recognizing the option of using absenteeism as a legitimate nondiscriminatory reason to rebut a plaintiff's prima facie case); *Bailey v. Amsted Indus., Inc.*, 172 F.3d 1041, 1045 (8th Cir.1999) (nonattendance as a legitimate nondiscriminatory reason)

14. *McDonald v. Pennsylvania*, 62 F.3d 92 (3d Cir.1995) (employee unable to work for two months after surgery not disabled because inability to work was of limited duration).

15. *See, e.g., Buckles v. First Data Resources, Inc.*, 176 F.3d 1098 (8th Cir.1999) (regular and reliable attendance is a necessary element of most jobs); *Nesser v. Trans World Airlines, Inc.*, 160 F.3d 442 (8th Cir. 1998).

16. *See, e.g., Anzalone v. Allstate Ins. Co.*, 1995 WL 35613 (E.D.La.1995) (summary judgment on ADA claim seeking a "home" accommodation denied where duties did not require work in an office environment and similar accommodations had been granted to others).

17. *See, e.g., Milton v. Scrivner*, 53 F.3d 1118 (10th Cir.1995).

conduct is linked to a recognized disability.[18] And it may refuse to hire a disabled person in accordance with a generally applied policy against hiring persons with criminal records.[19]

§ 10.36 Essential Job Functions

A "qualified individual with a disability" must be able to perform all essential job functions with or without reasonable accommodation.[1] By definition, "essential function" means job tasks or responsibilities that are "fundamental" and not "marginal."[2] The legislation expressly states that "consideration ... be given to the employer's judgment as to which

18. *See* 42 U.S.C.A. § 12114(c)(4) (even if unsatisfactory performance or behavior is related to drug use or alcoholism, employer may hold employee to its regular workplace standards of conduct). Courts are permitted to distinguish between disability and disability-related misconduct. *See, e.g., Martin v. Barnesville Exempted Village Sch. Dist. Bd. of Educ.*, 209 F.3d 931 (6th Cir.2000); *Salley v. Circuit City Stores, Inc.*, 160 F.3d 977, 981 (3d Cir.1998) (holding that drug-related misconduct is a legitimate, non-discriminatory reason for termination); *Hamilton v. Southwestern Bell Telephone Co.*, 136 F.3d 1047, 1052 (5th Cir.1998) ("ADA does not insulate emotional or violent outbursts blamed on an impairment"); *Mararri v. WCI Steel, Inc.*, 130 F.3d 1180, 1181–83 (6th Cir.1997); *Palmer v. Circuit Court of Cook County, Ill.*, 117 F.3d 351, 352 (7th Cir.1997), *cert. denied*, 522 U.S. 1096, 118 S.Ct. 893, 139 L.Ed.2d 879 (1998) (summary judgment appropriate where employer's motive for firing plaintiff was a death threat against another employee, not her depressive and delusional disorder); *Williams v. Widnall*, 79 F.3d 1003 (10th Cir.1996) (ADA does not protect alcoholics from consequences of their misconduct); *Collings v. Longview Fibre Co.*, 63 F.3d 828, 832 (9th Cir.1995), *cert. denied*, 516 U.S. 1048, 116 S.Ct. 711, 133 L.Ed.2d 666 (1996) ("Courts have recognized a distinction between termination of employment because of misconduct and termination of employment because of a disability."); *Maddox v. University of Tenn.*, 62 F.3d 843 (6th Cir. 1995) (appropriate to distinguish between a discharge on the basis of misconduct—drunken driving by a college football coach—and a discharge on the basis of a disability—alcoholism); *Little v. FBI*, 1 F.3d 255 (4th Cir.1993) (affirming employer's right to fire employee for unacceptable behavior triggered by a disabling mental illness).

19. *See, e.g., Moore v. Board of Educ. of Johnson City Schs.*, 134 F.3d 781 (6th Cir.), *cert. denied*, 525 U.S. 929, 119 S.Ct. 336,

142 L.Ed.2d 277 (1998) (teacher with criminal record and psychiatric admission); *Harris v. Polk County, Iowa*, 103 F.3d 696 (8th Cir.1996); *Williams v. Widnall*, 79 F.3d 1003 (10th Cir.1996); *Collings v. Longview Fibre Co.*, 63 F.3d 828 (9th Cir.1995), *cert. denied*, 516 U.S. 1048, 116 S.Ct. 711, 133 L.Ed.2d 666 (1996); *Despears v. Milwaukee County*, 63 F.3d 635 (7th Cir.1995); *Maddox v. University of Tenn.*, 62 F.3d 843 (6th Cir.1995); *Leary v. Dalton*, 58 F.3d 748 (1st Cir.1995).

§ 10.36

1. 42 U.S.C.A. § 12111(8).

2. S.Rep.No. 101–116, at 26. *See also Laurin v. Providence Hosp.*, 150 F.3d 52, 59 (1st Cir.1998) (shift rotation among hospital nurses was an essential job function); *Malabarba v. Chicago Tribune Co.*, 149 F.3d 690 (7th Cir.1998) (rotating to perform all the duties related to particular machine an essential function of job); *Jones v. Kerrville State Hosp.*, 142 F.3d 263, 265 (5th Cir. 1998) (participation in training to learn how to restrain or subdue patients was an essential job function); *Barber v. Nabors Drilling U.S.A., Inc.*, 130 F.3d 702, 707 (5th Cir.1997) (whether oil rig worker with a back injury as "a qualified individual with a disability" turns on whether firefighting and other emergency tasks were marginal or essential job functions); *Cochrum v. Old Ben Coal Co.*, 102 F.3d 908 (7th Cir.1996) (physician-imposed physical restrictions prevented plaintiff from performing essential functions and precluded any reasonable accommodation employer could make); *Smith v. Blue Cross Blue Shield of Kansas, Inc.*, 102 F.3d 1075 (10th Cir.1996), *cert. denied*, 522 U.S. 811, 118 S.Ct. 54, 139 L.Ed.2d 18 (1997) (panic disorder prevented plaintiff from performing essential function of answering telephone inquiries about claims); *Turco v. Hoechst Celanese Corp.*, 101 F.3d 1090 (5th Cir.1996) (diabetic unable to walk, move or concentrate as required to perform duties of chemical process operator not a "qualified" individual because those functions essential to job).

functions of a job are essential.''[3] At least one circuit has allocated the question of whether a job function is an essential one to the jury.[4]

Written job descriptions, and perhaps advertisements, will be considered evidence of the essential functions of a particular job.[5] For example, in *Overton v. Reilly*,[6] the plaintiff was disabled by depression, which put a strain on his contacts with other people. He was transferred to a job in which the job description stated that his personal contact would be primarily with fellow employees. After his termination, the employee sued, and the employer argued that he was not qualified for the job because he could not work well with the public, an essential job function. The appellate court rejected that argument, finding that because public contact was not part of the job description, it was not an essential function of the job.[7] But an employee limited by his disability to performing one or two of several core duties is not qualified.[8] And even if the function impaired by the disability is not the plaintiff's principal duty, an inability to perform it renders him unqualified if the occasional duty is nevertheless essential.[9]

§§ 10.37–15.39 [Reserved]

F. "WITH A *DISABILITY*"

§ 10.40 Disability Defined

Section 12102 of the ADA defines "disability" as:

(1) a mental or physical *impairment* that *substantially limits* one or more of an individual's *major life activities*;

(2) a *record* of having such an impairment;

(3) being *regarded* as having such an impairment.[1]

The Supreme Court has cautioned that ADA requires that disabilities be evaluated "with respect to an individual" and must be determined based on whether an impairment substantially limits the "major

---

3. 42 U.S.C.A. § 12111(8). *But see McGregor v. National R.R. Passenger Corp.*, 187 F.3d 1113 (9th Cir.1999) (essential functions inquiry must be made on an individualized basis, so per se employer policy against any employee returning to work until "100% healed" violates ADA).

4. *See, e.g., Barber v. Nabors Drilling U.S.A., Inc.*, 130 F.3d 702, 707 (5th Cir. 1997) (whether firefighting and other emergency tasks were marginal or essential job functions is for the jury).

5. 42 U.S.C.A. § 12111(8); S.Rep.No. 101–116, at 28.

6. 977 F.2d 1190 (7th Cir.1992).

7. *Id.* at 1195.

8. *Miller v. Illinois Dep't of Corrections*, 107 F.3d 483 (7th Cir.1997) (blind correc-

tional officer capable of serving as switch-board or armory officer but unable to deal with emergencies, like a prison riot, not qualified).

9. *See Brickers v. Cleveland Bd. of Educ.*, 145 F.3d 846, 849 (6th Cir.1998) (school bus driver required to be able to lift disabled students in emergency situations); *Martinson v. Kinney Shoe Corp.*, 104 F.3d 683 (4th Cir.1997) (shoe salesman unqualified where his epilepsy rendered him unable to maintain security due to unpredictable recurrence of seizures).

§ 10.40

1. 42 U.S.C.A. § 12102(2).

life activities of such individual."[2] The Court conceded that "some impairments may invariably cause a substantial limitation of a major life activity,"[3] but "[t]he determination of whether an individual has a disability is not necessarily based on the name or diagnosis of the impairment the person has, but rather on the effect of that impairment on the life of the individual."[4] As a result, courts are reluctant to characterize any particular impairment as a per se disability under ADA.[5] And the fact that an impairment is considered to be a disability under a different set of criteria for some purpose other than the ADA has no bearing on the determination of whether an individual is disabled within the meaning of the ADA.[6]

§ 10.41 Prong One: "A Physical or Mental *Impairment*"

Courts employ a three step process for determining whether an individual is disabled within the first prong of the definition of disability.[1] First, courts consider whether the individual's affliction is a physical or mental impairment. Second, they identify the personal or work-related functions that the individual claims is limited by an impairment and determine whether they constitute a major life activity under the ADA. Third, tying the two statutory phrases together, they ask whether the impairment substantially limited a major life activity of the plaintiff.[2]

2. *See Sutton v. United Airlines, Inc.*, 527 U.S. 471, ___, 119 S.Ct. 2139, 2147, 144 L.Ed.2d 450 (1999).

3. *Albertson's*, 527 U.S. at ___, 119 S.Ct. at 2169.

4. *Sutton*, 527 U.S. at ___, 119 S.Ct. at 2147. *See also* 29 C.F.R. pt. 1630 app. § 1630.2(j); *Bragdon v. Abbott*, 524 U.S. 624, 118 S.Ct. 2196, 141 L.Ed.2d 540 (1998) (declining to consider whether HIV infection is a per se disability under the ADA).

5. *See Deas v. River West, L.P.*, 152 F.3d 471, 478 (5th Cir.1998), *cert. denied*, 527 U.S. 1044, 119 S.Ct. 2411, 144 L.Ed.2d 808 (1999) (declining to hold that seizures are a disability per se); *Baert v. Euclid Beverage, Ltd.*, 149 F.3d 626, 631 (7th Cir.1998) (insulin dependent diabetes is not a per se disability under the ADA); *Matczak v. Frankford Candy and Chocolate Co.*, 136 F.3d 933, 938 (3d Cir.1997) ("Some individuals suffer from relatively mild forms of epilepsy which cause nothing more than 'minor isolated muscle jerks'—so we cannot and do not conclude that all epileptics are substantially limited by the impairment."); *Burch v. Coca-Cola Co.*, 119 F.3d 305, 316 (5th Cir.1997), *cert. denied*, 522 U.S. 1084, 118 S.Ct. 871, 139 L.Ed.2d 768 (1998) ("Unlike HIV infection, the EEOC has not attempted to classify alcoholism as a per se disability, and we decline to adopt such a questionable position."); *Still v. Freeport-McMoran, Inc.*, 120 F.3d 50, 52 (5th Cir.1997) (holding that blindness in one eye did not automatically constitute a disability); *Bridges v. City of Bossier*, 92 F.3d 329, 336 n. 11 (5th Cir. 1996), *cert. denied*, 519 U.S. 1093, 117 S.Ct. 770, 136 L.Ed.2d 715 (1997) (rejecting argument that hemophilia is a disability per se); *Homeyer v. Stanley Tulchin Assocs., Inc.*, 91 F.3d 959, 962 (7th Cir.1996) ("A disability determination, however, should not be based on abstract lists or categories of impairments, as there are varying degrees of impairments as well as varied individuals who suffer from the impairments."). *But see Kells v. Sinclair Buick–GMC Truck. Inc.*, 210 F.3d 827, 830–31 (8th Cir.2000) (treating both insulin-dependent diabetes and muscular dystrophy as per-se impairments).

6. *See, e.g., Richards v. City of Topeka*, 173 F.3d 1247 (10th Cir.1999) (the fact that a collective bargaining agreement stated that pregnancy would be treated as a disability does not compel a finding that the employer regarded a pregnant firefighter as disabled).

§ 10.41

1. *See Bragdon v. Abbott*, 524 U.S. 624, 631, 118 S.Ct. 2196, 2202, 141 L.Ed.2d 540 (1998).

2. *Id.*

The ADA itself provides no explication of the terms used in its tripartite definition of "disability." Congress empowered federal agencies to implement and enforce the ADA by promulgating regulations to supplement the law.[3] Those regulations flesh out these terms to some degree, and the agencies have looked to decisions and regulatory interpretations under the RHA for guidance. The EEOC interpretation of "impairment" under both the ADA and RHA embraces any physiological disorder or condition, cosmetic disfigurement, or anatomical loss affecting one or more major body systems as well as any mental or psychological disorder, including mental illness, retardation, or specific learning disability.[4] EEOC specifically excludes from the definition of impairment physical characteristics such as eye color, hair color, left-handedness, or height, weight or muscle tone that are within "normal" range and are not the result of a physiological disorder.[5] Also excluded are pregnancy, common personality traits such as poor judgment or a quick temper, and environmental, cultural, or economic disadvantages such as poverty, lack of education or a prison record.[6] Chronic pain conditions have been allowed as "impairments."[7]

There is no general rule that medical testimony is always necessary to establish disability,[8] especially where the impairment is obvious to a jury–a missing limb, for example. The First Circuit has stated that "it is certainly within the realm of possibility that a plaintiff himself in a disabilities case might offer a description of treatment and symptoms over a substantial period that would [allow] the jury [to] determine that [the plaintiff] did suffer from a disability."[9] Thus, the need for expert testimony turns on the extent to which the alleged impairment is within the comprehension of a jury that does not possess a command of medical

3. 42 U.S.C.A. § 12117.

4. See 29 C.F.R. § 1630.2; 34 C.F.R. § 104.3. See also S.Rep.No. 101–116, at 22 (defining impairment to include any physiological disorder or condition, cosmetic disfigurement or anatomical loss affecting one or more of the following body systems: neurological; musculoskeletal; special sense organs; respiratory, including speech organs; cardiovascular; reproductive; digestive; genito-urinary; hemic and lymphatic; skin; and endocrine; and listing as illustrative the following: orthopedic, visual, speech and hearing impairments, cerebral palsy, epilepsy, muscular dystrophy, multiple sclerosis, infection with the Human Immunodeficiency Virus, cancer, heart disease, diabetes, mental retardation, emotional illnesses, specific learning disabilities, drug addiction and alcoholism); Tudyman v. United Airlines, 608 F.Supp. 739, 746 (C.D.Cal.1984) (finding body builder's "unique musculoskelital [sic] system and body composition" not an impairment because it is not the result of a "physiological disorder [ ]," "cosmetic disfigurement," or "anatomical loss").

5. See, e.g., Andrews v. Ohio, 104 F.3d 803, 810 (6th Cir.1997) (holding physical characteristics of excessive weight and lack of cardio-respiratory endurance and strength not impairments under the ADA); Daley v. Koch, 892 F.2d 212, 215 (2d Cir. 1989) (holding under RHA that personality traits of "poor judgment, irresponsible behavior and poor impulse control" could be described as commonplace and "in no way r[ose] to the level of an impairment").

6. See 29 C.F.R. pt. 1630 app. § 1630.2(h)

7. See, e.g., Marinelli v. City of Erie, 216 F.3d 354 (3d Cir.2000) (plaintiff's snow plow accident that left him with residual pain is properly understood as a "condition" that affects his musculoskeletal system); Plant v. Morton Int'l, Inc., 212 F.3d 929, 937 (6th Cir.2000) (holding a "back strain" to qualify as an impairment for ADA purposes).

8. See, e.g., Katz v. City Metal Co., 87 F.3d 26 (1st Cir.1996).

9. Id. at 32.

or otherwise scientific knowledge. A lack of medical testimony can be a factor cutting against a finding of an impairment.[10] Other courts have held that conditions and diseases that are "less technical in nature," such as chronic pain can be supported by plaintiff's own testimony.[11]

a. AIDS/HIV Infection

In *Bragdon v. Abbott*,[12] the Supreme Court held that a person with AIDS, as well as a person with asymptomatic HIV infection, would be covered under the first prong of the ADA disability definition—that is, an HIV + person has an impairment that substantially limits a major life activity—because of the resulting substantial limitation on procreation and intimate sexual relations. Although the Court refrained from holding that AIDS was per se a disability under the ADA,[13] the Court held that AIDS is an *impairment* from the moment of infection with the AIDS virus that substantially impairs reproduction, a major life activity.[14]

10. *See, e.g., United States v. City of Denver,* 49 F.Supp.2d 1233 (D.Colo.1999) (holding that a lack of physician testimony is but one factor in determining whether a plaintiff has met his burden to establish disability); *Colwell v. Suffolk County Police Dep't,* 967 F.Supp. 1419, 1425–26 (E.D.N.Y. 1997) (holding that "nothing in the ADA compels the conclusion that medical evidence is necessary to establish disability status"); *rev'd on other grounds,* 158 F.3d 635 (2d Cir.1998), *cert. denied,* 526 U.S. 1018, 119 S.Ct. 1253, 143 L.Ed.2d 350 (1999). *Cf. Schwimmer v. Kaladjian,* 988 F.Supp. 631, 640 (S.D.N.Y.1997), *aff'd,* 164 F.3d 619 (2d Cir.1998) (holding, in a section 1983 case, that medical testimony is more persuasive than the witness's own recapitulation of his injuries).

11. *See, e.g., Marinelli v. City of Erie,* 216 F.3d 354 (3d Cir.2000)

12. 524 U.S. 624, 118 S.Ct. 2196, 141 L.Ed.2d 540 (1998) (HIV + status constitutes a physical impairment that substantially limits a fecund woman's major life activity of reproduction).

13. *Id.* at 641–42, 118 S.Ct. at 2207. For example, if a particular plaintiff suffering from AIDS had no preexisting plans to engage in intimate sexual relations or procreation, the impairment would not substantially limit any major life activity of that plaintiff.

14. *Id.* at 635–37, 118 S.Ct. at 2203–04. This holding raises interesting issues when one considers discrimination of the basis of genetics. Should the ADA be interpreted to protect against discrimination on the basis of a diagnosed but asymptomatic genetic condition? EEOC adopted the view that the ADA does provide such protection in its 1995 policy guidance on the definition of

disability. To date, there are no published cases dealing with the issue. However, in *Norman-Bloodsaw v. Lawrence Berkeley Laboratory,* 135 F.3d 1260 (9th Cir.1998), employees challenged the employer's policy of routinely testing its employees for syphilis, pregnancy and the sickle-cell trait. The testing was conducted during routine medical exams without the employee's knowledge. The court dismissed the ADA claim because no job action was taken against any employee on the basis of the tests, a lack of evidence that confidentiality was inadequate, and the scope of the exams did not violate the statute. Justice Rehnquist, Thomas and Scalia dissented in *Bragdon,* in part because they believed that asymptomatic illnesses do not substantially limit any major life activities. In addition, Justice Rehnquist stated, "Respondent's argument, taken to its logical extreme, would render every individual with a genetic marker for some debilitating disease 'disabled' here and now because of some future effects." On February 8, 2000, President Clinton signed an Executive Order which prohibits the federal government from using genetic information in hiring, promotion, discharge and other employment decisions for all federal applicants and employees. There appears to be bipartisan support for federal legislation that would extend this protection to the private sector. In addition, some two dozen states have already enacted some sort of similar protection. *See generally* Mark A. Rothstein, *Genetic Discrimination in Employment and the Americans with Disabilities Act,* 29 Hous.L.Rev. 23 (1992); EEOC Commissioner Paul Steven Miller's speech given at the University of Maryland Law School, April 27, 2000, *Is There a Pink Slip in My Genes: Genetic Discrimination in*

Particularly relevant to communicable or contagious diseases like AIDS or tuberculosis is § 12113(b) which provides employers an affirmative defense to the prohibition against disability discrimination in the case of an individual who poses a "direct threat to the health or safety of other individuals in the work place."[15] "Direct threat" is further defined to mean a "significant risk" to the health or safety of the plaintiff or others that "cannot be eliminated by reasonable accommodation."[16] The existence of such a risk is determined from the perspective of the person charged with discrimination but must be "based on the objective, scientific information available to him and others."[17] In *Bragdon*, the First Circuit on remand rejected the direct threat defense posed by the defendant, finding that the universal precautions prescribed in the Centers for Disease Control's Dentistry Guidelines substantially reduced the risk of transmittal of the AIDS virus.[18]

It should be noted, however, that some courts have held under the RHA as well as the ADA, that a person with AIDS or HIV Infection, although recognized as having a disability, will not prevail if her impairment prevents her from proving that she is "otherwise qualified" for the position (the RHA term) or a "qualified individual with a disability" (the ADA phrase) even with reasonable accommodation.[19] But the prima facie "qualified individual" requirement refers to the plaintiff's ability to perform the essential functions of the position in question, not to the safety or health risks she may pose while performing those tasks. Thus these decisions improperly relieve the defendant of the burdens associated with the direct threat *defense* and improperly impose on the plaintiff

the Workplace, BNA Daily Labor Report No. 83, at E–1, April 28, 2000.

15. 42 U.S.C.A. § 12113(b). *See, e.g., Onishea v. Hopper*, 171 F.3d 1289 (11th Cir.1999), *cert. denied*, 528 U.S. 1114, 120 S.Ct. 931, 145 L.Ed.2d 811 (2000) (HIV + prison inmates posed a direct threat to fellow inmates and could be segregated for recreational, religious, and educational programs) (case under RHA); *Montalvo v. Radcliffe*, 167 F.3d 873 (4th Cir.), *cert. denied* 528 U.S. 813, 120 S.Ct. 48, 145 L.Ed.2d 43 (1999) (HIV + minor posed a substantial and direct threat to safety of others in a martial arts instructional program and no reasonable modification could sufficiently reduce this risk without fundamentally altering the nature of the program) (case under Title III); *Doe v. University of Md. Med. Sys. Corp.*, 50 F.3d 1261 (4th Cir. 1995) (HIV + neurosurgeon); *Bradley v. University of Texas M.D. Anderson Cancer Ctr.*, 3 F.3d 922 (5th Cir.1993), *cert. denied*, 510 U.S. 1119, 114 S.Ct. 1071, 127 L.Ed.2d 389 (1994) (HIV + employee not "otherwise qualified" under RHA to remain in surgical technician position because risk of transmitting the disease during surgery, while small, would have "lethal consequences").

See discussion of this defense in § 10.25, *supra*.

16. 42 U.S.C.A. § 12111(3).

17. *Bragdon*, 524 U.S. at 649, 118 S.Ct. at 2210.

18. *See Abbott v. Bragdon*, 163 F.3d 87 (1st Cir.1998), *cert. denied*, 526 U.S. 1131, 119 S.Ct. 1805, 143 L.Ed.2d 1009 (1999).

19. *See, e.g., Bradley v. University of Texas M.D. Anderson Cancer Ctr.*, 3 F.3d 922 (5th Cir.1993), *cert. denied*, 510 U.S. 1119, 114 S.Ct. 1071, 127 L.Ed.2d 389 (1994) (HIV + employee not "otherwise qualified" under RHA to remain in surgical technician position because risk of transmitting the disease during surgery, while small, would have "lethal consequences"). The Fourth Circuit has recently reached the same conclusion in the case of a neurosurgical resident who tested positive for HIV. *Doe v. University of Md. Med. Sys. Corp.*, 50 F.3d 1261 (4th Cir.1995). *But see Holiday v. Chattanooga*, 206 F.3d 637 (6th Cir.2000) (requiring defendant to make individualized determination of whether HIV + applicant for police force was otherwise qualified).

additional burdens in proving prima facie that she is a "qualified individual."[20]

In *McGann v. H & H Music Company*,[21] the Supreme Court without comment left intact a federal appeals court ruling that permits an employer to drastically cut its insurance coverage for treatment of AIDS.[22] After the plaintiff informed the employer that he had AIDS, the company reduced the lifetime benefits payable for AIDS-related claims from $1 million, the limit applicable to other illnesses, to $5,000. McGann sued in federal district court, claiming that his employer, the health administrator and the insurance company had violated § 510 of ERISA.[23] The Fifth Circuit held that employers had an absolute right to alter terms of the health plan because the level of health care benefits under an employer's plan is not a vested right under ERISA. The Eleventh Circuit issued a similar decision, holding that "ERISA does not prohibit a company from terminating previously offered benefits that are neither vested nor accrued."[24] Because ERISA does not proscribe discrimination in the provision of employment benefits,[25] these courts have concluded that it would warp congressional intent to construe ERISA § 510 "discrimination" to preclude lifetime caps.[26]

An EEOC "guidance" on the application of ADA and ERISA to health insurance acknowledges that "not all health-related plan distinctions discriminate on the basis of disability." The guidance concludes that "broad distinctions" applicable to a "multitude of dissimilar conditions" do not unlawfully make distinctions based on disability. For example, providing lesser benefits "for the treatment of mental/nervous conditions than is provided for the treatment of physical conditions" would pass muster under ADA. This attempt to harmonize ADA with ERISA § 510 also asserts, however, that "health-related insurance distinctions that are based on disability may violate the ADA." And it defines a plan provision as "disability-based" if it "singles out a particular disability, (e.g., deafness, AIDS, schizophrenia ... or disability in general....)"[27]

The distinctions drawn by the agency appear internally incoherent, since they brand welfare plan classifications as "disability-based" only

20. *See* discussion of the direct threat defense in § 10.25, *supra*.

21. 946 F.2d 401 (5th Cir.1991), *cert. denied*, 506 U.S. 981, 113 S.Ct. 482, 121 L.Ed.2d 387 (1992).

22. Of course nothing in ADA requires an employer to offer any health insurance, just as it need not offer a disability retirement plan, even if it offers retirement benefits based strictly on service.

23. Employee Retirement Income Security Act of 1974, 29 U.S.C.A. §§ 1001–1461. Section 510 makes it illegal to "discriminate against a participant or beneficiary for exercising any right to which he is entitled under the provisions of an employee benefit plan or for the purpose of interfering with the attainment of any right to which such participant may become entitled under plan...."

24. *Owens v. Storehouse, Inc.*, 984 F.2d 394 (11th Cir.1993).

25. *See Shaw v. Delta Air Lines, Inc.*, 463 U.S. 85, 91, 103 S.Ct. 2890, 2896, 77 L.Ed.2d 490 (1983).

26. *See McGann*, 946 F.2d at 407.

27. *EEOC Interim Guidance Upon Application of ADA to Health Insurance*, 3 EEOC Compl.Man. (BNA) No. 176, at N: 2301–2304 (June 8, 1993).

when they are extremely particular, or, on the other hand, general and comprehensive. Its position is also in tension with Section 501(c) of ADA, which provides that ADA may not be construed to restrict a health care provider from classifying or administering risks unless it does so as a "subterfuge" to evade the purposes of the Act.[28] As the word has been interpreted in a companion employment discrimination statute, the provider's right to classify risks would be used as a "subterfuge" only when the employer or administrator has an actual intent to circumvent ADA's ban on disability discrimination in an aspect of employment *unrelated* to fringe benefits—a showing which could rarely, if ever, be made.[29] Further, ADA's legislative history suggests that the statute was not intended to disrupt existing insurance underwriting practices and was intended to permit employers to offer policies that limit coverage for certain procedures or treatments.[30] An early lower court decision, however, adopts in substance a diluted EEOC definition of "subterfuge" which condemns disparate treatment based on disability under the ADA unless that treatment is justified by the particular disability's risks or costs.[31]

b. *Physical Impairment*

All medical conditions are covered, whether temporary or permanent,[32] contagious or not, chronic or acute, congenital or acquired. EEOC guidelines state that pregnancy is not an impairment,[33] and whether infertility qualifies as an impairment is an open issue. The ADA definition of disability does not require that the impairment be of any certain duration; the statute simply requires that a person have a physical or mental impairment "that substantially limits" one or more major life

28. 42 U.S.C.A. § 12201(c).

29. Compare the Supreme Court's construction of "subterfuge" as used in the Age Discrimination in Employment Act of 1967, 29 U.S.C.A. §§ 621–634, as announced in *Public Employees Retirement Sys. of Ohio v. Betts*, 492 U.S. 158, 109 S.Ct. 2854, 106 L.Ed.2d 134 (1989), discussed in Chapter 7, above.

30. *See* Spelfogel, *The Interaction of ERISA and the ADA*, 68 St. John's Law Rev. 459, 467–468 (1994).

31. *Mason Tenders v. Donaghey*, 1993 WL 596313 (S.D.N.Y.1993), 223 Daily Lab. Rep. (BNA), at AA–1 (Nov. 22, 1993).

32. *See Aldrich v. Boeing Co.*, 146 F.3d 1265 (10th Cir.1998), *cert. denied*, 526 U.S. 1144, 119 S.Ct. 2018, 143 L.Ed.2d 1030 (1999) (no per se rule that a temporary impairment is not a disability under the ADA). *But see Hamilton v. Southwestern Bell Tel. Co.*, 136 F.3d 1047, 1052 (5th Cir.1998) (plaintiff cannot show a disability where symptoms of post traumatic stress disorder were sporadic and temporary); *Ryan v. Grae & Rybicki, P.C.*, 135 F.3d 867, 870 (2d Cir.1998) (defining "substantially

limits" to exclude colitis as an intermittent condition with long periods of remission even though the disease is severe when symptomatic); *Zirpel v. Toshiba Am. Info. Sys., Inc.*, 111 F.3d 80, 81 (8th Cir.1997) (although speaking and breathing were hampered during actual panic attack, disorder did not substantially limit plaintiff's major life activities where attacks were infrequent and very manageable); *Robinson v. Global Marine Drilling Co.*, 101 F.3d 35, 37 (5th Cir.1996), *cert. denied*, 520 U.S. 1228, 117 S.Ct. 1820, 137 L.Ed.2d 1028 (1997) (several instances of asbestosis-related shortness of breath did not substantially limit major life activity of breathing); *McDonald v. Pennsylvania*, 62 F.3d 92 (3d Cir.1995); *Vande Zande v. Wisconsin Dep't of Admin.*, 44 F.3d 538, 544 (7th Cir.1995) (an intermittent, episodic impairment, like a broken leg, is not a disability).

33. 29 C.F.R. pt. 1630 app. § 1630.2(h). In *Richards v. City of Topeka*, 173 F.3d 1247 (10th Cir.1999), the court cited the EEOC regulation with approval, but did not reach the issue because plaintiff conceded that she was not substantially limited by her pregnancy.

activities. Conditions such as drug addiction and alcoholism are covered as physical impairments but are subject to exclusions discussed below. Courts have included within the concept of a covered "impairment" conditions that are not disabling in themselves but, like high cholesterol, require medical treatment that is disabling.[34] Also included are the side effects of courses of treatment, like chemotherapy, that result from underlying conditions that are unquestionably physical impairments.[35]

While a cosmetic disfigurement may not appear to impair any activities, the fact that an employer may use it to reject an applicant may make it an impairment.[36] The Supreme Court in footnote 10 of *School Board of Nassau County v. Arline*[37] referred to cosmetic disfigurement as an example of an impairment. The Court stated that "the effects of one's impairment on others is as relevant to a determination of whether one is handicapped as is the physical effect of one's handicap on oneself."[38]

In *Hodgdon v. Mt. Mansfield Co., Inc.*,[39] the Vermont Supreme Court reinstated the RHA claims of a chambermaid who lost her job at a ski resort because her dentures were too painful to wear. Her employer told her not to return to work without her teeth. The court found the plaintiff's lack of upper teeth a physical impairment because it is "a cosmetic disfigurement and an anatomical loss affecting the musculoskeletal and digestive systems," and that the employer regarded the plaintiff as handicapped, even though the cosmetic disfigurement did not limit any major life activity other than her ability to work, because the employer regarded the plaintiff as unfit to be seen by customers.[40]

In a relatively early decision under the Rehabilitation Act, a court held that an applicant for flight attendant position whose weight exceeded the airline's guidelines was not handicapped where the weight resulted from a voluntary body building program and the individual was not substantially limited in any major life activity.[41] But a court of appeals ruled that a refusal to hire because of "morbid obesity" is actionable under the RHA. The court found that by rejecting a mental health attendant for a hospital position because of its concern that her limited mobility might impede her ability to evacuate patients, the employer treated her impairment as substantially limiting one or more major life activities.[42]

---

34. *Christian v. St. Anthony Med. Ctr.*, 117 F.3d 1051 (7th Cir.1997), *cert. denied*, 523 U.S. 1022, 118 S.Ct. 1304, 140 L.Ed.2d 469 (1998).

35. *Gordon v. E.L. Hamm & Assocs., Inc.*, 100 F.3d 907 (11th Cir.1996), *cert. denied*, 522 U.S. 1030, 118 S.Ct. 630, 139 L.Ed.2d 610 (1997) (that holding is implicit in court's decision that the impairment did not "substantially limit" the particular plaintiff's ability to work); *Pritchard v. Southern Co. Servs.*, 92 F.3d 1130 (11th Cir.1996), *cert. denied*, 520 U.S. 1274, 117 S.Ct. 2453, 138 L.Ed.2d 211 (1997) (although depression by itself not disability, other symptoms related to medication for depression may be).

36. S.Rep.No. 101–116, at 24.

37. 480 U.S. 273, 107 S.Ct. 1123, 94 L.Ed.2d 307 (1987).

38. *Id.* at 283, 107 S.Ct. at 1129.

39. 160 Vt. 150, 624 A.2d 1122 (1992).

40. *Id.* at 164, 624 A.2d at 1129.

41. *Tudyman v. United Airlines*, 608 F.Supp. 739 (C.D.Cal.1984).

42. *Cook v. Rhode Island*, 10 F.3d 17 (1st Cir.1993).

The decision in *Cook* specifically rejected two defenses likely to be frequently litigated under the ADA. Defendant asserted, first, that § 504 does not reach "mutable" conditions, an argument that has reaped rich rewards for defendants under Title VII.[43] Without deciding the broad legal question raised, the First Circuit ruled that even assuming arguendo a general requirement that a covered impairment be immutable, that requirement does not apply to situations where the employer "responds to a perceived disability in a way that makes clear that the employer regards the condition as immutable." In any event, the court concluded that on the record the jury could have reasonably found that plaintiff's particular metabolic dysfunction associated with her morbid obesity was permanent.

The defendant also asserted the plaintiff's condition was outside the ambit of § 504 because it was voluntarily incurred. On this point the court responded that the statute contains no language suggesting that it is relevant how an individual became impaired or contributed to that impairment. In fact, the application of RHA to numerous conditions caused or exacerbated by voluntary conduct—the court cited 45 C.F.R. § 84,[44] and judicial decisions involving alcoholism, AIDS, diabetes, cancer in smokers, drug abuse, and various types of heart disease—suggest the contrary. But the Supreme Court's decisions in *Sutton v. United Air Lines, Inc.*[45] and *Murphy v. United Parcel Service*,[46] holding that impairments must be considered in their medicated or mitigated state, suggest that mutable impairments may not qualify an individual for ADA protection. The issue did not surface directly in either of those cases because the plaintiffs had mitigated their conditions through either corrective lenses (*Sutton*) or medication (*Murphy*)—and consequently could not be considered disabled within the meaning of ADA. But what of the plaintiff who could mitigate but has not mitigated a correctable impairment? Will she be disqualified from protection either because her impairment is mutable or because it does not substantially limit any major life activity?

The answer may lie in the treatment of mutable characteristics under Title VII. In *Willingham v. Macon Telegraph Pub. Co.*,[47] the Fifth Circuit wrote that "[e]qual employment opportunity may be secured only when employers are barred from discriminating against employees on the basis of immutable characteristics, such as race and national origin ... Hair length is not immutable and in the situation of employer vis a vis employee enjoys no constitutional protection ... We adopt the view, therefore, that distinctions in employment practices between men and women on the basis of something other than immutable or protected characteristics do not inhibit employment opportunity in violation of

43. *See, e.g.,* discussion of *Willingham v. Macon Tel. Pub. Co.*, 507 F.2d 1084 (5th Cir.1975), in Chapter 2.

44. App. A., Subpart A(3) at 377.

45. 527 U.S. 471, 119 S.Ct. 2139, 144 L.Ed.2d 450 (1999).

46. 527 U.S. 516, 119 S.Ct. 2133, 144 L.Ed.2d 484 (1999).

47. 507 F.2d 1084 (5th Cir.1975).

[Title VII]."[48] The effect of the court's holding was to require the plaintiff to get a haircut, a relatively minor action, or forego the job. The wearing of corrective lenses or a hearing aid, or taking a pill that does not have serious side effects, or ingesting food to which one has a known allergy[49] may be treated as the Fifth Circuit treated a haircut—as precluding liability if the plaintiff with a treatable or avoidable impairment does not mitigate or avoid the disqualifying condition.

c. Mental Impairments

These include any mental or physiological disorder, such as mental retardation, organic brain syndrome, emotional or mental illness and specific learning disabilities. Although the term is broad, it does not include environmental, cultural or economic disadvantages. And decisions have excluded inability to handle stress[50] or to get along with others[51] as covered mental impairments. Nor did the fact that supervisors considered the plaintiff difficult and insubordinate demonstrate that they perceived her as mentally impaired, despite a previous diagnosis and hospitalization for depression.[52]

d. Exclusions

1. Behavior Disorders and Conditions

A variety of behavior disorders (kleptomania, compulsive gambling, pyromania, etc.) and sexual conditions are expressly excluded from the definition of "disability."[53] Specifically excluded "sexual behavior disorders" include transvestism, pedophilia, exhibitionism, voyeurism, and gender identity disorders not resulting from physical impairments.

In *Smith v. City of Jacksonville*,[54] the Florida Commission on Human Relations ruled that a police lieutenant's transsexualism constituted a handicap.[55] The ruling stated that "factually" transsexualism met the Florida definition of handicap because transsexualism is a "medically cognizable condition with a prescribed course of treatment."[56] The purported basis for firing Smith was that she wouldn't be able to have effective working relationships with co-employees and that inmates

48. *Id.* at 1091–92.

49. *Cf. Land v. Baptist Medical Center*, 164 F.3d 423 (8th Cir.1999) (peanut-related allergy does not substantially limit eating or breathing).

50. See, *e.g., Mundo v. Sanus Health Plan of Greater New York*, 966 F.Supp. 171 (E.D.N.Y.1997).

51. See, *e.g., Soileau v. Guilford of Maine*, 105 F.3d 12 (1st Cir.1997).

52. *Webb v. Mercy Hosp.*, 102 F.3d 958 (8th Cir.1996). *But see Holihan v. Lucky Stores, Inc.*, 87 F.3d 362 (9th Cir.1996), *cert. denied*, 520 U.S. 1162, 117 S.Ct. 1349, 137 L.Ed.2d 506 (1997) (where employees complained about manager's hostility and physical and verbal abusiveness, and evidence showed he was experiencing stress-related problems, he could show at trial he was regarded as having a disabling mental condition that substantially limited his ability to work even if in fact his ability to work was not substantially limited).

53. 42 U.S.C.A. § 12211.

54. FCHR, Case No. 86–0985, June 10, 1992.

55. Daily Labor Reports, Current Developments, No. 43, March 8, 1993, at A–7.

56. *Id.*

would create problems.[57] The case is said to be the first in the United States in which a public employee has returned to work after being discharged for transsexualism.

Homosexuals, lesbians, and bisexual persons are not considered, under current medical or psychological diagnoses, to have either a mental or physical impairment by reason of their sexual orientation(s).[58] Such individuals were never covered under the RHA. Nevertheless, many people view homosexuality and bisexuality as an impairment and some legislators were concerned that gay, lesbian and bisexual individuals would be covered under the ADA solely by virtue of their sexual orientation.[59] The statute explicitly dispels this concern.

2. Drug and Alcohol Users

The ADA excludes applicants or employees who are current[60] illegal drug users from the definition of a "qualified person with a disability." The ADA also amends § 504 of the RHA to provide for the same exclusion of illegal drug users.[61]

But a person who has successfully completed a supervised drug treatment program or has otherwise been successfully rehabilitated and no longer uses illegal drugs, but whose addiction substantially limits a major life activity is protected.[62] Illegal use of drugs is defined to mean

57. *Id.* at p. A–8.

58. *The Labor Lawyer*, Volume 7, Number 1, Winter 1991, p. 25.

59. *See* H.R.Rep.No. 101–485(II), at 142.

60. *See* 42 U.S.C.A. §§ 12114, 12210. *See also Zenor v. El Paso Healthcare Sys., Ltd.*, 176 F.3d 847 (5th Cir.1999) (critical issue is whether the employee was a "current" user on the date employee was notified of the termination, not when the termination became effective); *Grimes v. United States Postal Serv.*, 872 F.Supp. 668, 675 (W.D.Mo.1994), *aff'd without opinion*, 74 F.3d 1243 (8th Cir.1996) (rejecting actual termination date as relevant point of inquiry where plaintiff had been arrested for drug possession in January but termination was not finalized until April). *But see D'Amico v. City of New York*, 132 F.3d 145, 150 (2d Cir.), *cert. denied*, 524 U.S. 911, 118 S.Ct. 2075, 141 L.Ed.2d 151 (1998) (time of discharge is relevant time, but the level of responsibility entrusted to the employee, the employer's applicable job and performance requirements, the level of competence ordinarily required to perform the task in question, and the employee's past performance record are all relevant to the resolution of whether an individual's problem is severe and recent enough to classify him as a current substance abuser); *Teahan v. Metro–North Commuter R.R. Co.*, 951

F.2d 511 (2d Cir.1991), *cert. denied*, 506 U.S. 815, 113 S.Ct. 54, 121 L.Ed.2d 24 (1992) (looking at the date the adverse employment action became effective).

61. *See* 29 U.S.C.A. § 706(8)(C).

62. *See* 42 U.S.C.A. § 12114(b). *But see D'Amico v. City of New York*, 132 F.3d 145, 150 (2d Cir.), *cert. denied*, 524 U.S. 911, 118 S.Ct. 2075, 141 L.Ed.2d 151 (1998) (the likelihood of relapse is relevant to the determination of whether an individual is otherwise qualified; firefighter's *history* of cocaine addiction disqualified him where his job could be dangerous to himself and others).

The "and no longer uses" caveat is critical. Any employee is "currently engaging" in illegal drug use, and therefore excluded from the "qualified person" definition, if she uses drugs periodically in the months prior to discharge even if at the time of discharge she is in rehabilitation and not using. *Shafer v. Preston Memorial Hosp. Corp.*, 107 F.3d 274 (4th Cir.1997). *See also Burch v. Coca–Cola Co.*, 119 F.3d 305 (5th Cir.1997), *cert. denied*, 522 U.S. 1084, 118 S.Ct. 871, 139 L.Ed.2d 768 (1998) (despite completion of treatment program, plaintiff's firing for alcohol-related performance problems upheld because his frequent inebriation held to fall short of permanent impairment).

drug use, possession, or distribution that is unlawful under the Controlled Substances Act.[63] This term does not include the use of drugs taken under supervision of a licensed health care professional.[64]

Under § 12114, employees can be required to conform with the Drug Free Workplace Act of 1988,[65] employers may prohibit the illegal use of drugs and alcohol use at the workplace,[66] and employers may require employees to take drug tests.[67] An employer may also "require that employees shall not be under the influence of alcohol or be engaging in the illegal use of drugs at the workplace."[68] Employers are not required to institute employee assistance programs or to give such employees an opportunity to rehabilitate. They may, in short, "hold an employee who engages in the illegal use of drugs or who is an alcoholic to the same qualification standards for employment or job performance and behavior to which [the employer] holds its other employees, even if any unsatisfactory performance or behavior is related to the employee's drug use or alcoholism."[69] But an alcoholic who is a "qualified individual with a disability" may be held only to the "same" standards as nonalcoholics. Thus an alcoholic states a claim of unlawful discrimination if he alleges that a policy against working under the influence was enforced against him more harshly because of his alcoholism, even though an alcoholic may otherwise be discharged summarily the first time he reports to work intoxicated.[70]

Other exclusions in § 12114 relate to current psychoactive substance use disorders and current psychoactive substance-induced organic mental disorders not the result of medical treatment.[71] If a person with a disability (epilepsy, AIDS, etc.) also uses illegal drugs, but the person is discriminated against on the basis of the covered disability (on the basis of epilepsy or AIDS) and not on the basis of the illegal use of drugs, the discriminatory action against the person is illegal under the ADA.[72]

A person who is dependent on alcohol remains covered under the ADA, and under § 504 of the Rehabilitation Act, as a person with a disability. By contrast a person who simply uses alcohol on a casual basis, and is not dependent, would not be considered to have an "impair-

63. 21 U.S.C.A. § 812.

64. *See* 42 U.S.C.A. § 12111(6).

65. 42 U.S.C.A. § 12114(c)(3).

66. 42 U.S.C.A. § 12114(c)(1).

67. 42 U.S.C.A. § (b). And an employer is not required to make accommodations in its drug-testing policy for former substance abusers who cannot comply with the drug testing procedures for reasons other than a disability as defined by ADA. *See Buckley v. Consolidated Edison Co. of New York, Inc.,* 155 F.3d 150, 156 (2d Cir.1998) (former substance abuser who could not comply with testing procedure due to neurogenic bladder, a condition concededly not a disability under the ADA, could not claim employer failed to make reasonable accommo-

dation). The same opinion also held that more frequent drug testing of former substance abusers does not violate the ADA. *Id.*

68. 42 U.S.C.A. § 12114(c)(2).

69. 42 U.S.C.A. § 12114(c)(4). *See also Despears v. Milwaukee County,* 63 F.3d 635 (7th Cir.1995) (demotion of alcoholic employee who lost his driver's license from job that required a valid license to a job that had no such requirement was not unlawful discrimination on the basis of disability).

70. *Flynn v. Raytheon Co.,* 868 F.Supp. 383 (D.Mass.1994).

71. 42 U.S.C.A. § 12114.

72. *Id.*

ment" and therefore fails the first necessary part of the definition of disability. Under the ADA, as under § 504, a person with a disability must be qualified to perform the job in question. For an alcoholic this means that the person must be able to perform adequately all the essential functions of the job, despite the alcoholism.

In *Golson-El v. Runyon*,[73] a federal court rejected the RHA claim of a Postal Service employee, a recovering alcoholic participating in an employee assistance program, who was fired for exceeding the number of absences set by a "last chance" agreement. The court stated that even though the employee was subject to the last chance agreement because of her alcoholism, the failure to meet the requirements of the last chance agreement, and not the alcoholism as such, was the reason for her termination.[74]

Persons having "a record of" drug or alcohol abuse, or are regarded as being disabled by alcoholism or addiction, are covered under the second or third definition of disability unless otherwise excluded. See §§ 10.44 and 10.45, *infra*.

§ 10.42   "That *Substantially Limits*"

A physical or mental impairment is not a disability under the first prong of the definition unless its severity results in a substantial limitation of one or more major life activities.[1] A person possesses an impairment that substantially limits one or more major life activities if she is "[s]ignificantly restricted as to the condition, manner or duration under which [she] can perform a particular major life activity as compared to the condition, manner, or duration under which the average person in the general population can perform that same major life activity."[2] For example, the litigation challenge plaintiffs face is showing

73. 812 F.Supp. 558 (E.D.Pa.1993), *aff'd without opinion*, 8 F.3d 811 (3d Cir.1993).

74. *Id. See also Salley v. Circuit City Stores, Inc.*, 160 F.3d 977 (3d Cir.1998) (employee fired for drug-and alcohol-related misconduct not protected); *Wallin v. Minnesota Dep't of Corrections*, 153 F.3d 681, 689 (8th Cir.1998), *cert. denied*, 526 U.S. 1004, 119 S.Ct. 1141, 143 L.Ed.2d 209 (1999) (rejecting alcoholic prison guard's disparate treatment claim where evidence showed he left a cellblock unlocked and other employees did not commit such egregious errors); *Mararri v. WCI Steel, Inc.*, 130 F.3d 1180 (6th Cir.1997) (employee fired for violating last chance agreement was not terminated "because of" a disability); *Collings v. Longview Fibre Co.*, 63 F.3d 828 (9th Cir.1995), *cert. denied*, 516 U.S. 1048, 116 S.Ct. 711, 133 L.Ed.2d 666 (1996) (employer did not violate ADA by discharging five employees who admitted that they had violated company drug-free workplace rules); *Maddox v. University of Tenn.*, 62 F.3d 843 (6th Cir.

1995) (alcoholic employee lawfully fired for the criminal conduct of driving under the influence and public intoxication).

§ 10.42

1. 42 U.S.C.A. § 12102(2).

2. 29 C.F.R. § 1630.2(j)(1). The Tenth Circuit held that where a plaintiff's ability compares favorably with that of the general population, even where the plaintiff's ability has been severely reduced due to a traumatic injury relative to plaintiff's abilities before the accident, plaintiff cannot show a substantial limitation. *See Bowen v. Income Producing Mgmt. of Okla., Inc.*, 202 F.3d 1282 (10th Cir.2000). *See also Hilburn v. Murata Electronics N.A., Inc.*, 181 F.3d 1220 (11th Cir.1999) (coronary heart disease an impairment but one that did not substantially limit plaintiff's ability to run, lift or work). *Hill v. Kansas City Area Transportation Authority*, 181 F.3d 891 (8th Cir.1999), *cert. denied*, __ U.S. __, 120 S.Ct. 981, 145 L.Ed.2d 932 (2000) (plain-

an impairment sufficiently severe that it substantially limits a major life activity, yet not so severe that after accommodation, it will still disable her from performing the essential functions of the job.

For example, a person who is paraplegic will have a substantial difficulty in locomotion; and a person with lung disease will have a substantial difficulty in the major life activity of breathing.[3] Some impairments are so readily accepted as substantially limiting that plaintiffs should have little difficulty with showing that they are disabled. The Supreme Court has stated that HIV+ persons are typically covered because of a substantial limitation in reproduction,[4] and that a plaintiff with monocular vision "ordinarily will meet the Act's definition of disability."[5] Nevertheless, a determination that an impairment substantially limits the plaintiff in one or more major life activities must be done on an individual case by case basis.[6] So while a particular affliction such as AIDS or monocular vision may be held to be per se an impairment,[7] no per se rules can be imposed regarding the "substantially limits a major life activity" clause of the ADA's definition of disability, or therefore on the ultimate question whether plaintiff is "disabled." It is clear that intermittent or episodic impairments do not substantially limit a major life activity, but courts are divided as to whether such ailments are not impairments, or whether they are impairments that do not substantially limit.[8]

tiff's hypertension, taking into account the combination of medicines required to treat it, did not substantially limit her ability to work); *Cody v. CIGNA Healthcare of St. Louis, Inc.*, 139 F.3d 595 (8th Cir.1998) (plaintiff's depression did not substantially limit the major life activities of eating or sleeping where evidence showed that plaintiff ate at least one meal a day and slept between 4 and 12 hours each night).

3. *But cf. Robinson v. Global Marine Drilling Co.*, 101 F.3d 35 (5th Cir.1996), *cert. denied*, 520 U.S. 1228, 117 S.Ct. 1820, 137 L.Ed.2d 1028 (1997) (although breathing is major life activity, climbing is not, and the only problem experienced by employee with asbestosis was shortness of breath while climbing stairs).

4. *Bragdon*, 524 U.S. at 639, 118 S.Ct. at 2205–06.

5. *Albertson's*, 527 U.S. at ___, 119 S.Ct. at 2169 (stating that monocular individuals will not have "an onerous burden").

6. *See, e.g., Mondzelewski v. Pathmark Stores, Inc.*, 162 F.3d 778, 784 (3d Cir.1998) (reversing district court for failing to conduct an *individualized* assessment of extent to which employee's back condition coupled with his personal characteristics substantially limited a major life activity); *Doane v. City of Omaha*, 115 F.3d 624, 627 (8th Cir.1997), *cert. denied*, 522 U.S. 1048, 118 S.Ct. 693, 139 L.Ed.2d 638 (1998).

7. In *Albertson's*, the Court stated that there is no dispute that monocular vision caused by amblyopia is a physical impairment. 527 U.S. at ___, 119 S.Ct. at 2167 (citing 29 C.F.R. § 1630.2(h)(1)). Nor was there a dispute in *Sutton* that severe myopia was a physical impairment. 527 U.S. at ___, 119 S.Ct. at 2146. In *Bragdon v. Abbott*, the Court found that AIDS is an *impairment* from the moment of infection with the AIDS virus. 524 U.S. at 636–37, 118 S.Ct. at 2204–05. See discussion of impairments in § 10.41.

8. *See, e.g., Moore v. J.B. Hunt Transp., Inc.*, 221 F.3d 944, 2000 WL 994327 (7th Cir.2000) (rheumatoid arthritis that merely slowed plaintiff's walking did not substantially limit the major lfe activity of walking); *Land v. Baptist Med. Ctr.*, 164 F.3d 423, 425 (8th Cir.1999) (peanut-related allergy does not substantially limit abilities to eat and breathe); *Hamilton v. Southwestern Bell Tel. Co.*, 136 F.3d 1047, 1052 (5th Cir.1998) (plaintiff cannot show a disability where symptoms of post traumatic stress disorder were sporadic and temporary); *Ryan v. Grae & Rybicki, P.C.*, 135 F.3d 867, 870 (2d Cir.1998) (defining "substantially limits" to exclude colitis as an intermittent condition with long periods of remission even though the disease is severe when symptomatic); *Zirpel v. Toshiba Am. Info. Sys., Inc.*, 111 F.3d 80, 81 (8th Cir.1997)

Contrary to regulations promulgated by all three federal agencies empowered to enforce ADA, significant direct evidence of Congressional intent, and the decisions of eight of the nine circuits that had considered the issue,[9] the Supreme Court held in *Sutton v. United Air Lines, Inc.*[10] and *Murphy v. United Parcel Service, Inc.*,[11] that the determination of whether a person is substantially limited in a major life activity must take into account mitigating measures. In *Sutton*, severely myopic twin sisters were rejected by United Airlines for the position of "global pilot" pursuant to a company policy that global pilots' uncorrected vision be no worse than 20/100. The Court rejected their ADA claims because with corrective lenses, the sisters had normal 20/20 vision; they could not, therefore, demonstrate that their mitigated impairment (myopia) substantially limited them in a major life activity. In *Murphy*, a truck mechanic whose position required him to drive commercial vehicles was fired when his employer discovered that his blood pressure exceeded Department of Transportation health certification requirements for drivers of commercial vehicles. With medication, the plaintiff's hypertension did not substantially limit a major life activity.

The Court stated that three separate ADA provisions forced the conclusion that mitigating measures must be considered when a court determines whether an ADA plaintiff has a disability within the meaning of ADA. First, the Court felt it significant that the language "substantially limits" is in the present indicative verb form: "A person whose physical or mental impairment is corrected by medication or other measures does not have an impairment that presently 'substantially limits' a major life activity."[12] Second, the definition of "disability" requires an individualized inquiry; courts should not be forced to "speculate" about how an "uncorrected impairment usually affects individu-

(although speaking and breathing were hampered during actual panic attack, disorder did not substantially limit plaintiff's major life activities where attacks were infrequent and very manageable); *Robinson v. Global Marine Drilling Co.*, 101 F.3d 35, 37 (5th Cir.1996), *cert. denied*, 520 U.S. 1228, 117 S.Ct. 1820, 137 L.Ed.2d 1028 (1997) (several instances of asbestosis-related shortness of breath did not substantially limit major life activity of breathing); *McDonald v. Pennsylvania*, 62 F.3d 92 (3d Cir.1995); *Vande Zande v. Wisconsin Dep't of Admin.*, 44 F.3d 538, 544 (7th Cir.1995) (an intermittent, episodic impairment, like a broken leg, is not a disability).

9. *See, e.g., Bartlett v. New York State Bd. of Law Examiners*, 156 F.3d 321, 329 (2d Cir.1998), *cert. granted, judgment vacated*, 527 U.S. 1031, 119 S.Ct. 2388, 144 L.Ed.2d 790 (1999); *Washington v. HCA Health Servs. of Texas*, 152 F.3d 464, 470 (5th Cir.1998), *cert. granted, judgment vacated*, 527 U.S. 1032, 119 S.Ct. 2388, 144 L.Ed.2d 790 (1999); *Baert v. Euclid Beverage, Ltd.*, 149 F.3d 626, 629–630 (7th Cir.

1998); *Matczak v. Frankford Candy & Chocolate Co.*, 136 F.3d 933, 937–938 (3d Cir.1997); *Arnold v. United Parcel Service, Inc.*, 136 F.3d 854, 859–866 (1st Cir.1998); *Doane v. City of Omaha*, 115 F.3d 624, 627–28 (8th Cir.), *cert. denied*, 522 U.S. 1048, 118 S.Ct. 693, 139 L.Ed.2d 638 (1998); *Harris v. H & W Contracting Co.*, 102 F.3d 516, 520–21 (11th Cir.1996); *Holihan v. Lucky Stores, Inc.*, 87 F.3d 362, 366 (9th Cir.1996), *cert. denied*, 520 U.S. 1162, 117 S.Ct. 1349, 137 L.Ed.2d 506 (1997). *But see Sutton v. United Air Lines*, 130 F.3d 893, 902 (10th Cir.1997) *aff'd*, 527 U.S. 471, 119 S.Ct. 2139, 144 L.Ed.2d 450 (1999). *Murphy v. United Parcel Service*, 141 F.3d 1185 (10th Cir.1998), *aff'd*, 527 U.S. 516, 119 S.Ct. 2133, 144 L.Ed.2d 484 (1999).

10. 527 U.S. 471, 119 S.Ct. 2139, 144 L.Ed.2d 450 (1999).

11. 527 U.S. 516, 119 S.Ct. 2133, 144 L.Ed.2d 484 (1999).

12. *Sutton*, 527 U.S. at ___, 119 S.Ct. at 2146.

als," rather than evaluate the particular "individual's actual condition" as mitigated or corrected.[13] Finally, the Court found it critical that Congress stated in the "Findings and Purpose" section of the ADA that "43,000,000 Americans have one or more physical or mental disabilities."[14] If Congress had meant to include persons whose disabilities were mitigated by corrective measures, the Court reasoned, that number is far too small.[15]

Justice Stevens, joined by Justice Breyer, wrote in dissent that Congress unambiguously intended to cover persons such as amputees even when mitigating measures such as prostheses has restored such individuals' abilities to perform all major life activities in a manner on par with non-amputees.[16] In Justice Stevens' view, the statutory language requires only an inquiry "into the existence of an impairment—present or past—that substantially limits, or did so limit, the individual before amelioration."[17] Calling the majority's conclusion that mitigation removes a person from ADA protection "counterintuitive,"[18] Justice Stevens posits that the various Congressional reports accompanying the ADA "make it abundantly clear" that mitigation is not to be considered by a court when determining whether an individual is disabled.[19]

Reading *Sutton*, *Murphy*, and *Albertson's* together makes it clear that a plaintiff must allege that her impairment *currently* and in its mitigated state substantially limits a major life activity.[20] If the plaintiff

---

13. *Id.*

14. *Id.* at 2147 (quoting § 12101(a)(1)).

15. *Id.* (citing a variety of data, including a report from the National Advisory Eye Council, United States Department of Health and Human Services, to the effect that more than 100 million people need corrective lenses to see properly).

16. *Id.* at 2153–54.

17. *Id.* at 2154.

18. *Id.*

19. *Id.* at 2154–55 (Stevens, J., dissenting). Consider these quotations from the legislative history:

Whether a person has a disability should be assessed without regard to the availability of mitigating measures, such as reasonable accommodations or auxiliary aids. For example, a person who is hard of hearing is substantially limited in the major life activity of hearing, even though the loss may be corrected through the use of a hearing aid. Likewise, persons with impairments, such as epilepsy or diabetes, which substantially limit a major life activity are covered under the first prong of the definition of disability, even if the effects of the impairment are controlled by medication.

H.R.Rep.No. 101–485(II), at 52.

The impairment should be assessed without considering whether mitigating measures, such as auxiliary aids or reasonable accommodations, would result in a less-than-substantial limitation. For example, a person with epilepsy, an impairment which substantially limits a major life activity, is covered under this test, even if the effects of the impairment which substantially limits a major life activity, is also covered, even if the hearing loss is corrected by the use of a hearing aid.

H.R.Rep.No. 101–485(III), at 28–29.

Moreover, whether a person has a disability should be assessed without regard to the availability of mitigating measures, such as reasonable accommodations or auxiliary aids.

S.Rep.No. 101–116, at 23.

20. *Sutton*, 527 U.S. at ___, 119 S.Ct. at 2146 ("A 'disability' exists only where an impairment 'substantially limits' a major life activity, not where it 'might,' 'could,' or 'would' be substantially limiting if mitigating measures were not taken"). *See Belk v. Southwestern Bell Tel. Co.*, 194 F.3d 946, 950 (8th Cir.1999) (finding plaintiff met *Sutton* requirements where he was required to wear a leg brace which limited his mobility). See also *Spades v. City of Walnut Ridge*, 186 F.3d 897 (8th Cir.1999) (police

has mitigated—and under this trilogy of cases, mitigation includes not only devices such as corrective lenses, medication, and hearing aids, but also any conscious or unconscious coping mechanisms the individual has utilized or learned to compensate for the impairment—[21] the plaintiff must show prima facie that limitations linger despite mitigation, or perhaps because of the mitigating measure, e.g., medication,[22] and that these lingering limitations continue to substantially limit one or more major life activities.[23]

§ 10.43 "One or More *Major Life Activities*"

The physical or mental impairment must result in a substantial limitation of "one or more major life activities." The Senate report describes major life activities as including sight,[1] hearing, speech, breathing, learning,[2] working, self-care (e.g. eating,[3] hygiene),[4] locomotion, and manual tasks.[5] The House report adds participating in community activities.[6] EEOC regulations state that other major life activities include, but are not limited to, sitting, standing, lifting,[7] and reaching.[8] In *Bragdon v.*

officer could function without limitation when receiving medication and counseling for depression, so not substantially limited); *Hill v. Kansas City Area Transportation Authority*, 181 F.3d 891 (8th Cir.1999), *cert. denied*, __ U.S. __, 120 S.Ct. 981, 145 L.Ed.2d 932 (2000) (hypertension not disability because controlled by medication and did not substantially limit plaintiff in any major life activity).

21. *See Albertson's*, 527 U.S. at __, 119 S.Ct. at 2168.

22. *Cf. Hill v. Kansas City Area Transportation Authority*, 181 F.3d 891 (8th Cir. 1999), *cert. denied*, __ U.S. __, 120 S.Ct. 981, 145 L.Ed.2d 932 (2000) (plaintiff failed to prove that the combination of medicines required to treat her hypertension rendered her regularly too drowsy to perform the essential function of staying awake).

23. *See Otting v. J.C. Penney Co.*, 223 F.3d 704 (8th Cir.2000) (surviving *Sutton* because despite medication and surgery, epileptic's seizures were not under control at the time of her termination); *Belk v. Southwestern Bell Tel. Co.*, 194 F.3d 946, 950 (8th Cir.1999) (finding plaintiff met *Sutton* requirements where he was required to wear a leg brace which limited his mobility); *Spades v. City of Walnut Ridge*, 186 F.3d 897 (8th Cir.1999) (police officer could function without limitation when receiving medication and counseling for depression, so not substantially limited); *Hill v. Kansas City Area Transportation Authority*, 181 F.3d 891 (8th Cir.1999), *cert. denied*, __ U.S. __, 120 S.Ct. 981, 145 L.Ed.2d 932 (2000) (hypertension not disability because controlled by medication and did not sub-

stantially limit plaintiff in any major life activity).

§ 10.43

1. *See also Albertson's,*, 527 U.S. at __, 119 S.Ct. at 2167 (seeing is a major life activity).

2. *See also Anderson v. General Motors Corp.*, 176 F.3d 488 (10th Cir.), *cert. denied*, 528 U.S. 976, 120 S.Ct. 424, 145 L.Ed.2d 331 (1999) (learning is a major life activity).

3. *See, e.g., Amir v. St. Louis Univ.*, 184 F.3d 1017 (8th Cir.1999) (eating, drinking and getting along with others are major life activities).

4. But not house cleaning other than basic chores such as dish washing or taking out the garbage. *See, e.g., Marinelli v. City of Erie*, 216 F.3d 354 (3d Cir.2000) (cleaning is only considered a major life activity to the extent that such an activity is necessary for one to live in a healthy or sanitary environment); *Colwell v. Suffolk County Police Dep't*, 158 F.3d 635, 643 (2d Cir.1998), *cert. denied*, 526 U.S. 1018, 119 S.Ct. 1253, 143 L.Ed.2d 350 (1999) (merely "performing housework other than basic chores" does not qualify as a major life activity); *Dutcher v. Ingalls Shipbuilding*, 53 F.3d 723, 726 (5th Cir.1995) (same).

5. S.Rep.No. 101–116, at 22.

6. H.R.Rep.No. 101–485, at 52.

7. Courts have rejected claims of disability based on an inability to lift small weights. *See, e.g., Marinelli v. City of Erie*, 216 F.3d 354 (3d Cir.2000); *Thompson v. Holy Family Hosp.*, 121 F.3d 537 (9th Cir.

Abbott, the Supreme Court held that reproduction is a major life activity.[9] The Tenth Circuit has held that sleeping is a major life activity, but concentrating is not.[10] The Second Circuit has rejected "everyday mobility" as a major life activity where the plaintiff was able to walk and travel, stating that a plaintiff cannot "tailor[] his definition of the major life activity to fit the circumstances of his impairment."[11] The court continued:

> The need to identify a major life activity that is affected by the plaintiff's impairment plays an important role in ensuring that only significant impairments will enjoy the protection of the ADA. An ADA plaintiff could considerably lessen the burden of making an individualized showing of a substantial limitation were he able to define the major life activity as narrowly as possible, with an eye toward conforming the definition to the particular facts of his own case. For example, while it might be hard to show that a very mild cough substantially limits the major life activity of "breathing," it would be far easier to make an individualized showing of a substantial limitation if the major life activity were instead defined more

1997) (per curiam) (holding that a woman that could only lift twenty-five pounds consistently, fifty pounds twice a day, and one hundred pounds once a day was not disabled within the meaning of the ADA); *Williams v. Channel Master Satellite Sys., Inc.*, 101 F.3d 346, 349 (4th Cir.1996), *cert. denied sub nom. Williams v. Avnet, Inc.*, 520 U.S. 1240, 117 S.Ct. 1844, 137 L.Ed.2d 1048 (1997) (twenty-five pound lifting restriction not significantly limiting; *Aucutt v. Six Flags Over Mid–America, Inc.*, 85 F.3d 1311, 1319 (8th Cir.1996); *Ray v. Glidden Co.*, 85 F.3d 227, 229 (5th Cir.1996). *But see Burns v. Coca–Cola Enterprises, Inc.*, 222 F.3d 247 (6th Cir.2000) (twenty-three pound lifting restriction, combined with evidence of plaintiff's age, experience and education, sufficed to show plaintiff was substantially limited in working).

8. 29 C.F.R. pt. 1630 app. at 347.

9. 524 U.S. at 639, 118 S.Ct. at 2205. *See McAlindin v. County of San Diego*, 192 F.3d 1226 (9th Cir.1999), *amended*, 201 F.3d 1211 (9th Cir.), *cert. denied*, ___ U.S. ___, 120 S.Ct. 2689, 147 L.Ed.2d 961 (2000) (sex and ability to interact with others are major life activities).

10. *Pack v. Kmart Corp.*, 166 F.3d 1300 (10th Cir.), *cert. denied*, 528 U.S. 811, 120 S.Ct. 45, 145 L.Ed.2d 40 (1999) (stating that the critical issue is whether the activity is significant within the meaning of the ADA, not whether it is significant to the individual). *See Colwell v. Suffolk County Police Dep't*, 158 F.3d 635, 643 (2d Cir. 1998), *cert. denied*, 526 U.S. 1018, 119 S.Ct. 1253, 143 L.Ed.2d 350 (1999) (sleeping a

major life activity). *Cf. McAlindin v. County of San Diego*, 192 F.3d 1226 (9th Cir.1999), *amended*, 201 F.3d 1211 (9th Cir.), *cert. denied*, ___ U.S. ___, 120 S.Ct. 2689, 147 L.Ed.2d 961 (2000) (concentrating and sleeping are major life activities).

11. *Reeves v. Johnson Controls World Servs., Inc.*, 140 F.3d 144, 150 (2d Cir.1998) (agoraphobia). *See also Sinkler v. Midwest Property Mgmt. Ltd. Partnership*, 209 F.3d 678, 684–85 (7th Cir.2000) (getting to and from work assignments is not a major life activity); *Colwell v. Suffolk County Police Dept.*, 158 F.3d 635, 643 (2d Cir.1998), *cert. denied*, 526 U.S. 1018, 119 S.Ct. 1253, 143 L.Ed.2d 350 (1999) (sleeping is major life activity, but driving, doing mechanical work on cars, performing housework other than basic chores, going shopping in the mall, skiing, and golfing are not); *Wyland v. Boddie–Noell Enterprises, Inc.*, 165 F.3d 913 n. * (4th Cir.1998) (driving is not a major life activity); *Deas v. River West, L.P.*, 152 F.3d 471, 479 (5th Cir.1998), *cert. denied*, 527 U.S. 1044, 119 S.Ct. 2411, 144 L.Ed.2d 808 (1999) ("awareness" is not a major life activity); *Martinez v. City of Roy*, 141 F.3d 1185 (10th Cir.1998) (recreational swimming is not a major life activity); *Heilweil v. Mt. Sinai Hosp.*, 32 F.3d 718 (2d Cir.1994), *cert. denied*, 513 U.S. 1147, 115 S.Ct. 1095, 130 L.Ed.2d 1063 (1995) (asthmatic employee whose condition was aggravated by a poor ventilation system was unable to work in a particular job assignment, but it did not generally limit her ability to breathe or work and therefore did not substantially limit a major life activity).

narrowly as, say, the major life activity of "breathing atop Mount Everest."[12]

Plaintiffs who plead working as the only major life activity that is substantially limited by their impairment have been resoundingly unsuccessful in ADA litigation, and the trio of 1999 Supreme Court cases hold no promise for such plaintiffs. The Court noted in *Sutton* that the use of working as a major life activity creates a nearly circular definition that presents analytical difficulties: If an individual has a physical or mental impairment that substantially limits his ability to perform his job, he arguably qualifies as disabled under the statute, assuming he is otherwise qualified for the job.[13]

The difficulty for plaintiffs who plead working as the major life activity arises at least in part from EEOC regulations that state "[w]ith respect to the major life activity of working, [t]he term substantially limits means significantly restricted in the ability to perform either *a class of jobs or a broad range of jobs in various classes* as compared to the average person having comparable training, skills and abilities."[14] Thus, the ability to perform a single, particular job does not constitute a substantial limitation in the major life activity of working. Indeed during the last couple of years, the most common ground for rejecting a plaintiff's contention that an impairment substantially limited his ability to work is a failure of proof that the condition prevented him from performing, in the words of the EEOC regulations, a class of jobs, or a wide range of jobs in various classes as compared to the average person with comparable training, skills and abilities.[15] Of course, the determina-

12. *Reeves,* 140 F.3d at 152.

13. *Sutton*, 527 U.S. at ___, 119 S.Ct. at 2151 (recognizing this "conceptual difficulty" but specifically declining to determine the validity of the EEOC regulations that deem working a major life activity). *But see School Bd. of Nassau County, Fla. v. Arline*, 480 U.S. 273, 283 n. 10, 107 S.Ct. 1123, 1129 n. 10, 94 L.Ed.2d 307 (1987) (recognizing working as a major life activity under the RHA).

14. 29 C.F.R. § 1630.2(j)(3). Courts have interpreted this "broad range of jobs" language to place a "more fact-specific burden of proof" on the plaintiff. *See, e.g., Quint v. A.E. Staley Manufacturing Co.*, 172 F.3d 1 (1st Cir.1999), *petition for cert. filed*, June 21, 1999 (citing 29 C.F.R. § 1630.2(j)(3)). Under the EEOC guidelines, courts may instruct a jury to first determine whether plaintiffs were substantially limited with respect to a major life activity other than working. If the jury finds plaintiffs were not so limited, the jury is to then consider whether plaintiffs were substantially limited with respect to working. *See* 29 C.F.R. pt. 1630, app. § 1630.2(j); *Davoll v. Webb*, 194 F.3d 1116, 1135 (10th Cir.1999) (such an instruction sets forth a logical framework for the jury to consider working and other major life activities and the factors associated with each).

15. *See, e.g., Sinkler v. Midwest Property Mgmt. Ltd. Partnership*, 209 F.3d 678, 685–86 (7th Cir.2000) (plaintiff's inability to drive in unfamiliar places did not disqualify her from a broad range of jobs); *Schneiker v. Fortis Ins. Co.*, 200 F.3d 1055 (7th Cir.2000) (plaintiff's inability to work in stressful situations due to depression precluded her only from working under one supervisor); *Doren v. Battle Creek Health System*, 187 F.3d 595 (6th Cir.1999) (tendinitis, ulcer, knee, feet, and back problems that prevented nurse from working with adult patients not shown to limit her ability to work with pediatric patients or perform other nursing positions); *Berg v. Norand Corp.*, 169 F.3d 1140 (8th Cir.), *cert. denied*, 528 U.S. 872, 120 S.Ct. 174, 145 L.Ed.2d 147 (1999) (diabetic plaintiff who started own business and became CEO of a construction company after she was terminated is precluded from demonstrating that she was substantially limited in working); *Tardie v. Rehabilitation Hosp. of Rhode Island*, 168 F.3d 538, 542 (1st Cir.

1999) (the fact that employer may have regarded plaintiff as unable to work more than 40 hours per week, and thereby unable to perform her particular job, does not mean that appellees regarded her as being substantially limited in the major life activity of working); *Colwell v. Suffolk County Police Dep't*, 158 F.3d 635 (2d Cir.1998), *cert. denied*, 526 U.S. 1018, 119 S.Ct. 1253, 143 L.Ed.2d 350 (1999) (doctor's restrictions on police officer's work schedule did not indicate a substantial limitation on officer's ability to work at a broad range of jobs); *Gutridge v. Clure*, 153 F.3d 898, 901 (8th Cir.1998), *cert. denied sub nom, Gutridge v. Midland Computer, Inc.*, 526 U.S. 1113, 119 S.Ct. 1758, 143 L.Ed.2d 790 (1999) (although plaintiff's carpal tunnel syndrome disqualified him from being a computer service technician, the fact that he was able to find a job as computer repair person defeated his ADA claim); *Patterson v. Chicago Ass'n for Retarded Citizens*, 150 F.3d 719, 725–26 (7th Cir.1998) (mentally ill teacher found to be disqualified only from small class of jobs—teaching mentally disabled students); *Swain v. Hillsborough County Sch. Bd.*, 146 F.3d 855, 858 (11th Cir.1998) (plaintiff failed to produce evidence to show that she cannot perform a broad range or class of jobs, making instead vague assertion that she is unable to perform any job that precludes her from having regular access to a restroom); *Baulos v. Roadway Exp., Inc.*, 139 F.3d 1147, 1151–52 (7th Cir.1998) (plaintiffs were unable to perform one particular job for them, driving sleeper trucks, and that this is insufficient to establish a disability under the ADA); *Witter v. Delta Air Lines Inc.*, 138 F.3d 1366 (11th Cir.1998) (pilot's assumed inability to work as pilot left numerous nonpilot jobs he could perform, so not substantially limited in working); *Foreman v. Babcock & Wilcox*, 117 F.3d 800 (5th Cir.1997), *cert. denied*, 522 U.S. 1115, 118 S.Ct. 1050, 140 L.Ed.2d 113 (1998) (heart condition alleviated by pacemaker did not disqualify plaintiff from an entire range or class of jobs); *Helfter v. United Parcel Service, Inc.*, 115 F.3d 613 (8th Cir.1997) (inability to perform jobs requiring sustained repetitive motion and heavy lifting did not render plaintiff unable to perform other classes of jobs in her geographical area); *Hileman v. City of Dallas*, 115 F.3d 352 (5th Cir.1997) (plaintiff with spastic colon that led to her morning tardiness at work failed to show her inability to work in substantially similar jobs); *McKay v. Toyota Motor Mfg., U.S.A., Inc.*, 110 F.3d 369, 373 (6th Cir.1997) (finding that the plaintiff's inability to perform repetitive-motion factory work did not restrict her ability to perform either a class of jobs

or a broad range of jobs); *Weiler v. Household Fin. Corp.*, 101 F.3d 519 (7th Cir. 1996) (employee suffering from stress and temporal mandibular joint syndrome allegedly exacerbated by particular supervisor not substantially limited in working when she admitted she could perform same job for another supervisor); *Williams v. Channel Master Satellite Sys., Inc.*, 101 F.3d 346 (4th Cir.1996), *cert. denied sub nom, Williams v. Avnet, Inc.*, 520 U.S. 1240, 117 S.Ct. 1844, 137 L.Ed.2d 1048 (1997); *Gordon v. E.L. Hamm & Assocs., Inc.*, 100 F.3d 907 (11th Cir.1996), *cert. denied*, 522 U.S. 1030, 118 S.Ct. 630, 139 L.Ed.2d 610 (1997) (chemotherapy treatments did not limit plaintiff's ability to perform a class or range of other jobs); *Bridges v. City of Bossier*, 92 F.3d 329 (5th Cir.1996), *cert. denied*, 519 U.S. 1093, 117 S.Ct. 770, 136 L.Ed.2d 715 (1997) (mild hemophilia that disqualified plaintiff from performing fire fighting jobs did not substantially limit major life activity because that field of jobs too narrow to constitute a "class of jobs"); *Aucutt v. Six Flags Over Mid–America, Inc.*, 85 F.3d 1311 (8th Cir.1996) (physical problems preventing plaintiffs from lifting more than 25 pounds were not shown to have significantly restricted their ability to perform other similar jobs, taking into account the severity and expected duration of the impairments); *Ellison v. Software Spectrum, Inc.*, 85 F.3d 187 (5th Cir.1996) (treatment for breast cancer that at most decreased employee's effectiveness in her current job did not disable her from performing the broad range or class of jobs referred to in 29 C.F.R. § 1630.2(j)(3)); *Taylor v. Albertsons, Inc.*, 74 F.3d 1250 (10th Cir.1996) (plaintiff suffering partial disability consisting of inability to perform certain repetitive motions not disabled because still capable of performing light-duty work and a range of jobs other than her own); *Wooten v. Farmland Foods*, 58 F.3d 382, 386 (8th Cir.1995) (impairment preventing plaintiff from performing narrow range of meat packing jobs not considered substantially limiting); *Bolton v. Scrivner, Inc.*, 36 F.3d 939 (10th Cir.1994), *cert. denied*, 513 U.S. 1152, 115 S.Ct. 1104, 130 L.Ed.2d 1071 (1995) (plaintiff failed to show that he was substantially limited in the "major life activity" of working because he had shown only that his shoulder injury rendered him incapable of performing a "particular" job, not a wide range of jobs); *Heilweil v. Mount Sinai Hosp.*, 32 F.3d 718, 723 (2d Cir.1994), *cert. denied*, 513 U.S. 1147, 115 S.Ct. 1095, 130 L.Ed.2d 1063 (1995) (claim of asthmatic employee fails because "An impairment that disqualifies a person from only a narrow range of

tion of whether an impairment substantially limits a plaintiff's ability to work must be made on an individualized basis, so where the plaintiff's lack of training, skills and abilities combine with an impairment such that the person is unable to perform a broad range of jobs, the plaintiff will be considered to be disabled under ADA.[16] And a plaintiff unable to prove substantial limitation in the ability to work may show that impact on other major life activities.[17]

§ 10.44 Prong Two: "A *Record* of Such an Impairment"

The "record of such an impairment" element of the ADA's tripartite disability definition[1] appears to be the least litigated of the three. Implementing regulations define potential plaintiffs as those who "ha[ve] a history of, or ha[ve] been misclassified as having, a mental or physical impairment that substantially limits one or more major life activities."[2] Thus, the "record of such an impairment" plaintiff must overcome the similar obstacles that face plaintiffs proceeding under the first definition of disabled (those claiming they have an actual disability), by proving their record "substantially limits a major life activity." And because the question whether a particular condition substantially limits such an activity should be answered only after the court considers the effects of mitigating measures,[3] circuit courts have denied "record of" claims by plaintiffs who experienced even serious impairments where such measures have alleviated or corrected the impairments.

In *Ellison v. Software Spectrum, Inc.*, for example, a plaintiff previously treated for breast cancer through a lumpectomy and radiation therapy could not show a record of an impairment that substantially limited a major life activity because she had been able to work with modifications throughout her treatment, and was ultimately completely

---

jobs is not considered a substantially limiting one"). *But see Criado v. IBM Corp.*, 145 F.3d 437 (1st Cir.1998) (depression substantially limited working).

16. *See Burns v. Coca–Cola Enterprises, Inc.*, 222 F.3d 247 (6th Cir.2000) (twenty-three pound lifting restriction, combined with evidence of plaintiff's age, experience and education, sufficed to show plaintiff was substantially limited in working); *Fjellestad v. Pizza Hut Corp. of America, Inc.*, 188 F.3d 944, 949, 954–55 (8th Cir.1999) (plaintiff created genuine fact issue that permanent impairment of upper right extremity and weakness in arms substantially limited her ability to work when she lived in rural area in which the impairment reduced her employability by 91% and her labor market access by 95% respecting all available jobs in state) (relying on 29 C.F.R. § 1630.2(i)(3)(ii) (specifying as factors in determining restricted ability to perform broad scope of jobs, number of jobs that impairment precludes, geographic area to which individual has reasonable access, and

individual's job training, experience and expectations)). *Mondzelewski v. Pathmark Stores, Inc.*, 162 F.3d 778 (3d Cir.1998) (plaintiff's sixth grade education, limited job skills, advanced age, and back injury eliminated plaintiff from a broad range of jobs).

17. *McAlindin v. County of San Diego*, 192 F.3d 1226 (9th Cir.1999), *amended*, 201 F.3d 1211 (9th Cir.), *cert. denied*, ___ U.S. ___, 120 S.Ct. 2689, 147 L.Ed.2d 961 (2000).

§ 10.44

1. 42 U.S.C.A. § 12102(2)(B).

2. 29 C.F.R. § 1630.2(k). *See, e.g., Davidson v. Midelfort Clinic, Ltd.*, 133 F.3d 499 (7th Cir.1998) (plaintiff with attention deficit disorder had a history of learning difficulties sufficient to establish a "record of" an impairment).

3. *See* discussion of the 1999 Supreme Court cases requiring mitigation in § 10.42, *supra*.

recovered.[4] Similarly, the Second Circuit has held that a record of surgery, a one-month hospital stay, and a six month recuperation period was "of too short a duration and too vague an extent to" establish a record of impairment without any particularized or specific limitations on the employee's ability to work.[5] The Eighth Circuit rejected a "record of" impairment claim despite evidence of five surgeries, work restrictions, and an inability to perform simple tasks.[6] Some of these results appear at odds with the Congressional intent to permit "record" claims by fully recovered plaintiffs, so long as the impairment initially caused a substantial limitation in a major life activity.[7]

§ 10.45   Prong Three: "Being *Regarded* as Having Such an Impairment"

The "regarded as" portion of the ADA was designed to combat erroneous stereotypes that employers may have about impairments that are not, in themselves, substantially limiting.[1] The ADA regulations define three ways to satisfy the "regarded as" test: (1) the individual may have an impairment that is not substantially limiting but is treated by the employer as constituting a substantially limiting impairment; (2) the individual may have an impairment that is substantially limiting only because of the attitudes of others toward the impairment; or (3) the individual may have no impairment at all but is regarded by the employer or other covered entity as having a substantially limiting impairment.[2] If the employer regards the employee as merely injured or

4. 85 F.3d 187 (5th Cir.1996).

5. *See Colwell v. Suffolk County Police Dep't*, 158 F.3d 635, 646 (2d Cir.1998), *cert. denied*, 526 U.S. 1018, 119 S.Ct. 1253, 143 L.Ed.2d 350 (1999). *See also Sanders v. Arneson Prods., Inc.*, 91 F.3d 1351, 1354 (9th Cir.1996) (three month impairment that left only minimal permanent effects did not establish substantially limiting prong).

6. *See Gutridge v. Clure*, 153 F.3d 898, 901 (8th Cir.1998), *cert. denied sub nom, Gutridge v. Midland Computer, Inc.*, 526 U.S. 1113, 119 S.Ct. 1758, 143 L.Ed.2d 790 (1999). *See also Hilburn v. Murata Elecs. No. Am., Inc.* 181 F.3d 1220 (11th Cir.1999) (excessive absenteeism over four year period due to heart problems did not establish record of impairment).

7. *See* H.R.Rep.No. 101–485(II), at 52 (1990) (stating that the "record of" prong covers "individuals who have recovered from a physical or mental impairment which previously substantially limited them in a major life activity"); S.Rep.No. 93–1297, at 38–39 (1974), reprinted in 1974 U.S.C.C.A.N. 6373, 6389 (noting that the "record of" prong in the Rehabilitation Act covers "persons who have recovered—in whole or in part—from a handicapping con-

dition, such as . . . cancer"); 29 C.F.R. pt. 1630 app. § 1630.2(k) (noting that the "record of" prong of the ADA "protects former cancer patients from discrimination based on their prior medical history").

§ 10.45

1. *See Harrington v. Rice Lake Weighing Sys., Inc.*, 122 F.3d 456, 459 (7th Cir. 1997); *Johnson v. American Chamber of Commerce Publishers, Inc.*, 108 F.3d 818 (7th Cir.1997); *Vande Zande v. Wisconsin Dep't of Admin.*, 44 F.3d 538, 541 (7th Cir.1995).

2. *See* 29 C.F.R. § 1630.2(l). *See, e.g., Holihan v. Lucky Stores, Inc.*, 87 F.3d 362 (9th Cir.1996), *cert. denied*, 520 U.S. 1162, 117 S.Ct. 1349, 137 L.Ed.2d 506 (1997) (plaintiff could be "regarded" as having a disabling mental condition even if that condition did not substantially limit a major life activity); *Katz v. City Metal Co.*, 87 F.3d 26 (1st Cir.1996) (whether or not plaintiff's condition after a heart attack substantially limited a major life activity, he presented a jury question on whether he was regarded as disabled); *Hodgdon v. Mt. Mansfield Co., Inc.*, 160 Vt. 150, 624 A.2d 1122 (1992) (ski resort might regard chambermaid with dentures as disabled even if her cosmetic im-

ill, however, ADA provides no protection–the ADA "is not a general protection of medically afflicted persons."[3]

The assertion that an employee is protected because the employee is "regarded as" being disabled "turns on the employer's perception" and is therefore "a question of intent."[4] A plaintiff must therefore adduce evidence that the employer actually believed the employee to be disabled within the meaning of the ADA.[5] This probably means that the employee must prove the state of mind of the supervisor or other decisionmaker, or perhaps someone who influences such a person.[6]

The Second Circuit reversed a grant of summary judgment in *Heyman v. Queens Village Comm. for Mental Health for Jamaica Community Adolescent Program, Inc.*,[7] on the "regarded as" theory. The plaintiff suffered from lymphoma, and the court found material issues of fact as to whether the employer regarded the plaintiff as significantly restricted in his ability to perform the major life activity of work. A previous employee had succumbed to the same illness after a long struggle that resulted in absenteeism and poor job performance. "A jury could find that defendants' experience of having allowed [the previous employee] to continue [to work] despite his lymphoma and the resulting inability to perform all of his duties led defendants to conclude that [the plaintiff], afflicted with the same disease, would likewise be unable to function fully and soon would become a workplace liability."[8]

The Third Circuit has crafted an affirmative defense for an employer who *negligently* misperceives an employee's limitations but was not

pairment did not in fact substantially limit a major life activity) (case under RHA). In *Sutton*, the Supreme Court described two ways an individual may fall within the statutory definition: (1) the covered entity mistakenly believes that a person has a substantially limiting impairment; or (2) the covered entity mistakenly believes that a person with an actual nonlimiting or mildly limiting impairment has a substantially limiting impairment. 527 U.S. at ___, 119 S.Ct. at 2149–50.

3. *Christian v. St. Anthony Med. Ctr., Inc.*, 117 F.3d 1051, 1053 (7th Cir.1997), cert. denied, 523 U.S. 1022, 118 S.Ct. 1304, 140 L.Ed.2d 469 (1998). See also *Harrington v. Rice Lake Weighing Sys., Inc.*, 122 F.3d 456 (7th Cir.1997) (no violation of ADA even where employer views employee as permanently ill but not disabled). Further, it has been held that while an employer may not discriminate on a "regarded as" basis, it also need not make reasonable accommodation for the disability the employer regarded the plaintiff as having. *Webber v. Strippit, Inc.*, 186 F.3d 907 (8th Cir. 1999), cert. denied, 528 U.S. 1078, 120 S.Ct. 794, 145 L.Ed.2d 670 (2000).

4. *Colwell v. Suffolk County Police Dept.*, 158 F.3d 635, 646 (2d Cir.1998), cert. denied, 526 U.S. 1018, 119 S.Ct. 1253, 143 L.Ed.2d 350 (1999) (citing *Francis v. City of Meriden*, 129 F.3d 281, 284 (2d Cir.1997)).

5. *Id.* See also *Sullivan v. River Valley Sch. Dist.*, 197 F.3d 804, 810–11 (6th Cir. 1999) (requesting current employee to undergo mental fitness tests did not establish the employer regarded employee as disabled); *Cody v. CIGNA Healthcare of St. Louis, Inc.*, 139 F.3d 595 (8th Cir.1998) (employer's request that security personnel attend meeting with depressed employee regarding medical leave did not demonstrate employer "regarded" employee as disabled when employer had reports employee was armed).

6. *Id.* See also *Standard v. A.B.E.L. Servs., Inc.*, 161 F.3d 1318 (11th Cir.1998) (stray comment by co-worker with no authority to make decisions for employer cannot evince an actionable stereotypical attitude); *Deas v. River West, L.P.*, 152 F.3d 471, 481 (5th Cir.1998), cert. denied, 527 U.S. 1044, 119 S.Ct. 2411, 144 L.Ed.2d 808 (1999) (perception of a co-worker insufficient to establish employer's state of mind).

7. 198 F.3d 68 (2d Cir.1999).

8. *Id.* at 73.

infected with stereotypes or prejudice against the disabled: "If an employer regards a plaintiff as disabled based on a mistake in an individualized determination of the employee's actual condition ... then the employer will have a defense if the employee unreasonably failed to inform the employer of the actual situation."[9] In *Taylor v. Pathmark Stores, Inc.*, the employer misread the employee's medical records as stating that the employee's disability was permanent. The employer argued that it should not be liable for "imperfections in its internal procedures" that caused correspondence from the employee (and his treating physician) to be overlooked by the decisionmakers regarding the employee's employment in the absence of any evidence of animus or prejudice towards the disabled.[10] Holding that the employee took the necessary steps to correct Pathmark's misperception, the circuit court found Pathmark responsible for the misunderstanding.[11]

Under EEOC regulations, plaintiffs who allege that they are regarded as having an impairment that substantially limits the major life activity of working must prove that the employer regarded them as being unable to perform a wide range of jobs.[12] In *Sutton*, the Court assumed arguendo that the EEOC regulations were valid[13] but held that the plaintiffs had failed to allege adequately that their poor eyesight was regarded as an impairment because they referred to only one job, that of global airline pilot. Because the position of global airline pilot was a single job, plaintiff's allegation did not support the claim that the employer regarded them as having a substantially limiting impairment.[14]

Similarly, evidence that an employer was willing to or did offer to transfer the plaintiff to another position will defeat the "regarded as"

---

9. *Taylor v. Pathmark Stores, Inc.*, 177 F.3d 180 (3d Cir.1999).

10. *Id.* at 192.

11. *Id.* at 193. *See also Deane v. Pocono Med. Ctr.*, 142 F.3d 138, 144 (3d Cir.1998) (en banc) (even an innocent misperception based on nothing more than a simple mistake of fact as to the severity, or even the very existence, of an individual's impairment can be sufficient to satisfy the regarded as prong).

12. *See* 29 C.F.R. § 1630.2(j)(3). *See also Lessard v. Osram Sylvania, Inc.*, 175 F.3d 193 (1st Cir.1999); *Zenor v. El Paso Healthcare Sys., Ltd.*, 176 F.3d 847 (5th Cir.1999) (where plaintiff presents no evidence from which a reasonable jury could conclude that the defendant perceived plaintiff's addiction as substantially impairing his ability to work in a broad range or class of jobs, plaintiff failed to establish that he was regarded as suffering from a disability within the meaning of the ADA); *Taylor v. Pathmark Stores, Inc.*, 177 F.3d 180 (3d Cir.1999) (evidence of an employer's erroneous perception that an employee cannot perform a wide range of jobs suffices to make out a regarded as claim); *Cline v.*

Wal–Mart Stores, Inc., 144 F.3d 294, 303 (4th Cir.1998) (where evidence showed that employer perceived plaintiff as unable to perform job of night shift maintenance supervisor, court proceeded to "determine[] whether the night maintenance supervisor's position qualifies as a class of jobs or a broad range of jobs in various classes, as opposed to a single, particular job"); *Witter v. Delta Air Lines, Inc.*, 138 F.3d 1366 (11th Cir.1998).

13. *Sutton*, 527 U.S. at ___, 119 S.Ct. at 2151.

14. In *Welsh v. City of Tulsa*, the plaintiff argued that he was handicapped under the RHA because he was perceived by the city as having an impairment that substantially limited his ability to work as a firefighter. The court stated that although the implementing regulations define a major life activity to include working, "this does not necessarily mean working at the job of one's choice." An impairment that an employer perceives as limiting an individual's ability to perform only one job is not a handicap under the act, the court said. 977 F.2d 1415, 1419 (10th Cir.1992).

claim. Under these facts, the employer apparently perceives the employee as being unable to perform one particular job, not a class of jobs or a broad range of jobs within various classes. Consequently, the employer could not regard the employee as being substantially limited.[15]

The Ninth Circuit has held that a jury must decide whether a grocery store manager who was referred to his employer's employee assistance program ("EAP") because of his "aberrational behavior" was "regarded as" disabled and terminated in violation of the ADA.[16] The court found material issues of fact as to whether the employer regarded its manager as disabled based on meetings about his "problems," referral to the EAP program, and doctor's reports diagnosing depression and anxiety. The Second Circuit has held that referral to an EAP is not sufficient standing alone to establish that an employee was regarded as disabled.[17]

Employees disciplined or terminated solely due to their failure to meet a weight or other physical standard cannot state "regarded as" claims. In *Andrews v. Ohio*, the Sixth Circuit reasoned that "[b]ecause a mere physical characteristic [such as moderate obesity] does not, without more, equal a physiological disorder, where an employee's failure to meet the employer's job criteria is based solely on the possession of such a physical characteristic, the employee does not sufficiently allege a cause of action under these statutes."[18]

Section 12114(b)(3) protects employees who are erroneously regarded as engaging in the use of illegal drugs.[19] As with other "regarded as" claims, the plaintiff must prove that the employer perceived her as

15. *See Lessard v. Osram Sylvania, Inc.,* 175 F.3d 193 (1st Cir.1999); *Sherrod v. American Airlines,* 132 F.3d 1112 (5th Cir. 1998); *Miller v. City of Springfield,* 146 F.3d 612, 615 (8th Cir.1998) (city did not regard applicant for employment as police officer as having psychological impairment that substantially limited a major life activity, such that officer would be disabled under ADA, where applicant was employed by city as a dispatcher at the time she applied to be a police officer and continued to be employed by the city for about a year after that rejection).

16. *Holihan v. Lucky Stores, Inc.,* 87 F.3d 362 (9th Cir.1996), *cert. denied,* 520 U.S. 1162, 117 S.Ct. 1349, 137 L.Ed.2d 506 (1997).

17. *Cody v. CIGNA Healthcare of St. Louis, Inc.,* 139 F.3d 595 (8th Cir.1998). *See also Krocka v. City of Chicago,* 203 F.3d 507 (7th Cir.2000) (although defendant required police officer to participate in an employee monitoring program due to his depression, defendant allowed him to work without restrictions, defeating plaintiff's regarded as claim).

18. *Andrews v. State of Ohio,* 104 F.3d 803, 810 (6th Cir.1997) (noting that several of the plaintiffs had "not alleged anything more about a 'perceived impairment' than that they ... exceeded the [highway patrol] weight limit and that they ... failed to meet the [highway patrol] fitness criteria"). *See also Francis v. City of Meriden,* 129 F.3d 281 (2d Cir.1997) (although employee is not required to allege that his obesity was a disability to prevail on a regarded as claim, he must allege that that the employer regarded him as suffering from a disability).

19. *See, e.g., Buckley v. Consolidated Edison Co. of New York, Inc.,* 127 F.3d 270, 273 (2d Cir.1997), *vacated en banc on other grounds,* 155 F.3d 150 (2d Cir.1998) (stating that committee reports make clear that "[i]n removing protection for persons who currently use drugs, the Committee does not intend to affect coverage for individuals who have a past drug problem or are erroneously perceived as having a current drug problem") (quoting H.R.Rep.No. 101–485(II), at 77).

having an impairment that substantially limits a major life activity.[20]

§§ 10.46–15.59   [Reserved]

G.   MEDICAL EXAMINATIONS AND INQUIRIES

§ 10.60   In general

The ADA bars questions by the employer to all applicants—disabled or not—regarding the existence, nature, or severity of a disability, before the employer makes an offer of employment.[1] Indeed, ADA imposes a blanket prohibition on all pre-offer medical examinations and disability inquiries;[2] an employer may make pre-offer inquiries into the ability of an applicant to perform job-related functions only.[3] As the Tenth Circuit has explained, Congress intended to curtail all questioning that would identify persons with disabilities, so that according nondisabled applicants standing to sue when asked pre-offer questions about disabilities serves to enhance and enforce Congressional intent.[4] If a claim may rest on the mere pre-offer asking of the question, without evidence that the question led to a denial of employment or diminution of terms of employment,[5] the ADA approach departs from that under Title VII, where a pre-hire question geared to race, sex, religion or national origin is unlawful only when shown to have adversely affected the plaintiff's terms or conditions of employment.[6]

Post-offer physical examinations and medical inquiries are permitted[7] only if required of all employees and all medical information is kept

---

20. *See, e.g., Nielsen v. Moroni Feed Co.,* 162 F.3d 604, 610 (10th Cir.1998) (failing to carry burden despite evidence that decision-makers were concerned about a perceived addiction to prescription painkillers).

§ 10.60

1. *See* 42 U.S.C.A. § 12112(d)(2).

2. *Id.* at (d)(2)(A).

3. *Id.* at (d)(2)(B). Several courts have held that an employer may request a medical release before rehiring a former employee. *See Harris v. Harris & Hart, Inc.,* 206 F.3d 838, 842–43 (9th Cir.2000) (the ADA does not prohibit defendant from making inquiries to determine what accommodations, if any, would be necessary for a former employee with a known disability); *Grenier v. Cyanamid Plastics, Inc.,* 70 F.3d 667 (1st Cir.1995) (same).

4. *See Griffin v. Steeltek, Inc.,* 160 F.3d 591, 594 (10th Cir.1998), *cert. denied,* 526 U.S. 1065, 119 S.Ct. 1455, 143 L.Ed.2d 542 (1999) (standing to sue accorded to nondisabled plaintiff alleging that he was not hired as a result of his answers to the employer-defendant's impermissible medical inquiries). *Cf. Fredenburg v. Contra Costa County Dept. of Health Servs.,* 172 F.3d 1176,

1182 (9th Cir.1999) (plaintiffs need not prove that they are qualified individuals with a disability in order to bring claims challenging the scope of medical examinations or inquiries under the ADA); *Roe v. Cheyenne Mountain Conference Resort, Inc.,* 124 F.3d 1221, 1229 (10th Cir.1997) (same).

5. *But see Armstrong v. Turner Indus., Inc.,* 141 F.3d 554 (5th Cir.1998) (employer's alleged violation of ADA section prohibiting pre-offer medical examination and inquiry was not compensable injury in fact, and nondisabled applicant thus lacked standing to seek legal or equitable remedy based on such alleged violation in absence of some cognizable injury in fact of which alleged violation was legal and proximate cause).

6. *See* § 3.2, *supra.*

7. Despite this policy of ADA, it has been held that state workers' compensation benefits may be denied because of a false response to a pre-employment inquiry about disability that violates ADA. *Caldwell v. Aarlin/Holcombe Armature Co.,* 267 Ga. 613, 481 S.E.2d 196 (1997). The majority wrote that the applicant's proper response to a pre-offer disability inquiry is to pursue ADA remedies rather than lie.

confidential in separate medical files.[8] Employment offers may be made conditional upon the results of the examination.[9]

Employers can require current employees to submit to a medical exam or respond to medical inquiries as a condition of continued employment if the examination or inquiry is job-related and consistent with business necessity.[10] For example, in *EEOC v. Prevo's Family Market, Inc.*,[11] a grocery store was justified in requiring an HIV+ produce worker to submit to a medical examination where the exam was deemed necessary to protect the health and safety of co-workers and customers. The grocery store produced evidence that produce workers often cut or nick their hands, and the employee failed to provide sufficient medical evidence that he posed no safety threat.[12]

The Act neither prohibits nor authorizes testing for illegal drugs— such tests are not considered prohibited, pre-offer medical examinations under ADA.[13]

§§ 10.61–15.64 [Reserved]

H. HARASSMENT AND HOSTILE WORK ENVIRONMENT CLAIMS

§ 10.65 In general

Although it is unclear whether a claim for disability-based harassment exists, every circuit to consider the issue has assumed arguendo that a plaintiff can pursue such a claim.[1] If such a claim is cognizable,

---

8. 42 U.S.C.A. § 12112(d)(3). A public employer's post-offer testing may implicate the employee's Fourth Amendment privacy rights, and private or public employer testing that is imposed on the basis of sex, race, or national origin may violate Title VII, even if not ADA. *See Norman–Bloodsaw v. Lawrence Berkeley Laboratory*, 135 F.3d 1260 (9th Cir.1998) (nonconsensual testing for sensitive medical information pursuant to general employee health examinations).

9. 42 U.S.C.A. § 12112(d)(3).

10. 42 U.S.C.A. § 12112(d)(4)(A). See *Martin v. Kansas*, 190 F.3d 1120 (10th Cir. 1999). Employees enjoy this protection against non-job-related medical inquiries even if they are not in fact "disabled" within the meaning of the ADA. *Cossette v. Minnesota Power & Light*, 188 F.3d 964 (8th Cir.1999); *Fredenburg v. Contra Costa County Dep't of Health Services*, 172 F.3d 1176 (9th Cir.1999); *Griffin v. Steeltek, Inc.*, 160 F.3d 591 (10th Cir.1998), *cert. denied*, 526 U.S. 1065, 119 S.Ct. 1455, 143 L.Ed.2d 542 (1999).

11. 135 F.3d 1089 (6th Cir.1998).

12. *Id.* at 1094–95. *See also Watson v. City of Miami Beach*, 177 F.3d 932 (11th

Cir.1999) (tuberculosis tests for all police officers, and a fitness for duty medical examination for a police officer acting paranoid, hostile, and oppositional, were job-related and consistent with business necessity); *Hennenfent v. Mid Dakota Clinic, P.C.*, 164 F.3d 419, 422 & n. 3 (8th Cir. 1998) (dismissing disabled physician's ADA claim without prejudice to allow physician to reconsider his refusal to submit to a job-related medical exam); *Wyland v. Boddie–Noell Enterprises, Inc.*, 165 F.3d 913 (4th Cir.1998) (no ADA violation to require driver to undergo quarterly drug screens where testing was job-related and necessary for a business purpose); *Porter v. U.S. Alumoweld Co., Inc.*, 125 F.3d 243, 246 (4th Cir. 1997) (employee returning after back injury must submit to physical exam).

13. 42 U.S.C.A. § 12114(d)(1).

§ 10.65

1. *See Anthony v. City of Clinton*, 185 F.3d 873 (10th Cir.1999) (assuming without deciding that claim exists); *Walton v. Mental Health Ass'n*, 168 F.3d 661, 666–67 (3d Cir.1999) (same); *Wallin v. Minnesota Dep't of Corrections*, 153 F.3d 681, 687–88 (8th

courts will likely import Title VII case law on the elements of sexual and racial harassment and employer responsibility for harassment by various kinds of agents and non-agent employees.[2]

§§ 10.66–15.69 [Reserved]

I. DISCRIMINATION ON THE BASIS OF ASSOCIATION

§ 10.70 In general

ADA expressly prohibits discrimination against an individual "because of the known disability of an individual with whom the qualified individual is known to have a relationship or association."[1] For instance, an EEOC regulation takes the position that an employer cannot make an adverse employment decision based on the "belie[f] that the [employee] would have to miss work" in order to care for a disabled person.[2]

The Tenth Circuit has established the prima facie case: (1) the plaintiff was "qualified" for the job at the time of the adverse employment action; (2) the plaintiff was subjected to an adverse employment action; (3) the plaintiff was known by his employer at the time to have a relative or associate with a disability;[3] (4) the adverse employment action occurred under circumstances raising a reasonable inference that the disability of the relative or associate was a determining factor in the employer's decision.[4] If the plaintiff in an ADA association discrimina-

Cir.1998), *cert. denied*, 526 U.S. 1004, 119 S.Ct. 1141, 143 L.Ed.2d 209 (1999); *Moritz v. Frontier Airlines, Inc.*, 147 F.3d 784, 788 (8th Cir.1998) (same); *Keever v. City of Middletown*, 145 F.3d 809, 813 (6th Cir.), *cert. denied*, 525 U.S. 963, 119 S.Ct. 407, 142 L.Ed.2d 330 (1998) (implicitly recognizing ADA hostile work environment claim in affirming summary judgment for employer); *McConathy v. Dr. Pepper/Seven Up Corp.*, 131 F.3d 558, 563 (5th Cir.1998) (if claim is cognizable, it would be modeled after claim under Title VII). Indeed, our research has discovered no case that disclaims the theory.

2. *See, e.g., Walton*, 168 F.3d at 667 (utilizing Title VII elements based on similarities between Title VII and the ADA).

§ 10.70

1. 42 U.S.C.A. § 12112(b)(4).

2. 29 C.F.R. § 1630.

3. *Abdel–Khalek v. Ernst & Young, L.L.P.*, 1999 WL 190790 (S.D.N.Y.1999) (denying summary judgment where plaintiff showed that management knew of daughter's disability).

4. *Den Hartog v. Wasatch Academy*, 129 F.3d 1076, 1085 (10th Cir.1997). *See also Morgenthal v. American Tel. & Tel. Co.,*

Inc., 1999 WL 187055, at *2 (S.D.N.Y.1999) (noting that the implementing regulations state that "this provision is intended to protect any qualified individual, whether or not that individual has a disability"); *Dollinger v. State Ins. Fund*, 44 F.Supp.2d 467 (N.D.N.Y.1999) (state insurance auditor stated discrimination claim under ADA against state employer by alleging that he was isolated by his co-workers and employer and consistently denied promotions in place of less qualified employees based on his association with person living with HIV. Two circuit courts have affirmed summary judgment to the defendant where the plaintiff failed to carry the last element—that the adverse employment action occurred because of the plaintiff's association with a disabled person. *See McGuinness v. University of N.M. Sch. of Med.*, 170 F.3d 974, 980 (10th Cir.1998), *cert. denied*, 526 U.S. 1051, 119 S.Ct. 1357, 143 L.Ed.2d 518 (1999) (although plaintiff presented evidence that defendant knew plaintiff had a child with cerebral palsy, he failed to show that such awareness was a "determining factor" in the decision to make him repeat the first-year program); *Rogers v. International Marine Terminals*, 87 F.3d 755, 760–61 (5th Cir.1996) (affirming summary judgment where plaintiff failed to show that he

tion establishes these elements, the burden shifts to the defendant to articulate a legitimate, nondiscriminatory reason for the adverse employment action[5] Once such a reason is articulated, the burden shifts back to the plaintiff to prove that the employer's stated reason is pretextual and that the employer intentionally discriminated against plaintiff.[6]

Implementing regulations state that the association provision of the ADA covers "family, business, social or other relationship or association" between the qualified individual and an individual with a known disability.[7] Thus, this provision "is not limited to those who have a familial relationship with an individual with a disability."[8] As the Tenth Circuit noted in *Den Hartog*, the provision was intended to cover situations where a qualified individual was discriminated against because the employer assumes, without foundation, that the employee's association with a person with a disability, such as HIV, will require the employee to have to miss work or frequently leave work early or both, in order to care for the disabled person.[9] This provision was not, however, intended to cover employees who violate a "neutral employer policy concerning attendance or tardiness,"[10] or poor work performance.[11]

§§ 10.71–15.74 [Reserved]

J. RETALIATION

§ 10.75 In general

Both the RHA[1] and ADA[2] prohibit retaliation, even when the complainant is adjudged not to be a qualified individual with a disability.[3] The pertinent ADA section provides: "No person shall discriminate

---

was terminated *because of* a relative's disability).

5. *See Den Hartog*, 129 F.3d at 1085 (citing *McDonnell Douglas Corp. v. Green*, 411 U.S. 792, 802, 93 S.Ct. 1817, 1824, 36 L.Ed.2d 668 (1973)).

6. *Id.*

7. 29 C.F.R. § 1630.8.

8. *Id.*

9. *See Den Hartog*, 129 F.3d at 1082 (citations omitted); *see also Rogers*, 87 F.3d at 760; *Tyndall v. National Educ. Ctrs., Inc. of Cal.*, 31 F.3d 209, 214 (4th Cir.1994); *Braverman v. Penobscot Shoe Co.*, 859 F.Supp. 596, 604 (D.Me.1994) ("§ 12112(b)(4) was intended to apply, for example, to . . . an employer's discharge of an employee who volunteered at an AIDS clinic due to the employer's fear of contracting AIDS.").

10. *Den Hartog*, 129 F.3d at 1082 (noting that the ADA only requires that "job applicants or employees, but not their relatives or associates, need be reasonably accommodated") (citations omitted). *See also Tyndall*, 31 F.3d 209 (plaintiff's claim that

she was fired because her employer feared she would need time off to care for her disabled son failed because of past poor attendance record).

11. *Ennis v. National Ass'n of Business and Educ. Radio, Inc.*, 53 F.3d 55 (4th Cir.1995) (plaintiff failed to meet prima facie burden of showing she was a "qualified individual" due to her poor work performance).

§ 10.75

1. *See Hiler v. Brown*, 177 F.3d 542 (6th Cir.1999); *Hoyt v. St. Mary's Rehabilitation Ctr.*, 711 F.2d 864 (8th Cir.1983); *Rothman v. Emory Univ.*, 828 F.Supp. 537 (N.D.Ill. 1993) (former law student who suffered from epilepsy stated claim against law school under Rehabilitation Act by alleging that law school officials harassed him in retaliation for complaining about violations of Act).

2. *See* 42 U.S.C.A. § 12203.

3. *See, e.g., Krouse v. American Sterilizer Co.*, 126 F.3d 494 (3d Cir.1997) ("By its own terms, the ADA retaliation provision

against any individual because such individual has *opposed* any act or practice made unlawful by this chapter or because such individual made a charge, testified, assisted, *or participated* in any manner in an investigation, proceeding, or hearing under this chapter."[4] Retaliation claims brought under the ADA and RHA are treated the same as Title VII retaliation claims.[5]

To establish a prima facie case of retaliation under ADA, then, a plaintiff must prove that she engaged in a protected "opposition" or "participation" activity; her employer took an adverse employment action;[6] and a causal connection exists between the protected activity and the adverse action.[7] If an employee establishes a prima facie case of retaliation under the ADA, the burden shifts to the employer to advance a legitimate, non-retaliatory reason for its adverse employment action.[8] The employer's burden at this stage is relatively light: it is satisfied if the defendant articulates any legitimate reason for the adverse employment action; the defendant need not prove that the articulated reason actually motivated the action. If the employer satisfies its burden, the plaintiff must convince the factfinder both that the employer's proffered explanation was false, and that retaliation was the real reason for the adverse employment action.[9]

As under Title VII, the complainant with an "opposition" (as opposed to "participation") claim must have a good faith, reasonable belief that the employer engaged in actionable conduct,[10] and the em-

protects 'any individual' who has opposed any act or practice made unlawful by the ADA or who has made a charge under the ADA"). *See also Barker v. International Paper Co.*, 993 F.Supp. 10 (D.Me.1998) (to establish a prima facie case of employment retaliation for aiding or encouraging his disabled wife, a fellow employee, to exercise her rights under the ADA, employee had to show that: (1) he aided his wife in an ADA-protected activity; (2) he was subjected to an adverse employment activity; and (3) there exists a causal link between the protected activity and the employment decision).

4. 42 U.S.C.A. § 12203 (emphasis added).

5. *See Standard v. A.B.E.L. Servs., Inc.*, 161 F.3d 1318 (11th Cir.1998); *Krouse v. American Sterilizer Co.*, 126 F.3d 494, 500 (3d Cir.1997); *Penny v. United Parcel Service*, 128 F.3d 408 (6th Cir.1997); *Stewart v. Happy Herman's Cheshire Bridge, Inc.*, 117 F.3d 1278, 1287 (11th Cir.1997); *Soileau v. Guilford of Me., Inc.*, 105 F.3d 12, 16 (1st Cir.1997); *Barker*, 993 F.Supp. 10.

6. A change in shifts constitutes an actionable change in the terms, conditions, or privileges of employment where new shift, referred to by co-workers as the "punishment shift," left less free time for plaintiff

and required him to work every Saturday night. *Mondzelewski v. Pathmark Stores, Inc.*, 162 F.3d 778, 787 (3d Cir.1998).

7. *See Eckles v. Consolidated Rail Corp.*, 94 F.3d 1041 (7th Cir.1996), *cert. denied*, 520 U.S. 1146, 117 S.Ct. 1318, 137 L.Ed.2d 480 (1997); *Barker*, 993 F.Supp. 10.

8. *See Kiel v. Select Artificials, Inc.*, 169 F.3d 1131, 1134 (8th Cir.), *cert. denied*, 528 U.S. 818, 120 S.Ct. 59, 145 L.Ed.2d 51 (1999) (finding insubordination to be a legitimate nondiscriminatory reason for firing deaf employee).

9. *See Krouse v. American Sterilizer Co.*, 126 F.3d 494, 500–01 (3d Cir.1997) (citing Title VII cases). *See also* § 2.40 for discussion of Title VII retaliation cases.

10. *See, e.g., Standard v. A.B.E.L. Servs., Inc.*, 161 F.3d 1318 (11th Cir.1998) (plaintiff's retaliation claims fail because his belief that he was disabled within the meaning of the ADA was groundless); *Talanda v. KFC Nat'l Management Co.*, 140 F.3d 1090 (7th Cir.), *cert. denied*, 525 U.S. 869, 119 S.Ct. 164, 142 L.Ed.2d 134 (1998) (restaurant manager could not have reasonably believed that he was opposing unlawful discrimination when he refused to move worker with missing teeth from front counter position when worker was not precluded

ployee's conduct in opposition must be reasonable.[11] Close temporal proximity is usually necessary[12] but may not be sufficient[13] to prove that the adverse employment action is causally connected with the protected activity.

§§ 10.76–15.79   [Reserved]

K. PROCEDURE AND REMEDIES

§ 10.80   The EEOC's Role

The EEOC's primary goal is to educate businesses regarding their responsibility under the ADA. The EEOC offers assistance in explaining key provisions of the ADA and has responsibility for enforcing compliance with Title I of the ADA.[1] The procedures for processing charges of discrimination under the ADA are the same as those under Title VII of the Civil Rights Act of 1964.[2] Employers covered by Title I of the ADA may be covered by other federal requirements that prohibit discrimination based on a disability.[3] The ADA directs the agencies with enforcement authority for these legal requirements to coordinate their activities to prevent duplication and avoid conflicting standards. EEOC and the Office of Federal Contract Compliance in the Department of Labor (the OFCCP) have issued a joint regulation establishing procedures for complaints against employers that are also federal contractors.[4] The joint EEOC–OFCCP rule provides that a complaint of discrimination on the basis of disability filed with the OFCCP under § 503 will be considered a charge filed simultaneously under the ADA if the complaint falls within the ADA's jurisdiction.[5]

§ 10.81   Administrative Prerequisites

Title I incorporates by reference the two-step administrative and judicial enforcement scheme of Title VII of the 1964 Civil Rights Act,[1] described in detail in Chapter 4 above. Accordingly, Title I ADA plain-

---

from other jobs and move did not constitute a demotion).

11. *See Talanda*, 140 F.3d 1090.

12. *See, e.g., Davidson v. Midelfort Clinic, Ltd.*, 133 F.3d 499 (7th Cir.1998) (employer's adverse action must follow fairly soon after employee's protected expression); *Krouse v. American Sterilizer Co.*, 126 F.3d 494 (3d Cir.1997) (employee who was placed on leave 19 months after he filed an EEOC charge failed to establish causal link).

13. *See Kiel v. Select Artificials, Inc.*, 169 F.3d 1131, 1136 (8th Cir.), *cert. denied*, 528 U.S. 818, 120 S.Ct. 59, 145 L.Ed.2d 51 (1999) (causal link eroded by employee's intervening unprotected insubordination). *See also Hamilton v. Southwestern Bell Tel. Co.*, 136 F.3d 1047, 1052 (5th Cir.1998) (impliedly limiting protected activity by holding that the ADA does not insulate

emotional or violent outbursts blamed on an impairment, because the rights afforded under the ADA "are a shield against employer retaliation, not a sword with which one may threaten or curse supervisors").

§ 10.80

1. Bureau of National Affairs, Special Supplement, Daily Labor Report, No. 18, 1/28/92, S–4.

2. 42 U.S.C.A. § 12117(a).

3. Special Supplement, *supra*, note 1 at S–4.

4. *Id.* at S–39.

5. *Id.* at S–39.

§ 10.81

1. 42 U.S.C.A. § 12117(a).

tiffs must file a charge with EEOC within 180 or, in "deferral" states that prohibit disability discrimination at least as stringently as ADA and have comparable procedures and remedies, 300 days of an ADA violation. In addition, they must file a court complaint within 90 days after receiving a notice of right to sue from EEOC. As under Title VII, therefore, courts have had to determine what employer conduct constitutes the "trigger" that starts the clock running on the 180– or 300–day period.

This question arose in the context of applying the "continuing violation" theory to an ADA claim. In June 1992, a month before Title I of ADA went into effect, the employer ranked the plaintiff low among all foreman shortly after, and allegedly because, he had just completed an alcohol treatment program. A year later, after ADA applied, the company relied on these rankings in deciding not to return him to work following a layoff. Following Supreme Court Title VII precedent (subsequently largely overruled by provisions of the 1991 Civil Rights Act),[2] a circuit court concluded that the trigger for filing an EEOC charge was the June 1992 alleged discriminatory ranking, not the 1993 decision based on that ranking which adversely affected plaintiff's employment. Because the 1992 conduct pre-dated the effective date of Title I, it could not be the subject of a valid charge.[3]

§ 10.82 Judicial estoppel

To obtain government or private insurance disability benefits, claimants are routinely required to affirm in applications, and sometimes testimony, that they are partially or wholly disabled. Regardless of their success in securing disability benefits, some claimants concurrently or subsequently assert claims under ADA. Employers have argued that ADA plaintiffs are "judicially estopped" from contending that they are "qualified," in the ADA sense of being able to perform the "essential functions" of their previous job, by their affirmations to the contrary in the government administrative or private benefits process; and more broadly that any prior application for benefits, even one that takes no position about the claimant's ability to perform his previous job, is a per se bar to the ADA action.[1]

The Supreme Court has rejected these arguments, holding that while a plaintiff's previous statements regarding her disability are relevant, a plaintiff is not per se barred from pursuing an ADA claim merely

---

2. *Lorance v. AT & T Technologies*, 490 U.S. 900, 109 S.Ct. 2261, 104 L.Ed.2d 961 (1989). Section 706(e)(2) of the Civil Rights Act of 1991 overruled *Lorance* in part by allowing the subsequent employment consequences of an alleged discriminatory act, as well as the act itself, to trigger the applicable 180–or 300–day EEOC charge filing period. *See* § 4.3, *supra*.

3. *Huels v. Exxon Coal USA, Inc.*, 121 F.3d 1047 (7th Cir.1997).

§ 10.82

1. Technically, the "judicial estoppel" setting presented by parallel administrative and judicial proceedings is inapplicable where an employee takes inconsistent positions within the same litigation. In that setting, the assertion of inconsistent positions simply serves to undermine credibility. *Bradley v. Harcourt, Brace and Co.*, 104 F.3d 267 (9th Cir.1996).

because she has asserted in another forum that she is disabled.[2] Instead, when challenged, she must explain any discrepancy between statements she made while pursuing disability benefits and her ADA claim that she can, with our without reasonable accommodation, perform the essential functions of her job.[3]

Carolyn Cleveland applied for and received Social Security Disability Insurance ("SSDI") benefits under the Social Security Act ("SSA") after she suffered a debilitating stroke and was fired from her job at Policy Management Systems. During the SSDI application process, Cleveland stated that she was disabled and unable to work. Cleveland also filed an ADA claim alleging that her employer had terminated her without reasonably accommodating her disability.

The Court found that the representations Cleveland made in obtaining SSDI benefits were "context-related legal conclusion[s]," not factual assertions, so the standard doctrine of judicial estoppel was not implicated. Nor were the two statutes—SSA and ADA—so alike that a negative presumption was warranted; "there are too many situations in which an SSDI claim and an ADA claim can comfortably exist side by side." For example, the SSA concept of disability does not take into account reasonable accommodations. Accordingly, an ADA suit claiming that the plaintiff can perform essential job functions with reasonable accommodation is not inconsistent with an SSDI claim that the plaintiff could not perform her job (or other jobs) without an accommodation. Moreover, the SSDI scheme embodies broad presumptions regarding an individual's ability to perform a job based on the disability, whereas the ADA focuses on the special individual circumstances that may allow a qualified individual to perform a particular job. Additionally, the SSA inquiry turns on the claimant's ability to work generally in the national economy, rather than to perform the essential functions of the particular job she held or desired. Finally, the simple passage of time between the prior proceeding and the commencement of the ADA action may be significant, as where a plaintiff unable (with or without accommodation) to perform the essential functions of the job she seeks becomes able to do so after recuperation.

The Court stated that an ADA plaintiff cannot "simply ignore" statements made in obtaining SSDI benefits. Rather, she must "proffer a sufficient explanation" of the apparent contradiction.[4] Cleveland explained her seemingly inconsistent statements by relying on contextual and temporal distinctions: she made statements in the SSDI forum

2. *Cleveland v. Policy Management Sys. Corp.*, 526 U.S. 795, 119 S.Ct. 1597, 143 L.Ed.2d 966 (1999).

3. *Id.* at 797–98, 119 S.Ct. at 1600.

4. *Id.* at 806, 119 S.Ct. at 1603–04 (citing lower court authority that a party cannot create a genuine issue of fact sufficient to survive summary judgment simply by contradicting his or her own previous sworn statement (by, say, filing a later affidavit that flatly contradicts that party's earlier sworn deposition) without explaining the contradiction or attempting to resolve the disparity). *See also Motley v. New Jersey State Police*, 196 F.3d 160, 165–66 (3d Cir. 1999), *cert. denied*, ___ U.S. ___, 120 S.Ct. 1719, 146 L.Ed.2d 641 (2000) (finding that plaintiff failed to proffer a satisfactory explanation of his previous statement that he was "totally and permanently disabled").

without regard to reasonable accommodations at a time when the statements were accurate. The Court remanded for fact-finding regarding the legitimacy of Cleveland's explanatory statements.[5]

Cleveland may allow defendants to carry their initial burden as Federal Rule of Civil Procedure 56(c) summary judgment movants earlier and more easily than in a case where they must cite discovery materials to show that plaintiff has failed to raise a genuine issue as to her "qualified individual with a disability" ("QID") status. Where the plaintiff has made apparently inconsistent statements in a prior proceeding, the moving defendant need merely point to plaintiff's previous statements. In response, the plaintiff will be required to raise a genuine issue of material fact regarding his QID status. Under the applicable Rule 56(c) standards, this means that the plaintiff will have to come forward with all potentially admissible evidentiary material that would tend to persuade the trial judge that a reasonable jury could find her able to perform the essential functions of her job, with or without accommodation, by a preponderance of all the evidence and notwithstanding her prior apparently inconsistent statement.[6]

Apart from the possible problems plaintiff may encounter in proving an issue of fact where plaintiff has made a prior inconsistent statement in an administrative proceeding, ordinary claim and issue preclusion stemming from a previous judgment may obstruct the ADA claim. Where, for example, a plaintiff did not commence her action under ADA until after she had received a judgment in an action under the Family Medical Leave Act, her ADA action was held claim precluded because it arose from the same transactional nucleus even though it involved additional facts and a new legal theory. Plaintiff argued that she should not have had to wait to assert her FMLA claim until after she had exhausted the administrative remedies prerequisite to her action under ADA. The court observed, however, that plaintiff could have sped up that exhaustion by demanding a right to sue letter from EEOC after 180 days; alternatively, if she wished to afford EEOC more time, she could have filed her FMLA claim but asked the trial court to stay that action pending plaintiff's receipt of a right to sue letter on the ADA claim.[7]

§ 10.83 Remedies

For ADA remedies in the employment setting, refer to the discussion in Chapter 4 on remedies under Title VII, made applicable to ADA claims by the Civil Rights Act of 1991. A few procedures and remedies issues particular to ADA that have emerged in recent years are separately discussed below.

5. *See also Motley*, 196 F.3d at 164 & n.4 (acknowledging the fact-intensive nature of the estoppel inquiry).

6. *See Moore v. Payless Shoe Source, Inc.*, 187 F.3d 845 (8th Cir.), *cert. denied*, 528 U.S. 1050, 120 S.Ct. 589, 145 L.Ed.2d 490 (1999) (plaintiff failed to overcome prior statement to SSA for lack of evidence that she could perform essential functions of her prior job).

7. *Churchill v. Star Enterprises*, 183 F.3d 184 (3d Cir.1999).

Remedies that may be required of an employer who is found to have discriminated against an applicant or employee with a disability include "compensatory damages, punitive damages, back pay, front pay, restored benefits, attorney's fees, reasonable accommodation, reinstatement and job offers."[1] Compensatory and punitive damages, however, are available only where intentional discrimination is proved.[2] Damages may be awarded to compensate for actual monetary losses, future monetary losses, mental anguish and inconvenience. Punitive damages may be available if the employer acts with malice or reckless indifference.[3] However, punitive damages are not available against state or local governments. In cases alleging a failure to reasonably accommodate plaintiff's disability, compensatory or punitive damages may not be awarded to the charging party if an employer can demonstrate that "good faith" efforts were made to provide reasonable accommodation.[4] As under Title VII, the total amount of punitive damages and compensatory damages for future monetary losses and emotional injury for each individual is limited, based upon the size of the employer, using the following schedule:

Number of employees	Damages will not exceed
15–100	$ 50,000
101–200	$100,000
201–500	$200,000
500 and more	$300,000

It has been held that an employee may not avoid the ADA damages caps by relying on a violation of that statute as the sole federal law violation

§ 10.83

1. Bureau of National Affairs, Special Supplement, Daily Labor Report, No. 18, 1/28/92, S–4. *See, e.g., Doane v. City of Omaha*, 115 F.3d 624 (8th Cir.1997), *cert. denied*, 522 U.S. 1048, 118 S.Ct. 693, 139 L.Ed.2d 638 (1998) (ordering police officer reinstated).

2. Special Supplement, *supra*, at S–39. Thus where the sole evidence reflected in a pretrial order concerned employer acts and omissions that had an adverse impact on disabled persons, rather than animus against the disabled or acts of disparate treatment directed against the plaintiff, compensatory damages for emotional distress were unavailable. *Tyler v. City of Manhattan*, 118 F.3d 1400 (10th Cir.1997).

3. *See, e.g., Otting v. J.C. Penney Co.*, 223 F.3d 704 (8th Cir.2000) (punitive damage award reinstated on evidence that store manager made no effort whatsoever to explore any possibility that would allow plaintiff to return to work with her ladder-climbing restriction); *Cline v. Wal–Mart Stores, Inc.*, 144 F.3d 294, 306 (4th Cir.1998) (finding Wal–Mart liable for punitive damages based on supervisor's ignorant and callous

remarks regarding plaintiff's mental abilities but finding amount excessive and offering plaintiff a remittitur or new trial as required by the Seventh Amendment as construed by *Hetzel v. Prince William County, Va.*, 523 U.S. 208, 118 S.Ct. 1210, 140 L.Ed.2d 336 (1998)). The Supreme Court has held that outrageous conduct is not prerequisite to a punitive award under the similarly worded provision authorizing punitive damages in actions under Title VII, also added by the 1991 Civil Rights Act, provided plaintiff proves the malicious or recklessly indifferent state of mind of high employer agents. Kolstad v. American Dental Association, 527 U.S. 526, 119 S.Ct. 2118, 144 L.Ed.2d 494 (1999), discussed in § 4.26, *supra. Kolstad* was applied in an ADA action in *EEOC v. Wal–Mart Stores, Inc.*, 187 F.3d 1241 (10th Cir.1999) (reasonable jury could have concluded that managers knew they risked violating federal law, and good-faith defense fails because employer had not educated its employees about nondiscrimination policy).

4. Special Supplement, *supra*, at S–39.

underlying a § 1983 "and laws" claim.[5]

5. *Holbrook v. City of Alpharetta, Ga.*, 112 F.3d 1522 (11th Cir.1997). *See* § 2.50 for a more general discussion of the criteria used to determine if a § 1983 "and laws" claim is displaced by the detailed procedural or remedial provisions of another federal statute that the plaintiff hopes to use as the predicate for the § 1983 claim.

Chapter Eleven

COSTS AND FEES: FEDERAL RULE OF CIVIL PROCEDURE 54(d), THE CIVIL RIGHTS ATTORNEY'S FEES AWARDS ACT AND FEDERAL RULE 68

Analysis

A. RULE 54(d) COSTS TO PREVAILING PLAINTIFFS OR DEFENDANTS

§ 11.1   In General

Unlike attorney's fees under Title VII or § 1988, which as we shall see are ordinarily awardable only to prevailing plaintiffs, either side that prevails is presumptively entitled to costs under Fed.R.Civ.P. 54(d). Indeed the argument has been rejected that a losing Title VII plaintiff may be assessed costs only on the same terms as she should be assessed fees—that is, when the claim was frivolous, unreasonable, or without foundation.[1]

The awarding of costs lies within the sound discretion of the district court and may be denied where the award would be inequitable.[2] Citing that discretion, a district court has cut in half a large award of costs to a defendant law firm that prevailed after lengthy litigation involving its alleged unlawful denial of partnership on the basis of gender. The court took into account that the case was "close"; that it presented important issues of public concern and had been pursued by the plaintiff at great financial cost; and that the plaintiff was of modest means while the defendant was a large corporate firm.[3]

The "costs" recoverable by any prevailing party are limited, however, to items specified by a separate federal statute, 28 U.S.C.A. § 1920. These include clerk and marshal fees, fees by court reporters for transcripts "necessarily obtained for use in the case;"[4] printing disbursements and witness fees; specified docket fees; and fees for court-appointed experts and certain interpreters. Most important, "costs" as used in Rule 54(d) do *not* include the prevailing party's attorney's fees. This is consistent with the ordinary "American rule" which, as explained by the Supreme Court, calls for each side to pay its own lawyer, win or lose, unless there is specific statutory authority for fee shifting.[5] It is to such fee-shifting statutes that we now turn.

§§ 11.2–16.4 [Reserved]

B. INTRODUCTION TO THE CIVIL RIGHTS ATTORNEY'S FEES AWARDS ACT

§ 11.5 In General

The Civil Rights Attorney's Fees Awards Act (the "Act"), a 1976 amendment to 42 U.S.C.A. § 1988, permits a discretionary award of attorney's fees, in a "reasonable" amount, to prevailing parties, other than the United States,[1] in any action or proceeding pursuant to 42

§ 11.1

1. *See, e.g., Cosgrove v. Sears, Roebuck & Co.*, 191 F.3d 98 (2d Cir.1999); *Croker v. Boeing Co.*, 662 F.2d 975 (3d Cir.1981). And plaintiff's modest means do not suffice to overcome the presumption that costs are to be awarded to the prevailing party, although misconduct by the prevailing party or plaintiff's clear inability to pay might. *See, e.g., Cherry v. Champion International Corp.*, 186 F.3d 442 (4th Cir.1999).

2. See, e.g., *Friedman v. Ganassi*, 853 F.2d 207 (3d Cir.1988), *cert. denied*, 488 U.S. 1042, 109 S.Ct. 867, 102 L.Ed.2d 991 (1989).

3. *Ezold v. Wolf, Block, Schorr and Solis–Cohen*, 157 F.R.D. 13 (E.D.Pa.1994).

4. Some courts have taxed at least part of the costs associated with videotaping a deposition, *see Morrison v. Reichhold Chems., Inc.*, 97 F.3d 460 (11th Cir.1996), *Barber v. Ruth*, 7 F.3d 636 (7th Cir.1993), *Echostar Satellite Corp. v. Advanced Communications Corp.*, 902 F.Supp. 213 (D.Colo.1995), despite the argument that those costs are not the fees of a "court reporter" for a "stenographic transcript." Depositions are compensable as costs where court finds they were reasonably necessary. *Zotos v. Lindbergh Sch. Dist.*, 121 F.3d 356 (8th Cir.1997).

5. *Alyeska Pipeline Serv. Co. v. Wilderness Soc'y*, 421 U.S. 240, 95 S.Ct. 1612, 44 L.Ed.2d 141 (1975).

§ 11.5

1. So the United States as prevailing plaintiff cannot recover fees under § 1988, while the United States as losing plaintiff may be assessed fees per the Equal Access

U.S.C.A. §§ 1981, 1982, 1983, 1985, and 1986, as well as Titles VI and IX.[2] The purpose of the award is to enable plaintiffs to attract competent legal counsel; perhaps that is why fees have been denied for lawyers' public relations efforts on behalf of their clients.[3] The Act parallels separate statutory authority to award attorney's fees to prevailing parties in actions under the Rehabilitation Act of 1973,[4] the Age Discrimination in Employment Act,[5] the Equal Pay Act,[6] the Clean Water Act,[7] the Fair Labor Standards Act,[8] and under Title VII.[9] In fact, over a hundred separate statutes allow for court awarded attorney's fees. The principles governing eligibility for and computation of awards are largely interchangeable among these statutes.

Although a plaintiff must receive at least some relief on the merits in order to become a "prevailing party" eligible for fees, success on a "significant issue," even if it is not a "central" one, will suffice.[10] But opinion is divided as to whether fee eligibility depends upon the plaintiff's having prevailed on a claim under one of the § 1988-referenced federal statutes, rather than a related claim under state law.[11] A plaintiff

to Justice Act, § 11.15, *infra*, in circumstances where private defendants would not be subject to fee liability under § 1988.

2. But not state law discrimination claims where no federal claims are advanced. *See Paz v. Long Island R. Co.*, 128 F.3d 121 (2d Cir.1997).

3. *Halderman v. Pennhurst State Sch. & Hosp.*, 49 F.3d 939 (3d Cir.1995).

4. 29 U.S.C.A. § 794(a).

5. 29 U.S.C.A. § 626(b) (incorporating standards from the Fair Labor Standards Act, 29 U.S.C.A. § 216(b)). Textually, the ADEA and the FLSA differ from the other statutes in that they require fees to be shifted as the result of "any judgment" awarded to a plaintiff, with no reference to the concept of "prevailing party." See 29 U.S.C.A. § 626(b) of the ADEA, incorporating 29 U.S.C.A. § 216(b) of the FLSA. Nevertheless, a circuit has imported all the restrictions surrounding the "prevailing party" showing into fee disputes arising from judgments under the ADEA. *See Salvatori v. Westinghouse Elec. Corp.*, 190 F.3d 1244 (11th Cir.1999), *cert. denied*, ___ U.S. ___, 120 S.Ct. 1172, 145 L.Ed.2d 1081 (2000) (plaintiff who obtained judgment on merits of ADEA claim but no monetary or punitive relief denied fees); *Nance v. Maxwell Fed. Credit Union*, 186 F.3d 1338 (11th Cir.1999) (fees denied when plaintiff proved defendant's conduct violated ADEA but could not prove consequent injury and accordingly received no relief).

6. 29 U.S.C.A. § 206(d) (incorporating standards from the Fair Labor Standards Act, 29 U.S.C.A. § 216(b)).

7. 33 U.S.C.A. § 1365.

8. 29 U.S.C.A. § 216(b).

9. 42 U.S.C.A. § 2000e-5(k).

10. *See Shrader v. OMC Aluminum Boat Group, Inc.*, 128 F.3d 1218 (8th Cir. 1997); *Texas State Teachers Ass'n v. Garland Indep. Sch. Dist.*, 489 U.S. 782, 109 S.Ct. 1486, 103 L.Ed.2d 866 (1989); *District of Columbia v. Patterson*, 667 A.2d 1338 (D.C.App.1995), *cert. denied*, 519 U.S. 1058, 117 S.Ct. 688, 136 L.Ed.2d 612 (1997) (remanding to determine if plaintiff could establish prevailing party status with respect to claims other than the 4th Amendment claim as to which the appellate court held she had not prevailed).

11. *Contrast Williams v. Hanover Hous. Auth.*, 113 F.3d 1294 (1st Cir.1997) and *Exeter–West Greenwich Reg'l Sch. Dist. v. Pontarelli*, 788 F.2d 47 (1st Cir.1986) (attorney's fees recoverable even where plaintiff technically prevails only on state law claim, provided dispositive state law question is closely connected with the federal claim) *with National Private Truck Council, Inc. v. Oklahoma Tax Comm'n*, 515 U.S. 582, 115 S.Ct. 2351, 132 L.Ed.2d 509 (1995) (plaintiff not prevailing party). *Cf. Bridges v. Eastman Kodak Co.*, 102 F.3d 56 (2d Cir.1996), *cert. denied sub nom. Yourdon, Inc. v. Bridges*, 520 U.S. 1274, 117 S.Ct. 2453, 138 L.Ed.2d 211 (1997) (plaintiff who prevailed on merits but recovered no back pay under Title VII, yet who obtained $20,000 compensatory damages on related state law claim, is "prevailing party" eligible for attorney's fees and costs under Title VII).

adjudged to be a prevailing party should ordinarily receive a fee award absent "special circumstances," such as the plaintiff's egregious misconduct.[12] These circumstances are rarely found.[13] But *pro se* plaintiffs who also happen to be attorneys have been ruled ineligible for a fee award.[14] And a plaintiff who recovers only nominal damages, although a prevailing party, may be entitled to no fee award if those damages represent only a slight degree of success achieved in the litigation.[15]

To achieve success on a "significant issue" and thus "prevail" so as to be eligible for fees, the plaintiff need only obtain some relief, by settlement or otherwise, which changes his legal relationship with the defendant and is more than merely technical or *de minimis*.[16] In general,

12. *See, e.g., Patricia P. v. Board of Educ. of Oak Park*, 203 F.3d 462 (7th Cir. 2000) (under IDEA, even if the private school placement is appropriate, plaintiff can be denied fees where she did not cooperate in making the child available for evaluation)*; Lee v. American Eagle Airlines, Inc.*, 93 F.Supp.2d 1322 (S.D.Fla.2000) (denying prevailing plaintiff attorney's fees due to egregious misconduct of counsel during trial); *Christiansburg Garment Co. v. EEOC*, 434 U.S. 412, 98 S.Ct. 694, 54 L.Ed.2d 648 (1978). Cf. *Chaney v. New Orleans Pub. Facility Mgmt., Inc.*, 1998 WL 87617 (E.D.La.1998) (denying prevailing party attorneys' fees in Title VII action, finding performance of plaintiff's attorneys did not merit attorneys' fees). Failure to mitigate damages is not sufficient misconduct to forfeit fees. *Bridges v. Eastman Kodak Co.*, 102 F.3d 56 (2d Cir.1996), *cert. denied sub nom. Yourdon, Inc. v. Bridges*, 520 U.S. 1274, 117 S.Ct. 2453, 138 L.Ed.2d 211 (1997). But a state court denied fees under § 1988 to plaintiffs who successfully attacked the Federal constitutionality of a state law enforced but not enacted by defendant municipality, on the ground that plaintiffs should have known that the municipality could not be independently liable for the unconstitutional state statute. *Minnesota Council of Dog Clubs v. Minneapolis*, 540 N.W.2d 903 (Minn.App.1995), *cert. denied*, 518 U.S. 1005, 116 S.Ct. 2524, 135 L.Ed.2d 1048 (1996). In the class action context, a plaintiff who had opted out of a class settlement and then litigated the claim and received exactly the same damages had the plaintiff remained in the class, was deemed not a prevailing and was denied attorney's fees. *See Rivera–Rosario v. United States Dep't of Agric.*, 202 F.3d 35, 36 (1st Cir.2000).

13. *See, e.g., Gumbhir v. Curators of Univ. of Mo.*, 157 F.3d 1141, 1146 (8th Cir.1998), *cert. denied*, 526 U.S. 1005, 119 S.Ct. 1143, 143 L.Ed.2d 210 (1999) (declining to deny an award because of litigation

conduct). *See also* Zimmer, Sullivan & Richards, *Cases and Materials on Employment Discrimination* 663–64 (2d ed. 1988).

14. *Kay v. Ehrler*, 499 U.S. 432, 111 S.Ct. 1435, 113 L.Ed.2d 486 (1991). *See also Doe v. Board of Educ. of Baltimore County*, 165 F.3d 260 (4th Cir.1998), *cert. denied*, 526 U.S. 1159, 119 S.Ct. 2049, 144 L.Ed.2d 216 (1999) (legal representation of disabled child by attorney-parent a "special circumstance" disqualifying child, an IDEA plaintiff, from award of fees).

15. *Farrar v. Hobby*, 506 U.S. 103, 113 S.Ct. 566, 121 L.Ed.2d 494 (1992). *See also Tyler v. Corner Const. Corp., Inc.*, 167 F.3d 1202 (8th Cir.1999) (treating a "nuisance settlement" as a special circumstance rendering unjust a fee award to prevailing party).

16. *See Hewitt v. Helms*, 482 U.S. 755, 107 S.Ct. 2672, 96 L.Ed.2d 654 (1987) (declaration that prison authority violated due process with no finding of liability because qualified immunity defense sustained, did not enable plaintiff to prevail; nor did the change of policy resulting from his suit because he did not benefit from change, having been earlier released from prison); *Rhodes v. Stewart*, 488 U.S. 1, 109 S.Ct. 202, 102 L.Ed.2d 1 (1988) (even judgment ordering prison to modify magazine policy respecting inmates did not make plaintiffs prevailing parties, because one was dead and the other released when policy change was made, so neither personally benefited from judgment). *Compare Barnes v. Broward County Sheriff's Office*, 190 F.3d 1274 (11th Cir.1999) (applicant who obtained injunction against pre-employment medical examination as violating ADA did not prevail because he did not directly benefit from judgment at time of its entry, despite possibility he might benefit from it in the future should he reapply for employment) *with Ensley Branch N.A.A.C.P. v. Seibels*, 31 F.3d 1548 (11th Cir.1994) (current employ-

if the relief plaintiff initially seeks is "of the same general type" as the relief eventually obtained, plaintiff may be considered a prevailing party.[17] An injunction requiring a company to correct a racially intimidating work atmosphere, for example, has sufficed as the predicate for a fee award to a plaintiff who lost on most of his individual claims of race discrimination.[18] But in applying this standard, courts have sometimes resorted to a highly subjective appraisal of plaintiff's original objective in bringing suit, denying fees where that objective was not obtained even when the suit was clearly a "catalyst" for action by the defendant that responds in part to the suit.[19]

A finding of a violation under § 1983 may lead to an award of nominal damages where the predicate constitutional violation is "absolute," that is not dependent upon the merits of the plaintiff's substantive assertions or the magnitude of injury resulting from a violation.[20] Such damages may now be available under Title VII, which provides for certain kinds of legal relief since its amendment by the Civil Rights Act of 1991.[21] Whether such nominal damages can serve as a springboard for § 1988 attorney's fees was the subject of conflict among the circuits.[22]

In *Farrar v. Hobby*,[23] the Supreme Court attempted to resolve this conflict, but did so somewhat oddly. It formally conferred prevailing party status on plaintiffs who recover only nominal damages, but did so under standards that fix the amount of a reasonable attorney's fee at

---

ees prevailed by eliminating race-conscious personnel decisions through judgment striking down affirmative action policies). *See also Jacobson v. City of Coates*, 171 F.3d 1162 (8th Cir.1999) (determination that one of two challenged ordinances was unconstitutional changed legal relationship between parties sufficient to entitle plaintiffs to attorney's fees under § 1988 despite trial court's characterization of victory as "technical" and "insignificant"); *LeBlanc-Sternberg v. Fletcher*, 143 F.3d 748, 759 (2d Cir. 1998) (plaintiffs directly benefited from and prevailed by obtaining injunction against zoning regulations that would impair their ability to conduct religious services); *Layton v. Elder*, 143 F.3d 469, 470–73 (8th Cir. 1998) (injunction obtained by plaintiffs mandating county to make its services available to them despite their disability effected material change in plaintiffs' relationship with county and accordingly they were prevailing parties eligible for fees).

17. *Lyte v. Sara Lee Corp.*, 950 F.2d 101 (2d Cir.1991).

18. *Ruffin v. Great Dane Trailers*, 969 F.2d 989 (11th Cir.1992), *cert. denied*, 507 U.S. 910, 113 S.Ct. 1257, 122 L.Ed.2d 655 (1993). *See also LeBlanc–Sternberg v. Fletcher*, 143 F.3d 748 (2d Cir.1998) (award of injunctive relief against only one defendant sufficient where injunction materially

alters legal relationship between parties by modifying defendant's behavior in way that directly benefits plaintiff).

19. *See, e.g., Cady v. City of Chicago*, 43 F.3d 326 (7th Cir.1994).

20. *Carey v. Piphus*, 435 U.S. 247, 98 S.Ct. 1042, 55 L.Ed.2d 252 (1978) (nominal damages available for denial of procedural due process).

21. *But cf. Walker v. Anderson Elec. Connectors*, 944 F.2d 841 (11th Cir.1991), *cert. denied*, 506 U.S. 1078, 113 S.Ct. 1043, 122 L.Ed.2d 352 (1993), which held nominal damages unavailable under, or at least not mandated by, the pre-amended Title VII.

22. *See, e.g., Romberg v. Nichols*, 953 F.2d 1152 (9th Cir.1992), *vacated by*, 506 U.S. 1075, 113 S.Ct. 1038, 122 L.Ed.2d 348 (1993) (nominal damages award of $1 creates prevailing party status); *Ruggiero v. Krzeminski*, 928 F.2d 558 (2d Cir.1991); *Scofield v. City of Hillsborough*, 862 F.2d 759 (9th Cir.1988); *Coleman v. Turner*, 838 F.2d 1004 (8th Cir.1988); *Nephew v. City of Aurora*, 830 F.2d 1547 (10th Cir.1987) (en banc), *cert. denied*, 485 U.S. 976, 108 S.Ct. 1269, 99 L.Ed.2d 481 (1988); *Garner v. Wal–Mart Stores, Inc.*, 807 F.2d 1536 (11th Cir.1987).

23. 506 U.S. 103, 113 S.Ct. 566, 121 L.Ed.2d 494 (1992).

zero when their degree of success is slight. The Court confirmed that "a plaintiff 'prevails' when actual relief on the merits of his claim materially alters the legal relationship between the parties by modifying the defendant's behavior in a way that directly benefits the plaintiff"; and it acknowledged that even a judgment for only nominal damages "modifies the defendant's behavior for the plaintiff's benefit by forcing the defendant to pay an amount of money he otherwise would not pay." But it then drained this conclusion of practical significance under most circumstances by adding that when a plaintiff, having failed to prove an essential element of a claim for monetary relief, recovers only nominal damages, "the only reasonable fee is usually no fee at all."[24]

In *Carey v. Piphus*,[25] the Court had found that nominal damages must be available for deprivations of "absolute" rights like procedural due process because of "the importance to organized society that those rights be scrupulously observed." After *Farrar*, however, it is difficult to understand how, where there is little or no actual economic or emotional injury, the Court contemplates that such rights will be enforced if attorney's fees are only theoretically and not practically available to plaintiffs who successfully prosecute suits for their violation.[26] One possibility is that lower courts will limit *Farrar* to its facts: no jury specification of the constitutional right violated and no specific jury finding that the defendant's conduct caused the plaintiff's (nominal) damages. In one case, for example, a jury specifically found that a municipality's policy regarding excessive police force resulted in $1 of harm to an otherwise unsympathetic plaintiff, and the city disciplined an officer and modified its policy during the litigation. Upholding a fee award of $66,535, the appellate court distinguished *Farrar*, concluding that the finding benefitted the department and the community and might have collateral estoppel effect in subsequent litigation.[27] These distinctions, however, seem a thin evasion of *Farrar*. Plaintiffs could create them routinely by requesting special interrogatories concerning the right violated and causation, and the jury would presumably find

---

24. *Farrar v. Hobby*, 506 U.S. 103, 113 S.Ct. 566, 121 L.Ed.2d 494; *McCardle v. Haddad*, 131 F.3d 43 (2d Cir.1997) (affirming fees award of 33 cents where only nominal damages were recovered); *Cartwright v. Stamper*, 7 F.3d 106 (7th Cir.1993) (fees denied because $5 nominal damages award so "de minimis" that plaintiff's success on several claims would have little deterrent effect).

25. *See* 435 U.S. at 266, 98 S.Ct. at 1054.

26. Fees might fail in this situation either because an award of nominal damages may be trivial in relation to the relief originally sought or because no nominal damages may be recoverable. *See, e.g., Kerr–Selgas v. American Airlines, Inc.*, 69 F.3d 1205 (1st Cir.1995) (nominal damages must be timely requested before a jury retires).

Cf. Walker v. Anderson Elec. Connectors, 944 F.2d 841 (11th Cir.1991), *cert. denied*, 506 U.S. 1078, 113 S.Ct. 1043, 122 L.Ed.2d 352 (1993) (a finding of a Title VII violation does not mandate an award of nominal damages, and therefore, if plaintiff achieves no other relief, does not qualify the plaintiff for prevailing party status). *But cf. Hashimoto v. Dalton*, 118 F.3d 671 (9th Cir.1997), *cert. denied*, 523 U.S. 1122, 118 S.Ct. 1803, 140 L.Ed.2d 943 (1998) (distinguishing *Walker* as a case where plaintiff only technically prevailed, and awarding fees, where plaintiff recovered non-economic relief in the form of an administrative order by EEOC directing defendant to take measures to prevent future instances of retaliation).

27. *Wilcox v. City of Reno*, 42 F.3d 550 (9th Cir.1994).

causation whenever it awarded damages, even nominal ones. Another evasive tactic has been specifically rebuffed: if the plaintiff's lawyer first asks for nominal damages at the end of trial, when things look bleak for his client, the plaintiff who then recovers $1, while technically prevailing, will fail to recover fees by virtue of *Farrar*.[28] But a small damages award is not necessarily conclusive on the issue of fees. Because there is no federal small claims court and no amount in controversy requirement in civil rights cases, the Seventh Circuit instructs courts to determine whether the plaintiff aimed high and fell short, in which case *Farrar* may deprive the prevailing plaintiff of a fee,[29] or whether it was simply a small claim and was tried accordingly.[30] Other courts resist a literal adherence to *Farrar*, awarding fees even where plaintiff's monetary recovery falls many multiples short of what she sought.[31] These courts follow Justice O'Connor's *Farrar* concurrence in weighing the difference between the judgment sought and that obtained, the significance of the legal issue on which plaintiff prevailed, and the lawsuit's public purpose.[32]

Another possibility, somewhat uncertain, is that the recovery of nominal damages may permit the § 1983 plaintiff to recover punitive damages otherwise warranted by a malicious or aggravated violation of procedural due process. But is there a more reliable general incentive for a lawyer to pursue a § 1983 case involving an "ordinary" constitutional or federal statutory violation in what promises to be a case of "mixed motives"—that is, where she anticipates that the defendant could carry the *Mt. Healthy City School District Bd. of Education v. Doyle*[33] burden of demonstrating that it would have subjected the plaintiff to the same loss or deprivation for a lawful reason or reasons wholly independent of a substantial federally unlawful motive? In those cases there is probably no constitutional or federal statutory "violation," and hence no possible monetary relief on the merits or, accordingly, attorney's fees.

On the other hand, what if the plaintiff from the outset seeks no compensatory or punitive damages, only declaratory relief or an injunction, and recovers one?[34] Has he not then achieved substantial, indeed entire success on the merits? And what if there are multiple claims? It is clear enough that a plaintiff's recovery of compensatory damages on

---

28. *Romberg v. Nichols*, 48 F.3d 453 (9th Cir.1995), *vacated by* 506 U.S. 1075, 113 S.Ct. 1038, 122 L.Ed.2d 348 (1993).

29. *Cole v. Wodziak*, 169 F.3d 486 (7th Cir.1999) (approving sharp reduction of fee where plaintiffs recovered less than 10% of what they demanded).

30. *See Hyde v. Small*, 123 F.3d 583 (7th Cir.1997) ($500 compensatory damages award did not, by itself, justify denial of fees).

31. *See Brandau v. Kansas*, 168 F.3d 1179 (10th Cir.), *cert. denied*, 526 U.S. 1133, 119 S.Ct. 1808, 143 L.Ed.2d 1012 (1999), and cases cited therein.

32. *Id.*

33. 429 U.S. 274, 97 S.Ct. 568, 50 L.Ed.2d 471 (1977).

34. *See, e.g., Phelps v. Hamilton*, 120 F.3d 1126 (10th Cir.1997) (where plaintiffs' suit resulted in the invalidation of a state statute and led to legislative action to correct the constitutional infirmity, success was not merely technical, and fees must be awarded). *See also Owner-Operator Indep. Drivers Ass'n, Inc. v. Bissell*, 210 F.3d 595, 598–99 (6th Cir.2000) (even where plaintiff gains only a declaratory judgment plaintiff can recover fees as prevailing party).

fewer than all of the claims not only makes him technically prevailing but also entitles him to attorney's fees, although only with respect to the hours reasonably expended in pursuit of the successful claim or claims.[35] Or suppose the plaintiff prevails on several claims, obtaining only nominal damages on each? In this situation the Fifth Circuit has ruled that the plaintiff is not a prevailing party, arguably inconsistently with even the niggardly approach of *Farrar*.[36] The decisions struggle to define whether a plaintiff's "primary" goal was recovery of substantial monetary damages or merely injunctive relief to vindicate constitutional rights; if the former, then a "reasonable" fee may be nothing at all where the defendant's conduct is altered but no monetary relief is obtained.[37]

Farrar leaves unresolved a related question: can one become a prevailing party without having obtained, in the Supreme Court's words, a "consent decree, enforceable judgment or settlement," but simply because the filing of a lawsuit proved to be the "catalyst" that brought about some of the lawsuit's objectives? This typically requires the plaintiff to prove that the legal action is causally linked to the relief obtained by settlement or defendant's unilateral action,[38] and that the defendant's change in position was required by law and not merely gratuitous.[39] One circuit, en banc, has rejected the catalyst theory,

35. See Blum v. Stenson, 465 U.S. 886, 104 S.Ct. 1541, 79 L.Ed.2d 891 (1984); cf. Texas State Teachers Ass'n v. Garland Indep. Sch. Dist., 489 U.S. 782, 790–91, 109 S.Ct. 1486, 1486–1492, 103 L.Ed.2d 866 (1989) (litigant need not prevail on all issues or even central issue, only a significant one, to prevail). See also Morales v. San Rafael, 96 F.3d 359 (9th Cir.1996) (where plaintiff suffered dismissal of § 1983 claim against municipal defendant but recovered more than $17,000 from individual police officer, Farrar inapplicable because those damages are not nominal, even though they were far less than plaintiff sought); Stivers v. Pierce, 71 F.3d 732, 751 (9th Cir.1995) (despite Farrar, plaintiff is prevailing party even though only partially successful in obtaining the relief or benefit sought through the litigation). See text infra, respecting the circumstances warranting fee reduction where plaintiff has not prevailed on all claims.

36. Peters v. Polk County Mem'l Hosp., 7 F.3d 229 (5th Cir.1993), cert. denied, 513 U.S. 807, 115 S.Ct. 53, 130 L.Ed.2d 13 (1994).

37. Compare Cramblit v. Fikse, 33 F.3d 633 (6th Cir.1994) (per curiam) (plaintiff deemed to have fallen short of ultimate monetary goals and hence is denied fees) with Friend v. Kolodzieczak, 72 F.3d 1386 (9th Cir.1995), cert. denied, 516 U.S. 1146,

116 S.Ct. 1016, 134 L.Ed.2d 96 (1996) (inmate plaintiffs awarded substantial fees after settlement expanding their access to religious services and sacraments upon court's determination that their "primary" goal was an injunction).

38. A defendant cannot defeat a plaintiff's right to attorneys' fees by taking steps to moot the case after the plaintiff has obtained the relief he sought, for in such a case mootness does not alter the plaintiff's status as a prevailing party. See, e.g., Young v. City of Chicago , 202 F.3d 1000 (7th Cir.2000); Morris v. West Palm Beach,, 194 F.3d 1203, 1207 (11th Cir.1999); National Black Police Ass'n v. District of Columbia Bd. of Elections & Ethics, 168 F.3d 525, 528–29 (D.C.Cir.1999); Associated Gen. Contractors of Conn., Inc. v. City of New Haven, 41 F.3d 62, 68 and n. 9 (2d Cir. 1994); Martinez v. Wilson, 32 F.3d 1415, 1422 n. 8 (9th Cir.1994); Dahlem v. Board of Education, 901 F.2d 1508, 1512 (10th Cir.1990); Grano v. Barry, 783 F.2d 1104, 1108–09 (D.C.Cir.1986); Bishop v. Committee on Professional Ethics, 686 F.2d 1278, 1289–91 (8th Cir.1982).

39. See, e.g., Owner–Operator Indep. Drivers Ass'n, Inc. v. Bissell, 210 F.3d 595, 597–98 (6th Cir.2000); Payne v. Board of Educ., 88 F.3d 392, 397 (6th Cir.1996); Johnston v. Jago, 691 F.2d 283, 286 (6th Cir.1982).

relying specifically on the quoted language from *Farrar*.[40] Other circuits, however, continue to embrace the theory, dismissing the quoted phrase as not pertinent to the situation *Farrar* actually addressed.[41] Often these circuits rely on language from *Hewitt v. Helms*[42] that "relief need not be judicially decreed in order to justify a fee award" when the suit produces "voluntary action" by the defendants such as a "change in conduct that redresses plaintiff's grievances."[43] Still another unanswered question is when, even in fully litigated settings, an award of fees may not be "equitable and just," in the words of § 1988, even to a plaintiff who clearly prevailed on the sole or essential issue in the case. In one decision, plaintiffs obtained declaratory and injunctive relief on their sole claim, a challenge to the constitutionality of a statute. The court nevertheless denied attorney's fees because the public official defendants had never tried to enforce the statute.[44] And even where the catalyst theory is recognized, the plaintiff must demonstrate, as *Hewitt* insisted, that the relief she obtained through defendant's change of position benefitted her personally.[44a]

It has been argued that the *Farrar* limitation, while applicable to all cases under the Reconstruction civil rights acts, is wholly inapplicable to "mixed-motive" cases under Title VII or the ADA. The argument is based on Section 706(g)(2)(B), added by the 1991 Civil Rights Act, which specifically authorizes an award of attorney's fees under those statutes even when the employer makes the "same-decision" showing—that is, where the plaintiff has had only partial success.[45] But an appellate court

40. *S–1 v. State Bd. of Educ. of N.C.*, 21 F.3d 49 (4th Cir.), *cert. denied*, 513 U.S. 876, 115 S.Ct. 205, 130 L.Ed.2d 135 (1994).

41. *See Morris v. West Palm Beach*,, 194 F.3d 1203, 1207 (11th Cir.1999); *Payne v. Board of Education, Cleveland City Schs.*, 88 F.3d 392, 397 & n. 2 (6th Cir.1996); *Stivers v. Pierce*, 71 F.3d 732, 751–52, 753 n. 10 (9th Cir.1995); *Marbley v. Bane*, 57 F.3d 224, 234 (2d Cir.1995); *Zinn v. Shalala*, 35 F.3d 273, 276 (7th Cir.1994)*; Beard v. Teska*, 31 F.3d 942, 951 (10th Cir.1994); *Baumgartner v. Harrisburg Hous. Auth.*, 21 F.3d 541, 548–50 (3d Cir.1994); *Little Rock Sch. Dist. v. Pulaski County Special Sch. Dist.*, 17 F.3d 260, 263 & n. 2 (8th Cir. 1994); *Craig v. Gregg County, Tex.*, 988 F.2d 18, 20–21 (5th Cir.1993); *Paris v. United States Dep't of Hous. and Urban Dev.*, 988 F.2d 236, 238 (1st Cir.1993). *See also Wilcox v. City of Reno*, 42 F.3d 550 (9th Cir.1994) (arrestee who was punched in the face by a police officer held entitled to attorney's fees, although he received only nominal damages, because the litigation also led to the city's disciplining of the officer and modifying its policy governing the use of force); *Dunn v. The Florida Bar*, 889 F.2d 1010 (11th Cir.1989), *cert. denied*, 498 U.S. 811, 111 S.Ct. 46, 112 L.Ed.2d 22 (1990) (where defendants had the ability to change their unlawful behavior but failed to do so until faced with litigation, plaintiff can recover fees under the catalyst theory). *Cf. New Hampshire v. Adams*, 159 F.3d 680 (1st Cir.1998) (denying fees upon finding that IDEA proceedings were not the catalyst for a settlement affording plaintiff additional services).

42. 482 U.S. 755, 107 S.Ct. 2672, 96 L.Ed.2d 654 (1987).

43. *See Morris v. West Palm Beach*, 194 F.3d 1203, 1207 (11th Cir.1999) (quoting *Hewitt v. Helms*, 482 U.S. 755, 760–61, 107 S.Ct. 2672, 2676, 96 L.Ed.2d 654 (1987)); *Owner-Operator Indep. Drivers Ass'n, Inc. v. Bissell*, 210 F.3d 595, 598 (6th Cir.2000).

44. *Soundgarden v. Eikenberry*, 123 Wash.2d 750, 871 P.2d 1050, *cert. denied*, 513 U.S. 1056, 115 S.Ct. 663, 130 L.Ed.2d 598 (1994).

44a. *See Hewitt*, 482 U.S. 755, 107 S.Ct. 2672, and subsequent lower court authority cited *supra*, this section.

45. Section 706(g)(2)(B) is codified at 42 U.S.C.A. § 2000e–5(g)(2)(B). *See Gudenkauf v. Stauffer Communications, Inc.*, 158 F.3d 1074 (10th Cir.1998) (plaintiff who prevails in a mixed motive case should ordi-

has rejected that argument, observing that both the decision to award and the amount of attorney's fees are discretionary under Section 706(g)(2)(B) just as under Section 1988, the provision construed in *Farrar*. And it wrote that plaintiff's rejection of a settlement offer is one factor the court may take into account in deciding the appropriate amount of a fee award.[46]

Recoverability of fees for services performed in a preliminary administrative proceeding depends in part on whether the proceeding is optional or mandatory. If the state or local administrative proceeding is mandated, as it is under most employment discrimination statutes including Title VII, fees for legal services performed in that hearing can probably be recovered in a subsequent Title VII action. This is because the state or local administrative proceedings in a deferral state, and the EEOC proceedings in any state, qualify as a "proceeding under this subchapter" within the meaning of Title VII § 706(k).[47] If the prior administrative hearing is optional, however, fees are generally not awarded because such a hearing is not considered an "action or proceeding to enforce" civil rights under the language of § 1988. For example, because a plaintiff is not required to exhaust his administrative remedies before bringing a § 1983 action,[48] services performed in administrative proceedings on § 1983 claims are not compensable under § 1988.[49] Sometimes, however, where the administrative work is "useful and of a type ordinarily necessary to advance the civil rights litigation," fees may be awarded.[50] In *Pennsylvania v. Delaware Valley Citizens' Council for Clean Air*,[51] the Court applied this exception so as to allow fees.[52] The

narily be awarded attorney's fees in all but special circumstances despite inability to recover money damages or obtain injunctive relief).

46. *Sheppard v. Riverview Nursing Ctr.*, 88 F.3d 1332 (4th Cir.), *cert. denied*, 519 U.S. 993, 117 S.Ct. 483, 136 L.Ed.2d 377 (1996) (also considering such factors as why other relief was not awarded, what public purposes where served, how ubiquitous and wrongful the defendant's conduct was, and the strength of the discriminatory motive and other motives—such as unsatisfactory actions of the employee—in influencing the termination decision, even though both played a part in it). *See also Norris v. Sysco Corp.*, 191 F.3d 1043, 1050–51 (9th Cir. 1999), *cert. denied*, ___ U.S. ___, 120 S.Ct. 1221, 145 L.Ed.2d 1121 (2000) (affirming award of attorney's fees in failure to promote claim where defendant proved that it would not have promoted plaintiff absent the unlawful reason); *Akrabawi v. Carnes Co.*, 152 F.3d 688 (7th Cir.1998) (denying attorney's fees where jury found discrimination but employer carried same decision showing); *Canup v. Chipman–Union, Inc.*, 123 F.3d 1440 (11th Cir.1997) (disallowing attorney's fees in mixed motive case).

47. *New York Gaslight Club, Inc. v. Carey*, 447 U.S. 54, 100 S.Ct. 2024, 64 L.Ed.2d 723 (1980). *See also Jones v. American State Bank*, 857 F.2d 494 (8th Cir. 1988) (extending *Carey* to allow fees for pre-suit administrative work even when the subsequent suit seeks only that remedy and no relief on the merits). *But see Chris v. Tenet*, 221 F.3d 648 (4th Cir.2000) (holding Contra *Jones*).

48. *See Patsy v. Florida Bd. of Regents*, 457 U.S. 496, 102 S.Ct. 2557, 73 L.Ed.2d 172 (1982).

49. *Webb v. Dyer County Bd. of Educ.*, 471 U.S. 234, 105 S.Ct. 1923, 85 L.Ed.2d 233 (1985). *See also Duello v. University of Wisc. Bd. of Regents*, 176 Wis.2d 961, 501 N.W.2d 38 (Wis.1993) (fees incurred in connection with successful internal grievance procedure not compensable under § 706(k) of Title VII).

50. *Webb*, 471 U.S. 234, 105 S.Ct. 1923, 85 L.Ed.2d 233.

51. 478 U.S. 546, 106 S.Ct. 3088, 92 L.Ed.2d 439 (1986) ("*Delaware I*") (applying § 304(d) of the Clean Air Act).

52. In *Brooks v. Georgia State Bd. of Elections*, 997 F.2d 857 (11th Cir.1993), the

Delaware I Court found that post-judgment administrative proceedings, held to enforce a consent decree, were "crucial to the vindication of [plaintiff's] rights," and concluded that the attorney's services performed for those proceedings were compensable.

But it remains unsettled whether, or under what circumstances, a plaintiff who achieves complete merits relief through settlement or decision in pre-litigation administrative proceedings may pursue a judicial action seeking only compensation for the attorney's fees she incurred in the pre-suit proceedings. After all, in the leading case upholding an action for fees incurred in prior administrative proceedings under Title VII, *New York Gaslight Club, Inc. v. Carey*,[53] the plaintiff's action for fees was coupled with a claim on the merits. Yet the Eighth Circuit subsequently extended *Carey* to encompass Title VII actions brought solely to recover fees incurred in prior administrative proceedings. In *Jones v. American State Bank*,[54] the parties settled plaintiff's pregnancy discrimination claim during the administrative proceedings, but the state deferral agency denied attorney's fees as unavailable under state law. The Eighth Circuit affirmed the federal district court's award of fees under Section 706(k). It reasoned that because, as the Supreme Court stressed repeatedly in *Carey*, the state deferral agency proceeding was mandated by Title VII and complementary to the federal statutory scheme, the administrative proceeding constituted an "action or proceeding" for which fees might be awarded within the meaning of § 706(k).

In so holding, the Eighth Circuit treated *Jones* as distinguishable from a post-*Carey* Supreme Court decision, *North Carolina Department of Transportation v. Crest Street Community Council*.[55] There the Supreme Court erected a distinct barrier to recovering attorney's fees for services performed in optional administrative proceedings followed by fees-only lawsuits under any of the *civil rights* statutes for which fees are recoverable under *42 U.S.C. § 1988*. The plaintiffs in *Crest* objected to racially discriminatory aspects of the state's plan for a new highway, alleging that the plan violated Title VI,[56] one of the statutes listed in § 1988. The state transportation department agreed that the plan would constitute a prima facie violation of Title VI, and the parties ultimately

court awarded a plaintiff fees with respect to his attorney's preclearance work under § 5 of the Voting Rights Act of 1965 before the United States Justice Department, where the district court conditioned plaintiff's remedy on the results of those administrative proceedings. The court considered the preclearance work "useful and ordinarily necessary to the litigation" within the meaning of *Webb* because the judicial decision turned on the preclearance outcome. 987 F.2d at 860. It also relaxed the *Delaware I* requirement that the administrative legal work be "crucial" to the vindication of adjudicated rights "to mean not much more than that it be relevant to those rights and related to terms of the judgment." *Id.* at 864. For similar reasons, post-judgment monitoring of consent decrees is compensable under § 1988. *See Delaware I*, 478 U.S. at 559–60, 106 S.Ct. at 3095; *Eirhart v. Libbey–Owens–Ford Co.*, 996 F.2d 846 (7th Cir.1993); *Miller v. Carson*, 628 F.2d 346, 348 (5th Cir.1980).

53. 447 U.S. 54, 100 S.Ct. 2024, 64 L.Ed.2d 723 (1980).

54. 857 F.2d 494 (8th Cir.1988).

55. 479 U.S. 6, 107 S.Ct. 336, 93 L.Ed.2d 188 (1986).

56. Title VI of the Civil Rights Act of 1964, codified in 42 U.S.C.A. §§ 2000d—2000d–4a, prohibits discrimination based on race, color, or national origin in federally funded programs or activities.

negotiated a compromise plan. But the agreement made no provision for attorney's fees, other than to reserve plaintiff's rights to them, so the plaintiffs later instituted an action under § 1988 for fees incurred during the state proceedings and ensuing negotiations. The Court in *Crest* held that, regardless of whether negotiations following the filing of an optional administrative complaint under Title VI are themselves "proceedings to enforce" that statute, § 1988 does not authorize the recovery of fees incurred in *any* pre-suit administrative proceedings unless a judicial action is filed that also seeks relief on the merits.[57]

The Court in *Crest* relied on language in § 1988, absent from Section 706(k) of Title VII, stipulating that fees may be awarded only "in the action or proceeding to enforce" the listed civil rights laws, including Title VI. It concluded that the judicial action in which fees are sought, and not just the pre-litigation administrative agency proceedings for which they are sought, must qualify as an "action or proceeding to enforce a provision" of Title VI (or any of the other civil rights statutes listed in § 1988).[58] And it further concluded that a judicial action for fees alone could not be considered an action "to enforce" such a provision. Accordingly, it insisted that *under § 1988*, an award of fees for pre-suit administrative agency work is authorized only if a party prevails on a *merits-based* claim under one of the referenced civil rights statutes in a *judicial action* filed concurrently with, or subsequent to, the administrative proceedings. *Crest* did, however, recognize that if the ensuing judicial action meets this definition of a "proceeding to enforce" a § 1988 statute, a court "may still award attorney's fees for time spent on administrative proceedings to enforce the civil rights claim prior to the litigation."[59] In fact, so long as the civil rights plaintiff files a judicial action seeking merits relief, she may recover in that action fees for whatever attorney's work at the administrative stage was "useful and of a type ordinarily necessary to advance the civil rights litigation to the stage it reached before settlement"–regardless of whether the underlying administrative proceeding is characterized as a "proceeding to enforce" one of the § 1988 statutes.[60]

---

57. In this respect *Crest* sweeps more broadly than an earlier post-*Carey* decision, *Webb v. Dyer County Board of Education*, 471 U.S. 234, 105 S.Ct. 1923, 85 L.Ed.2d 233 (1985). As observed above, in *Webb*, the court held that attorney's services performed in an optional state administrative proceeding invoked by the plaintiff before filing an action under *§ 1983* are not compensable under § 1988. The *Webb* opinion reasoned that the administrative proceeding conducted before the § 1983 judicial action was not itself a "proceeding to enforce" that statute (By contrast, *Crest* describes *Carey* as holding that "mandatory state employment discrimination proceedings *are* proceedings to enforce *Title VII*." 479 U.S.

at 11 (emphasis added)). But *Webb* did not require, as *Crest* does, that the ensuing judicial action in which attorneys' fees are sought for services rendered in pre-suit administrative proceedings or negotiations must itself be a "proceeding to enforce"; nor does it require that to qualify as such a proceeding, the judicial action must invariably concern relief on the merits as well as fees.

58. *Crest*, 479 U.S. at 14, 107 S.Ct. at 341.

59. *Id.* at 15.

60. *Id.* (quoting *Webb*, 471 U.S. at 243, 105 S.Ct. at 1928).

Carey and *Crest* have distinctly variable tactical implications, recognized in those opinions. The prospective Title VII, ADEA, ADA or other employment discrimination plaintiff, operating under the *Carey* regime, may be less reluctant to reach a merits-only settlement at one or more of the mandated administrative stages, even if the parties fail to reach agreement as to fees. That is because *Carey* suggests, as *Jones* holds, that in a subsequent judicial action under those statutes she may seek fees alone. On the other hand, under the *Carey* opinion and *Jones* holding, prospective plaintiffs and their lawyers will feel less pressure to reach complete settlements in pre-suit proceedings under those statutes. By contrast, under *Crest*, prospective civil rights plaintiffs and their lawyers may bypass optional administrative proceedings entirely and resort immediately to suit unless they perceive a real possibility of advantageous and complete resolution, including fees, in a pre-suit forum. This tendency may be exacerbated by separate authority, discussed in Chapter 12, holding that adverse fact-findings by quasi-judicial administrative tribunals may have issue preclusive (collateral estoppel) effect in subsequent proceedings under § 1983.

That *Carey* survives *Crest* on *Carey*'s own facts—i.e., a Title VII judicial action combining a merits claim with the claim for fees—is supported even by a recent Fourth Circuit opinion that relies on *Crest* to reject the *Jones* extension of *Carey* to fees-only employment discrimination lawsuits. In *Chris v. Tenet*,[61] the court held that a fees-only action does not lie under § 706(k) of Title VII. The court reasoned that where a Title VII plaintiff sues for fees only, the trial court lacks subject matter jurisdiction to award fees. It explained that a special Title VII jurisdictional grant in § 706(f)(3) refers only to legal proceedings in a court of law to enforce the substantive guarantees of Title VII and does not extend to an action solely for fees incurred during Title VII administrative proceedings. It also quoted the Supreme Court's observation in *Crest* that it is entirely reasonable to limit the award of attorney's fees to those parties who, in order to obtain relief, found it necessary to file a complaint in court.[62] But the Fourth Circuit did distinguish *Carey*, observing that the plaintiff there had originally sought merits relief in addition to attorney's fees.[63]

Indeed, there is much to be said for the Eighth Circuit view in *Jones* that *Carey* survives *Crest* even where the employment discrimination plaintiff does *not* seek relief on the merits, only fees for work done in prior proceedings. Not only does the Title VII fee provision, § 706(k), lack the "proceeding to enforce" language of § 1988; it mandates the plaintiff's prior resort to EEOC and, if available, state or local administrative proceedings. While the Supreme Court in *Crest* was critical of some of *Carey*'s policy justifications, the opinion sedulously refrains from overruling *Carey*, and for good reason: the textual and structural differences distinguishing Title VII from § 1988 with respect to fees are more

---

61. 221 F.3d 648 (4th Cir.2000).

62. *Id.* at 654 (quoting *Crest*, 479 U.S. at 14, 107 S.Ct. at 341).

63. *Chris*, 221 F.3d at 653–54.

fundamental and deserve greater decisional weight than *Carey*'s passing reference to policy. Further, while it is true, as the *Chris* opinion recounts, that the plaintiff in *Carey* initially presented a merits claim, the Supreme Court's opinion made little of that. Instead it stressed the permissive language of § 706(k)—allowing courts to award fees in "any action or proceeding under this subchapter"—and the Title VII mandate that putative plaintiffs initiate such proceedings in state or local antidiscrimination agencies and the EEOC.

Fees may be awarded *pendente lite* when a plaintiff achieves some durable interim relief on the merits, for example an injunction that works some permanent change in the legal relations between the parties.[64] More generally the Supreme Court has approved the award of fees pendente lite to a party who has obtained some relief on the merits at trial or on appeal.[65] But plaintiffs did not acquire prevailing party status by virtue of obtaining an injunction pending appeal that merely preserved the status quo in a circuit that determines the propriety of such injunctions principally by balancing the equities and harms attendant on granting or denying relief, rather than by weighing the merits.[66] And attorney's fees for preliminary injunctive relief have been denied where the injunction is ultimately reversed on appeal, the party having obtained that injunction then being regarded as not having prevailed.[67]

Attorney's fees may be awarded for services necessary to implement or enforce a consent decree that resulted from earlier, successful litigation.[68] And a prevailing party may also recover, to the degree of her success, fees for services rendered in an unsuccessful judicial action if she ultimately prevails in a subsequent related judicial action.[69]

To calculate the amount of a "reasonable" award of attorney's fees the court must arrive first at a "lodestar" figure that represents a reasonable hourly rate multiplied by the number of hours reasonably

64. *See Hanrahan v. Hampton*, 446 U.S. 754, 100 S.Ct. 1987, 64 L.Ed.2d 670 (1980). *Cf. Gotro v. R & B Realty Group*, 69 F.3d 1485 (9th Cir.1995) (even contingent fee litigant who has not actually incurred the obligation to pay for his lawyer's work in obtaining remand of improperly removed case may recover those fees from the defendant as "actual expenses, including attorney's fees, incurred" within the meaning of 28 U.S.C.A. § 1447(c)).

65. *Hewitt v. Helms*, 482 U.S. 755, 107 S.Ct. 2672, 96 L.Ed.2d 654 (1987). *But cf. District of Columbia v. Patterson*, 667 A.2d 1338 (D.C.App.1995), *cert. denied*, 519 U.S. 1058, 117 S.Ct. 688, 136 L.Ed.2d 612 (1997) (civil rights plaintiff who obtained hearing after seizure of property, but ultimately failed to show the unconstitutionality of the forfeiture statute that facilitated the seizure, and therefore did not recover the property or obtain any other tangible bene-

fit of the kind she sought, not "prevailing party").

66. *LaRouche v. Kezer*, 20 F.3d 68 (2d Cir.1994).

67. *N.A.A.C.P. v. Detroit Police Officers Ass'n*, 46 F.3d 528 (6th Cir.1995). *See also Krocka v. City of Chicago*, 203 F.3d 507, 517–18 (7th Cir.2000); *Webb v. Ada County*, 195 F.3d 524 (9th Cir.1999) (denying fees despite plaintiff's victory at a preliminary stage of litigation where plaintiff ultimately lost); *Board of Educ. of Oak Park v. Nathan R.*, 199 F.3d 377, 382 (7th Cir.), *cert. denied*, ___ U.S. ___, 121 S.Ct. 65, 148 L.Ed.2d 30 (2000); *Hunger v. Leininger*, 15 F.3d 664, 670 (7th Cir.), *cert. denied*, 513 U.S. 839, 115 S.Ct. 123, 130 L.Ed.2d 67 (1994).

68. *Eirhart v. Libbey–Owens–Ford Co.*, 996 F.2d 846 (7th Cir.1993).

69. *Cabrales v. County of Los Angeles*, 935 F.2d 1050 (9th Cir.1991).

expended on matters on which the plaintiff prevailed.[70] Both the reasonable hours and reasonable rates questions are committed to the discretion of the district courts,[71] although elements of legal analysis integral to their decisions are reviewable de novo.[72] Fees sought by the plaintiff that are attributable to attorney time clearly devoted only to unsuccessful claims will be deducted from the overall request.[73] And a high number of hours in a case with a relatively modest claim for compensatory damages has been sharply reduced.[74] But where a party prevails on only one of multiple legal claims rooted in the same factual nucleus, fees should not be reduced automatically.[75] Instead, so long as the plaintiff has obtained "excellent" relief, he should recover a fully compensatory fee encompassing all hours reasonably expended on the litigation; less than "excellent" but still "substantial" relief may warrant a fee reduction in proportion to plaintiff's overall degree of success.[76] By not reducing the fee award simply because the plaintiff fails to prevail on every contention, this approach encourages plaintiff's counsel to advance alternative grounds for relief as authorized by F.R.C.P. 8(e). Similarly, time should not be deducted for unsuccessful but reasonable arguments made in support of a successful claim.[77]

The circuit courts appear to be in accord that time spent in establishing the prevailing party's entitlement to a fee award under § 1988 is itself compensable.[78] But such requests for "fees-on-fees" are themselves subject to reduction in proportion to the degree by which the "merits fees" award was discounted, as a percentage of merits fees claimed. For example, where plaintiffs recovered 87.2% of the fees claimed for work

70. *Blum v. Stenson*, 465 U.S. 886, 897, 104 S.Ct. 1541, 1548, 79 L.Ed.2d 891 (1984); *Hensley v. Eckerhart*, 461 U.S. 424, 103 S.Ct. 1933, 76 L.Ed.2d 40 (1983). *See also Quaratino v. Tiffany & Co.*, 166 F.3d 422 (2d Cir.1999) (overturning district court's abandonment of lodestar approach); *Coutin v. Young & Rubicam Puerto Rico, Inc.*, 124 F.3d 331 (1st Cir.1997).

71. *See, e.g., Zuchel v. City of Denver*, 997 F.2d 730, 743 (10th Cir.1993).

72. *See, e.g., Oviatt v. Pearce*, 954 F.2d 1470, 1481 (9th Cir.1992).

73. *See Gumbhir v. Curators of Univ. of Mo.*, 157 F.3d 1141 (8th Cir.1998), *cert. denied*, 526 U.S. 1005, 119 S.Ct. 1143, 143 L.Ed.2d 210 (1999) (requested attorney's fees were reduced by nearly 90% where plaintiff prevailed on only one claim with modest compensatory damages); *Daniel v. Loveridge*, 32 F.3d 1472 (10th Cir.1994).

74. *Gumbhir*, 157 F.3d at 1146.

75. *See Roberts v. Roadway Exp., Inc.*, 149 F.3d 1098 (10th Cir.1998) (fee award not subject to reduction where unsuccessful race claim was necessarily related to successful retaliation claim); *Jenkins v. Mis-*

souri, 131 F.3d 716 (8th Cir.1997); *Shrader v. OMC Aluminum Boat Group, Inc.*, 128 F.3d 1218 (8th Cir.1997) (where successful claim is interrelated to unsuccessful claim, court should not separate hours spent on separate claims).

76. *Hensley v. Eckerhart*, 461 U.S. 424, 103 S.Ct. 1933, 76 L.Ed.2d 40 (1983); *Goos v. National Ass'n of Realtors*, 74 F.3d 300, 302 (D.C.Cir.1996). But the court may not calculate attorney fees by means of a purely mathematical comparison between the number of claims pressed and the number prevailed upon; rather, the appropriate inquiry concerns whether the claims on which the employee prevailed are related to those on which he or she did not. *Brodziak v. Runyon*, 145 F.3d 194 (4th Cir.1998).

77. *See Jaffee v. Redmond*, 142 F.3d 409 (7th Cir.1998).

78. *See, e.g., Jenkins v. Missouri*, 170 F.3d 846 (8th Cir.1999) (where plaintiff class prevailed on appeal and was awarded attorney's fees on appeal, class was entitled to attorney's fees for defending against defendant's petitions for rehearing of appeals); *Clark v. City of Los Angeles*, 803 F.2d 987, 992 (9th Cir.1986) (citing cases).

related to the underlying merits of the action, a reduction of 12.8%, their lodestar award for the fees incurred in petitioning for those fees was also disallowed by 12.8%.[79] The court distinguished a caution by the Supreme Court that merits fees should not be reduced simply because the trial court failed to reach or rejected alternative legal *grounds* (as opposed to *claims*) advanced by a prevailing plaintiff.[80] In fees-on-fees situations the prevailing plaintiff would have an incentive to gild the lily, and the losing defendant little incentive to challenge improper billing entries, if defendants had to pay 100% of the plaintiff's attorney's fee work in situations where one could reasonably expect only a modest trimming of the underlying merits fees.

Even with respect to claims on which the plaintiff prevailed, fees may not be awarded for hours that are "excessive, redundant, or otherwise unnecessary."[81] The court will carefully scrutinize plaintiff's counsel's time records in the post-judgment hearing on attorney's fees to determine which hours were reasonably necessary to the outcome on successful claims.[82] Where EEOC successfully prosecuted a disparate treatment claim on behalf of the plaintiff, who joined the action to assert state law claims on which she did not prevail, a circuit court ruled that she was entitled to attorney's fees only with respect to the additional contribution, if any, by her attorney to the EEOC's successful efforts.[83] The court viewed most of the private attorney's services as redundant or unnecessary. But where, in another case, the court halved the hours for which compensation was requested to account for duplication in services rendered by plaintiff's two counsel, it was an abuse of discretion also to cut the rate of hourly compensation on the theory that "the actual rate was the combined rates" of each counsel: that "corrected twice for a single problem."[84]

The Court in *Blum v. Stenson*[85] held that the lodestar is based on market rates in the relevant community, and therefore fees awardable to nonprofit legal services organizations may not be limited to actual costs. Similarly, fee awards may compensate for the work of law clerks and paralegals, again at market rates.[86] To say that the lodestar rate is based on rates prevailing in the relevant community masks two difficult subissues: *which lawyer's* rate in a diverse legal community where lawyers of differing experience, special skills, and reputation enjoy different degrees of market power; and *which community's* rate where a lawyer from one community performs services in another with a signifi-

79. *Thompson v. Gomez,* 45 F.3d 1365 (9th Cir.1995).

80. *Id.* (citing *Hensley v. Eckerhart,* 461 U.S. 424, 103 S.Ct. 1933, 76 L.Ed.2d 40 (1983)).

81. *Hensley v. Eckerhart,* 461 U.S. 424, 103 S.Ct. 1933, 76 L.Ed.2d 40 (1983).

82. *See Miller v. Woodharbor Molding & Millworks, Inc.,* 174 F.3d 948 (8th Cir. 1999) (per curiam) (fees were inadequately documented because they failed consistently or specifically to identify the substance or content of the billed tasks).

83. *EEOC v. Clear Lake Dodge,* 60 F.3d 1146, 1154 (5th Cir.1995).

84. *Carter v. Sedgwick County, Kan.,* 36 F.3d 952, 956 (10th Cir.1994).

85. 465 U.S. 886, 104 S.Ct. 1541, 79 L.Ed.2d 891 (1984).

86. *Missouri v. Jenkins,* 491 U.S. 274, 109 S.Ct. 2463, 105 L.Ed.2d 229 (1989).

cantly different prevailing market average. *Blum* seems to rest on the premise that the appropriate market rate for § 1988 purposes is "the opportunity cost of that time, the income foregone by [the lawyer in] representing this plaintiff."[87] It follows that an established billing rate of the prevailing party's lawyer deserves significant weight. Thus a district court erred in compensating the prevailing plaintiff's counsel in an excessive force case at the lower rate that the defendant city paid lawyers to defend those cases.[88]

But what if the rate of the prevailing party's lawyer, a member of a firm in a large urban city, is significantly greater than the rate of a hypothetical counterpart lawyer in the smaller city where the bulk of the legal services were rendered? Using the opportunity-cost premise, the Seventh Circuit held that the (in that case, higher) rate set by the market for the prevailing party's counsel is presumptively appropriate in calculating the lodestar. No burden was placed on the prevailing party to show that she could not have obtained comparable representation at the lower rates prevailing in the smaller community. Instead, the court placed the burden on the losing party to demonstrate that a lower rate would more accurately reflect the winning lawyer's opportunity cost, for example by showing that he ordinarily commands the high rate claimed in only a small percentage of the total number of hours he "sells" in a year, devoting the balance to court-fixed contingent fee litigation. In that event, the court concluded, his true "market-clearing price" may be considerably less than the hourly fee that a few of his clients were willing to pay.[89]

Another difficult task facing a court in calculating a lodestar is to identify the issues on which plaintiff prevailed and in turn the number of hours counsel reasonably expended on those issues. In this sense degree of success is a critical component of the ultimate fee award. But a lodestar-based fee award need not be proportionate to the amount of damages a plaintiff recovers with respect to a successful issue.[90]

Attorney's fees may be augmented to compensate for delay in payment (as distinct from risk of nonpayment or "contingency"—to be discussed below). Risk of delay is compensated "either by basing the award on current rates or by adjusting the fee based on historical rates

---

87. *Gusman v. Unisys Corp.*, 986 F.2d 1146 (7th Cir.1993).

88. *Trevino v. Gates*, 99 F.3d 911 (9th Cir.1996), *cert. denied*, 520 U.S. 1117, 117 S.Ct. 1249, 137 L.Ed.2d 330 (1997).

89. *Id.*

90. *Riverside v. Rivera*, 477 U.S. 561, 106 S.Ct. 2686, 91 L.Ed.2d 466 (1986) (upholding attorney's fee award of $245,456 where recovery under federal civil rights statutes was only $13,300); *McKenzie v. Cooper, Levins & Pastko, Inc.*, 990 F.2d 1183, 1185 (11th Cir.1993) (after a reduction to eliminate an enhancement for con-tingency, appellate court approves a fee award of over $121,000 where the back pay recovery was only $8600; *Grant v. Bethlehem Steel Corp.*, 973 F.2d 96 (2d Cir.1992), *cert. denied*, 506 U.S. 1053, 113 S.Ct. 978, 122 L.Ed.2d 132 (1993) (affirming an award of over half a million dollars in attorney's fees where plaintiffs had settled for only $60,000. *But see Migis v. Pearle Vision, Inc.*, 135 F.3d 1041 (5th Cir.1998) (reversing fees award that equaled six and on half times the compensatory award where plaintiff succeeded on only one of eight claims).

to reflect its present value."[91] Nor does the Eleventh Amendment bar that adjustment in an action against a state.[92] Such fees constitute an item of "costs" under the language of § 1988 and may therefore be recovered from a state even in federal court, notwithstanding the Eleventh Amendment.[93]

Additional adjustment factors to the lodestar include the novelty and difficulty of the questions presented, the extent to which the demands of the case preclude other legal employment, the undesirability of the case, awards in similar cases, and the experience, reputation, and ability of the attorneys. Circuit courts have been reluctant to approve reduction in the amount of an award below the lodestar because of erroneous "billing judgment" by a plaintiff's lawyer in spending considerable time pursuing a claim that a district court considered relatively simple.[94] These adjustment factors may refine but cannot substitute for the basic multiplication of a reasonable billing rate by the number of hours reasonably expended on successful claims. Similarly, the attorney's fee award may not be limited by a contingent-fee arrangement that yields a lesser sum than the lodestar.[95]

In *Evans v. Jeff D.*,[96] the Court approved the practice of compulsory waiver of attorney's fees by settlement. FRCP 23 requires district court approval of class action settlements. Parties are free to negotiate the terms of a settlement and may waive statutorily authorized attorney's fees.[97] The Court held that § 1988 does not interfere with that freedom. The Civil Rights Act of 1991 leaves *Evans* intact.

Venegas v. Mitchell,[98] treats the effect of a § 1988 fee award on the plaintiff's contractual arrangement with his own attorney. It holds that § 1988 does not invalidate a contingent fee agreement providing for payments substantially in excess of the reasonable fee recoverable from the defendant. That is, § 1988 controls only the relationship between the losing defendant and the prevailing plaintiff, not between the plaintiff and plaintiff's own attorney. Although under general § 1988 principles plaintiff's own portion of a recovery may not include amounts she has agreed to pay her attorney that exceed the "reasonable" amounts recoverable as attorney's fees from the defendant, *Venegas* also rein-

91. *Missouri v. Jenkins*, 491 U.S. 274, 109 S.Ct. 2463, 105 L.Ed.2d 229 (1989).

92. *Id.*

93. *Hutto v. Finney*, 437 U.S. 678, 98 S.Ct. 2565, 57 L.Ed.2d 522 (1978). The specific abrogation of immunity in § 1988 recognized in *Hutto* survives the Supreme Court's decision in *Seminole Tribe of Fla. v. Florida*, 517 U.S. 44, 116 S.Ct. 1114, 134 L.Ed.2d 252 (1996), because Congress acted pursuant to § 5 of the Fourteenth Amendment. *See* Chapter 12.

94. *Quaratino v. Tiffany & Co.*, 166 F.3d 422 (2d Cir.1999) (reversing district court's halving of lodestar through "billing judgment" approach); *Robinson v. City of*

Edmond, 160 F.3d 1275 (10th Cir.1998) (reversing fee reduction because district court viewed case as "fairly" simple).

95. *Blanchard v. Bergeron*, 489 U.S. 87, 109 S.Ct. 939, 103 L.Ed.2d 67 (1989).

96. 475 U.S. 717, 106 S.Ct. 1531, 89 L.Ed.2d 747 (1986).

97. And failure to broach issue of attorney's fees during settlement negotiations can operate as a waiver of such an award. *See Wray v. Clarke*, 151 F.3d 807, 809 (8th Cir.1998).

98. 495 U.S. 82, 110 S.Ct. 1679, 109 L.Ed.2d 74 (1990).

forces a plaintiff's capacity to secure counsel of her choice by upholding the integrity of the private fee agreement. On the other hand, the plaintiff's attorney's fee award under § 1988 may not be absolutely limited by a contingent-fee arrangement that calls for a lesser sum than the lodestar.[99]

Previously, a prevailing plaintiff was not entitled to have its expert witnesses compensated by the losing party, absent contractual or statutory authority stating otherwise.[100] In *West Virginia Univ. Hosps. v. Casey*,[101] the Court held that § 1988 does not authorize the recovery of expert witness fees. They are limited to the amount designated for all witnesses, $30 per day. The Civil Rights Act of 1991, which includes expert fees as a part of an attorney's fee award under Title VII, reverses *West Virginia Univ. Hosps. v. Casey* in part. The Act authorizes expert fees in actions or proceedings to enforce provisions of § 1981 and § 1981a, but not § 1983.[102] Of course the Supreme Court has already included certain related costs, e.g., those for law clerks and paralegals, as part of the attorney's fees recoverable under § 1988.[103]

§§ 11.6–16.9 [Reserved]

C. LODESTAR MAY NOT BE ENHANCED FOR "CONTINGENCY," OR RISK OF LOSS

§ 11.10 In General

There is a strong presumption that the lodestar represents a reasonable fee, and any upward or downward adjustments may take into account only those factors not used in arriving at the lodestar.[1] In any event the lodestar may not be adjusted upward by a "multiplier" to compensate for an attorney's risk of loss, or "contingency"—as distinct from the loss caused by delay—unless perhaps evidence is produced to show that the possibility of an enhanced fee was required in order to

---

99. *Blanchard v. Bergeron*, 489 U.S. 87, 109 S.Ct. 939, 103 L.Ed.2d 67 (1989). *But see In Time Prods., Ltd. v. Toy Biz, Inc.*, 38 F.3d 660 (2d Cir.1994) (award must be reasonably related to a hypothetical fee arrangement that the prevailing party could have made with an attorney, which court set at a 33% contingency).

100. *Crawford Fitting Co. v. J.T. Gibbons*, 482 U.S. 437, 107 S.Ct. 2494, 96 L.Ed.2d 385 (1987).

101. 499 U.S. 83, 111 S.Ct. 1138, 113 L.Ed.2d 68 (1991).

102. This problem can be compounded if courts conclude, as the Eleventh Circuit has, that § 1983 is the sole vehicle for asserting § 1981 claims against state actors. *See Butts v. Volusia County*, 222 F.3d 891 (11th Cir.2000). One district court finessed

its way around this result by holding that where the underlying claim is based on § 1981, the action should be deemed brought under § 1981 for purposes of eligibility to recover expert fees, even if the vehicle for asserting the § 1981 right is § 1983. *See Webster Green Thumb Co. v. Fulton County*, 112 F.Supp.2d 1339 (N.D.Ga.2000).

103. *Missouri v. Jenkins*, 491 U.S. 274, 109 S.Ct. 2463, 105 L.Ed.2d 229.

§ 11.10

1. *See Hensley v. Eckerhart*, 461 U.S. 424, 103 S.Ct. 1933, 76 L.Ed.2d 40 (1983); *Pennsylvania v. Delaware Valley Citizens' Council for Clean Air*, 478 U.S. 546, 106 S.Ct. 3088, 92 L.Ed.2d 439 (1986) ("*Delaware I*").

attract counsel.[2] The Court in *Delaware II* rendered a 4–1–4 decision on the issue of the availability of contingency multipliers. As a result of this splintered decision, lower courts are attempting to implement the views of Justice O'Connor. Justice O'Connor would allow an enhancement for risk when an applicant has shown that: (1) the relevant market compensates for risk, and (2) but for the enhancement, he would have faced "substantial difficulties" in securing counsel in the relevant market.

The D.C. Circuit, en banc, reversed two of its prior panel decisions establishing the availability of enhancements for the D.C. market.[3] The D.C. Circuit interpreted the opinions of the plurality and Justice O'Connor in *Delaware II* as both requiring that a multiplier be made available only when a plaintiff would have encountered "substantial difficulties" in securing counsel without a risk enhancement. The plurality and Justice O'Connor disagreed, however, on "when" and "how" to apply a multiplier. Because of this disagreement, the D.C. Circuit viewed it as impossible to implement the "substantial difficulties" test. Concluding that no middle ground existed for contingency enhancements, the court held that they would not be available in Washington, D.C.

Previously, the courts in the D.C. and Ninth Circuits had looked to how the relevant market or locality treats contingency claims on an across the board, predetermined basis (instead of examining riskiness of lawsuits on a case by case basis). The Ninth Circuit still approves lodestar enhancement upon the finding of two factors: (1) the relevant legal market adds a premium for contingency (100% in *Bernardi*); and (2) absent such an enhancement the plaintiff would have encountered substantial difficulty in securing counsel.[4] Plaintiff in *Fadhl* satisfied her burden by presenting over thirty-five affidavits from local attorneys which established that a 100% contingency multiplier was necessary to ensure future contingency representation in San Francisco. A 100% enhancement must be applied to multipliers awarded in future lawsuits in the San Francisco market unless new evidence or legislation is presented warranting otherwise. This presumption in favor of a predetermined multiplier greatly eases plaintiff's evidentiary burden.

The circuit courts have taken three general approaches with contingency awards. As noted above, the D.C. Circuit completely bars contingency multipliers.[5] The Fourth, Sixth, Seventh, and Ninth Circuits have affirmed contingency awards.[6] The majority of the circuits, however,

2. *Pennsylvania v. Delaware Valley Citizens' Council for Clean Air*, 483 U.S. 711, 107 S.Ct. 3078, 97 L.Ed.2d 585 (1987) (O'Connor, J., concurring) ("*Delaware II*").

3. *King v. Palmer*, 950 F.2d 771 (D.C.Cir.1991) (en banc), *cert. denied sub nom. King v. Ridley*, 505 U.S. 1229, 112 S.Ct. 3054, 120 L.Ed.2d 920 (1992), *reversing King v. Palmer*, 906 F.2d 762 (D.C.Cir. 1990) and *overruling McKenzie v. Kennickell*, 875 F.2d 330 (D.C.Cir.1989).

4. *Bernardi v. Yeutter*, 942 F.2d 562 (9th Cir.), *amended by* 951 F.2d 971 (9th Cir.1991); *Fadhl v. City San Francisco*, 859 F.2d 649 (9th Cir.1988).

5. *See King v. Palmer*, 950 F.2d 771.

6. *See Craig v. Secretary, Dep't of Health & Human Servs.*, 864 F.2d 324 (4th Cir.1989); *Fite v. First Tennessee Prod. Credit Ass'n*, 861 F.2d 884 (6th Cir.1988); *Skelton v. General Motors Corp.*, 860 F.2d 250 (7th Cir.1988), *cert. denied*, 493 U.S.

explicitly limit the availability of contingency multipliers to "exceptional cases" only.[7]

The Third Circuit has announced stringent standards for enhancing the lodestar amount by a contingency multiplier and in each of the following cases has refused to approve one.[8] Before enhancing a fee award, the Third Circuit requires a plaintiff to satisfy four evidentiary factors: (1) how the relevant market treats contingency fee cases differently from hourly fee cases; (2) the degree to which the market compensates for risk of nonpayment; (3) the multiplier cannot be more than is necessary to secure counsel in the market as well as the case; and (4) absent such an enhancement the plaintiff would have encountered substantial difficulty in securing counsel.[9] The Third Circuit will not presume such factors, but insists on expert testimony (and perhaps a costly econometric study) to demonstrate them.

A decision of the Supreme Court, *Burlington v. Dague*,[10] appears to have ended this debate in favor of flatly precluding contingency enhancement. Although the underlying claims at issue were brought under modern environmental statutes, the Court's opinion and citations to cases, including *King v. Palmer*,[11] in which fees were sought under § 1988 or Title VII, strongly suggest that the holding will apply to fee applications under the latter statutes as well.

What if, as a result of *Dague* or otherwise, a putative plaintiff cannot attract counsel? Section 706(f)(1)(B)[12] authorizes the court, upon application and under such circumstances as it deems just, to "appoint an attorney" for a complainant and authorize commencement of the action without fees, costs, or security. And what if the court is unable, after diligent effort, to locate a lawyer willing to take the case without up-front compensation? There is authority that § 706(f)(1)(B) may be read to require the coercive appointment of counsel; this reading is partly justified by the fact that the unwilling lawyer may ultimately be compensated as the result of a statutory award of attorney's fees if his client prevails.[13]

810, 110 S.Ct. 53, 107 L.Ed.2d 22 (1989); *Bernardi v. Yeutter*, 942 F.2d 562.

7. *See, e.g., Rode v. Dellarciprete*, 892 F.2d 1177 (3d Cir.1990); *Hendrickson v. Branstad*, 934 F.2d 158 (8th Cir.1991); *Smith v. Freeman*, 921 F.2d 1120 (10th Cir.1990); *Norman v. Hous. Auth.*, 836 F.2d 1292 (11th Cir.1988); *Leroy v. City of Houston*, 831 F.2d 576 (5th Cir.1987) *cert. denied*, 486 U.S. 1008, 108 S.Ct. 1735, 100 L.Ed.2d 199 (1988).

8. *E.g., Kelly v. Matlack, Inc.*, 903 F.2d 978 (3d Cir.1990); *Rode v. Dellarciprete*, 892 F.2d 1177; *Blum v. Witco Chem. Corp.*, 888 F.2d 975 (3d Cir.1989) ("*Witco II*"); *Blum*

v. Witco Chem. Corp., 829 F.2d 367 (3d Cir.1987) ("*Witco I*").

9. *Rode v. Dellarciprete*, 892 F.2d 1177.

10. 505 U.S. 557, 112 S.Ct. 2638, 120 L.Ed.2d 449 (1992).

11. 950 F.2d 771.

12. 42 U.S.C.A. § 2000e–5(f)(1)(B).

13. *See Scott v. Tyson Foods, Inc.*, 943 F.2d 17 (8th Cir.1991); *Bradshaw v. United States Dist. Ct.*, 742 F.2d 515 (9th Cir.1984) and *Bradshaw v. Zoological Soc'y of San Diego*, 662 F.2d 1301 (9th Cir.1981). *Cf. Howard v. Military Dep't*, 5 F.3d 537 (9th Cir.1993).

§§ 11.11–16.14 [Reserved]

D. PREVAILING DEFENDANTS

§ 11.15 In General

While a prevailing plaintiff is ordinarily to be awarded attorney's fees in all but special circumstances, the Supreme Court in *Christiansburg Garment Co. v. EEOC*[1] has interpreted § 706(k) to preclude attorney's fees to a prevailing defendant unless the plaintiff's action was "frivolous, unreasonable, or without foundation." This appears to mean that a fee award to a prevailing defendant is unwarranted where the plaintiff's claim, although plainly flawed, is colorable.[2] The plaintiff's failure to establish a prima facie case, the unprecedented nature of a claim, the defendant's offer of a settlement, or the dismissal of an action before trial all figure in determining whether a claim is sufficiently frivolous, unreasonable, or groundless to justify taxing attorney's fees against a plaintiff. If the defendant can show that a plaintiff asserted a claim in subjective bad faith, the case for awarding the defendant his attorney's fees is stronger. But the circumstances warranting fees to a prevailing defendant must be truly exceptional, so much so that a trial court does not abuse its discretion in denying such fees even if no reason is stated for the denial.[3] And where EEOC is the plaintiff, it is not even enough for the defendant seeking attorney's fees to show that EEOC failed to present credible evidence of discrimination. In such a case the defendant has the even more difficult burden of demonstrating that EEOC should have "anticipated at the outset that none of its evidence of discriminatory conduct was credible" or unreasonably believed that it had made adequate efforts to conciliate.[4] It is difficult to imagine a situation in which the defendant could carry that showing.

If the standard for prevailing plaintiffs announced in *Farrar* were the test of whether a defendant is a "prevailing party," the defendant might qualify for fees when the plaintiff voluntarily dismisses her suit with prejudice even before a decision on the merits by motion for summary judgment or at trial. Such a dismissal does, after all, alter the legal relationship between the parties to the benefit of the defendant. But a circuit court observed that the *Christiansburg* opinion reflects the Supreme Court's mandate that separate, more stringent standards gov-

§ 11.15

1. 434 U.S. 412, 98 S.Ct. 694, 54 L.Ed.2d 648 (1978).

2. *Sayers v. Stewart Sleep Ctr., Inc.*, 140 F.3d 1351 (11th Cir.1998); *EEOC v. Reichhold Chems., Inc.*, 988 F.2d 1564, 1570–71 (11th Cir.1993). *See also E.E.O.C. v. L.B. Foster Co.*, 123 F.3d 746 (3d Cir.1997), *cert. denied*, 522 U.S. 1147, 118 S.Ct. 1163, 140 L.Ed.2d 174 (1998) (where plaintiff's proof would suffice if credited, claim cannot be considered as frivolous); *AFSCME v. County of Nassau*, 96 F.3d 644 (2d Cir.1996),

cert. denied, 520 U.S. 1104, 117 S.Ct. 1107, 137 L.Ed.2d 309 (1997) (reversing fee award against plaintiff that prevailed on a narrow claim closely related to a broader one on which it failed).

3. *Maag v. Wessler*, 993 F.2d 718 (9th Cir.1993).

4. *EEOC v. Bruno's Rest.*, 13 F.3d 285 (9th Cir.1993). *See EEOC v. Hendrix College*, 53 F.3d 209 (8th Cir.1995) (upholding award where EEOC was found to have failed to investigate before filing action).

ern for the fee eligibility of prevailing Title VII defendants. To show the frivolousness, unreasonableness, or groundlessness demanded by *Christiansburg*, the court concluded, the defendant must ordinarily have prevailed on a motion for summary judgment on the merits.[5] On the other hand, denial of a defendant's summary judgment motion does not necessarily prevent its recovering attorney's fees under the *Christiansburg* standard if plaintiff should have realized, from subsequent pretrial discovery, that his claim was groundless.[6] And the prevailing defendant eligible for fees under *Christiansburg* may, like the prevailing plaintiff, also recover the reasonable fees and expenses incurred in proceedings to collect the underlying fee award should plaintiff decline to pay it.[7]

The Equal Access to Justice Act,[8] unlike § 1988 and its Title VII counterpart,[9] provides for fee awards to prevailing defendants when the plaintiff's claim is merely groundless but not frivolous, if the unsuccessful plaintiff is the U.S. government. The circuit courts are in conflict concerning whether EAJA is available in actions under statutes (like the Reconstruction Acts and Title VII) that have their own fee-shifting statutes.[10] The circuits that have visited the issue thus far have allowed a prevailing defendant to recover fees from the government under the ADEA which has no fee-shifting provision for prevailing defendants.[11] And even where EAJA applies, a defendant employer will not be entitled to fees if the evidence presented by EEOC as plaintiff, although seriously flawed, is supported by anecdotal evidence.[12]

The *Christiansburg* test has been applied to govern the award of attorney's fees against unsuccessful intervenors. The Supreme Court characterized as "particularly welcome" a union's intervention challenging a proposed settlement of a sex discrimination action in order to protect "the legitimate expectations of ... [male] employees innocent of any wrongdoing."[13] The decision encouraged intervention by holding that intervenors would be liable for plaintiffs' costs of defending a settlement only when the intervention is "frivolous, unreasonable, or

---

5. *See, e.g., LeBlanc–Sternberg v. Fletcher*, 143 F.3d 765 (2d Cir.1998) (where plaintiff survives a 12(b)(6) motion to dismiss, a motion for summary judgment and a post-trial motion for judgment as a matter of law, plaintiff's claim is not frivolous as a matter of law); *Marquart v. Lodge 837, Int'l Ass'n of Machinists and Aerospace Workers*, 26 F.3d 842 (8th Cir.1994). *Cf. Walker v. City of Bogalusa*, 168 F.3d 237 (5th Cir. 1999) (awarding defendant fees for plaintiff's failure to produce evidence of defendant's discriminatory purpose or adverse impact).

6. *Flowers v. Jefferson Hosp. Ass'n*, 49 F.3d 391 (8th Cir.1995) (per curiam).

7. *Vukadinovich v. McCarthy*, 59 F.3d 58 (7th Cir.1995).

8. 28 U.S.C.A. § 2412(d).

9. 42 U.S.C.A. § 2000e–5(k).

10. *Compare Nowd v. Rubin*, 76 F.3d 25 (1st Cir.1996) (case under ADEA) *and Gavette v. Office of Personnel Mgmt.*, 808 F.2d 1456, 1463 (Fed.Cir.1986) (yes) *with Escobar Ruiz v. INS*, 787 F.2d 1294, 1296 (9th Cir.1986) (no).

11. *See EEOC v. O & G Spring & Wire Forms Specialty Co.*, 38 F.3d 872, 881–83 (7th Cir.1994), *cert. denied*, 513 U.S. 1198, 115 S.Ct. 1270, 131 L.Ed.2d 148 (1995); *EEOC v. Clay Printing Co.*, 13 F.3d 813, 815 (4th Cir.1994) (assessing attorney's fees against the EEOC in an ADEA case).

12. *EEOC v. O & G Spring and Wire Forms Specialty Co.*, 38 F.3d 872 (7th Cir. 1994), *cert. denied*, 513 U.S. 1198, 115 S.Ct. 1270, 131 L.Ed.2d 148 (1995).

13. *Independent Fed'n of Flight Attendants v. Zipes*, 491 U.S. 754, 764, 109 S.Ct. 2732, 2738, 105 L.Ed.2d 639 (1989).

without foundation."[14] In effect, then, intervention becomes *per se* a "special circumstance" that warrants denial of a fee award to a prevailing plaintiff. The Civil Rights Act of 1991 leaves this approach intact. In actions under the ADEA, several circuits have required prevailing defendants to show not that plaintiff's claim was objectively frivolous, but that it was brought in bad faith.[15]

§§ 11.16–16.19 [Reserved]

E. RULE 68 OFFERS OF JUDGMENT

§ 11.20 In General

Federal Rule 68 authorizes the defendant, at least 10 days before trial, to "offer to allow judgment to be taken against [it] . . . for the money or property . . . specified in the offer, with costs then accrued." It then provides that, if the offer is not accepted and a judgment obtained by the plaintiff "is not more favorable than the offer, the offeree must pay the costs incurred after the making of the offer." On its face, then, Rule 68 merely relieves a defendant who makes such an offer that is not accepted by the plaintiff and equaled or exceeded by a final judgment from what would otherwise be its liability for the "costs" routinely taxable under Federal Rule of Civil Procedure 54(d) in favor of prevailing parties in any federal civil action. Such an offer is valid even when it is conditioned upon acceptance of its terms by all plaintiffs, and a settlement agreement counts as a "judgment" that triggers the cost-shifting permitted by Rule 68.[1]

Rule 54(d) costs, however, are relatively minor, as they are universally understood not to include attorney's fees. The real bite of Rule 68 in civil rights and employment discrimination actions results from the interplay of that rule with the provisions in Title VII and § 1988 that call for an award of "a reasonable attorney's fee *as part of the costs.*"[2] Importing the underlined language into the word "costs" as it appears in Rule 68, the Supreme Court in *Marek v. Chesny*[3] held that a defendant's offer of judgment in a civil rights action governed by statutory provisions for attorney's fees can shift what would otherwise be the losing defendant's liability for the prevailing plaintiff's attorney's fees, as well as ordinary costs. Specifically, a Rule 68 offer that meets the requirements of that Rule relieves the losing defendant of liability for the plaintiff's post-offer attorney's fees as well as her ordinary costs of litigation. This holding greatly increases the defendant's incentive to make a Rule 68

---

14. *Id.* at 761, 109 S.Ct. at 2736–37.

15. *Turlington v. Atlanta Gas Light Co.,* 135 F.3d 1428 (11th Cir.), *cert. denied,* 525 U.S. 962, 119 S.Ct. 405, 142 L.Ed.2d 329 (1998) (citing cases).

§ 11.20

1. *See Lang v. Gates,* 36 F.3d 73 (9th Cir.), *cert. denied,* 513 U.S. 1017, 115 S.Ct. 579, 130 L.Ed.2d 494 (1994).

2. Section 706(k) of Title VII; 42 U.S.C.A. § 1988, final sentence.

3. 473 U.S. 1, 105 S.Ct. 3012, 87 L.Ed.2d 1 (1985).

offer, and the Civil Rights Act of 1991 leaves *Marek* intact. The *Marek* holding goes well beyond actions under the Reconstruction Civil Rights statutes governed by § 1988. In *Lyte v. Sara Lee Corp.*,[4] the court held that attorney's fees are a part of the "costs" shifted by a defendant's offer of judgment under FRCP 68 in actions under any statute that allows fee awards as a part of "costs," which would include those under Title VII, EPA, and ADEA.

The defendant's offer, to avoid liability for costs and fees to the prevailing plaintiff, must, in the words of Rule 68, include the plaintiff's "costs then accrued," that is, up until the time of the offer. The "costs" that must be included in the offer—like the "costs" mentioned in the subsequent phrase of Rule 68 that shifts liability for attorney's fees if the offer is rejected—have been held to include the amount of the plaintiff's attorney's fees accrued at the time of the offer. This is because a prevailing plaintiff would, absent an offer, ordinarily be entitled by judgment to an award of attorney's fees for pre-offer work.[5] Accordingly, those fees, together with ordinary costs, must be added to the judgment to calculate the total received by judgment that the offer must equal or exceed to shift post-offer costs and fees under Rule 68. Where an offer no longer exceeded, in fact was slightly less than, the amount of plaintiff's judgment once pre-offer attorney's fees were added to the judgment, the Rule 68 requirement that the offer equal or exceed the judgement was held not met and the defendant was therefore subject to the usual assessment of costs and fees owed a prevailing plaintiff, including those incurred after the making of its offer.[6]

In another case, the offer promised not only "costs then accrued," as prescribed by Rule 68, but also "reasonable attorney fees as determined by the court."[7] The Ninth Circuit construed the language of the offer to authorize a district judge's award of attorney's fees for plaintiffs' counsel's preparation of a fee petition *after* they accepted the offer, even though under Rule 68 costs, and hence, under *Marek*, fees, are halted by a successful offer. The court indicated that if the defendant had offered to pay only plaintiff's "costs then accrued," the offer would have clearly and unambiguously limited plaintiff's fees to the full extent that *Marek* and Rule 68 permit. The decision points up the necessity for defendant's counsel to draft tightly worded offers that not only meet Rule 68's strictures but also stay within them. A majority of circuits that have confronted the question held that any waiver of or limitation on attorney's fees in actions under statutes providing for the recovery of fees by prevailing plaintiffs must be "clear and unambiguous."[8] Similarly, a

4. 950 F.2d 101 (2d Cir.1991).

5. *See Scheeler v. Crane Co.*, 21 F.3d 791 (8th Cir.1994) (diversity case under Iowa civil rights statute).

6. *Id.*

7. *Holland v. Roeser*, 37 F.3d 501 (9th Cir.1994).

8. *See, e.g., Ellis v. University of Kan. Med. Ctr.*, 163 F.3d 1186, 1199–1201 (10th Cir.1998); *Muckleshoot Tribe v. Puget Sound Power & Light Co.*, 875 F.2d 695, 698 and n. 5 (9th Cir.1989); *Jennings v. Metropolitan Gov't of Nashville*, 715 F.2d 1111, 1114 (6th Cir.1983) (silence in settlement agreement does not waive plaintiff's right to pursue fees under § 1988). *See also*

circuit court has ruled ineffective a Rule 68 offer that failed to apportion the offer among the multiple plaintiffs. By advising only that the offered sum was "to be divided among all three plaintiffs," the offer failed to give the notice each required to evaluate whether to accept.[9]

The inclusion of attorney's fees in the Rule 68 post-offer "costs" that the plaintiff may be precluded from recovering assumes that the underlying fee statute includes "attorney's fees" within the definition of "costs." That is the case with most fee statutes, including § 1988, its counterpart under ADEA, and the principal Title VII fee provision, Section 706(k). By contrast, since the "mixed-motive" remedies section of Title VII, Section 706(g)(2)(B), refers to "costs" and "attorney's fees" distinctly and separately, attorney's fees will not be counted as part of the post-offer Rule 68 "costs" a plaintiff is barred from recovering where the entitlement to fees flows only from that section.[10]

Likewise, at least one circuit has held that attorney's fees are not shifted as part of costs in ADA actions because the text of the ADA does not define attorney's fees as part of costs.[11] In an ADA action, "the court or agency, in its discretion, may allow the prevailing party ... a reasonable attorney's fee, including litigation expenses, *and* costs."[12] Under this section, then, Congress did not define costs to include fees for the purposes of the ADA. Therefore, an offer that mentions only "costs" and is silent on the issue of fees cannot relieve the defendant of its statutory liability for fees.[13]

Can Rule 68 be used not just to relieve the defendant of cost and fee liability to a prevailing plaintiff but as the basis for an award of costs and fees to a prevailing defendant? If so, Rule 68 could serve as the prevailing defendant's end run around the *Christiansburg Garment* test—it would become eligible for attorney's fees simply by submitting what proves to be a shrewd offer of judgment, without having to show the groundlessness, frivolousness, or subjective bad faith the Supreme Court has required. A court of appeals, citing the text of Rule 68, has rejected this argument, confirming that the provision, while a one-way street available only to defendants, helps them only if the plaintiff prevails, and then only with respect to the plaintiff's costs and fees.[14]

Courts have generally held that Rule 68 offers of judgment may not be revoked during the 10 day period set by the Rule.[15] Moreover,

El Club Del Barrio, Inc. v. United Cmty. Corps., Inc., 735 F.2d 98, 100 (3d Cir.1984); *cf. Valley Disposal, Inc. v. Central Vt. Solid Waste Mgmt. Dist.*, 71 F.3d 1053, 1058 (2d Cir.1995). *But see Wray v. Clarke*, 151 F.3d 807, 809 (8th Cir.1998); *Elmore v. Shuler*, 787 F.2d 601, 603 (D.C.Cir.1986) (plaintiff must show that settlement agreement does not waive § 1988 fees and possibly even reserve that right affirmatively).

9. *See Gavoni v. Dobbs House, Inc.*, 164 F.3d 1071 (7th Cir.1999) (tort action).

10. *Sheppard v. Riverview Nursing Ctr.*, 88 F.3d 1332 (4th Cir.), *cert. denied*, 519

U.S. 993, 117 S.Ct. 483, 136 L.Ed.2d 377 (1996).

11. *See Webb v. James*, 147 F.3d 617 (7th Cir.1998).

12. 42 U.S.C.A. § 12205 (emphasis added).

13. *See Webb v. James*, 147 F.3d 617, 622–23 (7th Cir.1998).

14. *EEOC v. Bailey Ford, Inc.*, 26 F.3d 570 (5th Cir.1994).

15. *See Webb v. James*, 147 F.3d 617 (7th Cir.1998); *Richardson v. National R.R. Passenger Corp.*, 49 F.3d 760, 764 (D.C.Cir.

recission may not be an available remedy for mutual mistakes because the mandatory language of Rule 68, requiring that the clerk "shall enter judgment" upon the filing of an offer, removes discretion from the trial court as to whether to enter judgment upon the filing of the accepted offer.[16] Relief from a judgment entered as a result of a Rule 68 offer and acceptance may be available under Rule 60. Rule 60(b) provides in relevant part that "[o]n motion and upon such terms as are just, the court may relieve a party or a party's legal representative from a final judgment order or proceeding for the following reasons: (1) mistake, inadvertence, surprise, or excusable neglect; . . . (3) fraud (whether heretofore denominated intrinsic or extrinsic), misrepresentation, or other misconduct of an adverse party; (4) the judgment is void; . . . or (6) any other reason justifying relief from the operation of the judgment."[17]

1995) (all federal courts to consider the issue have treated Rule 68 offers as generally irrevocable during the 10 day period) (citing *Colonial Penn Ins. Co. v. Coil*, 887 F.2d 1236, 1240 (4th Cir.1989); *Fisher v. Stolaruk Corp.*, 110 F.R.D. 74, 75 (E.D.Mich.1986); *Radecki v. Amoco Oil Co.*, 858 F.2d 397, 402 (8th Cir.1988) (in dicta)). See also Charles Alan Wright, Arthur R. Miller & Richard L. Marcus, *Federal Practice and Procedure*: Civil 2d, § 3004 (1997)

(the courts have agreed with one of the drafters that Rule 68 offers cannot be withdrawn once served).

16. *See Webb v. James*, 147 F.3d 617, 621 (7th Cir.1998); *Mallory v. Eyrich*, 922 F.2d 1273, 1279 (6th Cir.1991).

17. *See Webb v. James*, 147 F.3d 617, 622 (7th Cir.1998).

Chapter Twelve

PROCEDURAL ASPECTS OF LITIGATING UNDER CONTEMPORARY EMPLOYMENT DISCRIMINATION LEGISLATION

Analysis

§ 12.1　Federal Subject Matter Jurisdiction

Federal court jurisdiction proceeds from 28 U.S.C.A. § 1331, the federal question jurisdictional statute. For cases arising under §§ 1981 or 1983, Congress also added a separate statute, 28 U.S.C.A. § 1343, which provides for original jurisdiction in "any civil action" brought to "redress the deprivation, under color of State law, ... of any right ... secured by the Constitution ... or by any *Act of Congress providing for equal rights* of citizens." (emphasis added). The Court read this language to give jurisdiction only where the right being abridged is one granted in the Constitution or in a statute intended to secure equal rights, not simply any civil right.[1] Narrow construction of § 1343 had major significance when § 1331 had a $10,000 amount in controversy requirement; since the elimination of that requirement for federal questions in December of 1980, civil rights plaintiffs have pleaded jurisdiction under § 1331 alone, or in combination with § 1343. There appears to be little advantage to invoking § 1343 as the basis for federal subject matter jurisdiction in civil rights claims.[2] Cautious civil rights lawyers nevertheless plead both § 1343 and § 1331 as distinct bases to support original and, under 28 U.S.C.A. § 1441, removal, federal court subject matter jurisdiction over §§ 1981 and 1983 claims.

Contemporary employment discrimination statutes contain their own express authorizations of federal subject matter jurisdiction, although again it is not clear what these add now that § 1331 has been shorn of its amount in controversy requirement.[3] A fine, sometimes barely discernible line separates issues classified as going to subject matter jurisdiction under these statutes, and therefore determinable at the threshold by the court, and issues classified as part of plaintiff's claim, and therefore determinable (on demand) by a jury.[4]

§ 12.1

1. *Chapman v. Houston Welfare Rights Org.,* 441 U.S. 600, 99 S.Ct. 1905, 60 L.Ed.2d 508 (1979); *Maine v. Thiboutot,* 448 U.S. 1, 100 S.Ct. 2502, 65 L.Ed.2d 555 (1980).

2. But see text immediately below.

3. *See, e.g.,* Title VII § 706(f)(3), 42 U.S.C.A. § 2000e–5(f)(3).

4. *Compare Scarfo v. Ginsberg,* 175 F.3d 957 (11th Cir.1999), *cert. denied,* ___ U.S. ___, 120 S.Ct. 1267, 146 L.Ed.2d 217 (2000) (whether the defendants, corporations and their owner, constituted a "single employer" subject to Title VII is a quasi-

The plaintiff should take care, however, especially when she also asserts claims under state law, to allege that her federal law claim "arises under" the predicate Reconstruction Act or employment discrimination statute. The Supreme Court has long insisted that in order to invoke federal subject matter jurisdiction under § 1331, the plaintiff's right to relief must be created by or at a minimum depend heavily on the construction of federal law.[5] The allegations of a right under federal law may not be "wholly insubstantial and frivolous" (for example, negated by recent authoritative precedent) or "immaterial" (for example, a federal claim "tail" wagging a "dog" composed of multiple state law claims of greater magnitude).[6] The Court has shown reluctance to recognize federal question jurisdiction of the district courts based on allegations that a federal statutory standard defines one of the elements of a claim that exists solely by virtue of state law.[7] Similarly, a defendant may not remove an action (on the basis of a federal question) where plaintiff's state law complaint refers to Title VII merely for such definitional purposes.[8]

This authorization for federal subject matter jurisdiction does not of course dispense with the necessity of securing personal jurisdiction over each defendant both constitutionally and under Federal Rule 4(k), as amended in December 1993. Whether a district court must first decide subject matter jurisdiction before considering personal jurisdiction depends upon whether either inquiry raises difficult or novel questions. In *Ruhrgas v. Marathon Oil Co.*,[9] the district court was faced with a very difficult and arduous subject matter jurisdiction inquiry; it chose to bypass the tough issue and dismiss the removed case on personal jurisdictional grounds, an issue that was considerably more straightfor-

jurisdictional question that determines whether Title VII applies and therefore must be decided by the court, which must answer it affirmatively before a jury may determine the related element of plaintiff's claim, i.e., whether 15 or more "employees" worked for such a "single employer") with *Garcia v. Copenhaver, Bell & Assocs.*, 104 F.3d 1256 (11th Cir.1997) (plaintiff must show that defendant is an "employer" as an element of her prima facie case under ADEA, so the issue goes to the merits and should be decided by a jury at trial).

5. *See, e.g., Louisville & Nashville R.R. v. Mottley*, 211 U.S. 149, 29 S.Ct. 42, 53 L.Ed. 126 (1908).

6. *Bell v. Hood*, 327 U.S. 678, 66 S.Ct. 773, 90 L.Ed. 939 (1946). But the immateriality or insubstantiality of a purported federal law claim is an exception to the general requirement that a federal court exercise federal subject matter jurisdiction over claims that the plaintiff has squarely based on federal law. In *Bell* , the Supreme Court offered examples that in effect branded a claim "insubstantial" only if it had been ruled legally insufficient rather recently by

a court of considerable authority, and "immaterial" only if the federal claim or claims were slight in number, weight, or relief sought in relation to one or more state law claims. Accordingly, a federal court that finds a claim the plaintiff pleaded under federal law to be legally insufficient should ordinarily dismiss it not for lack of federal subject matter jurisdiction but for failure to state a claim on which relief can be granted. *Id.* From time to time, however, lower courts reverse the presumption, demanding that the plaintiff's federal law claim be affirmatively substantial. *See Lovern v. Edwards*, 190 F.3d 648, 654–656 (4th Cir. 1999) (dismissing for lack of subject matter jurisdiction a claim because plaintiff's rights were not "directly and sharply" implicated by defendant's challenged conduct).

7. *See Merrell Dow Pharmaceuticals Inc. v. Thompson*, 478 U.S. 804, 106 S.Ct. 3229, 92 L.Ed.2d 650 (1986).

8. *Rains v. Criterion Sys., Inc.*, 80 F.3d 339 (9th Cir.1996).

9. 526 U.S. 574, 119 S.Ct. 1563, 143 L.Ed.2d 760 (1999).

ward. The Fifth Circuit reversed, finding that subject matter jurisdiction was more fundamental and must in all cases be considered at the threshold. The Supreme Court reversed, acknowledging that while in most instances subject matter jurisdiction will not present difficult questions and should be the threshold inquiry, when subject matter jurisdiction presents novel or challenging questions, and the personal jurisdictional inquiry presents no complex issues of state law, a court may proceed to decide the personal jurisdiction issue first. Although *Ruhrgas* involved a removed case, the holding appears equally applicable to cases brought to federal court in the first instance.

§ 12.2   Appellate Jurisdiction of the Federal Circuit Courts

Title 28 U.S.C. § 1291 in terms limits the jurisdiction of the courts of appeals to review of all "final decisions" by a federal district court. The interpretation of "final decision" is narrow and strict. For example, even a district court order dismissing a claim, but fewer than all the claims against a party,[1] or dismissing a party, but fewer than all the parties,[2] is usually not a "final decision" under § 1291 and accordingly is

§ 12.2

1. *See Hill v. Henderson*, 195 F.3d 671, 674–678 (D.C.Cir.1999) (holding, on purported appeal from dismissal of one claim, that district court's subsequent transfer of remaining Title VII and ADEA claims to a district in another circuit furnished no reason for exception to general rule that a dismissal of fewer than all claims is a nonfinal and hence not immediately reviewable decision). Most circuits to have addressed the issue are in accord that reviewability of pre-transfer orders lies instead in the circuit to which transfer was made. *See Hill*, 195 F.3d at 674–678; *EEOC v. Northwest Airlines, Inc.*, 188 F.3d 695, 700 (6th Cir. 1999); *Chaiken v. VV Publishing Corp.*, 119 F.3d 1018, 1025 n. 2 (2d Cir.1997), *cert. denied*, 522 U.S. 1149, 118 S.Ct. 1169, 140 L.Ed.2d 179 (1998); *Mackensworth v. S.S.Am. Merchant*, 28 F.3d 246, 249–252 (2d Cir.1994); *Tel-Phonic Servs., Inc. v. TBS International*, 975 F.2d 1134, 1138 (5th Cir.1992). The majority rule, by temporarily withholding review of the order dismissing fewer than all claims, may eliminate need for appellate review anywhere it plaintiff is satisfied by the outcome in the transferee court and avoids piecemeal appeals in two courts. *But see McGeorge v. Continental Airlines, Inc.*, 871 F.2d 952 (10th Cir.1989) (circuit court in transferee district held it lacked appellate jurisdiction to review dismissal order of district court in transferor district, citing 28 U.S.C. § 1294(1), which provides that "appeals from reviewable decisions of the district ...

courts shall be taken to ... the court of appeals for the circuit embracing the district"). The majority approach, by contrast, would not consider a pre-transfer dismissal order a "reviewable decision" within the meaning of § 1294, and therefore would not consider review of that decision restricted to the court of appeals for the circuit where the transfer order was issued. *See, e.g., Hill*, 195 F.3d at 675.

2. *But see Reuber v. United States*, 773 F.2d 1367 (D.C.Cir.1985) (where district court dismissed one party but then transferred remaining part of action to another district in another circuit, plaintiff held able to appeal the dismissal to transferor circuit court as a final judgment, apparently on the assumption that the dismissal order would eventually become final when the transferee district court disposed of the rest of the case). The decision is in tension with the general rule that orders of one district court made before transfer are reviewable by the circuit court embracing the transferee district court, an appeal which would only ripen, however, upon the issuance of one or more final decisions (or their fungible equivalent under § 1291) by the transferee district court. *See Chapple v. Levinsky*, 961 F.2d 372, 374 (2d Cir.1992); *Carteret Sav. Bank, FA v. Shushan*, 919 F.2d 225, 228 (3d Cir.1990); *Magnetic Eng'g & Mfg. Co. v. Dings Mfg. Co.*, 178 F.2d 866, 870 (2d Cir. 1950) (Hand, J.). As for the orders granting transfer themselves, they are not, under § 1404, final appealable orders or, ordinarily, reviewable collateral orders. *See Ukiah*

not appealable at that time unless the district court expressly determines "that there is no just reason for delay" and accordingly enters partial judgment under Federal Rule of Civil Procedure 54(b).

If, however, a federal district court certifies in an order that a nonfinal or "interlocutory" decision involves a "controlling question of law as to which there is substantial ground for difference of opinion," and that immediate review "may materially advance the ultimate termination of the litigation," the appellate court may, in its discretion, permit an immediate appeal from that order.[3] In addition, 28 U.S.C. § 1292(a)(1) provides (except where direct review is available in the Supreme Court) for "interlocutory" review of any nonfinal decision granting, continuing, modifying, refusing or dissolving an injunction, or refusing to dissolve or modify them.

Apart from those limited express statutory authorizations for immediate review of nonfinal decisions, case law stemming from *Cohen v. Beneficial Industrial Loan Corp.*[4] provides for review by the federal circuit courts of a narrow class of nonfinal "collateral orders" that are both separable from the merits of the cause and the immediate review of which is deemed important for one or more of several different reasons of policy. One such recognized "collateral order" exception permits interlocutory review of many orders denying a § 1983 defendant's motion to dismiss or summary judgment motion based on the defense of qualified immunity. The immediate reviewability of an order denying Eleventh Amendment immunity, is another instance of the "collateral order" exception. There is also a nascent but discernible doctrine of pendent appellate federal subject matter jurisdiction that may, very rarely, afford interlocutory review of nonfinal decisions that are very closely related to immediately reviewable "collateral orders." The nonfi-

---

Adventist Hosp. v. FTC, 981 F.2d 543, 546 (D.C.Cir.1992), *cert. denied*, 510 U.S. 825, 114 S.Ct. 88, 126 L.Ed.2d 55 (1993). But those orders may usually be challenged by a petition for writ of mandamus, if only for abuse of discretion or perhaps mere legal infirmity, in the court of appeals for the circuit of origin. *See In re Scott* 709 F.2d 717, 719 (D.C.Cir.1983) and 15 Charles Alan Wright, Arthur R. Miller & Edward H. Cooper, *Federal Practice and Procedure* § 3855 (1986 & Supp. 1999) (collecting cases). Thus they are immediately "reviewable orders," within the meaning of 28 U.S.C. § 1294, by the court of appeals embracing the transferor district court. Perhaps for that reason transfer orders have usually been held nonreviewable in the transferee circuit. *See TEC Floor Corp. v. Wal–Mart Stores, Inc.*, 4 F.3d 599, 602 (8th Cir.1993); *In re Briscoe*, 976 F.2d 1425, 1426 (D.C.Cir.1992); *Moses v. Business Card Express, Inc.*, 929 F.2d 1131, 1136 (6th Cir.), *cert. denied*, 502 U.S. 821, 112 S.Ct. 81, 116 L.Ed.2d 54 (1991); *Reyes v.*

Supervisor of the DEA, 834 F.2d 1093, 1095 (1st Cir.1987); *Roofing & Sheet Metal Servs. v. La Quinta Motor Inns*, 689 F.2d 982, 986–87 (11th Cir.1982); *Linnell v. Sloan*, 636 F.2d 65, 67 (4th Cir.1980); *Purex Corp. v. St. Louis Nat'l Stockyards Co.*, 374 F.2d 998, 1000 (7th Cir.), *cert. denied*, 389 U.S. 824, 88 S.Ct. 59, 19 L.Ed.2d 77 (1967). *But see Nascone v. Spudnuts, Inc.*, 735 F.2d 763, 773 n. 9 (3d Cir.1984) (transferee court after final judgment may determine whether it in fact has venue); *American Fid. Fire Ins. Co. v. United States Dist. Ct.*, 538 F.2d 1371, 1377 n. 4 (9th Cir.1976) (declining writ of mandamus to review transfer order on ground that transferee circuit could review transfer order after final judgment); *Magnetic Eng'g & Mfg. Co. v. Dings Mfg. Co.*, 178 F.2d 866, 868–870 (2d Cir.1950) (Hand, J.) (transfer as well as pre-transfer orders reviewable by transferee circuit).

3. 28 U.S.C. § 1292(b).

4. 337 U.S. 541, 546, 69 S.Ct. 1221, 93 L.Ed. 1528 (1949).

nal and hence ordinarily nonappealable orders may be entertained on interlocutory review if they raise issues so "inextricably intertwined" with the appealable "collateral order" (e.g., the order denying a state's Eleventh Amendment immunity or a § 1983 defendant's motion based on qualified immunity) that "review of the former . . . [is] necessary to ensure meaningful review of the latter."[5]

§ 12.3　Venue

Venue for employment discrimination claims under Title VII, the Age Discrimination in Employment Act, the Equal Pay Act, or the Americans With Disabilities Act is provided for expressly by the statutes creating those claims. Because the defendants in these cases are commonly far-flung corporate employers, rather than municipalities or counties existing within one district only, it is not surprising that these statutes afford broader venue choice than does the general federal venue state, 28 U.S. C. § 1391, applicable to civil rights claims. Venue for a Title VII claim, for example, lies "in any judicial district in the State in which the unlawful employment practice is alleged to have been committed, in the judicial district in which the employment records relevant to such practice are maintained and administered, or in the judicial district in which the aggrieved person would have worked but for the alleged unlawful employment practice, but if the respondent is not found within any such district, such an action may be brought within the judicial district in which the respondent has his principal office."[1]

The Reconstruction Civil Rights Acts, most notably 42 U.S.C. § 1981 and 1983, make no explicit provision for venue. Venue for actions presenting even one of these federal question claims therefore lies in the first instance in the districts provided by the pertinent subsection of the general federal venue statute, 28 U.S.C. § 1391(b). Plaintiff's choices will include under § 1391(b)(1) any district , if any, in which all defendants "reside."[2] In most civil rights actions, even where there are

---

5. *Swint v. Chambers County Comm'n,* 514 U.S. 35, 51, 115 S.Ct. 1203, 131 L.Ed.2d 60 (1995). Applying that standard, an appellate court that rejected state officials' Eleventh Amendment defense also declined to hear their objection to plaintiff's standing, because "we may resolve the Eleventh Amendment immunity issue without reaching the merits of standing." *Summit Med. Assocs., P.C. v. Pryor,* 180 F.3d 1326, 1335 (11th Cir.1999), *cert. denied,* ___ U.S. ___, 120 S.Ct. 1287, 146 L.Ed.2d 233 (2000). *See also Moniz v. City of Ft. Lauderdale,* 145 F.3d 1278, 1281 (11th Cir.1998) (because qualified immunity issue could be resolved without reaching the merits of appellants' challenge to plaintiff's standing, the jurisdictional standing issue not within pendent appellate jurisdiction).

§ 12.3

1. Title VII § 706(f)(3), 42 U.S.C. § 2000e–5(f)(3).

2. It should be kept in mind that § 1391(c), in turn, identifies each district in which a corporate defendant "resides" for purposes of subsection (b)(1). The district where an individual defendant "resides" within the meaning of subsection (b)(1) is not self-evident, either. A majority of the circuit courts to have confronted the issue have concluded that an individual's "residence" for venue purposes equates with his "domicile," a more restrictive concept used to determine a basis of constitutional personal jurisdiction and citizenship for purposes of federal subject matter jurisdiction under 28 U.S.C. § 1332. *See Manley v. Engram,* 755 F.2d 1463, 1466 n. 3 (11th Cir. 1985) (citations omitted).

multiple defendants, they are likely to all reside in the same district, so that subsection (b)(1) will afford a venue choice. Let us suppose, however, that this choice is not tactically appealing to plaintiff, or that not all defendants reside in the same district, so that subsection (b)(1) affords no choice at all. The plaintiff will always be able to fall back on the choice or choices provided by subsection (b)(2), namely, the district or districts in which "a substantial part" of the claim arises. In the typical civil rights case, where the alleged unlawful conduct is entirely within the district that embraces a local government subdivision, (b)(2) gives the venue choice of the district in which plaintiff was subjected to the alleged civil rights violation and in which it caused him injury. If there is but a single defendant, both (b)(1) and (b)(2) would typically give the same venue choice, because the district where a government entity or individual official defendant resides will also likely be the district in which all, or at least a part, of the claim arose.

But plaintiff may have commenced either a civil rights or employment discrimination action in state court. That is possible because state courts enjoy concurrent subject matter jurisdiction over those claims.[3] Quite commonly defendants will believe it tactically advantageous to defend such claims in federal court, before a judge virtually always tenured for life and before a usually more rural jury pool distributed in a district that surrounds but is not limited to urban population centers. Defendants will be able to remove to federal court any action containing even one federal civil rights or employment discrimination claim, under the authority of 28 U.S.C. § 1441(a) and the first sentence of § 1441(b). In that situation, original federal venue lies in only one district: the federal district embracing the state court from which the action was removed. § 1441(a).

So far we have been speaking only of the appropriate federal venues originally selected by the plaintiff. Once plaintiff lays venue in a federal judicial district, or defendant removes an action that the plaintiff filed in state court to the federal judicial district in which that state court sits, either party may have an opportunity to move to transfer venue to another federal judicial district. 28 U.S.C. §§ 1404 and 1406 provide for transfer *from* a federal judicial district where both personal jurisdiction, and original venue (under § 1391, or under a special statutory venue provision like Title VII's, or after removal under § 1441(a)), are proper—transfer per § 1404[4]—or where personal jurisdiction, or venue, or both are faulty—transfer per § 1406.[5] But transfer under either § 1404 or § 1406 is possible *to* only those federal judicial districts in which the action might originally have been brought, which the Supreme Court has construed to mean any district that would have had good personal jurisdiction and venue at the time the plaintiff filed in the original

---

3. *See* § 12.5.

4. *Ferens v. John Deere Co.*, 494 U.S. 516, 110 S.Ct. 1274, 108 L.Ed.2d 443 (1990) (§ 1404 used only where both venue and personal jurisdiction are correct).

5. *See Goldlawr, Inc. v. Heiman*, 369 U.S. 463, 82 S.Ct. 913, 8 L.Ed.2d 39 (1962) (§ 1406 permits transfer from district lacking personal jurisdiction).

federal district.[6] Moreover, before transferring, the district judge must find that the proposed transferee district is more convenient to parties and witnesses than the original, transferor district, and that a transfer would be in the interest of justice. See §§ 1404, 1406.

Does the specification of particular venues in Title VII preclude the district judge from exercising his usual discretion under §§ 1404 or 1406 to transfer the action to another district that would be more convenient (and that also has sound personal jurisdiction and venue)? No. Even if the plaintiff has filed originally in a district specified by Title VII, the district court may transfer under the usual standards for transfer under § 1404, i.e., upon determining that the proposed transferee district also had good personal jurisdiction and venue at the time the action was filed and will be more convenient to parties and witnesses and that the transfer will be in the interest of justice.[7]

Whether transfer will be granted, however, especially on defendant's motion, is quite a different matter. The plaintiff's forum choice "should not be disturbed unless it is clearly outweighed by other considerations."[8] Once, however, transfer is ordered, it is reviewed only for "a clear abuse of discretion."[9] A more complicated question is how to obtain review of an order granting transfer. (An order denying transfer is manifestly not a "final decision" within the meaning of 28 U.S.C. § 1291 and hence is not reviewable by the court of appeals superintending the original federal judicial district until and unless the party who sought transfer suffers an adverse, appealable final judgment.) An order granting transfer has been held to be neither a final appealable order at the time entered nor reviewable under the "collateral order" exception that would permit immediate federal appellate interlocutory review by the court of appeals for the circuit superintending the district court that ordered transfer.[10] The district court to which transfer is ordered will generally be unable to review the order that transferred the action to it because of the doctrine of "law of the case."[11] Nor, where transfer is ordered to a district in another circuit, will most transferee circuits review the transferor district court's order granting transfer.[12] One

6. *Hoffman v. Blaski*, 363 U.S. 335, 80 S.Ct. 1084, 4 L.Ed.2d 1254 (1960).

7. *Ross v. Buckeye Cellulose Corp.*, 980 F.2d 648, 655 (11th Cir.1993), *cert. denied*, 513 U.S. 814, 115 S.Ct. 69, 130 L.Ed.2d 24 (1994).

8. *Robinson v. Giarmarco & Bill*, 74 F.3d 253, 260 (11th Cir.1996); *Howell v. Tanner*, 650 F.2d 610, 616 (5th Cir.1981), *cert. denied*, 456 U.S. 918, 102 S.Ct. 1775, 72 L.Ed.2d 178 (1982).

9. *Richardson v. Alabama St. Bd. of Educ.*, 935 F.2d 1240, 1248 (11th Cir.1991); *Howell*, 650 F.2d at 616.

10. *See Ukiah Adventist Hosp. v. FTC*, 981 F.2d 543, 546 (D.C.Cir.1992), *cert. denied*, 510 U.S. 825, 114 S.Ct. 88, 126 L.Ed.2d 55 (1993). Still, on rare occasion,

courts of appeals for the circuit superintending the court ordering transfer will entertain petitions for writs of mandamus to review those orders. *See In re Scott* 709 F.2d 717, 719 (D.C.Cir.1983) and 15 Charles Alan Wright, Arthur R. Miller & Edward H. Cooper, *Federal Practice and Procedure* § 3855 (1986 & Supp. 1999) (collecting cases).

11. *See Chrysler Credit Corp. v. Country Chrysler*, 928 F.2d 1509, 1518 (10th Cir. 1991).

12. *See TEC Floor Corp. v. Wal–Mart Stores, Inc.*, 4 F.3d 599, 602 (8th Cir.1993); *In re Briscoe*, 976 F.2d 1425, 1426 (D.C.Cir. 1992); *Moses v. Business Card Express, Inc.*, 929 F.2d 1131, 1136 (6th Cir.), *cert. denied*, 502 U.S. 821, 112 S.Ct. 81, 116 L.Ed.2d 54

possibility is that the party who unsuccessfully opposed transfer will move after transfer in the transferee district for "re-transfer" back to the transferor district. The denial of that motion would be reviewable, after final judgment, by the circuit court embracing the transferee district.[13]

§ 12.4 Supplemental (Including "Pendent") Jurisdiction

Supplemental or pendent claim jurisdiction allows a plaintiff who has a federal claim against a nondiverse defendant[1] in federal court to append a transactionally related state law claim against the same defendant. For the past half-century the Court has authorized some form of pendent jurisdiction, recognizing that in its absence the plaintiff would be forced to litigate the distinct but related federal and state claims in two fora or to abandon the federal forum. The Court fully articulated the article III criteria for pendent claim jurisdiction in *United Mine Workers of America v. Gibbs*.[2] For a federal court to have constitutional power to entertain the state law claim, that claim and the federal law claim on which jurisdiction is founded must arise from a "common nucleus of operative fact"; the claims must be such that the plaintiff would normally be expected to try both in one judicial proceeding; and the federal claim must be "substantial."

The *Gibbs* opinion did not allude to the settled understanding that federal subject matter jurisdiction requires not just a constitutional foundation—in this case, Article III—but also a Congressional authorization or acceptance of that jurisdiction as manifested in a federal statute. But the court did identify several factors that a federal trial court, having concluded that it has constitutional power to hear both claims, should take into account in deciding whether, in its discretion, to dismiss the state law claim. It observed that the doctrine's justification "lies in considerations of judicial economy, convenience and fairness to liti-

(1991); *Reyes v. Supervisor of the DEA*, 834 F.2d 1093, 1095 (1st Cir.1987); *Roofing & Sheet Metal Serv. v. La Quinta Motor Inns*, 689 F.2d 982, 986–87 (11th Cir.1982); *Linnell v. Sloan*, 636 F.2d 65, 67 (4th Cir. 1980); *Purex Corp. v. St. Louis Nat'l Stockyards Co.*, 374 F.2d 998, 1000 (7th Cir.), *cert. denied*, 389 U.S. 824, 88 S.Ct. 59, 19 L.Ed.2d 77 (1967). *But see Nascone v. Spudnuts, Inc.*, 735 F.2d 763, 773 n. 9 (3d Cir. 1984) (transferee court after final judgment may determine whether it in fact has venue); *American Fid. Fire Ins. Co. v. United States Dist. Ct.*, 538 F.2d 1371, 1377 n. 4 (9th Cir.1976) (declining writ of mandamus to review transfer order on ground that transferee circuit could review transfer order after final judgment); *Magnetic Eng'g & Mfg. Co. v. Dings Mfg. Co.*, 178 F.2d 866, 868–870 (2d Cir.1950) (Hand, J.) (transfer orders reviewable by transferee circuit). The majority rule may turn on the recogni-

tion of the transferee circuit that courts of appeals for the transferor circuit may entertain petitions for writs of mandamus to review those orders, as indicated in one of the previous footnotes.

13. *See Nascone v. Spudnuts, Inc.*, 735 F.2d 763, 765–66 (3d Cir.1984); *Purex Corp. v. St. Louis Nat'l Stockyards Co.*, 374 F.2d 998, 1000 (7th Cir.), *cert. denied*, 389 U.S. 824, 88 S.Ct. 59, 19 L.Ed.2d 77 (1967).

§ 12.4

1. If all the requirements of the diversity statute, 28 U.S.C.A. § 1332, are met, the federal district court is *required* to accept original jurisdiction over all claims, state as well as federal, whether or not they are related. *Cemer v. Marathon Oil Co.*, 583 F.2d 830 (6th Cir.1978).

2. 383 U.S. 715, 86 S.Ct. 1130, 16 L.Ed.2d 218 (1966).

gants"—a later case, *Carnegie–Mellon*,[3] added "comity" to the list—and if these are absent "a federal court should hesitate to exercise jurisdiction over state claims." The *Gibbs* opinion specifically mentioned two examples of situations in which the trial judge should consider declining to exercise otherwise available pendent jurisdiction: where "the state issues substantially predominate, whether in terms of proof, of the scope of the issues raised, or of the comprehensiveness of the remedy sought"; and where there are "reasons independent of jurisdictional considerations, such as the likelihood of jury confusion in treating divergent legal theories of relief," that would warrant separate trials of the state and federal claims. *Carnegie–Mellon* read *Gibbs* as conferring substantial discretion on the trial courts to assert *or decline* jurisdiction over pendent claims, guided only by the ultimate values of judicial economy, convenience and fairness to litigants, and comity.

The *Gibbs* authorization of pendent claim jurisdiction might have remained were it not for Congressional dissatisfaction with the Court's ultimate rejection of a parallel doctrine, pendent *party* jurisdiction. The situation arises when a plaintiff tries to append to a substantial federal question claim—for example, a claim under § 1983, Title VII, ADEA, or any of the other federal statutes prohibiting employment discrimination—a claim under state law against *another defendant*, again where the requirements of complete diversity of citizenship are lacking. The question is whether, even assuming the state law claim bears a sufficient factual nexus to the federal law claim to meet the *Gibbs* test of constitutional power, a court should exercise jurisdiction over a party "not named in any claim that is independently cognizable by the federal court."[4]

In *Finley*, the Court stated that "the Gibbs approach would not be extended to the pendent-party field" because "a [federal statutory] grant of jurisdiction over claims involving particular parties does not itself confer jurisdiction over additional claims by or against different parties." At the same time, the Court reaffirmed pendent claim jurisdiction as declared by *Gibbs*. The burden was on Congress, in other words, to spell out its willingness to confer subject matter jurisdiction to the full extent of its constitutional power with respect to pendent parties, though not with respect to pendent claims.

After *Finley*, a federal courts study committee recommended that Congress enact express statutory authority for pendent and other forms of ancillary jurisdiction. As part of the Judicial Improvements Act of 1990 Congress adopted a new statute[5] that provides for supplemental jurisdiction. As it relates to employment discrimination claims based on federal law, the first sentence of § 1367(a) declares that the federal district courts "shall have" supplemental jurisdiction "over all other claims that are so related" to the foundational federal law claims "that

---

3. *Carnegie–Mellon Univ. v. Cohill*, 484 U.S. 343, 108 S.Ct. 614, 98 L.Ed.2d 720 (1988).

4. *Finley v. United States*, 490 U.S. 545, 109 S.Ct. 2003, 104 L.Ed.2d 593 (1989).

5. 28 U.S.C.A. § 1367.

they form part of the case or controversy under Article III of the United States Constitution." Since the *Gibbs* test for constitutional power was an interpretation of Article III, this part of the new statute provides statutory confirmation for the *Gibbs* "common nucleus" approach to pendent claim jurisdiction. The second sentence of § 1367(a) changes the result of *Finley* by providing: "Such supplemental jurisdiction shall include claims that involve the joinder or intervention of additional parties." Thus there is now express statutory authorization for pendent party jurisdiction on the same relaxed "common nucleus" standard that *Gibbs* and § 1367(a)'s first sentence provide for pendent claim jurisdiction.[6]

But does this statute, the impetus for which was a desire to respond to *Finley* by providing congressional authorization for supplemental jurisdiction in pendent party situations, also, inadvertently or by design, liberalize the scope of pendent claim jurisdiction by restricting the circumstances under which federal judges may decline to exercise it? One such suggestion emerges from the first sentence of § 1367(a), which states that the district courts "shall have" supplemental jurisdiction over all state law claims that show the *Gibbs* relationship to the foundation claim based on federal law. When the Court in *Gibbs* sketched the contours of pendent jurisdiction, it carefully eschewed any such mandatory language.

A second such suggestion emerges from § 1367(c). This subdivision authorizes district courts to decline to exercise supplemental jurisdiction only in four specifically enumerated circumstances, rather than, as under *Gibbs*, for any reason not comporting with judicial economy, convenience, fairness or comity. The first three circumstances roughly track the particular examples mentioned in *Gibbs*: (1) the putative supplemental claim "raises a novel or complex issue of State law"; (2) it "substantially predominates over" the federal question claim on which federal subject matter jurisdiction is initially founded; and (3) the court has already dismissed the claims that gave it original jurisdiction—in *Gibbs* terms, the federal question claims proved insubstantial.[7]

But the fourth appears to restrict the district judges' discretion to decline supplemental jurisdiction somewhat more than the open-ended *Gibbs* reference to generalized considerations of efficiency, fairness, and federalism: the trial court may decline pendent jurisdiction only "(4) in *exceptional* circumstances, [when] there are other *compelling* reasons." (emphasis added). Taking their cue from the structure of the limited subdivision (c) exceptions to the supplemental jurisdiction that subdivision (a) says the district courts "shall have," lower courts have ruled

---

6. *See Ammerman v. Sween,* 54 F.3d 423 (7th Cir.1995) (upholding supplemental jurisdiction over state law assault claim against co-employee as sufficiently related to Title VII claim against employer).

7. *See Patel v. Penman,* 103 F.3d 868 (9th Cir.1996), *cert. denied,* 520 U.S. 1240,

117 S.Ct. 1845, 137 L.Ed.2d 1048 (1997) (district court properly exercised discretion to refuse supplemental jurisdiction over state law claim after dismissal of § 1983 claims and all Fair Housing Act claims, and state law claim substantially predominated over remaining constitutional claims).

that § 1367 creates a presumption in favor of supplemental jurisdiction unless one of the specific subdivision (c) exceptions applies.[8] On this reading of the statute the range of a district judge's discretion to decline to exercise supplemental jurisdiction has been so narrowed that a decision to do so may be overturned by mandamus.[9] But the pertinent House Report seems to deny this result. It states that § 1367 merely "codifies" the *Gibbs* factors, overrules *Finley* and allows for pendent party jurisdiction.[10]

§ 12.5   State Court Jurisdiction

Under the Supremacy Clause of the U.S. Constitution, state courts have a duty to enforce federal rights unless Congress, by declaring federal court jurisdiction to be original *and exclusive*, affirmatively divests state courts of their competence to hear such claims. None of the Reconstruction Civil Rights Acts, or the modern employment discrimination statutes, asserts that the original jurisdiction of the federal courts is exclusive. Accordingly, the Supreme Court has held that state courts have full concurrent jurisdiction over federal employment discrimination claims.[1] And they must exercise that jurisdiction without discrimination when it is properly invoked. The only "valid excuse" for refusing to do so is reliance on a neutral procedural policy that the state court applies to all kinds of claims, including those under state law—and occasionally even such a reason may be overridden if deemed inconsistent with a policy of federal law.[2]

Because of this concurrent jurisdiction, a plaintiff may choose to bring her employment discrimination claim in state or federal court.[3] The reasons for filing in state court are varied and depend on the environment of the state system under consideration.[4] For example, the

8. *Executive Software North Am., Inc. v. United States Dist. Court for Central Dist. of Cal.*, 24 F.3d 1545 (9th Cir.1994); *Growth Horizons, Inc. v. Delaware County*, 983 F.2d 1277 (3d Cir.1993).

9. *See Executive Software*, 24 F.3d 1545.

10. H.R.Rep.No. 713, 101st Cong., 2d Sess. 29 (1990) reprinted in 1990 U.S.C.C.A.N. 6802, 6875.

§ 12.5

1. *Howlett v. Rose*, 496 U.S. 356, 110 S.Ct. 2430, 110 L.Ed.2d 332 (1990) (§ 1983). Similarly, the Court has upheld concurrent jurisdiction in Title VII cases. Nothing in the legislative history indicating Congress' anticipation that most Title VII cases would be brought in federal court overcomes the presumptive jurisdiction of the state courts. Nor does the fact that a Title VII right to sue arises only after review by both state administrative agencies *and* the federal EEOC affect the question of what judicial forum should entertain the action. *Yellow Freight v. Donnelly*, 494 U.S.

820, 110 S.Ct. 1566, 108 L.Ed.2d 834 (1990).

2. *Howlett*, 496 U.S. 356, 110 S.Ct. 2430, 110 L.Ed.2d 332.

3. To capitalize on eased claim requirements, a plaintiff may wish to sue under a state civil rights statute, in either state or federal court. For example, the Minnesota Supreme Court has held that the Minnesota Human Rights Act's definitions of "discriminate" and "sexual harassment" relieve a plaintiff of the burden of making the *Oncale* showing, mandatory to prove a claim under Title VII, that same-sex sexual harassment was "because of sex." *Cummings v. Koehnen*, 568 N.W.2d 418, 424 (Minn.1997). *See* discussion of *Oncale* in § 2.22(a), *supra*.

4. For an excellent comprehensive discussion of the factors involved in choosing between state and federal court, see Steven H. Steinglass, *Section 1983 Litigation in State Courts*, Part B (1994).

assumed sympathies of a particular state court judge or jury pool, relative to predictions about the counterpart federal judge or jury, may attract the plaintiff; an elected state judge's potentially greater susceptibility to public opinion may be particularly important here. Other factors in deciding between state and federal court fall into three general categories: choice of law considerations, procedural or administrative differences, and doctrinal limitations on the federal courts.

The choice of law considerations are two-fold. First, a plaintiff who has not conclusively determined to bring suit under § 1983 may find that state law provides rights of action more congenial from the standpoint of proof or remedies.[5] Federal courts would only be able to entertain such state law claims (assuming they were not accompanied by claims under federal law and accordingly eligible for federal "supplemental" jurisdiction under 28 U.S.C. § 1367) if all plaintiffs and defendants happen to be of diverse citizenship and the sum of the claims against each defendant exceeds $75,000, thereby satisfying 28 U.S.C. § 1332(a)(1). Second, where a plaintiff is determined to pursue an employment discrimination claim, she must predict whether, on each likely determinative issue not yet authoritatively construed by the Supreme Court, a state or federal judge will offer the more favorable interpretation. For instance, if the plaintiff expects to use claim or issue preclusion offensively, he may more often prefer federal court, where offensive preclusion has received somewhat greater acceptance. Similarly, the employment discrimination plaintiff may find a more favorable construction of federal law in a state court exercising concurrent subject matter jurisdiction over that claim.[6] For the defendant, of course, these considerations weigh in the decision whether to remove once the plaintiff opts for a state forum.

5. A few examples will illustrate such substantive differences in state versus federal civil rights and employment discrimination claims. Title VII and cognate employment discrimination statutes have been construed by the federal courts to permit liability only against the employing entity, not individual defendants like supervisors, managers, or co-workers. See Chapters 2, 7, 8, 10, *supra.* State courts are free to, and sometimes do, construe their own human rights statutes (which would-be Title VII plaintiffs must usually exhaust as a prerequisite to suit) differently. *See Gordan v. Cummings,* Cum. 99–254 (Me. Sup.Judicial Ct. 2000) (relying on federal law decisions that limited employer liability in harassment cases as showing a need for the liability of individual defendants). *See also Zanni v. Medaphis Physician Servs. Corp.,* 240 Mich.App. 472, 612 N.W.2d 845 (2000) (permitting 31–year-old claimant to proceed with claim of "reverse" age discrimination, a theory generally rejected under the coun-

terpart federal Age Discrimination in Employment Act and which is limited to claimants at least 40 years old). *But see Reilly v. Alcan Aluminum Corp.,* 272 Ga. 279, 528 S.E.2d 238 (Sup.Ct. 2000) (declining to imply private damages action under state law for age discrimination or to create for age discrimination a public policy wrongful discharge exception to the doctrine of employment at will); *Carrisales v. Department of Corr.,* 90 Cal.Rptr.2d 804, 988 P.2d 1083 (Cal.Sup. Ct. 1999) (plaintiff's co-workers not personally liable under California Fair Employment and Housing Act, consistent with federal law); *Reno v. Baird,* 18 Cal.4th 640, 76 Cal.Rptr.2d 499, 957 P.2d 1333 (1998) (same re supervisors).

6. *But see Alberte v. Anew Health Care Servs Inc.,* No. 96–3325, 232 Wis.2d 587, 605 N.W.2d 515 (Sup.Ct.2000) (following the "vast majority" of federal courts that had rejected individual liability under the federal Americans With Disabilities Act).

State and federal court procedural and administrative differences also figure in the calculus. For example, less congested state court calendars may attract the plaintiff with the prospect of an earlier trial date. And if interim relief is important, plaintiff may choose a state system, which typically will support a larger number of judges who may decide such requests more quickly than their federal court counterparts. A party who prefers less judicial pretrial intervention may opt for state court to avoid the ever increasing involvement of federal district judges mandated by Rule 16 of the FRCP.[7] A state court may use a more liberal limitations accrual approach than the stringent one adopted by the Supreme Court (at least for a claim under state law),[8] and in federal law cases may apply a state law tolling rule more liberally than would a federal district court. Also, a plaintiff might have better odds in state than in federal court of surviving a motion for summary judgment if the state court does not follow the Supreme Court's *Celotex Corp. v. Catrett* and *Anderson v. Liberty Lobby* decisions that ease the defendant's burden in making the motion and increase the plaintiff's burden in resisting it.[9]

State courts also frequently offer more liberal relation back where plaintiff has named a "Doe" defendant.[10] State court policy may allow discovery to proceed in situations where federal courts would stay discovery—for example, while an immunity question is being resolved.[11] State rules of evidence may be more, or less, favorable than the federal

7. See, e.g., Richey, *Rule 16 Revised, and Related Rules: Analysis of Recent Developments for the Benefit of Bench and Bar,* 157 F.R.D. 69 (1994).

8. *See Romano v. Rockwell Int'l, Inc.,* 14 Cal.4th 479, 59 Cal.Rptr.2d 20, 926 P.2d 1114 (Cal.1996).

9. These decisions are discussed in § 12.25, *infra.*

10. *See, e.g., Wayne v. Jarvis,* 197 F.3d 1098, 1102–04 (11th Cir.1999), *cert. denied,* ___ U.S. ___, 120 S.Ct. 1974, 146 L.Ed.2d 804 (2000) ("John Doe" pleadings cannot be used to circumvent limitations statutes because replacement with named party effectively constitutes change in party sued, not "mistake" that can related back under F.R.C.P. 15(c)(3)(B)); *Barrow v. Wethersfield Police Dep't,* 74 F.3d 1366 (2d Cir. 1996), *modifying* 66 F.3d 466 (2d Cir.1995) (plaintiff's amendment substituting named officers for "John Doe" defendants not permitted to relate back when plaintiff was unable or unwilling to comply with court's directive, issued within the limitations period, to name individual officer defendants; in effect, decision narrowly reads 1991 amendment to F.R.C.P. 15(c), extending relation-back period where original pleading reflects a "mistake" concerning a defendant's identity as not applicable where unnamed defendant's identity is unknown) *Jacobsen v. Osborne,* 133 F.3d 315, 321 (5th Cir.1998) ("John Doe" complaint reflects no mistake that could relate back under Rule 15(c)(3)(B), but rather an inability to identify defendant); *Cox v. Treadway,* 75 F.3d 230, 240 (6th Cir.), *cert. denied,* 519 U.S. 821, 117 S.Ct. 78, 136 L.Ed.2d 37 (1996) (same); *Worthington v. Wilson,* 8 F.3d 1253, 1257 (7th Cir.1993) (lack of knowledge as to identity of defendant cannot be cured by relation back under 15(c)). *But see Varlack v. SWC Caribbean, Inc.,* 550 F.2d 171, 174–75 (3d Cir.1977) (implicitly holding before 1991 amendments to the Rule that plaintiff's lack of knowledge as to defendant's identity is a curable "mistake").

11. *Cf. Troupin v. Metropolitan Life Ins. Co.,* 169 F.R.D. 546 (S.D.N.Y.1996) (declaring in Title VII case, as a matter of federal common law, a "self-critical analysis" privilege that shields from discovery the evaluative, narrative, and analytical, but not the factual material of an employer's internal reports on diversity planning and results of employee survey). It is unclear if such decisions will be viewed to reflect substantive federal policy that is obligatory through Supremacy Clause preemption on state courts hearing federal employment discrimination and civil rights claims.

rules.[12] And state courts do not uniformly allow a defendant to limit his

12. Claims under the Reconstruction Acts and modern employment discrimination statutes are "federal question" claims within the meaning of 28 U.S.C.A. §§ 1331 & 1343; as such, federal rather than state common law governs questions of evidentiary privileges when those claims are brought in federal court. *See* Fed.R.Evid. 501. Most federal courts have rejected the physician-patient privilege, although many states recognize it. *See Patterson v. Caterpillar, Inc.,* 70 F.3d 503 (7th Cir.1995). On the other hand the Supreme Court has recognized a psychotherapist-patient privilege, one that is also recognized in some form by all fifty states. *Jaffee v. Redmond,* 518 U.S. 1, 116 S.Ct. 1923, 135 L.Ed.2d 337 (1996). In finding protection of confidential psychotherapist-patient communications sufficiently important to outweigh the ordinary need for probative evidence, the Court indicated it was obeying the Rule 501 command that federal courts "continue the evolutionary development of testimonial privileges." Further, it upheld the privilege broadly beyond psychiatrists and psychologists to include communications made to all licensed social workers. It recognized only the narrowest of possible exceptions, for example, in circumstances where a therapist's disclosure would be essential to avert serious harm to the patient or others.

Numerous courts have held that a plaintiff waives the psychotherapist-patient privilege by placing his or her medical condition at issue, particularly if the plaintiff seeks emotional distress damages. *See, e.g., Schoffstall v. Henderson,* 223 F.3d 818 (8th Cir. 2000); *Jackson v. Chubb Corp.,* 193 F.R.D. 216, 225 (D.N.J.2000); *Sarko v. Penn–Del Directory Co.,* 170 F.R.D. 127, 130 (E.D.Pa. 1997); *Vann v. Lone Star Steakhouse & Saloon,* Inc., 967 F.Supp. 346, 349–50 (C.D.Ill.1997); *EEOC v. Danka Indus., Inc.,* 990 F.Supp. 1138, 1142 (E.D.Mo.1997).

The requirement of Federal Rule of Civil Procedure 35 that an order directing a physical or mental examination of a party may be made only upon "good cause shown" is more restrictive than the counterpart rules of some states. *See O'Quinn v. New York Univ. Med. Ctr.,* 163 F.R.D. 226 (S.D.N.Y.1995) (refusing to order plaintiff to undergo a medical examination despite what the court termed her "boilerplate" allegation of "mental anguish, emotional distress, and humiliation"). *But cf. Lahr v. Fulbright & Jaworski, LLP,* 164 F.R.D. 204 (N.D.Tex.1996) (ordering plaintiff to submit to mental examination with respect to Title VII prayer for compensatory damages for emotional distress and related state law tort claim).

The Supreme Court has facilitated the admissibility of expert scientific testimony under Federal Rule of Evidence 702, holding that the trial judge may evaluate the validity of the reasoning and methodology underlying such testimony and admit it even if it did not enjoy widespread "general acceptance" in the relevant scientific community. *Daubert v. Merrell Dow Pharmaceuticals Inc.,* 509 U.S. 579, 113 S.Ct. 2786, 125 L.Ed.2d 469 (1993) (district court acts as gatekeeper and must determine that scientific evidence is relevant and reliable to be admissible). *See also Jenson v. Eveleth Taconite Co.,* 130 F.3d 1287 (8th Cir.1997), *cert. denied sub nom. Oglebay Norton Co. v. Jenson,* 524 U.S. 953, 118 S.Ct. 2370, 141 L.Ed.2d 738 (1998) (psychological testimony relating defendant employer's actions to emotional distress damages of plaintiff admissible under *Daubert*). While the *Daubert* decision only addressed scientific testimony, the Court subsequently applied the *Daubert* holding to technical and other specialized knowledge in *Kumho Tire Co., Ltd. v. Carmichael,* 526 U.S. 137, 119 S.Ct. 1167, 143 L.Ed.2d 238 (1999), holding that the *Daubert* reliability factors such as testing, peer review, error rates, and "acceptability" in the relevant scientific community, can be utilized by a district court in assessing the reliability of an engineering expert's testimony "to the extent relevant." *See also Sheehan v. Daily Racing Form,* 104 F.3d 940 (7th Cir.), *cert. denied,* 521 U.S. 1104, 117 S.Ct. 2480, 138 L.Ed.2d 989 (1997) (statistician's analysis of and affidavit about employer list showing ages of employees slated for retention did not meet *Daubert* standards for admissibility due to failure to account for relevant variables and other defects reflecting lesser degree of care than would be used in scientific work).

But neither F.R.E. 702 nor *Daubert* allows the admission of expert testimony that is not helpful to the jury or draws inferences or reaches conclusions that the jury is competent to reach without the expert's testimony. *See, e.g., Nichols v. American Nat'l Ins. Co.,* 154 F.3d 875, 884 (8th Cir.1998) (plain error to admit testimony that is a thinly veiled comment on a witness' credibility).

A district court's decision on admissibility of any evidence, including expert testimony, is reviewed for an abuse of discretion. *See Munoz v. Orr,* 200 F.3d 291, 301–302 (5th Cir.), *cert. denied,* ___ U.S. ___, 121 S.Ct.

exposure to large fee awards by using offers of judgment as authorized by FRCP Rule 68.

Federal doctrinal limitations, mostly jurisdictional or quasi-jurisdictional, may also encourage filing in state court. State courts may, for example, impose looser standing requirements. Unless the parties are completely diverse and over $75,000 is at stake, a state law claim similar to its federal employment discrimination counterpart but construed more liberally on a procedural point may survive only in a state court.[13] Further, state courts may provide the only avenue for damages relief against a state in view of the Supreme Court's rather restrictive interpretations of the Eleventh Amendment—although the state as such may no longer be sued under § 1983 in either state or federal court. A given state may authorize attorney's fee awards to be enhanced for contingency, at least on state law claims, contrary to the apparent view of the Supreme Court respecting claims under the Reconstruction Acts or Title VII.[14] And a plaintiff may choose state court because his action includes a colorable but tenuous pendent state law claim that a federal court might construe more narrowly because of its duty to decide in accordance with its prediction of the resolution that would be reached by the state's highest court.

§ 12.6 Removal

Because state courts enjoy concurrent jurisdiction over claims under modern employment discrimination statutes, it is important to consider whether the defendant may defeat plaintiff's initial forum choice by removing such an action from state to federal court. Almost any claim arising under the Reconstruction Acts, Title VII, ADEA, ADA and EPA is, at least when pleaded alone, removable under 28 U.S.C.A. § 1441(a). That statute provides for the removal of "any civil action ... of which the district courts of the United States have original jurisdiction" to the federal district court that embraces the venue of the pending action in state court.[1] Since original jurisdiction in virtually all actions in which an employment discrimination claim is asserted could have been founded

45, 148 L.Ed.2d 15 (2000) (no abuse of discretion to exclude testimony of expert who failed to consider significant variables other than national origin and gender); *General Elec. Co. v. Joiner,* 522 U.S. 136, 118 S.Ct. 512, 139 L.Ed.2d 508 (1997) (reversing Eleventh Circuit which applied a more stringent standard of review; "while the Federal Rules of Evidence allow district courts to admit a somewhat broader range of scientific testimony ... [after *Daubert*] than would have been admissible under *Frye,* they leave in place the 'gatekeeper' role of the trial judge in screening such evidence").

13. *See, e.g, Romano v. Rockwell Int'l, Inc.,* 14 Cal.4th 479, 59 Cal.Rptr.2d 20, 926 P.2d 1114 (Cal.1996) (regarding employ-

ment discrimination claim under California law, rejecting strict federal interpretation of "trigger" date for statute of limitations, under which charge-filing period begins to run when employee learns he will be discharged, holding instead that the clock does not start running until the employee is actually discharged).

14. *Rendine v. Pantzer,* 141 N.J. 292, 661 A.2d 1202 (N.J.1995). *See* § 11.10, *supra,* for the Supreme Court's dim view of contingency enhancement under the Civil Rights attorney's Fee Act, 42 U.S.C.A. § 1988.

§ 12.6

1. Except as otherwise provided by Congress. *See* 28 U.S.C.A. § 1441(a).

on § 1331,[2] the federal courts must also entertain these federal law claims, and, under § 1367, may also hear state law supplemental claims as well.[3] The first sentence of § 1441(b) confirms that because such actions contain at least one claim based on alleged violations of a federal constitutional or statutory right, they are "removable without regard to the citizenship or residency of the parties."[4]

As amended in 1991, § 1441(c) provides expansive authorization for the defendant to remove the "entire case," even when the federal civil rights or employment discrimination claim "is joined with one or more otherwise non-removable claims or causes of action."[5]

In *City of Chicago v. International College of Surgeons*,[6] the Court held that removal jurisdiction could be exercised over supplemental state law claims even when those claims called for a deferential review of state administrative findings. The Court clarified first, that when there is at least one federal claim (a claim arising under federal law under § 1331), all other transactionally related claims within the case fall within the federal court's supplemental jurisdiction as defined by § 1367.[7] Second, the Court rejected any suggestion that an exception to § 1367 exists for claims requiring a review of administrative findings.[8] Noting that district courts routinely conduct deferential review pursuant to their original jurisdiction over federal questions involving federal administrative actions, the Court stated that "[n]othing in § 1367(a) suggests district courts are without supplemental jurisdiction over claims seeking precisely the same brand of review of local [or state] administrative determinations."[9] The issue that must be decided by a district court, then, is whether the claim challenging the state administrative finding is properly within the district court's supplemental jurisdiction. The Court ac-

---

2. *See* § 12.1, *supra.*

3. A case falls with § 1331 original jurisdiction when, under the "well-pleaded complaint" rule, the plaintiff's own cause of action is based on federal law, *see Louisville & Nashville R.R. Co. v. Mottley,* 211 U.S. 149, 152, 29 S.Ct. 42, 43, 53 L.Ed. 126 (1908). Thus, a case may not be removed on the basis of a federal defense, at least when Congress has not completely preempted the field of law, such as ERISA. *See Rivet v. Regions Bank of La.,* 522 U.S. 470, 476–77, 118 S.Ct. 921, 925–26, 139 L.Ed.2d 912 (1998) (holding that although artful pleading doctrine may allow removal where federal law completely preempts a plaintiff's state-law claim, the affirmative defense of claim preclusion will not support removal jurisdiction) (citing *Metropolitan Life Ins. Co. v. Taylor,* 481 U.S. 58, 107 S.Ct. 1542, 95 L.Ed.2d 55 (1987) (ERISA) and *Avco Corp. v. Aero Lodge No. 735, Int'l Ass'n of Machinists and Aerospace Workers,* 390 U.S. 557, 88 S.Ct. 1235, 20 L.Ed.2d 126 (1968) (Labor Management Relations Act)).

4. Because the claim retains its federal character after removal from state court,

the characterization of the limitations period remains a question of federal law. Thus the same statute of limitations applies whether the § 1983 claim is heard in state or federal court. *Kuhnle Brothers, Inc. v. County of Geauga, Ohio,* 103 F.3d 516 (6th Cir.1997).

5. Subsection 1441(c) goes on to provide that, upon removal, "the district court may determine all issues therein, or, in its discretion, may remand all matters in which State law predominates."

6. 522 U.S. 156, 118 S.Ct. 523, 139 L.Ed.2d 525 (1997). *See also Lacks v. Ferguson Reorganized Sch. Dist. R–2,* 147 F.3d 718, 721 (8th Cir.1998), *cert. denied,* 526 U.S. 1012, 119 S.Ct. 1158, 143 L.Ed.2d 223 (1999) (relying on *Int'l Coll.* to uphold removal of case involving claim challenging school board's administrative finding).

7. *Id.* at 164–65, 118 S.Ct. at 529–30.

8. *Id.* at 166–67, 118 S.Ct. at 530.

9. *Id.* at 166, 118 S.Ct. at 530.

knowledged, however, that district courts, after exercising subject matter jurisdiction, may be "obligated not to decide state law claims (or to stay their adjudication) where one of the abstention doctrines ... applies."[10]

To grasp the rationale of these cases, recall that § 1441(a) sets out the threshold precondition to removal: that the action brought in state court be one "of which the district courts of the United States [would] have original jurisdiction." The scope of a federal district court's *original* jurisdiction includes not only questions based on federal law under § 1331, however, but also related state law claims under § 1367(a) and (c), as amended in 1990.[11] Section 1367(a) extends federal courts' supplemental jurisdiction to state law "claims that are so related to" the federal question claim or claims on which original jurisdiction is founded that they "form part of the same case or controversy under Article III." Further, the second sentence of § 1367(a) extends that supplemental jurisdiction to such transactionally related state law claims even when they are asserted against different *parties*, i.e., parties against whom the plaintiff asserts no claim under federal law. As a result, common state tort law claims like intentional infliction of emotional distress and negligent retention [of a supervisory or managerial employee] may be filed as "pendent," in the pre–1990 terminology, or "supplemental," in the argot of the current § 1367(a), to the federal question claim on which federal jurisdiction is founded, provided only they are transactionally related to the degree that Article III requires under the Court's opinion in *United Mine Workers v. Gibbs*.[12] Finally, § 1367(c) serves as a discretionary check on the jurisdiction available under subsection (a). It authorizes the district courts to decline jurisdiction over related state law claims where there are novel or complex state law issues; where state law predominates; where all claims founded on federal question jurisdiction have been dismissed, for example for failure to state a claim or on summary judgment; or under "exceptional circumstances" that present "compelling reasons" to decline to hear the state law claim.

Thus the federal district court in *International College* could adjudicate the state law claims challenging the administrative findings of the Landmark Commission under § 1367. And the mere presence of claims that are forbidden to the district court by a waivable defense such as Eleventh Amendment immunity (*Schacht*) or claim preclusion (*Rivet*) will not defeat the initial removal of the entire case because the court will then dismiss the claims that it is without power to hear.

Viewed in this light, what are the "otherwise non-removable claims" that 28 U.S.C.A. § 1441(c) says may be removed as part of "the entire case"? Essentially they are state law claims that are either insufficiently related, within the meaning of Article III or § 1367(a), to a jurisdictionally foundational federal question claim, or are sufficiently related but subject to discretionary dismissal under § 1367(c). The facial contrast

---

10. *Id.* at 174, 118 S.Ct. at 534.

11. See § 12.4, *supra.*

12. *Gibbs* is discussed in § 12.4, *supra.*

between § 1441(c) and § 1367(a) might suggest that the scope of federal removal jurisdiction in these situations is broader than the scope of federal original jurisdiction—in other words, that the employment discrimination defendant sued in state court has more recourse to federal court for ultimate trial and disposition of an entire action containing loosely related or unrelated state law claims than does the plaintiff who might wish to commence such an action in federal court. The contrast disappears, however, if the part of § 1441(c) that purports to authorize federal courts to hear removed state law claims that are "not otherwise removable" (because they are not part of the same Article III "case") is unconstitutional.[13] The only remaining respect in which federal question removal jurisdiction under § 1441 appears to exceed federal question original jurisdiction under § 1331 as supplemented by § 1367 is that § 1441(c) does not cabin the district judge's discretion to decline removal jurisdiction to the four circumstances spelled out in § 1367(c).

In the foregoing discussion we have been assuming, as is often true with employment discrimination claims between parties who have dealt with one another first-hand within one state, that not all requirements of the federal diversity statute, 28 U.S.C.A. § 1332, are satisfied. If, however, all plaintiffs are of diverse citizenship from all defendants, and if more than $75,000.00 is at stake, a federal court must exercise removal jurisdiction under § 1441(a) over *all* claims in the action, including those based on state law, whether or not they are interrelated.[14] Removal in "pure" diversity actions—those in which there is *no* claim founded on a federal question—is also possible,[15] but is limited by the second sentence of § 1441(b), which renders removal unavailable if any of the properly joined and served defendants is a citizen of the forum state.

Section 1446(b) provides that defendants must file a "notice of removal ... within thirty days after the receipt by the defendant, through service or otherwise, of a copy of the initial pleading." There had been some dispute whether the clock began to run when the defendant received a courtesy copy of the complaint without prior formal service of summons. The Supreme Court held that the thirty day time period does not begin to run unless a formal service of summons either precedes or accompanies the defendant's receipt of a copy of the complaint.[16]

---

13. To this extent, § 1441(c) would appear to be authorizing federal subject matter jurisdiction that breaks even the flexible bounds of Article III as declared by the Court in *Gibbs*. See 136 Cong.Rec. S17581 (daily ed. October 27, 1990) (analysis by Sen. Grassley) (suggesting that the removal court must remand an insufficiently related state law claim).

14. *See, e.g., Cemer v. Marathon Oil Co.*, 583 F.2d 830 (6th Cir.1978) (affirming that district court lacked discretion to dismiss state law claims where requirements of diversity are met).

15. *See Scheeler v. Crane Co.*, 21 F.3d 791 (8th Cir.1994) (civil rights employment claim under Iowa law).

16. *Murphy Bros., Inc. v. Michetti Pipe Stringing, Inc.*, 526 U.S. 344, 119 S.Ct. 1322, 143 L.Ed.2d 448 (1999).

§§ 12.7–12.9 Reserved

B. THE ELEVENTH AMENDMENT

§ 12.10 In General

Prior to the adoption of the Eleventh Amendment, the Supreme Court had interpreted the case and controversy language of Article III, § 2, which defined federal subject matter jurisdiction to include suits "between a State and Citizens of another state," to permit federal suits between those two parties based on pure diversity.[1] In response to that decision, Congress promptly enacted the Eleventh Amendment, ensuring some degree of state sovereign immunity in federal court.

The Eleventh Amendment provides that the "Judicial power of the United States shall not be construed to extend to any suit in law or equity, commenced or prosecuted against one of the United States by Citizens of another State, or by citizens of any foreign state." Applicable only to actions in federal court, the Eleventh Amendment bars suits against a state government by citizens of that state, other states, and foreign states.

The Supreme Court has expanded the scope of the Eleventh Amendment beyond its textual confines to apply to diversity actions involving state citizen plaintiffs, to federal questions, and to pendent claims. Coverage was extended to federal question jurisdiction in *Hans v. Louisiana*.[2] Based on the principle of sovereign immunity, the Court in *Hans* held that the Eleventh Amendment bars suits against a state government by its own citizens. Since by hypothesis original federal subject matter jurisdiction in an action against a state by one of its own citizens must be based on a federal question, one effect of *Hans* is to bar even federal question claims for damages that are asserted against a state by one of its own citizens. Further expansion occurred in *Pennhurst State Sch. & Hosp. v. Halderman*,[3] in which the Supreme Court held that the Eleventh Amendment bars federal courts from determining pendent state law claims.

The Supreme Court has limited the Eleventh Amendment to actions against the state, state officials sued in their official capacity, units of state government, or where a money judgment will be satisfied out of state funds. It does not immunize local government units as such.[4] Nor does the Eleventh Amendment bar a state court from exercising jurisdic-

§ 12.10

1. *Chisholm v. Georgia*, 2 U.S. (2 Dall.) 419, 1 L.Ed. 440 (1793).

2. 134 U.S. 1, 10 S.Ct. 504, 33 L.Ed. 842 (1890).

3. 465 U.S. 89, 121, 104 S.Ct. 900, 919, 79 L.Ed.2d 67 (1984).

4. *See e.g., Lincoln Co. v. Luning*, 133 U.S. 529, 530, 10 S.Ct. 363, 363, 33 L.Ed. 766 (1890) (counties); *Workman v. City of N.Y.*, 179 U.S. 552, 574, 21 S.Ct. 212, 220, 45 L.Ed. 314 (1900) (cities); *Mt. Healthy City Sch. Dist. Bd. of Educ. v. Doyle*, 429 U.S. 274, 97 S.Ct. 568, 50 L.Ed.2d 471 (1977) (municipalities, school districts); *but cf. Florida Dep't of Health & Rehabilitative Servs. v. Florida Nursing Home Ass'n*, 450 U.S. 147, 101 S.Ct. 1032, 67 L.Ed.2d 132 (1981) (state agencies protected).

tion over another state,[5] or bar the United States government from suing a state in federal court.[6]

The Eleventh Amendment will generally not bar suit, even if it otherwise applies, where the relief sought is wholly prospective, or the state has consented to federal suit, or a congressional act overrides the immunity. Although the state in its own name enjoys Eleventh Amendment protection, the ability to bring suit against a state official (other than in her individual capacity) depends primarily on the type of relief sought. Under the fiction of *Ex Parte Young*,[7] the Eleventh Amendment does not act as a bar to federal suits naming a state official as defendant so long as the relief sought is truly prospective. Under *Edelman v. Jordan*,[8] the Eleventh Amendment permits official capacity actions against individual state agents for prospective relief, even when implementation of the judgment would adversely impact the state treasury, but bars similar actions for relief a court deems retrospective, including compensatory damages and back pay.

State law, which should be borrowed as a matter of federal law so long as not inconsistent with federal policy, defines whether an official is considered an officer of the state and therefore immune from federal suit. Courts will interpret whether state law requires a state or local treasury to pay judgments rendered against its officials. In *Carr v. City of Florence, Alabama*,[9] Alabama law regarded the defendant, a county sheriff, as a state officer. The court presumed that the defendant was a state official because the plaintiff failed to present "clear evidence" that any judgment would be paid out of the local treasury rather than a state treasury. Under Florida law, however, a sheriff is considered a county official.[10] As a result, there is no presumption immunizing him. Instead, the defendant sheriff must provide evidence that the judgment would come from state funds rather than a local treasury. In some cases the characterization of the employing entity will be functionally rather than categorically defined. Thus sheriff's officials otherwise clearly county employees received Eleventh Amendment immunity from damages for actions in their official capacity when the court found that they were

5. *Nevada v. Hall*, 440 U.S. 410, 421, 99 S.Ct. 1182, 1188, 59 L.Ed.2d 416 (1979).

6. *United States v. Mississippi*, 380 U.S. 128, 140–41, 85 S.Ct. 808, 814–15, 13 L.Ed.2d 717 (1965).

7. 209 U.S. 123, 159–60, 28 S.Ct. 441, 454, 52 L.Ed. 714 (1909). *Seminole Tribe of Florida v. Florida*, 517 U.S. 44, 116 S.Ct. 1114, 134 L.Ed.2d 252 (1996), generally reaffirms the vitality of *Ex Parte Young* as permitting prospective injunctive relief against state officials for federal statutory, as well as constitutional, violations. But it also renders the *Young* exception unavailable where the plaintiff complains of the violation of a federal statute that contains its own detailed, administrative remedial scheme and remedies more limited than the full powers of a federal court, including

contempt, that would be brought to bear in an action pursuant to *Young. See* the discussion of *Seminole* and its implications *infra* this section. Lower federal courts have also ousted *Young*-based federal court injunction suits against state officials where there is no specification of threatened enforcement action by the defendants. *See, e.g., Children's Healthcare is a Legal Duty, Inc. v. Deters*, 92 F.3d 1412 (6th Cir.1996), *cert. denied*, 519 U.S. 1149, 117 S.Ct. 1082, 137 L.Ed.2d 217 (1997).

8. 415 U.S. 651, 94 S.Ct. 1347, 39 L.Ed.2d 662 (1974).

9. 916 F.2d 1521 (11th Cir.1990).

10. *See Hutton v. Strickland*, 919 F.2d 1531 (11th Cir.1990).

acting as an arm of the state;[11] but sheriffs acting as county rather than state agents could be sued for damages in federal court.[12]

The circuit courts consider a variety of factors in determining whether a state instrumentality like a local government, college or authority is entitled to Eleventh Amendment immunity. These include degree of local autonomy and control, the performance or not of central governmental functions, the instrumentality's power to sue or be sued, its separate corporate status, its ability to take property in its own name, and its capacity through bond-levy or taxing authority to raise its own operating funds.[13] The dominant factor has been whether the funds to satisfy a judgment would be derived from the state's treasury, and the Supreme Court agrees that liability for a money judgment is "of considerable importance."[14] An earlier Supreme Court decision, in denying immunity to a bi-state entity created under the Compact Clause, asserted that the touchstone is whether, under state law, a state will bear *financial* responsibility for an adverse judgment against the entity.[15] But the Court has subsequently clarified that a state subdivision's formal, legal responsibility for a judgment suffices to confer the immunity, even if the subdivision will be indemnified by a third party. It is the entity's "potential legal liability, rather than its ability or inability to require a third party to reimburse it, or to discharge the liability in the first instance, that is relevant."[16]

11. *See, e.g., Scott v. O'Grady*, 975 F.2d 366 (7th Cir.1992), *cert. denied*, 508 U.S. 942, 113 S.Ct. 2421, 124 L.Ed.2d 643 (1993) (while evicting tenants ancillary to a foreclosure action).

12. *See, e.g., Franklin v. Zaruba*, 150 F.3d 682 (7th Cir.1998), *cert. denied*, 525 U.S. 1141, 119 S.Ct. 1033, 143 L.Ed.2d 42 (1999) (Illinois law); *Ruehman v. Sheahan*, 34 F.3d 525 (7th Cir.1994) (Illinois law).

13. *See, e.g. Carter v. City of Philadelphia*, 181 F.3d 339 (3d Cir.), *cert. denied*, 528 U.S. 1005, 120 S.Ct. 499, 145 L.Ed.2d 385 (1999) (district attorney's office not an arm of the state for Eleventh Amendment purposes because the state would not pay judgments against the office and it was funded by defendant city, not treated as surrogate for the state under state law, and enjoyed considerable autonomy in its operations).

14. *Regents of the Univ. of Cal. v. Doe*, 519 U.S. 425, 429, 117 S.Ct. 900, 904, 137 L.Ed.2d 55 (1997); *Callahan v. City of Phila.*, 207 F.3d 668, 670 (3d Cir.2000) (dictum) (describing most significant factor as whether a judgment against an agency would be paid from the state's treasury); *Becker v. Univ. of Nebraska*, 191 F.3d 904, 908–909 (8th Cir.1999) (conferring 11th Amendment immunity in ADEA case on state university to protect state treasury

from liability that would have had "essentially the same practical consequences as a judgment against the State itself" ... (quoting *Doe*, 519 U.S. at 429–430).

15. *Hess v. Port Auth. Trans–Hudson Corp.*, 513 U.S. 30, 44–47, 115 S.Ct. 394, 403–404, 130 L.Ed.2d 245 (1994). The dissent in Hess would alternatively have conferred immunity if a state exercises political or governmental control over the defendant. *Id.* at 410–411 (O'Connor, J. dissenting). *See also Duke v. Grady Mun. Sch.*, 127 F.3d 972 (10th Cir.1997) (school district not an arm of the state where state would not be liable for a judgment against the district). *See Jones v. Washington Metro. Area Transit Auth.*, 205 F.3d 428, 432 (D.C.Cir. 2000) (permitting agency created by Congressional compact, and subscribed to by two states and the District of Columbia, to claim the immunity, in an ADEA case after *Kimel*, in order to protect the governments' treasuries).

16. *Regents of the Univ. of California v. Doe*, 519 U.S. 425, 429, 117 S.Ct. 900, 904, 137 L.Ed.2d 55 (1997). *But cf. Champagne v. Jefferson Parish Sheriff's Office*, 188 F.3d 312 (5th Cir.1999) (state agency enjoys the immunity more because it was state funded and within the government executive branch than because it had capacity to sue and be sued).

Even when the Eleventh Amendment otherwise applies, the action is against the state itself and the relief is characterized as retrospective, the Eleventh Amendment will not bar suit if a state is held to have consented to be sued in federal court. The Court has held that Congress intended no such consent when it enacted § 1983 in 1871, apparently because it was not until the Court's decision in *Monell* in 1978 that § 1983 was held to apply to cities or counties, let alone states.[17] In any event, the status of § 1983 under the Eleventh Amendment has been mooted by the Court's ruling that a state, when sued its own name or through an official capacity action seeking damages against one of its officials, is not a "person" suable under § 1983.[18] Accordingly, regardless of the relief sought, the state as such is simply not a proper § 1983 defendant in actions brought in either state or federal court. A court of appeals decision extends this principle by holding that a federal court may not remedy a civil rights violation by awarding a defendant county contribution against its state, notwithstanding a general right to contribution under § 1983.[19]

In *Will v. Michigan Dep't of State Police*,[20] the Supreme Court held, however, that a state official can be a defendant "person" within the meaning of § 1983, even when sued in her official capacity, to the extent that the relief sought against her is of the "prospective" kind allowed under the Eleventh Amendment jurisprudence exemplified by *Ex parte Young, Edelman*, and *Milliken*.[21] The *Will* bifurcated definition of the statutory term "person" as applied to the individual state official is evidently driven by and devolved from the 11th Amendment, yet in turn that definition renders the 11th Amendment largely beside the point in § 1983 actions against a state.

In one unusual situation where *Will* would ordinarily bar the § 1983 action of its own force, the Eleventh Amendment may still be important. A state might neglect to raise the *Will* objection until the case is on appeal. Since *Will* in essence furnishes a defense of legal insufficiency rather than lack of subject matter jurisdiction, defendant's failure to raise that defense during trial might result in its waiver.[22] Whether the Eleventh Amendment objection, in contrast, is deemed a matter of subject matter jurisdiction or a waivable, affirmative defense is unclear. The Court in *Edelman* indicated that the immunity was a jurisdictional bar that can be raised for the first time on appeal,[23] and, in a later case, that a defendant whose Eleventh Amendment dismissal motion fails may

17. *See Edelman* as explained by *Fitzpatrick v. Bitzer*, 427 U.S. 445, 456, 96 S.Ct. 2666, 2671, 49 L.Ed.2d 614 (1976); *cf. Quern v. Jordan*, 440 U.S. 332, 99 S.Ct. 1139, 59 L.Ed.2d 358 (1979), reaffirming *Edelman* on a different rationale.

18. *Will v. Michigan Dep't of State Police*, 491 U.S. 58, 109 S.Ct. 2304, 105 L.Ed.2d 45 (1989).

19. *Harris v. Angelina County, Tex.*, 31 F.3d 331 (5th Cir.1994).

20. 491 U.S. 58, 109 S.Ct. 2304, 105 L.Ed.2d 45 (1989).

21. *Id.* at 71 n.10, 109 S.Ct. at 2312 n.10.

22. *See* FRCP 12(h)(2).

23. *Edelman*, 415 U.S. at 677–78, 94 S.Ct. at 1362–63; *see* FRCP 12(h)(3).

seek immediate interlocutory review.[24] However, in *Wisconsin Dep't of Corr. v. Schacht,*[25] the Court stated that the immunity was subject to waiver and that a court could exercise subject matter jurisdiction if the state does not assert it—hardly a characteristic of a defense grounded in subject matter jurisdiction.

Sharply to be distinguished from § 1983 claims against a state, and from "official-capacity" actions against an individual state officer, are "personal-capacity" suits intended to establish the officer's individual liability. To the extent she is sued personally, a state official is a § 1983 "person" liable for all otherwise appropriate relief, including damages.[26] Further, as in similar suits against city or county officials, the plaintiff need not prove that the defendant's challenged conduct was undertaken as a matter of state "policy"; it suffices to prove that, acting under color of state law, she deprived the plaintiff of a federally protected right. On the other hand, unlike the entity or entity official defendant in an "official-capacity" suit, the personal-capacity defendant may invoke the affirmative defense of qualified immunity to avoid the relief of damages.[27]

The Court has articulated increasingly strict standards for ascertaining whether Congress has abrogated the states' immunity from retrospective relief in federal court, demanding unmistakable specificity and clarity.[28] The clear statutory statement the Court now demands as evidence of an intent to abrogate must reference "either the Eleventh Amendment or the States' sovereign immunity," rather than simply a class of defendants that expressly or by construction includes the states.[29] The Civil Rights Remedies Equalization Amendment of 1986[30] meets this test, expressly overriding what would otherwise be state immunity so as to permit federal courts to award retroactive relief,

24. *Puerto Rico Aqueduct and Sewer Auth. v. Metcalf & Eddy, Inc.,* 506 U.S. 139, 113 S.Ct. 684, 121 L.Ed.2d 605 (1993). The immediate reviewability of an order denying Eleventh Amendment immunity is an instance of the "collateral order" exception to the usual rule, under 28 U.S.C. § 1291, that limits the jurisdiction of the courts of appeals to "final decisions" of the federal district courts. But under *Swint v. Chambers County Comm'n,* 514 U.S. 35, 51, 115 S.Ct. 1203, 131 L.Ed.2d 60 (1995), other, nonfinal and hence ordinarily nonappealable orders may be addressed on interlocutory review of the denial of an Eleventh Amendment motion only if they raise issues "inextricably intertwined" with the appealable (e.g., Eleventh Amendment) decision, so that "review of the former . . . [is] necessary to ensure meaningful review of the latter." Applying that standard, an appellate court that rejected state officials' Eleventh Amendment defense also declined to hear their objection to plaintiff's standing, because "we may resolve the Eleventh Amendment immunity issue without reaching the merits of standing." *Summit Med. Assocs., P.C. v. Pryor,* 180 F.3d 1326, 1335 (11th Cir.1999), *cert. denied,* ___ U.S. ___, 120 S.Ct. 1287, 146 L.Ed.2d 233 (2000).

25. 524 U.S. 381, 389, 118 S.Ct. 2047, 2052–53, 141 L.Ed.2d 364 (1998).

26. *Will,* 491 U.S. 58, 109 S.Ct. 2304, 105 L.Ed.2d 45.

27. *Hafer v. Melo,* 502 U.S. 21, 112 S.Ct. 358, 116 L.Ed.2d 301 (1991).

28. *See, e.g., Atascadero State Hosp. v. Scanlon,* 473 U.S. 234, 238, 105 S.Ct. 3142, 3145, 87 L.Ed.2d 171 (1985).

29. *See, e.g., Dellmuth v. Muth,* 491 U.S. 223, 230, 109 S.Ct. 2397, 2401, 105 L.Ed.2d 181 (1989); *Welch v. Texas Dep't of Hwys. & Pub. Transp.,* 483 U.S. 468, 478, 107 S.Ct. 2941, 2948, 97 L.Ed.2d 389 (1987) (explicitly overruling *Parden v. Terminal Railway of Ala. State Docks Dep't,* 377 U.S. 184, 84 S.Ct. 1207, 12 L.Ed.2d 233 (1964)).

30. 42 U.S.C.A. § 2000d–7.

under, among other statutes, Title IX. And because Congress, citing its legislative authority under section five of the Fourteenth Amendment, amended Title VII to provide expressly for the liability of state (as well as local) governments, the Court in *Fitzpatrick v. Bitzer* found a valid Title VII override of the states' Eleventh Amendment immunity.[31]

But no matter how specifically Congress purports to override Eleventh Amendment immunity, the Supreme Court has held, in *Seminole Tribe of Florida v. Florida*,[32] that it lacks power to do so when it is acting only pursuant to the Commerce Clause, as distinct from the Fourteenth Amendment. Thus while *Ex Parte Young* still allows federal

---

31. *Fitzpatrick*, 427 U.S. 445, 96 S.Ct. 2666, 49 L.Ed.2d 614. Since *Fitzpatrick*, however, the Supreme Court has announced more stringent restrictions on Congress' power to abrogate the states' Eleventh Amendment immunity, even when it does so expressly, by legislating under section five of the Fourteenth Amendment. *City of Boerne v. Flores*, 521 U.S. 507, 117 S.Ct. 2157, 138 L.Ed.2d 624 (1997). The "congruence and proportionality" test of *Boerne* is discussed in Chapter 2 in connection with its holding that Congress lacked authority under the Fourteenth Amendment to apply the Religious Freedom Restoration Act to state or local governments. One circuit has reaffirmed the authority of *Fitzpatrick* notwithstanding *City of Boerne*, and even extended *Fitzpatrick* by specifically holding the disproportionate adverse impact provisions of Title VII, not just its core disparate treatment principle, as within Congress' § 5 authority. In *In Re Employment Discrimination Litigation Against the State of Ala.*, 198 F.3d 1305 (11th Cir.1999), the Eleventh Circuit acknowledged some "incongruence" between Title VII and the 14th Amendment because proving the disproportionate adverse impact of a neutral employment practice does not demand the same kind of proof of discriminatory intent that is essential to show a violation of the 14th Amendment's Equal Protection Clause. Nevertheless, the court deemed the disparate impact mode of proof, as devised by the Supreme Court in *Griggs v. Duke Power Co.*, 401 U.S. 424, 91 S.Ct. 849, 28 L.Ed.2d 158 (1971), and subsequently elaborated by case law and the 1991 Civil Rights Act amendments to Title VII, as preventative rules that target the same core injury, intentional discrimination, as the 14th Amendment. Further, the court observed that under Title VII, employers can defend practices that have disproportionate adverse impact merely by showing the practice job related and consistent with business necessity; they need not show the "compelling interest" that the Religious Freedom Restoration Act, struck down in *Boerne*, required to justify legislation adversely affecting religious free exercise. Hence the court viewed the "means" evidenced by Title VII's disparate impact proof mode as "neither incongruent with the purpose of preventing intentional discrimination in public employment, nor disproportionate to the injury to be avoided." 198 F.3d at 1323–1324. The *In Re Employment Discrimination Litigation* decision, however, was issued shortly before the Supreme Court decided *Kimel v. Florida Bd. of Regents*, 528 U.S. 62, 120 S.Ct. 631, 145 L.Ed.2d 522 (2000), discussed below, and the reasoning of *Kimel* may undercut the Eleventh Circuit's conclusion upholding under § 5 the disparate impact provisions of Title VII.

After *Boerne*, there has been considerable ferment in the lower federal courts respecting the validity of Congress' attempts to override Eleventh Amendment immunity under a number of civil rights statutes other than Title VII. The Supreme Court has resolved the circuit split concerning the 11th Amendment's application to claims against states based on the ADEA. In *Kimel v. Florida Bd. of Regents*, 528 U.S. 62, 120 S.Ct. 631, 145 L.Ed.2d 522 (2000), the Court held that Congress, while expressly purporting to overrule the states' immunity, did not do so validly. Applying the *City of Boerne* "congruence and proportionality" test for "appropriate" § 5 legislation, the Court concluded that ADEA prohibits considerable "rational" age discrimination not prohibited by the 14th Amendment as construed. Nor could ADEA be appropriate as reasonably prophylactic legislation, because viewing the legislative record of ADEA, the Court viewed its extension as "an unwarranted response to a perhaps inconsequential problem" of age discrimination by the States.

32. 517 U.S. 44, 116 S.Ct. 1114, 134 L.Ed.2d 252 (1996) (overruling *Pennsylvania v. Union Gas Co.*, 491 U.S. 1, 109 S.Ct. 2273, 105 L.Ed.2d 1 (1989)).

court suits for truly prospective relief against state officials, *Seminole* effectively extends *Hans v. Louisiana*'s ban on federal court suits (whether brought by citizens or noncitizens of the defendant state) against the states themselves. Even when those suits are based on federal question claims, the states are immune unless Congress in creating a given claim expressly overrode Eleventh Amendment immunity in a valid exercise of its Fourteenth Amendment, § 5 authority. In the wake of *Seminole*, lower federal courts have denied jurisdiction over private actions against states in federal court when they have concluded that the underlying statute is enacted pursuant only to Congress' authority under the Commerce Clause.[33] And the Supreme Court impliedly

33. The Supreme Court has confirmed the judgment of every circuit that considered the question that Congress may not validly abrogate the states' immunity from private suits under the Fair Labor Standards Act in federal court brought against them in their own name, even when brought in the state's own courts. *See Alden v. Maine*, 527 U.S. 706, 712, 119 S.Ct. 2240, 2246, 144 L.Ed.2d 636 (1999). Such suits may accordingly be brought, if at all, only by the Secretary of Labor on behalf of the United States. *See Abril v. Virginia*, 145 F.3d 182, 189 (4th Cir.1998); *Mueller v. Thompson*, 133 F.3d 1063, 1064 (7th Cir. 1998); *Powell v. Florida*, 132 F.3d 677, 678 (11th Cir.), *cert. denied*, 524 U.S. 916, 118 S.Ct. 2297, 141 L.Ed.2d 158 (1998); *Quillin v. Oregon*, 127 F.3d 1136, 1138 (9th Cir. 1997); *Close v. New York*, 125 F.3d 31, 36 (2d Cir.1997); *Mills v. Maine*, 118 F.3d 37, 48 (1st Cir.1997); *Aaron v. Kansas*, 115 F.3d 813, 814 (10th Cir.1997); *Raper v. Iowa*, 115 F.3d 623, 624 (8th Cir.1997); *Balgowan v. New Jersey*, 115 F.3d 214, 217 (3d Cir.1997); *Moad v. Arkansas State Police Dep't*, 111 F.3d 585, 587 (8th Cir.1997); *and Wilson–Jones v. Caviness*, 99 F.3d 203, 211 (6th Cir.1996), *amended on denial of reh'g*, 107 F.3d 358 (1997). Of course a private plaintiff FLSA suit against a state official seeking prospective relief only may still lie in federal court per *Ex Parte Young*.

In *Alden*, the claim brought against Maine in its own courts was based on the Fair Labor Standards Act, validly enacted pursuant to Congressional authority under Article I of the Constitution. Thus *Alden* does not specifically address whether the immunity of states from suit on federal claims in their own courts holds even when the predicate federal law statute was enacted pursuant to Congress' 14th Amendment, § 5 authority. Yet the reasoning of the opinion–that the states enjoyed immunity from suit in state court without their consent before the founding of the nation, and nothing in the Constitution alters that immunity–admits of no exceptions. After all,

Congress' 14th Amendment, § 5 ability to override what would otherwise be a state's 11th Amendment immunity from suit in federal court merely limits the force of an amendment to the Constitution, the Eleventh; it does not speak to the state's immunities predating the Constitution itself.

The circuits have held that there is no Eleventh Amendment immunity for suits brought under the Equal Pay Act, because that Act could have been passed pursuant to Congress's § 5 Fourteenth Amendment powers. *See O'Sullivan v. Minnesota*, 191 F.3d 965 (8th Cir.1999); *Anderson v. State Univ. of N.Y.*, 169 F.3d 117 (2d Cir.1999), *vacated for reconsideration after Kimel*, 528 U.S. 1111, 120 S.Ct. 929, 145 L.Ed.2d 807 (2000); *Varner v. Illinois State Univ.*, 150 F.3d 706 (7th Cir.1998), *vacated for reconsideration after Kimel*, 528 U.S. 1110, 120 S.Ct. 928, 145 L.Ed.2d 806 (2000); *Ussery v. Louisiana*, 150 F.3d 431 (5th Cir.1998); *Timmer v. Michigan Dep't of Commerce*, 104 F.3d 833, 838–40 (6th Cir.1997). One such decision was issued after and despite *Kimel. Hundertmark v. Florida Dep't of Transp.*, 205 F.3d 1272 (11th Cir.2000) (per curiam) (declaring that EPA's legislative record reflected findings of substantial gender-based workplace wage discrimination, acknowledging that such findings did not extend to the public sector, but asserting that no such findings are necessary because gender discrimination is a national problem).

Similarly, the circuits have concluded that states are not immune from federal court suits brought to vindicate rights granted by Titles VI and IX. *See, e.g., Fuller v. Rayburn*, 161 F.3d 516, 518 (8th Cir.1998) (Title VI); *Lesage v. Texas*, 158 F.3d 213, 217 (5th Cir.1998), *reversed on other grounds*, 528 U.S. 18, 120 S.Ct. 467, 145 L.Ed.2d 347 (1999) (Title VI); *Franks v. Kentucky Sch. for the Deaf*, 142 F.3d 360, 363 (6th Cir. 1998) (Title IX); *Crawford v. Davis*, 109 F.3d 1281 (8th Cir.1997) (Title IX).

affirmed such cases in *Florida Prepaid Postsecondary Educ. Expense Bd. v. College Saving Bank*, holding that Congress lacked the authority to abrogate states' immunity under the patent laws.[34] Thus, any question whether private plaintiff actions based on statutes passed solely pursuant to Commerce Clause authority and providing for exclusive federal court jurisdiction—antitrust, bankruptcy,[35] copyright,[36] patent, and cer-

---

Most circuits considering states' immunity to ADA suits in federal court prior to the Court's decision in *Kimel* had found that Congress expressly and validly abrogated their immunity. *See Garrett v. University of Ala. Bd. of Trustees*, 193 F.3d 1214 (11th Cir.1999); *Dare v. California*, 191 F.3d 1167, 1174 (9th Cir.1999), *petition for cert. filed*, Feb. 24, 2000 (holding that in enacting Title II of the ADA, Congress validly abrogated state sovereign immunity pursuant to its 14th Amendment Section 5 powers); *Martin v. Kansas*, 190 F.3d 1120, 1127 (10th Cir.1999) (holding that Congress's statutory abrogation of 11th Amendment immunity in ADA was a valid exercise of its Section 5 power to enforce the 14th Amendment); *Muller v. Costello*, 187 F.3d 298, 307–11 (2d Cir.1999) (holding that Congress successfully abrogated the states' immunity under the ADA); *Kimel v. State Bd. of Regents*, 139 F.3d 1426 (11th Cir.1998), *cert. granted sub nom., Florida Dep't of Corrections v. Dickson*, ___ U.S. ___, 120 S.Ct. 976, 145 L.Ed.2d 926 (2000) and *cert. dismissed*, ___ U.S. ___, 120 S.Ct. 1236, 145 L.Ed.2d 1131 (2000); *Coolbaugh v. Louisiana*, 136 F.3d 430, 432–38 (5th Cir.), *cert. denied*, 525 U.S. 819, 119 S.Ct. 58, 142 L.Ed.2d 45 (1998) (holding that "the ADA represents a proper exercise of Congress's Section 5 enforcement power under the 14th Amendment"); *Clark v. California*, 123 F.3d 1267, 1270–71 (9th Cir.1997), *cert. denied sub nom. Wilson v. Armstrong*, 524 U.S. 937, 118 S.Ct. 2340, 141 L.Ed.2d 711 (1998). See also *Torres v. Puerto Rico Tourism Co.*, 175 F.3d 1, 6 n. 7 (1st Cir.1999) (declining to address issue but stating in dicta "we have considered the issue of Congress's authority sufficiently to conclude that, were we to confront the question head-on, we almost certainly would join the majority of courts upholding the [abrogation] provision"); *Crawford v. Indiana Dep't of Corr.*, 115 F.3d 481, 487 (7th Cir. 1997). *But see Alsbrook v. City of Maumelle*, 184 F.3d 999 (8th Cir.1999), *cert. dismissed*, ___ U.S. ___, 120 S.Ct. 1265, 146 L.Ed.2d 215 (2000) (holding that Title II of the ADA was not a valid exercise of Congress's 14th Amendment Section 5 powers); *Brown v. North Carolina Div. of Motor Vehicles*, 166 F.3d 698, 702–10 (4th Cir.1999), *petition for*

cert. filed, Sep. 8, 1999 (holding that states' 11th Amendment immunity was not validly abrogated because Congress exceeded its Section 5 enforcement power in forbidding states, under the ADA, from charging a fee to disabled persons to cover the cost of accessibility programs).

Post-*Kimel* decisions, however, decide the issue the other way. *See Lavia v. Pennsylvania Dep't of Corrections*, 224 F.3d 190 (3d Cir.2000); *Stevens v. Illinois Dep't of Transp.*, 210 F.3d 732 (7th Cir.2000), *petition for cert. filed*, June 30, 2000; *Erickson v. Board of Governors*, 207 F.3d 945 (7th Cir.2000), *petition for cert. filed*, June 26, 2000 (abrogating *Crawford v. Indiana Dep't of Corrections*, 115 F.3d 481 (7th Cir.1997)). *See also Little Rock Sch. Dist. v. Mauney*, 183 F.3d 816 (8th Cir.1999) (Congress expressly and validly overrode states' immunity from actions under IDEA). The Supreme Court has granted certiorari to decide the issue. *See University of Alabama Bd. of Trustees v. Garrett*, ___ U.S. ___, 120 S.Ct. 1669, 146 L.Ed.2d 479 (2000). This is the third time the Court has granted certiorari on this issue, but certiorari was dismissed when the other two cases settled.

34. 527 U.S. 627, 119 S.Ct. 2199, 144 L.Ed.2d 575 (1999). Despite Congress' unmistakably clear attempt to abrogate the immunity under the patent laws, the court held it lacked the authority to do so pursuant to the commerce clause or legislation.

35. *See In re Sacred Heart Hosp. of Norristown*, 133 F.3d 237 (3d Cir.1998) (barring a suit against a state in bankruptcy court); *In re Estate of Fernandez*, 123 F.3d 241, 243 (5th Cir.), *amended*, 130 F.3d 1138 (5th Cir.1997); *In re Creative Goldsmiths of Washington, D.C., Inc.*, 119 F.3d 1140, 1145 (4th Cir.1997), *cert. denied sub nom. Schlossberg v. Maryland Comptroller of Treasury*, 523 U.S. 1075, 118 S.Ct. 1517, 140 L.Ed.2d 670 (1998); *In re NVR, LP*, 189 F.3d 442 (4th Cir.1999), *cert. denied sub nom. NVR Homes, Inc. v. Clerks of the Circuit Courts*, 528 U.S. 1117, 120 S.Ct. 936, 145 L.Ed.2d 815 (2000); *In re Tri–City Turf Club, Inc.*, 203 B.R. 617 (Bkrtcy. E.D.Ky.1996); *In re Lush Lawns, Inc.*, 203 B.R. 418 (Bkrtcy.N.D.Ohio 1996); *In re York–Hannover Devs., Inc.*, 201 B.R. 137,

tain environmental statutes among others—may proceed against states or state instrumentalities in *any* forum has been answered by the Court—Congressional Article I attempts to make states amenable to suit will inevitably fail.

To an as yet uncertain degree, the *Seminole* decision also curtails federal court actions against state officials, the most common vehicle for enforcing compliance with federal law. The Court subjected an *Ex Parte Young* claim against Florida officials to its more general doctrine that disfavors implied private rights of action under federal statutes.[37] It seems unlikely, however, that either *Seminole* holding will have any effect on the vast majority of actions under § 1983, namely those based on a violation of the federal constitution.[38] Even before *Seminole*, it was clear that no § 1983 claim (based on a federal constitutional violation or an "and laws" claim based on violation of a federal statute) lies in any forum against a state in its own name. Such claims failed when brought in federal court because the Fourteenth Amendment Congressional override in § 1983 is insufficiently express.[39] Subsequently, in 1989, the Court held more broadly that no § 1983 claim against a state in its own name lies in any court, state or federal, because the 1871 Congress did not intend the defined defendant "person" to include a sovereign state.[40]

So the more vital, and shaded question is whether the second *Seminole* holding—that *Ex Parte Young* claims against state officials based on predicate violations of federal statutes may be precluded if the particular predicate statute contains a detailed or comprehensive remedial scheme that omits private rights of action—will restrict § 1983 (or *Bivens*)[41] claims against state (or federal) officials. Constitutionally-based claims against those officials should not be at all impaired. Unlike the statute at issue in *Seminole*, § 1983 expressly authorizes a private judicial action for damages and equitable relief. The same 1989 decision that deemed states *eo nominee* as unsuable non-"persons" specifically

140 (Bkrtcy.E.D.N.C.1996); *In re Midland Mechanical Contractors, Inc.*, 200 B.R. 453, 457–58 (Bkrtcy.N.D.Ga.1996); *In re Burke*, 200 B.R. 282, 286 (Bkrtcy.S.D.Ga.1996); *In re Martinez*, 196 B.R. 225, 230 (D.P.R. 1996). *But cf. In re Headrick*, 200 B.R. 963 (Bkrtcy.S.D.Ga.1996), *aff'd*, 146 F.3d 1313 (11th Cir.1998), *cert. denied*, 527 U.S. 1043, 119 S.Ct. 2410, 144 L.Ed.2d 808 (1999) (by filing proof of bankruptcy claim, state waived immunity).

36. *See Chavez v. Arte Publico Press*, 157 F.3d 282, 291 (5th Cir.1998), *vacated for reconsideration in light of College Sav. Bank and Florida Prepaid Postsecondary Educ. Expense Bd.*, 180 F.3d 674 (5th Cir. 1999) (*Seminole* condemns Congress's effort to force unconsenting states into federal court as the price of doing business regulated by the Lanham and Copyright Acts). *See also College Sav. Bank v. Florida Prepaid Postsecondary Educ. Expense Bd.*, 527 U.S.

666, 119 S.Ct. 2219, 144 L.Ed.2d 605 (holding state immune under Lanham Act).

37. The Court found the suit displaced by the extremely limited, but specific remedial provisions of the Indian Gaming Regulatory Act, which did not include private judicial actions.

38. And at least one circuit has found that *Seminole* has no effect on claims brought under §§ 1981 and 1985 as well. *See Ellis v. University of Kansas Med. Ctr.*, 163 F.3d 1186, 1195–98 (10th Cir.1998).

39. *Quern v. Jordan*, 440 U.S. 332, 99 S.Ct. 1139, 59 L.Ed.2d 358 (1979).

40. *Will v. Michigan Dep't of State Police*, 491 U.S. 58, 71, 109 S.Ct. 2304, 2312, 105 L.Ed.2d 45 (1989).

41. *Bivens v. Six Unknown Named Agents of Fed. Bureau of Narcotics*, 403 U.S. 388, 91 S.Ct. 1999, 29 L.Ed.2d 619 (1971).

referenced *Ex Parte Young* in noting that § 1983 does subject state officials sued in their official capacity to prospective relief to cure constitutional violations.[42] Subsequently, the Court held state officials liable in damages under § 1983 for constitutional violations when named in their personal capacities.[43] Put otherwise, however important *Ex Parte Young* may have been in 1908 as the source of an implied private, judicially enforceable claim against state officers behaving unconstitutionally, § 1983 now stands as an independent source of that claim.

Bivens actions (for constitutional violations by federal officials) are somewhat more vulnerable to implied preclusion a la *Seminole*. First, no statute expressly provides a private judicial action for such claims. Second, it might be argued that § 1983, by providing a right of action for constitutional violations against state actors, precludes a similar claim against federal actors. But that argument, fully aired by the *Bivens* dissent, was rejected by a majority of the Court. And because the federalism/state sovereignty undertone of *Seminole* is missing in the *Bivens* context, it seems even more doubtful that *Seminole* should be read to overrule that quarter-century-old precedent sub silentio.

But what of § 1983 "and laws" claims—those that use the remedial vehicle of § 1983 to vindicate violations of other federal statutes?[44] After all, those claims, asserting an implied private right of action based on federal statutory violations, are commonly directed against state officials—just like the claim at issue in *Seminole* under the Indian Gaming Regulatory Act against the governor of Florida. Nevertheless, the effect of *Seminole* on such claims should be felt, if at all, only at the margins. Even before *Seminole*, the Court had developed a line of authority that precludes an "and laws" claim if the detail or comprehensiveness of the predicate statute's remedial scheme makes it unlikely that Congress would favorably countenance a supplementary private judicial action under § 1983. *Seminole*, then, may come into play more as authority for a strict application of this implied remedial preclusion doctrine than as an independent limitation on § 1983 claims based on the violation of federal statutes.

Attorney's fees in civil rights and employment discrimination cases are wholly outside the strictures of the Eleventh Amendment. Under 42 U.S.C.A. § 1988, such fees are considered compensation for "expenses incurred in litigation seeking only prospective relief," instead of "retroactive liability for prelitigation conduct."[45] attorney's fees against a state are available to the prevailing party based on his degree of success on any "significant" issue that "changes the legal relationship between [the plaintiff] and the defendant."[46] In addition, such an award can include

---

42. *Will*, 491 U.S. at 71 n.10.

43. *Hafer v. Melo*, 502 U.S. 21, 112 S.Ct. 358, 116 L.Ed.2d 301 (1991).

44. These claims, and their possible preclusion if a court deems the remedial scheme of the predicate statute sufficiently

detailed or comprehensive, are discussed in § 2.50.

45. *Hutto v. Finney*, 437 U.S. 678, 695, 98 S.Ct. 2565, 2576, 57 L.Ed.2d 522 (1978).

46. *Texas State Teachers Ass'n v. Garland Indep. Sch. Dist.*, 489 U.S. 782, 792,

prejudgment interest, or a fee enhancement, for delay in payment based on current market rates rather than those rates relevant at the time the legal services were rendered.[47]

The Eleventh Amendment as construed in *Seminole*, then, prohibits federal courts from exercising jurisdiction over private party suits under Article I statutes against states sued in their own names. But may the states be sued on such statutes in their own courts? In *Alden v. Maine*,[48] the Court held that Congress cannot, by legislating pursuant to its Article I powers, override the immunity that a nonconsenting state enjoyed before the Constitutional Convention from suits in its own courts. Thus a nonconsenting state or state subentity may not be sued by a private party on federal claims, any more than on state claims, in its own courts.[49] Accordingly, unless a state waives its immunity from suit in its own courts or the federal courts, the judicial means of compelling a state to obey a federal statute enacted solely on Congress' Article I authority are rather limited. First, an aggrieved party may seek compensatory relief if she can prevail on the relevant federal official to bring suit against the state in federal court in the name of the United States, an option existing before and indirectly reaffirmed by *Alden*.[50] Second, a private party may bring suit herself in federal court by naming as defendant a state official and contenting herself with prospective relief under the umbrella of *Ex Parte Young*, to the extent that a *Young* claim based on a federal statute survives implied preclusion under the second holding of *Seminole Tribe*. Third, she may sue in federal court for compensatory relief against the state official in his individual capacity, although in such an action the relief must be sought from the officer personally, and not from the state treasury.[51]

§§ 12.11–12.14 Reserved

C. STANDING

§ 12.15 In General

Article III of the U.S. Constitution confines the federal judiciary to hearing actual "cases or controversies." The contemporary, judicially

---

109 S.Ct. 1486, 1493, 103 L.Ed.2d 866 (1989).

47. *Missouri v. Jenkins*, 491 U.S. 274, 109 S.Ct. 2463, 105 L.Ed.2d 229 (1989).*See Jones v. Washington Metro. Area Transit Auth., See Jones v. Washington Metro. Area Transit Auth.*, 205 F.3d 428, 432 (D.C.Cir. 2000) (Congress expressly and validly abrogated states' Eleventh Amendment immunity respecting prejudgment interest on back pay in enacting Title VII).

48. 527 U.S. 706, 119 S.Ct. 2240, 144 L.Ed.2d 636 (1999).

49. *Id.* at 712, 119 S.Ct. at 2246. The Court distinguished *Nevada v. Hall*, 440 U.S. 410, 99 S.Ct. 1182, 59 L.Ed.2d 416 (1979), wherein the state of Nevada was sued in a California state court. The Court explained that the Constitution did not reflect "an agreement between the states to respect" one another's sovereign immunity; only an agreement between states or the principle of comity could immunize one state from suit in another's courts. *Alden*, 527 U.S. at 738–39, 119 S.Ct. at 2259–60.

50. *See Alden*, 527 U.S. at 756, 119 S.Ct. at 2267.

51. *Id.* at 757, 119 S.Ct. at 2267–68.

elaborated jurisprudence of standing, however, has both constitutional and "prudential," that is, judicially self-imposed, components. All these elements of standing are treated by the Court as jurisdictional, and as such a federal court will usually decide a defendant's challenge to standing at the outset of a case, often on the basis of the plaintiff's pleadings.[1] Further, upon challenge by the defendant, the burden is on the plaintiff to prove the requisite jurisdictional facts. Standing is thus a potentially crippling roadblock to a federal court plaintiff who is unable to demonstrate the substantive requirements of standing doctrine without benefit of discovery.[2]

The constitutional dimension of standing doctrine requires that the plaintiff allege personal "injury in fact" that is "fairly traceable" to the allegedly unlawful acts of the defendant and "likely to be redressed" by the requested relief.[3] The injury in fact requirement ordinarily requires the plaintiff to allege and show personal harm that is "(a) concrete and particularized, and (b) actual or imminent, not conjectural or hypothetical."[4] An asserted right to have the government act in accordance with law is not sufficient. It has sometimes been held that even the stigmatizing injury of racial discrimination is insufficient unless plaintiffs have

---

§ 12.15

1. Despite the characterization of standing as "jurisdictional" for purposes of the original subject matter jurisdiction of the federal district courts, a federal circuit court may lack pendent appellate jurisdiction to conduct interlocutory review of a standing issue presented together with a nonfinal decision that is eligible for interlocutory review under the "collateral order" exception to the usual rule, under 28 U.S.C. § 1291, that limits the jurisdiction of the courts of appeals to "final decisions" of the federal district courts .. The immediate reviewability of an order denying Eleventh Amendment immunity, for example, is an instance of the "collateral order" exception. But under *Swint v. Chambers County Comm'n*, 514 U.S. 35, 51, 115 S.Ct. 1203, 131 L.Ed.2d 60 (1995), other, nonfinal and hence ordinarily nonappealable orders may be addressed on interlocutory review of the denial of an Eleventh Amendment motion only if they raise issues "inextricably intertwined" with the appealable (e.g., Eleventh Amendment) decision, so that "review of the former ...[is] necessary to ensure meaningful review of the latter." Applying that standard, an appellate court that rejected state officials' Eleventh Amendment defense also declined to hear their objection to plaintiff's standing, because "we may resolve the Eleventh Amendment immunity issue without reaching the merits of standing." *Summit Med. Assocs., P.C. v. Pryor*, 180 F.3d 1326, 1335 (11th Cir.1999), *cert. denied*, ___ U.S. ___, 120 S.Ct. 1287, 146 L.Ed.2d 233 (2000). *See also Moniz v. City of Ft. Lauderdale*, 145 F.3d 1278, 1281 (11th Cir.1998) (because qualified immunity issue could be resolved without reaching the merits of appellants' challenge to plaintiff's standing, the jurisdictional standing issue not within pendent appellate jurisdiction).

2. *Allen v. Wright*, 468 U.S. 737, 104 S.Ct. 3315, 82 L.Ed.2d 556 (1984).

3. *Id.*

4. *Lujan v. Defenders of Wildlife*, 504 U.S. 555, 559, 112 S.Ct. 2130, 2136, 119 L.Ed.2d 351 (1992) (citations, footnote, and internal quotations omitted). *See also Rizzo v. Goode*, 423 U.S. 362, 96 S.Ct. 598, 46 L.Ed.2d 561 (1976); *City of L.A. v. Lyons*, 461 U.S. 95, 103 S.Ct. 1660, 75 L.Ed.2d 675 (1983). Thus a lawyer who objected that his ability to practice law might be impeded by a religious sign over the entrance to a county courthouse (because he would not represent clients whose cases would be heard there) lacked standing where his practice was based elsewhere, he had never seen the courthouse in question and had no plans to open an office in that county, and could identify no case which had required or would require his presence there. *Doe v. County of Montgomery*, 41 F.3d 1156 (7th Cir.1994). But the Supreme Court has held that on a motion to dismiss, general factual allegations of injury may suffice. *National Org. for Women, Inc. v. Scheidler*, 510 U.S. 249, 255, 114 S.Ct. 798, 803, 127 L.Ed.2d 99 (1994) (citing *Lujan*).

personally been denied equal treatment.[5] Even where a serious, personal, economic or non-economic injury is properly alleged, the injury must be "fairly traceable" to the challenged government conduct—a constitutional requirement of causation.[6] Finally, even if a plaintiff properly alleges injury to herself or her class that is traceable to the defendant's conduct, she still lacks standing if the requested relief is unlikely to redress that injury.[7]

The issue of standing most often arises in employment discrimination cases when "testers" are used to ferret out evidence of unlawful discrimination in hiring and job referrals. The chief argument against standing in such cases is that the tester—the person, usually well qualified, who on behalf of EEOC or a private organization promoting equality of opportunity in employment presents himself to the employer or employment agency—has suffered no concrete injury for lack of any bona fide interest in an advertised position. The key question is whether the Title VII right sought to be enforced in a given case describes an aggrieved person in terms sufficiently broad to embrace the particular plaintiff. How the answer may varying depending upon the identity of the plaintiff and the relief sought is nicely illustrated by a District of Columbia Circuit's panel opinion.

The plaintiff group in *Fair Employment Council of Greater Washington* included two African-American employment testers—"equipped with fake credentials intended to be comparable" to those of the two white testers with whom they were paired—and the Fair Employment Council. The defendant employment agency had allegedly denied the African-American testers employment referrals that it gave to the white testers. An alleged "pattern" of racial discrimination against other applicants for referral assertedly made it more difficult for the plaintiff Council to carry out its goal of promoting equal opportunity in the community.

The court first rejected both the testers' and the Council's claims under § 1981. The testers, the court found, could not state a claim under that statute, which gives a cause of action only to persons deprived of what would otherwise be a legal right to make or enforce a contract. The testers could not have enforced a contract offering them employment because they had to make material misrepresentations of fact about their intentions to secure employment in order to induce the defendant employment agency to make referrals. What they really lost was only "the opportunity to enter into a *void* contract—i.e., a contract that *neither* party can enforce." That, the court wrote, "is not an injury cognizable under Sec. 1981, for a void contract is a legal nullity."[8] As

5. *Allen*, 468 U.S. 737, 104 S.Ct. 3315, 82 L.Ed.2d 556.

6. *See Simon v. Eastern Ky. Welfare Rights Org.*, 426 U.S. 26, 38, 96 S.Ct. 1917, 1924, 48 L.Ed.2d 450 (1976).

7. *Allen*, 468 U.S. at 752; *Goode*, 423 U.S. 362, 96 S.Ct. 598, 46 L.Ed.2d 561.

8. *Fair Employment Council of Greater Washington v. BMC Marketing Corp.*, 28 F.3d 1268 (D.C.Cir.1994). *But cf. Watts v. Boyd Properties*, 758 F.2d 1482 (11th Cir. 1985) and *Meyers v. Pennypack Woods Home Ownership Ass'n*, 559 F.2d 894 (3d Cir.1977), *overruled on other grounds by Goodman v. Lukens Steel Co.*, 777 F.2d 113

observed above,[9] the Council's § 1981 claim failed on prudential standing grounds. Only direct victims of an unlawful denial of the right to make or enforce a contract have standing to assert claims under that statute.[10]

The court was more equivocal about the standing of the individual testers to assert claims under Title VII. While expressly declining to decide whether testers lack standing because they have no bona fide interest in an employment position,[11] the court wrote that in general the Title VII scheme is more analogous to the Fair Housing Act provisions found to support standing in *Havens* than to the stricter requirements of § 1981. Nevertheless, the testers' claims were barred. Their claim for damages failed because only equitable relief was available under Title VII for violations that occurred before the effective date of the Civil Rights Act of 1991. To be eligible for prospective relief, they would have had to make "sufficient allegations that they are threatened with ... future illegality." That they could do only by showing a likelihood that the defendant agency would infringe their Title VII rights again, not simply that they would continue to suffer the ill effects of its alleged past violations. And how could they make such a case on the pleadings, even before discovery? It would be sheer "speculation" for them to allege that a future violation of their rights was probable, because that would depend—as it always will—upon matters within the defendant's control and knowledge.[12]

The Council fared somewhat better. Constitutional injury in fact was satisfied by its allegations that the defendant's conduct impaired the Council's ability to assist minorities in finding jobs, thereby undermining the effectiveness of its outreach efforts. Further, Title VII's plaintiff definition provided prudential standing "to the extent that the effects of ... [the defendant's] discrimination have perceptibly impaired ... [the plaintiff's] programs." The court reached this conclusion in reliance on the language of Title VII that authorizes suit by any "person claiming to be aggrieved" by an unlawful employment practice.[13] Under such a statute, a person injured by conduct that violates its own or another's rights—that is, a person who suffers Article III injury in fact—also survives the prudential restrictions on standing. If the distinctions drawn by this decision ultimately prevail, EEOC's testers may ultimately be found to have standing to sue with respect to discriminatory job referrals, but not discriminatory refusals to hire.[14] Yet a considerably

---

(3d Cir.1985), *aff'd*, 482 U.S. 656, 107 S.Ct. 2617, 96 L.Ed.2d 572 (1987) (according fair-housing testers standing to sue under §§ 1982 and 1981, respectively, although not squarely addressing question whether the testers had suffered legal injury within the meaning of those statutes).

9. *See* text *supra*.

10. *Fair Employment Council*, 28 F.3d at 1280.

11. *Id.* at 1280 n.1.

12. *Id.* at 1272. *See also Goff v. Harper*, 60 F.3d 518 (8th Cir.1995) (because recurrence of alleged violation was speculative, irreparable injury requirement for injunctive relief lacking).

13. 42 U.S.C.A. § 2000e–2(b).

14. *See Sledge v. J.P. Stevens & Co.*, 585 F.2d 625, 641 (4th Cir.1978), *cert. denied*, 440 U.S. 981, 99 S.Ct. 1789, 60 L.Ed.2d 241 (1979) (tester plaintiffs not harmed by refusal to hire for lack of serious

greater number of circuits have upheld Title VII standing by focusing on the significant differences in text and purpose between § 1981 and Title VII. The former protects only the right without regard to race to enter into and enforce a contractual relationship; the latter, prohibiting a wide range of discriminatory employment practices, accords a substantive right to "any person claiming to be aggrieved" to be free from practices that attempt "to limit, segregate or classify" applicants and which "in any way ... would deprive or tend to deprive any individual" of employment opportunities. Thus while a tester's lack of interest in actually working for the defendant will limit the nature and extent of his injuries and consequently appropriate relief, it does not preclude relief for humiliation, embarrassment and like injuries that typically stem from discrimination.[15] Standing for testers under § 1981 also suffers by comparison with cases that have upheld standing for § 1983 plaintiffs who challenged race-based denials of public accommodations that they sought solely in order to initiate litigation.[16] The public accommodations tester actually uses, or attempts, to use those accommodations; the § 1981 tester, by contrast, is not attempting to form a contract or therefore to exercise the limited[17] right protected by that statute.

A related question concerns the standing of those who argue that a defendant having no direct employment relationship with the plaintiff interfered with the plaintiff's employment relationship with a third party. The circuits that have directly confronted the question have recognized standing in this situation.[18] These courts reason that while

interest in job, and hence lack standing); *Parr v. Woodmen of the World Life Ins. Soc'y,* 657 F.Supp. 1022 (M.D.Ga.1987) (plaintiff held ineligible to prosecute suit when court found he was not genuinely seeking employment but instead simply manufacturing the basis for a Title VII violation; the statutory provision in question, 42 U.S.C.A. § 2000e–2(a) (1), created a right to nondiscriminatory hiring, a violation the court found the plaintiff could not have suffered) and *Hailes v. United Air Lines,* 464 F.2d 1006 (5th Cir.1972) (in dictum denying possibility of suit against an employer that published an advertisement containing an unlawful discriminatory preference if the plaintiff had been a mere reader of the advertisement rather than, as was the case, a reader who actually applied for employment; the particular Title VII provision at issue, 42 U.S.C.A. § 2000e–3(b), did not specifically define the person aggrieved).

15. *Kyles v. J.K. Guardian Sec. Servs., Inc.,* 222 F.3d 289, 300 (7th Cir.2000). *See Anjelino v. New York Times Co.,* 200 F.3d 73, 91 & n. 25 (3d Cir.1999); *EEOC v. Mississippi College,* 626 F.2d 477, 482–83 & n. 7 (5th Cir.1980), *cert. denied,* 453 U.S. 912, 101 S.Ct. 3143, 69 L.Ed.2d 994 (1981); *EEOC v. Bailey Co.,* 563 F.2d 439, 452–454

(6th Cir.1977), *cert. denied,* 435 U.S. 915, 98 S.Ct. 1468, 55 L.Ed.2d 506 (1978); *Waters v. Heublein, Inc.,* 547 F.2d 466, 469–470 (9th Cir.1976), *cert. denied,* 433 U.S. 915, 97 S.Ct. 2988, 53 L.Ed.2d 1100 (1977); *Gray v. Greyhound Lines, East,* 545 F.2d 169, 176 (D.C.Cir.1976). *See Trafficante v. Metropolitan Life Ins. Co.,* 409 U.S. 205, 209, 93 S.Ct. 364, 366–67, 34 L.Ed.2d 415 (1972).

16. *See Pierson v. Ray,* 386 U.S. 547, 558, 87 S.Ct. 1213, 1219–20, 18 L.Ed.2d 288 (1967) and *Evers v. Dwyer,* 358 U.S. 202, 79 S.Ct. 178, 3 L.Ed.2d 222 (1958) (both upholding standing to test right to use unsegregated public accommodations).

17. *Kyles v. J.K. Guardian Sec. Servs., Inc.,* 222 F.3d 289, 304 (7th Cir.2000).

18. *See, e.g., Bender v. Suburban Hosp. Inc.,* 159 F.3d 186, 188 (4th Cir.1998); *Christopher v. Stouder Mem'l Hosp.,* 936 F.2d 870, 874–75 (6th Cir.), *cert. denied,* 502 U.S. 1013, 112 S.Ct. 658, 116 L.Ed.2d 749 (1991); *Zaklama v. Mt. Sinai Med. Ctr.,* 842 F.2d 291, 294–95 (11th Cir.1988); *Gomez v. Alexian Bros. Hosp. of San Jose,* 698 F.2d 1019, 1021–22 (9th Cir.1983); *Spirt v. Teachers Ins. & Annuity Ass'n,* 691 F.2d 1054, 1062–63 (2d Cir.1982), *vacated on other grounds,* 463 U.S. 1223, 103 S.Ct.

the Title VII defendant must be a defined "employer," the plaintiff need not be an "employee" but instead is referred to in the statute as a "person aggrieved." (For the same reason the statute applies to defendant labor unions and employment agencies, which also have no direct employment relationship with a plaintiff.) The plaintiff attempting to invoke "*Sibley* standing" must show that a defined Title VII "employer" used a position of power and control over a third party to wrongfully interfere with that party's employment relationship with the plaintiff.[19]

Unions have had no difficulty gaining standing to protest discrimination against their members,[20] and standing under Title VII has been liberally granted to employees who can show some personal harm resulting from their association with co-employees.[21] But where the Title VII plaintiff has himself suffered no personal injury, standing is typically denied. In *Childress v. City of Richmond, Va.*,[22] the Fourth Circuit, in an equally divided en banc decision, affirmed a district court's denial of standing to white male officers seeking to recover under Title VII for an

3565, 77 L.Ed.2d 1406 (1983); *Sibley Mem'l Hosp. v. Wilson*, 488 F.2d 1338 (D.C.Cir. 1973). *See also Graves v. Lowery*, 117 F.3d 723, 728 (3d Cir.1997) (discussing standing per *Sibley*). *But cf. Fields v. Hallsville Ind. Sch. Dist.*, 906 F.2d 1017, 1018–1019 (5th Cir.1990), *cert. denied*, 498 U.S. 1026, 111 S.Ct. 676, 112 L.Ed.2d 668 (1991) and *Diggs v. Harris Hosp.–Methodist, Inc.*, 847 F.2d 270, 271–272 (5th Cir.), *cert. denied*, 488 U.S. 956, 109 S.Ct. 394, 102 L.Ed.2d 383 (1988) (finding no direct employment relationship, but not directly passing on standing per *Sibley*).

19. *See Sibley*, 488 F.2d at 1342. While courts that recognize *Sibley* standing are clear that the plaintiff need not have a direct employment relationship with the defendant, they do tend to require that the plaintiff have such a direct relationship with the third party. That relationship may be shown, however, through a test that considers the economic realities of employment but also relies on the degree of the third party's control over the plaintiff's conduct. *See, e.g., Alexander v. Rush N. Shore Med. Ctr.*, 101 F.3d 487, 492–493 (7th Cir. 1996), *cert. denied*, 522 U.S. 811, 118 S.Ct. 54, 139 L.Ed.2d 19 (1997); *Cobb v. Sun Papers, Inc.*, 673 F.2d 337, 341 (11th Cir.), *cert. denied*, 459 U.S. 874, 103 S.Ct. 163, 74 L.Ed.2d 135 (1982); *Spirides v. Reinhardt*, 613 F.2d 826, 831–832 (D.C.Cir.1979).

20. *See, e.g., International Woodworkers of Am. v. Chesapeake Bay Plywood Corp.*, 659 F.2d 1259 (4th Cir.1981); *International Woodworkers of Am., Local 5–475 v. Georgia–Pacific Corp.*, 568 F.2d 64 (8th Cir. 1977); *Air Line Stewards & Stewardesses Ass'n, Local 550 v. American Airlines, Inc.*,

490 F.2d 636 (7th Cir.1973), *cert. denied*, 416 U.S. 993, 94 S.Ct. 2406, 40 L.Ed.2d 773 (1974).

21. *See, e.g., Maynard v. City of San Jose*, 37 F.3d 1396 (9th Cir.1994) (upholding plaintiff's standing to sue for retaliation against him based on his association with members of racial minorities); *Parr v. Woodmen of the World Life Ins. Co.*, 791 F.2d 888 (11th Cir.1986) (standing for plaintiff to complain of discrimination based on an interracial marriage); *Stewart v. Hannon*, 675 F.2d 846, 848–850 (7th Cir.1982) (whites have standing to complain that blacks excluded as school principals); *EEOC v. Mississippi College*, 626 F.2d 477, 481–3 (5th Cir.1980) (same re failure to recruit or hire black faculty); *Waters v. Heublein, Inc.*, 547 F.2d 466, 469–70 (9th Cir.1976) (same re lower pay for black employees); *Rosenblatt v. Bivona & Cohen, PC*, 946 F.Supp. 298 (S.D.N.Y.1996) (white attorney fired allegedly because employer objected to his marriage to a black woman); *Chandler v. Fast Lane, Inc.*, 868 F.Supp. 1138 (E.D.Ark. 1994) (white plaintiff permitted to challenge discriminatory hiring and promotion practices directed only against African–American employees). *But see Childress v. City of Richmond, Va.*, 134 F.3d 1205 (4th Cir.) (en banc), *cert. denied*, 524 U.S. 927, 118 S.Ct. 2322, 141 L.Ed.2d 696 (1998) (denying standing under Title VII to white male police officers claiming that sexually and racially derogatory remarks aimed at women and blacks harmed them by chilling teamwork).

22. 134 F.3d 1205 (4th Cir.) (en banc), *cert. denied*, 524 U.S. 927, 118 S.Ct. 2322, 141 L.Ed.2d 696 (1998).

alleged hostile work environment or retaliation created by the city's discriminatory and hostile treatment of women and blacks. In concurrence, Judge Luttig explained that the difference between the court's Title VII standing analysis in *Childress* and that employed by the Supreme Court in the Title VIII case *Trafficante*, is found in the different language employed in the statutes. Title VIII's term "aggrieved person" is broadly and expressly defined in the statute as "any person who claims to have been injured by a discriminatory housing practice."[23] Title VII, on the other hand, uses the term "aggrieved person" but contains no definition. By defining the term in Title VIII, the Fourth Circuit reasoned, Congress "statutorily eliminated" all prudential standing requirements in Title VIII cases.[24] Conversely, by failing to define the term in Title VII, Congress impliedly infused the "term of art" "aggrieved person" with all of the prudential limitations on standing. The white male plaintiffs had not themselves been the direct victims of discrimination but were instead asserting the rights of third party victims, and prudential limits denied standing.

Contrast this with the Seventh Circuit's 1982 decision in *Stewart v. Hannon*,[25] holding that a white employee could be aggrieved by the lack of black employees in the workplace if that produced "the loss of important benefits from interracial associations," described by the court as a personal loss. The Seventh Circuit cited *Stewart* with approval in *Bermudez v. TRC Holdings, Inc.*,[26] where, however, it expressed doubts about allowing nonminority plaintiffs to recover for an allegedly hostile environment based on an employer's negative treatment of minorities.

Standing in a Title VII retaliation case has generally been limited to those persons who engaged in participation or opposition activities.[27] In *Karcher v. Emerson Electric Co.*, for example, a plaintiff was permitted to maintain a retaliation claim for emotional distress damages she suffered when her husband co-worker was dismissed after she filed a charge of discrimination against the employer. The court recognized plaintiff's claim despite the absence of a tangible employment detriment to her, because she suffered an injury ultimately traceable to her own protected participation.[28] In the converse situation, however, standing was denied to a spouse who alleged that he was retaliated against because of protected activity engaged in only by his wife.[29] And the claim of a police officer that he was retaliated against for opposing discrimination by other officers against citizens was not cognizable because he could not have reasonably believed that he was opposing an unlawful employment (as opposed to law enforcement) practice.[30]

23. § 810 (a) of the Fair Housing Act, codified at 42 U.S.C.A. § 3602(i)(1).

24. *Childress*, 134 F.3d at 1209–10.

25. 675 F.2d 846, 850 (7th Cir.1982).

26. 138 F.3d 1176, 1180 (7th Cir.1998).

27. See the discussion of retaliation under Title VII generally in § 2.40, *supra*.

28. 94 F.3d 502 (8th Cir.1996), *cert. denied*, 520 U.S. 1210, 117 S.Ct. 1692, 137 L.Ed.2d 820 (1997).

29. *Holt v. JTM Indus., Inc.*, 89 F.3d 1224 (5th Cir.1996), *cert. denied*, 520 U.S. 1229, 117 S.Ct. 1821, 137 L.Ed.2d 1029 (1997).

30. *Wimmer v. Suffolk County Police Dep't*, 176 F.3d 125 (2d Cir.), *cert. denied*,

§ 12.16 Standing After Bankruptcy Filed

A state appellate decision raises an interesting standing issue regarding the relationship between a plaintiff's previously filed bankruptcy case and a subsequent employment discrimination case. In *United Technologics Corp. v. Gaines*,[1] the plaintiff's Chapter 7 bankruptcy case was closed before [or shortly after] she filed a tort action based on conduct that preceded her bankruptcy petition. Once the bankruptcy case was closed, the tort defendant moved to dismiss under the applicable state real party in interest provision, arguing that the bankruptcy trustee owned the claim under federal bankruptcy law. The plaintiff responded by successfully petitioning in bankruptcy court to reopen her bankruptcy case and name a new trustee. The new trustee and the plaintiff agreed, and the bankruptcy court ordered, that any legal action on the tort claim would be prosecuted in the name of the debtor—although the proceeds of any favorable judgment would accrue to the trustee, as the representative of the debtor's estate.

Despite this agreement and order, the tort defendant contended in state court that the new trustee, not the alleged tort victim, owned the claim. It was undisputed that upon the initial filing of the bankruptcy petition, federal law[2] had effected an instant transfer to the trustee, notwithstanding any contrary provision of state law, of all the debtor's legal and equitable interests, including pending or inchoate claims for relief. The tort defendant argued that after this transfer occurred by operation of law, the agreement between the new trustee and the debtor, blessed by the bankruptcy court, amounted to a partial assignment of the claim that violated a state statute prohibiting the assignment of a personal cause of action.[3] Accordingly, defendant moved to substitute the new trustee for the tort plaintiff-debtor as real party in interest.[4] After the trial court denied the motion, the state appellate court reversed. It agreed with defendant that although the federal statute effecting transfer of the debtor's claim to the trustee preempted contrary state law provisions respecting ownership of the claim, it did not alter the ordi-

528 U.S. 964, 120 S.Ct. 398, 145 L.Ed.2d 310 (1999).

§ 12.16

1. 225 Ga.App. 191, 483 S.E.2d 357 (Ga. App.1997). *But cf. Dennis v. Dillard Dep't Stores, Inc.*, 207 F.3d 523, 525–526 (8th Cir.2000) (defendant granted leave to amend answer in Equal Pay Act case to assert affirmative "factor other than sex" defense; *Pulliam v. Tallapoosa County*, 185 F.3d 1182, 1189–96 (11th Cir.1999) (defendant who failed to plead "mixed motives" defense in answer preserved it by raising defense in pretrial order). *See also Harris v. St. Louis Univ.*, 114 B.R. 647, 649 (E.D.Mo. 1990) (debtor lacked standing to sue former employer under Title VII and ADEA); *In re Davis*, 158 B.R. 1000 (Bkrtcy.N.D.Ind.1993)

(filing of complaint where debtors lacked standing and failed to substitute trustee as real party in interest warranted Rule 11 sanctions).

2. 11 U.S.C.A. § 541.

3. *See* O.C.G.A. § 44–12–24.

4. *See* O.C.G.A. § 9–11–17(a), providing that no action shall be dismissed because not prosecuted in the name of the real party in interest until a reasonable time after objection has been allowed for, among other things, substitution of the real party in interest. This provision echoes the language of F.R.C.P. 17(a), which would be relevant in similar situations arising in the course of employment discrimination or civil rights actions filed in federal court.

narily prevailing state law rules prohibiting the trustee from assigning that claim thereafter.

The result in *Gaines* binds a plaintiff asserting a state law tort claim to state law limitations on assignability, despite contrary arrangements made during bankruptcy proceedings. It is of course quite possible that this holding does not affect claims under the federal employment discrimination or civil rights statutes. For one thing, the federal law provision automatically transferring ownership of the claim from the alleged victim to the trustee upon the filing of a petition in bankruptcy might not apply because of conflicting policies particular to the federal employment discrimination or civil rights statutes.[5] Second, even assuming the bankruptcy code provision automatically transferring ownership of the claim to the trustee does apply, and the trustee then assigns the claim to the plaintiff to the extent necessary for her to prosecute in her own name, those same federal policies might preempt state anti-assignment laws and uphold the assignment. Third, even if the trustee acquires the claim under the bankruptcy laws and assigns its prosecution to the plaintiff, and if federal civil rights policies do not pre-empt state anti-assignment provisions, many states do not prohibit the assignment of personal claims.

Assuming, however, that the *Gaines* reasoning may permissibly be extended to federal employment discrimination claims, the practical consequences to the debtor plaintiff in a state prohibiting assignments of personal claims may be grievous. First, the defendant would presumably be free to argue to the jury that any damages were suffered by, and any recovery will accrue to, the trustee, and, in turn, the victim's creditors— an argument not calculated to arouse jury sympathy for the plaintiff when it assesses liability or damages. Second, the alleged victim's share, if any, of whatever recovery is achieved despite this obstacle would potentially be substantially less than the victim could obtain in an action prosecuted in her own name, because that recovery would have to be distributed to the victim's creditors in accordance with the disposition of the bankruptcy proceeding. The authors are advised that the action in *Gaines* was in fact dismissed shortly after the appellate decision requiring the action to be prosecuted in the name of the new trustee.

To reduce these potential risks, plaintiff's counsel should ask the client early in the representation if the client has filed for bankruptcy. If so, but she has not scheduled the employment discrimination or civil rights claim, counsel should seek leave of the bankruptcy court to amend the asset schedule (or, if the bankruptcy case has already closed, petition to reopen the case and amend that schedule) to list the claim. Provided the claim is listed, the plaintiff may regain standing by persuading the

---

5. *But see Harris* and *Cain v. Hyatt*, 101 B.R. 440, 442 (E.D.Pa.1989) (both applying the ordinary automatic transfer provision so as to divest employment discrimination plaintiffs of standing). To same effect *see* *Walker v. Anderson Electrical Connectors*, 742 F.Supp. 591, 595 (N.D.Ala.1990), *aff'd*, 944 F.2d 841 (11th Cir.1991), *cert. denied*, 506 U.S. 1078, 113 S.Ct. 1043, 122 L.Ed.2d 352 (1993) (dictum).

trustee to "abandon" it,[6] either affirmatively or, once the bankruptcy case is closed, by operation of law.[7] In this way, even if the trustee declines to abandon the claim affirmatively, the plaintiff may prosecute a listed federal statutory claim in her own name as real party in interest once the bankruptcy case closes,[8] thereby avoiding the multiple tactical disadvantages inherent in prosecuting the case in the name of the trustee. Likewise, an employment discrimination defendant should inquire at the outset of investigation or discovery whether the plaintiff has filed a bankruptcy petition. If she has, but has not listed the claim in question (or has listed the claim but the bankruptcy case has not closed), the defendant should move to dismiss any pending action on real party in interest grounds. The plaintiff may respond, of course, by amending the asset list to include the claim, or, if the case has closed, by petitioning to reopen the bankruptcy case and the amending the list. But unless and until the trustee, either affirmatively or by operation of law, abandons the claim, the defendant may reap the significant tactical advantages attendant upon forcing the plaintiff to prosecute in the name of the trustee. In a jurisdiction with anti-assignment legislation and where there is no authoritative precedent exempting federal civil rights or employment discrimination claims from the automatic bankruptcy transfer, employment counsel on either side would be well advised to consult a bankruptcy expert to help steer these potentially perilous shoals.

§§ 12.17–12.19 Reserved

D. MOOTNESS

§ 12.20 In General

Because standing is a threshold jurisdictional or quasi-jurisdictional doctrine that bars the doors of the federal courthouse, the burden of its relatively restrictive application to constitutionally based claims for injunctive relief has been felt by plaintiffs. But the same Article III imperatives that underlie the standing doctrines are said to continue throughout the course of federal litigation under the rubric of the companion doctrine of "mootness," which may be thought of as standing redux. Mootness stops an action in its tracks either "when the issues

---

6. "Abandonment" is a procedure allowed for and strictly controlled by the Bankruptcy Code, 11 U.S.C.A. § 554; its detailing workings are beyond the scope of this book. *See Harris*, 114 B.R. at 649 on plaintiff's regaining standing after trustee abandons claim.

7. For abandonment to happen automatically under 11 U.S.C.A. § 554 upon the closing of a bankruptcy case, the asset must have been properly scheduled, either originally or through an amended asset schedule. There is authority finding it an abuse of discretion for the bankruptcy court to

deny that leave to amend. *Bittel v. Yamato Int'l Corp.*, 70 F.3d 1271 (6th Cir.1995) (unpublished opinion).

8. And plaintiff's counsel can safely refrain from filing the federal statutory claim until the bankruptcy case is closed. The limitations periods pertaining to the federal claims will be tolled from the time the bankruptcy petition is filed, so that the plaintiff need not file until 60 days after the bankruptcy case is closed. 11 U.S.C.A. § 108.

presented are no longer 'live' or the parties lack a legally cognizable interest in the outcome."[1]

In *Franks v. Bowman Transp. Co.*,[2] the Court permitted the sole named plaintiff in a previously certified Title VII subclass to pursue retroactive seniority relief on behalf of unnamed class members even though by then he lacked a personal interest in that relief and the unnamed plaintiffs would likely have other opportunities to obtain review of that issue. The Court thus appeared to accept that in a class action under Federal Rule of Civil Procedure 23, the concrete presentation sought to be assured by the "injury in fact" element of standing/mootness doctrine is met not by the named plaintiff but by the allegations on behalf of the class—they have a life of their own that survives his exit from the lawsuit.[3]

The question remained whether the federal courts' willingness to entertain the claims of unnamed class members after the mooting of the named plaintiff's claim was dependent on whether, as in *Franks*, the mooting event occurred only after the class had been certified. The Court has answered that question in the negative, permitting putative class members to obtain judicial review of rulings denying class certification issued after the mooting of the sole named plaintiff's claim. And it has permitted these appeals regardless of whether the named plaintiff's claim was mooted by his own favorable judgment on the merits—in which case it could be said that he still retains at least an economic interest in the statutory attorney's fees available to a prevailing party— or simply by expiration, as when a prisoner challenging parole release guidelines is released pending appeal.[4]

When a case becomes moot on appeal, the ordinary appellate court response is vacatur of the judgment below. The principal reason is that the judgment loser should not suffer the adverse res judicata or collateral estoppel effects of that judgment when, for reasons beyond its control, it is denied appellate review.[5] But where the parties render a case moot by settling their controversy on appeal, the equitable considerations favoring vacatur of the judgment under review evaporate and vacatur is not justified.[6]

§§ 12.21–12.24   Reserved

§ 12.20

1. *Powell v. McCormack*, 395 U.S. 486, 489, 89 S.Ct. 1944, 1947, 23 L.Ed.2d 491 (1969).

2. 424 U.S. 747, 96 S.Ct. 1251, 47 L.Ed.2d 444 (1976).

3. *Id.* at 754, 96 S.Ct. at 1259.

4. *See*, respectively, *Deposit Guaranty Nat'l Bank v. Roper*, 445 U.S. 326, 100 S.Ct. 1166, 63 L.Ed.2d 427 (1980) and *United States Parole Comm'n v. Geraghty*, 445 U.S. 388, 100 S.Ct. 1202, 63 L.Ed.2d 479 (1980).

5. *See United States v. Munsingwear, Inc.*, 340 U.S. 36, 71 S.Ct. 104, 95 L.Ed. 36 (1950) (referring to mooting that occurred "through happenstance"); *Associated Gen. Contractors of Conn., Inc. v. New Haven, Conn.*, 41 F.3d 62.

6. *U.S. Bancorp Mortgage Co. v. Bonner Mall Partnership*, 513 U.S. 18, 115 S.Ct. 386, 130 L.Ed.2d 233 (1994).

E. SUMMARY JUDGMENT (F.R.C.P. 56), SETTLEMENT, AND JUDGMENT AS A MATTER OF LAW UNDER F.R.C.P. 50(a) ("DIRECTED VERDICT") AND 50(b) ("J.N.O.V.")

§ 12.25 In General

Federal Rule of Civil Procedure 56 allows for summary judgment when, after opportunity for discovery, it appears that there is no genuine issue concerning the existence of a fact "material" under the substantive law, and that the moving party is therefore entitled to judgment as a matter of law. For most of the Rule's history, the party that most commonly moves for summary judgment—a defendant attacking an element of the plaintiff's case—had the burden of adducing evidence that virtually negated the fact plaintiff would have the burden of proving at trial. In *Celotex Corp. v. Catrett*,[1] however, the Court reallocated the burdens respecting the existence of a genuine issue: it placed it on the party resisting the motion if, as is usually the case, that party would bear the ultimate trial burden of persuasion on the targeted issue. Thus a defendant in a personal injury action may, by mere argument that the plaintiff has failed during discovery to turn up evidence tending to support any of the indispensable elements of her case (negligence or causation, for example), cast on the plaintiff the obligation to present such evidence in opposition to the motion.

In *Anderson v. Liberty Lobby*,[2] the Court ruled that the evidence produced at the summary judgment stage must be sufficient to sustain the verdict at trial *by whatever standard will be required to support the burden of proof at trial*. Thus the public official plaintiff suing the press for libel must provide sufficient evidence to convince a reasonable fact finder of *New York Times* malice by a "clear and convincing" evidentiary standard. Mere production of some evidence of such malice will not sustain the denial of defendant's motion for summary judgment. Of course in civil rights and employment discrimination cases, the plaintiff's burden on prima facie elements is the ordinary "preponderance of the evidence" standard. Therefore once the defendant properly makes the motion per *Celotex*, or by offering independent evidence of its own that suggests plaintiff cannot create a genuine issue about a material fact, the plaintiff can resist summary judgment only by producing admissible evidence–relevant,[3] reliable evidence that is either not hearsay or for

§ 12.25

1. 477 U.S. 317, 106 S.Ct. 2548, 91 L.Ed.2d 265 (1986).

2. 477 U.S. 242, 106 S.Ct. 2505, 91 L.Ed.2d 202 (1986).

3. For example, the Sixth Circuit reversed a trial court's decision, based on relevancy, to exclude a particularly offensive racially derogatory document circulated around the workplace with the supervisor's knowledge. *Robinson v. Runyon*, 149 F.3d 507, 513–15 (6th Cir.1998). The appellate court noted that even where a Title VII plaintiff proceeds not with direct evidence but rather via the inferential *McDonnell Douglas/Burdine* mode of proof, courts "must be mindful not to cripple a plaintiff's ability to prove discrimination indirectly and circumstantially by evidentiary rulings that keep out probative evidence because of crabbed notions of relevance" (internal quo-

which the Federal Rules of Evidence provide an exception.[4]

tation omitted). The court affirmed, however, the district court's exclusion of a hangman's noose which was displayed in the workplace for a short time period because the incident occurred over a year before the plaintiff's alleged harassment.

Because judges ruling on summary judgment motions can ordinarily consider only potentially admissible evidence, they must take into account the evidentiary rules that will govern relevance and the probative value/prejudicial effect balance at trial. In employment discrimination and civil rights cases, testimony about discrimination directed against other members of plaintiff's group commonly raises disputes about these issues. *See Heyne v. Caruso*, 69 F.3d 1475, 1479 (9th Cir.1995) (testimony of prior discriminatory acts against members of plaintiff's protected group by the particular employer agent alleged to have discriminated against plaintiff particularly probative of that agent's state of mind); *Palmer v. Board of Regents*, 208 F.3d 969, 972 (11th Cir. 2000) (affirming trial court's ruling that evidence of discriminatory acts by other decisionmakers in other departments was too remote to be relevant to motive of the decisionmaker at bar and accordingly was properly excludable as having greater prejudicial effect than probative value); *Roy v. Austin Co.*, 194 F.3d 840, 843 (7th Cir.1999) (approving trial court's use of general proposition "that showing disparate treatment by a different supervisor does not normally further a plaintiff's ability to make out a discrimination claim under Title VII."). *Beachy v. Boise Cascade Corp.*, 191 F.3d 1010, 1014 (9th Cir.1999), *cert. denied*, ___ U.S. ___, 120 S.Ct. 1425, 146 L.Ed.2d 316 (2000) (to be relevant, the discrimination must evince hostility towards "a well-defined and protected group such as persons of a particular race" gender, national origin, religion, age or disability, and because of that group's status; employer agent's irritation with or hostility to such persons based solely on their work habits is not probative of unlawful discriminatory animus). *See generally* § 3.10, *supra*, on other anecdotal evidence and statistical evidence about discrimination against plaintiff's group that has been considered relevant to proof of discrimination against the plaintiff herself.

4. *See McMillian v. Johnson*, 88 F.3d 1573, 1583–85 (11th Cir.1996), *aff'd on other grounds*, 520 U.S. 781, 117 S.Ct. 1734, 138 L.Ed.2d 1 (1997), which construed the ambiguous passage on the subject in *Celotex*, 477 U.S. at 324, to mean that although evidence need not be reduced to a form that would be admissible at trial, it must be of the kind that would be admissible in substance. For example, where a letter produced in opposition to summary judgment would be inadmissible hearsay if offered at trial, the plaintiff could nevertheless rely on its contents to raise a genuine issue of fact where there was reason to believe that the writer could testify to its contents at trial. *Offshore Aviation v. Transcon Lines, Inc.*, 831 F.2d 1013, at 1015–1016 (11th Cir. 1987). By contrast, the panel in *McMillian* would not permit otherwise inadmissible hearsay statements to raise a genuine issue of fact where they would still be inadmissible when offered at trial. While those statements would be admissible at trial for impeachment purposes, the panel ruled that potential impeachment evidence could not be considered as substantive evidence to raise a genuine issue about the fact targeted by the motion.

In contrast, the Fifth Circuit has read Rule 56(e) to preclude the use of unsworn or handwritten statements. For example, in *Watts v. Kroger Co.*, 170 F.3d 505, 508–09 (5th Cir.1999), a Title VII sexual harassment case, the court held that several handwritten statements by plaintiff's co-workers that were signed but not sworn, notarized, or in the form of affidavits, were not competent summary judgment evidence for the purposes of Rule 56(e). The court rejected plaintiff's arguments that the touchstone for consideration is the ultimate admissibility of the evidence at trial. Similarly, in *Duplantis v. Shell Offshore, Inc.*, 948 F.2d 187, 191–92 (5th Cir.1991) the court relied on Rule 56(f): If the party opposing summary judgment has evidence which has not yet been reduced to admissible form but is germane to the existence of a genuine issue of material fact, then it is proper for the party opposing summary judgment to move for a continuance "to permit affidavits to be obtained or depositions to be taken or discovery to be had." The court acknowledged that *Celotex* gave "some indication" that the nonmoving party's Rule 56(e) evidence might not have to be in strictly admissible form. But it interpreted *Celotex* as merely dispensing with the necessity of full depositions, allowing other documents listed in Rule 56(c), such as "answers to interrogatories, and admissions on file, together with affidavits," to suffice as material that may resist the motion. The court stated that if unsworn statements or unauthenticated documents were allowed at summary judgment, courts would "get bogged down in a

This potentially admissible evidence may be in the form of affidavits, documents, deposition testimony, interrogatory answers, admissions or otherwise, but it must be sufficient taken as a whole for a reasonable jury to find plaintiff's way on that fact by a preponderance of the evidence. Still, plaintiff's own affidavit can suffice to resist a motion for summary judgment.[5]

In Title VII and ADEA cases, the defendant may rebut the element of discriminatory intent by showing neutral, non-discriminatory reasons

needless examination of the hypothetical ways the nonmoving party's evidence might be reduced to admissible form by the time of trial." Because unsworn statements and unauthenticated documents are not the kind of evidence described in Rules 56(c) and 56(e), and it was not the district court's duty to examine whether and how it might be reduced to acceptable form by the time of trial, the district court should disregard such evidence at summary judgment.

At the summary judgment stage, trial courts are forced to make a not-so-easy forecast of what would be admissible at trial, and their forecasts are sometimes invalidated by appellate courts. *Wright-Simmons v. City of Oklahoma City*, 155 F.3d 1264, 1268–69 (10th Cir.1998) is a case in point. When deciding a summary judgment motion, the district court did not consider a report, prepared by the defendant's personnel department in connection with its internal investigation of an employee's complaints about racial harassment, which concluded that the complaining employee's supervisor engaged in racial harassment. But the appellate court concluded that the failure to consider such a report constituted reversible error, relying on F.R.E. 801(d)(2)(B) (evidence is not hearsay if it "is offered against a party and is … a statement of which the party has manifested an adoption or belief in its truth") and on evidence that the employer acted on the report when it sought the supervisor's resignation.

In *Stewart v. Henderson*, 207 F.3d 374, 377–378 (7th Cir.2000), the question was whether the trial court should have admitted evaluative statements made by others about the plaintiff that were contained in the affidavit of a supervisor-decisionmaker that he relied upon in recommending the adverse action plaintiff challenged. Referencing the Title VII substantive principle, see § 3.10, *supra*, that the employer's legitimate nondiscriminatory reason need only be sincerely held rather than correct, accurate, or wise, the court held that the affidavit was properly considered by the trial court in granting summary judgment. It was not hearsay, in short, because it was

offered not for the truth of the matter asserted but instead to demonstrate that the supervisor-decisionmaker changed his opinion based on that of the evaluators. And "regardless of whether the committee members were correct" in their perception that plaintiff's application evinced an "adversarial quality that would be detrimental in the position," "their statement is relevant to show … [the supervisor-decisionmaker's] state of mind when he made his [negative] recommendation." Similarly, in another case where evidence offered in opposition to summary judgment was germane to the state of mind of defendant's decisionmakers, it was not offered to prove the truth of the matter asserted, was therefore not hearsay as defined by F.R.Evidence 801(c), and could accordingly be considered. *Wright v. Southland Corp.*, 187 F.3d 1287, 1304 n. 21 (11th Cir.1999). Other times, of course, district courts correctly predict admissibility on difficult questions of evidence law. *See, e.g., Zaben v. Air Products & Chemicals, Inc.*, 129 F.3d 1453, 1455–57 (11th Cir.1997) (affirming trial court's exclusion of hearsay statements after an arduous double hearsay analysis under F.R.E. 801, 802 and 805).

Sometimes evidence law prohibiting hearsay confronts the principle of *Johnson v. Jones* that a § 1983 individual defendant official may not appeal a district court's summary judgment order denying him the defense of qualified immunity on the sole ground that the pretrial record reveals a genuine issue of fact requiring trial. One circuit has held that in this situation, *Johnson* precludes interlocutory appellate jurisdiction even when, in the view of the circuit court of appeals, the decision denying summary judgment depended on "the rankest type of inadmissible hearsay." *Ellis v. Washington County*, 198 F.3d 225, 229(6th Cir.1999), *cert. denied*, ___ U.S. ___, 120 S.Ct. 1720, 146 L.Ed.2d 642 (2000).

5. *Danzer v. Norden Sys., Inc.*, 151 F.3d 50, 57 (2d Cir.1998) (recognizing that disregarding a plaintiff's own affidavit would substantially alter the Rule 56(c) convention that all inferences must be drawn in favor of nonmovant).

for the employee's discharge. The plaintiff must then produce evidence that the defendant's explanation is pretextual. The Supreme Court denied certiorari in *Hardin v. Pitney–Bowes*,[6] where the Sixth Circuit had granted summary judgment on that issue. Justice Rehnquist dissented vigorously from the denial of certiorari, maintaining that summary judgment is never appropriate on issues of intent. Circuit courts have continued to uphold summary judgment on the ultimate intent question that lies at the heart of the individual disparate treatment case, consistent with the *Celotex* and *Anderson* standards. They have applied those decisions to require that the plaintiff, to survive summary judgment, must do more than offer some evidence that an employer's assertion of non-discriminatory intent was false, or even a pretext for unlawful discrimination; rather, the plaintiff must present evidence *sufficient* to enable a *reasonable* jury to find such pretext by a preponderance of the evidence, the plaintiff's ultimate burden at a trial.[7]

An example illustrates the risk faced by a plaintiff resisting summary judgment after the Supreme Court's restatement in *St. Mary's Honor Ctr. v. Hicks*,[8] of the trial burden on "pretext."[9] The Seventh Circuit, applying *St. Mary's*, has held that an ADEA plaintiff, to counter employer evidence of a legitimate nondiscriminatory reason in opposing a summary judgment motion, need only "produce evidence from which a rational factfinder could infer that the company lied"; it was not essential, in other words, for the plaintiff to offer other, affirmative evidence of pretext, for example, that similarly situated employees were treated differently.[10] But because, under *St. Mary's*, such a showing would merely permit, not require, the factfinder at trial to find intentional discrimination because of age by a preponderance of the evidence, plaintiff takes a risk in limiting his summary judgment showing to evidence that attacks the employer's asserted legitimate reason.

In the case at hand, for example, the court viewed the plaintiff's evidence that the employer had lied about its stated reason as insufficient to avoid summary judgment, apparently because it believed that a jury acting reasonably could not find such a lie by a preponderance of the evidence submitted on the motion.[11] The lesson for plaintiff's counsel seems to be that although *St. Mary's*, and therefore summary judgment practice, may *require* only one kind of evidence of pretext (e.g., evidence that the employer lied), plaintiff acts at her peril even on summary judgment if she withholds other available evidence of pretext. This is because, now that *Anderson* has equated the summary judgment standard with that required for directed verdict, her evidence in response to

6. 451 U.S. 1008, 101 S.Ct. 2345, 68 L.Ed.2d 861 (1981) (denying certiorari).

7. *See, e.g., Healy v. New York Life Ins.*, 860 F.2d 1209 (3d Cir.1988), *cert. denied*, 490 U.S. 1098, 109 S.Ct. 2449, 104 L.Ed.2d 1004 (1989), where the Third Circuit reversed its prior adherence to Justice Rehnquist's position, and *Alphin v. Sears Roebuck*, 940 F.2d 1497 (11th Cir.1991).

8. 509 U.S. 502, 113 S.Ct. 2742, 125 L.Ed.2d 407 (1993).

9. *St. Mary's* is discussed in detail in § 3.10, *supra*.

10. *Anderson v. Baxter Healthcare Corp.*, 13 F.3d 1120 (7th Cir.1994).

11. *Id.*

a defendant's summary judgment motion must meet the same preponderance-standard *weighing* she will encounter at trial, notwithstanding the Supreme Court majority's rhetorical protestations to the contrary.

Even when, as is so frequently the case in employment discrimination and civil rights litigation, the issue on the motion concerns a defendant's intent or other state of mind, summary judgment is, contrary to an older school of thought, now clearly available.[12] The Supreme Court apparently recognizes the propriety of summary judgment grants even on the issue of malice.[13] Summary judgment would therefore also seem available to dispose of claims for punitive damages, in cases where they are alleged to be dependent on a wrongful state of mind.[14]

The tilt toward the defendant in the summary judgment decisional calculus ushered in by *Celotex* and, especially, *Anderson*, has altered settlement dynamics both before and after the motion is decided. A defendant who is able and chooses to make the bare-bones initial supporting showing permitted by *Celotex* can make the motion rather inexpensively. Yet once the defendant makes the motion, *Anderson's* insistence on *enough* evidence to enable a reasonable jury to find for the plaintiff *by a preponderance* places great pressure on the plaintiff to respond by offering all or virtually all evidence that he has unearthed during the course of discovery that is likely to raise a genuine issue about the fact targeted by the motion. This process is quite expensive, but once complete represents a significant advance investment on the plaintiff's preparation for trial.

After the motion is made, then, plaintiffs are perhaps more likely than they were before *Celotex* and *Anderson* to settle to avoid the greater costs of resisting and the greater risk of losing the motion. On the other hand, if the motion is made and denied, plaintiff's price to settle is probably higher than in pre-*Anderson* days, for three reasons. First, the judge, by denying the motion, has pre-certified it as one a reasonable jury might find plaintiff's way by the required trial quantum of evidence. Second, there is less risk than previously that the plaintiff will suffer judgment as a matter of law, now that the Supreme Court equates the summary judgment standard with the standards for directed verdict and judgment notwithstanding the verdict. Third, the plaintiff's demand must now account for front-loaded, full-scale pretrial preparation costs that he has probably already incurred in order to resist the motion. Of

12. *See Crawford–El v. Britton*, 523 U.S. 574, 600–601, 118 S.Ct. 1584, 140 L.Ed.2d 759 (1998) (observing also that even if plaintiff can prove the wrongful state of mind, defendant may prevail on the qualified immunity defense by showing that the law was not clearly established when defendant acted). *See also Borgo v. Goldin*, 204 F.3d 251 (D.C.Cir.2000) (triable fact questions remained as to whether supervisor acted with reverse discriminatory motive); *Kimberlin v. Quinlan*, 199 F.3d 496, 502 (D.C.Cir.1999), *petition for cert. filed*, June 30, 2000 (summary judgment possible on question of defendant's motive to interfere with plaintiff's First Amendment rights) (citing *Crawford-El*).

13. *See Anderson v. Liberty Lobby*, 477 U.S. at 254, 106 S.Ct. at 2513.

14. *See* § 4.25, *supra*, on the standard announced in *Kolstad v. American Dental Ass'n*, 527 U.S. 526, 119 S.Ct. 2118, 144 L.Ed.2d 494 (1999) governing punitive damages in litigation under Title VII.

course even if the motion is granted, the defendant may still have some reason to negotiate, given the possibility of a meritorious plaintiff's appeal.[15]

Despite the Supreme Court's observation in *Anderson* formally equating the directed verdict and summary judgment standards, it is not inevitable in practice that the same evidence sufficient to resist summary judgment will also suffice to authorize or uphold a verdict. In general, the F.R.C.P. 50(a) and (b) motions for judgment as a matter of law (corresponding, in former terminology, to the motions for directed verdict and j.n.o.v.) should only be granted when the court determines that there is insufficient evidence from which a jury reasonably could find (directed verdict) or could have found (j.n.o.v.) an issue favorably to the party that bears the burden on an issue by the applicable quantum of evidence—normally, a preponderance. A common test used by the lower federal courts in a wide variety of cases to assess such sufficiency is whether there is "substantial evidence" on the issue in question, defined as "evidence of such quality and weight that reasonable and fair-minded men [sic] in the exercise of impartial judgment might reach different conclusions."[16] But to some uncertain degree this formulation implicitly assumes that directed verdict or j.n.o.v. will sometimes be warranted despite the admission of evidence supporting the proponent's position when that evidence is "overwhelmed by contrary proof."[17] The Fifth Circuit applied these tests to the burden the Supreme Court placed on the ADEA plaintiff[18] of proving that age had a "determinative influence" on the challenged employment decision. In dictum, the Fifth Circuit concluded that evidence tending to show that the employer's proffered neutral explanation is false—sufficient under *St. Mary's* to resist summary judgment under Rule 56 because it would permit a fact-finder to determine that the false explanation was a pretext for age discrimination—may nevertheless in some cases fail to support a verdict if that evidence is not "substantial" in the sense used to decide Rule 50 motions for judgment as a matter of law.[19] Another circuit's formulation, somewhat more respectful of the jury's fact-finding role, limits the rule 50 inquiry as follows: " 'whether the evidence presented, combined with all reasonable inferences therefrom, is sufficient to support the verdict [by the requisite preponderance of the evidence] when viewed in the light most favorable to the party against whom the motion is directed . . . In other words, we are limited to assessing whether no rational jury could

---

15. *See Sheng v. Starkey Laboratories, Inc.,* 117 F.3d 1081 (8th Cir.1997) (affirming validity and enforceability of agreement settling Title VII action even though parties executed it after a district court order, of which they were unaware, granted defendant's motion for summary judgment). Presumably defense counsel can guard against such a possibility by providing in a draft or oral settlement agreement that a condition of the accord's finality is that any pending summary judgment motion not be granted in the interim.

16. *Boeing Co. v. Shipman,* 411 F.2d 365 (5th Cir.1969).

17. *Neely v. Delta Brick and Tile Co.,* 817 F.2d 1224 (5th Cir.1987).

18. *Hazen Paper Co. v. Biggins,* 507 U.S. 604, 113 S.Ct. 1701, 123 L.Ed.2d 338 (1993).

19. *Rhodes v. Guiberson Oil Tools,* 82 F.3d 615 (5th Cir.1996) (en banc).

have found for the plaintiff.' In doing so, 'this court may not step in and substitute its view of the contested evidence for the jury's.' "[20]

In perhaps its most significant plaintiff-friendly employment discrimination opinion in decades, the Supreme Court has now resolved the post-*St. Mary's* debate, and the general standard governing FRCP 50 motions, consistent with the jury-respectful approach taken by the majority of the circuit courts. As the discussion that follows explains, however, the decision will probably have even more significant impact in the resolution of the vastly greater number of motions for summary judgment in employment discrimination and civil rights case and civil litigation generally.

In *Reeves v. Sanderson Plumbing Prods., Inc.,*[21] a case under the Age Discrimination in Employment Act ("ADEA"), the Court, taking note of the differing *St. Mary's* passages, wrote that the jury may find the ultimate fact of discrimination on a prohibited ground simply from (1) *evidence* establishing a prima facie case, coupled with (2) "sufficient" *evidence* that the employer's asserted legitimate nondiscriminatory explanation is false. The Court considered this approach consistent with general evidence law: "the factfinder is entitled to consider a party's dishonesty about a material fact as 'affirmative evidence of guilt' "; and once the employer's asserted reason is rejected, unlawful discrimination "may well be the most likely alternative explanation."[22] Of course, as *St. Mary's* had held, the jury may properly find liability in such a case only if properly charged that it must, from these two kinds of evidence, make dual *findings*: (1) that the reason or reasons offered by the employer for taking the adverse action against plaintiff were not its real reasons, *and* (2) that the employer's real reason was in fact the unlawful ground prohibited by statute—e.g., race, sex, or age. But the Court disapproved the circuit cases that had required plaintiffs to adduce *evidence* not only that the employer's asserted legitimate reason was false but also sufficient, independent *evidence* that the employer's actual reason was an *unlawful* one.

That of course still left the Court to explain what it meant by the required "sufficient" or "enough" evidence that an employer's proffered legitimate reason is false. On this point the Court was refreshingly precise. Resolving a long-standing uncertainty as to the general standard for directed verdict (now the Federal Rule of Civil Procedure 50 motion for "judgment as a matter of law") in the federal courts, the Court wrote that a trial or appellate court should consider the entire record, not merely evidence favoring the non-moving party–i.e., in the *St. Mary's* context, the plaintiff.[23] But it stressed that the deciding court must draw all reasonable inferences in favor of the nonmovant, refraining from making credibility determinations itself or weighing the evidence. And it

20. *Mathur v. Board of Trustees,* 207 F.3d 938, 941 (7th Cir.2000) (internal citations omitted).

21. 530 U.S. 2097, 120 S.Ct. 2097, 147 L.Ed.2d 105 (2000).

22. *Id.* ___, 120 S.Ct. at 2108–09.

23. *Id.* at ___, 120 S.Ct. at 2109–10.

clarified that in order to avoid intruding on that jury function, the court "must disregard all evidence favorable to the moving party [the defendant, in the *St. Mary's* setting] that the jury is not required to believe ...That is, the court should give credence to [all] the evidence favoring the nonmovant [plaintiff] as well as [only] that 'evidence supporting the moving party that is uncontradicted and unimpeached, at least to the extent that that evidence comes from disinterested witnesses.' "[24] Accordingly, as long as plaintiff's counsel substantially impeaches or contradicts defendant-favorable evidence, a court will not consider that evidence in determining whether to uphold a plaintiff's verdict.

In elaborating these Rule 50 standards, the Court relied heavily on *Anderson v. Liberty Lobby*,[25] its most recent principal guidance on deciding motions for summary judgment. Indeed the Court repeated the *Liberty Lobby* observation that the inquiry under the summary judgment and directed verdict (judgment as a matter of law) motions is "the same." So it now appears settled in cases under ADEA (and, as discussed below, under Title VII) that it is possible for a disparate treatment plaintiff to survive summary judgment and proceed to trial, *or* to survive a motion for judgment as a matter of law during trial or after a favorable verdict, provided only it has offered evidence establishing the minimal, *McDonnell Douglas* prima facie case and "sufficient" evidence of the falsity of the employer's asserted legitimate nondiscriminatory reason. See cases cited in § 3.10, *supra*. The plaintiff need not also have presented evidence of an employer decisionmaker's ageist, racist or sexist remarks, or evidence that a similarly situated comparator who was younger or of a different race, sex, religion, or national origin received more favorable treatment. (Although such additional evidence had been presented in *Reeves*, the opinion made clear that only *McDonnell Douglas* prima facie evidence, plus "sufficient" evidence that the employer's stated reason is false, is necessary to permit a jury to reach the ultimate conclusion that the employer relied on an unlawful factor.) And in considering when evidence of falsity suffices, the trial court should take into account only evidence favoring the plaintiff and unimpeached, uncontradicted testimony favoring the defendant.

Summary judgment (and, even more directly, judgment as a matter of law) should accordingly now be granted only in the presumably rare case that a court, considering such evidence alone, determines that a jury could not rationally find (or could not have rationally found) by a preponderance of that evidence the ultimate fact of unlawful race, sex, religious, national origin, or age discrimination, despite its acceptance of the prima facie case and the falsity of the employer's stated legitimate, nondiscriminatory reason. The Court observed that this could happen where, for example, the record "conclusively revealed" affirmative evidence that the employer's challenged decision was taken for a different nondiscriminatory reason—as where the employer gave the false, nondis-

---

24. *Id.* at ___, 120 S.Ct. at 2110.   **25.** 477 U.S. 242, 106 S.Ct. 2505, 91 L.Ed.2d 202 (1986).

criminatory explanation to conceal a lawful but embarrassing reason, or a reason unlawful under some law other than Title VII or ADEA. Or, the Court added, judgment as a matter of law may be warranted where the employer presents "abundant and uncontroverted independent evidence" that it did not act on an unlawful ground *and* the plaintiff "created only a weak issue of fact as to whether the employer's reason was untrue." As Justice Ginsburg observed in her concurring opinion, conclusive demonstrations by unimpeached and uncontradicted evidence that discrimination could not have been the employer's actual motivation will be "atypical." Accordingly, in her words, a plaintiff will have to produce evidence beyond the two minimally required categories–the *McDonnell Douglas* prima facie showing and evidence that the employer's stated nondiscriminatory reason is false–only in "uncommon" circumstances. Consequently, "the ultimate question of liability ordinarily should not be taken from the jury once the plaintiff has introduced" the two minimally required categories of evidence.

It seems apparent from the *Reeves* opinion that the Supreme Court intends these rules to apply to cases under Title VII, not just to cases under ADEA. See § 3.10, *supra*. Citing and adopting the approach taken by the courts of appeals, the Court assumed arguendo that the Title VII, *McDonnell Douglas* evidentiary framework for cases based on "circumstantial," as opposed to "direct" evidence, as that framework was elaborated in *St. Mary's*, was "fully applicable" to the ADEA case at hand. This conclusion follows logically as well. The Court repeated its statement from *Hazen Paper Co. v. Biggins*[26] that in ADEA actions, the plaintiff must show that his age played not just a role but had a "determinative influence" on the outcome of the employer's decision-making process. In Title VII cases, by contrast, the statute as amended in 1991 provides that a plaintiff need only prove that race, sex, religion or national origin was a "motivating" factor in the employer's decision. It is therefore to be expected that Title VII plaintiffs should be able to survive Rule 56 summary judgment motions and Rule 50 motions for judgment as a matter of law at least as readily as ADEA plaintiffs will be able to under the standards announced in *Reeves*. More broadly, the general Rule 50 (and by extension rule 56) standards announced in *Reeves* will likely be held applicable to the other employment discrimination and civil rights claims considered throughout this book, and indeed to civil litigation generally. The Court has usually hewed to a "transsubstantive" approach to the Federal Rules of Civil Procedure, construing and applying them uniformly without regard to the nature of a particular claim except where the Rules themselves specifically provide otherwise. Furthermore, its discussion in *Reeves* relied and elaborated on authority arising from ordinary civil litigation.[27] The application of

26. 507 U.S. 604, 610, 113 S.Ct. 1701, 123 L.Ed.2d 338 (1993).

27. For example, the Court cited *Boeing Co. v. Shipman*, 411 F.2d 365 (5th Cir. 1969), cited *supra* this section, as part of its discussion requiring federal trial courts, in deciding Rule 50 motions, to consider only evidence favoring the resisting party (usually the plaintiff) plus the uncontradicted and

summary judgment to employment discrimination "pretext" cases is discussed more fully in § 3.10.

§ 12.26　Settlement

The Supreme Court's approach to summary judgment heavily influences settlement dynamics, as discussed above. When a settlement agreement is intended by the parties to dispose of all issues between them, the failure of a party to raise an issue during settlement negotiation can constitute waiver of the issue.[1] Parties who desire the option of invoking a federal court's subject matter jurisdiction to enforce an agreement settling a federal court employment discrimination or civil rights action should take pains to have the agreement embodied in a court order or judgment or prevail on the court to reserve jurisdiction pending implementation of the agreement.[2] Courts ordinarily employ normal state law contract principles in deciding whether to enforce agreements settling litigation under federal employment discrimination laws.[3]

§ 12.27　Appeal

Courts reviewing trial errors in employment discrimination cases have applied the "harmless error" standard predominant in civil cases. Under that standard, the court need only conclude "with fair assurance" that the judgment was not "substantially swayed" by the error below.[1] In different circumstances, appellate courts will attempt to satisfy themselves of that in different ways. Erroneously admitted evidence may have represented a very small part of otherwise "one-sided" evidence supporting a verdict.[2] The court may deem the inadmissible matter of "minor importance."[3] Or the appellate court may consider that the district court sufficiently instructed the jury that they were not misled by erroneously admitted evidence.[4]

One Supreme Court decision in 2000, *Weisgram v. Marley Co.*,[5] expands the potential for circuit courts of appeals to enter judgment as a

unimpeached evidence favoring the movant (usually the defendant).

ty to enter into agreement on client's behalf).

§ 12.26

1. *See, e.g, Wray v. Clarke*, 151 F.3d 807 (8th Cir.1998) (failing to raise issue of attorney's fees constitutes waiver).

2. *See Kokkonen v. Guardian Life Ins. Co.*, 511 U.S. 375, 114 S.Ct. 1673, 128 L.Ed.2d 391 (1994) (rejecting the proposition that a federal court that failed to retain jurisdiction over a primary controversy has "ancillary" jurisdiction to hear a separate action to enforce a settlement agreement reached in the underlying action).

3. *See Hayes v. National Serv. Indus.*, 196 F.3d 1252 (11th Cir.1999) (applying Georgia law on scope of attorney's authori-

§ 12.27

1. *See Taylor v. Virginia Union Univ.*, 193 F.3d 219 (4th Cir.1999) (en banc), *cert. denied*, ___ U.S. ___, 120 S.Ct. 1243, 146 L.Ed.2d 101 (2000) (citing cases).

2. *See Alexander v. Fulton County*, 207 F.3d 1303, 1329–1330 (11th Cir.2000).

3. *Lubbock Feed Lots, Inc. v. Iowa Beef Processors, Inc.*, 630 F.2d 250, 271 (5th Cir.1980).

4. *Alexander*, 207 F.3d at 1329.

5. 528 U.S. 440, 120 S.Ct. 1011, 145 L.Ed.2d 958 (2000).

matter of law pursuant to Federal Rule of Civil Procedure 50 in favor of a verdict loser when the appellate court determines that the verdict is unsustainable because evidence supporting it was erroneously admitted.The Court held that a federal appellate court may itself enter judgment as a matter of law, without remanding for a new trial, either where it views the evidence presented at trial as originally insufficient to support a verdict, as in *Neely v. Martin K. Eby Construction Co.,*[6] or, as in *Weisgram,* where the jury's verdict becomes insufficient only after the appellate court rules that evidence supporting the verdict was improperly admitted.

But the Court's decision in *Reeves v. Sanderson Plumbing Prods., Inc.*[7] later in the same year significantly tightens the standard for the grant of a Rule 50 motion by either a federal trial or appellate court. *Reeves,* discussed in detail in §§ 3.10, 7.1, and in the section immediately above, severely limits an appellate court's freedom to affirm a trial court's grant of a Rule 50 motion or to order judgment as a matter of law itself so long as the jury could reasonably have reached its verdict by reference solely to all the evidence favoring the verdict winner and only the unimpeached and uncontradicted evidence favoring the verdict loser.

§§ 12.28–12.29 Reserved

F. CLASS ACTIONS

§ 12.30 In General

Claims of systemic disparate treatment or of neutral practices having a disproportionate adverse impact will often be advanced through class actions. In theory, maintenance of actions in class form should expedite the presentation of evidence on behalf of large numbers of claimants. In fact, after receiving class actions quite hospitably in the early years of the Act,[1] federal courts have erected substantial barriers to class certification through interpretations of Federal Rule 23.

The most formidable obstacle was declared by a Supreme Court decision construing the "commonality" and "typicality" requirements of Rule 23(a)(2) and Rule 23(a)(3). *General Telephone Co. of the Southwest v. Falcon,*[2] precludes named plaintiffs complaining of discrimination in one term and condition of employment (for example, promotion) from representing persons complaining about the same kind of discrimination with respect to other terms and conditions of employment (for example, hiring). The Court stressed that the requisite commonality and typicality

6. 386 U.S. 317, 87 S.Ct. 1072, 18 L.Ed.2d 75 (1967).

7. 530 U.S. 133, 120 S.Ct. 2097, 147 L.Ed.2d 105 (2000).

§ 12.30

1. Some of the facilitative features of Title VII class actions, and the procedural relief they afford to individual class members who would otherwise have to perfect all of that statute's preconditions to suit, are discussed in Chapter 4, above. *See also* Chapter 7, on the FLSA "opt in" procedures mandated for class-made claims under ADEA.

2. 457 U.S. 147, 102 S.Ct. 2364, 72 L.Ed.2d 740 (1982), discussed in § 4.9, *supra.*

must extend to defendant employer practices, not merely the general type of discrimination—race, gender, religion, or national origin—alleged.

Employment discrimination and civil rights cases are classic examples[3] of the kind of class action permitted by Rule 23(b)(2): where "the party opposing the class has acted or refused to act on grounds generally applicable to the class, thereby making appropriate final injunctive relief or corresponding declaratory relief with respect to the class as a whole." So where class treatment is denied in these cases it is usually because the claims fail to meet one or more of the compound requirements of Rule 23(a):

(1) "a class so numerous that joinder of all members is impracticable"[4];

(2) "questions of law or fact common to the class";

(3) "the claims ... of the representative parties are typical of the claims ... of the class";

(4) "the representative parties will fairly and adequately protect the interests of the class."

As for Rule 23(a)(4), the Court in *Falcon* did note that named plaintiffs complaining of one term or condition of employment could represent class members complaining of another where the employer used a common testing procedure or where different kinds of employees could be shown to have suffered discrimination "in the same general fashion," *e.g.*, through "entirely subjective decision making processes" or at the hands of the same employer personnel.[5] Nevertheless, many lower courts have taken a grudging approach to class action certification since *Falcon*. In any event, in applying the Falcon tests, district courts find it extremely challenging to obey the Supreme Court's separate admonition[6] that they avoid considering the merits of the underlying

3. *See Amchem Products, Inc. v. Windsor*, 521 U.S. 591, 117 S.Ct. 2231, 138 L.Ed.2d 689 (1997) (case under Rule 23(b)(3)).

4. Where the plaintiff class is not sufficiently numerous–e.g., if 20 or fewer plaintiffs compose the putative class–they may join their claims under the far more permissive standard of Federal Rule of Civil Procedure 20. That rule permits joinder provided only that the claimants assert rights to relief arising out of the same transaction or occurrence and at least one question of law or fact common to all persons proposing joinder. *See Alexander v. Fulton County*, 207 F.3d 1303, 1324 (11th Cir.2000) (common allegations of systemic pattern or practice of race-based discrimination arising from same series of transactions, coupled with discriminatory character of defendant's conduct, suffices, even though plaintiffs suffered different effects–promotion denials, transfers, assignments, or discipline–

resulting therefrom); *Grayson v. K Mart Corp.*, 79 F.3d 1086, 1097 (11th Cir.), *cert. denied sub nom. Helton v. Kmart Corp.*, 519 U.S. 982, 117 S.Ct. 435, 136 L.Ed.2d 332 (1996) (a unified policy, plan or scheme of discrimination satisfies Rule 20 commonality requirement); *Mosley v. General Motors Corp.*, 497 F.2d 1330, 1332, 1334 (8th Cir. 1974) (the discriminatory character of defendant's conduct, apparently even without the kind of common policy or scheme often required for Rule 23 class action certification under *Falcon*, can satisfy the commonality requirement of Rule 20).

5. *Falcon*, 457 U.S. at 159 n.15, 102 S.Ct. at 2371 n.15. *See also Bazemore v. Friday*, 478 U.S. 385, 106 S.Ct. 3000, 92 L.Ed.2d 315 (1986).

6. *Eisen v. Carlisle & Jacquelin*, 417 U.S. 156, 177, 94 S.Ct. 2140, 2152, 40 L.Ed.2d 732 (1974).

claim when deciding class certification.

Plaintiffs' counsel have tried to comply with the Court's strictures by assembling class-representative complements composed of applicants, employees and former employees complaining of varied terms and conditions of employment, with each named plaintiff offering to represent a discrete subclass. Defendants routinely reply with objections and motions asserting the existence of conflicts among the proposed subclasses and challenging plaintiffs' adequacy to represent them. When these motions succeed and class certification is denied, they may doom the class action as a practical matter, since orders denying certification are appealable only at the discretion of the appellate court after certification by the district court.[7] Even when defendants' objections are not sustained, they usually necessitate extensive discovery and briefing about the propriety of certification that can rob the class action of its intended expedition and efficiency.

Now that the Civil Rights Act of 1991 permits compensatory and punitive damages in claims under Title VII and the Americans with Disabilities Act, employer representatives have suggested that class treatment would be inappropriate in such cases because issues concerning individualized relief would predominate over issues of liability common to the class.[8] Formally, however, there is no such "predomination" requirement for class certification under Rule 23(b)(2), only under Rule 23(b)(3), which has sometimes successfully been invoked to support class action treatment for mass torts.[9] Although the Supreme Court recently underscored that high individual stakes and significant disparities among class members' demands for relief in mass tort cases may undermine the predomination necessary for (b)(3) certification, the same

---

7. *See* 1998 amendment to Rule 23 adding § 23(f). *See* text, *infra.*

8. *See, e.g., Allison v. Citgo Petroleum Corp.*, 151 F.3d 402 (5th Cir.1998) (plaintiffs' Title VII and § 1981 disparate impact claims for money damages and constitutional right of both parties to jury trial, as now provided under Civil Rights Act of 1991, rendered case unsuitable for class certification). District courts have reached varying conclusions on the effect of the 1991 Amendments on class action suits. *See, e.g., EEOC v. McDonnell Douglas Corp.*, 960 F.Supp. 203 (E.D.Mo.1996); *Morgan v. United Parcel Serv. of Am., Inc.*, 169 F.R.D. 349 (E.D.Mo.1996); *Griffin v. Home Depot, Inc.*, 168 F.R.D. 187 (E.D.La.1996); *Zapata v. IBP, Inc.*, 167 F.R.D. 147 (D.Kan.1996); *Bremiller v. Cleveland Psychiatric Inst.*, 898 F.Supp. 572 (N.D.Ohio 1995); *Arnold v. United Artists Theatre Circuit, Inc.*, 158 F.R.D. 439 (N.D.Cal.1994).

In 1997, the Supreme Court decertified a 23(b)(3) "settlement only" class because the court found numerous conflicts of inter-est among group members, as well as differing issues and claims. That decision, *Amchem Products v. Windsor*, dealt with a mass tort (asbestos) but it may have effects on employment class actions as well. Employment classes after 1991 may have many of the same qualities. For example, individual claims for back pay or front pay may undercut the class' cohesiveness. High stakes could induce individual plaintiffs to seek to control the litigation. Representing both current and former employees could make adequacy of representation questionable.

9. *See Amchem Products, Inc. v. Windsor*, 521 U.S. 591, 117 S.Ct. 2231, 138 L.Ed.2d 689 (1997). Where plaintiffs' claims require case-specific fact inquiries surrounding each alleged discriminatory practice, they have failed Rule 23(b)(3)'s predomination requirement, which is more demanding than the commonality requirement of Rule 23(a). *Allison*, 151 F.3d at 420; *Jackson v. Motel 6 Multipurpose, Inc.*, 130 F.3d 999, 1006 (11th Cir.1997).

opinion specifically distinguished the requirements of (b)(2).[10] And while the Court also discussed the requirement of Rule 23(a)(4), elaborated in *Falcon*, that the named class representatives fairly and adequately protect class interests, the Court's (a)(4) concern in the mass tort setting focused on the divergence of remedial goals between currently asbestos injury claimants who desired immediate compensation and those who had been exposed but were not yet suffering provable injury and who therefore sought delayed compensation through the creation of a massive fund.[11] By contrast, while civil rights and employment discrimination class members would seek damages in varying amounts for compensatory or punitive damages or both, these individual relief questions have typically been handled by bifurcating the systemic treatment class action into a second, remedial stage following an initial determination on liability.[12]

Class actions certified under 23(b)(3) must provide putative class members the option of excluding themselves from the suit.[13] Normally, 23(b)(1) or 23(b)(2) classes are mandatory, which means that the absent class members cannot opt out of the class. Most federal appellate courts have allowed district courts to provide opt out rights to some or all of the absent class members included in a mandatory class in limited circumstances. They have acted under the authority of Rule 23(d),[14] which permits a court, inter alia, to enter orders "determining the course of proceeding." For example, the District of Columbia Court of Appeals allows opt outs from mandatory classes in two situations: (1) if the court finds that the assumption of cohesiveness underlying the certification of a mandatory class is inapplicable to the individual class members claims for money damages, then it may fashion a hybrid class where class members have a limited right to opt-out to individually pursue their money damage claims; and (2) if the court finds that particular plaintiffs' claims are unique or sufficiently distinct from the claims of the class as a

10. *Id.* at 4644, 4641.

11. *Id.* at 4644.

12. *See* § 4.9, *supra*.

13. *See* F.R.C.P. 23(c)(2).

14. Rule 23(d) allows "the court [to] make appropriate orders: (1) determining the course of proceedings or prescribing measures to prevent undue repetition or complication in the presentation of evidence or argument; (2) requiring, for the protection of the members of the class or otherwise for the fair conduct of the action, that notice be given in such manner as the court may direct to some or all of the members of any step in the action, or of the proposed extent of the judgment, or of the opportunity of members to signify whether they consider the representation fair and adequate, to intervene and present claims or defenses, or otherwise to come into the action; (3) imposing conditions on the representative parties or on intervenors; (4) requiring that the pleadings be amended to eliminate therefrom allegations as to representation of absent persons, and that the action proceed accordingly; (5) dealing with similar procedural matters." This authority is limited, however. The Eleventh Circuit vacated two class communication orders as an abuse of the district court's discretion because the nationwide advertisements and mass mailings, issued before class certification, and made pursuant to the communications orders, were causing "serious and irreparable harm to the [defendant's] reputation and to its relationship with its employees." Communication with putative class may be made before certification, but districts "must strive to avoid authorizing injurious class communications that might later prove unnecessary." *Jackson v. Motel 6 Multipurpose, Inc.*, 130 F.3d 999 (11th Cir. 1997).

whole, then it can permit opt outs on a selective basis.[15] In any case, once reasonable opt out procedures are put into place and approved by the court, and putative class members are notified of the procedures, any deviation from the procedures justifies the court denying that opt out election.[16]

The Supreme Court had held that orders denying class action certification are not appealable before final judgment on the merits, even as it recognized that this decision would often induce a plaintiff to abandon his claim.[17] However, the Congress modified Federal Rule of Civil Procedure 23 in 1998 by adding section 23(f). It provides specific authority for a permissive interlocutory appeal of an order granting or denying class certification, subject to the discretion of the court of appeals. Appeals must be made within 10 days of entry of the class certification order, and provides for no stay of the action unless otherwise ordered. The rule took effect on December 1, 1998, and governs proceedings in civil cases commenced after December 1, and in pending proceedings "insofar as just and practicable."[18]

§§ 12.31–12.34 Reserved

G. CLAIM AND ISSUE PRECLUSION IN ACTIONS UNDER TITLE VII AND THE RECONSTRUCTION CIVIL RIGHTS ACTS

§ 12.35 Overview

An increasingly important procedural issue is the extent, if any, to which court actions will be barred by prior agency or court determinations.[1] EEOC reasonable cause determinations cannot prevent timely filed Title VII actions from being heard on the merits. Nor will the decisions of state or local administrative deferral agencies have preclusive effect on subsequent Title VII actions: it would make no sense to preclude a federal court when EEOC is merely required to give those

15. *See Thomas v. Albright*, 139 F.3d 227, 234–35 (D.C.Cir.), *cert. denied*, 525 U.S. 1016, 119 S.Ct. 539, 142 L.Ed.2d 448 (1998) (reversing the district court's decision allowing opt outs where neither prong of the test was met).

16. *See, e.g., Grilli v. Metropolitan Life Ins. Co.*, 78 F.3d 1533, 1538 (11th Cir.), *cert. denied sub nom. Coulter v. Metropolitan Life Ins. Co., Inc.*, 519 U.S. 1040, 117 S.Ct. 608, 136 L.Ed.2d 533 (1996) (denying late opt out elections where purported electors did not satisfy excusable neglect standard); *In re Painewebber Ltd. Partnerships Litig.*, 147 F.3d 132, 135 (2d Cir.1998) (same).

17. *Coopers & Lybrand v. Livesay*, 437 U.S. 463, 98 S.Ct. 2454, 57 L.Ed.2d 351 (1978).

18. *See* Amendments to Federal Rules of Civil Procedure, 118 S.Ct. 399 (April 24, 1998). Some state courts also permit interlocutory review of orders denying class certification. *See* § 12.5, *supra*.

§ 12.35

1. It is clear that no preclusion doctrines, statutory or common law, operate in the absence of an underlying judgment or administrative finding. *See Carver v. Nall*, 172 F.3d 513, 515 (7th Cir.1999) (settlement of union grievance proceedings before the Illinois State Labor Relations Board (ISLRB) did not have res judicata effect precluding deputy sheriffs' § 1983 suit). Thus, a settlement agreement that has not been integrated into a consent decree is not a judgment and cannot trigger preclusion.

decisions "substantial weight."[2] Resolving a conflict in the circuits, and reaching a result consonant with *University of Tennessee v. Elliott*,[3] the Supreme Court has held that the unreviewed administrative determinations of state or local agencies do not preclude private plaintiff actions under ADEA, either.[4] An ADEA lawsuit brought by EEOC, in contrast, will generally preclude private relief.

When, on the other hand, a state administrative determination is reviewed by a state court, a judgment of non-liability may bar a Title VII action in federal court by force of the Full Faith and Credit Act,[5] at least where the judicial review was sought by the employee.[6] *Kremer*, declining to create a Title VII exception to the preclusion required by the terms of § 1738, holds that a federal court presented with a Title VII claim must give the same deference to the state appellate judgment as would a court of the rendering state under the state's principles of preclusion.[7] Consistent with *Kremer*, a state court judgment reviewing a state administrative determination will be accorded the same preclusive effect in a federal court ADEA action that it would receive in the courts of the state.[8] Preclusion under the applicable *state's* law is, however, an important precondition to *Kremer* preclusion; where the state law does not bar subsequent federal employment discrimination suits, *Kremer* will not bar federal court relitigation.[9] Nevertheless, *Kremer* stands as a warning to prospective Title VII plaintiffs that they may lose their Title VII claim by seeking state judicial review of an adverse agency determination.

Kremer has been extended by some lower courts to reach the situation where the *employer* seeks state court review of the administrative agency decision.[10] This approach is questionable. Employment dis-

---

2. *University of Tennessee v. Elliott*, 478 U.S. 788, 106 S.Ct. 3220, 92 L.Ed.2d 635 (1986). *But see Mitchell v. Albuquerque Bd. of Educ.*, 2 F.3d 1160 (10th Cir.1993), *cert. denied*, 510 U.S. 1045, 114 S.Ct. 693, 126 L.Ed.2d 660 (1994).

3. 478 U.S. 788, 106 S.Ct. 3220, 92 L.Ed.2d 635 (1986). *Elliott* is discussed in § 12.38, *infra*.

4. *Astoria Fed. Sav. & Loan Ass'n v. Solimino*, 501 U.S. 104, 111 S.Ct. 2166, 115 L.Ed.2d 96 (1991).

5. 28 U.S.C.A. § 1738.

6. *See Kremer v. Chemical Constr. Corp.*, 456 U.S. 461, 102 S.Ct. 1883, 72 L.Ed.2d 262 (1982). Usually, as in *Kremer* itself, relitigation is barred by issue rather than claim preclusion. This is because most state courts reviewing underlying agency decisions have appellate jurisdiction to review only claims brought under their own state anti-discrimination laws, not claims asserted under Title VII. Some circuits have applied preclusion regardless of which party sought the review. *See Trujillo v. Santa Clara County*, 775 F.2d 1359 (9th Cir.1985);

Hickman v. Electronic Keyboarding, Inc., 741 F.2d 230, 232 n. 3 (8th Cir.1984); *Unger v. Consolidated Foods Corp.*, 693 F.2d 703, 710 n. 11 (7th Cir.1982), *cert. denied*, 460 U.S. 1102, 103 S.Ct. 1801, 76 L.Ed.2d 366 (1983), and *cert. denied*, 464 U.S. 1017, 104 S.Ct. 549, 78 L.Ed.2d 723 (1983).

7. 456 U.S. at 485, 102 S.Ct. at 1899.

8. *See, e.g., Hogue v. Royse City, Texas*, 939 F.2d 1249 (5th Cir.1991).

9. *See Brye v. Brakebush*, 32 F.3d 1179 (7th Cir.1994); *McNasby v. Crown Cork & Seal Co.*, 888 F.2d 270 (3d Cir.1989), *cert. denied*, 494 U.S. 1066, 110 S.Ct. 1783, 108 L.Ed.2d 784 (1990).

10. *See, e.g., Zanders v. National R.R. Passenger Corp.*, 898 F.2d 1127 (6th Cir. 1990); *Trujillo v. County of Santa Clara*, 775 F.2d 1359 (9th Cir.1985); *Hickman v. Electronic Keyboarding, Inc.*, 741 F.2d 230 (8th Cir.1984); and *Gonsalves v. Alpine Country Club*, 727 F.2d 27 (1st Cir.1984). In *Zanders* the court even precluded the Title VII claim where the *employer* instituted state court proceedings not based on employment discrimination. 898 F.2d at 1130.

crimination claimants in most states—those designated by EEOC as "deferral" jurisdictions—are required by Title VII itself to institute state administrative agency proceedings as a prerequisite to the effective filing of a charge with EEOC and therefore ultimately as a condition of prosecuting a Title VII claim in state or federal court.[11] If preclusion of the Title VII claim follows from an employer-instituted review of a state administrative proceeding that Title VII requires the potential plaintiff to commence, the employer in those states may avoid a judicial defense of Title VII claims by its own unilateral action whenever the agency finds for the claimant. The Supreme Court has repudiated a similar result under Title VII or ADEA in two decisions after *Kremer*.[12]

Against this background, *University of Tennessee v. Elliott*[13] creates an awkward dichotomy; it rejects preclusion based on judicially unreviewed state agency proceedings that underlie Title VII actions, but allows such preclusion in actions under the Reconstruction statutes. The plaintiff in *Elliott* presented both types of federal claims to the federal court, but found himself precluded only on the civil rights claim.

Federal courts have also barred Title VII claims by according preclusive effect to prior federal judgments in actions arising out of the same employment setting. In *Woods v. Dunlop Tire Corp.*,[14] for example, a Title VII claim was barred by res judicata because plaintiff had failed to raise that claim in a previous action that challenged her termination under the Labor Management Relations Act ("LMRA"). The Court invoked the broad, contemporary approach to claim preclusion, observing that it is "the identity of facts surrounding the occurrence which constitutes the cause of action" that triggers res judicata, even if the legal theories advanced in the two actions are distinct. That the short statute of limitations on the labor claim ran before EEOC had finished administrative processing of plaintiff's claim did not persuade the court to relieve plaintiff of the ordinary consequences of federal common law preclusion. The court noted that plaintiff could have demanded a notice of right to sue from EEOC 180 days after filing her EEOC charge, or if necessary sought a stay of the LMRA action pending completion of EEOC proceedings, and then amended the LMRA complaint to include a claim under Title VII.

In the class action employment discrimination setting, however, the Supreme Court has somewhat eased the subsequent sting of an adverse federal court judgment. Federal common law accords preclusive effect to judgments rejecting pattern-type discrimination claims in subsequent actions asserting the same theory. But adverse class action or group-

11. See discussion of state and federal administrative agency proceedings under Title VII in Chapter 4, above.

12. See § 12.38.

13. 478 U.S. 788, 106 S.Ct. 3220, 92 L.Ed.2d 635 (1986).

14. 972 F.2d 36 (2d Cir.1992), *cert. denied*, 506 U.S. 1053, 113 S.Ct. 977, 122 L.Ed.2d 131 (1993). *See Churchill v. Star Enter.*, 183 F.3d 184 (3d Cir.1999) (precluding ADA claim based on judgment in prior Family Medical Leave Act action alleging illegal termination based on disability, because plaintiff could have joined ADA claim with FMLA claim in prior action despite necessity of pursuing administrative remedies under ADA).

based judgments (e.g., rejecting claims of disparate treatment against protected group members or claims alleging the disproportionate adverse impact of a neutral practice) do not bar the claims of individual class members alleging disparate treatment à la *McDonnell Douglas/Burdine*.[15] Moreover, when a court denies class action certification, individual class members' claims may still be timely, because the filing of a class action has been held to toll the 90–day period for filing suit until the denial of certification.[16]

§ 12.36   Claim and Issue Preclusion Defined

42 U.S.C.A. § 1738 requires the federal courts to give state court judgments the same preclusive effect that other courts in that state would. A federal court applying that statute may therefore have to consult the preclusion law of any of the fifty states. As a representative introduction to the modern law of claim and issue preclusion prevailing among the states, this Chapter will refer to the widely followed Second Restatement of Judgments, which is also the model for the contemporary federal common law of preclusion.

a.   *Claim Preclusion*

Claim preclusion, or res judicata, refers to the preclusive effect of prior adjudications on entire causes of action asserted in subsequent litigation. A "valid final adjudication of a claim precludes a second action on that claim or any part of it."[1] The essential elements a defendant must plead and prove to preclude a claim, therefore, are : (1) a final judgment "on the merits" in the prior action; (2) identity of claims in the two actions; and (3) identity or privity between the parties in those actions.[2] In addition, for the first judgment to be "valid," it must have been rendered by a court of competent jurisdiction.[3]

Identity not only of claims but of parties in the two actions is required; in the subsequent litigation, the same plaintiff or someone in privity with him must be suing the same defendant or her privy.[4] Under

15. *See Cooper v. Federal Reserve Bank of Richmond*, 467 U.S. 867, 104 S.Ct. 2794, 81 L.Ed.2d 718 (1984).

16. *Crown, Cork & Seal Co. v. Parker*, 462 U.S. 345, 103 S.Ct. 2392, 76 L.Ed.2d 628 (1983).

§ 12.36

1. *Baker ex rel. Thomas v. General Motors Corp.*, 522 U.S. 222, 233 n. 5, 118 S.Ct. 657, 139 L.Ed.2d 580 (1998).

2. *Frank v. United Airlines, Inc.*, 216 F.3d 845, 850 (9th Cir.2000).

3. *Jang v. United Technologies Corp.* 206 F.3d 1147, 1149 (11th Cir.2000).

4. *See, e.g., Andrews v. Daw*, 201 F.3d 521, 525–526 (4th Cir.2000) (government official sued under § 1983 in original action in his official capacity not in privity with

himself when subsequently sued, also under § 1983, in his individual capacity, so plaintiff not precluded); *De Llano v. Berglund*, 183 F.3d 780 (8th Cir.1999) (§ 1983 action against university employees involved in plaintiff's termination not precluded by plaintiff's adverse judgment in Title VII action against university for lack of privity between defendants); *Tice v. American Airlines, Inc.*, 162 F.3d 966 (7th Cir.1998), *cert. denied*, 527 U.S. 1036, 119 S.Ct. 2395, 144 L.Ed.2d 795 (1999) (pilots not precluded from asserting ADEA claim despite prior suit challenging same employment policy because their interests were neither adequately represented nor "virtually represented" in prior litigation); *Delew v. Wagner*, 143 F.3d 1219 (9th Cir.), *cert. denied*, 525 U.S. 1015, 119 S.Ct. 538, 142 L.Ed.2d 448 (1998) (§ 1983 suit arising from alleged

the Second Restatement, claim preclusion is divided into the Rule of Merger and the Rule of Bar, depending on whether the plaintiff (merger) or defendant (bar) succeeded in the initial litigation.[5] The general Rule of Merger is that

> [w]hen a valid and final[6] judgment is rendered in favor of the plaintiff:
>
> (1) The plaintiff cannot thereafter maintain an action on the original claim or any part thereof, although he may be able to maintain an action upon the judgment.[7]

This prohibition against a plaintiff's "splitting" her "cause of action" is sweeping. In particular, so long as the first forum had subject matter jurisdiction to entertain the unasserted claims and provide the same remedies,[8] merger precludes the plaintiff from bringing a subsequent action based on the same real-life transaction or event, either to obtain greater or different relief from that sought originally or to assert a distinct legal theory,[9] or to bring forth new or different evidence or arguments.[10]

police misconduct in the investigation of motor vehicle was not barred by prior wrongful death suit; § 1983 defendants differed from wrongful death defendant); *Headley v. Bacon,* 828 F.2d 1272, 1279–80 (8th Cir.1987) (litigation against city officials sued in their personal capacity under § 1983 not precluded by prior litigation against them in their official capacities under Title VII) . *See* Restatement (Second) of Judgments § 36 cmt.e (determination in action against public official sued in official capacity binding on government but not on official personally). *But see McGuinness v. Regents of Univ. of N.M.,* 183 F.3d 1172 (10th Cir.1999), *cert. denied,* 528 U.S. 932, 120 S.Ct. 332, 145 L.Ed.2d 259 (1999) (defendant university regents successfully invoked claim preclusion in ADA action based on prior judgment in favor of university's medical school, with which regents were in privity).

5. Restatement (Second) of Judgments [hereinafter, "Restatement"] § 17.

6. For the purposes of both claim and issue preclusion, a judgment is final from "the date of its rendition, without regard to the date of commencement of the action in which it is rendered or the action in which it is to be given effect." *Id.* § 14. The definition includes trial court judgments on appeal, until and unless reversed.

7. Restatement (Second) of Judgments § 18.

8. *Id.* § 26(1)(c) (exception to § 24 definition of "claim")

9. Thus, a federal § 1983 action challenging the constitutionality of land use regulations was precluded by a prior state court action where plaintiff could have asserted their constitutional arguments. *See Wilkinson v. Pitkin County Bd. of County Comm'rs,* 142 F.3d 1319 (10th Cir.1998) (per curiam).

10. Restatement (Second) of Judgments §§ 18, 24. *See, e.g., Jang v. United Technologies Corp.* 206 F.3d 1147, 1149 (11th Cir. 2000) (after suffering dismissal of Americans With Disabilities Act claim for want of an EEOC notice of right to sue, plaintiff precluded from asserting same claim in new action after obtaining right to sue letter). Preclusion applies where both the prior and current claims were based on federal law, *see Rivers v. Barberton Bd. of Educ.,* 143 F.3d 1029 (6th Cir.1998) (barring Title VII claim) and where plaintiff splits what for claim preclusion purposes is a "single" cause of action by bringing state law claims in one suit and then, after obtaining an administrative notice of right to sue, bringing a federal claim for relief. *See Heyliger v. State Univ. & Cmty. College,* 126 F.3d 849, 855–56 (6th Cir.1997), *cert. denied,* 522 U.S. 1117, 118 S.Ct. 1054, 140 L.Ed.2d 117 (1998) (observing that plaintiff could and should have requested right to sue letter and, upon receipt, amended state court complaint to add federal law claim); *Brzostowski v. Laidlaw Waste Sys., Inc.,* 49 F.3d 337, 339 (7th Cir.1995) (plaintiff precluded for bringing state law claim first, federal law claim later); *Woods v. Dunlop Tire Corp.,* 972 F.2d 36, 41 (2d Cir.1992) (explaining how plaintiffs may preserve both state and federal law claims by filing the

The general Rule of Bar, in contrast, is triggered by "a valid and final personal judgment rendered in favor of the defendant"—it too prevents "another action by the plaintiff on the same claim."[11] Bar precludes in fewer situations than does merger, because it is subject to an exception for judgments rendered on certain procedural grounds. The first-action outcomes that do not bar include dismissals based on lack of jurisdiction, venue, nonjoinder, misjoinder, failure to satisfy a precondition to suit, prematurity, initial voluntary dismissals, and any grounds of termination that, according to the forum state's or federal court's procedural law or rules, do not bar another action on the same claim.[12] The exception is often said to apply to judgments "not on the merits." This terminology is misleadingly overinclusive, because in contemporary practice repetitive voluntary dismissals as well as involuntary dismissals for failure to state a claim, for untimeliness, or for failure to prosecute or obey court rules or orders all trigger bar even though they plainly do not determine the factual substance of the plaintiff's claim.

A threshold prerequisite for claim preclusion, therefore, is that the claim sought to be precluded in a subsequent action be the same as that asserted in a prior action. In sharp contrast to earlier, more technical and limited definitions, Restatement § 24 provides that the claim capable of extinction (by merger or bar) includes "all rights of the plaintiff to remedies against the defendant with respect to all or any part of the transaction, or series of connected transactions, out of which the action arose."[13] So long as the two actions stem from the same core of real-life events, claim preclusion is possible: the same claim is presented even if

former, seeking a stay pending conclusion of Title VII administrative process and receipt of notice of right to sue, and then amending complaint to add Title VII claims). In *Herrmann v. Cencom Cable Associates*, 999 F.2d 223, 226 (7th Cir.1993), discussed below, Judge Posner elaborated on the ways that plaintiffs required to obtain an administrative clearance before filing a federal employment discrimination claim could avoid preclusion even if the clearance is unavailable when the limitations period expires on companion federal or state law claims arising out of the same transaction and occurrence.

11. *Id.* § 19 (emphasis added).

12. *See id.* § 20 (1) and (2). For a representative list of first-action dismissal grounds that do not usually bar another action on the same claim, see FRCP 41(a)(1) and 41(b). The grounds specifically listed there include only initial voluntary dismissals and involuntary dismissals based on the dilatory defenses of jurisdiction, venue or failure to join a necessary or indispensable party. But the Federal Rule goes on to provide that an order dismissing on any other ground operates as an "adjudication upon the merits"—that is, the order

bars unless it "otherwise specifies." The Restatement, by including dismissals for prematurity or failure to satisfy a precondition to suit among the grounds that do not bar relitigation of the claim even where the dismissal order is silent on that point, thus bars on fewer grounds than Federal Rule 41 would suggest. A federal court using the Restatement as its guide for fashioning a federal common law of preclusion would accordingly not bar on those two grounds despite the contrary implication of the Federal Rules. Compare Restatement §§ 20(2) with 20(1)(c). The same result follows if F.R.C.P. 41(b) itself is read to except from bar dismissals based on prematurity. *See Criales v. American Airlines, Inc.*, 105 F.3d 93 (2d Cir.), *cert. denied*, 522 U.S. 906, 118 S.Ct. 264, 139 L.Ed.2d 190 (1997) (relying on *Costello v. United States*, 365 U.S. 265, 81 S.Ct. 534, 5 L.Ed.2d 551 (1961) as support for construing F.R.C.P. 41(b) to deny bar effect to dismissals for failure to comply with a prerequisite to a determination on the merits, and accordingly holding Title VII action based on timely EEOC charge not barred by dismissal of separate Title VII action based on untimely charge).

13. Restatement (Second) of Judgments § 24.

the plaintiff proceeds on different legal theories,[14] offers different supporting evidence, or seeks different or additional relief.[15] On the other hand, a prisoner's § 1983 damages claim predicated on unconstitutional conditions of confinement is spatially and temporally distinct from his habeas claim challenging an underlying criminal conviction. Accordingly, the § 1983 claim will not be claim precluded by a previous habeas determination—for res judicata purposes, these are different claims.[16]

The definition of claim identity prevents the relitigation not only of causes of action actually raised and adjudicated but of any causes that could have been raised with respect to the same real-life transaction. Thus in the lexicon of modern preclusion, claims based on state law and federal law arising from the same police arrest or employment discharge are considered part of the same transaction; if either is not raised in the original action it may be precluded in subsequent litigation, provided, as would usually be the case, the first forum had subject matter jurisdiction to entertain both claims.[17] Only if the second proceeding is significantly predicated on spatially or temporally distinct real-life events will it normally be considered a separate claim free of the preclusion defense.[18]

These principles are easier to state than to apply. Take, for example, *Herrmann v. Cencom Cable Assoc., Inc.*[19] There the Seventh Circuit Court of Appeals defined "transaction" under the Restatement as follows: "[the] two claims are one for purposes of res judicata if they are

14. *See N.A.A.C.P., Minneapolis Branch v. Metropolitan Council*, 125 F.3d 1171 (8th Cir.1997), *vacated on other grounds*, 522 U.S. 1145, 118 S.Ct. 1162, 140 L.Ed.2d 173 (1998) (action brought under state constitution by class of schoolchildren alleging that council's housing policies deprived them of adequate education was barred by previous action by class of minority persons living in low-income housing alleging that council's policies violated Fair Housing Act; "[t]he same cause of action framed in terms of a new legal theory is still the same cause of action"); *Brzostowski v. Laidlaw Waste Sys., Inc.*, 49 F.3d 337 (7th Cir.1995) (ADEA claim arising from discharge precluded by judgment in action asserting discharge violated employment contract).

15. *See* comments to Restatement § 24.

16. *See Rhodes v. Hannigan*, 12 F.3d 989 (10th Cir.1993).

17. *See* § 26(1)(c), Restatement (Second) of Judgments. *But see Humphrey v. Tharaldson Enters.*, 95 F.3d 624 (7th Cir. 1996) (civil rights claims barred even though state agency where plaintiff first sought relief lacked jurisdiction over those claims); *Davis v. City of Chicago*, 53 F.3d 801, 803 (7th Cir.1995) (precluding federal law claim that § 1983 plaintiff failed to assert when he invoked state court review of local administrative agency determination, even though it was not clear that state court would exercise jurisdiction over the § 1983 claim); *Misischia v. Pirie*, 60 F.3d 626 (9th Cir.1995) (res judicata invoked because § 1983 plaintiff did not seek judicial review in state court of administrative agency decision).

18. *See, e.g., Frank v. United Airlines, Inc.*, 216 F.3d 845, 2000 WL 791209 *4–5 (9th Cir.2000) (flight attendants' claims challenging weight policy under Title VII not claim precluded because based on alleged violations arising after date of postjudgment settlement and because it challenged a different, post-judgment policy); *Pleming v. Universal–Rundle Corp.*, 142 F.3d 1354 (11th Cir.1998) (summary judgment against employee on prior discrimination claim, involving one hiring decision, did not have res judicata effect so as to bar current claims based on two other hiring decisions occurring after filing of prior claim); *Perkins v. Board of Trustees*, 116 F.3d 235 (7th Cir.1997) (no preclusion of Title VII claim alleging employer refused to permit plaintiff to sit for civil service examination based on prior adverse judgment on plaintiff's Title VII claim that employer had refused to permit him to sit for another such examination two years before).

19. 999 F.2d 223, 226 (7th Cir.1993).

based on the same, or nearly the same, factual allegations."[20] The plaintiff, after being discharged by the defendant, filed a charge of discrimination with the EEOC. A few months later the plaintiff also filed suit in federal court against the defendant under the continuation of benefits provision of ERISA ("COBRA"). On defendant's motion, the district court granted summary judgment in the defendant's favor. After obtaining a right-to-sue letter from the EEOC, plaintiff then instituted a Title VII action against the defendant. The district court held the action precluded (by merger) because the claim under ERISA and the Title VII claim should have been brought in one lawsuit.

The plaintiff appealed and the Seventh Circuit reversed. The court of appeals, Judge Posner writing, held that although the proceedings stemmed from a common fact—the discharge of the employee—the Title VII claim concerned primarily events before, and the COBRA claim primarily events after, the discharge. The factual overlap was therefore insufficient to constitute one claim for purposes of res judicata.[21] On the other hand, the court hypothesized a situation in which an employee has an employment contract that protects her from being fired without cause. After the employee is fired, the employee brings suit alleging that the termination was in violation of both the contract and Title VII. In this situation, the "two claims would be the same for purposes of res judicata because, although they would not have identical elements, the central factual issue," whether the employee was fired for cause, would be "at the center of litigation of both claims."[22]

A subsequent appellate decision presents slightly variant facts that may fall between the categories sketched in *Hermann*. A federal employee filed suit alleging that his nonselection for promotion violated Title VII. The employee then filed a class action asserting that the employer had a policy of retaliating against employees who had filed discrimination complaints by denying their subsequent personnel grievances. The Eleventh Circuit upheld a district court decision that the class action was barred by res judicata because it involved the same parties and arose from the same nucleus of operative facts as the discrimination claim.[23] Here the events at issue in the two actions both concern conduct during the term of the plaintiff's employment, in contrast to the situation in *Hermann*. But the alleged retaliation occurred subsequent to the alleged discrimination, and the two claims concern somewhat different employer conduct. Is the retaliation claim barred because it would not have arisen "but for" the underlying claim of discrimination, a measure of claim identity expressly rejected by *Hermann*? A somewhat better rationale for the result is that plaintiff would probably have been allowed to amend his federal court complaint alleging unlawful discrimination to add a

20. *Id.* at 227.

21. *Id.* at 226.

22. *Id.*

23. *Stephens v. Department of Health and Human Servs.*, 9 F.3d 121 (11th Cir. 1993), *cert. denied*, 512 U.S. 1236, 114 S.Ct. 2740, 129 L.Ed.2d 860 (1994).

claim of unlawful retaliation without being required to initiate separate administrative proceedings on the latter claim.[24]

Because administrative exhaustion in Title VII actions is not a jurisdictional element, but rather a condition precedent, a dismissal of one suit for failure to obtain an EEOC right-to-sue notice, for example, would bar a second suit arising from the same operative facts because the first suit would be decided "on the merits."[25]

b. *Issue Preclusion*

Issue preclusion prevents the relitigation not of entire claims but only of particular, actually litigated, issues that were identifiably and necessarily determined by a prior judgment. The general rule of issue preclusion is that "[w]hen an issue of fact or law is actually litigated and determined by a valid and final judgment, and the determination is essential to[26] the judgment, the determination is conclusive in a subsequent action ... whether on the same or a different claim."[27] Therefore, in contrast to claim preclusion, an issue must have been actually litigated to enjoy preclusive effect in subsequent litigation.

The issue must have been the same,[28] although sometimes courts will reach that conclusion by inference.[29] Of course to find issue identity, the court applying issue preclusion must be able to ascertain from the first order or judgment that the same issue was actually determined and how it was determined. That is clearly more difficult, for example, in the

---

24. See Chapter 4 on Title VII Procedures.

25. *See Rivers v. Barberton Bd. of Educ.*, 143 F.3d 1029 (6th Cir.1998). *But see Criales v. American Airlines, Inc.*, 105 F.3d 93 (2d Cir.), *cert. denied*, 522 U.S. 906, 118 S.Ct. 264, 139 L.Ed.2d 190 (1997) (dismissal of Title VII action because EEOC charge untimely does not bar separate action based on timely charge).

26. *See, e.g., Gammage v. West Jasper Sch. Bd. of Educ.*, 179 F.3d 952 (5th Cir. 1999) (precluding ADA claim based on state court finding that plaintiff had not notified employer of disabling condition, a finding essential to judgment approving her nonrenewal). *But cf. Zamarripa v. City of Mesa*, 125 F.3d 792 (9th Cir.1997) (Arizona trial court's pretrial finding that defendant's confession was voluntary was neither judgment nor essential to eventual acquittal, and, thus, could not have collateral estoppel effect in subsequent civil rights action alleging that his confession to crime had been coerced).

27. See § 27 Restatement (Second) of Judgments. It may be wondered why issue rather than claim preclusion would be invoked if the issue common to the two actions were re-presented in a claim that meets the Restatement § 24's broad concept of claim identity and hence is subject to claim preclusion. The reason is that some prerequisite of claim preclusion other than claim identity might be lacking. For example, the original judgment may not be "final" or, in the "bar" situation, a judgment may fall within a § 20 exception for procedurally-grounded judgments deemed "not on the merits."

28. *See Phelps v. Hamilton*, 122 F.3d 1309 (10th Cir.1997) (prior state trial court ruling finding some prosecutions of protestors were brought in bad faith did not have collateral estoppel effect regarding whether subsequent prosecutions were brought in bad faith).

29. *Compare Bechtold v. City of Rosemount*, 104 F.3d 1062 (8th Cir.1997) (a finding in prior state court action that plaintiff's termination was proper implies that it was nondiscriminatory so as to defeat subsequent action under age Discrimination in Employment Act) *with McClendon v. Indiana Sugars, Inc.*, 108 F.3d 789 (7th Cir.1997) (Title VII plaintiff's attempted use of offensive issue preclusion fails in part because issue decided in his favor in state unemployment compensation proceedings did not necessarily show that employer's proffered reason for discharging him was a pretext for unlawful discrimination).

case of a general verdict for plaintiff in a case presenting more than one claim, or a general verdict for defendant on any claim, than where the plaintiff prevails on a single claim. Moreover, the second court must be able to ascertain that the common issue was determined favorably to the party invoking preclusion.[30] And any error in refusing to apply the doctrine will be held harmless if the issue has little relevance to a material issue in the discrimination or civil rights action in which preclusion is asserted.[31]

The Second Restatement of Judgments contains a number of exceptions to the general rule of issue preclusion.[32] Most of these are necessary to temper the judicial development that permits issue preclusion, unlike claim preclusion, to be invoked "nonmutually," that is, *by* (but not against—Due Process forbids that) a nonparty to the prior proceeding.[33] The most important Restatement escape from § 1738 issue preclusion in actions under Title VII and the Reconstruction civil rights acts permits relitigation if

> [t]here is a clear and convincing need for a new determination of [an] issue ... because the party sought to be precluded, as a result of the conduct of his adversary or other special circumstances, did not have an adequate opportunity or incentive to obtain a full and fair adjudication in the initial action.[34]

Thus, subject only to the restraints imposed by the Second Restatement's flexible exceptions, a defendant not party to a prior action may assert issue preclusion "defensively" against a plaintiff who was a party to that action[35] or in privity with such a party.[36] Further, a plaintiff not

30. *See, e.g. Johnson v. Watkins*, 101 F.3d 792 (2d Cir.1996) (§ 1983 false arrest and malicious imprisonment claim not precluded because arrestee had been *acquitted* of the charge for which he had been arrested) (applying New York law).

31. *Biggins v. Hazen Paper Co.*, 111 F.3d 205 (1st Cir.), *cert. denied*, 522 U.S. 952, 118 S.Ct. 373, 139 L.Ed.2d 290 (1997).

32. *See* Restatement (Second) of Judgments §§ 28, 29.

33. *See Bills v. Aseltine*, 52 F.3d 596, 604 (6th Cir.), *cert. denied*, 516 U.S. 865, 116 S.Ct. 179, 133 L.Ed.2d 118 (1995) (permitting § 1983 defendants to assert collateral estoppel nonmutually based on jury's finding, through ascertainable answers to special interrogatories, against plaintiff and in favor of co-defendant).

34. Restatement § 28; *see Kremer v. Chemical Constr. Corp.*, 456 U.S. 461, 480, 102 S.Ct. 1883, 1896, 72 L.Ed.2d 262 (1982). In addition, "[a] party precluded from relitigating an issue with an opposing party ... is also precluded from doing so with another person unless the fact that he lacked full and fair opportunity to litigate the issue in the first action or other circumstances justify affording him an opportunity to relitigate the issue." Restatement § 29.

35. *See Blonder–Tongue Laboratories v. University of Ill. Found.*, 402 U.S. 313, 91 S.Ct. 1434, 28 L.Ed.2d 788 (1971). In an unusual defensive preclusion context, the police officers convicted in federal court of violating Rodney King's civil rights after their state court acquittal on felony assault charges were unable to avail themselves of one of the standard exceptions to issue preclusion. The officers sued the City of Los Angeles to recover their costs in defending a subsequent civil suit King brought against them. The City was relieved of the obligation to pay for that defense because the court found that their convictions on federal criminal charges showed they had acted with actual malice in effecting King's arrest; and malice forfeited their entitlement to a City-paid defense. They were estopped from denying that they had acted with actual malice even though that finding, which the court deemed implicit in the federal criminal conviction, had been at least implicitly rejected by the prior state court verdict of acquittal. *Allen v. City of L.A.*, 92 F.3d 842 (9th Cir.1996).

party to the prior proceedings may assert issue preclusion "offensively"[37] —although again, because of Due Process, only against a defendant who was a party, personally or through a privy, to the earlier litigation.

§ 12.37 Title VII

In *Kremer v. Chemical Construction Corp.*,[1] the Supreme Court held that Title VII, like § 1983, contains no express or implied exemption from the mandate of § 1738,[2] so that in Title VII actions federal courts are required to accord state court judgments full preclusive effect.

In 1975 Rubin Kremer lost his engineering job with Chemical Construction Corporation after being laid off. After several attempts to be rehired, Kremer filed a discrimination charge with the Equal Employment Opportunity Commission (EEOC) under Title VII. Pursuant to Title VII, the EEOC referred the charge to a state administrative agency for proceedings under the parallel state antidiscrimination laws. The state agency made a finding of no discrimination and this finding was upheld on administrative appeal. Kremer then sought review of the administrative decision to the state's intermediate appellate court, which affirmed.[3] Thereafter, a District Director of the EEOC made the determination that "there was no reasonable cause to believe that the charge of discrimination was true and issued a right-to-sue notice."[4] Kremer nevertheless instituted a Title VII action in federal district court. The defendants moved to have the claim dismissed on the ground that the state-court decision precluded relitigation in federal court, and the district court ultimately dismissed Kremer's complaint. The court of appeals affirmed and the Supreme Court granted certiorari.

As in *McCurry* and *Migra*, the Court in *Kremer* framed the issue as "whether Congress intended Title VII to supersede the principles of comity and repose embodied in section 1738."[5] The Court noted that although Title VII requires the EEOC to give "substantial weight" to state proceedings, including presumably state judicial proceedings, that

---

36. *See Tyus v. Schoemehl,* 93 F.3d 449 (8th Cir.1996), *cert. denied sub nom. Miller v. Schoemehl,* 520 U.S. 1166, 117 S.Ct. 1427, 137 L.Ed.2d 536 (1997) (alderman challenging vote dilution allegedly violative of Voting Rights Act held issue precluded based on decision in prior action brought by voters challenging same district boundaries); *Shaw v. Hahn,* 56 F.3d 1128 (9th Cir.1995), *cert. denied,* 516 U.S. 964, 116 S.Ct. 418, 133 L.Ed.2d 336 (1995) (§ 1983 plaintiff attacking her peremptory, allegedly race-based exclusion from a civil jury in prior action held to have been in privity with plaintiffs in that action who unsuccessfully challenged her exclusion under *Batson v. Kentucky,* 476 U.S. 79, 106 S.Ct. 1712, 90 L.Ed.2d 69 (1986), on theory that she shared identity of interest with them as a matter of law; plaintiff accordingly bound by determination against prior plaintiffs on

that issue). *But see Unimex, Inc. v. United States Dep't of Hous. & Urban Dev.,* 594 F.2d 1060, 1061 n.3 (5th Cir.1979) (per curiam) (suit against official sued in official capacity cannot have collateral estoppel effect in subsequent suit against him in his personal capacity).

37. *See Parklane Hosiery Co. v. Shore,* 439 U.S. 322, 99 S.Ct. 645, 58 L.Ed.2d 552 (1979).

§ 12.37

1. 456 U.S. 461, 102 S.Ct. 1883, 72 L.Ed.2d 262 (1982).

2. *Id.* at 476, 102 S.Ct. at 1895.

3. *Id.* at 463–64, 102 S.Ct. at 1888.

4. *Id.* at 465, 102 S.Ct. at 1889.

5. *Id.* at 462, 102 S.Ct. at 1887.

direction is simply a floor on the level of deference required, not a ceiling as suggested by the dissent.[6] Accordingly, the Court held that in actions under Title VII, as under the nineteenth century civil rights acts, § 1738 requires federal courts to give as much[7] preclusive effect to court judgments as would other courts of that state.[8]

6. *Id.* at 470 n.8, 488, 102 S.Ct. at 1892 n.8, 1901. The *Kremer* majority distinguished federal court review of state court proceedings, the issue there, from federal court review of state administrative agency proceedings. (The *Kremer* dissent, by contrast, viewed the state appellate court's affirmance of the agency's finding as merely a continuation of the state agency proceedings. *Id.* at 490, 102 S.Ct. at 1902 (Blackmun, J., dissenting)). The majority thus laid the foundation for one of the holdings in *University of Tennessee v. Elliott*, 478 U.S. 788, 106 S.Ct. 3220, 92 L.Ed.2d 635 (1986), discussed below, asserting in dictum that "it is clear that [judicially] *unreviewed administrative* determinations by state *agencies . . . [under Title VII]* should not preclude [federal court] review [of federal claims under statutes that mandate prior resort to state administrative agencies] even if such a decision were to be afforded preclusive effect in a State's own courts." *Kremer,* 456 U.S. at 470 n.7, 102 S.Ct. at 1891 n.7 (emphasis added). The Court would later expand that holding from *Elliott* to permit federal court actions under the Age Discrimination in Employment Act notwithstanding a contrary state administrative determination. *Astoria Fed. Sav. & Loan Ass'n v. Solimino,* 501 U.S. 104, 111 S.Ct. 2166, 115 L.Ed.2d 96 (1991).

Justice Stevens, also dissenting, redefined the issue as whether the state judicial review of the agency proceedings involves a substantive review of the claims presented at the agency level—in which case the judgment would be entitled to preclusive effect—or a more deferential "arbitrary and capricious" standard—in which case the judgment would have no preclusive effect. *Kremer,* 456 U.S. at 507, 102 S.Ct. at 1910 (Stevens, J., dissenting). Although the majority stated that "[t]here is no requirement that judicial review must proceed de novo if it is to be preclusive," it did seem to require that the state court's holding must at least "constitute a finding 'one way or the other' on the merits of petitioner's claim." *Id.* at 480 n.21, 102 S.Ct. at 1896 n.21.

In a footnote, the Court cited several cases indicating that the state-court review in *Kremer* was a review on the merits. *Id.* In *Bray v. New York Life Ins.,* 851 F.2d 60 (2d Cir.1988), the United States Court of Appeals for the Second Circuit held that a state court dismissal on statute of limitation grounds of an appeal from an administrative determination of no probable cause served to preclude a relitigation of those issues in federal court under Title VII and § 1981. *Id.* at 61. Citing *Kremer,* the court concluded that "[b]ecause New York treats a dismissal on statute of limitation grounds as a final judgment on the merits for res judicata purposes," the state court judgment served to preclude relitigation in federal court. *Id.* at 64.

7. *Kremer,* 456 U.S. at 476. If state law would not accord a prior state court judgment preclusive effect in other courts of that state, neither would § 1738 give the judgment preclusive effect in a subsequent Title VII action in federal court. *See Pavon v. Smith Transp. Co.,* 192 F.3d 902 (9th Cir.1999) (under Oregon law, Title VII claim dependent upon proof of discriminatory intent not part of same "claim" as prior unpaid wage state court action that required only evidence of failure to pay off wage due, so no preclusion even though both claims arose from common events); *Dici v. Pennsylvania,* 91 F.3d 542 (3d Cir. 1996) (state court affirmance of workers compensation ruling on fact issues not issue preclusive in subsequent Title VII action because workers compensation and Title VII legal issues differed and a Pennsylvania state court would not give preclusive effect even to fact issues under those circumstances); *McNasby v. Crown Cork and Seal Co.,* 888 F.2d 270, 271 (3d Cir.1989), *cert. denied,* 494 U.S. 1066, 110 S.Ct. 1783, 108 L.Ed.2d 784 (1990) (denying preclusive effect in a Title VII action to a state court judgment because the judgment would not be entitled to preclusive effect in other courts of that state).

8. *See Heyliger v. State Univ. and Cmty. College Sys. of Tenn.,* 126 F.3d 849 (6th Cir.1997) (federal court Title VII action precluded by adverse state court judgment arising from same termination decision), *cert. denied,* 522 U.S. 1117, 118 S.Ct. 1054, 140 L.Ed.2d 117 (1998); *Bechtold v. City of Rosemount,* 104 F.3d 1062 (8th Cir.1997) (plaintiff's ADEA claim collaterally estopped by finding in his prior state court action that his termination was proper, implying it was also nondiscriminatory).

The Court observed that prior decisions, including *McCurry*, which insisted that the person to be precluded had received a "full and fair opportunity to litigate," did not define the extent of that requirement.[9] The Court in *Kremer* did, holding that "where we are bound by the statutory directive of section 1738, state proceedings need do no more than satisfy the minimum procedural requirements of the Fourteenth Amendment's Due Process Clause in order to qualify for the full faith and credit guaranteed by federal law."[10]

The *Kremer* majority opinion apparently limits its holding by emphasizing that "[n]o provision of Title VII requires claimants to pursue in state court an unfavorable state administrative action."[11] That is, an important undercurrent to the Court's opinion appears to be the idea that the petitioner/employee in *Kremer* was precluded only because he went beyond Title VII's mandated administrative agency exhaustion by pursuing the state law employment discrimination claim to the state appellate court. Nevertheless, some lower courts have downplayed the "voluntary" nature of the state-court review and have purported to give preclusive effect to state-court judgments even when it was the defendant employer, not the employee, who appealed the administrative finding.[12]

In one such decision, the employee, as required by Title VII, filed a state law claim with the appropriate state administrative body, which found liability. The employer appealed to state court, which reversed. The state agency appealed that ruling and an appeals court reversed and reinstated the agency's determination of liability. At the same time, the employee filed an action in federal court alleging violations of Title VII, § 1983 and § 1981, seeking remedies beyond those available through the state agency. The Ninth Circuit approved a district court decision dismissing the action as precluded by the state court decisions.[13] The court acknowledged that the *Kremer* plaintiff's resort to state court was voluntary, but it also noted the Supreme Court's statement that "the finality of state court judgments should not 'depend on which side

---

9. *Kremer*, 456 U.S. at 480–82, 102 S.Ct. at 1896–98.

10. *Id.* at 482, 102 S.Ct. at 1898. In *Clark v. Clark*, 984 F.2d 272 (8th Cir.), *cert. denied*, 510 U.S. 828, 114 S.Ct. 93, 126 L.Ed.2d 60 (1993), the United States Court of Appeals for the Eighth Circuit held that the due process requirement of *Kremer* does not require a state court specifically to address each contention raised by a litigant in order for that decision to have preclusive effect. *Id.* at 273. In *Clark* the plaintiff raised several constitutional contentions in her state-court action claiming title to real property. The state court ruled against the defendant, but failed to address any of the plaintiff's constitutional arguments in its opinion. Plaintiff then brought suit under § 1983 in district court seeking an injunc-

tion. The district court dismissed the suit and the plaintiff appealed. *Id.* The court of appeals affirmed, holding that due process does not require "any particular technique of opinion-writing [and that] [c]ourts frequently reject by implication arguments urged by parties." *Id.*

11. *Kremer*, 456 U.S. at 469, 102 S.Ct. at 1891.

12. *See Zanders v. National R.R. Passenger Corp.*, 898 F.2d 1127 (6th Cir.1990); *Trujillo v. County of Santa Clara*, 775 F.2d 1359 (9th Cir.1985); *Hickman v. Electronic Keyboarding, Inc.*, 741 F.2d 230 (8th Cir. 1984); and *Gonsalves v. Alpine Country Club*, 727 F.2d 27 (1st Cir.1984).

13. *Trujillo*, 775 F.2d at 1359–63, 1369.

prevailed in a given case[].' "[14] The Ninth Circuit also found that the Supreme Court's 1985 decision in *Marrese v. American Acad. of Orthopaedic Surgeons* (holding that the preclusive effect of a state-court judgment is determined solely by reference to applicable state law principles)[15] dictated that regardless of whether the federal plaintiff's trip to state court was voluntary, § 1738 mandated that the state-court judgment be given the same preclusive effect it would enjoy in courts of the state.[16]

These lower court decisions seem to miss the Supreme Court's point. That *Kremer* was not concerned with which side prevailed in state court does not diminish the significance of its emphasis that the employee in *Kremer* chose the state judicial forum voluntarily, not by compulsion of federal law. There is something manifestly unfair, and hence seemingly contrary to Due Process[17] as well as the law of preclusion, about permitting the employer to deprive the employee of a federal judicial forum on a federal claim simply by seeking judicial review of a state administrative proceeding that federal law required the employee to initiate. The Supreme Court's apparent recognition of this unfairness, and the supremacy of federal law in such situations, is implicit in two post-*Kremer* decisions that declined to preclude plaintiffs' Title VII or ADEA claims as the result of administrative proceedings that federal law obliged them to exhaust.[18]

§ 12.38 Federal Common Law Preclusion: State Agency to Federal Court

In *University of Tennessee v. Elliott*,[1] the Supreme Court reached divergent conclusions about the preclusive effect of unreviewed state agency factfinding on federal court actions under, respectively, Title VII and the Reconstruction civil rights acts. The Court held that state agency factfinding not judicially reviewed has no preclusive effect on Title VII claims.[2] By contrast, the Court did fashion a federal common-law rule of issue preclusion for state agency factfinding in actions under the Reconstruction civil rights statutes.[3]

---

14. *Id.* at 1364 (quoting *Kremer*, 456 U.S. at 470, 102 S.Ct. at 1891 (footnote omitted)).

15. 470 U.S. 373, 105 S.Ct. 1327, 84 L.Ed.2d 274 (1985).

16. *Trujillo*, 775 F.2d at 1363.

17. *See Logan v. Zimmerman Brush Co.*, 455 U.S. 422, 102 S.Ct. 1148, 71 L.Ed.2d 265 (1982) (once state creates a claim and hence a contingent property right of the plaintiff, it may not adopt procedures that effectively ensure that the claim will fail).

18. *See University of Tennessee v. Elliott*, 478 U.S. 788, 106 S.Ct. 3220, 92 L.Ed.2d 635 (1986) (Title VII plaintiffs); *Astoria Fed. Sav. & Loan Ass'n v. Solimino*, 501 U.S. 104, 111 S.Ct. 2166, 115 L.Ed.2d 96 (1991) (ADEA plaintiffs). *Elliott* is discussed in the text immediately following.

§ 12.38

1. 478 U.S. 788, 106 S.Ct. 3220, 92 L.Ed.2d 635 (1986).

2. *Id.* at 796, 106 S.Ct. at 3225. This holding was extended to federal court litigation under the Age Discrimination in Employment Act in *Astoria Fed. Sav. & Loan Ass'n v. Solimino*, 501 U.S. 104, 111 S.Ct. 2166, 115 L.Ed.2d 96 (1991).

3. *Elliott*, 478 U.S. at 798, 106 S.Ct. at 3226.

In 1981 the University of Tennessee informed Elliott that he was being discharged for poor work performance. He requested an administrative hearing to determine the validity of the discharge but also filed a federal action under Title VII and § 1983 alleging that the discharge was racially motivated. The administrative law judge found no racial motivation behind the discharge,[4] and Elliott did not appeal this result to state court. The university moved the federal court for summary judgment on the basis that the state administrative agency factfinding precluded any further action on the Title VII or § 1983 claims.[5]

The Supreme Court, reinstating a summary judgment granted by the trial judge, first noted that § 1738 was inapplicable. Section 1738 does not cover state administrative factfinding; by its own terms it requires prior state "judicial proceedings" like those in *McCurry, Migra,* and *Kremer*.[6] Yet federal courts have frequently devised federal common-law rules of preclusion.[7] The Court accordingly defined the issues as whether it should fashion a common law rule of preclusion "first with respect to respondent's Title VII claim, and next with respect to his claims under the ... Reconstruction civil rights statutes."[8]

In regard to the Title VII claim, the Court referred to the directive in 42 U.S.C.A. § 2000e–5(b) that EEOC must accord state administrative factfinding "substantial weight."[9] The Court stated that "it would make little sense for Congress to write such a provision if state agency findings were entitled to preclusive effect in Title VII actions in federal court."[10]

---

4. However, the administrative law judge did feel that the discharge was too harsh a response to the petitioner's poor work performance and ordered that the petitioner merely be transferred to another position with the university. *Id.* at 791, 106 S.Ct. at 3222.

5. *Id.* at 792–94, 106 S.Ct. at 3222.

6. *See* § 12.38.

7. *Elliott,* 478 U.S. at 794, 106 S.Ct. at 3224.

8. *Id.* at 794, 106 S.Ct. at 3224.

9. *Id.* at 795, 106 S.Ct. at 3224. *See, e.g., Heyne v. Caruso,* 69 F.3d 1475 (9th Cir. 1995) (overruling trial court's exclusion from evidence of a state antidiscrimination agency's finding of probable cause).*But see Beachy v. Boise Cascade Corp.,* 191 F.3d 1010, 1014 (9th Cir.1999), *cert. denied,* ___ U.S. ___, 120 S.Ct. 1425, 146 L.Ed.2d 316 (2000) (state agency's determination of insufficient facts to continue investigating inadmissible in jury trial; in effect such a determination amounts to final ruling of no probable cause, and as such entails a much greater risk of unfair prejudice than a more tentative agency determination finding probable cause to believe violation occurred). Similarly, EEOC's own probable cause determination is usually admissible in a subsequent judicial action under Title VII,

because its probative value outweighs its potential prejudicial effect, a determination within the discretion of the trial judge. *See* text *infra. But see Walker v. NationsBank,* 53 F.3d 1548 (11th Cir.1995) (noting that EEOC determinations routinely admissible in bench, not jury trials).

The IDEA requires federal courts to give state administrative proceedings "due weight." *See Board of Educ. of Hendrick Hudson Central Sch. Dist., Westchester County v. Rowley,* 458 U.S. 176, 206, 102 S.Ct. 3034, 3051, 73 L.Ed.2d 690 (1982) ("the fact that § 1415(e) [of the IDEA] requires that the reviewing court "receive the records of the [state] administrative proceedings" carries with it the implied requirement that due weight shall be given to these proceedings"). This does not mean however that a district court may adopt the state findings wholesale; the judge must conduct an independent examination of the evidence. *See Doe v. Metropolitan Nashville Pub. Sch.,* 133 F.3d 384 (6th Cir.), *cert. denied,* 525 U.S. 813, 119 S.Ct. 47, 142 L.Ed.2d 36 (1998).

10. *Elliott,* 478 U.S. at 795, 106 S.Ct. at 3225 (citing *Kremer v. Chemical Constr. Corp.* 456 U.S. 461, 470, 102 S.Ct. 1883, 1891, 72 L.Ed.2d 262 (1982)).

In addition, the Court cited *Chandler v. Roudebush* as supporting the view that state administrative findings are not entitled to preclusive effect in Title VII actions.[11] *Chandler* held "that a federal employee whose discrimination claim was rejected by her employing agency after an administrative hearing was entitled to a trial de novo in federal court on her Title VII claim."[12] The Court felt that it would be inconsistent with the decision in *Chandler* to deny Elliott a trial de novo on his Title VII claim. It therefore held that in actions under Title VII, unreviewed state administrative factfinding has no preclusive effect either under § 1738 or federal common law.[13]

The decision in *Elliott* concerned an attempt by an employer to use a favorable administrative finding to preclude a subsequent federal suit against that employer under Title VII. Several lower courts have refused to limit the *Elliott* Title VII holding, which concerned a defendant employer's attempt to invoke collateral estoppel, by giving preclusive effect when the Title VII *plaintiff* invokes the doctrine offensively.[14] The United States Court of Appeals for the Third Circuit, for example, has held that the *Elliott* condemnation of Title VII administrative preclusion by defendants also serves to prevent the offensive use of issue preclusion "in a Title VII action by an employee who has previously filed a successful [administrative] claim."[15] These courts have relied on *Elliott's* broad language, which denied preclusive effect to unreviewed state administrative determinations unfavorable to defendants, without indicating specifically that the Court also recognized the normal Title VII policy of affording claimants unimpeded access to a judicial forum;[16] or they have noted that the employer bore a heavier burden of persuasion on the common issue in the earlier proceeding, so that estoppel would be unfair.[17] But at least one court has found otherwise, in part by finding

11. *Id.* at 795, 106 S.Ct. at 3225 (citing 425 U.S. 840, 96 S.Ct. 1949, 48 L.Ed.2d 416 (1976)).

12. *Id.* at 795, 106 S.Ct. at 3225.

13. *Id.* at 796, 106 S.Ct. at 3225. This *Elliott* holding has recently been applied notwithstanding an employer's argument that the particular agency that rendered the finding on the common issue was "an actual court" because it enjoyed quasi-adjudicatory powers. The Fourth Circuit held that the existence of such powers did not transform the agency into a court for preclusion purposes, noting that either party could have petitioned a court for enforcement of the agency's decisions. *Rao v. County of Fairfax, Va.,* 108 F.3d 42 (4th Cir.1997).

14. *See, e.g., Herron v. Tennessee Bd. of Regents,* 42 F.3d 1388 (6th Cir.1994), *cert. denied,* 515 U.S. 1102, 115 S.Ct. 2246, 132 L.Ed.2d 255 (1995); *Roth v. Koppers Indus., Inc.,* 993 F.2d 1058, 1062–63 (3d Cir.1993); *United States v. Board of Educ. of Piscataway,* 798 F.Supp. 1093, 1100 (D.N.J.1992);

Gallo v. John Powell Chevrolet, Inc., 765 F.Supp. 198, 207–08 (M.D.Pa.1991); *Johnson v. Halls Merch., Inc.,* 1989 WL 23201, at *2 (W.D.Mo.1989); *Caras v. Family First Credit Union,* 688 F.Supp. 586, 589 (D.Utah 1988).

15. *Roth v. Koppers Indus., Inc.,* 993 F.2d 1058 (3d Cir.1993).

16. *See Roth,* 993 F.2d at 1062.

17. *See Herron,* 42 F.3d 1388. Of course an employer in an administrative proceeding under state law may often bear the burden of demonstrating some sort of "cause" or "just cause" for termination or other adverse employment action. If plaintiff proceeds to court under Title VII, and produces only inferential, *McDonnell Douglas*-type evidence of race, gender, religious or national origin discrimination, then she, rather than the employer, would bear the burden of persuasion on the ultimate issue of unlawful discrimination; and the employer would bear only a production burden to raise the defense of a legitimate nondis-

Elliott distinguishable because the plaintiff is more favorably situated in terms of Title VII policies.[18] Moreover, given the Court's other holding in *Elliott*, that Reconstruction Act plaintiffs, unlike Title VII plaintiffs, are vulnerable to defensive issue preclusion based on prior, optional administrative proceedings, § 1983 plaintiffs should be able to use preclusion offensively (subject to the exceptions in Restatement § 28) when they have prevailed in those proceedings.[19] Finally, it should be noted that a state (or federal) administrative agency's decision may, like that of an arbitrator,[20] be admissible in the employment discrimination lawsuit even if it is denied preclusive effect.[21]

criminatory reason. *See* the *Burdine* and *St. Mary's* decisions discussed in Chapter 3. In such a case it may therefore be unfair to permit the plaintiff, based on the prior administrative proceedings, to invoke issue preclusion against the employer on the issue of "cause" or other issues impliedly decided as a result. *McClendon v. Indiana Sugars, Inc.*, 108 F.3d 789 (7th Cir.1997) (offensive issue preclusion in Title VII action fails in part because plaintiff had lesser burden of proof in prior administrative proceedings). If, on the other hand, the plaintiff offers "direct" evidence of unlawful discrimination, the *defendant*, per Title VII § 703(m), must persuade that it would have taken the same employment action for a reason or reasons (e.g., "just cause") independent of the unlawful one. In such a case, at least, it is not shifting any burden of persuasion to preclude the employer from relitigating the issue of cause, on which it must carry the persuasion burden in both proceedings.

18. *Driscoll v. Greene County Sch. Dist. and Phil Brock,* No. 94–71 (M.D.Ga.1995) (precluding defendants from relitigating state administrative agency's quasijudicial, unreviewed findings concerning facts related to Title VII defenses, and adhering to that decision on reconsideration). One of the authors was co-counsel for plaintiff in *Driscoll.*

19. See text *infra.*

20. *Alexander v. Gardner–Denver Co.,* 415 U.S. 36, 94 S.Ct. 1011, 39 L.Ed.2d 147 (1974), discussed in § 4.6 above.

21. The clear majority of circuits hold that the admissibility of EEOC determinations in jury trials depends on F.R.E. 403 probative value/prejudice balancing and is within the discretion of the trial judge. *See Lathem v. Department of Children and Youth Servs.,* 172 F.3d 786 (11th Cir.1999) (no cause determination was properly excluded as too prejudicial); *Paolitto v. John Brown E. & C., Inc.,* 151 F.3d 60 (2d Cir. 1998) (no per se rule of admissibility); *EEOC v. Ford Motor Co.,* 98 F.3d 1341 (6th Cir.1996) (no error in refusal to admit EEOC determinations in either bench or jury trials); *Hall v. Western Prod. Co.,* 988 F.2d 1050, 1057–58 (10th Cir.1993); *Barfield v. Orange County,* 911 F.2d 644, 650–51 (11th Cir.1990), *cert. denied,* Barfield v. Lamar, 500 U.S. 954, 111 S.Ct. 2263, 114 L.Ed.2d 715 (1991); *Johnson v. Yellow Freight Sys., Inc.,* 734 F.2d 1304, 1309 (8th Cir.), *cert. denied,* 469 U.S. 1041, 105 S.Ct. 525, 83 L.Ed.2d 413 (1984); *McCluney v. Jos. Schlitz Brewing Co.,* 728 F.2d 924, 929–30 (7th Cir.1984); *Walton v. Eaton Corp.,* 563 F.2d 66, 75 & n. 12 (3d Cir.1977) (en banc); *Cox v. Babcock & Wilcox Co.,* 471 F.2d 13, 15 (4th Cir.1972) (admissibility within discretion of district court). *But see EEOC v. Manville Sales Corp.,* 27 F.3d 1089, 1095 (5th Cir.1994), *cert. denied,* 513 U.S. 1190, 115 S.Ct. 1252, 131 L.Ed.2d 133 (1995); *Plummer v. Western Int'l. Hotels Co.,* 656 F.2d 502, 505 (9th Cir.1981) (appearing to adopt a per se rule that a plaintiff may introduce an EEOC probable cause determination in a Title VII lawsuit); *Gilchrist v. Jim Slemons Imports, Inc.,* 803 F.2d 1488, 1500 (9th Cir.1986) (same). *But see Beachy v. Boise Cascade Corp.,* 191 F.3d 1010, 1014 (9th Cir.1999), *cert. denied,* ___ U.S. ___, 120 S.Ct. 1425, 146 L.Ed.2d 316 (2000) (state agency's determination of insufficient facts to continue investigating inadmissible in jury trial; in effect such a determination amounts to final ruling of no probable cause, and as such entails a much greater risk of unfair prejudice than a more tentative agency determination finding probable cause to believe violation occurred).

In bench trials, EEOC determinations are routinely admissible. *See Bell v. Birmingham Linen Serv.,* 715 F.2d 1552, 1554, n. 4 (11th Cir.1983), *cert. denied,* 467 U.S. 1204, 104 S.Ct. 2385, 81 L.Ed.2d 344 (184); *Garcia v. Gloor,* 618 F.2d 264, 272 (5th Cir. 1980), *cert. denied,* 449 U.S. 1113, 101 S.Ct. 923, 66 L.Ed.2d 842 (1981); *Peters v. Jefferson Chemical Co.,* 516 F.2d 447, 450 (5th Cir.1975); *Smith v. Universal Servs., Inc.,*

§§ 12.39–12.44 Reserved

H. INTER–ACTION AND INTRA–
ACTION PRECLUSION

§ 12.45 In General

Ordinarily, a plaintiff will be required to assert all available Title VII and Reconstruction Act claims arising from the same real-life events in the same judicial action. State courts have subject matter jurisdiction concurrent with federal courts to entertain both Title VII and Reconstruction Act claims. Accordingly, the jurisdiction exception to claim preclusion[1] is inapplicable and a final, prior state court judgment on one of these federal statutory claims should preclude asserting any other such claim in a federal court. Similarly, a prior final *federal* court judgment on one of those claims would usually preclude the subsequent prosecution of any other such claim in another federal action, per the federal common law of preclusion.

Nevertheless, there will be situations in which a subsequent action would not be claim precluded. For example, there may be no final judgment in the first action before the second action is commenced; the parties may have agreed that the plaintiff may split her claims; the second action may be adjudged to be based on a different "claim"; or, most obviously, the second action is brought by a different plaintiff against the same employer or civil rights defendant, thereby destroying identity of parties. In such cases the second action may proceed, although common issues will then be subject to *issue* preclusion.

Of course, as is always true when for some reason claim preclusion fails, the court in the second action must take care to invoke issue preclusion only to the degree that its distinct requirements and exceptions demand. A decision involving successive Title VII actions by different employees against the same employer makes the point. Two female employees commenced separate actions alleging discriminatory rejection for promotion to the same supervisory position in favor of a less qualified male. Coworker 1, whose action first proceeded to judgment, prevailed on bench determinations that (1) the employer's stated reason for preferring the male was a pretext for gender discrimination and (2) she, rather than the male or coworker 2, was best qualified for the lone supervisory position. In the second action, coworker 2, after establishing a prima face case which the employer rebutted by asserting the same ostensibly legitimate nondiscriminatory reason, asked the court to estop the defendant from denying that its rejection of her was pretextual. The

---

454 F.2d 154, 157 (5th Cir.1972). In *Walker v. NationsBank,* 53 F.3d 1548 (11th Cir. 1995), the court observed that EEOC administrative determination letters have been held routinely admissible in bench, but not in jury trials; those determinations, the court wrote, vary significantly in their degree of detail and quality, and have the potential to create unfair prejudice in the minds of jurors.

§ 12.45

1. See § 12.38, *supra,* concerning Restatement § 26(1)(c).

employer objected, and asked the court to estop the plaintiff from denying that coworker 1 was best qualified and that only she, not coworker two, was eligible for a remedy.

The court of appeals ruled that the plaintiff could (offensively) estop the employer from denying pretext, but that the employer could not (defensively) estop the plaintiff from relitigating who among the three candidates for the position was best qualified.[2] On issue (1), pretext, the standard for prerequisites of collateral estoppel were in place: the party against whom estoppel was asserted, the employer, was a party to action 1; the pretext issue was identical; that issue was litigated and determined; and the determination of the pretext issue was essential to the judgment in favor of coworker 1. Further, no exception to issue preclusion pertained, because the employer had received a full and fair opportunity with ample incentive to defend the first action in a tribunal that afforded no lesser procedural advantages than the second.

By contrast, the court rejected the use of defensive issue preclusion by the employer on the issue of which of the candidates was best qualified. It is a fundamental requirement not only of issue (as well as claim) preclusion but also due process that only parties to the action in which the prior judgment was rendered, or their narrowly defined privies, can be precluded, because only they have had an opportunity to litigate. Coworker 2 was not a party to the action that first came to judgment. Nor was she represented in it, actually or virtually, by coworker 1, whose interests were indeed adverse in the sense that only one of the plaintiffs could be deemed entitled to the promotion.

Suppose a plaintiff first brings an equitable suit under Title VII, triable only to a court, then a legal, jury-triable action under § 1981 or § 1983, and that, for one of the reasons given above, claim preclusion does not bar or merge the claims. If an adverse bench determination of an issue common to the two lawsuits could preclude relitigation of that issue in the subsequent action at law, a party could lose the right to jury determination of that issue when the legal claim is tried. In *Parklane Hosiery Co. v. Shore*,[3] a securities law case, the Supreme Court held that the ordinary rules of issue preclusion applied despite the consequent loss of the jury trial right. Presumably the same result obtains when the two actions presenting the common issue involve employment discrimination claims.

But sometimes legal and equitable claims are presented in the same action. By hypothesis there is no prior judgment, so *Parklane*-type preclusion does not apply. In this setting the Court does preserve the right to jury trial at the risk of inconsistent determinations of the common issue. In *Lytle v. Household Mfg., Inc.*,[4] the Court held that an adverse ruling on the common issue as part of a district judge's dismissal

2. *Meredith v. Beech Aircraft Corp.*, 18 F.3d 890 (10th Cir.1994).

3. 439 U.S. 322, 99 S.Ct. 645, 58 L.Ed.2d 552 (1979).

4. 494 U.S. 545, 110 S.Ct. 1331, 108 L.Ed.2d 504 (1990).

(ultimately reversed on appeal) of a Title VII claim could not preclude the jury from deciding the same issue differently in deliberating on the § 1981 claim. This holding was in accord with decisions that had condemned prior bench determinations of issues common to legal and equitable claims because the judicial ruling would, as law of the case,[5] bar relitigation of the common issue and in turn effectively deprive a party of a Seventh Amendment or statutory right to jury trial.[6] And where a jury decides, for example, the amount of a back pay award, the judge in a subsequent bench trial is bound by the jury's determination.[7]

The problem of mixed legal and equitable claims should arise less often in the employment context because of the Civil Rights Act of 1991, which amended Title VII. The Act provides that Title VII claims of intentional discrimination, like claims under § 1981 or § 1983, are triable to a jury. The problem should persist, and *Lytle* and *Parklane* remain pertinent, primarily when the Title VII plaintiff challenges only a neutral practice (alleging its disproportionate adverse impact), a claim triable solely to the court even under the Civil Rights Act of 1991. That plaintiff would be well advised, if desirous of preserving jury trial on a related Reconstruction Act claim, to present both claims in the same action, so that *Lytle* would protect the right to jury trial. Alternatively, if separate actions are permissible despite the restrictions of claim preclusion, and are tactically desirable or necessary to fulfill procedural prerequisites or avoid limitations problems, the plaintiff may still avoid the effect of *Parklane* by pressing for a judgment on the jury-triable Reconstruction Act claim before another court adversely determines the equitable Title VII claim.

---

5. The "law of the case" doctrine is a softer form of claim or issue preclusion within one civil action (and therefore not dependent on a prior final judgment) that rests on the premise that an issue once decided and not overturned by a subsequent appeal should, if presented a second time in the same case and court, be decided consistently with the first ruling. For the most part, the parties, having not challenged the ruling when able to do so on an initial appeal, are deemed to have waived the right to challenge that decision subsequently, subject only to an intervening change in the law or a showing that the previous decision was clearly erroneous and manifestly unjust. *See Kimberlin v. Quinlan*, 199 F.3d 496, 500 (D.C.Cir.1999), *petition for cert. filed*, June 30, 2000. While the question is not free from doubt, it has been held that the doctrine applies not just when an issue has been decided by an appellate court ruling at a previous stage of the case but also on remand to a district court where its previous ruling was not challenged, reviewed or decided on an initial appeal. *Id.* at 500. *Compare Crocker v. Piedmont Aviation, Inc.*, 49 F.3d 735 (D.C.Cir.), *cert. denied*, 516 U.S. 865, 116 S.Ct. 180, 133 L.Ed.2d 118 (1995) ("law of the case" not applicable where party failed to appeal appealable issue on first appeal or present it on remand to district court but raised it for first time on second appeal, so only possible bar to appellate court's consideration of issue on second appeal would be a species of equitable waiver).

6. *See Beacon Theatres, Inc. v. Westover*, 359 U.S. 500, 79 S.Ct. 948, 3 L.Ed.2d 988 (1959); *Curtis v. Loether*, 415 U.S. 189, 94 S.Ct. 1005, 39 L.Ed.2d 260 (1974).

7. *See, e.g., Troy v. Bay State Computer Group, Inc.*, 141 F.3d 378 (1st Cir.1998) (state law claim was triable to a jury, but Title VII claimant was limited to a bench trial for claim that accrued prior to the 1991 amendment).

I. THE PRECLUSIVE EFFECT OF EMPLOYMENT DISCRIMINATION CONSENT JUDGMENTS ON NONPARTIES

§ 12.50   In General

A 5–4 Supreme Court majority held in *Martin v. Wilks*[1] that non-minority employees who object to a consent judgment adverse to their interests are not required to intervene in a Title VII action but instead may collaterally attack the judgment in independent actions. Since the Court had several times recognized that employers are principally motivated to adopt "voluntary" affirmative action programs, or settle pending lawsuits by consent agreements, in order to avoid the costs of extended litigation, the *Wilks* decision appeared to remove much of the incentive for these arrangements. But the Civil Rights Act of 1991,[2] discussed below, substantially overrules *Wilks*, striking a balance between the minority plaintiffs' interest in comprehensive, efficient litigation involving all parties and the interest of nonminority persons potentially affected by a group-based decree.

The Act responds to the Court's decision in *Wilks* by foreclosing many collateral challenges, typically by whites or males, to employment practices adopted under the authority of litigated or consent judgments. These attacks customarily assert that the underlying judgments unlawfully provide group-based, reverse-discriminatory relief to minority or female applicants or employees, including those not shown to have suffered discrimination at the hands of the defendant employer. The Court in *Wilks* permitted such attacks even when the attackers knew about the underlying litigation but did not try to intervene. It relied on the familiar due process principle that a judgment cannot bind a litigant who was not a party or privy and therefore lacked an opportunity to be heard.[3] Yet the 1991 Act purports to bar the white or male challengers from later challenging decrees entered under the federal[4] antidiscrimi-

---

§ 12.50

1. 490 U.S. 755, 109 S.Ct. 2180, 104 L.Ed.2d 835 (1989).

2. Pub.L.No. 102–166, 105 Stat. 1071.

3. *See, e.g., Parklane Hosiery v. Shore,* 439 U.S. 322, 327 n. 7, 99 S.Ct. 645, 649 n. 7, 58 L.Ed.2d 552 (1979); *Hansberry v. Lee,* 311 U.S. 32, 40–41, 61 S.Ct. 115, 117–118, 85 L.Ed. 22 (1940).

4. The Act does not explicitly provide protection to consent judgments or orders entered under *state* discrimination laws. Andrea Catania and Charles A. Sullivan argue, however, that although § 703(n)(1)(B) does not mention subsequent challenges to decrees based on state law, "the drafters probably did not intend to allow state-based claims against court ordered restructuring in the workplace[ ]." Andrea Catania & Charles A. Sullivan, *Judging Judgments: The 1991 Civil Rights Act and The Lingering Ghost of Martin v.*

Wilks, 57 Brooklyn L.Rev. 995, 1035 (1992). "Such a view ... would tend to eviscerate the whole purpose of the [Act]." *Id.*

Another effect of § 703(n)(1)(A) is that state court consent judgments or orders under *federal* discrimination laws are given preclusive effect if the requirements of § 703(n)(1)(B) are met. *Id.* at 1033. This effectively alters and expands for the covered consent decrees the sphere of influence of 28 U.S.C.A. § 1738: so long as the requirements of the Act have been met, federal courts must give preclusive effect to state-court judgments even if courts of a state would deny preclusive effect to the consent decree, which they probably would if the challengers were not party to the prior proceedings. *See supra* § 12.36 (discussing party identity requirement of claim preclusion).

nation laws if they had a reasonable opportunity, after adequate notice, to raise their objections during the primary proceedings and failed to intervene, or if they were adequately represented in those proceedings by a similarly situated litigant.[5]

On the other hand, the Act also makes it more difficult for the parties to the primary lawsuit—the minority or female plaintiffs and the defendant employer—to achieve assurance that a judgment in their litigation will effectively end the controversy among all relevant parties. They will have to give actual notice to identifiable incumbent employees who might be adversely affected by a proposed judgment that, for example, commands group-based goals or quotas for a training program or promotion or adjustments to seniority. And when such notice is given, the Act leaves intact another of the Court's 1988 Term decisions[6] that generally[7] relieves intervening challengers from liability for the attorney's fees incurred by the primary parties in defending the group protection features of the proposed underlying judgment.

The difficulties faced by the primary parties are even greater with respect to contemplated relief—goals or quotas concerning hiring or, in the case of a union defendant, membership—that will affect nonminority employees who are not readily identifiable and accordingly cannot be given actual notice. In those situations the primary parties, if they seek a durable, comprehensive judgment, will have to join as additional parties persons or groups who will be deemed adequate representatives of the absentees likely to be affected by the judgment.

---

5. Pub.L.No. 102–166, § 703(n)(1)(A)-(B), 105 Stat. 1071. Section 703(n)(1)(A)-(B) reads:

(A) Notwithstanding any other provision of law, and except as provided in paragraph (2), an employment practice that implements and is within the scope of a litigated or consent judgment or order that resolves a claim of employment discrimination under the Constitution or Federal civil rights laws may not be challenged under the circumstances described in subparagraph (B).

(B) A practice described in subparagraph (A) may not be challenged in a claim under the Constitution or Federal civil rights laws—

(i) by a person who, prior to the entry of the judgment or order described in subparagraph (A), had—

(I) actual notice of the proposed judgment or order sufficient to apprise such person that such judgment or order might adversely affect the interests and legal rights of such person and that an opportunity was available to present objections to such judgment or order by a future date certain; and

(II) a reasonable opportunity to present objections to such judgment or order; or

(ii) by a person whose interests were adequately represented by another person who had previously challenged the judgment or order on the same legal grounds and with a similar factual situation, unless there has been an intervening change in law or fact.

Id.

Paragraph (2) explains that paragraph (1) shall not alter the standards for intervention under FRCP 24, apply [directly] to the rights of the parties to the underlying action in which the judgment was entered, or prevent challenges to judgments procured by collusion or fraud.

6. *Independent Fed'n of Flight Attendants v. Zipes*, 491 U.S. 754, 109 S.Ct. 2732, 105 L.Ed.2d 639 (1989).

7. The Court had saddled such a challenger with liability only when its position was "frivolous, unreasonable, or without foundation." 491 U.S. at 768 (Blackmun, J., concurring) (quoting *Christiansburg Garment Co. v. EEOC*, 434 U.S. 412, 98 S.Ct. 694, 54 L.Ed.2d 648 (1978)).

On balance, then, the Act makes it riskier for a putative challenger to wait to attack such a judgment until after it is entered and he is denied hire or promotion pursuant to its terms. Further, it encourages his intervention in the underlying action by continuing to shield him from liability for the plaintiff's attorney's fees in most cases. In these respects the Act affords indirect support for group protection remedies in the context of completed or, in the case of a consent judgment, partial litigation. But in cases that involve proposed group-based hiring or membership remedies, the primary parties may still be reluctant to enter into consent judgments for fear that they cannot locate and join as parties adequate representatives of all potentially affected nonminority persons; these persons would then remain free to attack the judgment collaterally. To that extent, the Act moderately discourages the group-based remedy.

Appendix

RESEARCHING EMPLOYMENT DISCRIMINATION LAW AND PRACTICE ON WESTLAW®

Analysis

Section 1. Introduction

Employment Discrimination Law and Practice provides a strong base for analyzing even the most complex problem involving employment discrimination law and practice. Whether your research requires examination of case law, statutes, expert commentary or other materials, West books and Westlaw are excellent sources of information.

To keep you abreast of current developments, Westlaw provides frequently updated databases. With Westlaw, you have unparalleled legal research resources at your fingertips.

625

Additional Resources

If you have not previously used Westlaw or have questions not covered in this appendix, call the West Group Reference Attorneys at 1–800–REF–ATTY (1–800–733–2889). The West Group Reference Attorneys are trained, licensed attorneys, available 24 hours a day to assist you with your Westlaw search questions. To subscribe to Westlaw, call 1–800–344–5008 or visit the West Group Web site at **www.westgroup.com**.

Section 2. Westlaw Databases

Each database on Westlaw is assigned an abbreviation called an *identifier*, which you use to access the database. You can find identifiers for all databases in the online Westlaw Directory and in the printed *Westlaw Database Directory*. When you need to know more detailed information about a database, use Scope. Scope contains coverage information, lists of related databases and valuable search tips. To access Scope, click **Scope** after you access the database.

The following chart lists Westlaw databases that contain information pertaining to civil rights and employment discrimination law. For a complete list of civil rights and employment discrimination law databases, see the online Westlaw Directory or the printed *Westlaw Database Directory*. Because new information is continually being added to Westlaw, you should also check Welcome to Westlaw and the Westlaw Directory for new database information.

Selected Employment Discrimination Law and Practice Databases on Westlaw

Database	Identifier	Coverage
Federal and State Case Law Combined		
Federal & State Case Law	ALLCASES	Begins with 1945
Federal & State Case Law–Before 1945	ALLCASES–OLD	1789–1944
National Disability Law Reporter	NDLRPTR	Begins with 1990
Federal Case Law		
Federal Case Law	ALLFEDS	Begins with 1945
Federal Case Law–Before 1945	ALLFEDS–OLD	1789–1944
Federal Civil Rights–Cases	FCIV–CS	Begins with 1789
Federal Civil Rights–Supreme Court Cases	FCIV–SCT	Begins with 1790
Federal Civil Rights–Courts of Appeals Cases	FCIV–CTA	Begins with 1891
Federal Civil Rights–District Courts Cases	FCIV–DCT	Begins with 1789
Federal Labor & Employment–Cases	FLB–CS	Begins with 1789

Database	Identifier	Coverage
Federal Labor & Employment–Supreme Court Cases	FLB–SCT	Begins with 1790
Federal Labor & Employment–Courts of Appeals Cases	FLB–CTA	Begins with 1891
Federal Labor & Employment–District Courts Cases	FLB–DCT	Begins with 1789

State Case Law

State Case Law	ALLSTATES	Begins with 1945
State Case Law Before 1945	ALLSTATES–OLD	1821–1944
Multistate Civil Rights Cases	MCIV–CS	Varies by state
Individual State Civil Rights Cases	XXCIV–CS (where XX is a state's two-letter postal abbreviation)	Varies by state
Multistate Labor & Employment Cases	MLB–CS	Varies by state
Individual State Labor & Employment Cases	XXLB–CS (where XX is a state's two-letter postal abbreviation)	Varies by state

Federal Statutes, Regulations and Court Rules

Federal Civil Rights–Code of Federal Regulations	FCIV–CFR	Current data
Federal Civil Rights–Federal Register	FCIV–FR	Begins with July 1980
Federal Civil Rights–U.S. Code Annotated	FCIV–USCA	Current data
Federal Labor & Employment–Code and Regulations	FLB–CODREG	Varies by source
Federal Labor & Employment–Code of Federal Regulations	FLB–CFR	Current data
Federal Labor & Employment–Federal Register	FLB–FR	Begins with July 1980
Federal Labor & Employment–U.S. Code Annotated	FLB–USCA	Current data
Federal Rules	US–RULES	Current data

State Statutes, Regulations and Court Rules

State Statutes–Annotated	ST–ANN–ALL	Varies by state
Individual State Statutes–Annotated	XX–ST–ANN (where XX is a state's two-letter postal abbreviation)	Varies by state
State Administrative Code Multibase	ADC–ALL	Varies by state
Individual State Administrative Code	XX–ADC (where XX is a state's two-letter postal abbreviation)	Varies by state

Database	Identifier	Coverage
Individual State Court Rules	XX–RULES (where XX is a state's two-letter postal abbreviation)	Varies by state

Federal Administrative Materials

Americans with Disabilities Act Technical Assistance Manuals	ADA–TAM	Information Booklets: 1991 Manuals: 1992
Equal Employment Opportunity Commission (EEOC) Multibase	FLB–EEOC–ALL	Varies by source
Federal Labor & Employment–Equal Employment Opportunity Commission Decisions	FLB–EEOC	Public sector: begins with July 1969 Private sector: begins with April 1994

State Administrative Materials

California Fair Employment and Housing Commission Decisions	CA–FEHC	Begins with 1978
California Occupational Safety and Health Appeals Board Decisions	CA–OSHA	Begins with 1974
Chicago Commission on Human Relations Decisions	CHICIV–ADMIN	Begins with 1992
Illinois Human Rights Commission Decisions	ILCIV–ADMIN	Begins with 1991
City of New York Commission on Human Rights Decisions	NYCCIV–ADMIN	Begins with 1970
Ohio Civil Rights Commission Decisions	OHCIV–ADMIN	Begins with 1980
Washington Public Employment Relations Commission Decisions	WALB–ADMIN	Begins with 1984
West Virginia Education and State Employees Grievance Board Decisions	WVLB–ADMIN	Begins with 1994

Legal Periodicals, Texts and Practice Manuals

ADA and People with Mental Illness, The: A Resource Manual for Employers	ABA–DISMAN	1994 edition
ADA Update	ADAUP	Begins with January 1997
American Bar Association Disability Law Texts, Combined	ABA–DIS	Varies by source
Civil Rights–Law Reviews, Texts & Bar Journals	CIV–TP	Varies by publication
Employment Discrimination Coordinator	EDC	Current data
HR Series Fair Employment Practices	HRS–FEP	Current through the August 2000 supplement
Into the Jury Box: A Disability Accommodation Guide for State Courts	ABA–DISJURY	1994 edition

Database	Identifier	Coverage
Labor & Employment–Law Reviews, Texts & Bar Journals	LB–TP	Varies by publication
Mental Disabilities and the Americans with Disabilities Act: A Practitioner's Guide to Employment, Insurance, Treatment, Public Access and Housing	ABA–DISGUIDE	1994 edition
Regulation, Litigation and Dispute Resolution Under the Americans with Disabilities Act: A Practitioner's Guide to Implementation	ABA–DISIMPL	1996 edition
Sexual Harassment: Federal Law	SEXHARASS	1997 edition

Other Legal Materials

Westlaw Topical Highlights–Labor & Employment	WTH–LB	Current data

West Legal Directory®

West Legal Directory–Civil Rights	WLD–CIV	Current data
West Legal Directory–Employment Law/Employee	WLD–EMPLE	Current data
West Legal Directory–Employment Law/Employer	WLD–EMPLR	Current data
West Legal Directory–Labor Law	WLD–LAB	Current data

News and Information

Andrews Employment Litigation Reporter	ANEMPLR	Begins with November 1996
BNA Employment Policy & Law Daily	BNA–EPLD	Begins with June 1993
BNA Labor Relations Reporter: Individual Employment Rights Newsletter	LLR–IERN	Begins with September 1986
Daily Labor Report	BNA–DLR	Begins with January 1996
Discrimination Law Update	DISCRIMLU	Begins with January 1997
Government Employee Relations Reporter	BNA–GERR	Begins with January 1986
Labor News	LBNEWS	Varies by source
National Association of Attorneys General (NAAG) Civil Rights Update	NAAGCRU	Winter 1996–Spring 1997
Public Employment Law Notes	PEMLN	Begins with January 1997

Section 3. Retrieving a Document with a Citation: Find and Hypertext Links

3.1 Find

Find is a Westlaw service that allows you to retrieve a document by entering its citation. Find allows you to retrieve documents from anywhere in Westlaw without accessing or changing databases. Find is available for many documents, including case law (state and federal), the *United States Code Annotated*®, state statutes, administrative materials, and texts and periodicals.

To use Find, simply access the Find service and type the citation. The following list provides some examples:

To Find This Document	**Access Find and Type**
Price Waterhouse v. Hopkins, 109 S. Ct. 1775 (1989)	**109 sct 1775**
Henningsen v. WorldCom, Inc., 9 P.3d 948 (Wash. App. 2000)	**9 p3d 948**
42 U.S.C.A. § 1983	**42 usca s 1983**
29 C.F.R. § 1604.6	**29 cfr 1604.6**
Minn. Stat. Ann. § 363.03	**mn st 363.03**
18 Pa. Cons. Stat. Ann. § 2501	**pa st ti 18 pa csa s 2501**

For a complete list of publications that can be retrieved with Find and their abbreviations, consult the Publications List after accessing Find.

3.2 Hypertext Links

Use hypertext links to move from one location to another on Westlaw. For example, use hypertext links to go directly from the statute, case or law review article you are viewing to a cited statute, case or article; from a headnote to the corresponding text in the opinion; or from an entry in a statutes index database to the full text of the statute.

Section 4. Searching with Natural Language

Overview: With Natural Language, you can retrieve documents by simply describing your issue in plain English. If you are a relatively new Westlaw user, Natural Language searching can make it easier for you to retrieve cases that are on point. If you are an experienced Westlaw user, Natural Language gives you a valuable alternative search method.

When you enter a Natural Language description, Westlaw automatically identifies legal phrases, removes common words and generates variations of terms in your description. Westlaw then searches for the concepts in your description. Concepts may include significant terms, phrases, legal citations or topic and key numbers. Westlaw retrieves the 20 documents that most closely match your description, beginning with the document most likely to match.

4.1 Natural Language Search

Access a database, such as Federal Labor & Employment–Cases (FLB–CS). In the text box, type a Natural Language description such as the following:

must an employer provide time off work for employee religious observance

4.2 Next Command

Westlaw displays the 20 documents that most closely match your description, beginning with the document most likely to match. If you want to view additional documents, use the Next command, click the **Document** arrow or **Doc** at the bottom of the page or click the right arrow in the left frame.

4.3 Natural Language Browse Commands

Best Mode: To display the best portion (the portion that most closely matches your description) of each document in your search result, click the **Best Section** or **Best** arrow at the bottom of the window or page.

Standard Browsing Commands: You can also browse your Natural Language search result using standard Westlaw browsing commands, such as citations list, Locate and term mode.

Section 5. Searching with Terms and Connectors

Overview: With Terms and Connectors searching, you enter a query, which consists of key terms from your issue and connectors specifying the relationship between these terms.

Terms and Connectors searching is useful when you want to retrieve a document for which you know specific details, such as the title or the fact situation. Terms and Connectors searching is also useful when you want to retrieve documents relating to a specific issue.

5.1 Terms

Plurals and Possessives: Plurals are automatically retrieved when you enter the singular form of a term. This is true for both regular and irregular plurals (e.g., **child** retrieves *children*). If you enter the plural form of a term, you will not retrieve the singular form.

If you enter the nonpossessive form of a term, Westlaw automatically retrieves the possessive form as well. However, if you enter the possessive form, only the possessive form is retrieved.

Automatic Equivalencies: Some terms have alternative forms or equivalencies; for example, *5* and *five* are equivalent terms. Westlaw automatically retrieves equivalent terms. The *Westlaw Reference Manual* contains a list of equivalent terms.

Compound Words, Abbreviations and Acronyms: When a compound word is one of your search terms, use a hyphen to retrieve all forms of the word. For example, the term **along-side** retrieves *alongside, alongside* and *along side*.

When using an abbreviation or acronym as a search term, place a period after each of the letters to retrieve any of its forms. For example, the term **n.l.r.b.** retrieves *nlrb, n.l.r.b., n l r b* and *n. l. r. b.* Note: The abbreviation does *not* retrieve *national labor relations board*, so remember to add additional alternative terms to your query such as **"national labor relations board"**.

The Root Expander and the Universal Character: When you use the Terms and Connectors search method, placing the root expander (!) at the end of a root term generates all other terms with that root. For example, adding the ! to the root *discrimin* in the query

misdemeanor /s discrimin!

instructs Westlaw to retrieve such terms as *discriminate, discriminating, discriminated* and *discrimination*.

The universal character (*) stands for one character and can be inserted in the middle or at the end of a term. For example, the term

withdr*w

will retrieve *withdraw* and *withdrew*. Adding three asterisks to the root *elect*

elect* * *

instructs Westlaw to retrieve all forms of the root with up to three additional characters. Terms such as *elected* or *election* are retrieved by this query. However, terms with more than three letters following the root, such as *electronic,* are not retrieved. Plurals are always retrieved, even if more than three letters follow the root.

Phrase Searching: To search for an exact phrase, place it within quotation marks. For example, to search for references to *Title VII*, type **"title vii"**. When you are using the Terms and Connectors search method, you should use phrase searching only if you are certain that the terms in the phrase will not appear in any other order.

5.2 Alternative Terms

After selecting the terms for your query, consider which alternative terms are necessary. For example, if you are searching for the term *admissible*, you might also want to search for the term *inadmissible*. You should consider both synonyms and antonyms as alternative terms. You can also use the Westlaw thesaurus to add alternative terms to your query.

5.3 Connectors

After selecting terms and alternative terms for your query, use connectors to specify the relationship that should exist between search terms in your retrieved documents. The connectors are described below:

Use:	To retrieve documents with:	Example:
& (and)	both terms	**age & discrimin!**
or (space)	either term or both terms	**sex! gender**
/p	search terms in the same paragraph	**hostile /p environment**
/s	search terms in the same sentence	**disparate /s treatment**
+s	the first search term preceding the second within the same sentence	**burden +s prov! proof**
/n	search terms within "n" terms of each other (where "n" is a number)	**vicarious! /3 liab!**
+n	the first search term preceding the second by "n" terms (where "n" is a number)	**wrongful! +3 terminat!**
" "	search terms appearing in the same order as in the quotation marks	**"bona fide occupational qualification"**

Use:	To exclude documents with:	Example:
% (but not)	search terms following the % symbol	**age % gender**

5.4 Field Restrictions

Overview: Documents in each Westlaw database consist of several segments, or fields. One field may contain the citation, another the title, another the synopsis and so forth. Not all databases contain the same fields. Also depending on the database, fields with the same name may contain different types of information.

To view a list of fields for a specific database and their contents, see Scope for that database. Note that in some databases not every field is available for every document.

To retrieve only those documents containing your search terms in a specific field, restrict your search to that field. To restrict your search to a specific field, type the field name or abbreviation followed by your search terms enclosed in parentheses. For example, to retrieve a California case titled *Soldinger v. Northwest Airlines,* access the California Labor & Employment Cases database (CALB–CS) and search for your terms in the title field (ti):

ti(soldinger & northwest)

The fields discussed below are available in Westlaw databases you might use for researching tort law issues.

Digest and Synopsis Fields: The digest (di) and synopsis (sy) fields, added to case law databases by West's attorney-editors, summarize the main points of a case. The synopsis field contains a brief description of a case. The digest field contains the topic and headnote fields and includes the complete hierarchy of concepts used by West's editors to classify the headnotes to specific West digest topic and key numbers. Restricting your search to the synopsis and digest fields limits your result to cases in which your terms are related to a major issue in the case.

Consider restricting your search to one or both of these fields if

- you are searching for common terms or terms with more than one meaning, and you need to narrow your search; or

- you cannot narrow your search by using a smaller database.

For example, to retrieve federal cases that discuss age as a bona fide occupational qualification, access the Federal Civil Rights–Cases database (FCIV–CS) and type the following query:

sy,di(age /p "bona fide occupational qualification" b.f.o.q.)

Headnote Field: The headnote field (he) is part of the digest field but does not contain topic numbers, hierarchical classification information or key numbers. The headnote field contains a one-sentence summary for each point of law in a case and any supporting citations given by the author of the opinion. A headnote field restriction is useful when you are searching for specific statutory sections or rule numbers. For example, to retrieve headnotes from federal cases that cite 42 U.S.C.A. § 2000e–2, access the Federal Civil Rights–Cases database (FCIV–CS) and type the following query:

he(42 +7 2000e–2)

Topic Field: The topic field (to) is also part of the digest field. It contains hierarchical classification information, including the West digest topic names and numbers and the key numbers. You should restrict search terms to the topic field in a case law database if

- a digest field search retrieves too many documents; or

- you want to retrieve cases with digest paragraphs classified under more than one topic.

For example, the topic Civil Rights has the topic number 78. To retrieve federal cases that discuss age discrimination in the context of civil rights, access the Federal Civil Rights–Cases database (FCIV–CS) and type a query like the following:

to(78) /p age /3 discriminat!

To retrieve cases classified under more than one topic and key number, search for your terms in the topic field. For example, to retrieve recent cases discussing sexual discrimination, which may be classified to Civil Rights (78), Constitutional Law (92) or Federal Civil Procedure (170A), among other topics, access the Federal Labor & Employment–Cases database (FLB–CS) and type a query like the following:

to(sex! /3 discriminat!) & da(aft 1998)

For a complete list of West digest topics and their corresponding topic numbers, access the Key Number Service or the Key Number Center.

> *Note*: Slip opinions, cases not reported by West and cases from topical services do not contain the digest, headnote and topic fields.

Prelim and Caption Fields: When searching in a database containing statutes, rules or regulations, restrict your search to the prelim (pr) and caption (ca) fields to retrieve documents in which your terms are important enough to appear in a section name or heading. For example, to retrieve federal statutes regarding unlawful employment practices, access the Federal Labor & Employment–U.S. Code Annotated database (FLB–USCA) and type the following:

pr,ca("unlawful employment practice")

5.5 Date Restrictions

You can use Westlaw to retrieve documents *decided* or *issued* before, after or on a specified date, as well as within a range of dates. The following sample queries contain date restrictions:

da(1999) & "title vii"

da(aft 1995) & discriminat! /s "national origin"

da(10/13/1999) & exhaust! /s administrat! /s remed!

You can also search for documents *added to a database* on or after a specified date, as well as within a range of dates. The following sample queries contain added-date restrictions:

ad(aft 1995) & discriminat! /s age

ad(aft 2/1/1998 & bef 5/15/1998) & injunct! /s relief remed!

Section 6. Searching with Topic and Key Numbers

To retrieve cases that address a specific point of law, use topic and key numbers as your search terms. If you have an on-point case, run a search using the topic and key number from the relevant headnote in an appropriate database to find other cases containing headnotes classified to that topic and key number. For example, to search for cases containing headnotes classified under topic 78 (Civil Rights) and key number 158 (Sex Discrimination), access the Federal Civil Rights–Cases database (FCIV–CS) and enter the following query:

78k158

For a complete list of West digest topic and key numbers, access the Key Number Service or the Key Number Center.

> *Note*: Slip opinions, cases not reported by West and cases from topical services do not contain West topic and key numbers.

Section 7. Verifying Your Research with Citation Research Services

Overview: A citation research service is a tool that helps you ensure that your cases are good law; helps you retrieve cases, legislation or articles that cite a case, rule or statute; and helps you verify that the spelling and format of your citations are correct.

7.1 KeyCite

KeyCite is the citation research service from West Group.

KeyCite for cases covers case law on Westlaw, including unpublished opinions.

KeyCite for statutes covers the *United States Code Annotated* (USCA®), the *Code of Federal Regulations* (CFR) and statutes from all 50 states.

KeyCite Alert monitors the status of your cases or statutes and automatically sends you updates at the frequency you specify when their KeyCite information changes.

KeyCite provides the following:

- Direct appellate history of a case, including related references, which are opinions involving the same parties and facts but resolving different issues
- Negative indirect history of a case, which consists of cases outside the direct appellate line that may have a negative impact on its precedential value
- The title, parallel citations, court of decision, docket number and filing date of a case
- Citations to cases, administrative decisions and secondary sources on Westlaw that have cited a case
- Complete integration with the West Key Number System® so you can track legal issues discussed in a case
- Links to session laws amending or repealing a statute
- Statutory credits and historical notes
- Citations to pending legislation affecting a federal statute or a statute from California or New York
- Citations to cases, administrative decisions and secondary sources that have cited a statute or federal regulation

7.2 Westlaw As a Citator

For citations not covered by KeyCite, including persuasive secondary authority such as restatements and treatises, use Westlaw as a citator to retrieve cases that cite your authority.

For example, to retrieve state cases citing the law review article "The Meaning of Discrimination: Why Courts Have Erred in Requiring Employment Discrimination Plaintiffs to Prove that the Employer's Action

Was Materially Adverse or Ultimate," 47 U.Kan.L.Rev. 333 (1999), access the Federal Labor & Employment–Cases database (FLB–CS) and type a query like the following:

adverse /s ultimate /s 47 /5 333

Section 8. Researching with Westlaw—Examples

8.1 Retrieving Law Review Articles

Recent law review articles are often a good place to begin researching a legal issue because law review articles serve 1) as an excellent introduction to a new topic or review for a stale one, providing terminology to help you formulate a query; 2) as a finding tool for pertinent primary authority, such as rules, statutes and cases; and 3) in some instances, as persuasive secondary authority.

Suppose you need to gather background information on whether an employer can enforce English-only language restrictions in the workplace.

Solution

- To retrieve recent law review articles relevant to your issue, access the Labor & Employment–Law Reviews, Texts & Bar Journals database (LB–TP). Using the Natural Language search method, enter a description like the following:

can an employer enforce english only language restrictions in the workplace

- If you have a citation to an article in a specific publication, use Find to retrieve it. For more information on Find, see Section 3.1 of this appendix. For example, to retrieve the article found at 73 Tex. L. Rev. 871, access Find and type

73 txlr 871

- If you know the title of an article but not which journal it appeared in, access the Labor & Employment–Law Reviews, Texts & Bar Journals database (LB–TP) and search for key terms using the title field. For example, to retrieve the article "Take Me Higher and Higher: Ugly Religious Harassment Nets Huge Award," type the following Terms and Connectors query:

ti(ugly & religious & harassment)

8.2 Retrieving Case Law

Suppose you need to retrieve state case law dealing with whether an employer must accommodate an employee's request for time off for religious observances.

Solution

- Access the Multistate Labor & Employment Cases database (MLB–CS). Type a Natural Language description such as the following:

must an employer accommodate an employee request for time off for religious observance

- When you know the citation for a specific case, use Find to retrieve it. For more information on Find, see Section 3.1 of this appendix. For example, to retrieve *Krushinski v. Roadway Express, Inc.*, 626 F. Supp. 472 (M.D. Pa. 1985), access Find and type

626 fsupp 472

- If you find a topic and key number that is on point, run a search using that topic and key number to retrieve additional cases discussing that point of law. For example, to retrieve cases containing headnotes classified under topic 78 (Civil Rights) and key number 151 (Religious Discrimination), type the following query:

78k151

- To retrieve cases written by a particular judge, add a judge field (ju) restriction to your query. For example, to retrieve cases written by Judge Posner that contain headnotes classified under topic 232a (Labor Relations), type the following query:

ju(posner) & to(232a)

8.3   Retrieving Statutes and Regulations

Suppose you need to retrieve federal statutes and regulations specifically addressing fair labor standards.

Solution

- Access the Federal Civil Rights–U.S. Code Annotated database (FCIV–USCA). Search for your terms in the prelim and caption fields using the Terms and Connectors search method:

pr,ca("fair labor standard")

- When you know the citation for a specific statute or regulation, use Find to retrieve it. For example, to retrieve 29 C.F.R. § 1606.2, access Find and type

29 cfr 1606.2

- To look at surrounding sections, use the Table of Contents service. Click a hypertext link in the prelim or caption field, or click the **TOC** tab in the left frame. You can also use Documents in Sequence to retrieve the section following § 1606.2, even if that subsequent section was not retrieved with your search or Find request.

- When you retrieve a statute on Westlaw, it will contain a message if legislation amending or repealing it is available online. To display this legislation, click the hypertext link in the message.

Because slip copy versions of laws are added to Westlaw before they contain full editorial enhancements, they are not retrieved with the update feature. To retrieve slip copy versions of laws, access the United States Public Laws database (US–PL) or a state's legislative service database (XX–LEGIS, where XX is the state's two-letter postal abbreviation). Then type **ci(slip)** and descriptive terms, e.g., **ci(slip) & discrimination**. Slip copy documents are replaced by the editorially enhanced versions within a few working days. The update feature also does not retrieve legislation that enacts a new statute or covers a topic that will not be incorporated into the statutes. To retrieve this legislation, access US–PL or a legislative service database and enter a query containing terms that describe the new legislation.

8.4 Using KeyCite

Suppose one of the cases you retrieve in your case law research is *Meiri v. Dacon*, 759 F.2d 989 (2d Cir. 1985). You want to determine whether this case is good law and to find other cases that have cited this case.

Solution

- Use KeyCite to retrieve direct history and negative indirect history for *Meiri v. Dacon*.

- Use KeyCite to display citing references for *Meiri v. Dacon*.

8.5 Following Recent Developments

As the employment discrimination law specialist in your firm, you are expected to keep up with and summarize recent legal developments in this area of the law. How can you do this efficiently?

Solution

One of the easiest ways to stay abreast of recent developments in employment discrimination law is by accessing the Westlaw Topical Highlights–Labor & Employment database (WTH–LB). The WTH–LB database contains summaries of recent legal developments, including court decisions, legislation and materials released by administrative agencies in the area of labor and employment law. Some summaries also contain suggested queries that combine the proven power of West's topic and key numbers and West's case headnotes to retrieve additional pertinent cases. When you access WTH–LB, you will automatically retrieve a list of documents added to the database in the last two weeks.

*

Table of Cases

D

E.E.O.C. v. Pape Lift, Inc., 115 F.3d 676 (9th Cir.1997)—§ **4.25, n. 36;** § **7.25, n. 22.**

E.E.O.C. v. Penton Indus. Pub. Co., Inc., 851 F.2d 835 (6th Cir.1988)—§ **8.22;** § **8.22, n. 2.**

E.E.O.C. v. Prevo's Family Market, Inc., 135 F.3d 1089 (6th Cir.1998)—§ **10.60;** § **10.60, n. 11.**

E.E.O.C. v. Reichhold Chemicals, Inc., 988 F.2d 1564 (11th Cir.1993)—§ **2.30, n. 2;** § **11.15, n. 2.**

E.E.O.C. v. Romeo Community Schools, 976 F.2d 985 (6th Cir.1992)—§ **8.10, n. 1.**

E.E.O.C. v. Sears, Roebuck and Co., 857 F.Supp. 1233 (N.D.Ill.1994)—§ **7.16, n. 13.**

E.E.O.C. v. Sears, Roebuck & Co., 839 F.2d 302 (7th Cir.1988)—§ **3.20, n. 29, 33;** § **4.40, n. 11;** § **8.15, n. 3.**

E.E.O.C. v. Shell Oil Co., 466 U.S. 54, 104 S.Ct. 1621, 80 L.Ed.2d 41 (1984)—§ **4.4, n. 12.**

E.E.O.C. v. Snyder Doors, 844 F.Supp. 1020 (E.D.Pa.1994)—§ **2.40, n. 22.**

E.E.O.C. v. Staten Island Sav. Bank, 207 F.3d 144 (2nd Cir.2000)—§ **10.12, n. 16.**

E.E.O.C. v. State of Illinois, 69 F.3d 167 (7th Cir.1995)—§ **2.3, n. 17.**

E.E.O.C. v. Steamship Clerks Union, Local 1066, 48 F.3d 594 (1st Cir.1995)—§ **3.35, n. 3.**

E.E.O.C. v. Tortilleria La Mejor, 758 F.Supp. 585 (E.D.Cal.1991)—§ **2.3, n. 58.**

E.E.O.C. v. United Parcel Service, 94 F.3d 314 (7th Cir.1996)—§ **2.23, n. 13.**

E.E.O.C. v. Wackenhut Corp., 939 F.2d 241 (5th Cir.1991)—§ **4.8, n. 9.**

E.E.O.C. v. Waffle House, Inc., 193 F.3d 805 (4th Cir.1999)—§ **4.6, n. 11, 28;** § **4.8, n. 3.**

E.E.O.C. v. Wal–Mart Stores, Inc., 187 F.3d 1241 (10th Cir.1999)—§ **4.26, n. 54, 62;** § **10.83, n. 3.**

E.E.O.C. v. Wal–Mart Stores, Inc., 156 F.3d 989 (9th Cir.1998)—§ **4.26, n. 60.**

E.E.O.C. v. Watergate at Landmark Condominium, 24 F.3d 635 (4th Cir.1994)—§ **2.3, n. 30.**

E.E.O.C. v. Western Elec. Co., Inc., 713 F.2d 1011 (4th Cir.1983)—§ **7.5, n. 20.**

E.E.O.C. v. Westinghouse Elec. Corp., 725 F.2d 211 (3rd Cir.1983)—§ **4.3, n. 26.**

E.E.O.C. v. White and Son Enterprises, 881 F.2d 1006 (11th Cir.1989)—§ **2.30, n. 1, 5;** § **8.10, n. 1.**

E.E.O.C. v. Wilson Metal Casket Co., 24 F.3d 836 (6th Cir.1994)—§ **4.9, n. 32.**

E.E.O.C. v. Wyoming Retirement System, 771 F.2d 1425 (10th Cir.1985)—§ **4.25, n. 19, 36.**

E.E.O.C. v. Yenkin–Majestic Paint Corp., 112 F.3d 831 (6th Cir.1997)—§ **3.10, n. 78.**

Egbuna v. Time–Life Libraries, Inc., 153 F.3d 184 (4th Cir.1998)—§ **2.3, n. 58, 62.**

Eilam v. Children's Hosp. Ass'n, 173 F.3d 863 (10th Cir.1999)—§ **3.2, n. 21.**

Eiland v. Trinity Hosp., 150 F.3d 747 (7th Cir.1998)—§ **3.2, n. 19.**

Eirhart v. Libbey–Owens–Ford Co., 996 F.2d 846 (7th Cir.1993)—§ **11.5, n. 52, 68.**

Eisen v. Carlisle and Jacquelin, 417 U.S. 156, 94 S.Ct. 2140, 40 L.Ed.2d 732 (1974)—§ **4.9, n. 9;** § **12.30, n. 6.**

Elbaz v. Congregation Beth Judea, Inc., 812 F.Supp. 802 (N.D.Ill.1992)—§ **2.10, n. 3.**

El Club Del Barrio, Inc. v. United Community Corporations, Inc., 735 F.2d 98 (3rd Cir.1984)—§ **11.20, n. 8.**

Ellert v. University of Texas, at Dallas, 52 F.3d 543 (5th Cir.1995)—§ **2.22, n. 44.**

Ellis v. NCNB Texas Nat. Bank, 842 F.Supp. 243 (N.D.Tex.1994)—§ **3.10, n. 78.**

Ellis v. Ringgold School Dist., 832 F.2d 27 (3rd Cir.1987)—§ **4.25, n. 25.**

Ellis v. United Airlines, Inc., 73 F.3d 999 (10th Cir.1996)—§ **7.7, n. 34.**

Ellis v. University of Kansas Medical Center, 163 F.3d 1186 (10th Cir.1998)—§ **11.20, n. 8;** § **12.10, n. 38.**

Ellis v. Washington County and Johnson City, Tenn., 198 F.3d 225 (6th Cir.1999)—§ **12.25, n. 4.**

Ellison v. Brady, 924 F.2d 872 (9th Cir.1991)—§ **2.22, n. 77, 138.**

Ellison v. Premier Salons Intern., Inc., 164 F.3d 1111 (8th Cir.1999)—§ **7.16, n. 3.**

Ellison v. Software Spectrum, Inc., 85 F.3d 187 (5th Cir.1996)—§ **10.43, n. 15;** § **10.44;** § **10.44, n. 4.**

Elmore v. Shuler, 787 F.2d 601, 252 U.S.App.D.C. 45 (D.C.Cir.1986)—§ **11.20, n. 8.**

Emmel v. Coca–Cola Bottling Co. of Chicago, 95 F.3d 627 (7th Cir.1996)—§ **4.26, n. 47, 68.**

Employment Discrimination Litigation Against State of Ala., In re, 198 F.3d 1305 (11th Cir.1999)—§ **2.3, n. 20;** § **3.35, n. 10, 19, 20;** § **12.10, n. 31.**

Engineering Contractors Ass'n of South Florida Inc. v. Metropolitan Dade County, 122 F.3d 895 (11th Cir.1997)—§ **4.40, n. 16, 19, 24, 34;** § **4.45, n. 8.**

Ennis v. National Ass'n of Business and Educational Radio, Inc., 53 F.3d 55 (4th Cir.1995)—§ **10.23, n. 6, 13;** § **10.70, n. 11.**

Ensley Branch, N.A.A.C.P. v. Seibels, 31 F.3d 1548 (11th Cir.1994)—§ **11.5, n. 16.**

Ensley Branch, N.A.A.C.P. v. Seibels, 20 F.3d 1489 (11th Cir.1994)—§ **4.40, n. 38.**

I

J

M

Maine v. Thiboutot, 448 U.S. 1, 100 S.Ct. 2502, 65 L.Ed.2d 555 (1980)—§ **5.3; § 5.3, n. 1, 41; § 6.5; § 6.5, n. 1; § 12.1, n. 1.**

Maitland v. University of Minnesota, 155 F.3d 1013 (8th Cir.1998)—§ **4.40, n. 19; § 4.45, n. 3, 4.**

Maitland v. University of Minnesota, 43 F.3d 357 (8th Cir.1994)—§ **4.20, n. 14.**

Majeske v. City of Chicago, 218 F.3d 816 (7th Cir.2000)—§ **4.40, n. 19, 23.**

Malabarba v. Chicago Tribune Co., 149 F.3d 690 (7th Cir.1998)—§ **10.26, n. 9, 14, 31, 32, 33, 34; § 10.36, n. 2.**

Malarkey v. Texaco, Inc., 983 F.2d 1204 (2nd Cir.1993)—§ **2.40, n. 25; § 4.10, n. 6.**

Malik v. Carrier Corp., 202 F.3d 97 (2nd Cir.2000)—§ **2.22, n. 132.**

Mallett v. Wisconsin Div. of Vocational Rehabilitation, 130 F.3d 1245 (7th Cir. 1997)—§ **5.3, n. 27.**

Mallinson–Montague v. Pocrnick, 224 F.3d 1224 (10th Cir.2000)—§ **2.22, n. 125.**

Mallory v. Eyrich, 922 F.2d 1273 (6th Cir. 1991)—§ **11.20, n. 16.**

Malloy v. Monahan, 73 F.3d 1012 (10th Cir.1996)—§ **4.26, n. 24.**

Malone v. Eaton Corp., 187 F.3d 960 (8th Cir.1999)—§ **2.22, n. 140.**

Mangold v. California Public Utilities Com'n, 67 F.3d 1470 (9th Cir.1995)—§ **7.7, n. 34.**

Manley v. Engram, 755 F.2d 1463 (11th Cir.1985)—§ **12.3, n. 2.**

Manning v. Metropolitan Life Ins. Co., Inc., 127 F.3d 686 (8th Cir.1997)—§ **2.40, n. 43; § 5.2, n. 68.**

Mantolete v. Bolger, 767 F.2d 1416 (9th Cir.1985)—§ **10.6, n. 6.**

Manzer v. Diamond Shamrock Chemicals Co., 29 F.3d 1078 (6th Cir.1994)—§ **3.10, n. 73; § 3.11, n. 33.**

Marable v. Walker, 704 F.2d 1219 (11th Cir.1983)—§ **4.26, n. 25, 42.**

Marafino v. St. Louis County Circuit Court, 707 F.2d 1005 (8th Cir.1983)—§ **2.31, n. 15, 19.**

Mararri v. WCI Steel, Inc., 130 F.3d 1180 (6th Cir.1997)—§ **10.35, n. 18; § 10.41, n. 74.**

Marbley v. Bane, 57 F.3d 224 (2nd Cir. 1995)—§ **11.5, n. 41.**

Marbury v. Madison, 5 U.S. 137, 2 L.Ed. 60 (1803)—§ **4.40; § 4.40, n. 47.**

Marcantel v. Louisiana, Dept. of Transp. and Development, 37 F.3d 197 (5th Cir. 1994)—§ **3.10, n. 53; § 4.40, n. 1.**

Marcing v. Fluor Daniel, Inc., 826 F.Supp. 1128 (N.D.Ill.1993)—§ **4.25, n. 38.**

Marcum v. Consolidated Freightways, 225 F.3d 659 (6th Cir.2000)—§ **10.23, n. 3.**

Mardell v. Harleysville Life Ins. Co., 31 F.3d 1221 (3rd Cir.1994)—§ **1.1, n. 27; § 3.10, n. 87.**

Marek v. Chesny, 473 U.S. 1, 105 S.Ct. 3012, 87 L.Ed.2d 1 (1985)—§ **3.35, n. 59; § 11.20; § 11.20, n. 3.**

Marinelli v. City of Erie, Penn., 216 F.3d 354 (3rd Cir.2000)—§ **10.41, n. 7, 11; § 10.43, n. 4, 7.**

Marquart v. Lodge 837, Intern. Ass'n of Machinists and Aerospace Workers, 26 F.3d 842 (8th Cir.1994)—§ **11.15, n. 5.**

Marrero–Rivera v. Department of Justice of Com. of Puerto Rico, 800 F.Supp. 1024 (D.Puerto Rico 1992)—§ **6.10; § 6.10, n. 39.**

Marrese v. American Academy of Orthopaedic Surgeons, 470 U.S. 373, 105 S.Ct. 1327, 84 L.Ed.2d 274 (1985)—§ **12.37; § 12.37, n. 15.**

Marshall v. American Hosp. Ass'n, 157 F.3d 520 (7th Cir.1998)—§ **2.31, n. 19.**

Marshall v. Switzer, 10 F.3d 925 (2nd Cir. 1993)—§ **5.3, n. 27.**

Martin v. Barnesville Exempted Village School Dist. Bd. of Educ., 209 F.3d 931 (6th Cir.2000)—§ **10.23, n. 1; § 10.35, n. 18.**

Martin v. Cavalier Hotel Corp., 48 F.3d 1343 (4th Cir.1995)—§ **2.50, n. 9.**

Martin v. Heckler, 773 F.2d 1145 (11th Cir.1985)—§ **5.2, n. 49.**

Martin v. Kansas, 190 F.3d 1120 (10th Cir. 1999)—§ **10.20, n. 15; § 10.60, n. 10; § 12.10, n. 33.**

Martin v. PGA Tour, Inc., 204 F.3d 994 (9th Cir.2000)—§ **10.12, n. 5.**

Martin v. United Way of Erie County, 829 F.2d 445 (3rd Cir.1987)—§ **2.4, n. 2; § 2.5, n. 7.**

Martin v. Wilks, 490 U.S. 755, 109 S.Ct. 2180, 104 L.Ed.2d 835 (1989)—§ **4.8; § 4.8, n. 11; § 4.40, n. 52; § 4.45; § 4.45, n. 11; § 12.50; § 12.50, n. 1.**

Martincic v. Urban Redevelopment Authority of Pittsburgh, 844 F.Supp. 1073 (W.D.Pa.1994)—§ **7.7, n. 21, 34.**

Martinez, In re, 196 B.R. 225 (D.Puerto Rico 1996)—§ **12.10, n. 35.**

Martinez v. City of Roy, 141 F.3d 1185 (10th Cir.1998)—§ **10.43, n. 11.**

Martinez v. Wilson, 32 F.3d 1415 (9th Cir. 1994)—§ **11.5, n. 38.**

Martini v. Federal Nat. Mortg. Ass'n, 178 F.3d 1336, 336 U.S.App.D.C. 289 (D.C.Cir.1999)—§ **4.5, n. 5; § 4.26, n. 33.**

Martinson v. Kinney Shoe Corp., 104 F.3d 683 (4th Cir.1997)—§ **10.36, n. 9.**

Maschka v. Genuine Parts Co., 122 F.3d 566 (8th Cir.1997)—§ **2.50, n. 11.**

Mason v. Stallings, 82 F.3d 1007 (11th Cir. 1996)—§ **10.20, n. 6.**

Mason Tenders Dist. Council Welfare Fund v. Donaghey, 1993 WL 596313 (S.D.N.Y. 1993)—§ **10.41, n. 31.**

Moreno v. Consolidated Rail Corp., 99 F.3d 782 (6th Cir.1996)—§ **10.5, n. 9.**

Morgan v. Ford, 6 F.3d 750 (11th Cir. 1993)—§ **2.50, n. 12.**

Morgan v. Hilti, Inc., 108 F.3d 1319 (10th Cir.1997)—§ **10.23, n. 6, 12.**

Morgan v. United Parcel Service of America, Inc., 169 F.R.D. 349 (E.D.Mo. 1996)—§ **12.30, n. 8.**

Morgenthal ex rel. Morgenthal v. American Telephone & Telegraph Co., Inc., 1999 WL 187055 (S.D.N.Y.1999)—§ **10.70, n. 4.**

Moritz v. Frontier Airlines, Inc., 147 F.3d 784 (8th Cir.1998)—§ **10.28, n. 5; § 10.65, n. 1.**

Morris v. American Nat. Can Corp., 952 F.2d 200 (8th Cir.1991)—§ **4.25, n. 14.**

Morris v. City of West Palm Beach, 194 F.3d 1203 (11th Cir.1999)—§ **11.5, n. 38, 41, 43.**

Morris v. Oldham County Fiscal Court, 201 F.3d 784 (6th Cir.2000)—§ **2.40, n. 40, 44.**

Morris v. State of Kansas Dept. of Revenue, 849 F.Supp. 1421 (D.Kan.1994)—§ **5.2B; § 5.2B, n. 3.**

Morrison v. Reichhold Chemicals, Inc., 97 F.3d 460 (11th Cir.1996)—§ **11.1, n. 4.**

Morrissey v. Boston Five Cents Sav. Bank, 54 F.3d 27 (1st Cir.1995)—§ **7.1, n. 18.**

Morrocco v. Goodwill Industries of Northwest North Carolina, Inc., 1993 WL 268625 (M.D.N.C.1993)—§ **2.31, n. 17.**

Morse v. University of Vermont, 973 F.2d 122 (2nd Cir.1992)—§ **10.5, n. 10.**

Moses v. American Nonwovens, Inc., 97 F.3d 446 (11th Cir.1996)—§ **10.25, n. 18, 35.**

Moses v. Business Card Exp., Inc., 929 F.2d 1131 (6th Cir.1991)—§ **12.2, n. 2; § 12.3, n. 12.**

Moses H. Cone Memorial Hosp. v. Mercury Const. Corp., 460 U.S. 1, 103 S.Ct. 927, 74 L.Ed.2d 765 (1983)—§ **4.6, n. 29.**

Moskowitz v. Trustees of Purdue University, 5 F.3d 279 (7th Cir.1993)—§ **7.25, n. 29.**

Mosley v. General Motors Corp., 497 F.2d 1330 (8th Cir.1974)—§ **12.30, n. 4.**

Mosley v. Pena, 100 F.3d 1515 (10th Cir. 1996)—§ **4.10, n. 8.**

Moteles v. University of Pennsylvania, 730 F.2d 913 (3rd Cir.1984)—§ **3.3, n. 21.**

Motley v. New Jersey State Police, 196 F.3d 160 (3rd Cir.1999)—§ **10.82, n. 4.**

Mouton v. Metropolitan Life Ins. Co., 147 F.3d 453 (5th Cir.1998)—§ **4.6, n. 20.**

Moyo v. Gomez, 40 F.3d 982 (9th Cir. 1994)—§ **2.40, n. 36.**

Moyo v. Gomez, 32 F.3d 1382 (9th Cir. 1994)—§ **2.2, n. 2, 9.**

Mozee v. American Commercial Marine Service Co., 963 F.2d 929 (7th Cir.1992)—§ **4.20, n. 3.**

Mt. Healthy City School Dist. Bd. of Educ. v. Doyle, 429 U.S. 274, 97 S.Ct. 568, 50 L.Ed.2d 471 (1977)—§ **3.11, n. 15, 25; § 5.2; § 5.2, n. 19, 43; § 11.5; § 11.5, n. 33; § 12.10, n. 4.**

Muckleshoot Tribe v. Puget Sound Power & Light Co., 875 F.2d 695 (9th Cir.1989)—§ **11.20, n. 8.**

Mueller v. Thompson, 133 F.3d 1063 (7th Cir.1998)—§ **12.10, n. 33.**

Mulhall v. Advance Sec., Inc., 19 F.3d 586 (11th Cir.1994)—§ **8.4, n. 12.**

Muller v. Costello, 187 F.3d 298 (2nd Cir. 1999)—§ **10.20, n. 15; § 12.10, n. 33.**

Muller Optical Co. v. E.E.O.C., 743 F.2d 380 (6th Cir.1984)—§ **8.20, n. 3.**

Mullin v. Raytheon Co., 164 F.3d 696 (1st Cir.1999)—§ **7.7, n. 34.**

Munday v. Waste Management of North America, Inc., 126 F.3d 239 (4th Cir. 1997)—§ **2.40, n. 43; § 2.50, n. 8.**

Mundo v. Sanus Health Plan of Greater New York, 966 F.Supp. 171 (E.D.N.Y. 1997)—§ **10.41, n. 50.**

Mundy v. Palmetto Ford, Inc., 998 F.2d 1010 (4th Cir.1993)—§ **2.22, n. 43.**

Mungin v. Katten Muchin & Zavis, 116 F.3d 1549, 325 U.S.App.D.C. 373 (D.C.Cir.1997)—§ **2.50, n. 8, 14.**

Munoz v. Orr, 200 F.3d 291 (5th Cir. 2000)—§ **3.20, n. 19; § 12.5, n. 12.**

Munsingwear, Inc., United States v., 340 U.S. 36, 71 S.Ct. 104, 95 L.Ed. 36 (1950)—§ **12.20, n. 5.**

Murphy v. Cadillac Rubber & Plastics, Inc., 946 F.Supp. 1108 (W.D.N.Y.1996)—§ **2.40, n. 5.**

Murphy v. United Parcel Service, 141 F.3d 1185 (10th Cir.1998)—§ **10.42, n. 9.**

Murphy v. United Parcel Service, Inc., 527 U.S. 516, 119 S.Ct. 2133, 144 L.Ed.2d 484 (1999)—§ **10.25, n. 8; § 10.35, n. 6; § 10.41; § 10.41, n. 46; § 10.42; § 10.42, n. 11.**

Murphy Bros., Inc. v. Michetti Pipe Stringing, Inc., 526 U.S. 344, 119 S.Ct. 1322, 143 L.Ed.2d 448 (1999)—§ **12.6, n. 16.**

Murray v. New York University College of Dentistry, 57 F.3d 243 (2nd Cir.1995)—§ **9.5, n. 9.**

Murray v. Thistledown Racing Club, Inc., 770 F.2d 63 (6th Cir.1985)—§ **2.20, n. 4; § 3.10, n. 9.**

Murrell v. School Dist. No. 1, Denver, Colo., 186 F.3d 1238 (10th Cir.1999)—§ **5.3, n. 35; § 9.5, n. 10.**

Muzquiz v. W.A. Foote Memorial Hosp., Inc., 70 F.3d 422 (6th Cir.1995)—§ **2.3, n. 48.**

Myers v. Hose, 50 F.3d 278 (4th Cir.1995)—§ **10.26, n. 22.**

N

N.A.A.C.P., Detroit Branch v. Detroit Police Officers Ass'n (D.P.O.A.), 46 F.3d 528 (6th Cir.1995)—§ **11.5, n. 67.**

U

V

W

Y

*

Index

†

0–314–25403–X

9 780314 254030

90000